Gladewater High School, 1922

Kilgore High School, 1913

Gregg County, Texas
Family Histories

Gregg County Courthouse, 1897-1932

Compiled by the
Gregg County Genealogy Society

Table of Contents

Introduction & Acknowledgements ... 3

Dedication 4

Reflections on Another Time 5

Gregg County Genealogy Society 7

Veterans 7

Towns 11

    Longview 12

    Gladewater 16

    Kilgore 18

Communities 18

Events 28

    Longview Race Riot of 1919 28

    Dalton Gang Bank Robbery 29

    The Oil Boom 29

    The Great Texas Balloon Race 30

Places & People 30

Patrons 39

Biographies 77

Index 288

M.T.

M.T. Publishing Company, Inc.
P.O. Box 6802
Evansville, Indiana
47719-6802
www.mtpublishing.com

Graphic Designer:
Thalita A. Floyd-Wingerter

Copyright © 2004
Gregg County Genealogy Society

The materials were compiled and produced using available information; M.T. Publishing Company, Inc. and the Gregg County Genealogy Society regret they cannot assume liability for errors or omissions.

Library of Congress
Control Number: 2004112560

ISBN: 1-932439-14-5

Printed in the
United States of America

Limited Edition of 750 copies
of which this
book is number ___262___.

Gregg County, Texas Family Histories

Sponsored by the
Gregg County, Texas Genealogical Society

Less than 500 additional books are available so do not miss this opportunity to purchase extra copies for your children and grandchildren!

Now that you have had the chance to review the exceptional quality of this book, we would like to extend an opportunity for you to order copies for your family members to treasure for years to come. If you are interested in ordering additional copies please fill out and mail in the order form below. Due to the limited supply, do not hesitate, send in your order today!   *Order online and save!

Free Shipping Through January 15, 2005

Gregg County, Texas Family Histories	Qty	Price	Total
Deluxe Standard Edition		$57.50	
Shipping/Handling $6.50 for the first book and $4.00 for each additional book		$6.50	
Indiana Residents Add6% ($3.84) Sales Tax per book		$3.84	
		TOTAL	

Check ❑   Mastercard ❑   Visa ❑

For credit card orders only, you can call
1-888-263-4702

_____
Name on Credit Card

_____
Credit Card # (include 4-digit # for MC)   Expiration Date

For Office Use Only

Check # _____   Amount _____

GREGG COUTNY, TEXAS
FAMILY HISTORIES
Order Form

_____
Your Name

_____
Address

_____
City   State   Zip

(_____)
_____
Daytime Telephone

_____
E-mail

Mail order form and payment to:
Gregg County, Texas Family Histories
M.T. Publishing Company
P.O. Box 6802
Evansville, IN 47719-6802
www.mtpublishing.com

Introduction and Acknowledgments

A concentrated effort has been made to give an account of the peoples of Gregg County, but as always, much remains untold. This book is an effort to promote, generate interest in, and preserve the history of Gregg County families.

This is not just a book about the first settlers of Gregg County. The book is about those first settlers, those first years and all the newcomers since that time. Everyone who has lived here is a part of the history of Gregg County. To those who failed to submit family histories, we can only say we wish you had. To each person who contributed in any way, the Gregg County Genealogy Society says "Thank you" for helping us to make this book possible — the people who submitted stories and pictures, who typed, who sold and bought patron pages. A special "Thank you" to the Gregg County Historical Museum for sharing their pictures with us.

I would like to commend Marybelle Tutt for her unswerving patience and devotion to this project as our chairwoman. Again, a profound thanks go to those who worked tirelessly on this project from the beginning to its end. Every effort has been made to exercise accuracy and fairness in keeping with the policy laid out to us by the publisher in the beginning. We apologize for any errors that may have occurred.

Linda Hughey Laminack
President, GCGS

Dear Reader:
1875 – A family huddled together beneath their wagon, the crisp fall air settling around them in the dark of the pine-covered hills. The baby whimpered, an older child mumbled in her sleep, and nearby a too-hungry dog snarled at a sound he heard in the pitch of night. The mother of the family — too worried to sleep and too tired not to — pulled her family closer together, wrapping them tighter in the quilt that she had carefully stitched together last spring back in Georgia.

The quilt — with its faded blues and browns and grays and purples — is a scrap of a petticoat, a remnant from a worn shirt, a piece of a once-favorite skirt, a corner of curtain. Pieced together, stitch after stitch, though, it is more than parts, it is even more than the sum of it parts, for it is a symbol of warmth, of protection, of homes old and new. To this traveling, frontier family seeking a new life, this quilt is a symbol of possibility.

Perhaps that quilt, or one very like it, hangs on the wall of your home, Reader, or lies carefully folded in a trunk in your attic. Perhaps your ancestors handed it down, decade after decade, until it came to rest with you.

Reading this book is like seeing a quilt. In these pages you will see scraps of stories, remnants of lives, pieces of people. This book is too brief to tell whole stories, and human lives are too full to be captured on pages. The people in this book were brave and fool-hardy, rich and poor, successful and some not as successful as others. They were doctors and farmers, teachers and ministers, housewives and nurses. Some may have been beautiful and others only so in the eyes of their mothers. They have fought in wars, lived through epidemics, and watched the world change from the days of quilts and covered wagons to computers and the Internet, from home-grown remedies to heart replacements.

But like the quilt, wrapping a family in its warmth, they were there, playing their part in the history of Gregg County, Texas, and the world.

This book – like a quilt – was pieced together. Individuals and families submitted stories to be edited by a committee. Like a quilt, this book took time — two years, actually. Both the number of people involved and the length of time add to the possibility of error. For things that are incorrect, please accept our apologies. May the stories that entertain and inspire you be like a quilt on a cool night — symbols of warmth, of place, of homes old and new, of possibility.

Marybelle Bolger Tutt
Book Chairman

Dedication

Have you ever thought about the fact that each of us is a unique individual who has never existed before and will never exist again? We are each a fink in a chain that ties all generations of a family one to another.

I am certain that all genealogists have a deep appreciation of and respect for each and every one of our ancestors. Just imagine, if only one of them had died before creating the link that eventually led to us, we would not exist today.

We are the result of the struggles, adventures, joys and sorrows of the many different people who are our connections to the past. How can we not be grateful for our very existence and revere those who have made that existence possible?

Never should we judge our ancestors for anything they did. They were the products of their times. To understand those "times" we must study history as we conduct our genealogical searches. Many years down the line, descendants will be appreciating us for the family histories we will have compiled to be passed down to them. No facts will be hidden from them; perhaps some findings will be in fine print, so to speak, but all will be there. Even health information and causes of death will have been included, possibly forestalling problems for them.

Not only will future generations have the results of our research, they will also have our personal life stories. They need to know more about us than just our birth and death dates. We must tell them what happened in between, how we lived as well as how we have felt about life. Knowing our views, our beliefs, and personal philosophy of life might possibly inspire our future "links" to conduct their own lives accordingly (assuming that we are God-fearing, decent, law-abiding citizens of this universe).

Now, let's all get busy completing the legacy we will leave to future generations. Thus, we eventually will become the revered ones!

Suzy B. Burt
GCGS Member

(From the Gregg County Genealogy Society Newsletter, Volume 12, Number 9, September 1995, p.1)

If

If you could see your ancestors, all standing in a row,
Would you be proud of them, or don't you really know?
Some strange discoveries are made in climbing family trees.
And some of them, you know, do not particularly please.

If you could see your ancestors, all standing in a row,
There might be some of them, perhaps, you wouldn't care to know.
But there's another question which requires a different view.
If you could meet your ancestors, would they be proud of you?

Anonymous
(From the Red River County, Texas
Genealogical Society quarterly, August 1991)

Reflections on Another Time

The following articles are reflections on times past in Gregg County. They are from different perspectives and locations. Pearl Smith Echols describes her Grandfather Killingsworth's old pre-civil war farm and farm life in north Gregg County. Pigeon (Mrs. Leck) Wood relates the hustle and bustle of the Oil Boom and its impact on the Greggton area of Longview in the western part of the county.

A Grandpa's House

By Pearl Smith Echols

I will give a short sketch of Grandfather Killingsworth's house as I remember it. It was located about five miles north on what is now called the Judson Road going north from Longview then called Summerfield Road on account of the only church in the surrounding area of East Texas. There was a Presbyterian Church at the Settlement of Pine Tree, so called from an enormous pine tree near the Postmaster's house, where the post office was. This church was too far for Grandfather to attend, although he was a Presbyterian. He joined this Methodist Church, so all the family became Methodist.

This house was a four-room log and plank house with attic. The kitchen off a few yards from the main building, this was the regulation of building to protect the main houses from fire. Another small room stood away from the kitchen. It was the store room where the groceries were stored that were hauled yearly from Shreveport, later from Jefferson and then from Marshall. The main staple articles were sugar, coffee, tea, rice, cheese and seasonings. Grandpa milled his own flour, meal, and made the lard and meat for this large family, in-laws, out-laws, besides the slaves, which numbered about one hundred when they were freed. There was also a shoe shop, a blacksmith shop, gin and grist mill where four and meal were ground. Back some distance was the slave quarters, all this I remember from childhood.

The house stood on a hill top back of the kitchen, at the foot of the hill a spring branch flowed. There a pond was made for the ducks and geese. Also, where the water ran swiftly, a deep trough was made into the tiresome journey up and down from those who prepared the meals, unless some of us young fry were near to run to the spring up and down the hill. Molly and I ran gladly to bring whatever Aunt Jane or Aunt Fanny wanted.

Out to the south of the house were the barn, cribs and stalls and carriage house for Grandma's beautiful carriage, all silver handles, satin lined, fringe and glass doors. I never saw her get into it but have heard that there was room for her only on the back seat on account of her enormous hoop skirt. Grandpa sat on the front seat with the Negro driver. I suppose the other members got to church the best way they could…maybe horseback.

The old house, original floors and rafters, burned some ten years ago. It then belonged to a great, great-grandson of Grandpa's. The graves of Grandfather and Grandmother and the mother of Elbridge, Lee and Julie are there. This great grandson has put a strong fence around the graves, but they are now in a field.

Our Yankee Kinfolks

After the death of Anderson Killingsworth, John Sweet's father, in Roane County, Tennessee, Mary Sweet Killingsworth moved to Montgomery County, Illinois, with her son, Stephen, and his wife, Nancy Hart Killingsworth. Her daughter Mary Killingsworth Allen and husband, William Allen, and their three sons, William, Rufus, and Jesse Killingsworth Allen (killed in an Indian war in Oregon) and two daughters had moved to Montgomery County, Illinois from Tennessee.

Generations of the Allen family are recorded in Montgomery County and Sparta, Illinois.

(Excerpts from *East Texas Heritage* by Nancy Ruff, January 13, 1985, narrative by Pearl Echols and research records.)

Willow Springs and Pine Tree in 1930

As seen through the eyes of an "Okie," Pigeon (Mrs. Leck) Wood, in 1984

Written for Pine Tree Junior High students Tammy Burt and Eliska Smith, to be part of their (award-winning) History Fair project

When the depression hit in 1929 I lived in Seminole, Oklahoma. My daddy, along with thousands of other men, set out to look for jobs to try to provide for their families. This trek led most of them to the piney woods of East Texas, where there were rumors of a new oil field being explored.

Daddy stopped at a place called Willow Springs, which originally consisted of a small grocery store, a blacksmith shop, and a cotton gin that was abandoned early in the boom. These were located at the intersection of Highway 80, Pine Tree Road and Cherokee Street. Three or four homes were between these and the railroad tracks. By the time Daddy arrived there were several lumber yards, oilfield supply houses, as well as other businesses necessary to develop oil fields. Because ninety percent of the heavy freight, pipe, steel, etc. was shipped from all over the United States to Willow Springs, it became known as the "hub of the East Texas oil field." The pipe, derrick steel, lumber, etc. was then transferred by trucks and wagons pulled by huge oilfield mules to all parts of the "oil patch" and as far south as Overton, Arp, Troup and Carlisle (Price).

Now that jobs were becoming available a new problem was finding food and shelter. Longview had a few rooms-for-rent and three or four small hotels but these had long since been occupied by the first men to arrive. Newcomers had a choice of sleeping in their cars (if they had one) or on a cot or pallet on the ground (most had brought quilts with them). A grove of pine trees about one block towards the railroad tracks on Supply Street (near Topburger) became known as Pine Tree Hotel since dozens of men slept here under the trees. Their food was whatever they could get at the small grocery store, mostly potatoes, bacon or whatever could be fried over an open fire. Sometimes they had crackers and cheese. This was the way of life but they didn't complain to us back home.

As cold weather approached, the men began moving in the old abandoned gin for whatever shelter it might provide. This was located just behind the building where Cammack Drug and Western Auto were located until recently.

Arkmo Lumber Company was built about one-half block south on Cherokee Street; here my daddy was lucky enough to find work. Daddy ways lucky enough to share a bedroom with the son of a co-worker, Grady Jones. Mrs. Jones cooked for him until we could move. In nearby houses lived other Jones families who arranged to use less space in their homes. Each family fixed two or three rooms with several beds in each, which were rented for $2.00 or $2.50 per week. In order to enable more men to get out of the weather, some of them slept crosswise. This allowed four to occupy one bed. Later, the Jones women, along with several others, started cooking for men – hence the old oil field boarding house. Some of that hospitality must have rubbed off, for these piney woods are still full of wonderful people today.

Along with winter weather came the rains. It rained almost every day for more than a year. Sometimes it would take days to get one load of pipe twenty-five or thirty miles.

After several months Daddy was able to build us a small, three room "shot gun" house. By the time we arrived, the present Greggton business district was filled with small cafes, dry goods stores, barber shops, news-stands, drug stores and even a two-story hotel, which stood where the post office was formerly located. Also within several months some twenty to twenty-five huge oilfield supply stores sprang up between Highway 80 and the railroad tracks. Freight was unloaded through the Willow Springs depot, which was an old caboose.

B.F. Walker, L.T. Campbell and Chief Davis were among the owners of trucking and wagon camps. They transported the oilfield supplies as far as Overton, Arp, Carlisle and Troup.

As more jobs became available, the community grew. Small shotgun houses along with many tent-houses lined every nook and cranny of Willow Springs. There was only walking room between many of them but families were happy to be back together again. Of course, modern conveniences such as bathrooms, or even running water, did not exist.

Now that families were reunited there was the problem of education. Pine Tree by this time had managed to add one or two classrooms to the original one room, but kiddos were everywhere. As soon as possible, a frame building was built near the railroad tracks between Cherokee Street and Avenue A. In this six room building could be found pupils from first through third grades. Since Pine Tree only taught

through junior high, students attended high school in Longview. Somewhere along the way the Presbyterian Church allowed the school to use their Sunday School rooms for classrooms. As fast as money could be appropriated another addition was made here and there. It has almost grown into a "Pine Tree Empire".

Along with education, our thoughts turned toward the churches we had left behind. The Pine Tree Presbyterian Church was so far away most people in Willow Springs couldn't attend, as there were few cars. Around 1931 the Jones Memorial Methodist Church, presently Greggton Methodist Church, was erected near the Willow Springs school. It contained a small auditorium and two small classrooms. Within the next year the auditorium to the First Baptist Church was built. Here we attended church when sawdust was used as a floor. Look at that church now!

As mentioned before, transportation was a big problem. The narrow farm roads were deep sand in summer and deep mud in winter. It could take two and a half to three hours to get to Longview because so many cars got stuck in the sand or mud. We all had to help push each other's cars so we might pass. After some time we learned we could go up to the little red caboose and ride the train to Longview for 25 cents. That was a luxury we took advantage of.

Speaking of luxuries, through the next several years Willow Springs boasted of three nice theaters (one at a time). But for some unexplained reason each of them burned (not the same year) between ten and twelve o'clock on Saturday mornings. Along with theaters we also had two hotels, an airport which later became a golf course, and many, many small businesses. About 1934 or '35 fire destroyed the whole business block where the Kettle and Jim's Trim now stand. Through the years Lebus built a huge machine shop that covered the area now occupied by the new East Texas Bank and Trust building. During the war all this was burned down when someone accidently turned over some gasoline.

In the forties Mr. Denny Wren and Mr. Sam Hall, co-owners of a drug store, were instrumental in securing our first post office; this was a small room in the back of

their drug store. Since there was already a Willow Springs post office in far south Texas, we had to change our name. Thus Greggton was born. Somewhere along the way, Mr. Bun Rodden dug a deep well where the water tower now stands and put in our first water system.

Twice in the early years Willow Springs was cited in *Ripley's Believe It Or Not*. First, it stated how many million dollars worth of freight and such had been processed through Willow Springs where an old abandoned caboose was used for a depot. Second, they noted that Willow Springs, or maybe Greggton by then, was the only town in the United States that had a volunteer fire department, a fire station but no fire truck or water system. This was true.

One other luxury we were blessed with about 1931 was our own doctor, E.O. Watkins. Dr. Watkins was known for his countless acts above and beyond the call of duty. He would borrow a mule or horse from one of the companies and ride in whatever necessary, even freezing rain, as far as the Big Woods (six or eight miles) to treat a seriously ill patient.

A few months after we were settled in our new home I got a job in Ethel's Boarding House, where we served family style meals to approximately one hundred regular customers each day. They were mostly oil field men who worked both far and near. Each morning we packed eighty-five to one hundred sack lunches for those on the move. Bologna or any other lunch meat that might spoil could not be used. My work began at 4 a.m., and ended about 9 or 9:30 at night when the men all made it in and were well fed. This was a good job, I thought.

The "boom people" have seen many changes, some good, some bad. But one has only to take a tour of the Greggton and Pine Tree area to see the progress and prosperity that is now enjoyed by thousands.

To sum it all up, what we now enjoy has come through caring, love, devotion and "millions" of hours of hard work. If we, the older generation, had nothing else to be proud of, we have only to look at our teachers, pupils and anyone else concerned with the growth and maintenance of the greatest school on earth... Pine Tree!

Gregg County Genealogy Society

Cannot find your ancestors? Come join the other seekers. The Gregg County Genealogy Society was chartered in 1984 as a support group for researchers of family and local history. Officers were Rachael Garner, Marybelle Tutt, Doris Anderson, Shirley Cantrell Tuttle, and Lloyd Stanley.

The objectives of the Society are to bring together persons interested in researching family and local history; to collect and publish genealogical and historical material of Gregg County and surrounding areas; to sponsor educational programs; and to share research methods and ideas. The group also encourages the donation of genealogical and family history books to the public library. The organization purchases genealogical and historical publications for the use of the general public. These materials are housed in the Longview Public Library on Cotton Street in the Mary Lee Robbins Room set aside for genealogical research.

The organization meets at the Longview Public Library on the first Tuesday of each month to share stories and experiences and hear presentations about techniques for everything from searching to conserving and archiving found items. The meetings are open to the public. Members receive a monthly newsletter that includes tips, events, and how-to articles on genealogy along with information about the month's program.

The 2003 officers were Linda Laminack, president; Willie Williams, vice-president; Loretta Storey, secretary; and Janice Doss, treasurer; for 2004: Linda Laminack, president; Mary Ann Smith, vice-president; Lolita Lloyd, secretary; and Janice Doss, treasurer.

Publications available from the Society:

All the cemetery books have a surname index, maps and the location of the cemetery.

Gregg County, Texas Cemeteries, Volume I (sold out). Gum Springs, Magrill, Summerfield (Old and New), White, Winterfield and George.

Gregg County, Texas Cemeteries (with Harrison County), Volume II. Alpine, Elmira Chapel, Judson, Killingsworth, Memory Park, New Providence, Richardson-Teague, Cain, Cole, Koon-Dickard, Dollahite, Forest Hills, LaGrone Chapel, Old LaGrone, Noonday, Whitehorn, Old Davis-Friendship, Old Young and Roe-Page.

Gregg County, Texas Cemeteries (with Rusk and Smith Counties), Volume III. Danville, Elderville, Fambrough Family, Florey Family, Kilgore City, Kilgore Memorial Gardens, Mount Moriah, Mount Sylvan, Parmer, Peatown, Old Union, Utzman-Barnett, Walnut Grove, Fortson, Hickory Grove and Thompson.

Gregg County, Texas Cemeteries, Volume IV. Greenwood and Grace Hill, both in Longview. Greenwood is Longview's oldest cemetery, already established when deeded to the town in 1877. Grace Hill was established in 1904.

Gregg County, Texas Cemeteries, Volume V. Camden, Fisher, Gay, Hunter, Lakeview, Mitchell, Moseley, Rock Springs, Rosedale, Sparkman-Reddick-White Oak, Wood, Old East Mountain, Gladewater Memorial Park, Mings, Alsup, Sabine Valley and Old Sabin Valley.

Gregg County, Texas Obituaries from Longview Newspapers 1921-1931. Obituaries from *Longview Daily Leader* 1921-1923, and *Longview Daily News* 1924-1931. These newspapers are no longer in existence and some issues were not available.

Forman's Funeral Home Book, Longview, Texas, Vol. I, 1931-1934 and Selected Obituaries from Longview, Texas Newspapers 1931-1934. This book covers the turbulent period of the early oil boom days when many new people had moved to the area. These funeral home records cover: birth date and place, parents and their birth place, attending physician, minister, place of burial and survivors of the deceased.

Forman's Funeral Home Book, Longview, Texas, Vol. II 1934-38. Continues the early oil field period including several New London School explosion victims. Same information about deceased as above.

Veterans

As this book goes to press, thousands of American military personnel are serving in a war in Iraq. Daily, newspaper headlines and TV news give us the numbers of deaths of soldiers. Unfortunately, "war fatigue" (as it is called), our inability to make sense of those numbers, or our own inattention mean that we do not often realize the meaning of those numbers. A soldier's death in a Humvee accident in Iraq means an empty place at a family supper table will never be filled. A Reservist's death in a desert attack means a co-worker's laughter will never be heard again. A Marine's death in a city whose name we can't pronounce means a Little League team lost a coach.

On the court house lawn in Gregg County, Texas, there stand several memorials – a tribute to those who gave their lives in the service to the country, a statue honoring all veterans as well as one honoring the Confederate soldiers, a plaque dedicated to World War I veterans. As with deaths we hear about on the evening news, the names listed on those memorials may seem very distant. History has faded their meaning. But a soldiers death in the Civil War, meant that an Earpville farmer did not come home to tend his crops, his hungry children had to grow up too fast. An officer's death in World War II meant a promising young businessman didn't return home to Kilgore. A Marine's death in Vietnam meant a once happy Longview family never felt whole again.

World War I Memorial

On these pages we honor the veterans of Gregg County.

Gregg County Cemeteries are the final resting place of many more men and women who are veterans of all wars. It would be impossible to list them all.

Confederate Veterans Buried in Gregg County, Texas

Grace Hill Cemetery, located at Marshall Avenue and McCann Road in Longview

Boring, J.W. (1832-1885)

Brown, I.L. (1847-1902) – Mississippi Cavalry

Key, William H. (1844, Bossier Parish, Louisiana-1917) – Pvt. Co. B, 18th Reg. Louisiana

Finch, John Landrum (1832, Spartanburg, South Carolina-1911) – Pvt., 2nd South Carolina Cavalry

McDuffie, Moses David (1843-1928, Gregg County)

Payne, Wm. B. – Co. H, 1st Kentucky Cavalry

Vance, Arthur H. (1834-1912)

Mt. Sylvan Cemetery, located on the first dirt road off FM 2767 near the Smith County line

Choice, Tully, (1922-1897)

Florence, Sim(s) J. (1829, Georgia-1890) – Pvt., Co. K, 3rd Texas Cavalry

Fowler, Littleton Morris (1844, San Augustine, Texas-died Henderson, Texas) – served in 4th Cavalry under John F. Camp, Generals Johnson, Bragg and Hood

Bass, John E. (died 1900) – 1st Sgt., 11th Texas Infantry

Mt. Moriah Cemetery, located on the old Gladewater Highway and Goforth Road, three miles northwest of Highway 31 from Kilgore

Goforth, Rueben (1841-1882) – Co. G, 10th Texas Cavalry

Wilkins, Mortimer (1844-1925) – Pvt., Co. F, 17th Texas Cavalry

White Cemetery, located at Fort Drive and Bentwood in Pine Tree

Little, S. Miles (1823, Tennessee-1905) – Co. G, 23rd Tennessee Regiment

Magrill Cemetery, located on Cotton Street in Longview

Moore, G.W. (1838-1914) – Pvt., Co. G, 10th Texas Cavalry

Sparkman-Reddick Cemetery

Reddick, William (born Tennessee)

Danville Cemetery, located near Kilgore on FM 2087, south of Highway 349

Barber, P.B. (83 years old) – Pvt., Co. F, 10th Regiment, Texas Cavalry

Spinks, James Monroe (1839-1928, Danville) – Pvt., Co. G., 10th Texas Cavalry; guide for Ector's Brigade

Kilgore City Cemetery, located on Harris Street, off Highway 42

Borders, William R. (1841-1922) – Co. I 1st North Carolina Cavalry

Keener, Lawson Jefferson (1840, Union Springs, Alabama-1888) – Lt., Co. I, 7th Texas Infantry; courier, scout and guard at Camp Ford, Tyler, Texas

Tutt, Richard H. – Pvt., Co. I, 19th Texas Regimental Infantry

Peatown Cemetery, located two miles north of Junction 2104 and the Elderville Road, behind the Peatown Christian Church

Holloway, Wm. Carroll (1844, Georgia-1898) – Pvt., Co. B, Parson's

Utzman Family Cemetery, Danville, Gregg County

Utzman, Jacob (1838-1904)

Greenwood Cemetery, located at Fourth and Magrill Streets in Longview

Allison, Dr. Jonathan Nicholas (1828, Virginia-1884)

Ansley, Wesley Sole (1844, Georgia-1922) – Pvt., Co. B, Texas Infantry, Granbury's Brigade; volunteered at age 16, mustered in at Marshall, Texas; was Commander of Camp No. 587, Sons of Confederate Veterans, 1907-1918

Brown, Bluford Washington (1831, Bibb County, Alabama-1897) – Co. F, 44th Alabama Infantry Division; returned home to raise a company of cavalrymen; Lt. under Capt. Willis Cleveland, Livingston's Regiment, Clanton's Cavalry Brigade

Brown, John William (1836, Albemarle County, Virginia-1905) – organized a company of soldiers in Rusk and other counties; Col., 7th Texas Infantry Division

Bruner, William Isaac (1830, Vicksburg, Mississippi-1895) – Lt. to the Capt., Co. C, 3rd Regiment, Mississippi Infantry Division

Burke, Archibald T. (1829, Georgia-1882) – Col., Co. F, 7th Georgia Regiment

Butts, Charles M. (1857-1895) – Co. B, 3rd Texas Cavalry

Campbell, Thomas Duncan (1831, Tennessee-1909) – Pvt., Captain Sutton's Co., Texas Cavalry Unit, Graham's Texas Rangers; father of Texas Governor Campbell

Catterton, Benjamin N. (1846, near Charlottesville, Albemarle County, Virginia-1916) – Pvt., Co. B, 39th Virginia Battalion

Durham, D.D. (born Kemper County, Mississippi) – Pvt., Independent Co. 59, 2nd Lt., 46th Regiment, Mississippi

Echols, Robert Finis (1846, Shelby County, Texas-1916) – Cpl., Co. I, 35th Regiment, Texas Cavalry

Flewellen, Thomas Archeleus (1829-1893) – Capt., Civil Department; enlisted in Tyler, Texas

Harrison, M.A. (1828-1905)

Hill, Richard Cabell "Dick" (1823-1907)

Howard, Jackson Conner (1847, Harrison County, Texas-1922, Longview) – Co. A, 3rd Texas Regiment; courier; enlisted at Gilmer,

Confederate Memorial

Veterans Organizations of Gregg County

American Legion
Post 140
Chartered 16 July 1934

Military Officers Association
of America (ROA)
Chartered 1989

Fleet Reserve Association
Piney Woods Branch 239
Chartered 21 March 1997

Northeast Texas Women Veterans
WAVES Ago Unit 61 of WAVES National
Chartered 8 November 1988

Marine Corps League
Det. 959
Chartered 16 August 1996

Veterans of Foreign Wars
Post 4002
Chartered 5 January 1945

Disabled American Veterans
Oil Capital Chapter

Dedicated to All Gregg County Veterans

Last of the Confederate veterans.

Texas; first mayor of Longview; sheriff when local bank robbed by Dalton gang; city marshall; lived at 213 E. Tyler Avenue

Howard, L.L. "Luke" (born Harrison County, Texas) – Co. A, 3rd Texas Cavalry, commanded by Col. Greer; later served under Gen. Ben McCollough and also Gen. Ross

Kelley, T.A. – Sgt., Co. F, Alabama Volunteers

Kennard, Thomas E. (1848, Alabama-1928, Longview) – Co. K, 34th Texas Cavalry; lived on South Green Street

Kilgore, John T. (1841, Coweta County, Georgia-1885) – Gregg County judge

Lane, William T.

Letcher, Lafayette

Levy, Richard B., Sr. (born Portsmouth, Virginia) – Pvt., Independent Signal Corp, 1st Co.; he was a Gregg County judge

Lewis, Bennett or **Benjamin Franklin** (1847, Decatur, Georgia-1926, Dallas, Texas) – Pvt., Col. Sims' Regiment under Capt. Coachman

Luckett, Charles Joseph (1836-1908) – Maj., Co. C, 2nd Texas Cavalry, Quartermaster Department

Mobberly, Samuel H. (1842, Kentucky-1910) – 1st Kentucky Infantry, Col. Ben Hardin Helms; he built the Mobberly Hotel in 1884

Murrell, George W. – Co. D, 4th South Carolina Infantry

Northcutt, William George (1837, Cobb County, Georgia-1909) – 1st

Sgt., Co. K, 60th Georgia Regiment; served under Capt. Howell, Gen. Stonewall Jackson, Gen. Joseph E. Johnston and Gen. Hood; scout to Gen. Johnston

O'Bryan, Dr. Andrew Franklin (1836, South Carolina-1916) – served as physician/surgeon in army; practiced medicine in Longview for many years

Perry, Green P. (died 1921) – Pvt., Co. D, 9th Texas Cavalry

Poe, John T. (1836-1917) – 1st Sgt., Co. F, 4th Texas Cavalry

Rucker, James Howard (1822, Tennessee-1888) – Capt., Co. D

Smith, John Tyson (1846, Anniston, Alabama-1916) – Texas Infantry under Gen. McGruder and Gen. Kirby Smith

Standsbury, L.D. (M.D.) (died in Longview)

Tankersley, A.B. (1833, Georgia-1887) – Maj., CSA; Baptist minister

Tate, Thomas Marvin (1830-1911) – enlisted in 1861 as gunsmith

Taylor, Andrew S. (1844, Amite County, Mississippi-1890) – Co. A, 3rd Texas Regiment; attorney and surveyor; surveyed the boundary lines for Gregg County in 1873

Terry, James H.

Weir, Richard N. or **W.** (1826 or 1836-1889) – Pvt., Co. C, 14th Texas Cavalry; Clerk, Quartermaster Department, 5th Texas Cavalry

Whitehead, James M. (died 1882) – served in Walker's Division

Wingfield, W.W.

Womack, Albert Alonzo (1844-1910) – Pvt., Co. A, 3rd Texas Regiment, Lane's Rangers

Young, W. Francis "Frank" (1841-1925) – Capt., Co. E, 10th Texas Cavalry

(Courtesy of Barbara Gilbert, President, R.B. Levy Chapter 1070 (Longview), United Daughters of the Confederacy. Also: *Gregg County, Texas Cemeteries*, Volumes I, III and IV; and Gregg County, Texas, obituaries, Longview newspapers, 1921-1931.)

Others known to have died in Gregg County, but their place of burial is not known:

Haskine, Joe M. (died in Longview) – Pvt. Co 3, 28th Texas Cavalry

Kelly, T.A. (died in Longview) – Pvt., Co. F, Alabama Volunteers

Laird, Dickson Henderson (1833-1917, Kilgore) – Pvt., Co. B., 3rd Texas Cavalry

Lane, J.A. (died at Longview) – Co. A, Milton's Light Artillery, Florida

Mayfield, W.S. (died in Longview) – Pvt., Co. H, 4th Texas Cavalry

Magrill, John R. (died in Longview) – courier in the CSA

Mitchell, A.S. (died in Longview) – Capt. Quarles' Regiment, 42nd Division, Tennessee

Phillips, B.F. (died at Gladewater) – Co. B, 35th Texas Cavalry

Reynolds, John Franklin (died at Kilgore) – Pvt., Co. B, Texas Reg., Ector's Brigade

Roe, John G. (died at Longview) – Pvt., Co. F, 11th Infantry

Tutt, Gabriel Hans (1831) – Barton's Co. G, 10th Texas Volunteer Cavalry

Tutt, Pierce B. (1835) – Graham's Co. I, 19th Texas Volunteer Infantry

Tutt, Thomas Neeley – Rapley's Arkansas Sharpshooters

Victory, J.T. (1845-1923, buried in Gladewater) – Pvt., Co. D, 1st Texas Regiment

Resident of Gregg County who was killed and buried at battle site:

Allison, Thomas Jefferson, Sr. – Co. C, 10th Texas Cavalry

To the honor of all veterans.

Right: Honoring all who have given their lives in the line of duty.

Towns

Gregg County has been home to many communities and settlements. Some have disappeared and are left only to memory while others have merged into the bigger towns. The boundaries and time frames have blurred or were never very distinct. Often oral tradition has been the only recollection of these places. Each location was unique and has had an impact on the foundation and continued growth of Gregg County from the earliest Indians to the children of the twenty-first century. The recording of what is known about these communities and the people who settled in them will serve to keep memories alive.

Gregg County

Gregg County was formed by an act of the Thirteenth Texas Legislature on 12 April 1873. The bill to form a new county was introduced by B.W. Brown, farmer and lay minister of Summerfield Methodist Church. Brown was a representative from Upshur County to the Texas legislature. The portion of the county north of the Sabine River was taken from Upshur County and the portion south of the river was taken from Rusk County. The original name chosen for the county was Roanoke, but Gregg was chosen. This name was in honor of Confederate General John Gregg. Andrew Taylor surveyed the new county lines for three dollars a mile.

The need for a new county was obvious to most of the inhabitants. Gilmer to the north and Henderson to the south were the closest seats of government. People needed to be closer to the courthouse to purchase marriage licenses, record deeds and wills, serve on a jury, as well as any other legal matters.

The Gregg County Commissioners (John F. Witherspoon, chairman; T.A. Harris, secretary; and John Page, Solomon Awalt, William Welborne, Britton Buttrell, and H.G. Williams) met 27 May 1873, to set out lines for the precincts. A voting place was established for each precinct: one, Longview; two, Walker's store, three, Davenports Mill, four, Welborne's store; five, Gladewater. The election lasted four days in order that all voters could get to the polls. Longview was chosen as the county seat over Awalt by 524 votes to 125.

T.K. Coleman and T.A. Flewellen offered the county a house on Center Street free of cost to use until a permanent building could be built. The first courthouse was built on block nine donated by the Texas and Pacific Railway Company. Local business men and merchants pledged lumber and shingles to use on the first courthouse to free people from taxes until after the building was constructed. The current one is the fifth one to be built on the same block.

The Texas New Yorker [17 October 1877] described Gregg County in glowing terms: "Gregg County, situated in the northeastern part of Texas and East of Smith county, is a section of country well worthy of notice, lying as it does in one of the richest agricultural districts of the southwest, where the climate is unexcelled for health and productiveness. It has an area of three hundred square miles and is watered by the Sabine river…[I]t has in abundance of all the valuable wood…climate is mild…[T]he county is not subject to epidemics and the diseases are few and generally controlled. As an evidence of its healthfulness, we will state that several physicians have abandoned the practice of medicine…

Iron ore abounds…Lignite coal is to be found in abundance along the Sabine river…[T]he soil is generally good, there is but little poor land in the county. We are certain there is not a survey of one hundred and sixty acres but that a man could make a good living on by using industry…."

On the Courthouse steps.

The 1880 United States Population Schedule listed the total population of Gregg County as 8,530 — 3,817 white and 4,713 colored. There were a total of 999 farms with 13,767 acres of cleared land. Cotton and corn were the principal crops.

From 1880 to 1930, Gregg County followed the trend for its three towns. Farming was the primary occupation. The county increased in population at a slow but steady rate. The discovery of oil changed the face of the county forever. In just a matter of weeks population grew from 16,000 to more than 100,000. A new courthouse and jail were built. The Gregg County Memorial Hospital (Good Shepherd) was built. Schools were suddenly over-crowded and new buildings were necessary to house the flood of students.

The county suddenly in the midst of depression was bursting at the seams. Although there have been set backs for Gregg County and her people through the last few decades, most have been overcome by the creativity and perseverance of the citizens. Gregg County, along with its people, has continued to develop and grow right into the twenty-first century.

The history of the County and its area are well-documented from the boom days into the twenty-first century. There are many sources including: the newspapers have been microfilmed and are accessible at local libraries and newspaper offices; filing cabinets of information are also available at the libraries; many churches and schools have documented the history of their institutions.

Longview

After the Civil War the railroad continued its march west. A line had been run as far as Marshall, Texas, before the war and the next stop would be at the future Longview. The Southern Pacific decided to by-pass Earpville. The Company chose to run the tracks about a mile to the west and laid out a new town — Longview.

Ossamus Hitch Methvin deeded one hundred acres to the Southern Pacific on 7 April 1870, for one dollar and in October he deeded an additional five hundred acres for $500.00. The town name is believed to have been chosen as a result of the view from Rock Hill (now 415 North Center Street) where Methvin's house was located.

A post office was opened on 27 January 1871, before there was regular mail runs by the train. O.H. Pegues was the first postmaster.

For two years track construction was delayed because of financial needs. This unfortunate event for the railroad would be a very fortunate event for Longview. As the westward most point of the line the town acted as a funnel and received an economic boost. Cotton growers came to Longview to ship their cotton. Businesses sprang up around the site. On 17 May 1871, Longview became the first incorporated town in future Gregg County.

The plat for the town was filed in Upshur County Deed Book Volume O, page 67 on 12 November 1871. The streets were to be one hundred feet wide with alleys being thirty feet wide. Blocks for the business section were to be 400 by 150 feet.

Another major event occurred in 1871. Twenty-year-old James Stephen Hogg, a future governor of Texas arrived in Longview to start a tri-weekly newspaper. This enterprise only lasted two months before Hogg moved to Quitman. In 1872, the weekly *Longview New Era* would be in print. J.L. Terry was the publisher. Over the years there would be numerous newspapers printed including the current *Longview News Journal*.

In any new settlement churches and schools were established quickly. These institutions represented permanence. The railroad gave land to set up churches. First Baptist Church was organized in 1871 by seventeen charter members. This congregation has met at the same location since that time — the corner of Fredonia and Church Streets. First Presbyterian Church was begun in 1872 with sixteen members at the corner of Center and Methvin Streets. First Christian Church was located downtown originally on land donated by the railroad at the corner of North Green and Methvin. Twelve people made up the original congregation. First Methodist Church has its origins in the Earpville Methodist, but this church would move downtown to join the other churches

Even before public schools, education was also a priority. Misses Molly and Sarah Teague, Miss Callie McCall and Mrs. Leak along with the Masons operated private schools. Professor J.M. Green opened the Longview Male and Female Academy. Around 1910, the Longview Independent School District was formed. Earlier, the county had been divided into common school districts. Schools were built for both white and black students. In 2004, there are three colleges/universities located in Longview.

LeTourneau University is a non-denominational evangelical Christian institution. Kilgore College-Longview Center is an outgrowth of Kilgore College. The University of Texas Center Longview is the most recent addition to the city.

The fledgling town was typical of a western frontier town — rough and tumble and the streets were not considered safe after dark. There were thirty-two saloons many of which ran some sort of gambling. Longview was several miles from the

Gregg County Lumber Camp

East Texas oilboom

nearest law enforcement officials who were in Gilmer. Newspapers report the disruptive behavior including robbery, beatings, and murder.

In 1873, Gregg County was established by taking portions of Upshur and Rusk Counties. Longview won the election over Awalt to become the county seat.

In 1874, according to the tax records, there were 27 liquor dealers, two foot peddlers, one billiard table, one pigeon hole table, one bagatel table, eight barrooms, four boarding houses, four physicians, 24 merchants, nine hotel keepers, two one horse-peddlers, one livery stable, two fortune tellers, a photograph/artist and a barber chair.

A major fire in 1877 consumed half of downtown, but the town rebuilt, replacing the wooden buildings with brick, and continued to grow. By 1882, there was a 450-seat opera house and three newspapers. Kelly Plow Company had moved to Longview from Marion County and was the main industrial plant. In 1903, Graham Manufacturing Company built a crate and box factory next to Kelly. The railroads continued to be a major factor in the economics of the town. Cotton, the major agricultural crop, was shipped from the railway.

During the late 1800s and early 1900s, Longview had electricity supplied by Longview Electric Light and Power Company. A public water system was installed. A street car line joined Longview proper and Longview Junction. Youngsters enjoyed stealing a ride from one place to the other. The Lacy Telephone Company set up business and would later by bought out by the Bell System. In 1892, the Texas Dental Association listed two dentists in Longview, N.C. Ogilvie and J.A. Thornton.

Longview had the excitement of a bank robbery in 1894 when Bill Dalton and his gang robbed the First National Bank.

In the early part of the twentieth century Longview was a generally quiet rural cotton and lumber center. Four events took its toll on the community. First, in 1919, racial tensions exploded into a riot. Several black residences and businesses were burned and one African-American was killed. Governor William Hobby called out the National Guard who remained until the situation was under control. Second, economically the area was hurt by fluctuations in cotton prices and by the dwindling timber supply. The biggest blow to Longview was the loss of the Texas and Pacific division offices. Third, in 1929, these offices were moved to Mineola taking about 700 employees and their families. Fourth came the national catastrophe, the Great Depression.

Then, on 26 January 1931 — the discovery of oil!! Immediately the entire county was a boomtown. Longview profited by being the county seat. Business blossomed, the courthouse stayed open extra hours, and every conceivable place someone could sleep was filled. Construction

Fredonia Street, Longview

Longview

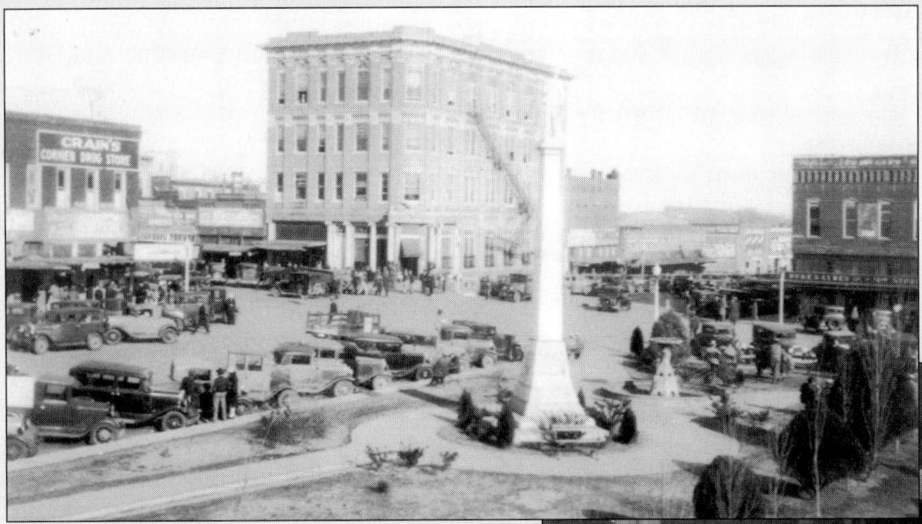
CRAIN'S
CORNER DRUG STORE

Bodie Park in downton Longview.

Below: Longview Post Office

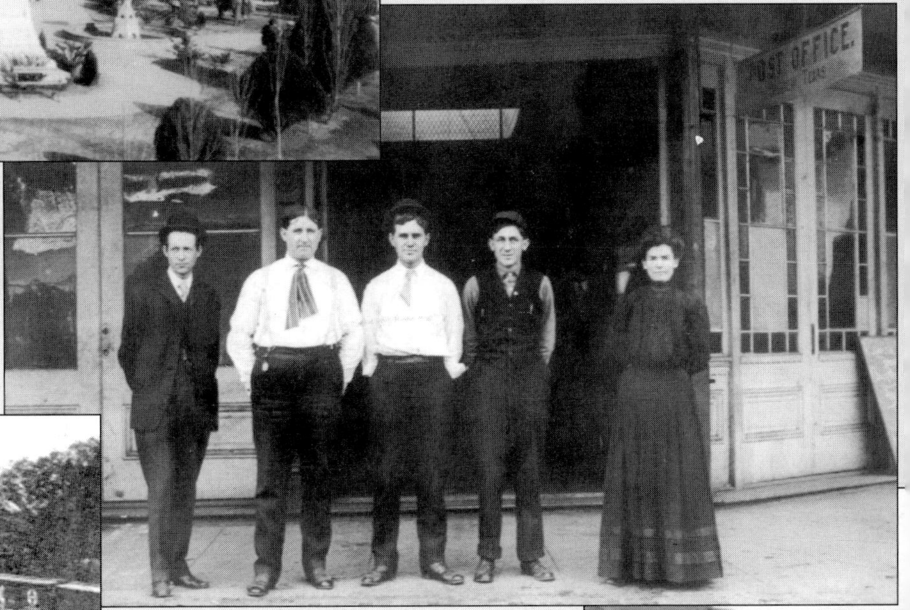
POST OFFICE.

Below: Cotton gin, Longview

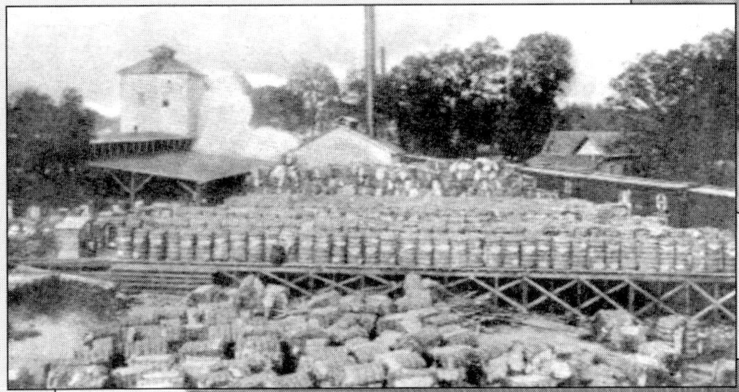

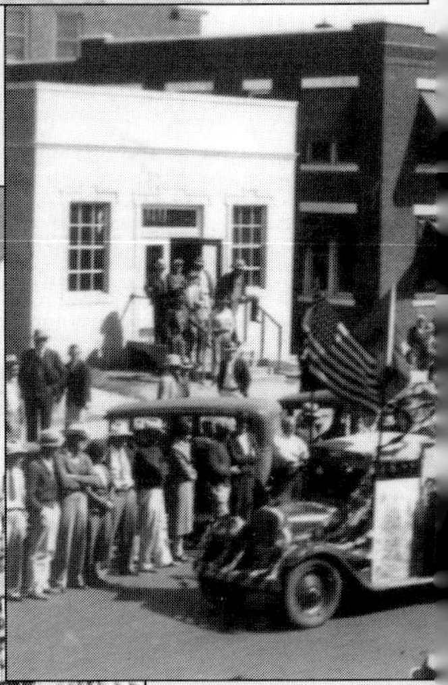

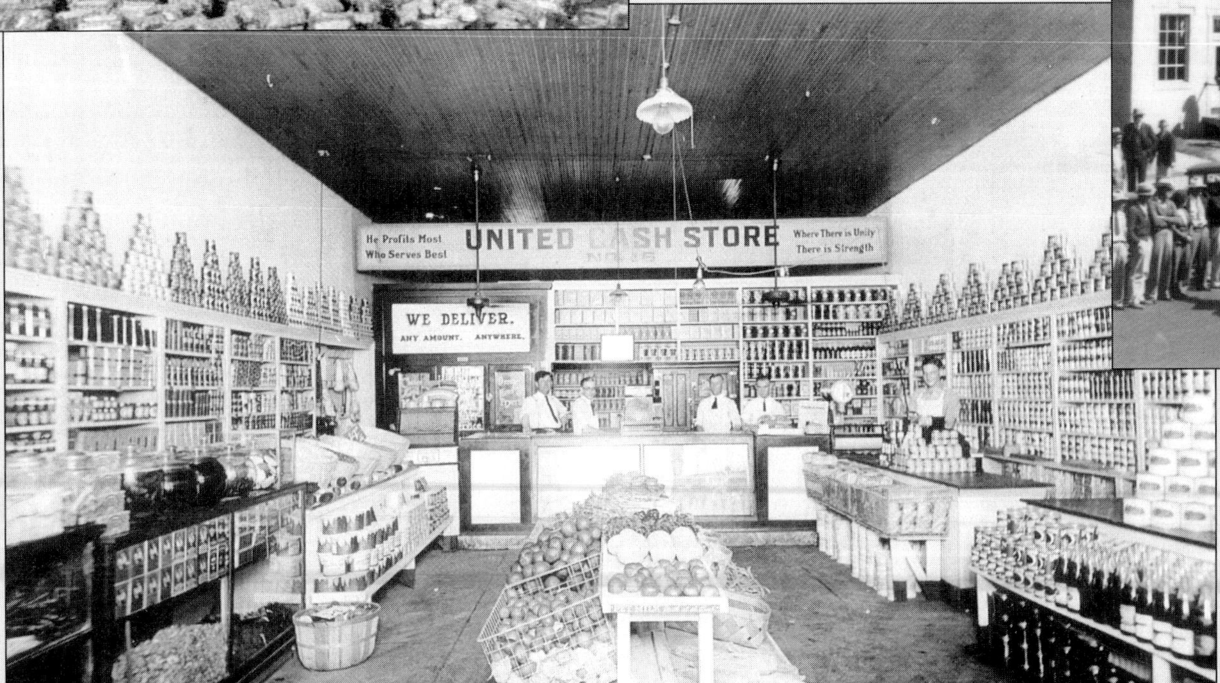
He Profits Most
Who Serves Best
UNITED CASH STORE
Where There is Unity
There is Strength
WE DELIVER.
ANY AMOUNT. ANYWHERE.

Left: United Cash Store, 1920s, downtown Longview

Longview Cannibals

Longview's Friendly Trek participants

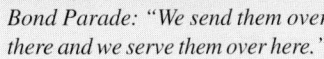

Bond Parade: "We send them over there and we serve them over here."

Right: World War II parade

Longview

was begun on a new Courthouse in 1932. New schools were built to house the tremendous influx of new students.

The citizens of Longview became more and more civic minded in the early part of the twentieth century. The Longview Chamber of Commerce was founded in 1916; the Longview Rotary Club in 1920. In 1926, the city became home to the East Texas Chamber of Commerce, defeating bids by the larger towns Tyler and Palestine.

During World War II Longview continued to grow. Pipelines were laid to move oil to the east for the war effort. The United States Government built Harmon General Hospital thanks to the efforts of Carl Estes. This project began about four months after the war started.

After the war R.G. LeTourneau bought the hospital and turned the grounds into LeTourneau Technical Institute that would become LeTourneau University. LeTourneau also opened LeTourneau Industries. This plant built large earth moving machinery. Eastman Kodak opened Texas Eastman Chemical Plant. Lake Cherokee was built for water for the city and pleasure. Schlitz Brewery, later bought by Stroh's Brewery, opened.

By the year 2000, Longview had become a regional medical center with Good Shepherd Hospital and Longview Regional Hospital. These hospitals are capable of major medical procedures from heart surgery to neo-natal care.

The town continued to increase its borders. Through the years many of the surrounding communities have been absorbed. Pine Tree and Spring Hill Independent School districts are now in the city limits along with Longview Independent School District giving Longview three large school systems. Besides being home to LeTourneau University, Kilgore College operates a branch in the city as does the University of Texas at the Longview University Center.

Longview boasts three museums. The Gregg County Historical Museum is housed in the historic Everett Building in downtown Longview. The building was designed by architect Samuel J. Blocker. Originally built as the Citizens National Bank in 1910, it was presented to the Gregg County Historical Foundation in 1979. The Everett Building is listed in the National Register of Historic Places and has an Official Texas Historical Marker chartered in 1970. Located in downtown Longview, the Longview Art Museum houses a collection

of paintings, drawings, prints and sculpture focusing on artists primarily of the Southwest, especially Texans. The R.G. LeTourneau Museum contains personal memorabilia of R.G. LeTourneau (1888-1969). The museum houses scale models of many of his inventions as well as a display of the first offshore oil drilling platforms. This is located on the LeTourneau University campus.

First National Bank, now the Gregg County Historical Museum.

Longview has a designated Historic District. The Nuggett Hill neighborhood is defined by Marshall Avenue on the north, North Sixth Street on the west, Padon Street on the south and Teague Street on the east. This architecturally significant area of 400 acres contain 45 buildings. There are also numerous historical markers in the city.

Longview has a number of activities. Artistic groups include a community theater, an opera repertory company, a symphony orchestra, and a ballet theater. The city also hosts two festivals, the Great Texas Balloon Race in July and AlleyFest in June.

Population in 2000 was approximately 77,636.

Gladewater

Red Rock was located on the Sabine River and was important as a ferry crossing. This village was one of several that would eventually make up Gladewater. A post office was established in 1849 by Isaac Vanoy. Claiborne D. Holbert operated a store.

Gladewater is on the boundary between Gregg and Upshur counties. It was founded by the Texas and Pacific Railway Company in 1873, on land bought from Jarrett Dean who had arrived in the county before 1850, and Anderson White who had also come about 1850. Both men deeded land to the railroad for five dollars. A community called St. Clair, two miles to the east, moved to Gladewater when the railroad announced that the only mail stop in the area would be there; residents from Point Pleasant, also bypassed by the railroad, moved to Gladewater.

During the Civil War Anderson White operated a hat factory. The first post office at Gladewater was established on 22 August 1873. The town's name probably originated from its proximity to Glade Creek, a stream that rose in a rather barren region called the Glades. Residents agreed to the name at a public meeting with the name Gladewater winning over St. Clair.

In the area around Gladewater lumbering was a major activity, although farming was also important. Cotton was the major crop. In 1908, the town had ten stores, one bank owned by J. Roy Knox, two blacksmith shops, two hotels, a gin, a sawmill, and a planing mill. A telephone system had been installed by Dr. T.J. Allison, Jr. Gladewater continued to grow slowly until 1931 and the oil boom.

L.J. Everett owned the first car in Gladewater. This event took place in 1910.

Gladewater, 1913

Gladewater

Left: Gladewater School

Middle: Gladewater's first class

Bottom: Gladewater Broadway Elementary, 1937-1938. First Grade Classs – Miss Simpson, Teacher. Some of the children are Robert Spruell, Jack Adams, Cullen Warren, Elestial Ledbetter, Eddy Craig, Francis McMichael, Glen Smith, J.W. Ward, Kelton Brewer, Barbara Watkins, Billie Francis Clark, Mima Jean Wood, Harry McKain, Harold Womble, Dorothy Hall, Darrell ??, Loraine Sanov (?), Billy Tugwell, Dick Edwards and Vonseal Spencer. (Submitted by Diane Warren.)

On 7 April 1931, the first Gladewater oil well blew in. It was located one mile outside town in the Sabine River bottom. Oil production led to a population increase during the 1930s from about 500 persons to around 8,000. In 1940, after the oil boom, Gladewater had a population of 4,454. Important annual festivals include the Roundup Rodeo in June and the Arts and Crafts Festival in September.

C.B. Dansby School, Kilgore

Kilgore

Kilgore is located in south central Gregg County. The area was first settled before the Civil War by planters from the old South, but the city was not founded until 1872, when the International-Great Northern Railroad built a line between Longview and Palestine. The railroad bypassed the New Danville area, and the company platted a new town, which they named for Constantine Buckley Kilgore, who sold the 174-acre town site to the railroad and urged many of the businesses of New Danville to move there. Many of the businesses did follow. The Danville Masonic Female Institute did not change locations, but the principal of the school moved to the new town and opened his own school, the Alexander Institute. The school later would move to Jacksonville, Texas, and become Lon Morris College.

The New Danville Presbyterian Church followed and did not become First Presbyterian Church until the 1930s.

A post office opened in 1873, and by 1885 Kilgore had two steam gristmill-cotton gins, a church and a district school; the estimated population was 250. Thompson Brothers was the first store in Kilgore, operating from 1873 until 1882. F.D. Oberthier opened the Kilgore State Bank in 1906, and an independent school district was formed in 1910. By 1914, the town had two banks, Baptist and Methodist churches, a newspaper, two cotton gins, several general stores, a drugstore, an ice cream parlor, a hotel and a reported population of 700.

The discovery of the surrounding East Texas oilfield in the fall of 1930 transformed Kilgore into a boomtown. Within days thousands streamed into the town. Four days after the Kilgore discovery well blew in, *The Kilgore Daily* was in print, quite a phenomena for a town that had not even had a weekly newspaper. People lived in tents and shacks, camping in every available vacant space. Honky-tonk bars sprouted up around the town; schools and other public institutions were overwhelmed. The city incorporated in February 1931. J. Malcolm was elected the first mayor. Kilgore became important for production and processing of the oil as well as supplying service. Numerous wells were drilled in the city itself, and at the height of the boom there were over 1,100 producing wells within the city limits. On part of one downtown block in the early 1930s stood the greatest concentration of oil derricks in the world; the area came to be known as the "World's Richest Acre."

Kilgore is the home of Kilgore College, the home of the famed Kilgore Rangerettes. The town boasts two outstanding museums: the East Texas Oil Museum that pays tribute to the oil industry and the Rangerette Museum. Both museums are on the college campus.

Communities

Agistha

Agistha was on the northwestern edge of the site of present Longview Gregg County. The settlement was probably established in the 1890s. A post office opened there in 1899 and closed in 1901. Around 1900 the community had a general store and a number of houses. The community disappeared from maps by 1920.

Awalt

Awalt, among the earliest settlements in Gregg County, probably settled in the late 1840s, was located about two miles south of Pine Tree Cumberland Presbyterian Church, near the site of the present western edge of Longview. The community was named for Solomon Awalt, who was the first minister of the church. A ferry known as Awalt's Ferry operated nearby on the Sabine River during the Civil War era. Awalt suffered the same fate as many communities when the new railroad bypassed it in the 1870s. An election determined the new county seat; Awalt lost the election to Longview. The town ceased to grow. Many residents apparently moved to the new community of Willow Springs nearer to the railroad. Awalt had disappeared by 1900. The entire vicinity is now part of the Greggton area of Longview.

Bethel

Bethel, a mile and a half northeast of Gladewater, was established in the mid-1840s and grew up around the Bethel Baptist Church. The church later became the present First Baptist Church of Gladewater. A school was founded and continued to operate until the early twentieth century. The community, however, began to decline after the Civil War and disappeared around the 1870s as it merged with Gladewater.

Big Head Village

According to early settlers Big Head Village was a Cherokee Indian settlement located on Rabbit Creek. Rabbit was believed to be the name of an Indian chief. An 1850 plat of S.S. Barnett's land indicated a site called "Big Head Village." The village was near a spring known as the Gum Springs. When the earliest settlers arrived at what is now the Danville area, near Kilgore, the area around the spring was cleared for use.

Kilgore

Kilgore, 1931

Left: Kilgore School

The King Cotton Gin in Kilgore near Sabine Street, c. 1917.

Bodie

Bodie, a farming community just southwest of Longview in east central Gregg County, was named for Gabriel Augustus (Bodie) Bodenheim. Bodenheim was mayor of Longview from 1904-1920 (minus one two-year term). The community was established around 1900 as a station on the International-Great Northern Railroad. In the mid-1930s, the settlement had a church, several stores, a mill and a number of houses.

Boring-Leake Cemetery

Although there is no documentation of a community by any name near the Boring-Leake Cemetery, there were probably settlements near including Earpville. (The site of the cemetery was in the vicinity of the railroad crossing near Second and Third and Cotton Streets, 2004.) A predominately Methodist church located at the site by about 1846. J.T. Magrill deeded the property to the Methodist Episcopal Church South in 1852. Two early pastors were the Reverend Robert D. Wyche and Dr. Job Taylor. The congregation moved to the Earpville Community in 1860. The cemetery that had been located next to the church remained in use for a number of years. Most of the graves were moved to the newly laid out Longview Cemetery (21 April 1877), now known as Greenwood Cemetery. By 1942, there were two marked graves at the location – Lucy C. Mobley, died 15 August 1870, and David W. Sherrill, died 31 August 1896.

Bozeman's Corner

Bozeman's Corner, north of Gladewater, was one of the many communities that sprang up during the oil boom of the 1930s. At its height in the mid-1930s, the settlement had several stores and a number of houses. It began to decline around the time of World War II, and after the war the area was annexed by Gladewater.

Calhoun

Calhoun was probably founded in the 1850s and was located on or near Rabbit Creek in the southern portion of the county, near the site of the present western edge of

Kilgore. Maps show a settlement in the area in the mid-1850s, and a post office operated there from 1853 to 1855. Calhoun disappeared after the Civil War.

Camden

Camden was located on the south bank of the Sabine River in the far eastern section of what is now Gregg County. The place was originally known as Walling's Ferry after John Walling, an immigrant to what was then Mexican Texas. Walling, who owned and operated a ferry at the location, arrived in Mexican Texas by 1835. In the Rusk County deed records, Book A, page 72, on 13 July 1844, Walling was granted a license to own and operate a public ferry across the Sabine. Fees charged to use the ferry were a wagon with three yokes, fifty cents; two-horse wagon, thirty cents; loose horses, three cents; cattle, sheep and hogs, two cents each.

The ferry was on the road from Port Caddo to communities in Rusk County. Steamboats came up the Sabine River to Camden.

The heyday of Camden was the 1850s. There was a post office (established in 1847) and a church, and a telegraph line ran though the village. Masonic Lodge 135 was chartered in 1854. There are remains of a cemetery believed to have been associated with a Christian Union Church.

Two famous visitors have been noted at Camden. Reportedly Sam Houston spent the night there on 10 December 1832. Houston was on an errand to negotiate with the Cherokee Indians for President Andrew Jackson. Robert E. Lee crossed the river at Camden in 1846, on his way to join General Zachary Taylor's army.

All that remains of the original community are some of the grave stones in the cemetery.

Cemetery at Camden, 2004

Camp Switch

Camp Switch, on the Missouri Pacific Railroad between Kilgore and White Oak in central Gregg County, was established before 1880. The small settlement was originally known as Camp or Camps, but the name was changed to Camps Switch for the nearby railroad siding. In 1884, Camps was listed as a station on the Texas and Pacific Railroad line.

Carter's Mill

Carter's Mill was six miles west of Longview near the site of present White Oak in central Gregg County. It was probably established after the Civil War. A post office operated there from 1877 until 1881. At its height in the early 1880s, the small settlement had a general store, a mill and a number of houses.

Clarksville City - St. Clair - Point Pleasant

Clarksville City is on U.S. Highway 80 between Gladewater and White Oak in northeast Gregg County. St. Clair, located in what is now Clarksville City, is believed to have been settled as early as 1827. St. Clair appeared on an early railroad map.

The first settlers arrived in the area before 1845. There was a stagecoach stop at the home of William W. Walters, which was later owned and operated by Warren P. Victory. Though first known as Gilead, the post office was named Point Pleasant in 1852. It closed in 1867. The community withered when the railroad bypassed it in 1873 and Gladewater was established. With the advent of the East Texas oilfield in 1930, so many homes, businesses and oil company camps and offices sprang up along the highway that it was called the Main Street of Texas, and street numbers were designated from Longview to Gladewater. The area around George W. Clark's home on the site of the old stagecoach stop became known as Clarksville.

A movement to incorporate, spearheaded by several oil companies and the L.W. Pelphrey Company, a general contractor specializing in oilfield construction, culminated in a vote to establish Clarksville City on 14 September 1956. Pelphrey was elected mayor and served until his death in August 1961. The bypassed portion of Old Highway 80 is named Pelphrey Drive in his honor. A Texas historical marker for the old community of Point Pleasant is at the city hall.

Claybank

Claybank, four and one-half miles east of Kilgore, was probably established after the Civil War. A post office operated from 1897 until 1902. Around 1900, the small settlement had a general store and a number of houses. By the early 1920s, the community no longer appeared on maps.

Cotton Plant - Iron Bridge

Iron Bridge, originally known as Cotton Plant, was on the Sabine River six miles south of Longview. Cotton Plant was advertised in broadsides in 1839 and had a post office from 1850 to 1866. Haden Edwards received a license on 7 July 1843 from Rusk County to set up a ferry on the Sabine River at a place called Cotton's Crossing. Edwards advertised lots for sale at Cotton Plant and Fredonia, two towns he planned to develop. In 1857, there was a United States Post Office in Cotton Plant, Rusk County.

A new post office called Iron Bridge was opened in February 1876, and by 1884 the community had a shingle mill, two steam gristmills, two churches, a public school and an estimated population of 150. The post office closed in 1891, and the community received mail from Elderville. In 1905, Iron Bridge had a school for twenty-five white pupils and another for 104 black pupils. The schools had closed and the community was no longer listed on maps by the 1930s.

Earpville

Another early community in what would become Gregg County was Earpville. The village was located generally near the corner of Highway 80 and Alpine Road, although a General Land Office map of 1893 had Earpville near the intersection of Alpine Road and Tryon Road. The location was on a stage route that ran from Louisiana to Starrville, Smith County.

Earpville was allegedly begun by James Earp (supposedly an uncle of the infamous Wyatt Earp). Earp gave up farming and opened a store in the area about 1860.

The Teague House

There was a church, a store and a stage stop along with several houses. The church was lead by Dr. Job Taylor, a physician. Dr. Taylor had earlier been at the church near the Boring Leake Cemetery. This church would move to downtown Longview in 1873 to become the Methodist Episcopal Church, South, the forerunner of First Methodist Church, Longview. In 2004, the only structure remaining from the Earpville era is the Teague House. Latimus and Mary Teague were not the first owners. Goin C. Richardson is believed to have built the structure as early as 1860. It is on Teague Street near the intersection of Highway 80 East. The Teague Family Cemetery is nearby in Longview's Teague Park.

Easton

Easton is on Farm Road 2906 ten miles southeast of Longview in extreme southeastern Gregg County and northeastern Rusk County. Most of the site, first known as Walling's Ferry and then as Camden, is near a bluff on the south bank of the Sabine River. In 1885 the Texas, Sabine Valley and Northwestern Railway built a line through the area but by-passed Camden and set up a station where a new community, Easton, began. By the late 1880s a large sawmill was in operation there. In 1890 reported businesses in Easton were the Buchanan and Company general store and a lumber and shingle plant. The population was listed at seventy-five. The community declined, and most of the remaining white inhabitants moved away. By 1940, Easton was a predominantly African-American community.

A post office first opened in 1883 with William P. Gladney as postmaster, but later closed. In March 1949, a post office was again established, after which the town soon incorporated.

Edwardsville - Peatown

Edwardsville was located on what is now Farm Road 2011 west of the Gregg County Airport. The land was purchased by Haden Edwards in August 1839, and patented in July 1849. It was purportedly named for Haden Edwards' son, Haden Harrison Edwards.

In 1855, Haden H. Edwards sold land to Elbert Dickson and John Watson for use as a school and church. Later, Watson donated more land for use by the school, church and cemetery. The first church was made of logs and was a Union Church (community), followed by a Methodist church, and then a Baptist church. All had short lives. A Christian Church chartered a congregation with twelve members in 1875. This church is still in existence.

Edwardsville never had a post office. The population received their mail at Danville.

Later, the area would be known as Pea Town. This local name became popular in 1860, the year of a drought when many crops had failed. A field in the area had the good fortune to have a very good crop of peas, consequently appeared the sayings "You can go to town for your peas" or "this place should be called Peatown."

The *Texas New Yorker* in 1877 wrote, "the lands are good and it [Pea Town] has a population of intelligent and industrious people."

Peatown School

Elderville School

Elderville

Elderville is off State Highway 322 just west of the Gregg County Airport. It was established in the late 1840s and originally named for one Colonel Brown, an early settler. Portions of the extended community were known at various times as Brown's Settlement, Brown's Bluff, or the Colonel Brown Community.

Willis Wilson settled in the area about 1850. He established a plantation along the Sabine River. With slave labor he grew cotton that was shipped on barges and riverboats.

A post office called Brown's Bluff opened there in 1874. Around 1875, its name was changed to Iron Bridge. Georgian H.T. Elder moved to Gregg County in 1882. He set up a sawmill and commissary for mill hands in the area and in 1887 the name of the community was changed to Elderville. The Post Office was housed in the Blackburn-Lucy General Store. By 1890, the community had a steam gristmill, a cotton gin, three churches, two schools, a general store and an estimated population of 200. By the early 1920s, Elderville reported ninety-six inhabitants and four businesses. After World War II much of the area became part of the Gregg County Airport.

In 1883, a school for African-Americans was established in the Elderville Community School District and included students from Pleasant Green, Elderville, Post Oak and Easton. Originally called Greenville, the name was changed to Gregg County Training School. Later, the name was changed to Ned E. Williams in honor of Williams, who was largely responsible for the school being built as well as the first principal. The school closed in 1969 when it was consolidated with the Longview Independent School District.

Footes

Footes, a farming community four miles southwest of Longview in east central Gregg County, was established by 1882. That year the owners of the Sabine Mills Lumber Manufacturing Company, located at Footes, placed a notice in the *Longview Democrat* newspaper. It also served as a station on the International-Great Northern Railroad. In the mid-1930s, the community had two stores and a number of houses.

Fredonia

Fredonia was on the south bank of the Sabine River in northern Rusk County. The site is now in central Gregg County on Farm Road 2087 and Interstate Highway 20.

Edwards received a large land grant in the Nacogodoches area from the Mexican government Texas. He had failed as an Empresario (a person who had agreed to set up settlers on land granted to him from the Mexican government). He had tried to foment a rebellion near Nacogdoches using the Cherokees to try to establish an independent republic named Fredonia.

Moving further into eastern Texas, Edwards advertised the sale of lots – two thousand of them. He planned to establish a town called Fredonia. Fredonia was located on land that Edwards acquired through a first-class head right. He filed the survey for the site on 20 March 1838, and in 1843, Edwards was issued a patent for a league of land. He proceeded with his plans without a patent and on 14 November 1839, he issued a broadside printed in Nacogdoches advertising the sale of lots in each of two new town sites on the Sabine. According to the advertisement, the planned towns were Fredonia, some sixty miles north of Nacogdoches, and Cotton-Plant, about forty miles from Fredonia. The territory, "lately occupied by the Northern Indians," was a tract that had been claimed by the Cherokees who first entered Texas in 1819-20. Edwards received a patent for the league including the site of Fredonia on 10 February 1843. On July 7, he was issued a license to operate a ferry across the Sabine at Fredonia, at a spot then known as Cotton's Crossing.

Fredonia was located on a road from north and south to Gilmer and Nacogdoches. The north road crossed the Shreveport-Tyler Road (Red Rock Road) near Pine Tree. Very little documentary evidence of the town has been found. No plat of Fredonia can be found, nor one showing the "2,000 lots" advertised in Edwards' 1839 broadside. Outlines of the town can be seen on early maps of the Edwards league. Deed records in the Rusk County Courthouse confirm the existence of Fredonia. Although there is no plat, various street names can be found by reading documents and maps.

By the 1850s, Fredonia had developed into a thriving town. It had three warehouses, principally for cotton, forty to fifty buildings including houses, and a cemetery. A post office operated there from 1849 to 1855 and from 1856 to 1859. Waide and Wilson owned a successful general store. Records for steamships exist, including the arrival of the *Buffalo* in 1848

Fredonia's advantage was that the location already had a well-known river crossing, Fredonia Crossing. In 1871, the Texas legislature granted the authority to operate the ferry to J.H. Jones and Henry Miller. In May 1884, the commissioners' court of Gregg County contracted for construction of the Fredonia Bridge. The bridge was used well into the twentieth century when a new bridge was completed in 1955 on the Old Longview-Kilgore Highway, Farm Road 2087. In 1870, the town was not listed in the post office directory. After the Civil War, a new settlement named Fredonia, formed by freed blacks, grew up about two miles south of the original town site.

Greggton - Willow Springs

Willow Springs was located in east central Gregg County. It was established around 1873 as a station on the Texas and Pacific Railway. In 1877, the community was described as a flag station with a depot four miles west of Longview.

In 1920, the town had a population of 180. It boomed after oil was discovered in the area in the early 1930s. The community's name was changed to Greggton in the early 1930s. A post office was established there on 20 November 1932, and discontinued 31 May 1960, when the services were transferred to Longview.

Greggton was named for the county by R.L. Hall. During the 1950s the community was annexed by Longview.

Harmony Grove School

Harmony Grove

Harmony Grove was in the north part of Gregg County between Seven Pines and Judson. The land for the school was donated by D.G. Sparks. During the oil boom the school grounds were fenced to keep the students from getting in the way of the oil drillers. The school would consolidate with Judson. For a time the consolidated school was known as Judson Grove.

Hughey

Hughey, on State Highway 42 and Farm Road 1252, six miles southwest of Longview in central Gregg County, was established around 1850. The community had at least two cotton gins. The gin owners were Williams Martin and John Hilbern. Martin's gin was used primarily for his cotton and was not for hire.

The small settlement boomed briefly in the 1930s after oil was discovered in the East Texas oilfield. At one time Hughey had a school, a Baptist church and several stores. The community later declined, and in the early 1990s only a few scattered dwellings remained at the site.

Judson - Lawrenceville

Judson is located in northeastern Gregg County, generally in the area of Judson and Seven Pines Roads. It developed around a Missionary Baptist church established in 1883 at a school known as Lawrenceville. Hiram and Georgia Whatley organized the church and gave land to build a building. The church (now the First Baptist Church of Judson) was named after Baptist missionary to Burma, Adonirum Judson.

Judson School, founded between 1873 and 1893. Thought to be the first building in what is now the Longview Independent School District.

The first school at this location was called Lawrenceville and was near the southwestern edge of the current Judson Middle School football field. Hiram Whatley taught at the school. The only public record that identifes the town is a Gregg County deed record mentioning a

Lawrenceville Cement Company. In 1870, the company sued C.W. Adams for a debt. An 1888 election place in Precinct 2 was at Lawrenceville School.

At one time the school was called Judson Grove after the Judson School had incorporated with the nearby Harmony Grove School. Judson School District combined with the Longview School District and moved all the high school students to the Longview facilities.

A post office operated at the community from 1890 until 1906. The first postmaster was Francis Whitehurst who operated the post office out of his house. By 1896, the community had Methodist and Baptist churches, two sawmills, a cotton gin, a school, a shingle mill, a blacksmith and an estimated population of 300. In the mid-1930s, Judson still had two schools, two cemeteries, several stores and a sawmill. The post office reopened and is still in operation in 2004. Judson Middle School and Mozelle Johnston Elementary school occupy the original grounds.

The Junction

In 1872, Longview gained another rail line. This track would run south and was to be about a mile east of the Texas and Pacific terminus in Longview (on Fredonia Street between Cotton and Tyler Streets). The exact date of the first junction depot is not documented, but an 1881 picture showed a modest building in what still appeared to be a rural setting. The area around this became known as the Junction, or the Longview Junction even though it was outside the Longview town limits. Soon another business area began to thrive. Throughout the 1880s, the railroad companies made improvements in the facility—a round house, a new well, the depot waiting room and platforms were improved with new floor and benches. In 1903, the Texas and Pacific made plans to build a two-story brick depot, an idea that upset the people of Longview. Telephone service was added in 1883.

The first Roman Catholic Church, St. Anthony, was built at the Junction in 1883. The Second Baptist Church (no longer in existance) was built on the north side of the I. and G. N. tracks. The Kelly Methodist Church (now First Methodist Church) organized the Junction Chapel.

There were five schools at the Junction, one Catholic and four private

Sam Mobberly built his famous Mobberly Hotel in 1884. The Mobberly

Main Street (Highway 80), Greggton

was supposedly known as the best hotel between New Orleans and El Paso. There were other hotels as well as boarding houses for the convenience of travelers and workers.

In 1904, Mayor Gabriel Augustus Bodenheim and the city commissioners annexed the area that included the Junction. This was a political move because at that time a Texas state law required a population of 5,000 for state approval for a town to sell city improvement bonds. Longview proper had less than 3,000.

As Longview continued to grow the Junction terminal lost its identity as a community as it merged with the town, but the train station is still there.

Killingsworth

Early records indict only that the Killingsworth Community was located north of the Sabine River. It was probably near the corner of Judson Road and Pliler-Precise Road, located at a site near what is now the northern edge of Longview, and was among the earliest settlements in Gregg County. Little is known about the origins of the community. It was probably named for John Killingsworth and his family, who settled in the area around 1850. A pay school reportedly was there by 1847. The school was believed to have been run by a Professor Gray (first name unknown). The Killingsworth Family Cemetery still marked the site in 2004.

Lakeport

Lakeport, an incorporated community on State Highways 149 and 322, just north of the Gregg County Airport and south of the Sabine River, is a residential development established after World War II. The community incorporated in the early 1970s. In 2004, there are a number of businesses, a church and a bank in Lakeport.

Liberty City - Hog Eye - Sabine

Liberty City is on State Highway 135 and Farm Road 1252, a mile north of Interstate Highway 20 in west central Gregg County. It was an established community before the Civil War. Portions of the extended area were known at various times as Mount Mariah and as McCary's Chapel, after two churches, and as Goforth after a local family. From 1902 to 1903, a community post office called Hog Eye operated in the home of B.F.

Chapman. Chapman had wanted to call the post office Sabine after the local school, but that name was already in use for another post office in another part of the state, and he chose Hog Eye instead. Sources suggest that the name came from either a local hog thief or a popular fiddler's tune. During the oil boom of the early 1930s the name was changed to Liberty City.

Little Beaumont

Little Beaumont, an oilfield community, was between Pine Tree Road/FM1845 and Spring Hill Road/Highway 300. Residents were oilfield families who moved up from the Beaumont, Texas, area with the opening of the East Texas oilfield. The community, like many others in Gregg County, has lost its identity.

Lewis Chapel Community

Lewis Chapel Church is located in north Longview at the corner of Airline Road and Church Street. The land was given to the Colored Methodist Episcopal Church by J.W. and Olive Newsom. Records also indicate the area was called Lewis Chapel Community. The oldest known pastor was S.J. Hynson who was there about 1915. The Lewis Chapel School was closed about 1943. The Lewis Chapel Cemetery is located near by.

New Danville

New Danville was believed to have been named by the Barnett family after Danville, Kentucky, the place they had lived before coming to Texas. Eventually

Gum Springs Presbyterian Church, New Danville, built in 1858 and burned in 1978.

the village would be known as Danville. Although never a platted community, at its height there were stores, saloons, a blacksmith shop, a cotton gin along with the church and school.

The church, Gum Springs Presbyterian Church founded in 1848, would later move into Kilgore and become the First Presbyterian Church there. The Gum Springs Church was named after a spring that was reputedly an Indian campground or village. The first building was made of logs and burned in 1857. A two-story frame building was erected on the site and was used until it burned in 1978. There is a large active cemetery at the location.

A Masonic Lodge was organized on 3 January 1852. The Masons and the Methodists would be responsible for early education efforts. The first school met in homes, followed by a co-educational school. The school was approved by an act of the Fifth Legislature of Texas in January 1854. This would give way to the New Danville Masonic Female Academy that would remain active as a day and boarding school until it moved to Kilgore in the 1870s. This school was the forerunner of Lon Morris College in Jacksonville, Texas.

A post office was begun as Rabbit Creek on 19 January 1850. The name would be changed to New Danville under Postmaster William P. Chisum.

The downfall of the thriving community was the railroad. C.B. "Buck" Kilgore offered the railroad gold to settle a few miles to the west. Many of the people, businesses and, most importantly, the school moved to the new town of Kilgore.

North Chapel

North Chapel, a farming community near Interstate Highway 20 two

Danville School

Pine Tree School, 1907

Back row, left to right
1. Alto Harris
2. Willie Fisher
3. Mr. Pace, teacher
    4. Feenie Bolton
    5. Lawrence Morgan
    6. Vonnie Harris
       7. Tom Harris
       8. Nina Stevens
       8. Clara Harris
         10. Ida Bolton
         11. Etta Bolton

Middle row, left to right
1. Ida Dee Harris
2. Marvel Fisher
3. Pat Fisher
4. Herbert Fisher
5. Josie Jones
    6. Mattie D. Fisher
    7. Rosie Thompson
    8. Annie Mae Little
    9. Ruth Calloway
    10. Ina Wood
       11. May Bolton
       12. Pearl Calloway
       13. Gertie Morgan
       14. Gladys Fisher
       15. Annie Mae Everett
         16. Mae Fisher
         17. Johnnie Lee Feemster
         18. Rembert Stevens
         19. J. B. Everett
         20. Clarence Everett

Front row, left to right
1. Jane Calloway
2. Loraine Fisher
3. Frank Harris
4. Lynn Smith
    5. Dick Calloway
    6. Henry Pace
    7. Marshall Pace
    8. Perry Fisher
       9. Sam Stevens
       10. Leck Wood
       11. Raz Calloway
       12. Kid Wood
         13. Jasper Morning
         14. Jerry Lee
         15. Howard Everett
         16. Tommy Everett

miles north of Kilgore, was probably established before 1900. In the mid-1930s, the small community had a school, a church, a store and a number of houses. After World War II the school was closed, and many of its residents moved away.

Omega

Omega was a rural community eight miles northeast of Longview on U.S. Highway 259 in northeastern Gregg County. It was probably established as early as the 1830s. A Civil War era map shows the road from Jefferson to Red Rock passed through Omega. By the mid-1920s, it had a number of houses and a school, which it shared with nearby Bethlehem in Upshur County. The school was consolidated with the Judson School in 1923. At various times several stores operated in the area. The Port Bolivar Iron Ore Railway had a train station and siding at a gin in Omega. After the railroad abandoned the line, a single car was pulled from Omega to Longview on Saturdays by a Model T Ford adapted to use on the rails. The community had a post office from 1853 until 1907. William O. Baker was named the first postmaster. During the 1930s oil boom a promoter, "Cyclone" Johnson, tried to change the name to Johnsonville.

About 1932, the Federal Aviation Administration set up a series of guidance beacons from Fort Worth to Atlanta, Georgia, to guide passenger airplanes. A tower in C.E. Plummer's backyard is one of a few that still stands. Plummer maintained the tower when he was in high school.

Although there are Texas highway signs that note Omega, the George Family Cemetery is the only physical part of the community that remains.

Phillipi

In 1852, there was a school located between Pine Tree and the later-to-be-established town of Longview. The community is thought to have had a pay school taught by Hamilton McNutt.

Pine Tree

William Welbourne purchased land in the Pine Tree area before arriving there in 1840. He would be the first postmaster of the little community. Welbourne's son William Lewis Welbourne owned the store where the post office was located.

Church tradition says the community was named for the large pine tree under which the first church services were held. The Pine Tree Cumberland Presbyterian Church was chartered in the Marshall Presbytery on 10 October 1847. It is the oldest organized church in present Gregg County. Joseph Castleberry gave three acres of the land to Cumberland Presbyterian Church for use as a school and church in 1948. Solomon Awalt was the first minister.

A log church was erected in 1850, followed by a two-story frame building in 1852. The building was used as a pay school and the Masonic Lodge Number 86. In 1858, a polygonal frame building was built that was there until 1932. In 1859, Dr. J.N. Allison built a large two-story brick house that still stands on Dundee Road. This house was considered to be a part of the Pine Tree Community.

During the Civil War Joseph M. Sparkman owned a shoe manufacturing business near Pine Tree. A slave given to him by his father-in-law was a shoemaker. He taught others how to make boots used by the Confederate Army.

Asa Castleberry operated a cotton gin at Pine Tree around 1900. At first the gin was powered by steam. After a year Castleberry used horse power to operate the gin.

This area would become incorporated with Greggton and later with Longview.

Pleasant Green

Pleasant Green is a rural community on Farm Road 349 one mile west of Gregg County Airport. It was established after the Civil War by emancipated slaves. The Pleasant Green Baptist Church, founded in 1871, served as the focal point of the community. In 1909, a larger frame building replaced the original church. In the

Pleasant Green Baptist Church – organized in 1871; built in 1909.

early 1990s, only the church and scattered dwellings remained at the site. Descendents of the original settlers still lived in the area.

Point Pleasant - Gilead

Point Pleasant, also known as Gilead, was located on old U.S. Highway 80 a half mile east of Moody Creek in northwestern Gregg County. It was founded about 1850, when a post office opened as Gilead. The name was changed to Point Pleasant in 1852. William W. Walters, who served as postmaster from 1858 to 1860, supposedly operated a stagecoach station during the town's early years. The community also contained the Possum Trot School and Moseley Cemetery. When the railroad came through the area in the early 1870s, it bypassed the town. The post office closed in 1871. Reportedly, about forty-eight families received their mail at Point Pleasant.

The Ridge

The Ridge, also known as Freedman's Ridge, is at the junction of Farm Roads 449 and 2751, two miles southeast of Omega in northeastern Gregg County. It was predominately home to emancipated slaves after the Civil War. The Pleasant Hill Colored Methodist Episcopal Church (later the Christian Methodist Episcopal Church), founded in 1870, served as the focal point of the community along with the Masonic Lodge. The church is still an active congregation. There is a cemetery alongside the church. Oral tradition about the church says it was founded before the Emancipation Proclamation. Land for the church building was given by J.W. and Olive Newsom in September 1877. The settlement was named for its location on a small rise. In 1911, the Port Bolivar Iron Ore Railway was built through the community, linking it with nearby Longview.

Roach

Roach was a short-lived community seven miles west of Longview near the site of what is now White Oak in north central Gregg County. A post office operated there from 1881 to 1882. At one time the community had a sawmill and a general store.

Rock Springs

Rock Springs, on the Old Kilgore Highway four miles south of Gladewater in northwestern Gregg County, was established by settlers from Arkansas in the late

Rock Springs School, built about 1848.

1840s and was originally known as Little Arkansas. An historical marker notes the site of a pay school, built by donated labor by settlers from Tennessee in 1849. The building was used not only as a school, but as a church and community meeting place. The building, which was used for church and Grange meetings as well as political rallies, is the oldest reliably dated building in the county. The schoolhouse was named Rock Springs for a nearby stream at a rocky ledge, and the community later adopted the name. An historical marker notes the site of the school built by donated labor in 1849. The building was used not only as a school, but as a church and for community meetings. The one-teacher school continued in operation until the 1930s when it was consolidated with Gladewater schools.

A cemetery is adjacent to the schoolhouse. The legend is that a housekeeper for the Brasher family was the first grave there before the Civil War as well as other unmarked graves. The cemetery adjoins an acre of land donated by Joel Smith on 20 July 1885 to Gregg County for a free public school house in the Prairie Creek school community. The land had been purchased by Smith's mother Charlotte Chisum Smith (widow of John W. Smith) and three of her sons, Samuel, Matthew and Melton, from Williams Roberts and Ira Johnson in what was Rusk County at that time. The earliest marked grave was an Infant Smith, daughter of Joel and Martha Dewberry Smith, born and died 18 July 1861. Another early grave was their daughter Arabella Smith (11 December 1866-3 October 1872). The first known fence was built about 1889 as this is the date on the cemetery gate. A new fence was built in 1955.

The first cemetery association was formed in the 1930s with W.G. Smallwood, Sam Smith and Mrs. Coma Timmons as trustees. This lasted a few years and was reorganized in 1955 with Doyle Brewer,

Sam L. Vernon and John Smith, trustees. B.P. Walker was elected president of the association with Mrs. Mable Brewer, secretary, and Mrs. Coma Timmons, treasurer, for a five-year term. The Rock Springs Cemetery Association is still active and holds a homecoming picnic and fund raiser the first Sunday in June each year.

Rolling Meadows

Rolling Meadows, on Farm Road 2087 just north of Kilgore, is a residential development established in the late 1970s. The community incorporated in the early 1980s.

Sabine Mills

Sabine Mills was a short-lived post office community near the site of what is now Rolling Meadows seven miles south of Longview in southeastern Gregg County. A post office operated there from 1878 until 1880. The small community, apparently the site of cotton or saw mills, was still shown on maps in 1882.

Seven Pines

Seven Pines, a farming community on State Highway 300 a mile north of Longview and twelve miles southeast of Gilmer on the Gregg-Upshur county line, was established around 1900 and named for seven large pine trees at the site. The area boomed when oil was discovered in the East Texas oilfield in the early 1930s; by the mid-1930s it had a number of stores and a population of several hundred, mostly oilfield workers. In subsequent years the town dwindled to a few businesses and the seven pine trees were cut down.

Shell Camp

Shell Camp was an oil boomtown near the Shell Oil Company drilling operations northwest of Kilgore in the East Texas oilfield in Gregg County. The community was one of a number of such settlements, or camps, that were built by the major oil companies or larger independents during the oil boom of the 1930s to house their employees.

Shiloh

The Shiloh Baptist Church just outside the White Oak area was founded in 1871. Gideon Christian, a slave owner from South Carolina, came to East Texas in 1860 and brought thirty-two slaves with him. After the Civil War a number of the ex-slaves, who also used the surname Christian, became landowners in the area. The church was established with the help of John Baptist, an African-American farmer and preacher. The church was the center of the community. A school was established shortly after the war. The one-room building was demolished in the late 1880s and classes were held at the church. In 1920, a two-room building was built and in the 1930s, a brick building was built. The school was closed in 1966 with the beginning of integration.

Spring Hill School

Spring Hill

In 1887, the Spring Hill School was built near a stream that came from a spring in a cliff. This was about two miles from the present school site. A two-story school-church building was built in 1897. A two-room building was erected in 1915, and with the oil boom in 1931, a larger building was needed. At this time there was no place for teachers to live. The board of trustees resolved this problem by building a teacherage on the school grounds. A modern Spring Hill Independent School District still occupies the land in 2004. Much of the area has been incorporated into the Longview city limits.

Summerfield

The Summerfield Methodist Church was organized prior to the Civil War on what is now Tryon Road in north Gregg County. Reverend B.W. Brown lived in the neighborhood and served as a pastor of the church. Brown, a state representative for Upshur County, was instrumental in the creation of Gregg County.

I.O. Clifton founded the Summerfield High School.

The Second Session of the Fourteenth Legislature of Texas passed an act on 9 March 1875, that read, "…unlawful for any person or persons to dispose of any intoxicating or spiritual liquors, by sale or otherwise, within two miles of the Summerfield High School, Gregg County."

In 1877, Summerfield was described has "having a neat church, a good school, and one of the best and most tastefully kept graveyards to be found in any county, as they have a man hired to keep it in perfect order." (*Texas New Yorker*)

Swamp City - Crews

Crews was also known as Swamp City, probably because of its location near the swamps of the Sabine River in Gregg County. It was named for Dr. C.C. Crews, a dentist in Longview. Crews donated the land on which the Crews Baptist Church was built. The town was founded by 1931, when its population was reported as 300. Oil provided the main industry and occupation of the inhabitants.

Teneryville

Teneryville, a community in northern Gregg County, was founded in 1931, when the Lathrop oil well came in. The town was named for G.B. Tenery, on whose land the oil was discovered. The site was part of Longview by the early 1990s.

Tryon - Winterfield

Tryon, a farming community east of U.S. Highway 259 North in what is now northeastern Longview in eastern Gregg County, was established in the 1850s and is said to have been named for Trion, Georgia, the original home of some of its early settlers. The Henderson family that arrived from Georgia had attended a school named Tryon and a church called Alpine. In 1881, the Alpine Presbyterian Church was organized at the community. Summerfield School was already in operation when many of the families arrived after the Civil War. The name of the school was changed to Tryon and Alpine Presbyterian Church was built.

The sanctuary of the Alpine Church was to have been where the cemetery is located but it was decided that the land was too rocky to dig a well. The cemetery was begun by the A.B. Wilkes family when their two-year old granddaughter, Maudie Dickard, died on 18 December 1881. A week later Nancy Jane (Mrs. A.B.) Wilkes died and was buried there. Families in the community asked to use the burial spot, also, and in 1885 the Wilkes's deeded the cemetery to the church.

Winterfield Methodist Church, located south of the Alpine Church, is also part of

Tryon School, c. 1914

the community. The Winterfield Cemetery is located across the road from the Church. The cemetery began on the farm purchased in 1879 by July G. and Martha Howard Garner. Land was set aside for a family cemetery upon the deaths of the Garners' nephew, Joel S. Bright, and niece, Jessie L. Webb, in November 1887. This family cemetery eventually became a community graveyard with more than 500 graves. The cemetery was maintained by family members until 1971, when the Winterfield Cemetery Association was organized. The site continues to serve the community (1996).

Winterfield Methodist Church Historical Marker: "This Church traces its origin to Methodist Camp Meetings held here in the farm community of Winterfield as early as the 1870s. The site of the camp meetings, which drew settlers from Gregg, Upshur, and Harrison Counties, was set aside in the early 1880s for worship purposes. Two small 1880s church buildings, sanctuaries erected here in 1929 and 1957, and other facilities including an education building have served the church. The congregation sponsors a number of outreach programs and activities and continues to provide civic and religious leadership for the community. Sesquicentennial of Texas Statehood 1845 – 1995"

Warren City

Warren City, on Farm Road 2275 in northwestern Gregg and southeastern Upshur counties, was founded and incorporated in 1952. It was named for the Warren Petroleum Corporation, which manufactures natural gas and is the town's main industry.

White Oak

During the 1880s, about 12 to 15 families lived in the White Oak area. Some of the men were employed at one of the three sawmills. As more families arrived in the area the need for a school became clear and a one-room building was built by T.J. Tuttle and J.E. Shelton. This building burned in 1885 and was replaced by one built by the same two men. Land was donated by Caleb Bumpus and Pleas Harris. The 1885 school was constructed between two white oak saplings. John Bumpus suggested the place be called White Oak. A larger building was built in 1912 — this time with two rooms. A Baptist church was established in the sawmill community about 1889.

Gregg County Events

Longview Race Riot of 1919

The Longview Race Riot occurred during the Red Summer, as May to October of 1919 has been called. It was the second of twenty-five major racial conflicts that occurred throughout the United States during these months. In 1919, Longview, a rural cotton and lumbering community in northeast Texas, had a population of 5,700; 31 percent were black. Racial tension was especially high immediately before the riot because two locally prominent black leaders, Samuel L. Jones and Dr. Calvin P. Davis, had urged black farmers to avoid local white cotton brokers and sell directly to buyers in Galveston. Then an article in the July 10 issue of the Chicago *Defender*, a sensationalistic nationwide black newspaper, described the death of a young black man, Lemuel Walters, in Longview. The article reported that Walters and an unnamed white woman from Kilgore, Texas, were in love and quoted her as saying they would have married if they had lived in the North. Walters, according to the article, was safely locked in the Gregg County Jail until the sheriff willingly handed him over to a white mob that murdered him on June 17.

Jones, a teacher in the Longview school system and a local correspondent for the Chicago *Defender*, was held responsible for the article, and on Thursday, July 10, he was accosted and beaten, supposedly by two brothers of the Kilgore woman. News of the article and of the attack on Jones inflamed tempers of both races, and about 1:00 a.m. Friday a group of twelve to fifteen angry white men drove to Jones' house. They were surprised by gunfire as they entered his yard and returned the fire as they fled. Three of the white men suffered superficial birdshot wounds, and a fourth man, who had sought shelter under a house, was found by blacks and beaten severely. Some of the white men went to the fire station and rang the alarm to attract more recruits; others broke into a hardware store to get guns and ammunition. An undetermined number then returned to Jones' house and found it empty. The mob set fire to this house, to the home of Calvin P. Davis, a black physician, to other black residences, and to a black dance hall in which they suspected the blacks had stored ammunition.

Early Friday, July 11, County Judge E.M. Bramlette and Sheriff D.S. Meredith telephoned Governor William P. Hobby, who ordered eight Texas Rangers to Longview and placed three Texas National Guard units in East Texas on alert. The rangers, however, could not arrive until Saturday morning, and Bramlette wanted troops in Longview before sundown Friday. Therefore, he called Hobby a second time, and the governor ordered 100 guards-

Believed to have been taken during the race riots.

men to Longview immediately. The guard headquarters was located on the courthouse square. On Saturday evening Marion Bush, Dr. Davis's father-in-law, was killed after he fled from Sheriff Meredith, who was either offering him protective custody or attempting to arrest him. Bush's death led Mayor G.A. Bodenheim to request more aid from Hobby. Hobby responded by dispatching an additional 150 guardsmen to Longview and by placing the city and county under martial law, beginning at noon on Sunday, July 13. Hobby put Brig. Gen. R.H. McDill in command of the guardsmen and rangers. McDill ordered a curfew in Longview, prohibited groups of three or more people from gathering on streets, and ordered all Longview citizens, including county, precinct and city peace officers, to turn in all firearms at the county courthouse.

At his request local officials named a citizens' committee to work with the military officers. The committee passed resolutions expressing disapproval of the shooting and burning and pledged their support to the military authorities. The rangers arrested seventeen white men on charges of attempted murder; each was released on $1,000 bond. Twenty-one black men were arrested, charged and sent to Austin temporarily for their own safety. Nine white men were also charged with arson. Not one of the whites or blacks was ever tried. Tension had subsided by Thursday to such a degree that Hobby ordered an end to martial law at noon Friday, July 18, and the citizens were allowed to pick up their firearms at noon Saturday. (Written by Ken Durham.)

Dalton Gang Bank Robbery

On 23 May 1890, the Dalton Gang road into Longview. Two members of the gang, brothers Jim and Bill Nite, had been working a sawmill north of Longview, and a third man, newcomer Jim Bennett, claimed to be a stock broker. The fourth man was Bill Dalton. They rode straight to the First National Bank. Jim Bennett stayed in the alley next to the bank and Bill Nite waited out front. Jim Nite and Bill Dalton entered the bank and put a note in front of bank president Joseph Clemons. Clemons handed over $2,000.00 and several hundred dollars worth of unsigned bank notes. The two robbers took the bankers as hostages.

Bank customer John Welborn, who had entered the bank while the robbery was in progress, and bank employee Josh Cooke, who was in the alley at the time, both gave the alarm about the robbery.

Gang member Jim Bennett, waiting in the alley, immediately began shooting. George Bukingham, who was in a nearby saloon, ran into the alley waving a pistol and was immediately shot and killed by Bennett. City Marshall Muckleroy heard the shooting and ran from the courthouse. He was shot and wounded by Bennett. Charles Learned, a local citizen, was shot and later died from his injuries. An unknown person who had joined the fray killed Bennet.

One story is that Dalton and the Nite brothers rode off with the bankers behind them on their horses. The hostages were dropped off about fifteen minutes later and walked back to town. Another source states Joe Clemmons prevented the cash reserve from being stolen by locking the vault as soon as he realized a robbery was in progress. Joe fled from the bank. In the alley he jumped in a large vat that contained lime. While the vat offered protection, he would die two years later as a result of inhaling the lime.

A posse was formed and rode off in pursuit. They were unsuccessful at apprehending the robbers. Bill Dalton would be killed in Indian Territory where he had tried to pass some forged Longview bank notes. Jim and Bill Nite were found in Guadalupe County, Texas; in a shoot-out with the law, Bill was killed and Jim wounded.

Jim Nite was returned to Longview where he stood trial and was sentenced to twenty years in jail. Later, he was freed on parole and killed in a gun fight in Oklahoma.

The Oil Boom

Oil was discovered in East Texas on 3 September 1930. The discovery well was drilled by C.M. "Dad" Joiner in an area that had been condemned by geologists. This first well was a mile south of the Gregg County line in Rusk County. Numerous earlier attempts at finding oil in East Texas had proved unsuccessful. The United States was in the worst depression of its history, but East Texas was booming. Other early discoveries were the Ed Bateman No. 1 near Kilgore and the J.E. Farrell-W.A. Moncrief No. 1 near Longview. Thousands of people were there to watch the oil blow in. The oil producing area was about forty-three miles long and an average of five miles wide and covered about 135,000 acres. Growth moved with amazing speed. During one week in October 1930, wells were being completed at an average of more than one an hour.

This production was unregulated and, as a result, there was a glut of oil. The price fell to ten cents a barrel. New wells were often allowed to flow freely, sometimes for days, partly due to lack of proper equipment. The Texas Railroad Commission, overseers of oil production in the state, recognized the waste because of overproduction and issued an order limiting withdrawals to 400,000 barrels a day. The Federal Court restrained the order on the grounds that the Commission had no jurisdiction over physical waste.

In August, hundreds of operators urged a general shutdown. Governor Ross Sterling ordered the field shut down to prevent threatening riots and violence and called in the National Guard to maintain

Mule teams used for hauling during the oil boom.

order. The Federal Courts were again appealed to and another restraining order was issued. It took nineteen proration orders and another Federal Court decision before the National Guard was withdrawn in December 1932.

Change in Gregg County was literally overnight. Many of the established residents had been worried about having enough cash to pay their taxes for the year, but lease hounds spread over the county quickly buying leases and rights for cash. As news of the original discovery spread around the country, Gregg County filled with hundreds for people seeking work. Every rooming house and hotel was filled. Private homes rented rooms. People set up tents and camped in cars. One hotel rented rooms in eight hours shifts. Many people slept in churches. Longview's population tripled in four months.

The 1931 spring was very rainy. Most county roads were not paved and turned to muddy swamps. Mule teams were used for the heavy hauling in many places. Miss Cora Mackey, county school superintendent, was faced with the problem of hundreds of new students. Other public facilities, law enforcement and health care were overwhelmed. Communities, old and new, had to deal with vice. Honky-tonks sprang up. Gambling and prostitution flourished. Gregg County was wide open to every conceivable crime. Captain Manuel T. "Lone Wolf" Gonzaullas and the Texas Rangers were sent in to control the crowds. Kilgore

East Texas Oil Field, Kilgore

had no jail. Gonzaullas stretched a 100 foot long chain down the aisle of an abandoned church and padlocked prisoners to the chain.

Eventually the situation leveled out. At the time of the boom, Longview was an established small city with a solid political base. Kilgore and Gladewater settled in to the surge of growth to become prosperous towns. Many people took their new-found wealth and moved away. Others stayed and spent the money in Gregg County.

The Great Texas Balloon Race

In 1978, the Great Texas Balloon Race was born from an agreement between Dr. Bill Bussey, D.D.S., a hot air balloon pilot, and Frankie Parson Riggins and Mary LeTourneau, Longview Mall managers. Bussey hung a Longview Mall banner on his hot air balloon to advertise the Mall opening and flew over Longview. Two years later, Bill Stoudt and Stroh's joined forces with the Longview Mall and the first-ever Balloon Glow was held on the Mall's south parking lot. The "balloon glow" was an instant success and became a regular feature at succeeding balloon races.

In 1985, the event outgrew the Mall parking lot and organizers moved the launch site to the Stroh Brewery grounds. The race was not held from 1987-1989, but returned with a new site at the East Texas Regional Airport where the event continues to be held.

"The Key Grab" is the most exciting race. Each pilot has one chance to guide their ball to a 12 inch ring on top of a twenty-foot tall pole and win the cash prize. As the race continues to grow in popularity, other events include children's activities, family entertainment, music concerts and food booths.

Places & People

Atkinson Pickle Factory

James Henry Atkinson, born in 1872 in McConnersville, Morgan County, Ohio, served as a teacher and by 1910 was a principal in Richland, Keokuk County, Ohio. By 1920, he had moved to Iowa, married Hattie Fisher and was the manager of a canning company in Brighton Township in Washington County, Iowa.

Sometime around 1921 he had relocated his family to Ada, Oklahoma, and operated a canning factory there. In late 1927, the merits of Longview, Texas, must have appealed to him and he opened a can-

ning company that later was the Atkinson Pickle Factory. The business was located at Green Street and the railroad tracks. The address later became 400 IGN Avenue. James and Hattie took up residence at 106 E. College Street.

On the evening of 23 July 1930, after an illness of three months, at the age of 58, James died in the Medical Arts Building at Dallas at 7 p.m. and was buried at Grace Hill Cemetery, Longview. Surviving children were Mary, Fred, Jewel and Helen.

Hattie continued to operate and manage the pickle factory. In 1933, at the age of 22, Fred was listed in the Longview City

Directory as an employee at the Atkinson Pickle Factory. By 1937, Hattie gave up managing and became the secretary-treasurer. M.D. Abernathy had been hired as manager and Fred was the superintendent. Later, Marvin D. Abernathy became the secretary-treasurer and helped the canning plant grow, which in turn was a ready help to the area farmers to find a market for their cucumber crops. Mr. Abernathy went on to serve as manager of the East Texas Exhibit Association and Director of the Longview Chamber of Commerce.

By 1941, the Atkinson Pickle Factory was called A A Canning Company, with

Fred as foreman and Marvin Abernathy as secretary-treasurer. Hattie, at the age of 55, was no longer with the company.

Before Hattie died on 1 May 1943, at the age of 57, the pickle factory had been sold. Fred was employed as a flight instructor at Jones Army Air Field in Bonham, Texas.

Camp Normal Industrial Institute

The Institute was a vocational institute for blacks. Israel Scott White, a Longview born attorney, became upset at the neglect of black patients in the local segregated hospitals run by whites. He persuaded the directors of the Camp Normal Institute to incorporate their institution into a hospital. White drew the plans for the hospital and found a black physician, Dr. Obra Jesuit Moore, to serve as administrator.

Cherokee Trace

The Cherokee Trace was a well-known landmark and boundary in early Texas. The trail was believed to have been established by the Cherokee Indians to create a link to other Cherokees who lived in eastern Oklahoma in the 1820s and 1830s. The Trace was probably used as a road for whites coming into Texas during the same time. A map dated 1850 showed New Danville on the road from Gilmer to Henderson. This road closely paralleled the Trace. The Official Texas Historical Marker (24 April 1970) for the Cherokee Trace is on FM 21 six miles northwest of Pittsburg, Camp County, Texas. The marker states: "...A tribesman with a keen sense of direction pulled buffalo hides behind his horse to press down the tall grass. Groups of Indians followed blazing trail, removing logs and underbrush, and marking fords. Others located springs and good camping places. After the road was established the Cherokees planted roses and honeysuckle which still mark the old trace..."

The Graham Manufacturing Co., Inc.

Buying fruit? Should you choose that sold in a basket or in a box? The East Texas basket manufacturers hope you choose a basket.

The Graham Manufacturing Co., Inc. began producing fruit and vegetable baskets, hampers and crates in 1901 in Longview, Texas, with Mr. Graham as president. In a 1926 advertisement, H.G. Simpson was serving as company president, T.E. Lacy as vice-president and treasurer and H.W. Norton as secretary and manager. East Texas farmers supplied the company with gumwood, usually sweet gum, but sometimes black gum. The farmers often hauled their wood to the factory with the rest coming by rail.

The logs were sawed into blocks up to 66 inches in length. These blocks were moved to a steam oven for about 24 hours. Each block was then placed on a rotary cut veneer machine to be sliced into thin layers. These layers were cut into strips and stapled into baskets. The middle of the block was sawed up to become crates. The drying process took two days to complete. Bushel and half bushel baskets were the principal products of East Texas basket factories.

Fruit and vegetable growers in Arkansas, Missouri, Illinois, Colorado, Utah, Idaho, Washington and Colorado purchased their containers from the East Texas market.

Harmon General Hospital

Less than four months after the United States entered World War II, Longview civic leaders, led by Carl Estes, publisher of the *Longview Daily News*, and by Grady Shipp, director of the Longview Chamber of Commerce, secured an army general hospital for the city. The hospital was built just outside the southern city limits on 156 acres of the James A. Holloway farm. Construction began in May 1942, and the facility opened with 1,525 beds in 119 buildings on 24 November 1942. The hospital ultimately had 2,939 beds in 157 buildings and a total of 232 barrack-type buildings connected by 3-1/2 miles of enclosed walkways. The facility was named after Col. Daniel Warrick Harmon, who had served in the Army Medical Corps thirty-six years at the time of his death in 1940. Col. Gouverneur V. Emerson, a twenty-six-year Medical Corps veteran, commanded the hospital from its opening until the deactivation process began.

In addition to the permanent hospital staff of over 700 who worked in the hospital's ten medical sections, Harmon also housed 270 Women's Air Corps personnel and two or three training hospitals of 300 people each. In addition, it housed German prisoners of war, perhaps as many as 200, during its last six months of operation. (A favorite past time of Longview citizens was to sit outside the fence and watch the Germans as they played tennis.) At its peak period, Harmon Hospital had a community of 4,000 to 5,000 staff, trainees and patients served by a railroad spur and depot, bank, chapel, newspaper, Western Union office, library and post exchange.

The hospital specialized in central nervous system syphilis and psychiatry, and was designated as a center for tropical and dermatologic diseases. As a result of these specialties it was unusual to have patients on the seriously ill list. Over 73 percent of the patients in 1944 and 1945 were admitted due to disease, less than 15 percent for battle wounds, and 12 percent for injuries. Only thirty-eight deaths occurred among the 23,405 military personnel treated at Harmon.

In June 1944, Harmon was recognized as a hospital for the special treatment of central nervous system syphilis. Patients

Harmon General Hospital, 1940s

School Days

Right: Unidentified school

Below: Longview Lobos, Basketball District Champions, spring 1957.

Above: Miss Minnie Poe's 3rd grade class, 31 May 1899.

Left: Unidentified school

School Days

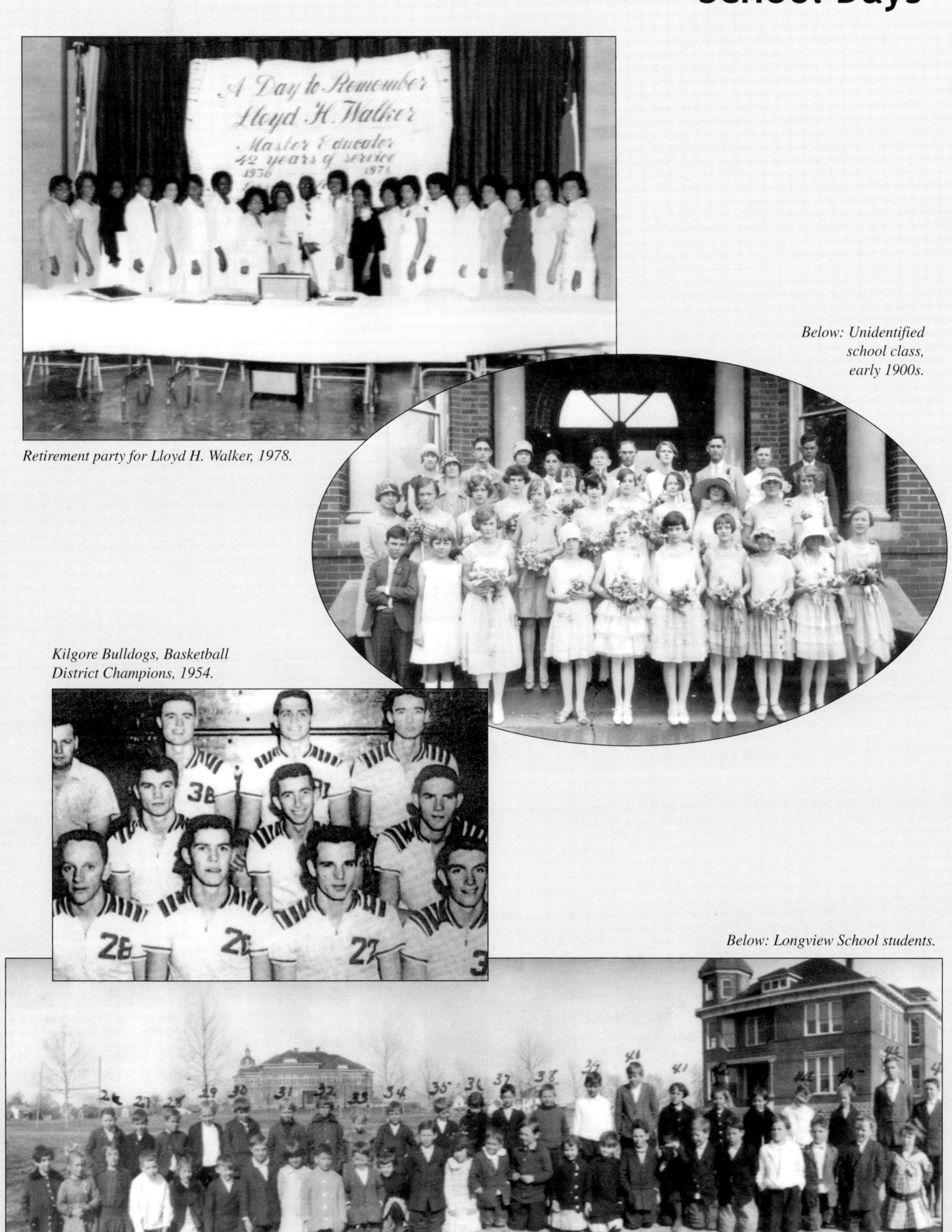

Retirement party for Lloyd H. Walker, 1978.

Below: Unidentified school class, early 1900s.

Kilgore Bulldogs, Basketball District Champions, 1954.

Below: Longview School students.

with the disease could choose either the traditional thermal therapy or they could volunteer for the malaria therapy. The volunteers were inoculated with malaria by anopheles mosquitoes, and resulting temperatures of 105 to 106 degrees killed the syphilis. Patients were then treated for malaria with quinacrine, which suppressed malaria but did not cleanse the blood of the plasmodia. Working closely with the Syphilis Center was the Laboratory for Imported Malarial Studies, which used malaria patients to determine which native species of mosquitoes could transmit malaria. These mosquitoes were used in the fever therapy. Colonel Emerson encouraged his staff to use other innovative medical techniques and drugs. Harmon developed an enteric-coated penicillin capsule months before the technique appeared in medical journals. Surgery was performed only if absolutely necessary, and early walking was encouraged. Harmon's pathological laboratory was recognized as the most efficient in the Eighth Service Command. Harmon physicians spoke to local, state and national medical societies, and they had thirty-three medical research papers accepted for publication in 1944 and 1945.

Harmon provided various recreational and entertainment opportunities for the patients — a gymnasium, tennis courts, swimming pool and bicycle trips. The hospital provided performances by USO-sponsored celebrities, by a patient band and orchestra, and at a movie theater. Harmon contributed significantly to the patriotism generated during the war. East Texas citizens contributed their time, money and household items to various needs at the hospital. Dozens of ladies volunteered as Red Cross Gray Ladies to provide games and reading material to the patients and to write letters for them. Other women formed the Red Cross Motor Corps, which ran errands for the patients and took them on outings. Harmon helped Longview to continue the economic and population growth begun a decade earlier in the East Texas oil boom. The hospital brought to Longview, for the first time, large numbers of people from outside the South. The Federal Housing Administration designated Longview as a Defense Housing Area, an act that enabled the city to construct houses and apartments during the war.

In October 1945, the process of closing the hospital began. The last patient was released and all wards were closed on December 6. In February 1946, Christian industrialist R.G. LeTourneau acquired the 156-acre hospital and all equipment and auxiliary buildings from the federal government for an industrial training school for veterans. The site today is the main campus of LeTourneau University. The hospital chapel has been refurbished as a memorial to the hospital personnel and patients. The chapel was awarded a Texas state historical marker in 1999. It is also a wedding site for many of the University's students. *(Written by Ken Durham.)*

Kelly Plow Company

The Kelly Plow Company began in 1843, when John A. Stewart started making plows in a shop in Marshall, Texas. In 1848, Stewart moved his business to a popular campsite for wagoneers, four miles west of Jefferson, Texas. Stewart, joined by his brother-in-law Zachariah Lockett, made plows and operated a general repair shop. George Addison Kelly joined the company in 1852. The firm became Kelly and Stewart in 1858. Kelly became the sole owner in 1860, the same year that he developed the Blue Kelly Plow, which later became so widely used in Texas that "Kelly" became a household word and "Blue Kelly" was synonymous with plow.

During the Civil War the Kelly Plow Company was a part of the arsenal for the Confederacy. By 1866, the enlarged business began to manufacture its own iron by smelting East Texas ores in a furnace two miles west of Kellyville.

The plant burned in 1880, and Kelly transferred the salvage to Longview in 1882. The new plant was built at what is now the corner of High and Cotton Streets. General agricultural implements were added to the line of products in 1882, and in 1907 the plant produced a full line of steel plows and tillage implements. In 1910, Kelly Plow was heralded as the largest and best-equipped factory of its type west of the Mississippi.

Robert Marvin Kelly (who would become the president of the Longview Chamber of Commerce) succeeded George Kelly in 1909 as president. LeGrand D. Kelly, another son, was co-manager and secretary-treasurer until his death in 1941. George A. Kelly, Jr. and LeGrand D. Kelly, Jr. managed the business in 1945. For a century the one-family business supplied plow tools to five generations of Texas farmers. The plant was in operation until the 1970s.

Kilgore College

Kilgore College in Kilgore, was established in 1935 through the efforts of citizens of Kilgore Independent School District and operated from 1935 to 1946 under the direction of the school district's board of trustees. In January 1946, invitations were issued to neighboring school districts to join a union district for junior college purposes. Seven districts accepted: Sabine (1946), White Oak (1946), Leverett's Chapel (1946), London (1947), Overton (1947), Gaston (1948) and Gladewater County Line (1951). A board representing these school districts would operate the college.

The College offers preparation for students who continue their education at four year schools as well terminal technical and vocational programs, and an adult education program in the evening division. The college's men and women participate in intercollegiate competition in football, basketball, golf, tennis and track as a member of the Texas Junior College Football Federation and the Texas Eastern Conference. The Kilgore Rangerettes, a nationally known precision drill corps of sixty-five coeds, was organized in 1940.

In the fall of 2000, Kilgore College enrolled 4,000 students, of whom 2,214 were full-time, taught by 145 full-time faculty members. Most of the student body comes from East Texas; in the fall of 2000, just over half came from Gregg County. The campus has hosted the Texas Shakespeare Festival since 1986. The East Texas Oil Museum, dedicated on 3 October 1980, the fiftieth anniversary of the discovery of the East Texas oilfield, is located on the campus.

The Kelly Plow Works, Longview

Kilgore Rangerettes

The Kilgore Rangerettes, the first women's precision drill team in the world, began in 1940 under the direction of Gussie Nell Davis, a physical-education teacher. College President B.E. Masters wanted an organization that would attract more female students, provide half-time entertainment for football games and promote physical activity. Masters brought Davis from Greenville, Texas, where she had established a high school drill team in 1928. She enlisted the help of local oil millionaire Liggett Crim to pay for the Rangerettes' initial costs.

The group made its debut at a football game in September 1940. Its fame instantly spread outside Kilgore, and within a year the Rangerettes had traveled to New Orleans to represent the region's oil business at the Lions International convention. The Rangerettes began appearing not only in East Texas but internationally as well. They are regular participants in such events as the Macy's Thanksgiving Parade and the Rose Bowl Game. The Rangerettes have made six international tours.

Members are selected each August at a two-week tryout camp, during which as many as 150 applicants vie for some thirty openings. Normally, sixty-five students make up the team, but only forty-eight members actually perform at one time. Their trademark routine is the high kick.

The Rangerettes have continued to wear essentially the same costume that includes a blouse, arm gauntlets, a belt and a short circular skirt in red, white and blue. A white hat and boots complete the look. The only alteration has been a slight shortening of the skirt.

Kilgore College opened a Rangerette Showcase on its campus in 1979. The exhibit, housed in the college's physical education building, features costumes, props and other memorabilia. A sixty-seat theater in the building provides films and slide shows on Rangerette performances.

Kilgore's Richest Acre

The "worlds richest acre" had twenty-four oil wells drilled in a half block of Commerce Street. Only one well still stands as a marker of the boom days. An historical marker also notes the spot.

Lake Cherokee

Lake Cherokee is on Cherokee Bayou in the Sabine River basin twelve miles southeast of Longview in southeastern Gregg and northeastern Rusk counties. The lake is owned and operated by the Cherokee Water Company to supply water for municipal, industrial and recreational purposes. Construction on the dam began in February 1948, and was completed on 19 November 1948. The lake has a capacity of 46,700 acre-feet and a surface area of 3,987 acres. The city of Longview diverts water for municipal use. The Southwestern Power Company circulates water from the lake for condenser cooling of the steam-turbine generating units at the Knox Lee Power Plant.

When the lake first opened people from surrounding areas participated in a lottery to determine who would get lots around the lake. Today, Lake Cherokee is a permanent home to many people and a weekend recreation spot for others who enjoy fishing, water skiing and swimming.

LeTourneau University

LeTourneau University, a private, non-denominational, evangelical Christian institution, is located on 162 acres in Longview, Gregg County. In 1946, Robert Gilmour LeTourneau, a noted Christian industrialist, and his wife, Evelyn, founded the school in the recently abandoned Harmon General Hospital, a World War II installation that they discovered when they visited East Texas in search of a site for a new manufacturing plant. With the help of Carl L. Estes, publisher of the *Longview News*, and other civic leaders LeTourneau was able to purchase the 156 acres and 220 buildings of the hospital from the United States government for only one dollar. They were not to receive clear title to the property for a ten-year period, during which the government could reclaim the property in an emergency. They agreed that no buildings were to be removed during that time and that on the premises they would establish a trade school for war veterans.

The state of Texas issued a charter to LeTourneau Technical Institute of Texas on 20 February 1946, and classes began on 1 April 1946. The institute accepted only male students, most of whom were veterans. During the first two years of operation the school was divided into an academy that offered the junior and senior years of high school and a college division that offered two-year trade school courses and a four-year course in technology. Students worked on a plan by which one-half attended classes three days each week while the other half worked at the LeTourneau plant. The alternate-day scheduling continued until 1961.

On 20 July 1961, LeTourneau Technical Institute became LeTourneau College, a coeducational, four-year college offering bachelor's degrees in engineering, technology and various fields of the arts and sciences. Also, at this time a master plan was developed, and permanent steel and brick buildings began to replace the old wooden barracks, which were either sold and moved or razed. The first permanent structure to be built was Tyler Hall, a men's residence hall, in 1962, followed by the Margaret Estes Library in 1963 and the Hollingsworth Science Hall in 1965.

In 1970, during the presidency of Harry T. Hardwick (1968-75), LeTourneau received accreditation from the Southern Association of Colleges and Schools. Hardwick also led in establishing a series of local and national public-relations organizations and saw the completion of the Longview Citizens Resource Center and the R.G. LeTourneau Memorial and Student Center.

Richard LeTourneau (son of the founder) returned as president from 1975 to 1985. He made personal computers available to faculty and students. Also, he completed nine major construction projects, including three new residence halls and an aviation facility at the Gregg County Airport.

This physical expansion of the campus reflected a growing student enrollment, which grew from 500 in 1964 to more than 2,500 in 2004. LeTourneau attracts students from almost all fifty states and from more than thirty foreign countries. In 1985, LeTourneau joined the Christian College Coalition in an effort to participate in student exchanges and other benefits. Other changes include changing the name of the college to LeTourneau University; initiating an adult-education program at sites in Longview, Austin, Bedford, Tyler, Dallas and Houston; beginning a teacher-certification program in secondary education; and offering the M.B.A. degree. Under President Dr. Alvin "Bud" Austin's leadership, the quality of the faculty increased as LeTourneau continued to combine technology and engineering and a solid liberal arts program with a strong Christian commitment. *(Written by Ken Durham.)*

Longview Community Center

The 1934 establishment of the Texas Federation of Women's Clubs created a force in Longview for women to pull together to improve their community. Ten

women's clubs combined to convince the Gregg County Commissioners Court to build the Longview Community Center. By 1936, a lot had been purchased at the corner of Whaley and Second streets and a frame building had been installed as a temporary meeting place. The community center was dedicated in May 1939. The member clubs provided furnishings for the permanent building and gained sole responsibility for managing the facility. The county commissioners support the facility monetarily and provide a part-time employee to help with the maintenance of the building. The federated clubs and others use the building for meetings. Seminars, recitals, rehearsals and school groups provide rental income. The Longview Community Theater holds performances throughout the year. The building was recorded as a Texas Historic Landmark in 1994.

Longview University Center

The Longview University Center is located at 3201 North Eastman Road. This branch of the University of Texas-Tyler currently offers courses in nursing, business, technology, liberal arts, math and sciences, and education. Graduate degrees offered include business administration, nursing, educational administration, public administration, engineering and tech-

nology. Students receive instruction from on-site professors, though Interactive Television, from the Internet or from a combination of these methods.

Magnolia Hotel

The Franklin Pecks came to Longview along with the railroad. Franklin Peck was a telegraph operator. After his death, his wife, Elizabeth Dodson Peck, operated a small hotel near the Junction. She purchased the Magnolia Hotel at the corner of Cotton and Center Streets. In the late 1870s, after Franklin Peck's death in 1877, Elizabeth married a second time to G.M. Tabler. She continued to manage the hotel until 1918, when her daughter Sharlie Peck and her husband, J.W. Dalston, took over. Their son, R.T. Dalston, managed the hotel from 1929 until 1935. The hotel was bought by the city of Longview and was razed to make room for a new city hall and central fire station. The hotel was known for the magnolia trees on the lawn and its good food. The charge for the best room and bath was never more the $2.50, even during the oil boom.

John Magrill and Magrill Plaza

John Magrill came to Upshur County (now Gregg County) from Alabama around 1846 with his brother Samuel D. Magrill.

John was appointed Confederate Postmaster of Earpville on 24 January 1862. He served as a courier in the Confederate States Army. In 1872, he sold land in what was later known as Longview Junction to the IGN Railroad. Magrill Street in Longview was named for him. In the 1800s, John was a dealer in groceries and provisions with his son-in-law William T. Whitelock.

Magrill Plaza, located in Longview, is a square bounded by First, Padon, Green and Grove Streets. John Magrill donated the land to all of the Negroes in Longview on which to build a church. The church was to be for all denominations. Today it is a public park.

Mattie's Ballroom / Reo Palm Isle

With the end of Prohibition and beginning of the oil boom, East Texas gave way to honky-tonks and night spots. Some unsavory and some respectable. Mattie's Ballroom at the corner of Farm Road 2987 and Highway 31 would become one of the many established at the time. The Reo is a landmark for Longview. The club featured not top country-western stars, but rising stars. A young Elvis Presley played there in the early 1950s. After 68 years, due to unforeseen circumstances, the Reo Palm Isle was forced to close in March 2004.

Mobberly Hotel

The Mobberly Hotel was built in 1884 by Sam H. Mobberly. After Sam H. Mobberly's death in 1910, the hotel continued to be run by his son Sam, Jr. The hotel was across the street from the Junction Railroad Station. The opulently furnished three-story building was the scene for grand balls, wedding receptions and other social gatherings. Each room had crystal chandeliers that were lit by kerosene. The rooms were furnished with carved poster beds and marble-topped washstands. There was a fireplace in each room. The furnishings were cherry and walnut. A circular staircase went from the grand ballroom to the second-floor parlor. The parlor contained an ebony piano. The other furniture in the parlor was made of cherry and ebony. A unique feature of the hotel was its battery-operated callboard. Guests could be notified when they were needed as well as provide room service calls.

The Mobberly was considered to be one of the best hotels between New Orleans and El Paso. The building passed its peek and was empty when it burned in 1961.

Port Bolivar Iron Ore Railroad

The Port Bolivar Iron Ore Railroad was chartered on 14 December 1910, to connect Longview with an area rich in iron ore near Hughes Springs in Cass County, a total of fifty miles. L.P. Featherstone planned the line to transport ore to Port Bolivar on the Gulf and Inter-State Railway, and by ship to Philadelphia, where he had made a contract for its sale. The capital stock was $50,000. The principal place of business was Longview. The members of the first board of directors were L.P. Featherstone, Fox Winnie and Eugene A. Wilson, all of Port Bolivar; L.C. Luckel and W.D. Myers, both of Houston; W.C. Brothers of Galveston; Lewis L. Featherstone of Beaumont; Murrell L. Buckner of Dallas; and T.B. Stinchcomb of Longview. In 1912, the railroad built thirty miles of track between Longview and Eno. On 1 July 1914, the Gulf, Colorado and Santa Fe leased the line for a period of five years at $40,000 a year. World War I halted further extension of the road. The line was abandoned in 1927.

Post Office Murals

Longview and Kilgore are privileged to have Post office murals created during the Great Depression to help keep artists earning money and as a way to bring art to the people. This was one of President Franklin D. Roosevelt's alphabet programs to help stay unemployment during the Great Depression. In 1933, President Franklin D. Roosevelt initiated the Public Works of Art Project, which paid 3,700 artists to decorate public buildings nationwide. Forty artists participated in the Texas program, which lasted six months before its funding ran out in the spring of 1934. A more permanent program soon followed and it was responsible for the creation of the post office murals. Between 1934 and 1943, about ninety-seven murals were done in sixty-six Texas post offices and federal buildings. By the 1990s, eight of those murals had been destroyed or lost. Texas' regional history and early settlement were chosen as subjects. Agriculture was chosen for Longview, and oil for Kilgore.

Markham Hospital

Markham Hospital, located at 418 South Center Street, was founded in 1923 by Dr L.N. Markham, physician and surgeon. It operated as a 25-bed private facility until his death in 1951. Louis Northcutt Markham was born in Longview in 1884. He attended Jacksonville Baptist College and graduated from Tulane Medical School in 1907. After his death his family continued to operate the hospital until 1971. Dr. B. Reid Clanton, Markham's son-in-law, established a pediatric practice in the hospital from 1957 until 1971.

There were 45 employees in all, including 16 doctors, 8 nurses, cooks, clean-up ladies and general help. Markham supplied living quarters to a staff of eight

The Rembert Theatre, 204 E. Cotton Street, Longview, as it appeared in 1929. One of the first Warners Brothers "talkies," Desert Song, *was showing.*

nurses, in addition to delivery room, emergency room, operating room, and lab and X-ray facilities, as well as facilities to treat contagious diseases. In 1930, the hospital received a complete remodeling job, including new paint throughout and new flooring. During the oil boom, Dr. O.W. Elkins referred to the oil boom increasing the population at the time that Markham served the city. After Dr. Clanton retired, the building remained empty. In October 1986, the hospital was razed. A landmark was lost to Longview.

Early Movie Theaters in Longview

In the 1920s, M. Tracy Flanagan was hired to manage the Rembert and sometime in 1927, he sold a half interest in the Rembert and the Elk, the only other theatre in Longview, to East Texas Theatres, Inc., a subsidiary of Jefferson Amusement Company in Beaumont. Jefferson Amusement was owned by Sol Gordon and his son Julius, who owned and operated about 70 theatres in Texas.

In 1927, Longview had two theaters, the Rembert and the Elk – and the Elk only operated intermittently until after the East Texas oil boom that increased population enough to provide a much larger movie going audience.

W.A. "Tony" Lanagan came from Beaumont to Longview in 1927 to manage the Rembert Theatre for Sol Gordon. Vaudeville, minstrel shows, touring acting companies that performed plays and even local dance recitals were offered as amusement. Later, silent pictures were added, which killed the vaudeville shows. Tony became part of the movement of union employees and introduced "talkies" to Longview. In late

1929 and early 1930, when the depression hit, it lured the unemployed to other parts of the country. Every Tuesday night was dish night at the Rembert and every patron was handed a dish to take home.

The old Elk Theatre was remodeled and opened full time as the Liberty. The Strand was operating at 104 South Fredonia. Neither theater had much seating capacity and were used to show low-budget quickie films that kept actors under contract and filled out the booking programs. Then the Rita opened.

Tony invented "grocery nights" in which he gave away baskets of groceries. This not only fed people who couldn't afford food, but promoted the local stores.

Tracy Flanagan opened the Arlyne, naming it after his wife. Ground was broken at 224 E. Methvin on 10 October 1938. The Arlyne was complete with art deco and air conditioning. When the work was almost complete, the *Longview Daily News* announced in a front page story that W.A. Lanagan was to head the Arlyne. Formal opening was planned for 24 May 1939. Opening day, the Longview High School Band led a parade through downtown. Grady Shipp, manager of the Chamber of Commerce, pushed the button to light up the building and trigger the giant searchlights. Don Cave, an interior decorator from Houston, had won the first ticket with a bid of fifty-five dollars. Tickets were 40 cents.

Remodeling work took place on the Rita and the Rembert just before the war broke out. New air conditioning, carpet, seats, projectors and paint made the places just like new. In early

1940, it was announced that *Gone with the Wind* would be seen throughout the country on a "road-show" basis, which meant that it would only be shown in a limited number of theaters on a reserved-seat basis. The cost of a ticket was much more in comparison with regular admittance. The Arlyne was inspected by an MGM official and chosen to show the movie. Attired in their best for this gala event, Longviewites loved it as much as they had in Atlanta or New York.

Longview became the scene for a big troupe of celebrities that came for the Fifth War Loan Drive. There was Johnny Mack Brown, Chill Wills, Gail Storm, Anne Jeffries, Rod Cameron, Bonita Granville and Edward Arnold. Other movie stars to visit the theaters were Tom Mix, Lee "Lasses" White, Jimmy Wakely, Dorothy Lamour and Gene Autry.

After World War II, movie attendance declined when the large military presence located at Harmon Hospital began to leave. Longview was not large enough to attract the "A" stars like Bob Hope, but we got Leo the Lion, who growled at the beginning of all MGM films.

The advent of television sealed the fate of movie houses like the Arlyne, Rita and Rembert. Ticket prices ranged from nine cents for children to 50 cents for a ticket after 6 p.m. at the Arlyne. Tony retired shortly after 1948, but came out of retirement to manage the River Road Drive In Theatre until he died in 1956. *(Information from Mayo Lanagan, son of Tony Lanagan.)*

Strand Theatre, 104 S. Fredonia Street. A crowd of Longview children eagerly await the start of a Saturday matinee in the early 1930s.

Gregg County, Texas
Family Histories

Patrons

Church of Jesus Christ of Latter-day Saints

Although The Church of Jesus Christ of Latter-day Saints has a long history in East Texas, it got its start in Longview as a Sunday School class, beginning in 1941. The class met first in the home of Zelda Alexander, next in the home of Sister Merrill, and then in the Labor Temple, where North Fredonia intersects U.S. Highway 80.

Church records show Howard Norton as Sunday School Superintendent in 1943.

Longview continued to show up as a Sunday School in the church directory until 1950, when it was listed as Longview Branch. The church address was given in the 1950 church directory as Labor Hall, with William B. Poesy as branch president.

To build the first chapel on South Green Street, the men cut timbers and made some of their own lumber. The women prepared food and served it hot to the men at the sawmill. Lumber was also used from two old houses. The members from Longview worked many hours on the church, as well as men from all over the district who donated time and labor. The women did what they could also. Joseph Lindsey was the supervising carpenter.

While making a tour of the Texas-Louisiana mission, Elder Bruce R. McConkie of the First Council of the Seventy (later an apostle in the church) held a meeting in Longview on 20 November, 1949, at which time he dedicated the chapel

of the Longview Branch. The released mission president, Glenn Grosbeak Smith, and the incoming mission president, Benjamin Leon Bowring, and their wives were also present at the dedicatory services.

Elder McConkie told the members that they "would see the walls of the chapel overflow." The walls did "overflow" as was predicted. Membership in 1957 was 400. Two houses on property that joined the land where the chapel was built were purchased to serve as classrooms.

When the branch was formed, there were about 50 members, including Bill Poesy, Charles Poesy, Annie Myers, Zelda Alexander, Blanche Denton, Beatrice Myers, the Mayo family, Ira E. Moss, Johnnie Bell Holly, and the Harry Edwards family. From Kilgore were Bertha Abbot, Gillian, Robert Dawson, Edna Cole, Joseph Hall and James Hall as members. The Longview Branch also included members from Nacogdoches and Lufkin.

The Longview Ward was established 18 October 1953, and it was in the Dallas, Texas Stake from 1953 until 1958. The Dallas Stake was created 18 October 1953, with Irvin K. Addison as stake president. Members in Longview had to travel to Dallas to attend stake meetings.

The Longview ward was in the Shreveport Louisiana Stake from 1958 until 1969, when it became a part of the Texas East Stake.

On 26 January 1958, Elder Spencer W. Kimball and Elder Harold B. Lee organized the Shreveport Stake, with J. Milton Belisle as stake president. President Belisle served only a short time and was succeeded by Karl Anthony Snow.

The Texas East Stake was organized on 9 November 1969, with the stake center in Gilmer, and members of the East Texas area, including Longview, were placed in this new stake. Gerald Christian Knackstedt was sustained as first president of the Texas East Stake. With the release of President Knackstedt in June 1974, Darrell C. Vickers was sustained as stake president.

With the completion and dedication of the new building located at 1700 Blue Ridge Parkway in Longview in 1978, the stake center was moved from Gilmer to Longview and renamed the Longview, Texas Stake.

On 28 November 1972, the church's committee on expenditures authorized the purchase of a 6-acre tract of land for the building of a new meeting house in Longview. The purchase was completed on 19 January 1974, for $45,353.00. Plans for the erection of a two-ward meeting house and stake center were authorized the following July. Bids for construction of the building were opened on 7 August 1974, and the low bidder was R.S. Bowers Construction Company of Salt Lake City, Utah. Six days later, the church committee on expenditures accepted the low bid and authorized the building.

A fund-raising social was held in Longview on 16 August 1974, and raised the last of the starting funds, which were mailed to Salt Lake City.

In September, a superintendent and his assistant arrived in Longview, and ground work started at the building site on Blue Ridge Parkway. A groundbreaking ceremony was held there on 28 September 1974. On 13 November the first footings were poured.

Final inspection on the completed building was held on 15 May 1976, and it was accepted by the Church.

A second Longview ward, indicating the continuing growth of the church, was organized July 1978, with Kent LeGrand Josephson as Bishop, Joe A. Rice as first counselor and Richard Oanschow as second counselor. Membership in the Longview ward,

Church of Jesus Christ of Latter-day Saints

Aerial view of construction of Church of Jesus Christ of Latter-day Saints.

Following President Loudon, Max J. Conlin was sustained as the new stake president, and his counselors were Charles R. Kennard and Charles A. Wagley.

Both the Longview First and Longview Second Wards were organized on 23 July 1978. Louis Muckleroy was the first bishop of the Longview First Ward, and Murray Conley and Daril Sparks served as his counselors. Kent Josephson was first bishop of the Longview Second Ward, with Joe Rice and Richard D. Ganshaw as counselors.

A third Longview ward was created in December 1980.

Longview Fourth Branch (Spanish) was organized on 10 March 1996, with Julio Merlos as branch president, with

before the second ward was created, was 688, with 248 families, 18 High Priests, 55 Elders and 7 Seventies.

Dedication of the building was held 9 July 1978. Presiding and conducting the meeting was the first president of the Longview Stake, Darrell C. Vickers. A stake choir sang "Oh How Lovely Was The Morning," and the invocation was given by Kent Josephson. The stake choir sang "After These Many Testimonies." Speakers were Gerald C.F. Knackstedt, former stake president; Max Martin, former bishop, and Louis K. Muckleroy, bishop of the Longview First Ward. The choir and congregation sang a song, and then Vernon Woodbury, first counselor in the Longview, Texas Stake, spoke. President Vickers was the concluding speaker and gave the dedicatory prayer. The stake choir sang "Bless This House," and William E. Grubbs gave the benediction. Conducting the stake choir were June Starks and Albertine Fowler, and the choir was accompanied by Debra Owens.

The total cost of the chapel in Longview was $1,050,000. It has a seating capacity of 1,800 with a full size basketball court. The building has 25,000 square feet.

In the last three years, the church building has undergone extensive renovations to update its facilities.

President Vickers was released on 12 August 1979, and Kent Josephson was sustained as the new stake president with Von W. Freeman and Norman Facer as counselors.

On 16 July 1983, the Longview, Texas Stake was divided, and the Gilmer, Texas Stake was organized with Von Freeman being sustained as the stake president of the Gilmer Stake, with Gary L. Hart

Church of Jesus Christ of Latter-day Saints, Longview, Texas

and Teddy R. Austin as his counselors. Max H. Martin was sustained as a new counselor in the Longview Stake.

President Josephson was released 17 January 1988. The new stake president was John F. Woodman with Kenneth Bell and William D. Craig as counselors. President Bell was released in 1994, when he moved to Utah from Longview, and Charles W. Schroeder was sustained as a counselor. President Woodman served until 18 January 1998, when he was released.

Charles W. Schroeder was sustained as stake president on 18 January 1998. His counselors were Charles R. Kennard and Max J. Conlin. President Schroeder's wife, Carolyn, passed away 4 January 1999, and he was released for family reasons on 17 January 1999.

Sustained as the new Stake President was Arthur Loudon, with Charles R. Kennard and Max J. Conlin as his counselors. President Loudon served until January 2000 when he moved to Louisiana.

Javier Alba and Norberto Herrera serving as counselors. Last minutes of a sacrament meeting for the fourth branch were recorded 23 May 1999, and the branch was merged with the third ward.

Some of the men who have served as bishop of the Longview Ward are William (Red) Posey, Harry Nimtz, Arley Barksdale, William E. Grubbs and Max Martin.

First Ward bishops include Louis Muckleroy, Robert Grebe, William E. Grubbs, Arthur Loudon and William D. Craig.

Men who have served as bishop of the Longview Second Ward are Kent Josephson, Joe A. Rice, Richard Ganshaw, Richard Johnston, Charles W. Schroeder, Peter Rouche, Michael B. Hill and Robert Ellsworth.

Bishops of the Third Ward have been Brian Christensen, Glenn Erwin, Max Conlin, Charles Wagley and Robert Johnston.

Units presently in the Longview Stake are the three Longview Wards, Marshall, Henderson, Nacogdoches and Lufkin.

First Baptist Church, Longview

An artist's rendition of the first building.

In 1872, a group of seventeen people met in a private home in Longview to organize a Baptist church. Reverend David Snodgrass, an itinerant Baptist preacher was the organizing minister; the first meetings were held in the homes of members. The Texas and Pacific Railway Company donated two lots at the corner of Fredonia and South Streets and a white frame building was erected in the 1870s.

The first pastor was Dr. A.E. Clemmons (1874-1881) of Tennessee by way of Marshall, Texas. His evangelistic efforts drew many people from the town into the church membership. It was a joyful group who worshipped in the building for almost thirty years.

In 1899, Dr. A.B. MacCurdy, a native of Scotland, came from Pennsylvania to pastor the church. He was the leader during the construction of the second building, a red brick structure completed free of debt and dedicated in 1901.

When the red brick building could no longer hold the crowds, a cream-colored brick church was built on the same site. This building served the members for

thirty-seven years as a house of worship. It became a favorite meeting place for all the people of Longview and was shared generously for civic affairs.

Under the leadership of Dr. John L. Whorton the church added three educational buildings and started three missions. The missions all later became churches: Mobberly Baptist Church, Valley View Baptist Church and Northside Baptist Church.

In 1945, Dr. W. Morris Ford became pastor. Under his guidance the church grew and the need for a new building was seen. This beautiful modified gothic structure housed a sanctuary, a chapel and children's building.

In 1957, nearly one hundred faithful members left to begin a mission which is now Oakland Heights Baptist Church.

Over the years interest in missions has extended to all parts of the world. Volunteer teams have gone to Russia,

Dr. John Lacy Whorton

Dr. W. Morris Ford

The red brick Sanctuary 1901

Kenya, Mexico, France, Guatemala, Belize and Brazil as well as many places in the United States to share their love of Christ.

A four-hundred-page history of the church was published in 1991. Many wonderful stories and pictures are included in this book. Copies are available for check out in the church library and at area public libraries. All members from 1871 to 1991 are listed in the appendix.

Over the years, twenty-eight pastors have served the congregation. The present pastor is Tim Watson, a young man who continues a line of consecrated ministers leading the church in preaching the Gospel of Christ here and around the world.

Right: The cream colored Sanctuary, 1912.

First Baptist Church, 1954

To God Be The Glory.

Pastors of
First Baptist Church
Longview, Texas

Rev. David Snodgrass	Organizing
Dr. Andrew E. Clemmons	1875 to 1881
Dr. Albert Bell Vaughn	1881 to 1883
Dr. William Harrington Dodson	1883 to 1886
Dr. George Washington Griffin	1887 to 1890
Rev. Adoniram Judson Wharton	1890 to 1891
Rev. A.E. Puthuff	1894
Dr. William Thomas Tardy	1894 to 1896
Rev. Franz Marshall McConnell	1896 to 1898
Dr. Alexander Bowles MacCurdy	1899 to 1902
Rev. Robert T. Winnifred Merrill	1902 to 1904
Rev. Asa A. Duncan	1904 to 1909
Rev. James Rankin Magill	1909 to 1910
Rev. James Eaton Hughes	1910 to 1914
Dr. Russell Johnson Pirkey	1914 to 1917
Dr. Asa A. Duncan	1917 to 1919
Rev. William Hutcheson Joyner	1919 to 1921
Rev. Oscar Lee Smith	1921 to 1925
Rev. John Lacy Whorton	1925 to 1930
Rev. Arthur A. Dulaney, Sr.	1930 to 1932
Dr. John Lacy Whorton	1932 to 1941
Rev. G. Kearnie Keegan	1941 to 1944
Dr. W. Morris Ford	1944 to 1972
Dr. William C. Everett	1972 to 1976
Dr. Charles L. Holland, Jr.	1977 to 198–
Dr. Kenneth Lane Hall	1987 to 1993
Dr. Harry Lucenay	1994 to 2001
Rev. Timothy E. Watson	2003

Elmira Chapel Cumberland Presbyterian Church
"The Church of the Helping Hand"

Elmira Chapel Cumberland Presbyterian Church was organized in 1897 to meet the educational and spiritual needs of the Spring Hill community north of Longview. The church's roots go back to 1887 when Spring Hill School was established in a one-room schoolhouse located near a bluff with a spring running below. This site was a short distance east of the present day intersection of Gilmer Road and Birdwell. Shortly afterward the Pine Tree Cumberland Presbyterian Church began sponsoring Sunday school classes in the schoolhouse. By 1891 Rev. W.M. Allen drove by horse and buggy from Marshall to preach once a month at Pine Tree on Sunday morning and in the afternoon at Spring Hill. These services continued and Spring Hill became a mission congregation or a "chapel" sponsored by the Pine Tree Church.

On 28 October 1897 the session of the Pine Tree Church decided it was time for the Spring Hill mission to become a separate congregation and a new church was born. James Rodden Castleberry donated 33 acres of land for the new congregation so the church and the school moved north to their present locations. James and his brother Richard operated the Castleberry Brothers lumber mill and timber holdings. Materials were also donated for building a five room manse and a two story church/school. The community provided the labor for the construction. The first floor of the building served as the church and the second was the public school.

The new church was named Elmira Chapel in memory of Elmira Pierce Castleberry, a charter member of the Pine Tree Church and the mother of the Castleberry brothers. Rev. J.M. Robertson became the first resident pastor in 1897, while also serving the Pine Tree Church. Later, when the school outgrew its space, Elmira Chapel provided land for the construction of a one story frame building in 1910.

The fortunes of the church, the school and the community changed dramatically when on 13 March 1931, oil was discovered in a well drilled on church land, one of the first in Gregg County. This enabled the church to build a brick sanctuary in 1931, a brick educational building in 1934 and a brick manse in 1935. A total of ten wells were drilled on the church's property. As a result the congregation was able to share its wealth by assisting other churches and supporting overseas mission work.

Elmira Chapel was the only church in the rural Spring Hill community until 1932. As other denominations established congregations they were welcomed and a spirit of co-

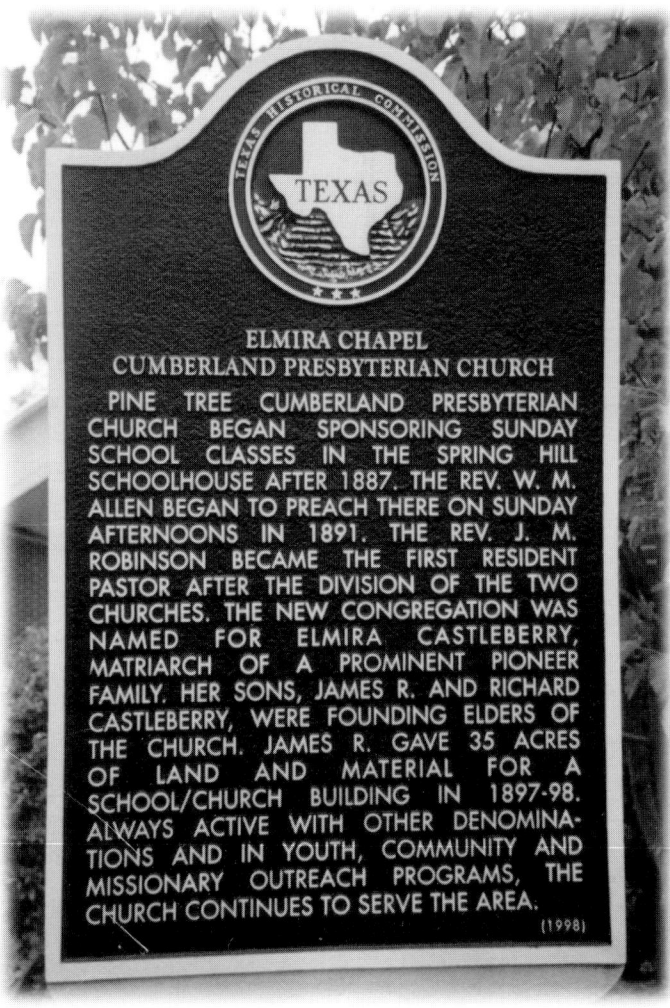

Elmira Chapel Cumberland Presbyterian Church historical marker.

operation prevailed. From the beginning Elmira Chapel and the Spring Hill School worked together serving the community with many people involved in leadership roles at both the church and the school. Throughout its history Elmira Chapel has been a serving congregation, participating in a number of local ministries and supporting overseas missions. Education, outreach, music and cooperation are the hallmarks of "the church of the helping hand."

First Pentecostal Church

Lewis Edwin Brown and his wife, Margaret, were early pioneers of Longview. Civic-minded, they often allowed groups, such as the circus, to set up tents on their acreage in the southeast section of the city. A religious group asked to use the property located on 13th Street between Cotton and Oden Streets for an Apostolic revival. They built a brush-arbor where they held services every night for several weeks in the summer of 1920. Among those attending the services were the Browns and their daughter, Annie Lou Nelms. When the Apostolic group left, Annie continued conducting services under the brush-arbor. Her first congregation consisted of her husband, William "Mark" Nelms, and their children, Marguerite, Madeline and Marcus; her parents and their youngest son, Paul; and a neighbor, Mrs. Gillock. With winter approaching, Mr. Brown realized they could not continue meeting under the arbor and deeded the lot at 208 South 13th Street to Annie. Annie and her family, including her father, known as "One-Arm Brown," built a small frame structure without a floor. He called it *Annie's Church,* but Annie called it *Jesus' Church.*

Annie Lou Brown Nelms

Preachers often came during the summer to preach revivals and many people would attend, but most of the time the only congregation remained Annie's family and neighbors. There were many times when it was only Annie, her children and her mother. Even when it rained, the family dressed up and went to the church and prayed, sang and worshipped as though others were present. Although there are no known records from this time until 1938, it is known that Annie Lou Nelms kept the church going and she remained a faithful member until her death in December 1972.

First Pentecostal Church, 210 South 13th Street, Longview, Texas

In a business meeting 2 December 1938, the church was called the Re-Organized Local Church of the Pentecostal Assemblies of the World (later called P.A. of W.), with Charles E. Sparks elected chairman and Mrs. R.F. Gillock, secretary. Mrs. Annie Nelms was elected secretary of P.A. of W., with Mrs. Gillock as treasurer.

Another business meeting was held 3 December 1938, to elect deacons and trustees to hold the property at 13th and Oden streets in trust for the P.A. of W., which had been occupied by the Pentecostal Assemblies of Jesus Christ. Those elected were Annie Lou Nelms as deacon and trustee, W.I. Brown and Charles E. Sparks, who replaced L.E. Brown (deceased). Elder Sparks was authorized to go before a Notary Public to have the above recorded. A receipt dated 5 December 1938, verified Charles E. Sparks appeared before C.C. Grayson, Notary of Gregg County, Texas. On this same date, Rev. E.D. Norman was elected pastor of P.A. of W. Rev. Charles E. Sparks was elected assistant pastor on 13 December 1938. J.J. Morrison became pastor between 1938 and 1948.

Annie Lou Nelms, as sole remaining Longview executive officer of the Pentecostal Assemblies of the World, deeded the property at 210 South 12th Street on 26 November 1948, to L.L. McClellan, W.M. Nelms, E.A. Camp, J.N. Hopkins and E.E. Geter, trustees for the Assembly of the Church of Jesus Christ of Longview, Texas. Rev. Richard F. Nichols, from New Castle, Indiana, continued as pastor until July 1962. The original building was torn down and a

new, larger building was erected in 1951. A brick addition was added on the south side of the building in 1958.

Rev. A. Odell Johnson, formerly from Missouri, was elected pastor, August 1962. He retired from this position in August 1965, because of illness. Rev. Robert E. Stark was pastor from then until 1970; Rev. Peurifoy was pastor in 1970; Rev. Aldon Phillips pastored next, followed by Rev. Donald Fulgium.

The First Pentecostal Church members voted to merge with The First United Pentecostal, 1901 Alpine Street, Longview, in January 1974, with Rev. Fulgium as pastor until his resignation, October 1978. Marguerite Ellen Nelms Grimes and Madeline Annie Nelms Terry, daughters of Annie Lou Nelms, were members of the church at this time. Over the years, Marguerite served the church as song-leader, secretary-treasurer and trustee. Madeline Terry is the last surviving member of the original congregation.

Other pastors elected were Thomas J. Bebee, 9 November 1978; Joe Shaw, 12 August 1980 until 1983; Earl Langham, 1983 until his death, 3 February 1988; Jerry Hovatter, 1988 to 1991; Leon Cross, April 1991 to April 1992; Kevin Prince, 1992 to 29 January 2003; and James Renfro, Jr., 20 January 2003.

The building erected in 1951 at 208 South 13th Street is still in use by a Pentecostal group, known as True Love Turning Point Church. *(Compiled by Mr. and Mrs. A.O. Johnson, assisted by the memory of Madeline Terry and documents in her possession.)*

First Presbyterian Church
Longview, Texas
1873 -2003

Known as "The Friendly Church in the Heart of the City," the First Presbyterian Church of Longview, Texas, will, in 2003, celebrate its 129th year of ministry on the same site. The coming of the railroad in 1871 marked the arrival of many pioneers coming to the Longview area eager for a church of their choice. Dr. W.K. Marshall, of Marshall, Texas, organized the First Presbyterian Church in 1873. The first church building was completed in 1874, on land donated by deed to four trustees of the Old School Presbyterian South, Longview, Texas. This land was on the corner of what are now Methvin and Center Streets. This plot of land was donated for the building of a church by the Texas and Pacific Railroad, which also gave land for First Christian, First Baptist and First Methodist Churches. O.H. Methvin, the founder of Longview, owned 100 acres of land in what is now the downtown area, which he used for his cornfield. After he sold his land to the Southern Pacific Railroad for one gold dollar, the railroad gave the four denominations land for the building of their churches. O.H. Methvin is buried in Longview's Greenwood Cemetery, the oldest municipal cemetery in town, his grave marked by a Texas Historical Marker. Another marker honors his memory on the walkway in front of the Gregg County Courthouse.

The first church building, which fronted south (Methvin Street), welcomed, in 1874, Rev. Dr. J.W. Wiggins as its first full-time pastor for $30.00 per month. The church was a white frame, of rectangular shape, with a portico, four columns and a high steeple in which hung the bell that still calls our worshipers today. The bell originally came from Walnut Grove Plantation south of the Sabine River, and was used to call the workers from the fields. The first little church was now within walking distance of the three other churches,

each established within three years of each other. By this time, where cotton and cornfields once covered the land, business blocks and neat cottages began to spring up. The First Presbyterian had seven pastors during the years 1874 to 1900. Although respect for preachers was sometimes great, payment never was.

The second church was built in 1900 on the same site. It was of red brick, English Gothic Style with two front entrances, stained glass windows, a tall steeple to house the original bell, and a manse next door. The second church had nine pastors, including Robert McAlpine Hall from 1921 through 1929, whose decendants are active in the church today. During the years of this church, the four churches often joined for socials on the lawn of the courthouse, and used this area also for Sunday School during the very hottest weather. It is interesting to note that First Presbyterian Church and the Gregg County Courthouse were both built on a foundation of quarried rock from the summit of Rock Hill, the highest elevation in the area (where the water tower stands today north east of the courthouse). The Gregg County Courthouse was built on

property across from First Presbyterian in 1875, and a new courthouse replaced it in 1897, serving Longview until 1932. In 1919, Longview saw its first paved roads, and the town's population was 5,173.

In 1938, some progress was made toward a new church home and educational building. The planned building would cost $70,000 and seat 600. It would be of Gothic Style, light colored brick with stone trim, beautiful stained-glass windows, and, of course, a very tall steeple for our special bell. The church was growing rapidly when Rev. Arthur Finley Fogartie accepted his call in 1939. Under his guidance, members saw the cornerstone laid in October of 1940, and a huge open house for the completed sanctuary, chapel, parlor, classrooms, and Fellowship Hall was joyfully held. The third church in 2003 has had five spiritual leaders: Dr. Fogartie, Dr. Thomas Hardy Talbot (1946), Dr. Stephen Lucas Cook (1963), Dr. William Daniel O'Neal (1977), Rev. Jonathan Edward Jehorek (1996). The First Presbyterian Church was honored with a Texas Historical Marker in 1994. *(Written by Carolyn C. Lindsey, Historian.)*

First Presbyterian Church, Longview, Texas

First United Methodist Church
Longview

Bell tower, 2004, a downtown landmark since 1952. (Submitted by Van Craddock.)

First United Methodist Church has a rich history that actually predates Longview. From that humble beginning in the log "meeting house" of the 1850s, First Methodist today serves 2,300 members with modern facilities covering a downtown city block.

Since 1874, when the railroad deeded land to what was then called the Methodist Episcopal Church South, First Methodist has shared the "Good News" from its present site at Fredonia and Whaley streets in downtown Longview.

The original one-room log meeting house was located at the east end of what is now College Street. In addition to the Methodists, other congregations used the log house as well. The property was deeded to the Methodist Episcopal Church South in 1853.

The log house eventually was abandoned and a frame building erected at Earpville. Early Methodists told the story about hogs occasionally disturbing the services by squealing and grunting under the building. (Long poles were stored under the building to move the animals before each service).

In 1874, a new brick church building (one of the first brick churches in Texas)

was built on the present downtown site. The church grew rapidly and in 1894 built its first parsonage.

By 1900, that structure had been outgrown. A new building was constructed thanks to the efforts of member G.A. Kelly, who organized the fund drive and served as architect and contractor. In gratitude, the church was named Kelly Memorial Methodist Church.

With the oil boom came more growth. A $60,000 education building was added and the church boasted 1,900 members. In 1936, at the Kelly family's request, the church was renamed First Methodist.

In 1950, bids were taken for a new sanctuary. Final service was held in Kelly Memorial on July 9th that year. The congregation met in the Arlyne Theatre during construction of the new facility, which was opened on 2 March 1952.

The First Methodist sanctuary was opened for services on 2 March 1952. (Submitted by Van Craddock.)

The half-million dollar children's building was dedicated in September 1956, and in the late 1950s the School for Little Children became a reality. A major youth/office wing was opened in the 1980s.

In October 2002, First Methodist consecrated its 19,252-square-foot Faith Center "to the glory of God." Part of a $5.6-million "Building in Faith" building and renovation program, the center includes a fellowship hall seating 700, kitchen, basketball court, stage, office and smaller meeting room.

Also included in the "Building in Faith" program were remodeling of the sanctuary, new 52-rank pipe organ, remodeled children's building and nursery, and conversion of the former fellowship hall into a music suite.

First Methodist has a place for everyone. There are active, vibrant ministries for adults, youth, singles and seniors. Sunday

worship is 8:30 a.m., 10:50 a.m. and 6 p.m. A nursery is provided for all activities. At this writing, Dan L. Miller is senior pastor; associate pastors are David Lindwall and Jerry Turner.

First Methodist's Faith Center, 2004, consecrated "to the glory of God" in October 2002. (Submitted by Van Craddock.)

First Methodist's mission statement says, in part, "We believe that the primary task of the church is to reach out into the world and bring persons in Christ's church; to relate them to God; to nurture them and equipment them to live as disciples ..."

For more than 150 years, First United Methodist Church has been "Stepping Out in Faith" by sharing God's love in Longview and around the world.

Known for many years as Kelly Memorial, this building served the congregation from 1900 to 1950. Shown at far right is Baracca Hall, completed in the fall of 1909. (Submitted by Van Craddock.)

A worship service in the First Methodist Sanctuary, 2003. (Submitted by Van Craddock.)

First United Pentacostal Church

First United Pentecostal Church, 200 Melba Avenue, Gladewater, Texas

The roots of the Gladewater First United Pentecostal Church, 200 Melba Avenue, go back to 1920 when Rev. Jessie Havard conducted a revival in the Rock Springs School House, located about three miles south of Gladewater just off the Old Tyler Highway on the Old Kilgore Highway. James Crawford Vernon was the teacher at this school. He was also a doctor and minister.

In October 1920, this group of people met in the Friendship Community Baptist Church for a revival. They also held services in the home of James and Nancy Warren in the community.

Soon C.W. "Charlie" Pounders gave land in the Friendship Community for the Pentecostal believes to build a church. The church was built in 1920-1921 and they called it "Mars Hill." This property was located on the corner of the Old Tyler Highway and County Road 3110. James T. (Jim) Warren had a team of mules and a log wagon. He cut the timber and hauled the logs to the sawmill to be made into lumber for the new building. The men of the community joined together and the "Mars Hill" church became a reality. On the corner, joining the church property, was Lane's Store and some small tourist cabins. Rev. Scott Sharp was the first pastor. Another pastor was Rev. Lewis Morrison. By 1931, Rev. E.J. Briggs was the pastor and continued there for the next eight years.

By the mid to late 1930s, some of the families of the church had moved into Gladewater to find means other than farming to support their families. They began having services under a big oak tree at the home of Lonnie and Fannie Hosch. The big oak tree still stands at 208 LaFayette Street behind Gladewater National Bank.

Shortly thereafter, a building on the corner of North Main and West Gay Avenue, formerly the "First And Last Chance Café," was rented. They continued having services at this location until the present building was constructed.

In March of 1941, the property on 200 Melba Avenue was purchased to build the church. The "Mars Hill" church building was torn down and the materials, including the windows and the floor joists, were used to build the present building. From pictures of the Mars Hill Church, the construction of the present building was a replica of the Mars Hill Church. The brick, new windows and other improvements came much later. Rev. L.J. Hosch, Sectional Elder of the Pentecostal Assemblies of Jesus Christ, was overseer for the construction of the building.

The Pentecostal Assemblies of Jesus Christ and The Pentecostal Church Incorporated merged in 1945 forming the United Pentecostal Church International.

The new church building was completed by late 1941. Rev. U.A. Massey was the first pastor in this new location. Ethel Moore Proctor was the first church secretary. Some of the former pastors were Rev. J.T. Warren, Rev. Eldridge Lewis and Rev. L.L. Stevens.

Rev. C.B. Warren became pastor of this congregation 12 April 1960. Since his pastorate began, the church building has been completely remodeled, ajoining properties were purchased and a nice fellowship hall and classrooms have been built.

Gladewater First Baptist Church

First Baptist Church, probably the oldest church in the area, dates back to 1844-45 when the church was located in the Bethel Community, one and one-half miles northeast of Gladewater. After holding a brush arbor meeting, a Reverend Raymond organized the Bethel Baptist Church. Charter members included: Mr. and Mrs. Mase Mosley, Mr. and Mrs. Jarrett Dean, Mr. and Mrs. A.M. Phillips, Mr. and Mrs. B.M. Bozman, Mr. and Mrs. J.K. Armstrong. Also listed were Mr. and Mrs. P.M. Brown, Mr. and Mrs. O.B. Talley, and Mrs. A.E. Jeter. After the Civil War, a frame building replaced the log building. They changed the name of the church to New Bethel Baptist Church.

For some twenty to thirty years, no information was kept concerning pastors. Since there was no regular pastor, preaching was at irregular intervals. A man known as Brother Ferrell was pastor of the church during the Civil War years (1861-1865). Other pastors who served during the early years (only last names are known for some of these men) were Brother H.B. Pender, Brother J.R. Christian, Brother Ray, Brother Goode, Rev. J.R. Christian (second pastorate). Also serving were Dr. McClelland, Rev. Oscar Ferrell, Rev. Daniels, Williams, Gilliam, Rouse, Hayes, Drewry, L.A. Willingham, Sam Dollahite, Green, Elder, L.M. Martin and Glenn Nefus.

L.J. Everett donated three lots (the present church location on Dean and Upshur Avenue), and a frame building was constructed on this property. They changed the name of the church to First Baptist between 1888-1894.

When Dr. G.E. Ellis was called as pastor in 1931, he moved to Gladewater with his wife, Maude, and children, Carlton and Eldene. Evidence of growth during his pastorate was the addition of almost three hundred members in eighteen months.

Members voted to demolish the old church and erect a larger Spanish style building in 1932. Dr. Ellis continued as pastor until his retirement in 1944.

In 1938, Maye Bell Taylor was sent by the Foreign Mission Board of the Southern Baptist Convention, to serve in Brazil. The church voted to support her financially, and continued to do so until her retirement in 1973. A scholarship to honor her was set up with funds from the sale of the church lake lot. Maye Bell died in 1983, leaving money in her will for this scholarship. It continues to be given in her memory each year to provide education for a seminary student in Recife, Brazil.

Ben R. Stripling came to Gladewater with his wife Lorene, son Paul and daughter Carolyn, when he accepted the pastorate in 1944. The next minister, Irby D. Bates, his wife Virginia, and children, John and Ann, joined the church in 1957. A new auditorium was built in 1962. B.F. Risinger, wife Jan, and sons, Mark and Andrew, came to Gladewater in 1971. The Family Life Center was constructed in the 1970s. Dr. Prentis McGee, wife Faye, and children, David, Susan, Donna and John, joined the church in 1980, when he became pastor.

In April 1982, the Pulpit Search Committee invited Dr. Larry Aultman to preach. He, his wife Donna, and children Jessica and Joel, accepted the call and served the church from 1982 to 1987.

Two scholarships were established during his tenure: the Eloyse Bruce Scholarship (for students attending East Texas Baptist College) was instituted in her memory in 1986. In April 1987, the Phillips Scholarship was set up through a gift of $5,000.00 at the death of Mrs. Jewel Phillips. The memorial was given in honor of her parents, Mr. and Mrs. Alfred Mason Phillips, founding members of the first church organized in the Bethel Community.

Roy Taylor, wife Dora, and children, Michael and Melissa, moved to Gladewater when he accepted the pastorate in 1988. Aubrey Pate, and wife Norma, came to our church in 1989, when he became Minister to the Senior Adults.

In 1995, the church celebrated its 150th birthday (sesquicentennial). The church invited former staff and members to help celebrate this event. They blessed all with messages and encouragement, both in word and in music.

Ellis Hayden, wife Jackie, and children, Brigette, Jamie and Lance, came to Gladewater in April 1998, after he accepted the pastorate. He continues in that position as this is written, March 2004. The church has organized three missions: Emmanuel Baptist Church in White Oak, the Union Grove Mission (Union Grove Baptist Church) in 1950 and the Greenway Mission (Highway 271) in 1952. This church, known as Gladeview Baptist Church, is now located on Culver Street.

First Baptist Church conducted a "United We Build" Program in 1999 to raise funds to renovate our facilities. A total of 1.3 million dollars has been raised to date. We are presently waiting (not too patiently) to begin this process. When finished, it will be handicap accessible and refurbished in every area. *(Written by Georgia Ruth Johnston.)*

FIRST BAPTIST CHURCH
GLADEWATER, TX

Celebrating 160 years of Ministry
1844 to 2004 and beyond

BAPTIST SUNDAY SCHOOL, GLADEWATER, TEXAS,
1922

Oakland Heights Baptist Church

In 1956, a mission committee was formed by the First Baptist Church of Longview. Rev. David A. Day was hired as the church planner. Bramlette Elementary School was the sight of the first Sunday service on 25 August 1957. The first deacons were Ben Hauk, Wayman B. Norman, J.R. Shaw, Cecil Ware and John Williamson.

Land was secured near the corner of Judson Road and Eden Drive from Mr. and Mrs. J.O. Akin. The church continued to meet at Bramlette until the first building was completed in August 1958. The building included a chapel and a two-story west education wing that faced Eden Drive. Judson Road was not curbed nor did it have four lanes, and Eden Drive was a narrow black-topped street.

It became officially the Oakland Heights Baptist Church on 1 January 1961. During this time Thomas Welch, Jr. was the Sunday School director who led the education program.

David Day resigned, and Don Berry came as the next pastor. To accommodate the growth to 559 members, a three-story education building was completed on the east side of the chapel. Don Berry stayed until 1963.

Dr. Lavonn Brown came as the third pastor in January 1964. During Dr. Brown's tenure the large sanctuary facing Judson Road was constructed and dedicated in December 1966. Dr. Brown served until January 1970.

Dr. Gene Petty became the fourth pastor and served from 1970 until 1975. During these years the area around the church began to experience commercial growth and the church became well established.

Thomas J. Monroe became the fifth pastor in March 1976, and served until February 1984. During this time the Family Life Center was built across Judson Road and was completed in 1980.

After retiring from First Baptist Church in Greggton, Brother and Mrs. James Dixon came to Oakland Heights. In 1980, Brother Dixon became the Minister of Pastoral Care.

The sanctuary built in 1966.

Dr. William Jack Fritts came as pastor in August 1984. During his ministry Oakland Heights increased in mission ministry, and the mission statement, "To know Christ and to make Him known," was developed. In September 1992, Dr.

Fritts felt that the goals he had set when coming to Oakland Heights had been accomplished and submitted his resignation.

Dr. Earl Powell served as pastor from October 1993, until June 1996.

In February 1997, Rev. Thomas Rae Roberson came from Moscow, Idaho, as the eighth pastor. He is a Bible scholar with emphasis on evangelism and missions.

In 1995, Brother Dixon felt a need to retire from his responsibilities, and David Lawson accepted the job as Pastor of Pastoral Care.

Mother's Day Out was begun in 1971, and it evolved into the Child Development Center. In 1980, the Family Life Center staff began the Summer Day Camp and the fall After School Care.

Oakland Heights has always had an excellent music program that included many talented volunteers. During the beginning years Dr. Wayman Norman directed the music and Jessie Norman was the pianist. The long time organist, Carl Bradley, spent a great deal of time getting the pipe organ made. He later upgraded it and added Rogers electronic pipes.

In September 2003, Oakland Heights sponsored a mission called Life Point. At least sixty people from Oakland Heights went to support this new concept led by the former youth minister, Brian Shobert.

We are blessed with overflowing parking lots and many other growth needs with a membership of 2,550. The steady growth and central location of Oakland Heights furnish the potential of continued ministry to Longview and the surrounding territory.

The 1958 chapel and first education wing.

Right:
In 1962 a three story education wing was added on the east side of the chapel.

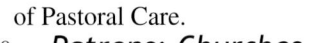

Pine Tree Cumberland Presbyterian Church

Pine Tree Cumberland Presbyterian Church, 1805 Pine Tree Road, Longview, Texas, 2003

On 10 October 1847, a group of people gathered together sheltered by the branches of a large pine tree. They were preparing to create an enduring symbol of their faith in God – they were organizing a new church.

This group became the charter members of the Pine Tree Cumberland Presbyterian Church. Those fifteen were John Rodden, Mrs. Amelia Rodden, J.T. Echols, Mrs. Martha Echols, Mrs. Ann E. Awalt, Jessie Freeze, Margaret Freeze, Milton Starnes, Ann Starnes, Benjamin Fuller, Mary Fuller, James R. White, J.W. Barnes, J.T. Castleberry and Mrs. Elmira Castleberry.

The organizing pastor of this church was the Reverend Solomon F. Awalt. He served as pastor of the church from 1847 until 1872. Rev. Awalt died in 1890 and was buried somewhere in the West. However, by order of the Marshall Presbytery, his body was moved to the Fisher Cemetery in the Pine Tree community in 1904.

One of the first concerns of the new church was the erection of a permanent structure to serve as both a house of worship and as a school. Joseph Castleberry deeded three acres of land to "Cumberland Presbyterian Church" to be used "for church and school purposes." An additional three acres of land was donated in 1850 by a Mr. Hamilton. A small log building was built in 1850 and was used for both church services and school classes until 1857 when it was replaced by a hexagon-shaped frame building. This served as church, school and landmark for 74 years.

In 1932, a brick building replaced the old hexagonal structure. It contained a large sanctuary, nine Sunday school rooms, an assembly room, kitchen and pastor's study. The first service in the new building was held on Thanksgiving Day, 24 November 1932. The total cost of the structure was around $8,750. It was dedicated debt-free on 11 December 1932.

Until 1932, there was no division between church and school property. Along with the oil boom came the need for larger educational facilities. The church deeded half of its property to the Pine Tree Schools. This property is the site of the present Pine Tree Intermediate School.

A new educational wing was added to the structure in 1950 giving the building its present form. Many improvements to both the interior and exterior have been made through the years. Notable among these are the beautiful stained glass windows, installed in the sanctuary in 1981-1982, made by church members Betty Peterson, Mabel Toler, Lucille Stevenson and then pastor Charles Petty.

Today, 156 years after the founding, the Pine Tree Cumberland Presbyterian Church remains a vital part of its community serving the spiritual needs of all ages and groups. It stands as a monument to the faith of those who gathered under the branches of a pine tree to begin a church. It is the oldest church in Gregg County and is also one of the oldest Protestant churches in continuous operation in the state of Texas.

Pine Tree Cumberland Presbyterian Church, 1857

Bethel Baptist Church

The Rev. Richard Perry and nine deacons organized this church in 1874. Services were held under a brush arbor on land donated by Rev. Perry and his wife, Betty, until a sanctuary was erected later that year. A Sunday School was formed in 1875. A new church building was erected in 1884 and in 1906. In 1890, a women's missionary society and a youth association were formed. The sanctuary built in 1906 was replaced by a fourth sanctuary in 1956. A junior missionary society was organized in 1958. Bethel is the oldest predominantly Black Baptist church in Longview and was the only brick (Black) Baptist church in the Texas-Louisiana district for a number of years. Sightseers would often tour the church and comment on its stained glass windows and pulpit furniture. Rev.

E.C. Hawkins was called to pastor in May 1952, and under his administration the present sanctuary was built. The Rowena Brown Fellowship Hall was added to the sanctuary in 1972. Mr.

Bethel Baptist Church, 323 South Court Street, Longview, Texas

Bethel Baptist Church, Longview, 1906

Marion Johnson donated property located on Luckett Street to Bethel and the Church later purchased property in front of the Church, from Court Street to High Street. An historical marker has been placed at the present location. Through the 129 years of Bethel's existence, nineteen pastors have served the congregation.

St. Mark Christian Methodist Episcopal Church

In the year 1867, before Gregg County was pruned out of Gregg and Upshur counties, the first black church in Longview, Texas had its beginning. Our fore parents worshipped under a brush arbor beneath a cluster of pine trees at the corner of North First and Padon Streets. For four years they worshipped under the arbor, then the record states that the late John Magrill of the white Methodist Church South deeded one acre to the blacks for the purported price of forty specie, which being interpreted means coin money.

On 18 July 2003 St. Mark participated in the unveiling of an historical marker at the site that has since been adopted as a park. We learned that the price of forty specie was recorded because Mr. Magrill faced persecution from whites for being sympathetic to ex-slaves. Instead, an offering of less than five dollars was taken, the actual amount paid.

Our church was organized by the late Rev. R.A. Hagler, the first building being a two-story box house, forty feet wide and sixty feet long, the upstairs used for meetings of the UBF lodge. They worshipped there until 1893 when it was torn down and a new building erected.

The first parsonage was built in 1916 but later burned. The church was repaired in 1918. The second parsonage was built in 1945. In 1946 the church was again remodeled and a fellowship hall added. In 1957 the church was once more repaired. In February 1972 St. Mark moved into its present structure at 1100 Sapphire St., under the pastorate of the late Rev. David V. Patton.

The autobiography of the late Bishop M.F. Jamison states that he was assigned to the Marshall and Longview stations as their first pastor. There were five members in Marshall and eight in Longview. He was later moved to Dallas, whereupon some of the members cried. There he founded Evening Chapel, later Boll Street, later Cedar Crest.

The late Rev. O.T. Womack, one of the founders of Texas College was also a pastor at St. Mark. He was married to our first organist.

St. Mark has four schools, one park and a recreational center named for members. *(Compiled and written by Evelyn Garrett Williams, church historian.)*

St. Mark CME Church, Longview, Texas

Foster Middle School
Longview, Texas

Foster Middle School, Longview

Foster Middle School, 410 South Green in Longview, Texas, has a rich historical background and is the only school building in Longview to be honored with an Official Texas Historical Marker.

The new city of Longview had only private schools until the first public school was built in 1880 on the corner of Green and Tyler Streets, followed by a larger building on the southeast corner of Green and College Streets in 1885. The Longview Independent School District was created by a special act of the 31st Texas Legislature in March 1909. The district contained 1,300 students drawn from a population of about 8,000, according to the Longview Chamber of Commerce.

In 1927, construction of the main building of what was then called Longview Senior High School was begun and completed in 1929, representing an investment of $130,000.

The architect was Elmer J. Withers of Forth Worth. Located on 6.3 acres, the original building contained sixteen classrooms, a homemaking room, library, clinic, office and auditorium and was built of multi-colored brick with wood frame windows and a red clay tile roof. The dedication read, "to the cause of education" and it has continuously served that purpose since its construction. At various times it has housed elementary classes in addition to high school and junior high students, as well as also serving as a center of community activity

With the East Texas oil boom, school enrollment increased from 1,970 to 4,400 in just two years, forcing the construction of a new high school on East Whaley Street in 1932 and converting this campus into a junior high school. Known as Longview Junior High, it was renamed as Henry L. Foster Junior High School after a former educator and superintendent of schools, when a second junior high school was built in 1957. The name was changed to Henry L. Foster Middle School in 1976, when the ninth grades were relocated to the newly constructed Longview High School campus and the sixth grades were transferred to the middle school campuses.

Serving approximately 800 students a year since 2000, the campus has grown to include a separate annex built in 1946, a library built in 1974, a band hall with attached gymnasium and the former Nicholson Memorial Library building which houses a magnet school for gifted and talented students from throughout the district.

Foster Middle School was recognized with an Official Texas Historical Marker in 1992 for the significant role as a historical educational facility it has played and continues to play in the lives of thousands of students.

Pine Tree Independent School District

Pine Tree Schools Celebrate 150 Years of Education, 1847-1997

Students attending school in 1907 either walked, rode a horse or possibly carpooled with a horse and wagon. A nearby spring and well supplied the drinking water to go with lunches they brought in tin pails from home.

Looking back 150 years, PTISD grew out of the Cumberland Presbyterian Church, still located in its original site on Pine Tree Road. The founders discussed ideas for organizing the church and school under the shade of a cluster of pine trees in October 1847.

The pastor was Rev. Solomon F. Awalt, a pioneer of Cumberland Presbyterianism. He left Tennessee in 1846 with his wife on their journey to the tiny Texas community of Pine Tree where they were to be reunited with her parents. On the way, they made stops in Alabama and Jefferson, Texas, organizing new churches in each location before continuing on their way.

The Pine Tree Presbyterian Church is the oldest church in Gregg County. One of the first concerns in organizing was to build a structure to serve as a church and school. Joseph Castleberry deeded three acres of land to the church for this purpose.

A small log cabin for both church and school was built in 1850, and was used until it was replaced by two separate buildings in 1857. A hexagon-shaped building was constructed for the church and a two-story building for the school.

The Masonic Lodge made major contributions to the early development of the school and was housed on the upper level of the school building, as shown in the 1907 photo pictured here, with Pine Tree classes held on the lower floor. Later, an extra room was built which made an "L" shaped structure off the original frame building.

Since the school could not be supported tuition-free, it was at first a "pay school." Prior to the Civil War and as late as 1870, Pine Tree was the leading school of the East Texas area. Many boarding students from adjoining communities and even other counties attended the school.

When the railroads came in 1872, more people moved into the area, and as neighboring communities grew, they organized their own schools. Gregg County was formed in 1873. The area was previously Upshur County.

From 1873 until 1931, Pine Tree had an average attendance of 100 pupils and three teachers, but the discovery of oil in 1931 changed that. Population rose quickly when the oil boom hit, and to keep pace with the enrollment, a shotgun building was erected in front of the two-story school and another shotgun building with six classrooms was built on the south side of Highway 80 near the railroad tracks.

With the oil boom came money and in 1932 the first brick structure was opened for grades 1-8. It contained 12 classrooms and an auditorium. Much more was to come. *(Reprinted with permission from the Cutlass, Vol. 36 No.4, 2 May 1997.)*

Since that time, the district's reputation for quality education has attracted steady enrollment. In September 2003, Pine Tree Independent School District consisted of seven campuses with a total enrollment of 4,671 students. Pine Tree Schools are accredited by the Texas Education Agency and by the Southern Association of Schools and Colleges. *"The Tradition of Excellence Continues!"*

Pine Tree students, in front of the school as it looked in 1907. (l.-r.) Back: Alto Harris, Willie Fisher, Mr. Pace (the only teacher in 1907), Feenie Bolton, Lawrence Morgan, Vannie Harris, Tom Harris, Nina Stevens, Clara Harris, Ida Bolton and Etta Bolton. Middle: Ida Dee Harris, Marvel Fisher, Pat Fisher, Herbert Fisher, Josie Wood, Mattie D. Fisher, Rosie Thompson, Annie Mae Little, Ruth Calloway, Ina Wood, May Bolton, Pearl Calloway, Gertie Morgan, Gladys Fisher, Annie Mae Everett, Mae Fisher, Johnnie Lee Feemster, Rembert Stevens, J.B. Everett and Clarence Everett. Front: Jane Calloway, Loraine Fisher, Frank Harris, Lynn Smith, Dick Calloway, Henry Pace, Marshall Pace, Perry Fisher, Sam Stevens, Leck Wood, Raz Calloway, Kid Wood, Jasper Morning, Jerry Lee, Howard Everett and Tommy Everett. (Photo Courtesy of Pine Tree ISD.)

St. Mary's School
A History of Catholic Education in Longview

St. Mary's School represents over half a century of Catholic education in Longview. It is the outgrowth of St. Anthony's School which opened in 1948, staffed by the School Sisters of Notre Dame headquartered in St. Louis, Missouri. This downtown location on Sixth Street, a part of St. Anthony's Parish, served the needs of area children for many years. As Longview flourished and grew, so did Catholic education.

With the continued growth of the parish, the facilities of St. Anthony's School became inadequate; further expansion at the existing site was impossible since the adjoining property was unavailable for purchase. Bishop T.K. Gorman of Dallas suggested considering expanding the parish school facilities elsewhere. Deciding to build on a new site, Monsignor Edward Shopka, (Szapka) then pastor of St. Anthony's, sought to purchase a 47-acre tract of land, entirely undeveloped and outside the city limits, for the construction of a new school. Organizing the support of parents, parishioners and community friends to raise the funds necessary for this new school, he successfully brought the project into being. Ground was broken at this site on Hollybrook and Ridgewood 17 December 1967; the new St. Mary's School was dedicated 8 December 1968. Constructed at a cost of $325,000, it contained 20,000 square feet of floor space, including eight classrooms, administrative offices, library, science lecture room, teachers' lounge, kitchen and cafetorium with a stage and seating for 450 people. Completely carpeted and air conditioned, it was considered one of the finest schools in the Diocese of Dallas. It also featured many acres of playground and ball field space.

The need for another parish became evident as the city of Longview grew north to include the new school property, and city population increased. In 1980, a new church was dedicated on this campus. The parish of

St. Mary's Catholic School

St. Mary's was established under the pastoral leadership of Father (now Monsignor) John Brennan in 1982. Prior to that, in order to enhance the physical education program at the school and provide a parish facility for athletic and fitness activities, a gymnasium was built and dedicated to Monsignor Shopka, whose foresight and sound financial management contributed so much to the development of Catholic education in the community. By 1987, more classroom space was clearly needed, so a four classroom annex was built adjacent to the original school building. One wing of this new building could be expanded into a single large room; it housed the band program for a number of years. When this space was needed for classroom use, a portable building was erected for the band.

These enlarged school quarters were sufficient for some time. But in 1996, Father Gavin Vaverek, pastor of St. Mary's Parish, initiated a fund drive to provide still more space for the expanding school. In 1998 a large parish center was dedicated. In addition to meeting rooms and a dining facility for parish use, the building houses the new school cafeteria, kitchen, stage facilities, science and computer labs, and five classrooms for the upper elementary program. A covered walkway was added connecting the original building, the gym and the parish center; at the same time, the original school building was renovated. The former cafetorium became an enlarged library, adult reading room, and computer lab for the lower elementary students. In addition, administrative offices were relocated and enlarged.

Today, St. Mary's offers quality education for grades preschool through eight in a Catholic environment and excellent facilities. Students of all faiths are welcome. The program focuses on religion, and offers academic instruction that exceeds state requirements. The program includes language development, mathematics, science, social studies, music, art, phonics, physical education and Spanish. Accelerated reading and the Diocesan Spelling Bee enhance the lower elementary program.

Upper elementary students continue the same core curriculum, adding special interest groups in Spanish, cooking, calligraphy, and Chess Club. The athletic program offers basketball, soccer, volleyball, intramural coed flag football, and track and field. Students also participate in the Presidential Physical Fitness Program, the Sports-a-Thon, and fall and spring relays.

In the Fine Arts music program, students may participate in choir and band. Fourth grade students receive recorder instruction; piano and instrumental lessons are available for all students. The art program covers basic design and history, offering hands on experience at all levels in a variety of media.

St. Mary's is part of a rich tradition of Catholic education in the United States. The first Catholic school opened in St. Augustine, Florida, in 1606. Now there are nearly seven thousand Catholic elementary schools in the country, with an enrollment of almost two million students. Catholic schools were the first to educate students in Louisiana, California, Kansas, North Dakota, Ohio, Kentucky and the District of Columbia. Catholic schools of the District of Columbia were peacefully integrated three years before the Supreme Court ordered the integration of public schools. *(Written by Judy Morris.)*

St. Mary's Catholic Church

Spring Hill Independent School District

In 1887, a group of citizens met and made provisions to build a school house. The site selected was south of the present Spring Hill community. A small building was erected near a spring in a nearby cliff, hence the name of Spring Hill. Sixty-five students were enrolled and Jim Christian was the first teacher. In 1897, a new frame two-story building was erected where the Elmira Presbyterian Church now stands. The first floor was used for the church and the second for the school. J.R. Castleberry donated 35 acres of land and the materials needed for the building. Later, the church deeded two acres of land to the school.

About 1910, a new one-room building was constructed and a second room and porch were added in 1915. Misses Nettie and Nannie Crane were employed. From 1931 to 1933, two frame buildings were built to provide for growth due to the discovery of oil. In 1932, a brick building was constructed. Seven grades were taught and the older students were transported to the high school in Longview. In 1934, a brick teacherage was completed on campus and female teachers were required to reside there. Grades were added, one each year, until 1940-41 when Spring Hill was classified as a four-year high school.

As student enrollment increased, more space was needed. In 1936, a second floor was added on top of the brick building; a cafeteria was added in 1937 and in 1941, a library. In 1950, a shop building along with a kindergarten and a music room, football stadium, athletic field house and swimming pool were built. In 1964, a new high school was built and this currently houses the junior high school. The junior high school built in 1974 now houses the middle school. In 1975, the Louie L. Williamson Auditorium, gym and band hall were constructed. A new wing was added to the elementary building in 1980, and also to the present junior high in 1983. Further growth of the District led to the construction and dedication of a new primary school in the year 2000, as well as updating and refurbishing other buildings on campus.

Superintendents who have served the District are W.A. Hearne, R.G. Hensley, Louie L. Williamson, C.C. Dowell, Tom Fox and Mike Crossland. Currently, the 2003-2004 student enrollment is 1,724 served by 140 teachers and administrators and 86 auxiliary staff.

Spring Hill ISD, Longview, 1933

School was different in the early 1900s. There was no janitor but two children were named each day to sweep the classroom during the afternoon recess. Each child felt special to be selected for this chore. To keep the grounds, students pulled weeds and picked up the trash. Everyone pitched in and the teacher built the fire each morning in the big stove using wood stacked on the porch of the school. There was no cafeteria or snack bar — everyone carried lunch in a "dinner bucket", usually a syrup pail with holes punched in the top for ventilation. Sausage or ham with biscuits and a baked sweet potato or a homemade teacake provided a tasty lunch.

Most small schools had only three trustees. Applicants for a teaching job came directly to each trustee to interview for a position. Most applicants were female and many of them only had two years of college.

Basketball was the popular sport and of great interest to the community. The games were played on a gravel court in front of the Presbyterian Church. Tall, long-legged farm boys made a good team. Neighboring schools of Pine Tree, White Oak, Judson and Harmony Grove were the opposing teams. The spectators stood along the sides of the court and cheered loudly.

A primitive school bus began to take high school students into Longview. This privately owned bus charged the school a fee per student for the transportation. In the early '30s there were only three high schools in the county — Longview, Kilgore, and Gladewater. When oil was discovered in East Texas in 1931, changes began to happen. As more students came to the area, schools furnished the buses and all 8th through 11th grade students were sent into Longview. Area schools began to grow and at present, there are seven public high schools in Gregg County — three of which are in the city of Longview.

Spring Hill is proud of the heritage and history of the school and community. The achievement and recognition earned is recognized state-wide. As an elderly gentleman who led the singing at church would say, "let's make old Spring Hill ring!" If that man were here now, he would say that old Spring Hill has rung out loud and clear. May it ever go forward and upward. *(Based on information provided by Spring Hill ISD and alumni.)*

Aaron Burleson Chapter
Daughters of the American Revolution

![Aaron Burleson DAR Chapter 50th Anniversary Tea photo]

Aaron Burleson DAR Chapter 50th Anniversary Tea
Those pictured were members attending the 50th Anniversary Tea.

The National Society Daughters of the American Revolution, founded in 1890, is a service organization dedicated to service to the Nation. Its objectives are Historic Preservation, Promotion of Education and Patriotic Endeavor. The President General is the official spokesman for the National Society.

The Aaron Burleson Chapter of the Daughters of the American Revolution was organized in Longview on 1 February 1946, by Mrs. Curtis W. Meadows with twenty-six members.

Aaron Burleson II was born in 1749 in Buncombe County, North Carolina. He assisted in establishing American Independence while acting in the capacity of minuteman. Aaron Burleson II was killed in 1784 by the Indians while crossing the Clynch River in Tennessee.

Many of the descendants of Aaron Burleson II proved worthy of their heritage. They attained distinction as lawyers, ministers, statesmen, editors, authors, educators, doctors, businessmen and soldiers.

Members of the Aaron Burleson Chapter recognize good citizens from area schools each year, award a scholarship to a graduating senior, recognize an outstanding ROTC graduating senior, promote Constitution Week throughout the area and recognize community leaders for historical preservation.

Chapter meetings are held on the first Tuesday of each month.

The East Texas Symphonic Band

Great band music returned to Longview and East Texas in 1988 when the East Texas Symphonic Band was formed under the leadership of its musical director, Dr. James Snowden. Since that beginning the East Texas Symphonic band has performed at least three concerts each year.

Although mostly composed of adults, the East Texas Symphonic Band has also included talented high school and college musicians. Because membership is by audition or by recommendation from the player committee, the band has been able to maintain a high level of excellent musicianship.

One of the things that makes the East Texas Symphonic Band unique is that some of their concerts are presented to the public free of charge. This is possible because of generous donations from individuals and corporate sponsors who enable the band to purchase music and defray some of its expenses.

It is the goal of this group of musicians to raise the awareness and appreciation of wind band music in the East Texas area by offering formal concerts and informal celebrations of what has been called "the people's music." They also try to provide motivation and encouragement to young people so that they, too, will make music a permanent part of their lives.

One example of the splendid concerts the band presents occurred on 11 September 2002, when the band gave a special "Tribute to America" concert on the anniversary of the September 11th attack on America. During this standing-room-only performance, the audience spontaneously began singing with the band and the mass choir that had joined the band for the evening. Together, the entire assembly shared in singing patriotic music and celebrating the greatness of America. This event was so moving that it was repeated again the next year.

The East Texas Symphonic Band began an annual custom of presenting Christmas dinner concerts in 1999. Traditionally, it is held in early December as a start to the Christmas season.

Another popular event the band hosts is the annual "Pops in the Park" concert. This free concert, performed at Teague Park in the bandstand, occurs near Memorial Day each year and recalls the days of city municipal bands by offering movie music, marches and a tribute to the Armed Forces.

The East Texas Symphonic Band was recognized in 1997 by being asked to perform at the 50th Anniversary Clinic and Convention of the Texas Bandmaster's Association in San Antonio, Texas. The East Texas Symphonic Band was the first-ever "community band" invited to play at such an event.

Throughout the region the East Texas Symphonic Band has been hailed as the "band for all the people." One concert attendee even went so far as to say, "I can't relate to some music but this band plays the music I know." Another declared that the band plays "music for the regular folks." Such comments reflect that the East Texas Symphonic Band is indeed fulfilling its aim and its mission.

East Texas Symphonic Bank, 11 September 2002 Concert.

Prelude
Longview Symphony Guild

In 1967, the Longview Symphony was founded. Dr. Landon A. Colquitt was the first President of the Board. Dr. James Snowden, the first conductor, held that position for ten years.

In 1972, the Junior Service League of Longview (now The Junior League) formed "The Women's Society of the Longview Symphony League" (TWSLSL). Mrs. Neal Hawthorne held the formation event at her home. Junior Service League member Barbara Tomberlain was given the Women's Society placement. As such, she was liaison to the Longview Symphony's Board of Directors.

In 1974, when Marvin Mikeska, Sr. was Board President of the Longview Symphony League, he and his wife, Josephine, and Grace and Ben Franklin Martin, Jr. attended the American Symphony Orchestra League National Convention in Memphis, Tennessee. Mr. Martin was immediate past President of the Longview Symphony League at that time.

The Mikeska and Martin wives went to all the women's meetings at the Convention to gain a better insight into what TWSLSL volunteers should be accomplishing. At one of the meetings, the Miami, Florida, group announced that they gave the name "PRELUDE" to their organization because it showed their purpose in one word. (Very loosely translated, it meant to them "doing preliminary work so the Symphony can play.") Grace Martin asked the Miami ladies if they would allow their Longview, Texas, counterpart to use the same name, and they heartily agreed.

That is how TWSLSL became "PRELUDE." Mrs. Martin was President, Mrs. Landon A. Colquitt was Vice President, and Mrs. W.D. Northcutt, Jr. was Secretary at that time. Other Prelude Board Members were Mrs. Reid Clanton, Mrs. C.C. Holloway, and Mrs. J.M. Knox. Prelude dues were two dollars per year in 1974.

Earlier that year, women involved in promoting the Longview Symphony (TWSLSL) took aprons and "rolling pins" to a clay working meeting and made small objects of clay to be sold in their booth at the Longview Spring Art Festival held in Teague Park. Mrs. Robert Daniel was craft chairman. The clay was professionally "fired" and then the members had a painting session to color their clay objects. Shortly thereafter, they had donated quilts and other handmade objects for sale in a storefront in old Jefferson, Texas, during the May Pilgrimage. Wanda McGowen was chairman of that project.

In July 1975, The Longview Symphony and Prelude were offered a formal fashion show by a well-known specialty store. This news "jump-started" everyone because the show was to benefit the Symphony's Maintenance Fund and it needed money. The fashion show was held as part of a formal dinner dance with the Big Band and Swing Orchestra (from the now defunct Ambassador College at Big Sandy). This large and well-attended event on October 4th was called "Wine, Women, and Song." Mrs. Kathryn Lawrence was the chairman.

Prelude's members melded into the Maintenance Fund Drive and gave unique purses as incentives to be earned by women working in the drive who attained their financial goals. Sixty purses were made and earned. Shirley Snowden painted and decoupaged musical designs on wooden purses found by Grace Martin. For several years, it was a prestigious badge of courage and success to carry one of the decoupaged purses. The purses were medium, round, and done in white with black musical designs and vice-versa.

For the U.S. Bicentennial, Prelude had a two-day festival, Bicentennial Fun Fest and held at Teague Park. Grace Martin of Prelude opened her husband's empty antique house (which borders the park at 322 Teague Street). She placed her antiques from the Dr. Shipp estate in the house and held a benefit House Tour for the Symphony. Admission was one dollar per person.

All over Teague Park there were special events and activities for the public. Mr. and Mrs. Jerry M. Jones were chairpersons of the event, assisted by Mrs. Mamie Key, Prelude President, and Jack T. Buchanan, President of the Longview Symphony League. Prelude members staffed a mini-museum of historical artifacts in the National Guard Armory on the East end of the park. Booths and concession stands contributed to the fund raising.

Prelude's Christmas Corner was started by Mary Murdoch in 1981. It was held in the Longview Community Center. The next year, Ava Avant Welge was Chairman of that gift show. The third season of Christmas Corner was moved to the brand new Maude Cobb Center where it has been held yearly to raise big money for the Longview Symphony. The first year they made $1,200.00, now they pledge $22,000.00 and give more when possible.

Now Prelude has been given an added identity as "Prelude, Longview Symphony Guild." Prelude president for 2003-2004 is Mary Murdoch.

Prelude members pictured represent the sixty women who worked on the Symphony's Maintenance Fund Drive in 1975 and earned purses for reaching their financial goal. (l.-r.) Seated: Mrs. Ben Franklin Martin, Jr., Mrs. E.L. Lee, Mrs. Marvin Mikeska, Sr., Standing: Mrs. B. Franklin Martin, Sr., Mrs. R.H. Smith, Mrs. S. Bommarito.

Zonta Club of Longview

Zonta International is a world-wide service organization of executive women in business and the professions working together to advance the status of women. Zonta began in 1919 in Buffalo, New York, U.S.A. Zonta is a Sioux Indian word meaning honest and trustworthy.

In 2003, Zonta International includes sixty-nine countries. The Zonta Club of Longview, with 103 active members, is the largest Zonta Club in the world. The local club was chartered in March 1955, and has been a vital force in Longview since it was organized on 22 April 1955. Charter members included Marguerite Bolls, Helen Boring, Dr. Mary Childress, Elizabeth Crim, Gwen Farmer, Maureen Galyon, Margaret Hill, Anna Hudson, Mary Belle Hughey, Margaret Lanier, Mamie Key, Johnnie McBride, Emogene Nabors, Katie Dee Todd, Alta Rita Welch, Freda West and Leila Wood.

Zonta is a classified service club and fund raising for service projects is a major undertaking. The monies raised are returned to the community entities. Early fund raising programs included selling candy, cookbooks, Christmas cards and gadgets such as the slice-a-slice bread slicer along with rummage sales of donated items. Some money from these early fund raising efforts was used to purchase a gas oven, at a price of $413, for the Community Center. Other early service projects included contributions to health agencies and a scholarship in the amount of $100.

Eventually, members of the club were receptive to the idea of one major fund raiser and the first Antiques Show & Sale was held 24-26 January 1975, at the Gregg County Fairgrounds with tickets selling for $1.50 for the 3-day event. Julie Barron served as general chairman for the first and second Antiques Shows. There were 50 antique dealers from 10 states and over 3,000 people attended that first show. Lunch and dinner were served at nominal prices, featuring home-cooked food prepared by Zonta members.

The Antiques Show & Sale became an annual affair. Following the five years at the Fairgrounds, the show was moved to the SPJST Lodge. On 23-25 January 1979, there were 38 dealers present and admission to the show was $2.00. In 1985, Maude Cobb Activity Center was the location selected for the show. The kitchen equipment at Maude Cobb was provided by the Zonta Club. In 1989, there were 60 dealers at the 14th Annual Show. A champagne preview opened the show on Friday night. A book was published consisting of the most requested pie recipes made famous by the Zontians who furnished pies for the tea room.

In March 2004, Zontians held the 30th Annual Antiques Show & Sale and the famous tea room where dealers and patrons of the show indulge in the delicious Zonta pies.

The Antiques Show & Sale has been the major fundraiser of Zonta Club for the past thirty years and the profits from the shows have been used to meet needs of the community. A portion of the service funds each year is used for scholarships. There are four Z Club scholarships for deserving members in the Z clubs of participating schools. One scholarship for $1,000 is given for a Young Woman of Public Affairs. The Mary Belle Hughey and the Emeritus Scholarships

Zonta of Longview

"Most Requested"
PIE BAR RECIPES

Zonta Pie Girls: Evelyn Maness, Mary Belle Hughey and Lillie Mae

for $1,000 each are given for deserving women furthering their education.

Many of the service projects each year have been to meet a one-time need in the community. In 1975, Zonta presented the keys to a new station wagon to Gregg/Harrison Mental Health and Mental Retardation Center. Gregg/Harrison MHMR purchased the R.G. LeTourneau home to be used for girls. Zonta was involved in providing the furnishings for the house. Zonta also supplied the funds to fully equip the kitchen at Maude Cobb Activity Center and furnished the Information Desk for the new Longview Public Library.

The Women's Center, Hope Haven Shelter for Women & Children, CASA, Literacy Council, Gregg Home for the Aged, Habitat for Humanity, The Salvation Army, Gregg County Early Childhood Development Center, Rainbow Room, Buckner Children & Family Services, Longview Community Ministries, Crisman Preparatory School, and other deserving community organizations have all benefited from Zonta support.

The Zonta Club, always committed to advancing the status of women, has supported activities for women in Longview through the Career Conference for high school girls in the area, the Working Women's Conference, and the Women in Longview Day.

Membership in Zonta gives a sense of pride to the individual to be a part of the accomplishments of the club.

1970 Centennial Parade, showing off Pat Ferchill's surrey. (l.-r.) Mrs. Clarence Richardson, Mrs. Harold Turner, Mrs. Tom Nelson, Mrs. O. Thomas Welch, Sr., Mrs. E.L. Lee, Mrs. Fred Boatner.

Lions Club of Judson

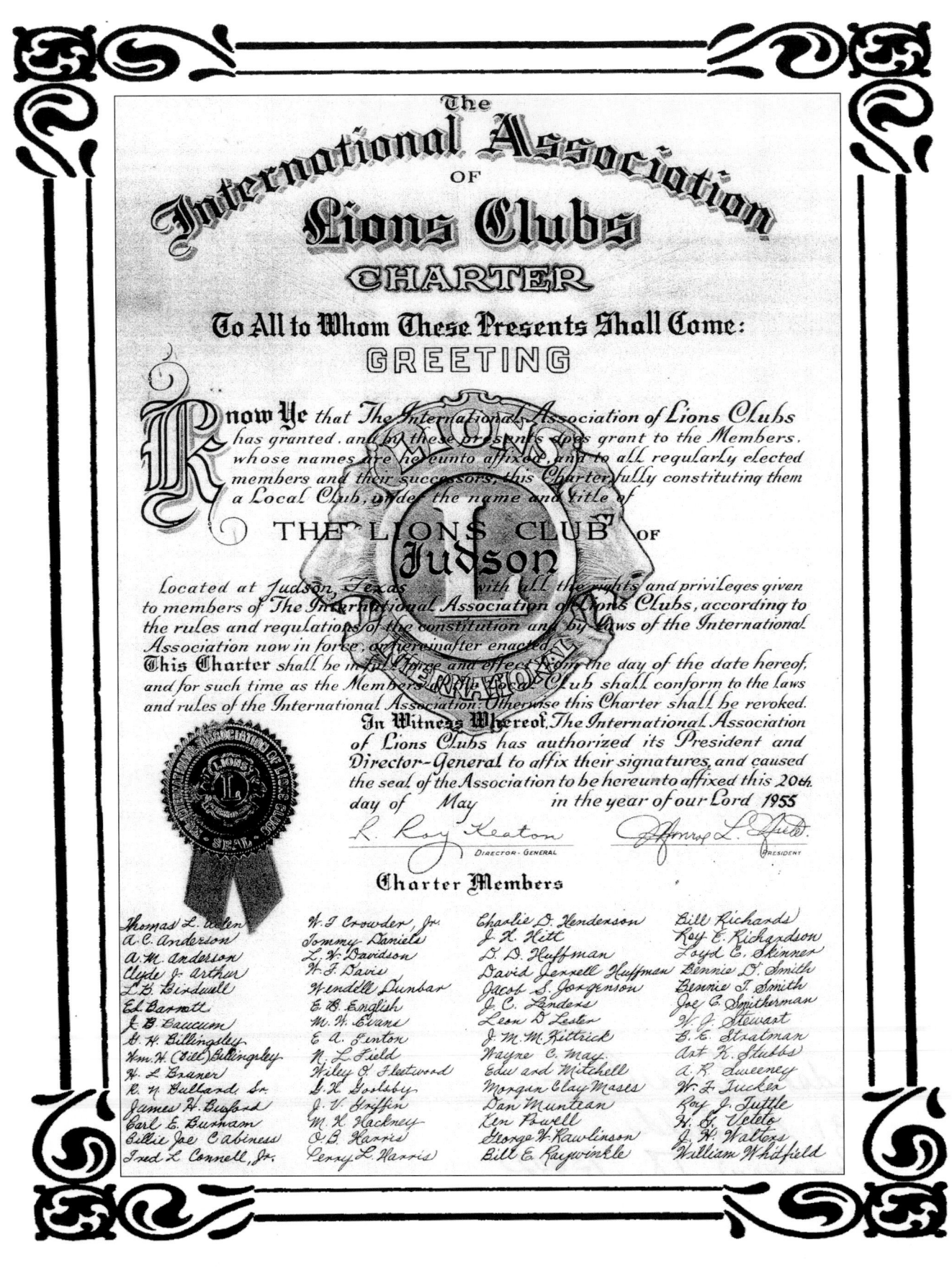

Judson Lions Club was organized 20 May 1955 with 45 members. We now have 31 members. We meet the second and fourth tuesday night at 7:00 p.m. each month at the Judson Community Center. Our main project is the concession stand at the Judson football stadium on Tuesdays and Thursdays. We are co-sponsor with other civic groups running the bingo at Contessa Inn. We are responsible for renting the Community Center. Each year we work with the school nurses at Doris McQueen, Mozelle Johnston and Judson to buy eyeglasses for students who need help. We send to camp at Kerrville, Texas children who are handicapped or have diabetes. We have disaster relief for disasters such as tornadoes, floods, etc. Students collect canned goods for needy families at Christmas. We collect eyeglasses and aluminum cans to be recyled. We have an annual chilli supper at Judson, and sponsor the county's annual Lions barbeque for Kerrville Camp. Things we have done in the past years include purchasing two leader blind dogs; putting lights up on the highway intersection at Judson; providing a picnic table and water fountain at the little schoolhouse at Mozelle Johnston; purchasing musical instruments for Mozelle Johnston school students; offering a garden for the blind at Maude Cobb Civic Center; providing the women's shelter with playground equipment; harvesting vest in Longview and yamboree in Gilmer; purchasing FFA animals; co-sponsoring the painting of Judson's mascot in the gym; co-sponsoring the scoreboard at the Judson football field; highway trash pick up; sponsoring Boy Scouts and Girl Scouts; giving an annual teachers' appreciation luncheon; supporting the American Cancer Relay; refinishing tennis courts at Judson; and paving the road between the community building and little schoolhouse. When there is a death in the community, the Lions Club takes ice to the home of the deceased. We build handicapped ramps at homes and provide monetary gifts as needed.

Judson Lions Club Membership

Marty Bentson, Mitch Billingsley, Tracy Briley, Billy Cabbiness, James Cammack, Charles Davis, Paul Dotson, Joyce Flanagan, Carroll Flournoy, Traci Francis, Terry Hamilton, Barry Henderson, Hoy Herrin, Lou Jorgenson, Jerry McKenzie, Ronnie McKinney, Kathy Mears, Don Orgeron, Wayne Prince, Reggie Roard, Robbie Robertson, Sandy Sandberg, Mary Sandberg, Ron Smith, Steve Smith, Bill Stack, Joe Thompson, James Tipton, Becky Whitenack, Brian Whitenack and Debbie Sadler

Captain William Young Chapter
National Society, Daughters of the American Revolution

Captain William Young Chapter of the National Society, Daughters of the American Revolution was organized 26 May 1939, in Longview, Gregg County, Texas. Since that time members have bought genealogy books to help other people find their ancestors. Friends and family of members began donating funds to buy genealogy books in memory of loved ones. Eventually, books were placed in locked cabinets at the Nicholson Library.

When the City of Longview built a new state-of-the-art library, Captain William Young Chapter donated all its books and family history pamphlets to the library. This was a huge gift! The genealogy which the chapter gave was appraised at $100,000.00, the library's largest donation from a non-profit volunteer organization. The genealogy is in a special room of the library named for our chapter's late member, Mary Robbins. These materials are fully accessible to the public for genealogy research during library service hours.

An interesting recent program given by our chapter on 17 May 2003, was a version of an "Antiques Road Show" where all DAR chapter members in Gregg County gathered at the Cherokee Club and displayed their artifacts. Local antique dealer Mrs. Billie Sue Turner gave assessments of the heirlooms.

An explanation of the Chapter's namesake follows: The gravestone of Captain Young, five miles from Greenville, South Carolina, says: "Died November 7th, age 63 years. He joined the Continental Army when 16 and served 'till its close.' A true patriot, an honest man, enjoyed in all eminent degree the respect of all who knew him." The old stone house built by him is still standing.

Captain William Young Chapter, NSDAR Charter Members

Margaret DeLoach Adams, Mae Dee Castleberry Allison, Charleen Elder Bagwell, Stella Goforth Bagwell, *Geraldine Van Allen Barbee, *Amelia Castleberry Belding, *Effie Rule Durham Bivins, Annie Lee Taylor Brown, Jessie Mae Prothro Brown, Annie Mae DeLoach Campbell, Emma Inez Watts Coghlan, Gay Keener Cole, Ethel DeLoach Crawley, Carrie Bruce Flewellen, Bettie Calvin Griffith, Camilla Charlotte Halliday, Antoinette Flewellen Hanivasy, Virginia Kelly, Kate Womack Lacy, *Mary DeLoach Levy, Erminie Northcutt Marshall, Lorraine Calvin Martin, Vesta Echols McWhorter, Fannie Mae Burlew Morgan, *Kathleen Jones Moore, Pearl Florence Moore, Bernice Northcutt, *Dolly Northcutt, Emma Northcutt, Josephine Still Northcutt, Lynne Smith Norton, Mary Maude Morgan Parker, Neina Mead Robbins, *Ida Sparks Rule Shaw, *Ann Castleberry Miller Smith, Margaret Martin Spangler, *Ruth Sparkman Sterling, Ida Northcutt Taylor, Louise Shaw Taylor, Georgia Van Landingham, Martha Cuberley Veale, *Lillie Lawrence Walker and *Mabel Brown Walker. The asterisk in front of a name means organizing member. *(From DAR 1939 Charter.)*

The Gladewater Music Club

A group of Gladewater ladies met in the home of Mrs. H.L. (Lillie Mae) McKaig for tea and a musical program in the spring of 1938. They decided to organize a music club. When they met again, the Gladewater Music Club was born. Forty-eight members signed the charter on 19 May 1938, at the home of Mrs. J.J. (Lavon Wood) Traughber, who is the only surviving member of the group. The newly federated club became a member of the Federated Music Club, Third District. The 1939-1940 Directory listed fifty members. In 1940, the club sponsored a musical program each day of National Music Week. Each year this week is observed in cities, churches and schools, to promote American artists, to uphold high standards and to make America the music center of the world. In 1942, the custom of presenting children of Music Club members began. In 1943, the children presented a program for the club. Many familiar names appear on these programs, as many children were afforded the opportunity to perform before an eager, attentive and proud audience. This program often highlighted National Music Club Week, which was also observed in schools and churches. These were continued until the 1960s.

The club gave support to the growing public school music program in Gladewater schools, as well as outreach to the churches. They continued as an outstanding club through the 1950s and '60s. In the 1970s, many women returned to the workplace, some members died and membership dropped to about a dozen ladies. Mrs. McKaig continued to have a yearly meeting in her home, as she had done since the organizational meeting. Mrs. E.D. (Vivian) Dillard, refusing to let the club die, served as President, Program Chairman, Reporter and in other offices as needed, holding the small group together until the membership began to grow.

A scholarship program was begun in the 1990s. Three students, interested in continuing the study of music in college, received scholarships in 2003. Today, 2004, there are 41 members in the club. "How to Write your own Gilbert and Sullivan Operetta," by Anna Russell, will be presented by members of the club at the meeting of the National Federation of Music Clubs in Galveston, Texas, in 2005. The club continues to dedicate itself "to bringing the spiritualizing force of music to the inner life of our town and nation." *(Written by Georgia Ruth Johnston.)*

The Longview Symphony

The Longview Symphony Orchestra has provided fine classical music for residents of Longview and its neighbors for 35 years. The orchestra started as an amateur group with a few conservatory-trained musicians volunteering their time. Today, the orchestra, all professionals, draws performers from Shreveport and Nacogdoches as well as from Longview.

Early directors included James Snowden, Longview High School band director, and Dr. Frank Carrol, Dean of Music at Centenary College. Tonu Kalam became a member of our symphony family in 1988. This talented director commutes from Chapel Hill, North Carolina, where he is a tenured full professor of music and is conductor of the symphony at the University of North Carolina. Kalam was trained as a composer and pianist at Harvard University and the University of California at Berkeley. He appears as guest conductor throughout the United States and Europe. Despite his heavy metropolitan agenda, he is as devoted to Longview's musicians and music lovers as they are to their maestro.

Local banks host receptions following four or five concerts a year to bring together area musicians and supporters of all the fine arts. Since 1967, the Longview Symphony League, comprising 30-plus members, has provided support for the orchestra. These members give time and money to manage the stage set-up, newsletters, publicity, fundraising, ticket sales and whatever else it may take to keep the orchestra hiring the best musicians available. A Longview Symphony Foundation began in 1978. The annual event has grown into a popular civic attraction as well as a major fundraiser for the symphony.

The Longview Symphony takes pride in sponsoring two youth concerts and orchestras for school-age children throughout the area. Some of the musicians visit the schools and demonstrate their instruments. KTPB radio, broadcasting from Kilgore College, tapes and replays the adult concerts and provides pre-concert notes from the conductor. The philanthropic potential of this group, for all the arts, has shown itself to be unlimited. Here is a common sentiment in our part of the pine thicket: "How can a town no larger than Longview have such a wonderful, world-class symphony?" Thank God, we do. *(Submitted by Joy Ellis Mitchell.)*

R.B. Levy Chapter 1070
United Daughters of the Confederacy

The Col. R.B. Levy Chapter, 1070 was chartered 4 April 1907, into the United Daughters of the Confederacy. The original group was formed in 1905 and known as Gregg County Chapter 753, Daughters of Confederate Veterans. The chapter chose the Levy name in honor of R.B. Levy, a native of Massachusetts, who served in the Signal Corp during the War Between the States. Levy later settled his family in Longview and served as the first County and District Clerk. The first Chapter President was Mrs. Viola Bivins, who served for 44 years, including two years as President of the Texas Division, UDC. Between 1905 and 1910, under her leadership, the chapter raised the necessary funds to erect a Confederate monument, which was dedicated 3 June 1911, and stands on the Gregg County Courthouse lawn. In 1999, the current membership, under the leadership of President Barbara Gilbert, raised $10,000 for the monument's cleaning and repair. The unveiling of the restored monument took place 26 April 2000. Among those attending the ceremony were nieces and a nephew of R.B. Levy and grandchildren of Mrs. Bivins. The R.B. Levy Chapter is dedicated to Historic, Benevolent, Education, Memorial and Patriotic objectives. Through the years the chapter has awarded annual scholarships to local and state students, erected and dedicated grave markers, researched and recorded multi-county and state cemeteries, preserved original military flags, and donated time and goods to various area schools, churches, museums, libraries, cemeteries, genealogical and community service organizations. As the R.B. Levy Chapter approaches its 100th anniversary, it remains dedicated to collecting and preserving material for a truthful history of the War Between the States for future generations. We are indebted to the founding and past members of the chapter for their diligence in this work.

Right: Confederate Monument, Gregg County Courthouse lawn, Longview, Texas

General John Gregg Chapter #958
Sons of Confederate Veterans

On 18 June 1997, several members of the Texas Division SCV gathered in Longview, Gregg County, Texas, to charter a new camp. Early meetings indicated that General John Gregg would be the name of the camp. There were several obvious reasons why he would be the choice. He was an admired general in the Confederate Army, and a statesman who helped frame the Confederate Constitution. Gregg County bears his name.

The SCV members wanted to remember General John Gregg again. The charter members named are Gary Fletcher, Bill McCay, Barney Hilburn, John Barrett, Ronald McCutcheon, William David Berry, Talmadge Booth, Hunter Hines Hilburn, Wesley Whatley, Aubrey Brashear, Kenneth Baum, O.L. Kimbrough, A.L. Blanton, Warren Hunt, M.D., Dick B. Lindley, Robert Lindley, James D. Wallace, Jimmy Middlebrooks, John Hardin, Dan Duggan and Bruce Engleman, with Sam Mercer as associate member. These men wanted to honor General John Gregg and perpetuate his memory. *(Submitted by Barney Hilburn.)*

John Tilley Edwards Chapter
Daughters of the Republic of Texas

The chapter was organized on 5 February 1965, by Winona Banks Perkins, the first president. She died 28 August 2003. There is still one living charter member, Eleanor Muse. The chapter is active with 47 members. It encourages the study of Texas history by giving historical programs in area schools, by announcements in the paper, and conducting essay contests. The group also promotes the celebration of Texas Honor Days and the displaying of the Texas flag.

John Tilley Edwards Chapter,
Daughters of the Republic of Texas, 1965

Samuel Paul Dinkins Chapter
Daughters of the American Revolution
Kilgore, Texas

The Samuel Paul Dinkins Chapter, Daughters of the American Revolution of Kilgore, Texas, was organized by Octavia Jones Gentry and named for her great-great-great grandfather. The chapter was officially confirmed on 25 April 1952.

NSDAR Motto
"God, Home and Country"

Shakespeare Club

The Shakespeare Club, the oldest club in Longview, was organized in 1897 in the home of Mrs. E.R. Boring, and it continues to the present, giving monthly reviews of important literature.

Both state and nationally federated, the club celebrated its Golden Jubilee in 1947 and was honored as a Pioneer Club. In 1996, the club celebrated its century of existence. The charter members were Virginia Kelly, Emma Boring, Jessie Bramlette, Mrs. S.B. Fambrough, Lucy Elmore, Mrs. Tom Cox, Mrs. J.C. Howard and Vesta Echols McWhorter.

Active in community service, the 1900 group brought books to form a nucleus for the first library, and they continue to contribute to the present library's literary efforts.

A major project at the end of World War I was the planting of a Memorial Avenue of pecan trees along Highway 80. The trees were later moved and replanted in front of the Gregg County Courthouse as a Memorial Grove. Members of the club carried pails of water to the trees to insure their successful transplanting.

In 1932, the club held a bridge tournament called a George Washington Tea for the benefit of the library fund. It was a "book tea" given at the opening of the Nicholson Memorial Library.

Members make presentations of current and classical literature including fiction, biographies, drama, poetry and short stories.

"WOW"

Funny, everybody has the same reaction.

*Available
from $1,200 to
$1,000,000*

HEARTS ON FIRE®

THE WORLD'S MOST PERFECTLY CUT DIAMOND™

Your Exclusive Hearts On Fire Jeweler

2501 Judson Rd   Northloop Plaza   Longview

903-758-GEMS (4367)

Jim
Bartlett
Fine Jewelry

Longview Coca-Cola Bottling Company, Inc.

You all know what Coca-cola is. The Coca-Cola Company is the world's largest producer of soft-drink concentrates, syrups and juices, and distributes it to authorized bottlers throughout the world. Soft drink brands are Coke, Diet Coke, Sprite, Cherry and Vanilla Coke, and Tab and the company also makes fruit juices sold under the name of Minute Maid. Fifty-nine percent of syrups are sold to company-owned and independent bottlers in the United States and overseas. Sixty-two percent of the Coca-Cola Company's business is from overseas.

KO is the NYSE symbol for Coca-Cola USA. Coca-Cola Enterprises (CCE) was put in place to buy up independent bottlers throughout the nation. CCE wanted Longview CocaCola because they already had bought seven bottling plants surrounding Longview's franchise territory and had to drive through Longview territory in order to serve their own. CCE owned Shreveport, Tyler, Marshall, Sulphur Springs, Henderson, Nacogdoches, Lufkin and Crockett. In 1996, Longview Coca-Cola was ranked number one in the State of Texas in sales per capita, and number 18 in the nation. At the time, there were more than 450 bottlers in the nation. During that timeframe, Longview Coca-Cola had 385 per capita, which means that some people drank so much Coca-Cola product that it was the equivalent of every man, woman and child drinking more than one eight-ounce Coke every day for one year. CCE finally made Longview Coca-Cola an offer it couldn't refuse and it was sold in May of 2000.

In order for you to understand the Coca-Cola Company's humble beginnings, here is some history. John Smith Pemberton, a Confederate veteran, invented Coca-Cola in 1886, but it wasn't Coca-Cola until it had a name and it got that from Frank Mason Robinson, a Yankee and veteran of the Union army. He got his inspiration for naming the new syrup after two of its ingredients, the coca leaf and the kola nut. Robinson changed the "K" in kola to a "C" for uniformity's sake, put in a hyphen, and then wrote out a label in long hand in the careful Spencerian script that would become the best known trademark in the world.

In 1887, two men by the names of Lawndes and Veneable purchased Coca-Cola for $283.29 in cash for the physical assets, inventory, ingredients, advertising materials and equipment, including a 40-gallon copper kettle and mixing paddles. Pemberton died in 1888 at age 57.

In 1888, Asa G. Candler took control of Coca-Cola. He paid approximately $3,500.00 for it. Since Frank Robinson had influenced him to buy the business, Candler named him General Superintendent of Asa G. Candler & Company. For about 15 years, from the time of its inception, Coca-Cola remained a fountain, by-the-glass drink only. Robinson knew that Coca-Cola had to be advertised in order to take hold. In 1888, he helped put the drink on the map by passing out "sampling" tickets around Atlanta, good for two free drinks of Coca-Cola in a glass. Business got so good that Candler, in 1891, decided that he needed to borrow money to expand...as

much as $50,000.00. He opted to go public. So, Coca-Cola of Atlanta was incorporated with 1,000 shares at a value of $100.00 each. Candler took half, gave 10 shares to Frank Robinson, and offered 490 shares for sale. Candler asked to have shares sold in New York, Philadelphia, etc. Only 75 shares were sold to F.W. Prescott, a Boston broker. Most Yankees did not know the drink because it was mostly Southern. That meant only $7,500.00 was raised in fresh capital, so Candler was stuck with the Coca-Cola Company and faced the reality of having to grow it by himself!

The Coca-Cola formula consists of seven ingredients, namely sugar, caramel, phosphoric acid, glycerine, caffeine, coca and kola extracts, and the seventh item known as the "secret" or "X" (unknown) ingredient that is a secret blend of flavoring oils. When employed at the Fountain Sales Division of The Coca-Cola Company in Atlanta, sales trainees were taken to the syrup plant there and allowed to see and taste the secret ingredient. It came in stainless steel drums, looked whitish in color and tasted like a cross between cinnamon and lemon extract. Candler could produce a gallon of syrup for less than $1.00, sold one gallon of syrup for $2.00 wholesale, and a druggist made a profit of $6.40 on a gallon of syrup (128 ounces of syrup in one gallon x 50¢ a drink = $6.40).

Benjamin Franklin Thomas and Joseph Brown Whitehead, two young Chattanooga, Tennessee, lawyers, approached Candler for the rights to put the soft drink in bottles. At first Candler resisted because he thought it was unsanitary because of the pop bottle closure used. However, a mechanical engineer from Baltimore perfected and patented the bottle crown that allowed for great advances in machinery and sterilization of bottles. In view of these developments, Candler agreed to give bottling rights to Thomas and Whitehead for the whole United States. However, before Thomas and Whitehead got underway, Joseph Biedenharn of Vicksburg, Mississippi, in 1894, became the first person to sell Coca-Cola in bottles. Thomas took the Northeast, Whitehead took the South. Thomas first built a plant in Chattanooga. Whitehead didn't have much money and in the spring of 1900, formed a partnership with John Thomas Lupton, a man who had made a small fortune during the patent medicine era selling black drought and other concoctions for the Chattanooga Medicine Company. For a half share in Whitehead's region of the country, Lupton put up $2,500.00. Whitehead moved to Atlanta and used the money to open the first Coca-Cola Bottling Plant in the soft drink's home town. In 1909, there were 397 Coca-Cola plants in the United States. Thomas, Whitehead and Lupton became Parent Bottlers, which meant that they actually ended up recruiting potential bottlers to go into the Coca-Cola business. In actuality, this meant that the "parents" paid the Coca-Cola Company 92¢ a gallon for syrup, then turned around and "resold" it to the actual bottlers at a generous markup – usually $1.20 a gallon. It was all done on paper. Thomas, Whitehead and Lupton were fast becoming millionaires.

Benjamin F. Martin, Minerva Sanger, Joe Sanger, Mamie Sanger, and children of Joe and Minerva.

In 1919, the Earnest and Bob Woodruff group, investment bankers of Atlanta, purchased Coca-Cola from the Candler family for 25 million dollars. During World War II, Bob Woodruff stated that every American serviceman and woman of any rank, and anywhere in the world would be supplied Coca-Cola. Mr. Woodruff had portable bottling plants shipped overseas to backup this promise. Woodruff had a 30,000-acre plantation in Georgia where he invited "big shots" like Eisenhower and Nixon and celebrities like Bob Hope and Edgar Bergen. Mr. Woodruff hosted box lunches and quail hunts for these people, as well as big lavish banquets for them.

The Longview Coca-Cola Bottling Company, Incorporated

The Longview Coca-Cola Bottling Company started bottling in 1912. The first owners of the Longview franchise were two men by the name of Fitzgerald and Echols, These two sold on a yearly contract to Clyde Prall during 1915 to 1918. On 18 September 1918, Thomas H. Sweeney from Roanoke, Virginia, purchased the Longview franchise from Prall for $17,849.59 and held it for 6-1/2 years. He paid $11,400.00 cash down and assumed a $6,449.59 note at 8% for one year. The Longview Cigar and Brokerage was included in the sales transaction. The bottlers first line contract stipulated a price of $1.30 per gallon for Coca-Cola syrup and this price held constant for many years. Records show that in 1924 he owed J.T. Lupton on four notes in the amount of $2,500.00 each. Sweeney was Benjamin Franklin Martin, Sr.'s first cousin. Sweeney's wife, Eva, had a brother named Sam Woodson who was married to Ruby Lupton of Roanoke, Virginia. Sweeney had two sons, Thomas, Jr. and Payton Sweeney. It was because of the Lupton connection of Sweeney's wife that he got in on the ground floor of the Coca-Cola business.

In 1920, Benjamin Franklin Martin of Lanexa (New Kent County), Virginia, was single and recently discharged from the Army after having served in World War I in France. He arrived in Longview on Thursday, 12 January 1920, the same day as R.S. McCarley of the McCarley Jewelry Store and they stayed at the same boarding house. Martin kept a diary. His train stopped at Junction Depot and he got off. He later went to Downtown Train Depot, where he should have gotten off in the first place. Martin went to work for Sweeney and was a route salesman for eight years, in charge of the Carthage, Texas, route. On 18 May 1920, an entry in his diary said he cut his finger and Dr. Northcutt took a stitch. He also worked in the plant's bottling line. He told his son that when he first went to work at the plant soda water outsold Coca-Cola eight cases to one. Popular flavors of the day were peach, banana, strawberry, orange, lemon and creme soda. The franchise territory of Longview Coca-Cola consisted of Gregg, Panola, and parts of Rusk and Upshur counties.

In 1925, Thomas Sweeney decided to leave Longview for a Coca-Cola plant he could purchase in Brownsville, Texas. He reasoned that Longview had limited possibilities

Longview Coca-Cola Bottling Company, Inc.

since a lot of timber had been cut out and the railroad round-house had moved from Longview to Mineola. B.F. Martin asked Sweeney if he would sell to him and finance the sale. Sweeney said he would not finance. Martin approached the Longview banks and was turned down on the grounds that they considered Coca-Cola unproved and a back-alley business. They probably would have jumped at financing a cotton or corn crop instead.

Franklin Martin, Sr. saw an advertisement in a bottler's magazine by James Sang, of Beaufort, South Carolina, who wanted to purchase a soda water bottling plant. Martin immediately contacted him outlining the opportunity in Texas and Mr. Sang soon arrived by train to have a look at the Longview Coca-Cola Bottling Plant. He liked what he saw and lent Franklin, Sr. the money to purchase a 1/3 interest and "Jimmy" Sang kept a 2/3 interest for himself. The purchase price was $42,185.00 – $40,000.00 plus a $2,185.00 note on a Dixie bottling machine. On 5 November 1925, the Longview Coca-Cola Bottling Company was incorporated and a charter was granted to run for 40 years to B.F. Martin, Lorraine Calvin Martin and James Sanger. Mr. Sang (who changed his name to "Sanger") was a bachelor and left his interest to his several nieces and nephews.

When the East Texas oil boom hit in 1931, the town of Longview went wild! The Coca-Cola Bottling Plant was forced to bottle 24-hours a day and the old machinery was constantly breaking down. Thomas Sweeney heard about the oil boom in this area and wisely bought royalty interest in the oil field. A case of Coca-Cola sold for 80¢, and $1.40, including deposit. Syrup for bottler's use sold for $1.30 per gallon as set out in a Coca-Cola bottler's first line contract. In 1933, General Manager, B.F. Martin, Sr., brought his younger brother, Malcom Montreville Martin, of Lanexa, New Kent Country, Virginia, aboard to head up the maintenance department. Malcom Martin had previously accompanied Mr. Sweeney to Brownsville to work for him in the plant there. The original location of the Longview plant was at the northeast corner of Cotton and Center streets. The location was across the street from Kelly Plow Company and the Magnolia Hotel which was owned by the Turley Dalston family. The building was owned by Dr. Cole and adjoined

Bunch's Mule Lot on the east. That part of the building not occupied by Longview Coca-Cola was rented to Eason Grocery and a feed and seed store. The building has been beautifully restored by Mr. Roland Hug.

In 1935, Longview Coca-Cola moved to a new state of the art building designed by architect Percy Zimmerman. The new location at 340 W. Tyler was across the street from Jack Riddle's Silver Garden Restaurant, which would cook your wild game for you and served wine and beer. They made the best hamburgers and sold fire works seasonally. They sold a prime T-bone steak for $2.00 at that time. In the old days, on Saturdays, the plant employees, both white and black, would order hamburgers from Riddle's and get in huge crap games. This practice continued until stopped by management at the suggestion of law enforcement. Longview Coca-Cola had the reputation of producing the best tasting Cokes in the country which was due to filtration of the water through sands. Mattie Casteberry of Mattie's Ballroom fame sent a thank you letter to Longview Coca-Cola every year in gratitude for her company's good business relations with Longview Coca-Cola.

B.F. Martin served as general manager of Longview Coca-Cola until about 1942. After he retired as general manager, the plant had three outside-the-family managers, Bill Clafferty, J.B. Thompson and Mel Rathert. Then there were the inside-the-family general managers, Harold Hedges, Charles V. Stephenson, Charles A. Stephenson and Michael Hedges.

In 1998, Longview Coca-Cola purchased the Schlitz/Stroh beer distribution center located at 1403 West Cotton Street from Bill Stoudt and operated from there until the plant was purchased by Coca-Cola Enterprises (CCE) Division of Houston in May of 2000. The CCE made Longview Coca-Cola an offer it couldn't refuse. The Longview territory is now served out of Tyler. The building on Cotton Street, last occupied by Longview Coca-Cola Bottling Company prior to the sale, has most recently served as a Columbia Space Shuttle Debris Collection Staging Area.

Before Longview Coca-Cola was sold to CCE, Frank Stephenson of Daytona Beach, Florida, was Chairman of the Board and Benjamin Franklin Martin, Jr. was President and CEO. And this is what happened during the 88-year Dynasty of The Longview Coca-Cola Bottling Company, Incorporated.

Horaney's

In August 1940, Harry S. Horaney started a feed and seed store at 207 N. Court Street, Longview. Through the years the business became more than a feed and seed store.

Harry and Albert Horaney

Albert Horaney started working in the business as soon as he was old enough. As he became older and became more involved, he would add new items. In 1958, Albert married Betty Barkett and she became a part of the business.

Albert's mother, Lorene, worked at the store until her death in 1973. Harry continued until his death in 1977.

Albert and Betty's sons, Al and Ron, worked at the store after school until their graduation from Kilgore College. They both became part of the family working full time, from unloading boxcars to taking care of customers.

When a fire consumed the 40 year-old R.B. Cook and Co. Feed Store in Gilmer, Texas, Albert knew it was time to pack up and move. Albert had always worried about the wooden floors in the original building. So, in November 1993, the old store was closed and moved to 301 W. Methvin. The warehouse was already on Methvin, so the new store was added to the warehouse.

In the 1940s, Horaney's became a community gathering place as well as a store. The business got larger as the town grew. More customers came to shop and visit. The town evolved out of its rural heritage, the people changed and the store carried new merchandise.

Albert liked to say in 1940 his dad ran a feed store that sold to farmers. Then things changed and the store progressed to seed, then hardware. In the early 1950s, Horaney's started selling roses, which led to chemicals and insecticides, tools and garden equipment. Horaney's today sells to farmers, ranchers and homeowners.

Ironically, although his father founded the store, Albert witnessed just about every moment, every event at this historic store. He was there from being a child and walking from school to help his dad.

He also remembered how very cold the original store was. Albert used to think how tough his dad had to be to survive in the early days. He also remembered seeing poor people walk in hungry and seeing his dad reach in his pocket to give them what he could. This, too, has been passed down to each generation.

When Harry opened the business, Longview's population was only 13,700, the oil boom was new, and the nation was preparing for war. When Albert opened the new store the population was near 80,000.

Horaney's was and is run by a family continuing the legacy left by Harry and Albert Horaney. Horaney's today, as in the past, is dedicated to serving its customers. Albert died in 1996, leaving Betty, Al and Ron to continue.

Wandering through the store reminds people of the old store and old times. You can still find lard cans, Saturday night tubs, andirons, cast iron, wood burning stoves, teakettles, canning supplies, kerosene lamps, cork stoppers and so much more.

Deer hunters and bird lovers, fisherman and lawn owners can find their sup-

Albert and Betty Horaney

plies as well as a complete organic area for the organic gardener.

Farmers and ranchers can also still find whatever they need. Need a cow bell for the football games? Come to Horaney's.

Betty is still at Horaney's each day overseeing the operation of the business. Ronnie is also there and now has a wife and four children that Betty likes to think will continue when she is no longer here.

Al is living in Tyler and has a wife and son. He has taken the knowledge his dad and mother taught him and opened his own store just like his dad operated. He, too, will pass his own store to his son.

Betty says that Horaney's will always give to its customers the personal service it was built on. She invites you to come in and browse, and you will like what you see. If you can't find something, ask, and she or Ron will try to find it for you.

The business is open Monday through Friday from 7 a.m. to 6 p.m. and Saturday 7 a.m. to 2:30 p.m.

The Horaneys – generations 2, 3 and 4.

301 West Methvin

Phone: (903) 753-3661

Pegues-Hurst Motor Co.
Your Ford Dealer Since 1915

What started as a livery stable by J. Garland Pegues has become the third oldest Ford dealership in Texas. On 2 August 1915, a factory sales agreement was executed with Ford Motor Company and remains in effect to this day, some 90 years later.

Pegues-Hurst history has seen five locations and they are as follows:

1st – 1913-1915: 229 E. Tyler (current Bank One parking garage)

2nd – 1915-1922: southeast corner of Tyler and Green (later occupied by Johnny Cace Restaurant)

3rd – 1923-1953: southwest corner of Methvin and Green (currently the drive-in bank for Bank One)

4th – 1953-1967: northeast corner of Marshall Avenue and McCann Road (building still stands)

5th – 1967-Present: 200 Spur 63, southeast corner of Cotton and Spur 63

Julian H. Hurst went to work for Pegues Motor Co. in 1916 at the age of 15, and became a full partner in 1945 with the death of J.G. Pegues when the name was changed to Pegues-Hurst Motor Co. After returning from World War II, where he was a pilot and flight instructor, Julian G. Hurst, son of Julian H. Hurst, went to work for the dealership, and became the dealer in

Julian Hurst, Julian G. Hurst and James H. Hurst with photograph of J.G. Pegues.

Left: Present location, 200 Spur 63, south of Highway 80, 1967-Present.

Methvin and Green, 1923-1953

Left: Tyler and Green, 1915-1922

1969 upon the death of his father. He remained in that position until his death in 1978. James H. Hurst, son of J.G. Hurst, became the dealer in 1978 to the present.

The original Model T Fords arrived by rail boxcars completely disassembled, with the wheels stacked and the chassis upended to the walls of the boxcars. J.G. Pegues, Julian H. Hurst and others would unload the cars, place the bodies on the chassis and drive them to the auto agency for final assembly, which took half a day, to get them ready for sale.

Rader Funeral Home

The story of LeRoy Rader Funeral Home, Inc. begins in Illinois in the late 1920s, when LeRoy Rader decided he wanted to be a mortician.

His parents were not able to help with his schooling, so he managed to move to Chicago, Illinois, where he enrolled in the Worsham School of Embalming. He worked a night job and attended school during the day.

After graduating from the 'embalming school,' he returned to southern Illinois and tried to find work in a funeral home. He could only find a part time job. LeRoy was in love with his high school sweetheart and he knew that if he hoped to get married he would have to find a job.

He arrived in Shreveport, Louisiana, still looking for work. He inquired at Wellman Funeral Home and they explained that their staff was full, but they had a spare room above the funeral home. He could sleep nights there while looking for work.

He eventually went to Paris, Texas, and landed a job at Roden Funeral Home. A few months later, he went back to Illinois, married his sweetheart and they moved to Paris and lived above the funeral home, in a furnished apartment.

Their son, Charley, was born in Paris in 1932. After a few years in Paris, LeRoy found a job in Longview, with the Welch Funeral Home. He worked in Longview for a couple of years and then was asked to manage the Everett and Welch Funeral Home in Gladewater.

In 1938, LeRoy Rader and Thomas Welch organized a partnership and opened the Welch and Rader Funeral Home in Kilgore. At that time, there were eleven other funeral homes in Kilgore. The next year they dissolved their partnership and LeRoy became the sole owner of Rader Funeral Home, Kilgore, Texas.

In 1953, his son, Charley, and Charley's wife, Betty, were students at North Texas State University. In addition to being a full time student, Charley had a job working at the *Denton Record Chronicle* newspaper.

LeRoy called Charley home one weekend and asked what he intended to do after he graduated from college. Charley replied that he planned to come home to Kilgore and work in the family business.

LeRoy explained that there was not enough business to support two families in Kilgore, but there was a funeral home for sale in Longview. Betty and Charley said, "Thank you, but we are not sure we want to live in Longview." On the way back to Denton, they decided they better check out the opportunity in Longview; they say now it was the best decision they ever made.

LeRoy purchased Rains and Talley Funeral Home on Fredonia Street in downtown Longview. Betty and Charley left Denton in December 1953, and moved to Longview. The Raders first lived upstairs over the funeral home, then moved into an apartment where the new Gregg County jail now stands.

Charley attended mortuary school in Dallas, and he and Betty returned to Longview in the spring of 1955, and have been active citizens in the community since that time.

Rader Funeral Home was located on North Fredonia Street, in the former Stinchcomb residence that had been converted into a funeral home in 1939.

In 1970, the Rader's began construction on the current funeral home building at 1617 Judson Road. At that time, Judson Road was a two lane oil-top road.

In 1981, Betty and Charley's son, Charles, graduated from Mortuary School in Dallas. The third generation of Rader's was at work in Longview. In 1986, their daughter, Lynn Martin, came to work at the funeral home doing public relations and advertising.

In 1989, the Rader's decided to expand with a locally owned cemetery. Charles located an area in North Longview on Seven Pines Road and after securing the necessary permits, the Raders started what is now Rosewood Park Cemetery.

Today, after serving the Longview community for over 50 years, Rader Funeral Home in Longview continues to be locally owned and operated by the Rader family.

Rader Funeral Home, 1953

Right:
Rader Funeral
Home, 2003

Texas Bank and Trust

Originally chartered as First State Bank of Longview, the bank opened its doors on 4 March 1958, with the late J. Clyde Tomlinson, Sr. as chairman and Norman Taylor as president. The bank's first Statement of Condition reflected assets of $2,635,234. When trust powers were granted in 1962, the name of the bank was changed to Longview Bank and Trust Company.

In August of 1969, Rogers Pope joined the bank as vice president in the Commercial Lending Division, and in March of 1970, he was named president and chief executive officer of Longview Bank and Trust Company. In 1975, upon the death of Mr. Tomlinson, Mr. Pope was elected chairman of the board. In his words: "The dreams and goals of our bank's founders were to be a state chartered, independent, resourceful institution wholeheartedly committed to serving the community of Longview."

Longview Bank and Trust organized a bank travel club for its customers in early 1976. Under the direction of Senior Vice President Hazel Hickey, the travel club evolved into OMNIClub in 1982.

In August 1978, Longview Bank and Trust appointed its first student board of directors — a special group of seniors from Pine Tree High School and Longview High School, selected for one-year terms on the basis of leadership ability, enthusiasm, scholarship and integrity. The tradition of the student board continues, and has come to include Longview High School, Pine Tree High School, Spring Hill High School and Trinity School of Texas.

The bank began offering mortgage loans in 1982, and has since become one of the largest mortgage lenders in the East Texas region.

In 1980, Bob Dyer joined the bank as vice president in the Commercial Lending Division and was named president in 1983. Also in 1983, Longview Bank and Trust began to offer full trust services, and the bank's Trust and Investment Division has become one of the premier centers for trust services in East Texas, with assets exceeding $500 million.

Longview Bank and Trust Company celebrated its 25th anniversary in 1983. For that occasion, the bank commissioned a work by well-known artist and sculptor Henry Wedemeyer — six bronze relief panels that would cover the limestone base for the 20' x 30' American flag that would become the bank's hallmark. The panels of the monument depict Longview from its beginnings as a rural town to its status, in 1983, as a regional center for commerce and culture.

The first East Texas bank to offer major credit cards with local credit approval, LB&T announced its VISA and MasterCard programs in 1987.

Longview Bank and Trust opened the first commercial bank branch facility in Longview in 1988 when it acquired Oak Forest National Bank. In 1991, the bank opened its second branch — known as the Pine Tree Branch — at Loop 281 and Gilmer Road.

In February 1993, BSC Alliance Limited Company began operations with ownership vested in Longview Bank and Trust and three other East Texas banks. The company, now known as BSC Securities, LC, was organized to afford independent banks the opportunity to offer their customers innovative services by sharing the cost of thse services with other banks.

In 1995, Howard Hackney joined the institution as president of Longview Bank and Trust.

Within a six-year span, Longview Bank and Trust opened six new branches: Cushing, in 1996; San Augustine, in 1997; Pine Tree Convenience Center, in 1998; North Longview, in 1999; Marshall, in 2000; Gladewater, in 2001.

In 2003, the bank celebrated its 45th anniversary. Shortly thereafter, the name of the bank was changed to Texas Bank and Trust Company. In late 2003, the bank opened a branch in Tyler, and, in late 2004, opened a newly constructed Tyler branch.

Upon the retirement of Howard Hackney in 2004, Rogers Pope Jr. was named president and chief operating officer, having previously served as trust officer, general counsel, and executive vice president.

The identifying slogan of Texas Bank and Trust since 1975 has been "People Make the Difference." The bank has reiterated its familiar slogan every Sunday since 1977 with an article in the *Longview News-Journal* entitled, "People of our Community Who Make a Difference." The article has achieved recognition not only for the individuals featured, but also for the impetus it has given the projects and causes for which they volunteer.

The symbol of Texas Bank and Trust is known throughout East Texas. It represents the bank's three primary commitments — to individuals, to business and industry, and to the communities it serves. The equal parts of the symbol indicate the bank's concern for excellence of service to all. The symbol's unity and integrity reflect the bank's pride in being an East Texas-owned, independent bank. The bold Texas star at the center of the symbol represents the bank's proud heritage of strength, stability and tradition.

In Memory of our Mother and Grandmother
Mary Ellen Hillis
For her love of family and genealogy.

"I know for certain that we never lose the people we love, even to death. They continue to participate in every act, thought and decision we make. Their love leaves an indelible imprint in our memories. We find comfort in knowing our lives have been enriched by having shared their love."

Leo Buscaglia

Our mother, Mary Ellen Heidler Hillis, was born 26 June 1922, the only daughter of Alice Ethel Bennett and Maximillion George Heidler, in Ft. Worth, Texas.

Her father, Max, was born in Austria, now Carlsbad, Czechoslavakia, on 11 November 1889. He immigrated to the United States in 1907, at the age of 18, when he "absconded" with his college money to follow his dream to be an American cowboy. He settled in Cleburn, Texas, where he married Alice Bennett on 8 November 1920. He owned a produce distributorship in Ft. Worth until his death on 18 July 1955.

Her mother, Alice, was born 13 October 1896, in Erath County, Texas. She was an astonishing woman who began the first of several careers at age 18, teaching in a one-room schoolhouse. Alice then attended business school and was the first female secretary for Ft. Worth Power and Light. She also attended beauty school and operated her own beauty shop. As her parents began aging, she returned to school once again and received a degree as a registered nurse, working at Cook's Children's Hospital in Ft. Worth. She used her nursing skills to care for her parents at home and continued to work as registrar at Cook's until a stroke incapacitated her. She moved to Longview and lived with her daughter, Mary Ellen, until her death on 2 June 1980.

Mary Ellen grew up in Ft. Worth as an adored only child and beautiful young woman, graduating from Paschal High School. She continued her education at North Texas Women's University, where she received a teaching degree in home economics. She met Charles Lee Hillis, Jr. from Wylie, Texas, through one of her college roommates. "Chock" or "Red" was attending North Texas Agricultural College (A&M). The rest is history, as the saying goes. Mary Ellen immediately knew that Chock was the one for her because, as she later told her family, he made her "toes tingle." They were married in Weatherford, Texas, on 16 March 1942.

Mary Ellen Hillis – June 2002

Like so many World War II soldiers, Chock left a pregnant wife when he went overseas to fight for our country. Their first born, Charles Max, born 19 April 1943, was almost two before he saw his daddy for the first time. Mary Ellen and Chock wanted a dozen children! Or maybe that was just Mary Ellen? They lost no time after the end of World War II, having Vickie Anne, 20 January 1947, and John Leeton, 12 March 1948. They were living in Levelland, Texas, at this time. Chock was working for Stanolind Oil and Mary Ellen and her mother were running a 12-room boarding house (the only house they could find to buy when they got transferred) for all the oilfield personnel that could not find housing during that boom time. They then moved to Andrews, Texas, where Mary Ellen began her teaching career. They had given up on being able to have more children and had given away the high chair and

baby bed when Jana Alice was born on 29 October 1956. Leigh Ellen followed on 1 February 1960.

Chock, Mary Ellen and the five children were transferred, with now Amoco Production, to Longview in 1960. Mary Ellen began teaching home economics at Pine Tree High School, where she taught for 20 years.

Mary Ellen's calling was teaching. She was a patient teacher, a good listener, and saw and nurtured the good in students that others had given up on. Many a young girl learned to cook, sew and manage a household under the tutelage of Mrs. Hillis and fellow Home Economics teacher, Mrs. Audibert.

Mary Ellen retired from teaching to care for her mother and husband. Knowing she couldn't sit idle, she drew on her lifelong hobbies: crafts…crochet, knitting, rug hooking, painting, any kind of handiwork, and opened Craft Cottage with daughters Vickie and Leigh. Chock retired from Amoco after 30 years and they had several years to travel and enjoy their 14 grandchildren. They celebrated 42 wonderful years of marriage before cancer took Chock on 20 August 1986.

Mom continued as matriarch of the Hillis family for 17 years before her death on 19 July 2003, pursuing her passions: genealogy, family, cooking, Christmas and doll collecting. She was a member and officer of DAR, a volunteer in the genealogy department of the library, an active member of First Christian Church, a kind and warm-hearted friend and, most of all, a mother, grandmother and great grandmother who left a legacy of love best illustrated by her note in the "Hillis Heritage" cookbook:
"My Darlings,
Your family made you what you are. Not only did your genes come from 7 generations of your ancestors, but your family has given you your set of values, helped to develop your strengths, shown you love and support. I hope each of you has happy memories of family.
Love, Mom"

The Hillis family, July 2003 – In Memory of Mary Ellen Hillis.

In memory of
O.H. Methvin
Founder of Longview

**Methvin descendents:
Lauren and Shannon Dodson (8th generation)
and Beth Holloway Dodson (6th generation)**

Gregg County, Texas
Family Histories

Biographies

ADRIAN

Seated: James Fowler Adrian and wife Sarah Elizabeth (Pearson). Standing: daughter Nan and son Charles.

"Grandfather and Grandmother was of German and Welsh decent. Grandfather came to this country from Germany as a tailor, settled in York District, South Carolina, and raised a family of five boys and two daughters. Names of boys: John German, Robert DeKalb, Fleming Fowler, David Willber and William Harvey. The daughters married a McDonald and a Davidson and raised families. John G. died a bachelor, Robt. D. left home whilst young to go to New Orleans and was never heard from again. Fleming F. came to Alabama from Ga., raised a family. His oldest son came through with Cherokee Indians, where they then settled in the Territory, now Oklahoma, as interpreter for the tribe. His descendants are now in Van Zandt county and other parts of Texas. David W., the writer's father, married in Georgia, a McDonald and raised a family of five sons and one daughter. Names: John German, Robt. DeKalb, James Fowler, David Willber and William Harvey. Daughter Nancy Jane. Sons all in confederate war. John G. was killed at Battle of Gettysburg, Robert D. sickened and died at Lancaster, Ky., after Shilo Battle. James F. came through with gunshot wound from General Kilpatrick's Cavalry in King George County, Va. William H. came through safe but died of pneumonia in Wood county fifteen years ago. Nancy Jane died in Gregg County thirty years ago. D.W. and James F. still alive. D.W. 80 years and J.F. 82. All have raised families. Their generations are increasing to the fourth generation and the writer being the eldest living member of the family would ask as a favor that succeeding generations still retain the name German in memory of the nationality of their great-great grand kin.

I dedicate this short memorandum to the succeeding generations of the Adrian family."
J.F. Adrian – 6 April 1914

The Rest of the Story

"Grandfather" was John David Adrian, born circa 1750. "Grandmother" was Rachel Fleming, born circa 1755 to Robert and Pheroba Fleming. Rachel and David married in South Carolina circa 1773. David, an elder in Hebron Presbyterian Church in Franklin County, Georgia, died there circa 1825; Rachel died there circa 1830. The children of David and Rachel were John German; Elizabeth M., married Wil-

liam McDonald; Rachel, married John Davidson; Robert DeKalb; Fleming Fowler; David Wilbur; William M. Harvey; and Olivia, married Frederick M. Gowder.

The Georgia-born children of young David were John German; Robert DeKalb; James Fowler (see "James Fowler Adrian"); David Wilbur (see "Adrian Addendum"); Nancy Jane (1837-1881), married Arthur B. Wilkes; and William Harvey. John, James, David and William moved to Cherokee County, Alabama, from Georgia. James, who lived in Gregg County, Texas, for two years, and William moved to Wood County, Texas. David resided in Mississippi, moved to Pittsburg, Upshur County, Texas, and then to Gregg County.

William Harvey (1840-1902) and wife Mary A. Elizabeth "Lizzie" Chastain (1846-1919) had four children: James Costin (1868-1963), Mary E., Russell DeKalb (1874-1958) and Joseph David (1880-1962).
– Submitted by Ann Baggett Fournet

ADRIAN ADDENDUM

David Wilbur Adrian (1834-1920), son of David Wilbur Adrian Sr. and Miss McDonald, homesteaded land in 1876 on what is now Adrian Road in Longview, Gregg County, Texas. He and his wife, E.V.A. Williams (1841-1921), had five children: Henry D. (1861-1943); Leila (1866-1886); Benjamin J. "Ben" (1870-1951); Robert David "Bob" (1872-1944); and Sallie B. (1876-1903), who married William A. McWhorter (1861-1932) and later died in childbirth.

Henry and his first wife, Martha "Mattie" Mackey (1864-1915), had four children: Marvin E. (1885-1963), Mattie (1889-), Vester (1892-) and Ralph Dewey (1898-). The family resided in Cooke County, Texas. Living with them at the time of the 1900 census was Henry's brother Ben. Henry's second wife was Eliza (1862-). Henry, his wife Mattie and son Marvin are buried in North Dexter Cemetery in Cooke County.

Leila married Thomas P. "Tom" Smith; they lost an infant daughter (1885) then had a son, Hughie L. (1886-1900). Leila probably died when Hughie was born. He resided with his Adrian grandparents at the time the 1900 census was taken, in June, and died two months later.

Ella and Ben Adrian with sons Fred, top, and J.C., bottom – 1908.

Bob and Ala Adrian with children (l.-r.) Eugene, Robbie and Harold – 1908.

Bob and Ben worked the farm with their families until Ben bought land on Old Highway 80 near White Oak. During the East Texas Oil Boom, oil was discovered on his land, allowing him and his family to live out their days in relative leisure. Ben and his wife, Ella McCreary (1871-1961), had two sons, "J.C." Justin (1902-1954) and Frederick L. "Fred" (1904-2002). J.C. married Samantha "San" and had no children. Fred married Nina Bassett (1907-1981); their daughter is Jerilyn.

Bob and his wife, Alabama Frances "Ala" Whatley (1875-1957), daughter of Hiram Whatley and Georgia F. Stone, were not as fortunate as Ben and Ella. They continued the hard existence of cotton farmers while raising most of their food as well. They had four children: infant daughter (1901), Harold DeKalb (1902-1986), Eugene (1904-1993) and Robbie (1906-1984). The children attended the Tryon School, high school and college. (See "Eugene Adrian" and "Joe Baggett & Robbie Adrian.")

Harold attended Southern Methodist University and worked as business manager of Methodist Hospital in Dallas, Texas, for most of his career. He was well known in the medical community. He and his wife, Mary Louise "Mamie" (-1987), attended the First Methodist Church. They never had biological children but dearly loved their goddaughter, Mary Louise Turner, and their nieces and nephews. Harold was known as "Uncle Bubba." Robbie had christened him "Bubba" as a toddler when she couldn't pronounce "Brother." Uncle Bubba and Aunt Mamie provided treats and entertainment for two generations of Adrian descendants.

Ralph Guidroz and his wife, Joy (Baggett), Robbie's daughter, returned to the Adrian farm in 1990. Ralph researched, applied for and received the Family Land Heritage Certificate of Honor in 1993, awarded the family for a century or more of continuous ownership of a family agricultural enterprise. The land is still in use today for cattle raising. It continues to offer recreation and spiritual renewal for Adrian descendants and their friends.
– Submitted by Brenda Petro

ADRIAN ACRES

As a child, I only knew it in its extremes-
the intense white heat of Summer,
the bitter blue cold of Winter.
These extremes, coupled with the love of my people,

produced the love of this place that has stayed
with me all of my life.
These short week to two week stays
over 50 years' time, tattooed my memory with -
the love of family,
the history of my tribe,
the taste of the food and water,
the sound of the bob-white,
the groan of a swing holding beloved relatives
as they spun family legends,
the feel of hot, deep sand on my feet,
the smell of the oiled road banked by
black-eyed Susans,
the sweet smelling petunias in my grandmother's
flower garden.
Only as an aging woman did I come to delight
in the heady, cold-wine days of Autumn and
Spring.
Only when I came to care for my dying father
did I see the magnificence of Fall colors, the
abundance of pecans and the fun of gathering them.
Only when I came to live here did I know -
the birth of new life in Spring,
the greening of the trees,
the pink and white blossoms of the
peach, pear, apple,
the great pleasure of turning the earth
with tools and gloves,
then abandoning them to feel the dirt in my hands,
the peasant in me rejoicing in the promising fertility
as I planted and prayed for new life,
the triumph as it burst forth to provide
food for the soul in beauty or
for the body in nurturance.
What a gift - my ancestral home.
I'm the fourth generation to live here.
I live in leisure and comfort, but I remember-
the hard times of no air conditioning or
central heat,
carrying water from the well, a city
block away,
watching my grandmother cook on a
wood stove
using hand chopped wood,
going to the outdoor toilet, fearing the
spiders there.
My great-grandparents, my grandparents, my
parents
held this place in trust for me and mine.
They spent their energy, their time, their love,
and what little money they had
preserving this precious place - this sacred ground.
How I love it!
How it has shaped me,
How it has been my security
when I lived in other, less comforting places.

The Adrian home in 1938.

E.V.A. and David Adrian, circa 1900.

Will I be allowed to live out my days here?
Will my children and other relatives
be allowed to call it home for years to come?
Only God knows -
Only time will tell.
All I can do is continue to celebrate
my opportunity to live in the now
in this beloved place
with memories of all who have loved me.
I can pass on the love and the memories,
the faith to my children and to others I love.
I will thank and praise God.
– Submitted by Joy Guidroz (daughter of
Robbie Adrian and Joe Byron Baggett,
granddaughter of Ala Whatley and Bob
Adrian, great-granddaughter of E.V.A.
Williams and David Wilbur Adrian)

EUGENE ADRIAN

Eugene Adrian was born on 17 May 1904, in Longview, Texas. He was the second son of Robert David and Alabama Frances (Whatley) Adrian; Harold DeKalb was two years older. After the birth of a daughter, Robbie, the family was complete. Their lives were full of community, and church activities. Bob was a hard working farmer and his children helped with the myriad tasks associated with rural life. Gene seemed to relish this life and was the child that could be counted on to do extra chores, when needed. Apparently, his brother Harold was more studious and Gene loved activity. Twice in his life, Gene was asked to give up his schoolwork to help on the farm; therefore, he graduated from high school one year after his peers.

After high school, he attended SMU in Dallas, Texas. It was there that he met Gladys Lattimore. While attending college, he worked in a drug store. Gladys was taking business courses and waited for the streetcar in front of the store. She would often go in for a milk shake. After getting to know each other, they began to have tennis and movie dates. Unfortunately, their relationship was interrupted when, once again, Gene was called home to help on the farm. They corresponded, and when he returned to Dallas their romance blossomed.

On 6 June 1931, Gladys and Gene married, and shortly thereafter Shell Oil Company relocated them to Houston, Texas. Gene worked as an accountant for Shell and Gladys stayed home to care for their children, Marilyn, born 20 May 1937, and James, born 13 January 1941.

Their lives centered around church activities at Bering Memorial Methodist Church.

Gene was Chairman of the Board and Gladys was secretary of her Sunday school class. Their son Jim recalls many happy times with that church family.

In November 1959, Gene and Gladys welcomed Richard Lowke to the family when he married Marilyn, and Chellie Parrish in June 1960, when she married Jim. From these marriages, the family grew. They were proud grandparents to Robert, Mark and Michael Adrian and Adrienne and Kyle Lowke. Fortunately, they lived to see all of their grandchildren graduate from college and begin their lives. The great grandchildren, Hannah, James and Jeremy Adrian, Brock and Kelsey Lowke, and Huntington Stoinoff, are the legacy of their well-lived lives.

Gene and Gladys Adrian, center, with children Marilyn and Jim.

After thirty-five years of work, Gene and Gladys returned to Longview. Again, church was an important part of their lives. They attended Summerfield Methodist, the church that Gene's grandfather helped establish. In addition, Gene continued his strong work ethic by helping to start Tyrone Road Water Company. He was proud of this endeavor and continued to be active in the company until he died at the age of eighty-eight. Gladys lived on in their home on Adrian Road until she was eighty-eight and died in Austin, Texas, at the age of ninety.

Gladys and Gene Adrian, right, back row, with grandchildren. (l.-r.) Back: Robert and Mark Adrian. Front: Adrienne Lowke, Michael Adrian and Kyle Lowke.

Gene and Gladys are buried in the cemetery of their beloved Summerfield Methodist Church. Their children and grandchildren will never forget the examples of hard work, faith in God, love and devotion they set.

– Submitted by Jim and Chellie Adrian

JAMES FOWLER ADRIAN

James Fowler Adrian (born 15 April 1832, in Franklin County, Georgia; died 3 August 1918, in Wood County, Texas) was one of the third generation of Adrians led by John David Adrian (born about 1750 in Germany; died in 1825 in Franklin County, Georgia) that emigrated from the Alsace region of what was then Germany in the late 1700s with his wife, Rachel Fleming, and first was documented in New York District, South Carolina, in 1778 (according to descendant and researcher Jenelle Tuttle). J.F. tells of his family in the "Adrian" biography in this volume. How special it is to have such a history written in his own words!

What J.F., or Jim, did not elaborate on is that he served in the Alabama 48th Infantry from Cherokee County, Alabama, as a part of Law's Alabama Brigade that fought at Gettysburg and later was part of Lee's Army of Northern Virginia. Jim enlisted on 25 March 1861, was wounded in Virginia, and was discharged 30 August 1864, at the close of the war, as a 1st Lieutenant. He is mentioned, along with brothers and cousins, in Law's Alabama Brigade in the *War Between the Union and the Confederacy* by J. Gary Laine and Morris M. Penny.

Jim was married on 22 January 1857, in Cherokee County, Alabama, to Sarah Elizabeth Pearson (born in 1839 in Cherokee County; died 28 May 1924, in Golden, Wood County, Texas). They had eight children, five sons and three daughters. Charles Newton was the last child born to Jim and Sarah, and the only one born in Wood County; all the others were born while the family was still in Cherokee County. Before moving to Wood County, Jim and family resided in Longview, Gregg County, Texas for two years.

The Adrian children were Mary A. (born circa 1857), William Robert "Bob" (born 20 October 1859; died 12 March 1947), James Beauregard (born 28 July 1861; died 11 August 1929), Sallie F. (born circa 1863), Nannie B. (born in October 1866; died 7 November 1960), Van(n) Pomeroy "Brick" (born 3 June 1874; died in 1933), Luther P. (born 18 October 1876; died 25 March 1881), and Charles Newton (born 7 November 1878; died 21 September 1952).

Van married Cora Matilda Brooks. They were the parents of two daughters, Ruby Mildred and Amy Estelle. Van and Cora resided in the Sherman-Denison area of Texas. Ruby Mildred

Sons of J.F. Adrian: (l.-r.) Van Pomeroy "Brick" (1874-1933), James Beauregard (1861-1929), William Robert "Bob" (1859-1947) and Charles Newton (1878-1952).

(Tolbert) had three daughters: Amy Ruth (Wheat), Joyce Omega (Willard) and Jean Marie (Hanna). Amy Estelle (McMurry) had a son, John, and a daughter, Jill.

Jim and Sarah are buried along with children Nannie and Luther and several relatives in the Sand Springs Cemetery near Mineola in Wood County, Texas. Jim was survived by his wife, seven children, twenty-seven grandchildren and seven great grandchildren.

The compiler's lineage from J.F. is as follows: great great grandfather James Fowler Adrian, great grandfather Vann Pomeroy "Brick" Adrian, grandmother Ruby Mildred Adrian Tolbert and mother Amy Ruth Tolbert Wheat.

– Submitted by Bruce Edwin Wheat, Hoover, Alabama

WISE & ANNA AGEE

William Wisemon Agee was born in Newton County, Arkansas, on 28 August 1894, the son of William Nathan and Nancy Eller Christian Agee. He was the grandson of William Newton Christian, a Confederate soldier from Arkansas, and a fifth great grandson of the Huguenot, Mathieu Agee, who came to this country in 1700-1701 from France.

Anna and Wise Agee

Wise met and married Anna P. Lawson in Newton County. Anna was born in Newton County on 27 November 1895, the daughter of Thomas and Louretta Cowles Lawson. Anna had a beautiful voice and attended singing school. After their courtship, they were married on 19 January 1913, in Hasty, Arkansas.

They were successful farmers. They loaded their wagon with extra produce and eggs to take to town to barter or sell for coffee, sugar and items they could not raise. Anna was a beautiful seamstress, and Wise a hard worker.

On 8 January 1919, they loaded their wagon and moved from Arkansas to Oklahoma. In 1939, they made their move from Oklahoma to Gregg County. Wise worked as an oilfield switcher for Sells Petroleum Company.

Wise and Anna were faithful members of First Assembly of God Church in Kilgore.

Wise died 15 January 1980, at age 85. Anna died on 9 May 1997, at age 101. They are both buried in the Kilgore Cemetery.

Wise and Anna were the parents of four daughters and one son: Arphie Ralston, Frank Agee, Zella Allen, Flossie Hankins and Beatrice Jones, and the grandparents of twelve children.

– Submitted by J. Bolton

MYRTLE ISABEL BILYEU AKERS

Myrtle B. Akers, real estate executive with Ben Franklin Realty of Longview, Texas, was born in Shelbyville, Missouri, 8 May 1900. She was the daughter of Lon A. and Emma Virginia Copenhaver Bilyeu. She studied at Central Missouri State College and then at the University of Missouri in Columbia, Missouri. She taught school in Kansas City and discovered teaching was not to her liking. She returned to her home in Holden, Missouri, to become assistant manager of the Harrow-Taylor Butter

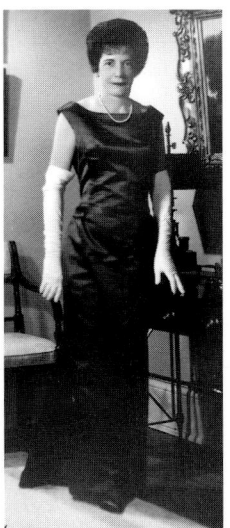

Myrtle B. Akers, 1965

Company, where she sailed around town in her new Buick that she bought with her own money.

In 1922, she married William Webster Akers of Holden, Missouri. In 1931, they decided to take their two young children and try their fate in the East Texas oil boomtown of Longview. They never looked back to Missouri. Longview became their life-long home.

Myrtle's education and her spirit of perseverance made her reach out for the business world in a time that most women stayed in the home, even though she and Webster added two more children to their family.

In 1936-1939, Myrtle became manager of the collection department of the Retail Merchants Association of Longview. And in 1939, she joined a group of medical doctors who founded Medical and Surgical Clinic. Myrtle was the Clinic Manager from 1939 until 1957. She was awarded an honor as the only woman in the United States to become a Fellow of Clinic Managers in 1958.

In 1958, she joined Franklin Martin in his real estate firm of Ben Franklin Realty. She remained for 20 years with Mr. Martin until her death in 1978.

During her business career, Myrtle served as chairman of the Longview Savings Bond Committee, Gregg County, Texas, 1963; advisory committee of the Longview Public School System, 1959; member of the Longview Civic Music; corresponding secretary of north Texas Dog Shows, 1962-1963; member of the national Association Real Estate Boards (president of the Longview Chapter Women's Council (1963-1964); member of the Business and Professional Women's Club (president, 1941); the service organization Pilots Club international (president, 1956-1957); and she served as the study chairman and was a member of the business women's circle (which met at night) at the First Presbyterian Church for over 40 years. Myrtle and her husband, Webster, were lifetime members and active in the First Presbyterian Church.

Myrtle and Webster Akers were blessed with four children: Dane Webster Akers, deceased in 1986; LaLita Yvonne Akers Taylor of Dallas, Texas; Shirley Lea Akers Fisher of Carrollton, Texas; and Patsy Ruth Akers McDonald of Dallas, Texas.

Myrtle and Webster Akers are buried in Memory Park Cemetery in Harrison County near Longview.

– Submitted by Patsy Akers McDonald

CLINTON ALEXANDER: Global with Roots Firmly in Gregg County

Being born in Germany does not mean a person cannot be a native of Gregg County. Clinton Douglas Alexander was born at Landstuhl Army Hospital in Germany. He actually only lived in Gregg County from 1986-1992 (the years of junior and senior high school at Spring Hill ISD). However he has always felt East Texas, especially Spring Hill, to be home.

Gregg County roots are very deep for the Alexander family. Clinton and his sister Cynthia Kay Alexander, who was born at Eglin Air Force Base, Okaloosa County, Florida, are descendents of James Henry Alexander and Amanda Tinsley McFarland. They moved to the Spring Hill community in 1910 but had been living in Gregg County since the end of the 19th century. Before that time Harrison County was their home. J.H. came to Texas from Alabama and Amanda from Arkansas.

Clinton and Cynthia's mother is Barbara Gail Tekell. Her maternal grandparents, R.K. (Randolph Keets) and Mattie Myrtle Johnson, relocated their family to Spring Hill in 1924 with a move from Rusk County. The Tekell side of the family, R.Q. and Katie Bell Tekell, came to Gregg County from Navarro County during the oil boom in 1931.

Capt. Alexander serving the troops Thanksgiving 2003, a military tradition.

Grandparents Robert Douglas "Doug" Tekell and Mattie Arlene Johnson provided a rural retreat at their Spring Hill home and farm for these global military children.

His military roots go back to grandfather James Clyde Alexander who was stationed at Treasure Island Naval Base in San Francisco, California, during World War II. James was on a mine sweep detail between California and the Hawaiian Islands while in the Navy. During that time he met and married Laura Fay Potts from Henryetta, Oklahoma, who, at that time, was in nursing school at UCLA Berkley.

During the period of the Vietnam War Michael Erwin Alexander, Clinton's father, be-

came an Air Force officer in the administrative field. Mike's military career lasted twenty years. He, as his father James had done 40 years before, returned to Gregg County to continue his career following military service.

Clinton set a plan in motion for his military career by applying for an Army ROTC scholarship. He used that scholarship to attend The Citadel, the Military College of South Carolina. The day after graduation Second Lt. Alexander reported to Ft. Knox, Kentucky, for armor training.

While stationed at Ft. Stewart, Georgia, Clinton married Victoria Wachtel of Raleigh, North Carolina. Their daughters Mattie Elizabeth and Ashley Erwin are named after Gregg County ancestors.

Clinton is an Army captain stationed at Ft. Hood, Texas. Capt. Alexander has distinguished his career while at Ft. Hood, Texas, with two commands. The first was commander of C Troop, 10th Cavalry. The reactivation of Charlie Troop in 2001 was the first time for this company to form up since being deactivated at the end of World War II. Originally this troop was known as the "Buffalo Soldiers" that patrolled the unsettled western territories. A second command followed in A Company, 2nd Battalion, 8th Cavalry. This March 2004, Clinton deploys to Baghdad, Iraq, to serve in the Operations Center of 2nd Battalion, 8th Cavalry.

– Submitted by Barbara Alexander

ISAAC ALEXANDER

Isaac Alexander, Methodist minister, youngest of fourteen children of David B. and Margaret (Gilmore) Alexander, was born on 24 July 1832, in Russell County, Virginia. When Isaac was one year old, his family moved to Tennessee. At sixteen years of age he became a Methodist. He grew up at Cumberland Gap and Strawberry Plains, where he later graduated from high school. From there he went to Emory and Henry College, where he received an M.A. at the age of nineteen.

After graduation from college, Alexander moved to Henderson, Texas, to teach at Fowler Institute. In 1855, he was ordained an elder in the East Texas Conference of the Methodist Episcopal Church, South, and promptly persuaded the conference to authorize him to open a female academy in Tyler. He married Miss Hall, the daughter of the Methodist preacher in Jamestown, Smith County, and opened a school in his wife's home. Alexander taught school and preached in Gilmer. In 1860, he was hired as principal of the four-year-old New Danville Masonic Female Academy. He kept this school open through the war. His wife and many of his students died in the yellow fever epidemic in 1864. In 1873, Alexander, the academy, and most of the population of New Danville moved to the new railroad town of Kilgore, where the academy reopened as a coeducation facility named Alexander Institute under the sponsorship of the local Methodist congregation. Alexander remained as principal when the school, which later became Lon Morris College, was turned over

to the East Texas Conference in 1875. In 1890, he resigned as president of the Institute (though he remained a member of its board until his death) and moved once more to Henderson. There he married Mrs. Margaret Lockens. Two children were born to them. At Henderson, Alexander taught for four years before entering the full-time pastorate. In 1911, he became chaplain of the Agricultural and Mechanical College of Texas, where he also taught history. Isaac Alexander died on 5 June 1919.

JAMES DAVID ALEXANDER

David Alexander was born (22 November 1939) and grew up in Gregg County. He attended White Oak Schools from kindergarten through the 12th grade (Class of 1958). He became one of White Oak's top students and one of Gregg County's most decorated high school athletes ever. He starred on State Championship teams in football, basketball and track and is reportedly the only Gregg County athlete ever to be selected first-team All State in both football and basketball. David still holds White Oak School records in these three sports, plus baseball. He attended Baylor University on a football and track scholarship and graduated with honors and a B.S. degree in math/physics in 1962.

During his 32-year career with NASA at the Johnson Space Center, he was vitally involved in putting men on the moon and in designing the Space Shuttle and its flights. David was recognized and honored as one of the leading rendezvous specialists. One of the rendezvous algorithms he derived in the mid-1960s reportedly is still used by military missiles. He was selected as Outstanding Citizen in the Johnson Space Center in 1993. After retiring in 1995 he and his first wife, Sandy, moved back to Longview.

Sandy also graduated from White Oak Schools and Baylor. She was an elementary teacher for 27 years and was recognized as one of the outstanding teachers in the Clear Creek ISD. Her parents, the late H.E. and Aline Bingham, were leading citizens in White Oak and Gregg County for many years. Sandy's older sister Janice (Canion) was an English teacher and Deputy Superintendent of the Longview ISD before retiring in 1999. Sandy lost her battle with recurrent breast cancer on 18 October 2000. The world is truly a better place because this beautiful person dwelt upon it for 59+ years.

James David Alexander, 1990

Two children were born to David and Sandy, Millicent (Milli) Alexander Jacks (born 30 August 1968) and David Gregory (Greg) Alexander (10 December 1970). Milli is an attorney in Fort Worth and the mother of two. Greg is a NASA computer scientist at the Johnson Space Center and the father of three.

David is also a Gospel quartet singer, songwriter, poet and Baptist deacon. He manages and sings baritone for a Southern Gospel quartet who ministers throughout the area. David has written 15 songs; 12 have been published. He also speaks periodically to school and other groups about his NASA experiences. Shortly after the Shuttle *Columbia* tragedy in March 2003, he was featured on Channel 7 TV and wrote articles for local newspapers.

Several months after Sandy died, David became acquainted with Virginia Ouzts, whose first husband, Samuel Ouzts, died of cancer in August 2000. Virginia was office manager for Longview's Union Tank Car Company for 28 years. She has two children, four grandchildren and one great-granddaughter.

David and Virginia were friends for about a year and a half, fell in love and were married on 11 January 2003, at Mobberly Baptist Church. They now reside at 219 Goodnight Trail, Longview.

JAMES HENRY & AMANDA (McFARLAND) ALEXANDER

The American ancestry of this Alexander family can be traced to Henry and Hester (Rush) Alexander of Lancaster County, Pennsylvania, and later to York District, South Carolina, and Shelby County, Alabama. Many of the family remained in Shelby County, Alabama; and descendants currently reside in and around Spring Creek/Calera, Alabama.

James Henry Alexander, the son of William M. and Catherine (Ferguson) Alexander, was born 28 October 1851, in South Carolina, probably York District. James migrated, with his mother, to Spring Creek, Shelby County, Alabama, circa 1855; then, with his sister, Mary, circa 1872, to Harrison County, Texas. He taught school in or near Marshall and married his student, Amanda Tinsley McFarland (1856-1940), on 27 December 1877, in Harrison County, where they resided until 1901. Amanda was born 24 March 1856, in Arkansas to J. Daniel and Elizabeth "Betty" (Shaddock) McFarland. In

James Henry and Amanda Tinsley (McFarland) Alexander, 27 December 1927.

1901 they purchased land and the previous Elmira Chapel Cumberland Presbyterian Manse in Spring Hill, Gregg County, Texas. They moved into this house, across the road from the church, with seven living children (Lizzy died in infancy, circa 1884): Eula Mae (Mrs. Ernest Holland, 1879-1962); Annie Jane (Mrs. Charles Green Stovall, 1881-1906); Katherine Elizabeth (Mrs. Frank Zollicoffer Ingram, 1886-1908); Lillie Dell (Mrs. Albert Henry Tubbs, 1888-1967); Willie Dee "Shug" (Mrs. Jesse Albert Braudaway, 1894-1985); Malcolm Erwin (1898-1981), married Rosie Mae Magrill; and Oscar Benjamin (1900-1966), married Stella Mae Thomas. The family became active members in the Elmira Chapel Cumberland Presbyterian Church and James served as Session Clerk (1910-1930); he was ordained as an Elder in July 1910.

Some time later, the family purchased a larger home and 100 acres to the east on what is now known as Spring Hill Road, where they raised crops and domestic animals. On 6 May 1930, James leased his mineral rights to B.A. Skipper which resulted in producing oil and gas wells.

Katherine Elizabeth (Alexander) Ingram died 19 February 1908, in Spring Hill, giving birth to George Alton Ingram. Frank Z. Ingram could manage his farming and the rearing of George Alton's older sister, Velma, and older half-brother, Roy; but, not a newborn. J.H. and Amanda took George Alton Ingram into their home and reared him as their own.

James Henry died in 1933 at the age of 82 and is buried in White Cemetery, Longview. His contemporaries said, "He was a very happy man with a great sense of humor, always looking at the bright side of life. He had a generous heart and was deservedly a popular man." James and Amanda's home was always open to anyone in need. Amanda was known for her kindness, always looking after the sick and needy; and, her fried pies were the best in Gregg County. Amanda continued to live in the home-place until her death in 1940. She is buried beside her husband in White Cemetery.

Many of their descendants lived their entire lifetime in Gregg County. Fourth, fifth and sixth generation Alexander descendants presently live in Gregg County, Texas.

– Submitted by Bettye Jo (Ingram) Hughes (great granddaughter of James Henry and Amanda Tinsley (McFarland) Alexander)

J.H. & AMANDA ALEXANDER: Descendants

James Henry Alexander (1851-1933) married Amanda Tinsley McFarland (1856-1940) on

(l.-r.) Back row: Frank Zollicoffer Ingram, 1881-1933, and Katherine Elizabeth Alexander, 1886-1908 (Mrs. Frank Z. Ingram). Middle row: Annie Jane Alexander, 1881-1906 (Mrs. Charles G. Stoval); James Henry Alexander, 1851-1933; Amanda Tinsley (McFarland) Alexander, 1856-1940; Lillie Dell Alexander, 1888-1967 (Mrs. Albert Henry Tubbs); and Eula Mae Alexander, 1879-1962 (Mrs. Ernest Holland). Front: standing, Willie Dee "Shug" Alexander, 1894-1985 (Mrs. Jesse Albert Braudaway) and seated in lap, Malcolm Erwin Alexander, 1898-1981.

27 December 1877. Three generations of their descendants presently live in Gregg County.

Eula Mae was born 7 October 1879; she died 1 July 1962. She married Ernest Holland (1881-1958). They owned and operated a general store in Pine Tree where they reared two adopted children: John and Eva Mae "Evie" (1912-1996).

Annie Jane was born 8 January 1881; died 18 June 1906. She married Charles Green Stovall (1875-1936), 1 March 1900. They had two children: Alice Lydia (1901-2001) and James Henry (1904-1912). Alice Lydia married Lewis William Eastland (1903-2001). They lived in Longview, were active in the CP Church and reared two sons: Robert Lewis and Charles Sidney.

Lizzy Alexander was born after 1881 and died at the age of three in Harrison County.

Katherine Elizabeth was born 17 December 1886; she died 19 February 1908. She married Frank Zollicoffer Ingram (1881-1933), 10 October 1904. They had two children: Lydia Velma (1905-1985) and George Alton (1908-1962). Lydia Velma married George Ernest McGrede, Sr. (1903-1955). They reared three children in Longview: Edith Eloise (1926-2004), Georgia Ruth (1928-1993) and George Ernest, Jr. George Alton Ingram, Sr. married Annie Florence (Walker) (1907-1992), 29 September 1928. He owned and operated service stations and reared four children in Longview: Bettye Jo, Mary Nell (1934-1996), Wanda Jean and George Alton, Jr. Alton and Annie were devoted members of the CP Church and Alton was ordained as an Elder.

Lillie Dell was born 1 August 1888; she died 4 October 1967. She married Albert Henry Tubbs (1884-1960), 12 May 1907. They owned a grocery/feed store in Longview, which was operated by their sons: Archie and Glenn. They had five children: James Archie (1909-1966),

Otis Dement (1912- 1914), Albert Glenn (1915-1990), Atha Grace and Joseph Malcolm (1927-1931).

Willie Dee "Shug" was born 17 December 1894; she died 20 October 1985. She married Jesse Albert Braudaway (1892-1961), 3 March 1915. They moved from Longview to Camp County where they farmed and reared five children: Audra Gladys (1916-1996), Malcolm Travis (1917-1980), James William "Bill" (1921-1988), Dorothy Alice (1924-1941) and Flora Dee "Fordie" (1926-1979).

Malcolm Erwin was born 15 July 1898; he died 9 February 1981. He married Rosie Mae Magrill (1899-1994), 5 May 1923. They lived their entire lives in Spring Hill where they operated a dairy farm and raised and trained horses. They were childless, but every child in the family claimed them and spent summers working on the farm, riding horses and swimming in Uncle Erwin's pond.

Oscar Benjamin was born 26 December 1900; he died 13 July 1966. He married Stella Mae Thomas (1904-1988). They reared one son, James Clyde "Pete" (1923-1980), who served in the Navy during World War II. Ben and Stella built a home where James and Amanda's original homeplace had stood and spent their retirement years there.

The Alexander men were very musically inclined. In the 1930-1940 era George Alton Ingram, Sr., Malcolm Travis Braudaway and James Clyde Alexander played together in a band – just for fun!
– Submitted by Sue Ellen (Hughes) Herbold (great-great granddaughter of James Henry and Amanda Tinsley (McFarland) Alexander)

ALLEN

Royal Polk "Roy" Allen (10 January 1888-31 March 1946) and Nellie Surat (Rolf) Allen (14 July 1890-26 February 1968) raised 10 children in the Greenhill community north of Mount Pleasant, Titus County, Texas. Roy was a carpenter and Nellie was a seamstress. All of their children except Margaret Kathryn moved to Longview.

Their first child, Winfred Vernet (19 August 1907-13 November 1978), was active in the First Methodist Church and served as an usher there for many years. He sold Chrysler and Plymouth automobiles. He and his wife, Florine (Cody) Allen, had two children, Vernette and Cody.

Russell Fleming Allen (born 11 August 1909, died 2003) married Zoie Mae Bradley (12 March 1905-13 July 1973) on 11 January 1931. He worked at an A&P Grocery in Mt. Pleasant. Zoie worked at Mrs. Vaughn's Beauty Shop. Their children are Elizabeth Nell (born 22 January 1932) and Jerry Ann (born 22 May 1935). Later, he worked for Babbling Brook Milk Company in Longview and co-owned a grocery store with Winfred from 1934-1936. Russell worked for Monsanto

Texas Hillbillies (l.-r.) Morris Allen, Jonnie Porter; Jerry Doggett, announcer; Durwood Goodson; Jimmie Allen; and Marvin Smith performing for KFRO radio about 1940.

Chemical Company in Karnack, Texas, during World War II. On 28 November 1974, Russell married Dura Smith. Dura has one child, Byron.

The third child, Horace Vaughn (5 March 1911-3 September 1963), served in World War II along with brothers, Woodrow Wilson and Morris Everett.

Margaret Kathryn was born 11 March 1913, and lived in Mount Pleasant with her husband, Allen LaPrade, until his death. They had two children, Bobby and Janis. Margaret worked at Piggly Wiggley until retirement. Now she makes quilts.

Woodrow Wilson (6 January 1915-23 January 1980) lived in Longview with his wife, Vaudis, and worked as a butcher most of his life.

Ala Jane was born 17 August 1917. She married Toy Sutherland and they had four children: Pat, Toy Jr., Nevil, and Pam. Jane is a seamstress.

Lucy Pearl (7 January 1920-27 October 1994) was married to Floyd Cordell. Floyd was a painter and paperhanger and Lucy often helped him. Their children are David, Nancy, Mary Ann and Sid.

Morris Everett "Mutt" was born 31 October 1922. He was a postman in Longview for many years after serving as a Field Lineman in World War II. He was a PFC in Battery B, 672nd Field Artillery Battalion from 14 April 1944 to 13 June 1946. He played most musical instruments by ear. He and his brothers performed as the "Texas Hillbillies" on KFRO radio. His wife, Florene "Flo" Hale, is buried with other family members in the Greenhill Cemetery outside Mount Pleasant.

Johnny James "Jimmy" was born 18 September 1926. He and his wife, Lil, live in

Roy and Nellie Allen with their 10 children

Shelbyville, Texas, where he is a Baptist minister. They have three children: Ray, Ricky and Lucy.

Dorothy Jean was born 14 July 1930, with her husband, Jack Little. They have three children, Allen, Mike and Gayle.

Roy's parents were John William Allen (15 March 1867-19 March 1926) from Moscow, Tennessee, and Mary Margaret "Mollie" Ellis (23 September 1868-24 February 1963) from Lynchburg, Tennessee. The couple eloped to Memphis, Tennessee, and then entrained for Mount Pleasant, Texas.

Nellie's parents were Walter Rolf (1860-1946) and Katy (1867-1932). Walter came to the United States from England in 1873 and became a citizen on 18 January 1937.
– Submitted by Morris Everett Allen

CHARITY ALLEN (CONAWAY)

Darlene McDonald Wilcox was born and reared in Kansas and moved to Gregg County in June of 1989. This was after she retired from the VA Medical Center in Dallas, Texas.

Darlene's maternal grandmother, Charity Allen, was born in 1860 in Rockford, Illinois. She was a descendant of John Alden and Priscilla Mullins. It has been said that Miles Standish, who was very shy, asked John, his best friend, to propose to Priscilla for him. John did, and ended up marrying her himself.

Charity moved to Kansas when she was 12 years old. As a young woman, she married John Conaway and they had eleven children. She said she grew into womanhood "by helping in the house, fighting prairie fires and setting broken bones." Not only did she mother and raise her own large family, but she also was called on to help her neighbors when they had problems. In the 1890s she became a midwife and delivered many babies, staying in homes where there were very contagious diseases. Sometimes she would be quarantined for days. Her five older children would stay home with their father, helping him and caring for the younger children.

During the raging epidemic of black diphtheria people were dying like flies. She and her spirited team were on the road for weeks. It is said not one of her patients died while those not under her care died by twos and threes. She always felt remorseful because she could not carry her cure to everyone. She had discovered a special formula for treating her patients.

Charity was a very kind and compassionate woman. She would prepare dinner for members of her church and invite them home for Sunday dinner. There was never an empty chair at her table. She was a very good cook, so people were always happy that they were invited to her Sunday dinners.

In 1925 Darlene's cousin, Tom Toothaker, delivered her, but Grandma Charity was standing ready to assist in the birth. Darlene's mother said that she was a "blue baby" as Darlene had a cord around her neck. Grandma never gave up when a baby was in distress and she worked until the baby was breathing as she should.

In her later years when Charity would come to visit and she would talk about her need to go home so she could feed and water the ducks, forgetting she no longer had any. She had difficulty remembering the present, but was really sharp when it came to telling stories about the olden days. She passed away on 24 December 1942, at the age of 82. She left a very large family who still remembers the many wonderful times spent at "Grandma's house".

– Submitted by Darlene McDonald Wilcox

WILLIAM EDWIN ALLEN

William Edwin Allen (1924-1964) was born in Scott County, Arkansas, to Permelia F. Thompson and Jasper James Allen. Permelia was the daughter of Lulah Fields Jameson and Steven Arthur Thompson. Lulah was the daughter of James B. Jameson of Kentucky and Victoria Gaines of Virginia. The Gaines family has been documented back through Richard Gaines, a soldier with Virginia troops (see *Index to Revolutionary Soldiers of Virginia*, Vol. 8, p. 174). Steven was the son of Sally O'Neil and James Henry Thompson of Mississippi.

Jasper was the son of William Andrew Allen of Scott County, Arkansas, and Sarah Ann Tedder of Pike County, Arkansas. William was the son of William Andrew Allen and Savannah (Vanna) Taylor. Savannah's parents were William W. Taylor (Alabama) and Nancy E. McMillan (Alabama). Sarah Ann's Parents were James A. Tedder and Delilah Pyburn, both of Pike County, Arkansas. James A. Tedder's parents were Farrington Tedder (North Carolina) and Elizabeth Meeks of Pike County, Arkansas. Elizabeth died young and Farrington married a widow, Mary Ann Saphonie Storey Burrell.

Jasper and Permelia were also the parents of Joanna Maxine Allen King and Mary Frances Allen Tuel. Jasper, Permelia and all three children are buried in White Oak, Gregg County, Texas.

William married Mary Alice Standridge, a.k.a. Thomas, 13 August 1942. Her parents were Venia (Vena) Blane McElroy of Perry County, Arkansas, and Ersle Wroten Standridge of Perry County, Arkansas. Ersle was also connected to the Rosemond family of Arkansas. Ersle was a past fiddling champion of Arkansas and wrote, sang and recorded songs under the

Starday record label. Vena was also a musician, singer, evangelist and one of the first lady realtors in East Texas. Vena was the daughter of Mary Louella Alverson and Walter McElroy. Family ties also include Gentry and Barnette families, who are believed to have Cherokee Indian links. Vena and Jesse Earl Thomas (Mary Alice's stepdad) came to Gregg County, Texas, during the oil boom. He and Carson Kennedy of Gladewater collected the oil workers money and banked it for them in Gilmer until the First State Bank of Gladewater was built.

William and Mary Alice had William David, Rosemary, and Thomas Andrew (Drew) born in Longview, Gregg County, Texas.

William was a successful home builder and real estate investor until his death 25 December 1964. Mary Alice shared his work as house designer and decorator. Her interests in real estate investment, creative art, and music has continued.

Additional information on these families are in the historical books of Scott and Pike counties of Arkansas, and the Lampassas and Burnet counties of Texas.

– Submitted by Rosemary Allen Thomas (Mrs. Galen Thomas), Pritchett, Texas

DR. J.N. ALLISON

Dr. Allison came to Texas from Virginia. He built a two-story brick house that still stands on Dundee Road. Dr. Jonathan Nicholas Allison, born 1828, Virginia, moved to Texas by 1859, settling in Upshur County, Texas. He was one of the earliest physicians in Upshur and Gregg Counties. The home he built near Longview in 1859, said to be a replica of his boyhood home in Virginia, is still standing. He married Joan R. Fisher, 1861, Upshur County, Texas. Their children were Joseph N., Jr, Mae Dee, Elmo P., Noell and Rupert.

DR. T.J. ALLISON

Dr. T.J. Allison was supposedly not related to Dr. J.N. Allison. Thomas Jefferson Allison, Sr. was the son of William and Martha Price Allison. He attended medical school in Augusta, Georgia. Dr. Allison married Mrs. Elizabeth Brown Smitherman, a widow with four children: Newton, Mary, Wiley and Robert. Elizabeth was the daughter of Hitson and Willie (Ray) Brown who were early settlers in Upshur County. Dr. Allison and his family arrived in Texas on Christmas Eve 1850, from Alabama. The Allisons, Browns, Samples and Killingsworths had traveled together by wagon train.

According to his son, Dr. Allison, Sr. was energetic, sociable and witty; he played the violin, and was a member of the Baptist church. Dr. Allison gave up practicing medicine after a few years in Texas and became a farmer. There were so few people in the area that practicing medicine was not profitable.

Thomas Jefferson and Elizabeth had seven children: Thomas J., Jr.; Willliam; Berry; Frank; Sophronia; Angeline; and Pugh.

When the Civil War broke out, Dr. Allison volunteered and served in Company C, 10th

Texas Cavalry, CSA. He visited his family twice after this, but in the winter of 1862, he left and they never saw him again. According to family tradition, his regiment was dismounted in May 1862. Dr. Allison was detailed to help bring the horses home. He was sick when he left the camp. After traveling only a few miles, he had to stop four miles south of DeSark, Prairie County, Arkansas, where he died 14 May 1862.

Elizabeth married Joe McCook in 1864. McCook was a blacksmith and widower with no children. She died 6 January 1866, of typhoid fever. Four of her children died of the fever the same year.

DR. T.J. ALLISON, JR.

Thomas Jefferson Allison, Jr. was born in 1850 in Alabama. He was a baby when his family arrived in East Texas. On 29 July 1875, he married Mary Ann Morgan of West Mountain, Upshur County. Mary Ann, daughter of Richard and Elizabeth (Elder) Morgan, was born 6 November 1857, in Texas. After marriage Allison decided he was not going to be a successful farmer, and turned to teaching. He taught at several locations and decided he was poorly equipped to teach, so he entered Ad-Ran College, Thorp Springs, Texas, 1882. He taught school, lead singing schools and worked as a surveyor. When a Dr. Shettlesworth moved into the community in 1887 to practice medicine, at age 32 Allison began to study medicine as a result of Dr. Shettleworth's influence. In his autobiography, Dr. Allison recalled that Dr. Shettleworth had been a pupil in Allison's first class at Mings Chapel. From September 1887 until February 1889, Allison studied medicine at the Louisville Medical School, Louisville, Kentucky. He decided to set up practice in Gladewater as there was just one other "old fashioned type" doctor there who did not even use a thermometer or a hypodermic syringe. Dr. Allison returned to Louisville in 1889 and graduated in 1890.

He practiced in Gladewater until 1926, then moved to Spanish Fort, Texas. He practiced there briefly until, in 1928, he decided at age 78 that he could be of little service to people and retired. He was a member of the Gregg County Medical Society, the Texas Medical Society and the American Medical Society. He was a member of the Church of Christ.

His hobbies were writing and walking. On his 85th birthday he walked twenty-five miles. Mrs. Allison died May 1935, Shelby County, Texas, and Dr. Allison in December 1938. They are buried in Nocona Cemetery.

Their children were Ada Dell, born 1876; Ida Dorinder, born 1877; Ela Lee, born 1878; Eula Lee, born 1880; Oma Marshall, born 1881; Minnie Elizabeth, born 1886; Virgil Clyde, born 1888; Ena Naoma, born 1890; and Ima Mae, born 1893.

ANDERSON

Glendon Sylvester Anderson was born 2 January 1937, in the Miller community of Arkinda, Little Ricer County, Arkansas, a son

William Edwin Allen   *Mary Alice Allen*

Laura, Eddy and Timothy, Wanda, Andy and Glen

of Glendon and Dora Georgia (Pond) Anderson. Glendon's nickname is "Andy;" he attended a one-room school, Winthrop and Foreman High Schools and received a GED in the Navy. He joined the Navy in 1955, and served aboard the USS *Coral Sea*. Andy received an Honorable Discharge from the Navy in 1965.

Andy first married Dorothy Letterman of Helena, Arkansas. Their one son, William Keith Anderson, was born 8 September 1960. Andy and Dorothy separated and then divorced in 1961.

While on leave in the San Jose area, Andy met Wanda Jean (Phillips) Williams. Wanda was born 3 April 1930, in Snow Hill, Hempstead County, Arkansas, a daughter of Floyd and Augusta (Stevenson) Phillips. Andy and Wanda had only been on a couple dates before they were married 29 March 1963, at the Golden Wedding Chapel in Reno, Nevada. Right after the wedding, Andy was away at sea for nine months.

Andy and Wanda have one son, Glendon Allen Anderson. Glen was born 27 May 1967, in San Jose, Santa Clara County, California. He was an Honor Roll student and graduated from White Oak High School. Glen attended Kilgore College and he graduated from Star College of Cosmetology. Glen resides in Dallas.

Wanda's first husband was Willis Edmond Williams Jr. and they had two sons. Kenneth Wayne Williams was born 31 June 1955, in Richard, Contra Costa County, California. Ken married So Yong Gerera and resides in Sunnyvale, California. So Yong has two children from a previous marriage, David and Lynn. Willis Edmond Williams III was born 22 January 1962, in Mountain View, Santa Clara County, California. Eddy married Robin (Bibb) Frost; they divorced. Eddy then married Laura Reed. Eddy and Laura have two sons. Timothy Matthew was born 5 December 1991, and Nicolas Tyler was born 13 July 2002. Eddy and family reside in Henderson, Texas.

The Andersons lived on Hidden Lake Drive in Sunnyvale from 1967 until 1972, when they sold and moved to Boysol Court in San Jose. Andy worked for the GM factory in Freemont from 1965 until 1975 and for Sunnyvale Lumber from 1975 until 1980. Wanda was a home-maker and a babysitter for neighbors. Wanda also bred Dachshunds. Summer vacations included camping, fishing, boating, canoeing and amusement parks and trips to Texas and Arkansas to visit family members.

Andy, Wanda, Eddy and Glen moved to White Oak, Texas, in 1980 and rented a duplex on Quail Drive for a few months before buying a house on Forest Drive. Wanda's parents lived a short distance away in Kilgore. Andy worked for White Oak School as a bus driver and maintenance man.

Andy and Wanda moved to Tanglewood Drive in 1996. Andy retired in August 2002. Andy and Wanda are now full time bowlers and enjoy the camaraderie of the senior leagues. Andy also enjoys working with wood and has built birdhouses, benches and wishing wells.

– Submitted by Glen Anderson, written by Eric Keenan

ARMSTRONG / JOHNSTON

John Kittle Armstrong (1806-1858), wife Sarah Poland Armstrong (1814- 1855), and several children came to the Gladewater area from Southern Alabama. They were probably the first white family to settle here. The Republic of Texas issued them a land grant in 1844. They had ten children. One of their sons, Martin A. Armstrong (1845-1899), married Mary Elizabeth Barnes (1848-1902).

Martin and Mary had several children, one being Dellah Armstrong (1866-1945), who married in 1881 O.G. "Ogie" Johnston (1859-1924). They built a home in 1882 just east of town on what is now Highway 80. Their daughter Augusta was born in 1883 (died in 1976), and son Charles "Bert" in 1890 (died in 1956).

Ogie Johnston served as a public officer for about forty years. He was the second county commissioner and the third Justice of the Peace for his precinct (an office he held for many years). After the death of Ogie, Bert and his wife, Mary "Pearle" Shirey Johnston (1890-1981), whom he married in 1920, lived with Dellah until her death in 1945. During this time, Bert and Pearle had three children: Robbie Nell, born in 1926; O.G., born in 1927; and Billy Ray, born in 1932.

Bert died 1 February 1956. His wife continued to live at the old family home site (Gladewater City Hall, the Winn Dixie building and the J.O. and Jerry Williams' homes are

Charles Bert and Mary Pearle Johnston, wedding photo, 1920

presently located on this property). She sold the estate to a local corporation as a commercial building site in the 1960s. Pearle then bought a home on Mustang Drive near her older son, O.G., and his family. Her son, Bill, who worked in Tyler, lived with her until he married in 1964. In 1975, she moved to Robbie Nell's home on Country Club Road. All three of her children lived near her in Gladewater, and took care of her until her death in 1981.

Robbie Nell married Robert R. Shepard (1928-1998) in 1953. They have two children: Janet Rhea, born in 1954; and Robert Ray, born in 1964. Janet married Steve Christian in 1985. Their daughters are Rachel, born in 1987, and Linnie, in 1989. Janet lives with her daughters in Jacksonville, North Carolina. Ray married Susan Oberg in 1997; they live in Plano, Texas.

O.G. married Georgia Ruth White in 1953. In 1982, they moved from their home on Mustang Drive to a new home on Country Club Road. Their daughters are Carol Ann, born in 1956, and Donna Lynn, born in 1959. Carol Ann presently resides in Carlisle, Pennsylvania. Donna Lynn is married to Joe Niehus; they live in Sherman, Texas. Their children are Katie Lauren, born in 1993, and Karlie Jo, born in 1995.

Billy Ray married Barbara Ann Holder in 1964. They have two children: Wesley Ray, born in 1966, and Wendy Gail, born in 1972. Wesley married Dianne Christian in 1995. Their daughters are Taylor, born in 1996, and Camryn, born in 2000. They live in Chandler, Texas. Wendy married John Stanley in 1997; they reside in Frisco, Texas.

– Submitted by O.G. Johnston

ATER-UTZMAN

Jennifer Alisse Ater Utzman was born on 14 August 1953, at Laird Memorial Hospital. Her parents are Stanley and Marita Ater. Her sisters are Kimberly and Stephanie Kelly. She is a 1971 graduate of KHS. She graduated from Kilgore College in 1973, and University of Texas at Tyler, which was called Tyler State College, in 1975. She received a Master's of Liberal Arts from Southern Methodist University in 1976. She began teaching at Foster Middle School in 1975. She and her mother, Marita Ater, taught together her first year. Marita was then transferred to Longview High. Jennifer then moved into her mother's old room and is still there. Jennifer has taught 6th grade world history, 7th grade Texas history, 8th grade U.S. history, and 8th and 9th grade speech in her 29 years at Foster Middle School.

Jennifer is a Past Grand Officer of the International Order of the Rainbow for Girls, Project Business Teacher of the Year for three years (Junior Achievement), and KETK Teacher of the Year in 1999. She is currently the secretary of the Rainbow Board, Treasurer of Alpha Delta Kappa (teacher sorority), Vice-President of Preceptor Omicron Epsilon (Beta Sigma Phi), Daughters of American Revolution, Order of the Eastern Stars, kindergarten teacher in Sunday School and Vacation Bible School at First Bap-

The Utzmans. Standing: Jessica-Alisse. Seated: Jennifer and Richard.

tist Church in Kilgore and is presently serving as President of the local unit of Association of Texas Professional Educators. Her time now is spent attending Rainbow functions all over the state with daughter, Jessica-Alisse, who is currently a state officer in Rainbows.

Jennifer's grandparents are Jesse Jewel and Nora Belle Johnson Ater of Overton, Arthur Leroy and Lillie Beatrice Byers Chanler, Sr. of Kilgore, Judge and Mrs. Flavius Josephus Johnson of Llano, and Mr. and Mrs. Homer Byers of Minden, Louisiana.

Jennifer married Richard Utzman, Jr. on 17 November 1979, after a year and a half of courtship. Richard was born on a naval base in Portsmouth, Virginia, where is father was stationed on the USS *Saratoga*. He graduated from West Rusk and Kilgore College. His parents are Richard Utzman, Sr. and Bernice Utzman of Overton. Richard's siblings are Tommy and Janet. Richard helps teach Sunday school and Vacation Bible School. He is Past Master of Rocky Mount Lodge # 63 in Overton and member of the Kilgore Rainbow Board.

Richard, Jr. was a welder by trade until he and Jennifer were hit by a drunk driver on 29 January 1984. Richard and Jennifer shared the same room for 53 days with special permission from Good Shepherd's board. Richard suffered from a broken hip, closed head injury and bruised kidneys. Jennifer broke her left leg and paralyzed her right arm. It took a year of physical therapy to regain almost all of the feeling. Richard has had two hip replacements. He has become a craftsman. He does stained glass, builds unique woodcraft items, birdhouses and has recently learned small motor repairs.

Richard and Jennifer's daughter, Jessica-Alisse Ater Utzman, was born on a stormy night. Longview Regional was on the back up generator for lights when she arrived in the world on 7 June 1989. She has attended Kilgore schools. She was the mascot at Maude Laird Middle School and is currently the freshman/J.V. mascot at Kilgore High. She is in the orchestra where she has played the viola for four years. She has played the piano for seven years. She has been involved with dance for 12 years. She has been an honor student for nine years. She is currently Grand Representative to Arkan-

sas/Kansas/Iowa/Minnesota in the International Order of the Rainbow for Girls. She will be receiving a floor office in June.

– Submitted by Jennifer Ater-Utzman

ATER-ZIMMERMAN

Stephanie Kelly Ater-Zimmerman was born 20 July 1961, to Marita and Stanley Ater. She attended Kilgore schools and graduated Kilgore High School in 1979, and Kilgore College in 1982. Kelly graduated from Baylor University in 1985. She taught at Arp Jr. High from 1985 to 1989. She was a stay at home mom with Zachry Ater Albertson Zimmerman, her first son, born on 27 November 1989, and niece, Jessica-Alisse Ater Utzman. She did not return to teaching until after her second son, Zane Austin Ater Zimmerman, born 12 February 1995, was four years old.

The Zimmermans. Standing: Zane and Zackry. Seated: Kelly and Dee.

She did teach a short time at First Baptist Church Child Development Center in the preschool department. Her next job was third grade at Chandler Elementary in Kilgore. She taught there from 1999 to 2004. She took on a new adventure and will be teaching 4th grade at Kilgore Intermediate in fall of 2004. Kelly is a member of Alpha Delta Kappa, a teacher sorority, and Beta Sigina Phi. She is also a member of Daughters of American Revolution and Association of Professional Educators.

Zachry is 14 years old. He has been in the Leap/GT program all eight years in school and was named outstanding student in history in the 7th grade at Laird Middle School. He plays golf, football and baseball. He says he is ready for high school. Zane is 9. He plays for the Ark-La-Tex Tornadoes, a select baseball team out of Shreveport, Louisiana, and also plays for Kilgore Boys Baseball Association. Zane was named MVP at the Regional Baseball Tournament. Both boys are honor students.

Kelly married Robert Dee Zimmerman on 20 December 1986. Dee is the son of Leland and Marguerite Zimmerman of Conway, Arkansas. Dee graduated from Vilonia High School, Vilonia, Arkansas, in 1978 and University of Arkansas in Monticello with a Bachelor of Science degree in Forest Management in 1982. Dee owns his own timber company, Zimmco Tim-

ber. He is a member of Kilgore Lions Club, Danville Masonic Lodge 4101 and currently coaches 9-10 years olds with the Kilgore Boys Baseball Association.

– Submitted by Kelly Ater-Zimmerman

STANLEY KELLY & MARITA ANN CHANLER ATER

Marita Ann Chanler Ater was born on 16 August 1933, to Arthur Leroy Chanler, Sr. and Lillie Beatrice Byers in the family home on Old Stone Road, Kilgore. Her parents came to East Texas, where her dad first worked in the oil fields, then later for Magnolia Oil Company. Her parents moved to Beaumont and Orange where her dad worked in the shipyards. After going with Stan to Buras/Triumph, Louisiana, she taught on an emergency certificate (5th grade). She began her teaching career at Foster Middle School (14 years teaching 7th grade Texas history, then moved to 8th grade American history and 9th grade world history. She was selected to be Social Studies Department Chairman at Longview High School in 1976. Here she taught American cultural studies, Texas history, economics, world history, psychology and sociology. She began the Jr. Historians in Longview in 1976 as a Bicentennial project and won first place in the state. She was also runner-up for Longview I.S.D Teacher of the Year. Her students were featured on the national news for innovative teaching ideas. In 1982, she moved to Kilgore where she taught Texas government, world geography, and political science. Jr. Historians continued here where they won first, second and third place in the state for six years. Marita was chosen Kilgore 1993 Teacher of the Year. She was the first teacher in Texas to win the Winfrey Award in Teaching Social Studies.

On retirement, Marita has had ovarian cancer three times and was able to take chemo – driving it into remission each time. Her grandchildren, children and her church activities at First Baptist Church keep her busy, as well as motivational speaking. Stan and Marita are parents of three daughters: Jennifer Alisse Utzman, Kimberly and Stephanie Kelly Zimmerman. Marita is a member of First Baptist Church, Alpha Delta Kappa (teacher sorority) and Civic Garden Club. She is also a board member of the American Heart Association and the East Texas Treatment Center and advisor for Rainbow for Girls where she has been a member for over 60 years. Her parents are Mr. and Mrs. Leroy Chanler, Sr. Her grandparents are Mr. and Mrs. Henry David Chanler, Mr. and Mrs. Homer Byers of Minden, Louisiana, and Mr. and Mrs. A.E. Dunn. Her sister is Janean Aaron of Arlington and brother is Arthur Leroy Chanler, Jr. (Dooger) of San Antonio.

Stanley Kelly Ater was born in Overton, Texas, on 22 December 1931. Stan's parents had moved to East Texas, where his dad worked for Gulf Pipe Line in the Overton area. Stan's maternal grandparents were Judge and Mrs. Flavius Josephus Johnson of Llano, Texas, and paternal grandparents were Mr. and Mrs.

Stan Ater family. (l.-r.) Back: Kimberly Ann Ater, Stan Ater, Marita Ater, Richard Utzman and Jennifer Utzman. Front: Dee Zimmerman, Kelly Zimmerman, Jessica-Alisse Utzman, Zane Zimmerman, and Zachry Zimmerman in his dad's lap.

Jonas Sanford Ater from Sweetwater, Texas. Stanley graduated from Overton High School in 1950, and Kilgore College. He received a Bachelor of Science degree from UT–Tyler in Industrial Technology – safety and management.

Stan and Marita were Kilgore College sweethearts. Stan had been awarded a football scholarship, but due to a knee injury, he decided to attend Kilgore College. Marita graduated from Kilgore High School in 1951, and was selected to be a Kilgore Rangerette in the summer of that year. The story telling of their first meeting was that after church on a summer night, Marita and two friends "circled the block" in downtown Kilgore in the area that included the Crim and the old post office. It seems Stanley stepped off the curb after coming from the Crim Theatre just as Marita approached the corner. The story told was that on the KC campus the next day, Stan saw Marita as they changed classes and said, "I think I need to give you driving lessons." A week later for their first date, they went to the movies and afterwards played miniature golf.

On many trips for Kilgore College with the Rangerettes and Band, Stan and Marita seemed to always run into one another. On a trip to Houston when the Shamrock Hotel was new, Stan and Marita were the first two who came to breakfast. Marita sat across from Stan and said he had the most beautiful blue eyes she had ever seen. It seems fate kept putting them in touch. Throughout the year, there were many sorority and fraternity parties and after-game receptions that they usually attended. The 1951-52 school terms included the Rangerette Revels and as the year ended, Rangerettes made plans to attend the Philadelphia Music Festival and to appear on the Ed Sullivan Show.

That summer (1952) Marita's parents went to Georgia to complete a contract for the pipe line that her dad worked for. While they were gone, Marita ran her dad's Sinclair Gasoline/Goodrich tire dealership for him. Her main helper was Jim Bob, a fine black man, who was able to nearly do everything needed except the bookwork, which was done by Marita. At the end of the summer, school began again. Marita and Stan were told he would be called into military service in a couple of months by the Rusk County draft board. Stan said he wanted to leave a wife and not a girlfriend so they made plans to be married. They married 30 September 1952, at Laird Hill Methodist Church. Stan was raised in the Methodist Sunday School in Overton, but attended the Episcopal Church in Henderson. Marita attended First Baptist Church in Kilgore.

Stan's call for service did not come as soon as they said. It was a mystery why Stan would be called at all at this time since he had no grade lower than a B, with almost all A's. It seems when his grades were filed, it wasn't discovered until several weeks later after basic training when Stan's dad, known as Mr. Jess, was having coffee with a Gregg County draft board member. As they talked, Mr. Jess discussed Stan's grades. A couple of calls later, they were told there was a mistake. Stan could get out. They called late on Sunday night to tell Stan that he could come home. Stan's reaction was "Do I have to take basic training again?" It seemed he would, so he decided to stay the full two years.

Stan served in the 4th and 5th armored division where, because of his mechanical knowledge and high marks at KC, he made Motor Sergeant. Stan's brother-in-law, a retired major, advised Stan not to go to officer's candidate school even though his grades qualified him. So Stan oversaw the vehicles and played service ball that included football, baseball and basketball. Stan was moved often and he trained ROTC units.

After Stan left for service, Marita continued to live with his parents. Marita and Stan's first child, Jennifer Alisse, was born 14 August 1953, at Laird Memorial Hospital. Their first Christmas away from home was in Ft. Knox, Kentucky. Their parents left their tree up and the presents were left to be opened until they arrived home in January.

Stan took a job with Gulf Oil. Marita and Jennifer moved to Buras, Louisiana, to join Stan on Easter 1954. They lived in Buras, Louisiana, for six years. Here Stan played semi-pro baseball. Kimberly was born on 22 November 956. Kimberly is a graduate of UT–Tyler in history and political science. She is now a graduate student and helps manage her father's business. Marita worked as a teacher for 5th grade and instructor for Delta Darlings twirl/Dance team. In 1960, they moved home after Stan took a job with Texas Eastman. The only job open was as a regular member of a crew. That was a long way from being a station engineer for Gulf Oil in Louisiana. They purchased a house on Howard Street in Longview. The family attended Mobberly Baptist Church. Stephanie Kelly was born 20 July 1960.

Marita decided to return to SFASU for a secondary degree. Their kids were in school at Jodie McClure and Foster Jr. High. Kimberly's 8th birthday was planned for 22 November 1963, but JFK was shot that day at noon. Marita was watching "As the World Turns" and folding diapers for Kelly. She fell on her knees and prayed for our president. He died at Parkland Hospital. One of the nurses on duty was Marita's sister Janean's roommate. They went on with the party, but not a word was spoken. Carol Coolidge had gotten a new T-bird that day and helped take the children to Eastman Park. They looked for a home in Kilgore and found a house on Edgewood Road. If they took up note of G.I. bill, the owner would reduce the cost by $1,000. They borrowed some, took some out of savings and bought the house for $25,000 in August of 1967. School continued for Marita with daily trips to SFASU. Finally, after graduation, she was hired to teach 7th grade Texas history at Foster Middle School for Principal Joe Bailey. She taught 7th, 8th and 9th grade for nine years, and then moved to Longview High School in 1976. Addijo Williams – Secondary Social Studies Coordinator – was Marita's mentor, a family friend and the greatest social studies teacher she had ever known. After Longview High, Marita then moved to Kilgore. She continued to take students on field trips and use innovative teaching ideas and sponsor Jr. Historians, finally retiring in 1998.

When Marita reflects back on her life and health, she knows she can overcome cancer and survive after having both knees replaced at the same time, brain surgery and several other surgeries. Marita tried to empower her students to think and make adult decisions, set short and long range goals and to develop a value system. She instills self-confidence and faith in her students. Marita believed in learning, earning and giving back by helping the disenfranchised. Stan retired as a supervisor after 38 years, being the last man to retire under Kodak before Eastman spun off. Stan also has had cancer twice and a heart attack. Marita retired after 32 years of teaching. They are completely and lovingly involved with the three grandchildren.

– Submitted by Stan Ater

DOTTIE MAE AVERY: Legacy of Love

Dottie Mae Fowler was born in Lindale, Texas, on 6 June 1906, to M.E. and Ola Lindsay Fowler. Dot liked to tell of their two-story farmhouse located in West Texas "out from town a piece," her father's surrey with the fringe on top and her own pony she rode to music lessons. Her favorite story was of her salvation ex-

Dottie Mae Avery

perience that occurred at a brush arbor revival meeting. The evangelist preached about hell; she didn't want to go. She accepted Jesus and was baptized in the creek.

Her high school days were spent in Dallas with her brother Harpee, the preacher at E. Grand Avenue Baptist Church. A women's society led by Mrs. Buckner gave her a scholarship to Southwestern Theological Seminary. She also attended Hattiesburg Women's College. Dot was sent out to do special Sunday School work, teaching a week at a time at various churches.

Before she even arrived at the church in Cotton Valley, Louisiana, W.O. Avery, a widower with a four-year-old son, felt God "tell" him that he would marry the visiting worker. Undoubtedly, he was her most attentive pupil, and she could not help but notice how handsome he looked in his white linen suit with his black hair. Since she was not allowed to date, the resourceful deacon volunteered to take her to her subsequent assignments, each time bearing gifts. When he presented her with an engagement ring, she would not answer his proposal until she "prayed through" to be certain of God's will. They were married in 1928.

News of the oil boom persuaded Mr. Avery to relocate Avery's Pharmacy and his family to Longview. Here they raised three sons, William Oliver, Jr. (1924-1965), Paul (1929-1992) and David (1932-). They were extremely active in the First Baptist Church where Dot served as the director of the Junior Department for forty years. The family entertained visiting preachers at their home for dinner, or at the drug store for "extra large" malts.

W.O., Jr. became a pharmacist like his father and grandfather, married Virginia Thorn, and reared four boys in Port Arthur: W.O. III, Danny, Tommy and David. Paul, an insurance salesman, wed Mary Vanita Harlow and had three daughters in Longview: Anne, Kathryn and Susan. David became a dentist and settled with his wife Patsy Homeyer in McKinney to raise their four children: Mark, Stephen, Karen and Tim. Dot's younger sister, Dorothy, lived with her while she was employed as Dr. Wharton's secretary. Dot considered Dorothy's children, Linda and Presley, her grandchildren as well.

After her husband's death in 1956, Mrs. Avery kept the pharmacy open for five more years. She then sold it and went to work at Longview Drug Store for 25 years, counting every customer a joy and every day a blessing. Often walking to and from the store, she worked six days a week until she retired at the age of 80. Her home was always the gathering place for warm family celebrations and chocolate chip cookies. She continued her hospitality at the rest home as the "self-appointed" greeter. She died at 92.

Dr. Wayman Norman called her a "matriarch of the church" where you could always find her sitting on the second row. For the family, she was a rock. Her 13 grandchildren and 20 great grandchildren could always count on her to write them regularly, keeping them informed

of family "news," and to pray daily for them each by name. Her loving legacy is a life well lived for Christ.

– Submitted by Kathryn Nealy

W.O. AVERY: Prescription for a Godly Life

"Longview in all her industrial and business expansion and attendant population growth, has produced no finer citizen over the past quarter of a century than was W.O. Avery." This assessment appeared in an editorial in the *Longview News Journal* 26 November 1956, the day following his death.

W.O. Avery

W.O. Avery was born in Ruston, Louisiana, in 1893 to W.S. and Maggie Avery. He had a brother, John, and three sisters, Mamie (Poole), Lennie (Owens) and Tressie (Deason). He attended Tulane University and received his pharmacy training in Macon, Georgia. During World War I, he was a sergeant in the medical corps.

In 1918, he married Jessie Taylor. The couple lost their first child, Margaret Alyce (1921-1924). A son, W.O. Jr., was born in March 1924, the same year they opened Avery's Pharmacy in Cotton Valley, Louisiana. Tragedy struck again and W.O. lost his wife.

Heaven smiled on Mr. Avery when, in 1928, he married a visiting Sunday School worker, Dottie Mae Fowler. They had two sons, Paul and David.

Attracted to Longview by the oil boom in 1931, W.O. and his father, also a pharmacist, relocated Avery's Pharmacy. He operated the downtown store at 101 E. Tyler for 25 years, during which time he never took a vacation. The occasional fishing trip was scheduled in the morning, followed by the druggist's long hours at the store: closing at 11:00 p.m. until World War II, 9:00 p.m. thereafter. If business duties called him out of town, he arranged such trips during the week so they would not interfere with church attendance. He broke his 15-year perfect attendance record when he went to his eldest son's wedding in Port Arthur. In 25 years, he missed church only three times.

He served his church in numerous positions: Business Men's Bible Class officer, Chairman of the Deacons for two years, and Chairman of the Preparation of the Lord's Supper for 20 years. A civic-minded businessman, he was active in the Chamber of Commerce, Lion's Club, Masons, American

Legion and was an organizer of the Longview Druggists' Association.

The aforementioned editorial captures the essence of his character… "As a husband and father, he set an example of devotion, hard work and high purposes which any man might be proud to emulate…As a Christian, he believed in living daily what he professed. No one was long in his presence without catching something of the spirit in which he lived and served. Many were his personal acts of charity…These qualities of true manhood, these attributes of good citizenship, were well known to the community because he consistently lived them before us daily. Truly Mr. W.O. Avery was the salt of the earth of which the Master taught – a life that has been a sweet savor among us and which will live on to cheer, to inspire, and to uplift all who have known him."

– Submitted by Susan Avery

MRS. W.O. AVERY

Since coming to Longview in 1970 and graduating from LeTourneau University, one of Mohan Jhass's most profound blessings was to cross paths with a very godly lady, Mrs. W.O. "Dot" Avery. Mrs. Avery was a true believer who loved and used "the Word." She was a pioneer in many Christian works at First Baptist Church; their first Sunday Bible Study was started by her.

Mrs. Avery "adopted" Mohan as her grandson when he married her granddaughter, Susan. Through the years of Mohan and Susan's marriage, Tiny Memo, as she was called, taught them many things by abiding in her faith. Mohan was often privileged to sit with her during her stay at the Colonial Village. From her he learned about persevering prayer, as well as about instant forgiveness, just as the Lord prays and forgives.

Tiny Memo never uttered an unkind word to any person. There was never a down day in her life. She carried a burden for all the unsaved. Believers at First Baptist Church miss her smile.

Daily she prayed for all those in her family by name, about fifty of them; that does not include a countless number of friends. She even wrote letters to all of them, even though they saw her in person regularly. Those who received her letters needed the Bible in hand for decoding, as every sentence was filled with scripture references.

The Jhass children, Jeremiah and Mary Grace, loved their great grandma. She never

Mohan and Mrs. Avery

missed an opportunity to share her faith with them. Mrs. W.O. Avery, "Tiny Memo," was a saint in her faith.

Mohan stated, "Every time I fall and fail, I recall her exhortation to come before the Lord and 'press through in prayer'. She taught me to love the Lord God our Father more and more."

– Submitted by Mohan Jhass

DAVID JESEY BAGGETT

David Jesey Baggett, one of three children of Mary Ann and David Jesey Baggett Sr., was born 10 April 1858, in Funny Louis, Catahoula Parish, Louisiana (now under Lake Louis). He first married Lettie Udora Mathews, on 24 February 1887. They were to have five children. Lettie was born in 1865, and died 28 February 1896.

The children of David and Lettie were Lewis Midelton, born 3 March 1889, and died 17 October 1932; David Lenard "Lenn," born 19 September 1890; Myrtle May, born 27 August 1892; Beulah Elis, born 27 February 1894, married Mr. Wynn; and Ader Bell, born 2 March 1895, and died 22 June 1896. David and the children were living in McLennan County, Texas, at the time of the 1900 census.

David supported the family repairing treadle sewing machines and other machinery. In 1920, he attempted drilling for oil with his son, Lenn, in Burkburnett, Wichita County, Texas. It was there that he suffered a heart attack and died on the 30th of October. Burial was in Old Armour Cemetery in Limestone County, Texas.

After the death of his first wife, David married Fannie Lucindy Petty on 26 February 1902, near Armour, Limestone County. Fannie, born 19 December 1868, in Chandler, Smith County, Texas, was one of seven children of Jane Birdwell (April 1832-June 1896) and Elisha Petty (11 July 1823-25 October 1907). David and Fannie were blessed with five children born in Coolidge, Limestone County: Jesey E. "Jess," born 31 December 1902, married Minnie Bell Osburn; Fannie "Faye"; Joa Byron "Joe"; Mary Ann Jane "Mollie"; and Ophealia Fay, born 18 July 1911, and died 11 January 1913.

The Baggett family. (l.-r.) Back row, children of the first family: Myrtle, Lewis and Beulah. Front: Jess, father David holding Mollie, Joe, mother Fannie and daughter Fannie in 1908.

Joe and Robbie Baggett with descendants at 50th anniversary celebration in 1982.

Fannie, born on 3 September 1904, married Paul Harris. At 99 years old, she lives in Lubbock, Texas, near her daughter and son-in-law, Josie Lee and Norman Berg, their two sons, Robert and Chuck, and younger descendants to the fifth generation. A hairdresser in her early years, Fannie later became a talented ceramic artist and teacher. She has held a lifelong membership in the Eastern Star.

Joe was born in Coolidge 24 June 1906. On 10 December 1932, in Gregg County, Texas, he exchanged wedding vows with Robbie Adrian (14 April 1906-4 August 1984). Joe died 29 December 1988. (See "Joe Baggett & Robbie Adrian.")

Mollie was born in Coolidge 7 December 1907. Julius Michael McKittrick (24 February 1903-19 September 1976) became her husband on 21 June 1942, in Judson Grove (now Longview), Gregg County. Mollie passed away 21 September 2002. (See "Mollie Baggett & Julius McKittrick.")

Times were difficult for the widow Fannie, after David died. She depended on her children for support. In 1936, Fannie and her daughter Mollie came to live in Gregg County. Their home was located on Judson Road across from the Judson Grove School, where Mollie would teach. Fannie went to her eternal reward on 22 July 1949, in Longview. Interment was on the 24th in Old Armour Cemetery.

– Submitted by Paul Guidroz

JOE BAGGETT & ROBBIE ADRIAN

Joa Byron "Joe" Baggett came to Gregg County in the early 1930s. The youngest son of David Jesey and Fanny Lucindy Petty Baggett (see "David Jesey Baggett"), Joe was born 24 June 1906, in Cooledge, Limestone County, Texas. His father died when Joe was fourteen years old while the family was living in Tehuacan, Limestone County. These were very tough times for the widow. Joe dropped out of school to support the family; later, he financially assisted his sister, Mollie, as she obtained her Bachelor of Science in Education degree from Texas Tech College in Lubbock.

Joe's job with Sun Oil Company brought him to Gregg County during the oil boom. He met Robbie Adrian in October 1932, and six weeks later married her in Gregg County on 10 December.

Robbie, the daughter of Robert David "Bob" Adrian and Alabama Frances "Ala" Whatley (see "Adrian"), was born 14 April 1906. She earned a teaching certificate after attending North Texas State Teachers College in Denton and taught in Longview and Pine Tree elementary schools.

Joe and Robbie's first home was rented from her uncle, Ben Adrian, near Old Highway 80 close to White Oak. They welcomed two daughters to this home: Joy, born 1 January 1934, and Robbie Ann, born 1 October 1935.

Regretfully, Joe and Robbie and their two daughters left Gregg County in 1939 when Joe's work took them to Indiana and Illinois. Joe Adrian was born to them 30 May 1947, in Opelousas, Louisiana. The family settled in Lafayette, Louisiana, in 1948, living there until 1970.

After 35 years of service, Joe retired from Sun Oil. All three children had completed college, married, started their own families and moved away, following their vocations. It was time to return to Gregg County and fulfill Joe's long-held dream to be a rancher-farmer.

In 1970, Joe and Robbie joined Harold and Mamie Adrian and Eugene and Gladys Adrian in establishing homes built on land they had inherited from Bob and Ala Adrian. All three couples were active in Summerfield Methodist Church and helped to start the Tryon Road Water Company.

Joy married Ralph Guidroz 21 November 1954, and Ann married Dan Fournet 1 April 1956; both marriages took place in Our Lady of Wisdom Chapel at Southwestern Louisiana Institute, now the University of Louisiana at Lafayette. Joe Adrian married Sarah Vinson in First Presbyterian Church in Lafayette 28 March 1970. All the men served in the U.S. Air Force.

Joy and Ann both were teachers. Joy later became a school and clinical social worker, after receiving her Master's at Louisiana State University in Baton Rouge in 1983. Since leaving the Air Force, Joe Adrian has had a successful career managing the production of computer boards for companies in six states.

Joe and Robbie's children hosted a fiftieth wedding anniversary celebration for them on New Year's Eve of 1982, at Summerfield Methodist Church. Among their descendants in 2004 are 25 grandchildren, plus two great grandchildren.

Robbie died 4 August 1984. Joe mourned his loss until he joined her in death 29 December 1988. Both are interred in Summerfield Cemetery.
– Submitted by Joe A. Baggett

SARAH VINSON & JOE ADRIAN BAGGETT

Joe Adrian is the son of Robbie Adrian and Joe B. Baggett, who were at one time residents of Gregg County, Texas (see "Joe Baggett & Robbie Adrian"). He married Sarah Frances Vinson on 28 March 1970, in Lafayette, Louisiana. Joe Adrian served as a pilot of B-52s and jet instructor pilot in the United States Air Force and retired as a captain in 1976. Upon leaving the Air Force he launched, and maintains, a distinguished career in the circuit board industry. Sarah worked in newspaper advertising and raised their two daughters, Gennifer Patricia "Tricia" and Margaret Vinson "Meg."

Gennifer Patricia Baggett was born in Enid, Oklahoma, on 31 August 1972. She married John Wayne Phelps on 19 October 1996, in Columbia, Missouri. Their son, Josiah Barron Glardon Nelson "Jeb" Phelps, was born on 4 February 2004, in Richmond, Virginia. Tricia is a Licensed Clinical Social Worker and serves as Clinical Director for the National Alliance for the Mentally Ill. John is a recent graduate of the University of Richmond School of Law and works as a disability rights attorney.

Margaret Vinson Baggett was born on 9 July 1978, in Austin, Texas. Meg currently works in the cosmetics industry and is close to completing her college degree in business management. Meg presently resides in North Carolina.

Sarah Vinson's parents are Mary Carlisle Sheegog and James Glardon "Don" Vinson. Mary was born in Hazard, Kentucky, in 1919. Don was born in Irvine, Kentucky, in 1918.

(l.-r.) Joe and Sarah Baggett, Tricia (Baggett) and John Phelps, and Meg Baggett.

Mary and Don married in Hazard on 16 September 1939. They had five children: Patricia, Sarah, Genevieve, Richard and John.

Don Vinson's family were both Huguenots and Quakers and settled in Maryland, North Carolina and Indiana. Family names include Hutchins, Howell, Brandon, Payne, Brasswell, Glardon and Cox. Don's earliest ancestor in America was Richard Coxe, who arrived on the *Godspeed* in 1607.

Mary Sheegog's family was from Kentucky and Virginia. Her mother's family came from Wales in the middle nineteenth century. Her father had both Irish and early American connections. Family names include Stephens, Jones, Morgan, Brawner, Carlisle, Springer and Hardin.
– Submitted by Tricia Baggett-Phelps

J.J. BAGWELL, JR.

John Judson Bagwell, Jr., and his wife Rosemary Clark Bagwell, moved to Longview 10 December 1970. They lived in Kilgore seven years prior to their move to Longview.

Bagwell family, 2003. (l.-r.) Peter and Deanne Rose, Jud and Tracy Bagwell, John and Rosemary Bagwell.

John was born 22 January 1932, in Longview, and has one sister, Mrs. Jane McCrea. He attended Riverside Military Academy, Gainesville, Georgia, in 1949 and 1950, and transferred to Baylor University where he graduated.

After graduation, he served in the Korean War as a military officer. When he returned to Gregg County, he formed his own investment and insurance business and was a real estate broker for many years. He had a great love for bass fishing.

Rosemary was born 24 October 1940, in Longview, and has two brothers, Bobby and David Clark. She graduated from Kilgore High School in 1958, and attended Kilgore College where she went to Business School. She lived and worked in Kilgore after college, then moved to Dallas. She returned to Kilgore after her marriage to John. Later, the family moved to Longview where they joined First Baptist Church. Rosemary was active in Junior League and Garden Club.

Their daughter, Mary Deanne Bagwell Rose, graduated from Pine Tree High School in 1981. After graduating from S.M.U. in 1986, she worked in education, and then started her own private practice of family therapy. She married Peter Rose in 1997,

Judson and "Tootsie" Bagwell, John Judson Bagwell, Jr.'s parents.

who works with autistic children at a Dallas High School. They adopted two children (siblings) from a children's home in St. Petersburg, Russia, in 2004.

John and Rosemary's son, Jud Bagwell, III, graduated from Pine Tree High School in 1989. He received a degree in Biology in 1995, and then started his own business after graduation. He participated in sports such as soccer, swimming and weightlifting. He married Tracy Gowan Bagwell in November 2000. They have one son, Jonathon Judson Bagwell.

John's parents, John Judson, Sr. and Charleen Elder Bagwell moved to Longview from Kilgore in 1935 where he had a radio and repair business, and later owned a record store, frozen food lockers and a hardware store. It was through the hardware store that they obtained the Johnson motor franchise and went full time into the boat and motor business about 1945. Judson worked in his business until his death in 2001. Charleen (Tootsie) Bagwell died February 1996. They are both buried in the Kilgore City Cemetery.

Joe and Mabel Clark, Rosemary Clark Bagwell's parents.

Rosemary's father, Joe Charles Clark, was a life long resident of Kilgore. He was a direct descendent of "Deaf" Smith who was a famous Texas scout. His wife Mabel Barton Clark was born in Cleveland County, Oklahoma. She moved to Kilgore in 1931 and she and Joe were married later. They became distributors for the *Dallas Morning News* until they retired. Joe died in May 1998, and is buried in the Danville Cemetery in Kilgore.
– Submitted by Rosemary Bagwell

BILLY JOE BAIRD

William P. Baird was born in Georgia in 1815. He married Mary Cox, daughter of William Bolin and Margaret Cox, on 2 November 1840, in Harris County, Georgia. William Bolin was the son of Revolutionary War veteran William Cox (South Carolina). William P. and Mary had two sons that served in the Civil War, William Jefferson and Benjamin W. Their son, John Thomas, was born in 1845 in Coffee County, Alabama. Around 1848 the Baird and Cox family moved to Upshur County, Texas.

John married Nancy J. Hoover, daughter of William and Nancy Ann Hoover, about 1869 in Upshur County. Their son, John Thomas Jr., was born 10 June 1876.

John Jr. married on 18 June 1902, Lula Mae Satterwhite, daughter of Joseph A. Satterwhite and Mary Elizabeth Snow, born 22 July 1881. Joseph was the son of Isaac W. Satterwhite, a Civil War veteran (Texas) and Martha Ann Stringer. Isaac was descended from Michael Satterwhite, a Revolutionary War veteran (North Carolina). Martha Ann, the daughter of Jefferson Stringer and Jane E. Pope, was descended from Revolutionary War veteran William Stringer (South Carolina). Jane E. Pope was a cousin of William Barrett Travis of Alamo fame. Mary Elizabeth Snow was the daughter of James and Elizabeth Snow; James was also a Civil War veteran (Texas).

John Jr. and Lula Mae had five children. Lorena Runette, born 7 November 1903, married Joseph Weldon Wheeler; Johnnie Lois, born 15 May 1905, married Frank Hart Marshal; John Thomas III, born 6 February 1912, married Helen Mathis; Billy Joe, born 27 October 1917; and Jack Forest, born 9 August 1920, married Mary Lee Epperson. Jack (Spot) will be remembered as the manager of Acme Brick Company in Longview for many years, as well as being known as the Professor of Possumology.

John Jr. was self employed, buying and selling mineral rights and royalties in the East Texas Oil Field. John Jr. and Lula Mae are buried in the Gilmer City Cemetery in Gilmer, Texas.

Billy Joe (Bill) graduated from Gilmer High School. He was attending the University of Texas when he joined the U.S. Navy in August 1941, assigned as Chief Store Keeper on the aircraft carrier the USS *Lexington*, stationed at Pearl Harbor. The *Lexington* left Pearl Harbor 48 hours before it was attacked on 7 December 1941. Surviving the sinking of the *Lexington* in the Battle of the Coral Sea, he was discharged in 1945.

Bill married Mary Virginia Bays 20 October 1946, in Marshall, Texas. She was born 18 December 1925, to Joel Hugh Bays and Verna Beatrice Buckner. Mary graduated from Marshall High School and St. Mary's School of Business.

Bill and Mary moved to Longview, Texas in 1949. Bill was self-employed as an independent landman. They joined the First Christian Church in 1950 and became active in the church, civic and cultural community.

In 1950, Bill was associated with F.R. Jackson and later served as Vice President when South States Drilling Company was formed. In

(l.-r.) Mary Baird, Barbara Ann Baird, Billy Joe Baird Jr. and Billy Joe Baird.

1962 he sold his interest in the company and became an independent oil producer associated with Morris Coats until Bill's death 7 May 1970. He is buried in Memory Park, Longview. Bill and Mary had two children: Billy Joe Jr. and Barbara Ann, born 13 May 1951, and 4 December 1953, in Gregg Memorial Hospital.

Bill Jr. graduated from Longview High School in 1969, attended the University of Texas, and graduated from Stephen F. Austin University in 1976. He married Dorothy Claire Drew, daughter of Carl William Drew and Adele Fieve, 12 January 1974, in Dallas, Texas. They have two children: Elizabeth Claire, born 7 April 1977, in Nacogdoches, Texas, and Drew William, born 2 April 1980, in Mexia, Texas.

Divorced in 1990, Bill remarried Kathleen Ann Christensen, daughter of Marcy John Sandau and Hilma Margaret Jenson, 6 October 2000, in Scottsdale, Arizona. He has one stepson, Clay Charles.

Bill is in the residential mortgage business in Scottsdale, Arizona. His daughter, Elizabeth, a graduate of University of Arizona with a Masters Degree, teaches at the South Carolina School for the Blind near Greenville. His son, Drew, a graduate of Guilford College in North Carolina, is employed in Greenville, South Carolina.

Barbara graduated from Longview High School in 1972, Kilgore Junior College in 1974, Stephen F. Austin University in 1975 and received her Master's degree in 1984. A Longview resident, she teaches at the Primary School in the Tatum School District.

After Bill's death, Mary went to work in the office of Dr. Henry C. McGrede. She remarried Wayne Bruce Dolive 12 July 1977, a widower with two sons, David Wayne and Brian Bruce.

– Submitted by Mary Baird Dolive

BALLOW/MACKEY

Sidney Love Ballow (28 June 1864), a tenant farmer with his parents, Steward and Artie Elizabeth, two sisters and two brothers, migrated to San Augustine, Texas, from Biloxi, Mississippi, in the early 1800s. He was blinded at the age of 31.

Mattie Lou Vail, parents Martin Luther and Melinda, came to Jamesville, Texas, in the early 1800s, migrating from Germany. There were eight children born of this marriage.

Sidney and Mattie were married 17 March 1917, and there were seven children born. Wil-

liam Wyatt (1919-1991) served in the Army in World War II and was a German prisoner for 19 months; he survived forced marches as a farm laborer before he and two other Americans escaped. Ernest Love (1923-1946) served in the CCC and in World War II; he was Japanese prisoner for five months before escaping. Andrew Wilburn (1925-1998) served in World War II as a Navy midshipman. Ira Willard (1927-1931) died of pneumonia. Edna Mae (1920-1992) was a homemaker. Eunice Marie (5 March 1946) lives in Lufkin, Texas.

The Mackeys: Faye, Kimberly Jo Hudspeth, Kerry Reece Mackey and Robert Kent

Audrey Faye Ballow-Mackey (28 May 1931) moved to Gladewater, Texas, in 1955. She graduated in 1949 from Woden High School. She worked at Martin's Drive and Nacogdoches Memorial Hospital, then moved to Dallas, Texas, in 1951 to work in teletype for Southwestern Bell Telephone, and as a bookkeeper for Parisian Fur Co. She returned to Stephen F. Austin State Teachers' College, living and working at Gibbs Hall Dormitory where she was a secretary for Dr. Lucille Norton and Dr. Karl Schleicher. She served as president of Gibbs Hall, Delta Psi Kappa, Sigma Gamma Sorority, W.R.A. and a member of Alpha Chi. She graduated in 1955 with a Bachelor of Science Degree, majoring in Physical Education — all levels. Audrey moved to Gladewater, Texas, to teach at Gay Avenue and Broadway Elementary Schools — grades 2-6. She received her Master's Degree in 1959 while teaching. After 12 years teaching elementary school, she went to Gladewater High School, coaching tennis, sponsoring cheerleading and teaching all physical education classes. In 1965 she married Norbert Reece Mackey of West Mountain. Three children were born in their 22-year union.

Kimberly Jo (5 April 1967) graduated from GHS in 1985, ranked 4th in a class of 135 She was a 12-year-member of Camp Fire Girls, receiving the Wo-He-Lo Medallion and was chosen "Youth of the Year" by the Chamber of Commerce. She was a four-year member of the National Honor Society, and participated in Band, Choir, Drama Club, and Who's Who in Band, Choir and Drama. She attended and received a degree in Music from Stephen F. Austin State

Brian Ray and Kimberly Jo Mackey Hudspeth and children, (l.-r.) Abigail Kay, Joshua Brian, Elizabeth Jean and Morgan Kimberly.

University, Nacogdoches, Texas. She married Brian Ray Hudspeth, son of the late Dr. Ray Hudspeth and Ermine Hall Hudspeth of Gladewater, Texas. She taught in Port Arthur Schools for two years before starting a family and moving back to Gladewater, Texas. They now live on the 4-H Farm in Henderson, Texas, with their "4-H children": Joshua Brian, Abigail Kay, Morgan Kimberly and Elizabeth Jean.

Robert Kent Mackey graduated 1987. He was active in football, golf and auto-mechanics. He was a member of FTA and Boy Scouts of America, receiving the Eagle Scout Award on his 16th birthday. He toured England and Gilwell Park with the Boy Scouts USA/England Friendship Tour. He went to work at Howe-Baker in Tyler, Texas, shortly after graduation and was there for 12 years.

Kerry Reece Mackey graduated in 1989, attended Stephen F. Austin State University, receiving a degree in Forestry; he worked for Stone Co., in Magnolia, Arkansas, three years before being called into the Ministry. He received his Masters Degree from Baptist Theological Seminary and is serving as a Senior Pastor at Fielder Road Baptist Church in Arlington, Texas. He and wife Stephanie and son Caleb Reece live in Fort Worth, Texas. While in high school, he was in football, band, track and field, on the golf team four years, while receiving his Eagle Scout Badge at the early age of 14. He served Troop 193 in all levels of leadership.

During this era, Faye served as a Director of the Chamber of Commerce for 15 years, a 30-year-member of Camp Fire Girls, and received the District Award of Merit and Silver Beaver Award from Boy Scouts of America for outstanding volunteer service. She was selected "Woman of the Year" in 1979, is a life member of the Texas State Teachers Association, National Education Association,

TAHPER, and Beta Sigma Phi (served as president of them all.)

She and her children were members of First Baptist Church of Gladewater, Texas, active in all phases of church activities.

– Submitted by Faye Mackey

REBECCA BARNES FAHLE / PAMELA BARNES HALL / KELLY BARNES HAND

Bobby C. Barnes (born 28 September 1929) has lived most of his life in Gregg County. However, he was born in Terrell, Texas. In the early 1930s, his parents Arthur D. Barnes (1908-1998) and Mable Rector Barnes (1910-2000) moved to Longview, Texas. Mable's mother was a Tutt, a longtime family residing in the Judson Community of Gregg County. These were the depression years, and his Dad's parents, C.A. and Ada Barnes, were already here. Arthur took a job with the city as foreman to lay bricks on the city streets. Bobby started school at age 5 at Northcutt Heights Elementary School. Before the year ended, however, the family moved to Gladewater, and Arthur went to work for the County running heavy machinery to build county roads. Bobby was in the 9th grade when they came back to Longview. He graduated from Longview High School and has resided in Longview since.

On 14 October 1957, he married Margaret Alice Webb, and they have three daughters: the twins, Pamela Elaine and Rebecca Jane, were born 14 October 1958, and Kelly Louise was born 19 September 1964. All three daughters are married and they all have daughters, eight collectively.

Margaret Alice, and twin sister, Marian Louise were born 20 January 1922, in Gregg County on the old Winterfield Road, which is now Tryon Road and in the city limits of Longview. In 1941 they moved to East Melton Street in town and never moved again. Margaret graduated from University of North Texas in Denton, Texas, and has lived in Longview her entire life. Margaret's father, Carey E. Webb (1896-1965), came to Longview from Dallas to take a job with the First National Bank when the old Dallas National Bank closed because of

the depression. Her mother, Elizabeth Blakely (1898-1986), followed in the spring. The Webb's remained in Longview.

Bobby, a certified Professional Landman, formed BOMAR Enterprises, Inc., an oil and gas exploration company. He semi-retired in 2001. Margaret retired from the Gregg County Historical Museum in 1999 as education coordinator after 13 years on the staff.

Pamela married Bradley Hall in August 1980. They have four daughters: Amber (born 1984); Audrey (born 1988), Adrienne (born 1990); and Alexis (born 1993). They live in Whitehouse, Texas. Rebecca married Steven Fahle in November 1982, and they have two daughters: Stephanie (born 1989) and Evelyn (born 1991). Kelly married Matthew Hand in August 1988, and they have two daughters: Haley (born 1990) and Madeline (born 1992). They currently live in Longview.

– Submitted by Bob Barnes

S. SLADE BARNETT

S. Slade Barnett, farmer and legislator, was born about 1807 in Kentucky. He married Talitha Cumi Woods in Kentucky. The family moved to Sabine County, Texas, sometime around 26 August 1838, when he received a conditional certificate for land in Texas. Barnett represented Sabine County in the House of the Fifth Congress of the Republic of Texas. He later moved to Rusk County, where he was elected a county commissioner in 1848, and a justice of the peace in 1850. On 15 July 1860, Barnett married Mary E. Kilgore in Rusk County. Two years earlier his daughter had married Constantine Buckley Kilgore. Barnett's estate was filed for probate in Gregg County on 10 August 1877.

J.A.V. BARTON & BRYAN MARSH ERWIN BARTON

John Andrew Virgil Barton was born in Millville, Rusk County, Texas, on 30 November 1853, the son of James Madison Barton (born 1816) and Emily Miller Erwin Barton (born 1830). Bryan Marsh Erwin was born in Starrville, Smith County, on 27 November 1857. They were married in Kilgore on 30 November 1875. J.A.V. Barton was a merchant and landowner, served in the Texas Legislature in the 1890s and was active, along with his wife, in the First Presbyterian Church of Kilgore, earlier known as the New Danville Presbyterian Church. The Bartons had ten children when Mr. Barton died in 1900. Mrs. Barton, with the help of her older sons, operated a mercantile business and managed farmland. After Mr. Barton's death, Mrs. Barton sold the home on Henderson Highway (the site of the present Fine Arts Building at Kilgore College) and moved her family to a Knowles Street residence, which was the former Alexander Institute dormitory and home of Dr. and Mrs. Isaac Alexander, founder of the Alexander Institute, a private co-edu-

Bob and Margaret Barnes family, September 2002.

Bryan Marsh Erwin Barton and J.A.V. Barton

cational school in Kilgore before the days of public education.

The Barton children were Augustin (Gus) Barton, an attorney and judge in Palestine; Dr. V. Henry Barton, a medical doctor in McAlister, Oklahoma; Philip E. Barton, a merchant and investor in Kilgore; Andrew Barton, a businessman in Fort Worth (died in 1918 of influenza during the influenza epidemic of World War I); Emily Belle Barton, married L.P. Griffin, Jr. in Kilgore; Julian W. Barton, banker and oil operator, Tyler; Josie B. Barton, married F.D. Obethier, Kilgore and Pittsburg; Jack C. Barton, banker at First National Bank, Longview; Pheriba Barton, married James H. Griffin, Sr., Kilgore; and Hugh Barton, banker and accountant, Fort Worth.

Mrs. Barton was revered by all who knew her for successfully raising a large family as a widow. She died in 1932, soon after the discovery of oil.

– Submitted by Helen Griffin

JOSEPH BEVILL BAUCUM, JR.

Joseph Bevill Baucum, Jr. was born 6 September 1937, to Joseph Bevill Baucum, Sr. and Helen Hines Baucum. J.B. Baucum, Sr. was a sales representative of Axelson, an oil field equipment company, and served on the Judson School Board. Helen taught in the Pine Tree and Judson Schools for 40 years. Joe graduated from Judson High School, Baylor University and Baylor College of Dentistry. In 1959, before entering dental school, he married Barbara Ann Glover. Barbara, the daughter of Millard Franklin Glover and Hattie Thomas Glover, was born 15 September 1938, at the Van Sickle

Barbara and Joe Baucum

Clinic. Dr. R.J. and Lina Glover Van Sickle were her aunt and uncle as were Paul and Ruth Akin.

After serving as a Captain in the Air Force, Joe returned to practice dentistry in Longview in 1965. Dr. Joe Baucum, the grandson of Dr. and Mrs. Henry Baucum and the great nephew of Dr. Arthur Bevill, served as President of the Gregg County Dental Society; President of the Cherokee Kiwanis; Deacon Chairman of First Baptist Church of Longview; and provided volunteer mission dental services along the border and in Mexico. In 1969, he was listed in *Who's Who in Texas Today*.

Barbara Glover Baucum, graduated from Longview High School, Baylor University, and completed a Masters of Education and a Mid-Management Certification from Stephen F. Austin University. She has served as President of the following groups: East Texas Dental Auxiliary; Alpha Delta Kappa, Theta Chapter (International Educators Sorority); Ivy League Garden Club; Judson Middle School PTA (Life Member Recipient). She has served on the boards of Junior League of Longview; Longview Museum of Fine Arts, Southside Day Care, and Crisman Preparatory School. As a member of First Baptist Longview, she has served on the Deacon Advisory Committee, Pastor Search Committee, Sunday School Director for 35 years, and volunteered on many mission trips. She also taught elementary and middle school math and science for 16 years.

Barbara and Joe count as their greatest accomplishment their two children, Robert Jayson Baucum, born 18 May 1963, and Stacy Elizabeth Baucum, born 26 February 1966. Jay Baucum graduated from Longview High School in 1981, and holds two degrees from Baylor University in Oral Communications and Business Administration. After working with Data Systems of Texas in Austin and as an Independent Rexall Showcase Distributor in Dallas, Jay married Molly Ann Davis, an Oklahoma University graduate. They are the proud parents of Davis Joesph Baucum, born 1 February 2000, and Andrew Thomas Baucum, born 16 April 2003. Presently, Jay represents a pharmaceutical company and Molly is a consultant with Price, Waterhouse, Coopers.

Stacy Baucum, an honor graduate of Longview High School in 1984, graduated with a degree in Finance from Baylor University in 1987. She then completed law school at American University in Washington, D.C. In May of 1991, she married Jean-Pierre Daccache of Paris, France. For five years, she practiced in Dallas with the Fulbright and Jaworski Law Firm and Jean-Pierre was involved in International Law. In 1999, they moved to Greenwich, Connecticut, where J.P. does International Financial Investments and Stacy volunteers with the Junior League of Greenwich and the International School of Dundee. They have two beautiful daughters, Lauren Elizabeth Daccache, born 6 December 1993, and Anna Marie Daccache, born 18 September 1997.

– Submitted by Joe Baucum

LINDLEY G. BECKWORTH, SR.

Lindley Garrison Beckworth, Sr., was born on a farm in the South Bouie community near Mabank, Kaufman County, Texas, 30 June 1913. He was educated in rural schools as well as Abilene Christian College, East Texas State Teachers College, Commerce, Texas, Sam Houston State Teachers College, Huntsville, Texas, and Southern Methodist University, Dallas, Texas. Beckworth taught school in Upshur County, Texas, for three years. He then attended the law department of Baylor University, Waco, and the University of Texas at Austin, was admitted to the bar in 1937, and commenced practice in Gilmer, Texas. He was a member of the state house of representatives from 1936 until 1938. He was elected as a Democrat to the Seventy-sixth and to the six succeeding Congresses (3 January 1939-3 January 1953). In 1952, Beckworth was unsuccessful for the Democratic nomination for United States senator. After losing the election he resumed the practice of law in Longview. He was then elected to the Eighty-fifth and to the four succeeding Congresses (3 January 1957-3 January 1967). He served as judge, United States Custom Court, New York City, 1967-1968. He later resumed the practice of law. He died at Tyler, Texas, 9 March 1984, and was buried in Rose Hill Cemetery, Tyler.

JOHN MAY BECTON

John May Becton, Presbyterian minister and teacher, was born in Craven County, North Carolina, on 9 January 1806, to Frederick Edwin and Fannie (May) Becton. John married Eleanor Sharp on 18 January 1827.

After converting from the Baptist religion to Presbyterianism in 1832, Becton was ordained at Mount Carmel Presbyterian Church in Tennessee, in April 1840. He arrived in San Augustine County, Texas, in the fall of that year, and his family came a year later. From 1840 until 1850, he taught school and organized Presbyterian Churches in East Texas, including the church at New Danville.

H e was appointed to organize a Presbyterian church on the first Sunday in October 1850. The Methodists were using the church on the first Sunday, so the Presbyterians had to wait until Monday. An outstanding pioneer Presbyterian minister, he is said to have "blazed the way for Presbyterianism in Texas." He organized several churches in the eastern region of Texas. He also taught at the San Augustine University and Nacodgoches University.

Becton died on 14 July 1853, at Danville and was buried there. The Presbyterian Historical Association designated his grave in the New Danville Masonic Cemetery a significant Presbyterian historical site.

MILTON & PATSY M. BELFLOWER

Patsy Ruth Miller was born in Van Zandt County 11 October 1927, to Martin and Opal Miller. The family moved to Longview in 1931. After graduating from Longview High School in 1945, Patsy attended North Texas State in

Milton and Patsy Belflower

Denton, Texas. After returning to Longview, she worked at the First Baptist Church as secretary to the Music Director.

Milton L. Belflower was born in Tifton, Georgia, 15 April 1926, to Irmon and Bertha Belflower. After World War II, Milton returned home to Valdosta, Georgia, after serving two years in the Navy. He heard about LeTourneau Technical Institute in Longview, Texas, so he made his first ties to Texas. After graduating from LeTourneau College in 1949 with a major in printing, he became a printing instructor.

Milton and Patsy met at the First Baptist Church in Longview where they were married 25 December 1950. Soon they moved to Commerce, Texas, where he received his B.S. Degree from East Texas State College in 1952. The growing family with two sons moved back to Longveiw where Milton worked in the LeTourneau College Print Shop until 1966. An apartment in the former Harmon General Hospital barracks on the campus became home.

In 1956 they bought farmland and built a home in Rusk County with a Longview address, Longview three-party line, and in the Kilgore School District. As the family grew, they became involved with the Kilgore sports activities. Dean Whitten from Kilgore encouraged Milton to apply for the position of instruction/manager, which consisted of setting up a printing program with a lab equipped for teaching and printing for the college. He was hired and remained in that position for 20 years.

The family continued to attend First Baptist Church in Longview, working and teaching. Patsy and Milton had five children, four of them born in Longview. Stephen was born in Commerce. Their oldest son, Kenneth, and Susan Eileen Stone were married 2 August 1975, the last wedding in the old auditorium of the First Baptist Church. Kenneth was born 1 November 1951, graduated from Texas A & M, is employed by Southern Baptist Mission Board in Phoenix, Arizona, and has four children. Stephen Douglas, born 28 January 1953, married Carolyn Sue Milford 28 June 1997; they have four children and two grandchildren. Edmund Wayne, born 7 June 1954, married Pamela Marie Hare 1 February 1976; they have two children. Ed works for Halliburton Oil Well Service Company. Pam teaches school in Whitehouse, Texas, where they

live. Spencer Lee, born 15 August 1957, graduated from Stephen F. Austin College, has one daughter, and owns S&H AC Contractors in Longview. Tina Ruth, born 21 June 1959, graduated from University of Texas in Austin in 1981 with a pharmacist degree. She married John Noe Tanguma 19 December 1981. They own Tan Bonita Photography located in Austin. Steve, Ed, Spencer and Tina attended Kilgore College. Steve and Sue work for Texas Eastman.

– Submitted by Milton and Patsy M. Belflower

H.E. BINGHAM

H.E. (Bill) Bingham, son of C.W. and Laura Shrum Bingham, married Aline Gregory, daughter of John and Gertrude Rogers Gregory, 16 February 1935. Bill and Aline established their home in White Oak and had two daughters, Janis and Sandra. Both graduated from White Oak High School and Baylor University.

Bill had one sister, Lola Latch. He moved from Upshur County to White Oak in the early 1920s. Aline had two brothers, Thomas and "Buddy," and four sisters, Claudia, Evelyn, "Tincy" and Rita.

Bill served twelve years as Gregg County Commissioner. A telegrapher for the railroad in the 1930s and 1940s, he later was an independent oil operator. Active in civic affairs in White Oak, he served on the school board and as mayor. He helped organize the Lions Club, which he served as president, and led in obtaining the charter for the White Oak State Bank. He and Aline were active members of the White Oak Baptist Church.

Aline was a housewife who taught numerous Bible classes and served in the White Oak Schools Parent-Teacher Association, which awarded her a life membership. She and Bill were named Mr. and Mrs. White Oak in 1986.

Bill died in 1991, Aline in 2002. Both are buried in the White Oak Cemetery.

In 1961, Janis married Donnie Canion of Smiley. Roger Bingham "Bing" Canion was

Bill, Aline, Janis and Sandra Bingham, Easter c. 1947.

born in 1962. That year the family moved from Smiley, where Janis had taught school, to Gregg County. Janis worked for Longview Schools as teacher and administrator for thirty-seven years. Donnie worked primarily for Gregg County, including service as deputy sheriff and probation officer, until his retirement in 1998. Both Janis and Donnie were active in civic work. He had a debilitating stroke in 1999.

H.E. "Bill" Bingham, c.1980

Janis earned a Master's degree from Stephen F. Austin State University and did post-graduate work at other institutions. Donnie earned a Bachelor's degree from the University of Texas at Tyler. Bing graduated from White Oak High School and Tarleton State University and earned a Master's degree from the University of Texas at Tyler.

Bing married Laci Laird of Kilgore in 2000. He is Director of Gregg County Juvenile Probation Department and Laci is an administrator at the East Texas Medical Center Behavioral Health Hospital.

In 1963, Sandy married David Alexander of White Oak. They had two children, Millicent and Gregory. The family lived in League City, where David was an aerospace engineer with NASA and Sandy was an elementary school teacher. In 1995, they retired and returned to Gregg County.

In 1996 Millicent married David Jacks. They live in Fort Worth and are the parents of David and Laura. Milli, a graduate of Baylor Law School, is a full-time wife and mother. She and David, a graduate of Lamar University and Southwestern Seminary, own a bookstore.

Greg married Catherine Duke in 1990. They live in League City, where Greg is a computer technician for Titan Corporation. He and Cathy, a graduate of Sam Houston State University, have two daughters, Caitlyn and Megan.

Sandy died of cancer in 2000, just hours before the birth of Milli's son.

– Submitted by Janis Canion

JAMES H. BIRDSONG

James H. Birdsong was born about 1822 in Sumter County, Georgia, the son of Joseph B. Birdsong and Sussanah Alurins, and died 29 July 1897. It is uncertain as to where they are buried. James H. Birdsong married Nancy Eunice P. Law (daughter of John Law and Sarah Maxey) on 1 November 1844, in Alabama. Nancy was born 1819 in Georgia, and died 27 May 1898.

James and Nancy were in Sumter County, Georgia, in 1850 with three children: Georgia, Monroe (James Monroe) and Thomas. They had moved to Pike County, Alabama, by 1860 and had added three more children: Sarah S., William H. and Amelia Emma. They were in Rutledge, Crenshaw County, Georgia, in 1870. By 1880 they were in Collin County, Texas.

James H. Birdsong was a farmer. He served with the 3rd Alabama Regiment, Company A during the Civil War. He enlisted as a private on 12 May 1862, and was appointed corporal in October 1863. He was captured 10 October 1864, at Cedar Creek, Virginia. James was listed as paroled at Appomattox. It is believed it was with General Robert E. Lee at Appomattox when he surrendered to General Grant.

The children of James H. and Eunice Birdsong were Georgia Ann, born 16 March 1846; James Monroe, born 22 November 1847; Thomas J., born 25 April 1850; Sarah S., born 1 November 1852; William Hopson, born 2 September 1854; Mary M., born 29 July 1856; and Amelia Emma, born 6 June 1858. All of the children were born in Georgia except Amelia Emma, who was born in Alabama.

JAMES MONROE BIRDSONG

James Monroe Birdsong was born 22 November 1847, in Sumter County, Georgia, and died 29 November 1929, in Kilgore, Gregg County, Texas. He is buried in Danville Cemetery. He married Elvy Ann Skipper, daughter of Sion Skipper and Mary Goins (Gains), 10 August 1868, in Crenshaw County, Alabama. She was born 9 March 1851, in Butler County, Alabama, and died 1929 in Kilgore, Gregg County.

In 1870 they were in Crenshaw County, Alabama. Sometime between 1870 and 1880 they moved to Gregg County, Texas. They are listed as living in Precinct 6 in the 1880 Gregg County census. They spent the rest of their lives in the Kilgore and Danville area. Fourteen of their sixteen children were born in Gregg County.

Their children were Homer F., born 1869; Ferdinand Lafayette "Fate," born 21 December 1870, and died 13 February 1939; William Monroe "Will," born 6 June 1873, and died 21 December 1952; Daniel Jefferson, born 5 February 1877, and died 1879; James Henry, born 30 September 1875, and died 2 February 1944; Thomas J., born 1878, and died 1880; Samuel Johnson, born 19 April 1879, and died December 1879; Robert Milton "Bob," born 18 October 1881, and died 11 April 1955; Thomas Franklin, born 3 January 1883, and 11 died July 1917; George Washington "Tige,"born 18 July 1885, and died 11 December 1961; Sarah Frances "Fannie," born 31 March 1887, and died 25 June 1971; Eunice Ann, born 18 February 1889, and died 8 June 1957; Oscar Prentice, born 16 March 1892, and died 10 August 1904; Exie

Augustus "Ex," born 31 January 1894, and died 31 December 1964; Fredrick Morris "Fred," born 24 May 1897, and died 2 September 2, 1971; and Maggie Morris, born 16 July 1905, and died 4 October 1918 (she was adopted after her parents were both killed).

Most of James Monroe and Elvy Birdsong's children married and had children born in Gregg County. Some of the descendants served in county offices or owned businesses in Gregg County. Some of the children were among the first to be involved in the East Texas oil fields.

ROBERT L. & JESSIE STOUARD BLAIR

A young married couple, R.L. and Jessie Mae Stouard Blair left the Clear Fork of the Brazos River in Stephens County, Texas, in the summer of 1937, bound for the East Texas oil field and a job. A daughter, Clara, and a son, Robert W., were born to them in Rusk County. In 1943, the family moved to the Gladewater area and made Gregg County their permanent home.

Jessie was born in Stephens County to a pioneer ranching family who descended from early Texas colonists, Lucinda Dyches and Burrel Eaves. Her great grandfather W.D. (Tom) Stouard came from Tennessee to the Fort Belknap area in the mid-1850s, where he became a Texas Ranger helping protect frontier Northwest Texas from the Comanche Indian raids. By 1882, he was ranching in Stephens County, raising horses and mules for sale to the U.S. government. After his death his son, John William, took over managing the ranch, which subsequently passed to his son, Jesse Lee Stouard. He and Etta Francis McLaren, whose family had come to Texas from Lawrence County, Tennessee, were the parents of Jessie Blair.

Robert L. Blair was born in Comanche County, Texas. His mother, Texanna Walker Blair, was the granddaughter of Dr. Samuel Walker who had migrated from Missouri to Texas after the Civil War and practiced medicine in Hamilton and Comanche Counties. His father, John Houston Blair, was descended from the Revolutionary soldier Samuel Blair and Samuel Blair, Jr., who served in the War of 1812 as a lieutenant in a Tennessee cavalry unit. After the Civil War, the Blair family migrated to Erath County,Texas, from Virginia by way of Tennessee and Georgia. In Tennessee the Blair's intermarried with the Burk-Bodine family, and in Georgia with the Mahan's.

Jessie and Robert Blair

In Gregg County, R.L. worked for Texaco Pipeline Company and eventually retired from this company with 39 years of service. In addition, he and Jessie ranched on 1,700 acres. This required the labor of the whole family and some hired help to bale hay, ride pasture, feed cattle, doctor sick animals and maintain the equipment. Along with her ranching activities, Jessie was a good cook and an accomplished seamstress, making much of the family clothing as well as clothes for the less fortunate.

Eventually, they downsized the cattle operation, and began breeding, training and showing registered Quarter Horses. R.L. and Jessie competed in horse shows past their 70th birthdays and collected countless trophies. Over the years they served as advisors and horse show judges for the 4-H Club. R.L. also served several terms as an Agriculture and Soil Conservation Committeeman and, in 1982, they were selected as the Gregg County Farm Family of the Year.

Both were active workers in their church and extended the hospitality of their home to countless others. After rearing their two children, they fostered several other young people. They were always glad to share their expertise and mentored others in raising and showing horses. They had great patience and took much pride in teaching their two granddaughters, Terry and Tammy Bates, daughters of Clara, to ride and show horses and spent many pleasant hours showing with them.

– Submitted by Clara Bates

BLALOCK: From Cumberland, England, to East Texas

THOMAS BLALOCK, SR. (1582) came to America, met and married his wife, Rachel, in Accomack County, Virginia in 1627. They had children Thomas Blalock, Jr., Rachel, William and John Blalock.

THOMAS BLALOCK, JR. (1628) married first Sarah Black and had children Thomas III, Elizabeth and Frances Blalock; then he married Anne Christian Scott in 1668 and had children Charles Richard, John William, Sr. and Anne Blalock.

JOHN WILLIAM BLALOCK, SR. (1671) was born in Accomack, Virginia (on the peninsula). He crossed the bay and secured a land grant in Hanover County, Virginia, where he married first Mary Terrell in 1691 – she died in 1697 leaving no children; he married second, Elizabeth Millington in 1698 in Hanover, Virginia. They had children John William, Jr., Elizabeth, William Millington, Richard and David Blalock. Daughter Elizabeth married Adam Smith of Brunswick County, Virginia. He and Elizabeth were closely connected with the Church of England in St. Paul's Parish.

RICHARD BLALOCK (1722), born in Louisa, Hanover County, Virginia, died in 1805, Cumberland County, North Carolina. He married Rachel Harden in 1745 in North Carolina and had children Charles, Richard, William, Sr. and Anne Blalock.

WILLIAM BLALOCK, SR. (1750), born in Albemarle, Virginia, died before 1790 in Cumberland County, North Carolina. He married Lucy Ann Womack in Granville County, North Carolina, and had children Charles, Hannah, William, Jr. and Sarah Blalock.

CHARLES BLALOCK (1778) married Sarah Ann Brazier in 1801 in North Carolina and had nine children: Lucy, Fannie, James Stuart, William, Rebecca, Elijah Brazier, Richard Womack, Sarah Jane and Charles Dickens Blalock. (*Note: This family moved to East Texas near 1899.*)

CHARLES DICKENS BLALOCK, born 13 December 1824, in Autauga County, Alabama, married Vashti Russell on 3 May 1849, in Harrison County, Texas. They had children Sarah Francis, John Wesley, Susan Elizabeth, Lucy Margaret, Richard Brazier, Nancy Alice, Charles Elijah, James William, Thomas Henry, Mary Ann, Marshall Manuel and Martha Ellen Blalock.

Charles Dickens Blalock served the country of the United States as a private in the Mexican War and fighting the Indians in the spring of 1846 in Wood's regiment and in Capt. E.M. Wilder's company, which were under the command of Zachary Taylor. He fought in the Battle of Monterrey. He was honorably discharged in May 1846.

MARSHALL MANUEL BLALOCK, born 30 September 1869, in Harrison County, Texas, married Lela Pearl McCook in 1875. She died in 1913 in Gregg County, Texas. He died in 1954 and they are buried in Gum Springs Cemetery, Longview, Harrison County, Texas. They had children Josephine, Melvina, Floy, Ida Ruth, James Dewey, Charles Thomas, Marshall Howard, Russell H. and Kate Blalock.

Marshall Manuel Blalock lived to be over 85 years old. His last years were spent living with his daughter, Josephine Cabbiness, and her family at 211 Northcutt Avenue, Longview, Texas, where he enjoyed seeing his grandchildren grow up and get married. He enjoyed the birth of his first four great grandchildren, watching them play on the front porch where he sat in an old wooden rocking chair. (*Note: This family was raised in Harrison and Gregg Counties.*)
– Submitted by Johnnie Mae Sundby (granddaughter of Marshall Manuel Blalock)

MARSHALL MANUEL BLALOCK & DAUGHTER JOSEPHINE MELVINA BLALOCK

Marshall Manuel Blalock was born 30 September 1869, Harrison County, Texas, and died in 1954 in Longview. He married Lela Pearl McCook, born 1875, died 1913 in Gregg County. They had the following children: Josephine Melvina, Floy, Ida May, George Dewey, Russell H. and Kate Blalock.

Josephine Melvina Blalock was born 29 October 1907, in Gum Springs Community, Harrison County, and died 13 September 1980, in Gregg County. She married Ralph Herman Cabbiness in 1923. He was born 10 December 1901, died in 1948, and is buried in Grace Hill Cemetery. They had the following children: Ralph Herman, Jr., Billy Joe, Patsy Sue, Margie Ann, Gaynelle and Milton Wayne Cabbiness.

They also raised a niece, Johnnie Mae Cabbiness. Ralph Herman Cabbiness, Jr. died at the age of two with pneumonia.

Billy Joe Cabbiness, born 5 February 1927, died 2 December 1981, married Betty Jane Smith, born 15 November 1928, on 3 October 1946, after he was discharged from the Navy. He served aboard a destroyer, the USS *Halford*, in the Pacific in and around Japan during the Vietnam War. He is buried in Judson Cemetery, Longview, Texas, alongside his infant daughter, Becky Jo Cabbiness, born 29 October 1952. They had the following children: Billy Ray, Brenda Jane, Bennie Ralph, Becky Jo and Bruce Wayne Cabbiness.

Billy Ray Cabbiness, born 9 May 1947, married 31 May 1969, to Janet Carol James, born 30 May 1947. They have no children.

Brenda Jane Cabbiness, born 15 September 1948, married Ronald Lester McKinney, and they live on a ranch north of Longview in Gregg County. They had children Kathryn May and Jeffery Kyle McKinney.

Bennie Ralph Cabbiness, born 29 October 1950, married first to Carla Ann Lloyd and had a son Jason Lloyd, and daughter, Amanda Dianne Cabbiness, who married Joe Herndon and has Katie and Olivia. He married second to Lynn Sunski Magee. She had David Thomas, who married Kendall Avery; Catherine Anne, who married Jeffery Scott Glunt; and Jennifer Lynne Magee, who married Kenneth John Fleitman. Jason Cabbiness married Kristen Kuehl.

Bruce Wayne Cabbiness, born 9 October 1954, married first Mary Phillips Lawrence. She had Pamela Renee Lawrence, who married Preston Green and they have Natalie and Taylor; second, married Robin Laney Seidel. She had Robert Joseph and Thomas Ray Seidel. Bruce and Robin had Briana Lynn Cabbiness, born 6 February 1992.

Patsy Sue Cabbiness, born 16 March 1928, still resides in the family home on Northcutt Avenue in Longview.

Margie Ann Cabbiness married Gaylon Snider and had Debbie, Pamela Sue, Terri Lynn, Gaylynne and Jason Glenn Snider. Debbie married Ralph Horridge and had Brooks, who married Mary Leon; and Haley Horridge. Pamela married Robert Meacham and had Jenny and Andrea. Terri married first Robert Powdrill and had Jeffery, Brent and Hillary; and second, Dr. William Simpson. Gaylynne married Garry Thomas and had Jessica. Jason married Kelly Whitfield.

Gaynelle Cabbiness married Fred Fitzgerald and had Freddie Ray Fitzgerald, who married Pamela Barnett and they have Freddie.

Milton Wayne, Sr. married Bonnie Brittain and had Milton Wayne, Jr., who married Carol Cearley and they have Milton Wayne III and Sterling Price Cabbiness; Marla Gayle Cabbiness married Michael Lewis. Marla has one daughter, Staci Nicole Cabbiness.

Johnnie Cabbiness married John Sundby and had Steve and Brian.
– Submitted by Brenda Jane McKinney

BLAND-ARNOLD

Abner Harrison Bland (1872-1954) and Fannie Wyatt Arnold (1872-1963) moved to Gregg County from Upshur County after their children all left home. They razed the house they lived in at Stamps Community and built a house in Longview to be near family members.

Abner Bland

Children, all born in Upshur County, Texas, of Abner and Fannie, are Mary Caroline, married Benjamin Mitchell; Roxie Pauline, married Marshall Green; David (died young); Howard Lee, married first Nellie Mary Jones and second, Alva Hamilton; Elton Ray, married Chloe Mizell; Harper Lee, married Hazel Camp; Exchier, married Maye Hendrix; Robert Lee, married Hazel Watson; and Lila Mae, married Robert Lee Mefford.

Ab Bland was born in Quitman County, Georgia, to James Presley and Mary Jane Belcher Bland. He died in Gregg County and is buried in the Mattox Cemetery, Upshur County. Ab was a farmer who raised sugar cane and would let no one cook the syrup off except himself. Syrup making was something the family looked forward to.

James Presley (1851, Alabama-1929, Upshur County, Texas) was the son of Harrison Jones Bland and Samantha Thompson. He married Mary Jane Belcher in 1871 in Barbour County, Alabama. Mary Jane's (1854, Georgia-1896, Upshur County) parents were Abner Belcher and Nancy Emiline Grubbs. James Presley and Mary Jane moved to Texas about 1895, along with their extended families the Culpeppers and Arnolds. Harrison was the son of William Bland (1772-1857) and Elizabeth

Fannie Arnold Bland

Wood (1776-1835). Harrison was a Baptist preacher. Abner Belcher's father was Obadiah Belcher (1830-1886).

Fannie was born in Abbeville, Alabama, to Sarah Caroline Culpepper and Jordan Arnold. Fannie and Ab married before they came to Texas. Fannie was a sturdy farmwife who washed in a washpot, milked the cows, brought in stove wood, cooked three meals a day for a dozen people, plucked geese to make mattresses and pillows, and took food to any relative or neighbor when they were sick.

Jordan Arnold (1846, Alabama-1918, Upshur County) was the son of Sarah Mims and Harrell Arnold. Jordan married Sarah Caroline Culpepper in 1866 in Henry County, Alabama. Sarah Caroline (born 1849, Henry County, Alabama) was the daughter of Joseph Culpepper and Sarah Ward. Joseph was a lieutenant in Company C, 25th Regiment, Alabama Militia during the Creek Indian War of 1836

Other surnames besides those mentioned include Grubbs, Parmer, Shepard, Shelton, Daniels, Harris and Riddell/Riddle.

– Submitted by Jennifer Lynn Wright

BOLES/STOVALL/SHEPPERD

James Henry "Jimmette" Boles was born 18 November 1869, Upshur County, Texas, and died 16 May 1934, Gladewater, Texas. Jimmette married first, about 1901, to Mollie Tubbs, born 26 October 1875, and died 26 December 1903, Gladewater, Texas. After Mollie Tubbs died, Jimmette married second to Mollie Stovall, who was born 12 November 1885, Gregg County, Texas, and died 12 December 1975.

Jimmette Boles owned a blacksmith's shop in Gladewater. This blacksmith shop was located where the Winnie Lee Shop was located, downtown Gladewater, on the corner of South Main and Sabine Streets. Jimmette's shop took on a new duty in 1910 when Mr. L.J. Everett bought the first car in Gladewater. Because Jimmette Boles always shoed the town's horses and kept them going, it seemed to make sense that he should take care of the first automobile in town. With only one car in town, Gladewater had no garages, so Mr. Everett would bring the car to Jimmette's shop for repairs. It didn't matter that he knew very little about cars, because no else did either. It was truly an event to see Mr. Everett drive through town. He always wore his driving goggles. Many people had to stop and hold their horses so the car would not scare them. Others cheered when the car went by.

Jimmette was the son of William Henry Bowles, born 1836, Mississippi. He died in 1900, Gregg County, Texas. William "Bill" Bowles married on 10 July 1857, in Texas, to Elvey Shepperd, born 5 June 1841, Davenport, Montgomery County, Alabama, and died in 1892, Gregg County. Both are buried in the Union Grove Cemetery near Gladewater. William was a veteran of the Civil War, and was a Corporal, 22nd Infantry, Company C, Texas State Troops. Elvey Shepperd was the daughter of Eleazor and Mary Ann (Butler) Shepperd.

Eleazor Shepperd was born 4 March 1815, Jefferson County, Georgia, and died December of 1851, Red Rock Community, Upshur County, Texas. Red Rock is now a part of Gladewater, Gregg County. Eleazor married on 5 September 1832, Montgomery County, Alabama, to Mary Ann Butler, born 20 March 1817, Edgefield District, South Carolina, and died 30 January 1891, Gregg or Upshur County, Texas. Mary Ann (Butler) Shepperd was the granddaughter of James Anthony Butler, born in 1740, Virginia, and died 16 May 1811, South Carolina. Butler was a veteran of the American Revolution. He fought in the Battle of Fort Sullivan, near Charleston, South Carolina. Some have joined the D.A.R. on his records. After the death of Eleazor Shepperd, his widow married William W. Allen, a descendant of Jane Anderson (sister to Elvey Anderson Shepperd). Jane and William Allen were the parents of Jane, born 22 April 1853. She married John Bumpus and they were the parents of William E. Bumpus and Margaret "Maggie" Bumpus, 1877-1963. Maggie married John Henry Bozman, 1873-1945. They were the parents of James Denzil Bozman, 1901-1987; Martha Ann Bumpus, married Miner Clements; and John Caleb Bumpus, born 24 October 1881.

Jimmette Boles had the spelling of his name changed from "Bowles," to "Boles." This was recorded at the Courthouse in Longview. Mollie (Tubbs) Boles, Jimmette's first wife, was the daughter of J.S. and P.J. Tubbs. J.S. Tubbs sold part of his land in a deed dated 28 August 1906, to A.H. Tubbs. A.H. Tubbs died on 17 September 1911, and the land was deeded to W.R. and his wife, Nora Sneed. W.R. and Nora Sneed sold this land to Missie E. (Bowles) Young, Jimmette's sister. Jimmette and Mollie (Tubbs) Boles were parents of an only child, Selmer John Boles, born 22 January 1903 in Gladewater and died 20 January 1968 in Gladewater, buried in Gladewater Memorial Park Cemetery.

Selmer married first to Annie Lee King, born 25 November 1902, Louisiana, and died 28 November 1983. Selmer and Annie divorced in December of 1942. They were parents of Odel Boles, Geneva Nell Scott, Thelma Lee McCary and Johnette Nathan Boles.

Jimmette Boles and his second wife, Mollie Stovall, were parents of an only child, James Elmer Boles, born 16 April 1923, Gladewater, died 29 November 1994, married first on 6 July 1947, Gladewater, to Elsie Fern Skelton, born 10 April 1930, Gladewater. Selmer married second to Jewel Yoder Bekal and they had two children. 1) Selmer Jimett Boles, born 29 July 1947, married 6 November 1969, to Brenda Aston, born 15 February 1949. They were parents of three children: John Phelps; Preston Courtney and Ciji Boles. 2) Mollie, born 5 October 1950, married first 19 October 1968, to Larry Speed and they had two children: Jennifer Adaine and Jeromey Dwight Speed. James and Elsie Boles were parents of 1) Elizabeth "Beth" Ruth Boles and 2) James Henry "Buzz" Boles, II. Beth

Boles was born 18 April 1948, married first 11 November 1967, First Methodist Church, Gladewater, to Kenneth Wayne Barrow, born 15 December 1946, Gladewater, son of Charles Austin and Margie Marie (Upchurch) Barrow. Beth and Kenneth had three children: Wayne Austin, born 2 July 1975; 2) Elizabeth Ashley, born 19 August 1980; and 3) Mollie Brock, born August 1980, a twin. Elizabeth and Kenneth divorced and Beth married second on 1 January 1990, to Ben Cranfield Shepperd, born 12 February 1948, Gilmer, Upshur County, Texas. Ben was the son of James Norton and Mary Joe (Cox) Shepperd. Owners of the Gilmer Abstract Company, both were killed in an airplane crash on 3 May 1968. Ben is a descendant of William Shepperd, Jr. and his first wife, Mary Barnes. Mary died in Alabama and William Shepperd, Jr., who was administrator of his father's estate back in Alabama, married Rebecca Porter, a widow. William and Rebecca came to East Texas about 1850. Elvey (Anderson) Shepperd, 1779-1860, widow of William Shepperd, Sr., 1777-1828, accompanied most of her ten children to the Republic of Texas in 1845. Eight of these children are listed on the 1850 census of Upshur County, Texas.

James Henry "Buzz" Boles, II was born 3 December 1950, Gladewater, Texas; he married first on 16 July 1971, Gladewater, to Sherry Lynn Dobbins, born 19 July 1952, Gladewater. They divorced in July of 1985. Buzz and Sherry were parents of Melissa Janelle Boles, born 26 December 1973. Melissa gave birth to 1) Michael Scott Noble, born 24 June 1993, son of Paxton Noble of Union Grove. But Paxton was killed in an automobile accident on 8 February 1993, before Michael was born. Melissa then married first in 1995, Gregg County, to Daniel Blalock, born 3 April 1977; they later divorced. Melissa and Daniel were parents of 2) Daniel Lee Blalock, born 5 September 1995, and 3) Zachary Todd Blalock, born 26 September 1996, all born in Gregg County. Melissa married second on 14 February 2002, Fort Hood, Texas, to Gene Paul Pope, Jr., born 19 March 1969; they live in Killeen, Texas.

James H. "Buzz" Boles married again on 6 August 1988, Longview, Texas, to Rebecca Jane "Janie" Howard, born 22 May 1946, Dallas, Texas. Rebecca is the daughter of James Calvin and Dorothy Ruth (Hooks) Howard McMichael. Janie had two daughters from a previous marriage, 1) Terri Townes Tyndell and Jill Townes Conway, both born in Clarksville, Texas. James Henry "Buzz" Boles graduated from Gladewater High School in 1969. He achieved the following degrees from Texas A&M at Commerce, Texas: BS, 1972, Industry and Technology; Master's, 1977, Vocational Education; and Doctorate, 1983, Educational Administration.

During high school he played drums in garage bands and held part time jobs. After college he went into Railroad Salvage at South Railroad Car Parts in Greggton, Texas, for three years. In 1975, he started teaching Metal Shop at Pine Tree High School. In 1978 he became assistant Principal at Pine Tree High School. In 1998 he became Vocational Director at Pine Tree High School and started his home inspection business on weekends. In 2003 he retired from public school employment and started inspecting homes full time.

James Henry "Buzz" Boles and his sister, Beth, often visited with their grandmother, Mollie (Stovall) Boles, and lived with her for a time. Mollie lived on the old Longview Highway, east of Moody Creek Bridge. Buzz was a regular visitor at the home of Helen and Perry Brown, a neighbor to his grandmother. Maude Wright, Helen's mother, was a cousin to James E. Boles. Maude and Sam Wright became owner of the farm that her mother, Missie E. (Bowles) Young, 1874-1943, purchased on 11 November 1911, after the death of her husband, Charles Leonard Young, 1866-1911. Buzz was also a frequent visitor to Maude and Sam Wright. Sam and Maude lived on the south side of the old Longview Highway and Mollie Boles lived on the north side of the old highway.

Mollie (Stovall) Boles was the daughter of Albert and Julie Stovall. Albert was born July of 1854, Mississippi, and married about 1877/78. Julie was born in August of 1853, Arkansas. They are found on the 1910 census records of Gregg County, Texas. Children listed were 1) William, born July 1879, Texas; 2) Mollie, born 12 November 1885; 3) Eva, born August 1888; 4) Julian, born August 1891; 5) Samuel, born August 1895; 6) John, born February 1892. (Also listed: Ruth, daughter-in-law, born March 1883, Texas; Emma Armstrong, daughter, born August 1877, widow, born Texas; Gertie Armstrong, granddaughter, born July 1896, Texas.) Living next door was John Wesley Mings and his wife, Sarah. There was a Charles Stovall that lived next door, born March 1875, Texas

Elvey (Anderson) Shepperd was born in 1779, Onslow County, North Carolina, where her family had been for several generations. In late 1779 Elijah Anderson, born c. 1850, and his wife, Lavinia Brack, moved to Richmond County, Georgia, with their large family. Their daughter, Elvey, married there on 22 February 1802, to William Shepperd, born about 1777. These families later moved to Jefferson County, Georgia, where Elijah, who was a revolutionary soldier, died before the Orphans Land Lottery of 1807, the year Lavinia entered her orphaned children in the lottery. William became a land owner in Jefferson County, Georgia, in 1821. The Andersons and Shepperds migrated to Montgomery County, Alabama, in the 1820s where William was killed by a Negro about 1828. Elvey, his widow, moved about ten miles south to Davenport, Montgomery County, Alabama, and later, in the fall of 1845, migrated with her family to the Republic of Texas. Elvey (Anderson) Shepperd died of cancer in April of 1860, and was buried in the Gay Cemetery just north of Gladewater but in Upshur County. Several years ago the Texas Historical Survey Com-

mittee [now The Texas Historical Commission], chaired by John Ben Shepperd, who was a descendant of Elvey, placed an historical marker on her grave. Elvey (Anderson) Shepperd was a descendant of three Mayflower ancestors: 1) Edward Doty, 2) Edward Fuller and 3) Samuel, son of Edward Fuller. Several have joined the National Society of Mayflower Families on the well-documented line.

(Note: Information contributed by family members, to a book titled *The Doty, Anderson, Shepperd and Allied Families*, by Carl V. Wright.) – Submitted by James Henry "Buzz" Boles, II

BOLGER-CRUESS

Robert Cruess (Bob) Bolger and Lillie Pearl Madden Bolger with their two children, Marybelle (age 10) and William (Bill) Robert (age 8), moved to Longview in 1948. Bob transferred from Mt. Pleasant, Texas, as a construction foreman for Southwestern Electric Power Company. He retired from the company with fifty years service and an outstanding safety record. He was a ham radio operator, member of First Baptist Church and a founding director of the SWEPCO credit union. His hobby was fishing. Bob could build almost anything.

Bob (1901-1973) was born in El Paso to Irish immigrants Samuel Robert and Isabella Cruess Bolger. Sam, an adventuresome man, was born 6 May 1866, Donnybrook, Dublin, Ireland, and died 18 April 1934, in Arizona where he was on one of his "strike it rich" ventures. Prior to his marriage Samuel Bolger, a mining engineer, had been to the United States. He returned home to marry his cousin, Isabella Cruess, in February 1898, in the Lockeen Church, County Tipperary. The couple lived in County Wicklow, Ireland, until about 1899, when Sam went to Mexico to work in a silver mine. Isabella followed him with their first child, Samuel Robert, Jr. (1899-1900). Isabella and baby Robin landed in Philadelphia, took a train to El Paso, Texas, where Sam met her in a wagon, and they went to San Jose del Sitio, Mexico, where Robin died of whooping cough. Isabella was the only English-speaking woman at the funeral.

Sam and Isabella traveled around New Mexico, Arizona, and Arkansas, before she settled in Mt. Vernon, Texas, in 1910. Sam continued to travel around the country in his quest for a mother lode. Besides Bob, the couple had five more sons: George Albert, Joseph William, David Edward, Rufus Hunt and Ruben Francis. All grew up in Mt. Vernon, Texas.

Lillie Pearl and Bob Bolger

Samuel Robert Bolger was the son of James Michael (son of James Peter Bolger, County Wexford) and Crosdella Elizabeth Cruess Bolger. James Bolger was a wine merchant and rectifying distiller at 49 William Street, Dublin.

Isabella Cruess (1873, Ireland-1955, Franklin County, Texas) was the daughter of Samuel Robert Cruess and Isabella Abernethy, who married 1863. Isabella Cruess was born in County Offaly at Lackah House, where her family had lived since before 1750. Isabella Abernethy (1832-1875) was the daughter of William H. Abernethy and Eleanor Horsman. William H. was born in 1795 in Ireland to William David Abernethy and Isabella James. Isabella James was the daughter of Mr. James and Margaret Spunner James (daughter of William Spunner of Shinrone).

Samuel Robert Cruess's occupation was gentleman farmer; he also bred and raced horses. He was born about 1816, and was the son of William Vere Cruess, Sr. (born 1795 at Lackah House) and Florence L'Estrange. William Vere, Sr. was the son of M. Thomas Cruess (1753-1796) and Mary Ann Hunt (1758-1802). Mary Ann was the daughter of William Hunt of Glangoal. M. Thomas Cruess was the son of M. William Cruess, born about 1722, and died 1782, at Lachah House.

Alternate spellings for Cruess in Irish records include Cruice and Cruise.

Descendents of Robert Cruess and Lillie Pearl include daughter Marybelle, who married Sid Tutt, and son Bill. Children and grandchildren of Marybelle and Sid are James (Jim) Sidney Tutt, Jr. and wife Margaret Ann Van Burkleo; Teresa Elizabeth Tutt and husband Troy Ware Cooper, Jr. and their daughter Teresa Sydney Cooper; Timothy (Tim) Bolger Tutt and wife Amy Beth Pritchard and children Benjamin Prichard Tutt and Mary-Austin Tutt; and Thomas (Tom) Mitchell Tutt and wife Karen Denise Pieratt and son Jonathan Thomas Tutt.

Children and grandchildren of Bill Bolger and Katherine Erin McKenna are Daniel (Dan) Patrick Bolger and Joellyn Democoeur and Elizabeth Shay Bolger and Daniel James Bolger; and Timothy (Tim) Robert Bolger and children Carlisle (Carli) Rose Bolger and Samuel Robert Bolger.

– Submitted by Bill Bolger

JAMES & PAT BOLTON

James Seguine Bolton, son of John Seguine and Carroll Bolton, was born in Kilgore, Texas, on 29 April 1961. He attended Kilgore schools until 9th grade when his family moved to North Carolina. While living in Kilgore James was involved in Boy Scouts and Kilgore Little League Baseball. After graduating from Cary High School in 1979, James attended East Carolina University.

In September 1987, James married Patricia Earp, daughter of John and Suveter Earp. Pat was born in Clayton, North Carolina, on 20 October 1961.

James, Pat, Josh and Courtney Bolton

James worked as Traffic Manager for the Telex Corporation for over 20 years and continued his career as Distribution Manager of Alcatel Corporation in Raleigh, North Carolina, for several years. He is now self-employed in home construction in the Raleigh area.

James and Pat are active church members in North Carolina. They are the parents of two children: Courtney Michelle, born 4 July 1991, and Joshua Seguine, born 31 October 1996.

– Submitted by James Bolton

JOHN AND CARROLL BOLTON

John Seguine Bolton and Sonja Carroll Jones Bolton were married 24 June 1960, in Kilgore. John, born in Cherokee County on 19 August 1937, is the son of the late Cherokee County Judge J.J. (Captain) Bolton and Bonnie Norwood Bolton of Rusk, Texas. After attending Tyler Junior College, John attended University of Texas-Arlington majoring in Industrial Management. He served in the U.S. Navy Airborne Early Warning Squadron 4, serving in the Hurricane Hunters in the Atlantic and Caribbean and is currently a member of the Hurricane Hunters Association.

Carroll and John Bolton

While their children were young, John served as coach for the Kilgore Youth Baseball league and as Cub Scout Master for his sons. He served one year as Chairman for the annual Boy Scout Fair.

After 35 years in the electronic industry, John retired from Memorex-Telex in 1993. John is the second great grandson of John Brownlow McCracken who came to Texas in 1839, and the great grandson of James Bolton, a Confed-

erate soldier from Texas. He is the third great grandson of William Bolton of Virginia, a Revolutionary War patriot. John is also the third great grandson of Revolutionary patriot Captain John Norwood of South Carolina who rode with the Swamp Fox, Francis Marion. John is a member of the Sons of the American Revolution, Sons of the Republic of Texas and Sons of the Confederate Veterans.

Sonja Carroll, born 30 October 1940, is the daughter of Jack and Bea Jones of Kilgore. She attended Kilgore schools and after marriage was a homemaker. The family lived in North Carolina several years. While living in Raleigh, Carroll worked in the Wake County School System.

Carroll is the second great granddaughter of William Christian, Confederate soldier from Arkansas, and Thomas J. Hise, Confederate soldier from Tennessee. She is the great granddaughter of Roland Jones and the second great granddaughter of Nicholas Barrett, both of whom were in the Oklahoma Land Rush in April 1889. Her fourth great grandfather, Conrad Hise, was a Revolutionary War Patriot, and her seventh great grandfather was the Huguenot, Mathieu Agee, who came to this county in 1700-1701 from France.

Carroll is a member of the Daughters of the American Revolution, the Huguenot Society and United Daughters of the Confederacy. She is a lifetime member of the Texas PTA and was listed in Outstanding Young Women of America in 1973.

John and Carroll are parents of three children: James, born 29 April 1961, in Kilgore; Kim, born 19 August 1963, in Dallas; and Kerry, born 19 August 1963, in Dallas. James and wife, Pat, live in North Carolina and are the parents of Courtney and Josh Bolton. Kim lives in Tennessee, and is the mother of three boys, Tyler and twins, Sawyer and Spencer Tsoumbos. Kerry and wife, Jeannie, live in Tennessee, and are the parents of Evan, Adam and Bryson Bolton. After retiring, John and Carroll have moved back to Kilgore. They are members of the First Christian Church of Kilgore where John is an active Elder of the church.

– Submitted by John Bolton

KERRY & JEANNIE BOLTON

Kerry Bolton, son of John and Carroll Bolton, was born in Dallas, Texas, on 19 August 1963. He moved with his family to Kilgore in 1970. Attending Kilgore schools, Kerry was involved in Boy Scouts and Kilgore Little League baseball. In 1975 his family moved to North Carolina. There Kerry attended Wake County schools and graduated from Cary High School in 1981. Kerry was active in the Cary High band and played drums for the band. After graduation, he attended Louisburg Junior College in Louisburg, North Carolina. His final year he was elected Homecoming King for the school. After graduating from Louisburg, Kerry attended North Carolina State University and graduated from Wake Technical College.

Kerry and Jeannie Bolton and (l.-r.) Adam, Bryson and Evan Bolton.

After being employed by the Telex Corporation for several years, Kerry went to work for Dell Computers in Austin, Texas, as a test design engineer. A year later, he was transferred by Dell to Nashville, Tennessee, to open their largest U.S. production plant.

While attending Louisburg College, Kerry met Jeannie Jones, daughter of Bruce and Frances Jones of Raleigh. Jeannie was born on 11 November 1963, in Raleigh, North Carolina. It was also in Raleigh that Kerry and Jeannie were married on 4 June 1988.

They are the parents of three boys: Evan Blake, born 11 December 1989; Adam Christian, born 5 May 1992; and Bryson Alan, born 29 June 1998.

– Submitted by Kerry Bolton

JAMES & KATIE BOND

James Bond (1888-1941) of Lincoln Parish, Louisiana, was the eldest of four surviving children of William Frederick Bond II and Theodocia Gallatt. After studies at Louisiana Tech, Jim fought in World War I. Two James Bonds in the same company necessitated his middle initial 'B' which he maintained throughout his career.

In July 1918, J.B. (Jim) Bond married Katherine (Katie) Beatrix Thurmon (1893-1971), an English teacher from Lincoln Parish, Louisiana, the eighth of nine children of Kate Broadwell Thurmon and William Mitchell Thurmon.

From 1920 to 1931, Bond operated an oil production company, Bond and Evans, in Pecos, Texas, following early drilling booms in Louisiana, West Texas and Arkansas. It was from El Dorado that Jim and Katie came to Longview, Texas, in 1931 with their son, William James (Billy) Bond (1924-2001).

Their first residence was the Longview Arms Apartments on West Methvin Street (currently the Longview Arms Bed and Breakfast), before building a home on the northeast corner of Seventh and Turner Drive in Nugget Hill, now an historic neighborhood. This remained their home until a 1938 divorce.

Among Bond's associates were the McWilliam brothers, who had extensive commercial and retail holdings. Bond joined them and Judge Megaughey in building the 6-story McWilliams Building on Green Street at Methvin. Bond maintained his offices there

J.B. Bond and Billy, circa 1933, on porch of house at 7th and Turner Streets, Longview.

until his death. Bond's associate and brother-in-law, Robert A. Thurmon, kept his office there until 1947.

Billy Bond returned from the Pacific in 1945 and assumed the name of Jim honoring his late father. He married Jane Allen (1928-1998) of Dallas in February 1946, a concert pianist who had studied at Southern Methodist University. They bought a home in the Green Acres Subdivision of Longview. Their son James Benjamin Bond (Jim) was born in January 1947. They lived there until their divorce in March 1949.

Jane Allen Ilan Bond and her son would visit the Thurmon family at 204 East South Street in Longview, where she would sometimes perform on the family piano, attracting an appreciative audience on the family's large, screened-in porch. Jane Allen married concert violinist Melvin Ritter of St. Louis in 1958. There were no children of that marriage.

In June 1950, William James (Jim) Bond married Yvvonne Lodell Deakins (1930-1974), a graduate from the business school of Southern Methodist University. Her mother was Kathryn Beatrice Deakins (1909-1988); her father was Homer Lodell Deakins (1901-1986), a longtime Chrysler/Plymouth dealer and cattle rancher in Longview.

Yvvonne (Yvvie) and Jim Bond lived in Dallas until their divorce in 1965. They had two sons: Mark Deakins Bond (Mark) (August 1956) and James Bradford Bond (Brad) (November 1959).

The grandchildren of J.B. Bond and Katie Bond remain close. Jim Bond resides in Michigan with his wife and three young children; Mark Bond lives in Atlanta and has a grown daughter; Brad Bond resides in South Carolina with his grown daughter and two younger sons. He has a grown son in Dallas.

– Submitted by Jim Bond

BOOTH

The early American ancestry of the Booth family traces to Robert Booth of Southampton County, Virginia. His grandson Reverend

Beverly Booth was a Revolutionary War Minuteman. The family migrated to Georgia, then to Texas. They settled north of Longview at Old Diana in 1851. Willis Early Booth moved to Longview when the Southern Pacific Railroad track was being completed. He was married to Anna Elizabeth Cain by the honorable Rev. Bluford W. Brown 31 December 1874. The couple had two children, Varina and Claudie, who died young. Anna died of childbirth complications 24 September 1879; all are buried in Greenwood Cemetery.

Willis Early established a hardware and buggy store downtown next to a livery store operated by his brother-in-law, J.D. Hoyler. He later had a hardware and furniture business on West Tyler Avenue.

On 18 November 1886, Willis Early married Woodie C. Woods, born 17 February 1860, Elderville, died 9 July 1930, Longview, buried Grace hill Cemetery. One of their sons, Aldo Booth, born 1898, was accidentally killed in an elevator accident during construction of the First National Bank Building at Fredonia and Tyler on 15 January 1912 (*Daily Times Clarion*, Vol. I, 16 January 1912).

Woodie's father, Caleb Nelson Woods, born 6 September 1817, Tennessee, died 7 October 1882, Elderville, was a charter member of Peatown Christian Church (historical marker at site). He was appointed by the State of Texas as Trustee of Peatown School in 1879. Woodie's mother was Anna Elizabeth Murchison, born 6 February 1827, North Carolina, died 3 June 1909, buried Peatown Cemetery. Willis Early Booth was born 27 January 1851, in LaGrange, Georgia, died 6 September 1915, Longview, buried Greenwood Cemetery. His son, J. Willis Booth, born 3 April 1891, married Gladys Laressa Adams of Elderville. Their picture, shown above right, was taken shortly after they married in 1918. After his World War I Army service, he became manager of Foreman's Furniture Store and Undertaking Parlor. In 1930 in the oil boom he went into business for himself. He operated the first motel in Longview and invested heavily in real estate, becoming the first president of the Longview Board of Realtors.

Gladys Adams Booth

He served on the City commission for four terms and was active in civic affairs. Following his death on 18 January 1963, an editorial in the *Longview Daily News* on 21 January 1963, said, "The name of Willis Booth was synonymous with progress" and recalled that "he was one of the first to advocate re-routing U.S. 80 from

James Willis Booth and Gladys Adams Booth

downtown Long-view to Marshall Avenue so as to expedite the flow of traffic through the city…making it possible for commercial development on Marshall Avenue…."

The children of J. Willis and Gladys Booth, all born in Longview, were Edwin Russell Booth, 15 November 1919–3 February 1998; Mary Elizabeth Booth, 21 May 1921–15 July 1988; Horace Kenneth Booth, 18 May 1926–30 July 1926; James Willis Booth, Jr., born 21 June 1927; and Talmadge Early Booth, born 16 December 1929.

Talmadge's parents were members of pioneer families of Gregg County. His great-great grandfather was Col. John Hamilton McNairy, born in Guilford County, North Carolina, in 1804. He moved to Shelby County, Texas, in 1837. He married twice and was the father of eleven children. His first wife was Sallie Leatherman, born Tennessee, died Mississippi, in 1836 on the way to Texas. His second wife was Susan (Susannah) Runnels, born Tennessee, 1824, died in Shelby County, Texas, in 1841. She was the daughter of Henry Runnels and Margaret (Peggy) Smith, who came from Tennessee to Texas in 1837.

Col. McNairy was one of two Regulators who, at the request of Gen. Sam Houston, signed the peace treaty for the Regulators to end the Regulator–Moderator War in 1844. Col. McNairy bought acreage in 1847 and moved to Coffeeville, Harrison County, Upshur County area (formerly all part of Shelby County).

He was instrumental in creating Upshur County and was the first State Representative from Upshur County in 1848. (Note: An area that later became Gregg County was still part of Upshur County at that time.) He was one of two State Representatives for Harrison County prior to Upshur County being formed out of Harrison County. He died at Coffeeville 7 January 1853. A state historical marker is located at his grave in the Old Coffeeville Cemetery, Upshur County, Texas.

Col. McNairy's paternal grandfather was Francis McNairy, patriot of Guilford County, North Carolina. John Hamilton McNairy is named after his grandfather, General John Hamilton, Revolutionary War, Battle of Guilford Courthouse, North Carolina.

Frances Monigold Liston Booth and Talmadge Early Booth

In 1950, Talmadge Booth graduated from Southern Methodist University, Cox School of Business. He established the Booth Insurance Agency in June 1950, and was awarded the Chartered Property and Casualty underwriter (CPCU) designation in 1963.

He married Frances Jo Birdwell in 1951. They had four children: Victoria Lynn, Robert Early, Stuart Lee and Leanne Elizabeth. Francis Jo died in 1981.

Talmadge married Frances Monigold Liston in 1983. She had one son, Thomas Walter (Pat) Liston.

Related Booth Family Line:
Adams Family

Lemual A. Adams, War of 1812 veteran, was born in Virginia in 1797. He married Elizabeth Brewer of Virginia in 1816. They lived in Maryville, Tennessee, prior to settling in Texas about 1845 near the Elderville Community. Neither Gregg County nor Longview existed then.

Lemuel, a cotton farmer, died in Elderville in 1892, and is one of only two War of 1812 Veterans (Tennessee Militia #SC25696) buried in Gregg County. His wife Elizabeth died in 1882 and is also buried in Peatown Cemetery. They had eleven children. (See detailed Adams Family paper at the Gregg County Historical Museum and the East Texas Historical Society paper at Longview City Library.)

William Russell Adams, born 5 August 1832, the sixth child of Lemuel Adams and Elizabeth Brewer, was a farmer and schoolteacher. He served as sergeant in the Confederate Army, Company H, 18th Texas Cavalry. He married Natilla "Tilla" McNairy 6 November 1859. She was born 10 February 1843, in Shelby County. William Russell Adams died 9

Francis McNairy house, prior to 15 March 1781

March 1887. Nattila McNairy Adams' father was Col. John Hamilton McNairy. Her mother was Susan Runnels, born 1824, Shelby County, and died in 1893 in Upshur County.

James Quincy Adams, son of William Russell Adams and Natilla McNairy, was born 27 September 1891. He was a farmer. On 24 September 1891, James Q. Adams married Judith Amanda Mercer, the daughter of Marion Mercer and Joanna Whittington Mercer. Judith, born 21 March 1871, was the second child born in Longview. John Quincy Adams, died 21 May 1936, is buried in Peatown Cemetery, Gregg County. Judith Amanda Mercer Adams died 24 April 1928, in Longview and is buried in Peatown Cemetery.

Gladys Laressa Adams, daughter of James Quincy Adams and Judith Amanda Mercer, was born 10 July 1894, in Elderville. She married James Willis Booth on 14 September 1918. She died 6 January 1993. She and her husband, who died in 1963, are buried in the Booth Family plot in Grace Hill Cemetery. She was a graduate of Texas Presbyterian Women's College (now Austin College) and taught school at Pine Tree. Mrs. Booth, a member of First Presbyterian Church, taught Sunday School for many ears and served as president of Women of the Church. She was past president of Shakespeare Club and a member of Daughters of American Revolution and United Daughters of the Confederacy, R.B. Levy Chapter. She was President of Longview High School PTA and first President of the City Council PTA.

– Submitted by Talmadge Booth

ELTON CLAY BOSWELL & AUDIE IMOGENE NULL

The East Texas oil boom of the early 1930s enriched more than bank accounts in the region—it brought a diverse group of people to Gregg County to work in the new industry. Major oil companies had offices in Longview. One employed by Humble from DeLeon, Texas, was Elton Clay Boswell. After working in the oilfields near Van, he met and married Audie Imogene Null of Grand Saline, Texas. Soon after their December 1937 marriage in DeLeon, they made their home in Longview.

Elton's father, John Thomas Boswell (born 13 October 1879), was one of 11 children of John W. Riley Boswell (born 22 March 1853) whose ancestry traces to England, 1650. Having come overland from Lafayette County (Oxford), Mississippi, the Boswells settled in DeLeon, Texas, Comanche County, where Tom Boswell married Clara Nabors (born 3 August 1887). They reared a large family. Tom died 15 March 1927; Clara died 25 November 1958. Both are buried in DeLeon, Texas, Cemetery. Elton was their oldest child.

Imogene's ancestors, the Nulls, originally of Dutch origin, came to America in the 18th century. From Philadelphia they migrated to the Carolinas, then on to Texas where some settled in Van Zandt County near Grand Saline. Imogene's parents, G. Cleveland Null (born 29

November 1890, died 7 August 1972) and Emma Ora Carroll (born 29 October1894, died 26 February 1955) and married 21 January 1912, and farmed land in the Jamestown, Texas, area near Grand Saline. Audie Imogene Null was born there 10 November 1914.

In his 38 years with Humble, Elton worked his way through the ranks to the position of Connection Foreman. His work took him through the oil fields of East Texas and to the Gulf coast where his expertise helped Humble produce some of the first off-shore wells. He had an outstanding job record and was well respected by all who knew him.

Imogene and Elton Boswell, 1962

Elton and Imogene's two children were Larry Joe Boswell (9 February 1941) and Gary Clay Boswell (17 March 1945). The family spent many happy hours fishing on Caddo Lake and participating in Scouting and Little League Baseball. Boswell Park in Longview was named in Elton's honor because of his pioneering support of Little League Baseball in Gregg County.

Boswell was an active supporter of Scout Troop 221, Larry's Scout group, and the Boy Scout Camp Tonkawa, and he was a member of Order of the Arrow. He proudly watched Larry achieve the rank of Eagle Scout as well as induction into Order of the Arrow. Elton was a 32nd Degree Mason and a member of the Hella Temple.

Before Elton's death in November 1965 (burial in Memory Park, Longview), he and Imogene had been married 28 years. Imogene worked for several years for Murray Jewelry, and she and family continued to be members of the Church of Christ which the family attended beginning at the Second and Whaley location downtown. It became the Alpine and Glover Church. Today, it is the Alpine Church of Christ.

– Submitted by Mrs. Elton Boswell

LARRY JOE BOSWELL & VIRGINIA ANN PLILER

Virginia Pliler (15 January 1943) and Larry Boswell (9 February 1941) were born and raised in Longview. Their lives entwined in high school, and they married on 13 April 1963, during their senior year in college. History repeated itself as they married in the same home in the Judson area where her parents Annie D. William (17 May 1907) and Fred M. Pliler (17 September 1902) were wed 31 years earlier on 21 April 1932.

The Boswell family, 2002. (l.-r.) Front: Christopher Boswell, Emma Ream, Virginia Boswell, Imogene Boswell, Larry Boswell, Rachel Boswell and Justin Boswell. Back: Michael Ream, Grayson Ream, Christi Boswell Ream, Shelli Boswell and Clay

Virginia, only child of the Plilers, is the fifth generation to live on the farm in Gregg County originally settled by her Killingsworth-Harris ancestors who came from Bibb County, Alabama, in 1851. Born at Markham Hospital, Virginia later attended Peggy Ann Private School and Judson schools where she was active as annual editor, honor society member, band member/twirler and Gregg County Fair Representative. In high school she met Larry Boswell and the rest, as they say, is history. Virginia went on to earn two degrees, graduating summa cum laude from North Texas State University.

Larry's parents, Imogene Null Boswell (10 November 1914) and Elton Clay Boswell (9 June 1906) moved to Longview as newly weds in 1937 during the Oil Boom. Larry was the oldest of two boys (Larry Joe, 9 February 1941, and Gary Clay, 17 March 1945) born to the Boswell family. Larry began his schooling at Mrs. Denton's Private School, then continued through graduation in Longview Schools. He attained the rank of Eagle Scout in scouting, played baseball, basketball, track and was All District First Team in football while playing for the Lobos. After earning his degree in Business/Psychology at NTSU, Larry and Virginia settled in the North Dallas area where she began to teach, was a Master Teacher consultant and was invited to be the keynote speaker for RISD Convocation. Larry began his 40-year career in insurance , serving the last 30 years as an officer and on the board of directors of an insurance company.

It's been said "you can't go home again," but the Boswells did it – twice. First in 1965, they returned to Longview and had two children, Clay Scott (26 May 1966) and Christi Lynn (25 July 1969), but in 1973 returned to Dallas. During the intervening years they had the good fortune to watch their children graduate from RISD Schools, earn several college degrees, marry and have children of their own. The Boswell family also came "home" to Longview many times to enjoy fun on the farm and good times with relatives. Then, in 1999 after 26 years

in Dallas, Larry and Virginia retired and returned to their roots on their 150-year-old family farm where they built a new home overlooking Virginia Lakes. They're home!
– Submitted by Larry Boswell

THOMAS ANDERSON BRAMLETTE

Thomas Anderson Bramlette, son of John Woodson and Nancy (Taylor) Bramlette, was born 26 March 1852, in Toccopola, Pontotoc County, Mississippi. His parents and grandparents (Jesse Hughes Bramlette and wife, Esther Wellborn) had moved from Alabama to Pontotoc County about 1836 when that county was in its infancy.

Thomas A. Bramlette spent the first 45 years of his life in Pontotoc County where he engaged in farming and also served as Clerk of the Chancery Court in the early 1890s.

On 25 February 1875, he married Annie Eliza Miller in Pontotoc County. The daughter of Ebenezer Erskine Miller and Margaret Clementine Lawrence, she was born 6 December 1852 in Pontotoc County where her parents and grandparents, Ebenezer and Margery (Reid) Miller had been early settlers. She received her education at Chickasaw Female College and was a schoolteacher before her marriage.

On 24 December 1896, Thomas A. Bramlette moved his large family to Longview. The family stayed with their cousins, the McClures, on Methvin Street until they bought a house on the southeast corner of Whaley and High Streets (now torn down).

While living in Longview, Thomas A. Bramlette engaged in the sawmill, cotton and cotton oil business and took an active part in local affairs. He served as president of the Longview School Board and was a member of the Board of Aldermen from 1903 to 1906 when Longview's first City Hall-Fire Station was built on Tyler Street. It was also during his term as Alderman that Grace Hill Cemetery was built, and he served on several committees involved in its development. It would later be the final resting place for him, his wife and many of their children and grandchildren.

Though brought up a Baptist, he had joined the Presbyterian Church after his marriage and became an active member. He was installed as Deacon of the First Presbyterian

Annie E. Miller Bramlette

Church of Longview in 1899, soon after coming to Longview, and served in that capacity until his death. He also served on the building committee for the second church building constructed in 1900.

Thomas A. Bramlette died 13 January 1912, in Longview. His wife died one year later on 19 January 1913. Both are buried in Grace Hill Cemetery. They were the parents of thirteen children:

1. Judge Erskine Miller Bramlette was born 14 November 1875, Tupelo, Lee County, Mississippi, died 13 June 1942, Longview, and is buried Grace Hill Cemetery. He was an early schoolteacher in Longview, was made principal of the Longview schools at the age of 21, a lawyer, judge and oil operator. On 22 July 1903, he married Jessie Olivia Boring (1876–1933) in Longview. She was the daughter of Emma Reancy Brown and Joseph Boring, born 28 May 1904, Longview; died 17 June 1985, Longview, and is buried Grace Hill Cemetery. A life-long resident of Longview, he was widely known as a landscape architect and designed many gardens in town. He donated the land for Bramlette Elementary School, built the Bramlette building in downtown Longview and developed Huntington Park.

2. Clementine Miller Bramlette, was born 11 September 1878, Pontotoc, Mississippi, and died 26 November 1941. She married 18 September 1900, in Longview, James Felix Hamman of Fort Worth. They had two children, both of whom died young: James Newton Hamman and Annie Clementine Hamman – all buried Grace Hill Cemetery.

3. John Edwin Bramlette, born 13 March 1878, Pontotoc, Mississippi, died 22 June 1923, Longview, and is buried Grace Hill Cemetery. Married 3 February 1904, in Longview, Josephine Helen "Dot" Keener, daughter of George and Lucretia Keener of Longview. They were the parents of three children: Josephine M. Bramlette, Kathryne Clementine Bramlette and John Edwin Bramlette, Jr.

4. Jesse Morgan Bramlette, born 11 September 1881, Pontotoc, Mississippi, died 25 May 1936. Married Hazel Branthoffer (1881–1979) of Greenville, Texas. Both buried Grace Hill Cemetery. No children.

5. Lawrence Miller Bramlette, born 11 February 1881, Pontotoc, Mississippi, died 22 January 1931, Longview, and is buried Grace hill Cemetery. Married 3 February 1904, to Dana Bass (1882–1974), daughter of Wyatt Roland and Marina (Howard) Bass of Longview. There were the parents of four children: Dana Bass Bramlette (1905–1998) who married Dr. Frank V. Mondrik (1907–1994), physician in Longview; Lawrence Miller Bramlette (1909–1916); Pauline Feagle Bramlette (1916–) who married Conan Westmoreland Cantwell (1907–1977) a Dallas attorney; and Jack Howard Bramlette (1920–1974) who married Joan Docherty.

6. Thomas Leander Bramlette, born 23 January 1883, Pontotoc, Mississippi, died 3 August 1929, Longview. Married 19 July 1910, Longview, Ada Chaney (1882–1932), daughter

of R.R. and France Ellen (Johnson) Chaney of Longview. They had one child: Annie France Bramlette (1912–2001), who married Dr. Lerone Edgar Wardlaw (1908–1989), an optometrist in Carthage, Texas, for many years. All buried Grace Hill Cemetery.

7. Annie Hibernia Bramlette, born 22 January 1885, Pontotoc, Mississippi, died 24 August 1959, Fayetteville, Arkansas, and buried beside her husband in Veteran's Cemetery, Fayetteville. Married 19 February 1908, in Longview, Chalmer Kirk McClelland (1877–1956), son of Robert Clement and Grace (Young) McClelland. They were the parents of five children: Ann McClelland (1908–2001); Chalmer Kirk McClelland, Jr. (1910–1992) who married Mary Josephine West; Clement Bramlette McClelland (1916–1989) who married Doris Alma Cook; James Edward McClelland (1919–2000) who married Maurice Ash; and Thomas Bramlette McClelland (1920–) who married Virginia Jane Cowan.

8. Floried Bramlette, born 19 July 1887 Pontotoc, Mississippi, died 14 November 1967, in Longview. Married 11 September 1906\7, in Longview, Dr. James Carlton Francis (1881–1957), son of John Woodson and Tennessee Virginia (Boyd) Francis of Cherokee County, Texas. Both are buried Memory Park Cemetery. Parents of three children: James Carlton "Bill" Francis, Jr., (1908–1990) who married Mrs. Edith Robinson Nevill (1921–1996); Dr. Thomas Bramlette Francis (1910–1998) who married Eugenia English Tunstall (1916–2000) of Crockett, Texas; and Floreid Francis (1916–1964) who married Henry Prather Burney, Jr. (1913–1970) of San Antonio.

9. William Howard Bramlette, born 18 April 1889, Pontotoc, Mississippi, died 9 March 1959, Jacksonville Cherokee County, Texas, and buried Resthaven Cemetery, Jacksonville. He married in Longview March 1920, Ione Perry Pegues (1891–1977), daughter of Emma Overton and Oliver Hazard Pegues, Jr., who was Longview's first postmaster. They were the parents of two children: Rev. William Howard Bramlette, Jr. (1923–); and Mary Ann Bramlette (1925–2001) who married William Lee Lasseter.

10. Paul Miller Bramlette, twin brother of Pauline Bramlette, was born 26 January 1891, Pontotoc, Mississippi, died 15 December 1967, in a Dallas hospital. He married 1 November 1912, in Longview, Claribel McCord (1891–1977), daughter of Judge Felix J. and Gabriella (Fuller) McCord, early residents of Longview. They had two children: Paula Bramlette, a life-long resident of Longview, born 16 August 1917, Longview, died 15 September 1992; and a child who died in infancy. All are buried Grace Hill Cemetery.

11. Pauline Bramlette, twin sister of Paul Bramlette, was born 26 January 1891, Pontotoc, Mississippi; died 16 July 1949, Longview and is buried in Grace hill Cemetery, Longview. She married 18 April 1912, in Longview, Balfour Feagle (1881–1934), son of W.M. and Alice (King) Feagle of Corsicana, Texas. He was a Longview optometrist and jeweler who owned Feagle Jewelry Store for many years. No children.

12. Nannie Mae Bramlette, 26 June 1892, Pontotoc, Mississippi, died 24 December 1979, in a Kilgore hospital and is buried in Memory Park Cemetery, Longview. She married 21 December 1915, in Longview, William Hughes Terrell (1878–1965), son of James Robert and Mary Penelope (Broyles) Terrell. Mr. Terrell was a pharmacist, who owned the Longview Drug Store for many years. After selling his store, he turned his hobby of picture framing into a business. They were the parents of two children: Jean Terrell (1918–) living Wilton, Connecticut, and William Robert "Billy Bob" Terrell (1929–1989), a Kilgore dentist for 42 years, who married Jane Fleetwood of Longview in 1945. Their children, Libby Terrell Laird and Bill Terrell live in Kilgore.

13. Frederick Leavenworth Bramlette, born 20 August 1895, Pontotoc, Mississippi, died 2 November 1950, San Antonio, Texas, and is buried Sunset Memorial Park, San Antonio. He married 28 November 1919, in Fort Worth, Texas, Grace A. Jones (1891–1973), the daughter of Dr. Jones of Pirtle, Texas. They had two children: Gloria Bramlette (1922–) who married Blair Plowman Labatt of San Antonio; Frederick E. Bramlette (1924–1976) who married Lida Lee Denney.

– Submitted by Floreid Francis Stevens (a great-granddaughter)

MONSIGNOR JOHN A. BRENNAN

Monsignor John A. Brennan was born in Waterford (home of the famous crystal), Ireland, one of eight children. His father, grandfather and great grandfather were named John, but this John decided not to continue the line, choosing instead the religious life of a priest. He arrived in the United States in September 1956, on the S.S. *Mauritania*. Monsignor was privileged to serve in Wichita Falls, Garland, Fort Worth and Dallas, Texas. In 1982, he was promoted from one of the largest parishes in the Diocese of Dallas and introduced to St. Mary's Catholic Church in Longview, where he spent twelve happy years as the first pastor. Blessed in associating with many Catholics and non-Catholics alike, he feels privileged to have served in the East Texas area. As he looks back now, perhaps those were the twelve happiest years of his life.

Presently, Monsignor Brennan has 36 years of perfect attendance in the Rotary Club. He feels energized by his fellow Rotarians in Longview, and wishes them and their families God's blessings.

One lasting mark Monsignor left on Longview would be Martha's Kitchen (a weekend soup kitchen). The Salvation Army served the poor, hungry and homeless from Monday to Friday, but they had no place to eat on Saturday and Sunday. Even though Monsignor had the largest parish in the Diocese of Tyler to run, a friend of his from Temple, Texas, encouraged him to establish Martha's Kitchen. And so it came to pass, thanks especially to the parishioners of St. Mary's. Many fine people from the community, both Catholic and Protestant, worked together to make it a tremendous success. The last two years that Monsignor was there, twenty thousand meals were served.

Msgr. John A. Brennan

His greatest achievement was introducing St. Mary's School to the computer age. Even though the cost was considerable, Monsignor felt it was necessary at that time. He is to be praised for his foresight.

After Longview, Monsignor spent nearly eight years as Chaplain at Mother Frances Hospital in Tyler, Texas. He ministered to the sick, approximately 97% non-Catholics, from 6 a.m. until after 5:30 p.m.

Monsignor feels that he was "promoted to Heaven" by being sent to St. Jude's Catholic Church (the patron saint of the hopeless) in Gun Barrel City, Texas. Their debt was approximately half a million dollars in the 65% Hispanic parish. The lowest weekend Mass attendance is 234 people.

Monsignor Brennan wishes all his friends and associates, whom he has met as he has traveled on his pilgrimage of faith, every happiness and success. "May God bless you all and may you all be in Heaven thirty minutes before the devil knows you're dead."

– Submitted by Msgr. John A. Brennan

LEO & SUSAN BRIAN

Leo Brian and Susan Cigainero Brian lived in the Spring Hill School district. They moved to Longview in 1970 from Tyler, Texas. Leo's parents were Leon Brian, Sr. and Eva Lorene Rathburn. He was born in 1934. Susan's parents were Albert Cigainero and Florine Whalen. She was born in 1936. Their children are Mark Wendell Brian and Karen Brian Edwards. Mark was born in 1956 and Karen in 1959.

Leo and Susan Brian

Leo was employed with Southwestern Bell Telephone Company. During his 34-year career, he held several positions. He was an Assistant and Scout Master in the Boy Scout program, member of Gregg County Genealogy Society and a volunteer for Meals on Wheels. Leo was a faithful member at Saint Andrew Presbyterian Church, serving as a session member and a volunteer for church projects.

Susan was employed at Saint Andrew Presbyterian Church and Tejas Girl Scout Council. She was a volunteer for Girl Scouts and Boy Scouts, Meals on Wheels, member of Gregg County Genealogy Society and a volunteer at the Longview Public Library. She was an active member at Saint Andrew Presbyterian Church, where the family held its membership.

After retirement Leo and Susan moved to Texarkana, Arkansas.

Mark is a Forestry Consultant, living in Nacogdoches, Texas. His wife is Mary Elizabeth Keese, born in Wharton County, Texas. They have two daughters, Judith Pauline (Mangrum) and Sarah Catherine, and a son, Matthew Elijah. Judith is married to Joel A. Mangrum and has a daughter, Jolie Ashling.

Karen is a Dental Assistant living in Texarkana, Arkansas. She married James A. Edwards. James was born in Indiana and is deceased.

– Submitted by Leo and Susan Brian

BLUFORD W. BROWN

Bluford Washington Brown, the son of Hitson Brown and Windford Ray, was born 31 January 1831, in Bibb County, Alabama. He was educated in Maplesville Academy. He married Nancy Caroline Cox on 8 November 1848. Nancy Cox was born 17 April 1832, in Bibb County, Alabama. When the Civil War began, Bluford Brown entered the Confederate Army as a first lieutenant of Company G, 44th Regiment, Alabama Infantry. He participated in numerous battles in Virginia. After the battle of Gettysburg, he was given leave to return home. While in Alabama, he was commissioned to raise a cavalry company, which was attached to the 8th Alabama Cavalry. After the war, upon returning home, Bluford Brown found that the Federal Army had looted his farm. Having lost everything, he managed to make a crop in 1865 and raise enough money to come to Texas in 1866. His parents and several siblings had moved to Upshur County in 1850 and settled northwest of Gladewater. Bluford Brown moved his family to the community of Summerfield. About 1885 he moved his family to Longview, where they lived on Whaley Street in what is now known as the Brown-Birdsong house. Bluford Brown served four terms in the Texas Legislature and was responsible for the creation of Gregg County. He was a delegate to the Democratic State Conventions of 1873, 1878 and 1880. Bluford W. Brown died 9 February 1897, and his wife, Nancy, died 7 January 1900. Both are buried in Greenwood Cemetery in Longview.

Bluford and Nancy Brown had eight children, Mary A., Martha, Emma Reancy, Oscar F., Isaiah Newton, Lula Frances, Walter Ney and Mittie Florence. Mary A. Brown married Thomas B. Stinchcomb and they had one son, Tad, who was a lawyer in Longview and married Mary Noel Mobberly. Martha Brown married W.G. Carroll. Emma R. Brown married Joseph W. Boring and had three surviving children, Jessie, Emory and Joseph. Jessie married Erskine Bramlette and Emory married Helen Joslin. Oscar Brown married Joanna R. Clark and had four children, Elmo, Fred, Ethel and Romaine. Isaiah Newton Brown married Iris Boyd and moved to Oklahoma. Lula Brown married Ed Crain, who had a drugstore in Longview. They had three surviving children, John Richard, Lillo and B.W., but John Richard died about the time he graduated from high school. Walter Brown moved to Houston and married Josie Rawls. Mittie Brown married Robert H. Bruce and had three children, May Dee, Carrie and Ingram.

ISAIAH BROWN

Isaiah Brown was born 5 October 1825, in Baltimore, Maryland, to Isaac Brown from New York, and Anna Westley (Wesley) from Baltimore. Isaac (1802-1896) and Anna (1802-1861) were married in 1825 in Baltimore. Isaac was a machinist and inventor of patented planing machines for the lumber business and trained Isaiah as a machinist, also.

Isaiah married Mary Ann Wilcox 2 July 1850, in Baltimore. She was born about 1835, to Peter Wilcox (1808-1861) and Julia Ann Ellender (1811-1887). Wilcox owned a prosperous butcher shop in the Baltimore Market Center. Julia Ann was born in Baltimore to Frederick Ellender (1778-1841) and Charity Grimes (1803-1861), who married 3 November 1803. He was a private in Captain Burke's Company, 6th Regiment, War of 1812, British Invasion of Maryland. Ellender's parents were German immigrants and industrious workers in building trades. Julia inherited nine brick houses from her parents.

Isaiah and Mary Ann's first child, Lewis Edwin Brown, was born 9 August 1851, Baltimore, and Anna was born in 1852, and named

Isaac Brown, c. 1883

after Isaiah's mother. Another daughter, Ida Cora, was born in 1862 in Illinois.

At the beginning of the Civil War, Isaiah and Mary Ann left Baltimore with the children. Isaiah joined the Confederate Artillery and served as a machinist in the Arsenal & Powder Mill at Pine Bluff, Little Rock, Arkansas, then on to Jackson, Mississippi, and then to Marshall, Harrison Counties, Texas, where he worked in the Powder Mill until the end of the war. A fourth child, Robert E. Lee, was born there in 1865. The family stayed in Harrison and Gregg County after the surrender and Isaiah bought property in Longview in 1875. He owned and operated a lumber mill in Hallsville. Not only a machinist, he was also a millwright and carpenter.

Anna Wesley Brown

Lewis Edwin married first to M. Methvin about 1877; she died before 1889. Lewis married second, 5 October 1890, Minnie "Margaret" Morris, born 12 September 1874, Mississippi. "Maggie," 23 years younger than Lewis, was the daughter of Daniel Boone Morris and Mary Emily (Mollie) Neighbors, who had removed from Alabama after the Civil War and bought a farm in Lansing Switch, Hallsville, Harrison County.

Anna married Frank DeLoy, a bookkeeper, in 1879. He died in 1885.

Ida Cora married James B. Davis, 7 February 1882. She married second to Louis W. Davis, 27 June 1889, Gregg County.

Mary Ann Wilcox Brown died about 1882.

Isaiah applied for a pension from the State of Texas for his service in the Confederate Artillery, citing "old age and chronic bronchitis" as his reason. He was 75 years old when the pension was granted: #7610, approved 20 September 1900. He stated that he had lived in Hallsville, Harrison County, since 1863, his occupation as machinist, and that he served in the Artillery Service under Col. Faulkner at Little Rock, Arkansas, was transferred to Mississippi under Col. Huger, and served throughout the war. He died the following year, 15 December 1901, at the residence of his son, Lewis Edwin Brown. He is buried at his old lumber mill.

– Submitted by Tamara Terry

JOHN GARLAND BROWN

Born in Albemarle County, Virginia, John Garland Brown and his wife Francine moved their family to Mississippi in 1840. Early in 1850 he visited his cousin Taylor Brown in Henderson and while there contracted to purchase an 1130-acre tract in northeast Rusk (later Gregg) County from Frost Thorne of Nacogdoches. This property was bordered on the south by where the East Texas Regional Airport is today and included what is now the town of Lakeport. Brown also owned 580 acres across the Sabine River.

After the Mississippi crops were gathered in 1850 in Browns moved their seven children and 15 Negroes to the farm near Cotton Plant which was where the junction of Texas highways 149 and 49 are today. The couple had two more children born in Texas.

Mr. Brown owned a gristmill on his farm. J.P. Waid, an engineer, built and operated the mil for a quarter-interest. There was no stream of water on the Brown farm large enough to furnish water power, but the mill was large enough to have a conveyor to carry the grain to an overhead supply bin. It had steam power furnished by a boiler obtained from Waid's brother, a riverboat captain. The mill ground both corn and wheat.

In 1861 John Garland Brown helped organize and train the first company of Confederate volunteers at Cotton Plant and was elected its first Captain. Too old at 51 to enter military service, he withdrew and his oldest son, John William Brown, was elected Captain and became a full Colonel by the war's end. The Sabine Grays mustered into Confederate service at Marshall on 7 October 1861, and became Company I, 7th Texas Infantry known as Gregg's 7th Texas Regiment.

In December 1862, John Garland Brown sold his farm to Joseph Cock, a former Mississippi neighbor who had fled to Texas to escape the Yankees. Brown bought Confederate bonds issued at Henderson with the proceeds from the sale.

In January 1863, the Brown family moved to the Becton Place at New Danville Located 7-1/2 miles to the west.

Francine died in September 1864. She had kept a diary that a descendant copied and bound in the late 20th century for distribution to family members. These diaries were in two volumes: one for the year 1861, and another for the period 1 January 1863, until her death in August 1864.

For the balance of the war Mr. Brown hauled salt from Steen's Saline, 14 miles north of Tyler to Harrison, Rusk and Upshur Counties, sometime returning to Tyler with loads of lumber. He kept two wagons hauling and furnished several Negroes working fulltime at the Saline.

When the war ended in 1865, the Negroes worked until the crops were gathered and were then set free. Brown was a 55-year-old widower with no land, no money, his bonds were worthless and he still had four children at home.

In December 1866, he married Mrs. Fannie Isabell Cock, the widowed daughter-in-law of Joseph Cock, who had two sons, aged 10 and 12, and 460 acres of land. She bore him three sons. They later purchased and moved to a 500-acre farm near what is now Longview and lived there until his death in 1891. He was buried beside Francine in Greenwood Cemetery in Longview. Fannie died in December 1908, and is buried at Grace Hill Cemetery in Longview.
– Submitted by Bev E. Brown (grandson)

L.E. BROWN & MARGARET MORRIS

Lewis Edwin Brown was born 9 August 1851, Baltimore, Maryland, to Isaiah Brown and Mary Ann Wilcox, who married December 1850. During the Civil War, the family left Baltimore, siding with the Confederacy, and arrived in Pine Bluff, Arkansas, by 1861, where Isaiah worked in the Arsenal. In December 1863, when Lewis Edwin was 12 years old, they came to Marshall where they lived in two rooms of the old male school house. Isaiah worked as a machinist in the Powder Mill at Marshall until the end of the war. He was also a millwright, carpenter and owned a sawmill in Hallsville, trades he passed on to his son, Lewis Edwin.

Lewis Edwin, called Ed, married first to M. Methvin, about 1877, in Harrison County. They had several children who all died young except for Frank Brown, who lived in Shreveport.

Ed married Minnie "Margaret" Morris, called Maggie, on 5 October 1890, in Hallsville; she was the daughter of Daniel Boone Morris, from Franklin County, Alabama, and "Mollie" Mary Emily Neighbors. Mollie was born in Benton County, Alabama, to Thomas Neighbors and Margaret Renfro, who removed to Tishomingo County, Tennessee, before 1860. Mollie was the third wife of D.B. Morris. Maggie was born 12 September 1874, in Mississippi, and soon after the Morris family bought a farm in Lansing Switch, Harrison County, Texas.

Margaret Morris, age 16.

Ed Brown, 23 years older than Maggie, was a man of small stature, only 5'2" tall. He had a saw mill and was an accomplished carpenter and cabinet maker. He built many houses in the Longview area, including the Finch House on Cotton Street. Ed lost an arm in a gin-mill

Maggie holding baby Peaches. (l.-r.) Standing: Henry Lewis, L.E. Brown and Annie. Front: William I. "Bill" and Donnie Leon.

accident, but claimed that he accomplished more with one arm than he ever did with two. He was affectionately called "One-Arm-Brown." He raised sheep for Maggie to use the wool for spinning and weaving cloth, and he did the same thing with cotton. They made mattresses out of the cotton and pillows out of down and feathers. Maggie had a spinning wheel and made all their clothes. Ed made all their shoes. He built the house they lived in at 1600 Timpson Street and all the furniture from exotic hardwoods. He raised pigeons and shipped them all over the country. They grew all of their own food. He invented what would be called a "deep freezer" to store their food in the basement. They created a "washerteria," a first in Longview, in their backyard building.

He and Maggie were Methodists until their daughter, Annie Lou Nelms, became converted to the Pentecostal religion. He donated the land and helped her build a church on 13th and Cotton Street, which he called Annie's Church.

L.E. Brown died 27 October 1935, in Longview at the age of 84. Margaret died 8 December 1950, in Longview. He and Maggie are both buried at the Gum Springs Cemetery.

Children of Lewis Edwin Brown and Margaret Morris Brown:

Annie Lou, born 19 August 1891, married William Mark Nelms;

Lewis Edwin, Jr., born 27 June 1895, married Lena Kennedy;

Donnie Leon, born 21 October 1897, married Sallie Turner;

William Isaiah, born 28 October 1899, married Elsie Hendricks;

Acme Elberta, born 2 December 1901, married Bernice Hemperly;

Tressie May, born 12 May 1904, died young;

Zellie Ineza, born 21 May 1905, died young;

Chester Adams, born 1 October 1909, married Eva Mae Akins; and

Paul Lee, born 7 September 1913, married Pearl Lee.
– Submitted by Hollis Xan Pugsley Carlson

L.E. BROWN: Memoirs

"I, L.E. Brown, came to Marshall, Texas, in Dec 1863 – Lived in 2 rooms in old Male College (now torn down).

My Father, Isaiah Brown, worked in the Powder Mill in the Machine Shop. After the Surrender, Captain Roberts and Major Alexander had all the powder gathered up and put in a Ravine and Blowed up to keep the children from getting hurt. This happened in 1865 about 2 weeks before the U.S. troops arrived in Marshall. About 1864, my Father arranged to get 3 barrels of flour and traded some to a lady for some home spun cloth to make us children some clothes.

The old Male School Bldg. stood about where the Marshall high school now stands. During this time it was not used as a school, but as a Reffige for people that came from other places.

There was no transportation. Only a small rail from Marshall to Caddo Lake where you could then get Steamboat transportation and travel by land was by Stage Coach. There were 3 Engines used on this small rail line from Marshall into Caddo Lake. The names of these Engines were Sam Houston, Ben Johnson, and Jay Bird. Engines were not numbered then as now. About 1865, these rails were taken up from Marshall to Caddo Lake and were then layed from Marshall to Shreveport, La. The town of Longview was layed off Dec 1870 and we moved to Longview in 1871. I have lived in Gregg and Harrison Co. since then. I have passed my 83rd Birthday."

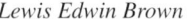

Lewis Edwin Brown

The School Experiences of L.E. Brown

"Just East of the Old Methodist Church on Shreveport road, I went to school to John Pierce. This was after the surrender. The boys favorite game then was "shinny." On one occasion I was stubborn & John Pierce, the teacher, made me stand up & that is one whipping I still remember. He whipped me across the shoulders & the stick stuck in my back.

There was no fire dept. in Marshall at this time – only Volunteer fireman. This was the only place I went to school while living in Marshall." (Written in 1934 at 1600 Timpson Street, Longview, Texas.)

MARY LOUISE BROWN

Mary Louise Delmas was born in El Paso, Texas, 29 July 1903. She was the second child and the first daughter of Adela J.E. Garcia and Emilio Charles Delmas. In baptism she received the name Catarina Amanda Luisa, being named for her paternal aunts. Although her birth certificate gives her name as Amanda Luisa, she was always known as Mary Louise.

One memory Mary Louise had was of the dedication of the first International Bridge joining El Paso and Juarez, Mexico, in November of

Mary Louise Brown

1909. Her father felt it important that she witness the historical event of the meeting of the presidents of the U.S., William Howard Taft, and Mexico, Porfirio Diaz, in the center of the bridge.

Mary Louise graduated from the 8th grade in Clifton, Arizona, and from Main Avenue High School (now Fox Tech) in San Antonio, Texas. She graduated from Physicians and Surgeons Hospital School of Nursing (later Baptist Memorial Hospital) in San Antonio.

When her mother passed away in 1923, Mary Louise's father passed the responsibility of raising her younger brother and sisters to her. The two older ones lived in a small apartment while Mary Louise remained in nursing school. The younger two spent some time in an orphanage and then lived with a family until Mary Louise completed her training.

Her life was one of long service in the medical field. Mary Louise worked for two doctors in San Antonio, a general practitioner and a pediatrician. In addition, she did private duty nursing in both San Antonio and Beaumont, Texas. Also in San Antonio, she was head of the Blood Bank at Baptist Memorial Hospital. Mary Louise was also trained as a clinical laboratory technician; in addition, she held membership in the Texas Society of X-Ray Technicians.

A patient by the name of Wilton Elmo Brown (q.v.) was hospitalized at P&S Hospital in 1923.

There he met young nurse Mary Louise Delmas, who was assigned to his care. So began the courtship of 'Boots,' as he was known, and Mary Louise; they were married 22 November 1926, in San Antonio.

Two daughters were born to this couple. Ellen Marie was born and died in San Antonio 16 November 1928. Exactly thirteen years later, Suzy (q.v.) made her worldly entrance in Beaumont.

Boots was diagnosed with myelogenous leukemia in 1942; he died 24 April 1943, in San Antonio where he was interred in Mission Burial Park South. His medical bills for a three-month hospital stay were so monumental that it took Mary Louise ten years to pay them off – but the deed was accomplished.

Mary Louise was a woman of many talents. She made beautiful, award-winning ceramics; she liked to sew, smock, knit, crochet, embroider and to read.

In 1979, Mary Louise moved to Longview to be near family. Then she began her final career, that of a babysitter. She passed to her eternal reward on 9 March 1993, a little over two years after entering a nursing home. Burial was beside her husband on 19 March 1993.

– Submitted by Amy Angel (granddaughter)

W.E. BROWN

Wilton Elmo Brown was born in Hillsboro, Texas, 27 October 1902, to James Isaac Brown and Docia Jane Hill. Somewhere along the line he acquired the nickname of 'Boots,' perhaps because he preferred wearing boots, rather than shoes. His family lived in Hillsboro, Smithville and New Braunfels, Texas, as well as Henrietta, Oklahoma.

To satisfy his parents, Boots attended Cumberland University in Lebanon, Tennessee. Although he received a Bachelor of Laws degree in 1923, he never actually practiced law. However, he did work for other lawyers, preparing briefs, etc.

After graduation, Boots was near San Antonio, Texas, when he was shot in the abdomen by a hitchhiker. This resulted in his hospitalization at Physicians and Surgeons Hospital, where he met his future wife. Boots carried the bullet and a piece of his undershirt internally for the rest of his life; this rendered him 'uninsurable' as well as unfit for military duty.

"Once there was a lovely lady" with younger siblings to raise. "Then there was this fellow" with no objection to taking on the task. So Boots and Mary Louise Delmas (q.v.) were married 22 November 1926, in San Antonio.

There were two daughters born to the Browns. Ellen Marie, born 16 November 1928, in San Antonio, died the same day; interment was in San Jose Burial Park in San Antonio. Suzy (q.v.) was born thirteen years later in Beaumont, Texas. The Browns were living in Houston, Texas, at the time, but returned to San Antonio early the next year.

After they were married, Boots began experiencing severe back pain. Exploratory surgery produced from his lower back area a 'sac' of hair, bones, teeth, etc., indicating that he was meant to be a twin; the other twin failed to develop.

Once when Boots ran a red light he was pulled over by a policeman. The officer remarked, "What's the matter with you, are you color-blind?"

W.E. Brown

Boots laughed and replied honestly, "Yes." Since he could not trust his own perception of color, he had to have help in choosing what to wear each day, and also when selecting gifts of clothing for his family. His most distinguishing feature was extremely long eyelashes that had to be trimmed so as not to scrape against his glasses.

During the oil boom days Boots worked in the Kilgore area. How nice it would be to have the details of that adventure!

While he was teaching diesel mechanics at Lackland Air Force Base in San Antonio, Boots was diagnosed with myelogenous leukemia. He died 24 April 1943, in San Antonio after a three-month hospital stay. In the city he was interred on the 26th in Mission Burial Park South.

Boots always looked for the good in everyone. He would give someone the shirt, or coat, off his back, and literally did so. Even if he had no idea where his own next meal was going to come from, he would give away his last nickel to help another person in need. What a grand legacy to leave his descendants!

– Submitted by Alan Burt (grandson)

LAWRENCE & GENEVIEVE BRYANT

Lawrence Derrill Bryant, Sr. was born 9 August 1931, to Carl and Julia Bryant at Kelsey community, six miles west of Gilmer, in Upshur County, Texas. He was baptized into The Church of Christ of Latter Day Saints on 12 May 1940. He grew up on his family's farm and attended Kelsey and Gilmer schools. He graduated from Gilmer High School in May 1949.

Lawrence joined the Navy in June 1949, and received his basic training in San Diego, California. He then attended Electricians School and was assigned to the USS Warrick AKA89 at the Supply Center in Oakland, California. While he was serving on the Warrick, the ship participated in the A-bomb test at Eniwetok. After the Korean War started, he spent the rest of his service time on the Warrick as the ship ferried supplies to Japan, Korea, Formosa, and Okinawa. The Warrick took part in the Inchon invasion during the early days of the Korean War.

In January 1953, he was discharged from the Navy and returned to Gilmer. He worked for a few months at Letourneau, Inc. steel mill in

Lawrence and Genevieve Bryant family, 1979.

Longview before taking a job as an electrician at Lone Star Steel Co. (LSS) in October 1953. On 14 February 1957, Lawrence married Genevieve Green, who had three daughters, Ann, Nan and Mary Williamson, from a previous marriage; Lawrence later adopted them. Lawrence and Genevieve had five more children: Beverly, Barbara, Julie, Kimberly and Lawrence Jr.

Lawrence moved to Longview in 1958, after a Wild Cat Strike at LSS caused him to lose his job. He worked for Coca Cola Co. in Longview as a vending machine serviceman until an arbitrator ruled he should not have been terminated from LSS. He was reinstated in his job with back pay.

Lawrence and Genevieve bought their first home at 1600 Sandlin in 1961. Lawrence continued to work at LSS until 1968. He then took a job with Continental Can Co., who made cans for Schlitz until 1974. When Schlitz started can production in 1974, he joined them. The company later became Stroh Container and, later still, American National Can Co. In May 1976, the family bought another home at 2501 Balsam in Longview.

In addition to raising eight children, Lawrence spent his spare time for many years raising a large garden at his father's farm in Kelsey. He retired from the can company in February 1995, at the age of 63. After retirement, Lawrence and Genevieve served as Ordinance workers in the Dallas Temple of The Church of Jesus Christ of Latter Day Saints. They served in that capacity for 5-1/2 years until he had to give it up because of bad knees. He had both knees replaced in 2000.

As of 2 October 2003, the couple still lives at 2501 Balsam in Longview. All of Lawrence and Genevieve Bryant's children are married; and they have 26 grandchildren and 15 great grandchildren.

– Submitted by Lawrence Bryant

BURKE

The Burke family move to Gregg County all began when Wendy J. Burke, MD came here in January 1988, from Memphis, Tennessee, to set up a practice in psychiatry. She and her son Julian Patrick Douthitt became quickly involved with Trinity Episcopal School and the Trinity School of Texas where he was enrolled. When asked to join the opera board at the beginning formation of the now Opera Longview, Wendy did not know that she would not see any of the performances for the next five years because she was working behind the scenes as stage manager and as President of the Board. An avid patron of the arts, she has supported the symphony, the ballet and the Shakespeare festival.

But it has not been all play. With her partner Gail McBride she formed Burke and McBride Investment Company in 1999.

The Burkes: Happy and Blessed.

Their first project was to move the old Church of Christ Scientist building from downtown Longview to a site off of Gilmer Road, where they remodeled it for an office for the psychiatric practice and a health network that has included psychotherapists, massage practioners and A Natural Choice, the complimentary medicine company they started with Lugene Rogers. In case they were not busy enough, they also built a fourplex condominium on Leisure Lane in 2001 into which LoIda and William Burke, Wendy's parents, moved. It was a happy move for the family to be in an area with all its assets; although, occasionally the Burkes have longed for the beaches of Florida, where they had been living.

Wendy's son and the Burkes' grandson, Julian, has grown into a man here in Longview and has now started his own business, Rafter J, which is an all around farm and ranch company building fences and hauling livestock around the area and across the country. The Burkes were also pleased about being in Gregg County because this is where their daughter, Wendy, met and married, on 1 November 2002, Keith Stack who has owned a construction company here for fifteen years.

Living in Longview has allowed the Burkes to enjoy close family ties, actively participating in the daily lives of their family, rich cultural experiences that are surprising for a town this size, and even rural life at the farm north of Longview with its cows, dogs, cats, horses and wonderful wildlife. They have started to volunteer at the Longview Museum of Fine Arts and, of course, are regular patrons of the library where they are trying to read at least all the mysteries.

– Submitted by Wendy J. Burke

RICHARD WESLEY BURNETT

Richard Wesley Burnett was born on 13 January 1898, in McLennan County, Texas. His family moved to Gladewater when he was two years old. Burnett joined the United States Navy and served during World War I. Afterward, he returned to Gladewater. He married Dale Jeter on 6 January 1924. With the East Texas oil boom, Burnett found his place in the business world. He began buying and trading oil leases as well as drilling for oil.

Burnett was an avid baseball fan. In 1935, shortly after his first success in the East Texas oilfield, he bought the Shreveport, Louisiana, franchise in the Class C East Texas League and moved it to Gladewater. The Gladewater Bears won the 1936 Texas League pennant; they won the league the next year. He had hoped to attract a major league franchise to Dallas. In 1948, he purchased the Texas Rebels of the AA Texas League for $550,000. A few weeks later, Burnett also purchased the Oakcliff ballpark for the Rebels' home park. He promptly renamed the Rebels the Eagles and the park Burnett Field. Burnett wanted to make the Eagles a pennant contender in the Texas League. In 1952, the Eagles won the league.

As a result of his successes as owner of the Eagles and his efforts to improve the conditions of minor league baseball, the *Sporting News* declared him the Minor League Executive of the Year in 1954. On 1 June 1955, Burnett, who was in Shreveport, Louisiana, to see his Eagles play a weekend series against Shreveport, suffered a heart attack and died. He was buried in Hillcrest Cemetery, Dallas.

AMY, TAMMY & ALAN BURT

Amy, Tammy and Alan, children of (q.v.) Sam and Suzy Burt, were born in Longview. They attended St. Mary's and Pine Tree schools. All were active in church, school and community activities. They are members of Texas First Families.

Amy was a Rotary Club exchange student to Austria in the summer of 1983. She graduated in 1984 from Pine Tree High where she was valedictorian, co-captain of the basketball team and active in debate and theater.

The recipient of a National Merit and other scholarships, Amy graduated from Texas A&M University in College Station with a B.S. in Agricultural Economics in 1988. While there, she was a member of Women's Chorus and also of their Octet. Amy pursued her doctorate in Ag Eco at A&M.

Amy and her husband, Fernando Angel, have three sons: Nando, Sam and Ben. In 1993 Amy and Fernando relocated to San Salvador, El Salvador. There she has been employed as a consultant for the U.S. Agency for International Development, as the agricultural sector specialist for FUSADES (the Salvadoran Economic and Social Development Foundation), and is now a consultant and policy advisor to the El Salvadoran Minister of Agriculture.

Alan, Tammy and Amy Burt

Tammy served as co-captain of Pine Tree High's Flag Corps. Active in numerous organizations, she held office in most. An award-winning UIL competitor and scholarship winner, Tammy graduated in the top-ten of her 1988 class.

In 1992 Tammy graduated Magna Cum Laud and with honors from TAMU with a B.B.A. in Accounting. That year she was one of 60 TAMU students selected to Who's Who Among American College Students. She was in the College of Business Administration Honors Program, the CBA Honors Association, Accounting Society, on the Honors Student Council, a member of Beta Alpha Psi National Accounting Honor Society and vice-president of the Business Student Council.

In 1991 Tammy was a summer intern with Marathon Oil Company in Lafayette, Louisiana. Since graduation, she has worked in California as a Certified Public Accountant for Ernst and Young as well as Ahem-Adcock-Devlin, and for San Bernardino Community Hospital-St. Bernardine Medical Center as Decision Support Coordinator. Presently she is the Chief Financial Officer of Hospice of the Valleys. Tammy and her husband, Bronco Ormuz, have a son, Brandon.

Alan, honor student, was active in city-league, church-league and school sports. He held membership and office in various school as well as church organizations. A 1989 Pine Tree High graduate, Alan earned a degree in mechanical engineering from Lamar University in Beaumont, Texas, where he pursued his Master's degree. Previously employed as Technical Support Analyst with Lamar University Media Services, he is currently Network Manager-System Administrator-Head of Desktop Support with Beaumont's Spindletop Mental Health Mental Retardation Services.

Early in 1990, while a student at Kilgore College, Alan was inducted into Phi Theta Kappa, the National Honor Fraternity for junior colleges. At Lamar he was a member of Chi Rho, the service fraternity of which his dad was a founding father at Texas Tech (the only two chapters are at Tech and Lamar).

– Submitted by Suzy & Sam Burt (parents)

SAM & SUZY BURT

That was a good year – 1941 – for that is when native Texans Sam Burt and Suzy Brown were born, he in Canyon and she in Beaumont. Son of Helen and Carl Burt, Sam was raised in Nazareth, while Suzy, daughter of Mary Louise (q.v.) and Wilton Brown (q.v.), grew up in San Antonio. Sam, a second-generation Texan, and Suzy, a third-generation Texan, are graduates of Texas Tech College (now University) in Lubbock. He is a chemical engineer, while she is a speech and hearing therapist.

That was another good year – 1965 – for that is when Sam and his bride Suzy became residents of Longview. Sam began working for Texas Eastman Company (now Eastman Chemical Company). During his 34-year career there, Sam held numerous responsibilities in various departments. Suzy was employed by the

Suzy and Sam Burt

Longview Independent School District. Prior to school integration, in 1966 she was one of five white speech therapists assigned to the then black schools.

Three children blessed the union of Sam and Suzy. They are (q.v.) Amy, Tammy and Alan.

Sam has been a faithful member of the Knights of Columbus, and also of Rotary International. Over the years, he has volunteered his time with coaching both basketball and baseball teams, assisting with Cub Scouts and also working with PTAs and Booster Clubs. In addition, he has been a member of several boards concerned with the good of the community (Capital Improvements Planning Board, Library Board). At present he is volunteer coordinator for Martha's Kitchen, a weekend soup kitchen sponsored by St. Mary's Church. He continues to serve his church in many other ways.

Suzy is an active member of Gregg County Genealogy Society. She is a charter member and treasurer of Catholic Daughters of the Americas Court St. Bridget. Organizations actively served in the past are Gregg County Children's Association, Deep East Texas A&M Mothers' Club and the Knights of Columbus Ladies Auxiliary. Suzy has worked with Girl Scouts, PTAs and various Booster Clubs as well. Chaperoning school and also church groups was a frequent activity. She currently serves the community by volunteering at Longview Public Library.

Suzy is a member of the R.B. Levy Chapter of the United Daughters of the Confederacy, based on the service of her paternal great-great grandfather, James Alexander 'Jimmy Cane' Hill (Florida). In addition, she is a member and the registrar of the John Tilley Edwards Chapter of the Daughters of the Republic of Texas, based on the service of her maternal great grandfather, Charles Francis Delmas. Charles also qualified Suzy for membership in Texas First Families.

Sam and Suzy are grateful to their respective revolutionary ancestors who assisted in establishing American Independence. Sam's are James A. Blackburn and Philip Fry (Virginia), Joseph Burt (North Carolina), plus Christopher Strait and Samuel Wherry (South Carolina). Suzy's are Abraham Anderson and Joshua Fowler (South Carolina), John Cantrell (North Carolina) and Nathan Horner (Maryland). The Burts feel privileged to be citizens of this great country founded on Christian principles. In God we trust!

– Submitted by Tammy Ormuz (daughter)

HARVEY J. BUTTS

Washington Lafayette Butts (1833-1870) came to Texas from Georgia in the 1850s. He married Mary Helen Angell (1843-1914) in 1861. They settled and farmed in south Gregg County (Rusk County at that time) near the present Ned Williams Road. Washington and Mary had four children: Harvey J. Butts was born in 1862, Sallie M. in 1864, Jesse J. in 1866, and Carrie M. in 1868.

Washington L. Butts and his wife, Mary, are believed to be buried in the Danville Cemetery.

Mary Angell Butts acquired a farm in the Elderville community near the Rusk-Gregg County line and she and her four children moved there in 1876.

Sallie M. Butts married Eugene Scott and lived in Longview. Jesse J. Butts never married and lived in Longview. Carrie M. Butts became Mrs. Massey and lived in Longview.

Harvey J. Butts (1862-1947) attended school at Peatown and acquired the family farm from his mother. The farm is still in the family and two of the great grandsons and their wives live on this acreage.

Harvey married Ethel Fambrough (1873-1911) in 1890. They had six children. Annie Helen Butts (1892-1966) married Jerry Joseph Lucy (1870-1932) in 1922. They lived with her father on the family farm in Elderville. They had four children: Ethel, born in 1933, lives in San Augustine.

Jesse Lafayette Butts (1899-1978) married Mary Catherine Price from Center in 1927; they lived in Longview and had no children.

Nellie Milam Butts (1903-1957) married Franklin McClure Reese in 1925; they lived in Longview and had no children.

Mary Ethel Butts (1906-1971) did not marry. She taught school in Longview and lived with her father and the Lucy family on the family farm.

Harvey J. Butts farmed until 1906, when he became a rural mail carrier out of the Elderville Post Office. His route included the Post Oak, Easton and Chalk Hill communities as well as Elderville. This was mostly horse and buggy work, but he did get to visit with a lot of people and get to know their problems and concerns. He retired from the Post Office in 1932 and went to work for Gregg County as a Right-of-Way Agent. This was during the oil boom and the county had started a major construction program to meet the needs of the new people and industries that came to the area.

For many years, Harvey served on the Elderville School Board and as Justice of the Peace. He was a member of the Peatown Christian Church and was an active Mason. He enjoyed the outdoors, particularly fox hunting. Harvey was an avid reader and loved to discuss politics. He was active in the leadership of the Elderville community.

Harvey J. Butts and his wife Ethel are buried in the Peatown Cemetery.

– Submitted by Ann Lucy

BYERS–CHANLER

Lillie Beatrice Byers was born in Aldon Bridge, Louisiana, 27 January 1914, to Homer and Margaret Alice Dunn Byers. She married Arthur Leroy Chanler, Sr. in a double ceremony in the pastor's home. Joining the Chanlers in the ceremony on 23 December 1930, were Claudine Delaney and Milton Frazier.

Beatrice Chanler

Leroy was born 13 August 1910. He was the son of Emma Caroline Chandler and Henry David Chanler. He was the tenth of ten children. His brother Dennis and wife Myrtis Chanler were the first of the Chanler family to move to East Texas. Leroy moved to Kilgore during the Oil Boom in 1932. He had worked in Greenwood hauling pulp wood and his next job was for his father-in-law, Homer Byers, who was an independent oil well driller and owned pulp wood trucks. He worked in Kilgore at the refinery, drilling rigs and then for Magnolia Oil Co. Beatrice came in July 1933, after caring for her brothers and sisters. They lived with Dennis and Myrtis on old Stone Road. This is where Marita Ann, their first child, was born on 16 August 1933. Their first apartment was with Mr. and Mrs. Redford, the police chief, by old City Hall in a large house made into apartments. The second apartment was on South Martin. Their third house was 600 block of Knowles where Marcia Janean was born on Christmas Eve of 1936. Some of their close friends were the Choice family, who were their neighbors. An unusual thing for the time was no running water. Outside well owners sold water at 35 cents a barrel to the citizens of Kilgore. Leroy went to work for J.J. Jenkins and lived in his rent house by the football stadium. Leroy was hurt there when the tongs came loose while he was on the derrick and knocked him into the machinery. Then the Chanlers bought a house and land off of Old Longview Highway. The large five-room house on the property had an efficiency apartment added to the house by Mr. Hankins for Leroy's family to live in.

They then bought a large, three-room shot-gun house and moved it to the adjoining property. Beatrice began working at G.F. Wackers, a nickel and dime store, in 1935. It was managed by Ray Duncan. The little Wackers was used for training. It was during this time that Leroy decided to go back to school and attended

KC and studied drafting and engineering. World War II intensified and the family moved to Beaumont where Leroy worked in the shipyard as an instrument pipe fitter with government clearance to work on sensitive materials. The family then moved to Orange in the Multi Max Village (government housing) on 309 Young Street. In 1946, the family returned to Kilgore. With the money that Leroy saved, he was able to buy the Sinclair/Goodrich Tire Service Station. The actual building was owned by Mayor Roy H. Laird. The address was 400 E. North Street. Leroy paid 2 cents for each gallon of gas sold as rent to Mr. Laird (gasoline sold between 25 and 35 cents a gallon). Beatrice worked at Beall's Brother and kept the books at the service station. Leroy went to work in Augusta, Georgia, on an atomic project on the Swanee River project. Marita ran the station and Kilgore College students worked with her while Leroy was away. Next he worked in Ohio for the Industrial Ohio River Atomic project. Arthur Leroy Chanler, Jr. (Dooger) was born after the war on 24 August 1949. Later that year, Leroy hurt his back again. At this time, Beatrice and Leroy were now living in a house bought from the Adamson family, a dear family friend. The Adamsons owned Sabine Machine and Supply. The six-room home was moved in and remodeled. Beatrice continued to work for J.C. Penney in the ladies ready to wear until she retired. Leroy died in 1 December 1980. Beatrice continued to live in the house until it burned in 1997. She now lives in Arlington with her daughter Janean Aaron. Leroy and Beatrice's children are Marita Ann, Marcia Janean and Arthur Leroy Chanler, Jr. (Dooger). Marita Ann married Stanley Ater and their children are Jennifer Alisse Utzman, Kimberly Ann Ater and Stephanie Kelly Zimmerman; and grandchildren are Jessica-Alisse Ater Utzman, Zachry Ater Albertson Zimmerman and Zane Austin Ater Zimmerman. Janean's children are Kristen and Fran Aaron and her only grandchild is Shirah Aaron. Dooger's children are Christopher Bryce Chanler and Candace Brooke Chanler.

– Submitted by Marita Ater

CABBINESS: From Virginia and Alabama to Texas

JOSHUA C. CABBINESS (born 15 July 1818) of Virginia married **SARAH A.E. MINGS** (born 14 April 1821) of Alabama on 18 October 1842, in Macon County, Alabama. They came to Texas between 1844 and 1849. Joshua died 10 December 1896. Sarah was the daughter of Jesse Daniel Mings (1705-1881) and Sarah Ann Elizer Riles (1799-1866) of South Carolina. She died 22 July 1897, and she and Joshua are buried in The Old Bethleham Cemetery, Upshur County, Texas.

JOSHUA and **SARAH CABBINESS** first settled in Upshur County, Texas, near Mings Chapel community that is located north of Gladewater and south of Gilmer, Texas. From there the large family has scattered to Oklahoma, California, Colorado, Gregg County and many other parts of the country. They had six children:

Old Bethleham Cemetery, Upshur County, Texas. Betty Cabbiness at Gravesite of Joshua C. Cabbiness and his wife, Sarah A.E. Mings Cabbiness, in Old Bethleham Cemetery, Upshur County, Texas.

1. **Mary J.** was born in 1844 in Alabama.

2. **Sarah Caroline** "Callie" was born 7 September 1849, in Upshur County, Texas, married John F. Ford about 1869, died 9 November 1930, and is buried in Old Bethleham Cemetery, Upshur County.

3. **Elbert Monroe** was born 6 December 1850, in Texas, married Mary Palistine Phillips, died 10 August 1942, in Caddo County, Oklahoma, and is buried in Gracemont Cemetery, Gracemont, Oklahoma.

4. **James R.** was born in December 1854, in Texas and married Lula W. Marshall on 7 July 1880, in Longview, Gregg County, Texas.

5. **Henry Daniel**, was born in Texas 22 May 1858, and married Ella D. Dunbar in Gregg County, Texas.

6. **Leoni F.** was born January 1866, in Texas and married Bettie L. Witcher in about 1859.

James R. Cabbiness and **Lula W. Marshall** had 10 children:

1. **Joshua** (5 March 1885-4 October 1915) married Ida Bullard.

2. **Mattie Dee** (29 April 1889-23 July 1942) married Benjamin Smith.

3. **Maude F.** (17 July 1891-3 January 1974) married Cody B. Culpepper. She is buried in Grace Hill Cemetery, Longview, Texas.

4. **Walter Laurence** (15 November 1893-26 July 1926) married Bessie Sanford.

5. **William Jennings Bryan** (15 December 1896-20 June 1949) married first, Ida Mae Blalock and second, Allyne Adkins. He is buried in Grace Hill Cemetery, Longview.

6. **Orline Sayer** (9 August 1898-6 October 1962) married Jess Franklin Johnson and is buried in Grace Hill Cemetery.

7. **Ralph Herman** (19 December 1901-1948) married Josephine Melvina Blalock and is buried in Grace Hill Cemetery.

8. Unknown

9. **Hershell** was born in 1882 and is buried in Grace Hill Cemetery.

10. **Hayden** was born 18 September 1903, and is buried in Grace Hill Cemetery.

James R. Cabbiness went to Oklahoma during the 1900s to find work when times were hard in Longview. While he was there, he lived with his brother, Elliott Monroe. In about 1920, he developed pneumonia and died. He is buried in Gracemont Cemetery, Caddo County, Oklahoma near Anadarko. His wife, Lula W. Marshall, remarried after his death to Hiram H. Carter. She is buried in Grace Hill Cemetery, Longview, Texas.

For further information on the family, see "Cabbiness: East Texas" in this book.

– Submitted by Betty Cabbiness

CABBINESS: East Texas

RALPH HERMAN CABBINESS, 10 December 1901, d. 1948, married Josephine Melvina Blalock, 1925, born 29 October 1907, d. 13 September 1980. They had Ralph Herman, Jr., Billy Joe, Patsy Sue, Margie Ann, Gaynelle and Milton Wayne. They also raised Johnnie Mae, who was the daughter of Josephine's sister, Ida Mae Blalock and William Bryan Cabbiness.

Ralph Herman, Jr. lived three years.

Billy Joe, 5 February 1927, died 1 December 1981, married Betty Jane Smith, 1946, who was born 15 November 1928. They had Billy Ray, Brenda Jane, Bennie Ralph, Becky Jo and Bruce Wayne.

Patsy Sue, 16 March 1929, never married.

Margie Ann, 13 August 1931, d. 8 February 1991, buried Rosewood Cemetery, Gregg Co., married Gaylon Snider. They had Debbie, Pamela, Terri, Gaylynne and Jason.

Gaynelle, 31 January 1933, d. 4 June 1977, buried Grace Hill Cemetery, married Fred F. Fitzgerald and had Freddie Ray Fitzgerald.

Milton Wayne, 17 July 1936, married Bonnie Brittain, who had Milton, Jr. and Marla.

Johnnie Mae (adopted), 25 May 1925, married first, Franklin Martin, second, John William Sundby, Sr. They had John Jr., Steve and Bryan.

BILLY JOE CABBINESS and Betty Jane Smith had Billy Ray Cabbiness, 9 May 1947, married Janet Carol James. He served in the Navy during the Vietnam War aboard the USS *Enterprise*.

BRENDA JANE CABBINESS, 15 September 1948, married Ronald Lester McKinney, who had Kathryn May and Jeffery Kyle.

BENNIE RALPH CABBINESS, 29 October 1950, married first Carla Lloyd and had Jason Lloyd and Amanda. He married second Lynn Sunski Magee (mother of David, Catherine and Jennifer).

BECKY JO CABBINESS, born and died 29 October 1952.

BRUCE WAYNE CABBINESS, 9 October 1954, married first Mary Phillips Lawrence (mother of Pamela Renee' Lawrence); second Robin Laney Seidel (mother of Robert Joe and Thomas Joe). They had Briana Lynn Cabbiness.

Of the grandchildren, several are married: **KATHRYN MAY MCKINNEY** married first Bill LaGrange, second Ruben Garza, and third Patrick McCarron; **JASON LLOYD**

CABBINESS married Kristen Kuehl; **AMANDA DIANNE CABBINESS** married Joseph Herndon and had "Katie" and Olivia; **PAMELA RENEÉ LAWRENCE** married Preston Green and had Natalie and Taylor; **ROBERT JOE SEIDEL**, unmarried father of a son, Jeffery.

DEBBIE SNIDER married Ralph Horridge and had Brooks, who married Alison Leon, and Haley Snider; **PAMELA SNIDER** married Bob Meacham and had Jenny, who married Quenton Carr, and Andrea, who married Marcus Schultz; **TERRI SNIDER** married first Robert Powdrill and had Jeff, Brent and Hillary, second Dr. William Simpson; **JASON SNIDER** married Kelly Whitlock; **FREDDIE RAY FITZGERALD** married Pamela Barnett and had Freddie Wayne; **GAYLYNNE SNIDER** married Garry Thomas and had Jessica; **MILTON WAYNE CABBINESS, JR.** married Carol Cearley and had Milton III, and Sterling Price; **MARLA GAYLE CABBINESS** married Michael Lewis. She has one daughter, Staci Nicole Cabbiness.

Other grandchildren: David Magee married Kendall Avery and had Christopher and Caroline; Catherine Magee married Jeffery Glunt and had Ron, Hannah, Jacklynn and Katelynn; Jennifer Magee married Kenneth Fleitman and had McKenzie and Anne.

– Submitted by Milton Cabbiness

BOB, JOYCE, JANA & JESSICA CAHILL

Bob Cahill and Joyce (Retort) Cahill established a home in Longview, Texas, on 2 September 1978, along with their two daughters, Jana and Jessica. Bob and Joyce were originally from Struthers, Ohio, where they both grew up.

Bob was the middle child of John and Georgina (Manhollan) Cahill. John was born to parents Charles and Rose Cahill on 2 January 1918, in Crenshaw, Pennsylvania. John was a private in the Army Infantry during World War II. He was captured by Rommell's forces in Africa and was held as a Prisoner of War in Germany for 27 months. Georgina (Manhollan) was the daughter of Charles and Cora (Fry) Manhollan, born on 3 February 1927, in Youngstown, Ohio. After John and Georgina married on 22 December 1945, John worked in the Youngstown steel mills. As a child Bob grew up with two siblings, older brother Jack and younger sister Alice, in Struthers. After graduating from Struthers High in 1966, Bob enlisted in the military. He served with Delta Company 1/26th Marines as a combat corpsman in Vietnam during 1968-1969.

Joyce (Retort) was the oldest daughter of Louie and Mary Retort of Struthers, Ohio. Louie Retort and Mary (Mediate) were first generation Americans from Italy. Louie was the second youngest child of 15, born to Joseph and Julia Retort on 8 August 1924. At the age of 15, he enlisted in military with the Army Air Corp. Louie served in World War II as a gunner. Mary (Mediate) was born in Hillsville, Pennsylvania, on 2 September 1921, to parents Frank and

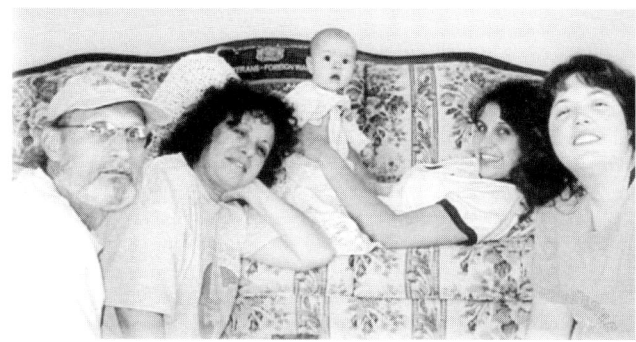

The Cahills: Bob, Joyce, Taylor, Jessica and Jana, September 2001.

Teresa Mediate. Mary worked as a beautician until marrying Louie on 6 September 1947. After marrying, Mary gave birth to three daughters, Joyce, Mary Lou and Roxanne. Joyce graduated from Struthers High in 1967 and worked as a billing secretary at Ohio Edison.

Bob and Joyce (Retort) were married on 12 April 1969, and celebrated the birth of their first daughter, Jana, on 16 December. Seven years later on 10 December 1976, Joyce gave birth to the couple's second daughter, Jessica. Two years later the couple made their move to their present home in Longview, Texas. In Texas, Bob graduated from Kilgore College Nursing School in 1986 and began a 14-year career as a Registered Nurse in the Gregg County area. Joyce worked for Wal-Mart in Longview as the invoice clerk for 19 years. Both of their daughters, Jana and Jessica, graduated from Pine Tree High School in Longview. In 2000, Bob, Joyce and Jana retired and currently live in Longview. Jessica works as a college speech instructor at area colleges and also resides in Longview with her husband Brandon Green and daughter Taylor.

CLAUDE PATRICK CALDWELL

Claude Patrick (Pat) Caldwell was born in Ireland 14 November 1899, in Abbeyleix, Queen's County. One of seven children, Pat was born Simon Claudius Caldwell to William Caldwell and Mary Anne Pinkerton. His wife Carmen Lorene Jenkins was born in Arkansas 10 March 1904, in Harrison, Boone County. She was the oldest of five children born to Oran Thomas Jenkins and Lora Ethel Jackson.

During World War I, from 1914 to 1918, Pat served in Britain's Royal Navy as a wireless operator on the Battleship *Barham* at the battle of Jutland May 31, 1916. At the end of the war, he was Honorably Discharged as a Telegrapher. He and his youngest sister Susan Frances Caldwell arrived in New York City in 1922 and shared an apartment with their older sister Catherine Mary Caldwell who came to New York City prior to World War I.

Pat attended Columbia University while in New York City. In 1925, he came to Dallas, Texas. Before coming to Dallas in the 1920s, Carmen attended grade and high school in Eureka Springs, Arkansas. She and Pat were married in Dallas 19 March 1928. Their twin daughters, Sharon and Shirley Caldwell, were born in San Antonio, Bexar County, Texas, 12 September 1930.

In the summer of 1941, the family moved from Dallas to Longview, Gregg County, Texas.

On 11 February 1943, at a term of the U.S. District Court of the Eastern District of Texas, Tyler, Texas, Claude Patrick Caldwell was admitted as a citizen of the United States of America (Certificate of Naturalization No. 54191873). "Name was changed from Simon Claudius Caldwell by decree of Court as a part of the naturalization 2/11/43."

During World War II, Pat served with the Texas State Guard. Claude Patrick Caldwell, T/5, Headquarters Detachment, 32nd Battalion, was Honorably Discharged from the Texas State Guard by reason of "civilian duties conflict" 5 December 1944, at Longview, Texas.

During World War II, Carmen belonged to the American Red Cross in Longview where she taught knitting. She also knitted mittens, scarves and socks for members of the military.

Pat, a Petroleum Engineer, was an employee of Magnolia Petroleum Company, a division of Socony Mobil Oil Company, Inc. He was superintendent of the East Texas lab during World War II. He retired from Socony Mobil Oil Company, Inc. in 1960 after 29 years of service. After retiring from Mobil, he worked for British American Oil Company in Marlow, Oklahoma, as superintendent of their gasoline plant.

Sharon and Shirley were graduated from Longview High School in 1947. In 1947, playing tennis for Longview High School, they reached the tennis doubles finals at the High School UIL State Meet held in Austin, Texas. In 1948, playing on a team composed of the top five Texas Junior Girls Singles Players, they won the Sears Cup in the United States Lawn Tennis Association Girls Intersectional Team Matches played on grass at the Philadelphia Cricket Club, St. Martins, PA. In the 1948 Texas Tennis Association's Ratings, they were ranked in Junior Tennis: No. 1 in Doubles, Sharon No. 3 in Singles, and Shirley No. 4 in Singles. In the 1948 American Tennis Association Ratings, they were ranked in Junior Tennis: No. 9 in Doubles, Sharon No. 15 in Singles, and Shirley No. 17 in Singles. In 1949, each was graduated from Kilgore Junior College, Kilgore, Texas, with a degree in Associate of Arts. In 1951, each was graduated from Stephen F. Austin State College, Nacogdoches, Texas, with a degree in Bachelor of Business Administration and each

received a Teachers Permanent Certificate (Permanent High School State Certificate) from the Texas Education Agency of the State of Texas.

Sharon married Wesley Lewis Whatley 24 November 1956, and they have always lived in Longview. They have one son, William Clayton (Clay) Whatley. Clay was graduated from Longview High School in 1979, and the University of Texas in Austin in 1983 with a degree in Chemical Engineering. Clay received a degree in Computer Science from the University of Texas at Tyler in 1987, and a Master of Software Engineering from Seattle University in 1992. He works for Boeing as a project manager and lives in Seattle, Washington. Sharon, a member of ACBL (American Contract Bridge League), is a Bronze Life Master. In 1992, after 25 years of service, Sharon retired from Texas Eastman as a Secretary in Public Relations.

Shirley worked for Smead & Harbour in Longview from 1952 to 1965. She moved to New Orleans the summer of 1965. In August of 1989, after 24 years of service, she retired from Amoco Production Company in New Orleans as a Lease Analyst, A&E-Land Data Department. In December 2003, she moved back to Longview.

Sharon and Shirley are members of the National Society Daughters of the American Revolution, Shirley belonging to the Louisiana Chapter, New Orleans, and Sharon belonging to the Aaron Burleson Chapter, Longview. They are also members of the Thomas Noble Chapter, National Society Daughters of the Ameri-

Carmen Lorene Jenkins, c. 1923

Claude Patrick Caldwell, c. 1943

Sharon Caldwell, c. 1948

Shirley Caldwell, c. 1948

can Colonists, New Orleans; the Robert Ruffin Chapter, National Society Colonial Dames XVII Century, New Orleans; and the Chalmette Chapter, U.S. Daughters of 1812, New Orleans.

Pat was an avid reader. At the time of his death 25 November 1970, he had been a resident of Longview 29 years. He was a member of Masonic Lodge No. 1182, Dallas, Texas; a member of Texas Petroleum Engineers; and a member of Trinity Episcopal Church. Survivors included his wife, Carmen Lorene Caldwell, Longview; two daughters, Sharon Caldwell Whatley and her husband, Wesley Lewis Whatley, Longview, and Shirley Caldwell, New Orleans; one grandson, William Clayton (Clay) Whatley, Longview; four sisters, Katherine Mary Caldwell, New York City; Susan Francis Caldwell Wood (Mrs. Arthur George), Dublin, Ireland; Margaret "Madge" Caldwell, Bray, Ireland; and Jennie Caldwell Jackson (Mrs. William), Longford, Ireland; and three nieces, Gwendolyn Wood Cookman, Ireland; Genevieve Wood Doherty, England; and Mary Wood Paterson, New Zealand. He was preceded in death by his parents and two brothers, Robert John and William George.

Carmen loved to sing and dance, play bridge and knit. At the time of her death 14 March 1993, she had been a resident of Longview 52 years. She was a member of Longview Chapter No. 610, Order of the Eastern Star, Longview, and the Louisiana Chapter, National Society Daughters of the American Revolution, New Orleans. She was a homemaker and a member of Trinity Episcopal Church. Survivors included two daughters, Sharon Caldwell Whatley and her husband, Wesley Lewis Whatley, Longview, and Shirley Caldwell, New Orleans; one grandson, William Clayton (Clay) Whatley, Seattle, Washington; and one sister, Elva Laura Jenkins, Little Rock, Arkansas. She was preceded in death by her parents and three sisters, Ethel Jenkins and infant twin sisters.

– Submitted by Shirley Caldwell

ROBERT ELISHA CALLAWAY

Robert Elisha Callaway came to Texas in 1849. The dates of the family births and deaths came from the family Bible. Robert Elisha Callaway was born in Baldwin County, Georgia, on 20 December 1820. His wife was Sarah Ann Elizabeth Walker, born on 29 October 1830, in Baldwin County, Georgia. They were married on 14 January 1846, in Georgia. Shortly after their marriage they started their journey to Texas. Their first child, Robert Merrell Callaway, was born in Alabama 9 March 1847. The next child was John Abington Callaway, born 9 July 1848, in Alabama. The first child of Robert Elisha and Sarah Ann Elizabeth Walker Callaway that was born in Texas was Margaret Ann Callaway, 25 May 1851. Next was Sarah Wicker Callaway, born 27 January 1853, then George Newton Callaway, born 17 October 1855; he died in 1858. Charles Ashley Callaway was born 27 August 1857, Mary Jane Callaway 4 July 1859, Sanders Eugene Callaway 21 May 1861,

Sallie Eliza Callaway 10 May 1863, and George Newton 8 February 1867. The Callaway family is in the 1850 census of Upshur County, Texas. Also in the 1860 and 1870 census, they were in Upshur County in the Spring Hill/Pine Tree District. There was a Callaway community in the area that may have been named after these Callaways since Robert Elisha Callaway was the first Callaway in the area per the 1850 census.

The community was located on Callaway Hill, near Farm Road 49, which was a way station on the road from Jefferson, Texas. The ferry, used for crossing the river, was a means of transportation and a trading center for the farmers. By 1855, there was a post office in the Callaway community. This area was also the voting district. There were several churches, a gin mill and a general store. The population had grown to about 265 people when the railroad decided to put the railroad tracks through Longview and, like a lot of small communities, the Callaway community started dying out.

Robert Elisha Callaway's family came to America from England during the civil war going on in England. He was a master mason in the Tuscumlum Lodge #86. He was a member of the Cumberland Presbyterian Church at Pine Tree. He served as session clerk from 1869 until his death in 1873. His son, John A. Callaway, also attended the church where he served as elder. Elmira Presbyterian was sponsored by the church at Pine Tree. John A. Callaway's son, Ollie, served as session clerk and was a deacon and an elder 1896-1906. He also served as superintendent of Sunday School. The son of Robert, John A., and his son, Ollie, were charter members of Elmira. Robert E. Callaway's son, Sanders Eugene, and his wife, Carrie Fisher Callaway, whose father, Jacob, was second postmaster at Pine Tree, had four children, one of which was R.E. Callaway. As time went by, most moved closer to Longview and joined First Christian Church. In 1955, R.E., Vera, his wife, and Elizabeth Ann went with a group from First Christian to form Woodland Christian. R.E. died in 1987, and his wife, Vera, and daughter, Elizabeth Ann Callaway McBroom, still live in the local area. There are many other relatives of these Callaway families still living in Longview.

– Submitted by C.J. McBroom, Jr. and his wife, Elizabeth Ann Callaway McBroom

LUTHER GRANVILLE CALVIN
(November 17, 1853–February 12, 1923)

Luther Granville Calvin was born 17 November 1853, in Ironton, Ohio, which is the county seat of Lawrence County. This area is on the banks of the Ohio River in Southern Ohio directly across the river from Huntington, West Virginia.

L.G.'s parents were Stephen Parker Calvin and Charlotte Jane Pollock Calvin. They had several sons. During the Civil War, L.G.'s father was a Lieutenant Colonel in the Union Army (5th Virginia Volunteer Infantry).

Ironton was predominately a German settlement and L.G. spoke fluent German. L.G.'s parents noticed his musical ability and had him

Luther Granville Calvin

formally taught classical music on piano, organ, and violin. His teachers in Ironton had previously learned their expertise from the best musicians in Cincinnati where a Musical Conservatory is located.

Verbal family history relates that L.G. Calvin and a cousin decided to take a trip to St. Louis, and while there determined to go to Texas by way of a river steamer. After debarkation at the port of New Orleans, they traveled by way of the Red River to Shreveport and through Big Cypress Waterway to Jefferson, Texas. They came overland to the settlement now known as Longview.

In Longview on 3 November 1880, L.G., a Presbyterian, married Lavonia "Vonie" Frances Tankersley, daughter of Absalom Tankersley and Elizabeth Sparkman Tankersley, who were charter members of the First Baptist Church in Longview. The bride's history was that when she was eight years old she migrated with her parents to Texas in a covered wagon from Jonesboro, Georgia, [Jonesboro was a focal point in the famous civil war novel, *Gone with the Wind*] with $800 in gold hidden in the tongue of the wagon, and camped at Longview's old Pine Tree Community site. An ongoing family tale is that Lavonia had vivid recollections of General Sherman's march through her home town of Jonesboro on his way to the sea. She related that the Yankee soldiers fed the citizens to keep them from starving.

For twenty-seven years, L.G. was manager of the grocery department of Womack & Perry Store, which also sold general merchandise such as hardware, nails, furniture, caskets, harnesses, plows and other provisions. Womack & Perry was located at the former site (1984) of the Hoffbrau restaurant on West Tyler Street.

L.G. and Lavonia had two sons who died in infancy (Granville Perry and Absalom). Their two daughters were Charlotte Elizabeth "Betty" Calvin and Vere Lorraine "Sis" Calvin. Betty Calvin married Leon Earl Griffith of Paris, Lamar County, Texas, on 20 November 1918. They became parents of twins, Lavonia Lorraine "Sugar" Griffith and Earl Calvin Griffith. The boy twin died at birth. Their daughter grew up and married James Nathaniel Adams, MD. The Adamses had two children, Darlina Calvin Adams (who is Mrs. Mike Clark of Flower Mound) and James Nathaniel Adams, Jr. of

Lavonia Tankersly Calvin

Longview. Darlina and Mike have two sons, Kyle and Kriss Clark. "Jimmy" Adams, Jr. and Donna Whitaker Adams have two sons, J.N. "Trey" Adams, III and Zack Adams.

On 12 August 1922, Lorraine Calvin married Benjamin Franklin Martin who had recently moved to Longview from Lanexa, New Kent County, Virginia. Their children are Benjamin Franklin Martin, Jr. of Longview and Charlotte Elizabeth Payne of Dallas. Charlotte's children are Madison Lee Oden of Houston, Martin Blair Oden of Dallas and Caroline Elizabeth Wylie of Houston.

During a robbery of the Clements Bank in 1894 by the Dalton gang, L.G. Calvin was standing in the doorway of Womack & Perry, when a hail of bullets struck a pile of bricks in front of the store. The bricks saved his life. After a change in ownership of Womack & Perry, Calvin worked for a while as salesman for Moore Brothers Wholesale Grocery in Tyler. He then purchased the W.T. Whitelock Grocery business from Whitelock's heirs in 1910 and called it L.G. Calvin Grocery. This is the former site (1984) of K. Wolens store at 100 South Fredonia Street. Calvin retired and sold his store to Harold Buchanan in 1917.

Lavonia Calvin was middle-aged when she was taught to play the piano by her husband, L.G. After this she became her husband's accompanist when he played the violin. Both their daughters inherited the Calvin musical ability. Lorraine also inherited two violins. One was from J.K. Polk Harris, Champion Fiddler of three states: Arkansas, Oklahoma and Texas. The other was the late Bernadine Teague's violin given to Lorraine by Latimus Teague during the mid-1930s. Lorraine sent her young son, Franklin, Jr., on his bicycle to get the instrument. Franklin, Jr. was so awed by the Teague House that when he grew up to be a realtor he bought the house in 1962.

L.G. Calvin was invited to be one of the musicians who brought music to Longview and Gregg County homes. At that time, it was the only form of entertainment in the area. Dr. W.D. Northcutt sang, and L.G. Calvin played the piano or organ, whichever was available at the home where the musicale was taking place. John Potter, a black man, played bass violin. The hostess of the musicale event always served a chicken dinner following the concert.

Accompanist for Mr. Polk Harris was Mr. L.G. Calvin. Mr. Harris was an early Gregg County settler who owned a rare violin. "Uncle Polk," the fiddler, had carried that violin with him through the Civil War. When L.G. Calvin's health began to fail, he sent his youngest daughter, Lorraine, then Mrs. B.F. Martin, Sr., to accompany "Uncle Polk" Harris on the piano while Mr. Harris played his fiddle. Polk Harris taught Lorraine all his old tunes and fiddling technique. This came easy to her because of her "God given" talent for music, which had been nurtured by instruction and encouragement from a doting father. She had been performing music at the First Baptist Sunday School and elsewhere since the age of three.

Polk Harris had been living in Abilene for many years and returned to Longview in ill health to live with his niece, Mrs. John Fisher. On his deathbed, he sent for Lorraine and personally presented his violin to her because of his close friendship with her father and because she had been his apt pupil. He had planned to will the instrument to her, but on second thought realized that possession was considered to be 9/10 the of the law. Polk Harris bought the violin in 1853.

Hand-carved on the back of the violin is the likeness of Paganini, the patron saint of all violinists and lettered around the sides of the instrument are the words "Ad Gloriam Paganini," translated, "To the Glory of Paganini."

A *Dallas Morning News* feature story and photograph of Lorraine Martin and the violin appeared 6 August 1922. As a result, she heard from many people throughout the state and nation who wanted to see the violin. Lorraine willed the Polk Harris violin to the Longview Symphony League. The violin given to Lorraine by Latimus Teague was donated by her in 1984 to the Gregg County Historical Museum.

The Victorian Teague farmhouse still stands in its original location in the community which was called Earpville in Upshur County, Texas. It was an older community than Longview and older than Gregg County. The house has a Texas Historical Medallion, has never been moved, and is one of the oldest houses in the City of Longview. The Teague House is located (where it is today in 2003) at 322 Teague Street in Longview, Texas.

"Betty" Calvin Griffith told her young nephew, Franklin Martin, Jr., whom she had interested in historical matters, that she had studied music from the Teague girls when she was a young girl and that the Teague House was considered very old at that time. "Betty" died at the age of 79 in 1964.

At the Calvin family reunion in Ohio, there were so many musicians in the Calvin families that they had their own orchestra. Lorraine played her violin in the Calvin orchestra when she and Franklin, Jr. attended the reunion at Salem, Ohio in 1964.

Lorraine played a baritone horn and her husband played bass horn in the Longview Municipal Band, sponsored by the Longview Chamber of Commerce, and was assistant director of that band from 1926 until 1932, She taught vio-

lin and voice. In keeping with the Calvin musical tradition, she organized string ensemble groups that were active throughout many years. For ten years, Lorraine played first violin with the Longview Symphony Orchestra and was generous with her financial gifts to this organization.

L.G. Calvin died on 12 February 1923, and is buried at Longview's Greenwood Cemetery beside his wife, Lavonia Tankersley Calvin, who died on 20 September 1934.

– Submitted by B. Franklin Martin

THOMAS MITCHELL CAMPBELL

Thomas Mitchell Campbell, governor of Texas, was born at Rusk, Texas, on 22 April 1856, the son of Thomas Duncan and Rachel (Moore) Campbell. He attended common schools at Rusk before entering Trinity University (then located at Tehuacana) to study law in 1873. Lack of finances forced him to withdraw after a year, but he got a job in the Gregg County clerk's office and studied law at night. In 1878, he was admitted to the Texas bar and began his practice in Longview. In the same year, he married Fannie Irene Bruner of Shreveport, Louisiana; they had five children.

Campbell practiced law in Longview until he was appointed a master in chancery for the troubled International-Great Northern Railroad in 1889.

Campbell distrusted monopolistic big business and sympathized with organized labor. He shared many of the reformist political views of his lifelong friend, former governor James Stephen Hogg. In 1897, Campbell resigned from the railroad, returned to private law practice in Palestine, and became active in Democratic party politics. He attended several Democratic conventions and subsequently, at Hogg's urging, decided to run for governor. Though Hogg died before the campaign got underway, Campbell used his endorsement and promised to resurrect his friend's antitrust policies. Campbell was elected governor in 1906.

In his two terms in office, 1907-1911, Campbell initiated a number of reforms involving railroad regulation, antitrust laws, lobbying restrictions, equitable taxation, and pure food and drug laws. Under his administration, the Robertson Insurance Law (1907) brought to a halt the insurance companies' practice of realizing large profits in Texas without investing policy reserves in the state. The most significant legislation during Campbell's administration centered on prison reform.

Governor Thomas M. Campbell's home.

Upon leaving the governorship, Campbell returned to private law practice in Palestine but remained active in Democratic politics. In 1916, he ran unsuccessfully for the United States Senate. In 1917, he served on the exemption board for World War I. He died in Galveston on 1 April 1923, and was buried in Palestine.

REVEREND BURRELL CANNON:
Inventor of the Ezekiel Airship

Burrell Cannon, born 16 April 1848, near Coffeeville, Mississippi, was the son of William and Margaret (Lamb) Cannon. From his father he received training as a machinist, blacksmith and cabinet maker. His training from Mississippi College was as a mechanical engineer.

He came to Longview in Gregg County about 1879, in his early 30s. He was ordained a Baptist minister before the age of 20, spoke several languages and was reported in later family stories to be a foreign missionary and Civil War veteran.

Cannon made his living as a sawmill operator, lured to Texas by cheap timberlands, while continuing to preach on weekends at various small country churches. His homebase was always Longview, although he and his family lived wherever he was cutting timber. He was operating a sawmill near Pine, Texas, (seven miles south of Pittsburg) at the turn of the century, an age obsessed with man's burning desire to fly like a bird.

For years, Cannon had been intrigued by the first and tenth chapters of the "Book of Ezekiel," in which he was convinced a flying machine was described in Biblical terms. By 1900, he had applied his mechanical engineering skills to that scripture and designed several wind-driven machines based on the "wheel within a wheel" concept, as described in the Bible. These included an airship and, in 1900, he convinced a group of Pittsburg businessmen to invest $20,000 in his project. Major prizes were being offered around the world for a successful man-carrying heavier-than-air machine, and Cannon and his investors no doubt believed his design would win the race.

The airship was constructed at the Pittsburg Foundry and Machine Shop. Interest in the project was so high that $25.00 shares of stock in the Ezekiel Airship Company were being sold and bought at $1,000 each! By the summer of 1902, the airship was completed and in late summer or early fall (there is no record of the exact date) a test flight was made in a pasture near the machine shop. Witnesses saw it rise up in the air, fly a short distance (later reported as being 167 feet) and, as the ma-

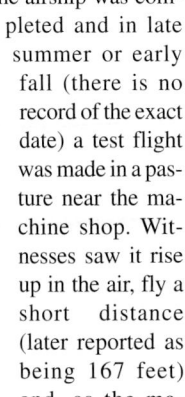

Rev. Burrell Cannon

chine was vibrating badly, the pilot cut the power and the airship came down. It actually flew, although historians have never claimed it was controlled flight and, for some unknown reason, the flight was not repeated. But it did fly in 1902!

In March 1903, the Pittsburg investors refused to put more money into the project, so Reverend Cannon took the machine on a lecture tour, the final stop to be the 1903 World's Fair in St. Louis, an event which offered huge prizes for a successful aircraft. Enroute to Texarkana on a flat railway car, a storm destroyed the airship. Family tradition says Cannon took one look at the wreckage and said "God's will be done. I want nothing else to do with this airship." In fact, a few months later he described in a letter his efforts to organize a company in Texarkana to continue developing the airship. This effort was apparently not successful.

He operated various sawmills for the next few years, but by 1908 was back in Longview, preaching where possible, and still inventing. A total of six patents are recorded in his name at the U.S. Patent Office, the last one for a complicated cotton-harvester just a year before his death in 1922.

On 16 June 1890, Cannon had married Amanda Elmina Haley Hinkle, a Longview widow with a 5-year-old daughter, Anna. To this marriage three other children were born. Two grandchildren presently survive Reverend Cannon, Lawrence Cannon Jr. of Marshall and Glenn Gordon of Longview. A number of Cannon's letters and those of his wife survive and provide much of the information in John Holman's book, *On the Wings of Ezekiel*, published in 2002 by the Northeast Texas Rural Heritage Museum in Pittsburg, where a full-size replica of the airship is displayed.

In 1910, still strongly committed to his belief that God was designing his airship, he resurrected his plans and organized the Security Airship Company of Longview, incorporated in Shreveport, Louisiana, on 28 September 1911. Prominent Longview businessmen backed the project and a factory was planned in which to construct the airships. Burrell Cannon had learned his lesson in Pittsburg, as the Security Aircraft Company was capitalized at $250,000 (instead of the $20,000 in Pittsburg) and a more generous stipend was prescribed for Cannon as living expenses while the ship was developed. President of the company was Dr. C.W. Lawrence; Cannon was Vice-President; J.J. Hudson was Secretary; and T.D. Coupland was Treasurer. Other investors were Otis Williams and E.M. Bramlette. Again, fever ran high and the stock sold rapidly.

Stock Certificate for Security Aircraft Company

Cannon left almost immediately for Chicago, where he engaged a machine shop to build the wheel mechanism, and perhaps a prototype of the airship. From 25 May 1911, until May of 1912, the Longview *News Clarion* ran five articles about the company, from its organization to the final word which was a re-print of a telegram received from an officer of the company (whose name was not listed in the newspaper) who had gone to Chicago to check on progress which said, "Wheels work perfectly. Come quick."

Family tradition says the airship was completed in Chicago, successfully flown by a man named Wilder, but crashed into a power pole on landing and was destroyed. There is no documentation for this story, and nothing further was found in any of the newspapers or other documents to indicate what happened. Thus the Security Aircraft Company became a part of this remarkable man's history.

After Amanda died in 1914, Cannon moved in with his daughter, Anna Gordon, in Longview. He continued to invent and received two other patents prior to his death on 9 August 1922. At the time of his death he was a beloved pastor, Sunday School teacher and Chaplain of the Longview Masonic Lodge. He is buried in Grace Hill Cemetery.

As Jay Miller, a noted aviation historian wrote, "It is to men like Burrell Cannon that we owe the honor of making the aviation age possible. Without their vision and dreams, and in spite of their unrequited efforts, aviation as we know it would not be possible." (Note 1: Details and documentation for statements in this article may be found in *On the Wings of Ezekiel, the Story of Reverend Burrell Cannon's Remarkable Airship,*

The Ezekiel Airship

published in 2002 by the Pittsburg/Camp County Museum Association. Note 2: James Dunn, a retired Longview engineer, now deceased, extensively researched the Security Aircraft Company and provided the facts about it.)

– Submitted by John Holman

CARLTON

Bill Carlton's grand-parents, the Carltons, were married in Missouri and came to Indian Territory (Walters, Oklahoma) about 1900. Asa Carlton hauled freight for a living and when the Ranger, Texas, oil boom started, he went into the oil field business. He hauled everything used to drill oil wells on eight-wheel wagon. Bill's father, Mike Carlton, and grandfather, Asa, were partners in the teaming business for several years, following the oil boom from town to town. They were in Pampa, Wink, Big Spring, Texas, and Hobbs, New Mexico, before coming to East Texas. In West Texas Asa and Bill had large draft horses to pull wagons and dirt equipment. When they came to East Texas they kept only some of the horses to pull wagons and to ride. They bought large Missouri mules from Ross Brothers Mule Sales at the Ft. Worth stockyard to pull the fresnoes, which were large pieces of equipment used to move dirt. The mules could take the summer heat and humidity better than the horses. To clear a location, trees were cut and Bill Carlton would place several pieces of dynamite under each stump to blow it out of the ground so the location could be leveled for drilling. About 1932 they had two small tin-covered houses that were placed on wagons and joined together. One was used for a bedroom and the other as the kitchen.

The mule skinners slept under the wagons with a tarp wrapped around to keep the rain out. It was not long until Bill leased some land from a Mr. Bumpas. It was 1/4 mile south of Fox City at the intersection of Highway 80 and Highway 42 (White Oak to Kilgore). He built a large cook shack to feed the single skinners. They stayed in the bunkhouse. There was a water well and a large flat rock with several washpans, soap, mirrors and combs. The skinners had to use these before the woman cook (called Uni) would let them in to eat. NO HATS AND NO VULGAR LANGUAGE WERE ALLOWED BY HER! The rules were strictly enforced. The skinner who broke the rule went to work without breakfast or a sack lunch. As you might guess, they did not challenge the cook's rules again.

Each oil company had a teaming contractor to do all their work. Bill Carlton did work for the Amerada Oil Company for many years. He sold out to Younger Brothers in 1937. The family moved to Kilgore, where he had the Brass Rail Bar and Poolroom. He sold that business in 1944, but he stayed in the dirt business with dump trucks, a dozier-dragline and 15 head of mules until his death in September of 1950, at the age of 47.

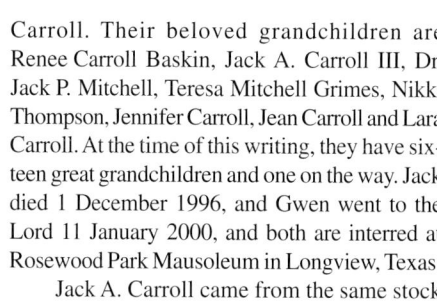
Mike and Bill Carlton, 1928

Mike left a wife, Mary Lucille, his oldest son, Bill, and twins Dolores Jean "Sissy" and Durold Dean "Sonny."

Bill Carlton went to the first grade at Bumpas School, which stood on Highway 42 at Camp Switch where White Oak Waterworks are now located. It was a shotgun building with doors opening on the side. It had three rooms with two grades in some of the rooms. The next year a new school was built, and Bill went to the second and third grades before they moved to Kilgore where he finished high school.

The Bumpas School closed and the children were bussed to White Oak. Bill Carlton's first sweetheart was Earlene Young. She went to Bumpas school also. He has never forgotten her although it has been 70 years.

After being away from East Texas for most of these years, Bill has come back home and now lives in Longview.

– Submitted by Bill Carlton

CARROLL

Jack Alexander Carroll was born in Unity, Pennsylvania, on 9 July 1917, the first child of five sons of Thomas Floyd Carroll and Jean Frances MacTavish. Jack relocated to Youngstown, Ohio, where he attended Youngstown University, and met and married Gwendolyn Blodwyn Ellis, daughter of David P. Ellis and Ruth May Thomas, in Wellsburg, West Virginia, 2 November 1940. In 1952, Jack and Gwen moved their family to Texas to work for Lone Star Steel where Jack was the Assistant Works Manager for 30 years. In 1984, Jack became founder and president of Mill Technology Inc. and PTM, Inc., both in Longview, Texas, where he supplied his customers with all the facets of complete pipe production facilities. Jack was recognized as an authority in the pipe mill industry. Jack and Gwen had five children that they held dear: Jack A. Carroll II, Charlotte Carroll Mitchell, Patricia Carroll Thompson, Donald Thomas Carroll and Charles David Carroll. Their beloved grandchildren are Renee Carroll Baskin, Jack A. Carroll III, Dr. Jack P. Mitchell, Teresa Mitchell Grimes, Nikki Thompson, Jennifer Carroll, Jean Carroll and Lara Carroll. At the time of this writing, they have sixteen great grandchildren and one on the way. Jack died 1 December 1996, and Gwen went to the Lord 11 January 2000, and both are interred at Rosewood Park Mausoleum in Longview, Texas.

Jack A. Carroll came from the same stock as Charles Carroll, the signer of the Declaration of Independence. His father was Thomas Floyd Carroll, born 1895 in Turtle Creek, Pennsylvania, the third child of mother Isabelle Dunseath McKeag and father Harvey Floyd Carroll, who was a tinsmith in Turtle Creek. Harvey's father was Salathiel J. Carroll, whose father was Thomas Carroll who died at the age of 35 years.

Gwen and Jack Carroll

Thomas Carroll's father was Daniel, who was a pioneer settler in what is now Jefferson, Pennsylvania. Salathiel began to learn the cooper's trade when fifteen years old, and after working for some years at that, he took up carpentry work. On 14 August 1845, Salathiel married Margaret Charlotte Peterson and they had three children, one of whom was Walter Lowrey Carroll who was the captain of the world's largest sternwheeler, the Sprague, that hauled coal from Louisville, Kentucky, to New Orleans, Louisiana. Margaret Charlotte Peterson was the daughter of Harvey Heth Peterson and Sarah Carroll. Harvey Heth Peterson was, for many years, a justice of the peace in Jefferson, Pennsylvania. He was also the county commissioner and was prothonotary (which was a chief clerk of any of various courts of law) for three terms. Harvey was born in 1796, and died at the age of 53 years. His parents were Gabriel and Margaret Charlotte Peterson. Gabriel Peterson commanded a company under Braddock, participated in the unfortunate battle at Braddock's Field and, afterward, joined General Washington in the Revolution. Gabriel and Margaret Charlotte lived to the respective ages of ninety-four and ninety-six.

The Carroll descendants are numerous in Turtle Creek, Pennsylvania, Youngstown, Ohio, and scattered throughout Texas.

– Submitted by Charlotte Carroll Mitchell

Hauling oil well casing with mule teams and eight wheel wagons.

RAY HELM & MARY NELL CARTER

The year was 1934 and the United States was in a time of critical economic depression. But for Dr. Ray Helm Carter (27 September 1906 to 6 March 1984) and his new bride, Mary Nell Young (born 31 May 1908, Lake Charles, Louisiana, to 5 February 1985), that was a year of happiness and adventure as they began their married life with a move to Longview, Texas.

Ray was born in Shamrock, Texas, to Horace Alexander and Eliza Jane (Caraway) Carter. Ray's grandparents were Robert Daniel and Mary Louisa (Helm) Carter from Tennesssee; and his great grandparents were Ewing Clayton and Margaret (Hopkins) Carter from Tennessee and Virginia.

203 East Methvin, Longview, Texas. This was the original Hurst Hospital of Dr. V. R. Hurst. It later became the Curtis Building and housed KFRO Radio before the building was demolished.

Ray H. Carter was a 1934 graduate of Baylor Medical School with a specialty in Eye, Ear, Nose and Throat. The move to Longview was specifically for an 18-month internship with Dr. V.R. (Vesse Reeves) Hurst, whose office and hospital were housed in the small three-story (including basement floor), red-brick building at 203 East Methvin Street, next to the present downtown Post Office building. Dr. and Mrs. Carter lived on the top floor of the hospital building, making a two-room apartment their first home. During their short time in Longview, they made lifelong friendships with J. Clyde Tomlinson, Sr. (later to become Mayor of Longview) and his wife, Mitt, and also with W.D. Northcutt, Jr. and his wife, Josephine. These three families owned adjacent lake house properties at Lake Cherokee for many years.

In 1935, the Carters moved to Marshall where for 35 years he was the city's only Eye, Ear, Nose and Throat physician, retiring in 1973. They were Baptists. They had three daughters: Carol Jane (Marshall, Texas), Raenell Craft (Longview, Texas) and Mary Claire Wood (Dallas, Texas).

The Carter family trail led back to Longview when, in 1964, Ray and Mary Nell's middle daughter, Raenell (14 October 1939), and husband, Russell Craft (9 April 1939), moved to Longview and made it home to the present time. They raised their four children in Longview and were charter members of Longview Christian Fellowship Church (1975). (See also "Russell & Raenell Craft.")
– Submitted by Russell Craft

RICHARD WATKINS CASTLEBERRY

Richard Watkins Castleberry, whose ancestor Heinrich Kesselberg came to America between 1683 and 1691 from the Rheinland, was born 12 February 1844, in Shelby County, Texas, to Aaron Trice Castleberry and Elmira Pierce. He died 3 March 1925, in Marshall, Harrison County, Texas. He married Mary Frances "Molly" Martin, daughter of Thompson J. and Margaret Martin, born 16 September 1846, in Alabama, on 6 October 1870, in Grayson County, Texas. Richard was a pioneer farmer of Gregg County living in the Pine Tree area. He moved to Kaufman County, Texas, but returned to Gregg County after 1880, where he farmed in Spring Hill. He later ran sawmills with his son-in-law Dennis Lawrence Magrill. Richard enlisted in the Confederate Army in March 1862, and served until the close of the war. He served three years and one month in Company C, 22nd Texas Regiment, Hubbard's Regiment, Walker's Division, an infantry division.

Richard was ordained an Elder in the Pine Tree Cumberland Presbyterian Church in 1872. He was a charter member and Elder of Elmira Chapel Cumberland Presbyterian Church in Spring Hill. He served as Superintendent of Sunday School at that church.

The children of Richard and Mollie Castleberry were Ada, born 22 July 1871, died 12 December 1871; Maggie, born 17 January 1873, died 11 November 1934, married Richard Tulle Magrill 22 October 1891, married (2) Jim Magrill 29 May 1909; Elmyra, born 12 December 1877, died 11 February 1962, married Dennis Lawrence Magrill 21 September 1893; Cora, born 17 November 1880, died 6 July 1956, married W.I. "Ike" Denson; Mary, born 8 July 1884, died 11 September 1915, married Claude Caesar Clemens about 1901; and George Aaron, 11 born March 1888, died 6 October 1965, married Lillian Belle Bussey 8 June 1918.
– Submitted by Anne Evers

CHEROKEE INDIANS

Cherokees were first reported in Texas in 1807, when a small band established a village on the Red River. A group of Indians requested permission from the Spanish to settle in Texas. The Spanish agreed because they wanted to use the Indians as a buffer against American expansion. By 1820, the Americans were competing with the Indians for the land. In early 1820, Chief Bowl, also known as Duwali, led some sixty Cherokee families into Texas. They settled first near present-day Dallas, but native Indians forced them to move further into eastern Texas into a virtually uninhabited region now in Rusk County.

The Cherokees had learned the importance, at least to the Americans, of having legal title to their land. They had repeatedly asked the Mexicans for a permanent land grant. In hopes of getting the Cherokees to aid against the onslaught of settlers from the United States, the Mexicans offered the Cherokees land for a price. The Indians had neither money nor legal expertise to gain a title.

When the Texas Revolution started in 1835, the Cherokees still did not have title to their land, and their loyalty to Mexico placed them in a doubtful position with the revolutionary government in Texas. The Cherokees addressed the problem by declaring themselves neutral in the conflict between Texas and Mexico.

The Texas revolutionary government, anxious to ensure Cherokee neutrality, sent Sam Houston to counsel with the tribe in the fall of 1835. Houston was an adopted member of the Cherokee tribe and became an influential supporter of the Cherokee people. In November 1835, acting on Houston's recommendation, the Texas government agreed to recognize Cherokee claims to the land north of the Old San Antonio Road and the Neches River and west of the Angelina and Sabine Rivers. The Texas government then appointed a commissioner to negotiate a treaty with the tribe. The result established a reservation for the Cherokees in East Texas and, although it considerably reduced their landholdings, the Cherokees agreed to the accord because they believed it finally gave them a permanent home. The reservation included the future Smith and Cherokee counties as well as parts of Van Zandt, Rusk and Gregg counties. Eight Cherokee leaders, including Duwali, signed the agreement in 1836, but the treaty was never ratified by the Texas government. Although a majority of the Cherokees had agreed to peace with the Texans, a militant faction of the tribe remained pro-Mexican, a fact that greatly hindered Texan-Cherokee relations.

The following year, 1837, Duwali consented to serve as the republic's emissary to the Comanches. Texas-Cherokee relations deteriorated again in 1838, however, when attacks on settlers in East Texas were blamed on a combined Cherokee-Mexican force. In the summer of 1839, a force of several hundred warriors led by Duwali met Texas forces in the Battle of the Neches near the site of present Tyler. More than 100 Indians, including Duwali, were killed, and the remaining Cherokees were driven across the Red River into Indian Territory.

JOHN I. CHOICE & CARRIE JANE CLINKSCALES

John I. Choice, born 8 January 1861, in Kilgore, married Carrie Jane Clinkscales, born 27 December 1868, in Kilgore. Carrie Jane's father, Frank B. Clinkscales, had lived most of his life in Starville in Smith County and was Sheriff of Smith County. At his death, his wife, Emma Stillwell Clinkscales, finished out his term of office.

John Choice became a rural mail carrier for the U.S. Post Office and a surveyor of Gregg County, and was also a founding member of the First Baptist Church of Kilgore.

John and Carrie had the following children: Harry Tully, married Olly Darby and moved to the Palestine, Texas, area where their only daughter, Jane Eleanor was born in 1921; Horace died at age 12; Frank C. never married but lived to be 71; Andrew Earl married Marybelle Crews;

Harry Tully Choice on horse; Horace standing behind baby Lorine; Frank, left front; John I. Choice and Carrie Jane Choice, seated; Andrew Earl, right front, about 1906.

Lorine died at age 3; John only lived 11 months; Ruth never married but was a school teacher at Kilgore Elementary for 35 years.

Andrew Earl, born 1898, and Marybelle, born 1903, married in Kilgore. Their children were Mavis Pauline, married Theodore McDaniel and settled in Carthage; Karry Augusta, married Marcene Nathan Holt; Earline, married Gerald Ray and settled in the Tyler area.

Andrew Earl became a rural mail carrier, like his father, and a builder of houses. After his father's death, he built his mother, Carrie, a home that still stands today at the corner of Choice and Knowles streets in Kilgore.

Earl was a member of the Masons and Marybelle a member of the Eastern Star. Earl died in 1967, and Marybelle lived until 1973.

Karry sought teaching and after attending Kilgore College, University of Colorado and receiving her Master's Degree at SFA, moved to Pecos where she taught for one year.

On 11 January 1943, Karry married Lt. Nathan Holt of the USAF in El Paso, and moved to Marfa, Texas, where they remained until Nathan was discharged. Moving to Carthage to pursue his law career, Nathan became a county attorney. In 1952, Karry and Nathan moved to Longview where Nathan took up private practice and was later elected First Assistant District Attorney, serving for 25 years and retiring in 1985.

Karry became Field Director for the Camp Fire Girls, serving the East Texas area for four years, after which time she took up a teaching post at South Ward, where she remained until retiring in 1985. Both Karry and Nathan were charter members of the Longview YMCA, Nathan teaching tumbling and Karry teaching tennis; both were involved in summer camps for the children they loved. Nathan died in December of 2000. Karry remains in Longview.

Daughter Kaaran earned her Ph.D. and married John Copes, and became head of the Physical Education Department of Angel State University in San Angelo, Texas. Kaaran died suddenly in 1973. Nathan M, Jr. lives in Austin, a retired programmer analyst for the Texas Department of Public Safety. Nate married Nancy Elliott, an elementary school teacher at Austin ISD. Nate and Nancy's children are Heath, a lieutenant in the Air Force; Greg, a doctoral student at the University of Texas in Austin, majoring in Aerospace Engineering; and Laura, a P.E. teacher for the Austin ISD.

– Submitted by Carrie Holt

ALBERT WHITMORE (A.W.) & NAN ROBERTS CHRISTIAN

Albert Whitmore Christian was the son of Edward Lewis Christian and Mariah McCollum Christian. He was born 25 July 1873, in Hopkins County, Texas. He was a descendant of Thomas Christian, the immigrant, who came to Virginia in 1657. Nan Roberts, his wife, was the daughter of William Perry Roberts and Margaret McDonald Roberts. Nan was born 10 February 1879, in Randolph County, Illinois, and her family moved to Hopkins County, Texas, when she was a small child. Her father was employed as a schoolteacher.

While living in Hopkins County, Albert met Nan Roberts, and they were married there 28 November 1897. In 1905, they moved to Longview, traveling by covered wagon. The trip took several days.

Albert W. Christian owned the first cleaning and pressing shop in downtown Longview. The shop was located on West Tyler, and he was in business there for many years. The family attended the First Baptist Church, and their children made many life-long friends there.

While living in Longview, Albert and Nan reared four children, who remained Longview residents as adults. The children were Chester Christian, who married Gertrude Howell; Ella Rhee Christian, who married Willard Lewis; Early Sessum Christian, who married Bennie Bruner; and Ila Mae Christian, who married Perry Lee Harris.

A.W. Christian in front of his shop on Tyler Street, Longview, Texas.

Albert Whitmore Christian died 4 November 1967, and Nan Roberts Christian died 16 July 1967. They are buried in Memory Park Cemetery in Longview.

– Submitted by Kathryn Harris Hines (granddaughter of A.W. and Nan Roberts Christian)

RANDLE CHRISTIAN

Almost four score and five years, after a "lot of slaves" bearing the surname Christian were brought to this area of East Texas, did a very young child begin to learn of her ancestor.

It began when the youngest great granddaughter of one of those slaves was denied access to the "Lord's Supper" at her family church.

One Sunday night at the Shiloh Baptist Church during the Lord's Supper service, the local Minister invited "all Christians to come now and take the Lord's Supper." Muriel Glenn Christian, not quite 5 years old, got up from her seat and started down the aisle of the church only to be detained. Muriel could not understand the detainment and felt an injustice had been imposed. She began to show irateness, but was restrained by her father, who gently led her out of the church. Shaking, with uncontrolled sobs, she insisted that she was "a Christian." She even asked her father if it was true.

Her father, Tommie Thadeus Christian assured her that she was a Christian and that the preacher meant, "Christians are those who have joined church." Tommie promised his "Baby," Muriel, that he would buy her some grape juice and tell her about her surname, Christian.

Thus the legend of her ancestors began.

Grandpa Randle Christian was born somewhere in North Carolina, around 1829, probably on a Christian Plantation. He migrated with his owners to South Carolina, then to Georgia, and on to Midway, Barbour County (presently Midway, Bullock County, near the town of Troy, Alabama). He became the property of a young slavemaster, Gideon Christian (probably Gideon, III).

Gideon "Gid" Christian of South Carolina, wife Carrie of Georgia, and their family along with from 30 to 32 slaves arrived in East Texas around 1855 or 1856. They settled in an area located in the southwestern section of Upshur County, Texas. Presently, the area is in the northwestern section of Gregg County, about four miles south of Gilmer, Upshur County, Texas, near the communities of East Mountain and West Mountain, and just north of White Oak, Texas. Formerly called Christian Settlement because all of its inhabitants wore the surname Christian, it is presently the Shiloh Community of Gregg County.

Grandpa Randle "was a pure Bushman African. He didn't sit on chairs, he would squat most of the time." "He had some brothers who came to Texas with him, and some sisters, too. His brothers were Butcher Christian, I and Alec. Ann was a sister. Butcher was born before leaving Alabama. Alec and Ann were born after the slaves were brought to Texas. Alec and Ann were sold to a 'Master Jones' (Tom might have been his name).... They took the name of Jones. They carried Ann off to the Blackland out west, but after several years she ran away and returned to the Settlement with two children. Her son was Simon Jones and a baby girl named Huldy Jones."

Muriel Christian learned later that in 1870 Randle Christian, at 41 years old, was a landowner with personal property valued at $200. He and his household resided in Precinct 2, Upshur County, Texas. Mail was received through the Coffeeville Post Office. The household included a housekeeper, Susan, a black female of 23 years; daughter, Channie ; son, Burger; daughter, Hulda; and sister, Ann Christian, all born in Texas.

"Grandpa Randle was first married to Miss Rebecca Jones Christian, who bore his children Ollive (Ollie), Channey (Channie), Burger and Hulda."

When the Shiloh Baptist Church, one of the oldest African American churches in East Texas, was organized in 1871, Randle Christian and wife, Rebecca Christian, their daughters, Ollive Christian Wilhite (Hardy) and Channey Christian Jones and husband, Alec (his brother) and his brother Butcher Christian and wife Christina were charter members of that newly organized church. Thus the settlement adopted the name of the church.

Grandpa Randle Christian died 13 March 1905, in Savannah, Texas, of old age.

Rebecca and Randle Christian's only known son, Burger Christian, married Miss Rachael (Snardy) Snoddy, 19 July 1887. Together they had seven surviving children. Rachael Snoddy Christian and Burger Christian's third son, Tommie Thadeus (named in honor of his maternal uncle, Tommie Snoddy and maternal grandfather, Thadeus Snoddy) Christian, married Miss Annie B. Jones 5 April 1913. They were the parents of seven children. Muriel Glenn Christian Jones (Boyce O.) was their youngest child and is the youngest great granddaughter, fourth generation, of the Randle Christian.

The heirs of Tommie Thadeus Christian (third generation) still own the land inherited from Randle Christian. The land has been passed on from preceding generations. Muriel G. Christian Jones has always resided in Gregg County and her present home is located less than nine miles from the property possessed by her ancestor, Randle Christian.

– Submitted by Muriel G. Christian Jones

DR. T.J. CLARK

Always wondering about her great-great grandfather, Flo Stevens of Longview shared this information from her research.

T.J. was the son of R.S. Clark and S.B. Clark, probably of Alabama. Dr. T.J. Clark deeded land in Upshur County in 1871, and married Virginia Beall Butrill on 22 February 1872, in Longview. According to the *Longview Democrat* in 1881, his sister, Miss Emma Clark, had a schoolhouse near the Presbyterian Church. The paper also mentioned that "Dr. Clark bought a lot fronting on Methvin, opposite the court house on which he will erect himself a dwelling house." In 1882, this same newspaper mentions Dr. T.J. Clark as a "jailer."

On 17 April 1886, *Texas New Era* has this story: "Escaped Jail, But Recaptured: "A negro man by the name of Henry with numerous aliases, was placed in jail last Wednesday, charged with assault to kill. In the evening when the jailer, Dr. T.J. Clark, went up to lock the prisoners in their cells, there being only two in jail, …Prisoner escaped, his and knocked the jailer's wife to the ground…she chased him with pistol but failed to fire. The jailer and wife were both badly bruised and shocked and both have suffered severely from the effects of the contest."

In the 19 July 1900, *Times-Clarion* this mention is made about him: "Dr. T.J. Clark's many friends will be glad to learn that his condition is somewhat improved." In the 1900 census he is listed as a farmer-invalid. By July 1902, he and his wife Virginia Beall Buttrill are both listed as deceased.

He was apparently a loving and generous husband as his great-great granddaughter has the receipt from the beautiful memorial grave marker that he had designed for his wife. Very little else is known about him; although, in 1990, there was a Confederate States of America sign at his memorial marker in Greenwood Cemetery, Longview, Texas. It is missing today. (*Note: Much of this information comes from the family Bible of Elbert Bartow Culpepper, given to him on 24 May 1881.*)

– Submitted by Eileen R. Vela (daughter of Martha Blanche Culpepper Roth)

CLANTON

Benjamin Reid Clanton, MD was born in Lancaster, South Carolina, 2 November 1912. He married Elaine Markham (see "Markham") 7 October 1941, in Longview. They had two daughters, both born in Longview: Virginia Elaine (born 1945) and Sara Finch (born 1949). Virginia Elaine married Jack Michael Covin, MD in 1965. Both Virgina and Jack's sons were born in St. Louis, Missouri: David Reid and Jonathan Scott. Sara married James Milton Cammack, Jr. in Longview in 1973.

Dr. Clanton was a long-time beloved pediatrician in Longview whose office was in Markham Hospital. Dr. and Mrs. Clanton are faithful members of First Baptist Church, Longview. They have both been active in all phases of church and civic life in Longview.

Dr. Clanton's father was Commodore Perry Clanton (1885-1945, South Carolina). C.P. Clanton's grandfather was William Marr Clanton, who married Emily Jane Hilton, and his great grandparents were Confederate soldier William Riley (1830-1910) and Amelia Young. C.P. married Sara Jane Bennett in 1906, in Lancaster, South Carolina.

Sara's mother was Sarah Lenorah Williams (1857-1924). Sara's maternal grandparents were Eli J. Williams (1830-1890) and Eleanor Jane Caskey (1828-1917).

Sara's paternal line can be traced to Thomas Bennett, who settled in Virginia prior to 1626. Her father was Benjamin Harrison Bennett (1850-1941). He married Sarah Lenorah

4 February 1880. Benjamin-r's parents were Confederate soldier James K. Bennett (1829-1984) and Lavensor Saperonia Sims (1832-1886). James K.'s parents were Simon Bennett (1799-1824) and Mary (Polly) Cauthen. Reubin Bennett (1757, Virginia-1847, South Carolina) served in the American Revolution in Raiford's Co., 16th Regiment and married Elizabeth Beckham (born 1756, North Carolina), daughter of William Beckham (born Granville County, North Carolina, and died in 1799).

Reubin Bennett, Sr. (died 1793, Warren County, North Carolina) married Mary Rogers (born in Surrey County, North Carolina) in 1755. Reubin, Sr. was the son of James Bennett, who was born in 1718, and lived in Isle of Wight and Brunswick Counties, Virginia. James was the son of Richard Bennett, Jr. and Anne. Richard Jr.'s parents were Richard and Anne Bennett; Richard, Sr.'s father was Thomas Bennett from Mulberry Island, Warwick County, Virginia, who was married prior to 1624 to Alice of Lawn's Creek, Isle of Wight County, Virginia.

– Submitted by R. Clanton

VAN CLIBURN

Van Cliburn is an American concert pianist. He performs works written primarily by romantic composers of the 1800s and 1900s.

Cliburn was born on 12 July 1934, in Shreveport, Louisiana. His full name is Harvey Lavan Cliburn, Jr. His mother, Rilda Bee Cliburn, began teaching him to play the piano when he was 3 years old. His family moved to Kilgore when he was small. Cliburn studied piano at the Juilliard School in New York City. He made his concert debut in Houston in 1947, but did not begin an active concert career until 1954. Cliburn first gained worldwide fame in 1958, when he won the Tchaikovsky International Competition for piano in Moscow. In 1978, he stopped giving concerts, but he resumed performing in public in 1989.

MARVIN & ARULA (LOCKETT) CLAY

Arula (Lockett) Clay (born 3 June 1919), one of Ira and Ora Lockett's six children, was the only of her siblings who had no college training. On 7 October 1939, she married Marvin Henry Clay (born 23 February 1914,

The Clay family, 1965. (l.-r.) Standing: Royce, Leon and DeQuence. Seated: Bennie, Arula and Marvin.

died 29 July 1987). Marvin was the son of Noah Clay (born 10 March 1887, died 14 November 1973) and Sudie (Coats) Clay (born 10 September 1887, died 19 January 1971).

Arula and Marvin had four children: Leon Madison (born 15 September 1940), Bennie (Clay) Moore (born 18 July 1943), DeQuence Ovide (born 2 February 1946) and Royce Edward (born 18. August 1949). Arula's father lived the adage: "Keeping busy keeps you out of trouble." She remembers being hired out to neighboring farms when their own harvest was completed. Before retiring from Gladewater Public School as a cafeteria worker (mid 1980s), she worked for Lacey's sewing factory on Highway 80 West and Jakie Cannon's laundry (owned by her uncle).

When they married, Marvin settled down and worked on the railroad. While working for Kelly Sides' Cement Plant, he was the community cement finisher and assisted with rebuilding Weldon School after it burned (1952). Marvin worked for Western Foundry in Tyler, Texas, and eventually retired from Good Shepherd Hospital in Longview, Texas (early 1970s). Marvin's cement craftsmanship can still be admired at the head of his younger brother's grave in Turner Town Cemetery. Marvin's outdoor adventures with Goalman Cannon and Watson (Bud) Davis provided a wealth of fodder for his artful story telling.

Committed Christians, Marvin and Arula were active members of St. James Missionary Baptist Church. Since an early age, Arula has sung in the choir. Marvin also sang in the choir, served on the deacon board and served as Worshipful Master of Master Mason Lodge #278 — like his father-in-law and grandfather-in-law had.

Arula and Marvin's youngest son, Royce, later served as chairman of the St. James deacon board. A graduate of Prairie View A&M, Royce served on the Gladewater City Council. He taught public schools in Longview and Austin. DeQuence served in the Vietnam War building roads and bridges for foot soldiers. He owned and operated Tri-C-Heavy Equipment Co. Bennie, a Jarvis Christian College graduate, taught public schools in Washington and Texas. Now retired, she teaches at Jarvis Christian College. She has spoken at churches throughout East Texas. Leon was the second black to serve on the Gladewater ISD School board. He retired from Exxon Oil.

Arula's fourteen grandchildren, dubbed "The Fabulous 14" are Denise (Clay) Price, Tyriska Turner, JaHarial Clay, Portia (Moore) Scott, Claudette Clay, DeQuence Clay Jr., Bridget Moore, Leon Clay Jr., Valencetta Clay, André Clay, Candice Clay, Royce Clay Jr., Jeremy Clay and Rachard Clay. Eight attended college, six hold college degrees, and three hold advanced degrees. Of the three who attended trade schools, one is a policeman and one owns D.C. Electric in Longview. Arula has 16 great grandchildren. At 84, she still lives in the Red Rock Community.

– Submitted by Leon Clay

MAUDE COBB

Maude Cobb ran a curbside newsstand on the corner near the post office for nearly 30 years. She was one of Longview's most familiar figures, and after her husband's death, provided her family's livelihood from her newspaper sales.

Whether it was winter, summer, stormy or sunny, Mrs. Cobb greeted customers seven days a week. She met regulars at the curb with their paper and change. During the East Texas oil boom, she steered newly arrived roughnecks and tool pushers to jobs with oil companies. She shared her meager earnings with the penniless, many of whom have never forgotten her. Mrs. Cobb is fondly remembered for her old-fashioned shawl around her head and her hard work. Friends provided her with a small kiosk to keep her out of inclement weather. She retired in 1962 at 81 years of age and died in 1964.

When the Longview Chamber of Commerce and the City of Longview were working to raise money for a convention center, a $330,000 contribution from Mrs. Cecile Moeschle, a Longview resident who had grown up in her grandmother's house, provided the boost needed to get the building named after Maude Cobb, her grandmother.

EDWARD WILLIAM COCK (1854-1952)

Ed W. Cock was born 28 February 1854, St. Mary Parish, Louisiana. Ed's parents were George Washington Cock and Fannie Isabella Hudson Cock. Ed moved to Holly Springs, Marshall County, Mississippi, with his parents in late 1855 or early 1856. This was the home of his grandfather Joseph T. Cock. Ed's brother Turner was born in Holly Springs, Mississippi, in 1856. Ed's father, George W. Cock died January 1857, in Holly Springs and is buried there in the City Cemetery. The 1860 Census shows Ed, his mother and brother living with grandparents Joseph and Sally Cock in Holly Springs.

Ed came to Texas with his mother, brother Turner, his grandparents Joseph and Sally Cock and Joseph's 42 negroes after the crops were gathered in 1862. This was during the Civil War, and Union troops had occupied Joseph Cock's home in Holly Springs. Joseph Cock purchased 1,000 acres of land in the Elderville community, Rusk County, Texas, on 13 December 1862, from John Garland Brown (who later became Ed's stepfather). Rusk County tax records in 1864 show Joseph with 1,000 acres of land, 42 negroes, 10 horses and 20 cows. Ed and his mother lived with grandparents Sally and Joseph Cock for four years. Ed's mother married John G. Brown (whose wife had died in 1864) on 20 December 1866, in Rusk County, Texas. In early 1867, Ed returned to Holly Springs, Mississippi, with his grandparents Joseph and Sally Cock, where he lived for approximately 3-1/2 years. (The Civil War had ended in 1865.)

The 1870 Rusk County Census shows Ed living with his mother and stepfather John G. Brown in the Elderville Community. Edward W. married Mary Ella (Mollie) Mitchell on 26 November 1879, in Gregg County, Texas. The

Mollie Mitchell and Edward William Cock

Elderville Community of Rusk County became part of Gregg County in 1873. Ed's mother gave him 100 acres of land in the Elderville Community where he lived and raised his family. In 1923, when daughter Kate went to Dallas to enter Business School, Ed and Mollie did not want to live alone, so they locked up their Elderville home and lived with daughter Ria and Star Dickson for two years in the Danville Community. Then it was back to their Elderville home for seven more years. Their son Pleas lived a half mile away. In 1932, Ed and Mollie again moved back to Star and Ria's at Danville, and lived in a small house in their yard for eight years. In 1940, Star and Ria Dickson moved to 1200 S. Martin Street in Kilgore, Texas. Ed and Mollie went along, moving soon to daughter Kate and Mabry Mistrot's home on Choice Street in Kilgore, Texas, where they lived through 1943. In January 1944, Ed and Mollie moved back to Ria and Star Dickson's, where Mollie died 28 June 1944. Ed spent his last eight years living for three months with Kate, then three months with Ria. Ed died 25 January 1952, at age 97 years, 11 months. He was buried at Elderville beside Mollie.

– Submitted by Wilson Dickson

GARTH COCKERELL

Garth Cockerell was born in 1919, in Eustace, Texas, to Dr. L.L. and Elizabeth (Earnest) Cockerell. His father was a practicing physician. Garth was a graduate of Athens High School and North Texas University. He served three years in the Army Air Force in World War II.

In 1943, Garth married Tina Colista Satterwhite in the White Oak Baptist Church, built on land given to the church by her parents, M.C. and Ada L. Satterwhite, long-time members of the community. Tina was born in White Oak, Texas, in 1923. When she was in first grade (1930), all seven grades in White Oak School walked through the woods to Tenneryville to watch the first oil well in Gregg County "blow in." Tina graduated from White Oak High School and Bish Mathis Business College. After finishing school, she worked as a secretary in the White Oak School System.

Garth and Tina came to Gladewater, Texas, in 1952. Garth was manager of McWilliams Furniture Company. Two years later, he established his own business, B&C Furniture Company. His son, Garth, now owns the business.

Garth and Tina Cockerell, 1987

The Cockerells became involved in organizations in Gladewater. Garth was a School Board Member for twelve years, served on the Gladewater Housing Board for twenty years, and was a Rotarian, Little League Baseball president and coach. In First Baptist Church, he taught Sunday school classes.

Tina (Nina) worked in the Gladewater Hospital Auxiliary; she received a "Volunteer of the Year" award. She was Chairman of the Auxiliary "Tasting Bee," president of Beta Sigma Phi Sorority, Cub Scout den mother, Camp Fire leader and Gladewater Music Club member for thirty-five years (president four years). In First Baptist Church, she was a member of the Handbell Choir, a thirty-year member of the Sanctuary Choir, treasurer of Women's Missionary Union and a faithful Sunday school member. She is on the Gladewater Cemetery Board.

Five children were born to this union; all five graduated from Gladewater High School. Sylvia, a graduate of TCU, married Mike Newman and lives in Shreveport, Louisiana. They have two daughters, Angela and Katie.

Gloria is a graduate of the University of Texas at Austin, and lives in Plano, Texas. She has two daughters. Cinnamon married Chad Nemec. They live in Austin, Texas, with their three children: Colista, Chili and Cezanne. Azure, married to Rudolph Reetz, lives in Richardson, Texas.

Garth, a North Texas University graduate, married Gayleen White. They live in Gladewater and have a son, Cameron, who is a Gladewater High School freshman.

Phillip, a graduate of TSTI in Waco, is married to Vicki Abernathy and lives in Shreveport. Their children are Clint, who attends TCU; Casey, who graduates this year from Loyola Prep School and will attend Ol' Miss this fall; and Candice, a Loyola Prep School junior.

Leslie, a Baylor University graduate, married Janis Ford. They live in Grand Prairie, Texas, with their two sons: Brian, an 8th grader, and Ben, a 5th grader.

Garth Cockerell died in 1988. A Garth Cockerell Memorial Scholarship is given each year to a Gladewater graduate.

– Submitted by Tina Cockerell

MARY LOU MELTON MCLENDON COE

Mary Lou "Quincy" Melton McLendon and her children moved to Gregg County in about 1891, following the untimely death of her husband, James Isum McLendon. Mary Lou was born 24 March 1855, and James Isum was born 2 March 1852, both in Georgia. They married 25 November 1873, in Dawson, Terrell County, Georgia. They moved to Texas about 1886, and settled in Graceton, Upshur County (just west of what is now U.S.Highway 259). Later, they moved to Gilmer where they owned and operated a sawmill. James Isum died 21 January 1891, in Upshur County, Texas.

Their children were (1) Idus Simpson McLendon, born 10 August 1876, in Terrell County Georgia, and died 9 September 1945, in Gregg County, Texas; (2) Augusta Eugenia McLendon, born 24 September 1878, in Terrell County, Georgia, and died March 1978, in Longview, Gregg County, Texas; (3) James Alpheus McLendon, born 8 March 1880, at Morris Station, Quitman County, Georgia, and died 27 May 1964, in Shreveport, Louisiana; (4) Harriet Mary Lou McLendon, born 11 December 1881, in Terrell County, Georgia, and died March 1918, in Gregg County, Texas; (5) Alice Cormie McLendon, born 29 October 1884, in Terrell County, Georgia, and died 10 December 1980, in Longview, Texas; and (6) Eliza Louvenia McLendon, born 31 July 1887, in Upshur County Texas, and died 5 May 1969, in Longview, Gregg County, Texas.

According to information obtained by a granddaughter, Autrie McLendon Fuller, from her Aunt Genie (Eugenia), Mary Lou first moved to a place on what is now Airline Road, just south of Summerfield Church and then purchased land that was known as the "Jimmy Killingsworth place," about 219 acres 1/2 mile west of Judson Road and south of Judson School. They remodeled the old two-story partial-hewn log house that was on the place and made it their home.

The acreage contained streams of running water, peach and apple orchards and other fruit and berries. There were walnut trees, hickories, chinquapins and large oaks. A cider-press was used to make apple cider, and they made soap of ashes taken from the wood stoves and fireplaces. The house was large, with two halls and

Mary Lou Melton
McLendon Coe

three porches. Six rooms were downstairs, and two rooms and a hall were upstairs. Several buildings outdoors provided storage, stables and shed for feeding and milking cows.

On 8 October 1898, a marriage license was issued to Benjamin F. Coe and Mrs. M.L. McLendon. Mr. Coe, a former Union soldier in the Civil War, had come from the North to Gregg County and boarded with the McLendon family. They were married until his death on 15 January 1914.

Mary Lou Melton McLendon Coe died of pneumonia on 8 February 1934, in Gregg County, Texas. She is buried at Judson Cemetery. On her grave marker is inscribed, "Strength and Honor are her clothing; and she shall rejoice in time to come. Proverbs 31-25."

COLEMAN

Jeff and Mary Ray Coleman's family had been a large one with thirteen children, but during the Civil War scarlet fever decimated Vernon. Louisiana. Mary died in the spring of 1862. Word of their mother's death reached Martin and Thomas in the Confederate Army. Both left camp and were reported AWOL. Thomas reached the Coleman home ahead of Martin. There he was told that Louisa Alabama, his 10-year-old sister, and Horatio Jefferson, his youngest brother, had died also, along with two of the Markham children.

Their relatives and neighbors said that they had returned from Louisa's funeral, and found Alice Ray dead. They told Thomas that, "Alice Ray was laid out and dressed for burial." Thomas had begun his medical training prior to entering the army. Leaving his horse still saddled, he rushed into the house to examine Alice. In his hurry, he slammed the door. The slamming shook the house and someone coughed. Thomas insisted that Alice had coughed, that she was alive.

The men, believing Thomas crazed with grief, attempted to prevent him from examining his sister. Thomas fought the men and " lifted her up, ran from the house, swung her across his saddle, and rode across the river to a campground where he nursed Alice back to health." Later, when he moved to Gregg County, then part of Upshur, Alice came with him and his wife.

After the war's end, Martin returned to Vernon to live, but Thomas attended medical school and never lived in Vernon again. Martin married Louisa Elizabeth Ledford "Miss Lu" by 1868; he was 29 and she, 19. Jeff made has home with the couple. Miss Lu was six feet tall with flaming red hair and a temper to match. Their first child, William "Willy" Coleman, was born 14 February 1869, in Vernon, next door to the Ledfords. When Martin and Jeff left for Texas, Lu, pregnant with their second child, and Willy returned to her parents' home. Mena Ethel Estella Coleman, her name chosen by her father, arrived on 19 October 1871, at the Ledfords.

Lu had no plans to go to Texas. About 1859, her father, Rev. Leford, had tried to avoid the coming War by moving his family to Texas, but one year of the Texas heat and cold drove the family back to Vernon. Lu remembered too well wrapping sacks around her feet to walk through the snow to school. Perhaps she had heard the old expression that "Texas was heaven for men and dogs but hell for women and horses."

– Submitted by Mary McLaughlin Aikman,
Kilgore, Texas

ISHAM JEFFERSON & MARY ELIZABETH RAY COLEMAN

Isham Jefferson "Jeff" Coleman and his son, Martin Turner Coleman, left Vernon, Jackson Parish, Louisiana, for the area later known as Gregg County, Texas in 1871. They planned to build a sawmill on Moss Lake off the Sabine River. Jeff, described as large-framed, dark-complexion, with dark eyes, always wore a long, long beard. Jeff, born 16 October 1803, the sixth child and fourth son of Revolutionary soldier Isham Coleman and Elizabeth Ann Roper of Dinnwiddie County, Virginia, unfortunately, did not live to see the sawmill built. Jeff died 16 January 1872, Gregg County, Texas.

Jeff chose to start his new business in East Texas since several of his children already lived there: his daughter, Martha Coleman Markham, wife of Louis S. Markham; a son, Dr. Thomas Marion Coleman, the first physician to register his medical license in Gregg County; and Alice Ray Coleman, his youngest daughter.

Later, other members of his family would call Gregg County home. Jeff's daughter, Georgia Coleman Graves, married Andrew J. Causey of the Sabine Community. Another son, William Goodwin Coleman, married and divorced Lavinia Wilkins, also a Sabine family. In 1931, Jeff's great grandson, James Mc Laughlin, Sr., moved to Kilgore to run the East Texas oil department of T.L. James, Inc. His son, James Mc Laughlin, Jr., later would serve as a Longview Police Chief.

Entering into a new business at age 68 was characteristic of the enterprising Jeff Coleman. Throughout his life, Jeff had been a "very sturdy, independent soul," who made his own way. At age 16, he left his family home, moved to Georgia, and later to Alabama, where he started accumulating a large store of worldly goods.

In Bibb County, Alabama, he married his cousin, Mary Elizabeth Ray, with the written permission of her parents, William and Elizabeth Ann Roper Ray; he was 20, she, 15. The Ropers were known as the "Preacher Ropers" due to the many Baptist ministers in that family. Elected a Justice of the Peace in his twenties, Jeff, with Mary's help, continued to prosper.

Jeff, served several terms as Justice of the Peace in Bibb and Talladega Counties. Always in search of greater opportunities for their growing family, Jeff and Mary moved to Talladega, Alabama, by 1840, and to Vernon, Jackson Parish, Louisiana, in 1847. They, like many other Southerners, followed the band of fertile red clay which could be farmed so productively from Georgia to Alabama to Louisiana.

Vernon, parish seat, was very prosperous in the 1840s and 1850s, and boasted seven colleges and many churches. Cotton accounted for the town's wealth and drew many settlers similar to Jeff and Mary. They joined the Mount Zion Baptist Church. Martin would marry Louisa Elizabeth Ledford, daughter of the Rev. William J. Leford, minister of Mt. Zion. The peace and prosperity of Vernon ended for the Colemans with the Civil War and fever epidemic. Mary Elizabeth Ray Coleman did not live to make the Texas move.

– Submitted by Charles Ronan McLaughlin,
San Anselmo, California

ISHAM JEFFERSON & MARY RAY COLEMAN: The Older Children

The older children of Isham Jefferson and Mary Ray Coleman follow:

I. William Goodwin Coleman, born 8 October 1821, Bibb County, Alabama; died c.1889, Huntsville, Walker County, Texas; married first Lavinia Wilkins; married second Cornelia S., born 1845, Texas, and had the following twelve children, all born in Texas: Mollie, 1867; Willie, 1869; Thames, 1871; Jeff, 1873; James S., October 1874; Charles S., January 1876; Frank, 1878; Bobb, October 1879; Eddie J., December 1881; Nora, November 1883; Lillie, November 1888; and Evonne, April 1891.

II. Martha Ann Elizabeth Coleman, born 27 August 1827, Bibb County, Alabama; died 21 May 1899, Denison, Grayson County, Texas; married Louis S. Markham, born 1832, died 1882, Gregg County, Texas; they had the following three children: Mary Elizabeth, died July 1862, Louisiana; Tommy S., died July 1862, Louisiana; and Dr. Louis Napoleon Markham, born 1856, Louisiana, died 1893, Texas, married first Laura A. Chapman, 1857-1881, Texas; married second Sarah Mayo Northcutt, 1863-1888, Texas; and he had Essie L. Markham 1876-1881, Texas; E.C. Markham, son, 1877, Texas; infant twins, 1882; and Dr. Louis Northcutt Markham, who married Princess Emma Finch and had Virginia Elaine Markham, who married Dr. Reid Clanton and had Virginia Elaine and Sarah Finch, and Princess Louise Markham, who married Ralph Matthew Dawson and had Donna, Rebecca Alice, Louis Markham, Carol Lynn and John Matthew.

III. Marilah Francis Coleman, born 18 December 1828, Bibb County, Alabama, died 20 October 1901, Jackson Parish, Louisiana; married William Murphy and had Mary Francis Murphy, 1858, Louisiana, and M.A. Murphy (daughter), 1867, Jackson Parish, Louisiana.

IV. John Washington Coleman, born 9 September 1830, Bibb County, Alabama; died 6 October 1830, Bibb County, Alabama.

V. Dr. Thomas Marian Coleman, born 19 November 1831, Bibb County, Alabama; died 29 September 1879, Gregg County, Texas; married Alice Lenora E. Johnson and they had (1) Nora C. Coleman, born 1873, Gregg County, Texas, died 1921, Texas, married Elbert C. Taylor 29 July 1892, Gregg County, Texas; (2) Annie, 1876-12 July 1881, Gregg County, Texas; and (3) Tommie M. "Birdie," born 1889,

died 1961, married William Dancy Sessums 10 May 1907, Gregg County, Texas.

VI. Mary Winifred Coleman, born 17 October 1833, Bibb County, Texas; died 18 August 1857, Vernon, Jackson Parish, Louisiana.

VII. Sarah Adaline Coleman, born 22 February 1837, Bibb County, Alabama; died 1883, married Samuel Horn, born 1835, Alabama, and had the following children: Robert T. Sanford, died 3 May 1862; (all the following born in Jackson Parish, Louisiana) Joseph A., 1862; Emma E., 1864; William W., 1866; E.R. (son), 1870; Lucy A., 1873; Alice, 1875; Mittie A.,1877; and Mattie J., 1879.

VIII. Georgia Ann Harrison Coleman, born 10 October 1839, Bibb County, Alabama; died 26 June 1913, Beaumont, Orange County, Texas; married first John Graves and had Sidney Eugene,1867; Lillian; Mattie; Maggie V.,1869; and Lela, all born in Louisiana; Lu, 1873, and John T., 1879, Texas; married second on 8 September 1887, Gregg County, Texas, Andrew J. Causey.

– Submitted by P.J. McLaughlin, Elgin, Texas

ISHAM JEFFERSON & MARY RAY COLEMAN: The Younger Children

The last five children of Isham Jefferson and Mary Ray Coleman's thirteen children follow:

IX. Martin Turner Coleman, CSA, born 18 February 1842, Talladega County, Alabama, died Texas, c. 1880; married c. 1868, Vernon, Jackson Parish, Louisiana, Louisa Elizabeth Ledford, born 21 March 1851, Alabama, died 5 November 1923, Antioch Community, Lincoln Parish, Louisiana and had (1) William Edgar Coleman, Sr., born 14 February 1869, Vernon, Jackson Parish, Louisiana, married Mrs. Beatrice Southern Parker and they had William Edgar, Louisa Marie and Thomas Alton; and (2) Mena Ethel Estella Coleman, born 19 October 1871, Vernon, Jackson Parish, Louisiana, died 4 July 1952, Shreveport, Caddo Parish, Louisiana, married George McLaughlin, born 15 January 1856, Bienville Parish, Louisiana; died 22 August 1903, Antioch Community, Lincoln Parish, Louisiana; they had six children: (a) Dora married John Roy Callaway and had George William and Betty Virginia; (b) Charles Fredrick married Jennie Kane; (c) George Lavell married Mrs. Sallie Edmiston Williamson; (d) James, Sr. married Elizabeth Howard James and had (1) Mary Elizabeth, who married and divorced John David Aikman and had Dora Ann Aikman, 1962-1980; and (2) James, Jr. married Gwenda Darlene Warrick and had James Patrick, who married Kelly Jean Wyatt and had Bailey Jean and Boone James, and Timothy David, who married Valerie Ann Astorudd and had Charles Ronan; (e) Milton Cannon married Mary Lee Jones; and (f) Willy Coleman, Sr. married Wilma Harris and had Willy Coleman, Jr., who married Dorothy Pearl McAllister and had Mark Coleman, Scott, Melissa Michell and David McLaughlin.

X. Horatio Jefferson Coleman, born 12 May 1844, Talladega County, Alabama; died 3 April 1862, Vernon, Jackson Parish, Louisiana.

XI. Louisiana Coleman, born 26 June 1846, Talladega County, Alabama; died 27 January 1896, Winn Parish, Louisiana; married 1869, Newton Hagler, born 16 October 1845, Ouachita Parish, Louisiana, died 18 July 1925, Jackson Parish, Louisiana; and had the following children, all born in Louisiana: (a) Rosalee, 1873; (b) Robert, 1874; (c) Francis Marion, 1876 (d) David G., 1878; and (e) Mary J., 1879.

XII. Louisa Alabama Coleman, born 3 March 1849, Vernon, Jackson Parish, Louisiana; died 16 April 1862, Vernon, Jackson Parish, Louisiana.

XIII. Alice Ray Coleman, born 27 September 1851, Vernon, Jackson Parish, Louisiana; died 7 May 1924, Grayson County, Texas, married 2 May 1880, Gregg County, Texas, James Bumpus, born September 1843, Texas; moved to Grayson County, Texas, and had Ethel May, 1881, and Nettie, December 1883.

– Submitted by Boone James McLaughlin, Montgomery, Texas

MARTIN TURNER COLEMAN

After Martin Turner Coleman and his father, Isham Jefferson Coleman, left for Texas, nothing was heard from them. One day in the spring of 1878, Ethel, 6 years old, and Willy, 9 years old, were playing in the front yard at the Leford home when a man rode up on a big horse. Strangers were rare. The man looked so different from their grandfather and uncles, who were all nearly seven feet tall, fair complexioned, with red or ginger hair. The stranger was short, dark and when he knocked at the door, his speech sounded funny – he was tongue-tied. The children heard him ask to speak with Lu, their mother, and saw him invited into the house.

Later, the stranger came out and walked over to Willy and said, "Willy, would you like a ride on my horse." Of course, Willy said yes and he was ridden around the yard. The stranger rode away. Ethel learned later that the stranger was her father, Martin Turner Coleman. He had come to ask Lu to come to Texas with him. He planned to travel with other Coleman and Ray family members who had formed a wagon train to travel to North Texas. Martin would drive Mrs. Graves' wagon. Lu refused to go with him.

Years passed with no word from Martin. The Rev. Leford died, his estate was divided, and Lu and her children needed a home. Lu's brothers, Franklin, Fuller and Alfred Ledford, all Baptist ministers, traveled to Marshall, Longview and into Red River County for news of Martin. The Coleman cousins who lived in Marshall sent them on to Longview. There, the Leford brothers were told that Martin, while driving his sister's wagon across a river, had been shot and killed. Whether the shooting was accidental or deliberate could not be determined. The brothers returned to Vernon satisfied that Lu was a widow. She married George Lawrence Wilder, a farmer and lay Baptist minister, as his second wife.

– Submitted by Bailey Jean McLaughlin, Montgomery, Texas

ELEANOR ADAM COLQUITT

Eleanor was born October 27, 1927, in Philadelphia, Pennsylvania. She was the only child of John Frederick Adam and Edna Eleanor Stricker Adam. At the age of five months Eleanor came to Dallas, Texas, with her mother, her father having been transferred to Texas by his employer, The John B. Stetson Hat Co. While en route to Dallas, she had been christened by a Lutheran minister.

Eleanor Colquitt

In Dallas, Eleanor grew up. She skated, rode her bicycle, learned to swim, went to the picture show with her mother, played with her friends and had a pleasant childhood. She attended the Highland Park public schools, graduating from high school in 1944, following which she enrolled at Southern Methodist University in Dallas and was awarded a B.S. degree in 1947. Her academic honors included being inducted into Alpha Theta Pi, the fore-runner of Phi Beta Kappa honorary scholastic fraternity, and selection into Mortar Board. Socially she was an active and enthusiastic member of Kappa Alpha Theta sorority. Eleanor made many friends at SMU, many of whom she has remained more than casually in contact with.

After graduation from SMU, she trained in medical technology at the UTMB in Galveston, Texas, and worked in this field until her marriage. On June 10, 1950, Eleanor married Dr. Landon A. Colquitt, a recent graduate in medicine from the UTMB. During the first decade of marriage, the trail of her husband's training and practice led her to Oceanside, California, then to McKinney, Odessa, Galveston and Houston, in Texas. Eleanor's first child was born in Oceanside, California, (a daughter, Carol, 1951) and two sons were born in Odessa (Landon, 1953, and John, 1955). In addition to being a caring and attentive wife and mother, she found time to begin a life time interest and participation in community activities affiliating with the Junior Service League, in Odessa.

Eleanor has lived in Longview, Gregg County, Texas, since 1959 when her husband started his medical practice in Longview. In addition to cheerfully continuing those duties attendant to being wife, mother and a household manager, she rapidly began to be involved in a wide variety of church, school and community activities and organizations. She was a

Camp Fire Girl leader from 1960 until her daughter advanced out of that age group; she taught a Sunday School class of intermediate boys at the First Methodist Church; and, she spent hours in the bleachers at ther sons' Little League Baseball games.

In 1962, her widowed mother moved to Longview and Eleanor cheerfully provided to her mother the necessary care and loving support that she needed until her death in 1979.

Eleanor was president of The Junior Service League in 1965-1966, and has been treasurer of the Sustainers of the JSL for 35 years. She has served on the administrative board of the First Methodist Church, been president of her Sunday School class six years, and for more than 30 years was chairlady of the sacristy committee, an assignment she enjoyed.

In 1968, at the request of Herbert Teat, Eleanor recruited the steering committee which evolved into the board of the Longview Symphony. With the help of her "recruits," she is responsible for Longview having a symphony orchestra. Eleanor retains membership in and is a regular attendant and participant in the 100-plus-year-old literary Shakespeare Club, the Magnolia Garden Club and the Heritage Bible Club. Now her greatest pleasure is playing bridge twice a month; one of her bridge clubs is in its 40-plus year of existence. This and any other pleasure she might gain is well deserved for half a century's labor being a tolerant wife, super-Mom and active participant in church and community activities – A Class Person, by any gauge or yardstick!

– Submitted by L.A. Colquitt

COONES: Music, Music, Music

Dorothy Hudgins Coones feels lucky to have been the only child born to Albert and Lottie Baker Hudgins on a farm six miles north of Nacogdoches, Texas. Lottie Baker's family was very musical, and Dorothy's uncle taught singing schools and she went with him. Dorothy does not remember when she could not read and sing gospel songs. When adults complained it was too hard to sing by shaped notes, her uncle would say "little girl, stand up and sing this." She was only five years old. The next year she started school at Central Heights. Miss Beach, her teacher, also played the piano, and Dorothy

Dorothy Hudgins Coones

took lessons from her and also passed first and second grades that year. After Miss Beach moved, her mother had her practice thirty minutes everyday. Finally, Pauline Pate came to Nacogdoches, and Dorothy took lessons for two years. When she was twelve, she was playing for Bonita Methodist Church. Later she transferred to Stephen F. Austin College's Demonstration High School so she could get choir and band music. College teachers taught all the classes. This was during World War II and the band director put all capable players from the high school in his college band. Dorothy played in the band for seven years and played the piano in the college swing band for four years. She finished with a B.A. degree in choral music and band at the age of 19 years old.

She started teaching music at South Ward Elementary School in Longview in 1946. Dorothy soon had a select choir of 30 fifth and sixth grade students. Madlyn Brannon was president of this group. Mrs. Clift Brannon found places, like the Lion's Club, where the group could sing. They sang successfully all over Longview. After Dorothy married and had four wonderful children, the Pine Tree principal called her to teach high school and junior high choirs. During that time, Dorothy wrote the words to Pine Tree's "Pirate Fight Song" in 1960. She had quartets with football men in the choir and girls' trios. Dorothy enjoyed doing programs for the PTA and showing off her groups. She decided to retire with 35 years of teaching in 1986, after having years of double classes with 680 students a day.

She played about 60 years for churches and nursing homes as well as 25 years for a Mellotone quartet with soloist Bud Fowler. Dorothy played many years with banjo player, Richard McDaniels, and 25 years with "Minnie Pearl and the Grinder Switch Belles." She has been the pianist for Central Baptist, Calvary Baptist, Macedonia Baptist and Greggton First Baptist Churches. Woodland Hills called her for help and Dorothy felt God put her there to play for them and it's been eleven years now. She also sings with the First Baptist "Saints Alive Choir," plays for Kilgore College and for Buckner's drama groups, and the "Gospel Chords" group in Gladewater. That is why this is titled "Music, Music, Music."

– Submitted by Dorothy Coones

GLADYS EDITH COUPLAND

Gladys Edith Coupland was born 30 September 1899, in Dodge, Texas, but spent her "growing up" years in Longview. Her parents, Thomas Dodson "T.D." Coupland and Martha White Sloan Coupland, nicknamed her "Gladden" for her lively, cheerful personality and positive outlook on life – qualities that stayed with her all her life.

Gladys received her education in the Longview schools, graduating from Longview High School with the Class of 1917 as salutatorian of that class. She attended Texas Women's College in Ft. Worth and the College of Industrial Arts (now Texas Women's University) in

Denton. When not pursuing studies at college, Gladys worked as a telegraph operator. It was in this way that she met her future husband, James Douglas Pitcock, of Tulsa, Oklahoma, who was also a telegraph operator at the time.

James Douglas "Doug" Pitcock and Gladys Coupland were married 7 May 1920, in Longview. They established a home in Tulsa, where Mr. Pitcock was a stockbroker for many years. Their children were Martha, born 23 September 1921 (married Virgil Roshto); Patricia, born 24 June 1925 (married Elmo Weyel); and James Douglas, Jr., born 21 April 1928 (married Eleanor Hall). Gladys and Doug moved their family to Houston about 1943, and except for a few years spent in Tyler, that remained their home until Gladys's death.

Gladys was an accomplished pianist. She taught piano to pupils in her home for more than sixty years and frequently played accompaniment for ballet productions. Always creative and artistic, she began taking art lessons at a college while living in Tyler, and in her fifties developed a passion for painting. Her oil paintings of flowers and landscapes were shown in several art shows in Houston, and she gave many works of art to her family and friends.

Gladys Edith Coupland, age 19, about 1918.

Gladys was proud to be able to trace her family roots in America back to 1635, to the earliest settlers of Newbury, Massachusetts, which was part of the Massachusetts Bay Colony, and also to the early days of Texas. Related to her interests in the arts and history, she was active in many organizations: Daughters of the Texas Republic, United Daughters of the Confederacy, Colonial Dames, Daughters of the American Revolution and various music and arts associations.

Gladys kept in contact with many childhood friends from Longview, and in 1967 attended the fifty-year reunion of the Longview Class of 1917. Gladys Edith Coupland died 5 January 1980, in Houston. Doug Pitcock died 11 July 1989, in Richardson, Texas.

– Submitted by Martha Pitcock Roshto (daughter)

LAURA HELEN COUPLAND

Laura Helen Coupland, the oldest child of T.D. Coupland and Martha White Sloan Coupland, was born 3 October l895, in New

Laura Coupland, age 16, about 1909.

Waverly, Texas. She grew up and attended schools in Longview, where her father owned a dry goods store. Laura graduated from Texas Women's College in Ft. Worth.

Laura, or " Aunt Lolly" as she was called by her nieces and nephews, never married, but led a full and active life as a teacher, missionary, musician, author and world traveler. She taught English and music in the public schools for many years, and wrote a simplified version of the classic *Moby Dick* that was published and used in elementary schools.

During the 1930s, Laura Coupland was a missionary (for the Baptist Church) and went to China to be a teacher in a girl's school. She was there during a civil war and had to protect her young students from danger during that time. When she returned from China, Laura traveled and spoke to various Baptist congregations in East Texas to solicit support in bringing one of her promising young Chinese students to the United States to live and receive a college education.

After a long and successful career teaching music, Laura Coupland spent her later years in Ft. Worth, where she passed away in 1976.
– Submitted by Shannon Teague (great grandniece)

THOMAS DODSON COUPLAND

Thomas Dodson (T.D.) Coupland was a Longview businessman and community leader in the early 1900s. The Coupland family planted their roots in East Texas in 1845 when Texas was a Republic, the same year it was admitted to the Union.

T.D. Coupland's grandfather, Andrew Jackson Coupland, came to Texas with some of his brothers from Alabama in 1845. T.D.'s father, Andrew Adams Coupland, was eight years old at the time. A.J. Coupland built a large log home and farmed 300 acres south of Rusk. He practiced law and was a Presbyterian minister. He was judge of Cherokee County for many years, at a time when that covered most of East Texas. His son, Andrew Adams Coupland, served in the Civil War in the 7th Regiment Texas Infantry.

Thomas Dodson Coupland was born 20 December 1872, on a farm in Cherokee County to Andrew Adams Coupland and Sarah Battle Carter Coupland. In his early childhood, the

Thomas Dodson Coupland (second from left) in front of T.D. Coupland Drygoods store, about 1909.

family moved to Smith County, near Troup, and he attended public schools there. T.D. wrote later in his life that he had often been asked about his alma mater, and his reply was "I hold no certificate written upon the perishable skin of a sheep, but only that carved upon the indestructible tablet of experience." Notwithstanding this, he became a successful businessman and community leader in Longview, and later in Winters, Texas.

Thomas Dodson married Martha White Sloan (born 25 September 1873 in Lyons, Iowa) on 20 December 1894, in Livingston, Texas. Before moving to Longview, they lived in New Waverly and Dodge, where T.D. was telegrapher and depot agent for the railroad. Their children were Laura, born 3 October 1895; Harold, born 5 March 1897; Philip, born 30 May 1898; Gladys, born 30 September, 1899; and Margaret, born 13 March 1901. All five children graduated from Longview High School.

From articles in *The Times-Clarion*, Longview's newspaper, it appears that the family moved to Longview between 1900 and 1906. T.D. was manager of Mistrot Brothers department store, eventually purchasing the store in 1907. "T.D. Coupland's" was one of the two major mercantile establishments in Longview for many years.

He was a member of the City Council for eight years, President of the Chamber of Commerce and served as President of the Board of Education for twelve years.

After his store burned down in Longview, T.D. relocated to Winters, in central Texas, in 1923, where he operated a variety store. In Winters he was Postmaster from 1931 to 1935, Secretary of the Board of Community Development and President of the Lions Club.

Thomas Dodson Coupland died 29 December 1937. Martha died 30 November 1935. Laura Coupland became a teacher, missionary to China and musician; Harold had a career in the Navy; Philip served in the Navy in World

War I and was a pilot in World War II; Gladys was a musician and an artist; Margaret raised her family in North Carolina. Gladys Coupland Pitcock attended the 50th reunion of the Class of 1917 of Longview High School in 1967.
– Submitted by Cindy Brasier (great granddaughter)

ROBERT BARTOW COUSINS

Robert Bartow Cousins, son of Isaac William and Mary Elizabeth (Bennet) Cousins, was born in Fayetteville, Georgia, on 21 July 1861. Cousins decided early in life to be a teacher.

He studied at the University of Georgia and earned a B.A. degree in 1882. He read law and passed the bar exam in Atlanta, but he continued to teach. He moved to Texas and taught Latin and Greek at the high school in Longview. He married Dora M. Kelly on 5 September 1885, in Longview. Dora and Robert had six children. He moved to Mineola where he was school superintendent for two years, and then to Mexia for sixteen years. In 1897-1898, he was president of the Texas State Teachers Association.

In 1904, Cousins was elected state superintendent of public instruction; under his leadership, between 1905 and 1910, several important educational reforms were introduced, including state accreditation, public school taxes and the upgrading of standards for teachers. In 1910, he became president of West Texas State Normal College (now West Texas State University) at Canyon, which he had helped establish. He and Joseph A. Hill coauthored a textbook, *American History for Schools* (1913), which was adopted by public schools in several southern states.

After the death of Cousins's youngest son at the age of thirteen, Cousins instituted the Gregg Cousins Loan Fund at West Texas State in the memory of his son. In the summer of 1918, he returned to Longview to go into business. The first women's dormitory at the college was built in 1920 and named in Cousins's honor.

He stay in Longview until 1921, when he became superintendent of the Houston public schools. In 1924, he accepted the presidency of the new South Texas State Teachers College (now Texas A&M University at Kingsville). Cousins remained in Kingville until he died on 3 March 1932. He was buried in Kingsville.

CRADDOCK

Van and Dorothy Craddock moved to Gregg County in 1946, but members of the Craddock family have called East Texas home since 1860.

A World War II veteran of the Army Air Corps (serving from 1942-46), Van Dorn Craddock Sr. and his wife, the former Dorothy Jane Latimer (married 24 February 1943), originally were from Red River County. In 1946, they moved to Gladewater where he was employed by Hall Lumber Company. On 1 July 1948, their son, Van Jr., was born in Gladewater's Hancock General Hospital.

In 1954, the Craddocks moved to Longview where Van Sr. became manager and sales representative for Builders Supply Company and later Standard Supply Company. The Craddocks joined First Presbyterian Church, and Van Sr. coached for many years in the Longview Boys Baseball Association. He died on 7 January 1988, at age 70. Dorothy remains active in her church and is a volunteer for the Gregg County Historical Museum.

Dorothy and Van Craddock, Sr., May 1980

The Craddocks' son, Van Jr., is a 1966 graduate of Longview High School. He married Bettye Herrington of Lufkin on 18 December 1970. Both are graduates of Stephen F. Austin State University. Van Jr. served in the United States Army in Vietnam in 1971-72, and after discharge from the military the Craddocks returned to Longview.

Van Jr., a long-time columnist for the *Longview News-Journal*, is director of communications at Longview's First United Methodist Church. He published a collection of his LNJ columns in a book titled *I Would've Been a Lumberjack but I Couldn't Hack It.*

Bettye is journalism instructor at Kilgore College. She is a 1998 recipient of the Minnie Stephens Piper Professor award for outstanding academic achievement. She is author of *The Golden Years:*

Chris Craddock, Cathy and Matt Tenner, Bettye and Van Craddock, Jr., 20 July 2002.

The First Half Century of Stephen F. Austin State University. It was her master's thesis and the first published history of SFA. The Craddocks are members of First Methodist.

Van and Bettye raised two children, Van Christopher (Chris) Craddock, born 27 September 1976, and Catherine Anne (Cathy) Craddock, born 6 July 1980, both at Good Shepherd Medical Center. Chris and Cathy graduated from LHS in 1995 and 1998, respectively.

Chris, a graduate of Kilgore College and the University of Texas at Tyler, is journalism teacher at Longview High School. Cathy, a graduate of Texas A&M University, married Matthew Richard (Matt) Tenner of Longview on 20 July 2002. She is an English teacher at J.J. Pearce High School in Richardson.

Originally from Wales, the first Craddock ancestors arrived in North Carolina by 1744. Head of that first household was Thomas Craddock Sr., who served in the North Carolina militia during the American Revolution. Several family members eventually relocated to Alabama, then to East Texas (Wood County) in 1860.

Craddock is from the old Welsh personal name Caradoc which means "amiable." The early Craddock coats of arms bore the motto 'Nee temere nee timide" (Neither rashly nor timidly").

– Submitted by Van and Bettye Craddock

RUSSELL & RAENELL CRAFT

Russell Craft (9 April 1939) was born in Lubbock Texas, to A.J. Craft (11 March 1909, Van Zandt County) and Mary Elizabeth (Russell) Craft Hiett (20 October 1912, Marshall, Texas). The Crafts lived in Longview from 1960 until 1986. Mary Craft married Ogie Heitt in 1965. On 26 January 1961, Russell married Raenell Carter (14 October 1939), daughter of Dr. Ray H. and Mary Nell (Young) Carter of Marshall. (See "Ray Helm & Mary Nell Carter.") Russell and Raenell lived in Austin and Jefferson before moving to Longview in 1964.

Russell Craft graduated from the University of Texas School of Pharmacy in 1962 and worked at Skaggs-Albertson's at South High and W. Whaley Streets. In December 1969, he entered partnership with Louis Morgan and Bob

Holbert, opening the Louis Morgan #4 Store in the new Chaparral Shopping Center at the corner of Judson Road and Johnson Streets. In 1975, Russell sold his interest in the store to Mike Holbert. Russell then managed the Pharmacy at the new Skaggs-Albertsons store at Loop 281 and McCann from 1976 until 1984, during which time he developed a full-time Consultant Pharmacist business serving twelve area nursing homes. In 1975, Russell Craft, Glenn Phillips and Lester Wooten became the founding Elders of Longview Christian Fellowship Church (LCF Church) at 2101 W. Marshall Avenue. The church purchased this property in July 1976. The land was originally part of the Rockwall family farm, and the original building had been erected as Youngblood's Chicken, then became Mickey Mantle's Country Cooking. Longview Christian Fellowhship School was founded in 1982 as a ministry of LCF Church. The name has since changed to Longview Christian School. With Grades K-12, it is the only school in the area accredited with the Association of Christian Schools International.

In 1984, Russell was ordained to the Gospel Ministry. In 1986, Russell and Raenell moved to Del Rio, Texas, and founded Del Rio Christian Fellowship Church (DRCF), which he pastored until returning to Longview in November 1994, as Associate Pastor of LCF Church. He became Senior Pastor of LCF Church in January 1996, and continues in that position to present. He has been a member of the Greggton Rotary Club, the Longview Ministerial Alliance, East Texas Pastors Association and Antioch-Oasis Ministers' Fellowship International.

Russell and Raenell Craft have four children: Kimberly Nell (born 10 November 1961, in Austin and a 1980 graduate of Longview High School), Russell Carter Craft (born 21 June 1963, in Marshall and a 1981 graduate of Longview High School), Leighann Elizabeth (born at Good Shepherd Hospital 17 April 1967, and a 1985 graduate of Longview Christian Fellowship High School) and Carol Claire (born at Good Shepherd Hospital 31 July 1968, and a 1986 graduate of Longview Christian Fellowship High School). As of 2003, the Russell Crafts are blessed with 18 grandchildren. Leighann Craft remained in Longview and married D. Paul Holloway on 11-28-1987. (See "D.T. Holloway.")

– Submitted by Leighann Craft Holloway

GLYN SHEPPARD CRANE & JUNE NELWYN KELLY

Glyn Sheppard Crane (born 24 August 1934, Little Rock, Arkansas) and June Nelwyn Kelly (born 30 August 1936, Shreveport, Louisiana) married 23 December 1955. With their son, Glyn Sheppard Crane, Jr. (born 23 July 1957, Shreveport, Louisiana), they moved to Longview in May 1959.

Glyn's parents are Ernest James Crane (born 24 October 1898, Hot Springs, Arkansas) and Leona Beatrice Goad (born 19 April 1901, Bradford, Arkansas). They were married 7 May 1920. June's parents, Buford Troy Kelly (born 10 February 1902, Sikes, Louisiana) and Cornie Louana Holmes (born 8 August 1899, Montgomery, Louisiana) of Shreveport and Bossier City, Louisiana, were married 21 May 1921.

A second son, Curtis Wayne Crane, was born 27 July 1959. A third son, Kelly, was born in 1964 in Longview. Glyn, Jr., Curtis and Kelly attended LISD schools. Glyn, Jr. graduated from Longview High 1975, Curtis 1977 and Kelly 1982. Glyn graduated from Kilgore College with an AA in Corrosion Technology and attended the University of Arkansas; Curtis graduated from University of Texas at Tyler with a BA in Accounting and earned his CPA; and Kelly graduated from University of North Texas in August 1987, with a BA in Chemistry & Biology and graduated in 1991 with an MA in Accounting/Finance.

Curtis married Lucretia Lynn Langston (born 27 May 1958, Palestine, Texas) 24 August 1979, in Longview, Texas. They have two sons, Austen Barrow Crane (born 4 March 1987, Longview, Texas) and Corbin Hodges Crane (born 30 May 1991, Longview, Texas). Lucretia Lynn Langston graduated from the University of Texas, Austin with a BA in Education in 1978.

Kelly married Janice Ellen Little (born 7 May 1967, Jefferson, Alabama) on 15 June 1997. Kelly and Janice have two children, Kathleen June Crane (born 15 October 1997, Shreveport, Louisiana) and Jackson Kelly Crane (born 28 June 1999, Shreveport, Louisiana). Janice Ellen Little graduated from Louisiana State University with a BA in Human Resource Management in 1991.

The Cranes are members and active in the First United Methodist Church of Longview. Glyn serves as trustee of the Sabine MHMR Board and is on the State of Texas Council. When first coming to Longview, Glyn was with Rader Funeral Home for a short time; the Longview Police Department, where he received many honors; and then went to work for Gregg County as Juvenile and Probation Officer. He worked for Tandy Corporation in the printing division, and later started his own company, Troy Business Forms.

June has been in the insurance industry since 1960, beginning as a Claims Secretary and working up to being a partner in D & H Insurance Agency. She was a member of the Independent Insurance Agents of Longview, the East Texas Insurance Association and the Federation of Insurance Women of Texas. She was the first woman elected officer of the Independent Insurance Agents of Longview; served in all offices for the local East Texas Insurance Association; and served on the state level for the Federation of Insurance Women of Texas.

– Submitted by June Crane

RAYMOND MARSHALL CROW

Raymond Crow, long-time resident of Longview, was born 16 September 1905, in Commerce, Hunt County, Texas, the son of Wroland Green and Sarah Annie Miller Crow. Raymond was the second of 12 children, and spent much of his childhood picking cotton on the blackland farms of Hunt County. W.G. Crow was a native of Dickson County, Tennessee; Sarah Annie Miller was born in Little River County, Arkansas. They moved their family from Commerce to Pirtle, Rusk County, in 1926. Raymond married Ivy Myrtle Moore of Pirtle in Longview on 30 September 1928. They were the parents of two sons, both born in Pirtle.

Raymond M. Crow, 1965

Raymond Crow, Jr., was born 4 July 1929. He died 29 August 1941, of diphtheria, in Longview.

Bobby Joe Crow was born 20 July 1935. After graduation from Longview High School, he was a career member of the U.S. Air Force.

Raymond, like his father and grandfather, was a carpenter and building contractor, and he moved his family to Longview in the late 1930s to take advantage of the growth brought about by the oil boom. In his latter years he concentrated on cabinet and finish work. He loved to fish and squirrel hunt in the Sabine River bottoms. He and Myrtle were active members of Mobberly Baptist Church in Longview, and she worked for many years at the downtown Perry Bros. variety store. Raymond died of a sudden heart attack while raking leaves on 6 December 1974. Myrtle arrived home from work and found him, still holding his lawn rake, seated on the back porch of their home. Myrtle moved to the Whaley Street retirement apartments after Raymond's death, and later moved to Illinois, to be near her son. She died in Fisher, Illinois, on 3 September 1992.

Bobby was married to (1) Martha Elizabeth White of Longview. They had two sons, Raymond Robert, who died shortly after birth, and Joe David Crow. (2) Marilyn Kilgore of Waco. They had one son, Michael Ray Crow. (3) Naomi Binnion of Champaign, Illinois.

Bobby died on 8 August 2000, in Fisher, Illinois. Like Raymond, he died of a sudden heart attack, and was found by Naomi when she arrived home from work. He had been very active in AMVets following his retirement from the military, having served in Spain, France, Vietnam and Thailand during his career. He served as Post Commander and Illinois State Commander of AMVets, where he was affectionately known as "Old Crow".

Raymond, Myrtle, Raymond Jr. and Raymond Robert Crow are buried at Pirtle Baptist Cemetery in Rusk County, Texas, beside Raymond's parents. Bobby is buried at Willowbrook Cemetery in Fisher, Illinois.

– Submitted by Ken Bickley,
Mineral Wells, Texas

CROWLEY-WATKINS

Robert Lee Crowley (born 24 August 1881, in Sunset, Montague County, Texas) and Cordelia Belle Watkins (born 6 March 1887, in Rosebud, Falls County, Texas) were married 18 October 1904, in Weatherford, Parker County, Texas.

Robert Lee Crowley and Cordelia Belle Watkins, Fiftieth Wedding Anniversary, 18 October 1954.

James Joseph Crowley and Martha Jane McKinney, parents of Robert, came from Murray, Kentucky, where they had a tobacco plantation. The children worked hard stripping leaves when they were young. During the Civil War [Joseph fought in the war.] the home was burned by the Union Army and many valuables were taken. The family was forced to relocate. They left Kentucky in 1880, and traveled to Texas by covered wagons and oxen. After a long cold trip, they settled in Sunset near Bowie and Jacksboro.

James Joseph Crowley's grandfather, Joseph, and three children, Joe, Elizabeth and Tom (who received a good education and became a lawyer in Oklahoma), sailed from Liverpool, England. Joseph's grandfather, William Crowley, was a needle maker in England and the family still has some of the needles in frames that are many years old.

Cordelia's parents, Monroe (Roe) Watkins (born 1840) and Nancy Jane Vaught Isbell (born 1845 in Alabama), married in 1860. Monroe fought in the Civil War, was captured by the North and was forced to fight for them before returning home. When he returned he and many other strong Texans fought the remaining Indians between Bexar and Bosque County. The incident is written about in Texas history books.

When he died he was almost one hundred years old. He is buried in Kopperel, Bosque County, Texas. The Crowleys had three children living in Longview. In 1957, they sold the farm in Covington, Texas, and moved to Gregg County. They started visiting here in 1946. They enjoyed the pines, neighbors and joined the Mobberly Church of Christ. They had ten children: E. Rufford, born 8 August 1908; Ardie, born 29 March 1911; Carl, born 12 April 1914; Robert, born 23 September 1917; Kathleen Brinkley, born 23 May 1920; Teen Sanders, born 16 July 1923; Frances Brogdon, born 18 July 1925; Evelyn Morton, born 19 June 1927; Dorothy Ruthven, born 17 April 1930; Wanda Bryant, born 15 May 1933. Only the last three are living. They had 33 grandchildren and 49 great grandchildren.

On 18 October 1967, the Crowleys spent their sixty-third wedding anniversary in Longview. Their request was to remain in Longview their final years. They are buried in Grace Hill Cemetery. Robert died on 5 March 1972, at age 90, and Cordelia died on 2 May 1968, at age 82.

Robert had one brother, Jack, sisters Molly Alsup, (Temple, Texas), Ruth Blodgett, (Childress, Texas) and Jennie Landtroop, (Post, Texas).

Robert always said, "I've lived beyond my days, seeing so much history, such as traveling in covered wagons and watching man land on the moon, on TV."

– Submitted by Dorothy Crowley Ruthven

CODY BRYANT CULPEPPER

First son of Elbert Culpepper, Cody Bryant was married to Maud Cabbiness who was a long-time employee of Perkins Department Store. Culpepper apparently began his young photographic career going from house to house telling people that they were getting ready to take pictures of their homes. Of course, this was the way to get everyone out to the porch to have their pictures taken! He later became a photographer in his own right and was the "official" photographer of Longview for many years. When asked why he became a photographer, he said, "well, I could do two things, take pictures and plow, and I didn't have a place to plow."

Cody Bryant Culpepper with camera.

He was the only photographer in Longview from 1915-1931. Culpepper photographed Longview for over half a century. His photographs can be found throughout historical publications, in many homes and in the Gregg County Historical Museum. From an article written by Nancy Ruff in 1990, she states that in 1908 he quit his job as a photo-grapher's "caller" and "farmed for a year until purchasing the Otho Dickerson photographic studio, located in a ten on unpaved and muddy Methvin Street." After about a year at that location, Culpepper moved his studio to where the Hurwitz building in downtown Longview is located. In 1913, his studio burned, and he relocated is business to the site of the current Texas Commerce Bank.

Culpepper left Longview for a few years, taking his passion, photography, to Vernon and Sweetwater, but decided that his home was Longview. He eventually moved his studio to his home on north High Street where he retired in 1960.

The Culpeppers. (l.-r.) Back: Emma Katherine Clark Culpepper, Katherine Inez Culpepper, Thomas Elbert Culpepper, Thomas Jefferson Culpepper, David Bartow Culpepper, Ernest Melton, Leta Belle Culpepper Melton, John Melton, Maud Cabbiness Culpepper and Cody Bryant Culpepper. Front: Martha Blanch Culpepper, Elbert Bartow Culpepper, Martha Etta Enox Culpepper, Nelwyn Melton, Hazel Culpepper and Florine Culpepper.

ELBERT BARTOW CULPEPPER

Elbert Bartow Culpepper moved to Texas around 1870, just after his mother passed away in Eufala, Henry County, Alabama. It appears that he came with one of his Arnold cousins. The family believes that he first went to Kerens, Navarro County, and then to Longview. This is credible because he met his wife, Martha Etta Enox, in Kerens where she was raised by her aunt Dearmore. (Martha Etta's parents, Araminta Pink Allen and Squire J. Enox, both died in Decatur, Wise County, when she was young.) Elbert Bartow Culpepper and Martha Etta Enox were married at the home of N.B. Dearmore on 23 October 1884, in Upshur County, probably Coffeeville.

He purchased 65 acres some time after 1895, on Springhill Road near Route 281, where he raised cotton, sugar cane and watermelons. His grandchildren remember crossing the road to break open a watermelon "without" their grandfather's permission.

Both Elbert and Etta joined the Primitive ("hardshell") Baptist Church in 1898 at East Mountain. The church always had a large all-day dinner on the grounds that included preaching and singing. Sunday dinner at the Culpepper's always had a huge spread, including fried chicken. As there were only two chairs with long benches on both sides of the table, the ten grandchildren had to wait until the grown-ups had eaten and often the only chicken left were the wings.

Apparently, when the preacher came to visit there was always a glass of wine offered. Etta even had many biblical passages written on a piece of paper (found in the family Bible) about the "appropriateness" of wine.

A granddaughter has vivid memories of going into Longview in her Granddaddy's wagon and returning home with large hunks of cheese that he purchased at Evan's store. She would be given a small slice of cheese and a stick of candy. Martha Blanche Culpepper Roth remembers when her Granddaddy returned home that everyone would get some cheese. Etta spoiled the grandchildren by always having teacakes in a lard can on top of the piesafe when the grand kids arrived. Also, as kids will do, they would sneak into the loft where Elbert kept the raw peanuts. They would eat them until they made themselves sick! Of course, they were caught and received a "peach tree switching!"

Sleeping quarters were also in short supply. Six of them shared two feather beds. Inez Culpepper Ferkovich and her three siblings had to share one bed – two heads at one end and two heads at the other. The granddaughters remember their Granddaddy going down the hall playing his Jews harp at daybreak. They knew it was time to roll out when the music hit their ears. Grandma always made scratch biscuits, sausage and scrambled eggs for breakfast.

Later in the day, after supper, they would all sit on the front "gallery." Living fives miles northwest of Longview — out in the country — it was so quiet all they could hear were crickets and an occasional car. Martha Blanch Culpepper Roth remembers knowing about what time her father, Tom, would be arriving from Shreveport, and they would start looking for his car lights from far away. Thomas Elbert Culpepper remembers reading the newspaper at night by the light of the gas fires from all of the old wooden oil derricks that surrounded the house.

During the late 1920s, Elbert and Etta bought a "Dependable Dodge" car. Etta would shift while Elbert steered and drove! They even drove to Shreveport to visit their son Tom (Thomas Jefferson Culpepper) and his family.

Elbert and Etta were the parents of four very fine children: Cody Bryant (Longview's "official" photographer for several years), Thomas Jefferson, Leta Belle and David Bartow. All were born in Coffeeville. Elbert and Etta are buried at Elmira Chapel Cemetery.

– Submitted by Eileen Vela, New Mexico

THOMAS JEFFERSON CULPEPPER

The second son of Elbert Bartow Culpepper, Thomas Jefferson Culpepper, was married to Emma Katherine (Kate) Clark. Kate was the daughter of Stella Maud Wood Clark and Thomas Britton Clark. Kate and Tom were married in Longview on 7 January 1916. Tom was known for being a member of the "Culpepper Quartet," a group that was composed of his brothers and sister — David Bartow (Bart), Cody Bryant and Letta Belle. They were invited to sing at various social occasions in town.

Tom and cousin Roger Arnold had another way to earn money. They spent one summer performing in the Culpepper Circus. Tom also went

Elbert Bartow and Martha Etta Enox Culpepper

The Thomas Jefferson Culpepper family

The Culpepper Quartet

into the photography business and helped support his brother Cody until Tom moved to Shreveport and later to Houston. Tom and Kate had four children: Katherine Inez, Martha Blanche, Thomas Elbert and Joseph Franklin.

Tom's sister, Letta Belle, married John Ernest Melton of Longview. Letta Belle died in McLean, Virginia, at the advanced age of 99.

David Bartow Culpepper first married Willa Koehler, and later in life married Teruko I. Bart lived much of his adult life in Houston. He made his living at first in the furniture business, and later in the insurance industry.

– Submitted by Eileen Vela, New Mexico

ROBERT STOKES DANIEL, JR.

Robert Stokes "Rusty" Daniel, Jr. was born 9 August 1914, the second of six children born to Robert Stokes and Edith Darlene Watson Daniel in Kerens, Navarro County, Texas. Robert's great grandfather, Josiah Goodson "Squire" Daniel, had moved his family from Alabama in 1855, settling in Wadeville just east of Kerens. In 1881, stock in the family general store in Wadeville was sold and Squire Daniel's sons Robert Hiram and Theophilus Smith opened Daniel–Price & Company Dry Goods in Kerens, which remained in business operated by the brothers, their sons and grandsons until 1932. The name is still visible on the side of the first building on the west side of Colket in the downtown business district.

Mr. Kalman Wolens of New York had selected Kerens to establish one of the first locations of what was to become a chain of department stores throughout Texas. Robert had graduated from high school in 1932 and on June 19th of the following year, he and long-time friend John Logan and a company driver moved that K. Wolens store to Gladewater to take advantage of the growing commerce that accompanied the oil boom. Rusty remembered that the streets were knee deep in mud and little housing was available. While the driver returned to Corsicana to participate in Juneteenth activities, the two young men set about arranging stock for business the next day. Because the building doors had no locks, they spent the first night in the store located in the middle of the 100 block

of West Commerce, property belonging to B.F. Phillips, Sr. The following morning Mrs. Phillips offered the boys accommodations in the upstairs of the Phillip's home at the southeast corner of U.S. Highways 80 and 271.

For the next few years Robert worked in every K. Wolens store in East Texas; he would fill in for managers on sick leave or vacation. During this time he became a charter member of Gladewater Jaycees and the Pineland Country Club. In 1940, he became the manager of the store in Henderson, Texas, and there met Elizabeth Malone who taught Home Economics at Henderson High School.

Elizabeth had been raised in Frisco, Collin County, Texas, the daughter of Francis David and Jessie Robertson Malone. The family of A.A. and Mariah Malone with infants Francis and Viola and Mariah's father, Francis W. Polser, arrived in Texas in 1885. The family traveled by train and wagon from Mosheim, Green County, Tennessee, settling in Walnut Grove, southwest of McKinney and east of Frisco. The Malones later acquired land in nearby Lebanon and later a farm in eastern Denton County, two and a half miles west of the original Frisco town site. Jessie's ancestor, Peter Teel, a colonist during the Republic of Texas, had settled in the Teel Settlement in Eastern Denton County.

Education was always to play an important role in Elizabeth's life – during the Depression will power and sheer determination had enabled each of the five Malone children to attend and graduate from North Texas State Teachers College (now the University of North Texas).

Robert and Elizabeth were married in her family home on 4 August 1941. They lived as newlyweds in Athens; Robert had been transferred to the K. Wolens store there, and Elizabeth taught Home Economics at Athens High School.

Robert entered the Army Air Force in May 1943, serving at the Post Exchange with the 5th Ferrying Group at Love Field, Dallas, Texas, and later at Bryan Field, Bryan, Texas. He received his discharge at Ellington Field, Houston, Texas, in October 1945.

Rusty rejoined the K. Wolens Company and was offered the store manager in Gladewater. Remembering the days that he had spent there during the boom, he was hesitant to accept the position feeling the town "too rough" to bring up a family. He reluctantly accepted the position, thinking he would quickly request a transfer. In December 1945, the family moved into an apartment on Virginia Drive which occupied the second floor of property owned by R.M. Wood. The Company had agreed to move the family's personal belongings, but because merchandise was needed for the store, space on company trucks was filled with goods to be sold and personal items waited in storage in the warehouses in Corsicana until the store could be fully restocked. Camp Fannin was still active with men being brought in to be discharged; it seemed that almost anything offered would sell, so the Daniel family

spent little time in their mostly unfurnished apartment. Hours were passed at the store and most meals were eaten out, either at the St. Clair Hotel on Pacific, the Buckhorn on Highway 80, the Green Hut or the Corral at the northwest corner of Highway 271 and Quitman Highway. K. Wolens frequently stayed open until midnight and the streets were always full of people and automobiles. Rusty was active in various civic and community affairs: he was a member of the Lion's Club and served as First Vice President of the Chamber of Commerce while future Texas Secretary of State and Attorney General John Ben Shepperd was President. Elizabeth was a member of the Three Arts Club and the family affiliated with the First Methodist Church.

Robert and Elizabeth Daniel, June 1991

Robert was transferred to Marshall in 1950. Robert Stokes III was born 15 November 1950, at Kahn Memorial Hospital in Marshall. Sondra had been born 3 December 1943, in McKinney while Rusty was in the service. Theresa had been born 14 January 1947, in Gladewater. After Rusty transferred to Cleburne, from September 1951, until January 1952, the family returned to Gladewater to establish their own business on 1 February 1952. They chose to return because of the excellent schools and friendly people of the church and community. The Daniels purchased the Peggy Ann Shop located in the old Everett Building at 109 East Pacific which had been owned and operated by sisters-in-law Stella Dickson and Mrs. E.L. Chevalier.

Deborah, their fourth child, was born two weeks later on 16 February 1952. Four years later Robert and Elizabeth changed the name of the business to *daniel's*. In June 1968, *daniel's* relocated to the newly remodeled building at 107 East Pacific, which had formerly housed Stuckey-Kincaid Department Store.

On returning to Gladewater, Rusty became a Rotarian and was a Paul Harris Fellow with 100% attendance for 39 years. He was chairman of the Camp Fire Association, Committeeman of Scouting, Webelo Sponsor of Cub Scouting, Red Cross Chairman and Sunday School Superintendent for a number of years. Elizabeth was active in the reorganization of the Gladewater Parent-

Teacher Association while the children were in school. She was the second president of the PTA City Council and served as President and held other offices of Three Arts Club and has been a member of Beta Sigma Phi Sorority since 1961. She was First Vice President of Key District Texas Federation of Women's Club for two years and is a member of R.B. Levy Chapter UDC, Daughters of the American Revolution, National Society Colonial Dames XVII Century, Daughters of American Colonists, Daughters of Republic of Texas, Colonial Order of the Crown, Plantagenet Society, Sovereign Colonial Society, Americans of Royal Descent and First Families of Texas.

The children finished Gladewater schools; all were members of the National Honor Society. Sondra was a member of the first story hour at the Gladewater Public Library and attended the first Kindergarten class offered by Gladewater Schools, 1949-50. Sondra, Theresa and Deborah were active in Camp Fire Girls and the high school tennis program; Sondra and Deborah competed in the UIL State Meet in Austin.

Robert III participated in school sports and Boy Scouts of America, attaining the Eagle rank. All four of the children graduated from the University of Texas in Austin. Sondra has made her home in Gladewater and works with her mother at daniel's serving as buyer and manager. Theresa married Robert F. McClure of Beaumont; they currently reside in Conroe. Their daughter Allison, a graduate of the University of Texas, married West Point graduate Captain Will C. Wright on March 1, 2003. Theresa and Robert's son Scott is currently a student at Baylor University. Robert III received a degree in Architecture from Texas and established his practice in San Diego in 1991. Deborah married Kenneth B. Meyer and resides in Houston. Their son Daniel is a senior at the University of Texas, and their daughter Kelly is a freshman. Rusty died 1 November 1991 – *daniel's* celebrated its 50th Anniversary in 2002.
– Submitted by Elizabeth M. Daniel

JESSE & MARGARET DANIELS

In 1860, Jesse Daniels (born 1830), a freed slave from the state of Georgia, migrated to the Longview, Texas, area. He settled in the Easton community where he found work at the local sawmill owned by a white man, George E. Prothro. Jesse was a hard worker who stood tall with natural ability and knowledge. He was made the first black foreman, supervising blacks and whites. With the help of God, and "Mr. Prothro," Jesse prospered and was able to purchase 825 acres of fertile land.

One day while Jesse was working at the sawmill, a white slaver arrived in town with several shackled black men and women. The year was 1861. Among the group was a female named Margaret. Margaret (born 1842) was a Mulatto from Tennessee. Her mother was black (and worked in the Big House) and her father was white. Margaret was captured by the slaver while she played outside the Big House with her fellow slave children. On the journey from

Tennessee to Easton, the slaver attempted to rape her; but a fellow male slave intervened and stopped him. A fight incurred with the black man being beaten to near death. The slaver stopped because a dead slave was worth nothing, and a beaten, crippled slave would lose over half his monetary value.

Mr. Prothro, Jesse and his co-worker overpowered the slaver. They unshackled and freed the poor humans.

Margaret and her fellow freedman were overcome with joy. With prayer and song, they thanked God. Their forced march from Tennessee to East Texas had weakened their bodies, minds and souls; but their spirits were intact. Black and white families came together with offers of food, lodging and clothes. The freedmen were given jobs in the sawmill, and the freedwomen were cared for by the womenfolk.

Jesse and Margaret fell in love and married. They had nine children. William (1861-1929), Jesse Jr. (1868-1923), Cullen David (1873-1951), Aaron (1863-1907), Oscar, Lenora, Mamie (1879-1926), Emma (1896-1975) and Margery were born to this union. Jesse rode tall in the saddle, looked all people in the eyes and ran his estate in a Christian manner. His custom was to arise early, saddle his favorite horse, and ride to his hog and cattle pen near the Sabine River. After feeding and watering his animals, he would return home for breakfast. On the day of his death, his horse returned with blood on the saddle. Immediately, a frantic search was undertaken. Jesse was not located. Days passed and hopes dampened. Several days later, Jesse's lean muscular body was discovered tied to a large Post Oak tree that stood adjacent to the hog pens. The blood stained rope that bound his corpse to the tree was double knotted. Even in death, his killers seemed afraid that he would regain his freedom. Jesse had been shot, hung, castrated, burned, whipped and dragged to death. Jesse's killers were never identified, but it was widely assumed that he was murdered because he was a black man with too much wealth and influence.

This is the lineage of Jesse and Margaret Daniels:

1) William's spouse was Janie Holt Daniels. He had one daughter Mable. In 1908, William became the first principle of Longview Colored High School. In 1956, the Northside Elementary school was renamed the Janie Daniels Elementary School.

2) Jesse, Jr. married Miss Virginia, and they had eight children (Willie, Fred, Eddie Lee, Noble, Dearcie, Sadie, Myrtle and Gracie). Jessie and Margaret's great grandchildren (Jesse, Jr. and Virginia's grandchildren) include Ollie Mae, Janie, Ernestine, Fred Douglas Jr., Rose Mael Alice Faye, Rubystein, Virginia, David, Ora D., Thelma, Noble, Johnny B., and Fannie M., Mary, Joseph and Sandra.

3) Cullen David married Eva Jane Hamilton (an early school teacher at Ned E. Williams High School) and had two children (J.C. and Dancy). His second wife was Lenora Peals. To this union was born ten children (Ona,

Algie, Glover, Roscoe, Cattrell, James, Inez, Norman, Ormond and Margery Louise). Jesse and Margaret's great grandchildren (Cullen's grandchildren) include Olen R., Loraine M., Patricia R., Dorothy H., Faye Jean, Olen O., Billye R., Cullen D., Wendell D., Oscar T., Perry E., Justine, Samuel Jr., Beatrice, Taylor D., Carol W., Ann D., Rose P., Annie C., Roscoe Jr., Evelyn, Robert D., Sherry D., Grace B., Lenora S., Cerella M., Erene D., Cottrell Jr., James A., Laverne, Doyle, Vickie A., Veronica, Alvin, Orma and Sheila.

4) Dr. Aaron married Mary Ellen Lewis, and had three children (Emma Ida, Lola Bell and Walter Charlsey). Their great grandchildren include Delmar, Dexter, Mack, Inell, Vastine, Alverstein, Wayne, Thomas, Don, Charles, Gerald, Wilma, Rochelle, Costelle and June.

5) Oscar's spouse and children are unknown.

6) Lenora married Uncle Craig.

7) Mamie married Uncle Timberlake and five children were born (Aaron, Audrey, Margaret Ardellue, Irmond Cecil, William D. and Ovis Robenia). The great grandchildren of Jesse and Margaret include Clarence L., Walter E., Myrtle R., Gladys M., Gwendolyn M., William D. Jr. and Lynda.

8) Emma Daniels married Uncle Rymes.

9) Margery Daniels never married.
– Submitted by Wendell David Daniels, M.D.
(great grandson)

EDWARD NEVON DAVIDSON

Edward Nevon Davidson was born 27 September 1925, at Grice, Upshur County, Texas, to T.J. and Bruce Cates Davidson. On 5 June 1947, Nevon married Patsy Louise Jean Blalack at East Mountain, Upshur County. Patsy was born 7 April 1930, at Glenwood, Upshur Country. She is the daughter of Nathan Armstrong and Alta Lera Willard Blalack. Patsy graduated from East Mountain High School. They were both very active in the East Mountain Baptist Church where Nevon was a deacon.

Nevon and Patsy moved to Seven Pines, Gregg County, in the spring of 1948. Nevon went to work for Greggtex Petroleum of Longview, later to become Warren Petroleum.

Nevon and Patsy are the parents of two daughters born while they were living at Seven

Edward Nevon and Patsy Blalack Davidson, 1983

Davidson family, 1995. (l.-r.) Back: Edwinna Fennell and Nevonda Chapman. Middle: Starlia Fennell, Derek Chapman and Patsy Davidson. Front: Edward Nevon Davidson.

Pines. Both girls were born in Gilmer, Texas. Nevonda Jean was born 14 November 1948, and Edwinna Lynn was born 7 September 1950.

In the fall of 1960, Nevon's company transferred him to Cleveland, Texas. They lived there for ten years. While living in Cleveland, Patsy was a homemaker and was very involved in school activities with their daughters. Patsy also did some work for the Cleveland City Library. Both daughters are graduates of Cleveland High School. Nevonda attended Kilgore Junior College. Nevonda married Vernon Luell Chapman, 31 May 1969, in Cleveland, Texas. Luell was born 7 August 1949, in Rusk County, Texas. He is the son of Robert Obie and Francis Ellen Huston Chapman of Laneville, Texas.

In the summer of 1969, Nevon and Patsy were transferred to Lovington, New Mexico, where Edwinna attended New Mexico Junior College. Edwinna married Gary Randall Fennell, 25 April 1981, in Longview. Randy was born in Longview, 27 March 1953. He is the son of Horace Randall and Doris Darline Larkins Fennell of Longview.

Nevon and Patsy longed to return to Longview. In September 1974, their wish came true — back to Longview to make their home in the Spring Hill Community. Nevon was transferred to Spear Plant in Kilgore, where he was the maintenance supervisor; and, later, Nevon was transferred to the Gladewater Plant in Warren City, where he was the Gas Tester. Nevon retired in 1986 after 39-1/2 years with Warren Petroleum.

Nevon and Patsy are the proud grandparents of two grandchildren. Derek Luell Chapman was born 30 August 1981, in Houston, Harris County, Texas, where he graduated from Cy-Fair High School in Houston. Starlia D'Lynn Fennell was born 15 September 1983, in Lovington, Lea County, New Mexico. She graduated from Spring Hill High School in Longview.

Nevon served in the United States Coast Guard. He loved to do refrigeration work, water ski, fish, whittle and travel in the motor home. Patsy loved to sew, water ski, play cards, travel in the motor home and cook – no one leaves her house hungry.

At Nevon's death the couple were married 55 years. Nevon died 28 July 2002, at the age of 76 at his home in Longview. He is buried at Sunset Memorial Cemetery in Gilmer, Texas. Patsy still lives in Spring Hill, where she enjoys all her family, church and friends.

– Submitted by Patsy Davidson

DAVIS

Jane Kemp was born in 1820, in Alabama, according to the 1900 Gregg County, Texas, census. She moved to the Longview area around 1840.

Jane Kemp lived on West Tyler Street in Longview and had 16 children. Of the 16, there is only record of one being born in Gregg County and her name was Victoria. Victoria was born in March 1860. Jane and her daughter worked as wash-women in order to support their family. They used the money earned to purchase their house on West Tyler Street.

Besides her children, one other family member, Edward Kemp, who was born in Longview in November 1876, also lived with Jane.

Jane's daughter, Victoria, married John Davis on 11 September 1884. To this union six children were born.

Their first daughter, Narciss, was born in October 1881. Narciss married William Miller on 9 November 1902. To this union eight children were born: the first child, Viola was born 28 April 1898, and died 12 November 1901; Willie May was born 5 May 1900, and died 19 January 1947; Victoria Bernice, or "Shug," was born 1 February 1910, and died 1 January 1998. Frankie Lyno, or "Bibby," was born 29 May 1912; she now lives in Greenville, Texas. Roberta Letitia, or "Teate," was born 9 June 1915, and died 27 March 1970. Clarence William, or "Bubba," was born 27 September 1918, and died on 5 September 1970. Barbara Letitia, or "Tito," was born on 11 August 1921; she now lives Sacramento, California. Narciss died on 10 June 1960.

Jane's second child, Letitia or "Tisha," was born in November 1883, and died 13 March 1973. She married Will Allen of Longview, on 2 September 1908. Jannie, or "Jane," was born in January 1890, and died in 1936. Roberta, or "Ruby," was born in May 1894, and died 20 November 1923. Susanna,

Letitia Davis sits in the living room of her home at 106 Grigsby Street, Longview, Texas.

or "Sudie," was born in 1895, and died on 25 October 1977. Davis married Arthur Lee Baker on 21 March 1914, and they had one son, Arthur Lee Baker, born in 1916.

Their last child, Alice, was born in 1900. There is no record of her death. John Davis died sometime after the birth of their last child in 1900.

Around 1920, the family bought two homes located at 106 and 108 Grigsby Street in Longview. The last record of Jane Kemp was found in the Gregg County land deed records, where she sold her house at 106 Grigsby to her daughter, Sudie, in 1930. There is no record of her death. Victoria Davis died 29 July 1949, in Longview, Texas.

The Davis family lived and worked in Longview. They attended Red Oak Baptist Church on Martin Luther King Boulevard. Most of the children of John and Victoria Davis are buried in their family plot at Grace Hill Cemetery on Marshall Street in Longview. Other family members buried there are Lear Davis (1898), Rosa D. Davis (26 December 1920–30 April 1938) and Ruby Elvira Davis (17 July 1898).

– Submittted by Fannie Anderson

GUSSIE NELL DAVIS

Gussie Nell Davis, founder of the Kilgore Rangerettes, daughter of Robert Augustus and Mattie Lavinia (Callaway) Davis, was born in Farmersville, Texas, on 4 November 1906. She attended public schools in Farmersville. She majored in physical education and received a B.A. degree from CIA (Texas Womens College) in 1927, and a M.A. from the University of Southern California in 1938. Davis began her career as physical education teacher and pep-squad director at Greenville High School. In 1928, she organized the "Flaming Flashes" twirl-and-dance group, one of the first drill teams in the nation.

She was hired by Kilgore Junior College to start a drill team to entertain the people during half-time so they would not want to leave. She more than succeeded. Davis was a consultant to drill teams, a judge of drill team competitions, a member of the National Drill Team Directors Association and Rangerettes Forever, and a member of the board of directors of Fiesta, International.

She was a member of the First Presbyterian Church, Kilgore. She was honored with Gussie Nell Day in Kilgore (1964) and in Farmersville (1970) and Gussie Nell Davis Day in Texas (1979). She was made Texas Woman of the Year by the Texas State Civitans (1969). Davis Hall, a dormitory at Kilgore College, is named in her honor (1969). She was named Women in Communications Headliner of the Year (1973) and Outstanding Alumna of Texas Woman's University (1978), featured in the Rangerette-Showcase Museum (1979), enrolled in the Greenville High School Football Hall of Fame (1980) and the Texas Women's Hall of Fame as arts nominee (1990), and given numerous commendations. She died in Kilgore on 20 December 1993, and was buried in Farmersville Cemetery.

HILTON JOYCEL & LILLIE ZELMODENE "DENE" (WADE) DAVIS

Hilton Joycel Davis and Lillie Zelmodene "Dene" (Wade) Davis moved to Longview in 1969 with their three children. They moved into their home the summer of 1971. The whole family are members of the Church Of Jesus Christ of Latter-Day Saints. Hilton was born 16 November 1926, in Pittsburg, Camp County. He graduated from Union Ridge High School in 1944. Hilton was an NIP for the Army in World War II – he served in Germany for two years. He attended Paris Junior College to earn a two-year degree in watch repair and jewelry man in 1949. He worked for 45 years in watch repair. Hilton and Dene co-owned the Thrifty Food Store, D & D Jewelers and MoDoeDay with Harold and Chessa Dixon. They sold their stores in 1982. Hilton went to work for Quest Pharmacy in 1995. He married 13 August 1953, to Lillie Zelmodene "Dene" Wade, born 25 April 1930. "Dene" graduated from Pittsburg High School in 1947. She went to Parkland School of Nursing in Dallas for two years where she earned her nursing degree in 1950. She worked as a surgical nurse for over thirty years at Pittsburg M & S Hospital. "Dene" passed away 16 July 2001, at the age of 71, in Gregg County.

Delton Wade Davis, born 23 February 1955, graduated Pine Tree High School in 1973. He served a two-year Italian speaking mission for the LDS church in Italy from 1974 to 1976. He graduated from Ricks College, Idaho, with a two-year degree. He has worked for Central Trucking for over twenty years.

Joycelyn (Davis) Ward was born 20 January 1956, in Pittsburg, Camp County. She graduated from Pine Tree High School in 1974. She received her Degree in Cosmetology in 1975. Joycelyn went to work for Pine Tree School Food Service in 1993. She married in the LDS Provo, Utah, Temple 1 June 1974, to Daniel Randy Ward, born 19 February 1951, in Gilmer, Upshur County. Randy graduated from Harmony High School in 1970. He is a self-employed paint contractor. They have four children: Daniel, 6 January 1976; Michael, 25 January 1977; Shawna, 1 September 1979; and Landon, 17 December 1985. Daniel is married, has two daughters and is expecting a third child in 2004. Michael is married and has one son. Shawna is a senior at Lamar University in Beaumont. Landon is a senior at Pine Tree High School. Tamara "Tammy" Denise (Davis) Zimmerman was born 9 December 1964, in Pittsburg, Camp County. She graduated from Pine Tree High School in 1983. She received her teaching degree in 1997 from Lamar University in Beaumont, Texas. She currently teaches early childhood at Hillcrest Elementary in Nederland. She married in LDS Salt Lake City, Utah, Temple 2 October 1987, to Michael John Zimmerman, born 19 April 1965, in Grants Pass, Josephine County, Oregon. He graduated from Timpview High School in Provo, Utah, 1983. He works for UPS in Beaumont. They have six children: Tamira, "still born" 26 January 1989, in Longview, Gregg County; Zachary, 27 April 1990, Longview, Gregg County; Aaron, 2 April 1992; Makinzie, 15 February 1994; Cassidie, 20 June 1996; Jacob, 8 November 1999. Their last four children were born in Nederland, Jefferson County.

Shawna Dene Davis was "still born" 9 April 1969, in Pittsburg, Camp County. (See "Daniel Randy & Joycelyn Ward" for additions to the Davis family history.)

LANNA ROSALIN DAVIS

Doy Herbert Davis was born 3 May 1930, in Pelican, DeSoto Parish, Louisiana. Doy Herbert Davis married Ulletta Ann Butler on 1 July 1949, in Mansfield, DeSoto Parish, Louisiana. Ulletta Ann Butler was born 10 October 1931, in Mansfield, DeSoto Parish, Louisiana. Doy Herbert and Ulletta Ann Butler Davis moved to Longview, Gregg County, Texas, May 1953. They had one son when they moved to Gregg County. Doy and Ulletta had two daughters, Lanna Rosalin Davis and Lauri Alicia Davis. Lanna Rosalin Davis was born 16 October 1954, at Markham Hospital in Longview, Gregg County, Texas. Lanna Rosalin Davis married James Clinton Pruett on 18 May 1974, at Mobberly Baptist Church in Longview, Gregg County, Texas. They had one son, Aaron Clinton Pruett, born 15 July 1977, at Good Shepherd Medical Center in Longview, Gregg County, Texas. Lanna Rosalin Davis Pruett and James Clinton Pruett were divorced in March 1978.

Lanna Rosalin Davis married Bruce Collier of Longview, Gregg County, Texas, on 1 December 1979. Bruce Collier was born 6 September 1952, at Markham Hospital in Longview, Gregg County, Texas. Lanna Rosalin Davis Collier and Bruce Collier had one daughter and one son. Courtney Blaine Collier was born 10 April 1981, at Good Shepherd Medical Center in Longview, Gregg County, Texas. Courtney Blaine Collier married Michael Myles Kittner on 15 June 2002, at Mobberly Baptist Church in Longview, Gregg County, Texas. Michael Myles Kittner was born 1 December 1975, in Alexandria, Louisiana. Clayton Barclay Collier was born 18 January 1986, at Good Shepherd Medical Center in Longview, Gregg County, Texas.

Bruce Collier adopted Aaron Clinton Pruett in February 1989, in Longview, Gregg County, Texas. Aaron changed his name to Aaron Bruce Collier. Aaron Bruce Collier married Stacy Lynn Klunkert on 18 December 1999, in College Station, Texas. Stacy Lynn Klunkert was born 18 April 1978, in College Station, Brazos County, Texas. Aaron Bruce Collier and Stacy Lynn Klunkert Collier are expecting their first child in January 2004.

All of the children of Doy Herbert and Ulletta Ann Butler Davis are active members of Mobberly Baptist Church. All of their grandchildren were raised actively attending Mobberly Baptist Church in Longview, Gregg County, Texas. Doy Herbert Davis retired from Texas Eastman Company in January of 1991, after 37 years of service. Ulletta Ann was a homemaker. Doy Herbert Davis died 8 January 2000, in Longview, Harrison County, Texas. He was buried at Rosewood Park in Longview, Gregg County, Texas.

– Submitted by Lanna D. Collier

LANNY BARTON DAVIS

Doy Herbert Davis was born 3 May 1930, in Pelican, DeSoto Parish, Louisiana. Doy Herbert Davis married Ulletta Ann Butler on 1 July 1949, in Mansfield, DeSoto Parish, Louisiana. Ulletta Ann Butler was born 10 October 1931, in Mansfield, DeSoto Parish, Louisiana. Doy Herbert and Ulletta Ann Butler Davis moved to Longview, Gregg County, Texas, May 1953. They had one son when they moved to Gregg County. His name was Lanny Barton Davis, born 27 October 1951, in Mansfield, DeSoto Parish, Louisiana.

Lanny Barton married Martha Elizabeth Cross of Gilmer, Upshur County, Texas. Lanny Barton and Martha Elizabeth Cross were married 7 September 1974, in Gilmer, Texas. Martha Elizabeth was born 9 August 1954, in Gilmer, Upshur County, Texas. Lanny Barton and Martha Elizabeth had two sons. Matthew Cameron Davis was born at Good Shepherd Medical Center in Longview, Gregg County, Texas on 31 May 1979. Matthew Cameron mar-

Davis family, December 1998. (l.-r.) Front: Aaron Levi Zimmerman, Zachary Loyd Zimmerman and Landon Keith Ward. Middle: Tamara "Tammy" Denise (Davis) Zimmerman, Cassidie Micheal Zimmerman, Michael John Zimmerman, Hilton Joycel Davis, Lillie Zelmodene "Dene" (Wade) Davis, Delton Wade Davis and Makinzie Joyce Zimmerman. Back: Daniel Randy Ward, Joycelyn (Davis) Ward, Michael Davis Ward, Shawna Lynn Ward, Daniel Arleigh Ward. Not in Picture: Jacob Ryan Zimmerman.

ried Karen Elaine Kouba on 18 August 2001, at Mobberly Baptist Church in Longview, Texas. Cameron Blake Davis was born 18 July 1989, at Good Shepherd Medical Center in Longview, Gregg County, Texas.

Lanny Barton and Martha Elizabeth, along with their children, are active members of Mobberly Baptist Church. After the marriage of Matthew Cameron, he and his wife Karen Kouba Davis moved to Allen, Texas.

Doy Herbert Davis retired from Texas Eastman Company in January of 1991, after 37 years of service. Ulletta Ann was a homemaker. Doy Herbert Davis died 8 January 2000, in Longview, Harrison County, Texas. He was buried at Rosewood Park in Longview, Gregg County, Texas.

– Submitted by Martha Davis

LAURI ALICIA DAVIS (MCGAUGHEY)

Doy Herbert Davis was born 3 May 1930, in Pelican, DeSoto Parish, Louisiana. Doy Herbert Davis married Ulletta Ann Butler on 1 July 1949, in Mansfield, DeSoto Parish, Louisiana. Ulletta Ann Butler was born 10 October 1931, in Mansfield, DeSoto Parish, Louisiana. Doy Herbert and Ulletta Ann Butler Davis moved to Longview, Gregg County, Texas, May 1953.

The Davises youngest daughter was Lauri Alicia Davis. Lauri Alicia Davis was born 10 November 1962, in Markham Hospital, Longview, Gregg County, Texas. Lauri Alicia Davis married Anthony Dale McGaughey on 18 August 1984, at Mobberly Baptist Church in Longview, Texas. Anthony Dale McGaughey was born 1 February 1959, in Lufkin, Angelina County, Texas. The McGaughey's had one daughter and twin sons. Their daughter, Emily Anne McGaughey, was born 21 April 1988, at Good Shepherd Medical Center in Longview, Gregg County, Texas. The twins, Mason Davis McGaughey and Madison Davis McGaughey, were born 8 January 1992, at Good Shepherd Medical Center in Longview, Gregg County, Texas.

All of the children of Doy Herbert and Ulletta Ann Butler Davis are active members of Mobberly Baptist Church. All of their grandchildren were raised actively attending Mobberly Baptist Church in Longview, Gregg County, Texas. Doy Herbert Davis retired from Texas Eastman Company in January of 1991, after 37 years of service. Ulletta Ann was a homemaker. Doy Herbert Davis died 8 January 2000, in Longview, Harrison County, Texas. He was buried at Rosewood Park in Longview, Gregg County, Texas.

– Submitted by Laurie McGaughey

WILLIAM H. DAVIS

James R. Davis was born about 1818 in North Carolina. He married Margaret Kirk who was born about 1819, also in North Carolina. Sometime after 1853 they arrived in East Texas in an ox drawn covered wagon. According to family stories they first settled in what is now Longview, but moved to Panola County, Texas, because of trouble with some Indians.

William H. Davis

James and Margaret had three children all born in Mississippi: Sarah Jane (1841-1911); James (1844), who was believed to have been killed in a logging accident; and William Henry (1849–1922, Gregg County).

William Henry married Amanda Elizabeth Reese 4 December 1871, in Panola County. They lived most of their forty-one years together in the northern part of Gregg County where William was a farmer. The couple were members of Winterfield Methodist Church and they, as well as many members of their family, are buried in the Winterfield Cemetery. After Amanda died, William married a widow, Almeda Darst.

Parents of Amanda Elizabeth Reese were John Reese and Sarah Phelps/Felps. Both were born in Georgia and died in Panola County.

Amanda Reese Davis

Children of William Henry and Amanda Davis: Sarah Jane (1872-1872); John William (1874-1925), married Etta Griffin 3 April 1910; James Reese (1876), married Corrinna Maud Bell 4 December 1901, Gregg County; Walter Henry (1878-1941), married Jimmie Virginia McCann 22 November 1903, in Gregg County; Margaret Ada (1880-1940), married George Washington Richardson 29 December 1898, Gregg County; Joseph Moore (1882), married Ethel Jenkins; Thomas Jefferson (1884-1972), married Jo Ann Harris; Amanda Pearl (1888-), married Thomas Robert Tutt 12 September 1909, Gregg County; Robert Dee (1891-1937), married Jewel Stovall 24 September 1911, Gregg County; and Katie Lee (1893-1925), married Charles Jesse Corley.

– Submitted by Ellis Crawford

JARRETT DEAN: From Alabama to Texas in 1845

Jarrett Dean was born 22 March 1813, Georgia, died 13 February 1883, Gladewater, Gregg County, Texas. He married 3 November 1836, Montgomery County, Alabama, to Mary Jane Phillips, born 16 May 1821, Montgomery County, Alabama, died 18 December 1871, Gladewater, Texas.

Jarrett was the son of John M. Dean, born 1784, aboard ship from Ireland to America. The Deans probably entered the port at Charleston, South Carolina, one of the oldest ports at the time.

John Dean was thought to have lived his younger years in Edgefield District, South Carolina which was Old District 96, and later married in South Carolina in c. 1805 to Nancy Mathis of Laurens County, South Carolina.

John and his brothers, Jarrett Dean, the elder, and James Minton Dean, migrated to Alabama from Georgia in about 1818, traveling with a dozen or so other family members.

John Dean was a veteran of the War of 1812; muster cards and payroll accounts from Twigs County, Georgia, were found that indicate that he helped build Fort Telfair in the fall of 1813 (recorded in the National Archives in Washington, D.C.). He served in the 3rd Company, #32, under Captain John Mirach and Lt. Henry Rell. The Deans came to Alabama shortly after the territory was opened up for settlement. John was one of the early land grantees. He purchased 80-plus acres of 27 October 1831, Section 26, T13, R16E, Montgomery County, Alabama.

John and Nancy Dean were parents of nine children. The oldest was Thomas Jefferson Dean. Several of his grown children migrated to East Texas and lived around Commerce, Texas, departing Alabama on 20 October 1869, and arriving in White Rock, Texas, which is near Greenville, on Christmas Day 1869. Daniel Dean, son of John, was born 18 December 1818, Alabama, died 8 July 1873, Bushey Creek, Anderson County, Texas. Daniel and his wife, Ann Jeter Hatley, and all but their son James Madison Dean, who was killed during the Civil War, all left Montgomery County, in the fall of 1872, arriving in Anderson County, Texas, by October of that year.

Malinda Dean, daughter of John and Nancy Dean, was born 31 August 1829, married in Alabama to George Washington Jeter, son of Eleazor and Anna (Moseley) Jeter. George and Malinda migrated to East Texas with other Moseley relatives and lived near Palestine, Texas

Mary Jane Phillips was the daughter of George Phillips, born 1786, Virginia, and his second wife, Elizabeth Talley, born 1790, Virginia. George and Elizabeth are listed on the 1850 census of Upshur County, Texas, as members of the Jarrett Dean household.

William Phillips, born 1807, a half-brother to Mary Jane Dean, and his wife, Mary "Polly" Shepperd, were residents of Montgomery County until they migrated to east Texas by 1840, where a son was born that year. Mary Jane probably wrote back to the Alabama relatives and said, "Y'all come to Texas!" And they did.

Jarrett Dean and his wife and his children, along with Anderson T. Wright, and his wife Sarah Ann (Barnes) Wright and their children, Hezekiah Barnes, a brother to Sarah Wright, and his wife Elizabeth (Phillips) Barnes, a sister to Mary Jane, and a family named Morgan all left Davenport, Montgomery County, and arrived in the Republic of Texas in the fall of 1845.

Jarrett Dean purchased 320 acres of land in the Hokit Grant for $75 on the 5 March 1854, in what is now Gladewater. His first home was a one-room house built of logs, with a fire place and shed room with a fire place separate from the main house which was used for a kitchen. On 30 December 1872, Jarrett Dean conveyed to the Texas and Pacific Railroad Company, for five dollars and further consideration, that said T & P Railroad Company would locate its railroad through said county of Upshur County, which was later a part of Gregg County, in such a manner as to pass through his land. John F. Dean, son of Jarrett, was born 27 September 1837, Montgomery County, Alabama, died 27 December 1868, Bryan, Texas. John was discharged from active duty in the Confederate Army on 5 March 1864; his record is recorded in the *History of the Tenth Texas Cavalry (Dismounted) Regiment, 1861-1865*, p.266.

Many of the early families lived near what was Point Pleasant, in what is now Clarksville City, just east of Gladewater. The first postmaster of Point Pleasant was John Kittle Armstrong, who was appointed in 1852. With the advent of the railroad people were drawn away from Point Pleasant and other small communities and gravitated to communities near the railroad. Citizens met under a large oak tree at the home of Jarrett Dean and his daughter, Bellona Dean Victory, and her husband, William Henry Victory to select a name for this small logging community. The name they selected was Gladewater, created in 1873, the same year that Gregg County was created (and so named Gregg after a Confederate General who lost his life leading his men to battle).

Dr. Thomas Jefferson Allison, Jr., an early doctor of Gilmer and Gladewater, wrote this in his autobiography in 1927: "The town was named Gladewater because its proximity of Glade Creek, which is a mile west of town. The stream is called Glade Creek, because it's headwaters are in a barren region called the Glades, which are located southeast of Pleasant Hill and west of Mings Chapel."

Other people that met under that oak tree to select a name for the community were the Bill Victorys, the John Jeters, Dr. and Mrs. Thomas Allison, Jr., the William Foshees, the Mason Phillipses and members of the Morgan family.

Mariah Amanda Dean (daughter of Jarrett) was born 10 October 1855, Upshur County, Texas, died 22 April 1942, Gladewater; she married first on 13 June 1878, to William Edward McFarlin. After his death Mariah married second on 29 August 1887, Gregg County, Texas, to James Franklin Wright, born 14 August 1840, Davenport, Alabama, died 30 July 1910, near Gladewater. Both are buried in Rosedale Cemetery, Gladewater.

James Franklin Wright served in Company A, Lane's Partisan Rangers, Texas Cavalry. He enlisted as a private on 16 July 1862, and served three years as a soldier in the Civil War. He was captured by the Union soldiers but escaped before they were able to put him in a prison camp.

James F. Wright came to the Republic of Texas in 1845 with his parents, Anderson T. and Sarah Ann (Barnes) Wright. Anderson was born in Georgia in 1811, and accompanied his family to Montgomery County, Alabama, in the 1820s when his father, William B. Wright, purchased land there in 1823. William B. Wright was born in 1787, Grandville County, North Carolina, died Polk County, Georgia, in 1856.

James F. Wright lived his early years on his father's farm in what is now Warren City, Gregg County. Anderson T. Wright, his father, purchased this 382 acres of land on 6 February 1849, in the Benjamin N. Hampton Survey and out of the Ross Survey, recorded Vol. B, p.328, Deed Records, Upshur County, Texas.

Anderson Wright died in about 1869. Sarah, his widow, was born in 1812, South Carolina, and died 10 October 1879. Both are buried in the Moseley Cemetery near Warren City.

James Franklin Wright and Mariah Amanda Dean McFarlin Wright were parents of (1) Lucy Vdell, born 16 November 1888, died 19 February 1914, Gladewater, married 1 May 1910, to William Ashby (Lucy died of childbirth); (2) James Samuel Wright, born 8 June 1891, Gregg County, died 31 August 1974, Gladewater; and (3) Martha "Mattie" Lillian Gosson.

James Samuel "Sam" Wright married Lillie Maude Young on 18 September 1912, Gladewater. They were sitting in a borrowed buggy when they were married by justice of the peace Ogie Johnston. Ogie Johnston was married 9 February 1882, to Della Armstrong, a descendant of Hezekiah and Elizabeth (Phillips) Barnes. Della was a cousin to both my parents.

Lillie Maude Young Wright was born 9 January 1896, Harleton, Harrison County, Texas, died 25 June 1977, Farmers Branch, Dallas County, Texas; both James and Lillie are buried in the Gladewater Memorial Park Cemetery. They were parents of eight children: (1) Helen Ynez Brown, born 8 September 1915, died 20 March 1996; (2) Maydean Hunt, born 19 May 1918, died 18 May 1940; (3) James Leonard Wright, born 10 November 1919, died 17 February 2001; (4) Nelwyn Louise Sims, born 10 November 1921, died 17 November 1986; (5) Franklin Leon Wright, born 1 August 1922, died 6 August 1953; (6) Ruby Olean Stewart Torres, born 13 February 1930; (7) Howard Glenn Wright, born 7 August 1933; and (8) Carl Venoy Wright, born 12 February 1935.

Maude and Sam Wright became owners of the Missie E. (Bowles) Young farm that Maude's mother purchased on 11 November 1911, near Moody Creek on Highway 80, Gladewater, Texas. Maude and Sam lived in Gladewater until his death. Maude then went to live with different children until her death in 1977. (Note: Information recorded in 1) *Ten Generations of the Wright Family in Two Parts* and 2) *The John Dean Family*, both compiled by Carl V. Wright.) – Submitted by David Dean Brown (great great grandson of Jarrett Dean)

REESE CALHOUN DEGRAFFENREID

Reese Calhoun DeGraffenreid was Representative to Congress from Texas. He was born in Franklin, Williamson County, Tennessee, 7 May 1859. DeGraffenreid attended school in Franklin and the University of Tennessee at Knoxville. He was graduated from Cumberland University, Lebanon, Tennessee, with a degree in law and was admitted to the bar in 1879. He opened a practice in Franklin and later moved to Chattanooga, Tennessee, for one year. He moved to Texas and helped in the construction of the Texas and Pacific Railroad. He began practicing law at Longview in 1883 where he was elected county attorney and resigned two months afterward. In 1890, he was an unsuccessful candidate for election to the Fifty-second Congress; but, was successfully elected as a Democrat to the Fifty-fifth, Fifty-sixth and Fifty-seventh Congresses and served from 4 March 1897, until his death in Washington, D.C., on 29 August 1902. He was buried in Greenwood Cemetery, Longview.

JAMES DAVID & ROSANNAH KEYS DENTON

James David and Rosannah Keys Denton moved to Longview in December 1994. Rosannah's father, Warren F. Keys Sr., was a businessman from Marshall who had started his first retail lumber business in Longview at 414 East Cotton Street in 1932. The business partner who ran Longview Lumber Company was Dee Plyler. Warren Keys and his wife, Maxie Edwards Keys, came over each week to monitor the operation. It was successful, and Mr. Keys opened another lumberyard in Marshall several years later. He also had retail lumber companies in Henderson, Texarkana and Shreveport at one time. Mr. Keys' father, John

James David and Rosannah Denton and sons, David, Tom and James.

Henry Keys, was the owner of a sawmill in Marshall, which his sons operated. When the sawmill ceased to operate, Mr. Keys' brother, Cecil Keys, became a part owner in Longview Lumber Company.

James David and Rosannah's three grown sons, James Keys Denton, Thomas Warren Denton and David Lee Denton, are living in other parts of the United States. James K. has a wife, Margaret Elizabeth, and daughter, Margaret Katherine, and the family residence is in Conroe, Texas. He also has two grandchildren, Kelsea and Garrett, from his step-daughter, Lauren, and her husband, Daniel Neal. James is a pilot for the United States Army. Thomas is living in Fort Payne, Alabama, and David is an attorney with the federal government in Washington, DC.

Previous to moving to Longview, Dave and Rosannah had lived in Egypt with their two younger sons for ten years and in Moscow, Russia, for another four years. While working overseas in those locations, Dave was employed as a petroleum geologist and country manager by Marathon Petroleum Company. Dave retired in December 1994.

– Submitted by Rosannah Denton

HAROLD DETEAU, Architect

Clarence Harold Deteau, a prominent architect in Longview, Texas, for 50 years was born in Waco on 20 November 1926, the only son of Paul Deteau, Jr., and Ollie Beatrice Carpenter Deteau. His grandfather sailed to Texas in the late 1800s from Alsace Lorraine, France.

Harold graduated from Waco High School in 1945, where he lettered in baseball, track and basketball, and was on the State Basketball Team. He was offered scholarships to Texas, A&M and Baylor, but was drafted. After basic training at Camp Fanning, he was shipped overseas to Liverno, Italy, as an Army medic.

During his service in Europe, he was a member of the Army basketball and softball team and played all over Italy and Europe, and was selected to the Army All-Star Team where he played on the MTO team in the Army World Series.

He returned to Waco after his discharge in 1947, attended Baylor University, then entered the school of Architecture at Texas Tech. There were 147 architectural students that started in his class and only 13 graduated with him in 1952.

Harold Deteau

During his studies at Baylor, he met and married Rita Pat McMeans in 1947. They were married for 22 years until her death in 1969 of leukemia. They had four children, Diana Kay, Richard Roland, Donna Gail and Denise Marie.

He met Shirley Hall Toler, a teacher in Pasadena, Texas, in 1970, and married her later that year and also adopted her three children, John Mark, Stephanie Kay and Bradley Alan. They have traveled extensively in the U.S., Europe, Canada, Central America and Mexico and still enjoy this pastime.

After graduation from architecture school at Texas Tech, he practiced in Sherman, Texas, until 1954. He moved his practice to Longview to work as a partner with W.L. Kelly, an engineer/architect. He has maintained a business in Longview for 50 years.

The numerous projects he has done over the many years include the First National Bank Building, numerous schools for the Longview School District, a dozen or more medical clinics, retail businesses, Stemco Mfg., schools in Hallsville, Tatum and Gilmer and 140 Gibson Stores. In 1967, he started the Wal-Mart chain after a meeting with Sam Walton in Longview. The many business chains he designed numerous projects for were Western Sizzlin, Roadrunner Convenience stores, over 50 projects for the Brookshire Food Stores and many custom residences.

Professional associations Harold Deteau was involved in were the Northeast Texas Chapter of the American Institute Of Architects, where he was a charter member and served as chapter director, state director and president; the Texas Society of Architects, where he was chapter representative to numerous state conventions; and the American Institute of Architects, where he has been a member since 1957. He is now a member Emeritus of all these organizations.

He is an active member of the First Baptist Church, was a director, a deacon, and donated his services to many building projects at First Baptist Church as well as other churches in the area.

His family is proud of his accomplishments in changing the landscape of Gregg County with his architecture for fifty years, his dedication to his family, his community service and his profession.

– Submitted by Shirley Deteau

DAVID WAYNE DOLIVE & BRIAN BRUCE DOLIVE

David Wayne and Brian Bruce, sons of Wayne Bruce Dolive and Billie Jean Hoke, were born in Gregg Memorial Hospital in Longview, Texas.

David was born 27 December 1954. He attended Trinity School of Texas and Bramlette Elementary School. He attended Junior High and through his junior year of high school at Spring Hill High School. David was a defensive lineman for the Spring Hill Panthers. He graduated from Longview High School in 1973. At Longview, David belonged to the Future Farmers of America, raising a show calf that won

David Wayne and Brian Bruce Dolive

him ribbons at the Harvest Festival. He was active in Boy Scouts, rising to the rank of Life Scout. He served as a Junior Deacon at First Christian Church, where he was on the basketball team that won the Four States Church League in 1966. David attended Texas A&M University in 1974 and 1975, and then returned to Longview to enter the work force. He graduated from the University of Texas at Tyler in 1987 with a B.S. degree in Computer Science.

David married Melanie Jeanne Perkins 21 November 1981, in Longview. Melanie was born in New Hampshire to John Cameron Perkins and Eveylyn Anderson. David and Melanie have three children: Evan Mathew, born 4 November 1982; Caitlin Christine, born 23 April 1986; and Haley Katherine, born 14 May 1993. They are members of the First Christian Church. Evan graduated from Tatum High School and attends Stephen F. Austin University. Caitlin and Haley attend the Tatum schools.

Brian was born 31 October 1959. He attended School For Little Children, Bramlette Elementary, Forest Park Junior High, and graduated from Longview High School in 1978. He was President of the Student Body and elected the first Mr. Lobo at Longview High. He played drums for the musical group, The Singsations. Brian played basketball for a church team that went to the State Finals in Dallas, Texas. He graduated from Texas A&M University in 1982, attended North Texas University School of Business, then graduated from Baylor College of Dentistry in 1987 with a D.D.S. degree. He was recognized for outstanding work in oral surgery. He practices general dentistry in Longview.

Brian married Peggy Elaine Payne 30 June1984, in Longview. Peggy was born in Honolulu, Hawaii, to Robert Daniel Payne and Betty Jean Bond Womack. Brian and Peggy have two children: Emily Jean, born 24 January 1990, and Daniel Bruce, born 1 March 1995. Emily attends Judson Junior High, while Daniel attends Hudson Pep Elementary. They belong to the First Baptist Church in Longview where Brian is a Deacon and the children are active in youth activities. Brian continues his early interest in sports and playing his drums.

– Submitted by David W. Dolive

WAYNE BRUCE DOLIVE

Dominque Dolive, son of Jean Dolive and Marie Savabos, came from Tilac, Gasgone, France, to Mobile, Alabama, about 1770. He married Marie Louise Baudain in 1772. Louis, the oldest of their six children, was born in 1773 in Mobile. There he married Louisa Le Fleau in 1801. Reuben H., second of their seven children, was born in 1805 in Mobile. He married Agnes Laurindine in 1825 in Baldwin County, Alabama. There, Silas Sedoin, third of their four children, was born in 1830.

Sedoin, who married Mary Lucretia May in 1858 in Baldwin County, served in the Civil War (Alabama). He and Mary had nine children, seven born in Baldwin County, and two in San Jacinto, Texas. Sedoin came to Texas by way of Galveston about 1877 and settled in San Jacinto County, where he was in the turpentine business. His son, Morgan Joseph, born in 1868, in Baldwin County, Alabama, remained in San Jacinto County, marrying Martha Jane Williams in 1882. They had seven children. Edward Daniel Dolive, third of their seven children, was born in 1892 in San Jacinto County on land his father owned which was across the road from Sam Houston's plantation known as Raven Hill.

Edward Daniel married Mattie Lee Kane in 1913 in Oakhurst, Texas. They had six children: Maurice, born 2 September 1915; Naneline, born 2 January 1917; Mary Lois, born 28 March 1919; Jim Morgan, born 10 August 1921; Don Edward, born 22 February 1924; and Wayne Bruce, born 23 September 1926. All were born in Staley, Texas. Edward was postmaster, deputy sheriff, cotton gin owner and general store owner for several years in Staley before moving to the State Fish Hatchery near Huntsville, Texas, in 1930.

Wayne Bruce grew up and went to school in Huntsville while living at the Fish Hatchery. He was president of his senior class, attended Boy's State and played on the basketball team that went to the State Tournament. After graduating from high school, Wayne joined the U.S. Marine Corps, serv-

ing with the 5th Division during World War II as a military policeman at Camp Pendelton, California, and as a surveyor on Guam for two years. After the War Wayne returned to Huntsville, attending Sam Houston State Teachers College before transferring to Texas A&M University, where he graduated with a B.S. Degree in Civil Engineering in 1950. In February 1950, he was employed by Tennessee Eastman Corporation, which later became Texas Eastman Company; he was the fourth person to be hired in Texas. Wayne retired in 1991, as a Senior Supervising Engineer, after having the privilege of seeing Eastman grow from virgin timber land into a major petrochemical plant. The company today is known as Eastman Chemical.

Wayne married Billie Jean Hoke, daughter of Weyman Jefferson Hoke and Edna Tadlock, on 27 May 1950, in Huntsville. They moved to Longview in 1950 and joined the First Christian Church. They were active in the church, civic and cultural activities of the community. Billie Jean grew up in Huntsville, graduated from high school in 1944 and from Sam Houston State Teachers College with a B.S. Degree in Business Administration in 1949. She received the Pennybacker award for academic excellence and extracurricular activities. She was elected to Who's Who in Colleges and Universities, and crowned Queen of the 1949 Coronation.

Billie taught in the School for Little Children at First Methodist Church, Longview. She later was the Business teacher at Spring Hill High School for several years. She served as President of the East Texas Chapter of The State Teachers Association in 1968. Billie died 11 May 1975, and is buried in Memory Park, Longview. Wayne and Billie had two sons, David Wayne and Brian Bruce.

Wayne married Mary Bays Baird 12 July 1977, a widow with two children: Billy Joe and Barbara Ann Baird. Mary made Wayne an instant grandfather with a three-month-old granddaughter, Elizabeth Claire Baird.
– Submitted by Wayne B. Dolive

LEONARD & LUDIE NARRAMORE DOSS

In December of 1919, Leonard Young Doss and his wife, Ludie Blanche Narramore Doss, had been deeded a farm by Leonard's parents, William and Martha Kansas Barrow Doss, "for the care and support of his parents." It was in Cass County and they expected to raise their children on this farm and spend the rest of their life there. The depression and the drought put a sudden end to these dreams. To feed his growing family, Leonard's only option was to follow

Leonard and Ludie Doss with their children, September 1955.

the oil boom, which he did. Eventually they ended up in Gregg County, Texas.

The Doss' seventh child, Carolyn Lajuan Doss (Kerns), was born in Greggton 2 November 1934. She was followed by Norma Jean Doss (Wilkinson), 12 July 1936; Wanda Lee Doss (Ashby), 15 July 1940; and Larry Noble Doss, 25 January 1943, all born in Gregg County, Texas.

The older children were Reba Onean Doss (Danvers), born 10 November 1921; Leonard Uland Doss, born 7 March 1924; and Dorothy Marie Doss, born 23 April 1926, in Linden, Texas; Hershel Lane Doss, born 18 October 1929, in Waskom, Texas, and Burl and Earl Doss, born 26 March 1932, in Henderson, Texas.

In their early years in Greggton they always had a garden, which was planted and cared for by Leonard; but, they did not have electricity or gas. Water was drawn from a community well, which was about two blocks down the street.

Leonard had a number of jobs but eventually went to work for Standard Tool, which was located on the east side of what is now Standard Street. The family then moved to a shotgun house on this same road. This was an oil topped road that ended where the railroad overpass is now located. It had a big oak tree in the middle and this was where the school bus picked up the children. In those years, Roy Travis was the bus driver.

Reba, the oldest child, married before she graduated from high school. Leonard Uland graduated from Pine Tree High school in 1942, and was the salutatorian of his class. After graduation he joined the Army. Dorothy moved to Corpus to be with Reba and married there. Hershel quit school to join the Navy and earned his diploma through them. Burl and Earl, the twins, graduated from Pine Tree High School. Both joined the Navy. Earl later graduated from Kilgore Junior College, and then Texas A&M University. Carolyn, Norma Jean, Wanda and Larry all graduated from Kilgore High School.

The family moved to Kilgore in 1951 as Leonard had obtained a job as foreman for Sabine Pipe and Supply. They joined the Eastview Baptist Church where Leonard sang in the choir and became a deacon.

(l.-r.) Top: David Wayne Dolive and Brian Bruce Dolive. Bottom: Billie Jean Dolive and Wayne Bruce

Because Leonard Uland was overseas during World War II when the youngest child was born, the whole family was never together at one time until October 1955, in Kilgore, Texas (when the above picture was taken). Strange as it may seem they were never all together again.

Leonard (born 6 August 1903) and Ludie (born 26 October 1902) were living in Kilgore, Texas, when Leonard died 19 March 1966. Ludie died two months later on 27 May 1966. Both are buried in Lakeview Memorial Gardens Cemetery in Longview, Texas.

– Submitted by Janice V. Doss

JOHN F. "BUCK" DOZIER & FLORENCE A. "TUMP" DOZIER

John Fletcher "Buck" Dozier (born 9 July 1881, died 27 May 1950) was born in the Winona area of Smith County. He was the son of James Thomas Fletcher and Mary Zelda Knowles Dozier. His mother was 1/8 Cherokee Indian, her grandmother having been Mahala Williamson Bird of the Cherokee Nation in Alabama.

Buck married Florence Addie "Tump" Wallace (born 24 April 1884, died 14 October 1970) the daughter of Civil War veteran Joseph Reid Wallace and Alice Morris of Mecklinberg County, North Carolina. They set up housekeeping on a sharecrop farm near Starrville, Texas, in 1907.

Born to them was Doris Irline, 8 October 1908, and John Raymond, 29 August 1910. They moved to the Browning Community in Smith County near Harris Creek where their second daughter, Mattie Lucielle, died at birth in October 1920. Wallace Duane was born 23 January 1923, after which the family moved to Holt's Chapel Community in Smith County where Laurance "Adrian" was born 10 November 1929.

In December 1934, the family moved to a 282-acre farm in Gregg County. The farm was owned by Buck's uncle, J.A. Knowles, and was located 5-1/2 miles west of Kilgore on the Tyler highway. The farm was one mile off of the paved road, and was promised to Buck and his family at Mr. Knowles' death if they would fence and maintain the land. John Raymond and Buck fenced the farm, with 5-year-old Adrian piling brush and dragging limbs. Wallace entered Sabine Schools. Buck and Tump were Missionary Baptists who lived their faith; Buck would not allow any drinking on the property. Their door was always open to friends and family, there was always enough for "another plate" at their table. Tump was renowned for her good cooking.

Irline married Garl Brewer and their children were Jon Garl, Wallace and Celita. Both Irline and Garl are buried in Killeen, Texas. Wallace and Jon Garl both reside in the Dallas area. Celita's whereabouts are unknown.

John Raymond married Elsie Huffman and they had one daughter, Elinor Jane Humphries, born 25 August 1944, who resides in Carthage, Texas. John Raymond was killed in battle 10 June 1944, during World War II, and is buried in Normandy, France.

Wallace served in the U.S. Marines during World War II. He died in July 2001, and is buried in Starrville Cemetery.

Adrian married Margaret Robinson in 1955. Their children are Laura Monique, born 3 November 1955; Laurance Arvell, born 14 October 1958, died 20 May 1959; Lee O'Neal, born 13 October 1960; and Linda Lee, born 12 October 1962. Adrian, his wife and children attended Sabine Schools and Kilgore College. Later, Adrian served 24 years as Trustee at the college. Adrian and Margaret made their home in the Liberty City Community near Kilgore. The boys are buried in the Starrville Cemetery.

Laura married Tim Rebouche of Dallas; they live in Austin, Texas.

Linda married Eddie P. Shawn and they had two sons, Phillip Michael, born 10 July 1998, and Will Alex, born 14 September 1999.

– Submitted by Margaret Dozier

CHARLES B. & JEWELL DRAKE

Charles Browning Drake was born in Forney, Kaufman County, Texas, on 18 March 1900, and was one of six children. His parents were Sidney J. Drake and Virginia Parrish Drake. He was educated in the Forney public schools. Because most of the town's banks' employees were serving in the military during World War I, the president of one bank asked and received permission from Charles' father to take him out of school before graduating to work in the bank. During this time in the bank he established an insurance business with George R. Jordan.

Jewel and Charles Drake, 1981

Charles married Jewell Kathryn Welch, a schoolteacher, on 10 June 1925, in Forney. She was one of eight children born to John W. Welch and Florette Haynes Welch. She attended public school in Kemp, and in the early 1920s attended Southwestern University in Georgetown, Texas. Two children were born to Charles and Jewell: Charles B., Jr. in 1927, and Bobby Wayne in 1931, both in Forney.

In 1933, the family moved to Longview, and Charles opened the Charles B. Drake Insurance Agency with offices in the Glover-Crim Building. Charles Jr. joined the agency upon his graduation from Texas A&M in 1949. He was called to active duty in the army in 1952, served in Ko-

rea in 1953-54, and was awarded the Purple Heart. Charles Sr. retired in 1953 and sold the insurance agency to Jim Brent of Dallas.

Jewell and Charles were charter members of the Wesley Methodist Church on South Mobberly Avenue, established about 1935. They were both active in the early growth of that church, and Jewell taught a ladies' class for many years. As president of the Longview Federation of Women's Clubs in 1939-40, Jewell was instrumental in the establishment of the Community Center in Longview. Charles was active in the Optimists' Club, serving as president in the late 1940s.

Their son Bobby Wayne died in 1934 and is buried in Forney. Their son Charles Jr. married Mary Eleanor Park on 29 July 1950, in Longview. They live in Everman, Texas, where their two sons, Jim Drake and Bill Drake, also live.

Charles and Jewell were married for 65 years. They lived in Longview until their deaths: Charles on 8 July 1990, and Jewell on 18 March 1999. Both are buried in Forney.

– Submitted by Charles B. Drake, Jr.

MARVIN HENRY DRYDEN

Marvin Henry "Chick" Dryden, born 15 November 1911, in Red River County, Texas, was the son of Robert Marvin and Myrtie Neal Dryden. He married Lillie Mae "Gay" Hawkins 12 May 1934, in Johntown, Texas. Gay was the daughter of William John and Mary Jane Askins Hawkins.

Chick worked for Humble Pipe Line Company. He worked all over the East Texas Oil field. He moved his family to Longview in 1946 and they lived on Judson Road. His two children attended Judson Grove School. The family attended First Baptist Church–Judson. In 1949, he was transferred to Cisco, where they lived for over two years; he was then transferred to Talco, Texas. From there, in 1953, he moved back to Longview – then to Odessa and Midland, where he retired. After his retirement he and Gay made one final move back to Longview, Texas. The company was then called Exxon. Chick and Gay lived in Longview until their deaths. Chick died 15 June 1981, and Gay died 22 October 1988.

Mary Yvonne Dryden, born 13 February 1935, was the first child born to Chick and Gay. She married Frederick Henry Stahl 12 May 1957, in Longview, Texas. Frederick was born 15 Au-

(l.-r.) Front: Marvin Henry, Lillie Mae and Charles Dryden. Back: Mary Dryden.

gust 1933. Their three children were all born in Longview, Texas. The first child, a daughter, Rebecca Lee Stahl was born 23 June 1959, and married Philip John Brunwald (1957) on 20 November 1981. Their children were Taylor Hawkins Brunwald, born 25 November 1988, in Ft. Bragg, North Carolina, and Hunter Fergusson Brunwald, born 25 March 1992, in Leich, Germany. Mary and Frederick's second child was Elizabeth Ann Stahl, born 4 May 1963, and married 11 May 1995, in Taos, New Mexico, to Michael Yeager. Elizabeth and Michael had William Michael Yeager, born 4 May 1998, in Taos, New Mexico. Their third child was Frederick Henry (Freddy) Stahl, Jr., born 5 November 1964.

The second child born to Chick and Gay was Charles Franklin Dryden, born 14 August 1932, and married 20 June 1957, in Longview Texas, to Alice Grace McWhorter, who was born 29 September 1937. Charles and Alice had three children. The first, Amecia Gaile Dryden, was born 2 September 1961, and married 10 December 1982, to Timothy Lee Clem, who was born 29 April 1959; their children were Samuel Travis Clem, born 7 August 1986, and Cyndell Grace Clem, born 9 September 1989. The second child of Charles and Alice was Daphyna Dawn Dryden, born 11 November 1963, and married 6 November 1982, to Wilburn Apple, who was born 21 January 1961. Their children are Nolan Stafford Apple, born 5 May 1986, Colton Tyrel Apple, born 25 November 1988, and Caitlin Cheyane Apple, born 30 June 1991. Their third child was Charles Franklin Dryden, Jr., who was born 16 August 1968, in Longview, Texas. He married Lisa Kaye Yockey 2 June 1983. Lisa was born 6 November 1967. Their children are Hannah Mae Dryden, born 29 December 1999, and Sophie Linn Dryden, born 28 August 2002.

Frederick Stahl served in the United States Army, Charles Dryden in the United States Navy, Wilburn Apple in the United States Navy and Philip Brunwald is career Army. Ancestors have served in the Revolutionary War, several served in the Confederate Army and some in the war with Mexico – to free Texas and receive land grants.

Rebecca Stahl Brunwald has a Master's in Psychology from Texas. Rebecca and Philip Brunwald both received Master's in Education from Northwestern State University in Natchitoches, Louisiana. Elizabeth Stahl Yeager, Chuck Dryden and Lisa Yockey Dryden all have degrees from Baylor University. Chuck graduated from Texas Tech Medical School and is now a Medical Doctor working the Emergency Room at Longview Regional Hospital.

Dawn Dryden Apple received a degree from University of Texas at Tyler and is working at Kilgore College. Wilburn Apple received a degree from LeTourneau. Michael Yeager a degree from Rutgers University in New Jersey
– Submitted by Mary Stahl

JOHN CARROLL DUDLEY

Kilgore became a town in 1872, named after Constantine Buckley "Buck" Kilgore who donated a 200-foot strip of land containing 15 acres. A town site was marked off and sold to individuals and businesses. By 1880, this small town was considered economically sound and was surrounded by many small farms bought by people who came to Texas from the southern states. One of those farmers was John Davis, who came to Texas sometime between 1851-1854 from Wilson County Tennessee.

He began to buy land in Northern Rusk County and made his first purchase in Rusk County. In the following years, he acquired several farms throughout the area. On 26 November 1879, he bought the 327-acre Pilsbury place for $1,000, which was located on the west end of the Henry Wells original survey in Rusk County. John Davis bought this property from R.W. Stone and wife, Ann M. Stone, who had also paid $1,000 for this property on 21 January 1875, but their payments were in four notes "each of said notes to be paid by the delivery of five bales of lint cotton, good, ordinary, weighing each 500 lbs."

This farm was both in Rusk and Gregg counties when John Davis sold it to his daughter, M.C. Russell, for $1,000 on 1 September 1881. When she died on 18 December 1884, the property was inherited by her three children, Mary Catherine (Kate) Russell, Burr Davis Russell and Henry Crew Russell.

John Carroll Dudley was born in Upshur County on 23 December 1861. He came to Rusk County about 1869 with his parents, William Carroll Dudley and Benneta Ann Andrews Dudley. Farming was his main occupation until he learned the carpentry trade from his father. He and Mary Catherine (Kate) Russell married on 10 February 1886, in Rusk County at her parents' home. They were living in Tyler in 1892 when the decision was made to move to Kilgore, build a house and farm the 327-acre farm Mary Catherine (Kate) and her brothers inherited from their mother.

The following letter was written on 18 October 1892, by John Carroll Dudley to his wife and in the letter he explains the beginning of construction, the site and who helped build the house. The site he chose was located in Gregg County.

"Kilgore, Gregg Co. Tex. Oct. the 18, 1892 Dear Wife: I resiaved your letter this morning. Was glad to heare from you. This leaves all well. Me and Ge. Meadows is haling lumber and will get all the lumber on the ground today that I will need now. I won't ceal over head yet. It will be a box hous with three roomes and a galery in front. It is rite west of where the old cabing youst to stand just outside the field on the ridge. The water will run everyway from the hous. I have got about half enouf boards sawed and the rest of the timber out. Burr hope me get the timber and your Pa and Burr will help me build I guess. If he can get a mule him and Burr will be up there Wenday morning. I want Nuben and Dasy shod up there. Send me five dollars by him if he comes. And if he does not, get Will to send a registered letter by the last of the weak. I have got enouf to pay for the nayles and the lumber I guess but I will have to pay for the halling and get home. I will be home a bout the midle of next weak if I can. I will close for the present. love to all, John Dudley."

Sometime around 1900, the house was completed with the addition of a dining room, fruit closet, kitchen, pantry, two bedrooms, two side porches and front porch.

The large double-walled frame house is a pier-and-beam structure sitting on a foundation of native iron ore rock. The piers are made of hand-hewn white oak logs which are still basically as sound and solid as the day they were installed. Like most houses built during this time period, the beams and flooring stand well off the ground (3 feet or more). This space gives ample floor ventilation as well as providing an area for storing potatoes, onions, etc. The dry, soft sand served as a play area for children.

A double fireplace vented by a common chimney is centrally located in the wall dividing the two front rooms. "A unique feature of the home is the wrap-around porch or gallery. This porch extends continuously along the south and west of the home. The ends of this porch terminate in single rooms known as "stranger rooms" having access only to the porch." The Dudley family utilized these rooms as bedrooms for the sons, visiting relatives and sometimes for the visiting Methodist parson.

The living room ceiling is covered with beaded boards. This same material was used to install wainscoting in two of the rooms. The wainscoting is three feet high and capped with the traditional chair railing.

The gable roof is very steep and was originally covered with wooden shingles. The house was painted white with turquoise blue trim. A white picket fence enclosed the yard.

John Carroll and Mary Catherine (Kate) Dudley bought the inherited portion of the farm from Henry C. Russell and wife, Minnie, on 19 January 1901. Burr Davis Russell and wife, Annie, also sold their part to them on 10 December 1902.

The Dudleys were the parents of eleven children. The youngest son died in 1924. The eldest son, Issac Alexander Dudley (named for the founder of Alexander Institute and Method-

John and Kate Russell Dudley family, taken in the front yard at the homeplace, summer 1918: (l.-r.) Mattie Gertrude (Mrs. Clarence Lee), Isaac Alexander Dudley, Annie Myrtle (Mrs. Sam Andrews), William Gardiner Dudley, Mary Catherine (Mrs. Mary Lovell), John Leon Dudley, Wayman Carroll Dudley, Benetta Inez (Mrs. Darry Meadows), Houston Russell Dudley and Kate (Mrs. H.A. McFadin). All are deceased.

ist minister), was made executor of the estate. The property was divided equally between the children with the youngest daughter, Kate Dudley McFadin, inheriting the family home and the 30 acres surrounding the home. She and her husband, Herschell A. McFadin, made it their home until their deaths in the 1980s. They were the parents of six children. Today the eldest McFadin daughter and her husband own the home and 17 acres surrounding the home.

Though farming was an important part of John Carroll Dudley's life he was well known as a carpenter in the area. The Methodist church and Baptist church buildings which burned on that historical Sunday during the oil boom were built by John Dudley as well as many homes in the Kilgore area. For short periods of time he would leave the farm in charge of his wife and children and travel to nearby towns to do carpentry work.

Dudley house, 2903 Dudley Road, Kilgore, Texas, 2004.

This farm had a large flower garden to the east of the house. More than once the story was told to grandchildren about how family members would come in 2-3 hours early from the fields to work in the flower garden. In fact, the John Dudley home had one of the first flower gardens in Kilgore, planted with roses, Easter lilies and an abundance of other varieties of seasonal plants. Since Kilgore didn't have anything like a florist in those days, the Dudleys would allow their garden flowers to be picked by members of the community to be fashioned into funeral wreaths. The flowers were picked and the wreaths woven on the front porch.

Truly, the John Carroll Dudley home, located two miles east of Kilgore on Dudley Road, Gregg County, Texas, and comprised of the original house completed in 1900 and 17 acres of land surrounding the home, is significant in the history of the East Texas area. This home typifies the lifestyle of the agrarian community that existed in the 1890s and the decades following the turn of the century. The architectural style of the house and the fact that it was constructed by the farmer-owner using his carpentry skills further enhances the need for and worthiness of commemoration.

– Submitted by Louise Raby

BARRY NAPOLEON DUFF & IDA BELL MOBBERLY

It is believed Barry Napoleon Duff arrived in Gregg County about 1916. He was born 20 July 1873, Alto, Richland Parish, Louisiana,

died 23 April 1953 in Lubbock, Texas, and was buried 25 April 1953, in Big Springs, Texas. He married Ida Bell Mobberly about 1918 in Gregg County, Texas. She was born in 1895 in Longview, and died in 1958.

The parents of Barry Napoleon Duff were William Hiram Duff of Wilkinson County, Mississippi, and Roseanna Paillett of Louisiana.

The lineage of Barry Napoleon Duff is as follows: grandparents were Edward Duff of Virginia and Louisiana, and Delila Thompson of Nasemond County, Virginia; great grandparents were John Duff, 1761, Culpepper, Virginia, and Elizabeth Strother of Rockingham County, Virginia; great great grandparents were John Duff of Virginia and Sarah Nash of Virginia; great great great grandparents were James Duff, born 1716, Virginia, and Mildred Tutt of Virginia.

– Submitted by Bonnie Duff-Neal Smith

JOHN MARTIN DUNCAN

John Martin Duncan, son of Franklin and Caroline (McAnnelly) Duncan, was born in Lawrence County, Tennessee, on 7 February 1851. In 1858, the family moved Texas. He studied law and, in 1872, was admitted to the bar at Jefferson in the office of Judge John C. Stallcup. Duncan established his practice in Longview, where he was elected county attorney of Gregg County in 1876, the year he married Allie Davis. From 1878 to 1882, he represented Smith, Gregg, Upshur and Camp counties in the Texas Senate. In January 1884, he moved to Tyler, where he formed a partnership with James S. Hogg.

JIMMY LEE & CAROL SUE (CLELAND) DUNN

Jimmy Lee and Carol Sue (Cleland) Dunn moved to Longview to settle in 1997. They lived, first, in an apartment and then found their home in 1998. Although this appears to be a short-term history with Gregg County, Jim has a lived in this area during several periods. He first worked for Dowell oilfield services in 1956-57 as a truck driver. He was hired out of the home office in Tulsa, Oklahoma. He worked at Texas Utilities on a Dow Chemical Company project in 1992-93. Jim and Carol lived in Marshall during 1995-96, while Jim worked as a chemistry instructor at Texas State Technical College. He returned to the University of Houston to complete his master's degree and again moved to East Texas to teach at the college. He retired from teaching in 2001, but taught part-time in 2002.

Why did these two move to East Texas? The hills and trees reminded them of their Tulsa, Oklahoma, childhood. Jim was born to Lee Roy Dunn and Ola Mae Smith on 25 September 1936. Lee Roy Dunn (25 April 1918–12 January 1982) married Ola Mae Smith (22 June 1921–23 February 2001) in Tulsa, Oklahoma, on 26 October 1935. Carol was the first of four children born to Pelham Jackson Cleland (29 September 1906–18 July 1984) and Nellie Angie Moss (27 January 1910–14 March 1958). Pelham and Nellie were married 4 April 1936, in Wagoner, Oklahoma.

Both Jim and Carol attended Daniel Webster High School in Tulsa, Oklahoma. They met after graduation and married on 14 June 1963. Jim worked at Ozark-Mahoning Chemical Company in Tulsa, and Carol worked at the Community State Bank. While at Ozark-Mahoning, Jim received a patent on a procedure to produce zirconium hexafluoride which was expected to be a replacement for stannous fluoride in toothpaste. The new product never gained acceptance.

One year later, the couple moved to Stillwater, Oklahoma, so that Jim could finish his chemistry degree at Oklahoma State University. After graduation Jim began work at The Dow Chemical Company in Freeport, Texas. Carol began working for the company that same year. Jim worked as a supervisor in various plants. He developed the corrosion inhibitors used in today's long-life automobile coolants. He was a team member in developing a better long chain alcohol analysis, fluid bed catalyst reactors and a procedure for the removal of 99% of all sulfur dioxide contaminants from the vent stacks of Texas Utilities electrical plant at Martin Creek.

Carol progressed from clerk to supervisor of marine scheduling and then to production planning. Carol received her B.S. from the University of Houston at Clear Lake City.

The couple have no children but enjoy visits from their many nieces and nephews. They are happy with the East Texas climate and their retirement home. The Dunn's take genealogical trips to Kentucky, Georgia, Arkansas, and Oklahoma. They are members of the Gregg County Genealogical Society.

– Submitted by Carol Sue (Cleland) Dunn

KEN & JEANETTE DURHAM

Ken Durham's connection to Gregg County goes back to 12 October 1860, when his maternal great-grandfather, William Edwards Paxton, wrote a letter to his wife Rebecca who was at home in Sparta, Bienville Parish. Paxton was taking his elderly mother to visit another son, who was a pioneer Baptist preacher in Central Texas. The interesting letter is headlined "Earpville, Tex," and the second sentence says, "I now write 63 miles west of Shreveport at a place called by the Texas waggoners 'Steal Easy'

The Durhams

— rather an uninviting name at least, but we have no alternative." Earpville predated Longview and was located in the area where Alpine Road and Teague Street intersect with Marshall Avenue. Ken donated the original letter to the Gregg County Historical Museum.

Kenneth Reuben Durham, Jr. and his wife, Mary Jeanette Davis Durham, moved to Longview in 1964. Shortly after each graduated from Baylor University, they married and taught school in Brownfield, Texas, until they moved to Longview where Ken had a job teaching history and political science at LeTourneau College. Ken's father was Dr. Kenneth R. Durham, who developed the largest dental practice in the Lubbock-South Plains area between 1928-1958. His mother was Eloise Hutchison Durham. Ken's grandparents were Rev. John P. and Minnie Estes Durham of Louisiana, and James S. and Eloise Paxton Hutchison of Arkansas and Louisiana.

A Japanese sniper killed Jeanette's father, Jack S. Davis, Sr., in 1944 in Burma, where he was serving with Merrill's Marauders. Both Jack and his wife, Alice Johns Davis, grew up in Dallas. Jeanette's grandparents were James D. and Mary Ella Long Davis of Rankin County, Mississippi, and Charles and Grace Brown Johns.

Ken was born 25 May 1938, in Tahoka, Texas, where he grew up and graduated from Tahoka High School in 1956. Jeanette was born 24 May 1940, in Dallas, where she grew up and graduated from Adamson High School in 1958. They met at Baylor University in the fall of 1958, became engaged the following fall and married on 26 August 1961. Three sons were born to this union: David Lawton on 5 April 1965, John Paxton on 11 May 1967, and Mark Hutchison on 30 November 1972.

David married Kim Brumit of Dallas, whom he met at Baylor. They have three children (Grace, Emma and Jeff) and serve as missionaries with SIM in Cochabamba, Bolivia, where David teaches at Carachipampa Mission School. John graduated with a degree in architecture from Texas Tech and works for Bank One in Chicago. John is a project manager for new-build banks in the Chicago-Lake Michigan area. He met Julie Jaffee in Chicago, and they have four children (Alexander Paxton, Hanna, Justin and Tess). Mark met Rebekah Holmes at John Brown University in Siloam Springs, Arkansas, and they have two children (Reuben and Joel). Mark teaches school in Longview.

After Ken and Jeanette graduated from Baylor and married, Ken earned his M.A. in history from East Texas State Teachers College (now A&M-Commerce) in 1963, and his Ph.D. in College Teaching–History in 1971 from North Texas State University (now UNT). Jeanette earned her M.Ed. in Early Childhood Education from UT-Tyler in 1981, after which she taught kindergarten in Longview. Jeanette retired in 1999 after teaching a total of twenty-one years, and Ken retired in 2001 after a forty-year teaching career, of which 37 years were at LeTourneau.

In several ways Ken has contributed a small amount to recording and preserving the history of

Longview and Gregg County. In 1980, the *East Texas Historical Journal* published his article on the Longview Race Riot of 1919, and in 2000 the *Journal* published his article on Harmon General Hospital. He also wrote *LeTourneau University's First Fifty Years*, which was published in 1995. Ken also researched and contributed information to the Texas State Historical Commission for the state historical markers at First Baptist Church of Longview and for Speer Chapel (formerly the Harmon General Hospital Chapel) on the campus of LeTourneau University. Summaries of Ken's articles on the race riot and Harmon Hospital and of his history of LeTourneau University appear in the *New Handbook of Texas* (1995). Ken also contributed entries to the *Louisiana Dictionary of Biography* (1988).

Ken's interest in the Civil War and in family history led him to research the Civil War letters of his great grandfather, William Edwards Paxton, and *Louisiana History* published his article in 1979.

Ken and Jeanette appreciate the quality of life Longview affords for raising children, and the friends they have formed at First Baptist Church, LeTourneau University and the Longview schools.

– Submitted by Ken and Jeanette Durham

DEWEY JACKSON & EDYTHE ELEANOR SPARKMAN EASTEP

Dewey was a self-employed businessman operating Eastep's Service Station, Eastep's Boat and Motors, and Eastep Package Store in Longview. Edythe was a housewife and partner in the operation of the businesses. They married 14 April 1956, in Longview. He was born in 8 May 1901, in Claiborne Parish, Louisiana, to Wesley Thomas Eastep and Lillie Mae Knighton. Dewey was a member of the First Christian Church, Longview Masonic Lodge No. 404, the Shriners, and Sharon Temple. He died 28 October 1981, in Longview.

Edythe was a member of the First Christian Church and Tuesday Workshop Membership Committee. She was also a volunteer for Bethany Home and Meals on Wheels. She was born 11 July 1922, in Waco, Texas, the daughter of Homer Ansel Sparkman, Sr. and Verna Louise Blount, and died 24 April 1992, in Longview. Dewey, Edythe and son John are buried at the Lakewood Memorial Gardens in Longview.

Edythe's children are Martha Ann Shipman, born 14 June 1946, in Oklahoma City, Oklahoma; Sara Jane Shipman, born 2 October 1948, in Anadarko, Oklahoma; Rebecca Sue Shipman, born 8 April 1951, in Anadarko, Oklahoma; and

Edyth Eleanor Eastep and Dewey Jackson Eastep

John Robert Shipman, born 6 October 1953, in Anadarko, Oklahoma, and died 1 February 1981, in Hughes Springs, Texas.

Martha is a retired elementary school teacher and past director of the Brazosport Bluebonnet Cloggers. She is director of the Holly Lake Cloggers and a member of the Down Home Cloggers of Longview. She married Deason L. Hunt Jr. 24 November 1965, in Nacogdoches, Texas. They have two children: Michael Allen Hunt and wife Kindal Shores Hunt of College Station, Texas, and Emily Kay Hunt Elliott of Lewisville, Texas, and granddaughter Kaylee Danielle Elliott.

Rebecca owns a Systems Consultant business in Lubbock, Texas, where she lives with husband Rick Akard. They have grandchildren Christian and Sean Akard of Lubbock.

Sara and her husband Paul Wallace live in San Diego, California, where she is Director of Administration for United SolarOvonics. She previously was an officer in the Untied States Navy. Her children are Stacia Obermeyer of San Diego, and Brian Garza of Colorado Springs, Colorado. Grandchildren are Alex and Austin Obermeyer of San Diego, and Briana Garza of Colorado Springs.

John's daughter is Kimberly Shipman Larkin of Harleton, Texas, and his granddaughter is Clara Guerro of Harleton.

– Submitted by Deason Hunt

Eastep Service Station, 1937. Dewey J. Eastep is on the right with suit and tie.

JAMES TEMPLETON ECHOLS (1808-1884) & MARTHA CYRENA HOUSTON ECHOLS (1809-1875)

James Templeton Echols (1808-1884) and his wife, the former Martha Cyrena Houston (1809-1884), were among the earliest settlers of what is now Gregg County. They were of the stock that pushed the frontier of the South westward in the 1700s and 1800s, on the move in every generation, until that frontier closed in East Texas. For information on their relatives and descendants, see the articles in this book on John Rodden, Robert Finis Echols, Eugene Osborne McWhorter and Eugene Rodden McWhorter.

James Templeton Echols, usually known as "Temp," was born in Georgia, the third of six known children of James Echols and his wife, the former Nancy Winbush. He was descended from John Echols (1650-1712) who in 1704 bought land in what is now Caroline County, Virginia.

Martha Cyrena Houston, usually called Cyrena, was born in Tennessee. She was a second cousin of General Sam Houston of Texas fame; her grandfather Matthew was a younger brother of General Sam's grandfather Robert. Cyrena's mother, Nancy Gillespie (died 1816), was of a family that was connected with the Houstons in western Virginia in colonial times and later in pioneering settlement of Blount County, Tennessee. Nancy's father William Gillespie (1737-1831), born in Northern Ireland, enlisted on 7 January 1777, as a patriot soldier in the 9th (previously 13th) Virginia regiment.

Temp and Cyrena were married in October 1840, probably in Shelby County, Alabama. Within a year, they had moved to Shelby County in the Republic of Texas. Their sons George and Robert Finis, known as Bob, were born there on 19 March 1843, and 30 July 1846, respectively. When Bob was barely a month old, Temp claimed 640 acres located 20 miles northwest of Shelbyville, near what is now Timpson, under a land grant issued to him by the Republic of Texas in 1844.

Four months later, in January of 1847, Temp sold his grant. By October, the little family had moved to the Pine Tree community in Upshur County—which had been formed from parts of Nacogdoches and Harrison Counties the preceding year and extended south to the Sabine River. On the tenth day of that month, Temp and Cyrena joined 13 others as charter members of Pine Tree Cumberland Presbyterian Church—the first organized church in the future Gregg County and the second oldest church of that denomination in Texas. The first elders were 39-year-old James Templeton Echols and 53-year-old John Rodden—father of Bob Echols's future father-in-law, Aaron Castleberry Rodden. Temp served as clerk of the session until 1869.

Temp Echols became a prosperous farmer who brought virgin forest into cultivation. According to the census of 1850, he was a merchant. On the side, he was also a music teacher. (Musical talent ran in the Echols family; some of George's descendants became professionals.) Among relatives in the area were Cyrena's younger brother Samuel A. Houston. Bob Echols

and his first cousin Luther Houston (fourth child of Samuel and his wife, the former Letitia Talbot) later married sisters: Amelia and Mary Rodden, known as Millie and Molly. Samuel later married Martha Jackson Echols, eldest child of Temp's older brother George W. Echols.

Temp Echols and his family lived in a two-story red brick house on top of a hill overlooking the Marshall-Tyler Road—presently in the 4200 block of West Marshall Avenue, immediately west of Loop 281 (Standard Street). The site is now that of a gas well at an address of 511 Hilltop Drive. The bricks for Temp's house were fired on the farm by his workers; brickmaking was a craft that had been traditionally cultivated in the Echols family. When Temp's house was demolished during the 1950s, the bricks were acquired by B.W. Crain, Jr., for use in building his home on the Kilgore Highway south of Longview.

After Temp and Cyrena died, George lived in the house for a time before moving to Fort Worth. Bob became a prominent farmer, cattleman, and businessman in Longview. James Templeton Echols and Martha Cyrena Houston Echols were buried in Fisher Cemetery. (Copyright 2004 by E.W. McWhorter)

– Submitted by Andrew G. McWhorter

ROBERT BRUCE & BILLIE ANNE ECHOLS

Dr. Robert Bruce and Billie Anne Echols came to Kilgore in July 1952 to begin his medical practice. He and Dr. Henry K. Crawley established the Kilgore Medical Clinic that summer at 320 E. South Street and practiced together until Dr. Crawley retired in 1984. Dr. Echols worked alone until he retired in 1995.

Dr. and Mrs. Robert B. Echols (Bob and Billie Anne), April 2003

Dr. Echols was born in Little Rock, Arkansas, on 23 June 1922. Dr. Echols received his B.S. in 1948 from the University of Missouri and his medical degree in 1950 from Washington School of Medicine, St. Louis, Missouri. He is the son of Harry Clyde and Vera Ellis Echols, who moved to Kilgore in 1955. Harry died in 1956. Vera lived until 26 December 1993. His great grandfather was George C. Echols from Alabama, who married Hannah Durham in Chambers County, Alabama, in July 1840. They were in Holly Springs, Mississippi, by the time Thomas Jefferson Echols (Dr. Echols' grandfather) was born in 1854. He

later moved to Arkansas, where he was a store-keeper and photographer.

Billie Anne Echols was born in 1927 in a small town in northeast Arkansas, named Reyno after her great grandfather, Dennis Wells Reynolds, who was a pioneer businessman and landowner there. Her parents were Dennis Wells Reynolds II and Clarissa Anne Lambert, who came from Tennessee. Samuel Ervin and Anna Golightly Reynolds were her grand parents; and James Madison and Elizabeth Ann Reynolds were great great grandparents, coming from Jackson County, Illinois. He was buried in Randolph County, Arkansas, in 1888 in the Old Reynolds Cemetery, out from Pocahontas. After Arkansas schools, Billie Anne received further education at Memphis, Tennessee, where she and Dr. Echols met and married in July 1951. He was interning at Baptist Memorial Hospital there.

Bob and Billie Anne's children are Bruce Alan Echols, M.D., Dallas; Bradley R. Echols, attorney in Longview; and Beverly Anne Stovall, a teacher in Rockwall, Texas. Grandchildren are Ross and Nicholas Echols, high school students at Pine Tree, Longview; Brittany Anne Stovall, entering her third year at SMU, Dallas; and Perry Daniel Stovall, who will be a junior at Rockwall High.

Harry Clyde Echols, III attended Kilgore College and married a Longview girl, Patricia Southerland. Harry Clyde is the son of Dr. Echols' brother, Harry, who was killed during World War II. They live in Houston, Texas, and have a son named Josh.

– Submitted by Bob and Billie Anne Echols

ROBERT FINIS ECHOLS (1846-1916), AMELIA RODDEN ECHOLS (1851-1895) & ALABAMA ZEIGLER ECHOLS (1857-1932)

Robert Finis Echols (1846-1916, known as Bob) and his wife, the former Amelia Ann Rodden (1851-1895, nicknamed "Millie") were representative of the children who grew up at the western pioneer edge of the Antebellum South. That generation helped their parents hack farms out of the Upshur County wilderness, fought a losing war for their country's independence, then joined with a wave of newcomers in building up the new town of Longview and participating in the resurgence of the South. For

Amelia Ann "Millie" Rodden Echols

information on Bob and Millie's ancestors and descendants, see the articles in this book on James Templeton Echols, John Rodden, E.O. McWhorter and E.R. McWhorter.

During the War Between the States, Bob Echols enlisted for military service on 13 February 1864, at the age of 17, stating his occupation as a farmer. When discharged at Navasota on 25 May 1865, he was a corporal in Captain W.H. Mullins's Company I in the 35th regiment of dismounted Texas Cavalry. Bob had fought in the successful defense of Texas against Northern invasion at Mansfield and Galveston. According to his discharge certificate, he was 5 feet 6 inches tall and had fair complexion, blue eyes and dark hair.

Bob Echols and Millie Rodden were married on 2 July 1868. She had turned 17 three months earlier, and he was almost 22. The young couple moved into a house on the farm of his parents, Temp and Cyrena Echols. It was located a few hundred feet south of the parents' house, which stood at what today would be 511 Hilltop Drive, fronting in the 4200 block of West Marshall Avenue in Longview. Bob and Millie remained active members of the church in which they had been reared, Pine Tree Cumberland Presbyterian. Their first child, Hugh Upshur Echols, was born on 18 August 1869. Judging by the content of letters Bob wrote a few years later, his main concerns at that time were his family, his crops and livestock, his church and his music. And judging from his penmanship, spelling, grammar, and style, he was well educated.

Bob Echols's house on Center Street at the southwest corner of Methvin Street in Longview.

On 21 July 1871, Bob's father executed a blanket right-of-way agreement in favor of the Southern Pacific Rail Road Company, allowing the track to be built across his extensive land holdings. Westward construction of the Southern Pacific had halted in February at the new town of Longview, which was incorporated in May. After the struggling SP was taken over by the new Texas and Pacific Railway Company, construction resumed in January of 1873. Early in February, the transcontinental TP track and its crowd of immigrant Irish workers excavating with wheelbarrows passed a couple hundred feet south of Bob and Millie Echols's house.

Meantime, Gregg County was created by taking 143 square miles from the southern tip of Upshur County. Against the intent of its advocates, the center of the new county turned out not at Longview but very close to the Pine Tree church and school, which were about a mile and a quarter north of Temp and Bob Echols' houses.

By this time, the community in that vicinity — or perhaps the southern part of it, along the Marshall-Tyler Road (now Marshall Avenue), in the vicinity of the Echols houses — had come to be called Awalt. It was presumably named after Solomon Awalt, who had been pastor of Pine Tree Cumberland Presbyterian Church from 1847 to 1872. In the first county election, at the end of June, 1873 the Awalt community made a bid to become the county seat, garnering 125 votes to Longview's 523. One of the five precincts of the new county was centered on Pine Tree or Awalt. In the election for the first justice of the peace for that precinct, Millie Echols's brother Aaron Jasper Rodden was defeated by Joseph Mark Sparkman by a vote of 205 to 356.

Bob and Millie Echols had seven children: Hugh Upshur (1869-1940, married Pearl Smith of Gregg County; six children), Fay Ann (born 1871, married her second cousin John Wicker Echols, a physician of McAlester, Oklahoma, whose father, William Homer Echols, was a son of Temp's younger brother John Herbert Echols; four children), Vesta Leila (1873-1945, married Eugene Osborne McWhorter; one surviving child), Ross (died at birth), Ola Nancy (1878-1963, married Sam C. Shipp of Kentucky, lived in Lebanon, Tennessee; one child), Fannie DeLoach (1880-1955, never married), and Robert Templeton (1883-1952, married Margaret Cofer of Gainesville; no children).

The growing Echols family moved into Longview, first to a house in what is now the 400 block of South High Street, then to one on Center Street at the southwest corner of Methvin Street. Each child completed the Longview public schools, received higher education, and was given a generous dowry at marriage.

While continuing to raise various crops, Bob Echols prospered especially in the cattle business. He operated mainly in a tract of several hundred acres running east along Harris Creek between

Robert F. "Bob" Echols and family at his house in Longview at Christmas time in 1915. Front row: Bob, daughters Ola and Amelia, grandsons James "Tince" Echols, Eugene Rodden McWhorter and Paul Echols. Back row: Son Robert T. and his wife Margaret, Bob's second wife Alabama Zeigler Echols, daughter Fannie, daughter-in-law Pearl Smith Echols, daughter Vesta Echols McWhorter, son-in-law Eugene Osborne McWhorter and son Hugh Upshur Echols.

West Marshall Avenue and the railroad, extending from the end of Gilmer Road to the present Spur 63 and thence north along Grace and Guthrie Creeks to McCann Road. Besides raising cattle of his own, Bob bought stock from others and from time to time loaded cattle cars for rail transport to the market in Fort Worth. In partnership with John Philip Zeigler (1863-1916), he also operated a meat market in Longview, located on Fredonia Street at the southwest corner of Methvin Street. Their slaughtering operations were conducted mostly at cattle pens located at what is now the west side of Spur 63 between Marshall Avenue and the railroad.

After Millie died in 1895, Bob married his partner's older sister, Alabama Zeigler (1857-1932), a close friend of Millie's who had never married. Her father, John P. Sigler (1814-1892), had arrived on a ship at Mobile as a young Swiss immigrant from St. Gallen. According to a family tale, he thought Alabama looked so beautiful after the long and arduous voyage that he thought its name would be a good one for his first daughter. He married Martha A. Sample or Samples (1832-1892) of Upshur County and moved to Longview in 1871. Bob and Alabama had one child, Amelia Alabama Echols (1899-1979), who never married.

Bob and Millie Echols' daughters about 1888: Vesta, Fay, Fannie and Ola.

Although residing across the street from First Presbyterian Church, Bob Echols long remained faithful to his Cumberland Presbyterian roots. He was ordained as elder like his father and father-in-law and transferred to the Longview congregation of that denomination. However, in 1906, the national Cumberland Presbyterian Church merged with the Presbyterian Church in the U.S.A., a Northern denomination. As a result, in 1909, several families of the Longview Cumberland congregation joined First Presbyterian—including Bob Echols, who remained an elder when he switched denominations.

The principal relic of Bob Echols's activities in Longview is Lake Lomond, a 40-acre impoundment of Harris Creek situated between Marshall Avenue and the railroad and extending from Lake Lamond Road to H.G. Mosely Parkway. ("Lamond" is a popular misspelling.) It was built in 1909 and 1910 by the Lomond Lake Corporation, which was formed for that purpose in 1908. The owners were Bob Echols, his son Hugh, and his friend Frank T. Rembert, a prominent Longview businessman. Named after Loch Lomond in Scotland, the lake was built on the western 80 acres of Bob's main tract and another 40 acres acquired from others farther west, extending beyond what is now Mosley Parkway. The corporation offered swimming, fishing permits, motor launch rides, and a pavilion for social events at a facility that fronted on West Marshall Avenue at the intersection of Gilmer Road. The corporation was dissolved in 1923, and ownership of the lake property passed to the McWhorter descendents of Bob's daughter Vesta.

After Bob's death, Alabama and her daughter Amelia moved to a house that still stands at 123 South Houston Street. After Alabama died in 1932, Amelia continued living there until about 1977, joined for much of the time by her sister Fannie.

Amelia Ann Rodden Echols was buried in her parents' plot at White Cemetery. Robert Finis Echols and his daughters Amelia and Fannie were buried in the McWhorter-Echols plot at Greenwood Cemetery. Alabama Zeigler Echols was buried in her grandfather's plot at Greenwood Cemetery. (Copyright 2004 by E.W. McWhorter)
– Submitted by Lottie McWhorter

MOLLIE MAXINE MCCOY EDMONDS:
The Real McCoy

Mollie Maxine McCoy Edmonds was born 8 February 1920, to Roxie Ray Rhodes and Charlie McCoy. Her parents met and married in Bagwell, Texas, around 1914.

After they married, they moved to Annona, in Red River County. Roxie and Charlie had five children: Rhodes and James Lawrence both died as infants, Charles Worth, 1912-1990, and twins, Mollie and Janie.

Charlie barbered in Annona for a few years, then moved his family back to Bagwell where he opened his shop in front of his house. At the age of ten, Mollie began giving haircuts in her father's shop. Standing on the top of a box to

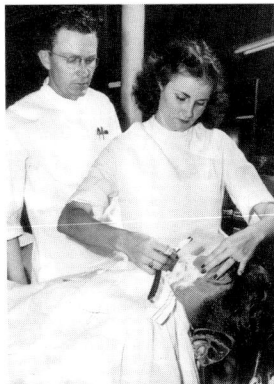

"Miss Mollie," 1945

reach her customers' heads, Mollie gained skill and experience in the barbering profession. As a young entrepreneur, Mollie would invite her friends over after school to give them haircuts. She recalls one schoolmate who gave him his sandwich in exchange for a haircut. The following article appeared in the Clarksville newspaper in 1930. "The little city of Annona, in Red River County, Texas, claims the honor of having within its confines the youngest barber in the state and perhaps in the world. Worth McCoy, 12 years old, son of Mr & Mrs Charlie McCoy, Worth has been "barbering" since he was 10 years old. He is an expert hair cutter and very adept with the razor. He has shaved as many as twenty-three men in one day."

Mollie barbered with her father for seventeen years and still owns her father's original barber chair, which has been in the family for over 80 years.

After World War II, a law was passed that required barbers to be state licensed. Typically a man's profession, "Miss Mollie" had to do some tall talking to gain admittance to the Dallas Barber College. Boasting "Irish pride" and determination, Mollie completed the course, graduated and was featured in the Dallas Times-Herald in 1949 as the first woman barber in Texas.

In 1938, Mollie married U.D. Humphrey. They had five children, Bobby, U.D. Junior ("Buddy"), Barbara, Judy and Melinda. Mollie supported the family while U.D., Senior went to barber school, then later put sons Bobby and Buddy through school at East Texas Barber School in Tyler.

"Miss Mollie," 2004

In 1951, U.D. and Mollie relocated to Longview and opened Mollie's Barber Shop on Highway 80.

U.D. and Mollie divorced in 1955, and Mollie continued to operate her shop.

Mollie and sons Bobby and Buddy all worked at Mollie's at various times. Mollie's Barber Shop is still open for business after 52 years with Miss Mollie still giving proper men's cuts.
– Submitted by Bobby Humphrey

ELDER

Originally from England, there are records of the Elder family in Virginia as early as 1664. In the latter part of the 18th century, Joseph Elder sold his land and moved to Georgia. His grandson, H.T. Elder, who later came to Texas, was born in Clarke County, Georgia, in 1851. The son of D.H. Elder, H.T. Elder was already married in 1870 according to the census of that year. His wife Sarah (Sallie) was born in Clarke County, Georgia, also in 1851.

In November 1882, H.T. arrived in Longview by train to visit relatives. Persuaded to move to Gregg County, he established a sawmill and commissary for mill hands in a small community, which was later named Elderville. He moved the sawmill to Kilgore after a few years. At that time he and Sallie became members of the First Presbyterian Church of Kilgore.

In the early days the H.T. Elder and Sons Lumber Company advertised that they dealt in yellow pine timber cut by hand and hauled by mules and oxen. H.T.'s sons, John and Frank Elder, Sr., later owned the sawmill. The lumber was shipped by train to destinations far and near. Some shipments went to the Gloor Ortman Lumber Company in Chicago, and others went to the Longview Casket Company. At that time Frank Elder, Jr., age 16, when not in school, had the task of checking the lumber onto the boxcars.

The Elders had eight children between 1871 and 1890, six of whom were born in Georgia: John Samuel, born 1871, married Camie Wilkins; Frank, Sr., born 1873, married Minnie Willoughby (Frank was nine years old when the family came to Gregg County by covered wagon.); Nancy Elizabeth, born 1875, married J.B. Walker; William Wesley, born 1877, married Victoria Spinks; Matilda Eudora, born 1880, married E.D. Skipper; James Z., born 1882, married Zipporah Harris; Henry Trip, Jr., born 1886, married Orion Choice; and Sallie Elder, born 1890, married Jim Hearne. Only Henry Trip, Jr. and Sallie were born in Texas. H.T. died in 1914, and ten years later when his wife died, she was survived by their eight children, forty grandchildren and sixteen great grandchildren.

Frank Elder, Sr. was educated in the public schools and at Alexander Institute in Kilgore, which later became Lon Morris College of Jacksonville.

Frank and Minnie Elder were parents of Charlene (Tootsie), married Judson Bagwell and lived in Longview; Frank Elder, Jr., married Gretta Treadwell and lived in Kilgore; and Jack D. Elder, married Winter Dickson and lived in Kilgore. All were born in Kilgore at home.

Elder family. (l.-r.) Back: Frank Elder, Jr., Minnie Willoughby Elder, Tootsie Elder Bagwell, Jack Elder holding Jack, Jr., Gretta Treadwell Elder and Judson Bagwell. Front: J.J. Bagwell, Jr., Jane Bagwell, Minette Elder, Frank Elder III and Meriam Elder. Winter Dickson Elder, Jack's wife, must have been taking the picture.

The grandchildren of Frank and Minnie Elder are J.J. Bagwell, Jr., Longview; Jane Bagwell McCrea, San Angelo; Meriam Elder Eakin, Tyler; Minnette Elder, Jamestown, New York; Frank Elder, III, Longview; Dr. Jack Elder, Jr., Longview; and Susie Elder Merritt, Kilgore.

Their great grandchildren are Deanne Bagwell Rose of Dallas; Jud Bagwell, Fort Worth; Beth McCrea Mayer, San Angelo; Winn McCrea, Marble Falls; Gretta Eakin Sharp, Edom; Joseph Eakin, Tyler; Carey Elder Kelley, Austin; Leon (Bo) Elder, San Diego, California; Kelly Elder Blakely, Dallas; Ginger Elder Cannon, Longview; Kristin Elder, Longview; Tiffany Elder Johnston, Kilgore; and Tara Elder Ford of Dallas.

There are 15 great great grandchildren of Frank and Minnie Elder.

Descendants of Frank, Sr. and Minnie Elder who are still residing in Gregg County are Winter and Jack Elder, Sr., Rosemary and J. Bagwell, Lee and Frank Elder, III, Jan and Jack Elder, Jr., Susie and A.P. Merritt, Jr., Ginger and Ron Cannon and sons and Tiffany and Bryan Johnston and children.

– Submitted by Meriam Elder Eakin

ELLIS

Barney Hobson Ellis was born at New Summerfield, Texas, 3 September 1898, and married Gertrude Dunnavant of Union Grove, born 15 January 1910. Children of this union were three daughters – Sally, Linda and Joy.

The youngest of eight children, Barney came to Longview in 1919 to care for his sick father and found employment with Texas & Pacific Railroad. His mother Margaret Ann (Dotson) Ellis's father, Josiah Dotson, had commanded forces in both battles at Manassas Junction (Bull Run) during the War Between the States. Barney's father, John Garrison Ellis, had farmed land as well as serving as justice of the peace. His grandfather and great grandfather had came to Texas early in the 1840s as Methodist missionaries to the Cherokee and Caddo Indians, along with settlers during the Republic of Texas days. Both were or-

dained in Alabama. Although John Wesley Ellis, Jr. returned to Georgia, the family has never been certain what came of John Wesley, Jr.

Mattie Gertrude Dunnavant came to Longview in 1929, leaving the family farm to seek her fortune in the big, booming city. Although valedictorian of her graduating class in Gladewater, she had no money for college. This brave lass worked as "Colonel" Culpepper's photography assistant, then as a dental hygienist for Dr. McKinnon before becoming a real estate partner with her husband – a career she successfully pursued for the rest of her life.

Ellis was a 32nd degree Mason and a member of the Scottish Rite. Barney Ellis served on the Longview Board of Realtors, as its president until his death. Ellis died of a heart attack on the 16th of September 1953.

Five years later Gertrude married Cecil Keyton, a local builder and developer from Neosho, Missouri. Together the two helped build "Forest Hills" and several ranching properties.

Sally married James Robert Dobbs, Jr. of Longview, who became an attorney in Tyler. The couple parented David Ellis Dobbs and Dianne Elizabeth Dobbs Daubler. Linda, a longtime teacher, married Jackie Lee Tucker of Spring Hill, a banker. Samuel Scott Tucker was born of this union. The couple settled in Plano. Joy returned to Longview during her mother's final illness in 1993. She and her children's father, B. Reagan McLemore III of Longview, had three children – Benjamin IV (d. 2002), Stephen Insley and Katheryn Keyton (Turner). Now a semi-retired college English teacher, Joy is married to Dr. O. Clayton Mitchell. The couple reside in her mother's old home on Iris Circle, built by Junius and Iris Flewelen in 1950.

– Submitted by Joy Ellis-Mitchell

EMBERLIN

The Emberlin family arrived in Gregg County in early 1932, with the newly discovered oil in East Texas. Roy Emberlin came as an employee of the Atlantic Oil and Refining Company. Roy's sister, Mabel, whose husband, John Handy, Sr., also worked for the Atlantic Oil Company, came to Gregg County. Mabel and John had a daughter, Elva, and a son, John, Jr. Like Roy, they lived in housing provided by the Atlantic Company near the Sabine River (called "the Bottom") and Murriel's Lake.

In June 1932, Roy married Lily Bryan from Oklahoma. They had a daughter, Darlene. Roy rode a horse in bad weather to operate the wells assigned him because the ground was low and there was an unusual amount of rain that year.

Fred Emberlin, Roy's brother, also came to East Texas with the Mercer Trucking Company. Fred and his wife, Dorothy, had two children, Patsy Ruth and Richard Lee. Roy's sister,

Minnie, and her husband, Whitey Gardner, with their children, Zelta, Lester Lee and Roberta, also moved to Gregg County. Whitey also worked for Mercer.

In 1942, Roy's parents, W.E. and Zora Emberlin, moved to Gregg County from Mineral Wells, Texas. Roy's dad, in prior years, had been a Teaming Contractor and hauled oil field equipment in fields in Texas, Oklahoma and Arkansas, by mule teams. In connection to their business they lived at Ranger and Mexia, Texas, for brief periods. He employed several men as well as his sons.

W.E. "Bill" Emberlin, Roy's brother, moved to East Texas and briefly worked for the Atlantic. In 1943, Bill Emberlin married Frances Woods of White Oak and had a son, Billy Carol. They later moved to Gilmer.

All the Emberlin children attended White Oaks schools. Darlene finished high school at Pine Tree. Billy Carol also attended Pine Tree and finished high school in Gilmer.

Darlene married Norman Whitehorn in 1950. They continued to live in Gregg County for about ten years before moving away. During those years Darlene was secretary to Mr. Anderson, Superintendent of the Judson Schools and the first Tax Assessor and Collector of Judson ISD. Norman worked for Shell Pipe Line and preached for many Churches of Christ throughout East Texas on weekends. Their children were born during this time. In 1960, they moved to Houston and from there to College Station in 1964. Norman received his doctorate. Darlene worked for A&M Consolidated School and Texas A&M University. They now live in Tyler and are both retired from Texas A&M. Norman holds an Associate Professor & Extension Specialist Emeritus and is an elder at the Rice Road Church of Christ. Their sons are Stan and Gary.

In 1983, Gary married Janet Miller of Beaumont. They live in the Pine Tree School District. Their children are Garrett, Alina, and Deanna. Gary, a graduate of Texas A&M, is now a designer of log homes for Satterwhite Log Home Company near Longview. He previously worked for Longview Bank & Trust. They attend the Reel Road Church of Christ where he is a deacon.

Roy and Lily Emberlin, June 6, 1932

Stan attended Florida College and Sam Houston State University and is an avid golfer. He lived in Longview and worked for the Western Co. until 1983. He married Kay Harding of Bryan in 1983, and now lives in Bryan, Texas, with children Zach, Ashley and Hunter. Stan works for Baskins Robbins Ice Cream Co. They attend the Benchley Church of Christ, where he sometimes leads singing.

They all proudly claim Gregg County as their roots.

– Submitted by Darlene Whitehorn

CARL LEWIS ESTES

Carl Estes, newspaper publisher and industrial leader, was born in New Market, Tennessee, on 10 November 1896, the son of Joseph Guinn and Della Marshall (Loy) Estes. He attended the public schools of Commerce and Denison and East Texas State Teachers College (now East Texas State University). He was editor of the college newspaper, which spurred his interested in journalism as a career. He worked as a foreign correspondent for the International News Service in Paris and Stockholm. He founded the *Tyler Telegraph* in 1930, and four years later bought the *Longview Daily News*, which later combined with the *Longview Morning Journal* as one newspaper. At Longview, he also owned and published two weekly newspapers, the *Longview Lens* and the *Greggtonian*. During the 1930s, Estes was publisher of the *Van Free Press*, the *Carthage Panola Watchman*, *East Texas Oil Magazine* (later the *Texas Oil Journal*), *East Texas Dairyman*, the *Wood County Record*, and the *Mineola Monitor*.

He served in the cavalry in World War I and was a lieutenant commander in the navy during World War II. He was active in the Democratic National Party. He returned to Longview after World War II and became instrumental in helping persuade a number of major industries to locate in the Longview area. Estes was a Mason and a Methodist. He married Margaret Virginia McLeod in Willow Grove, Pennsylvania, in 1943. He died at his vacation home in La Jolla, California, on 29 May 1967, and was buried in Memory Park, Longview, Texas.

DELL J. EVERETT

Dell Johnson Everett was the oldest son of Lafayette Johnson Everett and Martha Ann (Jeter) Everett. He was born in Gladewater on 10 January 1889. His father, L.J. Everett, was the owner and operator of the L.J. Everett Mercantile and Hardware Co. As a young man, Dell Everett studied music, singing in choirs and playing the clarinet. He was an enthusiastic horseman and, as he grew older, took charge of the horses and mules used for hauling in his father's business. He worked in his father's store and, in addition, had a job collecting laundry. An essay owned by the family and writ-ten by Dell describes his job of collecting laundry from people wishing to send their washing to a professional laundry. Dell collected the laundry in a horse-drawn wagon and loaded it on a train bound for Fort Worth. A professional laundry in Fort Worth washed and ironed the laundry and shipped it back to Gladewater by train within a few days.

In 1904, Dell's father bought the Citizens National Bank in Longview and moved his family to this city. The family kept their house in Gladewater and traveled back and forth to Gladewater whenever necessary. They lived in Longview at least until 1908 because Dell attended high school in Longview. The family has his report cards from 1904 through 1907 – all show attendance at Longview High School. Sometime between 1904 and 1908, Dell met Irma Mayfield, his future bride. The two young people lived in adjacent houses. Their letters mention being able to look at each other from their windows. Everett graduated from Longview High School in 1908. In the spring of 1908, he also spent some time working in Gladewater in his father's store. In 1909, he went to Baylor College (now Baylor University). Letters and diaries existing from that time tell us that, at Baylor, Everett went to moving pictures, walked young ladies home from church and drank cokes. While there Everett received many cards and letters from friends in East Texas, including cards from Irma.

Dell Everett and Irma Sue Mayfield (2 February 1891–25 July 1956) were married on 12 November 1912, in the house of Mr. and Mrs. Green Perry on Center Street in Longview. The Perry's were Irma's uncle and aunt. Green Perry was born about 1840 and died 16 November 1921. Mrs. Perry was the former Medora Womack of Marshall and the oldest sister of Irma's mother. Medora was born 28 February 1852, and died 2 January 1914.

Irma's parents were William Sidney Mayfield and Susan (Womack) Mayfield. W.S. Mayfield was an early East Texas dentist, hav-

Pictured at center is Dell J. Everett riding Red King in Gladewater Round-Up Rodeo parade.

ing studied dentistry in Pennsylvania. He was born in McNairy County, Tennessee, on 3 October 1844, and came to Texas as a child. Susan Womack was born in Marshall in 1856; and at the time of her death in 1900, had several siblings living near her home at 310 South Center Street in Longview. In addition to her sister, Mrs. Perry, another sister, Kate (Womack) Rembert (Mrs. F.T. Rembert) lived two blocks away at 414 Fredonia, and a brother, Alonzo Womack, lived with his family two blocks south on Center Street. Green Perry, Alonzo Womack and W.S. Mayfield were business partners in the Womack-Perry Co., a mercantile business located at the corner of Tyler and Cotton streets where Armadillo Willies stands today. W.S. Mayfield was a veteran of the War Between the States, having served with the Texas 4th Cavalry Battalion, Co. H, which conducted operations in the New Mexico Territory. This company apparently moved to Louisiana before the war's end because Mayfield's obituary states that he participated in the battles of Mansfield, Franklin and Pleasant Hill in that state before the war ended. W.S. Mayfield also served a term as Gregg County Clerk. In 1879, Mayfield opened a business with his brother-in-law, F.T. Rembert, which was known as Mayfield, Rembert and Co.

Dell and Irma lived their entire married lives in the house at 310 South Center where Irma had been born. Before and after the Everett's marriage, Dell worked in the Citizens National Bank. A 1920 census lists his occupation as a "bookkeeper at a bank." Later documents list him as Cashier. After the Citizens Bank closed, Dell was active in the business of the Gladewater Banking Co., a bank founded by his father. After his father's death in 1928, he served as the executor of his father's estate managing the Everetts' many business interests. Everett was active in civic affairs and sang in the choir of the First Baptist Church of Longview. He was one of the organizers of the Longview Municipal Band and played clarinet in that organization for many years. He also was an organizer of the Longview

Interior of Citizens National Bank. Pictured center, Dell J. Everett. Pictured right, L.J. Everett.

Saddle Club, in whose activities he was an active participant. In 1937, Everett bought land in Harrison County not far from downtown Longview; and in 1938, he built a state of the art stable to house his many three- and five-gated show horses. Everett rode and showed these horses in many area horse shows, sometimes entering a horse in every class of competition.

Dell J. Everett riding Red King.

In 1937, a number of Gladewater citizens formed the Gladewater Round-Up Rodeo Association with the goal of producing an annual rodeo in the Gladewater area. Dell Everett was among these men; and in addition to being a founder, he served on the Board of Directors of that organization until his death. In 1938, Everett purchased a "schooled parade horse" whose name as Red King. Everett and Red King appeared in all of the Gladewater Round-Up Rodeo promotional parades held to advertise the parade. Until his death in 1972, Everett rode Red King each night of the rodeo in the Rodeo Grand Entry Parade. Part of Red King's charisma was his ability to prance with the parade music and to rear and appear to cut-up on command. Gladewater citizens will remember his performances in rodeo parades of the 1940s, 1950s and 1960s. Irma and Dell J. Everett are buried in Greenwood Cemetery in Longview.

Irma and Dell Everett had one daughter, Dorothy, born 31 August 1916. Dorothy married Garland S. Rushing, M.D., a Longview physician and surgeon who was born in Arkansas and came to Texas in 1932. Dorothy and Garland had two children, Diana and Daphne. Diana lives in Longview, and Daphne is married to Robert S. Daniel, III and lives in Austin. The Daniel's have one son, James Rushing Daniel.

– Submitted by
Diana Rushing

L.J. Everett, about 1920

LAFAYETTE JOHNSON EVERETT

Lafayette Johnson "L.J." Everett (29 June 1863 – 4 May 1928) was born in Choctaw County, Alabama, the son of Josiah (23 No-

vember 1827 – 28 September 1864) and Tempa Bruner Everett (11 December 1840– 20 March 1898). It is believed that Josiah never saw his son, as he was serving in the Army of the Confederacy at the time of Lafayette's birth. Josiah enlisted 3 September 1862, as a Private in Company E, 3rd Alabama Infantry Regiment. He served in Virginia and died or was killed on 28 September 1864. His last resting place is unknown to the family. In 1874, Tempa and her son moved to Texas, along with other members of her community, including her brother and two of her husband's brothers who were married to her older sisters. Mother and son lived for a time in Longview, but as L.J. approached maturity, he gained employment with the Texas & Pacific Railway as a telegraph operator, living and working in Gladewater.

In Gladewater, or in nearby Union Grove, L.J. met and eventually married Martha Ann Jeter (20 November 1866–11 January 1964). Martha was the eldest daughter of Ann Elizabeth (Turner) Jeter (24 July 1838–31 January 1918) and Edmond Jeter. Martha's mother, Ann Elizabeth Turner, was born in Cowetta County, Georgia, and had come to Texas at the age of fourteen. Ann's parents were Benjamine and Elizabeth Turner. Martha was born in Union Grove. Edmond was a farmer and Baptist preacher.

L.J. and Martha were married on 19 December 1883. They lived in Gladewater in a house at the corner of North Main and Highway 80. The house occupied a site where a gas station stands today. After their second child was born, they built a larger house across the street where the drive-in bank stands now. This second house was a striking, two-story Victorian home with a wrap-around porch and it is well remembered by long-time residents of Gladewater.

Shortly after their marriage, the Everett's opened a hardware and mercantile store on Pacific Street in Gladewater. According to railway regulations, a railway employee could not operate a business in his own name, so the business was listed in the name of L.J.'s brother-in-law. The store was opened in 1888, and was known as the "J.T. Jeter Mercantile." In 1901, the name of the business was changed to "L.J. Everett Mercantile and Hardware Co." The store was successful and served the needs of the farming community; it was there that farmers could sell their cotton and buy such things as tools, sugar, cloth, etc.

Interior of L.J. Everett Mercantile & Hardware Co. about 1910. L.J. Everett pictured on the right; man on left unknown.

Martha Jeter Everett (Mrs. L.J.) riding side saddle in Gladewater Round-Up Rodeo Parade, about 1955.

There were three Everett children. The oldest child was a daughter, Katie Lea, born 4 October 1887 (died 1982). The oldest son, Dell Johnson, was born 10 January 1889, (died 5 April 1961); and a second son, Carl Bussey, was born 3 March 1889 (died 22 June 1934). L.J. Everett became the owner of the Citizens National Bank in Longview in 1904. This bank was located on Fredonia Street, and the building is owned and occupied today by the Gregg County Historical Museum. He moved his family to Longview for a time and his son, Dell, attended Longview High School, graduating in 1908. In 1911, L.J. opened the Everett Banking Co. in

Everett home on North Main in Gladewater, 1897-1965.

Gladewater adjacent to his store. Later, the Everett Banking Co. became the Gladewater State Bank. L.J. was bank president until his death in 1928.

The Everett grandchildren were Dorothy, daughter of Dell Johnson and Irma (Mayfield) Everett; and Carl Bussey Everett, Jr. and Jane Everett, children of Carl B. Everett, Sr. and Elizabeth Everett. Jane married Ward Stevenson of Orange, Texas.

L.J. Everett died in Shreveport, Louisiana, in 1928 in the aftermath of a stroke. Martha served as bank president for a time. The family has a picture of her riding sidesaddle wearing her riding habit; she is shown riding in a Gladewater Round-Up Rodeo parade. Martha died at the age of 97 in 1964. The Everetts are buried in Rosedale Cemetery in Gladewater.

– Submitted by Diana Rushing

ROBERT EDWARD FAULK

Robert Edward Faulk was born 5 August 1875, in Troy, Alabama, and died 14 December 1959, in Longview.

Robert married Mary Dell Sena Head on 24 December 1896, in Big Sandy, Texas. Mary Head was born 9 January 1877, in Troy, Alabama, to T.R. Head (born 1 December 1839, and died 4 August 1900, in Big Sandy) and Mable D. Beard Head (born 5 March 1837, and died 14 June 1898, Big Sandy). Robert Edward's parents were Phillip Marion (born 6 June 1833, Troy, Alabama, died 2 July 1911) and Mary Jane Rowden Faulk (born 10 April 1837, Troy, and died 24 January 1893).

The children of Robert Edward and Mary Dell Sena Faulk were Manilla Mae Faulk, born 4 May 1898, Big Sandy, Texas, and died 19 December 1913, Big Sandy; Fannie Clara (Faulk) Sellers, born 7 December 1899, Big Sandy, Texas, died 9 February 1991, Longview; Winnie Toy (Faulk) Richardson, born 28 November 1902, Big

Sandy, and died 21 November 1985, Spring Hill; Robert Grady Faulk, born 17 August l905, Big Sandy, died 20 January 1965, Dallas; Jessie Elree (Faulk) Richardson, born 6 November 1906, Big Sandy, died 10 August 1923, Big Sandy; Mable Dee Nellie Dee (Faulk) (McCranie) Green, born 13 October 1909, Big Sandy, died 23 January 1989, Georgetown, buried in Winterfield Cemetery, Longview; Lola Irene Elizabeth (Faulk) (Anderson, Stanley) Horn, born 17 November 1911, Big Sandy, died 18 December 1989, Longview; Ruby Lena (Faulk) Schloer, born 29 July 1914, Big Sandy, died 5 June 1982, California; and Thomas Leslie Faulk, born 18 October 1917, and died 18 February 1918, Big Sandy.

According to fragmented Faulk family history, it started from a province on the Rhine River lying between France and Germany. They migrated through Wilming-ton, North Carolina, to Alabama, Louisiana and Texas. They arrived in Big Sandy, Texas, sometime in the early 1890s. All were farmers at the time. Sometime in the late 1920s they moved to the Foster farm just over in Harrison County, just north of Page Road and east of Old Jefferson Road. Farming cotton, one or two bales a year, corn, gardening and raising their own beef and pork and chickens to live on. Sugar cured meat was the best at the time. They were both family-orientated and spent most weekends at Granny and Gramps' farm. Daughter Ruby served in the WACS, grandsons Elbert Sellers and John Sellers were in the Marines in World War II and Robert Charles Faulk served in the Army in Korea.

Around 1940, they gave up the farm and moved into town to 622 Louisiana Street, Longview, and lived out the rest of their lives with their gardens and flowers and family still visiting. All of the original family is gone now and Robert Charles Faulk carries on the family name with his son, Robby, and the other grandchildren the legacy. Family members belonged to Winterfield Methodist Church and are buried in the church cemetery.

– Submitted by Robert Charles Faulk

JESSIE THOMAS FEARS, 1880-1966

Jessie Arlee Thomas was the ninth child of Ezekiel Thomas and Vander Artimissie Clark Thomas. She was born and grew up in the Judson community just north of Longview in Gregg County. Along with her large family, she was a member of the Summerfield Methodist Church where she also played the pump organ. This is where she met her future husband, W.J. Fears, a minister of the Christian (Disciples of Christ) Church. He came to Summerfield to preach a series of meetings and Jessie played the organ for his services. They married on 1 April 1906, and immediately left by train for the Indian Territory (now Oklahoma) where he was a missionary. The next year they returned to Longview for the birth of their first child, Oren W. Fears. Af-

terwards, they moved to Panola County where they operated a grocery and general merchandise store in addition to Rev. Fears' duties as minister. Four more children were born during the ensuing years. Gracie Loucille was born in 1908 and died in 1910; Bettye Frances was born in 1911; Allyene Elizabeth was born in 1916; and Winston J. was born in 1921 and died in 1927. Later, they bought a farm in Rusk County and lived there a number of years before the death of Rev. Fears in 1926.

After the death of Rev. Fears, Jessie remained in Tatum, Texas, until 1937 when she returned to Longview and married William Robert Jones. They bought a small farm on Tryon Road and lived there for the rest of their lives. W.R. Jones died in 1961 and Jessie died in 1966. She is buried with her first husband Rev. Fears and their son Winston in the Tatum Cemetery.

Oren Fears married Veda Davidson and lived in Longview for many years before moving to Corpus Christi, Texas, where he worked for the Atlantic Richfield Oil Company. He returned to Longview in his last years where he died in 1994 and is buried in the Tatum, Texas, Cemetery. Oren and Veda had two children, Joe Wallace Fears, now of Corpus Christi, Texas, and Bonnie Fears Hays of Longview, Texas.

As a young woman, Bettye Frances Fears returned to Longview where she worked for a number of years at the M.E. Moses store and Sears. She also met and married Dallas F. Butter. They later left Longview for many years, but after retiring in 1969 returned. Frances and Dallas had one daughter, Virginia Butter Fields, the author of this article. Frances died in Longview in 2002.

Allyene Fears returned to Longview along with Frances and also worked at M.E. Moses before obtaining her beautician's license. Allyene first married W.H. Cook and lived in Pasadena, Texas, for many years. She returned to Longview in the 1950s to live near her mother and step-father in their declining years. Allyene's beauty shop was opened next to her house and as of 2003 is still in operation. Allyene's second marriage was to Atchley "Pete" Davidson. From her first marriage, Allyene had two children, Fred W. Cook of Longview, and Judy Cook Morris now of Amarillo, Texas.

– Submitted by Virginia Butter Fields

Faulk family, 1943-1944

Jessie Fears and W.J. Fears

WILLIS & RACHEL FINLEY

Willis Taylor Finley, son of Clyde Finley and Myrtle O. Inman, was born 12 February 1928, in Elmo, Independence County, Arkansas, and on 17 May 1958, married Rachel Faith Glasscock, daughter of Dewey Gadston Glasscock and Nina Bates, in Little Rock, Pulaski County, Arkansas. Rachel was born 5 March 1931, in Tunnel Hill, Catoosa County, Georgia.

Rachel and Willis Finley

Willis's ancestry can be traced back to Maryland. Willis's line of descent is from Charles Fenley (1689-1744) and Elizabeth Ann Harris (1690-1749) who lived and died in Prince Georges County, Maryland; John Finley (1725-1803) and Ann Norris (1738-1786) were born in Prince Georges County, and died in Greene County, Georgia – Eleven Finley (1769-1829) and Mary Taylor (1773-1839). Eleven was born in South Carolina; they both died in Independence County. John Finley (1809-1874) and Rosetta "Rosy" Bowen (1819-1872) were born in Georgia and died in Independence County. Eleven Norman Finley (1846- 1925) and Sarah Carter (1845-1911) were born in Independence County; Eleven died in Hardeman County, Texas, and Sarah died in Independence County. Norman Estis Finley (1879-1954) and Maryann "Addie" Walker (1881-1952) were born in Independence County, and died in White County, Arkansas – Clyde Finley and Myrtle O. Inman.

Rachel's line of descent is from Thomas Glasscock (1611-1662) and Jane Juett (1611-1683), born in England and died in Virginia – Thomas Glasscock (1645-1700) and Ann Nichols (1657-1713). Thomas was born in England and died in Virginia; Ann Nichols was born and died in Virginia. George Glasscock (1645-1714) and Million Downman (1683-1750) were born and died in Virginia. William Glasscock (1704- 1785) and Esther Ball (1712-) were born and died in Virginia. Dr. George Glasscock (1743-1787) and Martha Howard (1741- 1792) were born in Virginia and died in North Carolina – John Milton Glasscock (1765-1838) and Mary Caddell. John was born in Virginia and Mary was born in North Carolina; they died in Alabama – Benjamin Glasscock (1812-1883) and Margaret Tucker (1817-1901).

Benjamin was born in Georgia; Margaret was born in Alabama. They died in Alabama. Thomas Glasscock (1852-1925) and Nancy Sarah Elizabeth Laney (1960-1949) were born in Alabama; Thomas died in Alabama and Nancy died in Sweet Home, Arkansas; and Dewey Gadston Glasscock (1900-1964), born in Alabama, and Nina Bates (1895-1994), born in Georgia, both died in Little Rock.

Willis and Rachel were married in Winfield Methodist Church in Little Rock in 1958. They have been residents of Longview since 1975. They have two children: David Taylor Finley was born in 1960 and Carol Faith Finley was born in 1962, both at McConnell AFB, Sedgwick County, Wichita, Kansas.

David and Carol attended Pine Tree Schools in Longview and upon graduation attended Texas A&M University. David married Linda Ann Bottolfson in 1984 in the Faith Methodist Church in Spring, Texas. They have two children and live in Plano, Texas. David and Linda are both Engineers.

Carol married Jetre Alan "Jet" Schuler in 1988 in the First Methodist Church in Dallas, Texas. They have two children and live in Neenah, Wisconsin. Carol and Jet are Certified Public Accountants.

– Submitted by Willis Finley

JACOB & MARTHA BLANTON ALEXANDER FISHER

Christian Fischer, Amishman, born 1703/5, and his wife, Magdelena Yoder, immigrated from the Palatinate of Germany, November 1749, arriving on the *Phoenix* at the Philadelphia port and dropping the "c" from their name. Issue: Peter, married Barbara Souder, daughter of Henry Souder and wife, Barbara Stuaffer, Chester County, Pennsylvania; Christian, Jr., married Susannah Souder, sister to Barbara Souder; Magdelena, married John Zook; Barbara married Christian Detweiter; Anna married Christian Kauffman; and Veronica married Louis Riehl.

Peter Fisher and wife, Barbara Souder, a Mennonite born in Montgomery County, Pennsylvania, married by 1785. They left Pennsylvania c. 1802 and joined a Baptist settlement in Buncomb County, North Carolina. Peter Fisher died in Madison County, Alabama, in 1815, burial place unknown. Barbara Souder Fisher died 14 July 1831, and is buried in New Garden Cemetery close to Athens, Alabama. Issue: Jacob, born 1785, Lancaster County, Pennsylvania, married Martha Blanton Alexander, daughter of Col. Elias Alexander and wife, Nancy Agnes McCall, born 17 September 1796, in Rutherford County, North Carolina; David K. Fisher married Julia B. Camp, niece to Martha B. Alexander Fisher; John married Susan Spratt Garrison; George W. married Margaret T. Garrison, sister to Susan Spratt Garrison; Elizabeth married John F. Eckford of Alabama; Martha married William Bryson; and Susannah married Jacob Coffman.

Jacob Fisher and Martha Blanton Alexander married 2 February 1815, by her father in Rutherford County, North Carolina. They left North

Carolina and settled in Limestone County, close to Athens, Alabama, until 1850, when they came to Upshur (now Gregg) Co., Texas. They stopped for a brief visit with his brother, David K. Fisher, and wife, Julia, who had settled in Harrison County, Texas, near Marshall. Children of Jacob and Martha were Oliver Hazard Perry, married Caroline Hawkins 27 December 1841, in Alabama; William Decatur, married Martha D. Young in Texas, 26 January 1855; Henry Peter, married Madeline Clairmont, 1865; Julia Agnes, married Judge E.H. English of Little Rock, Arkansas, 30 September 1840; Martha Margaret, married Rev. Stokley Rowan Chadick 21 December 1847; Malinda Jane, married Andrew Montgomery 6 July 1843; Silas McBee, married Martha Killingsworth 23 September 1851; Ann Elizabeth, married George W. Fisher, 24 December 1846; Robert Donnell, never married; Jacob Lindley, married Josephine Howell 24 August 1851; Barbara Souder, never married; Mary Blanton, married W.W. Reyburn 26 May 1851; George Alexander, married Fanny Awalt 14 February 1867; and Joan Reinhardt, married Dr. John N. Allison 27 February 1861.

The children of Jacob and Martha who came to Texas were William Decatur, Henry Peter, Martha Margaret and husband Rev. Stokley Rowan Chadick, Malinda Jane and husband Andrew Montgomery, Silas McBee, Jacob Lindley, George Alexander, and Joan Reinhardt.

Jacob and family were members of the Pine Tree Cumberland Presbyterian Church and he served as Postmaster for the area. Some are buried in the Fisher Cemetery on Silver Falls Road in Pine Tree Community. Jacob and Martha Blanton Alexander Fisher rest there as well as some of the children and spouses.

Descendants of this last generation in Gregg County are too numerous to list, as are those scattered over the country. Information has been donated to the Gregg County Historical Society and can be found in the genealogical section of the library in Longview. (References: *Descendants and History of Christian Fisher Family*, compiled by John M. Fisher Family, 1957; *Fisher Family History*, Revised and Updated 1988 by Katie Beiler; *A Concise History of the Chadick Family*, compiled by Bill M. Taylor; *Alexander Kin*, compiled by Charles C. and Virginia Alexander, Vol. II; and research done by the author in Texas, Alabama, North Carolina and Pennsylvania.)

– Submitted by Grace Fisher DeuPree

JAMES W. FLANAGAN

James W. Flanagan was born in Albemarle County, Virginia, on 7 September 1805, the son of Charles and Elizabeth (Saunders) Flanagan. In 1815, the family moved to Kentucky. In 1826 in Kentucky, he married Polly Miller Moorman. Flanagan became involved in local politics, serving for twelve years as justice of the peace and a member of the circuit court of Breckenridge County.

Flanagan had been involved in several business ventures before he moved to Texas in 1843. In 1844, he moved to Henderson, where he opened a store, farmed, speculated in land and practiced law. His wife, Polly, died in 1844 at Henderson. He later married a widow named Elizabeth Ware.

A Whig in the 1830s and 1840s, and later a Republican, Flanagan was a friend and supporter of Sam Houston. In 1851-52, he served in the Texas House of Representatives and in 1855-58 in the Texas Senate. He advocated a state asylum for the insane and favored government-supported railroads. In 1856, he was a presidential elector; and in 1860, he was elected a delegate to a conference called by Houston concerning the upcoming secession of Texas from the United States. During the Civil War Flanagan was a Unionist sympathizer.

He was a delegate to the Constitutional Convention of 1866, but the document produced by this convention was rejected by the federal government and congressional Reconstruction was imposed upon the state along with most of the former Confederate states. J.W. Flanagan and son, Webster, were both delegates to the Texas Constitutional Convention of 1868-69. Flanagan was elected lieutenant governor in 1869 under Edmund J. Davis and Reconstruction, and his son was elected to the state Senate. J.W. Flanagan was elected to the United States House of Representatives as an at-large representative in 1869. Webster Flanagan replaced his father as president pro tem of the Senate. Flanagan served as a United States Senator, from 30 March 1870, until 3 March 1875. While serving as senator, Flanagan was appointed chairman of the Committee on Post Offices and Roads, the Committee on Education and the Committee on Labor.

After he left politics, Flanagan retired to his farm at Longview. His third marriage was to Elizabeth Lane. He had a total of eleven children. He died at Longview on 19 September 1887, and is buried in Henderson beside his first wife. He was a Baptist and an Odd Fellow.

FLEWELLEN

Thomas Archelaus Flewellen, the son of Thomas Flewellen and Frances M. Drake, was born 27 February 1829, in Upson County, Georgia. Thomas A. Flewellen married Victoria Monroe Thweatt on 17 October 1852, and in 1854 accompanied his father in a move to Camden, Arkansas. They stayed there less than a year and then moved to Smith County, Texas, northwest of Lindale. During the Civil War, Thomas A. Flewellen served in Company D, 13th Texas Volunteer Cavalry. Victoria Thweatt Flewellen died 5 June 1868, and is buried in the Flewellen-Thweatt Cemetery near Lindale. Thomas A. and Victoria Flewellen had three children, Junius Jefferson, Eliza Harris and Maria Antoinette. On 19 July 1870, Thomas A. Flewellen married Hettie Marshall of Henderson, Texas. About 1872, he moved his family to Longview and in 1878-79 he was mayor of Longview. He operated a store and is described in the city directory as a confectioner. Their home was at 206 South Center, which is now known as the Flewellen-Eason home. Thomas A. Flewellen

died 17 June 1893, and is buried in Greenwood Cemetery in Longview.

Junius Jefferson Flewellen was born 25 July 1855, in Smith County, Texas, and married Ada Johnson on 11 November 1877. Their home was at 307 South Green Street on the corner of South Street and Green Street in Longview. In 1879, J.J. Flewellen entered into business with R.G. Brown under the name Brown & Flewellen. They had a grocery store and sawmill in Longview. The partnership was dissolved shortly after 1900 and J.J. Flewellen then had a general store and entered into a partnership known as Castleberry & Flewellen. J.J. and Ada Flewellen had six surviving children, but one of these, Wilbur, died while attending medical school in Galveston. The other children were Nettie, Theo, Elizabeth, Junius and Eugene. Nettie married Emer Hamvasy, who owned a drugstore in Longview. Theo married Charles D. Smith, a lawyer in Beaumont. Elizabeth married Angus Miller and, after his death, married Lacy Eddins. Junius married Carrie Bruce and he developed the addition know as Iris Circle on Judson Road. Eugene married Margaret Showalter and was a businessman in Longview.

Eliza Harris (Aunt Didy) Flewellen was born 28 August 1853, and married Alonzo Womack on 3 November 1874. They had one surviving child, Kate, who married Thomas Edwin Lacy. The Womack-Lacy house was at 405 South Center Street in Longview.

– Submitted by Archie Colburn

FOIRRIESTIER

Newton J. and Martha Foirriestier married in Georgia. They moved to Union County, Arkansas, about 1860. Newton was a blacksmith, a trade handed down in the family. Their chil-

dren were John (1859), Mary (1862), George (1864), Adaline (1866), Martha (1868), Josephine (1870), William (1874) and Benjamin (1876). John was born in Georgia; the others were born in Arkansas.

George married Alice"Addy" Perkins in Union County, Arkansas, 4 February 1888. Addy was born in Arkansas to John Perkins from Missouri and Susan Glover from Alabama. The Perkins family settled in Ouachita Parish, Louisiana.

George and Addy had twin boys in September 1893, in Eldorado, Arkansas, James Lonnie and Alvin Fonnie. George died when the twins were small and Addy married Charles T. Williams. Alvin married Minnie Hawkins and James married Oma Elizabeth Williams 21 January 1913, in Hempstead County. Oma's parents were J.S. Williams and Mary Jane "Molly" Hamby Williams from Polk County. She had one brother, Riley, a half-brother, George Keadle and a half-sister, Idabell Johnson.

All three families moved to Cass County, Texas, between 1923 and 1926. They lived in the Union Hill area, the men all worked in the timber industry. Alvin Fonnie's wife Minnie died there and is buried in the Union Hill cemetery. Their children were Ethel and Iva Mae. He then married Oma Hawkins and they had one child, Norma Jean.

About 1930, all three families moved on to Gregg County. Alvin changed the spelling of his last name to Foistier. He and Oma are buried in Lamar County, Texas.

James and Oma lived on Old Highway 80 in a tent in Tent City for a short time before moving to White Oak, Highway 42 on the Bumpus place. (The children attended the Bumpus School.) They later moved to Pine Tree Road.
(Continued on page 150.)

(l.-r.) Back: Alvin Fonnie Foistier, Charles Thomas Williams (Lonnie and Fonnie's stepdad), James Lonnie Foirriestier and Oma Elizabeth Hawkins (sister to Minnie and Fonnie's second wife). Front: Minnie Hawkins Foistier (wife of Fonnie), Alice "Addy" Perkins Foirriestier Williams (mother of Lonnie and Fonnie), baby Ethel (daughter of Fonnie and Minnie), Oma Elizabeth Williams Foirriestier (wife of Lonnie) with their son Owen. About 1916.

FOSHEE

The Foshee family of America, which homesteaded in East Texas, descended from French Huguenots. They came from France and other European countries. The immediate family settled in this area before Gladewater and Gregg County were named. They came from Bibb County, Alabama, after living in Edgefield County, South Carolina. John Foshee arrived in America in the early sixteen hundreds. When he died in Virginia, he named his son, John, Jr., as guardian of his minor son Nathaniel. When Nathaniel reached his teen years, he enlisted in the Continental Army and served in the Virginia Militia. One of the sons of Nathaniel was Noah, born in 1791, who moved to Alabama. The son of Noah was James M. Foshee, who was the father of William Emmett Foshee. It was William Emmett who came to East Texas. William Emmett served his community as postmaster, justice of the peace, and as a business man. William Emmett Foshee married Mary R. Shepperd of the pioneer Shepperd family of East Texas. Their children were Minnie Florence Foshee Barker (1877-1955); Alfred Franklin Foshee (1878-1896); Mary Elizabeth Claudia Foshee (1880-1887); James Madison Foshee (1884-1946); Johnnie Virginia Foshee Bradley (1889-1967); Albert Martin Foshee (1892-1976); Edgar Leon Foshee (1894-1983); and Azar Beryl Foshee (1897-1949).

The above photograph is the historical marker at the Foshee homestead at 409 North Main Street in Gladewater, Texas.

This is where they were living when 'Grandma Oma' died in February 1937, only two and a half months after Billie Nell, the youngest child, was born. James died in February 1938, and 'Grandma Addy' died in March 1939. Their step-grandpa, Charles T. Williams, and the older children took care of the young children. 'Grandpa Williams' died in 1948. They are all buried in the White Oak Cemetery. James and Oma Foirriestier had eight children: Owen married Dora Warren (he spelled his name Foster); Essie married Hugh Morley, then Ed Fletcher; Lonnie Bryant "L.B." married Molly Morris; Ruby married Nash Odom; Alvin Fonnie "Buster" married Rita Kelley; Aline "Teenie" married Odell Warren Granger; Beval married John Kelley; Billie Nell married Lenn McDowell; Harold Mosley, Kenneth Carpenter. James and Oma Foirriestier had twenty-three grandchildren, most of whom were born in Gregg County and have lived in Gregg County all their lives. Alvin Fonnie "Buster" and Billie Nell are the only two still living. Most of the family are buried in the White Oak Cemetery. Buster is the last surviving heir to carry the Foirriestier name. Spellings for the name are Foirriestier, Foistier, Foster, Forrester. Other surnames connected to this family are Perkins, Glover, Williams, Hamby.

– Submitted by Sissy Tyl

HENRY L. FOSTER

Henry L. Foster, long time superintendent of Longview Schools, was born near Longview, 30 September 1891. His parents were Della Gomer Foster and R.D. Foster. He was educated in the Longview public schools and he received his B.S. degree in 1926 at San Marcos Teachers College, and did graduate work at University of Texas and at Colorado State Teachers College.

Foster was married in Hallsville, 4 June 1918, to Florence Black, daughter of T.P. and Fannie Black. Henry and Florence Foster had two children, Henry, Jr. and Florine.

Foster began his teaching career in Longview, in 1913, as principal of the First Ward School. After serving in World War I, he resumed work as principal of the Campus Ward School in Longview. In 1922, he was appointed principal of the Longview High School and a year later began his long career as superintendent of the Longview schools.

He was active in civic affairs. He served as a director of the First National Bank of Longview and a steward in the First Methodist church; was a member and president of the Rotary club; and served several years as a director of the Longview Chamber of Commerce. Foster was also a member of the National Educational Association, and served on the executive board of the State Teachers Association and as president of the East Texas division.

(l.-r.) Seated: Ann and Dan Fournet. Standing: John Fournet, Robbie Fournet Mahlman, Bill Fournet and Linda Fournet Olejnik.

DANIEL J. & ROBBIE ANN BAGGETT FOURNET

After their 1 April 1956 marriage, and graduation from Southwestern Institute the following summer, Daniel J. and Robbie Ann Fournet, began, in November of 1956 in San Antonio, Texas, a military life and career in the United States Air Force. Please see "Joe Baggett and Robbie Adrian" in this volume for Ann's early history and connection to Gregg County.

Dan completed multi engine pilot training in February of 1958, seventh in a class of eighty. The good standing allowed him a choice and assignment to the Military Air Transport Command, where he served for ten years. He was honored for combat service as a transport pilot during the Vietnam war.

The four children of Dan and Ann were born while Dan was on active duty. They are John Byron, born 14 November 1957 in San Angelo, Texas; William Daniel, born 26 June 1959 in Honolulu, Hawaii; Linda Ann, born 6 August 1963 in Lafayette, Louisiana; and Robbie Adrian, born 22 August 1966 at Fort Lewis Army Base in Tacoma, Washington.

Dan left active duty in October of 1966, moved with his family to California, and joined Pan American World Airways as a commercial pilot. He remained in the U.S. Air Force Reserves, and retired as a Lt. Colonel in 1977. As a commercial pilot and reservist, he continued Vietnam war service until that conflict ended.

In 1990 and 1991 Dan was recognized for civilian service for airlift support during the Gulf War. The family moved to Danville, California, in 1968 and remained in residence there, except for a brief assignment to Berlin, Germany, where Dan flew for the Internal German Service of Pan American World Airways.

Three of the four Fournet children are graduates of California Universities: John,

Forestry, University of California at Berkeley; Linda, Recreation, San Jose State University, and Robbie, Economics, University of California at Davis. William is a graduate of Louisiana Tech University, in Aviation.

In December of 1991, Pan American ceased operation, forcing what seemed like early retirement for Dan. In October of 1992, however, he was employed as a pilot by United Airlines and officially retired from that company and flying in March of 1998.

Dan and Ann continue to live in California with families. They are John and wife Carmen with daughters Jonelle (born in 1985), Linda (born in 1988), and Jacque (born in 1991); Linda with husband Mark Olejnik and sons Daniel (born in 1988) and Jacob (born in 1995); Robbie with husband Robert Mahlman and children Thomas (born in 1995) and Adrianne (born in 1999). William and wife Terri reside with sons Jason (born in 1997) and Trevor (born in 2002) in Cornelius, North Carolina.

– Submitted by John Byron Fournet

DR. JAMES CARLTON FRANCIS

Dr. James Carlton Francis, dentist in Longview from 1906 until the mid-1940s, was born in Rusk, Cherokee County, Texas, 8 August 1881. He was one of eight children born to John Woodson and Tennessee Virginia (Boyd) Francis, both of whom lived their entire lives in Cherokee County, and whose parents had moved there in the late 1840s from Tennessee.

Dr. Francis's family moved to Jacksonville, Texas, when he was a young boy where he attended the public schools and graduated from high school. He attended the Baptist College in Jacksonville before enrolling in Vanderbilt University Dental College, Nashville, Tennessee, where he graduated in May 1906. Two months later he opened a dental office in Longview, soon establishing an excellent practice both in the city and the surrounding towns.

On 11 September 1907, Dr. Francis was married to Floreid Bramlette in Longview. Born 19 July 1887, she was the eighth of thirteen children born to Thomas Anderson and Annie Eliza (Miller) Bramlette, who had moved their large family to Longview from Pontotoc, Mississippi, on Christmas Eve, 1896. Floreid attended the public schools in Longview, graduating from Longview High School in 1904. Throughout her life, Mrs. Francis was very active in church, civic and club work in Longview. She was a worker in the Presbyterian Church practically all her life, and as a member of the building committee, she had an active part in the construction of the present First Presbyterian Church. In 1928, she served as one of the first officers of the Woman's Chamber of

Floreid Bramlette Francis

Eugenia Tunstall Francis

Commerce of Longview, the first organization of its kind in Texas. She was an early president of the Longview Federation of Women's Clubs, and it was during her administration that the plan was developed for Gregg County to participate in the erection of the Longview Community Center. After retiring as president, she remained on the building committee until the structure was completed in 1937. She is credited as the inspiration for Longview's first Friendly Trek Homecoming, a city-wide festival, in 1939. A golfer, she was an early member of Pinecrest Country Club and was a member of the East Texas Ladies Golf Association.

During his early years in Longview, Dr. Francis was a member of the Longview Cannibals baseball team and the Masonic Lodge. He was a lifelong member of the Presbyterian Church and for many years served on the Board of Deacons of the First Presbyterian Church of Longview. He was a charter member and one of the organizers of the East Texas Dental Society and was a member of the Texas Dental Society.

In 1924, Dr. Francis moved his office to the Hurst Sanitarium on Methvin Street, east of the downtown post office. In 1934, his son, Dr. Thomas Bramlette Francis, graduated from Baylor Dental College and joined his father in practice. They remained at this location until 1940, when they built a new office at 205 S. Center Street. He and his son were associated for many years in the ownership of Francis and Francis, Dentists. Dr. J.C. Francis retired about 1947, due to failing health and eyesight.

Dr. Francis died 13 November 1957, at his home in Longview after a lengthy illness and is buried in Memory Park Cemetery. His wife died at Markham Hospital in Longview, 14 November 1967, and is buried beside her husband.

Dr. James Carlton and Floreid (Bramlette) Francis were the parents of three children, all born in Longview:

1. James Carlton "Bill" Francis, Jr., born 11 May 1908, died 24 September 1990, in Longview and is buried in Grace Hill Cemetery. He graduated from Longview High School in 1925 and later attended Texas A&M University.

He was a construction engineer and was a member of the First Presbyterian Church. He married 26 December 1954, in Mount Pleasant, Texas, Mrs. Edith (Robinson) Nevill (1921-1996). He adopted her only child, Les Nevill.

2. Dr. Thomas Bramlette Francis, born 21 March 1910, died 28 February 1998, in Longview and is buried in Rosewood Park Cemetery, Longview. He was a dentist in Longview from 1934 until 1980. He married Eugenia English Tunstall of Crockett, Texas on 27 November 1936, in Longview. They were the parents of two daughters, both born in Longview: Floreid Francis, born 3 February 1938, and Eugenia Francis, born 9 November 1942. (See "Thomas Bramlette Francis.")

3. Floreid Francis, born 16 September 1916, died 10 August 1963, in Longview and is buried in Memory Park Cemetery. She graduated from Longview High School in 1933 and attended the University of Texas in Austin, where she was a nominee for Bluebonnet Belle. She married 17 June 1937, in Longview, Henry Prather Burney, Jr. of San Antonio, son of Henry P. Burney, Sr. and Clare Denman. They were the parents of two children, both born in San Antonio: Clare Denman Burney, born 22 November 1939, and Henry Prather Burney, III, born 27 October 1942, and died 30 May 1969.

– Submitted by Floreid Francis Stevens (granddaughter)

DR. THOMAS BRAMLETTE FRANCIS

Dr. Thomas Bramlette Francis, dentist in Longview from 1934 to 1980, was born 21 March 1910, Longview, Texas. He was the son of Dr. James Carlton and Floreid (Bramlette) Francis. His father, a native of Cherokee County, Texas, moved to Longview in 1906, where he practiced dentistry for 40 years. His mother was one of thirteen children of Thomas A. and Annie (Miller) Bramlette, who moved to Longview from Pontotoc, Mississippi, in 1896.

He attended the public schools in Longview, graduating from Longview High School in 1928, Lon Morris College in Jacksonville, and Southern Methodist University before entering Baylor University College of Dentistry, Dallas, where he graduated in 1934. He returned to Longview and entered practice with his father at the Hurst Clinic on Methvin

Dr. Thomas B. Francis

Street. They were associated for many years in the ownership of Francis & Francis, Dentists. About 1940, they built a new office at 205 S. Center Street.

Dr. Francis was married on 27 November 1936, in Longview to Eugenia English Tunstall of Crockett, Texas. The daughter of Vicory Barker and Emma Virginia (English) Tunstall, she was born 8 October 1916, in Crockett where she grew up and graduated from high school in 1934. She moved to Longview in 1935 to live with her uncle and aunt, Oliver and Beecher (Tunstall) Daniel. She attended C.I.A. in Denton for one year. During her years in Longview she was a member of the First Presbyterian Church, the Junior League of Longview and was a charter member of the East Texas Dental Society Auxiliary.

Dr. Francis was a member of the East Texas Dental Society, serving as president in 1942, and the Texas Dental Association of which he was a member for over 50 years.

A lifelong member of the First Presbyterian Church of Longview, he served many years on the board of Deacons and as a ruling elder. He was a member of the board of trustees of the Longview Independent School District from 1952 to 1959, serving as president three years. He was also a member of the Masonic Lodge, the Civitan Club and the Rotary Club.

Dr. Francis retired from his dental practice in 1980 due to ill health, but was able to enjoy his retirement until his death on 28 February 1998, in Longview. Mrs. Francis died 6 November 2000, in Longview. Both are buried in Rosewood Park Cemetery. They were married for 61 years and had two daughters: 1. Floreid Francis, born 3 February 1938, Longview. She graduated from Longview High School in 1955, and received a BA degree from Southern Methodist University in 1959. She married 6 August 1960, at the First Presbyterian Church, Longview, to Dr. Alexander Calvitt Stevens, surgeon in Longview from 1959-1989. They are the parents of three children: Alexander C. Stevens, Jr., Thomas Huxford Stevens and Scott English Stevens.

2. Eugenia Francis, born 9 November 1942, Longview. Graduated from Longview High

School in 1960, and attended the University of Texas, Austin, and Southern Methodist University. She was married 22 June 1963, at the First Presbyterian Church, Longview, to Philip Martin Cartmell, Jr. of Shawnee Mission, Kansas. They had two children, Catherine Compton Cartmell (Kerr) and Thomas Philip Cartmell.

– Submitted by Eugenia Francis Cartmell

JOE & MYRTLE SMITH FREEMAN

Joe Freeman, son of Samuel Freeman and Vandorah "Dorah" Dean, was born in Martin, Franklin County, Georgia, 1 May 1881. His brothers were Rasial Mattison and Tom Gerome. Joe came to Gregg County, Texas, in 1898 with his mother and stepfather, Thomas W. Mitchell. The Mitchells lived on Center Street in Longview, and Mitchell operated a café. Joe's brother Tom and his sons, Carl and Raleigh Freeman, came, too.

Joe and Myrtle Smith Freeman, 1953

Myrtle Susan Smith, daughter of Robert Thomas Smith and Sarah Eveline Brannon, was born near Nashville, Tennessee, 23 February 1886. Her brothers and sisters were James Madison C.; William Henry; Frances Cordelia, who married Tom Freeman; Ivy Magnolia; Lester Louis; and Beulah Catherine. The Smiths arrived in the Judson community of Gregg County, Texas, from Franklin County, Georgia, about 1897 and bought a farm. Myrtle's brother William Henry stayed in Georgia.

Joe Freeman and Myrtle Smith were married in Longview on 6 December 1903. They made their home in the Judson Community where he farmed. For a number of years they lived on a farm adjacent to her parents, but about 1918 bought a farm from Bob Smith at the corner of Fuller Road and FM 1844 so the girls would not have to walk so far to attend Harmony Grove School. They were faithful members of Judson Baptist Church where Joe led the singing for many years. The family often attended "singings" held at various churches on Sunday afternoons. Once Joe brought home a pump organ and announced, "Sister is going to play the organ." Jewell watched those playing in church and learned to play by shaped notes. From that time, she always played when Joe led the singing.

Joe worked to support his three daughters: Jewell Violet "Sister;" Jodie Lavinna "Little'Un"

or "Buddy;" and Thelma Helen "Honeybaby;" he instilled a work ethic in them. When Jewell went to Jacksonville Baptist College in 1923, Joe cut firewood and hauled it to Longview to pay her expenses. Myrtle cooked, sewed and maintained an immaculate home while instilling Christian ideals and virtues in her daughters. In the 1930s, gas wells were drilled on their property and they knew prosperity for the first time. This enabled them to travel and to relax a little. Celebrating their Golden Wedding Anniversary with an open house at their home was a highlight for them.

Myrtle had a stroke and died in Longview on 7 July 1961. Joe died from a heart attack at home on 23 October 1961. Both are buried in Judson Cemetery. Jewell Freeman married William Carleton King; they made their home in Smith County where Jewell taught school. Lavinna Freeman married Daniel L. McQueen and Eugene S. Scott; she worked for the City of Longview for many years. Thelma Freeman married Rayford Fenton; she worked at Riff's Clothing Store in Longview. Joe and Myrtle had seven grandchildren: Daniel Cole McQueen; Beverly Ann McQueen; Norma Jo McQueen; Milton Ray Fenton; Mary Lynn Fenton; Patricia Ann Fenton; and Janet Louise King.

– Submitted by Janet King Bonner, Flower Mound, Texas

ROBERT H. FREEMAN / ISA DORA CHRISTIAN

Robert Hamilton Freeman, born 19 January 1876, and Isa Dora Christian, born 22 May 1878, were married on 3 February 1898.

Robert (Bob) Hamilton Freeman was the youngest child of William G. and Rachael Freeman. He was born in Tocca, Habersham County, Georgia, and came to East Texas with his parents in 1890.

"Dora" Christian was born in Crim's Chapel, Texas, in 1878, daughter of Thomas Harrison Preston Christian and Amanda Susan Lester. The Christians were married in Georgia and moved to the Crims Chapel area around 1870. Dora had six siblings: Ida, Jim, Susan, Georgia, Edgar and Ethel.

Bob and Dora lived in the communities of Crim's Chapel and Pirtle until sometime in 1916. From the time of their marriage, they farmed and Bob operated a cotton gin. After leaving Crim's Chapel, they lived in Longview for the remainder of their lives. There was an exception for a period of two years when Bob worked as Superintendent of the W.K. Henderson estate (radio announcer for Station KWKH in Shreveport) and the family lived in Shreveport.

In Longview, Bob worked primarily as a carpenter. He helped build the Crim's Chapel church and worked on many of the buildings and schools in Longview. He died on 18 January 1933.

Bob and Dora Freeman were the parents of seven children: Willie Irene (born October 1898), Belton Ward (born April 1900), Edgar Preston (born August 1902),

Carrie Lee (born October 1904), Mary Susan (born April 1908), Lila Vermelle (born January 1910) and Robert Homer (born September 1916). All were born in the Crim's Chapel and Pirtle communities, in Rusk County, Texas.

After Bob's death, Dora lived with her daughter Carrie until Carrie's death in 1960. She then lived with her daughter Mary Susan (Sue) Rothwell (see "John W. Rothwell & Mary Susan Freeman") and granddaughter, Billie Sue Garvey (see "Dr. A.B. Garvey/Billie Sue Rothwell"), until her death in 1970.

Bob and Dora are buried in the Crim's Chapel Cemetery in Rusk County.

– Submitted by Susan Evans

DAVID WAYNE FROST

As relative newcomers to Gregg County, the family of David Wayne Frost, Sr., arrived April 1973, from Corpus Christi, previously residing in Edinburg and McAllen. Wayne, born 7 July 1935, in Hill County to Henry Franklin Frost and Lena Mae Pierce Frost, received a petroleum engineering degree from Texas Tech University. Drafted into the army, he served for awhile at Augusta, Georgia, where he met and married Freida Hamilton Strauss 29 December 1959. She was born there 15 November 1937, to William Isadore Strauss and Marion Mosley Hamilton Strauss and was a recent graduate of Mercer University in Macon, Georgia.

After military duty, Wayne was hired by Sun Oil Company and he and Freida moved to his hometown of Edinburg where she taught school while he worked at the natural gasoline plant in Starr County. He was transferred to the Silver, Texas, plant near Colorado City where the couple was living in a company camp house when their first child, Sharla Elizabeth, was born. Briefly living in McComb, Mississippi, the family was back in the Rio Grande Valley living in the Sun Field Camp in Starr County when Shelly Lorene was born in Edinburg. Sun Oil decided to close the company camps, so moved the office and Frosts to McAllen where they bought their first house. David Wayne, Jr., was born there.

Nine years were spent in the Valley before Wayne was sent to Corpus Christi for a year then to Longview, where they lived for ten years. After a year in Shreveport they were transferred to Oklahoma City. They lived in the suburb of

The Frost family, 1980: Wayne, Sharla, Frieda, Shelly and David.

Edmond for ten years, returning to Longview 18 June 1993, after Wayne's retirement.

A home was purchased in the Pine Tree school district during the first Longview stint. The family was involved in the activities of the school, city and First Baptist Church, where Wayne was deacon vice-chairman, in choir and a Sunday School teacher, then director. He was on the Pine Tree School Board of Trustees, a ball coach, in Society of Petroleum Engineers and later served on several city commissions. He and Freida were Baylor University Parents of the Year 1990.

Besides teaching school, Freida sold real estate in Longview. She was the Gregg Association Women's Missionary Union Director, in Junior League, DAR, and was Phi Mu sorority alumni president in Oklahoma City, House Corporation president at OSU and the OKC Panhellenic Woman of the Year 1990.

Their girls were cheerleaders for Pine Tree and David played city and school ball. All three graduated from Baylor University. Sharla, Mrs. Michael Struffolino, and Shelly, Mrs. Eric Joseph, taught school in Richardson and Longview respectively before children were born. David became an attorney in Tyler where he and Lyndy Anderson Frost reside. Grandchildren are Elizabeth Anne, Michael Pierce and Lauren Hamilton Struffolino; Sydney Elizabeth, Sadie Lee and George Aaron Joseph; and Victoria Monroe, Caroline DeSpain and David Anderson Winslow Frost.

It is probable that some of Wayne's ancestors stopped for a time during the 1800s in this location. This is evident because two co-lateral ancestors, siblings of Mary Elizabeth Morse Frost, married in Gregg County. Kendall Q. Morse married Jane Rogers 10 October 1879. Sarah Dixie Morse married Jessie Zebelon Causey 20 November 1884, all four of their children were born here, and both are buried in Mt. Moriah Cemetery, Gladewater.

– Submitted by Freida Frost

DAVID WAYNE FROST, JR.

Although David Wayne Frost, Jr, lived in Gregg County for only ten years, he considers Longview his home, especially since his parents were residents there. David moved with his family to East Texas in April 1973, from McAllen, Texas, where he was born 6

David, Caroline, Victoria, Anderson and Lyndy Frost, March 28, 2005.

April 1968. He came by way of the Corpus Christi suburb of Portland, where the Frosts lived for just one year.

David is the son of Freida Strauss Frost and David Wayne Frost, Sr. and the younger brother of Sharla Frost Struffolino and Shelly Frost Joseph.

The children attended Pine Tree ISD schools where David started kindergarten. He was in Cub and Boy Scouts, Children of the American Revolution, and participated in YMCA camps, city and church league baseball, basketball and soccer, beginning in that last sport when it was first organized in Longview. In the Pine Tree school programs, he added football and track to his activities while continuing to be involved at First Baptist Church.

Sun Oil Company transferred Wayne and family to Shreveport where David attended Captain Shreve High School as a ninth grader. After living in Louisiana for almost a year, Wayne was then sent to the Oklahoma City office. The family settled in the suburb of Edmond where David excelled in sports for Edmond Memorial High School. His football team was District Champion; his basketball team was State Runner-up Champion; David was State High Jump Champion, and was All-state in all three sports. He was also a National High School Football All-American.

Although recruited by numerous colleges, he chose to accept a football scholarship from Baylor University, where he played wide receiver position for five years. He graduated with a degree in business and, during his fifth year, he was in a master's program, receiving the MBA degree in the fall of 1991.

During his Baylor years, he was a Scholar Athlete all four years of his active varsity time. The honor went to only three or four football players out of about 100. This accomplishment, of a GPA of 3.4 and up, came in spite of the time restraints of sports and his KOT fraternity responsibilities.

On 4 January 1992, he married Lyndy Karen Anderson, whom he had met at Baylor where she was sweetheart of his fraternity. She was born 27 March 1969, the daughter of Patricia Duke and Dr. Jerry Meitzen Anderson of Sherman, Texas. David and Lyndy resided in Dallas, where he had taken a position with the U.S. General Accounting Office and she taught school. After a couple of years with the GAO, David decided to attend the Texas Tech University Law School, while Lyndy taught school in Lubbock. Upon completion of that degree, magna cum laude, David became an associate of a law firm in Tyler, Texas.

The couple had three children, Victoria Monroe Frost, Caroline DeSpain Frost and David Anderson Winslow Frost. They were active members of First Baptist Church, Willow Brook Country Club and involved in community activities. Lyndy was in the Junior League and the family participated in fundraising runs and golf tournaments.

David had Pierce, Morse, Chapman and Frost ancestors who settled in East Texas dur-

ing the 1800s. The first two were here about the time of statehood and all were mostly farmers.

– Submitted by David W. Frost, Jr.

SHARLA ELIZABETH FROST-STRUFFOLINO

Even though Sharla Frost Struffolino now lives in the Dallas suburb of Coppell, she considers Longview her home. She was born on her mother's birthday, 15 November 1962, in Colorado City, Mitchell County, Texas, to Freida Strauss and David Wayne Frost, Sr. Wayne, a Petroleum Engineer with Sun Oil Company, was transferred several times.

Mike and Sharla Struffolino, Elizabeth, Michael and Lauren Struffolino.

The family was living in a company camp house in Silver at Sharla's birth. They moved to McComb, Mississippi, when Sharla was three months old and then to Wayne's hometown of Edinburg, Texas, when she was ten months, and then soon afterward to Sun Camp in Starr County. Sun then closed the company camps, moving everyone into McAllen where Sharla started kindergarten, as did her little sister, Shelly. David Wayne Frost, Jr. is their younger brother.

After six years in McAllen, Wayne was sent to Longview after a 15-month stay in the Corpus Christi suburb of Portland. In Longview, Sharla went to Pine Tree ISD schools from fourth grade until she graduated and went to Baylor university in Waco, Texas.

She was in Brownies and Girl Scouts, Children of the American Revolution, Girls' Softball, dance and gymnastic classes and went to YMCA camps. She took piano for twelve years and participated in guild and hymn festivals. Sharla became a cheerleader in the ninth grade, and later was a varsity cheerleader. She was in NHS, graduated in the top 5 percent of her class, was Miss Flame and 2nd Runner-up in the Miss Longview Pageant while being very active at First Baptist Church.

At Baylor she participated in activities for her sorority, Delta Delta Delta, graduating in 1985 with a degree in education. She later received her master's degree, magna cum laude, from the University of North Texas.

Sharla's teaching career of seven years was with Richard ISD and while living in Dallas, she met Michael Anthony Struffolino at Park

Cities Baptist Church and they married 3 December 1988. Michael was born 18 January 1963, son of Shirley Farmer and Charles Michael Struffolino of Houston.

Sharla was active in the Dallas Junior League, Baylor Women's Council, Delta Delta Delta Alumnae, Coppell Assistance League, PTO, Community Bible Study and leadership positions at church.

Mike graduated from the University of Oklahoma where he was in Lambda Chi Alpha Fraternity. He worked in management as an employee of IBM. He was a Baptist deacon, taught College Sunday School, played and coached several sports, and was involved with the YMCA guide program. He and Sharla had four children, Elizabeth Ann, Marion Rose (died at birth), Michael Pierce and Lauren Hamilton Struffolino.

Sharla had Pierce, Morse, Chapman and Frost ancestors who settled for a time in East Texas during the 1800s. The first two were here about the time of statehood and all were mostly farmers. Sophia (full-blood Cherokee Indian) and Hugh Pierce's son, George, and his wife, Elizabeth, came from Georgia to Rusk County before the 1850 census.

By the time of his death in 1854, his estate inventory indicated he had acquired a large amount of land and material possessions that were sold by his children who had moved to Central Texas.

– Submitted by Sharla Frost Struffolino

WILLIAM L. FULLER

William L. Fuller was born in Lee County, Alabama, 24 January 1867. He died 16 June 1956, in Longview and is buried in Judson Cemetery. He was the son of William M. Fuller and Elizabeth Gilmer or Gilmore. He married Vannie Smith, daughter of Riley D. Smith and Emily Emma Dean, in 1891 in Franklin County, Georgia. She was born 8 February 1876, in Gregg County, died 16 January 1947, in Longview and is buried in Judson Cemetery.

Will Fuller was a lifelong member of the Summerfield Methodist Church. Will moved to Hallsville with his parents, and at the age of two years old they moved to the Judson community. Will was an original member of the Longview volunteer fire company that formed in 1885. It was a horse-drawn hook and ladder. Will was a farmer and later was involved in the oil business. He and Vannie had two children: a daughter Willie L., known as Leedie, and, a son James Ollie Manuel. Leedie married Ex Birdsong and died in 1948. James "Mann" married Grace Jane Calloway. He was the Tax Assessor and Collector of Gregg County. James "Mann" died in 1956.

Will had two brothers, John Judson "J.Y." and Samuel H., and a sister, Mary F. John Judson married Rhoda Antenette Hamby. John Judson was known as a "Pioneer Farmer" of Gregg County. Mary F. married Bob Smith, brother of Vannie Smith Fuller. Many of the descendents still live in the Longview area.

– Submitted by Linda Williams

HENRY UDELL "HUGH" GARRETT

Rags in the motor. Sabotage! The downed P-47 smoked on the runway. "He's a goner!" the corpsmen shouted as they reached the wreckage. But pilot Hugh Garrett muffled the response, "I'm alive down here!" surviving with a broken shoulder.

Army Air Corps flying instructor Hugh Garrett joined the ferry group, transporting aircraft across the U.S. during World War II. Fondly known as "Pappy" to younger pilots, Garrett's 1946 crash ended his four-year military career.

Henry Udell Garrett was born in Bastrop, Texas, to Eddie and Belle Wyatt Garrett on 15 March 1907, moving to Bryan, Texas, after four years. He rode his uncle's horse to school, often barefooted. Life was rough, so he worked after school for Horlock Ice Industries. After eighth grade, Garrett left school, working full time. In 1923, he became foreman of one of Horlock's Houston plants.

In 1928, Garrett got his first taste of the "oil patch" working for W-K-M Company of Houston as assistant to the purchasing agent. In 1930, Gearench Manufacturing Company hired him as salesman and later as sales manager.

Garrett worked for Shell Refining Company and designed equipment for Guiberson Corporation of Dallas. Within two years he owned six gas lift patents.

When Garrett enlisted in the Army Air Corps in 1942, he spent his off hours doing what he did best…designing oil tools. By his discharge in 1946, he owned additional patents and a vision for the future.

His position with Guiberson awaited him; however, he took the big step, signing on with Longview's Olsco Manufacturing Company to manufacture his own specialized gas lift valve. Garrett's business soon outgrew Olsco's facilities, so he purchased a Houston plant, founding Garrett Oil Tools. By 1949, GOT exported its first tool shipment. "Just five years and four months after 'Hugh' Garrett entered the Olsco office in Longview with his hat in his hand, an idea in his head and little or nothing in his pockets, he found himself at the helm of a $1,500,000 organization – 'The World's Largest Manufacturer and Distributor of Gas Lift Valves.'" (*Men of Petroleum Progress*, 1952, page 54) Garrett enjoyed success in the Petroleum business until his death, 9 October 1979.

In the midst of his career, Garrett married Christine Dyche Garrett and raised three children, Betty Walden, John Garrett and Dorothy Bachtell. He grandfathered four boys, Douglas and Garrett Walden, and Michael and David Bachtell.

Henry Udell "Hugh" Garrett

Henry Udell "Hugh" Garrett

Though a powerful businessman and a busy, prolific inventor, Garrett valued his faith and family most. He made time to cheer at his son's Little League games, attend his daughter's piano recitals and join his wife in PTA activities. In his later years, he enjoyed an active role in the lives and talents of his four grandsons.

Garrett's humble beginnings birthed his determination to lovingly provide for his family and to improve his community. His vision and generous gifts to Longview's YMCA and his beloved First Baptist Church has provided buildings Longview will continue to enjoy for generations.

– Submitted by Dottie Bachtell

DR. A.B. GARVEY & BILLIE SUE ROTHWELL

Dr. Adam Burney Garvey, born 27 December 1920, and Billie Sue Rothwell, born 8 August 1926, were married in Longview on 14 March 1948.

Adam Burney (known as "Doc" or "Garvey"), son of Osborn Conrad Garvey and Minnie Elaine Burke Garvey, was born and raised in Livingston, Texas. After graduation from pre-dental school at John Tarleton College, he completed his dental training and graduated from the University of Kansas City Dental College. He lived in Longview from 1947 to 1950 when he entered military service. After three years in the U.S. Air Force, where he attained the commissioned rank of captain, he returned and opened his offices in Greggton. According to an editorial following his death in 1960, "Adults and their children as well, who knew Dr. Garvey appreciated the fact that he 'had a way' with children – a natural manner that gained their interest and trust. Such an attribute springs from a genuine understanding and dedication of heart to a worthy purpose and a good cause."

Doc was a member of the Longview First Christian Church, a trustee on the Board of Directors of the Longview Elks Lodge, member and one time President of the Longview Dental Society, member of the Gladewater Country Club and was active as a civic worker and community booster. As a member of the Longview Dental Society, he was instrumental in having fluoride added to the Longview public water system. Doc enjoyed many hobbies such as golf, boat racing and modifying his custom-made Studebaker Hawk automobiles.

Billie Sue Rothwell Garvey was the daughter of John William Rothwell and Mary Susan Freeman (See "John W. Rothwell/Mary Susan Freeman."), whose families had lived in the Longview area since the late 1800s. Billie Sue was born in Longview and moved to Mineola when she was two years old. She attended public school in Mineola where she was on the tennis team and the drum-major for the Mineola marching band. After graduation from high school, she attended the University of Texas in Austin, where she was a member of Alpha Delta Pi Sorority. Upon graduation in 1947, she returned to Longview where she met and married Adam Burney.

Billie Sue was a member of the First Christian Church and was employed as the Executive Director of the Mental Health Association in Gregg County until her retirement. She was also an avid golfer and an active member of the Cherokee Country Golf Association (where she served as President of the Ladies Association) until her death on 15 November 1999

Dr. and Mrs. Garvey had three daughters, Diane, Susan and Tina. Diane Garvey McFarland currently lives in Longview with her husband Malcom McFarland. Susan Garvey Evans lives in Temple with her husband John and three children, Alyson, Kiel and Kristen. Tina Garvey Denison lives in El Paso with her husband Gene and four children, Lindsey, Regan, Taylor and Kelsey.

Both Dr. and Mrs. Garvey are buried in Memory Park Cemetery.

– Submitted by Diane McFarland

GEISE–MCKINLEY

Although born on a farm in Sandyland, Arkansas, Jenny Frances Wagner Scherer Giese McKinley was always very proud of being a TEXAN. After all, she came to Texas at six weeks of age. She started school at five years because Greggton Elementary only had six students in the first grade. There were two new students: Joanne Rambo and Jenny Scherer. They started to school in 1934, and are still friends in 2003. They have dinner almost every Thursday night at the Butcher Shop in Longview.

In 1935, Jenny's family was transferred to the "Big Woods," and Jenny attended Judson Grove School from second grade through the

Jenny Frances Wagner Scherer in 1934.

ninth grade in 1942. This was the year the family was transferred to Burras, Louisiana. She started her sophomore year at Burras High School and got to take French. They moved again in November that year to Harlingen, Texas. She finished her sophomore year there and moved to the family farm in Sandyland, Arkansas

In May 1945, she graduated from Smackover High School and moved to Beaumont, Texas, where her mother was working as a welder in the Pennslyvania Ship Yards. Jenny attended Lamar Technical College. Then moved back to Kilgore, Texas, where she started classes at Kilgore College and made the Rangerettes the next year. A great memory from the Rangerette days was that on 7 December 1946, Kilgore College's football team and the Rangerettes participated in the First Junior College Rose Bowl. The Rangers lost the game, but the Rangerettes won the half time.

In September 1947, Jenny went to TSCW in Denton and graduated in August 1949. She then went to teach in Edinburg, Texas. She married Wayne Giese and had two children: Lara Lee Giese and Cindy Lou Giese. In 1957, the family moved to Moron, Venezuela. They lived about 40 kilometers out in the jungle on the beach. She then took a job teaching at the Escuela Privada de Venepal so that their family could have a house of their own. She was a trilingual teacher to children of nine different countries.

After four years, Jenny and daughters returned to Kilgore. She taught one year in Overton, Texas, then moved to Anaheim, California, where she could make a good living and raise her daughters.

After 27 years of teaching in California, getting a couple more degrees, working as a translator in the 1984 Olympics, diving with SeaLab III, competition square dancing in Dijon, France, and raising her two girls who both graduated from California State University in Long Beach, Jenny retired.

After all, 40 years was enough to teach. She moved to her home on Lake Cherokee, where she plays golf, paints, works with the Rangerettes Forever and is a member of the United Daughters of the Confederacy.

Oh, yes, she married a childhood friend, "Butch" McKinley in 1991, and they just keep rolling along.

– Submitted by Jenny Frances Wagner Scherer Giese McKinley

JESSE MARTIN GLASCO

Jesse Glasco was born 12 May 1818, in Tennessee. After coming to Texas, he married Louisa Earp, daughter of James Earp, in Earpville on 16 December 1846. In 1873, he was appointed by the General Land Office of Texas to settle a boundary dispute between Upshur County and the newly formed Gregg County. He also surveyed a road to be laid down between Longview and Gilmer – the salary for the job was fifteen dollars. He represented Upshur County in the Eleventh State Legislature in 1866. Jesse Glasco was interested in science, botany, mineralogy and

engineering. From 1859 to 1861, and 1867 to 1873, he was a meteorological observer for Upshur County for the Smithsonian Institute as well as collecting local reptiles, insects and Indian pottery for the Institute. He died 17 December 1886, and is buried in the Grice Community Cemetery, Upshur County.

MILLARD FRANKLIN GLOVER

Millard Franklin "Cap" Glover was born 29 October 1911, in Kilgore, Texas. His father was Jackson Franklin Glover, who ran away from his home in Alabama at the age of 14. During the Civil War, he came to East Texas, worked and eventually bought three hundred acres near Kilgore. He married Augusta Borders in 1890. Their first three children died of typhoid fever; later, they had five more children of which Cap was the youngest. After the death of his father, the family moved to Longview, where his mother established The Glover Hotel during the oil boom days. Young Cap worked at Glover Cleaners and later married Hattie Thomas on 3 September 1937, at The First Christian Church. Their attendants were Elaine Markham and Wendal Harper. Cap and Hattie had one daughter, Barbara Ann, who was born at the Van Sickle Clinic and delivered by her uncle, Dr. R.J. Van Sickle, the husband of Lina Hardin Glover. Hattie Thomas Glover was born 7 August 1916. She was the daughter of James Edward Thomas and Harriet Tweedle Thomas of Sulpher Springs. Jim Thomas, a landowner, traded cattle and horses and was very successful during World War I. He was active in the First Methodist Church and served as City Commissioner of Sulphur Springs for many years. With 13 children, the large Thomas home was a happy haven for the family and their many friends.

While working in the oil field equipment business, Cap bought apartments and Hattie, who had training in Dallas as a comptroller, began to keep the books. Later, Cap worked for Goodwin and Bass Chevrolet, winning many awards from General Motors. Both Hattie and Cap were members of First Baptist Church of Longview. They loved to travel and were able to have many wonderful trips abroad. Cap passed away on 26 February 2000, at the age of 90.

– Submitted by Barbara Baucum

GOODSON–PELPHREY

James Henry Goodson was born 9 January 1925, the only child of Henry Louis Goodson and Vera Elizabeth Warren. The Goodson family came to Gladewater, Gregg County in 1931. James met Wanda Minnette Pelphrey, born 6 November 1926, in 1938. Her family came to Gladewater, Gregg County, in 1931. They were childhood sweethearts. They married 27 December 1947, in Gladewater.

James graduated from high school in 1942. He was commissioned as an Ensign in the United States Navy, January 1945. After the war, he finished his pre-med courses at Texas A&M and was accepted at Southwestern Medical school in Dallas, July 1947. He graduated in

1951. He took his Internship and Ob-Gyn Residency at Parkland Hospital in Dallas. When he was a senior, he was an acting Intern in Ob-Gyn. When he was an Intern, he was acting resident in Ob-Gyn. He had found his place in Medicine. James became a skilled surgeon and clinician and his talents were recognized. He was appointed Chief Resident his last year of residency. That year the Professor at the Medical School retired and he was appointed Chairman and Interim Professor. This was the first of many accolades he was to later receive. James loved teaching. A colleague said, "Jim was a perfect example of what the word 'doctor' means. He was a teacher."

In 1955, James went into solo practice, an unprecedented move. He was appointed to the attending staff at Baylor Hospital in Dallas. He was Board Certified in 1959. He did so well on his orals, the examining committee and their colleagues recognized a bright future for him in Ob-Gyn. He later became an officer in the American College of Obstetricians & Gynecologists. He was President of the Dallas-Fort Worth Ob-Gyn Society, President of the Texas Association, Founding Father and President of the Southwestern Gynecologic Assembly, President of the Medical Staff, Baylor University Medical Center and was on the Advisory Committee.

In 1974, Baylor Hospital bought a 100-Watt Sharplan Laser. Without instruction he taught himself the intricacies of the laser. In a short time with his background in physics (he had excelled in Engineering Physics at A&M) and surgical skills, he felt comfortable using the laser surgery. He used the laser beam at its highest power giving him the ability to cut as a knife would. Realizing the danger lasers presented, he started courses in Laser Physics and Laser Safety. This led to an open invitation to teach at annual meetings of the American College of Obstetrics and Gynecologists. One of his greatest contributions was his invention to eliminate laser smoke during laparascopic surgery. The Laser Smoke Eliminator was patented in 1986. He was a skilled compassionate practitioner of medicine. He practiced 38 years. When he closed the office door for the last time, he said, "I wasn't through yet." He died four months later of cancer on 5 December 1993, in Dripping Springs, Hays County, Texas. He was buried in a white pine box in Wallace Mountain Cemetery, 7 December 1993.

– Submitted by Minnette Pelphrey Goodson

GOODSON–WARREN

Henry Louis Goodson was born 27 March 1885, in Simpsonville, Upshur County, Texas. He died 29 March 1956, in Tyler, Smith County, Texas. Vera Elizabeth Warren was born 9 September 1893, in Albany, Shackelford County, Texas. She died 17 March 1984, in Dallas, Dallas County, Texas. They married 28 December 1918, in Gilmer, Upshur County, Texas. Henry and Vera had one child, James Henry Goodson, born 9 January 1925. He died 5 December 1993, in Dripping Springs, Hays County, Texas. Henry's

grandfather, M. Hampton Goodson, was born circa 1813 in South Carolina and was killed in the Civil War. Vera descends from Robert Warren, born 14 July 1745, in Frailty, Charles County, Maryland. He died 28 October 1826, in Blount County, Tennessee. Robert established Warrensburg, Tennessee, on his land grant. He served in the American Revolution. Humphrey Warren, Sr. came to Maryland about 1662. They were English born and descend from William de Warren, the first Earl of Surry, who married Gundred, the daughter of William the Conqueror.

Alonzo Baber Boren, born 21 October 1830, in Georgia, married Sally Elizabeth Johnson, who was born 8 August 1843, also in Georgia. The Johnson and Boren family came to Upshur County, Texas, in 1850. The land they bought turned into "black gold." Their daughter, Daisie Lee, married James Rush Warren, Vera's father, who was appointed to the bench as a federal Judge in the early 1930s. The family was in Upshur County, Texas, in 1846. Gustavus Earickson Warren was born 1824 in Tennessee, and died in 1899. He was an early leader and prominent in the affairs of the County, serving as County Clerk from 1852-1869. He was a Captain in the Civil War and fought in the Battle of Yellow Bayou. James is a member of the Sons of the American Revolution and the Sons of the Republic of Texas.

The Goodson family came to Gregg County in 1931. Henry was Vice President of the First State Bank in Gladewater. James met Minnette Pelphrey, born 6 November 1926, in 1938. They were childhood sweethearts. James graduate from Gladewater high school in 1942. He enrolled at A&M as an aeronautical engineer. His dream was to fly. On his birthday in 1943, he enlisted in the Navy Reserves. The Navy sent him to Southwestern Louisiana Institute for one year, and then to Midshipmen's School at Cornel University in Ithaca, New York. He was commissioned an Ensign in the United States Navy, January 1945. Trained as a fighter director, he was the first of two to be sent to the Pacific Theatre for the invasion of Japan. After the war, he was stationed on the Destroyer Escort, USS *Lofberg* 759.

James came home in June 1946, and immediately enrolled at A&M to start pre-med courses. He took 20 hours a semester, finished in a year with a 92 grade point average. He was accepted at Southwestern Medical School in Dallas. Minnette transferred to Southern Methodist University her senior year to finish her degree while planning their wedding. They were married 27 December 1947. There were three children: Lasca Minnette, born 26 March 1949; James Rush, born 30 July 1959; and Courtney Anne, born 1 March 1961.

– Submitted by Lasca Longacre

GRAYBILL

Henry Graybill was born in Lancaster, Pennsylvania, about 1755. He moved to South Carolina previous to the American Revolution, where he served as an officer for that colony, and then under General Elijah Clarke in Georgia. Henry later settled in Georgia and is listed as one of the

Graybill family, children of Michael and Dora Graybill.

original settlers of Greene County and one of the founders of Hancock County. He served as surveyor, clerk of the superior court, court appraiser, grand juror, justice of the inferior court, road commissioner, State Congressman, and was elected four times by the Legislature as one of the electors of President and Vice-President. Henry is listed as one of the charter members of Powellton Baptist Church. He was also one of the first members of the Masonic Lodge in Georgia. Henry died in Hancock County, Georgia, in 1822.

Henry Graybill and his wife Mary (Polly) had six children: Phillip; Henry, Jr. married Mary Gregory; John married Ann Nancy Choice; Elizabeth; Martha; and Michael married Judith Butts, daughter of Thomas Clements and Sarah (Hunt) Butts.

Michael and Judith (Butts) Graybill had seven children: Jesse Goodwin Butts, John W., George, Michael (Don) Adoniram, Silas M., Sarah Tyler and Caroline Emily.

Jesse Goodwin Butts Graybill was born in Baldwin County, Georgia, on 9 October 1817. J.G.B. Graybill married Mary Frances Dickson, daughter of William and Lucy Dickson of Hancock County, Georgia, on 14 January 1841.

J.G.B. Graybill and his family moved to Danville in the late 1840s. The Graybill family came with other related families from Georgia. The men came overland. The women and children came later by ship into the port of Galveston. Mary Frances insisted upon bringing her piano, which was transported by wagon overland from Georgia.

J.G.B. and Mary had eight children: Leonidas Josephus, William, Mary Jopetra, George Washington, Frances, Michael Hamilton, Thomas and Jesse Julia (Cunyus). Only Frances, Michael Hamilton, Henry Thomas and Jesse Julia (Cunyus) reached adulthood.

J.G.B. was listed as one of the original officers of the Danville Masonic Lodge No. 101 established in 1851. He served in H Company, 9th Battalion, of the Texas Reserves during the Civil War.

J.G.B. Graybill died in Danville on 20 December 1894. Mary Frances Graybill died in Danville in July 1906.

Michael Hamilton Graybill married Dora Rosson, daughter of Thomas Jefferson and Ellen (Hale) Rosson, in Danville on 2 January 1889. They made their home in the Peatown Community. They had seven children: child died in infancy, 1889; Mary Ellen, born 1891, married Edwin Vernon Temple; John Frank, born 1893; Annie, born 1895, married Thomas H. Pennick; Michael Hal, born 1896; Lucy Virginia Juanita, born 1898; and Louise, married Abnott.

– Submitted by Tommy Harriss

BRANDON, JESSICA & TAYLOR GREEN

Brandon Green and Jessica (Cahill) Green established their home in Longview, Texas, on 10 June 2002. Brandon was born on 22 November 1974, to parents Manvel and Charlotte (Lane) Green.

Manvel was born the oldest child of three to parents Bo and Ruth (Powell) Green. Bo married Ruth on 10 March 1947. Manvel graduated from Linden-Kildare High School in 1967, enlisted in the Army and served in Vietnam from 1968-1969. Manvel married Charlotte (Lane) on 3 September 1971. Charlotte was born in Hughes Springs as the second child of six children to parents Charles and Jean (Dorflinger) Lane, who married on 2 August 1948. Charlotte graduated from high school in 1970. After Manvel and Charlotte married, they had three sons, Scott, Brandon and Kevin. Manvel currently works for the Cass County Road Commission, while Charlotte works for Linden-Kildare ISD.

After graduating from Linden-Kildare High School in 1993, Brandon headed off to college at Southern Arkansas located in Magnolia, Arkansas. Later Brandon transferred to Stephen F. Austin State University in Nacogdoches, where he graduated in 1999 with a Bachelor's of Science in Kinesiology.

Jessica was born in Youngstown, Ohio, to parents Bob and Joyce (Retort) Cahill on 10 December 1976. Bob was the middle child of parents John and Georgina (Manhollan) Cahill. John was a private in the Army Infantry during World War II and a prisoner of war in Germany for 27 months. John married Georgina (Manhollan) on 22 December 1945, in Youngstown, Ohio. Bob graduate from Struthers High

in 1966, and enlisted in the military serving with Delta Company 1/26 Marines as a combat corpsman in Vietnam during 1968-1969.

Joyce (Retort) was the oldest daughter of Louie and Mary (Mediate) Retort. Louie, the second youngest of 15 children, enlisted in the military at the age of 15 and served in World War II as a gunner. Mary (Mediate) married Louie on 6 September 1947. Joyce graduated from Struthers High School and worked at Ohio Edison until she married Bob on 12 April 1969.

In September 1978, they relocated to Texas with their two daughters, Jana and Jessica. Bob retired after a 14-year career as a Registered Nurse. Joyce is also retired after 19 years with Wal-Mart as the invoice clerk. Jessica graduated from Pine Tree High School in 1995. She graduated in 1999 with a Bachelor's of Arts in Speech Communication from Stephen F. Austin State University, and in 2000 with a Master's of Arts degree in Communication. Brandon and Jessica were married on 15 August 1998, and had their daughter, Taylor, on 6 March 2001. Brandon has coached football and baseball for several school districts and currently coaches at LindenKildare. In 2001, Brandon was part of the Lufkin ISID coaching staff that coached the varsity football team to a state championship title. Jessica worked as a full time speech communication faculty member at Stephen F. Austin State University. Currently, she is an instructor at area colleges. Together, Brandon, Jessica and their daughter Taylor Green reside in their home in Longview, Texas.

– Submitted by Brandon Green

JOHN PERRY GREEN: Five Years in Gregg County

John Perry Green moved his family to the Longview area in 1956, where he was employed as an industrial engineer by Garrett Oil Tool. "Johnny's" move to Longview was one of three five-year periods away from his farm in Bobo Community, near Timpson, Shelby County, Texas. He had worked in Houston for two large tool companies, Reed Roller Bit and Dixon Gun Plant, and taken engineering classes at the University of Houston in the evenings. In 1941, he was deferred by the Marines to train women to be machinists to make war materials.

John Perry Green was born 22 April 1921, in Timpson, Texas, to Nubern and Pearl Weir Green. On 27 December 1939, he married his high school sweetheart, Juanita Rhodes. She was born 5 August 1921, to William Thomas and Lydia Bowlin Rhodes. J.P. and Juanita had four children. Tempie Ann was fifteen, Jerry Glen was eleven, Barbara Jean "Jeanie" was nine, and Jack Michael "Mike" was four when they moved to Gregg County.

Tempie became a Longview Lobo band majorette, a Kilgore College Rangerette and Miss Congenial-

ity in the 1959 Miss Longview Pageant. Jerry played football for the Pine Tree High School, was a Boy Scout and a Greggton 4-H club member. He caught and showed a calf in the Houston Livestock Show. Jeanie was a Campfire Girl, was in the 4-H Foods Project and learned to swim at the Pine Tree pool. Mike played Little League Baseball.

Juanita served as the Organizational leader of Greggton 4-H Club from 1957 to 1960. They had 58 members and met at the Greggton Community Center. In 1960, Juanita took the census in the Pine Tree area, and later did recount work near downtown Longview.

Johnny was a charter member of the Industrial Engineers organization in Greggton/Longview. He coached and played on the Garrett Oil Tool baseball team. In 1957, they were the Longview Industrial Softball League Champions. Johnny maintained his ranch and home in Shelby County, going there every weekend. At age forty, he self-retired to his Wine Glass Ranch in Bobo. Where he had once produced tomatoes and cotton for market, and operated a dairy for five years, he built a poultry farm. The land was used for commercial cattle and registered quarter horse production. He lived out his years doing exactly what he wanted – living on the land he loved. J.P. and Juanita had thirteen grandchildren (nine boys and four girls) in 1994 when he died. J.P. is buried in the Tennessee Community Cemetery in Shelby County. Juanita now lives in the city of Timpson, but still maintains their country home.

Tempie and Jeanie graduated from SFA; Jerry attended A&M, volunteered for Vietnam, and he and Mike are Grade A Construction Superintendents for Texas and world companies. All live within five miles of their parents' farm and carry on the country life traditions of their ancestors.

For a more detailed account of the Green, Rhodes and related families, refer to *The History of Shelby County, Texas, 1988, Vol. I*, and *Timpson, Texas, Area History 1800-2002*.

– Submitted by Juanita R. Green

Brandon, Jessica and Taylor Green

John Perry Green family. (l.-r.) Standing: Mike Green, Jennie Green Rhodes, Tempie Green Pike and Jerry Green. Seated: John Perry Green and Juanita Rhodes Green.

HUBERT GREGG

Hubert Gregg was born 21 February 1889, in Nebraska. He came to Longview in 1931. In 1932, he began to support himself by selling peanuts. Known as the "Peanut Man," Gregg was blinded at age six by an illness. He was a fixture at summer league baseball games and Longview Lobo football games as well as around town. Gregg was a long-time supporter of Longview athletics. He was led by a guide dog and pulled a red wagon full of parched peanuts. The 3rd of April 1979 was proclaimed "Hubert Gregg Day" in Longview. The Longview ISD honored him in September 1985 in celebration of his fortieth year of selling peanuts at the football games. After his death, the school placed a brass plaque at the Lobo Football Stadium dedicated to his memory. Hubert Gregg died at age 102 on 27 May 1991.

JOHN GREGG

Gregg County was named for Confederate General John Gregg. He was born in Alabama 28 September 1828. At age 19, he had become a professor of language and mathematics. In 1847, he studied law. By 1852, he had moved to Fairfield, Freestone County, Texas. He set up a law practice and was later elected district judge. Gregg was chosen as a member of the Secession Convention and represented Texas at the Provisional Congress in Montgomery, Alabama.

John Gregg was an admired general in the Confederate army, and time and time again people would refer to him as the gallant General Gregg. General Robert E. Lee, General Pemberton and the Richmond, Virginia, newspaper reported that "the gallant General Gregg has fallen."

General Gregg was a statesman who helped frame the Confederate Constitution with the idea that the people needed the power to serve as a check on the central government. General Gregg returned to Texas from Montgomery, Alabama, to form a Confederate infantry unit. He fought many battles, was captured and became a P.O.W. He was exchanged for three Union lieutenants. He was then promoted to Brigadier General. In the battle of New Market, he led his men gallantly in battle. In October 1864, he was killed on the Darbyville Road. His wife and his body were carried back to Aberdeen, Mississippi, where he lies today.

"In 1873, when a new county was carved out of Rusk and Upshur Counties, it was remembered that early on, General Gregg believed in the independent people of Texas and their ability to govern themselves. Thus Gregg County was named."

– Submitted by Barney Hilburn
(member Sons of Confederate Veterans)

REV. & MRS. MILLER GREGORY

Rev. Miller Gregory organized the Central Baptist Church in the Longview Community Center in November 1949. In 1950, the church bought the old Nazarene Church building on the corner of 4th and Padon Streets. Later, the church was the first church in Longview to move

Rev. and Mrs. Miller Gregory

out on the Northeast Loop and was renamed the Eden Drive Baptist Church. Rev. Gregory pastored the church for 20 years.

Rev. Gregory was known to everyone in Longview in the '50s and '60s as "Brother Gregory" or "the preacher." He was a friend to everyone and respected by everyone. He was an "old time" minister of the gospel, who was 24 hours a day what he was in the pulpit.

Rev. Gregory was born in Smith County, Texas, 31 December 1909, the son of Heywood Gregory, a fruit grower and his wife, Jennie Miller Gregory, daughter of Dr. Franklin R. Miller of Tyler. Heywood Gregory's father, Jacob Gregory, came to Texas with the Cotton Belt Railroad from Waterloo, Kentucky. Jacob was a tool checker at the Roundhouse in Tyler. Jacob's wife was Barbara McFarland, daughter of John Wesley and Elizabeth Atkinson McFarland of Fentress County, Tennessee, and granddaughter of James McFarland and Barbara Young.

Irene Hitt Gregory, wife of Rev. Gregory, owned the South Green Bible Book Inn for 25 years. Irene was born 19 September 1914, in Choctaw County, Oklahoma, the daughter of Fred Hitt and Lillie Harris Hitt. Miller and Irene were married 12 July 1930, at Hugo, Oklahoma. Irene was descended from a family of Germans brought to Spottsylvania County, later Culpepper County, Virginia, in 1714 by Governor Spottswood to open iron mines. The first Hitt was Peter Hidte. The Hitts migrated to Laurens County, South Carolina, then into Alabama, coming to Smith County in the early 1850s.

Irene's grandfather was Alfred Hitt, who married Nancy Land. Alfred was the son of Alfred Hitt and Alice Jarman Hitt who came from Alabama in oxcarts. Alice Jarman was the daughter of Berry Jarman and Mary Wrenn, who also came to Smith County. Rev. Miller Gregory died 13 August 1982. Irene died 2 February 2002. Both are buried in White Oak City Cemetery. They had two children, Ronald H. Gregory, longtime piano teacher of Longview, and a daughter, Janet.

– Submitted by Ron Gregory

ROBERT JACKSON "JACK" GREGORY

"At 604," is how Robert Jackson "Jack" Gregory, Sr. begins most conversations when reminiscing about growing up in Longview.

Jack's mother, Worthy Pauline Burnett Gregory (born about 1895), was raised in Van Zandt County, Texas. Her grandparents, P.C. "Uncle Cal" and Susan Alvina Hill Burnett, were early settlers having arrived at Rocky Point community from Harrison County in 1852. Her father, William Preston "Press" Burnett, owned a hardware store in Wills Point.

On 24 December 1911, she married Samuel Benjamin "Ben" Gregory (born 10 November 1875) who was a city marshal from Edgewood, Texas. His parents, Marion Williamson Gregory and Rebecca Jane McManus Gregory, raised him in Van Zandt County. They were originally from Taxahaw, Lancaster County, South Carolina, before moving to Palestine, Texas, in 1886 and then to Wills Point.

Ben and Worthy had five children, Worth Benjamin (born 14 March 1914), Gerald Leroy (born 19 January 1916), Sybol Elizabeth (21 January 1918), Thalia Rebecca (born 23 November 1921) and Robert Jackson Gregory (born 5 September 1924). Ben traded Morgan horses at First Monday in Canton. Even though they were young, Worth and Gerald would go with him to help handle the horses. In 1926, while pursuing a suspect, Ben died of a heart attack. He was 50 years old.

With the insurance money, Worthy bought a large house at 604 E. Methvin Street (located between 3rd and 4th Streets) in Longview. Her father had relatives that lived in Gregg and Harrison counties. The house was in the Junction and close to workers on the Texas & Pacific Railroad. She rented rooms to support herself and her children.

When the railroad headquarters moved from Longview to Mineola, most of her boarders left. Times were hard and occasionally the children lived with other family members back in Edgewood. Sybol, Thalia and Jack went to Dallas to the Juliette Fowler Children's Home for a few years after the minister at the First Christian Church in Longview, Rev. James R. Wright, sent a letter of recommendation on Worthy's behalf. Jack can remember holding hands with Thalia through the fence that separated the boys from the girls at the Home as they ate watermelon seeds.

(l.-r.) Worth Gregory, Gerald Gregory and Jack Gregory, 1943, Claxton Studio, Longview.

Things picked up for the family when the oil industry boomed in the area. By 1932, all the children were back living at 604.

When Jack was attending First Ward Elementary School, his mother told him it was time to find a job. He started working for the *Longview News and Journal* selling newspapers on the street. He was 10 years old. On Saturday nights he would crawl into the lighted *Longview News and Journal* sign and sleep so he would be the first one to get papers on Sunday morning. He earned about $1 a week.

One day while turning somersaults on the hitching post in front of 604, Jack's friend, Tillman Perkins, told him that his dad, Melvin Shivers, was looking for a delivery boy at Junction Drug Store. Knowing he would make more money, he starting working there riding a bike delivering prescriptions to customers. He earned about $3 a week for this job and earned enough money to buy his mother an icebox. He also bought a new bike.

After attending First Ward, Jack attended Longview Junior High and Longview High Schools. He participated in all sports. He remembers sneaking out of a classroom window at the high school to see Dorothy Lamour who was in town selling war bonds. Other fond memories include waving at the "Sunshine Special" train that ran on the tracks behind their home as it blew its whistle before reaching the crossing of Methvin and 6th Street, swimming in T.P. (Texas & Pacific Railroad) Pond with his buddies, and talking to the hobos on "Hobo Island" at T.P. Pond

During World War II, Worth and Gerald were in the Army. Worth was in the Quartermaster Corps, and Gerald was in Field Artillery. When Jack turned 18, he joined the Army Air Corps. He went to several mechanic schools and was assigned to the 9th Bomb Group, as Assistant Crew Chief. This B-29 bomb group was shipped to the Mariana Islands (which include Guam, Saipan and Tinian) on a Liberty Ship in November 1944, debarking at Tinian Island. His plane was named the *T.N. Teeny* and was parked only a few hundred yards from the *Enola Gay*, the plane chosen to drop the first atomic bomb. Jack served there until the end of the war.

After returning to 604, Jack attended Kilgore Junior College and married Rubye Cute Miller on 31 August 1946, in her hometown of Dardanelle, Arkansas. He graduated from SMU with a BBA degree in 1949. Later taking night classes, he earned an MBA from Texas A&I in Kingsville. He started work for Humble Oil (Exxon) in 1951 and retired from there as an executive accountant in 1986.

Jack and Rubye had two children, Robert Jackson Gregory, Jr. (born 15 August 1949) and Beth Suzan Gregory (born 23 August 1953). Rubye died 28 November 2000, and is buried at Memory Park in Longview. Jack currently lives in Burleson, Texas, near his son, Jack, Jr. and daughter-in-law, Kaye Barker Lile Gregory. He has five grandsons: Jeremy and Nat Mitchell, and Collin, Ky and Cody Gregory. He also has

four great grandchildren: Raven and Reagan Mitchell, and Isaac and Ky Gregory, Jr. Jack plays tennis or jogs daily and is a member of the First Christian Church in Burleson.

– Submitted by Kaye Gregory

HENRY CLAY GRIFFIN

Henry Clay Griffin was born in Longview, Texas, on 28 July 1879, to Wyman Watson Griffin (1844-1888) and Susan Rilda Taylor (1852-1924), both from Illinois. His wife, Mary G. Martinez, was born on 8 February 1897, in Texas. Mary's parents, John Lasco Martinez (1874-1935) and Alfugia Cucca Refugio (1855-1957), were both from Mexico.

Henry and Mary Griffin, 1945

Henry and Mary were married in 1918 at Gregg County, Texas, and lived at 608 E. Methvin Street, Longview. Henry's work journal shows him working long days and hours for the Texas and Pacific Railroad from 1909 to 1917 and the City of Longview's Water Department through 1925. Working as a fireman for the railroad, he tended to the trains' steam engine boilers. The Water Department of the City of Longview borrowed Henry from the railroad to help with its boilers located at the city's old water plant near the Sabine River and the Missouri Pacific Railway near FM Road 2087. Henry continued to worked for the water department in construction work and general repairman and later as a meter reader. In 1927, the Griffin and Martinez families moved to Harrison County and settled in Marshall, Texas.

Henry's sister, Hattie May Griffin, (1882-1974) was married to John Richard Crain Jr. (1871-1915), son of Dr. John Richard Crain (1832-1871) and Mattie Patience Rogers (1833-1906) of Hallsville, Texas. Dr. Crain served as surgeon with the 7th Texas Infantry Regiment for the Confederate Army under Brigadier General John Gregg (1828- 1864). Gregg County, Texas, established in 1873, was named after General Gregg. In 1780, Dr. Crain's grandfather, Joel Crain (1762-1844), fought with six of his brothers in the American Revolution (1776-1783) for North Carolina Regiments.

The children of Henry Clay and Mary Griffin are Henry Clay Griffin Jr. (1918-1995), World War II, U.S. Army; Daniel Boone Griffin (1920-2002), World War II, U.S. Army Air Force; Mary Susan Griffin (1924-1984); Goldie Gray Griffin (1928-2000); and John Ross Griffin (1931-1988), all of Marshall, Texas; and Wyman Watson Griffin (1922-2003), World War II, U.S. Army, of Longview, Texas.

Henry died 12 October 1971, and Mary died 5 May 1973; both are buried at Colonial Gardens Cemetery, Harrison County, Texas.

LARKIN PORTER GRIFFIN, SR. & SARAH ELIZABETH GRIFFIN

L.P. Griffin, Sr. was born in 1858 in Cokesbury, South Carolina, and moved to Bethany, Louisiana, with his parents as a small child. Sarah Elizabeth (Sallie) Westmoreland Griffin was born in Bethany, Louisiana, in 1864. In 1894, L.P. Griffin moved his family to Kilgore and established a General Mercantile business on the corner of what is now Commerce and Main Streets (better known today as the "World's Richest Acre"). Mr. Griffin died in 1926, four years before the discovery of the great East Texas Oil Field. Griffin purchased the home of Captain J.M. Thompson (the father of Mrs. Lou Della Crim on whose land the second discovery well for the field was drilled), who then moved to Sherman to be actively engaged in the establishment of Austin College.

The Griffins were active in the Methodist congregation in Kilgore and raised a family of eight children: L.P. Griffin, Jr. was a farmer-rancher; Clyde worked as a rural route carrier; Josephine married a Baptist minister, W.D. Anderson, and helped him with his congregation near San Antonio; James was a merchant in Kilgore; Roy worked as a salesman for Hughes, Delay, & Allen Menswear in Tyler; Leon was a merchant and was active in real estate rental properties after the oil boom; Mays died at age 12 years; Sallie Mills Devereux-Sherwood was a veteran teacher for Kilgore schools and private piano teacher prior to her teaching career.

The Griffins were known for their loveable, gregarious personalities; their humor was irresistible and irrepressible.

Larkin Porter Griffin, Sr. and Sarah Elizabeth Westmoreland Griffin.

WILLIAM F. & SUSAN ANN STOKER GRIFFIN

William F. Griffin is the son of Jacob Griffin, born about 1782 in Nash County, North Carolina, and died about 1856 in North Carolina, and Temperance Floyd, born about 1796 and died about 1865 in North Carolina. Temperance Floyd was a daughter of Thomas Penuel and Mary (Beckwith) Floyd and sister to Dolphin Ward Floyd, Alamo defender, and John W. Floyd, who is buried in the Floyd Cemetery in Upshur County, Texas.

William was born 1821 in North Carolina, and died 23 April 1882, in Gregg County, Texas. He is buried in the Gilmer City Cemetery beside his daughter, Janie B. Griffin Johnson, and her infant. William married Susan Ann Stoker on 27 December 1846, in Troup County, Georgia. Susan, daughter of Arnold Stoker and Rebecca Leander Jones, was born April 1828, in Georgia, and died after 1927 in Texas. Susan is buried in the Gladewater Cemetery in Gladewater, Texas.

William and Susan lived in Georgia for several years. After many of Susan's family had moved to Texas, their family also moved to East Texas and settled in Gregg County, about two miles south of the Gregg County Courthouse. They were listed on the 1860 Marshall, Harrison, Texas, census with their four children. William was a farmer. The youngest, Janie, was born about 1858 in Alabama, so the family migrated to Texas after that time.

William and Susan had eight children: 1) John Early, born 8 December 1848, in Georgia, married 1873 in Texas to Radonia Alabama Lee, daughter of Nathan Lee and Sarah. John died 27 January 1927, in Upshur County, Texas, and is buried in Walnut Creek Cemetery; 2) J.D., born 1854 in Alabama; 3) Orra A. Griffin, born 4 December 1855, in Alabama, married Henry Levi Sewell. Orra died 10 August 1888, in Texas; 3) Janie B. Griffin, born about 1858 in Alabama, married 30 April 1878, in Gregg County, Texas, to William Richard Johnson. Janie died 12 July 1882, in Upshur County, Texas. William and Janie had one daughter, Nettie Belle Johnson, born 15 March 1878, in Longview, Texas. She married Alex Young Magrill, son of Alexander R. Magrill and Margaret C. Rucker, on 11 October 1898, in Gregg County, Texas. Alex, a railroad switchman, was killed instantly on 4 December 1920, in Longview, Texas, while switching railroad cars. Nettie later married Edward F. Winn. She died 24 June 1963, in Dallas, Texas; 4) Charles "Charley" T., born 20 December 1860, in Texas, married 17 December 1884, in Gregg County to Lou Cunyus. Charley died 13 August 1887, in Texas and is buried in the Peatown Cemetery in Gregg County; 5) William Elisha, born 9 September 1863, and died 11 October 188–. William is buried in the Gum Springs Cemetery; 6) Sudie R., born 1866 in Texas; 7) Fannie L., born 1869 in Texas. She married John L. Richardson 7 July 1888, in Gregg County, Texas; 8) Ella A. born 1873 in Texas.

– Submitted by Connie Wallace Perdue

WYMAN WATSON GRIFFIN

Wyman Watson Griffin was born 1844 in Pike County, Illinois, in Montezuma Township near the Illinois River. His wife Susan Rilda Taylor was born 1852 in Brown County, Illinois.

Wyman's parents were Lorenzo W. Griffin (1818-1862), born in Ohio, and Mary Westrope (1816-1905), born in Kentucky. Mary's parents were William Westrope (1783- 1825) and Mary Wicoff (1779- 1850). Mary's grandparents were John Westrope (1763-1781), a Revolutionary War lieutenant from North Carolina during 1778 to 1783, and his wife Hanna Bryan (1765-1802). Hanna's parents were William Bryan (1734-1780) and Mary Boone (1736-1819), sister to frontiersman Daniel Boone.

Lorenzo Griffin and his parents, Wyman Griffin (1788-1856), a cabinetmaker from Connecticut, and Sarah Watson (1793-1854) from Pennsylvania, arrived Illinois in 1838 from Ohio.

Wyman Watson Griffin enlisted in the Civil War's Union Army in February 1862, for the Illinois 28th Infantry Regiment, E Company. His service included the Siege of Cornith, Mississippi; the Battle of Hatchie River in 1862; the Siege of Vicksburg; the Battle of Jackson, Mississippi, in 1863; the Siege of Spanish Fort; the capture of Fort Blakely; and the Siege of Mobile, Alabama, in 1865. Immediately after the war in July 1865, there was fear that dissident exconfederates might join with Emperor Maximilian in Mexico and attempt to invade Texas. Wyman's duty at Brazos Santiago Island included the construction of the Major General Phil Sheridan Railroad. Consisting of 25,000 troops in the Brownsville, Texas, area, the railroad was completed late in 1865 and ran from the northern tip of Brazos Santiago Island, the shipping and receiving port for U.S. troops, 11 miles to Whites Ranch Landing on the Rio Grande River. Wyman was mustered out March 1866 in Brownsville, Texas.

Wyman and Susan were married 17 February 1870, at Cape Girardeau, Missouri. Susan's parents, James W. Taylor (1822-1870) and Nancy Jane Stine (1824-1880), came from

1920s Griffin homestead.

Kentucky. Susan's brother, Casper J. Taylor (1844-1862), a Civil War volunteer for the Illinois 129th Regiment Infantry, died in Bowling Green, Kentucky, of measles.

Gregg County, Texas, tax records show that a Watson Griffin was a resident in 1878. The 1880 Census records show Wyman Griffin as a laborer for the railroad. Wyman owned property where Longview's Teague Park and U.S. Highway 80 now exist. An 1883 agreement between W.W. Griffin and the railroad let the Texas and Pacific Railroad construct and maintain a water tank or pond on his land for railroad purposes.

In 1887, Wyman filed for a Civil War Pension based on disability, and then later died on 5 October 1888, in Valley City, Illinois, where he was buried. He was survived by his wife Susan (died 12 August 1924) and children Minnie Griffin (1873-1930) born in Missouri; Henry Clay Griffin (1879-1971); Hattie May Griffin (1882-1974); Daniel Boone Griffin (1884-1960) and Goldie Gray Griffin (1887-1930), all born in Gregg County.

– Submitted by Tony Griffin

JAMES LOUIS GRIGSBY

James Louis Grigsby (born 2 May 1905) of Ruston, Louisiana, and his young wife, Blanche Alice Mitchell (born 29 May 1911) of Shawnee, Oklahoma, came to Longview during the oil boom of 1930. They raised their family of four children: Frances Ellan Harrell, Betty Carolyn Feather, James Louis Grigsby, Jr., D.D.S. and Nelda Faye Strong. The children attended South Ward, Foster Jr. High and Longview High School.

The Grigsby family had two homes in Longview. They lived at 512 Ridgelea Street until Longview grew north past the depot into new developments, and then moved to 1907 Sunshine Sq. Later, 400 acres of land was acquired in Harrison County to be used for agriculture and ranching.

Louis Grigsby's career highlights include ten years as a Special Investigator for the Gregg County District Attorney; affiliation with the famed Texas Rangers during the tumultuous days of bootlegging, illegal gambling and chasing renegades like Bonnie and Clyde; owner of the Schlitz beer distributorship (1947-88); and commercial real estate management of the ware-

Susan Rilda Griffin and grandson Henry Clay Griffin, Jr., 1919

Louis and Blanche Grigsby

house district at South Cotton Street (later re-dedicated Grigsby Street).

Louis joined the U.S. Coast Guard during World War II. He was a charter member of Sharon Temple, Tyler, and rode horseback in the award-winning Shrine Mounted Patrol as the carrier of the American flag. He successfully influenced the moving of Joseph Schlitz Brewery to Longview and was member and president of the Wholesale Beer Distributors of Texas.

East Texas celebrated 22 November 1980, as Louis Grigsby Day.

Blanche M. Grigsby was a member of the Eastern Star and the American Diabetic Association. She was an avid needle pointer, a devoted wife and mother and a faithful children's worker at the First Baptist Church where all of the family regularly participated in membership and worship.

Blanche died 25 October 1971. Louis married Annie Lou Ray in 1980. His death came 19 October 1988. Louis and Blanche Grigsby are buried in Memory Park Cemetery.

The family has grown to 10 grandchildren, 23 great grandchildren and two great great grandchildren.

Frances Grigsby married Bill Harrell. Their son, Billy Bob, and wife, Connie Barclay, have daughters, Rebecca and Lindsay. Lindsay married Jason Flynt and they have a daughter, Macy. Second son, Michael Wayne, and wife, Denise, have two sons, Troy and Sam.

Carolyn Grigsby and husband, Robert Feather, have a son Robert Keith. Robert and wife, Lisa Sawyer, have daughters, Victoria and Susanna. Daughter, Sunni Feather and husband, Britt Brookshire, have Blake, Chad, Ross and Caroline.

Dr. James Grigsby and wife, Wilena Vick, had five children: Robyn married Mark Lowe and their children are Laura, Lindsey and Elizabeth; Matthew is deceased; Dr. Louis Grigsby and wife, Teri, have Staci and Jacklyn; Brent and Amanda Grigsby have Kaitlyn; and Trey and Amanda Grigsby are newlyweds.

Nelda Grigsby and Jim Wallace are the parents of Carolyn Ann and husband, Mark Walgren, who have daughters, Ellen and Laura. Aliceson Wallace and husband, Dr. Jeffrey Pinkerton, have John, Reed and Ali. Nelda is now married to Jack B. Strong of Longview.

– Submitted by Carolyn G. Feather

WILLIAM EDWARD & JOY HAMBERLIN GRUBBS

William Edward Grubbs, born in 1922, from Atlanta, Georgia, and wife Joy Hamberlin Grubbs, born on 3 December 1925, from Gilmer, Texas, moved to Longview, Texas, in 1951. They had married in Houston, Texas. They lived on Surfside Island at Freeport, Texas, where he was in the Coast Guard. After the War he worked for Post Army Engineers traveling from one Army Base to another.

They had three children when they moved to Longview on Highway 80 across from the Triangle Restaurant: Bill Jr., born 1945 in Gilmer; Jerry Mack, born 1946 in Gilmer; and Debby Jane, born 1950 in Gatesville, Texas. They later had twins, Tommy Ray and Tammy Kay, born 1963.

William went to college at LeTourneau. He worked for Skelley Oil Co., then Texas Eastman when the plant opened, where he was a foreman.

The family lived on Idylwood Drive, West Ann Drive, at Dundee Place on Dundee Road, and Fair Haven Street.

The children went to school at First Ward, South Ward, Valley View, Forest Park, Mozelle Johnston, Pine Tree and Longview High. All the children were in the band. Bill and Mack were also in a Swing Band under Mr. Rotundo, and Debby was a majorette.

Bill and Mack graduated from BYU in Provo, Utah. Bill majored in Marketing and Research and Mack in Business Management. Debby went to Ricks College in Idaho; she graduated at LDS Business College in Salt Lake City, Utah.

Bill, Jr. married Helen Patten from Logan, Utah. They live in Bountiful, Utah, and have six children, Jeffrey, Jennifer, April, Ryan, Emily and Stephanie. Jerry Mack married Kaye Walquist from Cedar City, Utah. They live in Bountiful, Utah, and have five children, Todd, Leslie, Julie, Trevor and Kimberly. Debby married James Plaster from Spokane, Washington. They live in Spokane and have five children, Angela, Lindsey, Camron, Brandon, and Tyler.

William and Joy Grubbs family. (l.-r.) Back: Jerry Mack, Tammy and Bill. Front: Debby, Tommy, Joy and William.

Tommy married Deidra Horn; they had two sons, Shawn and Shane. He later married Sarah Carson and had a daughter, Hannah. Tommy is now working in San Antonio.

Tammy married Paul Hane and their daughter, Tiffany, is at BYU. Tammy is now married to Bill Rice. They live in Longview.

The Grubbs are members of the Church of Jesus Christ of Later Day Saints on Blue Ridge Parkway. William served as Bishop twice, on High Council, in the Stake Presidency, was Stake Mission President and Stake Patriarch. Joy worked with the youth program for 35 years, held the Stake Young Women Presidency, was Ward Primary and Young Women's President, and Ladies Relief Society President for 13 years, worked closely with her children and school. She went to PTA convention for Mozelle Johnston School. She worked two years as a hair dresser.

The Grubbs have seen many changes in Longview: new buildings, a mall, new South Ward School and beautiful Longview High, and new streets and highways such as I-20. One change that is sad to see is the brick streets being taken up, but time changes everything.

The Grubbs still live in Longview and enjoy it.

– Submitted by William Grubbs

RALPH ROBERT & JOY BAGGETT GUIDROZ

Ralph Guidroz and Joy Baggett met while both were sophomores at Lafayette High School, Lafayette, Louisiana. Their senior year they started a "going steady" relationship that continued through their college years at Southwestern Louisiana Institute (now University of Louisiana at Lafayette). They married in 1954. (See "Joe Baggett and Robbie Adrian" for Joy's early history.)

Ralph descends from Acadians who came to Louisiana seeking religious freedom after expulsion from Nova Scotia, Canada, because they wouldn't convert to the Church of England. His mother, Eula Breaux (1904-1992), descended from Alexis Breaux, who arrived in Louisiana with his family in 1678 after spending some time exiled in Maryland. Charles Guidroz (1899-1976), Ralph's father, descended from the Acadian families of LeBlanc, Guerniere, Olivier, and from Abraham Guidroz, who emigrated from Berne Canton, Switzerland.

Charles and Eula had three children: Earl (1926), Theresa (1929) and Ralph (1933). After college and marriage, Ralph and Joy embarked on his Air Force career odyssey, beginning with short stays for training in San Antonio, Texas, and Tucson, Arizona. Ralph was assigned as a navigator at Ellington AFB, Houston, Texas, where Laura Ann was born (1956). Brenda Lynn entered the family (1957) in Biloxi, Mississippi, where Ralph was assigned to Keesler AFB. Later, in Topeka, Kansas, at Forbes AFB, Sara Ruth made her appearance (1959). Captain Guidroz left active duty service in August 1959.

After graduate school at the University of North Carolina at Chapel Hill where Ralph worked on a Master's degree in geophysics

At the wedding of Gwen Johnson and Paul Guidroz in 2002. Bottom left: Paul Guidroz and Kris Easter. Upper left: Ken and Brenda (Guidroz) Petro and daughter Robbie. Bride's right: Paul's daughters Mallory and Sydney Guidroz. Center, step below groom's left: Joy and Ralph Guidroz. Bottom right: Sara (Guidroz) and Francis Fontana and children Evelyn Joy, Michael, Peter and Amelia. Upper right: Laura (Guidroz) and Tom Leahy, daughter Erin in front of Tom, and Erin's husband Bryan Saylor.

Joy and Ralph Guidroz, center, with the Leahy family. Clockwise, beginning lower left: Jessica, Bill, T.D., Laura (Guidroz), Tom, and Sean Leahy, Bryan and Erin (Leahy) Saylor.

(awarded in 1964), the young family moved to Farmers Branch, Texas, where Ralph worked at Texas Instruments for the next seven years. Joy pursued training at Scottish Rite Hospital to teach children with dyslexia. She was a language therapist at the Greenhill School for five years.

In 1968, the family moved to Berkeley, California, answering the call to enter the work of evangelization in the Catholic Church. Ralph earned a master's in Applied Theology from the Graduate Theological Union. Their first son, Paul Robert, was born in Berkeley (1969).

August of 1969 found the family at St. Mary's Church, Govans, Baltimore, Maryland, where Ralph was Director of Religious Education and Evangelization. In 1970, John William completed the nuclear family.

The opportunity to return to Lafayette, Louisiana, came in 1974. Ralph worked for the Diocese of Lafayette for the next fourteen years, rising to the office of Vicar for Lay Development. In 1986, he became Executive Director of the Louisiana Catholic Conference (LCC), working as liaison between the seven bishops of Louisiana and the people of the Catholic Church. In 1988, Ralph was awarded the Pro Ecclesia et Pontifice medal by Pope John Paul II for outstanding service to the Catholic Church.

After the LCC pastoral office was closed by the new Archbishop in 1989, Ralph and Joy decided to return to Adrian Road in Gregg County to the property they'd inherited from Joe and Robbie Baggett. Joy obtained a position as Clinical Social Worker for Meadow Pines Hospital, where she worked until 1995. She then entered private practice, retiring in 2003. Ralph worked in evangelization at St. Joseph's (Marshall, Texas) and Christ the King (Kilgore). In 1996, he became Director of Evangelization at St. Mary's (Longview).

Adrian Road is still home base for visiting children and grandchildren. Ralph and Joy enjoy their visits. Life in Gregg County is good!

– Submitted by John Guidroz

RALPH ROBERT & JOY BAGGETT GUIDROZ: The Descendants

Laura Ann Guidroz, the first child and daughter of Ralph and Joy, was born 6 July 1956, in Houston, Texas. She was married in December of 1975, to Tom Leahy, born 14 August 1953. Their five children are Thomas Daniel, born 1 February 1978, at Camp Pendleton, California; Erin Nicole, born 27 March 1979, in Lafayette, Louisiana – she married Bryan Saylor on 17 April 1999; Sean Patrick, born 12 June 1980, in Glastonbury, Connecticut; Jessica Joy, born 13 August 1982, in Shreveport, Louisiana; and William Joseph, born 2 July 1984, in Texarkana, Texas.

Brenda Lynn Guidroz, second child and daughter of Ralph and Joy, was born 22 September 1957, in Biloxi, Mississippi. She was married in August of 1975, to Kenneth Petro, born 16 November 1956. Their two children, both born in Lafayette, Louisiana, are Jason Michael Charles, born 20 January 1976, and died in April of 2001, and Robbie Adrian, born 26 January 1989. The daughter of Jason and Laura Fink, born 29 April 1976, is Kealie Amera Petro, born 12 August 1998, in Lafayette.

Sara Ruth Guidroz, third child and daughter of Ralph and Joy, was born 16 May 1959, in Topeka, Kansas. She was married in August of 1981, to Francis Fontana, born 10 March 1956. Their four children, all born in Houston, Texas, are Peter Joseph, born 24 May 1986; Amelia, born 10 September 1988; Evelyn Joy, born 18 February 1992; and Michael Francis, born 27 May 1993.

Paul Robert Guidroz, fourth child and first son of Ralph and Joy, was born 14 January 1969, in Berkeley, California. He was married in March of 1989, to Holly Hill, born 8 January 1970; they divorced in 1996. Their two daughters are Mallory Michelle, born 13 September 1989, in West Monroe, Louisiana, and Sidney Elizabeth, born 29 January 1991, in Monterey, California. Paul was married in April of 2002, to Gwendolynn Denise Johnson, born 18 October 1968. Their son is Ethan Patrick, born 26 December 2003, in Plano, Texas.

John William Guidroz, fifth child and second son of Ralph and Joy, was born in October of 1970, in Baltimore, Maryland. He was married in May of 2002, to Kris Pitts Easter, born in June of 1967.

Ralph and Joy feel that God has truly blessed them with their children, grandchildren and great grandchild. They look forward to any future "blessings".

– Submitted by Laura Guidroz Leahy

GUTTRY

Carlos Byron (Carl) Guttry, was born 14 February 1895, in McNeil, Arkansas, to John Wilson Guttry (died 1919) and Murtilda Jane Sanders Guttry (1859-1938). He married Nancy McNeil and had three children, of which Carlos Byron (C.B.) Guttry, Jr. was the only survivor. Nancy died in 1923. Carl worked for Gulf Oil in Harmon, Louisiana, where he met Lala Sutherlin, born 18 July 1907, in Grand Cane, Louisiana, to Laura Agnes McDonald (1889-1982) and John Arthur Sutherlin

Ralph and Joy Guidroz, left of center, with descendants and other relatives at the wedding of son John and Kris Easter, center–back, in 2002.

Carlos Byron Guttry

(1886-1912). Her father, John Arthur, who died in a cotton gin accident, was the nephew of Judge E.W. Sutherlin and Dr. W.K. Sutherlin of Shreveport, Louisiana. Lala Sutherlin and Carlos Byron

Lala Sutherlin Guttry

Guttry married in 1926 when C.B., Jr., his son from his first marriage, was five years old. John Sutherlin (John S.) Guttry was born to them 25 May 1931.

In July 1931, Lala and Carl Guttry moved to Kilgore where Carl continued work for Gulf Oil and retired in 1960. They were active at St. Luke's Methodist Church in Kilgore where Lala taught Sunday School and John S.'s future wife, Lottie Lou Lipscomb (born 1934), was her student. Lala worked at Daiches Jewelry and as a dental assistant for Dr. Billy Bob Terrell in Kilgore and later in Long-view in the office of Drs. Wade Clendenen and W.D. Northcutt, III. She retired in 1984 at age 77, but continued making sour dough bread for her church and for neighbors and friends.

Growing up in Kilgore, John S. and Lottie became acquainted at an early age and began dating when he was nineteen and she sixteen. John S. attended North Texas State (now the University of North Texas) and the University of Texas Dental School in Houston, graduating in 1956 and joining the Air Force soon after. He was stationed in Narsarsuwak, Greenland, for a year; then he and Lottie married 28 September

The Guttry family, July 2003

1957. After spending nine months at Carswell AFB in Ft. Worth, John and Lottie settled in Longview, where he established his dental practice in August 1958.

Lottie attended Sweet Briar College in Virginia and graduated from U.T.–Austin with a bachelor of music degree in 1956. She later received a Master of Arts in English from Stephen F. Austin University, and a Doctorate from East Texas State (now Texas A&M University–Commerce). She taught at Kilgore College and at U.T.–Tyler and later owned the Sylvan Learning Center.

John S. and Lottie have three children: Melinda, John Dabney and Robert Byron. Melinda married Patrick Barge, an airline pilot. They have three children, Stephen Alexander, Caitlin Rebecca and Shaughn Patrick, and live at Lake Cherokee. John Dabney married Sherie Rivenbark in Orlando, Florida, and they live in Howie in the Hills where he works for Marriott in Orlando. They have three children: John Dabney, Jr., Rebecca Elizabeth and Rachel Lyn. Robert married Shannon Maledon. He practices dentistry in Longview and they have two children: Robert King and Mary Shannon Guttry.

– Submitted by Robert B. Guttry

HAFNER

Clynton Leroy Hafner was born in Neches, Texas, in January 1912. Clynton (Clint, as he was to be called later) married his sweetheart, Neva Inez Todd (born in Neches in August 1915), in 1934. Their first son, Clynton Leroy Hafner, Jr. (Leroy), was born in Jacksonville, Texas, in 1936. Their second son, William Kirk Hafner (Kirk), was born in Longview in 1948.

Clint and family transferred to Longview in 1939 with the Double Dip Ice Cream Company. Shortly after moving to Longview, Clint took employment with the Southwestern Electric Power Co. After a few years with the power company, Clint began working as a salesman for the Firestone Company store. Clint worked his way up to manager and lived and worked in Marshall, Texas, during 1940 and returned to Longview as manager in 1941.

In 1946, Clint and his Firestone District Manager, Charles Fuller, formed Fuller-Hafner Tire Service. Their first location was a Gulf Service Station at the corner of Sixth and Methvin Streets. The partnership later moved to the corner of Green and Tyler. In 1951, Hafner and Fuller dissolved their partnership and Clint opened Hafner Tire Service at the corner of Tyler and Highway 80 (West Marshall). The Tyler/80 location was the original location of the Firestone Store that Clint had managed, so in a sense he returned home. Clint operated as a Goodyear dealer at this location until his death in 1958. Neva helped with the bookkeeping at Hafner Tire Service, but otherwise was a stay-at-home mom. Neva died in 1953. Clint and Neva are buried at Memory Park in Longview.

Leroy attended Mrs. Denton's Private School for first and second grade, then Campus Ward Elementary, Longview Jr. High and graduated Longview High School in 1954. After attending Kilgore Jr. College for one year, Leroy graduated from Louisiana Tech in 1959 with a B.S. in Mechanical Engineering and later obtained a Master of Engineering degree from Texas A&M. Leroy worked at General Dynamics at Daingerfield, and then enjoyed a 33-year career at Texas Eastman Co. After retirement from Eastman in 1993, Leroy worked 5 years for Huntsman Chemical Co. at the Eastman plant

Leroy met Patricia Eugenia Doane at Louisiana Tech. They were married in 1959. Patricia and Leroy are active members of First Baptist Church, Longview. Patricia and Leroy have two children, Michael William, born in 1960, and Kathryn Malise Hafner Costlow, born in 1964; both were born in Longview. Michael was married in 1983 and has two daughters, Brittany and Cortney. Kathryn married in 1985 and has two daughters, Morgan and Madison. Michael and Kathryn both reside in Katy, Texas.

Kirk lived with his Aunt Verna Dyal in Bernice, Louisiana, until age 14, then came to Longview to live with Patricia and Leroy until he joined the Marines at the age 17. He served in Vietnam before being discharged and returning to the Longview area with his wife Donna. They have two children, Michael and Brenda.

– Submitted by Leroy Hafner

JAMES WALTER HAGLER

James Walter Hagler, son of Robert Velver and Nellie Mae Prickett Hagler, was born 8 February 1917, at Golden in Wood County, Texas, and died 14 January 2000, in Longview, Gregg County, Texas. He married Lucille Elizabeth Moore on 4 April 1941, in English, Red River County, Texas. Elizabeth, born 15 May 1918, in Avery, Red River County, Texas, was the daughter of James Moore and Nina Bryant Moore.

J.W. grew up in Golden, Texas, with cousins as his neighbors and classmates. He graduated from Golden High School as Salutatorian when there were 11 grades, and the next year, when they added the 12th grade, he graduated as Valedictorian.

J.W. Hagler received his college education from East Texas State University in Commerce, Texas. His undergraduate degree was in education with a double major in math and history. His master's was in education with administrative certification.

Commerce was where J.W. met Elizabeth Moore, whom he later married. After marrying, they then began teaching in small schools until J.W. accepted a teaching position at White Oak, Texas. After teaching there for a few years, J.W. moved to Danville where he was superintendent for one year prior to running for County Superintendent. He served 12 years as County Superintendent and then resigned to become Director of Special Services for the Longview Independent School District. J.W. was a big Lobo fan and attended all the football games, even after

J.W. Hagler

he retired, until he was too ill to go. Then he listened to the games on the radio at home.

J.W. began preaching in 1938 in Golden. For the next 52 years he continued to preach in numerous Churches of Christ in the East Texas area on a short-time basis. As a minister, he performed many marriages and funerals, as well as visiting the sick daily until his own illness forced him to retire. The last wedding he performed was for his granddaughter, Angela Gaye Wood, to Paul Noel McFarland on 8 December 1993.

In addition to his work in the church and public schools, J.W. was active in several service organizations. For over 50 years, he was a member of the Longview Lions Club, serving both as a president of the club and a district governor of Lion's International. J.W. received the Melvin Jones Award for outstanding service and also, just before his death, he received a 50-year plaque.

In November of 1999, J.W. received a 50-year award for being a member of the Grand Royal Arch Chapter of Texas, Kilgore Chapter No. 449, R.A.M. He was also active in the Boy Scouts of America, where he earned the Silver Beaver Award. And, he served on the board of directors for the East Texas Professional Credit Union for 25 years.

J.W. and Elizabeth had two daughters, Glenda Gaye Hagler Wood and Elizabeth Ann (Betty) Hagler Sistrunk. They had three grandchildren: Glenda had one child, Angela Gaye Wood McFarland; and Betty had two children, Traye Bradley Conway and Shelley Ann Conway Wagner. His children and grandchildren were all born in Gregg County, Texas.

– Submitted by Glenda Hagler Wood

HOWELL POPE & MARY EMMA HOLT HALE

Howell Pope Hale was a son of Texas pioneers Joel Blanton Hale and Mollie McHaney Hale. The family raised cotton on land in northern Rusk County at the Crossroads Community.

H.P. Hale married Mary Emma Holt, a daughter of Romaldus Edwin Holt of New London. She attended the Alexander Institute in Kilgore.

The Hales lived in northern Rusk County in the early days of their marriage and he worked briefly in Longview. Later, he bought a large tract of land in Gregg County on the north side of Kilgore, spanning an area from the present site of East Texas Council of Governments to Kilgore High School on Longview Street. In addition, he owned land in Gregg County lying parallel to the present Longview highway and in Smith County. He farmed cotton on all of his land until the discovery of oil in Kilgore. He later established Southern Hardware and Seed Co.

The Hales had three sons: Max Edwin Hale, Louis France Hale and Howell Holt Hale.

Max Hale worked in the Kilgore Post Office before he and his wife, Ruth, moved to Dallas in order to give their handicapped son better education and treatment for cerebral palsy. (Larry now resides at Marbridge Ranch near Austin where Max and Ruth now live.) Their daughter, Judy Lynn, and husband Ronald Anderson live in Kerrville. Their daughter, Julie, lives in Ohio with husband Bob Anderson and their son. The Hales also have a son, Eddie.

The Hales' second son, Louis France Hale, attended Kilgore College, East Texas Baptist College and North Texas State College where he earned a degree in Economics. He married Ethel "Jeanne" Denman of Henderson, and established their home in the Gregg County portion of Kilgore.

Howell Holt Hale, their third son, operated trucks for his own business and for Kilgore Ceramics. Holt married three times and had an adopted son, Mike Jones.

– Submittted by W.D. (Bill) Hale

LOUIS FRANCE & JEANNE DENMAN HALE

At the time of his death in May 2001, Louis France Hale was a prominent rancher, particularly interested in youth agriculture programs. He served as a trustee, board member, committee chairman, choir member and teacher of an adult Sunday School class at First Christian Church.

Jeanne, active at First Christian for many years, is still teaching the Young Adults Sunday School class she began almost 50 years ago (now called Young Adults Forever). She has been active in PTA at every grade level, city council, Kilgore Woman's Club and Christian Women's Fellowship. She was "Mrs. Texas 1957," "First Lady of Kilgore 2000," Outstanding Graduate of Henderson High School 2003, and received the first "Unsung Hero" medal of her church. She is a member of Mensa and Intertel high IQ societies.

The Hales' sons all live on land that has been in their family since 1856. The historic Hale-McHaney Ranch holds a state designation as a Family Land Heritage ranch.

The eldest, Louis F. Hale Jr., graduated from North Texas State University and teaches Language Arts at a middle school in Longview. A professional musician, he has written, recorded and performed Blue Grass music in Denton, Fort Worth, Dallas and East Texas. His wife, Nancy, operates the Senior Nutrition Center in Kilgore. Their son Louis III is a Kilgore College student and daughter Sarah, a Kilgore High School student, was an intern in the Shakespeare Festival Company in Kilgore in 2003.

The Hales' second son, William Denman "Bill" Hale, is a graduate of Texas A&M University. He is an elder of First Christian Church, has chaired committees and taught classes. He is County Commissioner of Precinct 1, Rusk County. He owns Box-H Cattle Co. in northern Rusk County. His daughter Amy and husband Jeff Lettice live in Seattle and expect their first child in December 2003. His son, Will (W.D., Jr.) attends Stephen F. Austin University.

Their third son, Howell Pope Hale II, retired from Getty Oil Co. He is an elder of First Christian Church. A talented artist, he specializes in pencil sketches of rural scenes. He built his own log home and his wife Anne, a CPA and real estate salesperson, helped him finish it. Their son, H.P. III, works as a Corrosion Technologist in Houston. Their younger son, Joel, is an honor roll student at Kilgore High School and plays competition tennis.

The Hales' daughter, Martha, and husband Duane Deen live in the Monroe Community. Duane is principal of Kilgore Heights Elementary School in Kilgore. Martha teaches Language Arts in middle school in Kilgore, and is active in church and civic affairs and with the Rangerettes Forever of Kilgore College – she served as president in 2003. Their son Justin graduates from Texas A&M in December 2003, and plans to stay for a Master's degree. Jared is an art student at Kilgore College and a member of Phi Theta Kappa honor society. Jesse is a student at Kilgore High School and plays competition tennis.

– Submitted by Jeanne Hale

HALL/MARTIN
November 27, 1863 – April 21, 1941
July 23, 1902 – September 12, 1998

Robert McAlpine Hall was born on 27 November 1863, in Talladega, Alabama, to Rev. William Hall and Sarah McAlpine Hall. Robert's education included Hampden-Sydney College in Virginia and the University of Texas. He graduated from Union Theological Seminary, Richmond, Virginia, in 1888.

In 1889, he married Hester Elizabeth Daniel (18 January 1868–11 January 1932) of Vicksburg and Victoria, Texas. Born to this union were Bessie McAlpine (6 January 1890– 26 March 1901), Alice Johnson (13 June 1897– 29 March 1901), Nellie Stevenson (24 June 1900–1982), and Ruth Evelyn (9 October 1906– 7 December 1994).

Robert held the degree of Doctor of Divinity, serving many Presbyterian churches. Pastorates were in Westminster Church, San Antonio, Ballinger, and First Church in Galveston, Goliad, Helena, Edna, Beeville in Texas, and Ashland and Blacksburg in Virginia. He

Rev. Dr. Robert M. Hall, 1921

Elizabeth Hall, 1891

was a Superintendent and an Evangelist in Texas. He served First Presbyterian Church in Longview from 1921 to 1929.

Dr. Hall's ministry was marked by two things: first, his unwavering determination to see things done decently and in order; and, second was his devotion to young people, seeing many of his hopes realized in the work being done at the Westminster Presbyterian Encampment, Kerrville, Texas, of which he was one of the founders.

Dr. Hall was the 5th president of the Longview Rotary Club and the only clergyman to that date.

Elizabeth rendered much service in the church, working with small children. She was a wonderful companion and mother. Her fields of talent were in art and music.

Ruth Evelyn married Malcolm Montreville Martin of Lanexa, Virginia, on 22 April 1925, and lived in Lanexa, New Kent County, Virginia. Born to this union were Elizabeth Lee, Mary Evelyn and Patricia Anne. In March 1935, they moved to Longview, Texas, in Gregg County.

Malcolm was affiliated with Coca Cola Bottling Company, of which his brother Benjamin Franklin was part owner. He also owned a Gulf Service Station on Highway 80. He served as Deacon and Elder and was an active member of the Men's Bible Class at First Presbyterian Church. He was a man of many talents and had a wonderful sense of humor. He was loving and giving to his wife, family and the community. He lived to see his home in the

Malcolm and Ruth Hall Martin, 1925

Nugget Hill addition listed in the National Registry of Historic Places of the United States Department of the Interior.

Ruth, Malcolm's devoted wife, was an outstanding Christian example of Christ's teachings with her family and community. She was noted for having her three little girls in Sunday School every Sunday and on time. Her talents were many: music, oil and china painting, handwork, Sunday School teacher, Circle chairman and volunteer.

Elizabeth "Betty" Lee married John Ronell Dunaway on 2 April 1945, and their children are Robert Lee, Carol Anne, James Roland and John Malcolm. Betty married Theodore Boone in 1962 and raised his two sons, the late Theodore Boone, Jr. and Michael Brett Boone. Betty has been an Independent Senior Sales Director with Mary Kay Cosmetics since 1980 and presently lives at the family home place in historic Nugget Hill where the families gather and remember the good old days. Betty is an active member of St. Michael and All Angels' Episcopal Church in Longview.

Elizabeth, Mary Evelyn and Patricia Martin, 1935.

Mary Evelyn married Zack Fall Mitchell of Walnut Grove, formerly Walnut Grove Plantation, of Elderville, Texas. Their sons are Ronald Hall and David Gardiner. Mary and Zack enjoy living at Walnut Grove Farm where three generations of Mitchell's were born. They are active members of First Presbyterian Church, Longview.

Patricia Anne "Pat" married Hugh Donald Taylor of Gladewater, Texas, and their children are Martin Duke, Samuel Alan and Mary Lee. Pat is an Independent Senior Sales Director with Mary Kay Cosmetics. Pat and Hugh are active members of First Presbyterian in Longview where Pat is a Stephen Minister.

Betty, Pat and Mary were baptized by Dr. Hall, their grandfather. All three were married in the First Presbyterian Church in Longview where "Grandpa" was pastor for eight years.
— Submitted by Mary Martin Mitchell

BOB & MARSHA HANKINS

Bobby Dale Hankins was born 22 November 1938, in Gladewater, Texas, the son of Jack and Flossie Hankins. Bob attended Kilgore Public Elementary Schools and graduated from

Seated: Marsha, Heather Michelle and Bob Hankins. Standing: Robert Wesley and Ryan.

Bellaire High School in Houston. He also graduated from the University of Houston.

Bob was the second great grandson of William Newton Christian, Confederate soldier from Arkansas, and the seventh great grandson of the Huguenot Mathieu Agee, who came to this country in 1700-1701 from France.

Bob married Marsha Funderburk in Odessa, Texas. Marsha was born 14 August 1950. They are the parents of three children: Ryan, Heather Michelle and Robert Wesley.

Bob served as area coordinator for Stran Steel until 1971 when he became President and owner of Tommy Service General Contractors. He served in that capacity until his death on 10 August 1998. He is buried in Sunset Memorial Gardens in Odessa, Texas.

Bob and family were members of the Sherwood Church of Christ in Odessa.
— Submitted by Marsha Hankins

JACK & FLOSSIE HANKINS

Jack Merrill Hankins was born in Okmulgee, Oklahoma, on 30 August 1913, the son of James Alexander and Weltha Jane Ledford Hankins. Jack's father, James Alexander, was born 20 December 1877, and died in 1933. His mother, Jane, was born 15 April 1884, in Cherokee, North Carolina. He was the grandson of Samuel Jackson Ledford and Nancy Tioletto Maney Ledford, a Cherokee Indian from North Carolina.

Jack married Flossie Elizabeth Agee on 1 December 1937. Flossie, the daughter of William Wisemon and Anna Lawson Agee, was born on 31 December 1918, in Hasty, Arkansas. She

Flossie and Jack Hankins

is the great granddaughter of William Newton Christian, Confederate soldier from Arkansas, and the sixth great granddaughter of the Huguenot Mathieu Agee of Manakintown, Virginia. Flossie is a member of the Huguenot Society of Texas. She graduated from Boynton High School in Oklahoma and attended Kilgore College.

Jack came to Gladewater in 1935 at the height of the oil boom in East Texas. After their marriage, the Hankinses made their home in Gladewater. Jack worked for Sells Petroleum Company until 1946 when he went to work for the Dia-Log Company. He worked as Sales Co-ordinator for Dia-Log until 1977 when he retired. Flossie worked in the medical field in Kilgore and in Houston until she retired.

They are the parents of one son, Bobby Dale Hankins. Bob was born 22 November 1938, in Gladewater and died 10 August 1998, in Odessa, Texas.

Jack and Flossie are the grandparents of three grandchildren: Ryan, Wesley and Heather Hankins.

The Hankins are members of the First Christian Church in Kilgore.

– Submitted by Mrs. Jack Hankins

JOANNE RAMBO HANKINS

Joanne Rambo Hankins was born in Iowa Park, Texas; her family moved to East Texas in 1932, and lived at Hill Top on Highway 80 in a tourist court. Later, they moved to Lafamo where they lived in a real house. One thing about the house – they tore off the back porch in order to drill a well right out the back door. Joanne was one of the two five-year-olds who started school at Greggton Elementary School in 1934. Here is where she met Jenny Scherer. The lives of these two girls would always be intertwined. Second grade was at Bumpus on Highway 42. Then to the "Big Woods" and the third grade at Judson. There was Jenny again. Fourth grade was Kilgore-Shell Camp School, fifth grade thru ninth grades were spent back at Judson. Here she and Jenny got to skip the 8th grade because they changed from 11 grades to 12 grades in Texas. Tenth thru 12th grades were in Kilgore, where she graduated in 1945. Next was Kilgore College, and becoming a Rangerette.

During World War II many girls wrote to servicemen they knew. Sister Billierae sent a photo of Joanne to a friend on the USS *Pensacola*, who showed it to his friend Johnny Hankins. Johnny thought Joanne was pretty cute, and asked if he could write to her. The correspondence romance began in 1944. Out of the Navy, Johnny went back to work for Bryon Jackson Tools and came to see Joanne in June 1946, for the first time.

In December 1946, school was turned out for one week so that everyone who wanted to could go to the First Junior College Rose Bowl in Pasadena, CA. The College "rented" a train, and the band, Rangerettes and others journeyed west. They traveled on Pullman coaches to Los Angeles. Joanne graduated from KC in June of 1947; she and Johnny were married on October 4th. They spent their honeymoon moving her to

Joanne Rambo Hankins,
Rangerette, 1945-47

California. While there, their first child, Shirley, was born. Johnny was then transferred to Odessa, Texas. As many have found in the oil business, you were moved around a lot. From Odessa, to Wichita Falls, where Starley was born, and then Tulsa, Oklahoma. Still working for Bryan Jackson Tools, the next stop was Maricaibo, Venezuela. Joanne and Jenny had plans to get together in Venezuela. But fate can ruin the best plans made. Johnny was killed in an auto accident in Barquisemeto, Venezuela, 29 May 1958.

Joanne and girls came home to Kilgore and family. She moved to a house beside her parents, and has lived in the same house since 1958. She raised her girls and sent them to school and college. Her daughter, Shirley, is a teacher in Austin. Unfortunately, cancer took Starley away in 2002. Joanne still lives on the ranch and works with the Rangerettes Forever. Joanne, Billierae and Jenny have dinner every Thursday night at the Butcher Shop in Longview. Real friendships do last.

– Submitted by Joanne Rambo Hankins

HARDY

Mr. and Mrs. Henry Leroy Hardy came to Gregg County in 1931 or 1932 with two daughters, Betty Louise and Virginia Lee. Mr. Hardy was born in Wesson, Mississippi, the youngest of seven children. He was born on 21 December 1897, and died on 16 January 1964. He served overseas in World War I (even thought he had to add a few years to his age since we have been told he was only 15).

Emma Evadna Sellers was born 18 February 1900, and died 2 November 1980. Her father was Marvin Bell Sellers, whose family was from Tennessee, and he married Cora Belle Fisher from Friendship, Arkansas, on 29 August 1897. They were the parents of five children; their oldest child, Isaac, died after being bitten by a rattlesnake when the family was living in a sod house on the prairie. Apparently, their fortunes improved when Mr. Sellers got into law enforcement. He was appointed Deputy with Indian Affairs. After that, he served as Sheriff in Cordell, Oklahoma, Deputy for the City of Sapulpa and Security Guard for the Railroad. He also worked for the McAlester Prison at one time, and was appointed Postmaster in 1906.

Henry Leroy Hardy met Emma Evadna Sellers in Oklahoma and they were married on 18 October 1922. Betty Louise was born 23 August 1925. Virginia Lee was born 17 September 1929. Both were born in the Marvin Sellers' family home in Sapulpa.

Some interesting information was revealed from old documents found recently about Mrs. Hardy being descended from the William Bland (also spelled Blann) family, who according to the Americana, are of English descent. Richard Bland was a delegate representing the State of Virginia in the First Continental Congress at Carpenter's Hall in Philadelphia. The Bland Home in Williamsburg, Virginia, was to be restored by the Rockefeller Foundation at the time the account was written in 1956. (Information may be found in *Lassings Field Book*, pages 280-287; *Bancroft's History, Vol. VI*, page 281; and *Spencer's History U.S., Vol. I*, Page 281.)

Unfortunately, we have very little information in our possession of the Hardy family. Henry's father was a photographer and died when Henry was a young boy. Mr. and Mrs. Hardy were involved in various businesses and work such as the oil fields in Borger, Wink, Snyder and Dallas, Texas, before coming to the Longview, Gladewater, Greggton and White Oak areas. Most people were struggling to feed their families during the Depression years. He operated an ice house (as shown in photo – note the sign on the ice house "Home Brew 5 cents"), a filling station next to Shirley's Grocery, and probably was most successful when he ran a recreation hall (pool and dominoes) on what was called "Old Sun Camp Hill," across Old Highway from Buckle's Drug Store; others were Clapps Grocery and Coy Hooks Barber Shop.

It was told that Betty Louise was the first baby to be brought to Borger, Texas, when tents were the homes of choice, though the sand wasn't their choice. Betty and Virginia went to White Oak School until 1941, just before Pearl Harbor, and then moved to Jefferson. Betty married William Calvin (Bill) Cornelius on 18 September 1943. He served in World War II, landing on Omaha Beach in the D-Day Invasion. When he

H.L. Hardy, wife Evadna and daughters Betty and Ginger, Highway 80, 1932.

was reported missing in action, Betty joined the WACS. He was reported to be a POW of the Germans on 13 June 1944, and was held for a period of about ten months. He came home safely. Betty died on 10 September 1982, and Bill died 25 August 2001. Betty and Bill have one daughter, Gina Perry. She and her husband, Chris, reside in Jefferson. Gina has one daughter, Melissa Skelton. Virginia married Bob Allen on 19 February 1949. Bob Allen served in the Korean War and also returned home safely. They have one daughter, Betty Nell, a Special Education Teacher, and two grandsons, Matthew and Mark Montgomery. They live in Cushing, Texas, and Matthew is beginning Kilgore Junior College.

– Submitted by Virginia Allen

CHARLES NEWTON "NEWT" HARRIS

Charles Newton "Newt" Harris was born 29 August 1858, in Cherokee County, Alabama. His family actually lived on the border of Cherokee County, Alabama, and Chattooga County, Georgia. He was a descendant of the Rev. John Harris (born in 1725), a Presbyterian minister of South Carolina. Newt was also a direct descendant of General Andrew Pickens and his wife Rebecca Calhoun Pickens of South Carolina, their daughter Mary Pickens having married the son of Rev. John Harris. The parents of Newt Harris were John Ewing Harris and Sabrina Morgan Harris. John Ewing Harris moved into Georgia as a young man.

Sarah Catherine Harris, a daughter of John Ewing and Sabrina Morgan Harris, married a man named Charles N. Henderson. The Harris and Henderson families were involved in the founding of the Alpine Presbyterian Church in Menlo, Georgia. Soon after the Civil War, Sarah and her husband moved to the East Texas area. They were among the founders of the Alpine Presbyterian Church in Longview. Sabrina Harris, now a widow, moved to East Texas with her son Newt in 1871. They were traveling with another married daughter and her husband, Mary Ann Harris and W.L. Sprayberry. During this trip, Mary Ann was drowned as they crossed a turbulent Mississippi River. Compounding this tragedy was the fact that Mary Ann had pinned to her petticoat the money for both families; so, Newt and his mother reached East Texas with very little financial backing to start a new life.

Charles Newton Harris and two of his McGrede grandchildren, about 1930.

Newt Harris began working at being a farmer, but from his mother's family he had learned about land speculation — that is, buying land and reselling it at a profit. As soon as he had enough money for a stake, this is what he began doing and did very well for himself and his family. On 19 October 1879, he married Martha Killingsworth, the daughter of James and Martha Oden Killingsworth. They lived first in Harrison County and moved into Gregg County early in the 1800s. Their children were John A. Harris (died in infancy); Emma Virginia Harris, who married Russ Pliler; Stella Harris, who married John Taylor; Jo Ann "Jodie" Harris, who married Thomas Davis; Charles "Charlie" Newton Harris II, who married Sadie Jane Brewer; Essie Francis Harris, who married George Ward; James Leslie Harris, who married Lula Essie Beard; and Novie Belle Harris, who married Henry McGrede. Charles Newton and Martha also unofficially adopted their niece Frances "Frankie" Killingsworth, who married Louis Bryan.

Martha Killingsworth Harris died 19 November 1908, and Charles Newton Harris died 19 April 1934. They are buried in the Old Summerfield Cemetery.

– Submitted by Kathryn Harris Hines (great granddaughter of "Newt" and Martha Killingsworth Harris)

JOHN WOMACK HARRISON

John W. Harrison was born in Marshall on 30 December 1892, to Chase Love Womack Harrison and Yancy Davis Harrison. He married Winnie D. Hamilton, who was born 3 February 1896, in Cherokee, Alabama. John and Winnie were married 24 September 1924, in Dallas by Dr. George W. Truett. After teaching school several years in Graham, Texas, the couple moved to Marshall with baby daughter Katherine.

In the summer of 1929, at the death of Mr. Harrison's uncle Frank Rembert, John W. and Winnie D., the young Harrisons, moved to 316 South Fredonia Street, Longview, to help Mr. Harrison's aunt Kate Womack Rembert, with her businesses and home. Soon, another daughter, Marjorie, was born. A year later, Ann Louise was born. Six years later in 1934, the Harrisons joyfully welcomed John W. Harrison, Jr.

The Harrisons became prominent and popular citizens of Longview. John W. Harrison was the science teacher in Longview High School from 1927–1939. After retiring from teaching school, he was elected to the school board. He belonged to the Rotary Club and Masonic Lodge. He was a director of First Federal Savings and Loan and headed the civil defense during World War II. After the war Mr. Harrison taught geology at Kilgore Junior College.

The Harrison home became a popular place for the young crowds to gather, roll the rugs up and dance. There were always wonderful refreshments on the dining room table with decorations appropriate to the holidays.

John W. Harrison and Winnie D. Hamilton Harrison, early 1920s

Mrs. Harrison saw to it that the children went to Sunday school and church at the First Baptist Church one block away. Mr. Harrison attended and supported the First Methodist Church. Mrs. Harrison planted azaleas all around the house the year before Mr. Harrison died. They were to be a surprise for him in the spring but he died March 7. The remaining azaleas still bloom every spring.

After Mr. Harrison's untimely death in 1955, Mrs. Harrison continued to live in the house until her death in 1989.

Katherine married Charles Campbell from College Station and now lives in Fort Worth. Their first daughter, Ann, was born in Longview; Margaret was born in Sherman, and son Brice was born in Midland.

Marjorie married Jim Bivins and has lived in Longview all her life except for her years at S.M.U. They have two children, Craig Harrison Bivins and Louise Durham Bivins.

Louise married David Murphy from El Dorado. They have two children, Katherine and Warren. Both Louise and David are deceased.

John, Jr. married Jean Ramey, and they own Ramey-Harrison Appliances. Like his father, John, Jr. has been a devoted member of the school board and Rotary Club. They stayed busy rearing four children, David, Carol, Kelly and Martha.

After being in the family since the 1870s, the house at 316 Fredonia is owned by John W. Harrison, Jr.

– Submitted by Catherine Harrison Campbell

LORY CHRISTOPHER (L.C.) HARROFF

Lory Christopher (L.C.) Harroff was born in Mena, Polk County, Arkansas, on 18 December 1913. He was the youngest of five children born to George Henry Harroff and Mary Ada Neeley Harroff. L.C. married Pauline Mae Reed on 10 March 1937, in Sevier County, Arkansas. He and his family moved to Gregg County in May of 1955. L.C. had followed his older brother, George Pierce, to Gregg County. L.C. found employment at the East Texas Steel Casting plant as a maintenance man. Pauline was born in Haskell County, Oklahoma, on 19 September 1920. She found work at the local hat factory as a molder.

L.C. and Pauline had seven children: Meayrene (born 26 January 1943), Iva Jean (born 14 July 1944), Barbara Ann (born 31 July 1946), Caroline Sue (born 19 August 1947), Scott Donald (born 20 June 1962), Samuel Kevin (born 18 October 1964) and Paula Elaine (born 15 September 1966). The last two children were born at Good Shepherd Hospital. The first four were raised in the Judson area of Longview. The last three children were raised in Gladewater where the family moved in 1968.

Lory Christopher Harroff, Paula, Scott, wife Pauline and Kevin Harroff, Gladewater, 1973.

L.C. died on 11 August 1974, in Gregg County at the Gladewater Hospital. Pauline died 16 September 1989, in Gregg County at Good Shepherd Hospital. They are both buried at the Owens Chapel Cemetery in Mena, Polk County, Arkansas.

– Submitted by Paula Carter

PAULA ELAINE HARROFF-CARTER

Paula Elaine (Harroff) Carter was born 15 September 1966, at Good Shepherd Medical Center in Longview, Gregg County, Texas. She is the seventh of seven children by Lory Christopher (L.C.) and Pauline Mae (Reed) Harroff. Paula and her family lived in the Judson area of Longview until the family moved to Gladewater in 1968.

Graduating with honors in 1985 from Gladewater High School, Paula was active in athletics as well as *The Bear Facts* school newspaper. She continued her education at Kilgore Junior College. In 1988, she received an Asso-

ciate of Arts Degree. After working for a few years, she returned to Kilgore Junior College and completed the Surgical Technology Program in 1993. Paula is currently a senior at the University of Texas at Tyler.

Her work history has taken her from the Winn-Dixie Grocery store in Gladewater, where she worked for ten years, to her current employment at Good Shepherd Medical Center in Longview. Starting out as a Certified Surgical Technologist, she worked in the scrub position for nine years and then was able to advance to the O.R. Materials Coordinator position, which she has held for the last two years. She has been employed by GSMC since January 1993.

Randy Eugene Carter and Paula married on 8 July 1990. Randy is the fourth of four children born to Howard Glenn and Gladys Marie (Dabney) Carter. He was born on 19 November 1965. They were wed at the home of James and Barbara (Harroff) Fears, in Longview, Texas. Barbara is one of Paula's four older sisters. Her brother, Scott Donald Harroff, gave her away at the wedding.

Anna Marie Carter was born on 1 September 1998, at Good Shepherd Medical Center in Longview, Texas. Anna has been a true blessing to the Carter and Harroff families. Anna is currently attending class in the Gladewater Independent School District.

Anna and her parents, Randy and Paula, reside in the home that was bequeathed to Paula when her mother, Pauline Harroff, died in 1989. This is the home that Paula grew up in.

– Submitted by Paula Elaine Carter

SAMUEL KEVIN HARROFF

Samuel Kevin Harroff was born on 18 October 1963, at Good Shepherd Medical Center in Longview, Gregg County, Texas. Kevin is the sixth of seven children of Lory Christopher (L.C.) and Pauline Mae (Reed) Harroff. The family lived in the Judson area of Longview before moving to Gladewater in 1968.

Kevin graduated form Gladewater High School in 1982. He was active with *The Bear Facts* school newspaper and voted All-District in Varsity Football. He continued his education by attending Kilgore Junior College in Kilgore, Texas.

He began working in the oil fields of East Texas while still in high school. His brother-in-law, Stephen Knighton, got Kevin his first job. Steve is married to Caroline Sue (Harroff), one of Kevin's four sisters. Still working in the oil fields, Kevin is currently a driller with a local company.

Lynette Faye (Phelps) and Kevin were married in 25 May 1985. Lynette was born on 23 February 1967, at Olaehe, Johnson County, Kansas. They had a son, William Christopher, who was born on 8 September 1986. Due to some complications, Christopher died the next day. He is buried at Memorial Park in Longview. On 3 May 1992,

Back: Kevin and Lynette Harroff. Front: Samantha and Kristen, 1997.

they were blessed with another child, Samantha Kay. Soon to follow was her sister, Kristen Michelle, on 15 November 1993. Samantha and Kristen currently attend school in the Gilmer Independent School District.

Kevin has always been a big fan of the Dallas Cowboys football team.

– Submitted by Kevin Harroff

SCOTT DONALD HARROFF

Scott Donald Harroff was born on 20 June 1962, in Santa Paula, Ventura County, California. His parents, Lory Christopher (L.C.) and Pauline Mae (Reed) Harroff, had him back in their home in Judson, Gregg County, Texas soon after. Scott is the fifth of seven children. The Harroff family moved to Gladewater in 1968.

Scott Harroff

After attending school in the Gladewater Independent School District, Scott graduated in 1980. He then continued his education at the DeVry Institute of Technology in Dallas. He graduated from DeVry in February 1982.

He worked in Longview with Rockwell International as a telecom engineer. He then starting working with MCI and was with that company for 12 years. Since 1997, he has been employed with Time Warner.

Scott's hobbies are sport fishing and motorcycles. He owns two bikes, one of which is a Harley-Davidson.

– Submitted by Scott Harroff

Paula Elaine Harroff Carter with daughter Anna Marie, 2001.

HAYNES-LINDER

James Martin Haynes was a pioneer farmer in East Texas. Mr. Haynes came to Texas in 1882 with his wife, Mary Ellen, and son, Marcus. He took an important role in the agricultural and industrial activities of Gregg County. He raised mule teams for the railroad on his farm in western Gregg County from 1911 until 1935. He saw great changes after the discovery of the Great Texas Oil Field. James M. Haynes accounted well for himself in the world, frequently lending a helping hand to his neighbors, especially during early pioneer times. He encouraged the adoption of practical farming methods, giving his support to the betterment of his beloved Gregg County.

John, Blane and Carolyn Linder with Brittany and Paige Linder.

Son, Marcus P. Haynes, has also been identified with farming activities and development of Gregg County. Mr. Haynes took over the Haynes Farm two miles east of Gladewater in Clarksville City in early 1930. Because his farm was in the fairway of the East Texas Oil Field, he had mineral interests that are still producing today. He married Mary Lester and they had two daughters, Willie and Helen.

Helen Haynes and husband, Roy L. Pierce, had two children, Don and Carolyn. Don passed away at age 14 of cancer. Helen lived on and operated the Haynes Farm after her father, Marcus, retired in the early 1960s. Helen was a lover of music, played the piano and wrote poetry. She passed away in 1973.

Carolyn Pierce married John G. Linder (died 1997). He worked for Sun Oil Company until his retirement. They have one son, John G. Linder, Jr. Carolyn took over the running of the Haynes farm in 1973, and lives a few hundred feet from where she was born. She has been very active in Gregg County. She served on the Gladewater School Board; served as president of the Gladewater Chamber of Commerce; served on the Haynes-Linder Farm, Gregg County, Texas, Camp Fire Girls Board; and testified before the U.S. Congress on behalf of the oil industry and royalty owners of Texas. She was nominated to the Texas Women's Hall of Fame. At the current time, she is serving as Alderman on the Clarksville City Council.

John, Jr. married Jennifer Blane Thomas in 1987. They have two daughters, Brittany and Paige. John has taken over the operation of the Haynes Farm. He is in the oil production business and still raises cattle on the Gregg County farm. Brittany and Paige Linder will the sixth generation to be associated with the history of Gregg County. The Haynes Farm, begun in 1911, has been a working farm with either agricultural products or cattle for all that time. Oil production was added in the 1930s. In 2011, the farm will celebrate its 100th year of production.

– Submitted by Carolyn Linder

MARTIN HAYS: Oil Magnate Sheriff of Gregg County

Martin Hays had been Sheriff of Gregg County since 1 January 1925, when the East Texas Oil Field was discovered in late 1930. A year later the Cranfill & Reynolds Martin Hays #1 well blew in, gushing oil onto the surface of his 550-acre lease comprising the W.C. Alvice Survey by Merrill's Lake, three miles south of Camp Switch. The estimated open flow of his first well (of eventually 93) was 30,000 barrels per day.

Sheriff Hays had led a quiet life of public service until the advent of the oil discovery. From his first election in 1910, until his election as Sheriff in 1924, he served as District Clerk and as City Marshal. The latter office included the offices of Chief of Police and Superintendent of Sanitation, as indicated in a Resolution of Thanks from the City Commission dated 9 December 1924, after receipt of his resignation from these offices to assume his title as Sheriff.

During his tenure as Sheriff, he was widely known and respected as a fair, gentle, but tough if necessary, lawman. He rarely was armed even when making an arrest; but the sudden influx of boomers and camp followers with the discovery of oil overwhelmed the tiny department, and Governor Ross Sterling sent the National Guard and the Texas Rangers to help maintain law and order in the beleaguered oil patch. In his last term, the boom years, Gregg County had no killings, and Sheriff Hays' office remitted $24,800 in excess income from its office to the State Treasury. His extensive holdings and the need to attend personal matters led Hays to forego

Martin Hays

running for a fifth term in 1932. His public service, however, continued with appointments to the Gregg County Draft Board and War Rationing Board during World War II, and service on the Longview City Commission in the 1930s.

Martin Presley Hays was born 15 September 1883, near Oak Hill in Rusk County, the son of Martin Van Buren Hays and Nancy C. Matthews Johnson Hays. To this couple were born John (November 1881-?), Martin, Jesse (12 June 1885–20 August 1908), Douglas (6 November 1888–9 April 1952), and Alice Pearl (13 January 1892–9 February 1987). Each parent had been previously married; Martin V.B. Hays and Feriby Isabella Shows had one son, William W. Hays. William and spouse, Emma (?), had two children, Anniebell (9 October 1898–28 February 1990) and Alice Pearl (22 January 1902–11 December 1986). The former married Asberry Talmage Hagood and moved to South Carolina, after having had five children in Texas. The latter married Joseph M. Graham and reared six sons in Longview.

Martin Van Buren Hays was born 17 June 1844, in Monroe County, Mississippi, to John T. and Alice B. McElroy Hays, the third of five known children. Alice died in the early 1850s and John T. married Sarah Blount 25 March 1854, in Bibb County, Alabama, where they had three more children. Martin Van Buren Hays served in Tarrant's Artillery Battery, CSA, and in 1880 or 1881, moved with his second wife, Nancy, to Rusk County, Texas.

Martin and Nancy were married on 13 January 1880, and were divorced in 1915 as a result of Martin's abandonment of the family in 1902. He had moved to the Confederate Veterans' home in Austin by 1914, where he died 23 May 1921.

Nancy was the daughter of Richard H. Matthews and his wife, Sarah (?), born 27 February 1859, in Tuscaloosa, Alabama. She married Frank Johnson 15 July 1875, and had one known child, Collier F. Johnson. In the 1880 Federal Census, Nancy was listed as a widow, aged 21. She married Martin V.B. Hays 13 January 1880, in Tuscaloosa, Alabama, and moved shortly thereafter with him to Texas. After her divorce, Nancy operated the Bodie Hotel at "The Junction" in Longview, where she was known as "the mother of the railroad boys." She died at home on North Fredonia Street, Longview, on 24 August 1931, and was buried along with her former husband in the Martin and Clara Hays lot in Grace Hill Cemetery.

Sheriff Martin Hays married Clara Ella Harris(s) 2 February 1908, and had one child, Hollis Beryl Hays, born 11 January 1909, and died 17 March 1910. The Hays later took in their niece Pauline Wood, who lived with them as a daughter from 1927 until her marriage to Robert Cargill in 1933. The former sheriff suffered a series of strokes beginning in 1950, and succumbed to them 11 April 1958. Clara survived him until 15 July 1975. Both lie in Grace Hill Cemetery. Clara's genealogy is outlined in a separate story in this volume.

Robert Cargill is deeply grateful to Floyd and Linda Lippeatt of West Blocton, Alabama, for providing the information presented here about Sheriff Martin Hays' ancestry.

– Written by Robert Cargill, Jr.;
submitted by Paula Kaplan

HEDRICK–ROACH

Billy Dean Hedrick (born 1931) and Anna Bess Roach (born 1933) eloped to Texarkana, Arkansas, and married in 1950. They have spent their entire married life in Kilgore, Gregg County, after growing up in adjoining Rusk County.

The Lem Hedrick (1888-1970) and Gertrude Blair Hedrick (1897-1973) family moved to Gregg County in 1934 from Stone County in Missouri after losing their farm during the Great Depression. Some of the children recall the sight of their cows being herded away. Lem continued some farming and also did pipelining in the East Texas Oil Field. Billy Dean was one of fourteen children born to that union.

Anna and Bill Hedrick and sons.

Anna Bess' parents, James Victor Roach, Sr. (1902-1998) and Bessie Staggs Roach (1908-1984), moved to Pistol Hill in nearby Rusk County in 1934 after working many years in the Collins Street Bakery at Corsicana, Texas. He worked until retirement in the East Texas Oil Field.

Bill and Anna Bess raised four sons in Kilgore, including the first set of triplets born in Rusk County. The sons, Bill, Dale, David and Don, all reside in Kilgore and are raising families there.

The firstborn son, Bill (born 1952), graduated from Kilgore High School, served in the U.S. Air Force, obtained a Bachelor of Science degree in Political Science from the University of Texas at Tyler, then chose professional photography as his vocation. He has won numerous awards in that chosen field. He also served as editor of the Texas Professional Photographer magazine. Bill owned a studio in Kilgore for 19 years. His hobby is flying and he owns his own airplane.

Bobby Dale (born 1953) is a graduate of Kilgore High School (1972) and Kilgore College. Dale was employed at Skillern's Drug as their youngest manager at that time. Later, he worked in different areas in the oilfield and plans to retire from Eastman Chemical. Dale married Laura Anne Wilson in 1973 and they have three children: Anna Marie, William Karl and Lisa

Michelle. At this writing, Anna Marie and her husband Steven Hamilton have a son, Christopher.

Byron David (born 1953) is a graduate of Kilgore High School (1972) and Kilgore College. He has spent his entire career as a self-employed plumber of his own company. David married Danette Compton in 1975. They are parents of two children: Bret Daniel and Brittany Katherine.

Bruce Don Hedrick (born 1953) is a graduate of Kilgore High School (1972), Kilgore College and East Texas State University. He has taught in the Kilgore ISD system his entire career, having taught from K through 12. An avid fisherman, Don and his wife have built their own home. Don married Jana Buck in 1980. Their two daughters are Jena Leigh and Leanne Joy.

– Submitted by Anna Hedrick

HENDERSON

William Reed "Pete" Henderson was born in Bonham, Fannin County, Texas, 31 October 1907; he grew up there and participated in most athletics and band. From 1925-27, worked for T&P Railroad as brakeman along with his father, the engineer, and his brother, who was the fireman. "Pete" also had a dance band and learned to fly a bi-plane during those two years. When the oil boom hit Electra, he went to work there for LeBus Rotary Tool Works until 1930, at which time they transferred him to Greggton. He returned to Bonham to persuade Alice Keeton to become his bride even though the depression was not the best time to start a home in a town that had folks sleeping on the courthouse lawn! They married in Honey Grove, Texas, at the Presbyterian Manse on 26 April 1931. By 1934, he became Shop Foreman at LeBus. In 1937, he took the same position at Standard Tool Machine Shop until 1940. From 1940-44, he became co-owner with Elmer Porter of the Greggton Machine Shop (the building still stands and is in use in 2003).

The couple had a daughter, Alice Reed, in 1932, and a son, Pete, in 1933. The family moved to Longview in late 1937, at which time they moved from the First Presbyterian Church to the First Baptist. From 1943 to 1945, he became tool pusher for Wampler Brothers Drilling Company and, after two years, he became a 1/3 partner. In 1946, he started Henderson Drilling Co., and later took his tool pusher, Lee Berwick, in as a minor partner. From 1955-57, he was an oil operator on a part-time basis as times became difficult for small independents. In 1956, "Pete" served on a committee in the Chamber of Commerce and was chosen Outstanding Independent Oil Operator. He began yet another "career" as a Deputy Sheriff in Gregg County until 1961. He then became Constable in Precinct 1 until 1973. During all these years he worked on his dream of becoming a Mason and attained the Scottish Rite. He also taught Law Enforcement classes at Kilgore Jr. College periodically during 1961-73. He spent 1973 and 1974 recuperating from a massive heart attack. In 1974, he decided not to allow the doctors' predictions of dying to occur and became a Civil Process

Server. This career lasted until November 1998, when he served the last paper on his "walker"! His health had been deteriorating for a few years.

Besides working, his great love was his Sunday School classes, horses and dancing. Alice also loved dancing, and they participated in Alicia's Dance Class and Club for 20 odd years.

On 23 November 1911, Alice Keeton was born in Fannin County, Texas, on the family farm. She grew up among eight siblings; she was active in church and school, playing piano and tennis (won regionals) and drama. She clerked and went to school in Commerce until she became Mrs. Henderson. Living conditions were not easy. She was an outstanding homemaker, seamstress and cook. Alice became active in PTA during the children's school years. She also loved her church family; they moved to the First Methodist in 1951, following their children there. She was active in the ladies' groups and Mr. Henderson served on the Board of Stewards for a time. Alice enjoyed gardening, also, and cherished her time with the Daughters of the American Revolution Chapter. She had a massive heart attack at age 59 which caused a major lifestyle change. She believed the dancing also helped her to live until 86 years of age, although other health problems curtailed most activities from age 78. "Pete" died at age 91. They are buried in the Memory Park Mausoleum.

– Submitted by Alice Furrh

HENDERSON–KILLINGSWORTH–ABNEY

Jasper Lewis Henderson was born 5 September 1898. He was the sixth of seven children born to James Lawson Henderson and Adella Dickard. His grandfather, Lawson Pursley Henderson, moved to Texas in 1869 from Cherokee County, Alabama, with his wife Talitha Cumi (Heitt) Henderson and their six children. Lewis Henderson's father and grandfather were staunch Presbyterians. Lawson Pursely, a charter member of the First Presbyterian Church in Longview, helped found the Alpine Presbyterian Church, north of Longview, in 1881. Lewis Henderson played on Longview's State Championship football team in 1915. After the death in 1924 of Lewis' first wife, Gladys Rebecca Killingsworth, daughter of Samuel Abney Killingsworth and his first wife, Donnie Cain, Lewis married Blanche Killingsworth in 1926, the daughter of Samuel Abney Killingsworth and his second wife, Florence Ann Leath Killingsworth.

Lewis had one child by his first wife, Gladys Killingsworth, Richard Lewis Henderson, born 4 December 1921, in Longview, Texas. Richard lives in Midland, Texas, with his second wife Elma Jean (Noble) Jarrett Henderson and is President of Rich-Air Properties. He was a pilot with the Eight Air Force in World War II, flying out of Great Britain. He has two children by his first marriage to Elizabeth Ann McHaney, Susan Elizabeth Askins and Richard Eanes (Rick) Henderson. He has three grandchildren, Kendall Smith, married to Russell Smith, Mason Askins and Cooper Askins, and one great granddaughter, Elizabeth Ann Smith.

Blanche Killingsworth Henderson, the second child of Samuel Abney Killingsworth and Florence Ann Leath Killingsworth, was born 30 August 1909, at the family home north of Longview, Texas. She recalls riding a donkey named July to attend school that was located at the Alpine Presbyterian Church community. Blanche Killingsworth joined the First Baptist Church, Longview, when she was 11 years old. She later taught Sunday School and was superintendent of the fourteen-year-old Sunday School department. She and Lewis Henderson had one child, Blanche Henderson, born 26 November 1939.

Lewis Henderson operated a sawmill on property north of Longview, just off Henderson Road. Later, he became a drilling superintendent for F.R. Jackson's oil company until his death in 1952 in Levelland, Texas. Blanche Killingsworth Henderson married Zach Abney, Jr. of Marshall, Texas, in 1960, and they lived in Longview until his death in 1984. In 1995 she moved to College Station, Texas, to live with her daughter, Blanche Henderson Brick, and her husband, Robert Brick. Blanche Brick is Division Chair of Social Sciences at Blinn College in Bryan; Robert is Division Chair of Natural Sciences. They have two children, Kathleen Brick, a science teacher in the Cypress Fairbanks School District in Houston, and John Brick, an attorney in Houston. John is married to Jamee Boutell Brick and has one daughter, Hannah Grace Brick.

Blanche Killingsworth Henderson Abney is a member of the First Baptist Church, Longview, the East Texas Historical Association, the Southern Historical Association and a major contributor to a family history of "Mary (Barry) and William Barry Henderson, Their Forebears and Descendants."

– Submitted by Blanche Henderson Brick

CHARLES NEWTON HENDERSON

The horrible, not so civil, war was finally over and the country was in the throes of the Reconstruction Period. Charles Newton Henderson, born 18 February 1832, at York County, South Carolina, but now living in Cherokee County, Alabama, had been through five years of terrible times. His faithful wife, Sarah Catherine Harris, had also gone through pretty terrible times. She had lost a baby in 1860, and had nearly starved before Charles came back from the war in 1865. They, at that time, had two children. He was a lieutenant in General Joe Wheeler's outfit and was so fond of the General that he named his first child for him. Since times were bad and carpet baggers

Charles Newton and Sarah Catherine (Harris) Henderson

and scalawags had overrun the country side, the decision was made to remove to Texas. Two brothers, Lawson Pursley and John Barry, were both living in Texas. John Barry ran an exchange of horses for the stagecoach line from Marshall to Jefferson, and Lawson ran a freight line.

The family made the trip to Texas with other family members by covered wagon, train, riverboat and horse drawn carriages. The riverboat sank and some lives were lost, including a sister of Sarah Catherine, Mary Sprayberry. Finally camping at the John B. Henderson home at Woodlawn, they sought out a place to live. They first moved to Wood County with some of the Harris kin. Two sons were buried there. They moved to Starville in Smith County briefly. Then they came to Gregg County. Charles Newton purchased land next to his brother Lawson Henderson's farm and began farming.

Charles Newton was a skilled farmer and having six sons was an advantage. He was one of the first to use barbed wire to fence his property, much to the chagrin of some neighbors.

Charles and Sarah, called Sallie, were charter members of Alpine Presbyterian Church. Faithful and true for the years they had together, they celebrated their 50th anniversary, with all their children present, in 1906. In a few days both had died. They are buried in Alpine Cemetery and their gravestone, the tallest in the cemetery, serves for both of them. They had ten children, seven growing to adulthood: Joseph Scippio, born 16 October 1860, married Mary Elizabeth Reynolds; William Harris, born 25 March 1866, married Lizzie Estelle Finley; Alice Ida, born 8 March 1868, married Robert Taylor Henderson; Thomas Newton, born 26 September 1874, married Augusta Eugenia McClendon; Arthur Albert, born 17 November 1876, married Birda Inez Bunt; Sidney Franklin, born 17 December 1878, married Mary Lou McClendon, married second to Lela Baggett Fox; and John Dewitt, born 8 December 1883, married Ruth Dickard. Many of their descendants still live in Gregg County.

– Submitted by David Hastie

LAWSON PURSLEY HENDERSON

Lawson Pursley Henderson was born 2 August 1824, and died 18 July 1921. He was the sixth in a family of 15 children born to William Barry and Mary Barry Henderson in York County, South Carolina. The family migrated to eastern Alabama in 1833.

Lawson married Talitha Cumi Hiett (born 20 April 1823) on 10 October 1849. They lived in Cherokee County, Alabama, until 1869. They and several family members then removed to Texas. Lawson and Talitha stopped for several years in Woodlawn, Harrison County, where Lawson's older brother, John Barry Henderson, lived. Lawson was a freighter, running a line from Jefferson to Marshall. Eventually, he bought land in Gregg County and said he would go no further than the railroad line ran. He purchased land about five miles north of Longview on what is now Sam Page road. The Wilson Henderson home now stands on the spot that Lawson Henderson chose.

Lawson Pursley and Talitha Cumi (Hiett) Henderson

Lawson was a charter member of Longview Presbyterian Church. He had previously been a charter member, with his wife, of Alpine Presbyterian Church in Menlo, Georgia. In 1891, they became charter members of Alpine Presbyterian Church in the Tryon Community of Longview. Lawson was elected one of the first elders and was always active in church life on the local and district levels.

Lawson and Talitha had six children to reach adulthood: Rebecca Jane (born 7 December 1851) married Curtis Mackey, Sylvester Fair (born 7 March 1853) married Arminda Smith, Ada Adelia (born 22 April 1858) married Josiah Wilkes, James Lawson (born 17 December 1859) married Adella Dickard, Robert Taylor (born 17 November 1865) married Alice Ida Henderson and Nancy Luella (born 6 July 1869) married John Monroe Morgan.

Lawson did not join the army of the Confederate States of America when, in 1861, so many marched off. A horse had fallen on him and severely injured his leg. He was 37 years old at the time. However, he worked hard for the Southern cause and his home was not spared from Union forces.

His descendants still worship at Alpine Presbyterian Church. Some of his sons, grandsons, great grandsons, and a great great grandson, Mickey Melton, have or are serving as elders.

Talitha Cumi, Lawson's wife of 41 years, died 26 February 1890. After her death, he married Miss Mary Morrison (born 26 October 1844). Mary died 20 May 1912. Lawson Pursley Henderson died 18 July 1921, at the home of his daughter, Jane Mackey. He was nearly 97 years old. He and his two wives are buried at Alpine Presbyterian Church Cemetery, Longview, Texas. Many of his descendants have lived into their ninth decade.

–Submitted by Mary Ruth Henderson Hastie

MORGAN BARRY HENDERSON

Morgan Barry Henderson was born 14 November 1900, to R.T. "Bob" and Alice Ida Henderson, the first son after five daughters. He was much loved and Grace, his older sister, said they were so overjoyed about having a brother that they had him riding in the buggy with them as soon as he could sit erect. They called him, "my brother." He was given two family names besides Henderson.

On 18 January 1924, he married Gladys Mae Culpepper (born 20 May 1903 to Charles Thomas Culpepper and Luisa Elizabeth

Ferguson). They had four children: Alice Elizabeth, born 20 October 1924, married Bryan Grimes; Armenda Jane, born 15 June 1927, married William Henry Boothe; Mary Ruth, born 5 April 1930, married George Hastie; and Morgan Barry, born 5 April 1930 (twin to Mary Ruth), married Tijuana Jordan.

Armenda Jane and William Henry Boothe had twin sons, Billy and Barry Boothe. Mary Ruth and George Hastie had three children: David, Daniel and Marilyn. Morgan Barry and Tijuana Jordan had one daughter, Laura Alice. Morgan Barry Henderson married second Shirley Potz Neilson.

Morgan Berry and Gladys (Culpepper) Henderson

Morgan Barry Henderson, Sr. was in the dairy business and settled on Airline Road. This was three miles north of the Gregg County Courthouse. The telephone company considered this area too far to provide telephone service. With the cooperation of his father, Bob Henderson, and neighbors, they put up their own line. Each family owned their telephone and helped pay for the poles and lines. It was Morgan's responsibility to keep it up and going. The same problem was experienced with the electric company. They worked hard, and it was hard work, to get the REA to come into being in Gregg County. This was a great help for rural people. At this time people on Judson Road had electricity, but Airline Road was 'in the country' three miles from the courthouse.

The three daughters became teachers. Elizabeth taught in Smith County and Tyler Independent School District; Jane was located in Gonzales, Texas, and Mary Ruth performed mission work in Guatemala and Mexico. Barry served in the Korean War as a waist gunner on a B-29. He later served as commissioner for Precinct 1 in Gregg County.

Morgan and Gladys were married for 45 years and lived at the same location all those years. After Morgan's death in 1969, Gladys moved to Tyler to be closer to her daughter and two sisters. They had moved to "The Haven" in 1948 to care for Morgan's father, R.T. Henderson. Gladys died in 1995. She and Morgan are buried in the Alpine Church Cemetery.
– Submitted by Jane Henderson Boothe

ROBERT TAYLOR "BOB" HENDERSON

The R.T. Henderson family began in 1891 when Robert "Bob" married his cousin, Alice Ida Henderson. They were both born in Alabama, he 17 November 1865, and she 8 March 1868. They had come to Gregg County, Texas, with their

families and settled first in the Tryon Community. After their marriage, they bought land that was located on what would later be called Airline Road. At that time, it was considered 'in the country,' and was so thought of for many years afterwards. It was only three miles from the Gregg County Courthouse.

The couple had nine children, only five living to adulthood. Willie Cumi, born 8 March 1892, married Oscar Watson Ward and second, J.P. Owens of Lindale. Willie and Oscar had two daughters, Margaret Alice and Dorothy Ruth. Nanny Alice "Alie Bob" was born 26 August 1893, and married Andrew Jackson Tuttle. They had seven children: Robert, George, Roy, Dan and daughters, Dimple, Polly and Nancy. Grace, born 18 September 1897, married Rowan A. Whatley. They had three children, R.A. Jr., Mary Alice and Leora. Morgan Barry, born 14 November 1900, married Gladys Mae Culpepper. They had four children: Alice Elizabeth, Armenda Jane, and twins, Mary Ruth and Morgan Barry. George Taylor, born 7 November 1902, married Hattie Belle Riley. They had two daughters, Betty Jean and Marion.

Bob Henderson was a progressive farmer. He planted a prized peach orchard early in the 1900s. In 1904, he took some of his peaches to the World's Fair in St. Louis and won a bronze medal for them. He planted cotton for some years; but when he learned that it was wearing out the land, he varied his crops with corn, peas, watermelons and other crops. The County Agent used his farm for special projects to teach other farmers crop rotation, terracing, etc.

Before his marriage, Bob was a deputy sheriff along with Alice's brothers, William, Sid and, later, John. He served as president of the Federal Land Bank organization of Gregg and Harrison counties and was very active in county agricultural activities. He was a trustee at Tryon School for several years. He also served for many years as Precinct Chairman for elections at Judson School.

Alice was a much beloved teacher at Judson and Indian Rock before their marriage. They were both charter members of Alpine Prebytrian Church and served it faithfully for all their years. They are buried in Alpine Church Cemetery.

At their 50th anniversary in 1941, there were 17 grandchildren present (one was born later) and one great grandchild. There are many descendants of this couple still in Gregg County.
– Submitted by Elizabeth Henderson Grimes

FORREST ALBERT HERNDON & ALMA CARTWRIGHT HERNDON

Alma Cartwright Herndon was born in Brown County, Texas, 4 June 1904. She was the second of five children. Her grandfather Ashcraft was an early settler and owned a large

R.T. and Alice Henderson in front of "The Haven," built before their 50th anniversary.

ranch in Brown County. His daughter, Frances Ashcraft, married a handsome young man, William Davis Cartwright, from Brownwood, Texas, where they continued to live. Alma had a high regard for education and was determined to receive her college degree. She received a tennis scholarship to the University of Texas. It was also necessary for her to work so she would teach for a year then go to school for a year. She accomplished her goal and was graduated from Howard Payne College. She and Forrest Herndon met at the wedding of friends. Her mother always found something wrong with her dates, so Alma postponed introducing Forrest to her parents, realizing she was falling in love, until one Sunday night in church. To her surprise her mother said, "he's a fine-looking young man, and he sang those hymns like he meant it." They were married in San Marcos, Texas, on 24 February 1929.

Forrest Albert Herndon was born in Warrensburg, Missouri, on 5 September 1900, the youngest of three children. His parents were Samuel Rodney Herndon and Scottie Malott. They moved to Cisco, Texas, when he was seventeen. He was an outdoorsman and active in sports. He received a degree from Cisco Junior College and was employed by Humble Pipeline Company until his retirement.

Forrest and Alma made their home in Cisco before moving to Longview, then settling in Kilgore after a year. Their first son was stillborn in Cisco, but within a few years they were blessed with a daughter, Darba Gay, then a son, Samuel Forrest. After World War II ended, they built a home in the historical Meadowbrook addition of Kilgore. In 1950, the family moved

Forrest and Alma Herndon

to Longview. Alma loved Bible study and always taught Sunday School. She was a loving homemaker, an accomplished seamstress, creative in decorating and working with flowers—always taking top ribbon prizes at the garden club shows. She was an avid reader and member of the Twentieth Century Club in Longview. She was nurturing and very unselfishly ministered to her mother and Forrest's mother in the final weeks of life. She also nursed her sister and Forrest's sister during their year's illnesses with cancer in her home. Alma and Forrest again faced grief when their son Samuel died of polio at the age of fifteen. Their deep reservoir of faith in God Almighty undergirded them. They again opened their home to their aging fathers, who became close companions until the time of their deaths. Alma and Forrest were a loving couple who honored each other in every way—celebrating their 60th wedding anniversary before Forrest died on 20 July 1989. Alma lived to be 96, dying 5 October 2000. Both are buried in Memory Park Cemetery in Longview, Texas.

– Submitted by Darba Jackson

JIMMIE HERNDON

Jimmie Herndon was born in Longview, Texas, on 19 June 1896, to Anna Brown and Albert Herndon. His mother, Anna, was born in 1874. There has been some conflict about Jimmie's father's first name. On his death certificate his father is listed as George Herndon, but on his application for a social security number filed by Jimmie, Albert Herndon was used.

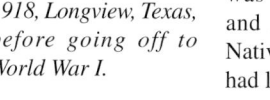

Private Jimmie Herndon, 1918, Longview, Texas, before going off to World War I.

No one knows where Anna Brown or Albert Herndon came from. The first record of Anna was on the 1910 Gregg County Census. It was said that Albert Herndon died in some sort of accident while working off shore. Anna had one sister, Eely Brown, who was born in 1873. Eley had one daughter, Katie Mae, who was born in 1894, in Longview. It was said that Anna and Eley were both Native American and had long black hair.

Anna Herndon married Captain Wheatley of Longview on 24 May 1902. Captain moved to Longview from Hughes Springs, Texas, which is about 60 miles north of Longview, and brought with him one daughter from a previous marriage named Alma, who was born in 1896. Anna gave birth to a daughter, Anna May, in 1907. The family lived in a house they owned on Walnut Street in Longview.

Willie May Herndon, Longview, Texas.

Eley married Jessie Hodge and moved to Dallas, Texas, where she raised Katie.

Jimmie Herndon went to school and worked in Longview until 1918, when he joined the U.S. Army and served during World War II. After his discharge from the Army in 1919, Jimmie returned to Longview and married his childhood sweetheart, Willie May Miller, on 11 August 1919.

Jimmie and Willie May lived on South Court Street and had three children: Jimmy Gerald, born 7 January 1921; James William, born 2 August 1922; and Jannie Marie, born 27 September 1924.

While living in Longview, Jimmie worked at the box factory. The Herndon children attended school in Longview until the family moved to Dallas in 1930. Soon after moving to Dallas, Jimmie and Willie May divorced. Willie May married Tommy Lawrence of Dallas, and Jimmie married Mary Estella Cox on 4 January 1955.

While in Dallas, Jimmie worked at the Melba Theater; and he and his wife, Mary, owned and operated a diner called the "Dolphin Inn." Mary died on 10 May 1967, and Jimmie brought her to Longview to be buried at Grace Hill Cemetery.

After Mary's death, Jimmie moved to Hughes Springs and lived until 1971 on the property which belonged to the family of his stepfather. After his health failed, he moved to Perris, California, with his children, Jimmy Herndon and Jannie Anderson. Jimmie died in Perris on 26 January 1972.

Jimmie's sister, Katie, married Robert Arnold, Sr. and had one son, Robert Arnold, Jr.

Katie died in Dallas in 1950, and her husband died in 1941. They are both buried in Dallas. Their son, Robert, lives in Perris, California.

The Herndons were active members of Bethel Baptist Church located on Harrison Street in Longview.

– Submitted by Tiana M. Cook

W.A. (BILL) & DALE HEWELL

William Albert (Bill) Hewell came to Longview, Texas, in 1933 from Wichita Falls, Texas, where he worked for a bank. He established a public accounting firm in Longview in 1933 with his office in the Chamber of Commerce building. In 1934, Bill met Dale Davis who worked at Pegues Motor Company. Dale was the daughter of Vera Combs and stepdaughter of T.M. Combs.

Bill and Dale were married on 17 March 1936, in Shreveport, Louisiana. Their good friends, Laura Virginia Wood and Charles Ellsworth (who later married), were their attendants. The Hewells' first home was on Young Street in Longview.

Bill was called into military service during World War II, serving in the Army Finance Corp stationed at Fort Benjamin Harrison in Indiana. While Bill was away, Dale worked in their public accounting firm, W.A. Hewell & Co. Both Bill and Dale were public accountants; they were awarded certificates by the Texas State Board of Public Accountancy in December 1946, and issued permits to practice as public accountants. Their certificate numbers are 736 and 737.

The Hewells resided on West Highway 80 until they moved to 715 Noel Drive in Mobberly Place in Longview in the early 1950s.

The Hewells' first child Sally Irene was born 29 March 1948, at Markham Hospital in Longview. She was followed by twins born 23 December 1952 — William Marvin (Bill) and Walter Robert (Bob).

The Hewell family attended First United Methodist Church in Longview, where Bill and Dale were active in the Men's Bible Class and Thelma Morgan Sunday School classes.

Their public accounting practice grew with the firm performing audits and preparing income tax and estate tax returns. Their firm had the first computer installation of NCR (National Cash Register) in the East Texas region.

From left to right: James William, Jannie Marie and Jimmy Gerald Herndon.

Bill and Dale Hewell

Bill served almost thirty years on the Board of Directors at Longview National Bank and was instrumental in the formation and growth of the bank's trust department. Dale was a member of the Garden Study Club and Longview Study Club, plus had membership in the KRD (Kan't Rate a Date) Club.

Sally, the oldest child, graduated as salutatorian from Longview High School in 1966, and received a BBA degree from Texas Christian University in 1970, graduating summa cum laude. She worked in Dallas with Price Waterhouse & Co. and became a CPA in 1972. Bill and Bob both graduated from Longview High School in 1971. Bill graduated from the University of Texas-Austin in 1975, and earned a graduate degree from UT in 1979. Bob graduated from Texas Christian University in 1975, and graduated from Texas Tech School of Medicine in 1977. Sally moved to Longview in 1977 with her husband Russell E. (Russ) Brown (also a CPA). Bill is an accountant in Dallas and Bob is a physician in San Angelo.

William Albert (born 17 July 1909) and Dale (born 27 June 1913) were living in Longview when he died 12 September 1991, and Dale died 2 September 1992. Both are buried in Memory Park Cemetery in Longview, Texas.
– Submitted by Sally Hewell Brown

HILLIS

The earliest known Hillis ancestor in America was Samuel Hillis, born in 1708 in Scotland or Ireland. He is named in the 1752 will of his father-in-law, Robert Luckey in Lancaster County, Pennsylvania. After Robert Luckey's death, Samuel moved his family to Rowan County, North Carolina, where he died, naming Revolutionary War soldier sons, Robert, Sampson and Samuel Jr., and three daughters in his will.

Stephen Henry Hillis and Murphy Hillis, sons of Dixon Naylor Hillis, grandsons of Samuel Jr., migrated from Van Buren County, Tennessee, to Texas in 1905. They lived at Clear Lake and then settled in the small community of Wylie, Texas.

Leeton Hillis came to Longview from Wylie in March 1946, as vice-president of Longview National Bank (now Regions Bank). Leeton was the son of Murphy Hillis and Flora Johnson Hillis, born 5 January 1899, outside McMinnville, Tennessee. Leeton never married and remained with Longview National Bank until his retirement in 1964. As far as anyone can tell, Leeton was never seen dressed in anything but a suit, tie and pastel dress shirt. He was a fairly conservative man. In contrast, his life-long passion was professional wrestling. Leeton would travel each Tuesday evening to the Dallas Convention Center, where he had front row tickets to the wrestling matches for 27 years, and drive back to Longview, ready for work Wednesday morning.

Leeton Hillis

Then in 1960, cousin Charles Lee Hillis, Jr. was transferred to Longview with Stanolind Oil Co. (now BP Amoco) from Andrews, Texas, bringing with him his wife, Mary Ellen Heidler Hillis, and five children: Charles Max, Vickie Anne, John Leeton, Jana Alice and Leigh Ellen. Charles Jr. was born in Wylie, Texas, on 6 November 1919, to Charles Lee Hillis (25 March 1889–1 May 1963) and Sally Poston Hillis (5 July 1894–16 March 1973), grandson of Stephen Henry (18 December 1866–5 January 1951) and Nancy Johnson Hillis (6 November 1870–16 November 1917). Stephen's parents were Dixon Naylor Jr. and Adeline Rhodes Hillis, and his grandparents were Dixon Naylor and Lydia Logue Hillis.

Charles Jr. graduated from high school in Wylie, then attended Arlington Jr. College (A&M) in Arlington, Texas, until January 1942, when he joined the army to fight in World War II. After graduating from Officer Training School as a second lieutenant, he was sent to the South Pacific

Charles Lee "Chock" Hillis, Jr.
and Mary Ellen Hillis, 1982

for 3-1/2 years, participating in the invasion of Lete in the Philippines, Iwo Jima and Okinawa before returning home as a captain. He was hired then by Stanolind Oil Co., working in Levelland and Andrews before coming to Longview. Charles retired from Amoco after 30 years.

"Chock," as he was called by his wife and friends, and Mary Ellen, daughter of Maximillion George Heidler (11 November 1889–18 July 1955) and Alice Ethel Bennett (13 October 1896–2 June 1880), raised their family in Greggton. All but the oldest child graduated from Pine Tree Schools where Mary Ellen taught home economics for about 20 years. They were active in the First Christian Church and many different service clubs. They were married 42 years until Chock's death on 20 August 1986. Mary Ellen continued to be active in Longview for another eighteen years until her death on 19 July 2003. Charles Jr. and Mary Ellen Hillis left quite a legacy in the East Texas area with 14 grandchildren, 11 great grandchildren and still counting. Both are buried in Lakeview Memorial Gardens Cemetery in Longview, Texas.
– Submitted by Jana Smith

JAMES STEPHEN HOGG

James Stephen Hogg, the first native governor of Texas, was born near Rusk on 24 March 1851, the son of Lucanda (McMath) and Joseph Lewis Hogg. After going to school in Alabama in 1866, he returned to Texas and studied law and worked as the typesetter in a newspaper office at Rusk.

He owned a paper in Longview for only three months before moving to Quitman, Texas, from 1871 to 1873, where he fought subsidies to railroads, the corruption of the Ulysses S. Grant administration and local lawlessness. He served as justice of the peace at Quitman from 1873 to 1875, then studied law. He married Sallie Stinson; four children were born to them. Hogg received his only defeat in a contest for public office in 1876, when he ran against John S. Griffith for a seat in the Texas legislature. He was elected county attorney of Wood County in 1878, and served from 1880 to 1884 as district attorney, where he became known as the most aggressive and successful district attorney in the state. In the national campaign of 1884, he succeeded in winning enough black votes from the Republicans to make Smith County a Democratic stronghold.

In 1886, he was elected attorney general of Texas. He was elected governor in 1890 on a platform that advocated the establishment of the Railroad Commission. While governor, from 1891 to 1895, Hogg did much to strengthen public respect for law enforcement. Always interested in the history of Texas, he succeeded in obtaining financial aid for a division of state archives and appointed C.W. Raines to supervise the collection and preservation of historical materials.

On 3 March 1906, Hogg died in the home of his partner, Frank Jones, at Houston. He was buried in Austin.

HOLLERS/DUKE/BLACK/YARBROUGH

Billie Joyce (Hollers) Jones was born 10 August 1926, in Travis County, Texas, to William Arthur Hollers and Stella Lassophene Duke, both of whom were born in Texas in 1903. William died in 1962 in Dallas, Texas, and Stella died in 1986 in Longview, Texas. Joyce had one brother, James Lemuel Hollers, who passed away in 1999 in Lufkin, Texas. He was married to Bobbie Jo Lawrence of Hallsville, Texas. They had a daughter, Deborah Kay Burrous, and a son, Richard William Hollers.

James Lemuel Hollers and sons by Mattie E. Mayes.

Joyce's grandfather, James Lemuel Hollers, was born in 1860 in Somerset, Kentucky, to Albert/Albertson Hollers and Amanda Black. They were both born in 1832 in Kentucky, and married in 1854. They left Kentucky in 1880, moving on to Missouri or Kansas. They acquired land in Pawnee and Woodward Counties, Oklahoma. Where they moved after that is not known. James Lemuel Hollers was a Methodist circuit riding preacher all over Central and West Texas. He was married three times and had children by each wife. He died in Riviera, Texas, in 1933.

Billie Joyce's grandmother was Mattie Elizabeth Mayes, whose parents were James Harvey Mayes and Missouri Hughes. They are both buried at Proctor, Texas. Joyce's grandfather, Robert Edward Duke, was born in 1875 to John William Duke and Catherine Elizabeth Packer. They were both born in Mississippi, and moved their family to Texas in 1876, where they settled in Comanche, Milam and Runnels Counties. Burial for both was in the latter county. Rob-

Billie Joyce Hollers Jones

ert Edward Duke married three times and had daughters by each of his wives. Joyce's maternal grandmother, Ellen Yarbrough, died when Joyce's mother was only about six months old and is buried at Jarrell, Texas. Robert Edward Duke is buried at Wichita Falls, Texas. John William Duke was the son of David Duke of Mississippi and grandson of John P. Duke of Morgan County, Georgia.

Joyce's maternal great grandparents, John Black and Elizabeth Shipley, were both born in Tennessee and died in Wayne County, Kentucky. The father of John Black was Nathaniel Black. Some members of the Black family who moved to Texas are buried in and around Cooke County.

Very little is known about Joyce's grandmother, Ellen Yarbrough, except that she was born in Alabama and died at a young age. Her father was A.C. Yarbrough, who lived in and around Cameron County, Texas, until about 1906; then he moved to San Saba, Texas, to be near some of his other children.

Glynda Gilley, daughter of Joyce, is married to Keith Cooper and they reside in Harrrison County, Texas. Keith is employed at Texas Eastman while Glynda works for the Hallsville Independent School District. They have two sons, Nicholas Allen Cooper and Phillip Ryan Cooper.

Johnny Wayne Cargile, son of Joyce is married to Paula Hubbard. They live in Coker, Alabama, with their son, Jonathan Wayne Cargile. Johnny is employed by Planit Solutions, Inc. in Tuscaloosa, Alabama.

Joyce has conducted an exhaustive, enjoyable 48-year search for her ancestry.

– Submitted by Joyce Jones

HOLLOWAY

The Holloway family was among the landed gentry of Great Britain living in Middlesex, Warwick, Oxford and Burks. Family tradition tells of three brothers who came to America. Thomas Holloway served in the Revolutionary War and died in North Carolina in 1835. His son David Holloway was born in 1783 in North Carolina and married Mary Polly Hardigree Whitakers in Greene County, Georgia, on 15 December 1807. He served in the War of 1812. He and Mary arrived in Camden, Texas, on 24 December 1848. Mary died 1 October 1849, and David on 24 July 1856.

Their son, James Pendleton Holloway (31 October 1818–9 July 1884), married Sarah Elder (20 December 1817–1899) on 5 January 1842, and arrived in Camden from Georgia in 1859. In 1872, they moved to the Longview area where they bought a farm one mile south of town, living there until his death. When the First Christian Church was founded in 1875, James P. and Sarah, as well as two of their children, were among the original twelve charter members, and James P. was an Elder and the first pastor. They had nine children.

Their second child was William Carroll (Billy), born in 1844. He served in the Confederate Army from 1861 to 1863, and after returning, married Rebecca Bassett (1854–1934) in 1870.

Rebecca (Mrs. W.C.) Holloway with children, 1904.

In 1872, they bought a farm south of Longview where LeTourneau University is located today. In order for Rebecca to get to town, W.C. took his axe and cut a road north connecting to the Marshall road where the stagecoach stop was located. It became known as Mobberly Avenue.

They had five children and as the number of children grew, a school building was erected on the corner of what are now Mobberly and Avalon, which was known as The Holloway School. W.C. was a charter member of the First Christian Church and served as its third pastor. They had nine children. He died in 1898.

In 1942, the United States government forced the sale of the Holloway farm for the location of Harmon General Hospital. A historical marker near the entrance to LeTourneau University pays tribute to the original Holloway farm.

Their fifth child was James Alton (5 May 1883–22 June 1946), who married Lizzie Harrison Methvin (19 October 1884–3 March 1957) in 1906. He owned and operated the Home Mercantile Company, which he changed to Home Furniture Company. Of their five children, the second was William Alton (28 August 1909–10 March 1989) who continued to own and operate the Home Furniture Company until he retired in 1958. He married MaeBeth McHaney (9 May 1912–8 February 1986) in 1931. Their three daughters, along with children and grandchildren, continue to live in Longview and represent eight generations of the Holloway family in this area.

– Submitted by Beth Dodson

D.T. HOLLOWAY

Delbert Thomas and Geraldine (Orendorff) Holloway moved from Amarillo, Texas, to Longview in 1969, and lived at 208 and 305 Broadway Street in the Pine Tree area for six years before moving to Hallsville in Harrison County, where they have remained to present. They have three sons: Kenneth Hugh "Kenny" Holloway (born 8 March 1953 and a graduate of Pine Tree High School), Leonard Russell "Rusty" Holloway (born 12 November 1962 and a graduate of Hallsville High School), and D. Paul Holloway (born 15 June 67 and a 1985 graduate of Hallsville High School). Kenny and Paul have both been employed by Texas Eastman Company for many years.

Delbert worked for Stemco Manufacturing Co. from 1969 to 1983. Gerry worked at American Bank from 1982-83. After 1983, Delbert and Gerry worked together designing and building homes, particularly in the Page and Smelley Roads and Sandy and Lori Small Lanes area.

Delbert was born 12 December 1929, to Sidney Omer and Erna (Yeager) Holloway in Haskell, Texas. Erna was of German heritage. The Omer Holloways had three sons, all raised in Haskell: Delbert Thomas, Crawford Omer (Amarillo, Texas) and Roy Coleman (Amarillo, Texas).

Gerry was born 30 December 1931, in Portales, New Mexico, to Ray Cooper Orendorff and Gladys Bertha (Kerr) Orendorff. The Orendorffs were previously from Hot Springs, Arkansas. Ray's mother's name was Lena Cadell, and Gladys' parents were Will and Ada (Mathis) Kerr. Ray and Gladys Orendorff's eight children were (from eldest to youngest): James Weldon, Lillian (Longview), Geraldine (Longview), Waynell, Donald Ray, Charles William, Eloise (Longview) and Larry Gene (Longview). None of the girls had second names.

Delbert and Geraldine Holloway's sons' families are as follows: Kenny Holloway has one daughter, Heather, and two granddaughters, Sidney and Sophie Grace; Rusty and his wife, Delores, have no children; Paul married Leighann Elizabeth Craft (born 17 April 1967, in Longview) on 28 November 1987. Paul has been employed at Texas Eastman Co. since 1987. He and Leighann are also on staff in Children's Ministry at Longview Christian Fellowship Church. They have five children: Lauren Elizabeth, Logan Paul, Rachel Leah, Allyson Kimberly and Ethan Thomas. (See "Russell & Raenell Craft" and "Ray Helm & Mary Nell Carter" for more information on Leighann Craft.)
– Submitted by Mr. & Mrs. Delbert T. Holloway

LOWELL HOLLOWAY

The Holloway story begins in Georgia where David Holloway was born in 1783. In early adulthood, he married his neighbor and sweetheart, Mary, and settled down to raise a family.

In 1848, when David was 65 years old, he was attracted to the new state of Texas. He, Mary and two married daughters began the long wagon trek to the rugged frontier state.

Upon arrival, David bought land and settled in a community of Georgians who had preceded him to Texas. David's son, James Preston, came from Georgia in 1859 to reunite the family.

James, age 41, and his wife, Sarah, 42, came with their eight children to take their place in the community on their newly purchased 665 acres.

Despite shouldering many responsibilities, James found time to travel about the countryside on horseback preaching the word of God. His eldest son, William Carroll "Billy," joined the Southern Confederacy at the age of 16 and became involved in the Civil War. In 1864, his brother, Robert, joined up and served in William's company. Robert died of complications from a fever. The war ended in 1865, and the soldiers returned home.

William Carroll married Rebecca Lee Bassett in Upshur County in 1870, and brought her home to the family. The community was located some fifteen miles southeast of what would later become Longview.

In 1872, William Carroll purchased a 650-acre farm two and one-half miles south of Longview. When his wife, Rebecca, remarked that there was no road to town, he set about creating one with his ax. The road later became Mobberly Avenue. They built a home on their land. Their eight children, six of whom survived to adulthood, were born there.

Lowell Holloway, Jr. and daughter, Kristi, dedicate the Historical Plaque honoring O.H. Methvin, founder of Longview.

Eventually, the brothers and sisters moved away. One of them, James Alton (born in 1884), completed business school in Tyler and became manager of a 5- and 10-cent store in Longview. At the age of twenty-two, he married Lizzie Methvin, granddaughter of O.H. Methvin, the founder of Longview. They built a home in Longview for which Lizzie helped pay by teaching shorthand.

In 1912, James Alton and a partner purchased a local general merchandize store. Later, James bought out his partner and converted the store into the Home Furniture Company.

James Alton was an active member of the local Christian Church that had been founded in 1875 with his grandfather as the first pastor and his father as the third. He was also a fervent booster of Longview and was so enthusiastic and outgoing it was often said he knew more people than anyone in the county.

James Alton stayed close to his five brothers and sisters who remained in the area. Following the death of their mother in 1934, at the age of 80, they divided the homeplace which was left to them. The land fronted on Mobberly Street, the main entry into town.

James Alton continued operating the furniture store until his death in 1946 at the age of sixty-five. For a time, his sons, William and James Lowell, managed the business. William subsequently bought out Lowell. Lowell took advantage of the opportunity to open his own furniture store in 1949 on the same site where Lowell Holloway Furniture is situated today.

Lowell had five children, the eldest being James Lowell, Jr., who also became associated with the store. Lowell Holloway, Jr. has four daughters: Marci (whose daughters are Amanda and Emily Worsham), Julie Dowell (whose daughter is Meghan), Laura and Kristi (whose daughter is Lizzie Kay Hall). He has a stepson, Rickey Fopay, and a stepdaughter, Monica Mott (whose daughters are Abby and Olivia). He is married to Shirley Holloway.

Kristi is married to Ben Hall. Their daughter, Lizzie, is the eighth generation of the family in Texas and is the namesake of Lizzie Methvin Holloway.

Thus, the Holloway story continues, marking a long and interesting history of people dedicated to the improvement and progress of Longview.
– Submitted by Mary Murdock

WEST HOSKINS

West Hoskins was born in Anderson County, Tennessee, 11 March 1819, to Jesse F. Hoskins Jr. and Bethena Johnson. He married Sarah Clay Ashurst in 1840, Union County, Georgia. Sarah was born 1819 in Kentucky. West died 6 March 1877, Panola County, Texas. Sarah died 10 August 1881, in Longview, Texas. Both are buried in Grace Hill Cemetery, Longview. (Jesse Hoskins Sr., grandfather of West, used the spelling "Hauskins" in all his journals).

West and Sarah lived in Georgia about 10 years where both sons, Joseph Martin and Jesse, were born. They moved back to Tennessee soon after 1850, then to Texas in 1853, and settled in Youngblood Community, Panola County. He became a large land owner, taught school, farmed and was active in a number of civic groups in the community and in Carthage.

Joseph Martin Hoskins was born 8 October 1841, died 13 August 1920; he married Margaret Ann Euphemia Reasonova 28 February 1861, in Panola County, daughter of Benson Reasonova. She was born 5 February 1844, in Shelby County, Texas, died 28 March 1928, in Longview. Both are buried in Grace Hill Cemetery, Longview. Joseph enlisted 26 April 1862, in Co. C and was a Private in Randall's Regiment. The obituary of Margaret Euphemia Hoskins referred to her as a prominent and beloved pioneer citizen of Longview and an active member of the First Presbyterian Church of Longview. She was survived by three daughters: Sarah Carter (married John H. Carter 16 September 1879, in Longview), Penelope Johnson (married Willie Johnson), and Mrs. R.M. Kelly (Arra Lee); grandchildren Walter Carter, Mrs. J.O. Talbot, Jack Johnson, George Kelly, Euphemia Kelly and Mrs. Herbert Fisher.

Jesse Hoskins was born 1843, died March 1885, and is buried in Grace Hill Cemetery, Longview; he married Virginia Holliday 12 September 1866, Panola County. The date of her death is unknown. They had one child, a daughter, Mary Pearl Hoskins, born 1870 in Gregg County, died at age 10 years. After the death of Virginia, Jesse married Ella (maiden name unknown). One child, a son, Oran West Hoskins, was born to this marriage in 1879. Oran was killed in a train wreck about 1906 at Memphis, Tennessee. He left 10-month-old twins, Jack and Joy. Evidently they died young as the Affidavit of Heirship of West Hoskins states that Jesse Hoskins was deceased and had no surviving heirs. Jesse enlisted in the Confederate States Army 27 April 1862. He was a Private in Capt. A.W. DeBerry's Company,

West and Sarah, Joseph and family, and Jesse and wife moved to Longview in the early 1870s and they were very prosperous business citizens of Longview. There are numerous transactions recorded in Gregg County Deed Records where West, Joseph and Jesse purchased and sold property and businesses within the city of Longview. Of these, West purchased lots on the corner of Methvin and Fredonia, the corner of Tyler and Center, a store building and contents on Tyler Street in 1875 next to a private bank owned by F.J. Harrison and Co., where he later built a brick building. Following his death, his sons sold the building to Dock and Oliver Pegues in 1882. West also owned a steam mill and Joseph owned a machine and tool mill. The residences of West and Joseph were located on the block bounded by Cotton, Green and Hoskins Streets. West died intestate and his sons sold a large amount of the property. At the time of his death he still owned several hundred acres of land in Panola County.

Pleasant Hill Hoskins, brother of West, came to Texas soon after 1840 and also settled in Youngblood about 1842. Ples was a school teacher and Minister of the Gospel. He donated land and built a church/school house in the community. His daughter Julia married J.W. Sparks in Panola County and they lived and died in Kilgore. They are buried in Kilgore Cemetery.

Burke J. Hoskins, brother of West, and family also moved to Longview and resided for about two years (1876-1879). Burke was a Methodist-Episcopal of the South Minister and a school teacher. He also served in the Confederate States Army.

The writer's great grandmother, Emily Hoskins Brooks, was a sister of West Hoskins. She and her husband, Reverend Frances Asbury Brooks, and family also moved to Panola County, Texas, in the early 1850s. Also, two other sisters, Malissa and Selina, and a brother, Milton Tate Hoskins, and their families moved there. Asbury Brooks was a Minister of the Gospel and a school teacher. His father, Stephen Brooks, was a Methodist Minister, was the first Mason Chaplain in Tennessee and served as a delegate in writing the constitution of Tennessee.

Some of the surviving descendants of Jesse Hoskins (Hauskins) Sr. have been meeting yearly for a reunion the second weekend of September in Anderson County, Tennessee, since 1937.

(Information obtained from wills, marriage records, death records, deed records and cemetery records of Anderson County, Tennessee, Panola County, Texas, and Gregg County Texas, and from the *Hoskins Family History Book* and family members through the years.)
– Submitted by Lula Marie Brooks Sullivan

MARIA HOUSTON

Maria, known as "The Tamale Lady of Northeast Texas", was born in Chihuahua, Mexico. She met John Houston, a mining engineer who had gone to Mexico to dig his fortune out of the mountains around Chihuahua. Maria, who had few needs, had a great many wants and she wanted John Houston. She swore that Houston would not go back to Texas without her, and so it was. Maria and John had four sons and adopted two more orphan boys who became her world when John returned to Mexico and vowed he would not come back to Texas until he found his fortune. Maria did not mind waiting for her husband because she had her boys. John was killed when terrorists dynamited the train he was riding on.

Maria, left without the support and comfort of a husband, had little money. After it was gone, all she had were her boys. Maria's good life was shattered. She and her boys worked hard together and never complained, but only earned just enough to live in a tarpaper shack, put food in their mouths and a mattress beneath their tired bodies at night.

Maria roamed the streets of Longview alone day after day, selling hot tamales from her humble little cart, refusing all help that anyone offered. Maria seldom smiled as the pain and sadness crushed her. Her boys fought constantly in school because of the snide remarks made about their mother. They had her pride and allowed no one to ridicule their mother. She had nothing to give them but pride, and sometimes they cried when they were alone, because Maria never worried about the faded shirts or patched trousers, but it hurt her to see their black eyes and split lips. Maria prayed daily that her boys would be with her forever.

World War I raged across Europe. Maria was bitter, sad and yet proud because the Army led her boys away from Longview and on to foreign soil. All six volunteered, the youngest lying about his age in order to serve. He even went AWOL from his unit to find his brothers and fight alongside them.

She waited patiently for the fighting to end and the happy return of her boys as she peddled her hot tamales in the oil fields and army camps that stretched from Texas to Arkansas, telling anyone who would listen about her boys. Maria knew when they returned she would be happy again.

The war came to an end and Maria waited for her boys in uniform, but only one man in uniform came. After he informed her that all her sons had been killed in action, the stranger reported that he would help her fill out the forms for the $10,000 insurance policies. In reply, Maria told him she had not sold her sons to the government, that the government could not buy them as it bought guns and ammunition and beef to eat. She turned from the man and walked slowly away. (Source: Calab Pirtle III, "Back Roads of Texas," *Dallas Times Herald*, Sunday, 29 May 1983.)

J.C. & BELLE HOWARD: True Longview Pioneers

Jackson Conner Howard was born in 1847, the year his parents, Abner Perry Howard and Elizabeth Caroline Conner moved to Texas from Taledega, Alabama, and bought 640 acres north of Hallsville. Entering the Confederate Army, Company A, 3rd Texas Regiment at age 15, J.C. served as both drummer boy and courier.

In 1870, he purchased farmlands and married Laura Buie with whom he had eight children. In 1891, the widower married Mary Belle Fowler and fathered four more children. Their homestead was on E. Tyler and First Street. Carnivals and tent shows that came to Longview would set up on the Howard property in the old corn patch. Across the street was the Opera House where famous Shakespearean actor, E.H. Southern once played, but the Howard children were much more taken with another act, "Amy the Fire-eater".

Mr. Howard served as the first mayor of Longview, county sheriff for 14 years, and city marshal for 4 years. It was during his term as sheriff that the infamous Dalton Gang robbed the pioneer town's only bank. He and his posse captured gang member Jim Nite in Oklahoma Territory. Mr. Howard later resigned to enter the cotton business and was proprietor of Howard Dry Goods.

Belle Howard cooked meals for her husband's prisoners, often saloon rowdies. After his death, she sewed for the public and made shrouds for the dead. As there was no public library, she began one in her home and was a founder of the First Methodist Missionary Society. She had graduated from Alexander Institute in Kilgore (later to become Lon Morris College) and after receiving her teaching certificate, taught English there. Mrs. Howard descended from Littleton Fowler (1803-1846), a circuit rider preacher who established the first Protestant church in Texas the year the state won independence from Mexico.

Two of their daughters remained in Longview, Vanita (Guild) and Gladys (Harlow). Vanita graduated as valedictorian from the first high school in Longview, in a class of 13. She

J.C. and Belle Howard

was an avid antique collector and active in the First Methodist Church. During the 1930s, Gladys worked as a proofreader in the Gregg County Clerk's office at night. When the oil boom brought hundreds of roustabouts with no place to sleep, they lined the courthouse halls. For protection, Gladys carried a pistol as she stepped over the bodies on her way home. She later married A.E. Clapp, an accountant for numerous oil barons and active in Rotary, First Methodist Church and a past President of Pinecrest Country Club. He had two daughters: Charlotte (Halbert) and Natalie (Graves). Gladys was active in the D.A.R, Shakespeare Club, and First Methodist Church. Her daughter, Mary Vanita Harlow (Avery) taught elementary music for L.I.S.D. for 30 years and remains active in the music ministry at First Baptist Church in the hometown of her forefathers.

– Submitted by Mary Vanita Avery

The following is a colorful account of the Dalton Gang bank robbery imbedded within an obituary:

Daily Leader
Monday, October 2, 1922

Pioneer Texan and First Mayor of Longview Dies. Jackson Connor Howard Was Sheriff When the Dalton Gang Robbed Local Bank.

An echo of the greatest day in the history of Longview and all Gregg County, a day when Longview fought the battle of the East Texas Alamo, was heard here early this morning upon the death of J.C. Howard, 74 years old, one of the pioneer Texans, first mayor of Longview, for fifty years a resident of Longview and Gregg county, for fourteen years sheriff of this county and for four years city marshal, holding that office until he resigned to enter the cotton business. He was one of the best known characters of Texas today.

Mr. Howard died at the family home at 213 E. Tyler Avenue early this morning... Funeral services were held this afternoon at the Christian Church.

Interment was made in Greenwood cemetery with Masonic honors. A procession half a mile long followed the silver-bound casket to the cemetery to pay a final tribute to this pioneer Texan. The city hall and other public buildings were closed part of the day.

During his fourteen years as sheriff, Mr. Howard took part in many posse hunts for criminals and was instrumental in finally breaking up the notorious Dalton gang of bank robbers. It was during his term as sheriff that Bill Dalton and three others of his gang, Jim Bennett, Jim Nite and Bill Nite, robbed the First National Bank here in May 1894. It was a day in which Texas history was made. It was the Alamo of East Texas and his legend has been handed down from father to son, and told at many a hearth side, of how Longview citizens rose to the defense of the bank and fought a battle in which hot lead flew like a hurricane.

Jim Bennett was killed in the shooting which occurred in the alley behind the bank, and three Longview citizens were wounded. Sheriff Howard was at the courthouse when the first shot was fired; he started for the scene of the fighting. When the robbers had been driven off, Bennett's body was strung to a telephone pole cross bar near the Texas & Pacific station.

Mr. Howard was born in Harrison County, near Cypress, 74 years ago. He was the son a Major Abner Howard of the Confederate Army. He married Miss Laura Buie in 1868 and moved to Gregg County fifty years ago. Upon the death of Mrs. Howard many years later, Mr. Howard married a Miss Fowler who survives him.

HUDGINS

Four generations of Hudgins lived, worked, matriculated and procreated in Gregg County, Texas, over a span of three centuries. Beginning in the early 1870s and continuing into the early 21st century, the Hudgins family presence has been evident in this second smallest county in the State of Texas. If one resided in the newly incorporated City of Longview during the mid-1870s, you would have been a friend, neighbor or business acquaintance of John Wilson Hudgins and his family.

John Wilson moved to East Texas from Tuscalossa County, Alabama, where he was born on 3 October 1848. His parents, Leonidas Green Hudgins and Lucretia Whitfield Hudgins, relocated to Alabama in 1846 from their birthplace in Person County, North Carolina. John Wilson married Jane Elizabeth Cook on 30 December 1875, in Henderson, Rusk County, Texas. The Hudgins family Bible records this marriage and the fact that Jane Elizabeth, born on 1 May 1852, moved from Medon, Tennessee, to East Texas in December 1872. The six children from this marriage were all born in Longview, Texas. These children, in order of birth were Lillian Lucretia, 24 October 1877, Richard Elice, 24 December 1879, John Wilson, Jr., 13 March 1882, Ada Elizabeth, 5 July 1884, Archie Lea, 14, 1887, and Maggie Bertice, 7 July 1892. Three of these offspring continued to reside in Longview into adulthood: Richard Elice, John Wilson, Jr. and Maggie Bertice (also known as Birdie). Of these three, only Richard Elice was married and had children who lived in Longview for most of their adult lives.

John Wilson, Sr. was a farmer who owned and tilled the soil on several hundred acres of land between Cotton and Young streets in the eastern

portion of Gregg County. Birth certificates of John Wilson's children also list his occupation as "tinner." This implies that he worked in tin and perhaps installed the roofs on some of the early homes in Longview. The United States Census of 1880 records that his mother, Lucretia, and Tennessee relatives of his wife, Jane Elizabeth, resided in their Longview household during that time. He died on 31 October 1900, and is interred in Gum Springs Cemetery east of Longview with his wife, who died on 17 June 1929.

The elder son, Richard Elice, married Carra Bonnie Barton, daughter of Robert Barton and Julia Ann Tutt. Carra was born on 24 October 1884, in Kilgore, Gregg County, Texas. Elice was a fireman on the Texas Pacific Railway in the days that wood and coal were the fuel that fired the boilers of the steam locomotives. His last run, before an accident forced his retirement, was from Texarkana to Fort Worth. A natural gas explosion in the Fort Worth hotel where he was staying over night in 1933 resulted in severe lung damage and, ultimately, his death on 26 October 1935. Elice and his wife Carra, who died on 19 March 1972, are buried in Gum Springs Cemetery.

Elice and Carra had three sons and a daughter, but only the two oldest sons, Archie and Earl, continued to reside in Longview. Archie Lee Hudgins was a fireman with the Longview Fire Department for many years. He had one son who was killed in an accident in the early 1950s. Archie is buried in Gum Springs Cemetery.

Richard Earl Hudgins, born 1 October 1909, was employed in retail and wholesale businesses in Longview until he joined the Railway Express Agency, later REA Express, in 1942. Earl married Geraldine (Gerry) Geneva Mobley in Longview on 4 June 1938. They had a son, Richard Elton Hudgins, and twin daughters, Judy Nan Hudgins and Julia Ann Hudgins. Earl died on 16 February 1985, and is buried in Gum Springs Cemetery. Gerry Hudgins and her daughters, Judy Lamb and Julia Landis, currently reside in Longview.

Richard Elton Hudgins, born in Longview on 9 October 1939, graduated from Longview High School in 1957. He received his bachelor degree from Texas A&M University in 1961, and was commissioned a Second Lieutenant in the United States Air Force (USAF). Richard married Octavia LeNeille Flemister on 1 July 1961, at the First Baptist Church in Longview. They have two daughters, Rebecca Elizabeth and Rachel Elise, who reside in Washington and Oregon, respectively. Richard retired as a Colonel from the USAF in 1983, and was subsequently employed by the Boeing Company in Seattle, Washington. After many years of living and traveling throughout the world, he retired in 2001, and now resides with his wife, LeNeille, in SaddleBrooke, north of Tucson, Arizona.

– Submitted by Richard Hudgins

HUGHEY

A.A. Hughey, Jr. was born 15 April 1930, to A.A. and Floria Estelle Ward Hughey in Emory, Texas. Junior was raised in Emory by Floria because she and A.A. divorced in 1932.

*John Wilson Hudgins and
Jane Elizabeth Cook*

At the age of 18, Junior joined the Army and received his discharge in April 1952. In June, he dove into a swimming pool, broke his neck and lived three days. A.A. had an auto accident on the way to the funeral and never got to attend the services. Junior was buried in Dallas.

The eldest of A.A.'s second family, Thomas Buford, born 31 October 1935 to A.A. and Callie Draper Hughey, had a learning disability caused by an accident at the age of 22 months that forced him to leave school after the eighth grade. Buford lived in Elkhart with A.A. when he died 28 August 1982, struck by a hit and run drunk driver. He's buried at Old Pilgrim's Cemetery in Elkhart.

After graduating from Leverett's Chapel in 1957, John Stacey, born 8 August 1937, enlisted in the Navy and married Wanda Owens. Their children were Steven, Scott and Kelly. They raised their children in Elkhart, Texas, where Stacey worked for Shell Oil Company. Stacey died 18 April 1976, and is buried at Old Pilgrim's Cemetery in Elkhart, next to Callie and Buford. Stacey has five grandchildren.

Roy Gerald, born 1940, graduated in 1959 and moved to Page, Arizona, to work on the Glen Canyon Dam with A.A. He married Charlotte Norris and they had one daughter, Ella Christine. Roy later married Loretta Wickman and had Selina, Stacy, Carla and Dena. Roy later married Ila Burkett Gardner of Longview, who died in 1981. Roy has eight grandchildren and two great grandsons. Roy works for RSI in Kilgore.

Linda Janelle, born 1946, graduated Leverett's Chapel in 1964, moved to Phoenix and married Ron Steinmetz; they had Callie Ann in 1965 and Ronald, Jr. in 1967. After returning to Longview, Linda married Jerry Laminack in May 1977, and had daughter Stacy. Linda works at the Longview Public Library in the Genealogy Department and is currently serving her second consecutive term as President of the Gregg County Genealogy Society. She is also Secretary for the Leverett's Chapel Exes Association. She has ten grandchildren.

After high school, Phillip Jerome, born 25 September1947, joined the Army and served his tour of Vietnam from 1967 to 1968; he returned to Longview and married Janice Davis. His second wife was Tricia Halliday of Elkhart, Texas, who died as a result of a motorcycle accident which afflicted Phillip with an aneurism that resulted in his death 20 July 1982. Phillip is buried at Woosley. There were no children from either marriage.

Sherry, born 1950, married Robert Wortham of Slocum, Texas; they had Katrina and Stephanie. Both Sherry and Bob became teachers, and Sherry later got her Master of Library Science Degree. Bob and Sherry have worked together in the Palestine, Grapeland and Slocum school districts their entire careers. Active in their church, they were Youth Ministers for several years. They have four grandchildren.

– Submitted by Sherry Hughey Wortham

A.A. HUGHEY

Aurbon Acey Hughey was born 5 May 1901, to Thomas Ace and Nancy Addie Fry Hughey in Point, Texas, the second of four sons: Earl, A.A., Herschel and Jesse. Ace's grandparents, Thomas Madison and Mary Jane Darnell Hughey of Georgia, came first to Garden Valley in Smith County in 1866, moved to Providence in 1873, and finally settled in Point. Mary Jane's grandmother was a full-blood Cherokee named Lucinda "Luskie" Acorn.

In 1931, A.A. married Floria Estelle Wade who bore a son named A.A., Jr. The marriage was a short one. Four months after his 22nd birthday and army discharge, on a warm day in June 1952, Junior broke his neck swimming.

On February 3, 1933, A.A. Hughey married Callie Draper, daughter of Marion LeRoy and Callie Spence Draper, in Emory, Texas. In 1939, A.A. joined the IBEW as a journeyman electrician. Thomas Buford, John Stacey and Roy Gerald were born while living in the Emory and Point area. When the war broke out in 1941, A.A. moved his family to Orange County, Texas, to work in the shipyards and, towards the end of the war, to Oakland, California, where both he and Callie worked as electricians in the shipyards. When the war ended, the family moved to Kilgore. A.A. went to work for the telephone company and, later, L.E. Meyers. Linda, Phillip and Sherry were born while living in the Kilgore area.

Union jobs were scarce in East Texas, so A.A. went wherever the union sent him. Callie raised her six children almost single-handedly. One year, during a bitterly cold winter, all six children were sick, A.A. was still looking for work and they were almost out of propane. The delivery man left the tank full, saying he would settle up when Hughey came home.

After 25 years, Callie and A.A. divorced. In 1963, while living in Phoenix, Arizona, A.A. married Lily June Caddell. Lily was born on the reservation in Ida Belle, Oklahoma, her great grandfather being Black Jack, the Renegade, and one of the last few Choctaw to be captured for the "Trail of Tears." In 1974, A.A. retired from the IBEW and bought property in Elkhart, close

A.A. Hughey family. (l.-r.) Back: Roy, Thomas Buford and John Stacy. Middle: Phillip Jerome and Linda. Front: Sherry Jean. Taken July 1965, Phoenix, Arizona.

to Stacey and Sherry, who lived in Slocum. Callie died 7 March 1976; Stacey died 18 April 1976; Phillip died 20 July 1982. A.A. bought eight acres from his daughter-in-law, Wanda, and farmed peaches so that Buford would have money after he died; but, Buford died 28 August 1982. Aurbon died of cancer 22 August 1983, and was buried at Woosley, a.k.a. Hughey Family Cemetery. Lily moved to Mountain Home, Idaho, to be near her sister, where she died in December 1997.

Both of Aurbon's grandfathers, Thomas Madison Hughey and James M. Darnell, were wounded serving the Confederacy and survived Appomatox. Ancestors who fought in the Revolutionary War are Dean, Hornbuckle, Cole, Hughey, Fry, Darnell, Noland, Hogg, Armour and Shook.

– Submitted by Linda Hughey Laminack

CALLIE DRAPER HUGHEY

Callie Draper was born 29 March 1915, in Paducah, Texas, to Marion LeRoy and Callie Spence Draper. Callie was premature and weighed only 3-1/2 pounds at birth. Callie Spence Draper, a six-foot tall schoolteacher, died on April 4th of kidney poisoning. Returning to Emory, Roy took his newborn daughter back to Emory, and took the job as jailer for Rains County, and the jail became home for Callie. When Roy moved to Corsicana to work, Callie remained with her grandmother, Annie Edmondson Draper Jennings, and step-grandfather, Andrew Burton Jennings, until 3 February 1933, when Callie married Aurbon Acey Hughey of Point, Texas.

Roy's second marriage to Olive produced M.L. "Billy," Doris Janel, Mamie Ruth and Jack. Billy married in Corsicana and became a fireman for the city. Doris married a man named Harachuck and remained in the Beaumont area; Mamie Ruth married a Wilson and settled in New Mexico. Jack married Goldie and settled the San Francisco Bay area, serving in the Merchant Marines during World War II.

Callie attended Rains School and graduated in 1932. Mama was 5'11" and played center for the basketball team. Until her teens, she wore her hair past her waist until it was discovered that the weight of the hair was the cause for her headaches.

Callie crocheted masterpieces. She once spent a year making a pansy-patterned bedspread so that an organization could raffle it for $200 dollars. The second she made is in possession of her daughter Sherry. Callie's creative abilities have passed to her daughters and grandchildren. They crochet, sew, tat, quilt and participate in different forms of arts and crafts. Callie was an exceptional seamstress. When she died 7 March 1976, she was working as a seamstress for the famed Hurwitz Man's Shop in downtown Longview.

Callie was known among CB-ers, as "East Texas Granny" and could "rachet-jaw" with the best. She spent many Saturdays and Sundays at gatherings all over East Texas.

Callie's great great great great grand-mother was Ann Holder Henson of Maryland, a full-blood Cherokee who lived to be over 102. She was a member of the "Jacobite" Indians because of their conversion to Christianity in North Carolina. Callie's grandfather, George C. Spence, served as Sheriff of Rains County from 1902 to 1903, and family rumor says he was a Texas Ranger. Her Uncle John Henry Spence spent his life in law enforcement and was a Texas Ranger. Both John and his brother Frank retired from the railroad as Special Agents. Roy Draper was jailer for Rains County many years and later retired from law enforcement in Beaumont.

Callie's grandfather, Timothy A. Draper, served as a Deputy Marshall in 1870 and 1880 in Scott County, Missouri, enumerating the census. Taking the 1890 census in Poplar Bluff, Missouri, he was shot and killed. Callie's Revolutionary War ancestors are Draper, Spence, Motley and Killett. Her great great great great grandfather, William H. Henson, was not only Benjamin Cleveland's aide-de-camp, but a good friend. At the end of the war, they settled together as neighbors.

– Submitted by Roy G. Hughey

WILLIS HINTON & WILLIAM H. HUGHEY

Willis Hinton and William H. Hughey were sons of Joseph P. Hughey, born 1793 in Oglethorpe County, Georgia, and Nancy Ligon, born 1798, daughter of Willis and Nancy Gaddy Ligon of Virginia.

In 1829, Joseph Hughey, returning from visiting relatives in Wilkinson County, Mississippi, contracted pneumonia and made it as far as Jasper County, where he died.

Nancy remained a widow until 1838, when she married Henry Baxter, born 18 May 1808, died 5 September 1896, in Kilgore.

Henry moved his family to Chambers County, Alabama, where Willis met Nancy Ann Atkins, born 26 January 1828, in Upson County, Georgia. He married Nancy 27 February 1845. She died on 16 August 1905. Willis died on 28 October 1873. Both are buried at Mt. Moriah Cemetery.

By 1851, Henry Baxter and Willis settled in a portion of Rusk that became Gregg. The settlement became known as Hughey Community. Located at Highway 42 and FM 1252, six miles southwest of Longview, the community grew in the 1930s during the oil boom. At one time, Hughey had a school, a Baptist church and several little stores. By the early 1990s, only a few scattered buildings remained. Gregg Home for the Aged now occupies the Hughey school.

Willis and Nancy had the following children: William W. Hughey, born April 1844, in Alabama, married 20 January 1880, to Mrs. Sarah. E. Gober, lived in Rusk County with daughter, Jimmie, born 1884; Josephus Brock, born 1846, married Sallie P. Barber in December 1869; Colista Ann, born 21 November 1851, died 5 February 1908, married Robert A. Curtis who died 20 January 1898 – both are buried at Mt. Moriah; Josephine, born 1854, was the first

born in Texas; Charles W. Hughey was born 15 January 1857, died 10 December 1899; James C. Hughey was born 21 February 1859, died 9 March 1881; Edna Ann Hughey, born 8 February 1861, and died 29 June 1903, married 12 December 1879, to James Brack Nicholson, born 11 December 1857, died 24 October 1923 (Edna and James' children were Daisy Bell Nicholson, married James S. Ward, and Norma Nicholson, married Asa Lanier.) – Edna and James are buried at Mt. Moriah; Thomas Hughey, born 1865, married 27 December 1884, to Bunnie Friddell and moved to Tyler – their children were Lawrence, Blanche and Curtis; John F. was born February 1869, married Mary Jane McFarland – their children were Achsah, Mary B., John W. and William R.

In 1900, Nancy, age 72, was living in Longview with John. After Willis died, Nancy and the remaining children, Charley, James, Tom and John, moved in with William, his wife Sallie E. and their children, Horace, Anna and Effa (1880 census, Precinct 4 of Gregg County), Joe B. and Sallie (Precinct 6) with Haywood, Annie Belle, Meshac and Sallie.

William H. Hughey was born 1821 in Morgan County, Georgia, and died in 1877 and is buried at Mt Moriah. His widow married 7 July 1877, to Walton H. Payne, Sr.

– Submitted by Selena Hughey

LARRY WAYNE HUNT

It was a bitterly cold December 1927 when Charles Logan Hunt and his family, consisting of his wife Syntha Evalene Cowan and seven children, made the last segment into Texas of the family migration that had begun in Virginia 120 years before. This migration route had taken the Hunt family through Kentucky, Missouri, Arkansas and Oklahoma. The destination of this last leg was the Lower Rio Grande Valley in extreme south Texas. Their first winter in Texas was spent in Raymondville planting onion sets by hand. That was the first farming experience in Texas for Larry's father, Clifford T. Hunt. Clifford was the middle child and had siblings Gordon N., Sedley M., Mabel A., Albert L., Gerald G. and Hugh J. All of the children were born near Spiro, Indian Territory, which later became Oklahoma in 1907.

Charles Logan was born in Taney County, Missouri, on 3 February 1867, and he was married in Spiro on 10 June 1902, to Syntha, born in Lawrence County, Missouri, on 1 January 1880. Occupations in the Spiro area were primarily agricultural, for family consumption and as income. The U.S. census of 1910 for Le Flore County, Oklahoma, lists the occupation for Charles Logan as farmer. This would be the early occupations entered into by all six of his boys.

Charles Logan was the oldest of seven; the others were Thomas M., Mary L., Mordilla, Lydia M., Susan F. and Noah J. Their father, William Jefferson, was born in Kentucky in 1839, and married to Susan J., who was born in Missouri in 1842. William J. and Susan J. were married in Missouri about 1866.

Charles Logan Hunt family. (l.-r.) Back: Sedley M., Charles Logan and Clifford T. Front: Albert L., Gerald G., Mabel A., Hugh J. and Syntha Evalene (Cowan).

William J. was the second child born to Thomas, who was born in Kentucky in 1815, and Mary "Polly," who was also born in Kentucky, in 1819. Their other children were Cynthia, John A., Nancy, Mary A., Lydia M. and James. All were born in Missouri except Cynthia and William J., who were born in Kentucky. Between 1850 and 1860, Thomas was again married, this time to Harriet Moss, and they later had four children: Monroe, George P., Ida B. and Burr H., all born in Missouri. The Homestead Final Certificate Number 5174, dated 7 February 1887, stated that on 18 October 1881, Thomas and Harriet settled on a homestead in Benton County, Arkansas, in the Bright Water Township, and had made payment in full.

The earliest of Larry's lineage to enter Texas was Garrett E. Boom, born July 1809 in Curaçao, West Indies. Because the ship he was on in the summer of 1832 wrecked at Paso Caballo near present day Port O'Connor, he entered what would later become the Republic of Texas. Garrett married Nancy Fletcher of Virginia. Their daughter, Mary Virginia, married John Bishop Newton of Fayette County, Texas, in 1859 at La Grange, Texas. Their son, Charles Wright, married Emma Eliza Dean in 1895 in Georgetown, Texas. Through this lineage Larry has proudly gained membership in The Sons of The Republic of Texas.

– Submitted by Larry Wayne Hunt, Gregg County Genealogy Society member

JAMES HARRISON HURST

James (Jim) Harrison Hurst was born in Longview on 17 November 1945, to Julian Garland (born 10 May 1925) and Jane Jo Medley Hurst (born 5 December 1923). (Both J.G. and Jane Jo were born in Longview – see "Julian Harrison Hurst" and "John Long Smith.") Jim married on 3 May 1969, Linda Sue Ray, also born in Longview on 21 October 1946, daughter of Helen Blount and L.C. Ray. L.C. died in 1987 and is buried at Lakeview Cemetery. Helen Ray continues to reside in Longview at Eden Place Apartments. Helen worked for both Dickinson/ Harrison and Northcutt Insurance Agencies and L.C. worked for the T&P Railroad.

Jim and his father, J.G., and grandfather, Julian Hurst, – three generations – all attended

James G., Jay H. and John R. Hurst

Mrs. Denton's School in kindergarten and first grade, and all attended Longview High School. And all three have been owner/dealers of Pegues-Hurst Ford Motor Company. (See "Pegues-Hurst Ford.") Julian began at age fifteen working for J.G. Pegues, and later bought into the company in 1945. He continued operating the company till his death in 1969, and then J.G. took over until he passed away in 1978, when Jim began managing the firm. Both J.G. and Jim have been accomplished pilots. J.G. was a flight instructor during World War II and continued flying as a civilian. Jim has over 6,000 hours, and both he and his dad have graciously flown many people for medical, funeral and other needs.

Jim's mother, Jane Jo, was well loved for her many charitable deeds. She was active in the American Cancer Society, Camp Fire Girls and the First Christian Church, where she taught Sunday School. She was the first Bargain Box Chairman of the Junior Service League. Jane Jo Hurst died 27 April 1969, and J.G. Hurst died 7 May 1978; both are buried at Grace Hill Cemetery.

Jim is a graduate of Texas Christian University and South Texas School of Law and Linda (Tweet) is a North Texas State University graduate. Both graduated from Longview High School, as did all three sons. Their youngest son, Jay Harrison Hurst, born 22 August 1979, was quarterback for the Lobos when the team almost won the 5A State Championship in 1997. Both Jay, who graduated in Psychology with a minor in business from Texas Christian University, and James Garland, born 21 November 1974, graduate of the University of Texas with a degree in Chemical Engineering and University of Houston School of Law, reside in Houston and they are continuing the family tradition of flying. John Russell, born 2 February 1977, who attended University of Texas, is now in Portland, Oregon, in the concrete business.

Jim and Tweet live in Huntington Park. Tweet collects antiques and enjoys painting. Jim enjoys flying and running and has won several medals in swimming.

– Submitted by James Harrison Hurst

JOHN HENRY HURST

John Henry Hurst was born in Niota County, Tennessee, on 14 September 1869, and came to Texas as a young man. He married Lena Walker, also born in Tennessee on 30 August 1872, on 24 February 1888, in Bonham, Texas. (The story told by Lena was that she was only 15 when they eloped by crossing the Red River into Oklahoma, which was then Indian territory, to get married. They spent the night with a farming couple and Lena slept with the farmer's wife, who kept her awake trying to talk her out of marrying. Her parents made them remarry with a real preacher when they arrived home.) J.H. and Lena Hurst moved to Longview the same year. All of their children were born here. J.H. began work as a station agent for the T&P Railroad. He later was vice president of the First National Bank and served on the school board. The family attended the First Christian Church where J.H. was a member of the church orchestra. J.H. Hurst died in 1943 and Lena Walker Hurst on 5 August 1962. They are buried at Grace Hill Cemetery, Longview, Texas

Mr. and Mrs. J.H. Hurst

The children of John Henry and Lena Hurst are Henry Eugene Hurst, born 14 December 1888; Edith Isabella Hurst, born 21 February 1892, and died 1972; John Russell Hurst, born 27 November 1893, and died 1968; Lewis Charles Hurst, born 4 January 1896; Julian Harrison Hurst, born 13 June 1901, died 26 September 1969, and married 18 July 1922, to Grace Smith, born 19 August 1903, and died 26 September 1969. (See "John Long Smith" and "Julian Harrison Hurst.")

The children of Julian Harrison and Grace Smith Hurst were Julian Garland Hurst and Clara Maude Hurst. Julian Garland Hurst, born 10 May 1925, and died 7 May 1978, married 5 December 1944, to Jane Jo Medley, born 5 December 1923, and died 26 April 1969. (See "Julian Harrison Hurst" and "James Harrison Hurst.")

The children of Julian Garland Hurst and Jane Jo Medley are James Harrison Hurst and Grace Anne Hurst. James Harrison was born 17 November 1945, and married 3 May 1969, to Linda Ray. Their children are James Garland Hurst, born 22 November 1974, John Russell Hurst, born 2 February 1976, and Jay Harrison Hurst, born 23 August 1979.

Grace Anne Hurst was born 2 March 1949, and married John Clyde Crank, born 19 October 1949. Their children are John Clyde Crank, II, born 26 August 1983, and Medley Jane Crank, born 24 April 1986.

Clara Maude Hurst, born 5 January 1932, married 2 February 1951, to William Burke Patterson, born 19 October 1931, and died 10 December 1970. (See "Julian Harrison Hurst" and "William Brant Payne.") The children of Clara and William Patterson are Grace Hurst Patterson, Julianne Patterson and William Burke Patterson, Jr.

Grace Hurst Patterson, born 30 October 1955, married 15 May 1982, to Dennis Wayne LaMaster, born 14 May 1958. Grace and Dennis have seven children and live in Longview: Laura Grace LaMaster, born 7 May 1983; Julie Katherine LaMaster, born 26 January 1987; Leslie Claire LaMaster, born 23 October 1988; Grace Elisabeth LaMaster, born 29 May 1991; John Clark LaMaster, born 18 December 1994; Jane Anne LaMaster, born 13 April 1997; and, Scott William LaMaster, born 27 December 2000.

Julianne Patterson, born 3 May 1958, married Pat Crabtree, born 2 February 1970; and married, second, Frank Setzer in June 1990. Julianne and Pat have three children: John William Crabtree, born 8 December 1981; Clara Elizabeth Crabtree, born 23 February 1983; and Evelyn Anne Crabtree, born 16 June 1984. All reside in Paris, Texas.

William Burke Patterson, Jr., born 25 December 1968, married Laura Gayle Harvey on 22 November 1992. The Patterson's reside in Baton Rouge, Louisiana, and have two children: Mary-Margaret Patterson, born 20 March 1995, and William Payne Patterson, born 29 October 1998.

– Submitted by Grace LeMaster

JULIAN HARRISON HURST

Julian Harrison Hurst was born in Longview on 13 June 1901, and married on 18 July 1923, to Grace Smith, born 19 August 1903, in Crockett, Texas, and moved to Longview at age 10. (See "John Long Smith" and "John Henry Hurst.") They died on 26 September 1969, and are buried at Grace Hill Cemetery, Longview, Texas. The children of Julian and Grace Smith Hurst are Julian Garland Hurst and Clara Maude Hurst.

Julian Garland Hurst was born 10 May 1925, and died 7 May 1978. He married on 5 December 1944, to Jane Jo Medley, born 5 December 1923, and died 26 April 1969. (See "James Harrison Hurst.")

Julian Harrison Hurst

Grace Smith Hurst

The children of Julian Garland and Jane Jo Medley Hurst are James Harrison Hurst and Grace Anne Hurst.

James Harrison Hurst was born 17 November 1945, and married 3 May 1969, to Linda Ray, born 21 October 1946. (See "James Harrison Hurst.") Their children are James Garland Hurst (22 November 1974), John Russell Hurst (22 February 1977) and Jay Harrison Hurst (22 August 1979).

Grace Anne Hurst was born 2 March 1949. She married on 10 May 1980, to John Clyde Crank (19 October 1949). Grace Anne and John Clyde Crank's children are John Clyde Crank, II (26 August 1983) and Medley Jane Crank (24 April 1986).

Clara Maude Hurst (5 January 1932) married 21 February 1951, to William Burke Patterson (19 October 1931) and died 10 December 1970. Bill Patterson and Clara Hurst were childhood sweethearts and attended Mrs. Denton's Private School together in kindergarten. Bill Patterson served as a Sergeant in the army at Ft. Hood, Texas. After return to Longview, he began work as a life insurance salesman with the Equitable Life Association, where he continued until his death in 1970 at age 39. He died of a heart attack while jogging in Long Park. A section has been named for him from Eden Drive to LeDuke – William B. Patterson Park. He was active in many civic affairs including the American Cancer Society and the Rotary Club and the Vestry of Trinity Episcopal Church. He is buried in Grace Hill Cemetery, Longview, Texas. Clara Hurst Patterson married second on 2 December 1972, to William Brant Payne. (See "William Brant Payne.")

The children of Clara Maude Hurst and William B. Patterson are Grace Hurst Patterson, Julianne Patterson and William Burke Patterson, Jr.

Grace Hurst Patterson (30 October 1955) married on 15 May 1980, to Dennis LaMaster (14 May 1958). They reside in Longview. Dennis is partner/manager of DLS Environmental, a hazardous waste company. They attend Longview Christian Fellowship and have seven children: Laura Grace LaMaster (7 May 1983); Julie Katherine LaMaster (16 January 1987); Leslie Claire LaMaster (23 October 1984); Grace Elisabeth LaMaster (29 May 1991); John

Clark LaMaster (18 December 1994); Jane Anne LaMaster (13 April 1997); and Scott William LaMaster (27 December 2000).

Julianne Patterson (3 May 1958) married Pat Crabtree on 2 February 1979; and married Frank Setzer in June 1990. Julianne and Pat had three children: John William Crabtree (8 December 1981); Clara Elizabeth Crabtree (23 February 1983); and Evelyn Anne Crabtree (16 June 1984). All reside in Paris, Texas. Julianne works for the Department of Human Resources and Frank for Farm Bureau as an appraiser.

William Burke Patterson, Jr. (25 December 1968) married on 22 November 1992, to Laura Gayle Harvey (26 February 1969). Burke is a Regional Vice President for American Funds. Laura was born in Wichita Falls, Texas, and is the daughter of Gayle Johnston Harvey and granddaughter of Helen and E.C. Johnston of Longview. The Pattersons reside in Baton Rouge, Louisiana, and have two children: Mary-Margaret Patterson (20 March 1995) and William Payne Patterson (29 October 1998).

– Submitted by Clara Payne

EARNEST & JESSIE BAKER HUSBAND

Earnest and Jessie Estelle Baker Husband were married in Lovelady, Texas, on 6 September 1928. Earnest Husband was born 20 February 1907, in Call, Newton County, Texas. He was the fourth child of Eligah Franklin and Ida Luticia Taylor Husband. Jessie Baker was born 4 November 1910, in Groveton, Texas, the first child of Nathaniel Beauregard and Polly Elizabeth Alfred Baker.

Earnest worked as a carpenter for Gulf Oil Company in Southeast Texas. He built houses in the oil field camps. This job kept him moving quite often before he brought his family to Gregg County. Earnest and Jessie's eldest child, Earnest Jr., was born 24 July 1929, in Trinity, Texas. Earnest Jr. married Suzanne Rigby in Odessa, Texas. Earnest and Sue have three children. Ida Louise was born 6 May 1932, in Call, Jasper County, Texas. Ida Louise married Dewey Jones in Las Vegas, Nevada. Ida and Dewey have three children. James Obed, 16 February 1935, and David, 25 January 1937, were born in Hull, Liberty County, Texas. James married Mavilene Redding in Longview, Texas. They have one daughter. David married Lillian Edith

Jessie and Earnest Husband

Garrison in Longview. They have two children. Polly Anne was born 8 December 1938, in Bloomington, Victoria County, Texas. Polly married Donald Woods in Dallas, Texas. She and Donald have two children.

By 1940, the family was living in Gladewater, Gregg County, Texas, where Wanda Joyce was born on 28 February 1941. Wanda Joyce married Wally Bluhm in Longview. They have two children; Paula and Paul (twins) were born 20 August 1944. Paul Larue died 17 November 1945, and is buried in White Oak Cemetery. Paula married David Cobb in Ingleside, Texas. They had one son. Matilda Omega was born on 7 October 1946. Matilda married Robert Washburn. They had one son. She later married Danny Brown in Midland, Texas. They now live in Houston.

When Earnest came to Gregg County, he went to work for Atlantic Richfield Oil Company working in the field "flowing" oil. He also did carpenter work to help feed and clothe his family. He and Jesse lived in Gladewater, and then White Oak until 1960, when Earnest was transferred to Ingleside, Texas. Earnest retired in 1971, and he and Jessie moved back to White Oak in 1980. Jessie died on 25 September 1988, and Earnest died 12 January 1992. They are buried in Lakeview Memorial Gardens in Gregg County.

Jessie came from a long line of Congregational Methodist ministers, and they attended Methodist and then Assembly of God churches. After they moved to Gladewater they were members of several Assembly of God churches, including a long time membership in the Southside Assembly of God Church in Longview. The church was located on Birdsong Street. Earnest and Jessie were both active members of their church.

– Submitted by David Husband

ABNER CLARK & MARTHA CAROLINE (JOHNSEY) INGRAM

Abner Clark Ingram was born 5 December 1836, in Georgia. He married Martha Caroline Johnsey, daughter of John Johnsey and Nancy Pardue, 25 December 1858, in Shelby County, Alabama. Martha was born 26 March 1840, in South Carolina, probably Chester District. Abner was a farmer.

Abner and Martha produced eleven Ingram children while residing in Spring Creek, Shelby County, Alabama. John Wright (1860-1923) married Isabella Jane Alexander (1859-1930), daughter of William M. and Catherine (Ferguson) Alexander. Isabella was a sister of James Henry Alexander (1851-1933). Clark Terrell (1861-1937) married Susan Jane Wyatt (1864-1922). Stonewall Jackson (1866- 1924) married Elizabeth Caroline Tamson "Carrie" Alexander (1875-1956). Carrie was a first cousin of James Henry Alexander (1851-1933). William Garrett (1868-1946) married Matilda Josephine "Mattie" Hopper, daughter of Gustavis C. and Rachel (Russell) Hopper. Samuel Davis (1870-Unk.) married Edna Edney. Martha Sydney (1872-1946) married Henry Harmon Alexander (1867-1952). Henry was a

Abner Clark Ingram

first cousin of James Henry Alexander (1851-1933). Mary Josephine "Jocie" (1874-1941) married William Daniel Schofield (1872-1902). L.C. Ransome (1876-Unk.) married twice to both unknown. A son (1879-1879) died in infancy. Lydia Elizabeth "'Liddy" (1880-1948) never married. Frank Zollicoffer (1881-1933) married (1) Maggie Freeman (1833-1904); (2) Katherine Elizabeth Alexander (1886- 1908), daughter of James Henry Alexander (1851-1933); (3) Margie M. Tucker (1889-1909); and (4) Allie Crawford (1995-1914).

Abner enlisted as a Private in Company G, 20th Regiment, Alabama Infantry, Confederate States Army on 9 September 1861, and served until the end of the war. He was captured numerous times. His last parole and exchange was 22 September 1864, at Rough and Ready, Georgia. While Abner was at war, John and Clark were kidnapped by Yankee soldiers, but were returned unharmed. All his children born after the Civil War were named for persons with whom he had served.

Martha died 10 June 1888, in Montevallo, Shelby County, Alabama. In 1892, Abner and his daughter, Jocie, called for "'letters of dismissal," from the Spring Creek Cumberland Presbyterian Church. Abner and his younger children removed to Gregg County, Texas, to join his sons, William and Samuel, who had migrated earlier. Martha and husband relocated to Mississippi. John, Clark and Stonewall remained in Alabama, having already started families.

Abner Clark Ingram died 5 January 1898, in Longview. He is buried at Alpine Cemetery.

Four of Abner's children relocated to Texas. William Garrett and Matilda "Mattie" (Hopper) Ingram had six children: Bonnie Rachel (1897-1983) married Robert Pierce Dickard (1885-1962); Aubrey Davis "Dat" (1898-1979) married Eliza Belle "Mam" Davis; Eva Mae (1903-2003) married John Robert "Bob"McGrede; Garland Gustavos (1907-1977) married Annie Dee Smith; Billee Franklin (1912-1981) married (1) Willie Opal Huffman (1915-1986) and (2) Lula Tanner (1920-1979); and Mattie Lee (1916-1982) married Alvie Tuney Wood. Mary Josephine and William Daniel Schofield had three children. Their first born son died in infancy. Mary Ethel (1898-1975) married (1) Otis Edgar Coleman (1916- 1944) and (2) Lonnie Henderson; and Alta Beatrice (1901-1987)

married Windell Clarence Kilpatrick (1899-1979). Lydia Elizabeth "Liddy" never married. Frank Zollicoffer and his descendants will be addressed in a separate article.
– Submitted by George Alton Ingram, Jr. (great grandson of Abner Clark and Martha Ingram)

FRANK ZOLLICOFFER INGRAM

Frank Zollicoffer Ingram was born 7 June 1881, in Spring Creek, Shelby County, Alabama, to Abner Clark and Martha Caroline (Johnsey) Ingram. He migrated to Gregg County in 1892 with his father four years after his mother's death. He married (1) Maggie Freeman, circa 1900. She was born circa 1883 in Gary, Panola County, Texas, and died circa 1904 in Longview, Gregg County, Texas. He married (2) Katherine Elizabeth Alexander, 10 October 1904, in Longview, Gregg County, Texas, daughter of James Henry and Amanda Tinsley (McFarland) Alexander. She was born 17 December 1886, in Harrison County, Texas, and died 19 February 1908, in Spring Hill, Gregg County, Texas. He married (3) Margie M. Tucker, 18 October 1908, in Longview, Gregg County, Texas, daughter of John and Mary (McFarland) Tucker. She was born April 1889, in Upshur County, Texas, and died in 1909 in Gregg County, Texas. He married (4) Allie Crawford 8 March 1914, in Gregg County, Texas, daughter of James and Lorena (Tincher) Crawford. She was born 27 December 1895, in Texas and died 29 December 1985, in Texas. Frank was named for Brigadier General Felix Kirk Zollicoffer, with whom his father, Abner Clark Ingram, had served in the Confederate Army. Frank was known to be short tempered and had the reputation as one of the best fighters in Gregg County.

Frank Zollicoffer Ingram

Marriages with Margie Tucker and Allie Crawford produced no children. Frank and Maggie Freeman had one son, Herman Roy Ingram. Roy was born 14 February 1902, and died 15 November 1945, in Longview. He married Minnie Mae Hopper (1901-1977), niece of Matilda Josephine "Mattie" Hopper (1876-1965), who married Frank's brother, William Garrett Ingram (1868-1946). Roy and Minnie Mae had four children: Audrey Mae (living) married Marvin Ray Edelman; Roy Charles (living) married Mary Katherine Satterwhite; Herman Roy (1926-1926) died at birth; and Billie Frank (living) married Sylvia Parrish.

Frank's marriage to his first cousin, Katherine Elizabeth Alexander, produced two children: Lydia Velma Ingram and George Alton Ingram, Sr. Velma was born 29 April 1905, and died 28 May 1985, in Longview. She married George Ernest McGrede, Sr. (1903-1955). George and Velma (Ingram) McGrede reared three children: Edith Eloise (McGrede) Roark (1926-2004); Georgia Ruth (McGrede) Hester (1928-1993); and George Ernest, Jr. (living). Velma married Thomas Earl Bonner after 1955. George Alton Ingram, Sr. was born 17 February 1908, in Spring Hill. His mother died during childbirth and he was reared by his maternal grandparents, James Henry and Amanda Tinsley (McFarland) Alexander. Alton married Annie Florence Walker, daughter of Alton Edgar "Jack" (1877-1939) and Mary Eula (Watson) (1885-1969) Walker, 29 September 1928, in Pine Tree. Alton and Annie Ingram reared four children: Bettye Jo (Ingram) Hughes (living); Mary Nell (Ingram) Bryant (1934-1996); Wanda Jean (Ingram) Hughes (living); and George Alton Ingram, Jr. (living).

Frank was a farmer and a member of the Cumberland Presbyterian Church. Frank Zollicoffer Ingram died 13 February 1933, in Longview. He is buried at Alpine Cemetery. Many of his descendants continue to live in Gregg County, Texas.
– Submitted by Sean Charles Ingram (great grandson of Frank Zollicoffer and Katherine Elizabeth (Alexander) Ingram)

GEORGE ALTON & ANNIE FLORENCE (WALKER) INGRAM, SR.

George Alton Ingram, Sr. was born 17 February 1908, in Spring Hill to Frank and Katherine (Alexander) Ingram. Katherine died in childbirth. Alton was reared by his grandparents, James and Amanda Alexander. Alton, who was thought to be stillborn, was wrapped in swaddling and set aside while Frank attended to Katherine's welfare. Alton's half-brother, Roy, was five years old and Frank tied their dog, trusted to return home safely, to Roy and sent him for help in the middle of the night. After traveling several miles through fields, forests and creek bottoms, Roy and the dog rode home with assistance. The mid-wife determined that Alton was alive and retrieved him from the swaddling clothes.

George Alton Ingram, Sr., 1955

Alton married Annie Florence Walker, daughter of Alton Edgar "Jack" (1877-1939) and Mary Eula (Watson) (1885-1969) Walker, 29 September 1928. Annie was born 26 April 1907, in Mangum, Greer County, Oklahoma. They made their home in Longview, where he owned and operated service stations. He was drafted for World War II, sold his properties, banked the proceeds and reported for duty at Shreveport. He had passed his initial examination, but was subsequently rejected as physically unable to serve. He was unable to repurchase any of his property, but found work in the Talco oil fields of Titus County. During this time they lived in Titus and Wood Counties. They returned to Longview in 1950 when Alton purchased a Magnolia station on Mobberly.

Alton and Annie were devout members of the CP Church, where Alton served as Deacon and Elder. They were loving, attentive parents, living and teaching a rigid code of ethics and morals. They reared four children: Bettye Jo, Mary Nell (1934-1996), Wanda Jean and George Alton, Jr.

Annie Florence Walker Ingram, 1978

Bettye Jo was born 25 June 1932, in Pine Tree. She married John William Hughes, 5 June 1949, at Elmira Chapel CP Church, Spring Hill. They presently enjoy retirement in Houston. Bettye and John had three children: Sue Ellen married Franklin Fredrick "Frank," Victoria; Dona Elyse married Gary George Sabin, Victoria; and Jay Weldon married Melanie Marie Mobley, League City.

Mary Nell was born 11 January 1934, in Greggton and died 6 February 1996, in McKenzie, Tennessee. There she married Billy Oneal Bryant (1923-1988) 26 December 1955, where they lived until death. They had no children.

Wanda Jean was born 30 August 1936, in Spring Hill. She married Charles Herbert Hughes (1932-1994), brother of John William Hughes, 11 November 1957, in Longview. They made their home in Austin until Charles' death. Wanda resides in a nursing home in Corpus Christi. They reared three children: Karen Lynn married Charlie Ray "B.J." Deleon, Roswell, New Mexico; Kevin Scott married Dietra Ann Mahler, Corpus Christi; and Keli Rianna is unmarried and lives in Los Angeles, California.

George Alton, Jr. was born 2 October 1946, in Mt. Pleasant, Titus County. He married (1) Susan Jean Wieber (living) 10 July 1965, in

George Alton and Annie Florence Walker Ingram, 1959

Longview. George and Susan had two children: Sean Charles married Kathryn Ann "Kathee" Garst, Scranton, Pennsylvania, and Dana Lea married Andrew Alan "Andy" Moody, Denver, Colorado. George Alton, Jr. married (2) Caryl Susan Shanholtz, 15 November 1991, in Rome, Italy. They make their home in McKenzie, Tennessee.

George Alton Ingram, Sr. died 13 July 1962, in Longview. Annie Florence (Walker) Ingram died 2 June 1992, in McKenzie, Tennessee. They are buried at White Cemetery, Longview.

– Submitted by Dana Lea (Ingram) Moody (granddaughter of George Alton and Annie Florence (Walker) Ingram)

FRANK RICHIE JACKSON & MARGARET LOIS KILLINGSWORTH

Margaret Lois Killingsworth was the third of five children born to Samuel Abney Killingworth and Florence Ann Leath, and was born 26 March 1914, at home in Gregg County, Texas. She grew up mostly on a family farm in North Gregg County, going to school in Longview and later moving into Longview to live around 1930. She finished LHS in 1931 and attended College of Industrial Arts in Denton, Texas, for one year before returning to Longview to work and meet her future husband.

Frank Richie Jackson was born in Pike County, Alabama, the third of six children born to Andrew Columbus Jackson and Laura Ann Richburg. He was born at home on 8 March 1903. He attended schools in Pike County and church at Antioch Primitive Baptist Church in Coffee County where his father was "tune hyster." He moved to Texas in 1930 before finishing high school and worked for Humble Oil Company during construction of the Longview pump station. He lived at the boarding house owned by the Killingsworths, met and married Lois on 14 January 1933, in Shreveport, Louisiana, with Lois' sister, Blanche, and her husband, Lewis Henderson, as their attendants.

Initially, Frank (nicknamed Jack by this time) and Lois lived in Longview. They soon moved to Gladewater where he was engaged in the fuel hauling business. Their first son, Frank Richie Jackson, Jr., was born 12 April 1936. They returned to live in Longview in 1937, and remained at 441 South Fredonia Street until 1952. At that time they moved to the new home they had built on their lake east of Longview on the

edge of Harrison County, Texas. Lois was a full-time homemaker and mother to three sons: Frank, Jr.; Jere Langdon Jackson, born 21 February 1941; and Andrew Craig Jackson, born 5 April 1946. Jere and Craig were born in Longview.

"Jack" was self-employed as an independent oil operator and drilling contractor, founding South States Drilling Company. Independently, he partnered with many other independents, including Roy L. Fisher, Sam Killingsworth and John Robbins, working throughout Texas, New Mexico, Louisiana, and Mississippi. His company operated six full-time drilling rigs with support staff of over 100 until 1959.

F.R. and Lois were active members of First Baptist Church, Longview, serving as teachers, superintendents, deacon and many other contributing capacities in their church. The three boys graduated LHS and Baylor University in medicine, college professor of history and insurance. F.R. died 27 November 1962, in Longview following a stroke. Lois assumed his oil operations until her death. She was elected to Longview City Council in 1972, distinguishing herself as the first woman to be elected to that governing body. She subsequently served as Longview's first woman mayor in 1973. She emphasized park development and beautification efforts for the city, and Lois Jackson Park is the memorial to her contributions to this city. She died suddenly on 22 December 1974, at home at the age of 59 of cardiac arrhythmia. Both F.R. and Lois are buried in Memory Park Cemetery in Longview.

– Submitted by Dr. Frank Jackson

FRANK RICHIE JACKSON, JR. & DARBA GAY HERNDON

Frank Richie Jackson, Jr. was born in Gladewater, Texas, on 12 April 1936. He was the first of three sons born to Frank Richie Jackson and Margaret Lois (Killingsworth) Jackson. In 1938, the family moved to Longview to stay.

Darba Gay Herndon was born at Laird Hospital in Kilgore, Texas, on 20 July 1934. She was the second of three children born to Forrest Albert Herndon and Alma Faye (Cartwright) Herndon. Their first child was a stillborn son. The Herndon's lived initially at Laird Hill, Texas, and subsequently moved to Kilgore in 1946, then to Longview in 1950.

Frank and Darba met during high school years. After graduation, Darba attended Kilgore College for one year and was a Rangerette. She then transferred to Baylor University in 1953. Frank finished Longview High School and entered Baylor University the same year. Though friends in school and at church, they first dated at Baylor. Darba graduated in 1956 with a B.A. in Music and Education, did graduate work at the University of Colorado, then taught first grade in Odessa, Texas. Frank graduated in 1957 with a B.A. in History and Pre-Med Studies, attended the University of Texas, and then Baylor Medical College in Houston. They married 21 June 1958, at the First Baptist Church, Longview. The couple lived in Houston for the remainder of the time at medical school and through internship at Jefferson Davis Hospital. Their first of four children, Samuel, was born 19 April 1959, while they were in Houston.

Frank, Darba and Herndon moved to Ft. Worth, Texas, for Frank's Family Practice Residency in 1962. Their second child, Laura Blanche, was born 13 December 1962. The family then moved to Portland, Oregon, for Frank's duty in the U.S. Air Force (USAF) and stayed from 1963-65. Their third child, Forrest Leath, was born 9 August 1965, in Portland. Frank was awarded the USAF Commendation Award for his outstanding service. The family moved to Longview in 1965 for Frank's private practice in Family Medicine. He practiced in four locations in Longview. Their fourth child, Frank Worth, was born 5 April 1973. Darba was a full-time homemaker/mother until 1987 when she became a residential real estate agent. All four children graduated from college. Laura developed carcinoma of the thymus gland and passed away 11 December 1992, at the age of 29.

Frank and Darba were both active in FBC, Longview, serving as teachers, deacon, choir and contributing as workers in other activities. Darba's interest and activities included family, Junior League, Garden and Book clubs, and as an active real estate saleswoman. Frank's interests and activities included family, hospital staff and medical societies, civic boards, reading and travel. They have three grandchildren: Lauralee Elizabeth Jackson, Forrest Milan Jackson and Margaret Frances Jackson. They lived for 32 years at 1900 Judson Road and moved to 2 Palisades in 1998. As of October 2003, Frank remains in active medical practice and Darba continues to be an active real estate agent.

– Submitted by Leath Jackson

LAURA BLANCHE JACKSON
13 December 1962–12 December 1992

Laura Blanche Jackson was born 13 December 1962, in Ft Worth, Texas, the second child of Darba Herndon Jackson and Frank Richie Jackson, Jr. Her family moved in 1963 to Portland, Oregon, while her father served in the USAF. They moved to Longview in 1965 where her father entered medical practice.

She attended Longview Public Schools – first at Mozelle Johnston Elementary, then Judson Middle School, and graduating from Longview High School in 1981. She was an

honor student and took part in many extracurricular activities. Her favorite was band, majorette and serving as head drum major her senior year. Her classmates honored her by voting her Most Beautiful Girl her senior year.

She entered Baylor University, Waco, Texas, in 1981, graduating in 1985 with a B.A. degree in communications. During her years at Baylor she was active in Kappa Kapa Gamma Sorority and Baylor Student Foundation. Following graduation from Baylor she moved to San Antonio where she was employed as full time staff in several statewide and local political campaigns based in San Antonio. She then accepted the position of Marketing Director of the San Antonio World Affairs Council. She held this position until her illness developed in 1991. She then moved back to Longview, receiving multiple medical treatments 1991-1992, including surgery, radiation and chemotherapy. Her courage and attitude during this time of difficulty inspired everyone and was a testimony to her deep spiritual strength and commitment to her Lord. She passed away 12 December 1992 – one day before her 30th birthday.

Her life was a joy to all whom she touched. She established instant rapport with everyone she met. Her positive nature was readily apparent. Three memorial scholarships have been established in her memory:

1. Laura Blanche Jackson Student Scholarship at San Antonio World Affairs Council to an outstanding high school senior;

2. Laura Blanche Jackson Oncology Nursing Award, established in Longview by the John Darby family, recognizing the outstanding oncology nurses chosen each year in Longview;

3. Laura Blanche Jackson Lectureship in World Issues at Baylor University, which annually brings speakers to the Waco campus to increase students' exposure to and knowledge of world issues and affairs, established by her parents and friends.

– Submitted by Worth Jackson

MONROE HOMER & MARY AUGUSTA MYERS JACKSON

Monroe Homer Jackson and Mary Augusta Myers Jackson planned to live in Sherman, Texas. One of eight children, Monroe graduated from Texas A&M University in 1929 with a degree in textile engineering. He worked for Poole Manufacturing in Sherman until the company closed. With the onset of the Depression, Monroe applied to the U.S. Postal Service, moving to Longview in 1931. He delivered special delivery letters, a gun strapped on his hip. Mail carriers were often robbed.

The Jacksons built their home on Mobberly Avenue and had two children, Sue, born in September 1936, and Tom, born in March of 1939. The Jacksons were active in the Camp Fire Girls and the Boy Scouts. Tommie, as she was known to all of her friends, served as camp counselor. Sue was elected the first "Queen of Camp Natowa." Tommie was well known around Longview for her beauti-

Monroe Homer Jackson

ful alto voice and sang all over East Texas for Chamber of Commerce banquets, service clubs, church and school functions. She also sang weekly on WFAA radio in Dallas.

During World War II Monroe was sent to Camp Howze in Gainesville, Texas. In 1947, they returned to Longview, buying a home on Travis Avenue. Tommie was president of the South Ward PTA and directed the South Ward Dad's Club Minstrels in the late 1940s. They were both active in Wesley Methodist Church. Monroe was on the Board of Stewards. Tommie served as Sunday School Superintendent, and was a member of the WSCS.

Sue often played the piano for Wednesday evening church services and was President of the Lon Morris Subdistrict of MYFs of East Texas. Tom was active in the Boy Scouts, was an avid model train enthusiast and a ham radio operator. Graduates of Longview High School, Sue attended Kilgore College and was a member of the Kilgore College Rangerettes. Tom attended Kilgore College, finishing his college work at North Texas State University. Sue now lives in Kilgore and Tom in Florida.

Mary Augusta Myers Jackson

The Jacksons were among the first original 500 shareholders with Cherokee Water Company. They built a home on Lake Cherokee and soon decided to move to the lake. They had a beautiful rose garden, iris garden and a huge vegetable garden each year. Many days found them trying to catch the "biggest bass" for a fishing contest sponsored by Loper's Sporting Goods. Tommie eventually won the contest!

Due to failing health, Monroe retired in 1964 as Superintendent of Mails. Offered

Laura Blanche Jackson

several postmasterships and a position as a postal inspector, he turned them down to stay in East Texas.

Monroe spent the rest of his days gardening and fishing until his death in 1974. Tommie lived in Kilgore until she became ill with Parkinson's disease and moved to Florida to live with Tom and his wife. She joined Monroe in 1985. Both are buried in the Kilgore Cemetery. They have children, grandchilden and great grandchildren living in Texas, Oklahoma and Florida.

– Submitted by Sue Jackson Hill

MONROE FRANKLIN JAMISON

Monroe Franklin Jamison was born into slavery in Georgia, on 27 November 1848. At age twelve he was sold to Robert Jamison of Talladega, Alabama. After he was freed, he started his career as a Methodist minister in Alabama. Monroe Jamison moved to Texas in 1872, settling in Marshall. Jamison, the best known of a group of circuit-riding ministers, was noted for his ability to preach in the "Alabama style," an old-fashioned jubilant style of preaching that appealed to the poor. He was always ready to defend his beliefs and to debate doctrine with clergy from other churches. Jamison joined the East Texas Conference of the Colored Methodist Episcopal Church under Bishop Isaac Lane in 1873, and was assigned to the Marshall and Longview stations. He married Minerva A. Flinnoy on 14 January 1874. In February 1875, he was appointed to serve in Dallas and built the first Colored Methodist Episcopal church in the city. At the 1876 Colored Methodist Episcopal annual conference in Dallas, Jamison was promoted to presiding elder.

In 1908, Jamison earned a Doctor of Divinity degree from Texas College. Later, he established other churches throughout the North Texas area. Jamison edited the *Christian Index*, the Colored Methodist Episcopal Church newsletter, and the *Christian Advocate*, the East Texas Conference newsletter. He was appointed bishop of the Colored Methodist Episcopal Church in 1910, and served until his death eight years later. In 1912, Jamison published an account of his life's work, entitled *The Autobiography and Work of Bishop M.F. Jamison ("Uncle Joe")*. He died 19 May 1918, and was buried in the Pleasant Hill Cemetery.

ELDORAS B. JENKINS

As native Texans and descendants of long-time Texans, the Eldoras B. Jenkins family became Gregg County residents in September 1959, as a teacher in Longview High School retiring in 1988.

In 1977, youngest daughter Rebecca joined the Curtis and L.L. Mackey family, who settled in north Gregg County in the 1870s, when she married Michael Mackey Melton, son of Lou Ann Mackey and Grady Melton, Jr., on 19 November 1977.

Lamar County's 1870 census listed the Thomas Jenkins family, with grandfather Dan Moody Jenkins being born 12 October 1870. In

1898, Dan married Minnie Castles and farmed in Hopkins County. Grandfather Clinton Hanson came from Magnolia, Arkansas, in 1897 on horseback to marry Minnie McDaniel in Hopkins County, farming later in Franklin County, Texas.

Doris Jean Crews was born 25 November 1926, in Smith County, Texas, to Ernestine Ham and Jesse Calvin Crews. The Ham family from Hartwell, Georgia, in 1898 and the Crews family from Perry County, Alabama, in 1901 came by train to north Smith County, settling in the Harris Chapel community.

Eldoras B. Jenkins, born in Hopkins County on 12 July 1927, to Eula Hanson and Charlie Jenkins, married Doris Crews of Red Springs, Smith County, on 5 June 1949.

Doris, Rebecca, Jeanna and Eldoras Jenkins, 1957.

After teaching in Slaton and Brownsboro, they moved to Longview in 1959. Daughters Jeanna, 14 February 1953, and Rebecca, 18 October 1954, were born in Tyler, Texas. Jeanna began first grade at Valley View Elementary in 1959 with Evelyn Petty as teacher and Rebecca also had her in first grade.

Doris was a stay-at-home mom who did substitute teaching. She started full-time at Valley View in 1960 and retired in 1982.

Jeanna and Rebecca went to Forest Park JHS and graduated from Longview High School in 1971 and 1973. Sarah Latch taught violin and they were in Longview's strings program for six years, becoming charter members of the first Longview Symphony Orchestra directed by James Snowden. Rebecca began playing the cello in the seventh grade.

Jeanna (in 1975) and Rebecca (in 1977) graduated from Baylor University. In 1976, Jeanna received her commercial art degree (B.F.A.) from North Texas State University, Denton, and has been a graphic designer in the Dallas area since then.

After marrying Mickey Melton, Rebecca taught kindergarten in Austin before moving to Longview in 1980. Since 1997, Rebecca has taught at Foster, Everhart and Hudson Prep Schools.

Three granddaughters are Ann Crews Melton, born 17 December 1980, valedictorian in 1999 at Longview High and Austin College graduate of 2003; Emily Mackey Melton, born 23 December 1982, LHS grad of 2001 and junior education major at Baylor; Elizabeth Michael Melton, born 16 September 1987, sophomore at LHS. Ann and Emily played in the Lobo band for four years and were majorettes, while Elizabeth played soccer and did drama since fifth grade.

The Jenkins family has been active members of Oakland Heights Baptist Church since 1959, and the Melton family is still active at Alpine Presbyterian Church.

– Submitted by Doris Jenkins

A.O. JOHNSON

Atha Odell Johnson was born 9 March 1926, in Dexter, Missouri. His wife, Jessie Lillian Morgan Johnson, was born 27 October 1927, in White Oak, Missouri. They were married 24 July 1946, in Piggott, Arkansas. They celebrated their 57th wedding anniversary July 2003.

To this union four children were born. Julia, 1952, Janis, 1954, Barbara, 1955 and Douglas, 1957. The girls were born in Dunklin County, Missouri. Douglas was born in Longview, Texas. The children attended school at South Ward, Jodie McClure, Foster Junior High and Longview High. Barbara attended Mrs. McNeal's private school her first year. Douglas served ten years in the Navy.

Julia has two sons, Eric and Darren Jackson, born 1975 and 1978. Janis has a daughter and son, Jessica and Daniel Camp, born 1985 and 1988. Barbara has a son, Preston Proctor, born 1986. All were born in Longview.

Odell and Lillian started out farming on his dad's farm in Dunklin County. In 1948, Odell went into the ministry. Leaving the farm in Missouri, they evangelized until 1952, when he became pastor of the Apostolic Pentecostal Church in Jefferson, Texas. In December of 1953, they left Jefferson to again evangelize. In January 1955, they came to Longview. He helped in the First Pentecostal Church at 208 South 13th Street, also preaching revivals in the surrounding area as well as out of state. In 1962, he became pastor of the church and held this position until 1965, when he became disabled.

In August of 1966, Lillian started work with the U.S. Postal Service. She first worked

(l.-r.) Back: Douglas, Lillian and Odell Johnson. Front: Barbara, Janis and Julia.

at the Annex building on West Cotton Street. Next was the Main Office downtown, then the Southside Annex on Mobberly Avenue, which is now the Main Office. She worked at the Downtown Station the last 16 years of employment, retiring 30 November 1990.

Odell's ancestors were father Gilford Johnson, born 1895, and grandfather Eli Johnson, born 1838, both in Henderson County, Tennessee; great grandfather Stephen M. Johnson, born 1815, and great great grandfather Sherwood Johnson, born 1795, both in South Carolina; grandmother Elvia Arrena Brigance, born 1857, Henderson County, Tennessee; great grandfather Henry C. Brigance, born 1824, Tennessee; great great grandfather Clinton Brigance, born 1798, possibly Sumner County, Tennessee; mother Luella Abernathy, born 1903, grandfather William Henry Abernathy, born 1873, grandmother Nancy Elmine Cheek, born 1876, great grandfather Solomon Cheek, born 1848, and great grandmother Mary Catherine Masters, born 1850, all in Bollinger County, Missouri.

Lillian's ancestors were father Albert Morgan, born 1904, Dunklin County, Missouri; grandfather George Morgan, born 1855, Jefferson County, Illinois; grandmother Nellie Auten, born 1872, Franklin County, Illinois; great grandfather Isaac Morgan, born 1815, Tennessee; great grandmother Eleanor Willoughby, born 1828, Tennessee; mother Freida Powers, born 1907, Stoddard County, Missouri; grandfather Luther Jesse Powers, born 1881, Missouri; grandmother Bertha Mifflin, born 1889, Kentucky; great grandfather George Washington Powers, born 1850, Kentucky; great grandmother Nancy Ann Pharris, born 1845, Missouri; great great grandfather Sydney Pharris, born 1821, Tennessee; and great great grandmother Charlotte Jane Lindsey, born 1820, Tennessee.
– Submitted by A.O. and Lillian Johnson

R.K. JOHNSON

In 1924, R.K. (Randolph Keets) and Mattie Myrtle Lindsey Johnson relocated their home from Rusk County, Texas, to Gregg County. Their farm at Crossroads, a small community near Kilgore, was not near the Crossroads School. Their two small daughters, Mattie Arlene and Edith Joyce, could not walk the long distance when they started to school.

R.K. and Myrtle made a trip to Longview. They made inquiries about farms in the area that might be for sale. When they learned about 30 acres very near the two-room school at Spring Hill, that seemed like the answer.

The big old farm house with a "dog-run" hall, front and back porches, and two fireplaces made the

Johnsons convinced this was for them. Two water wells, a barn and a nearby orchard made the place even more attractive.

A deal was made. For $1,200.00, the Johnson family had a new home. Thirty acres, a good farm house and all the mineral rights – what a deal! In 1924, the term mineral rights was not in the vocabulary in Gregg County.

School had begun, but Arlene was allowed to start late. A two-room country school did not have too many formal rules. The same teacher taught four grades in one room – only 14 children, total. The older children were in the other room. (The teacher at that time, Eva Mae Ingram (McGrede) – from a pioneer East Texas family, was 100 years old on 3 May 2003. She died a few months after that.)

Edith was younger, therefore, she started to school a few years later. Ada Louise Anderson (Brewton) was her early teacher. Ada was past 90 when she passed away a few years ago. Her family was a well-known Longview family.

Years later, Arlene and Edith graduated from Longview High School. Spring Hill did not have a high school at that time. All the Longview area communities bused into Longview High School. The discovery of oil in Gregg County brought a population explosion. Soon there were high schools in all the "now larger" communities. Both Edith and Arlene later taught in the Spring Hill Elementary School.

Edith's two sons, Ronnie Van Humphries and Jeffrey Lynn Humphries, graduated from Spring Hill. Arlene's two daughters, Barbara Gail Tekell and Martha Diane Tekell, also graduated from there. Arlene's four grandchildren, Cynthia Kay Alexander, Clinton Douglas Alexander, Shannon Leigh Giles and Robert Shawn Giles, were graduates of Spring Hill High. One of Edith's grandsons, Luke Van Humphries, finished there. Ronnie's two daughters, Sarah Jane and Katie Brooke, are still attending at Spring Hill in 2004.

Jeffrey's sons, Thomas Chad finished at Pine Tree, and Samuel Curtis (Curt) is still a student at Pine Tree. When the Johnson family moved to

Spring Hill there was only one church. They had been Methodist at Crossroads. There seemed to be no problem, however, in becoming a "go-to-church-every-Sunday" family at Elmira Chapel Cumberland Presbyterian Church.

R.K. was later a deacon and then an ordained elder. Myrtle taught children's Sunday School and worked in the "Missionary Society."

Edith and Arlene followed the same path as their mother. Each of their husbands, Thomas Calhoun (Cal) Humphries (deceased) and Robert Douglas (Doug) Tekell (deceased) were elders in the Elmira Chapel Church.

Both of Arlene's daughters, Barbara and Martha, are elders. Their husbands, Michael Erwin (Mike) Alexander (deceased) and Darrell Henry Giles, are elders. Edith's sons, Ronnie and Jeffrey, are elders.

At present, the church sponsors a pre-school program. Lee Ann Theis Humphries, Jeffrey's wife, is the director of the Elmira Chapel Discovery School.

It seems that a need to relocate in 1924 was a good choice for the Johnson family. The two-room school mushroomed. Today there are five campus sites in the Spring Hill School system. The high school is a 3A classification. Each year the enrollment seems to increase.

R.K. and Myrtle would be proud!
– Submitted by Arlene Tekell

BILLY RAY JOHNSTON

Billy Ray Johnston was born in Gilmer, Upshur County, Texas, in 1932. He is the son of Charles "Bert" and Mary "Pearle" Shirey Johnston. They lived directly across from Spencer Harris on East Broadway in Gladewater, Texas. Bill graduated from Gladewater High School (1951) and received a BBA degree from Baylor University (1955).

After graduation, he accepted a job with Texaco in New Orleans, Louisiana, in the accounting department. In 1956, Bill transferred to the Tyler Texaco office, working as an oil scout and later as a landman until 1967. He was vice-president-cashier at the Gladewater First State Bank until 1977 and president-manager of Gladewater Federal Savings and Loan, retiring in 1988. Bill now spends time working his sixty-acre farm on the Country Club Road, where he and his family have lived since 1967.

Barbara Ann Holder was born in Tyler, Smith County, Texas, in 1933 to Gaylard Wesley and Eldice Head Holder. She graduated from Tyler High School (1951) and Tyler Federal Institute of Business (1952), working as a secretary from 1952 to 1965. Barbara met Bill while working for Pan American Petroleum Company and he for Texaco; they were married in Tyler (1964). She worked for the Gladewater ISD as the high school registrar from 1987 to 1998.

Both Bill and Barbara are active in the First Baptist Church, having served on numerous committees. He held many offices, was an Adult Choir member, Sunday School teacher and is a deacon. She has taught Missions Friends, Girls in Action, Acteens, Vacation Bible School, helped with

(l.-r.) Front: Mattie Arlene Johnson Tekell and Edith Joyce Johnson Humphries. Back: Shannon Leigh Giles, S.H. 1992; Clinton Douglas Alexander, S.H. 1992; Cynthia Kay Alexander, S.H. 1989; Barbara Gail Tekell Alexander, S.H. 1962; Martha Diane Tekell Giles, S.H. 1962; Ronnie Van Humphries S.H. 1969; Jeffrey Lynn Humphries, S.H. 1972.

Billy Ray Johnston family. (l.-r.) Back: Wendy Johnston Stanley, Barbara and Dianne Christian Johnston. Middle: John Stanley, Billy Ray and Wesley Ray Johnston. Front: Taylor Marie and Camryn Dianne Johnston.

children's choir and has been teaching the kindergarten Sunday School class since 1969.

Bill is a past director of the Gladewater Chamber of Commerce, United Fund and East Texas Baptist University. He is a past president of the Lions Club, Starrville-Friendship Water Supply and the Gladewater Hunting and Fishing Club. He served on the Gladewater ISD Tax Board.

Bill and Barbara have two children, both born in Tyler: Wesley and Wendy. Wesley Ray (born 1966) graduated from Gladewater High School (1985), attended Kilgore College and graduated from Baylor University (1990) with a BBA degree. A CPA for Hibbs-Hallmark, Tyler, he married Dianne Marie Christian (1995). They have two daughters, Taylor Marie (born 1996) and Camryn Dianne (born 2000). Dianne graduated valedictorian from Penelope High School (1988), Hill County Junior College (1990) and Summa Cum Laude from Sam Houston State University (1992) with a BBA Degree. She is a CPA for Gollob-Morgan-Petty, Tyler. Wesley and Dianne live in Chandler, Texas, where all the family is active in the Chandler United Methodist Church and Wesley is a volunteer fireman.

Wendy Gail (born 1972) graduated valedictorian from Gladewater High School (1991), Magna Cum Laude and Phi Beta Kappa from Baylor University (1995) and Summa Cum Laude with a Ph.D. in School Psychology from the University of South Carolina (2001). She has been a Psychologist for the Grapevine-Colleyville ISD since 2001. Wendy married John Alexander Stanley (1997). They reside in Frisco, Texas; John is employed with MediQuip. He graduated from Gladewater High School (1991), attended Kilgore College, graduated from Baylor University (1995) with a BS degree and has an MS degree and Athletic Trainers Certification from the University of South Carolina (2000).

– Submitted by Barbara Johnston

DR. CAROL ANN JOHNSTON

Carol Ann Johnston, daughter of O.G. and Georgia Ruth Johnston, was born 7 January 1956, in Gladewater, Texas. She is a descendent of John

Kittle and Sarah Poland Armstrong, M.A. and Elizabeth Barnes Armstrong, O.G. and Dellah Armstrong Johnston, and Charles Bert and Mary Pearle Shirey Johnston, and her parents. Her grandparents, Charles Bert and Mary Pearle Shirey Johnston, lived in the O.G. and Dellah Armstrong home on Highway 80, directly across from Spencer Harris Machine Shop in Gladewater.

Carol Ann attended Gladewater schools, graduating fifth in her class (1974). She was a member of the band, National Honor Society (president of both her senior year) and was Betty Crocker Homemaker of the Year (1974). She received a B.A. Degree in English (1978), and an M.A. in English (1980; thesis – Flannery O'Connor and Simone Weil) from Baylor University, Waco, Texas. She attained an M.A. in English and American Literature (1983), and a Ph.D. in English and American Literature (Dissertation – "Heavenly Perspective: Thomas Traherne and Seventeenth-Century Visual Traditions") from Harvard University in Cambridge, Massachusetts (1992). While at Harvard, she was an Instructor and Teaching Fellow (Department of History and Literature and Department of English, 1983-1990). She also had the privilege of teaching with Nobel Prize in literature recipient Seamus Heaney, Poet in Residence.

Carol Ann was hired as an Instructor of English at Dickinson College in Carlisle, Pennsylvania (1990-92); Assistant Professor (1992-98); and Associate Professor with tenure (1998 to present). She teaches various courses in English, Medieval and Early Modern Studies, and American Studies.

Carol Ann was a Lecturer in the English Department of Baiko Jo University, Shimonoseki, Japan (1980-81). Also included in her International Teaching Resume are London, Ways of Seeing (Dickinson Summer Program in London, 1998); London, Culture of a City (2000); and Norfolk, History and Culture (2000; Director, Dickinson Program in England. She has many articles and poems in print. She also wrote an academic book entitled, *A Study of Eudora Welty's Short Fiction*, published by Twayne (1997). She has made scholarly presentations at the University of California, Fordham University, Dallas

Dr. Carol Ann Johnston

Poetry Society, American Studies Faculty Seminar, University of East Anglia; Southern Women's Writer's Conference in Rome, Georgia; Sixteenth Century Conference in St. Louis; Modern Language Association, New York; respondent for the Central Pennsylvania Consortium on Stanley Fish's talk "Criticism and the Law," at Franklin and Marshall; International Emblems Conference at the University of Glasgow, Scotland; and Kyushu Society of American Literature in Fukuoka, Japan. She was also Dramaturg for the Jean Cocteau Repertory Theater's New York Premiere of Seamus Heaney's, "The Cure at Troy" (fall 1997).

Grants and honors received: Francis Fellowship (1978-79), Beasley Scholarship (1978-1980), and Teaching Fellowship (1979-80; Baylor University); Harvard Graduate School of Arts and Sciences Fellowship (1981-1983); Radcliff Grant for Research abroad (1986); nominee for Levenson Teaching Award (1986, 1987, 1988; Harvard University); Choice Magazine Academic Book of the Year Award (1998); finalist, Dallas Poetry Society annual competition (2001); and Martha Porter Sellers Chair of Rhetoric and the English Language (2002; Dickinson College).

– Submitted by Dr. Carol Ann Johnston

O.G. JOHNSTON

O.G. Johnston was born in Gladewater, Texas, 30 May 1927, at the home of his parents, Charles Bert and Mary Pearle Shirey Johnston. He is a descendent of John Kittle and Sarah Poland Armstrong, Martin and Elizabeth Barnes Armstrong, O.G. and Dellah Armstrong Johnston, and his parents. His family lived directly across from the Spencer Harris Machine Shop on East Broadway (Highway 80). He received his education in the Gladewater schools, graduating in 1944. He was a member of the Gladewater High School Band, directed by Alto Tatum, and the National Honor Society. He received his B.A. Degree (1948) and M.A. Degree (1951) from Baylor University, Waco, Texas.

He began his teaching career in the Union Grove School District in 1951. He taught seventh/eighth grade for four years, before accepting employment as seventh/eighth grade mathematics instructor in the Gladewater District. Other positions held during his thirty-six year tenure at Gladewater were high school counselor (1964-69), principal at Weldon (during integration, 1969-1971) and assistant superintendent (1971-1985). In 1985, he was appointed superintendent of the Gladewater schools, serving in this capacity until his retirement in June 1991.

Georgia Ruth White was born in Dublin, Arkansas, (1930) to George Cleveland and Bessie Mae Anderson White. She graduated from high school in Clarksville, Arkansas (1948). She accepted a position as laboratory and x-ray technician at Bloom Clinic in Gladewater (1952). At First Baptist Church she met O.G. In December, she returned to the College of the Ozarks in Clarksville, receiving a B.S. Degree in May. She and O.G. were married in Clarksville in 1953, and returned to Gladewater to make their home.

The O.G. Johnston family. (l.-r.) Back: Carol Ann, Georgia Ruth and O.G. Johnston, and Joe and Donna Niehus. Front: Katie and Karlie Niehus.

Georgia Ruth returned to work at Bloom Clinic (August 1953), changed professions (1958), and began teaching in the Union Grove School District. She attended college, attained teacher certification, earned an M.A. Degree in Education from Stephen F. Austin College and Reading Specialist Certification from the University of Texas, Tyler. She accepted a position teaching sixth grade reading in the Gladewater schools (1971), later transferring to the high school to teach reading (1976). She also taught an Advanced Honors Reading Course, retiring in 1991.

O.G. and Georgia Ruth continued to be active in the First Baptist Church. He served on numerous committees, held many offices, directed the Youth Choir, was Interim Adult Choir Director, Adult Choir member, deacon, Training Union leader and Sunday school teacher. She was a member of Adult and Handbell choirs, Historical Committee, Women's Missionary Union, worked with Mission Friends, Acteens, Vacation Bible School, Youth Choir, ceramics and taught Sunday school. She is also a member of Delta Kappa Gamma (honorary teacher society). Both are Texas Certified Master Gardeners.

Gladewater citizens elected O.G. to the city council in 1968. He served eight years, and was mayor (1971 1976). He was elected to the Kilgore

College Board of Trustees (1980-1992), and served as president several years. He has lifetime membership in the Texas State Teachers Association; he was a member of the Gladewater Rotary Club, served as president one term, and is a Paul Harris Fellow.

They have two daughters. Carol Ann was born in Gladewater (1956). She graduated from Gladewater High School (1974), received a B.A. (1978) and M.A. Degree (1981) from Baylor University, and a Ph.D. in English Literature from Harvard University, Cambridge, Massachusetts (1992). (See "Dr. Carol Ann Johnston.")

Donna Lynn was also born in Gladewater (1959). She graduated from Gladewater High School (1978) and received a B.S. Degree from the University of Texas in Austin (1982). She has taught in the Buda, Leander and San Antonio (Northeast) school districts of Texas. She married Joe Lawrence Niehus in 1984. Their two daughters, Katie Lauren (1993) and Karlie Jo (1996), were both born in San Antonio. They presently reside in Sherman, Texas, where Joe is a radiologist and Donna enjoys being a homemaker. (See "Joe & Donna Johnston Niehus.")

– Submitted by Mrs. O.G. Johnston

ROBERT MARSHALL & MARION CECELIA JOHNSTON

Robert Marshall Johnston (born 25 July 1939) and Marion Cecelia Jones Johnston (born 10 October 1939) were married in Gilmer, Texas, 21 May 1960, and moved to Longview in 1970, after Cecelia purchased a home on her "coffee" break. They had three children at that time, Robert Marshall Johnston II (born 28 March 1961, in Bryan, Texas), Charles Michael Johnston (born 20 September 1962, in Bryan, Texas) and April Cecelia Johnston, now Bonds (born 3 April 1968, in Tulsa, Oklahoma). Jill Elizabeth Johnston, now Garner, was born in Gladewater, 25 May 1977. Robert II, Charles Michael and April all graduated from Pine Tree High School. Jill graduated from Spring Hill High School. Robert Sr. passed the CPA Exam in 1975, and received his bachelor's degree in 1990 from UT-Tyler. He was trying to get his degree before his children, but two had already graduated from college. Robert II graduated from UT-Tyler and Michael graduated from BYU. April later graduated from Texas A&M and University of Houston School of Pharmacy. Jill is currently a senior at UT-Tyler.

Robert Sr. and Cecelia were active in the community and in the Church of Jesus Christ of Latter Day Saints. They were foster parents for several years, fostering five children. Cecelia was active in adoptions and the Republican Party. Robert was one of the original members of the Longview Apartment Association and on the board of directors for several years for the

East Texas Association for Abused Families, as well as involved in alcohol and drug abuse programs in the community. As members of the Church of Jesus Christ of Latter Day Saints, which they joined in 1965, Robert and Cecelia have had many callings, including Sunday School and Primary Teachers, advisors in the young men's and the young women's programs, teachers in Relief Society and Priesthood, member of the High Council, Bishopric and Bishop. Robert II served a mission for the Church in New York, New York (Spanish), and Charles served a mission for the Church in Peru. Both speak and write Spanish.

Robert II married April Nanette Smith 29 June 1991. They have two children, Robert Marshall Johnston III (born 25 January 1994) and Victoria Nanette Johnston (born 21 March 1997), with a new baby girl expected toward the end of 2003. Rob and April live in Barnhart, Missouri.

Charles Michael married Rosa Elvira Solari (born 19 October 1962) on 18 July 1987, in Lima, Peru. They have two children, Christian Andrew Johnston (born 9 June 1988) and Juliana Michelle Johnston (born 3 May 1990). Mike and Rosa live in the Spring Hill area of Longview.

April Cecelia married Britt Gregory Bonds (born 31 March 1967) on 4 January 1992. They have two children, Reece Cameron Bonds (born 9 March 1995) and Lucas Avery Bonds (born 26 April 1998). They expect another child in May of 2004. They live at Hideaway, Texas.

Jill Elizabeth married Kristopher Wayne Garner (born 14 December 1975) 3 August 2002. They are both attending college and live in the Spring Hill area of Longview.

– Submitted by Robert M. Johnston

JACK & BEA JONES

Jack and Bea Jones came to Kilgore in 1942 at the height of the oil field boom. Jack, born 10 December 1917, is the son of the late Arthur and Florence Jones of Morris, Oklahoma. He is the grandson of Roland Jones and the great grandson of Nicholas Barrett, both of whom were in the Oklahoma land rush on 22 April 1889. He is the third great grandson of Conrad Hise, a Revolutionary War patriot from Tennessee.

Jack married Lois Beatrice Agee on 29 October 1939. Bea, born 14 December 1922, in Haskell, Oklahoma, is the daughter of the late William Wisemon and Anna Agee of Kilgore. Bea is the great granddaughter of William N. Christian, Confederate soldier from Arkansas, and the sixth great granddaughter of the Huguenot, Mathieu Agee, of Manakintown, Virginia. Bea is a member of the Huguenot Society of North Carolina.

Jack worked for Thompson Pump Company for many years and retired from Trico Industries. Bea worked in the P.T.A. of the Kilgore School District. They both held offices in their church throughout the years. Bea also worked for Max Daiches Jewelry. In the 1970s and 1980s, Jack and Bea were members of the local square dance club. They held many offices, both local and in the State Federation of Square and

Jack and Bea Jones

Round Dancers. They are one of the two couples who organized and began the JO-DA Square Dance Festival.

They are the parents of one daughter, Sonja Carroll, three grandchildren and eight great grandchildren. They are members of the First Christian Church of Kilgore.

– Submitted by Jack and Bea Jones

JAMES E. JONES

The James E. Jones family has been residents of Gregg County since 1954, when the family moved to Kilgore; but, both James Edward Jones and his wife, the former Josephine Tate, are from pioneer East Texas families. James' great grandfather, Thomas Jones, moved from Tennessee to Texas, settling in Panola County before his death in 1861.

Josie's father, Joseph Newell Tate, was born in Wood County, Texas, in 1890, and her mother, Mary Lucille Gossett, was born in Henderson, Rusk County, on 31 March 1908.

James was born at Brooks, a rural community in Panola County, on 28 January 1931, the seventh son and the ninth of ten children born to Thomas Orlander Jones and the former Alice Estell Hill. James' father died on 28 August 1939, about a year after a log fell on him. His mother struggled to maintain the family's farm at Brooks, but finally lost it.

James attended school through the sixth grade at Brooks and then attended two more years at Carthage before quitting to take odd jobs to support himself and his family.

Josie was born on 4 July 1931, in Henderson, Texas, the second of eight children for Joseph Newell Tate and Mary Lucille Gossett.

James and Josie were married 3 June 1949, in Henderson. James and Josie Jones are parents of six children:

1. Mary Mitchell Robinson, born 12 June 1950, at Lufkin, and now employed at a mailing firm in Dallas;

2. Judy Davis, born 14 February 1954, in Henderson. She now works as office manger for a doctor in Utah;

3. Ronnie Jones, born 5 July 1955, in Henderson. He lives in Austin;

4. Ed Jones, born 11 May 1959, in Kilgore, is a cybercrime detective with the Longview Police Departments;

5. Daniel Jones, who works as a computer analyst for Motel Six corporate headquarters in Dallas, was born 23 February 1961, in Kilgore. He lives in Dallas;

6. James Eugene Jones, born 27 January 1965 in Kilgore, is a computer consultant. He lives in Frisco near Dallas.

When James and Josie moved to Kilgore, he went to work for Kilgore Ceramics as a sprayer. Then, in 1966, he was employed by LeTourneau in Longview, where he learned to be a machinist. Two years later, he joined LTV, a manufacturer of airplane parts, at Gregg County Airport. Sixteen years later, when LTV closed its Gregg County plant, he went to the Grand Prairie LTV plant, working there during the week and coming home to Gregg County on weekends. He retired from LTV on 30 September 1992.

James and Josie joined the Church of Jesus Christ of Latter-day Saints in 1954, and were sealed as a family in the Mesa, Arizona, temple in 1964. His current church callings include building physical facilities representative, secretary of both High Priests and Elders Quorums, and ward missionary.

Josie suffered a fatal heart attack on 15 November 1992.

James married Ida Annelle Dugan on 1 September 1993. She was born in Randall County, Texas, on 3 December 1938.

– Submitted by Nell Jones

JACOB SYVERINE JORGENSON I

The Norwegian ancestry of Jacob Syverine Jorgenson dates back seven generations. He was the son of Jorgen Gustav Jorgenson (born 9 March 1874, died 29 March 1955) and Miss Christine Nelson (born 18 February 1881, died 3 March 1961). Born on 6 July ___, Jacob was raised with his eight brothers and sisters on the family farm at Clifton, Bosque County, Texas. He attended parochial schools and graduated from Clifton Junior College. Life was hard in this old Norse community; however, Jacob's pioneer spirit brought him to Gregg County in the early 1930s. He married Lurlie Dee Bechtold in May of 1933. Two children were born to this union: Geneva Jean (born 23 August 1935) and Raymond Earl (born 7 May 1937).

Jacob and Lurlie were charter members of First Lutheran Church in Longview, Texas. The charter was signed at the Armory building on the corner of High and Tyler streets on 27 October 1935. Their infant daughter Geneva Jean was the first Lutheran baby baptized on this historic day by the Reverend A.E. Schardt. Jacob found employment with Danciger Refineries. When the school at London, Texas, was destroyed by a natural gas explosion, men and trucks were dispatched to the area to help with rescue efforts. Later he traveled with Hudson Engineering working on government projects.

Known to most as '"Jake," he moved his family back to Longview in 1943. He went into business for himself as a cement contractor and completed a major job at Ambassador College in Big Sandy. Geneva and Raymond graduated from Judson Grove High School where Jake was a member of the school board and the Judson Lions Club. He loved gardening and beekeeping. Geneva married Ray Tucker (29 December 1952) and at this writing they have enjoyed fifty years of wedded bliss. They built their home at 307 Hollybrook Drive, a stone's toss from the Jorgensons at 200 Hollybrook Drive (formerly Airline Road address). At that time, Hollybrook was a mere dirt trail heading east toward present-day Fourth Street. Early residents of the area known as "Airline Estates" included Mrs. Waggoner, the Jorgensons, the Tuckers and the Morrisons. They agreed with Mrs. Waggoner that the name of their "dirt trail" should reflect the land's natural landscape of abundant holly and brooks. Early land owner John Finch sold the corner acreage to Jake and Lurlie and it was used as a "'cow pasture" and later divided and sold to facilitate an electrical substation and Summer Meadows Nursing Home. Jake's warehouse was relocated across the street on land purchased from Charlie Harris. The little yellow house that became a longtime landmark of the area was removed, along with the warehouse, after Jake's death. Jacob and Lurlie were married 29 years, but divorced due to marital strife. They both were remarried. Mr. Jorgenson passed away on 15 September 1996, at the age of 90 years. He was proceeded in death by his grandson Anthony Ray Tucker (born 6 July 1959, died 10 September 1982). Left to cherish their memory is an extended family of descendents and friends.

– Submitted by Renea Tucker-Click

GEORGE ERIC JOSEPH

There are long family connections with East Texas by the family of George Eric Joseph and Shelly Lorene Frost Joseph. His Joseph ancestors came from Lebanon and settled in the Jefferson area. His grandparents, Joe and Adal Joseph, had the Joseph Department Store in Jefferson, and their home presently is occupied by the Stillwater Inn Bed and Breakfast/Restaurant. Eric's father, George, was raised in that house as were his siblings, John, Ed and Helen. Upon graduation from Texas A&M University, George came back to East Texas, settled in Longview and worked in the oil business. He eventually started, with partners, his own company, Key Production.

George married Martha Virginia Pearce, daughter of David Fritz Pearce and Flo-

Martha and George Joseph, 1997

rence Elizabeth Truelove Pearce. Martha was raised on a farm in the Glenwood community of Upshur County along with her sister Pat and brothers, Jim and Bill. All were graduates of Spring Hill High School. George and Martha raised their children, Amelia "Amye" and Eric in Longview.

Eric, born 15 November 1961, became an outstanding golfer, winning the Texas Junior Championship and playing for Longview High and Texas A&M. After receiving his degree in Geology, he returned home and joined his father's oil firm. He served on the boards of several organizations and was president of the Pinecrest Country Club Board of Directors.

Shelly and Eric Joseph, Aaron, Sadie and Sydney, February 1999

He had met Shelly during his college days while she was still a student at Pine Tree High School where she was a cheerleader, sang in the P.T. Express and was a Homecoming Duchess. She was born 29 August 1964, in Edinburg, Texas, to Freida Hamilton Strauss and David Wayne Frost, Sr. The Frost family had moved to Longview in April 1973, from Corpus Christi. Wayne was a petroleum engineer and was transferred to Gregg County by Sun Oil Company. Shelly attended LSU-Shreveport for a year when her family moved to that city. She then transferred to Baylor University where she was active, along with her sister Sharla Elizabeth, in their sorority Delta Delta Delta. Their brother, David Wayne, Jr., also graduated from Baylor where he played varsity football.

After receiving her degree, she returned to Longview where she taught school for three years at G.K. Foster Elementary School. She and Eric had married 1 November 1988, at First Baptist Church where they later taught Sunday School, served on committees, he ushered, and she taught in the girls missions organizations. Besides church activities, Shelly was active in the Junior League and served twice as PTA President for Judson Middle School.

Their children are Sydney Elizabeth, born 11 May 1991; Sadie Lee, 12 November 1994; and George Aaron, January 2, 1999. At the time of this writing, both girls have participated in competitive cheerleading and Sydney was a cheerleader at Judson Middle School where she was also a Student Council Representative. They have also been active in church activities.

Shelly had Pierce, Morse, Chapman and Frost ancestors who settled in East Texas during the 1800s. The first two were here about the time of statehood and all were mostly farmers.
– Submitted by Shelly Frost Joseph

SHELLY LORENE FROST JOSEPH

Grandview Hospital in Edinburg, Texas, was the birthplace of Shelly Lorene Frost, 29 August 1964, as the daughter of Freida Hamilton Strauss and David Wayne Frost. Even though she was born in Wayne's hometown, the family was living at that time about 50 miles away in the Sun Oil Camp in Starr County near Delmita. As a petroleum engineer, Wayne was required to live in the camp near the gas plant. However, after many years of operating the camps, Sun decided to close them and moved the office into McAllen, when Shelly was about a year old. The family lived there about seven years and that is where Shelly started kindergarten at Calvary Baptist Church, as did her older sister Sharla, and then both went to Jackson Elementary School.

Wayne was then transferred to Corpus Christi and the family lived for about fifteen months across the bay in the suburb of Portland. From there, Wayne was sent to the Sun office in White Oak, so the Frosts moved to Longview in April 1973. All of the children attended Pine Tree schools, including younger brother David Wayne Frost, Jr., who started public kindergarten.

During her younger years, Shelly took dance, piano and gymnastics. She was in Brownies and Girl Scouts, Children of the American Revolution, Girl's Softball, went to YMCA camps and was Becky in the play "Tom Sawyer" in seventh grade. She was an active student in the choir program from middle school up, was in All-region Choir, PT Express ensemble, and also the youth choir and ensemble at First Baptist Church, where she and her family were very involved members. Shelly was in the PT Junior High Student Council and became a cheerleader in the eighth grade. She continued to be a cheerleader through her senior year, when she was also a duchess in the homecoming court.

The family moved to Shreveport for less than a year, then Wayne was sent to the Oklahoma City office where they lived in Edmond. In the meantime, Shelly followed her sister to Baylor University where they were both active

Martha and George Joseph with grandchildren Aaron, Sydney and Sadie Joseph.

in their sorority, Delta Delta Delta. She graduated with a degree in education.

On 1 November 1986, she married George Eric Joseph, son of Martha Pearce and George Joseph of Longview. As a geology graduate from Texas A&M, Eric had joined his father's oil company, Key Production. The couple resided in Longview where Shelly taught school for three years and then stayed home with their children, Sydney Elizabeth, Sadie Lee and George Aaron Joseph.

Shelly was in the Junior League, was Judson Middle School PTA President twice, and taught Sunday School at First Baptist Church, where they had married and continue to be active members.
– Submitted by Shelly Lorene Frost Joseph

JUDKINS

Mark Judkins and Brenda Beckman met at Brigham Young University in January 1982, in a beginning Latin dance class where they became friends and dance partners. Mark had learned the art of ballroom dancing while in high school, as well as the skill of putting a girl in lifts above his head. The previous summer he had danced with another partner in a talent show, and they looked just like the Fred Astaire/Ginger Rogers couple. Little did Mark know that Brenda was in the audience, dreaming that she could learn to dance like that. Brenda loved dancing in her youth, especially modern dance, but knew nothing about ballroom dance, thinking it was a dance just for the older generation.

Mark and Brenda on their wedding day.

Being on a back-up ballroom dance touring team, Mark had potential to represent BYU in different foreign countries in the coming year, but chose to serve a mission for the Lord's church instead, which normally lasts two years. Because Brenda's love for Mark grew over the months she got to know him, she was determined to learn all of the ballroom dancing she could while he was gone (to the Milwaukee, Wisconsin Mission), so she could match his abilities and be able to perform beautiful dances with him, like she saw in that talent show, when he returned. By the time Mark came home from his mission, she had moved up to the touring team as well as learned the art of being lifted up high in the air while dancing. There was one particular competition called the Open Cabaret that was put on twice a year at the University.

The Judkins family

Mark had tried to win this competition two times before with other partners, but never got to the finals. In March of 1984, Mark and Brenda entered the Open Cabaret and received first place, dancing to the song "Ice Castles." Six days later they were married.

Mark and Brenda were married 6 April 1984, in the Jordan River Temple in West Jordan, Utah. It was a cloudy spring day filled with family, friends, and a beautiful ceremony and reception. They bought their first home in Provo, Utah, and had three children there. Since that time, Mark went on to get his Bachelor's degree from BYU in facilities management, then a Master's degree in Human Resource Management from Utah State University in Logan, Utah. By that time Brenda had four more children, and their family lived in Orem, Utah.

It was always a goal for Mark to be an employee for the Church of Jesus Christ of Latter-Day Saints, the church in which he served his mission years earlier. He finally achieved his goal and filled a position in Longview, Texas, in April of 2000. He is the facilities manager for 25 meetinghouses in the Northeast Texas area and parts of Oklahoma and Arkansas, and has ten employees as well as two church-service missionaries.

This April Mark and Brenda will have been married 20 years. Their children range in age from four years to eighteen years. They feel that they have been blessed greatly, and are grateful for the time they have had living here in Texas. Getting here was not easy, and the first year here was almost like coming to a different country because of the climate, culture and accents. But it is home now, and they like it very much. Dancing is still a part of Mark and Brenda's life as they take advantage of the many dance events held at their church. They also enjoy teaching interested youth to dance and are planning a cabaret-type dance for the upcoming church dance festival.

– Submitted by Mark Judkins

GEORGE ADDISON KELLY

George Addison Kelly, son of Jacob and Anna (Gregg) Kelly, was born on 17 October 1832, in Greene County, Tennessee. About 1849, he moved with his father to Natchitoches Parish, Louisiana. Three years later he went to Jefferson, Texas, as mate on a steamship. Soon he became foreman over the slaves at the small iron foundry that John A. Stewart was operating at Four-Mile Branch west of Jefferson. Stewart's chief item of manufacture was a crude plow, but Kelly realized the possibilities of a large trade in cowbells and country hollow ware and persuaded the firm to make them. In 1854, he made a trip to Louisville, Kentucky, to learn better methods of manufacturing and brazing the bells. In Kentucky, he learned new methods of foundry work, and his experience proved extremely valuable to the firm. The foundry could not supply the constantly growing demand for sandy-land plows. In 1858, the business became known as Kelly and Stewart. When Stewart died in 1860, Kelly became sole owner of the plant.

In 1861, with the outbreak of the Civil War, Kelly, as captain, organized and equipped a company for the Confederate Army. When the Confederacy decided that he could provide greater services as a manufacturer than as a soldier, he was ordered to remain with his plant and make military supplies. After the war he was the owner of a weekly journal, *The Home Advocate*, published in Jefferson from January 1869, at least through January of 1871. The paper featured articles on Christianity, education, agriculture and the development of local businesses. The foundry and factory were partially destroyed by fire in 1882. Kelly moved what he was able to salvage to Longview and organized the Kelly Plow Company. He married Lucy Anne Stewart; the couple had three sons and four daughters. Kelly was a Methodist and Mason. For four years he was mayor of Longview. He died there on 2 October 1909, and was buried in Greenwood Cemetery.

KENNARD

Nathaniel Kennard arrived in Maryland from Ireland in 1720. His grandson, Nathaniel, was born in 1750 and served as a Lieutenant in the Revolutionary Army before marrying Ann Sandefur in North Carolina in 1790. Their son, James Jones, had a son, Charles Henry, who married Mary Jane Dupree in 1833 and came to Texas from Alabama in 1852, bringing their five-year-old son, Taylor Eliga, with them. T.E. attended primary school at Pirtle and a boys' school at Kilgore before joining the Texas Calvary in 1862 when he was 14 years of age. As a 16-year-old soldier, T.E. participated in the cavalry campaign battles through Louisiana that put an end to the last major effort by Union forces to invade Texas. He was wounded, but continued to fight.

After the Civil War, T.E. returned home to find all of his family missing. He located one sister living in Shelby County and settled near her before marring Sara Elizabeth Tatum in 1869. They lived in Rush County for several years before moving to Longview about 1873.

T.E. was in the mercantile business with J.R. Boring, and also had a sawmill. He served as the Longview postmaster during the Cleveland administration. He and Sara built the family home south of downtown Longview on "Kennard Hill" in 1886, where they lived until their deaths. They were very active in the Cumberland Presbyterian Church. Sara died in 1902, and T.E. in 1928, and both are buried at Grace Hill Cemetery.

Sara and T.E. had ten children: H. German, Zoe, D.C., Leo, Nona Pauline, Homer, Love, Taylor, Don and Elizabeth. Their fifth child, Nona Pauline, married Judson Holloway McHaney, prominent Gregg County judge, in 1903 after the death of her mother, Sara.

After their marriage Nona and Judson continued to live in the Kennard home and raise their own children as well as several of Nona's younger siblings.

OPHELIA KEY

Ophelia Key Stevens Dilley Brooks was born in the Canal Zone of Panama on 9 June 1914, to Frank Murray Key of New Brunswick, Georgia, and Abigail Cardenas of Caracas, Venezuela.

Ophelia Key was a great great granddaughter of Francis Scott Key, author of "The Star Spangled Banner." She had three brothers, Frances (Frank) Scott Key, Patrick Henry Key and George Edward Key. (As of this writing, Frank and George are still living and Patrick is deceased.)

Ophelia attended and graduated from Balboa High School, Balboa, Panama, Canal Zone, in 1932. In high school, she was known for her culinary arts and swimming and as an indoor baseball player. She also possessed the "gift of gab." During her senior year of high school, 1932, Ophelia married John Edward Stevens of Dover, New Hampshire. John was a radioman serving aboard the USS *Sacramento* stationed at the Panama Canal. In March of 1936, after moving to Dover, New Hampshire, their daughter Shirley Carole was born on 14 March 1936. The marriage was dissolved by divorce in 1937.

Ophelia Key and daughters Shirley and Judith, 1945

After this time, Ophelia took her daughter Shirley back to Panama where her brother Frank was still living. She got a job as a seamstress in the U.S. Army Post Exchange. While working at the Post Exchange, she met Orville Dilley as he was stationed at the U.S. Army Post located there. In 1941, Ophelia and Orville married and he was transferred to Camp Roberts, California. From Camp Roberts, California, they transferred to Camp Robinson, an Army post in Little Rock, Arkansas. While stationed in Arkansas, Judith was born 18 December 1942.

In 1943, Ophelia and Orville, by then a 1st Lieutenant in the U.S. Army, moved to Texas, where he was stationed at Camp Fanning, in Tyler, Texas. They resided in Kilgore with their two daughters, Shirley Carole Stevens, age 7, and Judith Florence Dilley, age 1 year.

Orville went overseas and was killed somewhere in France during the Battle of the Bulge on 3 February 1945. Ophelia remained in Kilgore with her daughters, where they went to school and graduated from Kilgore High School.

Ophelia married Bazzie Wilbur Brooks of Henderson, Texas, on 2 July 1962, in Kilgore, Texas, but moved to Longview a couple years later. He was employed by Trailmobile, Inc. Bazzie preceded Ophelia in death on 8 November 1986.

Ophelia was an avid swimmer and spent her days swimming at the local YMCA and attending her Senior Citizen's group at the Senior Center in Longview. Also, she was a member of the TOPs Club.

After graduating from high school, Shirley married Harold Edward Morrow, an accountant, of Birmingham, Alabama, in 1953. Their son, Steven Edward, was born, 1 July 1954, in Mobile, Alabama. The marriage was dissolved in 1956. On 1 April 1959, Shirley married James Anthony Isham, in Kilgore. James was a hospital corpsman in the U.S. Navy, and the family spent a great deal of time transferring from one naval base to another. Their daughter, Lisa Deanna, was born 13 August 1960, in Corpus Christi, Texas, and their son, Christian Anthony, was born 7 August 1962, Kilgore. The marriage between James and Shirley was dissolved 15 April 1982.

Christian is now a Lieutenant Colonel serving with the U.S. Marines Corp in Honolulu, Hawaii. And Lisa is in Asmara, Africa, teaching school at the International School of Asmara.

Judith married James Franklin Emmons of Kilgore, 1 June 1961, in Kilgore, Texas, after graduating high school. They moved to La Crescenta, California, where James went to work for the U.S. Postal Service. He had previously been discharged from the U.S. Navy. It was in La Crescenta where Mark Timothy was born on 21 June 1962. They were transferred back to Longview in late 1962. Their daughters, Kristi Diane, 17 December 1964, and Jamie Karol, 6 November 1968, were born in Longview. Mark is a welder by trade, and Kristi is a certified public accountant; they both reside in Longview. Jamie is in Dallas working as a real estate broker.

After raising their families, Judith and Shirley went back to school at Kilgore College in Kilgore. Judith received her nursing degree in 1976, and over the years was employed at several different nursing facilities in the Longview area. She retired from Laird Memorial Hospital, Kilgore, 31 January 2003.

Shirley became employed at Texas Eastman Division of Eastman Kodak in 1978, after completion of business school at Kilgore College. She retired from Eastman after 21 years on 1 December 1999.

Both Shirley and Judith are members of Aaron Burleson Chapter of Daughters of American Revolution.

Ophelia had nine great grandchildren: Vonda Lee Morrow; Lee Allen, Shelby Christine, Emily Katherine and Christian Anthony Isham; Michaela Grace Ellis; Tiffany Nicole, Mark James Emmons and Sarah Sustaita.

Ophelia died of congestive heart failure in Good Shepherd Medical Center, Longview, 26 July 1988. Both she and Bazzie are buried in Kilgore Cemetery, Kilgore.

– Submitted by Shirley Isham

CONSTANTINE BUCKLEY KILGORE

Constantine Buckley (Buck) Kilgore, judge, state senator and Confederate veteran, the son of Willis Kilgore, was born in Coweta County, Georgia, in 1835. He moved to Texas with his parents in 1846, and they settled in Rusk County. He attended the Fowler Institute, clerked for Timothy Pillsbury and was admitted to the bar after a year of study. Despite his opposition to secession, Kilgore volunteered during the Civil War in the Tenth Confederate Cavalry and was advanced to the rank of captain of Company G after reorganization of the regiment at Corinth. On the Kentucky campaign, Kilgore was made adjutant general of his brigade. He was wounded at Chickamauga, captured, and imprisoned at Fort Delaware from 1864 to March 1865. He returned to Rusk County after the war and resumed his law practice. He built a home at the terminal of the International-Great Northern Railroad in 1872. Kilgore had given the land to the railroad. The site later became the town of Kilgore, named in his honor. He represented the county at the Constitutional Convention of 1875. In 1877, he moved to Wills Point. In 1880, he served as a Democratic elector and, in 1884, he represented the Seventh District in the Texas Senate, where he was elected president pro tem. He resigned in 1886 to run for the Fiftieth Congress and later represented the Third District from March 1887 to March 1895. On 20 March 1895, he was appointed United States judge in Indian Territory (later Oklahoma) by President Grover Cleveland; he served in that office until his death. Kilgore was a Presbyterian and a Mason. He married Frances Barnett in 1858. He died in Ardmore, Indian Territory, on 23 September 1897, and was buried in the White Rose Cemetery at Wills Point.

KILLINGSWORTH

In 1850, before the Civil War began, word was that good land was to be had in Texas.

That news spurred John Sweet Killingsworth and his wife, Emmaline Abney, their family and servants to migrate from Bibb County, Alabama, to eastern Texas. His earlier ancestors had come to America in 1667. Before that the family line is traced back to England as far as 593.

The John Sweet Killingsworth Cemetery, 1997

John Sweet and Emmaline Abney Killingsworth were both born in Edgefield District, South Carolina. John's parents, Anderson and Mary Sweet Killingsworth, and their ancestors have been traced to the early settlers of Nantucket, Massachusetts, Quaker heritage. The Abneys settled in Virginia (Richmond), and then in South Carolina and later in Alabama.

Because John Sweet's parents moved from South Carolina to Roane County, Tennessee, around 1796, John grew up there, learning the silversmith trade. Later, he moved to Selma, Alabama, where he met and married Emmaline Abney (18 January 1820), and from there they moved to Bibb County where they had 13 children. They sold their farm in 1850 and started west in a cavalcade of settlers traveling overland in oxcarts and wagons with their children, servants, livestock and household supplies. Some accounts record over 100 people traveling in this group. They (along with the Hilton Brown family) traveled to Upshur County (now Gregg County), where John Killingsworth and his wife purchased a tract of 392 acres of land, of which 112 acres are still intact today and owned by descendants.

The Killingsworths built a settlement consisting of their home, a shoe shop, blacksmith

The James W. Killingsworths. (l.-r.) Seated: Eddie, Robert, Eliza (mother), unknown and Bennie. Standing: Rebecca, Clara, Alice, Lucy and Tera.

shop, gin and grist mills for flour and meal, and slave quarters. South of the house were the barn, cribs and stalls, and the carriage house. Emmaline and John lived on the land until their deaths (19 November 1881, and 21 October 1884). They are buried on the tract of land in their family cemetery. This home site and cemetery are still in the family.

On 3 November 1905, a family reunion at the cemetery site was held. Again on 28 November 1998, descendents gathered at the cemetery for a rededication ceremony and dinner on the grounds.

Many descendents of John Sweet and Emmaline Killingsworth still live on the original property and in and around Gregg County today.

KILLINGSWORTH-CARAWAY

Emma Agnes Killingsworth, fourth child of Samuel Abney Killingsworth and Florence Ann Leath Killingsworth, was born 9 November 1917, in Longview, Texas. She graduated from Longview High School in 1934, attended BMI Business College in Longview and became legal secretary for Fred R. Erisman, attorney. Later, Mr. Erisman was elected District Attorney of Gregg County, and she continued to work for him in the District Attorney's office. She married Archie Edwin Caraway on 19 July 1941, at the First Baptist Church in Longview, Texas. Three children, Agnes Kay Caraway, Abney Edwin Caraway and Laura Ann Caraway, were born to this marriage.

Archie Edwin Caraway was born 12 August 1912, in Lufkin, Angelina County, the eldest of two sons of Arch Caraway and Laura Kate Caraway. He was a graduate of Lufkin High School and received a Mechanical Engineering degree from Texas A&M University, College Station, Texas. After graduation, he was employed by Lufkin Foundry and Machine Company, which later became Lufkin Industries. He and Agnes lived in Odessa, Longview, Dallas and Lufkin. He was manager of Lufkin Industries for Texas, Oklahoma, Louisiana and Arkansas, and was transferred to the executive offices in Lufkin shortly before his death 12 May 1965.

Agnes Kay Caraway, oldest child of Agnes and Ed Caraway, was born 23 April 1944, in Lufkin. She graduated from Hillcrest High School in Dallas in 1962, and North Texas State University in Denton in 1966. She has one child by her first marriage to Grant Murrell, Laura Kay DeFrance, born 22 March 1967, who is married to Roland DeFrance. They live in Richmond, Texas, and have one child, Lauren Ruth DeFrance, born 21 July 2002. Agnes Kay Caraway married Walter Dildy, who is with David Weekly Homes, and they live in Dallas, Texas.

Abney Edwin (Bud) Caraway, second child of Agnes and Ed Caraway, was born on 8 May 1945, in Longview. He graduated from Hillcrest High School in 1963, and from Stephen F. Austin University in 1967. He lives in Austin, Texas, and works in real estate and property management.

Laura Ann Caraway, third child of Agnes and Ed Caraway, was born 11 May 1951, in Dallas. She graduated from Longview High School in 1969, and from Baylor University, Waco, Texas, in 1973. She is presently employed as a Senior Probation Officer in Dallas.

Emma Agnes Caraway taught Sunday School at Park Cities Baptist Church for 19 years before moving to Lufkin, and later to Longview. She is a member of First Baptist Church, Longview, and enjoys gardening and is an avid bridge player. She also enjoys spending time with her great granddaughter, her children, her granddaughter, her numerous nieces, nephews, great nieces and members of her extended family in Texas.

– Submitted by Laura Ann Caraway, Dallas, Texas

JOHN ALBERT KILLINGSWORTH & REBECCA GARNER

John Albert Killingsworth was born 14 November 1826, Bibb County, Alabama. He was the third of 13 children born to John Sweet Killingsworth and Emmeline Abney. Mary Rebecca Garner was born to William and Nancy Latham Garner on 3 March 1832 in Alabama

John Albert and Rebecca married at Bibb County, Alabama, on 3 February 1848. To this marriage was born 14 children – 7 girls and 7 boys. In later years the Killingsworths "adopted" twin boys who had lost their parents. Ten children were born in Alabama: James William, Henry Newt, Nancy Ellen, Margaret, Molly Antoinette, Sarah Jane, Leroy Lee, John L., Willey T. and Amanda Sweet; and four in Texas: Eudera Minnie, Samuel Abney, Isaac Gordon "Ike" and Ida R. Killingsworth.

In 1868, Albert and Rebecca traveled to New Orleans, where John Sweet Killingsworth and his eldest son, James A. Killingsworth, met them and brought them to Upshur County (now north Gregg County), Texas.

John Albert died 17 August 1906, and Rebecca Killingsworth died 16 April 1881. Both are buried in Old Summerfield Cemetery, Tryon Road, Gregg County, Texas.

– Submitted by Lois McCaleb

JOHN SWEET KILLINGSWORTH

John Sweet and Emmeline Abney Killingsworth were both born in Edgefield District, South Carolina. John's parents were Anderson and Mary Sweet Killingsworth. The Sweets have been traced through the books on heraldry in the libraries and to early settlers of Nantucket, Massachusetts, Quaker heritage.

The Abneys settled in Virginia (Richmond), and then in South Carolina and, later, Alabama. John's parents, Anderson and Mary Sweet Killingsworth, moved from South Carolina to Roane County, Tennessee, around 1811. John Sweet grew to manhood in Tennessee. At age 18, he enlisted in the American Army in December of 1814, immediately prior to the Battle of New Orleans, which ended the war. He was never sworn into regular service. He went to Lebanon, Tennessee, where he learned the silversmith's trade, which he followed for some years at that place. He went to Selma, Alabama, when it was a small village. He pur-chased a tract of land and constructed the first frame building (a board house) erected in Selma and was present and saw the first steamboat pass up the river.

John Sweet and Emmeline were married in Selma in 1820, and moved to Bibb County, Alabama, where they had 13 children and farmed until November of 1850. In 1850, they sold their farm to Emmeline's brother, Thomas Hamilton Abney, and started west in a cavalcade of settlers traveling overland in oxcarts and wagons with their children, slaves, livestock and household supplies. They, along with the Hilton Brown family, traveled to Upshur County (now Gregg County), Texas. John Sweet and Emmeline purchased a tract of 392 acres of land through Emmeline's nephew, Alexander Hamilton Abney, who was established in Gilmer, Texas, as a land trader, District Clerk and, later, Postmaster.

John and Emmeline built a settlement consisting of their home, a shoe shop, blacksmith shop, gin and grist mill for flour and meal, and slave quarters. Emmeline and John are buried on the tract of land in their family cemetery.

SAMUEL ABNEY KILLINGSWORTH & FLORENCE ANN LEATH

Florence Ann Leath was born 8 March 1885, at home in Harrison County, Texas. She was the ninth child of Josiah S. Leath and Margaret Ann Hiett. Both were from early settler families of East Texas, coming from Alabama after the Civil War.

Samuel Abney Killingsworth was born 20 October 1870, at home in Harrison County, Texas. He was the twelfth of fourteen children born to John Albert Killingsworth and Rebecca Garners. Both parents were from early settler families of East Texas, coming from Alabama after the Civil War.

Sam and Florence were married at the home of her parents in north Harrison County, on 21 November 1906. Her written account of the wedding included "104 grown people and a yard-full of children. Everyone was happy, there was singing, Louis Richardson playing the organ, and it lasted until 6 p.m."

They moved to Sam's farm in north Gregg County. To this marriage was born five children, three girls and two boys, between 8 September 1907, and 25 March 1921.

Sam worked as a farmer of cotton, corn, sugar cane, beef and dairy cattle, and horses. Florence was a full-time homemaker/mother to their five children until a horse accident, which injured Sam's neck severely. While he was confined to bed, Florence took on the management of the farming operation, was primary nurse to her recovering husband and continued with all family activities.

The family moved into Longview in 1931, opening a boarding house on Whaley and Center Streets for workers in the newly opened East Texas Oil Field. Sam and Florence then built their own family home at 441 South Fredonia, where they continued with boarders through 1937. They then returned to live on their farm in north Gregg County until 1943, when they again moved into Longview and remained there until their deaths.

Both were active members of First Baptist Church, Longview. Sam's retirement was spent mainly enjoying fishing and his family. He died at home on 7 July 1961. Florence continued to live in their home on Oxford Lane until her death on 2 July 1976. Her lifelong interest was in her family, yard and flowers, and she passed this love to all her children and grandchildren. She was preceded in death by two of her children, Samuel Hardy Killingsworth and Margaret Lois Killingsworth Jackson. Sam and Florence are buried in the family plot in Memory Park Cemetery, Longview. They were survived by three children — Blanche Killingsworth Henderson Abney, Emma Agnes Killingsworth Caraway and Charles Lee Killingsworth.

– Submitted by Agnes K. Caraway and Samuel H. Jackson

ORMAN & MARJORIE KIMBROUGH

Orman "Kim" Kimbrough III was born in Azle, Texas, on 24 March 1914, to Orman Kimbrough, Jr. and Linnie Moore Kimbrough. His father was a farmer and rancher. Working with cattle was one of Kim's greatest pleasures, and he will never forget their last cattle drive to the Ft. Worth stockyards from the Jacksboro-Azle area.

Marjorie Olson Kimbrough was born in Madison, Wisconsin, on 9 June 1923, to Kenneth Olson and Mildred Nusbaum Olson. Her father was a professor and Dean of the Medill School of Journalism at Northwestern University.

Orman graduated from Weatherford College and North Texas State University, and after working in the teaching profession and then in government service with the National Youth Administration, he enlisted in the Navy in World War II, and was stationed at Great Lakes Naval Base. Here he met Marjorie Olson, who was a student at Northwestern University, and courted her for 15 months and then married her before he was sent to the South Pacific until the end of the war.

Upon his discharge, he and Marjorie came to Texas to live, and witin six months, he was

Orman and Marjorie Kimbrough and their children, Kenny Kimbrough, Laurie Bruce and Lanny Kimbrough, taken on their 50th anniversary, June 12, 1994.

working for the Veterans Administration and was sent to Gregg County, Longview, Texas, 1 July 1946, to set up a veterans' training office. Orman and Marjorie have made Longview their permanent home.

During their more than fifty years here, Orman, familiarly known as "Kim," worked for several years with the VA, and then bought the Sinclair distributorship, which became his career for twenty years. Marjorie worked with him in the oil company as bookkeeper.

He was one of the first gasoline distributors to inaugurate the self-service gasoline pump concept; and, he established the town of Merry Christmas, Texas.

They raised three children: Orman "Lanny" Kimbrough IV, born on 9 February 1948; Kenneth Kimbrough, born on 23 March 1950; and Laurel Kimbrough, born on 28 May 1951. All the children went through the Longview public school system and went to Texas universities.

Kim went into the radio business in 1962, and after having part interest in several radio stations, he ended up with full ownership of KEES in Gladewater, and maintained that station until he sold it in 1982. He has been active in cattle, oil royalty and oil production, and has been Director of two banks and a Savings and Loan. For nearly 21 years, he was a member of the Longview School Board, and also served on the Gregg County Appraisal board.

Both Kim and Marjorie were active in their children's activities, coaching baseball and basketball, and associated with Boy Scouts and Campfire Girls. They served in the First Presbyterian Church, as teachers. Kim was a Deacon and Elder, and Marjorie directed children's choirs and sang in the chancel choir for 40 years.

Their oldest son, Lanny, graduated from Baylor Dental School, married Susan Henry from Corpus Christi, and moved to Odessa, Texas, where Lanny set up his practice of orthodontics. They raised two sons, Orman "Lance" Kimbrough V, and Kevin Kimbrough. In 1998, Lanny died of cancer.

Their second son, Kenny, graduated from Veterinary School at Texas A&M, and married Gindy Propes from Henderson. Kenny set up his veterinary practice in Longview, and he and Gindy raised three daughters: Kristy Kay, who has just married Derek McBride; Ginny Rae, who married Steven Walker and has two sons, Hayden and Garrett; and Julie Marjorie, who graduated in August 2003, from Texas A&M.

Their daughter, Laurie, is married to Robert Bruce, a Presbyterian minister, who is presently serving in Tyler. Bob has two children by his first marriage, Shannon, who is married to Michael Shappell, and Rob, married to Gretchen Giels with a son, Jake.

Laurie has two children by her first marriage, Casey Leanne Cox and Adam Michael Cox.

Kim and Marge are about to celebrate their sixtieth wedding anniversary, and feel that living their lifetime in Gregg County, in Longview, has been a great life, and a very wonderful place to raise their three children. And Kim has climaxed his life with the publishing of his book, *The Good Life*, which is his autobiography and tells of many of the trips that he and Marge have made, and delineates his genealogy.

– Submitted by O.L. Kimbrough

JOHN, JACOB SOLON & A.A. KING

Paulina and John King came from Bedford County, Tennessee, in 1844. Paulina (Landers) and John King had two children, Nancy (1845-1925) and Jacob Solon (1848-1927). The 1850 Rusk County Census includes the King family, which bought land near the Cherokee "Run Off" (1850 Tax Roll). Jacob Solon married first Juliana Ray and, second, Lula Viola Browning.

In 1870, at age ten, Lula Viola Browning (1862-1930) journeyed to Texas on a wagon train from Clearwater, Florida. Her father, Alexander Mead Browning (1843-1932?), a Confederate soldier, did not return from the Civil War. Five years later, believing her husband was dead and fearful for the welfare of her children, Lula's mother, Sarah Browning (1838-1885), swam a stream swollen by recent rains, carrying each of her five children to board a wagon train headed for East Texas. The family settled in Cross Roads, a small community near Kilgore.

A generation later, Sarah had married Erastus Parr, Lula had married Jacob Solon King, and Lula's older brother, Tom, was a Methodist preacher in Houston. One day when Tom entered his pastor's study, he found a frail, old bewhiskered man who revealed himself to be Tom's long-lost father, Alexander Browning. He told Tom about his capture in Spotsylvania and his imprisonment in Elmira, New York. Alexander had searched unsuccessfully for his family, and had finally tracked down his son. After his Texas visit, Alexander returned to his family in Florida and died a few months later. He is buried in Clearwater, Florida. A handwritten note on a family history reports: "No one can find a divorce decree on Sarah or Alexander. They were true

Asbury Alexander King

A.A. King's descendents, 1978.

Joe and Ola Mae Kuykendall

Methodists." (This family story is included in *The Family Saga: A Collection of Texas Family Legends*, edited by F.E. Abernethy.)

Jacob Solon King had ten children: Mossie, Dura and Willie May from his first marriage; Asbury Alexander, Lecta, Mamie, John, Solon, Esther and Myrtle from his marriage to Lula. Besides farming, Jacob Solon once taught in Kilgore's Alexander Institute (now Lon Morris College in Jacksonville). In 1890, the family moved from Crim's Chapel to Kilgore near present-day Kilgore High School. When Jacob Solon sold his best property to the school, he answered his family's protests: "To what better use could it go than for education?"

Asbury Alexander (A.A.) King (1883-1962) was born at Oak Hill in Rusk County with "love of the land" in his veins. He farmed and operated cotton gins in Smith and Gregg Counties. In 1908, he married Lottie Whittington, a school teacher from Elderville.

They had three children, Viola Della, John Solon (Jolly) and Edward Berry King. In 1916, he purchased a farm near Kilgore and cleared 1,000 acres for cotton farming.

He served as Gregg County Sheriff 1923-25, and a second term 1936-38. During his terms he combated moonshiners, the Ku Klux Klan, boom-time gambling and killings. King believed in keeping "a strong, upper hand" even though he became unpopular by closing "gambling houses" and "honky tonks" at midnight.

Once, he personally delivered a train car-load of criminals from Gregg County to the state penitentiary in Huntsville. His motive for accepting this dangerous job: "I loved the people of Gregg County and wanted to make it a better place in which to live."

His wife, Lottie, died in 1933 and he never remarried. Asbury Alexander King died 15 May 1962, and is buried next to his wife, Lottie Whittington King, in Kilgore. (See "Robert Dabney & Viola King Lipscomb" and "Guttry" histories.)

– Submitted by Dr. Lottie Lipscomb Guttry

J.W. & MARTHA JANE (KILPATRICK) KNOX

John W. "White" Knox and Martha Jane Kilpatrick produced nine children, seven of whom lived until adulthood. Their daughters were Annie, Alvah, Jennie and Lula (died at an early age). Their sons were Walter, Dee, Kirk, Robert Lane and a baby boy who died in infancy.

Annie and Alvah remained unmarried; and Jennie married Zack Little, but they had no children. Neither Walter nor Dee married. Kirk married Claudia (a twin) and they had a daughter, Martha, and sons, Murray, J.W., James D., Galen and Kenneth. Kenneth Lane married Mattie Lee Rhodes and they were the parents of sons, Robert Rhodes and Sidney Earl.

J.W. was a cattle farmer and maintained his gas leases with the help of his boys. Alvah, Annie and Robert Lane were schoolteachers, as was Lane's wife, Mattie Lee. Claudia was a businesswoman and the operator of a wash-a-teria. They all performed church work and community service. J.W. Knox and his family were Baptists and they married Methodists. They lived in Harleton, Texas.

(l.-r.) Front: J.W. Knox, Alvah Knox, wife, Martha Jane Kilpatrick Knox, Zack Little and Jennie K. Little. Back: Lula, Annie, Dee, Walter, Kirk, and Robert Lane Knox.

To date, all are deceased except the children and grandchildren. Sam and Judy Knox moved from Plano, Texas, to Longview, Texas. Sandra and Jim Martin live in Granbury, Texas. Galen and Kenneth Knox live in the Houston area. Joe and Debbie Knox also live in Longview.

– Submitted by Esther Mack Knox

KUYKENDALL

The Kuykendall ancestry has been traced back to Jacob Luursen (pronounced "Lier-son") who, with his wife Styntje (Christina) Douwes, left Amsterdam in 1646 on a West India Company ship. They arrived in New Amsterdam, New Netherlands (later New York, New York), in late 1646 or early 1647. They had only one son, Luur Jacobsen, born in 1650 in New Amsterdam. From him, all Kuykendalls, regardless of how they spell the name, can trace their ancestry. Luur added van Kuykendaal ("view of the vale") about 1705 in Virginia, becoming Luur Jacobsen van Kuykendaal. The van was dropped between 1750 and 1760 by third generation Kuykendalls.

John William Kuykendall brought his family to the new state of Texas in 1845 and settled in the Harmony Hill area of Rusk County. Grandfather Joseph A. Kuykendall was born in Rusk County in 1854. He moved his family to western Harrison County in 1901, and died there in 1930. His son, Joe Henry Kuykendall, was born in Rusk County in 1893, and moved with his parents to western Harrison County in 1901. He served in the Army during World War I and participated in several battles in France. In 1920, he married Tessie Reese, also of western Harrison County. To them three sons were born. Joe G. Kuykendall was born in Longview Sanitarium in 1926; Carroll was born in 1929; and Don was born in 1938. All three are graduates of the University of Texas at Austin, and all earned B.B.A. degrees in accounting.

Carroll and wife, Dee, live west of Cedar Hill in the Dallas area, and they have two married daughters. Both live in Dallas and have two children each. Don and wife, Linda, live in western Harrison County. They have a daughter, Julie, who lives in Longview. She has a daughter and a son. Their son, Mark, and his wife, Monica, live in Harrison County and have two sons.

Although Joe Kuykendall was born in Longview in 1926, he did not become a resident of Gregg County until 2 March 1957, when he married Ola Mae Cowart from Mississippi. She came to Longview in 1954 to teach at Valley View Elementary School. She taught there until retirement in 1987. Joe worked for an independent oil well drilling and well servicing company from 1956 until retirement in 1989.

Joe and Ola Mae's children are David, born 13 September 1961, and Lori, born 7 March 1963. David married Cheryl Krutza, a physical therapist from Carthage. They live in Harrison County at the site where his grandparents lived and where his father grew up. David is Director of the Physical Plant at LeTourneau University. He and his wife are parents of two children: Rachel Alyse, born 2 June 1999, and Emily Sarah, born 26 May 2001. Lori lives in Longview and works at Buckner Westminster Place.

– Submitted by Joe Kuykendall

LANAGAN

W.A. "Tony" Lanagan was born 17 November 1893, in Lake Charles, Louisiana. His father, John Antonio, was master of the tug *Isabel*, and his grandfather captained the schooner *Welcome*.

Eddie and W.A. "Tony" Lanagan in 1927 just after they arrived in Longview.

Tony Lanagan decided on a different career in 1903, when he saw "The Great Train Robbery." He grew up working in movie houses and came to Longview in 1927 to manage the Rembert Theatre. He introduced talking pictures to Gregg County in 1929.

The family initially was three children from a previous marriage – W.A. Jr., Ruby and John Mercer – and wife, Eddie Irene (Mayo), who he married 23 July 1927, in Beaumont. A third son, John Mayo Lanagan, was born to this marriage 13 July 1930.

Tony was an integral part of Longview entertainment for three decades, managing several theatres and opening the Rita and Arlyne theatres in 1935 and 1939. He was a Mason, director of the Longview Chamber of Commerce and

The Lanagan children, John Mayo, John Mercer, Ruby and Billy (Dr. W.A. Lanagan Jr.) photographed in 1933 on the scenery dock behind the Rembert Theatre. A housing shortage during the East Texas oil boom caused the family to live in the Rembert's backstage dressing rooms while the family home at 1125 Judson Road was being built.

30-year member of the Longview Rotary Club. Tony and Eddie Lanagan divorced in 1948. He later married Reba Bryant and had a fourth son, Tracy William, born 3 March 1952. Tony Lanagan died 3 November 1956.

After 1948, Eddie Lanagan worked 25 years at the *Houston Chronicle* and returned to Longview when she retired in 1975. She was a Good Shepherd Hospital Auxiliary volunteer and died 21 October 2000. She is buried in Forest Lawn cemetery, Beaumont.

W.A. Lanagan, Jr. (Billy) graduated from the University of Texas, served in the U.S. Coast Guard in World War II, married Mary Etta Massengill in 1941, and had three sons, Tony, Mike and Bill. He earned a doctorate in education and was Superintendent of Pine Tree ISD when he died suddenly in May 1964.

Ruby worked in Washington during World War II, returned to Longview and married Roy C. Cobb, a funeral director. They had one son, Robert Edward. She died 13 July 1984, and is buried in Memory Park cemetery, Longview, where Roy, Tony, Billy and Mary also rest.

John Mercer went to live with his birth mother, became a shipping executive and died in Portland, Oregon, 11 December 1988.

John Mayo Lanagan was educated at Longview High School, Kilgore College and Lamar University. He married Mary Janet Fort 11 March 1950. They had four children born in Longview: Judith Lynn, 9 October 1951; David Mayo, 19 October 1952; Elizabeth Sean, 4 November 1954; and John Matthew, 14 November 1955.

John Mayo was a reporter and editor for Longview newspapers, and did public relations work for Bell Telephone and Lone Star Steel Company, where he was public relations director for 22 years. He was a director and president of Hospital in the Pines, officer and director of the East Texas Chamber of Commerce and a founding director of the Texas Chamber of Commerce.

Tracy Willam Lanagan graduated from Longview High School and the University of Houston. He works in sales and married Jane Carol Stephens 3 June 1978. They have two children, Jena Renee and John William.

– Submitted by John Mayo Lanagan

AL & GLADYS LANCASTER

John Albert Lancaster, son of Ernest A. and Lola Elma Denman Lancaster, was born 11 October 1921, in Hutchinson, Reno County, Kansas. He married Gladys Nina Glasscock, daughter of Dewey Gadston and Nina Bates Glasscock, 11 October 1952, at her parents home in Little Rock, Arkansas. Gladys was born 4 August 1924, in Tunnel Hill, Georgia, at her grandparents', Tully Democrat and Luara Deck Bates, home. Al died on 26 October 1971, in Kilgore, Texas, and is buried in Pinecrest Memorial Park, Alexander, Saline County, Arkansas.

Al grew up in Westville, Oklahoma, and Gladys grew up in Little Rock, Arkansas. They met at the Boston Avenue Methodist Church when they were both living in Tulsa, Oklahoma. Gladys was transferred to Oklahoma City, Oklahoma.

After they married, they moved to Burkburnett, Texas, where Al taught Vocation Agriculture. In March 1953, he became an Assistant County Agent in Upshur County, Texas. Al had graduated from Oklahoma A&M College with a Bachelor of Science degree in Agriculture & Agricultural Education in 1943. Later, he earned a Master's degree in Agronomy from Texas A&M. He was an Agronomist with the Texas A&M Agriculture Extension Service. He worked for many years on location at Mt. Pleasant and at the Agricultural Research and Extension Center at Overton, Texas. They moved to Kilgore, Texas, in 1965.

After graduating from Little Rock Senior High School, Gladys worked as a secretary for Aetna Insurance Company. She then moved to Tulsa and worked for Standard Oil and Gas Company. Gladys became a full time mother, but later was employed by Mobley Company and the University of Texas Petroleum Extension Service in Kilgore.

During World War II Al served as a Tec 4 with the 155th General Hospital in the U.S. and European Theater (1943-1946).

Al and Gladys' first daughter is Emily Anne Lancaster, born 31 May 1956, in Longview, Gregg County, Texas; on 14 March 1981, in St. Luke United Methodist Church, in Kilgore, she married Michael Olen Brumfield, son of John Olen and Nettie Louise Newman Brumfield. Michael was born 30 November 1956, in McComb, Pike County, Mississippi. He is a graduate of Mississippi State University with an Mechanical Engineering degree and Master of Engineering from Louisiana Tech University. Mike is employed at Eastman Chemical. Anne graduated from Texas A&M with an Accounting degree. She worked for Amoco Oil Company and the City of Longview, and is now a full time mother. They have two daughters.

Al and Gladys' younger daughter is Jan Alberta Lancaster, born 25 November 1958, in Longview, Texas; on 23 January 1988, at St. Luke United Methodist Church, she married Jerald Wayne Lewis, son of Carroll Denman and Helen Jean Mount Lewis. Jerald was born 29 January 1960, in Mena, Polk County, Arkansas. He is a graduate of the University of Arkansas with an Electrical Engineering degree and is employed by Eastman Chemical. Jane graduated from Texas A&M with a degree in Marketing. She is employed by Texas Chemical as a System Analyst. They have two sons and a daughter.

– Submitted by Gladys Lancaster, Kilgore, Texas

LANDERS

Kathryn, Ray and Jo Ann Landers, the children of Jim and Effie Landers, grew up in their home on Judson Road and all attended Judson schools from first grade until graduation.

Kathryn was graduated in 1948 as Salutatorian of her class. Ray was graduated in 1960 as Valedictorian of his class; and, Jo Ann was gradu-

JoAnn Landers Miller, James Rayburn (Ray) Landers and Mary Kathryn (Kathy) Cabaniss

ated in 1961 as No. 3 and the highest ranking girl in her class. Effie was active in PTA all the years her children attended Judson. She and Jim supported the Band Parents Club and chaperoned trips when Ray was in the band. Jim was an avid sports fan and the Judson Blue Devils had no greater fan. He began attending football games when Judson had its first football team in 1937. Ray and Jo Ann played basketball, so Jim and Effie attended all the basketball games as well as the football games, where Jo Ann served as a cheerleader. Basketball was an early sport for Jim and Effie, as they both played when they were in school.

Kathryn attended East Texas State University, Kilgore Jr. College and North Texas State University before graduating in 1951 with a B.B.A. degree, just three years after her graduation from Judson. She taught one year at New London High School. In 1953, she began work in the Engineering Department at Texas Eastman Company, where she worked for Mr. John English. She was the secretary for Dr. R.J. Schrader while he was developing the Polyethylene Plant at Eastman. In 1956, Kathryn moved to Dallas where she worked for Mobil Oil Company. She was married on 29 July 1961, to Charles Davis Cabaniss. She continued working at Mobil until 1963 when their son was born. In 1978, Kathryn began working in the library at Lake Highlands High School and in 198–, she returned to the University of North Texas where she received her M.L.S. Degree. She retired as an elementary school librarian from the Richardson Independent School District in 1997. She still resides in Dallas with her husband. Their children are son Kevin and his wife Carol, and daughter Kristin. They have one granddaughter, Peyton, and two grandsons, Tanner and Trace.

Ray attended the University of Texas at Austin where he was graduated in 1964 with a B.S. degree. He began his career as a math teacher and 7th grade basketball coach with the Deer Park Independent School District. He moved up a grade as a coach each year until he became the Varsity Coach and remained that for eleven years. He then served as Athletic Director for the District. On 16 May 1993, he received his Doctor of Education Degree from the University of Houston. He served as Deputy Superintendent until his retirement in December 1998. In January 1999, Ray began his second career as a Financial Consultant and became a partner in Robertson, Landers and Associates with offices in Deer Park and Houston.

Jo Ann attended Kilgore Jr. College where she graduated as Salutatorian in the class of 1963. She then attended North Texas State University where she earned a B.B.A. degree in January 1965. She taught business courses at Lake Highlands High School in the Richardson Independent School District where Mr. A.M. Anderson, former Superintendent at Judson, was the Principal. Jo Ann met her future husband, Jerry Miller, while both were teaching at Lake Highlands. On 12 August 1968, Jo Ann received her M.Ed. with a concentration in counseling. Jo Ann and Jerry were married on 27 November 1968. After her marriage, she served as a school counselor at Lake Highlands Junior High School until their oldest son was born. Jo Ann is currently employed at a financial services firm. She and Jerry reside in Dallas and have two sons, Mason and Brandon.

– Submitted by Jo Ann Miller

JAMES CLARIENCE LANDERS & EFFIE BELL MATTOX

Jim Landers and Effie Mattox married on 26 November 1927, at 8:00 p.m. in the home of Dr. John L. Whorton, pastor of the First Baptist Church of Longview. A train ride took them to Dallas to begin married life. They resided in Dallas where their first child, Mary Kathryn Landers, was born on 6 May 1931. When she was six weeks old, the family moved to the East Mountain Community near Gladewater, Texas, to reside with Jim's family. He and his father, Christopher Columbus Landers, operated a grocery/service station. His mother, Amanda Killingsworth Landers, and Effie operated a boarding house for oil field workers who were drilling wells on the Landers property.

In early 1933, Jim and Effie built a new home on their farm that was located on Judson Road, where presently Loop 281 crosses. The farm included the land where Longview High School is built and the land on the west side where a strip mall is today.

Jim was reared in the East Mountain Community, but his great grandparents, John Sweet Killingsworth and Emmeline Abney, had come from Selma, Bibb County, Alabama, in 1851 and settled in a part of Upshur County that later became Gregg County. They are buried in the "JSK" Killingsworth Family Cemetery located on the Pliler/Boswell Ranch, Pliler-Precise Road, Longview, Texas. His grandparents,

Effie Mattox Landers and James Clarience Landers, 1983

John Albert Killingsworth and Mary Rebecca Garner, came to the area sometime between 1866 and 1868. They are buried in the Old Summerfield Cemetery at Summerfield Methodist Church. Jim's mother, Amanda, was the tenth child of their 14 children.

Effie was the daughter of George Starling Mattox and Mary Elizabeth Smith. She was born in the Judson Community and attended Harmony Grove School. Mary Elizabeth became a widow in 1919, when her husband was killed by a run-away team of horses. Lizzie, as she was affectionately known, reared her five daughters on the farm until they all married. Effie lived in the area until her death on 19 January 1987.

Jim worked on his farm and Effie was a true housewife. In 1936, Emmit and Una Mae Martin came to live on the farm. Emmit helped Jim in the fields and Una Mae, who was only 18 at the time, came to the house to help Effie.

The family increased on 24 May 1942, when a son, James Rayburn Landers, was born. Another daughter, Jo Ann Landers, was born in 17 July 1943.

The farm produced some cotton and corn, but it mostly produced food for the table. In the 1940s, Jim worked for W.W. Melton, a Continental Oil Company Distributor, and then operated a Conoco station on the Marshall Highway. In the early 1950s, Jim became a custodian for the Judson Independent School District. After Judson's consolidation with Longview ISD, he worked at Mozelle Johnston Elementary School until he officially retired in 1970. In 1972, he began to work again at Mozelle Johnston and worked there four hours a day until the day he died on 7 July 1992. He started work between 5:30 and 6:00 a.m. and got home about 11:00 a.m. He went to work on that July morning, came home at 11:00 for lunch, sat down in a chair and died.

Effie became a member of the Judson Baptist Church, now First Baptist Church of Judson, when she was a child. Jim became a member when they moved to the community. Effie was active in the Women's Missionary Union, Bible School, and could always be counted on to cook for special activities. Jim served the church as Treasurer, Sunday School Teacher for several different ages, custodian and was a Deacon for 50 years.

– Submitted by Kathryn Landers Cabiness

ENOCH LAWRENCE

From Bibb County, Alabama, Enoch and Ann Belvin Lawrence, with six of their ten children traveled to the Pine Tree area to visit friends and relatives, accompanied by their nephew John Wesley and Elizabeth Belvin Lawrence and their two children. Later, Enoch settled in Grey Rock, Titus County, and his nephew remained in what is now Gregg County where he became the first Precinct 3 Peace Justice and a strong businessman.

Enoch's initial visit led to the marriage of two daughters. In 1869, Cynthia Jane Lawrence married William James Rodden of the Rodden pioneer family. Three children were born: Caddie, Lawrence and I.P. William Rodden died at

Aaron Trice Castleberry III and Cynthia Lawrence Castleberry

Enoch's home in 1874 and was buried in the old Monticello Cemetery, Titus County.

In 1878, Cynthia married Aaron Trice Castleberry III (pictured), another pioneer family. To this union Maud was born. Aaron and his brother, James Rodden Castleberry, operated agriculture, retail lumber and lumber milling businesses under the name of "Castleberry Brothers." These brothers provided strong financial support to establish Gregg County and ensured continued growth of Gregg County.

In 1882, Agnes Lodeema (Deedie) Lawrence married James Rodden Castleberry. Three children were born: Mae Dee, James Herman (pictured with parents) and Joseph Jack. James and Deedie were active in the affairs of the Spring Hill community including donation of the land for Elmira Chapel Presbyterian Church. After the death of his wife, James continued to promote growth in Longview and singly raised his children.

Hollie Middleton Lawrence, Enoch's grandson, came to Gregg County in 1898 where he worked for his uncles, the Castleberry Brothers, in their lumber business in Gladewater. In 1903, Hollie married Lillie Iona Shelby of Franklin County. Later, they moved to Longview and raised their sons, Holly M. Jr., Fred Parker and William Warren.

Hollie, Sr. continued to work for James Castleberry until 1920. He established the "Lawrence Lumber Company" with his brother, Henry Winfred, on East Cotton Street. Hollie, Sr. was a deacon in the First Baptist Church of Longview, director of the Citizens National Bank and later director of the First National Bank. After retirement in 1931, he remained interested in the progress and development of Longview.

Hollie Lawrence Sr.'s brother, Garland Belvin, wife, Jessie Campbell Lawrence and

Agnes Lodeema Lawrence and James Rodden Castleberry, Mae Dee, James Herman and Joseph Jack

son, Garland Belvin, Jr., moved to Longview from Franklin County in 1935. Garland became a prominent farmer/dairyman. His son, G.B. Lawrence, Jr., became a homebuilder.

Another great grandson of Enoch Lawrence, Kemp G. Lawrence, and his wife, Patti Geers, moved to Longview with their daughter, Betsy Kim, in 1957 from Titus County. Two children were born in Longview: Nancy Elizabeth and Joey Kemp. Presently, all make their home in Longview. In 2003, a great great great grandson of Enoch and Ann Belvin Lawrence was born to Joey and Suzanne Taylor Lawrence. All Kemp's children and five grandchildren have graduated from or are presently enrolled in Pine Tree schools. All live near where Enoch Lawrence visited family, where Aaron and Cynthia Lawrence lived/died and where early Lawrence/Castleberry/Rodden families ran their farms and businesses.

– Submitted by Kemp Lawrence

HOLLIS LLOYD LAWRENCE JR.

Moving to the Gregg County area of Gladewater, Texas, was one of the best moves that Hollis and Ruth Lawrence ever made. Arriving in Gladewater about 1965, they bought the Ritz Pharmacy from Jake and Mary Beth Couch. At one time, during the oil boom, it was the Stancell Drug Store. What a thrill for the young couple with three sons: Hollis Dee, Michael Lloyd and Edward Joseph Lawrence. All three graduated from Gladewater High School and are members of the Sons of the American Revolution.

Hollis and Ruth Lawrence, 1951

Hollis Lloyd is the son of Hollis Lloyd Lawrence, Sr. and Julia Cordelia Gillespie of Carthage, Texas. Finishing high school in 1948, he entered the Air Force and served in French Morocco, North Africa. Returning home, he went to the University of Texas and received his Pharmacy degree, B.S.R.Ph. He is a Methodist, a Mason, a Kappa Sig and belongs to the Texas Pharmacy Association. Hollis is a member of the Sons of the American Revolution and traces his ancestry back to Scotland, Ireland and England to 1620. He is a collateral relative of William Penn, signer of the Declaration of Independence. John Wortham has honored his tenth generation great grandson of Middlesex County, Virginia, as being a member of the First Families of Virginia.

Ruth Neundorfer and Hollis Lawrence were married in Groesbeck, Texas, on 12 August 1951. She is the daughter of Col. O.J. Neundorfer (Ret.) of Albany, Georgia, and Ruth Edward (Eddie) Oliver of Limestone County, Texas. Her ancestry makes her a direct descendant of Andrew Miller, who came into Texas to join Austin's Colony and fight for Texas Independence. Her great great grandmother Celia Neal Miller was in the "run away Scrape" from Santa Anna.

She is a member of the Daughters of the Republic of Texas and a Methodist. Ruth also belongs to the Colonial Dames (ancestor Capt. David Peebles) and the Daughters of the American Revolution (ancestor Sylvanious Walker). She attended Southern Methodist University, where she was a member of Delta Delta Delta sorority, at Dallas, Texas. Advance Personnel Service was owned by her in Longview, Texas.

Hollis Dee Lawrence married Mary Lou Gipson of New London, Texas, and they have two sons, Jeremy Dee and Jonathan Chance Lawrence. Michael Lloyd Lawrence married Michelle C. Dossman of Eunice, Louisiana, and they have one son Christopher Michael Lawrence. Edward Joseph Lawrence has two children, Clay Edward and adoptive daughter Callye Renee Lawrence.

The strong legacy left to Hollis and Ruth Lawrence by their ancestors is their belief in God, to serve their country, work hard, be honest and to go forward with courage in keeping of this nation's freedom. May these convictions extend to the generations to come.

– Submitted by Ruth Lawrence

LEAGUE

George Marjoribanks, changed to Marchbanks, an exiled Jacobite Scotsman imprisoned by the British, arrived in Virginia on the *Elizabeth and Ann* on 14 January 1716. Later wed to Ann Echols, their children were John, George, Lucy, Sarah, William, Joseph, Ursula and Mary Ann.

Mary Ann Marchbanks was born about 1735, married James League about 1754, and died 5 November 1817, in Amelia County, Virginia. The will of James League is recorded in Amelia County, Will Book 8, page 120, March 1813.

A deed dated 21 November 1746, shows James League, Jr. and Mary Anna sold the 100-acre tract given to Mary Anna by a deed from her father, George Marchbanks.

James and Mary had numerous children, one of which, named Joab, was born 5 May 1759, in Amelia County, died 22 May 1829, and is buried at Clear Springs Church in Simpsonville, Greenville County, South Carolina. Joab received a land grant of 300 acres in South Carolina and married Patience Marchbanks. Their son, Joel, was born 8 September 1795, and died 1858 in Greenville County, South Carolina. His will is filed in Will Book B, page 107. Joel was a member of the 3rd Regiment, Astairs, South Carolina Militia. He married Nancy Jones.

Of this union, came Joel Perry League, born 7 February 1833, died 28 October 1862. Joel married Harriett Williams. Their son was

Luther and Minnie League with children, Lois League, John League, Earl League and Joe League.

Ciccero C. League, who married Angeline Fowler on 3 May 1877, in Carroll County, Georgia. Their son, Joe Luther Perry League, was born 17 June 1886, in Macon and died August 1961, in Longview, Texas. Joe Luther married Minnie Teressa Stephens, 9 December 1909. Luther was a farmer. As Luther and Minnie washed clothes together, their singing could be heard coming from the kitchen. Their daughter, Lela Lois, born 7 November 1911, married Thomas Cecil Nichols, 11 June 1932, and died 2 February 2003. Children were James Garland, born 19 March 1937, and died 1 January 1996, and Lanyta Dianne, born 26 June 1942.

Cecil worked for Kelly Plow Company in Longview, and then Humble Oil Company in Cisco, living in Humble Camp. Lois loved to cook and take care of her family and was a blessing to everyone she met.

James Garland married Linda Fay Evans, 4 September 1955. James worked at the Longview National Bank, but retired from Commerce Bank. They had James Garland, Jr. and Jon Mark. James Jr. married Rebecca Bowden, 9 June 1978. Their children are Christopher Jared, Kevin Scot and James Michael. John Mark married Debbie Sullivan, 31 August 1999. James Garland died 1 January 1996.

Lanyta Dianne married Milton William Evans, Jr., 21 November 1959. Their children are Danyta Kay, Lanyta Kayann, Danesa Gayle and Milton Todd. Lanyta married Ronald Dale Holloman, 23 May 1981. Their children are Ashley Kayann and Dustin Dallas. Ashley

(l.-r.) Earl League, Morgan League, Lois League, Bessie League and Joe League.

Kayann married Trinity Wade Grisham, 26 October 2002. Danesa Gayle married Ray C. Hanson, 7 September 1991, and of this union was born Branden Ray. Milton Todd Evans married Mary Oates, 11 April 2001.

– Submitted by Lanyta Dianne Nichols Evans,
Longview, Texas

ROBERT GILMOUR LETOURNEAU

Robert Gilmour LeTourneau was born on 30 November 1888, in Richford, Vermont, the son of Caleb T. and Elizabeth (Lorimer) LeTourneau. After an elementary education, he learned mechanics and engineering through correspondence courses. He was living in San Francisco at the time of the great earthquake. During the rebuilding he was introduced to the welding torch and throughout his career he was recognized as one of the pioneers in constructing machines entirely by welding rather than with rivets.

In 1909, at age twenty-one, R.G. moved to Stockton, California, where he began a dirt-moving business and built his own scrapers. He built the first all-welded scraper with electric motors to adjust the blade, and he invented the bulldozer blade that attached to the front of a caterpillar tractor. In 1932, he used rubber tires instead of steel wheels for the first time on heavy equipment. Not only was he mechanically creative, he established two unique employee programs as well: educational programs for employees to improve their skills and an industrial chaplain program.

The development of the self-propelled, scraper-earthmover in the late 1930s placed R.G. LeTourneau Inc. in the forefront of the earthmoving and heavy equipment industry just as World War II was beginning. In 1946, he moved his operations to Longview, Texas. Most notably, LeTourneau built mobile platforms for offshore drilling. He was referred to often as "God's Businessman" because he dedicated 90 percent of his company stock to the LeTourneau Foundation, which sponsored Christian missions in South America and Africa, and financed LeTourneau Technical Institute from its founding in 1946 until 1961.

He was a trustee of John Brown University, Siloam Springs, Arkansas, and a member of the board of reference of Wheaton College in Illinois. He was active in the Christian Business Men's Committee International, in which he served a term as president. LeTourneau died on 1 June 1969, in Longview and was survived by his wife, Mary Evelyn Peterson LeTourneau, and their five children.

ROBERT DABNEY & VIOLA KING LIPSCOMB

Viola King, daughter of Asbury and Lottie King (see "John, Jacob Solon & A.A. King" biography), graduated in 1926 from Longview High School and attended the College of Industrial Arts (now TWU) in Denton, achieving a BA degree. She took post-graduate courses at U.C.L.A. and the University of Colorado. While teaching English at Longview High School in 1932, Viola met her future husband, Robert

Dabney Lipscomb of Dallas, who was supervising construction of the new high school on Whaley Street.

Robert Dabney Lipscomb (1902-1954) was the youngest child of Dr. Cuvier Lipscomb (1840-1915). In 1861, Cuvier came with his family from Middleton, Mississippi, to Grapevine, Texas. Enlisting in the Confederate Army, Cuvier served under his cousin Major Khleber Miller Van Zandt in Company D, Seventh Texas Infantry in Marshall. After two years as private, he was promoted to hospital steward, which required him to perform surgery on wounded soldiers. He fought in the battles of Ft. Donelson, Shiloh, Corinth, Chickamauga and Atlanta. After the war he completed his medical degree at Virginia Medical College in 1865.

Robert Dabney Lipscomb and Viola King Lipscomb, about 1950.

In 1865, Dr. Cuvier Lipscomb settled in Denton, Texas, as the first practicing physician. His first wife, Mary A. Walden, died in 1880, leaving her husband and six sons. In 1890, he married Emma Belle Gregg. They had two children, Emma Belle and Robert Dabney Lipscomb.

Dabney Lipscomb studied architecture at the University of Texas at Austin, where he joined the Sigma Chi fraternity. After working for several architectural firms in Dallas and Austin, he obtained a position in the office of Mark Lemmon where he helped design the Tower Petroleum Building in Dallas, the Third Church of Christ Scientist in Dallas, seven schools in Port Arthur, Longview High School and the Cotton Bowl.

In spring 1932, while working in Longview, he met Viola King. Their friendship grew during the spring and summer. Because of the Depression, Mr. Lemmon had to close his office, causing Dabney to lose his position. That fall Viola and Dabney became engaged and were married on 4 February 1933. After their marriage Viola's father, Asbury A. King, offered Dabney the position of overseeing his oil properties in East Texas. The Lipscombs were active in St. Luke's Methodist Church in Kilgore, and Dabney served on the Kilgore ISD school board. A member of AIA, Dabney designed several Kilgore buildings during the 1950s, including Center Chevrolet, the Laird Hospital addition and Sabine School.

After a courageous battle with cancer, Robert Dabney Lipscomb died in Kilgore, 9 November 1954. In 1957, Viola married Hollis Kinsey, a Pepsi-Cola bottler, and moved to Tupelo, Mississippi.

Three children were born to Viola and Dabney Lipscomb: Lottie Lou (1934), Robert Dabney, Jr.(1937) and Diane King Lipscomb

(1939). In 1957, Lottie married Dr. John Sutherlin Guttry, who practiced dentistry in Longview (see "Guttry" history). Robert Dabney, Jr. (Bob) married Sandra (Cissy) Gehlen of Kilgore and lives in Georgetown; Diane married Max Kimmel of Kilgore and lives in San Marcos.

– Submitted by Viola King Lipscomb Kinsey

LITTLE, PICKETT & FULTON: The 1950s Gregg County Settlement

In the Texas oil fields of the 1930s, employment was fresh on the minds of most folks who were contemplating settling in the piney woods of Gregg County. World War II was ending with D-Day on the beaches of Normandy, 6 June 1944, and V-E Day (Victory in Europe), May of 1945. The August 1945 atomic bombing of Hiroshima and Nagasaki had brought Japan to her knees and removed the threat of further Japanese attacks and marked the surrender of Japan and the end of the war on 2 September 1945.

Industry boomed in Gregg County after the war with the advent of many new inventions and patents. The Industrial Revolution had modernized daily life while bringing the soldiers from the farmlands to the towns and cities. This trend continued from the 1940s into the 1950s, bringing courageous days as had not been seen since the East Texas Oil Boom that began settlements in and around Gregg County.

Florida native Harvey Little and his lovely wife, Irene Pickett, tied the noble knot of matrimony in 1949 in Houston Texas. Setting out for fame and fortune, Harvey brought his bride to Longview, Texas, in 1950 to pursue a home building and real estate business. The need for housing was great as most newcomers had to settle in the old World War II Harmon Army Hospital barracks located on the LeTourneau College Campus. Mr. R.G. LeTourneau operated a great industrial steel plant, called RG LeTourneau Incorporated, where he revolutionized earth-moving equipment and steel fabrication for the military.

Harvey's bride, Irene, a six-year World War II Veteran Army Captain and nurse, quickly helped Dr. John Wensley establish a medical clinic on Longview's south side where he also served as company physician for the Le Tourneau plant and Texas Eastman Kodak, two of Gregg County's major employers.

Irene influenced her family from McCaskill, Arkansas, to join her in Texas. Her brother, Winford Pickett, and his wife, Mamie Stone Pickett, and children, James Doye, Ross, Eugene, Ronnie, Syble and husband, Bob Youse, a LeTourneau College graduate, responded quickly by settling first on the LeTourneau Campus and later in Pinewood Park. Irene's father, Joseph Preston Pickett, widower of the late Mary Beaulah Hampton and a brother, "Chuck" Mearl A. Pickett and his wife, Easther Arlene Mouser Pickett, and five children, James, Jo Ann, Betty, Robert and Brenda Fulton joined them in Texas in 1958.

Among the Arkansan relatives that settled in Gregg County were the siblings of Mamie Stone Pickett: sister, Helen Stone, husband, Kenneth B. Rowland and children, Brenda, Gail and Dianne; brother, Harold Stone and wife, Delores Ann Cox and children, Debra, Jeffery and Mary Beth; and another sister, Bertha Stone, and husband, Leslie Fielding, and children, Naomi "Toppie," Patsy, Peggy, Jerry and Mike. Most of these families lived on the LeTourneau College Campus in the early days before relocating throughout the city of Longview. The children attended schools in Longview and Greggton, located west of Longview. Family gatherings were frequent and Grandpa Pickett, was happy to be reunited with his children, Irene and Chuck, who had served in World War II. Chuck had also served in the Civilian Conservation Corps in Salinas, California. Grandpa Pickett died in 1968 and was taken back to Arkansas for burial beside his beloved Beulah. This set a trend, and as retirement and death cast her shadows, one by one, the family returned to the lovely foothills and fertile lands of Southwest Arkansas. It is said, if you listen carefully on cool evenings in October after the sun sets, that you can hear dancing in the leaves and music as it falls upon the corn stalks near the vegetable patches of days gone by as the settlers rejoiced with happy, round-faced children for peaceful afternoons in the sunshine of Gregg County life.

– Submitted by Brenda Poole, Diana, Texas

ELIZA LOCKETT ROSS & JOHN ROSS

Because of the nature and intent of slavery, no records were forwarded out of that institution to freedom with the liberation of those who had been enslaved. Therefore, today's society must rely on oral historians for information through the Civil War and, for some, even a generation thereafter.

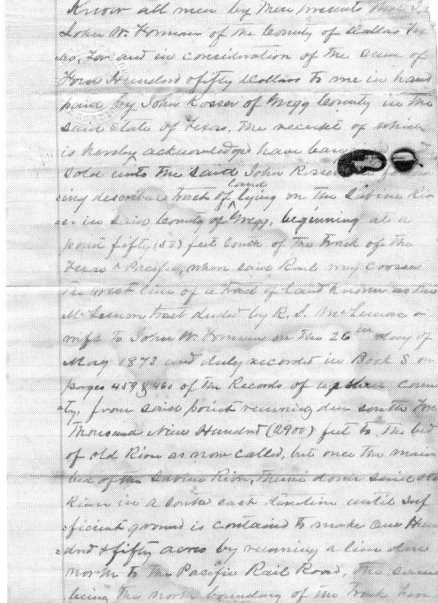
Deed of land purchase of John Ross and Eliza Lockett Ross.

According to sketchy documentation and the memory of community elders, Eliza (Lockett) Ross, who was born a slave in 1846 (died 10 April 1914), was one of the earliest black landowners in Red Rock Community, just west of Gladewater. Eliza Lockett Ross was known by all three names, which was unusual for a black woman in Texas in the early 1870s. She came to Texas from Hollie, Arkansas, and settled first in Henderson County. She and her husband, John Ross (died 12 October 1903), and their five children eventually settled in Red Rock. Some legal documents name John Ross as "John Rosser." The name discrepancy can be explained: Since the white man expected to be addressed as "sir," probably in response to being asked what his name was, he responded, "John Ross, sir," and it was interpreted and recorded as "Rosser." No documentation exists that explains why all children wore the name of Lockett and the mother and father wore Ross. The children were Essek Lockett (born 19 September 1865), William "Bill" Lockett (born 1869; died 1938), Nancy (Lockett) Barnes (born 1867; died 1945), Lenora (Lockett) Pouncy (born 4 March 1892; died 18 June 1953), and Laura Mitchell (no statistics).

More is remembered about Eliza than is remembered about John by those who live to tell the story. By the time Eliza passed away, she had amassed a respectable amount of land; and in 1876, had donated land for the organization of the St. James Baptist Church, the first to be established in the Red Rock community. Eliza Ross, Ruff and Margaret Cannon, Anderson Barnes,

Little-Pickett-Fulton families at the wedding of Bob Youse and Syble Pickett, May 9, 1958.

Henry Moland, Alex Hanson, Anderson Brown, Ben and Emma Powell, Willie and Eliza Dearion, Samuel Thompkins, Sandy and Florence Hawley, John Manuel Floyd Sr. and Perry Wilburn organized the church. The small congregation first met in Eliza Ross' home, then in a brush arbor, a box structure and a two-frame building. Today, St. James Baptist Church is the brick church that stands at the entrance into the community off Highway 80 across from the rodeo grounds. From these twelve families grew the thriving community of Red Rock as it stood through the 1970s and 1980s. The descendants of these families developed skills that made Red Rock self-sufficient, productive and a great contributor to the growth and development of Gladewater.

John Ross and Eliza Lockett Ross set the course for the community: the acquisition of land and the productive development of Red Rock that has continued and produced about seven generations of valuable citizens who still contribute to the American society. John and Eliza and most of those founding members who are now deceased are buried in the Red Rock Community Cemetery.
– Submitted by Bonnie Moore

ESSEK & MATTIE (WILSON) LOCKETT

Essek Lockett was the oldest child of Eliza and John Ross. It is believed that he was born in Hollie, Arkansas, but raised in the Red Rock Community. Essek continued the legacy started by John and Eliza of owning land. On 25 February 1888, Essek bought about 65 acres of land for $195.00 which ran along side his father's property – skirting Gregg and Upshur Counties. Essek also instilled in his children the value of land ownership, the privileges it afforded and the power it brought.

Mattie and Essek Lockett

Essek married Mattie (Wilson) Lockett (b. 6 March 1867; d. 25 April 1933) from neighboring Camp Community, now known as Shiloh. Their children were Ira Lockett (b. 2 November 1902; d. 1989), Ellison Smart Lockett (b. 12 February 1894; d. 6 January 1916), Oliver Lockett (b. 30 April 1895; d. 23 May 1956), Exora (Lockett) Williams (b. 2 November 1896; d. 18 January 1934), twins Della (Lockett) Hawley and Dell Lockett (no statistics), Corene Harper (no statistics), Asbury (Jam) Lockett (b. 15 March 1903; d. 28 March 1972), and Clemmie (Lockett) Coby (b. 18 April 1904; d. 22 May 1982).

Essek built his home. It is the oldest structure still standing in Red Rock at the end of Rodeo St. His youngest daughter, Clemmie, inherited the home and lived in it with her family. It is now rental property for her descendants. Essek donated a second parcel of land to the St. James Baptist Church which spots where the edifice stands today at the entrance to the Red Rock Community. Essek earned a living through cotton farming, vegetable crops and timber work. Simply because of his age, it is also believed that he must have worked the railroad. He served as deacon of the church, Worshipful Master of Lodge #278, was featured in the Louisiana Baptist Association yearly publication in 1914, and was named in the yearly reports of the Master Masons for several years.

His second son, Oliver, served in World War I. Witnessing the horrors of this war, Oliver became insane and ran away from the war. In an effort to hop a train, he lost a leg and part of his other foot. For several years he was institutionalized, until his father, Essek, and later his brother, Ira, were able to gain custody of him. He lived out long and prosperous years in the home and care of Ira Lockett. Clemmie's husband, John L. Coby, was the community barber. Della's husband, Robert, was the community rock layer. Ellison Smart died early as a result of an accident while trying to herd cattle to higher ground during a flood. He rode his horse into a low hanging tree limb and was knocked into raging waters.

Just one generation removed from slavery, at Essek's death on 11 September 1934, he owned the largest house in the community and 248 acres of land. He left a handwritten will with his oldest son, Ira, as its executor.

IRA G. LOCKETT

Essek and Mattie Lockett's oldest son, Ira, (2 November 1892–28 March 1989) married Ora Cannon (24 December 1894–27 January 1969) on 14 February 1915. Her parents were Ruff Cannon (4 October 1849–6 August 1929) and Margaret Cannon (16 June 1839–24 March 1924). (Ruff and Margaret were married 5 December 1877. Ruff was son of Rebecca (Allen) Cannon and Gilbert Cannon.) Ira and Ora's children were Connie Mae (Lockett) Loftis/Heleum (17 November 1915–18 May 1965), Ira Mae (Lockett) Taylor/Sparks (born December 1917; living in Arlington, Texas), Arula (Lockett) Clay (born 3 June 1919; living in the Red Rock Community), Reverend Bevin (B.W.) Lockett (29 January 1921–20 July 2001) whose widow, Thelma (Reese) Lockett, lives in Longview, Texas, Roscoe C. Lockett (18 March 1923; living with his second wife, Florence (Parker) Lockett, in the Ira Lockett home in Red Rock; his first wife, Efella (Davis) Lockett is deceased), and Ruby Lee Lockett (31 August 1924–30 July 1956). Ira, the oldest child, was the last to pass away. His wife Ora, the youngest of her siblings, was the last to pass away. She was a housewife and never held a job outside the home.

Ira continued the legacy of accumulating property with the philosophy that "They can't make any more of this." He became the most prominent citizen in the history of Red Rock. He raised six children and two became the first

Ira G. Lockett and Ora Lockett

college graduates from the community: Connie and Ira Mae graduated with teaching degrees from Jarvis Christian College. At his death, Ira had accumulated land that amounted to over 300 acres in Red Rock and Shiloh communities. He had successfully run three businesses: Lockett's Saw Mill in the 1930s, a syrup mill in the 1940s and 1950s, and Lockett's General Stores in the 1920s and again in the 1940s-1960s. He had established himself as a landlord of properties and had provided employment for other community members. He served as secretary as well as deacon for St. James Church. He was Worshipful Master of Master Mason Lodge #278, just as his father had been. He championed many political movements. (His biggest fight was against the city dump being placed in Red Rock – he lost.) Politicians sought his support because of his influence in the Black communities. He organized and served as president of The Red Rock Layman Civic Club in August 1957, as well as president of the Red Rock Cemetery Association. He was featured on the "Points of Interest" series hosted by Carlton Corbin on KLMG in the late 1970s or early 1980s and was often reported on in the *Gladewater Mirror*.

Ira, his wife, Ora, and three of their children are buried in the Red Rock Community Cemetery.
– Submitted by DeQuence Clay

ALICE LON

Alice Lon, from Kilgore was known for her petticoats and fame as "the Champagne Lady." These famous petticoats were her trade mark on the musical program The Lawrence Welk Showcase (ABC, 1955-1982). Alice's mother, Mrs. Lois Wyche of Kilgore, made all twenty-five of them. Alice would be the first of Welk's "Champagne Ladies." In July, the ultra-conservative Welk fired Lon for "showing too much knee" on the air. After hearing from so many fans, he tried to get Alice Lon to reconsider and return to the show, but she never did. She died in 1981.

DAVID & MARY LONG

David E. Long was born 7 April 1929, in Tulsa, Oklahoma, to Ernest and Mabel (Brumble) Long. His family moved to Fort Worth in 1938. In 1942, his family moved to Longview where his father worked for Premier Oil Refinery. David has two siblings: JoAnn (born 26 May 1932) and Sandra (born 22 August 1939).

David enjoyed his years in Longview. He and his friends would walk from 12th

David and Mary Long in 1949.

Street to the Sabine River and Clear Lake to fish and spend the night.

David graduated from Longview High School in 1947, attended Kilgore Junior College and Texas A&M, and graduated from Texas Tech in 1952 with an Industrial Engineering degree. David married Mary June Miller on 24 August 1950.

Mary June Miller was born in Canton, Texas, on 3 October 1930, to Martin and Opal Miller. The Millers moved to Longview in June 1931, when Mary was 8 months old. Longview was an oil boomtown. Martin went to work at the Longview Post Office and worked there for 34 years. Mary has four siblings: Nancy Elizabeth (born 23 May 1926), Patsy Ruth (born 11 October 1927), Jack Martin (born 28 June 1929), and Peggy Sue (born 8 January 1932).

Mary enjoyed growing up in Longview. She remembers going to the double feature movies on Saturday for nine cents. The present-day LeTourneau College campus is located where the Harmon Army Hospital was during World War II. Mary remembers seeing buses with German prisoners going down Mobberly Street.

Mary graduated from Longview High School in 1947 as valedictorian. She worked at the First National Bank of Longview until she married David on 24 August 1950. Dr. Morris Ford married them in the First Baptist Church of Longview. Mary and her three sisters were all married in the First Baptist Church of Longview and they all celebrated their 50th wedding anniversaries between 24 August 2000, and 21 July 2001. After David graduated from Texas Tech, the couple moved to Houston, Texas, in January 1952, where he worked for Reed Roller Bit Co. They have six children: James David was born 29 November 1951, in Lubbock, Texas; the children born in Houston, Texas, are Gary Martin (born 12 November 1953), Susan Kay (born 14 October 1955), Thomas Edward (born 15 December 1956), Karen Anne (born 12 June 1958) and John Alan (born 16 March 1961).

Mary was a homemaker until 1973. At that time, she began working at a bank to help put the children through college. After working 22 years at the bank, Mary retired in 1995. David retired in 1984. They continue to live in Houston.

– Submitted by David E. Long

ELIZA LONG

Eliza Long was born in Gregg County, Texas, in 1868, the daughter of Mr. and Mrs. Charlie Key. She passed away after a prolonged illness on 28 March 1963. She was a faithful member and worker in Bethel Baptist Church until her health failed. To the parentage of Eliza and James Long was born six children: Viola, Essie, Alice, Jimmie Lee, Emmitt and Daniel. After the death of James Long, Eliza and Archie united and to their union was born a daughter, Tessie Lee. Many of her grandchildren have contributed professionally to the educational and medical fields.

Eliza Long, 1868-1963,
wife and mother

The family acquired property on Gilmer Road, Longview, Gregg County Texas, that included both sides of the street and extended north past what is now Fairmont Street. This property was divided into portions so that each child received a portion. Ownership of property on Gilmer Road remains in the family to this day.

– Submitted by Lula Johnson

JERRY JOSEPH LUCY

Jerry Joseph Lucy was born in New York City in 1870. He made his way to Kilgore in the late 1800s and worked for the Elder family in the lumber business. He came to the Elderville community in the early 1900s and was a partner with George Blackburn in the lumber and ginning business, and later also associated with Gardiner Mitchell in that business. In 1906, he went into business for himself with a country store that also served as the Elderville Office and was Postmaster.

In 1922, Jerry Lucy and Annie Helen Butts married and made their home in the house of Annie's father, Harvey J. Butts. Annie Butts was the oldest of the six Harvey Butts' children and had dropped out of school when she was fourteen to care for her invalid mother and to provide a home for her father and be a mother for her brothers and sisters. At the time of her marriage, all her siblings were gone and only she and

her father remained in the family home. This soon changed; Jerry was born in 1924, Julia Ann in 1925, Dan in 1927, and Frank in 1928.

Jerry Joseph Lucy died in 1932 in the early days of the Depression and his store and Post Office closed the next year. He and Annie, who died in 1966, are buried in Elderville Cemetery.

Annie Lucy was left with four children and a failed business, but she was also left with a caring and loving father and five siblings and their families.

Mary Butts returned home in 1933 to teach in Longview and to help Annie. Harvey and Mary provided financial support and Annie maintained the household and mothered the children. Jerry, Julia Ann, Dan and Frank joined the Peatown Christian Church and were baptized in the"Blue Hole." They attended Campus Ward Elementary School, Foster Junior High and graduated from Longview High School.

Annie was very involved with her Church, the schools and the well-being of the Elderville community. During the Depression years, she worked with the County to provide a health service, Home Demonstration Club and a canning facility that allowed the community families to preserve the foodstuff they grew. She was involved with the community telephone system and promoted Elderville's involvement with the Rural Electrification Administration. She always said the REA changed our way of life more than anything else in her lifetime. She also served as Postmaster following the death of her husband until the Elderville Post Office closed.

Jerry, Dan and Thurman Wathen (Julia Ann's husband-to-be) were in service in World War II and Frank served in the Korean War.

Jerry (1924-2003) married Woodie Mackey from the Judson Community in 1946, graduated from Texas A&M and served Raines and Bowie Counties as County Agent until he returned to Longview in 1960 and started ranching in the Judson Community. Mary Beth was born in 1949, Rebecca Ann in 1953 and Jerry Lester in 1959. Jerry is buried in the Alpine Cemetery.

Julia Ann graduated from Texas State College for Women and married Thurman Wathen from Athens in 1947. Thurman graduated from Texas A&M and was employed by the Army Corps of Engineers. They retired to Roseburg, Oregon. Julia Ann and Thurman have three sons, Ben born in 1953, Dan in 1957 and John in 1962.

Lucy-Butts House, Elderville Community

Dan graduated from Texas A&M, was employed by Texas Eastman Company and married Ann Kincheloe in 1958. They have two sons, Dan Frank, born in 1959, and Stephen Harvey, born in 1960. Ann and Dan live in the Elderville Community on land that has been in he family since 1876.

Frank was a rural mail carried and a rancher. He has retired from the Post Office but continues to ranch. In 1974, he married Betty Nalley, a widow with three children: Leisa, born in 1956, Kevin, in 1957, and Jonathan, in 1971. Frank and Betty live in the Elderville Community in the original homeplace of the Harvey Butts family.

– Submitted by Dan Lucy

LUNDY/KIMBLE

Willie Alvin and Trula Sloan Williams moved to Longview, Texas, in 1956. Willie is a grand nephew of Hampton Kimble and a great grandson of Sam and Easter Lundy Kimble.

The Lundy and Kimble families were friends, and the men often worked together. The senior Lundy and Sam Kimble came to East Texas from Georgia. Sam was a Gandy Dancer and it is believed that Lundy was a Dancer also. Lundy was married to Easter and they had two sons at that time, Henry, born in 1859, and Lewis, born in 1861. The senior Lundy died in 1863, and Sam Kimble married Easter. The Kimbles had six children: George, born 1864, Hampton and Henderson, 1866, Lewis, 1867, Cornelia, 1874, and Aaron, 1877.

Although the Kimbles were residents of Queen City, Cass County, Texas, they were doing railroad construction in Longview, Texas. Henry Lundy took up permanent residence in Longview in the 1890s, and his half-brother Hampton joined him later. Soon after, Hampton married Minnie Lee, the daughter of Glass and Melinda Watkins of Atlanta, Texas. Hampton died 22 April 1929, and Minnie died 15 September 1965; they both are buried in Grace Hill Cemetery in Longview, Gregg County, Texas.

– Submitted by Willie A. Williams,
Longview, Texas

GEORGE & BENA THOMAS MACK

George Mack and his bride, Bena, arrived in the United States in 1910 from Berbera, Lebanon.

George grew up in a family of God-fearing people with honor, respect and love for other people.

Bena Thomas Mack and George Mack

George went to school long enough to learn the Lebanese alphabet, becoming very fluent using the Bible as his main learning tool, until the death of his father, Peter Butrous McChoil Mack, when George quit school at the age of 9 years old. In order to assist the family in making a living, George was a deep-sea diver and worked in the family orchards raising figs, olives and silk worms. George's widowed mother, Saydie, also known as Ida, came to America, living in the vicinity of Mineola, making friends with a very compassionate doctor who she visited in Shreveport, Louisiana. After Saydie returned to Lebanon in 1910, she and the doctor maintained a correspondence. Shortly after, Saydie booked passage for 17-year-old George and his 14-year-old bride, Bena Thomas. It was hoped that after the war, George would help Saydie return to America to live, but World War I made travel impossible for civilians.

Prior to Mr. Mack's arrival in Longview, a band of gypsies had been in the vicinity, causing much destruction and had been ejected by the citizens. Because of Mr. Mack's appearance, having olive complexion, dark curly hair and hazel eyes, the barbershops refused him service until he proved that he was an honorable person. Mack went to what was then called the "Nickel Store," bought a mirror and had Bena hold it while he cut his own hair. Mr. Mack became known as an honest man of his word and one who loved and feared God. Having known much hardship, Mr. Mack was always ready and willing to help his fellow man.

During his stay in Longview, George had a hard time finding a place to live until he met Mr. Finch, father of Eva Jean Blount, wife of Peppy Blount, who owned a row of houses by the railroad tracks that sat close to the depot. He was forever grateful to Mr. Finch, who showed such trust, respect, love and affection to George that it was never forgotten by either party.

George was drafted just as the war ended in 1918, but was not made a naturalized citizen for serving. He went to Texarkana to apply for naturalization. Years later, after they moved to Longview, it was discovered that Bena had not received naturalization through George's papers, so she applied for and received her naturalization from Tyler with tutoring from Dr. A.G. Thomas. One of his former employers was Tony Lama of El Paso, who was famous for his handmade boots. He had such high regard for George that he offered him a partnership, but George returned to the familiarity of home and settled in Marshall to work for Mr. Binotti in his shoe repair shop. Later, George owned his own shoe shop.

Mr. Binotti had a lovely tenor voice that could be heard as he and his wife were enroute to their home from work, their car windows down as his beautiful voice filled the air.

George and Bena had two boys and two girls, one of which was Dr. Sam Mack, a favored Longview doctor and oral surgeon, who died 18 October 2002. An infant granddaughter, Linda Sue Knox, died 29 November 1955, and her father, Sidney Earl Knox, died 2 May 1982.

– Submitted by Esther Mack Knox

L.L. MACKEY

Farmer, land conservationist, community leader, Christian and family man are all words that describe Lester Losson (L.L.) Mackey. Mr. Mackey was born 24 April 1886, to Curtis Mackey and Rebecca Jane Henderson Mackey of the Tryon community in northeastern Gregg County. Curtis Mackey died when Lester was two years old. The only son, Lester was soon responsible for helping his mother, his older sisters Cora and Jessie, and his twin sister Lula manage the household, pay for and run their 175-acre farm. Because of his responsibilities, Lester's formal schooling was limited – he went to school when the weather was too bad for farming – but he learned to work the land. At age 21, he raised four bales of cotton on some land given to him by his mother. Soon he began buying land on his own in the Omega and Judson communities.

L.L. and Winnie Mackey

On 24 October 1917, in Hallsville, Texas, Lester married Winnie Davis Woodall. Winnie Woodall Mackey was born 7 April 1893, in Harrison County, Texas, the daughter of William Troy Woodall and Irena Hope Woodall. She graduated from Sam Houston Normal School and became a school teacher. She retired from teaching when she married. The couple had four children: Lynelle Mackey (Meyer), born 28 November 1918; Woodie Mackey (Lucy), born 8 January 1925; Lou Ann Mackey (Melton), born 22 August 1926; and William Lester Mackey, born 22 May 1929, died 6 March 1995.

Mr. and Mrs. Mackey worked hard and prospered, eventually owning more than 3,000 acres of land. A successful cotton farmer, Mr. Mackey also owned and operated two cotton gins. In 1937, *Progressive Farmer* magazine named him its Master Farmer of the year. He was an innovator in the soil conservation movement – helping to organize the Upshur-Gregg Soil and Water Conservation District and serving as its chairman for 26 years. After World War II, as cotton faded in importance in East Texas agriculture, Mr. Mackey became a leader in the development of registered Hereford cattle and in permanent pasture improvement programs. Timber became an important part of his business and he served as a director of the Texas Forestry Association. Throughout his lifetime, he was a good steward of the land, using it to grow cotton, planting seedlings to produce timber and raising cattle upon it.

Mr. Mackey was involved in all aspects of community life. He served on the board of trustees of the Judson Independent School District. He had a 28-year perfect attendance record with the Longview Kiwanis Club, was a member of the Longview Masonic Lodge and was a Shriner.

A deeply religious man, L.L. Mackey was a lifetime member of Alpine Presbyterian Church, the church his parents helped found. Mr. Mackey became a deacon at age 24, served as an elder (later elder emeritus), was the Sunday School Superintendent, and on three occasions was named as a delegate to the Presbyterian General Assembly. He helped organize Camp Gilmont, a Presbyterian retreat located in Upshur County, where a building is named "Mackey Hall" in his honor

L.L. Mackey died 24 January 1973, in Longview, Texas. His wife, Winnie, passed away 21 July 1979. They are buried at Alpine Presbyterian Cemetery. The home they built in 1931 still stands today and remains in family ownership. Even though Mr. Mackey received many awards and honors, his children and grandchildren are proudest of the love and wise counsel they received from this great and good man, a true son of the East Texas soil.

– Submitted by Mary Kathryn Meyer

LESTER LOSSON MACKEY

In 1870, Curtis Mackey (1853-1888) was only seventeen years old when he and his younger brother left their Civil War-ravaged home in Cherokee County, Alabama, and began driving a team of mules and a wagon to Gregg County in East Texas. Settling in the northeast section of the county, he became a charter member and elder of Alpine Presbyterian Church in the Tryon Community and, along with his wife Rebecca Jane Henderson (1851-1939), raised four children. The children, Anna Cora (1880-1971), Jessie Naomi (1882- 1927), and twins Lula Cumi (1886-1972) and Lester Losson (1886-1973), contributed to Gregg County in many ways.

Anna Cora was a teacher in Gregg and Harrison counties for many years. She served as Gregg County School Superintendent during the years of the East Texas Oil Boom (1930-1939) and successfully managed the tremendous growth of both students and school facilities in the county. Cora was active in Delta Kappa Gamma and Alpine Presbyterian Church for many years. Jessie Naomi married William Claude Mackey in 1919, and Lula Cumi married Sam McKelvey in 1916.

Lester and Winnie Mackey

Lester Mackey married Winnie Woodall (1893-1979), a teacher from Harrison County, in 1917 and brought his bride to the family home on Tryon Road. He began to acquire land and eventually built his first home in the Omega Community, five miles north of Tryon. The Port Bolivar and Iron Ore Railroad ran right behind his home and guests would often sit on the back porch to wait for the train. cotton had become king in East Texas, and Lester owned a cotton gin next to the home in Omega and one in Harrison County. Many times during the harvest season, he would run the gin all night to accommodate the many wagons full of cotton that waited on the parking lot next to the gin. When the Omega school closed, Lester moved his family to be near Judson School and became a school trustee. He continued to acquire land in Judson and soon owned a large cotton farm there.

Lester Mackey became widely known as a farming and ranching leader across the state of Texas. He strongly believed in soil conservation and served as director of the soil conservation district for many years. With his love of the land as a guide, many innovative farming practices were begun and shared with other farmers and ranchers. He was named Progressive Farmer of the Year in Texas by *Progressive Farmer* magazine and was instrumental in bringing crimson clover to Texas. In addition to numerous other farm and ranch awards, Lester received accolades for his service in the Kiwanis Club, Longview Masonic Lodge and the Longview Chamber of Commerce. Lester was also an elder in the Alpine Presbyterian Church and was instrumental in the purchase and organization of Camp Gilmont, a Presbyterian Youth Camp that is still active today.

Winnie Mackey served on the council of the Home Demonstration Club for many years. She was an honorary member of Delta Kappa Gamma, an officer of the Women of the Church and active in the PTA. She was also an integral part of the various agricultural activities of her husband.

Winnie and Lester Mackey had four children who continue to live in the Judson Community in Gregg County. They are Nona Lynelle Meyer, who married Wilbur Meyer (1922-1991); Woodie Mackey, who married Jerry Lucy (1924-2003); Lou Ann, who married Grady Melton (1920-2003); and William Lester (1929-1995), who married Nancy Rountree. William Lester and Nancy have three sons who will carry on the Mackey name.

– Submitted by Beckey Moffett and Mary Beth Mann (granddaughters)

MADDEN-MOSELY

Lillie Pearl Madden was born in Titus County, Texas, in 1911, to William Harvey Madden and Mary Sylvester Moseley. Lillie Pearl married Robert (Bob) Cruess Bolger (see "Bolger-Cruess") in 1930 in Titus County. Lillie Pearl and Bob moved to Longview in 1948. They had two children: Marybelle married James Sidney (Sid) Tutt and William Robert (Bill), who married Katherine Erin McKenna.

William Harvey and Mary Mosely Madden

As the children were growing up Lillie Pearl was active in school activities serving as room mother, along with various P.T.A. offices (she was a life P.T.A. member). She was a member of First Baptist Church, as well as BXYZ and Saints Alive Choir (both senior adult groups). Lillie Pearl was a talented seamstress. She also hand-beaded many wedding books and bridal accessories.

William Harvey (Harve) Madden (born 1889, Georgia, and died 1942, Titus County, Texas) was the son of William Henry Madden and Sarah Roxanne Patterson. His family moved from Georgia to Arkansas, where he met his wife. Harve and Mary, along with their first born child, Amanda Ozella (1906), road the train to Texas about 1908. Harve tried farming at first, but then had a blacksmith shop in Mt. Pleasant until he died.

William Henry Madden was born 1834 in South Carolina, and died 1901 in Titus County. He was buried in the Tranquil Cemetery, Titus County. His family lived in Georgia where William Henry was a miller. His parents were Charles and Susannah (maiden name unknown) Madden, both born in South Carolina. William Henry married Sarah Roxanne Patterson in Arkansas.

Sarah Roxanne Patterson was the daughter of William and Letitia (unknown) Patterson. Sarah was born in South Carolina in 1859, and died in 1940 in Titus County. She is buried in New Hope Cemetery, Titus County. She married first to ___ O'Brian. After William Henry Madden died, she married Jefferson Davis Gober.

Mary Sylvester Moseley was born 1880 in Dallas County, Arkansas, and died 1967 in Titus County. She and Harve are both buried in the Masonic Cemetery, Mt. Pleasant.

Mary grew up in the hills of Arkansas. She had a third grade education; Harve could not read or write when they married, but she taught him how. Even though it was hard for her, she wrote regular letters to her children after they moved away. Because of her limited reading skills, she could never read patterns for crocheting or knitting, but was very skillful at reproducing the item by looking at the pictures. She gardened until well into her eighties and could grow anything.

Mary Moseley's parents were Jesse Moseley and Mary Fernetta Hasty. Jesse was born in 1851 in North Carolina, and died in 1932 in Arkansas. Jesse and Mary Fernetta married 1877, Dallas County, Arkansas. Born in 1856 in Arkansas, Mary Fernetta was the daughter of Benjamin Hasty and Polly Roden.

Jesse's parents were Amos Moseley, born about 1820, and Arcenith Rodgers; both were born in North Carolina. They moved to Arkansas just prior to 1860.

Benjamin Hasty's ancestry can be traced to James Hasty, born about 1700, probably in Ireland, and who died in 1767 in Virginia. Other names in the Hasty lineage include Asbury/Asberry, Warren and Cook.

– Submitted by Marybelle Bolger Tutt

MAGRILL

John Richard Magrill, born January 1820, and his brother Samuel Devall Magrill, born about 1821, came to Upshur County (now Gregg County) in 1846 from Alabama. The brothers were originally from Edgefield, South Carolina, and moved to Butler County, Alabama, prior to 1830. Their grandfather Richard Magrill was from Newry, Ireland, and died in South Carolina. Their father, Benjamin Magrill, died in Alabama.

The brothers both married in Lowndes County, Alabama, and moved with their families and mother to Texas. Their mother, name unknown, lived to an old age and died in Longview. John Richard Magrill married Elizabeth A. Thomas 10 November 1842. John was a farmer and served as Confederate Postmaster of Earpville. After the Civil War he was nominated as a candidate for County Commissioner. In his latter years, he was a grocer with his son-in-law William T. Whitelock. John acquired quite a bit of property around what is now Longview. In 1871, he deeded an acre, known as "The Grove," to the blacks of Upshur County to be used as a gathering place for religious services. This block at Padon and Green Streets in Longview is now known as Magrill Plaza. At about the same time, John deeded property for the erection of a Methodist Church in the present city of Longview. In 1872, John sold land in what was later known as Longview Junction to the IGN Railroad. This became part of the city of Longview, and Magrill Street was named for him. John died 14 March 1899. At that time he was the longest living resident of Longview.

Samuel Devall Magrill married Mary S. Curtis 26 June 1845. He was also a farmer in the Earpville area. He raised a large family in Upshur and Gregg Counties. Samuel was married three times, each time to a Mary. The second wife's surname is not known.

His third marriage to Mary E. (Orr) McKinley, 12 August 1873, was the first marriage recorded in Gregg County. Samuel died in June 1879, of typhoid fever.

The children of John and Elizabeth Magrill were William Benjamin, James Monroe (married Agatha B. Bassett), S. Elizabeth (married Dr. Leander Dexter Stansbury), Amanda C.

(married William T. Whitelock), John Richard and George F. The children of Samuel and Mary S. Curtis were John B., Alexander R. (married Margaret C. Rucker), Mary, Samuel Dee (married Alice Elisabeth Gardner), Margaret, Laura J., William E. and Alice. His children by his second wife were Dennis Lawrence (married Elmyra Castleberry), Richard Tulle (married Maggie Castleberry) and Dora. His children by his third wife were Martha ("Mattie") (married Wade Hampton Davidson) and Temperance Annie (married Thomas Alonzo McKee).

Occupations of the Magrills included farming, railroading, merchandising and sawmilling. The following served the Confederacy in the Civil War: John R. Magrill, Sr., William Benjamin Magrill, John B. Magrill and Dr. Leander Dexter Stansbury.

– Submitted by C.D. Magrill

MARKHAM

Virginia Elaine Clanton was born in Longview, 8 January 1919. Her parents were Louis Northcutt Markham, MD (1884-1951) and Princess Emma Finch (1889-1965); both were born and died in Longview. Dr. Markham was raised by his Aunt Dolly and Uncle Steve Forman after his parents died. He graduated from Jacksonville Baptist College and Tulane Medical School. He operated Markham Hospital, Longview, where he practiced medicine from 1923 until 1951. Princess Finch and Louis Markham married in 1913, Longview. They are buried in Greenwood Cemetery. She graduated from Baylor University in 1910.

Dr. Markham's father, Dr. Louis Napoleon Markham, born 1856, Louisiana, is buried in Fairview Cemetery, Denison, Texas, as is his second wife, Sarah Mayo Northcutt. They both have markers in Greenwood Cemetery, Longview. Dr. L.N. Markham graduated from Louisville Medical School, 1880, and did further training at Bellvue Hospital in New York City. Sarah was the daughter of William George Northcutt and Julia Ann Moore, daughter of Jeremiah Moore, Jr. and Susannah Scurry.

Princess was the daughter of Confederate veteran John Landrum Finch (1832, South Carolina–1911, Longview). He was a devoted member of First Baptist Church, Longview from 1872-1911. Her mother was Eugenia Althea Poole (1894-1937). Both are buried in Grace Hill Cemetery.

Parents of Louis N. were Rev. Lewis S. Markham (1812, Tennessee–1882, Longview) and Martha Ann Elizabeth Cole (1826, Alabama—1899, Denison); they were charter members of First Baptist Church Longview. Martha is buried in Denison but has a marker along side her husband in Longview's Greenwood Cemetery.

Sarah's parents, William George Northcutt (1837, Georgia—1909, Longview) and Julia Ann Moore (1836, South Carolina—1876, Longview) were charter members of First Baptist Church and are buried in Greenwood Cemetery. William served as Longview's mayor. He

established the first hardware store as well as owning a brick yard, monument works and manufacturing wagons.

John Finch was the son of John Smith Finch (1804-1862,) and Mary Coan (1896-1862). Both were born and died in South Carolina.

Eugenia Poole's parents were Merry Sedley Poole (1826, Louisiana–?) and Nancy Jane Kimberling(1832, Missouri–1851, Harrison County, Texas). Sedley Poole was born to Robert Poole (1784, South Carolina–1854, Harrison County, Texas) and Eliza Tines (died 1839, Harrison County). Nancy Jane's parents were Benjamin Franklin Kimberling (1801, Virginia –1854, Harrison County) and Emily Knight (1806–1876, Harrison County).

Parents of Lewis S. Markham were Thomas L. Markham and Elizabeth Campbell. She was a charter member of First Baptist Church. Elizabeth married second ___ Franks.

Martha Coleman was the daughter of Isham Jefferson Coleman (1803, Virginia—1872, Longview) and Mary Elizabeth Ray (1807, Georgia–1862, Louisiana). They married in 1823 in Alabama. Mary Elizabeth was the daughter of William Ray (born 1765, North Carolina) and Elizabeth (born 1874, Virginia). Parents of Isham J. Coleman were Revolutionary War soldier Isham Coleman (1758, Virginia–1825, Virginia) and Ann Roper (1763, Virginia—1825, Virginia), daughter of Charles Roper, Sr. and Ann.

– Submitted by Elaine Markham

MARTIN

The Martin family tree has been carefully maintained and celebrated for years in Navarro County, where its Texas roots first took hold.

George Wesley Martin, the eldest son of William Martin (who died 26 August 1870 in North Carolina), traveled by covered wagon with his widowed mother, Mary Elizabeth Young Martin, and her children, Bazely, Joe, Harriet, Bell and Caroline, from Smithfield, North Carolina, to Lexington, Tennessee, whereupon he married Martha Virginia Cunningham.

In 1871, the young couple joined a wagon train that was headed for Texas. After a stint in Lamar County, Texas, they pressed onto Navarro County, where their first son, William Jessie Martin, was born 17 February 1872. Ten additional children were born to George Wesley and Martha Martin, nine of whom survived: Nora, Dora, Joseph Elijah, Newt, John Robert, Dock J., Roy E. and Martha Virginia.

Daniel Donaho was born in 1805, possibly in South Carolina. He married a part-Choctaw girl, Anne Chance (born 1802), while living in Hinds County, Mississippi, in 1826. In order to avoid removal as part of the infamous Trail of Tears, Daniel and his young wife moved to Texas, some believe as early as 1829. On 3 September 1835, he received a Spanish land grant of 4,428 acres at Parkington Prairie in Liberty County.

Daniel and three of his brothers, Moses, William and Willie, fought in the Battle of San Jacinto.

Cora Blanche Anderson Martin and Arthur Pat Martin

Between 1847-1850, Daniel and Anne moved their family (Dan, Louis, Augustine, Travis Fanning, Blackston, Jarvis and Henry) to Navarro County. Despite their contributions to Navarro County, upon their deaths, Daniel and Anne were buried outside the fence of Cosgrove Cemetery – due to Anne's Choctaw lineage. Incensed by the injustice, great granddaughter Ollie Donaho Kiser was successful in getting the fence extended to include these two Texas pioneers.

On 11 November 1865, Travis Fanning Donaho married Sara H. Cockerall. Their family consisted of William Lee, Charles H., David T., Sallie Bell, Lula and Mollie.

The Martin and Donaho lines merged when two children from each family married one another. Dora Martin married William Lee Donaho and Sallie Bell Donaho married William Jessie Martin.

Sallie Bell bore William Jessie six children: Travis Wesley, Jessie Lee, Arthur "Pat", Essie, Chester and Tom. Arthur married Cora Blanche Anderson (both born in 1900) and brought the Martin name to Gregg County, Texas. By 1939, when tragedy struck, they were living outside Kilgore on the Smith County line with their children Arthur Glen, Cora Vemelle, Robert Newton and Emma Lee. Fourteen year-old Emma Lee and her mother were passengers in an automobile driven by Blanche's father, C.M. Anderson, when his car collided with another. Blanche Martin was killed instantly. Emma Lee was left unconscious for 14 days. Blanche's husband, Arthur, broken-hearted, never remarried.

Sisters Vernelle and Emma Lee married and raised their families in Kilgore. Vernelle married T. Ray Custer and had two sons, Tommy and Donald. Emma Lee married Vernon L. Ratliff and had two sons, Vernon Alan and Gary Wayne Ratliff.

– Submitted by Alan Ratliff

BENJAMIN FRANKLIN MARTIN, SR.
2 March 1893–29 September 1962

Benjamin Franklin Martin, Sr., Manager of Longview Coca-Cola Bottling Company, was one of eight children born to Thomas Smith Martin, Sr. and Mollie Morris Martin in Lanexa, New Kent County, Virginia. Franklin, Sr. was born 2 March 1893. He was not a relative of America's famous historic person, Benjamin Franklin. His parents just liked the name and gave it to him. The Martin parents lived in the historic county where George Washington married and where, earlier, Captain John Smith was saved by Pocahontas on an unnamed island in the Chickahominy River. Today, the island is within view of the Martin ancestral farm homesite in Lanexa and the homesite is owned by B.F. Martin's nephew, Thomas G. Martin, of Warrenton, Virginia.

When Franklin, Sr. was four years old, the family home that was on a high knoll overlooking the Chickahominy burned to the ground during sub-freezing weather. He and all his family were saved by a black family who took the Martins into their home for the remainder of the night. The Martin family temporarily moved into their general merchandise store down-the-hill, until the new house was built on the same site.

Franklin, Sr.'s brothers and one sister, in their order of birth, were Morris Billing Martin, Walter Coleman Martin, Thomas Smith Martin, Jr., Alice Bell Martin Horgan, Benjamin Franklin Martin, Sr., Herbert Esten Martin, Marshall Allan Martin and Malcolm Montreville Martin. The latter also moved to Longview, Texas, and married Ruth Hall. Their three daughters are Elizabeth Lee Martin Boone, Mary Evelyn Martin Mitchell and Patricia Anne Martin Taylor, all of Longview.

A fourth-grade drop-out by choice, Franklin Sr. couldn't stand the concept of Lanexa's one room schoolhouse. It was not interesting to him. At age ten, he started earning money. For a quarter, he ferried people, in a rowboat, across the wide, deep and swift Chickahominy River. He knew the value of money and said he kept every quarter until it rusted. When he was fifteen, Franklin, Sr. almost died of peritonitis and spent about three months recuperating from surgery at Johnson and Willis hospital in Richmond, Virginia. Of this episode, Franklin, Sr. said, "When I was laid out on a stretcher at Lanexa's freight depot awaiting a train to transport me to the hospital, someone looked down at me and said, 'he won't make it 'til morning.' I looked up and said, 'I bet I do.'" Franklin, Sr. recovered.

He and his younger brother Malcolm worked together on the family farm. They had a horse named "Charlie Horse," as well as one named "Nemiah" which they called "Nemo" for short. As an extra agricultural project, Franklin, Sr. and Malcolm raised a crop of watermelons, which turned out exceptionally delicious and filled a full railroad freight car. The car was purchased by a buyer for shipment to New York City. Then the buyer sent word that he wanted another freight car load of watermelons just like the first one shipped. Unfortunately, this was impossible because the boys first freight car load was also their entire crop.

Franklin was the only one of his brothers who went to World War I. He enlisted at age 24, and was inducted on 28 October 1917. He served in Company D, 51lth Engineers, and returned from France on the USS *Susquehanna*, which docked at Newport News, Virginia. He received his final discharge at Camp Lee, Virginia, on 19 June 1919.

A cousin of Franklin, Sr., named Thomas H. Sweeney of Roanoke, Virginia, owned the Coca-Cola Bottling Works in Longview, Texas. He wrote to his Aunt Mollie, mother of Franklin, Sr., to inquire if she had a son who might be interested in relocating to Texas to work for him. She told him that Franklin, Sr. might be interested since he was unmarried and just getting out of the Army. Franklin, Sr. came to Longview by train from Virginia. He arrived in Longview on Thursday, 12 January 1920. He said he got to his destination with a long, heavy suitcase and money borrowed from his brothers and sister. When he got off the train in Longview, which had a population of under 5,000 at the time, he was at Junction Depot and was so sad and blue that he felt like getting back on a train and going straight back home. "Where is Longview?" he asked. Someone told him that he hadn't gotten off at the main depot but at Junction Depot, and was not yet in Longview. "You have to get a mule car to get to the downtown station," he was told. This he did.

Franklin, Sr. reported for work at the Longview Coca-Cola Bottling Company where he was a truck delivery route salesman for about six years before becoming part owner. When Franklin, Sr. started the job, there was a ratio of eight cases of soda water sold to one case of Coca-Cola. No one was allowed to call it "Coke" which was, in those days, considered a dirty word. Bankers in Longview, at the time, thought the bottling business was "a back alley business," "a flash-in-the-pan," "fly-by-night" business, which they frowned upon. They thought its chances for success were "slim to none" and they would not lend money on a Coca-Cola plant. They would have lent money for a cotton or corn crop, which were the two principal cash crops, throughout East Texas at the time.

Franklin, Sr. told about driving his truck route to Carthage where a Coca-Cola warehouse was maintained. He had to go by way of Beckville and Tatum and said, "When I heard

Benjamin F. Martin, Sr., 1935

rain on the roof at night after I'd gone to bed, I dreaded getting up the next morning because I had to completely unload the truck case-by-case to lighten the load before crossing the creek bottom bridge and then I had to reload the truck after crossing.

Franklin, Sr. met his future wife, Lorraine Calvin, at the home of a Baptist Sunday School teacher, Mrs. A.D. Bush, who had a home party for her Sunday School pupils in 1921.

In his young days, Franklin, Sr. played the fiddle by ear. After being formally taught to play a horn by H.G. Munden, band director, he played the bass horn in the Longview Municipal Band (sponsored by the Longview Chamber of Commerce) from 1927 to 1932.

An avid hunter from his life in Virginia, Franklin, Sr.'s free time was spent hunting ducks, geese, quail, squirrels and dove in Gregg County and other places. He hunted deer and wild turkeys at the Tom Harris Deer Hunting Club in Mason County, and once killed a bear. He always kept one or two well-trained bird dogs. Most of his fishing was done at Dallas Caddo Club, of which he was a member, and at Cherokee Lake.

In the early 1920s, Thomas Sweeney decided that he would sell the Longview Coca-Cola plant and move to Brownsville, Texas, because, in his opinion, Longview had no future. Among other things, Thomas Sweeney reasoned that most all the timber had been cut out and there wasn't anything else left. He sold his home and farms and moved his wife, Eva, and two sons, Thomas, Jr. and Payton, to Brownsville where he purchased the Brownsville Coca-Cola bottling plant.

For a while it looked as though Thomas Sweeney had been right about Longview as it seemed that everything went downhill. Longview's economy suffered a severe blow when district personnel of the Texas and Pacific railroad were moved to Ft. Worth and the terminal was moved to Mineola. Longview had always been a railroad town and this change left its mark on the municipality. The removal took away from Longview many families and a large payroll of more than a million dollars. Then the Depression rolled in and a struggle for existence was right at home in Longview. There was a severe drought in the summer of 1930 which parched the meager crops. Many a business man locked his doors at night and wondered if he could make it through another day.

Franklin, Sr. wanted to buy the Longview plant, but his cousin could not see his way to owner-finance the Longview plant for him. Franklin, Sr. decided that he needed a partner with money for financing and saw in a bottler trade magazine where a James "Jimmy" Sanger of Beaufort, South Carolina, who was in the candy and confectionery business, desired to purchase a soda water plant. Franklin, Sr. contacted Mr. Sanger by letter and later traveled by train to South Carolina to see him. Mr. Sanger was interested enough to journey to Longview to have a look at the opportunity and he liked what he saw. Mr. Sanger lent Franklin, Sr. the

money to purchase a one-third interest in the Longview Coca-Cola plant and Mr. Sanger purchased the other two-thirds equity interest for himself. The purchase price was $42,185.00. Franklin, Sr., a minority stock holder, became manager of the plant on 20 October 1925. Eventually, Franklin, Sr. became the plant's largest single stockholder.

Things began to look up in Longview on 26 January 1931, when the Lathrop oil well was brought in 4.5 miles northwest of Longview. The City of Longview offered a $10,000.00 reward to the drilling crew that brought in an oil well in the Longview area. Bringing in the well was viewed by thousands of spectators. The great East Texas Oil Boom stretched to the limit the capacity of the Longview Coca-Cola Bottling Company in order to keep up with demand. The plant literally bottled twenty-four hours around the clock. This occasioned a need for a new bottling plant facility that was constructed in 1935 at 340 West Tyler Street.

For a few years after his arrival in Longview, Franklin, Sr. thought nothing in the State of Texas, or anywhere else for that matter, could match anything in Virginia. In later years, he became one of Texas' most outspoken boosters. The turnaround was complete. Nothing could match Texas in his mind's eye.

Since Franklin, Sr. went through the "School of Hard Knocks," he held an education in highest esteem. Thomas S. Martin, Jr., five years older than Franklin, Sr., seemed to be his role model older brother. Tragically, Thomas died of typhus fever at the age of twenty-three in his third year of medical school at Richmond, Virginia (after having graduated with honors in pre-med from the College of William and Mary). Franklin, Sr. also had one sister who had a college education. Esteeming education, Franklin, Sr. not only sent his son and daughter through college, he also sent a nephew to VMI in Virginia, and then through the University of Texas Law School in Austin, Texas. He sent a niece to TWU in Denton.

A self-made man, Franklin, Sr. was a member of the First Baptist Church in Longview and he was a Mason and a Shriner. Benjamin Franklin Martin, Jr., owner of Ben Franklin Realty in Longview, married his wife, Grace, on 6 October 1973, in Dallas, Texas. Franklin, Sr.'s daughter is Charlotte Elizabeth Martin Payne of Dallas. Her three children are Madison Lee Oden of Houston, Martin Blair Oden of Dallas, and Caroline Elizabeth Oden Wylie of Houston. Franklin, Sr. was one of the organizers and Charter Director of the Cherokee Lake project and remained a director until his death. He is buried beside his wife in Memory Park Cemetery in Harrison County near Longview.

DEWEY O. MATHIS

During the summer of 1945, the Dewey O. Mathis family moved from Lake Worth near Fort Worth, to Longview, Gregg County, Texas. The family consisted of Dewey, born 2 February 1909, near Baird in Callahan County, Texas, his wife

(l.-r.) Rebecca Ann Mathis, Dessie Lee Williams Mathis and Dewey Otto Mathis.

Dessie Lee Williams, born 18 March 1911, near Eros, Louisiana, their two children, James, a high school senior, and Sybil, a high school freshman, and his mother-in-law, Clara Williams.

Their trip to Longview was an arduous one taken at a time of gasoline rationing and the shortage of new tires. Three blowouts on the 1939 Dodge required the purchase of two used tires along the way and meant the family arrived in Longview with no spare tire.

Dewey's father was Alison Woodville Barrington Mathis, a farmer and native of Alabama who had moved first to Mississippi, then to Louisiana before venturing to west Texas. Dewey's mother was Susan Caledonia Davis, a native of Mississippi. After Dewey's birth, the family moved back to Louisiana where Dewey grew to manhood and married Dessie in Ouachita Parish in 1928. At the time they married, Dewey worked in an ice plant and was earning $1.00 a day.

When the family began growing, Dewey sought a better paying job and found one with a milk company in Monroe, Louisiana. In 1938, during the Depression years, Dewey lost his job and hitchhiked to Tyler, Texas, where he found work with another milk company. As soon as he had the money, he moved his family to Tyler. By this time, his father-in-law had died of a rattlesnake bite and his mother-in-law moved into the home with Dewey, Dessie, James and Sybil. The children were now nine and seven years of age and both in school. Dewey worked hard at his job and was promoted to manager of a new branch plant in Kilgore. In 1942, Dewey and Dessie were recruited to work for Consolidated Aircraft Corporation in Fort Worth manufacturing bombers for use in World War II.

Dewey was recruited by the manager of a Longview milk company in 1945, which prompted the move to Longview. In 1946, James graduated from high school and started college. In 1947, a third child, Rebecca, was born. Dewey became manager of the plant in Longview. Sybil graduated from high school in 1949 and worked for a local bank.

Son and daughter of Dewey and Dessie Mathis, Sybil Marie Mathis and James Otto Mathis, c. 1947.

Dewey decided in 1948 to try restaurant ownership, a venture that proved unsuccessful. He then went to work for another milk company. James graduated from college in 1951 and married Peggy Sue Miller, a 1947 graduate of Longview High School and one of four daughters of Martin and Opal Miller. Approximately six months later, Sybil married Don Reynolds, son of Henry Clay Reynolds and Frankie Lee Richardson.

Dewey became restless again and moved to Irving, Texas. He lived there a few years and decided to move back to Louisiana, which he had always considered "home." Rebecca married James Stevenson in 1968 in Monroe, Louisiana. Dewey and Dessie lived there until Dessie developed cancer and they moved back to Texas and lived with James. Dessie died in 1977. In 1979, Dewey also died of cancer. They are both buried in Huntsville, Texas.

– Submitted by Elizabeth Yielding

JAMES OTTO MATHIS & PEGGY SUE MILLER

James Otto Mathis and Peggy Sue Miller were married 21 July 1951, by Dr. W. Morris Ford at the First Baptist Church, Longview, Texas. Both graduated from Longview High School, James in 1946 and Peggy in 1947. They met in the church where they were later married.

James Mathis was born 29 July 1929, in West Monroe, Ouachita Parish, Louisiana. His parents were Dewey Otto Mathis and Dessie Lee Williams. Dewey was the son of Alison Woodville Barrington Mathis (known as A.W.B.) who was born in Alabama to Edmond Mathis and Nancy Wilkinson, and Susan Caledonia Davis who was born in Mississippi to Thomas Sidney Davis and Emma Elizabeth Hall. Before attending school in Longview, James had attended schools in West Monroe and Monroe, Louisiana, and in Tyler, Kilgore and Fort Worth, Texas. After graduating from Longview High School, he attended Kilgore College and the University of North Texas, receiving his bachelor's degree in 1951.

Peggy Miller was born 8 January 1932, in Longview, Gregg County, Texas. Her parents were Martin Marion Miller and Ruby Opal McWilliams. Martin was the son of William

Aaron Miller and Nancy Lucinda Chaney. Opal was the daughter of Marion Lafayette McWilliams and Eva Elizabeth Parsons. After graduating from Longview High School, Peggy worked briefly as a secretary for a sign company and then became secretary to one of the vice-presidents of a local bank. She continued in this position until the couple moved out of town.

Their first child, Linda Sue, was born 25 June 1952, in Longview, Gregg County, Texas. Shortly after her birth the family moved to Victoria, Victoria County, Texas, where James began his teaching career as an art teacher in Victoria Junior High School. Their second daughter, Elizabeth Ann, was born in Victoria on 26 February 1954. During the summer of 1955, the family moved to Andrews, Andrews County, Texas, where James initiated the art program in Andrews Junior High School. Their third child, James Allison Mathis, was born 4 May 1956, in Andrews.

The elder James earned his master's degree in school administration in 1956 at the University of North Texas. In the fall of 1959, he was appointed to a counseling position at Andrews Junior High School. During these years, Peggy was at home with the children.

James Otto Mathis and Peggy Sue Miller Mathis, July 21, 1951

In 1963, James resigned his position in Andrews to pursue his doctoral studies full time. The children were all now in school and Peggy took a secretarial position at Denton State School while James attended graduate school on a teaching fellowship and graduate scholarship at the University of North Texas. In 1964, Peggy became secretary in the Art Department at the university. James completed his doctorate in 1965 and secured a position as associate professor of education at East Central State University in Ada, Oklahoma. After two years there, he accepted an invitation to join the faculty of Sam Houston State University in Huntsville, Walker County, Texas. During his tenure there, he held several positions on university committees, chaired the University Senate, served as secretary and as president of Texas Counseling Association and was appointed to

(l.-r.) James Allison Mathis, Linda Sue Mathis and Elizabeth Ann Mathis.

the Texas State Board of Examiners of Professional Counselors for a six-year term by then Governor Ann Richards.

Peggy worked for 14 years as a secretary at First Baptist Church of Huntsville. She retired in 1988. James retired in 1989 and was named "professor emeritus" by the board of the Texas State University System. Since retiring, they have continued residing in Huntsville and pursuing their hobbies. Their three children enjoy successful professional careers. Linda has her doctorate from Texas A&M University and works at ESC Region IV in Houston. Linda lives in Katy with her husband Greg Combs and her two children, Melina and Greg, Jr., live and work nearby. Elizabeth teaches mathematics at a middle school in Huntsville, where she lives with her husband, Paul Yielding. The younger James is an optometrist and lives in Fort Worth where he is in private practice and works in research for a pharmaceutical manufacturer.

– Submitted by James O. Mathis

OBIE H. MAULDIN & ETHEL CHILDRESS (CHILDERS)

Obie Hendrick Mauldin was born in Harleton, Harrison County, Texas, on 14 February 1890, the third child of James Loden Mauldin and Medaline Easter Starr, and the grandchild of Nathaniel Whitfield Mauldin and Suzanna P. Loden. Obie met Ethel Childress (Childers) in a cotton field near Longview and a year later they married. Ethel was born 25 May 1894, to John Ellison Childers Jr. and Amanda Caroline Barnes. She was the seventh child in a family of ten children, all born in Corinth, Alcorn County, Mississippi. She was known as an attractive woman with dark hair and dark complexion. Ethel died 29 May 1924, and is buried in the Judson Cemetery. Obie died 15 May 1958, and is buried beside Ethel in the Judson Cemetery in Longview, Gregg County, Texas.

Obie and Ethel lived in the area of East Mountain where six children were born. The first child, Nathan, died at birth and is buried in the family plot in Judson Cemetery. The other five children born to this union include Jimmie Eleson Mauldin, born 8 November 1911, walked into the Fason Grocery Store at age 16 and saw Ceedie Elizabeth Fason. Ceedie was born in Jefferson, Texas, to William (Billy) Fason and Georgia Martin on 13 October 1918. Three years later, on 5 November 1932, they drove to Texarkana to be married. The trip was difficult, with three flat tires on the way and four flats returning home. They settled in Jefferson, Texas, where Jimmie operated Mauldin Brothers Lumber Company. Jimmie and Ceedie had three children — the first one was stillborn and is buried in Trinity Cemetery, Marion County, Texas. James Ellison Mauldin, born 30 March 1934, and Shirley Ree Mauldin, born 29 August 1939, completed their family. Jimmie died on 19 June 1972, and is buried in Trinity Cemetery, Marion County, Texas. Ceedie still resides in Marion County.

Novie Ree Mauldin, born 19 November 1915, married Horace (Whick) Gray Davis. They had Patsy Sue Davis, Jeannie Davis and Bennie Wayne Davis. In later years, she divorced Whick and moved to San Angelo, Texas. Novie, the only surviving child of Obie, resides in San Angelo with her husband, George Bundren.

James Cole (Coley) Mauldin was born 20 August 1917, and died 20 June 1985. Coley first married Eleanor Jean Smith and had two children, Janice and Melvin. He then married Margaret Woods, who brought a daughter, Jeanette, to the marriage. They had one son, J.W. Both Coley and Margaret are buried in Trinity Cemetery.

Preston "Peck" Leon Mauldin was born 6 April 1920, and died 30 July 1994. He married Marie Delphine Fason, born 20 September 1925, died 18 September 1996, and they had P.L. (Junior), Dianne, Christy and Larry. Both Peck and Marie are buried in Trinity Cemetery, Marion County, Texas.

Ida Mae Mauldin was born 20 May 1924, and died 13 June 1994, in San Angelo, Texas. She first married William Scott "Scottie" Hamilton. Their only child, Linda Jean Hamilton, survived only five months. In later years, Scottie and Ida Mae adopted Darlene Hamilton. Linda Jean and Scottie are buried in the Scottsville Cemetery, Harrison County, Texas. Ida Mae is buried in Judson Cemetery.

After Ethel Childers died, Obie married Mollie Whitley and moved to the country near Jefferson where he operated a grocery store. One child, Clarence Whitfield Mauldin, was born on 4 June 1928. Clarence married Elizabeth Shirey and they had Rocky and Ronald. Clarence died 6 August 1997, and is buried in Trinity Cemetery, Marion County, Texas. Elizabeth resides in Marion County, Texas.

There are many descendants from the Mauldin/Childers union who reside in Texas and the surrounding states.

– Submitted by James E. Mauldin, Sr.

JOSEPH E.J. MCALISTER

Joseph E.J."Joe" McAlister was born in Pittsburg, Texas, in 1880. He passed away in 1957. His last years were in Longview, Texas.

Joe ran away from home when he was 16 and hopped a train bound for New Orleans, Louisiana. He was caught by the railway guards and had a choice of being put off the train or caring for cattle on the cattle cars. The beef was bound for the port in New Orleans where they were to be put on a sailing ship bound for California. He chose to take care of the cattle. In New Orleans, he was offered the job of taking care of the cattle aboard ship. He took that job. When he arrived at the Horn of South America, he heard that he was to be shanghaied to go on to China. He jumped ship and hid out in the hills until the ship sailed. He returned to the U.S. on another ship. Joe later joined the army and fought in the Spanish American War of 1898. He was in the infantry in First Texas Company I. His commanding officer was General Fitzhugh Lee.

Joe told his son, Ed McAlister, about the war in Cuba. The Spaniards would kill wild hogs and skin them out and put the skins, heads and all, on and crawl through the bushes and tall grasses grunting like hogs. The men on guard duty were all told to shoot the hogs if they heard them because the Spaniards would sneak up and stab the guards to death. And, it did happen to some of them.

The commanding officer would go out of camp at night at one guard post and return to camp at another guard post. Joe McAlister was the only guard on duty that refused to let the officer just walk past without stopping him. He would point his rifle at the officer until the officer slowly advanced to be recognized.

Joe's company was on one side of San Juan Hill, parallel to Teddy Roosevelt's Rough Riders. They were unable to advance up the hill and were being beaten very badly. Teddy Roosevelt told his bugler to sound RETREAT! The bugler was excited, and probably afraid, and became confused. He accidentally blew CHARGE! The horses and riders charged up the hill trampling many of the enemy. The soldiers killed the rest. Because of a mistake made on the bugler's part, Teddy Roosevelt was able to ride to glorious victory!

Later in Joe's life, he had captain's papers and ran the ferry from the Long Beach area in California to Santa Catalina Island.

He married Itura Belew from Hallsville, Texas, and they had two daughters and one son, Ed. He was twenty some odd years older than his wife.

– Submitted by Mrs. Ed McAlister

CLARENCE E. MCGAW

Clarence Emory McGaw, a native of Bowie, Texas, was born on 16 January 1890, to Robert James McGaw and Cornelia Tomlinson McGaw, pioneer residents of the Bowie area. His grandparents were Robert W. McGaugh and Clementine McGaugh. The family moved to Nocona, Texas sometime around 1900. He was graduated from Nocona High School and graduated from the University of Texas in 1915, and was admitted to the bar that same year.

He served in World War I as a Sergeant, Company C, 4th Infantry, United States Army.

He sold law books for a period of time where he met Dorothy Bearce Richards in Des Moines, Iowa, and they were married 26 June 1927.

He moved his law practice to Longview, Texas, in May of 1931, from Ft. Worth, Texas.

Clarence E. McGaw

His family consisted of wife, Dorothy, daughter Grace, and sons, Clarence Jr. and two-month-old Robert William. Daughter Rose Marie was born twenty months later.

After practicing law here in Longview for four years, he was elected District Judge of the 124th District. He served from 1936 to 1940. In the early part of 1949, he established a law office in Snyder, Texas, where he practiced until 1959, when he returned to Longview after suffering a stroke.

He was a life-long member of the Baptist Church and for many years was a deacon and Sunday School teacher in the First Baptist Church of Longview.

He was a member of the Knights of Pythias Lodge, having been past Chancellor, Supreme Representative, and Chairman General of the Grand Lodge of Texas.

He received the Silver Beaver award for his work with scouting.

He was a member of the Gregg County Bar Association and the Texas Bar Association. He died at his home 1 November 1963, at the age of 73.

– Submitted by Bob McGaw

MCHANEY

James Cornelius and Mary Ann Wood McHaney came to Texas from Virginia about 1850 and settled in Rusk County, where William Edwin was born on 2 February 1852. Julia Barclay Holloway was born 10 February 1854, in Georgia and came to Texas at the age of three with her parents in a covered wagon. W.E. and Julia were married Christmas Eve 1871, in the Old Union Church 12 miles southeast of Longview. In 1882, they moved to Pirtle where they lived for ten years and where W.E. and his partner, John Wood, installed the first steam-powered cotton gin in this section of the state. In 1892, they moved to Longview where they bought a home belonging to Julia's grandfather, James P. Holloway, located one mile south of the courthouse on what is now Green Street, where they lived for 40 years. In 1907, W.E., along with his sons, established a large gin business on East Cotton Street. After World War I, they built electric gins at Greggton and Glenwood and operated a sawmill at Monroe.

In the early days, "Pappy" or "Uncle Buck" as he was fondly called, hauled produce, chiefly

Judge Judson Holloway McHaney, c. 1927

cotton, to Jefferson and Shreveport by wagon and brought back supplies of coffee, flour and sugar. W.E. helped establish and was a trustee of the Holloway School, an early school in southeastern Longview. He served as deacon and elder of the First Christian Church and was chiefly responsible for the building of the first parsonage. It was a familiar sight in Longview to see W.E. riding his jet-black mare up and down Green Street, as he continued to do in later years, amidst tooting car horns. During the Oil Boom of 1931, every available room of their house on Green Street was converted into living quarters to help newcomers find shelter and the front yard opened to "boomers" in tents. After Julia's death in 1934, "Pappy" moved to his farm located in what is now known as Pinewood Park, where he lived until his death in 1937. In 1936, he was invited to lead the Longview Centennial Fair Parade on horseback.

Of their eight children, the third was Judson Holloway McHaney, born 28 November 1876, in Rusk County, Texas. Judson studed law at Texas Christian University and was admitted to the bar in 1897 before beginning his law practice in Longview. On 25 November 1903, he married Nona Pauline Kennard in her family home, where they raised their own six children and Nona's younger siblings.

Judson served as Gregg County Judge from 1909 to 1916, and as County Attorney and District Attorney. He was very well liked and respected and never entered a race for office that he did not win. Judge McHaney was well known as one of the leading advocates for good roads for Gregg County, and it was under his administration that the first strip of asphalt was laid over the present roadway in Gregg County that became Highway 80. After 23 years in public office, he returned to private practice. Judson died 12 December 1931. Three of Judge McHaney's grandchildren, six great grandchildren and three great great grandchildren continue to live in Longview today.

– Submitted by Carol Holloway

WILLIAM EDWIN & JULIA HOLLOWAY MCHANEY

William Edwin (Billy) McHaney, son of Cornelius and Mary Ann Wood McHaney, was born 22 February 1852, Mt. Enterprise, Rusk

County, Texas. The McHaney family had moved, along with their slaves, to Rusk County from Henderson County, Tennessee, in 1849. Julia Holloway, born 13 February 1854, had moved to Rusk County (near what is now the Lake Cherokee dam) with her parents, Rev. James P. and Sarah Elder Holloway, along with their slaves, from Clark County, Georgia, in 1857. Billy and Julia were married at the Holloway home on 28 December 1871.

They began housekeeping on Billy's land, his portion given him by his father as the children married, at Bellview, Rusk County (now Pirtle, four miles south of Kilgore). Billy farmed his land and began a cotton ginning business with his Uncle John Wood. They established the first steam-powered cotton gin in Bellview, Rusk County.

William Edwin McHaney and Julia Holloway McHaney on their 62nd wedding anniversary, 1933.

Billy was a great outdoorsman, loving to fish and hunt. He was known particularly for his love of fox hunting, hearing the hounds make the chase. In his latter years, the young men of the community would invite him to go on their hunts and keep the fires going while they went out to seek the prey. He loved to entertain the grandchildren and their friends with his favorite fox hunting tales. In addition, he loved to tell about his father taking the boys of the family to Henderson to hear Sam Houston speak on the courthouse square. He described Houston as tall, always wearing a big black hat.

The McHaneys had eight children, two having died in early childhood at Bellview. The family moved to Longview in 1892 in order to receive better medical care and educational opportunities for the children. Their first child was Katie May, born 1874; Judson Holloway, born 1876; Annie Belle, born 1879; Vallie, born 1889; Will Eanes, born 1891; and Dee, born 1893.

W.E. was asked to lead the Gregg County Centennial Fair parade in 1936, along with Oliver Pegues. Both were pioneers of East Texas and in their eighties. They rode horseback through the streets of Longview bearing the United States and Texas flags. The McHaneys were charter members of the First Christian Church of Longview. He was responsible for hauling sand for the building on the corner of

Methvin and Green Streets. They and their family were loyal members of the church for their lifetimes. Besides her church activities, Julia McHaney and her daughters were active in attending the United Daughters of the Confederacy meetings, having lost a brother in the War Between the States.

The grandchildren lovingly remembered "Pappy" McHaney riding his gray mare from his home on South Green Street to town, hitching the horse on Fredonia at the First National Bank Building and visiting with the townsmen. He particularly enjoyed the new people that came to Longview during the oil-boom days.

– Submitted by Helen M. Griffin

SEXTON LANDO MCKINLEY & MARGURITE ELOISE VULGAMORE

Sexton McKinley and Margurite Vulgamore met in Wink, Texas, in the late 1920s. They were married there and came to East Texas prior to 1932.

Mack came to Gregg County working for Gulf Oil. First they lived near Kilgore on Highway 31 near Rabbit Creek. In 1935, Mack went to work for Tidewater Oil Company in 1935. The family lived in the Tenneryville area through 1942. Mack was transferred to Conroe, Texas, Venice, Louisiana, and then to Turnertown, Texas, in 1945.

Mack was in charge of the "south end" of the East Texas field for Tidewater. The kids went to school at Gaston. They moved to the Tidewater Camp at Kilgore in 1952. The county line ran right down the middle of their house. They slept in Rusk County and ate breakfast in Gregg County.

Mack became "Field Foreman" for all of Tidewater's holdings on both ends. His specialty was as "trouble-shooter" for drilling. If a well had a problem, especially the deep wells, they called for him. He was sent anywhere there was a "blowout" problem. Every well was like a child to him. He stayed with it from beginning to end with many long days and long nights sleeping in the car.

When he was transferred to Venice, Louisiana, Marge would not take the boys down there

The trouble shooters: solving a problem on a well: "Mack" McKinley, "Boots" Odom and "Jelly" McWherter.

because it was the end of the World War. During World War II, companies were doing lots of drilling down there. Mack had to keep the oil flowing – this was his contribution to the war effort.

He retired from Tidewater in 1969. Then, he worked as an independent contractor out of Shreveport. One of the people he worked with was Buddy Foggleson (Greer Garson's husband). In his work for them, he traveled to Montana, Wyoming and the Dakotas, drilling wells and doing whatever was needed. He continued to work until he was 85. He passed away at age 86 in 1990.

It was said of Mack, "Although he was a 'man of position,' he would jump in and do whatever was needed. He wouldn't ask anyone to do what he wouldn't." He was a man of very little education who worked himself up to the higher ranks of Tidewater. He was a hard man, but a fair one. No matter the differences with his men, they always respected him.

Marge raised the boys, worked in the flower shop and played bridge. She knew how to be a friend to everyone. She made everyone feel comfortable in her house. Marge participated in activities all over Kilgore, including her church, bridge club and camp activities. She was a "people person" and with her job at the flower shop, she met most of Kilgore and was liked by most who knew her.

MOLLIE BAGGETT & JULIUS MCKITTRICK

Mary Ann Jane Baggett, better known as Mollie, was the daughter of David Jesey Baggett and Fannie Lucindy Petty (see "David Jesey Baggett"). The youngest survivor of five children, Mollie was born 7 December 1907 in Coolidge, Limestone County, Texas. From there the family later relocated to Tehuacana, also in Limestone County.

Mollie earned her Bachelor of Science in Education from Texas Tech College in Lubbock. In 1936, Mollie and her mother came to live in Gregg County. Their home was located on Judson Road across from the Judson Grove School, where Mollie would teach.

Mollie, a "born teacher," taught for Judson Independent School District, which consolidated with Longview Independent School District. A fourth grade teacher, her favorite subject was geography. All through the years she enjoyed locating places on maps and globes. Mollie, who enjoyed teaching, retired in May 1973, after 38 years of service.

Mollie married Julius Michael McKittrick in Judson Grove (now Longview) 21 June 1942. He had been born 24 February 1903, in Alto, Texas. Julius owned and managed McKittrick Grocery at the intersection of Judson and Tryon Roads. In 1951, he became postmaster of the Judson Post Office located in a small corner of the store. After several years, Julius quit the grocery business and relocated the post office to a white building next door to their home. In that home they raised two children: Mary Louise, born 14 November 1943, and Peter Michael,

Children of David and Fannie Baggett in 1982. Seated: Joe. Standing (l.-r.): Fannie (Harris) and Mollie (McKittrick).

born 1 June 1949. There they also cared for elderly parents: Mollie's mother and, later, Julius's father. Julius passed away 19 September 1976.

A Sunday school teacher, Mollie helped her husband as assistant postmaster at Judson Post Office. She enjoyed doing recognition and appreciation programs. One of her favorite quotes to use was "Stir what you've got."

Mollie was quiet, energetic and creative. She was kind and loving, and a "lady" in all respects. She had high ideals and morals. If she couldn't say something nice about someone, she wouldn't say anything at all.

Mollie enjoyed watching musicals; her favorites were *Sound of Music* and *My Fair Lady*. In the last few years of her life, when someone would ask her how she was getting along, she would answer, "I'm as fit as a fiddle with all the strings broken."

Until the very end of her life, Mollie was aware of people and happenings around her. She went to be with her Lord on 21 September 2002, at the age of 94. Burial was in the Judson Baptist Cemetery. Mollie is greatly missed by her family and friends.

– Submitted by Mary McKittrick Woolley

JAMES ALPHEUS MCLENDON & BESSIE LEA ARNOLD MCLENDON

When James Isum and Mary Lou Melton McLendon and their family of five children left Dawson, Georgia, in 1886, they came to Texas and settled in Graceton in Upshur County. James Alpheus McLendon, the third oldest child, was six years old. They later moved to Gilmer.

Following James Isum's death on 21 January 1891, Mary Lou and the children moved to a 219-acre farm in the Judson community about five miles north of Longview.

Around 1900, James Alpheus, known as Al, bought 84 acres of the farm from his mother and built a large house on Judson Road.

Al and Bessie Lea Arnold, daughter of Joseph Council Arnold and Mamie E. Rees Arnold of Graceton, were married on 22 December 1907.

The couple's nine children (the oldest and youngest were girls with seven boys in between) were Mamie Eloise, born 30 September 1908; James Melton, born 9 August 1910; William Bryan, born 20 January 1912; Joseph Franklin, born 24 February 1914; Carl Lea, born 15 November 1916; Roger Neil, born 10 January 1918; Johnnie Louis, born 7 November 1920; Charles David, born 17 April 1917, and Bessie Allene, born 6 August 1932.

Al farmed, raising cotton mostly as a cash crop. Al and Bessie always had a large garden, raising most of their food for spring, summer and fall, and canning much food for winter. As the boys got older, Al would take them "out west" during cotton picking time to make the family a little extra money for winter.

He was also a carpenter and school bus driver for Judson schools. During 1941 and 1942, he helped construct several of the military bases around the county, including facilities at Sheppard Field at Wichita Falls, Fort Bliss at El Paso, Camp Fannin at Tyler, and Camp Wolters at Minerals Well, Texas, and Camp Livingston in Louisiana. He served in "holding the election" and was called for jury duty many times.

The family was associated with the Judson Baptist Church and before Al could afford a "Model T," the whole family would go to church in a surrey.

The children attended Judson school, with the older ones going to Longview High School. A high school was added at Judson later, and Johnnie, Charles and Allene graduated from Judson High School.

Four sons were in military service during World War II. Carl went into the Army in early 1941. He was sent to Europe and was in the thick of the war until 1945. Joe was a Navy Seabee, eventually being sent to Saipan-Tinian to build airstrips for the take-off of the Enola Gay to bomb Hiroshima, Japan. Johnnie went into the service in 1942 and was assigned to the Army Air Corps ground service. After many months of aircraft maintenance he was sent to the Pacific Area, landing on Saipan-Tinian about two weeks before the

McLendon family, 1948. (l.-r.) Back: Joe, Bryan, Carl and John. Front: Charles, Allene, Al, Bessie, Mamie and Melton.

Enola Gay took off on 6 August 1945. Bryan was drafted into the Army late in the war years and was in training during his term of service. When the bomb was dropped, Carl was in Europe with General Patton. Joe was on Okinawa, Bryan was in Washington state waiting to be shipped out and Johnnie was on Saipan-Tinian. When the war was over, Al and Bessie were relieved and thankful to see their four sons return safely home from the service.

Mamie married Elbert Whitehurst and they had three children: Geneva Inez, Ouida Florine and Mamie Ethlyn. Elbert died in 1936. Mamie married Julius Coggins, and they had a son, Gary Neal. Julius died in 1956. Mamie died 20 July 1957.

Melton married Juddie Annelle Reel and they had three children: Margie Nell, Patsy Elizabeth and James Melton, Jr. Melton died 23 May 1949.

Bryan married Eva Lillian Bussell. She died in 1933. He married Mary Alice Northen and they had four children: Frances Jane, Michael Bryan, Larry William and James Allan. Bryan died 13 July 1996, and Alice died 28 May 2002.

Joe married Gladys Opal Moody and they had two children, Judith Ann and Jo Carol. Joe died 7 October 1988.

Carl married Mary Florence Terry and they had three children: Mary Anne, Roger Terry and Donna Jean. Carl died 19 May 1960. Roger died 2 January 1933.

Johnnie married Geneva Jasmine Ivie, they had four children: Johnnie Randall, James Louis, Roger Glenn and Peggy Elaine. Geneva died 6 August 2003.

Charles married Carol Harrison Moore. They had two children, Charles Daniel and Nancy Carolyn. Carol died 6 January 1999.

Allene married Lloyd Edwin Roach, and they had five children: David Edwin, Linda Elaine, BeLinda Arleen, Gregory Mark and Lisa Gayle. Lloyd died 2 August 2002

Bessie died in Longview on 14 April 1961. Al died on 27 May 1964, while visiting his son, Charles, in Shreveport, Louisiana. Al and Bessie are buried in Judson Cemetery.

– Submitted by John L. McLendon

JAMES MELTON MCLENDON & ANNELLE REEL MCLENDON

James Melton McLendon, born 9 August 1910, was the second child and first son of James Alpheus McLendon and Bessie Arnold McLendon. He was called Melton, the maiden name of his paternal grandmother, Mary Lou Melton McLendon Coe. The family lived on their farm about five miles north of Longview near Judson. The children had the usual farm chores as they were growing up, including picking cotton, and they attended Judson School. Since Judson did not have a high school then, Melton went to Longview High School. In the graduating class of 1928, he was ranked fourth with an average of 91.11.

In 1930, Melton was in Fort Worth attending Brantley-Draughon College and working at

Annelle Reel McLendon and James Melton McLendon, Easter 1949

the Biltmore Parking Garage. On his return to Longview, he met Annelle Reel, daughter of William Henry Reel and Janie Ethel Prior Reel. Following a few months of courtship, they were married 9 December 1931.

They raised a crop for a year or two, moved to Fort Worth for a job, then back to Longview. In 1934, he started to work for R. Lacy, Inc., learning the business as he worked. Through practical experience and self-study, he worked his way up and became Gas Engineer for the company about 1945. In 1948, the family moved to a company house off the present West Loop 281.

Annelle kept house and took good care of the children. Margie Nell was born 13 November 1932; Patsy Elizabeth was born 25 October 1934; and James Melton McLendon, Jr. was born 19 August 1937. Annelle gardened, canned food and was the typical housewife who lived in the country near Longview. In 1942 she started working for Perkins Bros. Co., and later worked at Colonial Book Inn. In the early 1960s, she was hired to work in the Gregg County Clerk's office and later became Chief Deputy.

One vacation was in Galveston, but most were spent fishing on a lake or river. The family would pack food, cots and mosquito netting. A big block of ice was wrapped in a tarp then buried in the sand to keep it from melting until needed.

When Melton was called for the draft during World War II, he failed his physical examination because of a heart condition. His doctor referred to it as "leakage of the heart." He died 23 May 1949, of a heart attack at age 38. He is buried at Memory Park in Longview.

Annelle continued to work and be involved in the children's school and sports activities at Pine Tree. After graduations and marriages, she lived alone for a few years, then was married briefly to Wade Hampton Smith.

The family experienced a tragic loss when her son, Jim, died in 1991 at age 53.

For several years she shared a home in Longview with her daughter, Margie Lile. Now at age 90, she lives in Spring, Texas, where she and Margie moved in 1997 to be near her other daughter, Pat Teague.

– Submitted by Karen Lile Parker

ALICE ELVIRA HENDERSON MCWHORTER (1840-1931) & HER CHILDREN

Alice Elvira Henderson McWhorter (1840-1931) and her children were typical of the wave of migrants to Texas from older parts of the defeated South immediately after the War Between the States. This was a tide that blended readily with culturally identical stock by which Gregg County was originally settled in the 1840s and 1850s. For information on Alice's descendants, see the articles in this book on Eugene Osborne McWhorter and Eugene Rodden McWhorter.

Alice moved to Kilgore from LaFayette, Georgia, shortly after the settlement of the estate of her husband, Warren Osburn McWhorter (1836-1885), in November 1886. With her, or slightly earlier, came all seven of her children: William Andrew (1861-1932), Claude Fleming (1866-1919), John Barry (1868-1931), Eugene Osborne (1870-1954), Thomas Afton (1871-1954), Mary Frances (1873-1955) and Robert Warren (1876-1957).

Alice was the youngest of 15 children of William Barry Henderson (1787-1863, son of John and Mary McWhorter Henderson) and his wife Mary (1795-1888, daughter of John and Elizabeth Watson Barry). When Alice came to Texas in 1886, her widowed mother and all but one of her surviving brothers and sisters had already moved to Gregg and Harrison Counties, beginning in 1870. They came from the contiguous Walker and Chattooga Counties in northwestern Georgia and Cherokee County in northeastern Alabama. The William Henderson family was living in Cherokee County when Alice was born in 1840. Their house was still standing in 1985.

In 1881, Alice's mother Mary and 12 of her children, grandchildren and their spouses joined four other persons in organizing Alpine Presbyterian Church in the Tryon community north of Longview. Mary and seven others of that group moved their membership from First Presbyterian Church of Longview—including Alice's brother Lawson Pursley Henderson (1824-1921), who had been a founding member of that church in 1873. A Georgia obituary of Mary Barry Henderson in 1888 says she named the new Alpine Church in memory of Alpine Presbyterian Church of Alpine Community—now the town of Menlo—in Chattooga County. Mary and her husband William and four of their children had also been organizing members of that church in 1853. The Tryon community and school with which Gregg County's Alpine Church was closely associated were presumably named for the Trion community in Chattooga County. Alpine and Tryon, also spelled Alpin and Trion, are old Scottish place names.

Most of Alice Henderson McWhorter's ancestors—families including Barry, McWhorter, Winsley (Winslow), Moore, Watson, McDowell, and probably Porter and Irvine—came to the American colonies from Northern Ireland or Scotland during the 1700s. Her grandfather John Barry (1771-1844) was a son of Margaret Catherine Moore Barry of Spartanburg County, South Carolina, known as Kate (1752-1823), who won renown as a patriot heroine in connection with the Revolutionary War battle of Cowpens in 1781. Cowpens was the crucial victory that was dramatized fictitiously but accurately in Mel Gibson's movie *The Patriot* in 2000. The home where Kate Moore Barry grew up, Walnut Grove Plantation, is still standing, eight miles south of Spartanburg. Kate's husband Andrew (1745-1811) fought at Cowpens as well as King's Mountain, Fishing Creek and Musgrove's Mill. Alice McWhorter's grandmother Elizabeth Watson Barry (1774-1838), in turn, was a daughter of Samuel Watson (1729-1808) of what is now York County, South Carolina. He was a delegate to the provincial congress in 1775 and 1776, and became colonel of the New Acquisition District regiment of patriot horsemen, fighting at Stone Ferry and Hanging Rock.

Alice's husband Warren McWhorter—born in Pickens (now Oconee) County, South Carolina—was a farmer whose forebears came to America in the 1600s and 1700s, mostly from Northern Ireland and England. His ancestral names include Gaines, Posten (Poston), Willson, Calhoun, Featherstone, and Pendleton. Warren's grandmother Elizabeth Willson McWhorter (1776-1840) was a daughter of James Willson, who was one of the 12 patriots killed at Cowpens (versus nearly 900 redcoats and tories killed, wounded or captured).

Warren Osburn McWhorter
(1836–1885)

Alice and Warren were married on Christmas Eve 1860, and Will was born the following October. After making one crop, Warren enlisted in the Confederate army on 4 March 1862, in Summerville, seat of Chattooga County. He became first sergeant in Company B, Ninth Georgia Infantry Regiment, Anderson's Brigade, Hood's Division, Longstreet's Corps, Army of Northern Virginia. He was wounded in a hand at the Battle of Sharpsburg in September 1862. While on duty recovering and tending wounded at Gettysburg in July 1863, he suffered severe heat exhaustion from which he never fully recovered. After a furlough of several months, he returned to duty. On surrendering with General Lee's army at Appomattox, Warren was paroled on 10 April 1865, and walked home to Georgia, arriving on May 20. By the time Bob was born in 1876, the family had moved to a farm at LaFayette in Walker County. Warren was ordained as elder and served as Sunday school su-

perintendent at the Presbyterian Church in LaFayette.

When Alice Henderson McWhorter and her seven children moved from LaFayette to Texas in the winter of 1886-87, they settled together in Kilgore, where daughter Mary was enrolled in Alexander Institute. Later, the family moved to Omen in Smith County to enable the sons to attend Summer Hill Select School, conducted by Professor O.W. Orr. Alice kept boarders, and the six sons farmed and worked at odd jobs. Within a few years, the family moved to Longview. About 1900, shortly after Will and Claude were married, Alice's sons contributed to building a two-story colonial-style house for her, where she lived until her death at the age of 91. Extensively remodeled by Alice's grandson Eugene Rodden McWhorter as his residence in 1938, the house still stands at 405 South High Street. However, it passed out of the family in 1945. Alice was buried at Alpine Presbyterian Church cemetery.

William Andrew McWhorter (1861-1932) married Sally Adrian (1876-1903) of the Tryon community in 1899. In 1910, he married his first cousin, Mary Williams (1876-1936), daughter of Alice's sister Rebecca Jane. Will was a farmer and cattleman. He and Mary lived many years in the newly developed irrigation district at Balmorhea in Reeves County, Texas. He died childless and was buried in Alpine Church Cemetery, as were Sally and Mary.

Claude Fleming McWhorter (1866-1919) was the carpenter who supervised construction of the first sanctuary of Alpine Presbyterian Church in Gregg County in 1885, when he was 18 years old. Claude married Mabel Barnes (1879-1980, born in Ogden, Utah), in 1897 and made a railroad career in Palestine. Mabel and Claude had two children: Ruth McWhorter Mottley (1898-1966) and Laurence Stansel McWhorter (1901-1991).

John Barry McWhorter (1868-1931) served for a time around 1900 as Longview's city marshal—the town's entire police force. In 1905, he married Ellen Hudson (1877-1959). The couple resided in his mother Alice's house until John's death. Ellen and John had one child,

Alice Henderson McWhorter with her seven children in 1889. (l.-r.) Back: Tom, Mary, Will and Alice. Front: John, Gene, Claude and Bob.

Mary Alice (1906-1992), who was married to Thomas Shook Bell of Hallsville until he died in 1937, and later to Byron A. Crocker (1900-1975) of Sherman, Texas. Having begun teaching at Union Grove school when she was 18 years old, Mary Alice became principal of First Ward school in Longview and retired as principal of Valley View school. B.A. Crocker was city engineer and director of public works for the City of Longview. John and Ellen were buried in the McWhorter-Echols plot at Greenwood Cemetery in Longview.

Eugene Osborne McWhorter (1870-1954) married Vesta Leila Echols (1873-1945) of Longview. For more information, see the article on them in this book.

Thomas Afton McWhorter (1871-1954) was a Longview businessman, an elder in First Presbyterian Church, and a bachelor until 1916. In that year, he married Helen Ripy (1883-1960) of Lawrenceburg, Kentucky. They reared two sons: Frank Ripy (born 1918) and Thomas Osborne (1920-1978). In 1923, Tom and Helen moved with their two young sons from Houston to Magnolia, Texas, to manage 4,000 acres of timber land that he had acquired, and that eventually went into oil and gas production. In retirement, they moved back to Houston. Frank McWhorter married Elizabeth Morrow (1919-1991) of Houston in 1941. They reared two children: Robert Frank (born 1950) and Marian Helen (born 1954). In 1993, Frank married a childhood friend of Elizabeth's named Doris McClung McCleskey (born 1920) of Houston. Frank's brother Tom married Nancy Kay Coke, then Louise Day Thompson, and finally Ina

Alice Henderson McWhorter's house, still standing at 405 South High Street in Longview, shown about 1910 and 1938.

Killgore Rogers. Tom and Louise reared four children: John Charles Thompson McWhorter (1952-1977), Anne Stuart McWhorter Fanelli (born 1955), Thomas Duvall McWhorter (born 1957) and James Barry McWhorter (born 1965).

Mary Frances McWhorter (1873-1955) was organist at First Presbyterian Church of Longview in 1897 when she married the pastor, Samuel Mills Tenney (1871-1939). Both Mary and Sam became noted scholars and authors in topics pertaining to the Presbyterian Church. After serving as pastor of a number of churches, Sam helped establish the Presbyterian Historical Foundation at Montreat, North Carolina, and served as its first curator until his death, with Mary as his assistant. Both received the honorary degree of Doctor of Letters from Austin College at Sherman in 1938. (Sam was already a doctor of divinity.) They reared three children: Samuel McWhorter Tenney (1899-1939), Robert Paul Warfield Tenney (1901-1980) and Warren William Tenney (1903-1955).

Robert Warren McWhorter (1876–1957) married Jennie V. Melville (died 1981) in 1908. They lived in Palestine, where Bob became a railroad conductor and managed real estate investments. They had two children who died in infancy. Both Bob and Jennie V. were buried in Palestine. (Copyright 2004 by E.W. McWhorter) – Submitted by Eugene W. McWhorter

EUGENE OSBORNE MCWHORTER (1870-1954) & VESTA ECHOLS MCWHORTER (1873-1945)

McWhorter Park in Longview perpetuates the memory of Mr. and Mrs. E.O. McWhorter. They were active in business, social, and public affairs of Longview during the first half of the twentieth century. For information on their ancestors and descendants, see the articles in this book on Alice Henderson McWhorter, Robert Finis Echols, James Templeton Echols, John Rodden and Eugene Rodden McWhorter.

Eugene Osborne McWhorter (1870-1954), known as Gene, and Vesta Leila Echols (1873-1945) were married on Thanksgiving Day of 1900 in the parlor of her father's home on Center Street in Longview, catercorner from the southwest corner of the courthouse square. Vesta had been a member of the first graduating class of Longview High School and was a graduate of Ward's Female Seminary in Nashville, Tennessee, forerunner of Ward-Belmont College. She had also attended college in Weatherford, Texas, and studied art and china painting in Dallas.

The couple's first child, Warren Echols McWhorter, was born on 17 September 1901. Warren died of diphtheria in 1906. Meantime, with his brother Tom, Gene operated McWhorter Brothers Grocery Store, which closed as a result of the Bank Panic of 1907. During the same time, he was elected as a city alderman, serving from 1901 to 1907. In that capacity, he was instrumental in securing the city's acceptance of the privately established "Longview Cemetery" as a city cemetery in 1905, renamed Greenwood at that time.

Eugene Osborne and Vesta Echols McWhorter, about 1930.

From 1907 until 1912, Gene worked for his father-in-law, Bob Echols, in the meat market and cattle business. That period saw the birth of his second and final child: Eugene Rodden McWhorter (1909-1991), who also became known as Gene. At that time, the E.O. McWhorters were living in one of the two houses located at the southwest corner of the courthouse square, catercorner from Vesta's father's house. From 1912 to 1935, Gene was elected each two years as Gregg County tax collector.

Gene was chairman of the executive committee of the Gregg County Democratic Party for six years. For a like period, he served as secretary and treasurer of the board of trustees of Longview Independent School District. When the East Texas Chamber of Commerce was organized at Longview in 1926, Gene and Vesta were in charge of banquet arrangements by which hundreds were served on the courthouse lawn. Gene was later honored by that organization as their "man of the year." In 1939, he was elected to the Longview city commission, serving for a time as chairman—a position carrying the honorary title of mayor of Longview. Vesta, in turn, was a charter member of the following associations: the Longview Shakespeare Club, the local chapter of the United Daughters of the Confederacy, the Longview Art Club, the Longview Garden Club, the Longview Music Club, and the Captain William Young chapter of the Daughters of the American Revolution. She was a talented painter, leaving many oils and watercolors for her family to cherish.

Both Gene and Vesta were active members of First Presbyterian Church; he was ordained as a deacon and an elder, and she served as a Sunday school teacher and president of the Council of Church Women in Longview. As avid ballroom and square dancers, the couple took part in social events of Longview and were early members of Pinecrest Country Club.

Besides his employment as county tax collector, Gene continued as a cattleman and farmer, eventually acquiring three farms in Gregg County and another at Balmorhea in Reeves County, Texas. Beginning in the 1950s, he allowed the Greggton Lions Club to use part of one farm (which had belonged to Vesta's Rodden ancestors) for childrens' baseball fields. Gene's grandchildren later sold much of that farm to the City of Longview for McWhorter Park, which was named in memory of Gene and Vesta.

E.O. McWhorter also acquired both of the one-third shares of the Lake Lomond property—popularly misspelled as Lake Lamond—that had belonged to his brother-in-law Hugh Echols and his friend F.T. Rembert. Among other business enterprises, Gene established Lake Side Dairy at Lake Lomond in 1928. The dairy was operated by Gene's brother John and later by David Gore until it closed in 1942. The milking barn is still standing, used by the McWhorter family for storage, behind the business at 1302 West Marshall Avenue.

At some time around 1920, Gene moved with his wife and son to a house at 401 North High Street, on the northwest corner of High and Whaley Streets. (The lot remains in the family.) Gene acquired most of the property along the west side of that block of High Street and extending several hundred feet west along Whaley and Marshall Avenue, including several rental houses and a one-acre pond known as Pace's Pond. His final residence was at 405 North High Street.

Mr. and Mrs. E.O. McWhorter and their son Warren were buried in the McWhorter-Echols plot at Greenwood Cemetery. (Copyright 2004 by E.W. McWhorter)
– Submitted by William P. McWhorter

EUGENE RODDEN MCWHORTER (1909-1991) & LOTTIE WHERRY MCWHORTER (born 1913)

Eugene Rodden McWhorter (1909-1991) was a prominent engineering manager and landowner of Longview whose local roots sprang from pioneer times in the 1840s. For information on his ancestors, see the articles in this book on Eugene Osborne McWhorter, Alice Henderson McWhorter, Robert Finis Echols, James Templeton Echols and John Rodden.

The only surviving child of Eugene Osborne and Vesta Echols McWhorter, Eugene Rodden McWhorter was known as Gene like his father. He graduated from Longview High School in 1926 and entered the University of Texas as an engineering student. Due to hard times at home and the onset of the Great Depression, Gene dropped out at mid-term in January 1930—just in time to participate in the beginning of the East Texas Oil Boom. He immediately organized a natural gas distribution business to serve the booming Greggton area. After a couple years, he sold out to United Gas, worked for that company for a time in Kilgore, and then finished his electrical engineering degree at the University. He also took an additional year of business courses which were that era's equivalent of an MBA program. Resuming his career with United Gas in Beaumont, Gene became one of the earliest registered professional engineers in the state.

In the Beaumont office of United Gas Company, Gene fell in love with a pretty cashier named Lottie Maicel Wherry. They were married in 1935

Eugene Rodden and Lottie Wherry McWhorter at the wedding of their daughter Charlotte Vesta in 1974.

at that city's First Baptist Church, where Lottie had long been a member and Sunday school teacher. By that time, United Gas had transferred Gene to Orange, Texas, as district engineer.

Lottie was the third of six surviving children of Walter Thomas Wherry (1884-1947) and his wife, the former Laura Wellington Childress (1885-1968), both of them descended entirely from colonial Scotch-Irish stock like Gene's parents. Reared on a farm near Lebanon, Tennessee, Walter became a very successful independent oil operator at Spindletop and other fields of southeast Texas such as Sour Lake and Saratoga. When Lottie was born in 1913, the Wherry family was living in the bustling Spindletop oil field, where Walter operated a general store and boarding house and served as postmaster for the town of Guffey. After moving his growing family into a large house in Beaumont, Walter became active in civic and social affairs of that city. As a trustee of South Park Independent School District, he set in motion the establishment of South Park Junior College—which in time became Lamar University. Lottie graduated from that high school and college.

When United Gas Company transferred Gene home to Longview in 1936, he and Lottie bought the home of his grandmother, Alice Henderson McWhorter, at 405 South High Street, remodeling it extensively. Beginning in 1939, Gene participated in establishing Madaras Steel Company and building its revolutionary direct-reduction steel plant. The Madaras plant was located at what is now the north side of West Cotton Street immediately west of Lake Lamond Road—which at that time ended at the railroad and was called the Steel Plant Road. The year 1940 saw the birth of Eugene Warren McWhorter, who became known as Gene like his father and grandfather. (However, in this article, "Gene" refers to Eugene Rodden McWhorter.)

When World War II broke out, Gene turned his engineering talent to the construction and operation of Monsanto Chemical Company's Longhorn Army Ammunition Plant at Karnak. William Paul McWhorter, known as Bill, was born in 1942. Immediately after the war, Monsanto transferred Gene to an engineering management position at Clinton Laboratories of the atomic-bomb Manhattan Project, near Oak

Ridge, Tennessee. Gene's mother had died in the summer of 1945 after a long illness. His father accompanied Gene, Lottie, and the two boys to Oak Ridge, living with them there.

In 1946, Gene brought his family back to Longview. They lived with the senior Gene McWhorter in his house at 405 North High Street, continuing there for five years after E.O. McWhorter's death in 1954. E.R. McWhorter became one of the first local engineers to be employed by R.G. LeTourneau, then likewise one of the first to be employed by Texas Eastman Company in 1949. Meantime, Charlotte Vesta McWhorter was born in 1948.

After helping build the Eastman plant, Gene stayed on to help operate it, retiring in 1974. Besides his engineering vocation, E.R. McWhorter was active in development and management of his father's extensive real-estate and mineral holdings, which Gene and Lottie and their children acquired by inheritance and purchase from relatives. A lifelong member of First Presbyterian Church of Longview, Gene was ordained there as deacon and elder and served in many other capacities. Like his father, he served as a trustee of Longview Independent School Board. For more than 30 years, he was a member of the Rotary Club of Longview. In his early years, Gene enjoyed art and music, creating etchings and playing clarinet and saxophone. Later, his chief pastime was golf at Pinecrest Country Club.

Through the years, Lottie McWhorter worked as bookkeeper and office manager for the family real-estate and mineral interests. She has been an enthusiastic volunteer at First Presbyterian Church, serving among other duties as historian for many years. She has been a member of the Shakespeare Club, the Captain William Young Chapter of the Daughters of the American Revolution (serving as local regent and at the state level), the Longview Study Club and the Longview Garden Club. Her artistic interests have included portrait painting in oils. An avid historian and genealogist, Lottie was the chief compiler of two books on her husband's ancestry: *Some Descendants of David and Mary Poston McWhorter* (1978) and *Mary (Barry) & William Barry Henderson: Their Forebears & Descendants* (1987). Working alone, she also compiled *Jessie Ellen (Lynn) & Jackson Scott Childress: Their Ancestors and Descendants* (1991).

Eugene Warren McWhorter married Nancy Green of Longview in 1965, earned master's degrees in chemical engineering and marketing, and is now a technical market communications consultant in Longview. William Paul McWhorter married Maxine Mohon of Longview in 1965, became a physician, and lives in Eugene, Oregon. Charlotte Vesta McWhorter married Thomas Gardner Rundell of Wichita Falls, earned a master's degree in English, and lives in Dallas, where her husband is an attorney.

Eugene Rodden McWhorter died in 1991 and was buried at Grace Hill Cemetery. Lottie retired from her labors as family bookkeeper and

office manager in 2004. At this writing, she has six grandchildren and six great grandchildren. (Copyright 2004 by E.W. McWhorter)
– Submitted by Charlotte McWhorter Rundell

MEADOWS

James Kinchion Meadows, with his wife, Elizabeth Ann Dunnaway Meadows, came to the Rusk-Gregg County area from Louvale, Stewart County, Georgia, in 1879. At that time, they had seven children: Alice Corine, Jenea Augusta (Anna), George Franklin, Janie Lubreta, Charles Andrew Jackson, Mary Elizabeth (Dolly), Nathaniel Christopher Green (Kit) and Julia Elizabeth. After coming to East Texas, they had John Henry, Sam Edwin, Emma and Katie Belle. They, James and Eliza Ann, had been neighbors and had grown up in Louvale, Georgia.

James Kinchion Meadows and Eliza Ann Dunnaway were married 13 August 1861. James was the son of Jesse Green Meadows and Renvie Baldwin Meadows. He was born 18 September 1839, in Louvale, Stewart County, Georgia, and died 27 August 1888, and is buried in Pirtle Cemetery, Rusk County, Texas. Eliza Ann Meadows was born 26 November 1841 in Antiock, Stewart County, Georgia, and died 2 August ----. She is also buried in Pirtle Cemetery. She was the daughter of James Monroe Dunaway and Lucinda Cousins Dunaway.

Jenea Augusta (Anna) Meadows was born 21 August 1863, married on 19 February 1884, George Henry Crews and died 18 April 1947. She is buried Hickory Grove Cemetery.

Alice Corene Meadows was born 21 August 1862, and married John Wesley Peace and moved to Oklahoma.

George Franklin Meadows, born 1866, married 20 November 1892, Cordie Lee Crews. He died in 1935, and is buried in Danville Cemetery, Gregg County, Texas.

Charles Andrew Jackson Meadows was born in 1870, and married Paulina Lee Mercer. He died in 1951, and is buried in Winterfield Cemetery, Gregg County, Texas.

Mary Nancy Elizabeth (Dolly) Meadows was born 14 August 1872, Louvale, Stewart County, Georgia, married on 2 August 1893, Ferdinand Lafayette (Fate) Birdsong. She died 13 August 1963, and is buried in Danville Cemetery, Gregg County, Texas.

Nathaniel Christopher Green Meadows was born 20 May 1875. He married 1 March 1894, Naoma Utzman. He died of a heart attack while burning stumps in his pasture on 11 March 1954. He and his wife are buried in Danville Cemetery. They had seven children: Virginia Dare, Van Oliver (Bill), Chesley Hobson, Carrie Bell, Calvin Mays (Dick), James Kinchion and Stella Mae.

Virginia Dare (Darie) Meadows was born 2 February 1895, in Gregg County, Texas. He married Benetta Inez Dudley on 23 November 1921. They had seven children: Mary Virginia, John Dudley, Delores, Lucretia, Wayne Nathaniel, Shirley Jean and Glenn Curtis. He married second Irene Jones Faircloth. Darie died

14 February 1964, in Longview, Texas, and is buried in Memory Park Cemetery, Harrison County, Texas.

Van Oliver (Bill) Meadows was born 16 April 1897, in Gregg County. He served in World War I. He married Willie Mae Standard on 11 August 1928, in Longview, Texas. They had two children, Naoma Mae Belle, born 21 June 1929, and Mary Elizabeth, born 3 February 1932. Van Oliver died in Shreveport, Caddo Parrish, Louisiana, and is buried in Danville Cemetery.

Naoma married Artie Stanley on 27 June 1947. They had three children: Larry Gene, born 25 May 1948; Julie Kay, born 6 December 1951; and John Timothy, born 13 March 1958

Chesley Hobson Meadows was born 18 January 1899, married Fannie Mae England on 25 March 1928. He died 26 April 1987. They had no children. He is buried in Memory Park Cemetery, Harrison County.

Carrie Bell Meadows, born 15 September 1900, Gregg County, married Robert Barton 15 September 1922, and died 1 December 1966. They had one son, William Robert (Billy Bob). She is buried in Grace Hill Cemetery, Longview, Texas

Calvin Mays (Dick) Meadows, born 4 February 1905, married Alene Watkins 10 October 1936. They had one daughter, Nancy. Dick died 27 July 1966, and is buried Danville Cemetery.

Stella Mae Meadows, born 25 February 1909, married Arthur Quinn on 5 December 1925. They had five children: Arthur Donald, Pauline, Marion, Bobby Joe and Grace Lynn. She died 28 November 1986, and is buried in Danville Cemetery.

James Kinchion Meadows, born 19 October 1910, married Lottie Mae Moorman 1 January 1943. He died 2 Januray 1970. They had no children. He is buried in Danville.

Julie Elizabeth Meadows, born 24 April 1878, Stewart County, Georgia, married Waddie Dolphus Robertson on 1 November 1899, died 14 December 1959, and is buried in Danville.

John Henry Meadows born 8 August 1879 was killed accidentally in Forest Home Baptist Church 10 November 1897 and is buried Pirtle Cemetery.

Sam Edwin Meadows, born May 1881, married Tenza Minta Stroud 1 March 1905.

Emma Meadows, born 10 July 1884, Longview, Texas, married Daniel Francis Hays. Emma died 4 March 1948, in Elgin, Oklahoma.

Katie Belle Meadows, born 28 April 1885, died 19 September 1886, and is buried in Pirtle Cemetery in Rusk County.

There are many descendants scattered throughout East Texas from these families.

– Submitted by Elizabeth Meadows

DAVID SUTTON MEREDITH, JR.

David Sutton Meredith, Jr. was born in Longview on 22 July 1902. Judge Meredith graduated from Longview High School and attended the University of Texas. While he was a senior at the university, he was elected county judge of Gregg County, becoming the youngest county judge in the state of Texas.

Considered by many to have had one of the most brilliant legal minds ever to serve on the bench in Gregg County, Meredith had been engaged in the private practice of law after his retirement from the judge advocate general's staff of the United States Air Force and his subsequent appointment as an assistant attorney general under John Ben Sheppard. Few of the judgments he rendered as special district judge were ever reversed

He served from 1927 until 1928 as county judge and was elected district attorney in 1928, serving until 1931 when he resigned to enter the private practice of law with the late E.M. Bramlette.

In 1935, he was appointed judge of the special district court of Gregg County by Governor James V. Allred, was elected without opposition, and served until 1940 when he resigned to form a law partnership with Carroll and Leslie Florence in Gilmer.

He enlisted in the United States Army as a private in June of 1942, and was graduated from the Anti-aircraft Officers Candidate School at Camp Davis, North Carolina, in December of the same year. He was commissioned in the Judge Advocate General Corps in 1943, and went to Ann Arbor, Michigan, for special training. Upon completion of this training, he was sent to the Pacific theater of operations and served on the judge advocate staff throughout the remainder of the war.

On 21 December 1925, he married Lois Leland McGaughy of Gilmer. They had four children: David Sutton III, born 26 June 1928, died 12 November 1998; Corinne Leland, born 15 November 1932, died 30 December 1938; Henry McGaughy, born 10 December 1934; Will Gordon, born 6 August 1941.

David Sutton III married Ann Byrd McArthur of Fayetteville, North Carolina, 10 February 1951. They had two children, David Sutton IV, born 1 September 1952, and Lois Leland, born 7 February 1955. Henry McGaughy married Sara Ann Parker of Center, Texas, on 4 June 1966. They had three children: John McGaughy, born 29 May 1970; Steven Parker, born 23 July 1972; and Thomas Stuart, born 14 August 1980. Will Gordon married Margaret Jonelle Horner of Longview on 28 December 1962. They had three children: Leigh Ellen, born 1 July 1969; William Quinn, born 21 March 1972; and Van Patterson, born 19 June 1977.

Judge Meredith's father and mother were pioneer citizens of Gregg County. His father, David Sutton Meredith, was born in Meredithville, Virginia, in 1869. He came to Texas in the early 1890s and settled in Henderson. He married Minnie Burr Fisher in 1894, and they moved to Longview in 1895. He was a former Gregg County sheriff in the early 1900s. He also was a widely known merchant, being associated for many years with the F.T. Rembert Company. Mrs. Meredith, born 17 December 1870, was a native of Berlin, Maury County, Tennessee. She attended Tennessee Female College in Franklin, Tennessee, where she received a Bachelor of Arts and Master of Education degrees. She did postgraduate work at Peabody College, Nashville, and

then accepted a teaching position in the public school system in Henderson, Texas. She was a member of the United Daughters of the Confederacy and a charter member of the Standard Club, one of the first study clubs organized in Longview. Mr. Meredith died 14 March 1934, and Mrs. Meredith died on 29 January 1961. At the time of her death, she was the oldest member of the First Methodist Church in Longview. Both Mr. and Mrs. Meredith, Sr. are buried in Greenwood Cemetery in Longview. Mr. and Mrs. Meredith, Sr. had five children: Monroe Mays, born 23 December 1896, died 3 March 1898; Olivia Gee, born 20 July 1899; David Sutton, Jr., born 22 July 1902, died 21 January 1958; Perry Reynolds, born 25 September 1906; and Wilmer Thomas, born 27 August 1909.

– Submitted by H.M. Meredith

METHVIN

The first Methvin to come to America from Scotland was Nathan in 1790. His son, Richard R., moved from Georgia to Texas about 1825, purchasing many acres in Upshur County, bordered on the north by the Cherokee Trace, near what became Earpville. He was a wagon maker and had a livery stable on the corner where the main Longview Post Office stands now.

Richard's son, Ossamus Hitch Methvin, was born 10 March 1815, in Georgia and married Margaret Perreau (1819-1894) in New Orleans in 1835. They moved to East Texas about 1848, where he purchased land in what was still then Upshur County. This included the property on Rock Hill (Center Street north of the present Longview Court House) where he built his three-story home and from which came many of the stones used to build the first Gregg County Courthouse, the First Presbyterian Church and other local structures. The original Methvin cornfield, where the present Gregg County Court House stands, is home to an Official Texas Historical Marker commemorating O.H. Methvin, the "Founder of Longview."

On 7 April 1870, O.H. Methvin deeded the Southern Pacific Railroad one hundred acres of land for $1 "for the purpose of aiding there-in, and opening up and developing the sources of the country." It was from the porch of his house on Rock hill that the remark "What a long view!" was made, thus naming the new town. He died 1 February 1883, and is buried in Greenwood Cemetery in a grave marked by an Official Texas Historical Marker.

Mr. and Mrs. O.H. Methvin, 1800s.

O.H. Methvin, Jr. (6 November 1851–1910) married Anna Frances Crouch. He installed Longview's first public transit system, a mule drawn rail car, which ran until 1912. He also operated a restaurant in downtown Longview. They had seven children.

Their daughter, Lizzie Harrison Methvin (19 October 1884–3 March 1957) married James Alton Holloway (5 May 1883–22 June 1946) in 1906. Alton owned and operated the Home Mercantile Company, which he changed to Home Furniture Company. Of their five children, the second was William Alton (28 August 1909–10 March 1989) who continued to own and operate the Home Furniture Company until he retired in 1958.

William married MaeBeth McHaney (9 May 1912–8 February 1986) in 1931 and they had three daughters: Ann (1932), Beth (1935) and Carol (1951). Ann Holloway married Gilbert J. Moore in 1951 and had four children: Brad (1952); Doug (1953), who has a son Landon (1993); Elizabeth (1955); and Gilbert James III (1965). Beth married Bill W. Dodson in 1954 and had two children: Gary (1955) and Ann (1958). Gary has two daughters, Lauren (1990) and Shannon (1996). Carol married Jerry Bahadory in 1984. Lauren and Shannon Dodson and Landon Moore represent eight generations of the first Methvins in this area.

– Submitted by Gary Dodson

MARTIN MARION MILLER & RUBY OPAL MCWILLIAMS

Martin and Opal Miller moved to Longview, Gregg County, Texas, in 1931 when Martin got a job at the Longview post office, from which he retired after 34 years. Martin and Opal were both born in Texas. Martin said, "I was born March 11, 1902, on a farm near Murchison, Texas, on a cold, snowy day, and my father was in bed with the measles." His parents were William Aaron Miller and Nancy Lucinda Chaney. Martin had two brothers and five sisters: Sadie Agness, Katherine Mary, Ollie Margaret, Fred Eugene, Hattie Irene (Patsy), Preston Jesse and Helen Evelyn.

Martin's family moved quite often. Before he was four years old, the family moved to Alabama, where his father farmed and worked in a sawmill. In 1907, the family moved to a place between Ben Wheeler and Martins Mill, Texas. The year Martin was twelve, the family sold their crop and moved to Rockwall, Texas, where they picked cotton for several farmers. Then they rented a farm near Colorado City, Texas, and

Ruby Opal McWilliams and Martin Marion Miller

(l.-r.) Back: Nancy Elizabeth Miller, Jack Martin Miller and Patsy Ruth Miller. Front: Mary June Miller and Peggy Sue Miller.

made a good crop. They next moved to DeQueen, Arkansas, for about six months before moving back to Colorado City. In 1914, the family moved to Troup, Texas. It was in Troup that Martin's father died 14 January 1919, of influenza during the influenza epidemic. This left Martin, age sixteen and the oldest boy, as the one to take over the farm. At the time, the family consisted of Martin, his mother, four sisters and two brothers. Another sister was born seven months later. They made one crop at Troup and then moved to a farm nine miles north of Colorado City, where they lived for about three years.

About 1922, Martin made a trip to Canton, Texas, where he met Ruby Opal McWilliams, who, in his words, "was the prettiest girl I'd ever seen. She was on the porch of my cousin's house. I remember she had a bow in her hair." In 1923, the Miller family moved to Canton. Martin and Opal were married at Myrtle Springs, Van Zandt County, Texas, on 5 October 1924.

Ruby Opal McWilliams was born 5 May 1901, at Martins Mill, Van Zandt County, Texas. Her parents were Marion Lafayette McWilliams and Eva Elizabeth Parsons (Whiddon). Opal had four brothers and three sisters: Perry Joseph Linston, Nettie Bernice, Loyce Elora, Irby I., Maggie Oline, Marion Kellis and Gerald Reginald. She also had four half-brothers and four half-sisters. The McWilliams children were Virgil Andrew, Maude Katherine, William Warren, John Howell, Lela Clifton and Mary Ann Sousin. The Whiddon children were William Ernest and Lela Ann.

Martin and Opal had five children, the first two born at Martins Mill, the next two born at Canton and the youngest at Longview. Their children were Nancy Elizabeth, born 23 May 1926, married John Burns Smith 6 July 1951; Patsy Ruth, born 11 October 1927, married Milton Luther Belflower 25 December 1950; Jack Martin, born 28 June 1929, married Hallie Griffith (Casteel) 2 March 1960; Mary June, born 3 October 1930, married David Earl Long, 24 August 1950; and Peggy Sue, born 8 January 1932, married James Otto Mathis 21 July 1951.

Martin died 6 October 1989, and Opal died 7 April 1998. They are both buried in Memory Park at Longview, Texas

– Submitted by Linda Combs

WILLIAM MILLER

William Miller was born 25 December 1870, in Minden, Louisiana. He was the second son born to a German immigrant, also named William Miller. His mother's name is unknown. She was said to be of African American and Native American descent.

William's father was the descendant of the Muellers who lived in a small town outside of Minden, called Germantown, founded in 1835.

William Miller in Longview, Texas.

Around 1890, William moved to Longview, Texas. He met Narciss Davis, who was born in October 1881, in Longview, and they married on 9 November 1902. To their union eight children were born.

Viola was born 28 April 1898, and died less than three years later on 12 November 1901.

Willie May was born 5 May 1900. She married Jimmie Hern-don on 11 August 1919. Jimmie and Willie May lived on South Court Street in Longview and had three children: Jimmy Gerald, born 7 January 1921; James William, born 2 August 1922; and Jannie Marie, born 27 September 1924. Willie May died 19 January 1947.

Victoria Bernice, or "Shug," was born 1 February 1910. Victoria taught school in Marshall, Texas, from 1927-1929. She then moved to Dallas and married Claude W. Carpenter on 23 July 1930. Claude worked as a porter for Union Pacific Railroad. To this union one daughter, Claudette Alyce, was born on 17 October 1936. Victoria and Claude moved to California in the early 1950s. In 1997, a few years after her husband's death, Victoria returned to Longview, where she died on 1 January 1998.

Miller children and grandchild: (l.-r.) Victoria, Letitia, Willie Mae, Barbara, Frankie, William and Victoria's daughter, Claudette, Longview, Texas, 1941.

William and Narciss Miller visiting Los Angeles, California, around 1958.

Frankie Lyno, or "Bibby," was born 29 May 1912. Frankie married Judge Hutchings of Longview on 7 April 1934. They had one son, James, born 24 September 1931. They lived at 106 Grigsby and owned and operated Longview's Sunset Café. Judge died in 1991, and shortly after his death Frankie moved to Greenville, Texas, to live with her son.

Roberta Letitia, or "Teate," was born 9 June 1915. She met and married Judson M. Lucas on 5 July 1935. Roberta lived in Longview until her death on 27 March 1970.

Clarence William, or "Bubba," was born on 27 September 1918. He served in the United States Cavalry from 1942-1943, and returned to Longview after honorably discharging from the Army. Clarence lived in Longview until his death on 5 September 1970.

Barbara Letitia, or "Tito," was born on 11 August 1921. Barbara moved to Dallas around 1930, and met and married Harry Keppler on 20 April 1948. They had two sons, Harry, Jr. and Jacques. Barbara and her sons moved to Sacramento, California, around 1950, where she continues to live. Her husband and both of her sons preceded her in death.

William Miller worked for years as a teamster truck driver for Transfer Company and then as caretaker of Grace Hill Cemetery in Longview. He died 9 July 1964, and his wife, Narciss, died 10 June 1960. They rest side by side at Grace Hill Cemetery.

The Millers were active members of Bethel Baptist Church located on Harrison Road and all of their children attended school in Longview. On 15 April 2002, the family celebrated the birth of Ariah, the first born of the sixth generation to the Miller family.

– Submitted by Terri Cook

MITCHELL

In 1840, from Bonbrook Plantation, Cumberland County, Virginia, the prominent Willis Wilson and wife, Mary Anna, along with their children, Mary Anna, Maria Willis, Elizabeth and two baby Wilsons ventured to East Texas. There, on part of an old (Frost Thorn survey) Spanish land grant, they founded Walnut Grove Plantation, located north and west of the Gregg County Airport, so named for the many walnut trees that grow there. Before the Civil

War, Willis became seriously ill, so he took the family back to Bonbrook to attend to his estate. Before they could return, both parents (Willis and Mary Anna) died. After the Civil War, an uncle, Captain William Wilson, CSA, and his sister Elizabeth accompanied Mary Anna and her sister Elizabeth back to Walnut Grove.

Ethel Fall Mitchell, 1910

In 1879, Mary Anna married Dr. Pleas J. Mitchell who had come from Alabama with his brother, Walter. To Pleas and Mary Anna were born William Gardiner Mitchell and a sister Mary who, after her marriage to George Teague of Longview ended, moved to Dallas.

Mary Anna was a charter member of First Presbyterian Church, Longview that was built in 1874. At that time she gave the bell from Walnut Grove Plantation that was previously used to call in slaves. Today it is used to beckon worshippers. Later, she also founded Center Presbyterian Church in Elderville.

Only a few months old when his father died, William Gardiner grew up fast until, as a boy of ten, his mother, Mary Anna, turned Walnut Grove over to him. William, now a farmer, raised and harvested cotton, corn, sweet potatoes, cream peas, sugar cane, watermelons, trees, chickens, goats, cattle, horses, mules and hogs. Providing jobs in the Depression, he also owned and operated a sawmill and a cotton gin. A prominent citizen of Gregg County, he served as Grand Jury foreman during the days of "hot oil" investigations. A Rotary Club member, Elder in the Presbyterian Church and a School Board member, he also acted on a special committee to acquire land for Lake Cherokee. His mother, Mary Anna, was 85 when she died in 1940.

On 1 March 1909, William

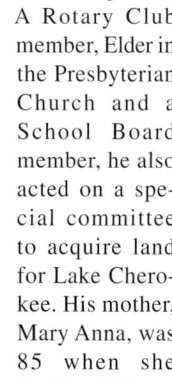

William Gardiner Mitchell, Sr., 1910

Gardiner Mitchell married Ethel Mae Fall, daughter of Dr. W.S. Fall and Mary, of Cherino and Henderson, Texas. To this union were born W.G. Mitchell, Jr. (married Grace Lee Martin, daughter of William C. and Florence), Willis Wilson Mitchell (Dick) (whose wife, Nell Mitcham, survives), Mary Ethel (who became Mrs. Ralph Kutzer of Bandera) and Zack Fall Mitchell (who married Mary Evelyn Martin, daughter of Malcolm M. and Ruth Hall).

In 1937, part of Walnut Grove was sold to become a large part of Gregg County Airport. Much of Walnut Grove has since been divided, but Walnut Grove Family Cemetery is still maintained on the large portion that remains. In 1982, the highway that runs through the farm was named Gardiner Mitchell Parkway in honor of William Gardiner Mitchell, Sr. Today, Zack and Mary reside at Walnut Grove, along with one of their sons, Ronald Hall, and his wife, Nancy Karen.

– Submitted by Mary M. Mitchell

MITCHELL-GEE

John Mitchell was born about 1797 in North Carolina, and died after 1880 in Gregg County. John was a farmer. He married Elizabeth (maiden name unknown), born about 1799 in North Carolina, and died in Texas. They had at least four children: Rebecca, John, James Milton and Frances.

(l.-r.) Willie Mae Tutt Rector, Mary Cansadie Mitchell Tutt and Susan Jane Gee Mitchell. In lap, Marjorie Tutt.

Rebecca was born about 1832 in Tennessee (no further information).

John Mitchell II was born 1834 in Tennessee, and died 1937 in Gregg County. He was buried in Winterfield Cemetery, Gregg County. John II married Susan Jane Gee, 20 May 1856, in Rusk County, Texas. John and Susan's children were Mary Cansadie (married William Thomas Tutt), James Milton, Hulda Elizabeth (married James Sidney Tutt), Martha A. John, Sarah L. and Susan Ellen.

James Milton married Mary _____. He was born about 1837 in Tennessee.

Frances was born about 1839 in Tennessee, and married _____ Smith. They had five children: Sarah, Carrie, Almedea, James and Jesse, all born in Texas.

Susan Jane Gee was born in Alabama about 1838. In 1908, she applied for a Confederate Veterans Widow's pension, which was approved. John Mitchell had served in Company G, 14th Texas Infantry, C.S.A., enlisting 23

March 1863, and was surrendered at New Orleans, Louisiana, 26 Mary 1865.

Susan's parents were Philip Gee (c.1820, South Carolina) and Huldah Cook (1816, South Carolina). Philip and Huldah were married in Jefferson County, Alabama. Philip had been a postmaster in Calhoun County. Alabama, and a charter member of Mt. Pisgah Baptist Church, Blount County. In 1850, they were living in Tallapoosa County, Alabama. In 1853, they bought a team of oxen and a wagon and moved to East Texas.

Huldah's parents were Elias Green Cooke and Martha B. Prater.

In 1861, Huldah filed a legal list of property that she owned free and clear of her husband.

Besides Susan Jane, Huldah and Philip had the following children, born in Alabama: Martha B., born about 1840; twins James and George William, born about 1843; John L., born about 1846; Lemuel Merrill, born about 1848; Phillip Jackson, born about 1849; and Robert M., born about 1853. Hershal was born about 1853, and Ann E. was born about 1855, in Rusk County, Texas.

– Submitted by Teri Tutt Cooper

BEN & MARY BLAND MITCHELL

In 1925, Benjamin Eustice Mitchell came to Longview, Texas, and purchased one hundred acres of land. This property is now known as the North West Hills Addition just west of McCann Road. He bought two mules, one horse, two cows and all equipment needed to operate a progressive farm. He had previously owned two farms in Upshur County, and after having made many improvements on them, had sold them for enough to purchase this one. With his wife Mary Caroline Bland Mitchell, son Eiland Callen, age 8, and daughter Carlene, age 5, he began to remodel the old farm house and build two new barns and a tenant house.

Ben cleared about 25 acres of wooded land to make room for cotton, corn and peas.

Ben Mitchell being presented a certificate as an outstanding farmer.

The peas were planted between the cornrows after the corn was laid by. Ben believed in leaving this world a better place for having been there. He believed in making use of every foot of ground and planted the terraces with McDonald blackberries (a walnut-sized berry). This was a money crop. People came either to pick berries on the halves or for twenty-five cents a gallon or a dollar for a syrup bucket full. Later, he planted several acres of strawberries that proved to be his best investment. Ben made enough money from the berries to run the farm for the year and to always have money in the bank. At times there would be 25-30 people picking berries. He had a large packing shed in the field where cars could drive out to buy the berries. He also had several acres of peaches.

One year Ben was a prominent Gregg County farmer who had been recognized by the county agent and county commissioners for taking part in the government plan of "Food-Fiber for Freedom's Fight." They rode horses to inspect the farms around the county.

Mary was a wonderful cook and homemaker. They had a large garden and twice a week Mary went to town to take produce, eggs and butter to the rooming houses.

In 1929, during the Great Depression, oil was discovered in Gregg County. "Lease hounds" were courting all landowners to try to buy mineral rights. Longview was no longer a quiet place. People were living in tents, barns or anyplace there was shelter.

Ben Mitchell took a car-load of daughter Carlene's friends out of school the day the Lathrop #1 was to be brought in. They were there to see the oil shooting a hundred feet high and hear the shouting for joy.

Ben sold the farm and purchased ten acres on Highway 80 adjoining the Grace Hill Cemetery. He built the Crystal Service Station and Garage out of beautiful crystals he had gotten in Arkansas and made into blocks.

The city made a street through his land. The street was named Tutt Street as there was already a Mitchell Street and daughter Carlene had married James Tutt. Ben and James built 14 rent houses on the street.

Benjamin E. Mitchell was a faithful member of First Baptist Church and the Business Men's Bible Class from 1929 until his death in 1971. At the time of his death he was the oldest member of the class, where he was faithful in attendence. He was known as an honest, loving Christian man and a friend to all. He made Gregg County and Longview a better place for being here.

Longview has been good to the family and Carlene Mitchell Tutt is proud to be a native daughter.

– Submitted by Carlene Mitchell Tutt

George Emmett and Margaret Moore family

MOORE

The Moores came to New Danville, Texas, in about 1847. William (born 1800) and Sarah (born 1804) came from Rhea County, Tennesse. They had seven of their own children (William, Thomas, James, Sam Houston, George Washington, Robert and Thomson) to make the trip with them. There were also six other Moores listed on the 1850 census with them; they must have been nieces and nephews. The Moores raised cotton and corn in Rusk County, Texas. A sister, Julia, was born in 1848.

George Washington Moore (born 12 June 1838) went to farming for himself about 1866 in Coffeeville, Upshur County, Texas, with his sister Julia and brother Robert living with him. William and Sarah must have died between 1860–1870. On 20 December 1875, George married Francis Lummus (born 1859) daughter of Robert Lummus (born about 1830). George (died 30 October 1914) and Francis (died 27 September 1889) owned farmland in Precinct 1, Longview, Gregg County, Texas. They had children James, Josphine, Calvin, Mary and George Emmit Moore. George and Francis are buried at Magrill-Moore cemetery on Cotton Street in Longview, Texas.

George Emmit Moore (born 18 October 1886) married Margaret O'Toole (born 1 June 1886) in Wichita Falls, Texas, 31 December 1905. He met Margaret while he was out in west Texas sharecropping. They were married while sitting in a horse-drawn cab at the falls. He brought Margaret back home to Gregg County. Margaret, daughter of Patrick O'Toole (born 18 February 1841, in Camlaugh, Ireland, died 27 February 1920, in Rineland, Texas) and Anna Dearker O'Toole (born 10 March 1855, West Virginia, died 20 May 1891). They had children Nettie, James Patrick, Frances, Dixie, Johnny, Margaret, Robert, Ethel, Charles, Emmit, Mary, Julia and William. George died 20 February 1973, and Margaret died 19 July 1970; both are buried at Magrill-Moore cemetery. This cemetery is either on or near land George Washington Moore once owned.

James Patrick Moore (born 31 August 1909) married Evie Leona Hitt (born 17 February 1911, in Naples, Texas), daughter of Jasper Price Hitt (born 7 November 1879, died 28 Oc-

J.P. and Evie Moore

tober 1959) and Zellar Khun (born 14 July 1886, died 20 May 1946). James Patrick Moore was in the Civilian Conservation Corps (C.C.C.). J.P. went to Colorado with the C.C.C., returning to Gregg County to meet Evie at Sand Hill, Texas, and marry. In about 1949, James Patrick Moore went to work for Kelly Plow in Longview. He worked there until he retired in 1976. Evie worked for M.E. Moses in Longview for 29 years (1960–1989). J.P. (died 13 February 1986) and Evie (died 9 September 1993) had four children: Jerry, Dixie, Ray and James Kenneth Moore. J.P. and Evie are buried in the Magrill-Moore Cemetery. Jerry married Brenda Ashcraft 20 September 1961. Their children are Pat, Joyce, Timothy and Jerrilyn. James Kenneth Moore married Fern Paul 23 June 1972. Kenneth and Fern had children David and Danielle. Danielle married Michael Conley 20 May 2000.

– Submitted by Fern Moore

JAMES MOORE, SR.

James Moore, Sr. brought the Moore family from Ireland to Tennessee, settling a piece of land that straddled the river just outside Knoxville, Tennessee. The family lived on the Tennessee side, using the Kentucky land for their cattle and the forest timber to build ships, which was the family's occupation.

For the next generation, Texas was to be the destination for the five oldest boys. Robert, Joe, James Melton, William and Thomas fitted a wagon with all the necessary staples, followed the Indian trails to Texas, settling at a location that would later become known as Big Sandy.

Robert married and moved to Pine Mills, leaving James in charge. In 1836 came the Texas Revolution, Joe remained behind while James went to fight. When James received his bounty land, he and Joe set up a trust company and a deeds office. William and Thomas moved to other parts of Texas.

In 1858, James married and moved to the Gladewater area where he began a lumber business.

In July 1859, James's son James Washington was born and a year later, Charlie. In his spare time, James played the violin at weddings, parties and dances. One night after playing for a dance, James started home but was shot and left for dead. His violin and money

James Moore

stolen, badly injured, he managed to get astride his horse and get home where he died three days later.

James' mother married William Humphreys and had two sons, Will and Robert. James hated his stepfather's use of his father's trunk. Because of William, James was sent away at age seven for schooling and training, but instead was worked from daylight to dark. In spite of it, James learned to read the Bible and sign his name. When he returned home at the age of 18 to a deteriorated home place, he learned that William had sold almost everything off after giving his own sons portions. Charlie had sold his shares and moved to Waco and all he owned of his father's original land grant was 240 acres. James went to work for the railroad cutting ties to make enough money to build a new home.

James W. Moore family, April 1919. (l.-r.) Back: Fred Moore, Ethel Moore, Vannie Lee, Charlie Lee, Arthur Eddins and Vickie Eddins. Front: James Washington Moore, Mary Jane Moore holding Evelyn Lee Burke, Birdie Eddins and Raymond Eddins.

The Sassar family from Alabama bought property adjoining James, and on 9 January 1888, James married Mary Frances Sassar. Vickie was born 26 May 1889; Vannie on 24 February 1892; James Winford, nicknamed "Fred," was born 28 November 1894.

"Fred" met Mary Ethel McCullough from Gilmer at an all day singing and married her on 21 August 1917. Fred was called to war and sent to San Antonio where he contracted influenza. Discharged in 1919, he returned home. Opal was born in 1919, Dorothy Fae in 1921, and James Warren in 1926. When Opal reached school age, the family moved to Tyler. Opal finished school in Gilmer.

When World War II broke out, Opal was working for the WPA and was persuaded to move to Dallas by North American Aviation to go to college and work, later becoming an Inspector with the company. During her tenure, suspicious things happened. Government agents on the night crew revealed sabotage and those involved were arrested for treason. When the war ended, Opal went to work for the telephone company, married Jimmy Mecey, had a son David, and transferred to Longview in 1963, retiring from SBC in 1984.

As an honor student, David was appointed to West Point but chose instead to go to Kilgore College on a music scholarship. After graduating col-

lege, David was injured badly and spent a year in recovery. During this time he started using a camera set up on a tripod on the patio. David is now one of the most noted photographers in the U.S.

– Submitted by Opal Moore Mecey

CURTIS & DAISY MORRIS

He was named Ralph Curtis Morris by his parents, Anna and Wade Morris, when he was born in Washington County, near Marietta, Ohio. His family called him Ralph, but after he graduated from high school and went to Ohio University in Athens, Ohio, he chose to go by his middle name and was thereafter known as Curtis Morris. At the University his social fraternity was Theta Chi. In subsequent years he was elected to several honorary fraternities as well.

Upon graduation, Curtis secured a fellowship for graduate study at the University of Colorado before going to Jonesboro, Arkansas, to teach in the State A&M College there.

When Curtis arrived at the school in 1926, he met a young lady teacher who had already been there a year teaching commercial subjects. Daisy Mildred Jones and Curtis Morris were married one year later in Mineral Wells, Texas. Following the 1927-28 school year, Curtis and Daisy removed to the University of Colorado where he began his pursuit of a doctorate.

Fate had a way of providing challenging opportunities to the Morrises and after a series of interruptions in his education, Curtis accepted the invitation of Walter Long, who was manager of the Austin, Texas, Chamber of Commerce. He filled the position of assistant to the manager. The young couple moved to Austin.

In 1929, the Morrises were to relocate again, this time to Center, Texas, where Curtis became manager of the local Chamber of Commerce. The next year he was tapped by the East Texas Chamber of Commerce to work for them in Longview. In 1930, Daisy, Curtis and baby Rosemary moved to Longview where they remained until 1949, when they departed for Houston.

While in Longview, Curtis and Daisy became parents again with the birth of Ralph Curtis, Jr. eighteen months after their arrival in town. They took an active role in community activities while in Longview. Curtis was voted an elder in the First Presbyterian Church and was elected Chairman of the Gregg County School Board. He was named chairman of the first City Planning Board of Longview. He was also a member of the Rotary Club.

While with the East Texas Chamber of Commerce, Curtis was "loaned" out to work on the "Tidelands Case" that was promoted on behalf of the interests of Texas in keeping for Texas the proceeds of the oils on the Tidelands off the Texas Gulf Coast. He spent considerable time in Washington, D.C., as a certified lobbyist on the "Tidelands Case." From 1941 to 1949, Daisy retired from club work and taught social studies and served as school counselor at Longview High School.

In 1949, the Transcontinental Gas Pipeline Company offered Curtis a position, and he and

Daisy moved to Houston where he served as vice president of the company.

In 1953, Curtis became the manager of the Washington, D.C., office of the American Gas Association, and he and Daisy relocated there where they would remain for 22 years.

They retired to Longview in 1976, and at once became involved citizens taking an interest in several organizations including the Gregg County Historical Museum and the Longview Symphony League, where they both served on the Board of Directors.

Rosemary Morris is married to Harold David Medley, Ph.D., who operated as President of the Delanese International Marketing Company in New York. Dr. Curtis Morris, Jr. served for many years as the Director of the Clinical Research Center, University of California Medical School, San Francisco. Curtis and Daisy were also parents to a foster daughter, Mary Ellen Cathey, who is the wife of Dr. H. Mark Cathey, director of the National Arboretum, Washington, D.C.

Curtis passed away in 1985. Daisy, at age 100, is currently confined to her residence because of declining health.

– Submitted by Dr. R. Curtis Morris

HENRY MORROW & JULIA LEE

Henry Olin Morrow was born in Dallas County, Alabama, 7 January 1892. Henry's parents were William Morrow and Minnie Martin Morrow. They had fourteen children: Zelpher, Willie, Irene, Mary Lou, Ada, Henry, Lee, Inez, Arch, James, Mattie Goldie, Flo-rence, Gladys and Johnnie. About 1899, they decided to move to Texas; they heard it was easier to make a living. In covered wagons, William, Minnie, all of their children and her parents, Henry Clay and Jennie Summers Martin, came to Texas.

The Morrows first settled in Harrison County, Texas. Henry Morrow, when about 26 years old, worked for the county. While driving a team of mules and a wagon full of gravel down Page Road, he saw the prettiest woman, Julia Ann Gertrude Lee. He courted Julia and they married on 8 December 1917. Julia was born on 12 December 1902, to George Thomas Lee and Dona Small. Dona's parents (James P. Small and RoxiAnna Hines) were one of the first pioneer families in Harrison County, Texas. James was also a brave Confederate Soldier. He enlisted 12 May 1862, at Troy, Alabama, with Company G, 59th Alabama. He was captured at Petersburg 17 June 1864, and sent to Elmira Prison. James was released 7 June 1865, after taking the Oath of Allegiance.

Henry and Julia Morrow

William, Minnie, Henry and Julia Morrow, with Dona Small Lee, moved to Gregg County, Texas. William and Minnie lived to see their children grown and many grandchildren. William Morrow died 13 September 1927, and Minnie died 22 July 1941. They are both buried in LaGrone's Cemetery. Henry and Julia Morrow had ten children: Gladys, Robbie, Cecil, Gertrude, Minnie, Faye, Louise, George, Robert and Ronnie. Henry and Julia celebrated their 50th wedding anniversary 8 December 1967. Henry died 18 April 1969, and Julia died 9 March 1986.

Their fourth child, Gertrude, with brown curly hair, blue eyes and a zest for life, had her eyes on the men in uniform. Gertrude married Aaron Paul, 8 April 1943, in Longview, Texas. He was a sergeant in the army during World War II. He was killed in action 31 March 1945, in Germany. Gertrude met his brother in 1946, William Paul. They courted, fell in love and were married on 22 April 1946. William was born to John Paul and Anna Maria Snyder on 25 February 1925, in North Hampton, Pennsylvania.

William and Gertrude Paul

William also served in World War II as a private in the Big Red I Unit. He had his legs severely wounded while invading Normandy Beach on D-Day, and went on to take a German bunker. He received a Purple Heart and Bronze Star for his heroic actions. William and Gertrude have four children: two daughters (Fern and Terry) and two sons (Aaron and John). Terry has two sons, Jeffery Martin and Corey Wayne McCurry. They all live in Gregg County, Texas.

– Submitted by Terry Paul McCurry, Longview, Texas

MORTON: From England, Mississippi, Tennessee, to Texas

William Arthur Morton, of Gregg County, Texas, was descended from George Morton, came from Bawtry County, Notts, England, to America about 1600, and settled near Plymouth, Massachusetts. He had one son named George Morton, born between 1612-1615, who married Miss Phebe Cooper. Their son Richard Morton, born between 1635-1645, died 3 April 1710, in Hatfield, Massachusetts, married Ruth Edwards. They had Thomas, John, Richard, Joseph, Abraham, Elizabeth, Ebenizer and Jonathan Morton.

Richard Morton, October 1704, married Mary Waite. They had two children, Abraham and Benjamin Morton.

Benjamin Morton, 20 October 1739, married Mary Dexter. They had Mary, Abraham, Benjamin, Jonathan, James, Azuba, Sarah, Maggy, Metta, Louisa and Eunice Morton.

Abraham Morton, 28 March 1762, married Phoebe Langford. They had Benjamin, Phoebe, Hannah, Abraham, Clark and Joseph Morton.

Benjamin Morton, born 1783 in Kentucky, married Delilah (last name unknown) in Tennessee. They had William, John Luke, Joseph and Frank P. Morton.

William and John Luke Morton were the first Mortons of this family to come to Gregg and Rusk County, Texas, from Tennessee about 1855.

William Morton, 16 April 1832, Tennessee, married Sarah E. (last name unknown). They had Laura E. Morton, buried in Mt. Moriah Cemetery, Gregg County, and Nolly Morton.

John Luke Morton, born in Maury County, Tennessee, about 1834, married Salina Hicks, 20 November 1856, in Rusk County, and died in 1899. Both are buried in Hickory Grove Cemetery, Rusk County, Texas. They had John William, Mary E., Jim, (twins) Sally and Sammy, Virginia, Richard Hubbard and George Will Morton.

John William Morton, 18 January 1858, Rusk County, died 12 August 1924, Rusk County, married Lou Treacy Ray, 13 December 1881, daughter of Gabriel Ray and Treacy Bateman. Their children were Lou Kinney, William Arthur, John Luke, Lenora Bell, Leila, Bonnie Bernice and Annie May Morton.

William Arthur Morton, grandfather of Betty Jane Smith Cabbiness, was born 28 February 1884, Crossroads, Rusk County, died 8 August 1944, in Longview, Gregg County, married Virginia Adele Reed, 24 December 1902, in Elderville, Rusk County. Virginia Adele Reed, the daughter of Solomon Reed and Nancy Walker, was born 15 November 1885, in Overton, Texas, died 5 April 1976, in Longview. They had Annie Lou Lorena, 1903, died 1904; Flora Lillian; Gracie Beatrice, 1907, died 1912; (twin) Robert Solomon, 2 February 1910, died in car accident 4 March 1932; (twin) Roy William, 2 February 1910, died 19 March 1971;

Five Generations: Reed-Morton-Cabbiness-McKinney-McKinney, from 1885 through 2001. (l.-r.) Virginia Adele (Reed) Morton, b. 18 November 1885, d. 5 April 1976; Flora Lillian (Morton) Smith, b. 23 May 1905, d. 2 October 1998; Betty Jane (Smith) Cabbiness, b. 15 November 1928, living; Brenda Jane (Cabbiness) McKinney, b. 15 September 1948, living; Kathryn May McKinney, b. 22 June 1969, living.

Josephine Evelyn, 29 July 1912, died 8 May 1981; Woodrow Wilson, 26 December 1917, died 23 August 1997; Ennis Melton, 30 August 1920, died 2000; (twin) Dimple Marjorie, 13 December 1922, died August 1995; (twin) Dorothy Marie, 13 December 1922, died 17 April 1998. Some of these children are buried in Hickory Grove Cemetery, Rusk County.

Flora Lillian Morton, 23 May 1905, married Richard Benjamin Turner Smith of Gregg County, who was the son of George Calloway Smith and Ida Leala Stephens Smith. Lillian died 2 November 1998, Longview. Both are buried in Judson Cemetery. They had Bennie Dongene Smith, married Gayle Turman of Tyler, and Betty Jane Smith, married Billy Joe Cabbiness of Longview. Their records are continued under the Cabbiness and Smith reports.

– Submitted by Vicki Buley

MUSTON

Robert N. and Sara Muston and family became residents of Gregg County in 1944. He was born in Eastland County, Texas. Sara was born in Clay County, Mississippi.

Robert, as a young man, moved to Mississippi, and was taught the art of making candy in Greenwood. After learning this trade, he bought the equipment, moved to West Point, Mississippi, in 1928, and opened his own candy store, Crown Candy Company. Sara was working at Pryor's Department Store, and they met and were married in 1929. He continued operating his candy compny until 1931, when the country was in a deep depression. Their first child, a son, Robert N. Muston, Jr., was born at that time.

As many families were forced to do during the depression years, the Muston family moved back to Texas where Robert found work in the oil fields of East Texas. He was employed by a major oil company in Cayuaga, Texas. The Muston's daughter Helen was born there in 1934. He left the Tidewater Company at that time, moved to Laird Hill, Texas, and remained there until 1944.

Robert went to work for Atlantic Oil Company, located at that time between White Oak and Longview. He remained in their employment for 38 years until he retired. His children attended Longview Schools, and the family was a member of First Baptist Church for 43 years.

Mrs. Muston was a homemaker, but for a time she also taught sewing classes for the Singer Sewing Center in the late 1940s. She also was a volunteer at Good Shepherd Hospital in Longview.

Robert, Jr., Sara, Helen and Robert Muston

Robert Nelson Muston, Sr. passed away in 1987. His wife, Sara Alice Hurst Muston, died in 1990. Their son, Robert Nelson Muston, Jr., joined his parents in 2001. Robert and Sara Muston are buried at Grace Hill in Longview.

Their daughter, Helen, presently resides in Kilgore. The Mustons have children, grandchildren and great grandchildren residing in Texas and Louisiana

– Submitted by Helen Muston Merrill

RON & PEGGY NADER

Ron Nader, the son of Matilda Asaff and Tom Nader, was born in Marshall, Texas. Matilda, who was from a small village in Lebanon, has her name inscribed on the wall at Ellis Island. Tom was born in Marshall.

Peggy Hunt Nader, the daughter of Reba Nell Duncan and Henry Maxwell Hunt, was also born in Marshall. Many of her ancestors were from the Marshall area.

Ron and Peggy Nader

Ron and his wife Peggy have lived in Gregg County for thirty-three years. He has practiced pharmacy for all those years, first working at K&B Drugs, then at Rite-Aid, and now at Eckerd Drugs. Although his career has kept Ron well occupied, he is an avid gardener, as is Peggy.

Peggy had an interest in the family-owned Duncan's Rainbow Floral in Marshall. After the flower shop was sold, she worked at Dillard's for Estee Lauder. When Peggy retired from the position at Dillard's, she began her pursuit of genealogy, searching for information on families she knew nothing about. One night her father came to her in a dream, asking her to search his side of the family. She states "such a comfort feeling is hard to describe." That is what really encouraged her to begin her search.

As a result of Peggy's research, she has discovered a number of ancestors who qualify her for membership in various lineage societies. Her Daughters of the Republic of Texas ancestor is John Patroan English, one of the first Anglo babies born in Texas (1819); proof of this was found in a Bible record as well as in an affidavit. Peggy's Daughters of the American Revolution ancestor is Judkins Hunt from Virginia. Her United Daughters of the Confederacy ancestor is Col. Wilkins Wallace Hunt, who fought at Gettysburg and Hatcher's Run. Her Colonial Dames ancestor is Henry Pope of Virginia.

On her father's side she is a sixth great granddaughter of St. Denis, who founded Natchitoches, Louisiana. Another Revolutionary War ancestor is Bailey Anderson. Peggy "had the honor" of being instrumental in securing a special marker for his grave in Elsian Fields in Harrison County, Texas.

Peggy has been regent of Aaron Burleson Chapter, Daughters of the American Revolution; she has been chaplain of R.B. Levy Chapter, United Daughters of the Confederacy; she has been vice-president of John Tilley Edwards Chapter, Daughters of the Republic of Texas; and she has been vice-president of the New England Colony Chapter, Colonial Dames of the Seventeenth Century. In addition, Peggy has been secretary as well as president of the Gregg County Genealogy Society; also, she was altar guild directress for St. Michael and All Angels Episcopal Church.

Peggy is the mother of one daughter, Martha DeLeice Looney, who was born in Shreveport, Louisiana. Dee's daughter is Heather Lauren Brown, born in Longview.

– Submitted by Peggy Hunt Nader

NELMS-BROWN

William "Mark" Nelms moved to Longview about 1916 and lived there the rest of his life with his wife, Annie Lou Brown. The son of William "Carroll" Nelms and Armintia Minervia Rhodes, who had removed from Hardeman County, Tennessee, after the Civil War, he was born 16 January 1886, Charleston, Delta County, Texas. After graduating from high school, he moved to Dallas to work where he was introduced to Annie by her brother, Lewis Edwin Brown, Jr. They married 19 March 1911, at the home of her parents, Lewis "Edwin" Brown and Minnie "Margaret" Morris. Annie grew up in Hallsville, graduated from high school and planned to become a teacher. After they married, they lived in Fort Worth where Mark worked as a brakeman for Texas & Pacific Railroad. Their first child, Marguerite Ellen, was born there 24 June 1913, and Madeline Annie was born 31 January 1915. They moved to Timpson Street, Longview, where Marcus Edwin Nelms, called Buddey, was born 22 April 1916.

The family bought a home on Oden Street; had a telephone, # 70, a radio and were among the first to buy a car. Mark belonged to the Masonic Lodge. He inherited an Apron from his father with the names of the previous owners recorded on the reverse: William Randolph Nelms, Abner Carroll Nelms and William Carroll Nelms. Annie was a member of Eastern Star until she got the Holy Ghost. She built a Pentecostal church on 13th Street and Oden in 1920 near their home and conducted services Sundays and Wednesday nights.

The Oden Street home was the birthplace of their other children: William Arthur, 12 September 1921; Calvin J., 15 January 1925; and Naomi "Ruth," 14 January 1926.

Mark eventually became conductor for T&P Railroad, until a spark caused him to lose an eye about 1928. He received a settlement, retired from the railroad and bought a farm on Cotton Street.

The neighborhood men often met to socialize in the backroom of the local barbershop. They drank some tainted Jamaica Ginger and became gravely ill. Mark had "Jake-Leg" as a result, but eventually walked with canes, dragging his feet.

Mark and Annie Nelms, Marcus, Madeline and Marguerite

Marguerite married 29 January 1929, to Henry Herman "Bitty" Grimes, while still in high school. They had two children, Billy Eugene, 1929, and Margaret Jane, 1937. Marguerite died April 2003, and is buried at Gum Springs Cemetery.

Madeline married 28 January 1931, to Robert Joe Terry, three days before she turned 16. They had three children, all born in Gum Springs: Bobby Joe, 28 October 1931; Carl Theron, 12 February 1933; and Gloria Juanita, 17 December 1934. On their anniversary in 2004, they celebrated their marriage of 73 years.

Marcus tragically drowned in a pond near the railroad terminal in Longview, 29 May 1934, when he was 18 years old. He was swimming with family and friends who could not save him from the undertow. He was buried at Gum Springs Cemetery.

William quit school at 14 and worked to help support the family. William married Francis Miller; they had two children: Joyce Ann, 1943, and Dewey Mark, 1945. William died 23 November 1992, of a heart attack and is buried at Gum Springs Cemetery.

Calvin served in the Navy during World War II. He married Billie Faye Ridings and had four children: Pamela, Ronald Calvin, Richard Wayne and Randall Lee. Calvin worked for Eastman Kodak Company. He died 17 January 1989, of cancer and is buried in Memory Park.

Ruth graduated from high school and worked for the telephone company. She married a soldier who died in World War II; Betty Jean was born in 1946. Ruth married Atha Allen Hill, 27 July 1948. Their children were Verna Sue, 1950; Martha Anne, 1952; and Carolyn Kay, 1961.

Mark and Annie moved back into the parsonage next door to the church they built on 13th Street. For a while, Mark sold real estate in a small office on Cotton Street.

William Mark Nelms died at their parsonage home, 1 August 1952, of Brights disease. Annie Lou Nelms died 11 December 1972, in Longview, from strokes. Both are buried at Gum Springs Cemetery.

– Submitted by Madeline Terry

LEON DOW (SLIM) NELMS

Leon Dow (Slim) Nelms, son of Walter Orvil Nelms and Carmen Estella Shott, was born 12 August 1929, in Waveland, Yell, Arkansas. The fourth of seven children, he grew up with lots of wonderful experiences. He graduated from Havana High School in 1948. He joined the Army and was assigned to the 7th Division, C Battery, 31st Field Artillery; he was stationed in Korea during the Korean War. Slim was a Staff Sergeant, at the end of his tour. When he came home, he married Mandy Lea Fredrick on 6 April 1955.

Mandy is the daughter of Jefferson Davis Fredrick and Beulah Irene Thomas; she was born 19 January 1937, in Waveland, Yell, Arkansas. Slim and Mandy came to Gregg County in 1955 soon after they married. They had family living in Gladewater, a sister and her husband, Thelma and Doyle Berry, and also an uncle and aunt, Tom and Lovisie Nelms.

Slim went to work for Doby Wilson, owner of G.M. Sales Company – they handled military surplus truck parts. The business was located on Highway 80 East, in Clarksville City, outside of Gladewater. He bought the business after Mr. Wilson died, then phased it out over several years. Slim and Mandy bought property on the Old Longview Highway in Gladewater and moved a home onto it. Slim did a lot of work to the home and Mandy loved to work in the yard.

Dow and Ann Nelms and four-week-old grandson Bradlee Hardy.

They started their family soon after arriving. Their children were born at the Leake Hospital in Gladewater; they had one son and two daughters. Walter Leon was born 26 February 1956; his last marriage was to Jill Dollison on 6 March 1995, and she brought to the marriage three children and many grandchildren. Barbara Ann married Brian Keith Hardy on 12 July 1976, at the Clarksville Baptist Church in Clarksville City. They went to live in Lawton, Oklahoma, where Keith was stationed at Ft. Sill. Barbara graduated from Lawton High School in May 1977, and Keith finished his tour of duty on the same day. They moved back to Gladewater and

Mandy Nelms (far left) with her children (l.-r.) Barbara Hardy, Sandra Nelms and Walter Leon Nelms.

The Hardys: Keith, Barbara, Brian, Kyle and Bradlee

bought the home place from Mandy and Slim. There they have raised their family. They had four boys, the first one was named Brian Keith after his father. Brian married Michelle Townsend on 23 December 2003; they are expecting their first son in June 2004.

The next son was Bobby Lee, who died after living 19 hours. He is buried at the Memorial Park outside of Gladewater. Benjamin Kyle came next and then, 12 years later, Bradlee Kent was born.

Sandra Lea married Billy Wayne Hammett on 15 July 1977. They had three boys. Michael Wayne was their first; he married Joni Lee Armstrong on 22 September 2001, and on 5 July 2003, they had their first baby, Levi Joel. Next came Ronald (Ron) Dow; he married Shawn Hood on 14 February 2002, who brought to the family the first girl, Stormy. And then came Brandon Lee. Sandra and Billy divorced, and she got remarried to Richard Nunn on 24 July 1987. Richard helped Sandra raise the boys; they divorced in 2000.

Slim and Mandy divorced in 1974; both remarried. Mandy married Crawford Smith on 22 November 1977; after seven years, they divorced. Mandy moved to Linden, Texas, to be closer to her daughter Sandra.

Slim married Jerry Ann Davis on 26 May 1979. She brought to the marriage two daughters, Kate Kunkell and Debra Roach, and two grandchildren, Mellisa and Tommy Kunkell. Slim and Ann decided to retire and in 1985; they moved back to Arkansas where he grew up. They have a home in the mountains. He is enjoying his retirement, fishing every day. Gregg County played a big part in the lives of the Nelms family and parts of the family will always be here.

– Submitted by Barbara Hardy

TRAVIS NEVELS

Travis Nevels was born 28 September 1906, in Jefferson County, Mississippi. His grandfather, Martin Simeon Nevels, fought with the 4th Mississippi Cavalry during the Civil War. In Shreveport, 19 September 1929, Travis married Doris Viola Edington (born 24 August 1910, Louisiana). She is a direct descendant of William Pelham Humphries, the disputed heir of the famous Spindletop Oil Field in Beaumont, Texas. Subject to legal battles for many years, the land (containing the Spindletop field and 7/8 of the city of Beaumont) was granted to Humphries, as a Texas colonist, by Mexico in 1835.

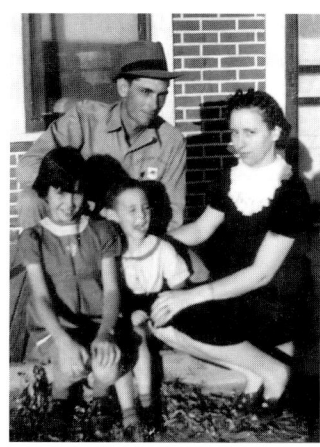

Travis Nevels and wife, Doris Viola, with daughter Marceal and son Travis Lloyd, 1936.

Travis, employed by Magnolia Oil Company as a driller, was transferred from Greenwood, Louisiana, to Kilgore shortly after daughter Gloria Marceal, was born 15 May 1930. In Kilgore he helped bring in the Daisy Bradford and other gushers in the East Texas Oil Field. With the coming of black crude, living accommodations were non-existent in the overnight boomtown; consequently, area churches allowed oilfield workers to sleep on their floors. Travis did so until he was able to buy a small tent for his family.

Eventually, they settled in Greggton in one of Magnolia's "shotgun" houses — very luxurious, they said, after the tent!! While living in Greggton, son Travis Lloyd was born 12 June 1935. Travis was then transferred to West Texas and followed the oil boom for ten more years.

In 1945, after 20 years with Magnolia, Travis retired and moved his family back to Gregg County. He bought an old country grocery in a rural community known as Seven Pines. Not surprisingly, he named his store "Nevels Grocery," and catered to the rural oilfield families living nearby. The old store was eventually torn down and a new one built, but unfortunately, it burned to the ground in 1967, Travis barely escaping with his life. Not discouraged, he moved an old building onto the site and "Nevels Grocery" didn't miss a beat! Travis operated his country store for 35 years. During this time, Doris fulfilled her life's dream to become a nurse. She graduated from nursing school with honors, was licensed by the State of Texas and followed her dream until she retired in the 1980s.

On 27 March 1994, Travis died at the age of 87 years. Subsequently, on 22 February 2002, Doris died at the age of 91 years. Both are buried in Lakeview Memorial Gardens Cemetery, Longview.

Daughter Marceal graduated from BMI School of Business in Longview, then married Cecil Camp in 1948. He owned and operated Cecil Camp Motor Company in Longview for 25 years prior to his death in 1986. Their daughter, Vicki Susan (Welch), was born in 1950; son, Steve Alan Camp, in 1953; and daughter, Joy Denise (Torrez), in 1959. After Cecil's death,

Marceal married Keith W. Clark in 1991. Keith died in February 2003, and at present, Marceal lives in Gilmer.

Son, Travis Lloyd, graduated from North Texas University in Denton, then married Patricia Zinser, a registered nurse, in 1956. Employed by Texas Instruments, Richardson, Texas, he later was transferred to Johnson City, Tennessee, where he retired after 35 years. He and wife, Patricia, have two children, a son, Travis III, born in 1957, and a daughter, Angela (Nicholas), born in 1964.

Other surviving descendants of Travis and Doris include ten great grandchildren and three great great grandchildren.

– Submitted by Marceal Nevels Clark

NICHOLS

In 1614, in Careby, England, William Hatcher was born. He died 1 April 1680, in Henrico County, Virginia. Known a "William the Immigrant," he was a member of the House of Burgess from Henrico County, 1644-45, 1649, 1652 and 1658-59. An outspoken man, William was forced to apologize in the House for the little respect shown to the officials of the Virginia Colony. In 1676, known for his notoriously high temper, he was involved with his neighbor, Bacon, in "Bacon's Rebellion" and fined 19,000 pounds of tobacco and caske and 8,000 pounds of dressed pork for uttering mutinous words. In 1636 and 1637, records show that William Hatcher received more than 650 acres on the Appomattuck River for the paid transport of more than seven people from England.

Home of Dr. John Hatcher, Careby, Lincolnshire, England.

William's sons were Edward, Henry and Benjamin. Henry died intestate. In a deed dated 1 April 1680, Edward and Benjamin conferred upon Henry's children, mares, heifers, guns and various household items, and to insure a peaceable settlement of the personal estate left by their father. Captain John Worsham presented accounts of Edward's estate, recorded 2 February 1711. Inventory was presented 28 September 1711, by MaryBeth Hatcher and recorded 5 November 1711.

Nancy, granddaughter of William and Anne Burton Hatcher, married Flayle Nichols of Bedford County, who served in the Revolutionary War. With land opening up, several members of the Hatcher, Nichols and other Bedford County families moved into what was to become East Tennessee.

Charlcie Nichols, Charles Nichols, Cecil Nichols and Mac Nichols

Another descendant of William and Anne was Sarah E. Hatcher, 23 February 1849. She married Robert Benjamin Hamilton Nichols, 29 August 1869. Robert was born 1840 in Georgia. He died in 1911, and Sarah in 1927 in Texas. Their son, Samuel John Wesley McCook Nichols, born in 1885, married Ivey Jewel Clark born 1882. Samuel died in 1963. Ivey Jewel died in Longview in 1925. Their son, Thomas Cecil Nichols, born 2 March 1912, married Lela Lois League, 11 June 1932. Thomas died 14 May 1954, in Cisco, Texas. Their children were James Garland Nichols and Lanyta Dianne Nichols.

James Garland married Linda Faye Evans, 4 September 1955. Their children were James Garland, Jr. and Jon Mark. James, Jr. married Rebecca Leigh Bowden, 9 June 1978. Their children are Christopher Jared, Kevin Scot and James Michael. Jon Mark married Debbie Sullivan, 31 August 1999.

Lanyta Dianne married Milton William Evans, Jr., 21 November 1959. To them were born Danyta Kay, Lanyta Kayann, Danesa Gayle and Milton Todd. Lanyta Kayann married Ronald Dale Hollomon, 23 May 1981. Their children are Ashley Kayann and Dustin Dallas. Milton Todd Evans married Mary Oates, 11 April 2001. Ashley married Trinity Wade Grisham, 26 October 2002. Danesa Gayle married Ray C. Hansen, 7 September 1991; they have one son, Branden Ray.

All of these descendants live in Longview, Kilgore and the surrounding communities.

– Submitted by Danesa Hansen

Cecil Nichols, Lois Nichols, James Garland Nichols and Dianne Nichols

WALTER REUBEN NICHOLSON

W.R. Nicholson was born near Kilgore, in the small community of Hughey, to John Wesley and Missouri Harris Nicholson. Before Walter was five, John W. moved his family to Hopkins County. Walter had a brother Edward and a sister Dora.

W.R. received his teaching certificate in August 1898, and began his teaching at Rock Springs School in Sulphur Springs. Later, he began working for the Van Fleet-Mansfield Drug Company as a traveling drug salesman. It was during this time that he met Ethel Cliff Jarrett of Pittsburg, Texas. They married 21 October 1906, in Mt. Pleasant, Texas. They had seven children: Dana Clare, Walter Ronald, Ethel Frances, Mary Virginia, John Walter (born and died on the same day in 1917), Ruth L. and Margaret A.

Nicholson Library, Longview.

He became a banker and industrialist in the oil field business. He was a member of the Board of Trustees of Southern Methodist University and of Lon Morris College, giving scholarships to SMU, Lon Morris and Texas State College for Women. The Little Chapel in the Woods is a small nonsectarian chapel on the campus of Texas Woman's University in Denton. An initial donation of $15,000 from the W.R. Nicholson family of Longview, Texas, served as seed money. Additional funds were raised by students, faculty and alumnae of the college. Nicholson also donated large sums of money to build a public library in Longview in memory of sons Ronald and J. Walter.

Walter Reuben Nicholson died 11 July 1959, and is buried in Grace Hill Cemetery, Longview. Ethel Cliff died 18 October 1970.

JOE & DONNA JOHNSTON NIEHUS

Donna Lynn Johnston, daughter of O.G. and Georgia Ruth Johnston, was born 27 November 1959, in Gladewater, Texas. She is a descendent of John Kittle and Sarah Poland Armstrong, M.A. and Elizabeth Barnes Armstrong, and O.G. and Dellah Armstrong Johnston, and Charles Bert and Mary Pearle Shirey Johnston, and her parents. Her grandparents, Charles Bert and Mary Pearle Shirey Johnston, lived in the O.G. and Dellah Armstrong home on Highway 80, directly across from Spencer Harris Machine Shop in Gladewater.

Donna attended school in Gladewater, graduating fifth in her class in 1978. While in high school, she was a member of the choir, the National Honor Society, cheerleader for three years and was chosen as Gladewater's participant in the Miss Gregg County Contest. She at-

The Joe Niehus family. Front: Karlie. Middle (l.-r.): Katie and Donna. Back: Joe.

tended Kilgore Junior College for one year before transferring to the University of Texas in Austin, where she received a Bachelor of Science Degree in 1982. During her senior year, Dr. Frank Guzak, her teaching supervisor, honored her by selecting her as a nominee for Student Teacher of the Year.

She began her teaching career as a sixth grade teacher in the Buda (Texas) School District, in 1982. She accepted a position to teach first grade in the Leander School District (Texas) at the beginning of the 1984-85 school year. Donna met her husband, Joe Lawrence Niehus, in Austin, and they were married on 23 June 1984, in Gladewater. They moved to San Antonio, Texas, in 1987, where Donna taught first grade and gifted/talented students in the Northeast School District until August of 1994.

Joe is the son of Judy Niehus and the late Larry Niehus of San Antonio. He graduated from Winston Churchill High School in San Antonio in 1976. He received a B.A. Degree from Texas A&M University at College Station in 1980. After his graduation, he worked for NCR before taking a job with Tex-Sys Incorporated. Joe attended the University of Texas in 1986 to finish his pre-med requirements. The University of Texas Medical School in San Antonio accepted him into the 1988 class, and he graduated in 1993. He also did his residency in radiology at the University of Texas in San Antonio. He was a member of the Alpha Omega Alpha Fraternity, was chosen as the recipient of the Bowen Vought Award (1993) and received a fellowship in radiology (1998).

Donna and Joe have two daughters born in San Antonio: Katie Lauren, born on 21 November 1993, and Karlie Jo, born on 8 August 1995. After Joe completed his medical training, the family moved to Sherman, Texas, where he began his practice with the Sherman Radiology Group. The girls attend school in the Howe Independent School District. Donna is a member of the Parent Teacher Organization and assists with projects at school. The family attends the First Baptist Church at Howe, Texas.

– Submitted by Donna Lynn Johnston Niehus

PATRICK NOON

Patrick Paul Noon was born in Seminole, Oklahoma, 27 September, 1942, and moved to Gainesville, Texas, with his parents, Elmer and Alice Noon, when he was four. He graduated from Gainesville High School and earned his Bachelor's degree at North Texas State University in August 1964. In September, he began his teaching career at Pine Tree High School where he taught social studies and served as assistant principal until his retirement 32 years later. He served as Student Council sponsor and led the organization to achieve state honors and hold state office. He directed the SFA summer Student Council workshops and for 30 years, he announced football games. He held offices in professional organizations related to the teaching profession. He worked part time for Bob Wheeley Real Estate in the 1970s. Summers found him working in Yellowstone National Park, for Phillips Petroleum, going to school, teaching summer school and traveling to Europe. When he retired from public school work, he reentered the real estate business with Coldwell Banker and served on the state board. In 2003, he received the Longview Realtor of the Year award.

In the fall of 1966, Janice Holley Stone came to Pine Tree where she taught girls' physical education and sponsored cheerleaders, pep club and Blue Jackets. She was born in Winnsboro, Texas, 12 December 1938, to B.D. and Tobie Holley. She graduated from Winnsboro High School and North Texas State University and began her teaching career in February 1960, in Houston. Before arriving at Pine Tree, she taught in Marshall, Jefferson County, Colorado, Daingerfield and Ore City. Summers, she worked as a counselor and assistant director at Camp Fern near Marshall, Texas, and directed the Camp Fire Girls' Camp Natowa. In May 1963, while teaching in Colorado, she married Roger Allen Stone who was born in Parrish, Alabama, 10 October 1943. They had one child, Joe Neal Stone, born 7 April 1964. Roger was a Sergeant in the U.S. Army's A Co., 2nd Bn, 7th Calvary Regiment, 1st Cav. Div. On 17 November 1965, he died in the Ia Drang Valley battle in Vietnam, about which Col. Hal Moore and Joe Galloway wrote the book *We Were Soldiers Once...and Young*. The book was made into a movie.

The Patrick Noon family

It was at Pine Tree that the young widow met Patrick Noon. They became friends, serving as sponsors for the Bucs, an organization originated by her in the fall of 1969. Romance blossomed and they were married 26 November 1969, at First Baptist Church Longview. Their son Joel Wayne Noon was born 10 May 1971. After Wayne's birth, 'holley' returned to Pine Tree to teach special education. In the fall of 1989, she became yearbook adviser which she continued until retirement in May 2002. Some of the books she advised earned top ILPC awards.

Both sons graduated from Pine Tree, Joe in 1982; Wayne in 1989. Joe graduated from Texas A&M and received his Master's from the University of Tennessee where he met and married Theresa Culberson on 2 May 1988. They had two sons, Dylan Cody Stone, born 10 December 1993, and Connor Harrison Stone born, 2 April 1996. They moved to Colorado where Joe worked for a company designing and building electrical curing systems for concrete and was a free lance writer.

Wayne received his degree from Baylor University and became a licensed real estate agent and broker. On 30 December 2000, he married Susan Renee Wallace, daughter of Bob and Shirley Wallace of Longview. Susan was born 10 July 1968. She graduated from Spring Hill High School and Stephen F. Austin University. She taught history and coached in Frisco, Texas, and Wayne worked as a commercial real estate research analyst. After their marriage, they moved to Longview where Wayne worked for Coldwell Banker before starting his own company, Noon and Associates, in the spring of 2004. Susan taught history at Pine Tree. Their first child, Rylee Mackenzie Noon, was born 2 March 2004.

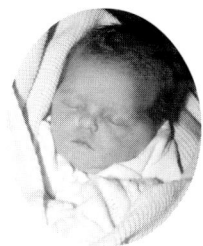

Rylee Mackenzie Noon

The Noon family managed concession stands for Longview Boys' Baseball for 15 summers. They were active members of First Baptist Church where Patrick served as a deacon and worked with a disaster relief team. 'holley' served as WMU director and both boys were active in the youth program.

Photography and canoeing were synonymous with 'holley' and she introduced the family to Caddo Lake where they canoed, boated and camped out. They became members of the Dallas Caddo Club where they spent many weekends, with Patrick joining 'holley' on a canoe/picture taking expedition or her helping him catch enough crappie for a fish fry. They often took folks on tours to show them the beauty of Caddo.

Although not native to Gregg County, they settled in and considered it home.

– Submitted by 'holley' Noon

NORMAN

Dr. Wayman Bowers Norman and Jessie Evelyn Jackson Norman moved to Longview with their one-year old son, Paul Jackson Norman, in July 1951. Melanie Ruth Norman, a Gladney baby, was added to the family in 1956. Dr. Norman, the son of Baptist minister Dr. McKinley Norman, was born in Louisville, Kentucky, in 1923, while Jessie Norman, daughter of Baptist minister Dr. C.B. Jackson, was born in Ghent, Kentucky, in 1924. The Normans met at Baylor in Waco and married in Greenville, Texas, in 1944. Jessie graduated cum laude from Baylor in 1945 while Dr. Norman graduated from Baylor in 1943 and Southwestern Medical in Dallas in 1946. After one year of rotating internship at Baylor hospital in Dallas, the Normans spent two years in the army – stationed in Denver, Colorado, and Omaha, Nebraska. After two more years in graduate study at Barnes Hospital in St. Louis and the Dallas V.A. Hospital, the Normans came to Longview where Dr. Norman practiced ear, nose and throat specialties for thirty-seven years.

Faithful Baptists, the Normans joined Longview First Baptist Church where they were active in the choir and teaching. Dr. Norman became a deacon and president of the Longview Downtown Rotary in 1954. In 1956, the Normans volunteered to help start Oakland Heights Baptist Church, serving as Music Minister and pianist for seven years. In addition, both taught classes. After serving twenty-five years, they returned to First Baptist where they presently are first-grade teachers and sing in the Sanctuary and Saints Alive choirs.

In the 1950s, Jessie served as president of the Gregg County Medical Auxiliary and became a charter member of the Longview Story League, remaining an active member until the present. Also, for three years she was a member of the Executive Board of the Baptist General Convention of Texas. In 1987, Dr. Norman helped found the East Texas Civil War Round Table (now called the History Club of East Texas) where he continues as a member. He served seven years on the Board of Directors of East Texas Baptist University, and for ten years was chairman of the Hollandsworth Scholarship for Baylor

Dr. Norman is a docent at the Gregg County Historical Museum where he has done over 300 videotaped oral history interviews. He is also a docent at the East Texas Oil Museum in Kilgore.

– Submitted by Dr. Wayman B. Norman

Wayman and Jessie Norman

DOLLY NORTHCUTT

Miss Dolly Northcutt was the oldest daughter of Eda Mauthe and Dr. W.D. Northcutt. Miss Dolly was born 1 February 1892, in Longview and died 4 March 1982. She is buried in the family plot at Grace Hill Cemetery.

Miss Dolly was honored in 1970 during Longview's Centennial Celebration as "First Lady of the First Century" for her outstanding contributions to its growth and development. After her mother's untimely death, Dr. Northcutt called on this twenty-year-old eldest daughter to manage his large household. Thus began her lifetime of service, not only to her family, but to her church, community and country.

She was an organizing member of Capt. William Young Chapter, Daughters of the American Revolution; organizing member and first president of the Longview Garden Club; organizing member of Longview Federation of Women's Clubs; assisted in establishing Longview's first library; member of R.B. Levy Chapter, United Daughters of the Confederacy; member of Longview Downtown Development Corporation; and founding member and served on the Board of Directors of Gregg County Historical and Genealogical Foundation. The first concept of Mrs. Rogers Lacy and Dolly Northcutt of a living museum of local heritage became a reality with the purchase and renovation of the historic Everett Building by the Foundation.

As a real estate developer, she designed and managed the Surrey Place subdivision, including Covington Drive and Winchester Lane.

In 1938, as a genealogist and historian, she compiled and published a book, *Northcutt and Allied Families*, in collaboration with her cousin Mrs. Paul B. Belding.

She was a life-long member of the First Baptist Church and served on the pulpit and building committees. She was the first historian of the church and saved many valuable documents.

– Submitted by Gordon Northcutt

DR. WILLIAM DAVIS & EDA MAUTHE NORTHCUTT: Descendants

Dolly was born 1 February 1892, in Longview and died 4 March 1982. She is buried in the family plot at Grace Hill Cemetery.

Leon, born 9 April 1893, was a representative of the Banker's Life Insurance Company of Des Moines, Iowa, a deacon of the First Baptist Church, a member Lion's Club and the Business Men's Bible Class, a Mason and Shriner. Leon married Bertha Fisher, daughter of Silas McBee Fisher and Juan Minerva Bumpas Fisher, 19 September 1921. Their son, William Fisher Northcutt, attended Longview High School, New Mexico Military Institute, the University of Texas and Yale University. During World War II, he was a Flight Engineer on a B-29 when, on 9 January 1945, his plane went down in the South Pacific. Leon died 27 February 1958, and is buried in Grace Hill Cemetery.

Ema moved out of the family home with her sister Dolly to 7 Covington Drive in 1932. She was a musician and played the piano for one Sunday School Department at the First Baptist Church for more than thirty years. Her hobby was needle work and she made many sweaters, caps and socks for the Red Cross during World War II. She was an organizing member of the Capt. William Young Chapter of the Daughters of the American Revolution.

Flossie was born 25 August 1895, and on 21 June 1919, married William Ridley Wheeler, son of Franklin Clay Wheeler and Amelia Ridley Wheeler of Shreveport, Louisiana. After serving in World War I, Ridley Wheeler he worked for the Southern Crude Oil Company in Shreveport. In 1930, he moved to Fort Worth, Texas, and became an Independent Oil Operator. Their children born in Shreveport are Barbara Frances and Ridley Northcutt Wheeler, who attended New Mexico Military Institute and Southern Methodist University. He served in the European Theater and the Southwest Pacific areas of World War II. Ridley married Gay Cole Howard. Their children are Sarah Northcutt Wheeler, who married William Magee, and Nancy Howard Wheeler, who married Robert Heller. W.R. Wheeler, wife Flossie and son Ridley Northcutt Wheeler are buried in Memory Park Cemetery in Longview.

William Davis Northcutt, Jr. married Josephine Still on 2 October 1932.

Eda Northcutt, born 3 August 1901, remained in the family home with her sister Jessie. Eda attended East Texas Baptist College and Baylor University. She taught elementary school in Longview and was an active member of the First Baptist Church.

Jessie Vada, born 29 May 1904, married Edward A. Brown. She was born 29 May 1904, attended the College of Industrial Art in Denton (Texas Women's University) and the University of Texas. She taught in the elementary school and, being a talented musician, taught private piano lessons. She was a member of the Daughters of the American Revolution and the First Baptist Church. Sons Arthur Northcutt and George Melvin Brown were born in Longview. In World War II, Edward (Ted) A. Brown, served in the Adjutant General's department. While stationed in Washington, D.C., twin daughters Barbara and Betty and son Bruce E. Brown were born.

Arthur Northcutt Brown married Janet Tienry of Fort Worth. They have two children, Suzanne and David Brown.

George Melvin is unmarried.

Bruce E. Brown married Pam Posey of Dallas and has two children, Emily and Alan Ridley.

Barbara Brown lives in Dallas and married Dr. Robert Munford.

Betty died in 1969.

– Submitted by LeGrand Northcutt

WILLIAM GEORGE NORTHCUTT

William George Northcutt was born in 1837, Cobb County, Georgia, and married Julia Ann Moore, daughter of Jeremiah and Susannah

Scurry Moore, in 1856. The couple left Georgia in 1869 in company with relatives, and moved to Harrison County, Texas, where he leased a saw mill and manufactured furniture. After the city of Longview was founded in 1870, the family moved into town to establish residence and the Northcutt Hardware and Furniture Company. William bought lots on the corner of West Tyler and North Center Streets and built the first two-story brick building in town for his business. Later, he and his sons built wagons, owned the brickyard where the first bricks in Longview were made and expanded the business to include paint manufacturing and ornamental tin works and a monument works where imported marble was finished and inscribed. Northcutt Hardware and Furniture Company was in continuous business at the same location from 1872 until it was sold in 1944.

W.G. Northcutt and his wife were charter members of the First Baptist Church where he served as deacon and trustee for thirty-eight years. Mayor of Longview twice, he served in 1888-89 and 1898-1900. He and his wife were parents of seven children: John Thomas, Jere E., William Davis, Sarah (Mrs. L.N. Markham), Jessie (Mrs. E.B. Protho), Dolly (Mrs. S.C. Forman) and Iba (Mrs. C.L. Taylor).

The third child, William Davis, was born 12 November 1861, in Cobb County, Georgia. He attended Preacher McClelland's School and entered Texas A&M College in 1877-78, the second year of the College. He was a graduate of the University of Louisville, Kentucky, Medical Department and practiced medicine for forty five years in Longview. Thirty-five of those years he was local physician and surgeon for the Texas & Pacific, International & Great Northern and Santa Fe Railways. He was a charter member of the Gregg County and Northeast District Medical Societies, and member of the Texas Medical Association and the American Medical Association. Dr. Northcutt was City Health Officer, a member of Longview Volunteer Fire Department, charter member of Longview Rotary Club, a Mason, served as City Alderman, served several terms as Mayor and was a member of First Baptist Church for over fifty years

He married Eda Mauthe, daughter of Jacob and Barbara Grund Mauthe, 12 May 1888. They had seven children: Dolly; Leon; Emma; Flossie (Mrs. W.R. Wheeler); William Davis, Jr.; Eda; and Jessie (Mrs. E.A. Brown).

In 1902, the Northcutts built a home at 313 S. Fredonia Street, Longview. The lovely Victorian house, recently restored, still stands.

Many of their descendants still live in Longview.

NUNNALLY-HOLLY

The marriage of Larry Stephens Holly and Nancy Teresa Nunnally was performed at First Baptist Church, Longview, 27 February 1982. Larry was born in Longview, and Nancy was born in Tarrant County, Texas. This union produced a son, David Randall Holly, 18 August 1983.

Larry attended Pine Tree Schools, was an Army veteran and became a licensed insurance

agent. He is currently a salesman for Kilpatrick Life Insurance Company, Longview. Nancy, a Gladewater schools graduate, attended Kilgore College and was listed in the 1969 *Who's Who Among Students in American Universities and Colleges*. A vocalist and graduate of Texas A&M Commerce (formally East Texas State University), she worked teaching school and in various financial institutions and tutored. She volunteered for numerous organizations, including the schools David attended. David graduated a Texas Scholar from Longview High School in 2002. He attends Kilgore College and works for CiCi's Pizza.

Larry's parents are Johnnie Mae Williams Holly, a seamstress, and Joe Franklin Holly, Jr. Nancy's parents are Dorothy Stephens Nunnally, a teacher, and John Henry Nunnally. Both fathers were in sales. John Nunnally is buried in Rising Star, Texas, and Joe Holly is buried in Odessa, Texas. Johnnie Holly Swafford is buried in Longview. Dorothy Nunnally Caffey resides in Gladewater, Texas. Dorothy and John's only son, Randall Jay Nunnally, a musician, died in April 1986, Gregg County, Texas.

– Submitted by Nancy Holly

ODOM

Thomas G. Odom and Arenva Leslie, both born in Georgia, married 23 December 1849, in Perry County, Alabama. They left Alabama in the early 1850s for Louisiana and then on to Texas. They settle in Shelby County where they farmed for a living with their six boys, Arron, William, Edgar, Henry, John and Moses.

Edgar married Sarah Wolf Bryan in Shelby County, 12 August 1885. Sarah Bryan's family came to Texas in the 1860s from Alabama. They had their own wagon train with family, slaves and animals. The Bryan's bought over 4,000 acres in Panola County. Edgar and Sarah farmed. They had five children: Charlie, Nannie, Kyle, Dixie and Edgar.

Charlie married Martha Waldrop; Nannie married J.C. Dailey; Dixie married H.G. Green; Edgar died as a child. Kyle Bryan (K.B. or Buddy), born 19 January 1891, married Ada Williams, born 8 November 1898, in Panola County on 25 April 1914. Her father's family came to Panola County from Tennessee. M.G. Williams, her grandfather, went to medical

K.B. and Ada Odom

school in Illinois, then on to Kansas for more training; this is where her father, John W. Williams, was born. They were in Panola County by 1860. Ada's mother was Mary Jane Rhodes from Rusk County, Texas.

K.B. and Ada Odom started their family in Panola County, but moved to Gregg County after only a few years. They did some farming, and Granddaddy (K.B.) bought and sold produce. During World War II, he worked for the WPA building rock buildings, fences and drainage ditches. Grandma worked her garden, quilted from a frame hanging from the ceiling, and did ironing for people, heating her iron on the stove until they finally got electricity. They had 13 children: Arron, 13 August 1914, died 21 February 1934; Baby Odom, 1 July 1916; Terrell Jack, veteran of World War II, died 14 October 1981; Nash Kyle, 21 May 1919, married Ruby Foirriestier March 1940, was a welder, died 3 April 1989 (they had six children); Johnny Edward, 6 June 1921, married Maxine and had four children; Samatha Jane, 2 April 1923, died 5 December 1992, married Thaxton Murry and had four children; Charlie Virgil, 6 March 1925, married Beatrice and had six children; Willie (Bill), 17 December 1926, died 15 October 1985, married Marie and had five children (he worked for Gregg County at the courthouse); Audry Arenva, 4 April 1928; Frank, 14 December 1929, died 6 March 1930; Jimmie Oree, 21 June 1931, married Robert Light and had one child; Thomas Henry, 4 June 1934, has three daughters and was a welder; and Richard Cole, 31 March 1938, was a barber and owned a boot shop on Gilmer Road (his wife, Marylyn, taught at Pine Tree grade school), had three children and died September 2001.

All of K.B. and Ada's children married and reared their families in Gregg County. They followed the old tradition of carrying of family names. All of the children were named after a family member. Some of these names are still being handed down. Surnames are Odom, Leslie, Bryan, Williams, Rhodes, Kyle and Cole.
– Submitted by Shirley Odom Gibson

ANNIE LANDRETH OGUNGBADE

Annie Landreth Jones Ogungbade, a native Louisianan, was born 20 August 1927, to Oscar Samuel, Sr. and Loueaser Young Daniels in Hosston, Louisiana. At an early age she was adopted and joined her adoptive parents, Andrew and Ida Ophella Beard Landreth, in Belcher, Louisiana. When Annie was ten, Andrew died, and Ida and Annie later relocated to Vivian, Louisiana. She has one son, Sammy Landreth, three grandchildren, five great grandchildren and a host of (12) brothers and sisters: Earnest Samuel, Rozzell Samuel, Billy Ray Samuel, Rose Samuel Joseph, Ruthene Samuel Neville, Beatrice Daniel Davis, James H. Young, Sr. and five deceased.

Annie attended Louisiana public schools until the ninth grade. Financial hardships then demanded her presence at work instead of school. Therefore, her departure from school re-

Annie L Ogungbade

sulted in her working to contribute toward family living expenses. Becoming acquainted with the workforce at an early age quickly taught her the value of hard work and perseverance.

Eventually, her marriage of 21 years to Adrew Leroy Jones, a retired Sergeant of the U.S. Army, led her to Longview, Texas, in 1970. After separation and divorce, she married Ladipo A. Ogungbade, which ended very quickly due to his passing away in 1976. Since her arrival, her work and contributions to the Longview community have been continual.

Ogungbade was among the first to be hired as a Ward/Unit Clerk at Good Shepherd Hospital. She worked on various medical floors and assisted with the daily operations of administrative patient care. Her duties included patient chart documentation, transcribing, requisitioning and coordinating discharge appointments. She worked as a unit clerk for ten years.

Upon leaving the healthcare industry, she pursued another career opportunity at Eastman Kodak, where she served as a building attendant. She was a dedicated worker and completed 12-1/2 years before she retired in November 1990.

After retirement and years of surviving the workforce, she decided to secure her high school diploma. At age 64, she completed her GED. After receiving her GED, she sought additional skills and training at Kilgore College in Office Technology.

As a non-traditional student, younger students surrounded her in her college classrooms. Nevertheless, she remained focused on her dream and maintained an "I can do it" attitude.

With a new education and office skills, Ogungbade decided to re-enter the workforce. She became a part-time employee with Senior Texas Employment Program (STEP). With STEP she has worked in a variety of administrative positions at the Harvey Johnson Community Center, Longview Independent School District and the Longview Public Library.

Possessing strong work ethics, Annie has demonstrated her willingness to volunteer and serve others. She has contributed more than 1,000 hours of volunteer work to Meals on Wheels distributor, Highway 80 Rescue mission meal preparation, assisting with AARP, RSVP, and the Harvey Johnson Jolly Seniors Association.

Always a strong woman of faith, she is an active member of the New Bethel Missionary

Baptist Church and is the corresponding secretary. As a former member of Mount Olive Missionary Baptist Church, Annie was very instrumental in helping to implement the Vision Food Share outreach program which provides hundreds with nutritious food at half the cost.

Life has taught her many lessons, and her advice to future generations is "Take advantage of all the opportunities and get all the education you can." She advises seniors contemplating whether to return to school or not…. "go for it!" As is evident of her accomplishments, Annie is a firm believer that "All things are possible with the help of God."
– Submitted by Annie Landreth Ogungbade

STELLA MAUD WOOD CLARK PALMER

Affectionately called by many "Mammy," she was born in Pirtle, Texas. Her parents were James Edwin Wood and Catherine Patience Berger Wood. She married the grandchild of one of Gregg County's pioneer families – Britton Buttrill and Ruth Emmaline McCord Buttrill. Their grandson, Thomas Britton Clark, was the son of Dr. T.J. Clark and Virginia Beall Buttrill. Maud and Tommie were married in Henderson, Texas, on 16 December 1896.

Thomas Britton, a carpenter, died an untimely death at the age of thirty-six, when he fell from a roof where he had been working. Having four children to raise, Maud worked in a chocolate factory and moved her family back to Pirtle where her mother, a widow, lived. She later returned to Longview and opened a small boarding house in her home. She took in railroad engineers who needed a place to stay. Her daughter remembers meeting one of her boarders, a railroad man, named Red Schaffer, who would often bring her gifts (Juicy Fruit gum) when he returned from his trips. Red was a friend of Reece Buttrill Clark, one of Maud's sons. Reece was nicknamed "Boots" from his railroad engineering job.

Maud remarried to Luther C. Palmer and moved to Dallas. In her eighties she chased her granddaughter, Eileen, around the yard. Maud died at the ripe old age of 97 in Houston, Texas. Rumor is that she was out dancing with her preacher at a church function the day before her death! Her husband has long since passed away.
– Submitted by Eileen Vela,
Las Cruces, New Mexico

F.D.G. & WILNA PARK

F.D.G. was born 25 September 1900, to Mary Bell Blackard Park and Samuel S. Park in Johnson County near Clarksville, Arkansas. He was one of thirteen children. He grew up on a farm and was educated in the Clarksville schools and at the College of the Ozarks (completed in 1920).

He moved to El Dorado, Arkansas, in 1921, attended El Dorado Business School and became employed by McWilliams Furniture Company in El Dorado.

He married Wilna Massey in Columbia County in the town of Waldo, Arkansas, on 14 November 1926. She was born to William Thomas and Lena Formby Massey on 19 March 1905, in Waldo. She had a sister and a brother. She attended Freed-Hardeman and David Lipscomb Colleges in Tennessee in the 1920. The couple resided in El Dorado until 1931 when they moved to Longview, Texas, during the East Texas oil boom.

In 1931, he became Secretary-Treasurer of the Johnston Formation Testing Corporation and the Arkansas Drilling Company, both owned by E.C. Johnston, Sr. Offices were on Judson Road in Longview.

In the 1940s, he was co-owner of Johnston-Park Drilling Company and Park-Thornton Drilling Company, operating out of the McWilliams Building in Longview. From 1947-1954, he owned and/or worked in various businesses including as General Manager of McCrary Motor Company (Lincoln-Mercury on West Tyler), at Park Motor Company (Dodge-Plymouth) in Carthage, Texas, and at Park-Hammond Texaco Service on West Tyler at Highway 80 in Longview.

Wilna was a homemaker during her married life. She was an active member of the Church of Christ in Longview. She was an early member of the 2nd and Whaley Church of Christ. Later she was a member of the Mobberly Avenue and Alpine Churches of Christ.

In 1954, the family moved to Odessa, Texas, where F.D.G. owned Park Oil Tools (agent for LeBus International Engineers). In 1965, he retired and they moved back to Longview.

F.D.G. and Wilna were the parents of four children. William Thomas was born 15 June 1928, in El Dorado, Arkansas. He married Fabia Brame in Oakdale, Louisiana, on 27 August 1955, and they now reside in Lafayette, Louisiana. They have two children, Tom (deceased) and Tracey Park of Lafayette.

Mary Eleanor was born in Longview, 9 November 1931. She married Charles Drake on 29 July 1950. They now reside in Everman, Texas. They have two sons, Jim and Bill Drake, both of Everman.

Samuel Jackson (Jack) was born 3 September 1937. He married Carol Clymore in Ponca City, Oklahoma, on 12 September 1959. They have two daughters, Shara Kipp and Brenda Alexander, both of Longview.

F.D.G. and Wilna Park

Jerald Gomer (Jerry) was born in Longview, 30 January 1941. He married Ann Curry in Longview, 4 April 1969. They reside in Longview. They have two children, David Park of Fort Worth and Kristi Park of Austin.

F.D.G. died 20 June 1977, in Longview; Wilna died 22 June 1990, in Longview. They were married 50 years. They are buried in Columbia Cemetery at Waldo, Arkansas.

– Submitted by Jerald G. Park

JOHNNIE LAWRENCE & REBA PATILLO

Johnnie Lawrence Patillo and his wife, Reba King, met and married in 1940. They lived with his parents in Longview, Gregg County, Texas. His parents were Joe Anderson Patillo and Octavia McEntire Patillo. His paternal grandparents were John and Margaret Patillo. John and Margaret Patillo had three sons: Almarine, Ed and Joe Anderson. They also had daughters – how many and where they are is unknown. John and Margaret lived in Longview. They donated land for McCabe Methodist Church, which was located in the 200 block of Nelson Street, Longview, Texas. This is the church the generations of Patillo's attended. The church later merged with Wesley United Methodist and is now known as Wesley-McCabe United Methodist Church.

Joe Anderson Patillo and his wife, Octavia, along with their son, owned and operated the Patillo Hotel, located at 107 E. Nelson Street, Longview. This hotel was across the street from another hotel known as the Nichol's Hotel, later bought by Y.D. Floyd. This was in the heart of Nelson Street, where many activities took place. The 1930s and 1940s brought many of the well-known Black entertainers to Longview and they took rooms at these hotels. To name a few would include Louis Armstrong and Count Basie. They performed at the Reo Palm Isle and in the black community's Cotton Club, which later became a movie theater. These were exciting times for this family and the Black people in Longview, Texas.

Joe Anderson bought cross-ties, in the Longview Junction area, near the railroad crossing in the Cotton Street area, for J.W. Tyre of Jacksonville, Texas. Joe's wife, Octavia, did maid work for two prominent families – Attorney Stinchcomb and Dr. Adams and his wife, Madge, on Fredonia Street, Longview, Texas. After this couple stopped working for others, they dedicated their time to operating the hotel business. Octavia died in the 1950s. Joe Anderson remarried to Ardelia Sowells and this union ended in his death in the 1970s.

Johnnie Lawrence Patillo was born 6 February 1917, in Longview, Gregg County, Texas, attended Longview Public Schools and was a student at Wiley College. For eighteen years, he was a noted jeweler and operated Patillo's Jewelry and Watch Repair Shop at 107 E. Nelson Street and, later, at his home on Walnut Street. He departed this life on 16 September 1959.

Reba King Patillo was born 28 March 1918, in Tenaha, Texas. She was the sixth child of eleven born to Sam King and Annie Greer

King. She received her education in the public schools of Tenaha and Timpson, where she graduated. She was a member of Friendship Baptist Church in Tenaha, Texas, until she joined McCabe Methodist Church, now known as Wesley-McCabe United Methodist Church. She did domestic work for the late Dr. Dworin and his family. She also worked for Longview Flower Shop, Fedway (now known as Dillard's) and Reagan's. She retired and enjoyed spending time with her family, until her death on 24 February 2000.

The descendents of this family are Dorothy Patillo Daniels – 15 August 1940, Joe Davis Patillo – 30 August 1942 and Johnny Lawrence Patillo – 11 February 1965. Mr. Joe Davis Patillo, son of Johnnie Lawrence and Reba Patillo, married Brenda Daniels Patillo. He retired from the U.S. Army and currently has a Private Detective business in Houston, Texas. Brenda works for Foley's. He is a product of the Longview Public Schools and she from the Houston Public Schools.

Mrs. Dorothy Patillo Daniels, widow of the late Algie Perry Daniels, is a retired school-teacher in the Longview public Schools. Both attended Longview Public Schools, and Dorothy is a graduate of Wiley College and Algie a graduate of Bishop College. Both colleges are in Marshall, Texas. Dorothy retired after 31 years employment at the local Social Security Office. She was the first Black female hired in the local office, in 1965, under the management of the late Russell D. Patterson. She works part-time at the Longview Public Library. Algie died 6 April 1995.

Mr. Johnny L. Patillo, son of Joe Davis Patillo, is married to Erica. Their children are Joseph, Danielle and Daneshia. Johnny is employed by Eastman in Longview, Texas. Johnny attended Longview Public Schools and Erica went to school in Georgia. They both served in the U.S. Air Force.

Thus ends the saga of a loving family and many treasured memories remain of the earlier years. The older generations passed the torch and life goes on. Keep the torch burning with lots of love in your heart for each other and for your fellow man. The Patillo's of yester-year are watching over each of us – Joe, Brenda, Dorothy, Johnny, Erica, Joseph, Danielle and Daneshia. God bless.

– Submitted by Dorothy Daniels

PATRICK

Elbert Vinson Patrick was born in Laurel, Mississippi, on 16 April 1902. His wife, Minnie Findley Patrick, was born 24 November 1903, in Hattiesburg, Mississippi. He grew up in Laurel and graduated from Laurel High School. After graduation, he went to Peoria, Illinois, to attend horology and jewelry school. His wife attended school in Hattiesburg and worked in a department store as a sales clerk. When first arriving in Texas, he worked as a watchmaker in Winnsboro but soon moved to Longview. He returned to Mississippi briefly for their wedding,

Elbert and Minnie Patrick at the Dallas Fair in the fall of 1932.

which took place on 8 June 1930. From 1931 to 1937, he was associated with the Feagle Jewelry Company as a watchmaker. In 1937, he started his own business in a location in the Wood Drug Store. Mrs. Patrick worked in the store with him until the birth of their only child, Linda Rae Patrick, on 15 January 1943.

In 1948, he opened a store at 204 N. Center which was E.V. Patrick Jewelry. He enjoyed fishing and gardening and also liked to travel. Mrs. Patrick taught a children's Sunday School Class at Wesley Methodist Church on Mobberly Avenue for many years. In their later years they enjoyed their granddaughters, Patricia Rae and Sherry Kay Plummer.

They remained in the jewelry business until a few years before his death on 17 February 1972. His wife remained in their home at 119 Garfield Street until failing health made it necessary for her to move near her daughter in Diana, Texas. She died 24 August 1979. They are buried at Grace Hill Cemetery on Highway 80 in Longview, Texas.

– Submitted by Linda Plummer

WILLIAM BRANT PAYNE

William Brant Payne was born 3 December 1930, in Sulphur Springs, Texas, to William Crogan and Vesta Evelyn Irons Payne. William B. (Bill) Payne married Ann Bridges (born 7 December 1930) on 23 December 1950, and they had five children. He was widowed July 1971. Bill is a graduate of Texas A&M University and the Wisconsin School of Banking. He married Clara Hurst Patterson (born 5 January 1932 (see "Julian Harrison Hurst" biography) on 2 December 1972. Clara is a graduate of Hockaday Junior College, where she was a friend of Bill's first wife, Ann Bridges. She also attended the University of Texas. Her first husband, William Burke Patterson died 10 December 1970. After her marriage to Bill Payne, she and her three children moved to Paris, Texas.

Three years later, in 1976, the family moved to Longview when Bill bought the Imperial 400 Motel and the Continental Inn, both on Highway 80. They bought the three-story W.R. Nicholson home on Hughes Street, built

around 1940, and ideal for the eight children. Bill built the Kilgore Ramada Inn. Also, he later owned the Fredonia Inn in Nacogdoches, the Contessa Inn in Longview and the Community Inn in Kilgore. Bill and Clara moved to Kilgore and lived for a year in one of the houses built by Earl Hollandsworth behind the Community Inn. They then moved to Longview in 1993, and now live in Huntington Park. Bill also owned three Holiday Inns in Shreveport and the International Inn on Interstate 20 in Longview. All motels have been sold and he is now retired.

They attend Longview Christian Fellowship and Clara teaches two Bible studies. She is a past president of the Junior League of Longview and the Junior Literary Club. She is a member of the Capt. William Young Chapter DAR and also serves on the boards of Longview Community Ministries and Love Overflowing. They feel very blessed to have twenty-two healthy grandchildren and one great grandchild.

The children of Ann Bridges and William Brant Payne are Katherine Ann, William Brant, Jr., Lee Bridges, James Alan and Timothy Andrew.

Katherine Ann Payne (13 March 1953) married 2 October 1977, to John Harville (8 April 1950). They reside in Paris, Texas. Kathy is a Special Education teacher. Johnny owns Fangio Body Shop. Their children are Emily Ann Harville (28 November 1978), married Gary Reynolds in 1996 and they had daughter Allie Blake Reynolds (22 March 1997) – Emily married second Micah Spence in December 2003; John Keller Harville (10 February 1981);

Wedding of Clara Hurst Patterson and William Brant Payne, 2 December 1972.

Wedding of Burke and Laura Harvey Patterson, the William Brant Payne family, 21 November 1992.

Molly Frances Harville (23 December 1982); and Sarah Ellen Harville (12 July 1986).

William Brant Payne, Jr. (2 August 1955) married January 1980, to Debra Boswell (23 October 1954). Brant is a Petroleum land man. He and his children reside in Longview. The children of Brant and Debra are William Brant Payne, III (4 August 1981); Michael Alan Payne (13 March 1983); Ann Bridges Payne (26 November 1985). William Brant Payne, Jr. married second to Pam Terry in 1988 and they have Austin Mitchell Payne (10 August 1988).

Lee Bridges Payne (22 January 1958) married 20 January 1982, to Donna (2 April 1960). They have a bed and breakfast (Payne Homestead) on the island of Vinalhaven, Maine. They have two children, Lee Francis Payne (15 September 1994) and William Collin Payne (2 February 1997).

James Alan Payne (20 January 1963) lives in Charleston, South Carolina, and is in the motel business.

Timothy Andrew Payne (10 May 1966) lives in Los Angeles, California, and is a casting director.

(Note: For the children of Clara Hurst and William Burke Patterson, see "Julian Harrison Hurst" biography.)

– Submitted by Brant Payne

ROSEMARIE PELPHREY-BOONE & MARTIN HAYDEN BOONE

Rosemarie Pelphrey was born 30 June 1923, Corsicana, Texas, to Nauty Byrd Wornel and Lasco Wheeler Pelphrey. The family lived in Breckenridge, Texas, where the flourishing L.W. Pelphrey Co. was established to build roads and bridges supporting the activities generated by the Ranger oil boom. The U.S. economy, along with the oil field, was making record gains. In 1929, the stock market crashed, the oil boom lost its momentum and L.W. Pelphrey Co. was forced into bankruptcy. Lasco, ever alert to revitalizing his company, realized the oil field in Gregg County, Texas, was the best opportunity. He moved his company, his key personnel, their families and his key equipment. In 1932, Lasco transported his wife and three daughters, Nauty Byrd, 11, Rosemarie, 9, and Minnette, 6, to Gladewater. Their longtime family maid followed in her car.

Rosemarie discovered East Texas was a different world. There were no wide vistas, no high skies and no strong winds to enjoy leaning against. Oak trees, tall pines and a plethora of flowering shrubs filled the spaces. Dirt roads, quagmires in the frequent rains, replaced roads of established Breckenridge. Gladewater Schools were mostly overcrowded. Rosemarie's grade met in a temporary wooden shack. In less than five years, beautiful brick schools were built. The most outstanding was the state-of-the-art high school. Vocational training and pre-college academic courses were offered.

Rosemarie remembers Ruth Ashton as an outstanding English teacher; her detailed instruction in diagramming sentences was a necessary background in Rosemarie's later studies (M.A. thesis in history). Another learning experience was membership in the award winning concert and marching band. Alto Tatum, genius leader of the band, gave the members a lasting appreciation of music, also building their self-confidence through extensive travel experiences. The New York's World Fair in 1936 was the highlight trip. Rosemarie was a Drum Majorette her senior year. Teenage years in Gladewater were fun and varied – Camp Fire Girls, Epworth League (Methodist), swimming at Lake Devernia, and dancing at Mattie's Ballroom to Chick Webb and Ella Fitzgerald, at Palm Isle to occasional big bands and at El Patio to a jukebox.

Rosemarie graduated in 1940, and matriculated at the University of Texas, Austin. The university was the ideal college experience. Rosemarie pledged Alpha Chi Omega and was Vice President in her senior year. World War II was declared in 1941. The difference was the young instructors were drafted and the professors taught classes. In her junior year Rosemarie met Martin Hayden Boone, Jr., a Navy V-12 premed student with the highest grade ever recorded in Organic Chemistry, who had already been accepted at the University of Pennsylvania Medical School in Philadelphia. After Rosemarie's graduation in 1944, they were married in September in Gladewater and left for Philadelphia where Martin began medical school. Rosemarie joined a medical research group studying oxygen intoxication. The group earned a Presidential citation for their contribution to the war effort. Martin was Secretary of his class all four years, graduating in spring of 1948.

Martin's internship and first year surgical residency, including special clinical instruction in hand surgery, was at Parkland Hospital in Dallas, Texas. Rosemarie was histologist for the Pathology Department. During the Korean War, Martin served in Germany and Rosemarie remained at Parkland. On completion of Martin's tour of duty, they moved to Midland, Texas, where Martin achieved his dream as a certified practitioner of Family Medicine.

Their children are William Allman, born 1953; Jane Devereux, born 1954; Rose Ann, born 1956; Benjamin Hayden, born 1959; and Julia Elizabeth, born 1962.

After 17 years, Martin and Rosemarie moved to Springfield, Missouri, to give Martin more family time. After a residency in anesthesiology, Martin was board certified and joined Professional Anesthesia Service as a partner. Rosemarie took her M.A. degree in History at Southwest Missouri State University and taught as associate teacher for six years.

Their grandchildren are Daphnie Leander Boone, born 1976 – father William Allman Boone; Michaela Boone Arradaza, born 1996 – parents Jane Devereux and Arthur Dioso Arradaza; Christopher Thomas Neu, born 1985, Michelle Ann Neu, born 1988, and Brian Andrew Neu, born 1989 – parents Rose Ann and Leo Thomas Neu III; Tyler Hayden Boone, born

1986 – father Benjamin Hayden Boone; Meghan Rose Wilson, born 1994, and Mitchell Reagan Wilson, born 1996 – parents Julia Elizabeth and William Wayne Wilson.

– Submitted by Nauty Byrd Mayer, Gladewater, Texas

PELPHREY-GOODSON

Wanda Minnette Pelphrey, born 6 November 1926, Breckenridge, Stephens County, Texas, to Lasco Wheeler Pelphrey and Nauty Byrd Wornel. Lasco descends from William Pelphrey, born 29 January 1764. He fought in the American Revolution. Nauty Byrd descends from Richard Wornel, who also fought in the American Revolution. After the war, the family moved to Kentucky. Indians killed him in August 1790, near Crab Orchard, Lincoln County, Kentucky. His son, William Richard, born 15 February 1790, died 8 December 1865. The family came to Texas in 1836, settling in Hill County. Minnette belongs to the Daughters of the American Revolution and the Republic of Texas, the Huguenot Society and many other hereditary organizations.

Lasco was a road and bridge builder. He followed the 1917 Ranger Oil boom for work. He was listed on Dun and Bradstreet before the Depression. P.B. Keller, brother of the famed Helen Keller was his business associate. "Black Thursday" was on 24 October 1929. The stock market crash devastated L.W. Pelphrey Company. Minnette remembers offering pennies from her piggy bank to help. When news of Gregg County's oil boom hit, Lasco saw a new beginning. The company moved to Gregg County in 1931. In May 1932, the family packed the Lasalle to start a new and exciting life in Gregg County. Minnette's first memory was the heavy perfume of damp, red clay dirt, pine trees and the smell of oil all mixed together.

James Henry Goodson was born 9 January 1925, Dallas County Texas, to Henry Louis Goodson and Vera Elizabeth Warren. They came to Gladewater in 1931. Henry was Vice President of the First State Bank in Gladewater. Minnette met James at a swimming party the summer of 1938. He had sun bleached hair and incredible blue eyes.

Minnette remembers saying to herself "when I grow up I am going to marry him." It was James' first year in high school; Minnette was in Jr. High. There were parties playing spin the bottle and post office. In high school they danced at Mattie's Ballroom, Palm Isle and El Patio. James had a 1941 blue Ford convertible. He played first chair trombone in Gladewater High School Band; Minnette was Drum Majorette (her senior year she was editor of *The Bear Facts*). It was an idyllic time. On 7 December 1941, Minnette was watching a picture show at the Gregg Theatre, when James came to get her. They spent the day listening to war news. James graduated from Gladewater High School in 1942. Minnette graduated in 1944. He went to A&M, she went to the University of Texas where she pledged Alpha Chi Omega sorority.

James died 5 December 1993, of cancer in Dripping Springs, Hays County, Texas. They moved there to build a house for Minnette.

James and Minnette married 27 December 1947. Their children are (1) Lasca Minnette, born 26 February 1949, married James Kinney Longacre, born 7 February 1947, on 20 May 1972, children Aubrey Sienna, born 1 August 1974, and James Evan, born 31 December 1976; (2) James Rush, born 30 July 1959; (3) Courtney Anne, born 1 March 1961, married James Ray Sjoerdsma, born 2 March 1990, children Paige Allison, born 15 September 1990, and Dustin James, born 24 June 1992.

– Submitted by Minnette Pelphrey Goodson, Dripping Springs, Texas

PELPHREY-MAYER

Lasco Wheeler Pelphrey, his wife Nauty Byrd Wornel and three girls, Nauty Byrd, age eleven, Rosemarie, eight, and Minnette, five, came to Gregg County in May of 1932. They had rented a wonderful house, perfect for the five of them, at 314 N. Main.

Pelphrey had moved his construction company some months before; then brought the family for a visit at Christmas. That winter the constant rain was terrible. The pavement stopped just west of Mineola. Trucks moving oil field equipment kept the dirt roads torn up.

The school had been inundated with children. Most classes were in hastily erected single wall shacks in the area now used for the Broadway school playground. They were warmed with stoves made from oil drums and fueled with natural gas.

By 1934, the family lived at the edge of town in a two-story building originally built for the office and dormitory for permanent employees. The tool shed became the kitchen; one office room became the living room-dining room. The other downstairs room became the office with a cot at night making a bedroom for the construction superintendent. The two upstairs rooms were bedrooms. Five rooms of furniture plus the office furniture fit into four rooms pretty well. The important thing was that the family was all together. They soon moved further out from town into a remodeled old farm house. An office and a large shop building were constructed on three and a half acres. The whole area was later incorporated as Clarksville City, and the loop cut off when Hwy. 80 was constructed was named Pelphrey Drive. Lasco became the first mayor.

The girls graduated from Gladewater High School and went to the University of Texas, Austin. Just before Nauty Byrd was to graduate, she had a blind date with a Field Artillery officer, Gordon J. Mayer, from Philadelphia, Pennsylvania. After a whirlwind courtship of fifty-three days, they were married at Old Post Chapel, Ft. Sill, Oklahoma, on 25 September 1943. She followed him from post to post until he was sent overseas, then she went back home to wait until the war was over.

Deciding they should live in Texas, Gordon enrolled at Kilgore College then transferred to Texas A&M, majoring in Civil Engineering.

He worked for the Texas Highway Department for twenty-three years. As a very gregarious and civic-minded person, he served as Lay Reader for St. Mark's Episcopal Church for twenty-five years and was Lay Eucharistic Minister in the Corporate Liturgy. He was regularly an officer of the church board, usually Senior Warden of treasurer. He was a 32'd Degree Mason, Scottish Rite; Hella Temple A.A.O.N.M.S., Dallas; Sharon Temple, Tyler and Gregg County Shrine Club.

For over thirty years he served as Percinct 3 general election judge, was a long-time director of the Gladewater Rodeo Association, member of the Lion's Club and often a director. He was a member of the board of directors of the Gladewater Municipal Hospital and four-times chairman. For over thirty years he was a member of the Chamber of Commerce, and in 1979, was named Gladewater's Outstanding Man of the Year by the Chamber.

Nauty Byrd has a Bachelor's Degree in English with a minor in Psychology from the University of Texas Austin. She has done graduate wok at the University of Houston, Stephen F. Austin University and SMU. She taught school for thirty-nine years; one year kindergarten, ten years first grade and twenty-eight years as Middle School Librarian.

Texas Federated Women's Clubs named her Key District Teacher of the Year 1973-1974. She was also named Texas Outstanding Clubwoman 1974-1976. She was a long time member and officer of the Three Arts Club. She is president of the Garden Club and a member of the Daleth Study Club.

The Former Students Association of Gladewater High School gave her the Outstanding Alumnus Achievement Award in 1991. She was president of the organization for its first three years.

In 1976, Nauty Byrd was active in Gladewater's Bicentennial Celebration. It was a lot of fun with period costumes, parades and parties. She, Elizabeth Osteen and Mildred Barker wrote and published two volumes of local history.

Nauty Byrd was raised a Methodist and Gordon a Catholic. They compromised and joined St. Mark's Episcopal Church, Gladewater. Now that Gordon is gone and St. Mark's closed, she has returned to First Methodist after sixty years.

Nauty Byrd, her daughter and granddaughters belong to Magna Charta Dames, Plantagenet Society, Colonial Dames of the XVII Century, Daughters of the American Colonists, Daughters of the American Revolution, Daughters of the Republic of Texas and Daughters of the Confederacy.

Gordon and Nauty Byrd have two children: Gordon J. Mayer, Jr., a Consulting Engineer in the Dallas Metroplex, and Patricia Milligan, a professor of Information Systems at Baylor University; two grandchildren: Mindy Milligan, a pre-med graduate student at Baylor, and Mitzi Milligan, a senior Bio-Medical Science Major at Texas A&M.

– Submitted by Patricia Milligan

PELPHREY-WORNEL

Lasco Wheeler Pelphrey, son of Samuel Pelphrey and Mary Alice Wheeler, was born 10 May 1892, in Mineola, Texas. He married Nauty Byrd Wornel, who was born 5 January 1895, to Elisha William Wornel and Minnie Heavel Stanley in Hill County, Texas.

Lasco's first enterprise was a bicycle shop in the barn. He bought so many parts that the company wrote they were sending a representative to call. This frightened Lasco, who did not know if what he was doing was legal. He scattered all the evidence and waited on the road to tell the salesman no one named Pelphrey lived anywhere around there.

Sam Pelphry was a master mechanic in charge of the railroad roundhouse in Hillsboro, Texas. He required his sons to build their own toys after drawing blueprints, listing material needed and costs. When Lasco wanted a car and had met all the requirements, his father went to Fort Worth and brought the chassis of a burned out car home on a flatcar.

All roads in Texas were county roads then. Lasco's first road work was picking up roots from the dirt brought in for the streets in Hillsboro. He hawked newspapers and did any other work he could find. He quit school in the tenth grade because it interfered with his business. (Later, when he was living in Dallas, he went to Draughn's Business College at night.) His day job was with Texas Power and Light building electrical sub-stations south of Dallas.

Nauty Byrd graduated from Hillsboro High School. That summer her family moved to Corsicana and she enrolled in high school there, taking courses she had not had. The next year she went to college in Thorp Springs. (In the 1930s, she went to Centenary College in Shreveport.) Always, she was a voracious reader.

Nauty Byrd and Lasco were married 12 June 1916. They lived in rooming houses in twenty-six towns in the next five years as he followed construction. He was subcontracting bridges from a distant cousin. They carried a trunk packed with dresser scarves, bedspreads and other amenities. Later she said she fixed each room as though they would be there forever.

When Lasco died, his partner said one could not drive in East Texas without using one of his roads, which included the first widening of Highway 80 from Gladewater to Longview.

– Submitted by Nauty Byrd Mayer

PERSON

The journey from Alabama to Texas in 1855 was no doubt an arduous one for John J. and Nancy Ellen Fulgham Person, who gave birth to a son, Joseph Crow Person, on 7 December 1855, in Nacogdoches, Texas. John Person was a farmer and preacher ordained at the Antioch Baptist Church in Centreville, Alabama.

They did not settle in Texas at this time (reason unknown), but returned to Bibb County (formerly Cahawba), Alabama, where they still owned property. He enlisted in the Army of the Confederacy and served as 1st Sgt., Co. F, 44th Alabama Infantry. It would not be until after the war that they would return to Texas, settling in Upshur County with their family. John and Nancy are buried in Morris Cemetery, Pritchett, Upshur County.

Joseph Crow Person and Alice Fisher, daughter of pioneer family Silas McBee Fisher and Martha Killingsworth Fisher, were married on 12 February 1875, in Gregg County, Texas. On 22 November 1895, they bought land in the William Castleberry survey close to White Oak from J.K. "Cap" and Eliza Rucker for $600.00, on which they farmed and reared their seven children. An adjoining 20 acres to the south was purchased around 1900. Alice Person died on 7 July 1929, about a year before the East Texas oil field was discovered. J.C. Person was employed for a time by the State and was also an elected Gregg County official. He died on 14 September 1939. All of the children of Alice and J.C. were born in Gregg County, with sons Louis being the eldest and Frank Clark being the youngest. Their five daughters were Gertrude (Mrs. Jose Munden), Emma (Mrs. Henry Ponder), Cassie (who died at an early age), Georgia (Mrs. Harry Munden) and Mattie (Mrs. Alvin J. Callaway). All members of the family are buried in Fisher Cemetery, with the exception of Louis who is buried at Grace Hill Cemetery in Longview.

– Submitted by James Sydney Person (only son of F.C. and Fannie Hill Person who currently resides in Longview)

PHILLIPS

Floyd Elmer Phillips was born 24 July 1892, in Hempstead County, Arkansas, a son of Joseph Marion and Daisy Dean (Smith) Phillips. He was not afforded the opportunity to attend school for very long, as he became the man of the house at age nine when his father died. Floyd married Augusta Lenora Stevenson, 3 February 1915, in Hempstead County. Augusta was born 26 March 1898, in Hempstead County, a daughter of Andrew Paul and Sarah Jane (Mitchell) Stevenson.

Floyd and Augusta had eight children. Rubye Evelyn was born 24 September 1916, and married Walter H. Bennett Sr. Walter died, and Rubye then married Harvey Wright, her high school sweetheart. Sybil Edna was born 13 August 1918, and married Percy Charles "Joe" Bauman. Joe died, and she then married Woodrow Wooldridge. Bonnie Mae was born 25 July 1920, and married Warren Keith Guy. Dillard J. was born 9 March 1922, and married

Augusta and Floyd Phillips

Faye Foster. Floye Anne was born 27 September 1924, and married James Robert Wyatt. Wanda Jean was born 3 April 1930, and married Willis Edmond Williams Jr.; they divorced. Wanda then married Glendon Sylvester Anderson. Ellen was born and died 13 December 1933. Bobby Joe was born 6 August 1935, and married Helen Little; they divorced. Bobby Joe then married Helen Johnson.

They family moved to Kilgore, Texas, in the late summer 1930, having heard about the oil boom. Floyd worked in the oil fields as a "roughneck" on the drilling rigs. Upon first arriving in Kilgore, the family lived in a tent between two huge oak trees for a few weeks until an old farmhouse became available to rent. A little later, Floyd bought his brother Ezra's frame house, which Floyd helped build, and also 100 acres of adjoining property on FM 1252. Floyd continued working for the oil companies as a pumper, well inspector and machinery maintenance man. Augusta canned fruits and sold fresh peaches from the orchard and used the money to furnish the house. They also kept boarders. Augusta made clothes and linens from the patterned material of flour sacks. Augusta enjoyed gardening and cultivated a variety of vegetables, flowers and plants. The children attended Sabine School in Liberty City. Floyd and Augusta were members of the First Baptist Church in Liberty City.

About 1960, Floyd built a brick house nearby and sold the frame house and lot. Floyd retired from the Atlantic Richfield Company. Floyd and Augusta moved into the Towne Oaks Apartments in Longview and sold their brick house in 1979. Floyd was a fifty-year member Mason with the Warren G. Harding Masonic Lodge 717 in Smackover, Arkansas. Augusta was a member of the Order of the Eastern Star Chapter 630.

Floyd died 14 September 1982, in Good Shepherd hospital and was buried in the Kilgore City Cemetery. Augusta stayed in the apartment for a couple months and then went to live with daughter Rubye. Augusta died 26 February 1984, in Good Shepherd Hospital and was buried beside Floyd.

– Submitted by Wanda Anderson,
written by Eric Keenan

PHILLIPS, MORGAN & SHEPPERD

Jack Loyce Phillips was born 11 February 1925, Gladewater, Gregg County, Texas. He married on 21 December 1946, to Barbara Gene Wampler, born 25 August 1926, Amarillo, Texas. Barbara was the daughter of Floyd and Goldie Marie (Roden) Wampler. Jack and Barbara are parents of Barbara Gail Phillips, born 18 August 1950, Longview, Texas, and Nancy Jane Phillips, born 20 September 1952. Gail, daughter of Jack and Barbara, married on 15 January 1972, to Stephen Charles Mizer, born 11 July 1949, Kansas City, Missouri; children of Gail are Ashley Gail Mizer, born 11 November 1974, Galveston, Texas; Stephen Jack Mizer, born 3 January 1978, Tyler, Texas; Whitney Phillips Mizer, born 21 October 1980, Tyler,

Texas; and Thomas Sutton Schoonover-Mizer, born 17 October 1990, Tyler, Texas. Nancy Jane Phillips, daughter of Jack and Barbara Phillips, married on 12 August 1972, to Curtis Mark Abernathy, born 30 June 1950, Carthage, Texas; he is the son of Curtis Quentin and Peggy Abernathy. Children of Nancy and Mark are Leslie Anne Abernathy, born 17 February 1975, Houston, Texas, married on 14 June 2003, Longview, Texas, to Burke Randall Johnson, born 18 March 1975, New Haven, Connecticut; Clay Madison Abernathy, born 26 June 1977, Longview, Texas, married on 24 May 2003, Longview, Texas, to Jaclyn Gail Pickens Martin, born 24 January 1977, Longview, Texas; and Nancy Claire Abernathy, born 10 October 1979, Longview, Texas.

Jack has served the Gladewater community for many years. He served as the mayor of Gladewater and was vice president of Independent Petroleum Association of America; president of the Gladewater Round-Up Rodeo for 22 years; president of the Lions Club; chairman of the board, First Methodist Church, Gladewater; a Mason, serving as Potentate of Sharon Shrine Temple, Tyler; and has been an active geologist and successful independent oil operator. Numerous oil fields bear his name and the name of his wife, children and parents. Jack is a worldwide sportsman and has hunted in North and South America, Canada and Africa.

Jack and his sister, Lavon Inez Phillips, were children of Loyce Phillips, a successful pioneer oilman. Loyce was born 14 October 1898, Gladewater, Texas, and died on 5 February 1975, Gladewater. Loyce married on 28 January 1922, to Inez Elizabeth Scarborough, born 9 November 1899, Cameron, Texas, died 8 July 1975, Gladewater, Texas; she and Loyce are buried in the Gladewater Memorial Park Cemetery. Lavon Phillips was born 26 October 1923, Gladewater, Texas, and married on 1 June 1948, to Verne Douglas Philips, born 3 November 1918. Verne was the son of Vincent Darby Philips, born 14 July 1885. Verne and Lavon were parents of Susan Scarle Philips, born 6 July 1952, Houston, Texas.

Loyce Phillips was the son of Azor Holbert Phillips, born 10 January 1877, Gregg County, Texas, died 4 May 1963, Gladewater, Texas, married on 29 December 1897, Gregg County, to Carrie Ellen Morgan, born 16 August 1875, died 19 December 1956. Both are buried in the Gladewater Memorial Park Cemetery.

Azor Holbert Phillips was the son of Alfred Mason "Mase" Phillips. Mase was born in the Republic of Texas on 31 December 1844, Jonesville, Harrison County, Texas, and died 10 September 1913, Gladewater; he was a veteran of the War Between the States, the Civil War. He served as a private in Company G, 35th Texas Cavalry, Terrell's Brigade, Kirby Smith's Division, trans-Mississippi Department. Mase enlisted at the age of 19, in Pittsburg, Upshur County, Texas, in 1863. His record was published in *Reminiscences of the Boys in Gray, 1861-1865*, p. 606.

Mase Phillips married in about 1867, Upshur County, Texas, to Mary Elizabeth Holbert, born 24 February 1851, Upshur County, Texas, died 29 September 1915, Gladewater, Texas. Mase came to Union Grove in about 1847 with his parents from Jonesville, Harrison County, Texas. Mase and Mary's first home was at the corner of Gay Avenue and Rodeo Drive in Gladewater. Mase had a store at Red Rock, a grist mill, a syrup mill, a saw mill and a cotton gin. He was active in community affairs and was a Mason, and he and Mary were charter members of The First Baptist Church in Gladewater.

Mary Elizabeth (Holbert) Phillips, Mase's wife, was the daughter of Clairborn Holbert and Matilda Talley. Matilda was the daughter of James Obie Talley and Mary "Polly" Kirkpatrick. Matilda died when Mary was quite young and Mary went to live with her uncle, Carrol D. Holbert. Clairborn Holbert was a veteran of the Confederate Army and both he and his brother Carrol each served in succession as postmasters at Point Pleasant, an early community now a part of Clarksville City, east of Gladewater.

Carrie Ellen (Morgan) Phillips was the daughter of Daniel McCowan Morgan, born 17 November 1839, died 11 April 1904. He married 5 August 1868, Sand Flat, Texas, to Mary J. Thorn, born 28 December 1849, Smith County, Texas. Daniel and Mary (Thorn) Morgan were parents of Adiline, Knox, Wendel, Carrie Ellen, Loufreshie, and Florrie. Daniel M. Morgan was the son of John and Margaret (Bowles) Morgan. John was born 26 November 1802, Georgia, died 21 September 1881, Upshur County, Texas; Margaret was born 15 September 1805, Georgia, died 24 December 1875, Upshur County, Texas. According to one family member, Lavon Philips, the Morgans came to Upshur County, Texas, from Piedmount, Alabama, in 1856. John and Margaret Morgan are buried in the Morgan Cemetery.

Alfred Mason "Mase" Phillips was the son of William Phillips, born 1807, Georgia, died 28 March 1862, Upshur County, Texas. He married on 28 September 1827, Montgomery County, Alabama, to Mary "Polly" Shepperd, born 12 April 1812, Richmond County, Georgia, died 27 March 1875, Gladewater, Texas. Both are buried in the Union Grove Cemetery. William and Mary (Shepperd) Phillips came to the Republic of Texas, arriving first in Harrison County, where they lived near Jonesville, Texas. Records were found where William Phillips sold 301 acres of land to J.J. Webster on 5 January 1846, recorded in Volume H, p. 583, Harrison County land records. This sale was made by William in preparations for his removal to Upshur County, Texas.

William and Mary Phillips came to Harrison County after 1837, but before 1 January 1840, where he received a land patent in November of 1840. William Phillips was the son of George Phillips and his first wife, whose name is unknown. George married his second wife, Elizabeth Talley, in Virginia. George and Elizabeth were members of Bethlehem Baptist Church, Pintlala, Montgomery County, Alabama. According to church records, they joined by letter in 1836. William and Mary Phillips were also members of that church. George Phillips was the father of the following: Milley Fendley, born c. 1804, Georgia; William, born 1807; Medea Ann Pouncy, born c. 1808, married Peter Pouncy, long-time minister at the Bethlehem church at Pintlala, Alabama; Mariah Bozman, born c. 1820, Georgia, married Benjamin M. Bozman (Mariah and Benjamin lived in Upshur County.); Mary Jane Dean, born 16 May 1821, Montgomery County, Alabama, married in 1836, there to Jarrette Dean, born 1813, Georgia; Laurina Moseley, born c. 1824, Montgomery County, Alabama; and Elizabeth "Betsey" Barnes, born 27 September 1828, Montgomery County, Alabama, married there to Hezekiah Barnes. Hezekiah was a land owner in what is now Warren City, near Gladewater. Hezekiah and his wife Mary are the progenitors of Robbie Nell (Johnston) Shepard, O.G. Johnston and Billy Ray Johnston, all of Gladewater.

George and Elizabeth (Talley) Phillips are found on the 1850 Census of Upshur County, Texas. Elizabeth is listed as deaf. They were members in the household of their son-in-law, Jarrett Dean. Mary and William Phillips were in Texas before other family members. It was Mary (Shepperd) Phillips that must have written to the Shepperd and Dean families back in Alabama and said, "Y'all come to Texas!" And they did.

Mary "Polly" (Shepperd) Phillips was the daughter of William Shepperd, born about 1777, died in about 1828, Montgomery County, Alabama. William married on 22 February 1802, Richmond County, Georgia, to Elvey Anderson, born 1779, Onslow County, North Carolina, died April of 1860 of cancer, Upshur County, Texas. Elvey, called Elvira in her probate records, was the daughter of Elijah Anderson, born 1757, Onslow County, North Carolina. Her mother was Lavinia Brack, born about 1763, Onslow County, North Carolina, died 1844, Montgomery County, Alabama. Lavinia's will was probated on 11 November 1844. Elijah and Lavinia Anderson went to Richmond County, Alabama, and later to Jefferson County, where Elijah died by 4 July 1807, the year his widow entered his children in the 1807 Georgia Orphans Land Lottery. Elijah Anderson was a veteran of the American Revolution. He was named in a deed in Onslow County, North Carolina, dated 8 April 1777. Elijah was the son of Elmore Anderson, whose land records dated 1763, Onslow County. Elmore wrote his will in Onslow County, North Carolina, on 21 February 1772, and named his son, Elisha Anderson, brother to Elijah. Elisha and Elijah married sisters. Elisha married Elizabeth Brack and Elijah married Lavinia Brack. Both men served as soldiers in the American Revolution, as did their father-in-law, Eleazor Brack. Eleazor was born in 1727, and died 11 October 1801.

Elijah Anderson brought his family to northeastern Georgia by 1779. Elijah's probate records of Jefferson County, Georgia, Minute Book B, p. 35, names his heirs. His widow, Lavinia (Brack) Anderson accompanied the Shepperds and Andersons to Montgomery County, Alabama, in the 1820s. In her probate records, dated 11 November 1844, a petition was filed to sell the land belonging to Lavinia located near Davenport, Montgomery County, Alabama. Another court action was filed on 28 December 1844 for the personal property, which sold at auction for $10,139.00.

William and Elvey (Anderson) Shepperd were parents of (1) Charity Bonham and (2) Elizabeth Brady, both of whom remained in Montgomery County; (3) William, Jr.; (4) Lavinia Moseley (Her husband Mason Moseley brought his family to East Texas by 1839 and lived just east of the present site of Gladewater; (5) Mary "Polly" Phillips; (6) Elijah Byrd Shepperd; (7) Elisha Eleazor Shepperd, born 4 March 1815, Richmond County, Georgia, died December 1851, Red Rock Community, Upshur County, Texas, married Mary Ann Butler, born 20 March 1817, died 30 January 1891, Upshur County, Texas, daughter of Thomas and Aletha (Barnes) Butler, came to the Republic of Texas in 1845 with the Shepperd family; (8) Alfred Fulton Shepperd, ancestor to John Ben Shepperd, former Attorney General of Texas (It was John Ben who was responsible for the placement of an historical marker on the grave of Elvey (Anderson) Shepperd in the historic cemetery, Gay Cemetery, Upshur County, Texas.); (9) Robert Alexander Shepperd; (10) Elvey, Jr. married Mathis B. Merchant; and (11) Allen Martin Shepperd. Eight of the Shepperd children and their families are listed on the 1850 Census of Upshur County.

In the fall of 1845, Elvey (Anderson) Shepperd and most of her grown children and their families, all migrated to The Republic of Texas, arriving in what was later, Upshur County and later, Gregg County, Texas. The historical marker that was placed on the grave of Elvey Shepperd gave that, "with the help of her sons, built one of the first homes in this area, a log cabin that stood for over 100 years."

Elvey Anderson Shepperd was a descendant of three Mayflower passengers, Edward Doty, Edward Fuller and Samuel Fuller, son of Edward. Several of her descendants have joined the Mayflower Society on her well-documented line. (Note: Information came from family records published in a book titled, *The Doty, Anderson, Shepperd, and Allied Families*, by Carl Venoy Wright, a descendant of Eleazor Shepperd and his wife, Mary Ann Butler.)
– Submitted by Jack Phillips, Gladewater, Texas

PHILLIPS–NELSON

Joseph Marion Phillips was born 5 February 1868, in Hempstead County, Arkansas, a son of James A. and Eliza Jane (Simms) Phillips. Joseph married Daisy Dean Smith 9 January 1890, in Hempstead County. Daisy was born 15 October 1873, in Hempstead County, a daughter of Albert and Rhoda (Pennington) Smith. Daisy was an orphan and all that is known about her parents comes from her Social Security record, which states her father was Albert Smith and mother

(l.-r.) Lillie, Ezra, Ethel, Floyd and Daisy Phillips

was Rhoda, last name unknown, and from information her son Floyd provided on her death certificate which states her father was a Smith and mother was a Pennington. John H. Tarpley was Daisy's guardian on her marriage record.

Joseph and Daisy had five children. Ethel Eliza was born 24 October 1890, and died 12 October 1932. Ethel married Lum Turner Hanson. Floyd Elmer was born 24 July 1892, and died 14 September 1982. Floyd married Augusta Leonora Stevenson. Lillie Gertrude was born 20 December 1894, and died 30 September 1960. Lillie married Guy P. Clark. Ezra Aaron was born 22 June 1897, and died 13 December 1989. Ezra married Elsie Gilmer. Oma Lee was born 10 January 1901, and died 18 September 1905.

Joseph and family resided near Spring Hill, Arkansas, in the Smackover community and farmed for a living. He was caught in the rain while riding a horse and became ill with pneumonia. Joseph died shortly thereafter on 11 January 1902. He was buried in the Bethany Cemetery near Spring Hill.

Daisy was widowed for the next several years and raised the children by herself. She married Joseph Franklin Nelson in 1909. Joseph went by the nickname "Gay" and was born 3 November 1862, in Illinois. Daisy and Gay had one son; Orlando Burl was born 8 March 1910, and died 3 July 1993. Orlando married Marie Dees.

Daisy and Gay moved from Smack-over, Arkansas, to Kilgore, Gregg County, Texas, in 1940. They lived in a two-room "shotgun" house behind her son Floyd's house on FM 1251. Daisy and Gay were raising her granddaughter, Ethel Dean Hanson. Daisy's daughter Ethel had given birth to twin girls. One of the girls, Martha J. Hanson, died a day after birth. Ethel died a month after giving birth.

Gay could hardly be seen without his smoking pipe in hand. Gay died 5 May 1946, in Kilgore, and his funeral was held in the Sabine Baptist church. Daisy lived in the "shotgun" house until about 1959, when she moved into the Kilgore Nursing Home at FM 1252 and Highway 42. Daisy did not believe in going to doctors and, therefore, never went to one. She had been losing her eyesight gradually for several years and was all but blind when she died. It was probably due to cataracts. Daisy died 1 January 1968, in the nursing home. Her funeral service was held in the East Sabine Baptist Church and she was buried beside Gay.
– Submitted by Rubye Wright

PLILER

The early Pliler settlers migrated to America from Germany in the 1700s. Most came in through Pennsylvania and later migrated to South and North Carolina. Their migration to Texas came through Alabama, Mississippi and Louisiana. One early ancestor, Conrad Pliler, Sr., fought in the Revolutionary War, and one of his son's descendants (Emanuel) formed the branch of Plilers living in East Texas.

Eleven children were born to the later namesake Conrad Russell Pliler and Mary Allen Williams. Four sons of this union, George Merriweather Pliler (19 July 1859), Robert Russell (8 September 1870), Marion Emanuel (26 June 1852) and Wiley (1853), migrated from South Carolina in the late 1800s to Texas, stopping in an area that was later incorporated into the township of Longview. Their descendants still populate East Texas.

Emanuel, George and Robert Russell Pliler, c. 1930

Large amounts of land offered at 25 cents an acre attracted the Plilers. Each brother acquired land in different areas. George Pliler (married to Margie Mittie Hayes) bought a sizable farm in the Gum Springs area in 1897 (bounded by Gregg and Harrison Counties), where he was a successful farmer and sawmill owner. The area is still populated by over 55 Pliler descendants today. Many of the Pliler clan attended a one-room school in Gum Springs. Emanuel and Wiley Pliler chose to settle on what is the south side of Longview today. That area around Pliler Street and off Mobberly then was very sparsely populated, being mostly fields and woods. Mobberly was a narrow, unpaved road.

Russell (Russ) bought large parcels of land off Judson Road which was then just a narrow wagon and buggy dirt road. His homestead included large farm lands and a cotton gin that operated for many years. He married Emma Virginia Harris (born 13 October 1883; married 1891), daughter of Charles Newton Harris and Martha Jane Killingsworth, in Longview. Russ was a colorful character who was generous with the families working his land and saw that their children attended school. He prided himself on his work, and his handshake closed many transactions.

The story goes that a man came to purchase one of Russ's cows. The cow was brought up, the two men shook hands, but the buyer continued to stand there. When he requested a receipt, Russ simply took hold of the rope and told the man the cow wasn't for sale after all.

The Plilers were musically talented. Russ was skilled on the piano and violin. The family piano came by wagon in 1901 to Longview and is still in the family. Russ's son, Fred, played the fiddle, and Emanuel played the guitar. They played for family gatherings and community get-togethers.

Two children, Fred Marshall Pliler (17 September 1902) and Doris Henri Pliler (4 May 1907), were born in Gregg County to Russ and Virginia Harris. Charlie Pliler, a nephew, also lived with the family for awhile. Fred farmed and worked the land adjacent to the Pliler homestead, and Doris settled nearby after marrying Noel F. "Buddy" Graves.

– Submitted by Mrs. Wiley Pliler

FRED MARSHALL PLILER & ANNIE D. REBECCA WILLIAMS

Fred Marshall Pliler (17 September 1902), son of early East Texas residents Robert Russell Pliler (9 September 1870) and Emma Virginia Harris (18 October 1883), grew up with his sister, Doris Henri Pliler, on the Pliler/Harris land in Gregg County, north of Longview — some of the same land settled by his great grandparents, John Sweet Killingsworth and Emmaline Abney, who migrated to Texas in 1854 from Bibb County, Alabama.

Fred built his home on Judson Road, and he and Annie D. Williams married in that home 21 April 1932. A graduate of SFA in Nacogdoches before her marriage, Annie taught in the then county schools at Sabine and Danville. She taught all grades and even served as principal. After her marriage, she was involved in the community as charter member and president of the Longview Fine Arts Club, member of the Garden Club, The Longview Home Demonstration Club and President/Lifetime Member of Judson PTA. She was a teacher of Alpine Presbyterian Sunday school classes as well as Women's Circle groups and the Thursday Bible Club. Annie D. was a wonder-

Fred, Annie D. and Virginia Ann Pliler, 1946

ful hostess, and she enjoyed entertaining relatives and friends in their home.

Fred worked as a cotton ginner, farmer and an independent road builder before being elected to three consecutive terms as County Commissioner, Precinct 1 (1944-1951). He built two lakes on his farm and actively studied the latest techniques for agricultural land use. He served as Deacon at Alpine Presbyterian Church and was active in Kiwanis Club. With his easy-going manner, broad smile and desire to serve, Pliler was extremely well liked by all who knew him. During his years as County Commissioner, he was instrumental in the development of Gregg County Hospital (now Good Shepherd) and Gregg County Airport. Once, when officials complained that the large trees around the courthouse had no squirrels, Fred saw to it that an overflow of Shreveport court house squirrels were brought to Longview.

Pliler died unexpectedly while serving in office (6 February 1951). Fred Pliler Memorial Park, near the site of Summerfield Methodist Church on Tryon Road, was dedicated in his honor on 12 February 1951.

The Plilers had a daughter, Virginia Ann (15 January 1943), born in Gregg County. After Fred Pliler's death, Annie D. Pliler married (1953) widower Haskell Lee Mallory (14 September 1903) from Mineola. He was a Fireman for the T&P Railroad and had no children from his previous marriage. Haskell Mallory died in September 1971. Annie D. Pliler Mallory died at the age of 88 on 8 November 1995, and is buried alongside Fred Pliler in the Alpine Presbyterian Cemetery in Longview.

– Submitted by Virginia Pliler Boswell

RATLIFF

In 1920, Dewey Ratliff, born 24 June 1898, and his young wife, Ora Beatrice Martin Ratliff, born 4 July 1898, were scratching out a living in Wood County, Texas. Dewey's parents, Lorenza "Lon" Ratliff (born 6 February 1871) and Aris Deney McIntyre Ratliff (born 28 February 1883) were divorced. Lon and his youngest son, Oscar, were living in

Danville School, 5th grade class, 1931 – Miss Annie D. Williams, teacher.

Vernon Leroy Ratliff, 1947

Wood County. Aris and Ima Lee (Lon and Aris' youngest daughter) were living with daughter Gaynell and son-in-law, Garland Baremore, in northern Wichita County. Lon and Aris' oldest daughters, Bessie and Elnora Ratliff, had married.

Garland Baremore, at age 27 in 1920, was finding success in the oil fields and convinced his younger brothers-in-law that they could do the same. By 1930, Dewey and Oscar were both working oil leases in Freestone County.

As they entered the Depression years, like most families, they huddled together. Dewey and his growing family lived with his mother and two sisters and their families. His father, Lon, moved west to Fisher County, where his grandmother, Mary Schwalbe Ratliff, lived.

By the 1940s, the Ratliff brothers, Dewey and Oscar, had followed the oil field to Gregg County. Oscar and his mother, Aris, shared a residence in Gladewater, and Dewey and Ora, with their children, Vernon Leroy and Shirley Maudine, settled in Kilgore where Dewey began his tenure with Delta Drilling Company.

Dewey's son, Vernon, followed in his footsteps. After returning from the Philippines, where he served in the U.S. Army during World War II, Vernon signed on with Delta Drilling Company. With a regular paycheck in his pocket, he purchased a brand new 1947 Ford, and by the spring of 1948, he had found his bride, Emma Lee Martin. They had two sons, Vernon Alan and Gary Wayne.

Vernon's son, Alan, continued the oil field legacy, working for Amoco Production Company before founding his own oil and gas consulting firm. He named his firm Woodbine in remembrance of his East Texas roots. Alan married Jonita Franks in 1976, and they had two children, Benjamin Alan and Jordan Michael.

Vernon's younger son, Gary, graduated from North Texas State University and now teaches diesel technology at Kilgore College in Longview. He keeps alive another family tradition with his passion for classic cars.

Vernon and Emily Ratliff and Dewey and Ora Ratliff are buried at Kilgore Cemetery. Aris Ratliff died 23 March 1968, and is also buried there. Aris (a.k.a., Lorissa) Deney McIntyre was the daughter of Duncan and Martha Ann Porter McIntyre of Falls County, Texas.

Oscar lived to be 90 years old. He eventually moved to Wink in west Texas and is buried in Roby Cemetery. Dewey and Oscar's father, Lon, and their grandmother, Mary Schwalbe Ratliff, died at Longworth in Fisher County, Texas.

The Ratliff family traces their genealogy back to Jacob Anderson Ratliff, a Civil War veteran who was born in Alabama. He moved to Texas, and in 1868, he married Mary Schwalbe, daughter of German immigrants. Mary was born in Grimes County, Texas, in 1848.

– Submitted by Jo Ratliff

LEONARD PHOUTS RAY & MARY FRANCES STRONG RAY

Reverend Leonard Phouts Ray, born 17 July 1851, was the son of Andrew Cannon Ray and Mary Wilmoth Athon. He was born in Talbot County, Georgia, and came to Texas in 1870, having come up the Mississippi River from New Orleans by boat, to the Red River, and landed at the Jefferson, Texas, harbor. He settled in Upshur County, near Gilmer, to be close to relatives who had come to Texas from Georgia earlier. He married Mary Frances (Fannie) Strong in 1873 in Pritchett, Upshur County. Fannie was born to William Benjamin Strong and Martha Winn Johnson Strong in Troup County, Georgia, on 5 November 1850. They had eight children, two of whom died as young children and are buried at Enon Cemetery near Gilmer.

Leonard Phouts Ray and Mary Frances Strong Ray

Leonard was a preacher-farmer, who moved his family and bought land on Judson Road about 1892. He established the New Providence Missionary Baptist Church on Judson Road in 1897 (at the site of the present New Providence Cemetery by the Village Shopping Center). After a windstorm destroyed the church building, the congregation moved to the Judson community, but kept the cemetery. Reverend Ray preached in many Baptist churches in the East Texas area until his death on 27 August 1917.

Children born to them were William Andrew, born 1875; Mary (Mamie), born 1880; James F., born 1882; H. Grady, born 1890; Grace, born 1893; and Helen, born 1896.

Fannie Ray took great pride in the fact that she was educated at the Looney School in Gilmer, a prestigious private school for boys and girls before the days of public education. Her professor was Dr. Isaac Alexander, who later was the head of the Alexander Institute, a private school in Kilgore in the 1800s.

– Submitted by Helen M. Griffin

REED: Tennessee to Gregg and Rusk County

VIRGINIA ADELE REED is descended from the **REEDS** of Scotland, North Carolina and Tennessee.

CLAYTON CLAYBORNE REED, born 1699 in Scotland, married Eliza Jane Patterson in 1700 in Scotland. Their son, WILLIAM, SR., 1742, married Sarah Jane Patterson, born 1740, Tennessee. Their son, WILLIAM, JR., 1763, of North Carolina, married Judith Silver. They had James, 1787; Clayborn, 1789; William III, 1791; Robert, 28 October 1796; Andrew, 1799; and John N., 1805, in Barron Co., Kentucky.

ANDREW REED, born 1799, died 1866 in Shelbyville, Bedford Co., first married Betsy Lane, b. 1797, d. after 1819. Both buried Reed Cemetery, Flat Creek Community, Shelbyville, Bedford Co. They had Cynthia, 17 December 1817, married James M. Stewart, died 22 March 1904, buried Reed Cemetery; and Claybourne Reed (unknown information).

Andrew's second wife was Malinda Elizabeth Coats, born 1797, Sumner Co., died 1866, Shelbyville. They had Wilson Carol, born 8 March 1822, died 30 March 1904, in Texas; William Martin, born 12 January 1828, died 15 January 1905, buried Reed Cemetery, Tennessee; Daniel David, born 4 May 1831, died April 1878; Margaret Catherine, born 9 April 1834, married Abraham Empson Smith Hanes, and died 1900, Bedford Co., buried Reed Cemetery, Tennessee; (twin) Eliza, born 1837, died 1905, Shelbyville; (twin) Emily, born 1837, died Arlington, Texas; Malinda Evelyn, born 12 January 1841, married Henry R. Coats, born 25 January 1868.

ROBERT REED, 28 October 1796, Lincoln County, Kentucky, was a minister who married Elizabeth (unknown), died 1864, Shelbyville. They had William, 1817; John A., 1819; Alfred, 11 March 1822; Andrew Jackson, 1824; Daniel, 1824; Isaac, 1827; Malinda Lucinda, between 1815-1820; Joshua, 1832; Patsy, 1833; Mary Ann, 1835; James Madison, 1841; and Alcey Elizabeth, 1842.

ANDREW JACKSON REED, 1824, Flat Creek, Shelbyville, died 6 August 1887, Henderson, Rusk County, Texas, buried Reed Cemetery at Reed's Switch, Overton. His first wife, Sophia Ellen McNew, 1829-1830, Holland, died between 1894-1899, Van Zandt Co., buried in Cana Cemetery, Canton. They had Amanda, 1848; Manuel Thomas, 1850; Ellen, 1856; Josephine, 1872; Samuel Dill, 1859; Andrew Jackson, Jr., 1860; Isaac Kansas, 1862; General Gano, 1865; Solomon, 1868; and Bell,

Andrew Jackson Reed and Sophia McNew Reed

Sophia Ellen McNew Reed, wife of Andrew Jackson Reed, with son, Bell Reed, his wife Dora Agnes Turner Reed holding their daughter, Girtrude Annie May Reed, and child, Delphia Tarver (in center).

1873. Andrew Jackson's second wife was Sarah "Sallie" Priscilla Hall (Byers), buried in Enoch Cemetery.

SOLOMON REED, 27 July 1868, Rusk County, died 14 January 1921, and is buried in Gum Springs Cemetery, Harrison County, Texas. He first married Nancy Ann "Nannie" Walker, born 12 February 1870, Rusk County, died 28 March 1918, Longview, Gregg County, buried Hickory Grove Cemetery, Rusk County. They only had one child, Virginia Adele Reed, born 15 November 1885, Overton, Texas. Solomon married second, Mary M. Callihan after 1918. He and Mary are buried in Gum Springs Cemetery, Harrison County, Texas.

VIRGINIA ADELE REED, grandmother of Betty Cabbiness, was born 15 November 1885, and lived most of her life in Rusk and Gregg counties. She married William Arthur "Bill" Morton. They had eleven children. (See separate article "MORTON: From England, Mississippi, Tennessee, to Texas.") She died 5 April 1976, in a nursing home in Longview, Gregg Co., Texas, but is buried in Hickory Grove Cemetery in Rusk County.
– Submitted by Betty Cabbiness

KARL REEH

Karl August Reeh (pronounced Ray) immigrated from his birthplace of Kassel, Germany, to the U.S.A. in 1909 at age 24. His parents had moved to Kassel from their home country of nearby Austria. His port of entrance was Galveston. He became employed as a machinist with the Texas & Pacific Railroad in Houston.

Karl married Mamie Frances Polk from the community of Genoa, which is outside Texarkana, Arkansas, in 1916. Their first child, Kathlyn, was born in Houston in 1917. T&P transferred Karl to Palestine, and it was there that their second daughter, Dorothy, was born in 1919. He was transferred to Longview in 1921, where the family lived on Pliler Street. It was there that their first son, Douglas, was born in 1922. Another daughter, Frances, was born there in 1924, and another son, Thomas, in 1929.

T&P went on strike nationwide around 1927, and it was then that Karl opened his first grocery store on Center Street, which he operated for about a year before going to work for the G.A. Kelly Plow Company and selling his store to the Plilers. The family moved closer to town in 1931 to 701 South Green Street, and it was there that their last offspring, Karl Joseph, was born on America's birthday, 4 July 1934.

During World War II, Karl served his country as a tool and die maker at North American Aviation in Grand Prairie, after which he returned to Kelly's in 1945. During the Korean Conflict, he was employed at Tempco, also in Grand Prairie, until the time of his death at age 69 in 1955. Although living in Grand Prairie during these periods, the family maintained their home in Longview since they knew these periods away were temporary and they would be returning.

In addition to Karl, Mamie and their three daughters are also now deceased. Kathlyn died at age nine of pneumonia.

Karl and Mamie Reeh

Dorothy graduated from L.H.S. in 1936, and was married to the late Bill Bales of Gladewater. They had three sons, Gary, Richard and Tom, all of whom graduated from Longview High School.

Douglas, "Floogie" his nickname at L.H.S., was well-known for his avid jitterbugging. He served in the army during World War II in North Africa and Italy. After returning from the military, he took journalism at Kilgore College, and graduated from radio school in Dallas in 1950. He spent some thirty years in radio and television broadcasting before entering the newspaper field. He and his wife, Florence, presently own and publish the *Timpson & Tenaha News*. They have five children, seven grandchildren, and four great grandchildren. Three of their children, Kathy, Daryl and Galen were born in Gregg County.

Frances graduated from L.H.S. in 1942, and was married to the late Douglas Davenport, who was from the Houston area. They had two children, June and Karl Douglas. After residing in several places around Houston, they finally settled down in Columbus.

Thomas (T. Reeh) graduated from L.H.S. in 1946, attended Kilgore College 1946-48, and graduated from the University of North Texas in 1952 with a B.A. in speech and English. "T," like "Floogie" before him, spent many hours on the

dance floor during his dating days. He was a pioneer in weight lifting in Longview. He founded a Kilgore College weight lifting team in 1948 and place third in the 181-pound division in the Southwestern AAU Championship. At North Texas in 1952, he placed second in the same event. He was an exhibition roller-skater and performed at stage shows, beauty pageants, etc. Thomas also spent some thirty years in radio and television broadcasting at stations in Gladewater, Marshall, Tyler and Shreveport, before entering the real estate business in Shreveport. After leaving the Gregg County area, he became known as Tom Reeh. He and his wife, Rebecca, own and manage Reeh Plaza and Reeh Rentals in Shreveport, where they have resided since 1954. They have been involved in many religious and civic activities through the years. Tom has been president of the Sunset Acres Homeowners and Renters Association (SAHARA) for several years. Tom and Rebecca have three daughters and seven grandchildren.

Karl Joseph (Tony) graduated from L.H.S. in 1952. He attended Kilgore College and graduated from Adams State College, Alamosa, Colorado, in 1956. He spent one year in the army in New York City and two years in Germany 1957-60. He received his Master's Degree in Library Science from the University of California in 1963, and then spent three years in the Peace Corps in Malaysia 1963-66. He worked in libraries in New Haven, Colorado, and San Mateo, California, from 1966-74. He presently lives in Berkeley, California, where he became interested in landscaping and has owned Rakes' Progress Landscaping with his partner since 1979. He is presently Commissioner of the City of Berkeley Disaster Council and President of the LeConte Neighborhood Association.

Although none of Karl Reeh's sons or daughters still reside in Longview, Douglas, Thomas, and the Bales boys, live close by and still maintain close relationships with many high school classmates. They always look forward to the Longview High School class reunions and cherish many fond memories from the "old stompin' grounds."
– Submitted by Thomas Reeh

REYNOLDS: A Family Remembered

In 1927, my grandparents, Hez Bussie and Daisy Darnell Reynolds, moved to a large farm they purchased in Gregg County. The farm is located three miles south of Gladewater on old Highway 135.

In 1931, Lady Luck presented them with a very big suprise when oil was discovered on their farm. Hez and Daisy had been hit hard by the Depression, like everyone else in our country, and times had been hard. The oil discovery was such a blessing and they were able to build a new home, buy a new car or two and other things they had only dreamed about before their "Windfall."

Hez and Daisy had eight children: Irene, Forrest, Bill, Lenord, Dock, Harmon, Elizabeth and Hughleen. Through the years they were blessed with twenty-one grandchildren, fifty-three great grandchildren and numerous great great grandchildren. As you can see, there will always be plenty of Reynolds descendents in Gregg County.

50th wedding anniversary of Hez and Daisy Reynolds. (l.-r.) Back: Mutt Amos (gr.s-i-l) holding son Dennis; Jack Mitchell (s-i-l); Lenard "Dick" (son); Z.D. "Dock" (son); C.C. "Bill" (son); Harmon (son); J. Forrest (son); Jackie "J.D.") (son). Middle: Faye Reynolds holding Randy; Earnestine Amos (gr.dr.); Betty Reynolds (gr.dr); Hughleen Reynolds Milsap (dr.); Leola Reynolds (gr.d-i-l) holding David; Marlene Mitchell (gr.dr.); Nova Reynolds (d-i-l); Irene Reynolds Mitchell (dr.); Barbara English (gr.dr.); Winnie Reynolds (dil); Elizabeth Reynolds English (dr.); Barbara Ray (gr.dr.); Marlene Reynolds (gr.dr.), age 16; L.E. "Bucky" Reynolds (gr.son). Front: Marvin Ray Reynolds (gr.son); H.B. Reynolds (grandfather); Daisy Dee Darnell Reynolds (grandmother) holding Sharon Milsap (gr.dr.); James Forrest "Butch" Reynolds (gr.son); Freddie Mac Reynolds (gr.son); Micheal D. Reynolds (gr.son); Bill Calvin Reynolds (gr.son).

Marlene's family, the Bill Reynolds family, and several aunts, uncles and cousins lived in the area near the Grandparents' home, they have lots of memories to cherish for the rest of their days. Marlene remembers the Easter egg hunts in the pasture and the woods, and the big fish fries where the fish that some of her uncles caught in the river were cooked. Those huge fish were enough to feed everyone in the community.

Now, Grandpa Hez was quite a storyteller. He would tell the grandchildren some really scary ghost stories about the "Haints," as he called them, that haunted the big house on his parents' farm in the Glenwood area where he grew up.

One annual holiday gathering, the Fourth of July celebrations that Marlene Frantz always remembers so vividly, was the all-day picnic, swimming in the river, games, etc. All of her kinfolks, friends and neighbors joined them at the same place on the Sabine river for this celebration. It was like a park, their own private place – not really, but it was great. She will never forget what fun they had; it was special. In those days, so long ago, there wasn't a lot of entertainment, so the family made the most of what they had.

Another holiday gathering that the family looked forward to was the Christmas party that Grandma and Grandpa Reynolds hosted for all of their children and grandchildren on Christmas Eve.

There are so many other precious memories, too numerous to write about in this short story, but it will give you readers an idea of how great it was to grow up in a large, loving family.

Many of the Reynolds family members have passed on, but there are still some left. They are now senior citizens, but still a close knit family with lots of great grandchildren to carry on in Gregg County and lots of other places in the world.

The picture of Hez and Daisy Reynolds' family was taken at their house (County Club Road and Highway 135) on their 50th wedding anniversary, 4 December 1947. They were married in 1897.

– Submitted by Marlene Reynolds Frantz

RICHARDS

David Richards, an Englishman, was born in 1768, and died 19 February 1847. His wife, Hanna Fletcher, was born in 1785, and died 13 January 1873. They had a son, David Marr Richards (born 12 January 1836, died 17 January 1907), who ran away from home in Virginia at the age of 14 and settled in Arkansas.

David Marr Richards married Louisa Christina Durr, who was born in Germany 23 June 1841 (died 11 November 1919). They moved from Saline or Sebastian County, Arkansas, to the backwoods community of Doe Branch, Arkansas (name later changed to Ferndale), 20 miles west of Little Rock, Arkansas. David Marr and Louisa Christina had nine children: William (Billy), Mary, John, Noah, Sam, Holland, Louisa Christina, Jacob (Jake), and Rachel.

Noah (born 11 May1870, died 2 February 1958) grew up in this backwoods community. He received a grade school education at Doe Branch, and later attended the university in Little Rock, where he obtained first and second grade teaching certificates. He taught in local area schools for seven or eight years and was a farmer. When he was in his mid-20s, the Klondike gold rush was in full bloom. He decided to go seek his fortune. So, with his savings carefully concealed in the bottom of his shoes, he started out for Alaska getting as far as Port Townsend, Washington, before hearing discouraging news and returning home.

Noah married Mary Hollan Mitchell Stephens (born 28 July 1870, died 8 April 1963). They had four children: Golda, Otho Elba, Ulan G. and Zula Marie. Mary Hollan had a daughter, Neylon Stephens, by a previous marriage. They moved to Longview in the fall of 1918, when Otho (born 5 April 1907, died 11 October 2000) was 11 years old. In April 1918, they rented land north west of White Oak and share-cropped for three years. The children attended the White Oak School. In 1921, they bought a 165- acre farm northwest of White Oak. In the fall of 1924, they traded the farm for a house in Longview. In 1934, they moved to a farm in Horatio, Arkansas, where they lived until September 1939. They moved back to Texas to the Judson area where they ran a chicken farm. After several years, they moved

back to Longview and lived on North 7th Street. Noah was a strong conservative Methodist and attended the Wesley Methodist Church and, later, the Methodist church on North 4th Street.

William Augustus (Gus) Mitchell (Otho's maternal uncle), helped Otho get a job on the Santa Fe Railroad. Otho went to work for the Santa Fe Railroad on 1 April 1926, and became a telegraph operator. He moved away from Longview for several years. In 1931, he moved back to Longview and worked as a telegraph operator for the Santa Fe in Longview for the next 20 years.

In 1932, he met Mavis Lucille Pumphrey (born 5 January 1915) at the First Baptist Church, Longview. They were married on 15 June 1933, in Bauxite, Arkansas. Lucille was from Pratsville, Arkansas, a small community west of Sheridan, Arkansas. Lucille worked for Elliott & Waldon, an abstract company in Longview, typing oil records. They lived in several apartments in Longview before buying a house at 605 Buchanan Avenue, where they lived until they left Longview in 1950. They were faithful members of the First Baptist Church, Longview.

They had two children, David Eugene (born 9 February 1940) and Ralph Wayne (born 8 January 1944). David and Ralph attended South Ward Elementary School. The family moved to San Augustine in December of 1950. Otho was the Santa Fe station agent there. Otho became a Deacon of the First Baptist Church, and he and Lucille started a church library. David was Valedictorian of his high school graduating class.

In 1958, they moved to Carthage, Texas. Otho was station agent for the Santa Fe in Carthage until he retired in July 1972. Otho and Lucille started a church library in the Central Baptist Church in Carthage. Otho was a deacon of Central Baptist Church.

David graduated from Baylor University with B.B.A. in Accounting. He worked as a National Bank Examiner for the Office of the Comptroller of the Currency, U.S. Treasury Department, for eight years. He was a loan officer for several banks in the Houston area, including M Corp and Allied. He later went to work for the Office of Thrift Supervision, U.S. Treasury Department.

David was one of the Founding Elders of Cypress Bible Church, Houston. He married (24 April 1965) Carol Daniels (born 13 July 1941). Carol graduated from Texas A&M, Kingsville, in 1963 with a B.A. in Business. They have two

Otho and Lucille Richards 50th Wedding Anniversary. (l.-r.) Carol, Laura, David, Randy, Lucile, Otho, Patsy and Ralph

children, Randy (born 4 October 1968) and Laura (born 16 October 1970). Randy graduated from Colorado Christian University, Denver, Colorado, with a B.B.A. and M.B.A. in Management. Laura graduated from University of Texas, Dallas, and is a Certificated Public Accountant.

Ralph graduated from Stephen F. Austin University with a B.B.A. in Accounting. He worked as a National Bank Examiner for the Office of the Comptroller of the Currency (OCC). He spent two years in the U.S. Army before returning to work with the OCC. He married (16 July 1966) Patricia "Patsy" Arlee Bush (born 21 August 1946). Patsy graduated from Southwestern University, Georgetown, Texas with a B.S. in Education. While with the OCC, Ralph and Patsy lived in Tulsa, Dallas, Austin, Oklahoma City, Midland, Houston, San Antonio and Amarillo. After 30 years of federal service, Ralph retired. Patsy first taught at Cyprus Community Christian School, Houston. Later she taught science at Mark Twain Middle School, San Antonio, and at Sam Houston Middle School, Amarillo. In 1998, Ralph and Patsy moved back to Longview, where Ralph was born. Patsy teaches 8th grade science at Pine Tree Junior High, Longview.

– Submitted by Ralph W. Richards

D.L. RICHARDSON SR.

Douglas (Duggar) Lafayette Richardson was born 21 June 1902, in Gilmer, Texas, and died 14 February 1978, Spring Hill, Texas. His parents were Jefferson Davis Richardson, born 31 July 1861, Glenwood, Texas, and died 3 October 1928, East Mountain, Texas, and Sallie Elizabeth Amos Richardson, born 25 December 1860, Georgia, and died 8 July 1939, East Mountain. Douglas married Winnie Toy Faulk on 4 November 1922, Seven Pines, Texas. Winnie was born 28 November 1902, Big Sandy, Texas, and died 21 November 1985, Spring Hill, Texas.

Winnie's parents were Robert Edward Faulk, born 5 August 1874, Troy, Alabama, died 14 December 1959, Longview, and Mary Dell Sena Head Faulk, born 9 January 1877, Troy, Alabama, and died 24 July 1968, Longview.

D.L. and Winnie moved from Big Sandy to Longview in the late 1920s. They lived on Magrill Street. D.L. worked for Southwestern Electric Power Co., L.E Myers Co. and drove a bus for City Bus Co. in the 1930s. He started a business for himself, D.L. Richardson Electric Service, and operated from home, 1707 Alpine Road. Winnie was a full time mother and housewife.

The couple built a new home in Spring Hill in 1958, where they lived until retirement and they passed away. Both are buried at Lakeview Memorial Gardens in Longview. D.L. and Winnie were members of First Christian Church in Longview. The Upshur County Discovery oil well on 6 May 1931, was drilled on D.L.'s father's land at East Mountain

D.L. and Winnie's children were Sybil Loraine (Richardson) Stacha, born 4 September 1924, Big Sandy, died 27 April 2000, Longview. She married Joe Stacha, Jr. from Clifton, Texas, on 7 February 1947. Joe Stacha was born 15 April 1923, Clifton,

D.L. Richardson family, 1932

died 8 July 2003, Longview. Joe and Sybil had one child, Waynette Elain Stacha, born 27 April 1948, Longview. She is living in Houston. Sybil graduated from Longview High School in 1942.

Douglas Laverne Richardson Jr., born 12 March 1931, Longview, is currently living in Duncanville, Texas. Douglas and his first wife, Ada Louise Dunnavant, were married in 1950 and had three children: Bobby Gene Richardson, born 12 July 1951 (lives in Longview); Carol Diane (Richardson) Roberson, born 19 June 1954, in Gladewater and lives in Tyler; and Debra JoRene (Richardson) Mills, born 16 November 1956, in Gladewater and still lives in Gladewater. Douglas and Louise were divorced in 1968, and Louise passed away in 1972. She is buried in Grace Hill Cemetery in Longview. On 14 March 1969, Douglas married Norma Jean Bowlin of Gladewater. They live in Nacogdoches, Texas. Douglas and Norma adopted a daughter, Sunni Michelle Richardson, who was born on 22 August 1971. Douglas, Jr. graduated from Longview High School in 1950. Douglas, Jr. has lived in Longview, Gladewater, White Oak, Nacogdoches, Duncanville, Wichita Falls, and has been living back in Duncanville since 1986. He took early retirement from Darr Equipment Company in 1988, after 37 years service.

– Submitted by Douglas L. Richardson Jr., Duncanville, Texas

LOUIS & NELLIE HEIDTMEN RICHKIE

Louis Richkie, born in Austria on 25 December 1880, met Nellie Heidtman, born in Taylorsville, Kentucky, on 26 September 1875, in Sulphur Springs, Texas, in 1903. They married there on 2 April 1905, lived in Corsicana, Texas, sixteen months, moving to Longview, Texas, in the late summer of 1906. Their children are two sons and three daughters: Frank Henry Heidtmen, 1897-1945; Colonel Ralph Malcom Heidtman, 1899-1977; Mary Richkie Finley, 1906-1991; Sara Richkie Whitehurst, 1909-2003; and Rosa Richkie Lamb, 1911.

Louie and Nellie Richkie share the distinction of being the only custom tailors ever in Longview. The first tailoring firm was a small frame structure on Bank Alley; next was the entire second floor of a brick build-

ing on the east side of Fredonia Street. Here the firm had grown to employ twelve or more professional tailors. For 56 years Nellie worked side by side with her husband.

Nellie Richkie died on 16 April 1961, Louie Richkie on 4 May 1964. They are interred in Memory Park.

Their lasting contribution to Longview is best described in an editorial titled "Louie Richkie" which appeared in the *Longview Daily News* on 7 May 1964: "Louie Richkie exemplified the truism that where there is a will there is a way. Coming to America from 'his native Austria while he was a young man of age (20 years), he was guided by destiny to Longview... He was a man of ambition and desire; these attributes spurred him onward as he worked tirelessly in the tailor shop he opened to achieve the goal of which he had dreamed before coming to this country.

"Louie Richkie was a quiet, modest, unassuming man who 'had aspirations of becoming a useful citizen and a successful businessman even before reaching maturity. It was this desire which brought him to Longview in 1906 – it was the same inspiration that kept 'him active in his advanced years.

"To him work was essential to a useful life. He could have retired many years ago and enjoyed the fruits of his labors, but he was not constituted that way. It was through his personal efforts that he built a successful business and acquired considerable property. As he improved his financial status, he continually invested in Longview's real estate. He wanted to do his part in building the town that had been good to him, which he loved and appreciated with citizenship in the United States. He never faltered in his faith even during the dark days of depression or when other hard times befell the community. This, in his own way, 'hand and hand with Nellie, was 'his means of expressing gratitude.

"Louie and Nellie Richkie were 'highly respected people possessing an ever widening circle of friends in varying strata of society. They did not know the meaning of ostentation, being content to live honorably, honestly, and simply. They were good people – good to family, friends, temples of worship and to the community. Although not generally known, their benefactions were manifold."

Though they are departed, their memory lives on in the hearts of their family.

– Submitted by Gayle Whitehurst Hansen

(l.-r.) Herman Whitehurst, Sara Whitehurst, Nellie Richkie, David Lamb (child), Rosa Lamb, Mary Finley, Wayne Finley and Louis Richkie

ROBBINS

The Robbins family has been active in the community, serving in various capacities in the civic, religious, educational, social, fine arts and philanthropic enterprises in Longview and the surrounding area. They have been active members of Trinity Episcopal Church, Longview, Texas. John Cyrl Robbins was Senior Warden several times and received a lifetime award when the vestry elected him Senior Warden Emeritus. Mary Lee Donaghey Robbins worked endless volunteer hours through the Women of Trinity. Betty Lloyd, Charles H. Davis, John Clinton, Dorothy and George Kennedy all served on the vestry and Endowment Board of Trinity Church. Betty Lloyd was Senior Warden twice, and John Clinton was Senior Warden and was instrumental in the building of the new sanctuary which was completed in 1994.

Mr. and Mrs. George Kennedy Sr.

The Robbins family has been involved in educational endeavors through the Trinity School of Texas (an Episcopal college preparatory school which encompasses pre-kindergarten through twelfth grade), the University of Texas at Tyler as well as the University's Long-view Center, and the Longview Public Library. Mary Lee Robbins devoted countless volunteer hours in the genealogical part of the library, and the Robbins family gave the genealogy room in the new library in her honor.

Good Shepherd Medical Center has also been a field of interest for members of the Robbins family. John C. Robbins, Jr. served on the original Good Shepherd Hospital board when it was under the leadership of the Episcopal Church, and Robbins/Davis family members served on the boards of the Good Shepherd Medical Center, and the Good Shepherd Foundation. The family also supported the Heart of Gold Campaign to start the hospital's acclaimed heart center and has participated in the numerous projects of the Medical Center.

The Longview Museum of Fine Arts and the Longview Opera have had the support of the Robbins family, and Dorothy Kennedy has served on the Museum's board as well as its advisory board.

– Submitted by Dorothy Kennedy

JOHN CYRIL ROBBINS (1897-1978)

This pedigree will show that the Robbins had been lords of manors from Thomas Robins

Mr. and Mrs. John C. Robbins

of Matson Manor, who purchased it in 1526, down to John Robbins (b. 1832, d. 1906) who sold Battramsley in 1866, a period of 340 years.

The Robbins family history starts with Thomas Robyns (Bourchier) of Matson Manor (Randwick, Co. Gloucester, England (b. 1465, d. 1520). He was of the Bilston family. He was successful in trade. (married heiress of Bourchier family of Berkeley). In 1643, when Charles I seiged Gloucester, the Robyns family of Matson Manor stood by the King. In 1669, John Robins (son of Henry) was appointed by Charles II to Stewardship of Bristol. The Steward left Matson and all his money to daughter Mary (married Bishop of Bristol, 2) Bishop of Hereford). William Robins married Dorothy Bacon. William bought Matson, but lost everything in 1765. Thomas Robins (b. 1715, d. 1815), a lawyer of Crewkerne and William's nephew, had three sons. Two sons, John (born 1746) and Thomas (1749) made fortunes in India. Thomas married, in 1784, Ann, daughter of William Sandby of the well-known banking house in the Strand, in England. Thomas bought Pylewell Park near Lymington, Hants. He had four daughters and three sons, leaving them all considerable fortunes. The residue of his property went to General Thomas William Robbins, of Castle Malwood, who died without issue. His second son, John Robbins (b. 1788, d. 1883), besides the fortune left to him by his father, was left the manor of Battramsley of the New Forest by his kinsman Philip Ainslie. He had hunting rights in the New Forest. John Robbins died as the result of a carriage accident near Battramsley in 1883. His only child, John Robbins (1832-1906), was left an orphan at age 6; he sold Battramsley in 1866. John Robbins' son, the Rev. Dr. John Robbins of the Anglican Church, married Ann Dunbar Abbot from the shipping magnate family of the Dunbar lines in Scotland. Ann Dunbar Abbot was descended from the Kings of Scotland. They had four sons. The oldest, John George Clinton Robbins, Sr., called Clinton, (b. 1867, d. 1948) was born in London, England. He had two sisters, Mary and Georgia, and three brothers, each named John. He came to America at the age of 16 to visit with family friends in the Dakotas to learn ranching. He returned to England at age 18 to attend church and parties. Still wanting to go the U.S., his father arranged for him to return with a close friend's son named Gresley. They were to go into ranching in Laramie, Wyo-

ming, where they started one of the first dude ranches in the state. It was known as the Robbins-Gresley Dude Ranch on the Medicine Bow River. The partnership desolved after five years and he bought a farm near Dona Ana, New Mexico. He married, 1897, Neina Mead (1866-1985), an American with ancestry of English and Holland Dutch traced back to colonial times.

Neina was the daughter of William Ecker Mead (1839-1909) of St. Louis, Missouri (son of Edward Mead, 1806-1885), and Theresa Holton Hoy Mead (1839-1873, at Chilicothe, Missouri), who married 1856. William's sister was the mother of the cowboy artist Charles M. Russell. Neina lived with her Aunt Sue Brown in San Miguel, New Mexico, where Neina taught school. Neina's Holland Dutch ancestor named Wolfert Ecker built "Wolfert's Roost," 1690, which was later bought by Washington Irving who named it "Sunnyside." The Eckers of colonial times are buried in Sleepy Hollow Church Cemetery in New York. Clinton and Neina had two children, John Cyril Robbins (1897, Dona Ana Co., New Mexico–1978, Longview, Gregg Co., Texas), and Dorothy Mary Robbins, (1899-1984). Clinton and Neina moved their family to a new farm in Las Cruces, New Mexico, in 1902. In 1905, they bought a farm and moved to Santa Cruz, California, on Monterrey Bay. Clinton's bank in San Francisco was wiped out with the earthquake and fire. He then bought a farm in Mesilla Park, New Mexico, and moved his family there.

Clinton started the Mesila Park Nurseries. He was county commissioner in Donna Anna Co. Clinton and Neina had a cabin in the mountains near Ruidoso where they would go in summer. In 1935, they moved to Longview, Texas.

John Cyril Robbins entered New Mexico A&M college in 1911 at the age of 14. He was a Second Lt. in World War I (1914-18), then returned to college and graduated with an agricultural degree, 1923. He was part owner of Buchanan (Ford) Motor Co. in Fabens, Texas (1920-30). He entered the oil business in 1930, forming the Southwest Drilling Co. He came to Longview in 1931. John Cyril married Mary Lee Donaghey, 1932, at St. James Episcopal Church, Mesilla Park, New Mexico. He started Robbins Petroleum Co. in Longivew. He was a member of Trinity Episcopal Church, Longview.

Mary Lee Donaghey was the daughter of John "Jno." Donaghey, banker (1864, Grayville, White Co., Illinois–1954, Trenton, Texas) and Emmie McDaniel Hendricks (1873, Easley, Pickens Co., South Carolina–1951, Trenton, Texas). Mary Lee graduated from the College of Industrial Arts, Denton, Texas, 1926, with a Bachelor of Science, and taught school in Farmersville, Texas. She moved to Fabens, Texas, in 1928 to teach there.

Mary Lee and John Robbins had three children. (1) Betty Joyce Robbins (1934, Longview, Texas) married in 1955, Longview, Texas, to Charles Henry Davis, (1930-1986), son of Roy and Ruth (Curtis) Davis of Longview, Texas. They were the parents of two children, Charles Robbins Davis, Jr. (1956) and Elizabeth Joyce

Davis (1958). Charles married Pamela Smith Davis, 1978, and had three children, Charles Robbins Davis, Jr. (1982), Wesley Christine Davis (1984) and Mary Brook Davis (1989). Elizabeth married Jimmy Franz, 1998. Upon the death of Charles Henry Davis, Betty Robbins Davis married, 1992, Bob Motley Lloyd (1929-2001). Bob had two sons, Donald Parker Lloyd (1956) and Kelley Sidney Lloyd (1965), who are Betty's stepsons.

(2) John Clinton Robbins (1935, Long-view, Texas) married Beverly Ann McLemore, 1956. They were later divorced. They had four children: Rebecca Lynn Robbins (1957, Longview); twins, Lila Gail Robbins (1959-1991) and Mary Susan Robbins (1959, Longview); and Beverly Ann McLemore (1961, Longview). In 1976, John Clinton married, second, Janna Little Boren (1944, Madill, Oklahoma–1998, Longview, Texas). She had two children by a previous marriage, both born in Oklahoma: Carrie Christine Boren (1970) and Dan Little Boren (1973), who spent their formative years in Longview, Texas. Their father, David Boren, served as Governor of Oklahoma and United States Senator. Janna Robbins died in 1998, and is buried in Memory Park Cemetery, Longview. John Robbins was an oil operator and President of Robbins Petroleum Co. in Longview.

(3) Dorothy Mae Robbins (1937, Longview) married, 1956, George Ernest Kennedy, Jr. (1934, Nacogodoches, Texas), the son of George Ernest and Lucy (Haden) Kennedy, Sr. Their children are George Ernest Kennedy III (1959, Longview, Texas), who married Marilyn Adcock, 1983 (children: George Ernest Kennedy IV, 1985; Stacia Michelle Kennedy, 1987; and Derek Robbins Kennedy, 1990), and Neina Mead Kennedy (1962).

– Submitted by Betty Lloyd

ROBERTS

Myra Lynn Ray Roberts was born in Longview on 23 September 1910, to Jim and Alice Ray who were Longview pioneers. She had an uncle who saw the Dalton Brothers riding out of town on Judson Road after the bank robbery. Myra Lynn was valedictorian of Longview High School. She and her three sisters graduated from Mary-Hardin Baylor. Her brother, Frank Ray, graduated from Texas A&M.

Myra Lynn married Meredith Earl Roberts on 15 September 1935, after his graduation from the University of Texas Law School. Both were always involved in community work. She taught Latin as well as English at Longview High School. After retiring from teaching school, she was elected to the Longview School Board and served as its president. She was also active in Longview Study Club, Longview Symphony Board and Lawyers Wives Club.

Earl Roberts, Sr., was born in 1908 and grew up on a Texas farm in Waxahachie. The eldest son, Earl attended the Masonic Home of Fort Worth, received a B.A. from Trinity University and a law degree from the University of Texas. Some of his honors at Texas were Senate Clerk and President of the Texas Baptist Student Union.

In 1940, Earl was elected the youngest District Judge in Gregg County. Besides his commitment to the community, he and Myra Lynn were very active in First Baptist Church. Both taught Sunday school and Earl served as a deacon for many years as well as teaching the Businessman's Bible Class.

Earl and Myra Lynn had three children: Earl Jr., Claire Lynn and James Franklin (Jim). All three were born at Markham Hospital, spent many years on their Judson Road farm while attending Longview schools and all graduated from Baylor University.

Earl Jr. married Betty Hull and they had two boys, Murray and David. Earl graduated from the University of Texas Law School and went into private practice with his dad. He served on many boards as well as being elected as mayor of Longview. Earl and Betty have been blessed with four grandchildren: Laura Cate, twins Cameron and Wythe, and Jonas Roberts.

Claire Lynn taught school for many years at Longview ISD and is now retired. She is active at F'irst Baptist Church and involved in Opera Longview and Kappa Kappa Gamma. Her children, during her marriage to Jerry Strickland Harris, are Miriam Harris Jones, Melissa Harris McDonald and Houston Exl Harris. Claire's grandchildren are Alexis and Julia McDonald and Harris Jones.

Jim married Judy Inzer from Eastland, Texas, in 1963. Jim and Judy have two boys, James and Jason. They are the proud grandparents of two grandchildren, Caroline and Mary Margaret Roberts

– Submitted by Claire Roberts

GEORGE STANTON ROBERTS: "The Piano Man"

George Stanton Roberts was born in Vernon Parish, Louisiana, on 13 December 1917. He is the son of Mary Ella Koonce and W.B. Hughes. Mary Ella was the daughter of James Phillip Koonce and Lillie Zelika Burr Koonce. W.B. is the son of Wilmuth Octavia Conerly and George Washington Hughes. All of these people were born in Louisiana.

George began playing piano at age four; yet, he became extremely ill. His mother placed nickels on his eyes to keep them shut, in case he died. However, having great faith, his mother and grandmother prayed for God's healing. They also prayed that whatever talent God would bless young George with would be dedicated to Him throughout George's life. Later, at age seven, George was elected church pianist. After high school he went to Louisiana State Normal Teacher's College. George went to Civilian Conservation Corp in 1937. He played for gospel quartets, and he even played the piano for 70,000 people in the Shreveport Municipal Auditorium. In 1939, George received a four-year scholarship to play the piano for the Northwestern College's Dance Band. Having no time to practice the piano, though, he majored in business, typing 155 wpm, as well as shorthand, doing the same speed.

When World War II began, George enlisted in the Navy and was sent to New Orleans. Afterwards, he was sent to the Naval Armory at Indianapolis, Indiana, to learn to code. From this experience, he wrote a song called, "Code Happy" which the Navy Glee Club performed. George began attending Unity Methodist where members befriended military personnel, and he eventually became their pianist. During wartime, George met and married Jane Beebe on 12 February 1944, in San Diego, California. After being overseas, George arrived home for the birth of his first child, Ellen, born 23 March 1945, in Indianapolis. George was honorably discharged when the war was over in September 1945, and became the secretary and pianist for a church in Oakland, California.

Returning to Louisiana to finish his education, he composed many sacred songs, plus his "Janie Songs" in honor of his wife. On 7 July 1950, George's second child, Marbeth, was born, about the time he finished college as well as going to seminary in Ft. Worth. In July 1972, George came to Longview, playing the organ for the Trinity United Methodist Church, as well as the piano for churches, weddings, receptions, civic functions, gospel singings, Rotary clubs, Sunday school classes, Friday and Saturday nights at Cace's Seafood and Steakhouse, and even for traditional, humorous, womenless weddings. "Beautiful Longview," which George wrote, was made the official song by the Longview City Council. George has fulfilled his commitment to God, remembering that he is here because of the prayers of his family. He has enjoyed sharing his musical talent with others, even the good people of Gregg County, playing all of his music by memory. As George's two daughters say, "When daddy sits down to play, he paints a picture. The keyboard is the canvas, his fingers are the brushes, and the Holy Spirit provides the paint."

– Submitted by Jane Bebee Roberts

JANE BEEBE ROBERTS

Jane was born in Portsmouth, Scioto County, Ohio. Her biography is in the *1986 History of Scioto County*, pp. 173-175. She descends from Samuel Beebe, who was born in England in 1633, and arrived in New London, Connecticut, in 1650.

Her grandfather, Edwin, was born in Athens County, Ohio, in 1854. Later in life he decided to take his wife, Mary, and son, Waldo, to Scioto County in the 1900s.

Stan and Jane Roberts, 1982

Jane also descends from Isaac Bonser, whose father, Joseph, and grandfather, Detner, died in the Revolutionary War. Isaac Bonser walked from Northumberland County, Pennsylvania, in 1795, and claimed land in the then Northwest Territory, now known as Scioto County. Isaac walked back to Northumberland, got his wife, Abigail Burt, their four children, Joseph, Jane, Hannah and Samuel, plus four more families, and was the first to arrive in Scioto County by flatboat 10 August 1796. Isaac's son, Joseph, born in 1791, was taken prisoner at Detroit in the War of 1812. He married Rebecca Patton in 1820 and had four children, Jane, Rhoda, Jasper and Ellen.

Jane married Richard Goodrich, and their son, Benjamin Franklin, married Lucinda Johnson. Richard's daughter, Ida Mae, married Charles Clinton Wood, and Charles's daughter, Margaret, married Waldo Putnam Beebe. Waldo's daughter, Jane, was born on 28 April 1924.

Jane was a member of Trinity Methodist Church, singing in children's choirs; later, she moved to Long Run in 1936. She was put into the 7th grade the first year the junior high system began. She was in the Girl's Glee Club, mixed chorus, a library helper, and played the clarinet in the band and orchestra. Jane graduated in 1942 at Valley Rural High School in Lucasville, Ohio.

When she went to Indianapolis seeking work, she met her future husband, George Stanton Roberts, stationed at Naval Armory. George transferred to San Diego, California, where Jane and George were married, 12 February 1944.

Jane went to Indianapolis, awaiting her first child, Mary Ellen, who was born in March of 1945. George was stationed again in California, separating from the Navy in September of 1945. Jane and her family lived in Oakland, but George needed his piano degree, so he chose Louisiana College. Off to Ft. Worth, Texas, for further studies, he and Jane welcomed Joan Marbeth into the world in July of 1950.

Jane became interested in family history and began learning the process. Upon moving to Midland, Texas, Jane became a member of the Permian Basin Genealogical Society and was on the board and co-editor of the newsletter.

Jane was also elected president for the first two years of the newly-organized chapter of Phi Sigma Alpha, winning first place nationally in three out of five categories the first year. The second year she received the "Woman of the Year" award from the District Chapters of Phi Sigma Alpha. She also became a Charter Member of the Midland County Genealogical Society. Jane, Stan, Ellen and Marbeth sang as a family quartet.

Jane's biography is in the 1971 and 1972 editions of *Personalities of the South*. Moving to East Texas, she became a member of the Gregg County Genealogical Society, serving as secretary. She was a charter member of the Christian Writer's League of East Texas. She served on board as secretary, treasurer, vice-president, and president. She has been a member of the Scioto and Athens County Genealogical Society and the New England Historic Genealogical Society.

Jane has served for twenty-five years as the assistant librarian at the Longview Texas Family History Center.

She is a Membership Chairman of "Friends of the Library," which gave a book in her honor to the local genealogical library. Jane has enjoyed every moment in her quest of family history, plus the fellowship of those she meets along the way.

– Submitted by Stan Roberts

DOSS CLIFTON & LILLIAN (LILLY) EDITH JARRELL ROBERTSON

Doss Clifton Robertson was born 6 January 1891, in Louisiana. His parents were James Clifton and Louisa L. Jones Robertson. James Robertson was born 18 May 1849; his place of birth is unknown. Louisa Jones was born 17 October 1855, place of birth also unknown. Doss Clifton married Lillian Edith Jarrell on 21 October 1915 in Hornbeck, Louisiana. Lillian's parents were Simeon Barton Jarrell and Laura (Dolly) West. Simeon was born 21 October 1871, in Winnfield, Louisiana, and Laura was born in 1877, in Hornbeck, Louisiana.

Doss and Lillian Robertson

Doss and Lilly had four daughters: Theda Lestine, Mildred Christine, Lillian Jarrelline and Ethel Pauline.

Theda Lestine (21 May, 1917–14 July 1993) married Amos Jackson Titus. They had one son, Amos Jackson Jr. He died just a few hours after his birth.

Mildred Christene (25 December 1918–24 January 1972) married (1) James Oscar Garrison (22 December 1915–10 September 1984) on 31 December 1938. They had two children. Lillian Edith was born 13 September 1940, in Centralia, Illinois; Lillian married David Husband, 4 September 1959, in Longview, Texas. They had two children, David Amos (born 15 August 1960) and Connie Lestine (born 26 May 1962). Mildred Christene and James Oscar Garrison's second child was Lou Clifton, (3 May 1942–21 February 1977). Lou was born in Gladewater, Texas. He died in Houston, Texas, and is buried in Oakwood Cemetery in Jefferson, Texas. Lou Clifton married Carol Gregg in 1967 in Longview, Texas. They had one son, James Ray Garrison (12 November 1967) who presently lives in Texas.

Mildred married (2) Richard Kester Swimm on 19 December 1944. They had four children: Charlotte Christene (born 13 October 1945), Ruth Ann (born 3 December 1947), Rickye Dossene (born 18 September 1951) and Richard Dee (born 14 January 1957).

Lillian Jarrelline (22 June 1920–14 October 1984) was married to Otis Lee (Jack) Collins (20 January 1916). They had four sons: Robert Lee, (born 14 August 1938), Tommy Joe (born 16 October 1940, died 1993 in Jackson, Mississippi), Arnold Dale (born 20 July 1942) and Jackie Ray (11 born April 1944).

Ethel Pauline, (22 January 1926–29 June 1993) was married to Robert Zimmerman of Illinois. She had no children.

Doss worked as a conductor for the Kansas City and Southern railroad while they lived in Louisiana. In 1931, Doss came to Kilgore with his family to work in the oil fields. They lived in a tent when they first came to Texas, and later lived in the Shell Camp in Gladewater, Texas. During the 1950s, Lilly worked for the Standard Coffee Company driving a delivery van.

Doss was a great fisherman. He loved to go to Caddo Lake in northeast Texas. He and his son-in-law, Richard Swimm, would go up to Long's Camp on Caddo Lake on a Friday night and sleep in the car so they could be there and ready to fish at first light. Three days before he died, he and Richard went to Long's camp, neither of them knowing it would be his last fishing trip.

Doss Clifton Robertson died 2 August 1960, and Lillian Edith Jarrell Robertson died 17 November 1983. They are both buried in Lakeview Memorial Gardens, Longview, Texas.

– Submitted by Lillian Husband

JOHN RODDEN (1794-1865) & AMELIA CASTLEBERRY RODDEN (1805-1851)

John Rodden (1794-1865, born in Virginia) and his wife, the former Amelia Castleberry (1805-1851, born in South Carolina), were part of the early rush of migrants to the Republic of Texas during the late 1830s. A few years later, John and Amelia helped found the Pine Tree community in what is now Gregg County. Their generation had come from the original southern states with their parents to settle the Indian frontier in central Alabama between 1810 and 1820. For information on their relatives and descendants, see the articles in this book on James Templeton Echols, Robert Finis Echols, Eugene Osborne McWhorter and Eugene Rodden McWhorter.

Aaron Castleberry Rodden (1822-1898)

The residence of Aaron Castleberry and Nancy McClelland Rodden, at about 2127 Gilmer Road in Longview, shortly before it was demolished in 1977.

John and Amelia were married on 3 January 1822, in St. Clair County, Alabama, which had been organized just three years earlier from what was Creek Indian territory until 1814. He was 27 years old, and she was barely 17. Amelia was the last of seven children of Aaron Trice Castleberry (born 1780) and his first wife, whose maiden name was Anderson. Amelia's grandfather, Richard Castleberry, born in Germantown, Pennsylvania in 1740, served as an officer under Nathaniel Greene in Georgia during the Revolutionary War, later drawing land in Baldwin County, Georgia, and marrying a girl named Ann Trice. Richard's grandfather, in turn, was Hendrick Casselberg, a Mennonite who came to America shortly before 1692, probably from the Palatinate in western Germany.

John and Amelia Rodden's first child, Aaron Castleberry Rodden—later known as Acey—was born on 19 December 1822, in Shelby County, adjacent to the southwest of St. Clair County. Over the next 16 years (judging from John's record in the 1850 Upshur County census), at least five more children were born to them in Shelby County: Mary in 1827, Nancy Jane in 1831, Anna Eliza in 1833, Joseph in 1835, and John Howard in 1838.

In January 1839, with their growing family, John and Amelia joined a wave of pioneers that flowed from Shelby County, Alabama, to Shelby County in East Texas (organized in 1837). Both counties were named for Isaac Shelby, a patriot hero of the Revolutionary War battle of King's Mountain and first governor of Kentucky. In both counties, the first courthouse was located in a place called Shelbyville. Earlier members of that wave from Alabama included Amelia's father, Aaron Castleberry, and his second wife, the former Sarah Craven, who moved to Texas before its independence from Mexico. It was either Aaron or his son by the same name to whom the Republic of Texas issued Headright Certificate Number 508 on 19 June 1838, for 2/3 league and one labor of land (2,952 acres and 177 acres respectively), based on entering Texas in 1835. That certificate was later used to claim 2,303 acres in present Smith County and 827.34 acres in present Camp County. John Rodden, in turn, received a third-class headright certificate (Number 439) for 640 acres on 3 October 1843, which he later ap-

plied to claim 640 acres in Wood County. Meantime, in 1841 in Texas, Amelia had borne William Jasper Rodden, who was apparently the couple's seventh and last child.

John and Amelia Rodden's eldest child, Aaron Castleberry Rodden, arrived in Texas nearly a year after his parents, on his 27th birthday in December of 1839. As a bachelor, he was entitled to a third-class headright certificate for 320 acres (Number 440), which was issued in 1843 on the same date as his father's certificate and later applied to claim 320 acres in Wood County. Acey was probably living in Shelby County when he married a girl named Dorothy R. Holt. According to his Bible, Dorothy was born 12 January 1828, and died on 30 October 1845, at the age of 17.

John and Amelia Rodden finally came to the end of their pioneering travels in Upshur County, Texas, which was organized in 1846 and extended south to the Sabine River at that time. On 10 October 1847, they were named first among the 15 charter members of Pine Tree Cumberland Presbyterian Church. Next were listed James Templeton Echols and his wife Martha Cyrena, and then Ann Elizabeth Awalt, the wife of the pastor, Solomon Awalt. Also among the founders were Amelia's older brother Aaron Trice Castleberry Junior and his wife Elmira. John Rodden and James Templeton Echols—known as "Temp"—were the congregation's first elders.

Amelia Castleberry Rodden died four years later, in 1851. Until his death 14 years after hers at the age of 70, John Rodden did very well as a farmer in Upshur County, acquiring extensive land holdings. John and Amelia Castleberry Rodden were buried at White Cemetery.

Since John's 24-year-old son Aaron Castleberry Rodden was not listed among the founding members of the Pine Tree church in 1847, he was probably still back in Shelby County at that time. It was evidently there that the young widower married Nancy McClelland (1829-1872, born in South Carolina) on 11 January 1848. He was 25 years old, and she was 18. By 1850, according to the census, they were living in Upshur County. On 11 April 1851, their first child was born: Amelia Ann Rodden, known as Millie. (She married Robert Finis "Bob" Echols, son of Temp Echols, and died in 1895.)

By this time, Acey and Nancy Rodden were living in the cabin where they would reside for the rest of their lives. Enlarged and improved through the years, it stood until 1977, a couple hundred feet northwest of the intersection of Gilmer Road and Toler Road. When the house was demolished by a real estate developer who left the site vacant behind commercial construc-

tion at 2127 Gilmer Road in Longview, it was the oldest building in Longview. At first, the land belonged to Acey's father, John Rodden. But on 30 January 1854, John gave Acey a 240-acre tract that included the house.

Seven more children were born to Acey and Nancy Rodden: William M. (1852-1897, married Stevanna Matlock), Mary Jane (1854-1946, known as Molly, who married Luther Houston, a first cousin of her brother-in-law Bob Echols), John David (1857-1860), James Howard (1859-1884), Aaron Jasper (1861-1938, married Lucy Henderson), Nancy Ella (1867-1888, known as Ella, married Fred Heffner) and Newton Wood (1870-1946, married Leona Walker).

When the War Between the States began in the spring of 1861, Acey Rodden was 38 years old. Despite his relatively advanced age, he enlisted as a private, serving in Company D of the 28th dismounted Texas cavalry, stationed in Marshall. On 6 July 1865, he was paroled by the Northern occupation forces and permitted to return home. While Acey was away during the war, his wife managed the family's farm very capably. The workers called her "Big Nancy."

When Nancy died in 1872 at the age of 42, she left four children at home for Acey to finish rearing; little Newt was not quite two years old. Acey continued to prosper in farming on land acquired from his father and others, so that he was able to give each of his children a substantial farm.

Acey Rodden was a master Mason of the Tusculum Lodge Number 86 of Pine Tree, which was chartered in January 1852. His children and grandchildren remembered him as a kind and gentle man who was an able mechanic and musician as well as a farmer. One of his projects was construction of a pipe organ for his home, with pipes made of papier-mâché. Another was a treadmill powered by a dog for operating a butter churn. According to a family story, one time while Acey was away, Nancy sold a wagon-load of his accumulated hardware to an itinerant scrap hauler. On his way home, Acey encountered the junkman, admired his load of useful parts, and bought it back without recognizing his own property.

When he died in 1898 at the age of 75, Aaron Castleberry Rodden was buried next to his wife Nancy in White Cemetery, near the graves of his parents. (Copyright 2004 by E.W. McWhorter)
— Submitted by David W. McWhorter

ROSSON

William Henry Harrison Rosson was born in Maury County, Tennessee, in 1817. He married Mary Elizabeth Scott, the daughter of James B. and Mary (Patton) Scott, in October 1839.

William Henry Harrison Rosson arrived in Texas in 1846, settling in Red River County. In 1848, he and Mary Elizabeth moved to Danville in what was then Rusk County. He purchased some 400 acres of farmland. Rosson was named Justice of the Peace and given the title "Squire." He sat at court, officiated as a minister and worked as a farmer.

On the 1850 Rusk County Census, William and Mary Elizabeth list five children: James

Madison, Thomas Jefferson, Rebecca Jane, Mary Elizabeth and Joseph Barkley.

In the late 1850s, Thomas Jefferson "Jeff" built the first cotton gin in the Danville area. It was a hand-fed machine powered by two mules. It was the first industry in Danville.

Jeff's days with the cotton gin were limited. When war broke out in 1861, both Jeff and James joined the Texas 10th Cavalry. Jeff was wounded four times during the war, once at the battle of Murfreesboro. He carried one bullet in his leg the rest of his life. Jeff was once left on an advanced picket post while his command was retreating during Sherman's march through Georgia. After several hours of solitary duty, he was told to retreat, also. Upon returning to headquarters, his Captain said, "Well, Jeff, you are the only Rebel in captivity that held Sherman's whole Army in check for four hours."

Upon returning from the war, Jeff and James bought their father's farm of about 1,000 acres. William Rosson bought a farm in Smith County and later moved to Starville.

Jeff married Ellen Elmira Hale on 26 December 1866. They had ten children: Dora married Michael Hamilton Graybill; Mattie Ellen married William Anderson; Henry H. married Louises Bryant; William Gregg married Vick Wilson; Thomas Percy died at the age of 21; John Hartwell married Della Parpal; Annie Virginia married J.F. Holht; Leila Nancy married Henry T. Booth; Della Tigner died at the age of three; and another child died in infancy.

Dora and Michael H. Graybill had seven children: Mary Ellen, who married Edwin Vernon Temple; John Frank; Annie, who married Thomas H. Pennick; Michael Hal; Lucy Virginia Juanita; Louise Abnott; and a child who died in infancy.

Jeff Rosson, or Uncle Jeff as he was know to almost every person in Gregg County, died at the age of 86 in 1928. It was a favorite joke among his friends to ask Mr. Rosson where he was during the great raid known as Sherman's March. He always answered, "Oh, where was I during that time? Why I was just in front of Sherman."
– Submitted by Susan Green

JOHN S. ROTHWELL & LILLIE K. SMITH

John Samuel Rothwell, born in 1848, and Lillie K. Smith, born in 1866, (both in Albemarle County, Virginia) were married at her home in Albemarle. They moved to Loneview after their marriage in 1891. The marriage certificate lists his occupation as farmer.

Their home was at 106 Teague Street. Their children attended the school of Miss Sally Teague. A receipt in the family Bible shows tuition for one semester for their daughter, Ruby, was $5.00.

John and Lillie were active in their church and community. *Times Clarion* newspaper articles say that "Ice Cream Socials" were given at their residence in May and July 1906 for the Ladies Aid Society. John's "Woodmen of the World" cemetery monument indicates that he was a member of that fraternal organization.

John Samuel was the son of John R. Rothwell and Sonora Anne White of Albemarle County. His grandfather, John P., served in the 7th Virginia Regiment from 29 August 1814, to 24 February 1815, in the War of 1812. Claiborne, his great grandfather, was born in 1740 and immigrated to the United States from England at an early age. He enlisted in the Virginia Volunteers in 1763, and received a land grant in 1791 for patriotic service during the Revolutionary War.

Lillie K. Smith was the daughter of Robert R. Smith and Eliza F. (Parrott) Smith of Albemarle County, Virginia. Her mother, Eliza Parrott, was the granddaughter of Sheriff William Parrott (1754-1855). William fought in the Revolutionary War and later served for many years as a court justice of Orange County, Virginia. He eventually became the high sheriff of Orange County and, later, became the senior court justice and first sheriff of Green County, Virginia.

Lillie's obituary says that she "was a member of several lodges and a faithful member of the Christian church and was one of the most popular ladies in all circles and dearly loved by all who knew her." The funeral took place at their home on Teague Street and was attended by "a great concourse of mourning friends."

John and Lillie had five children: Ruby Ann, Lucy Mae, Randolph, Alma and John William. (See "John W. Rothwell & Mary Susan Freeman.")

John passed away on 2 September 1918, and Lillie's death followed on 25 July 1920. Both John S. and Lillie are buried in Grace Hill Cemetery in Longview.
– Submitted by Tina Denison

JOHN W. ROTHWELL & MARY SUSAN FREEMAN

John William (Bill) Rothwell and Mary Susan (Sue) Freeman were married on 1 January 1925, in Longview.

Bill was born in Longview on 1 February 1898, to John Samuel Rothwell and Lillie K. Smith Rothwell. (See "John S. Rothwell & Lillian K. Smith.") He served in the Navy during World War I and, according to letters written to his mother during this time, was stationed in both France and the United States Naval Base in Cardiff, Wales.

Sue was born 12 April 1908, in Pirtle, Texas. Her parents were Robert H. Freeman and Isa Dora Christian Freeman. (See "Robert H. Freeman & Isa Dora Christian.") Sue was an active homemaker, mother and member of the Ladies Railroad Auxiliary. She enjoyed many handicrafts including painting, knitting, crocheting and sewing.

Bill and Sue lived in Longview until 1929 where Bill worked for the Texas and Pacific Railroad. They moved to Mineola in 1929 when the terminal was moved to Mineola. Bill worked for the railroad until he lost a leg in a railway accident in 1945.

They then returned to Longview to operate a drug store in the Greggton area and lived in Longview the remainder of their lives. Eventually, Bill was able to demonstrate his ability

to function on an artificial leg and he resumed his work for the T&P Railroad as a passenger conductor until his death on 2 October 1956.

They were the parents of one daughter, Billie Sue Rothwell (see "Dr. A.B. Garvey & Billie Sue Rothwell"), born 8 August 1926, in Longview.

After Bill's death, Sue lived with her daughter, Billie Sue, and three granddaughters until her death in May 1977. Bill and Sue are buried in Memory Park, Longview.
– Submitted by Susan Evans

GLEN PAXTON RUFF

Glen Paxton Ruff was born on 22 July 1905, in Ninnekah, near Chickasha, in the Oklahoma Territory only two years before Oklahoma became the forty-sixth state of the United States. He attended Oklahoma State University. His father, Harvey Paxton Ruff (1872, Searcy County, Arkansas – 1942, Enid, Garfield County, Oklahoma), ran for State Representative, Enid District No. 1, on the Republican ticket, stating in his campaign ad, "I favor a Pay-As-You-Go System of State Government." His youngest son, Hudson Ruff, remembered that he was a delegate to the Republican Convention in Chicago. "Harv," as he was called, had moved from his birthplace in Searcy County, Arkansas, to Texas where he was the postmaster at Childress, Texas. He married on 31 December 1899, the last day of the nineteenth century, in Richmond, Fort Bend County, to Mary Laura Braswell (1883–1962), daughter of Randolph Braswell (1851, Rocky Mount, Nash County, North Carolina – 1926, San Antonio, Bexar County, Texas) and Laura Bell Smith (1853, Boone County, Missouri – 1950, San Antonio, Bexar County, Texas). Mary Braswell Ruff was an educated woman, receiving her master's of education from West Texas State College at Canyon, Texas, and working both as a home demonstration agent with the United States Department of Agriculture and as a schoolteacher.

William Riley Ruff and Paralee Robertson Ruff

The Ruffs descended from the South Carolina Ruffs, who emigrated from Germany and were living in Newberry County, South Carolina, at the time of the First Census of the United States in 1796. A researcher identifies Godsend Ruff (c. 1754–1824) as our subject's earliest known ancestor and cites three tracts of land surveyed and certified for Godsend Ruff in Craven County, South Carolina, in May 1772, and then on 25 May 1774. These three tracts were granted from King George II of Great Britain to Godsend Ruff. To qualify to receive a grant, the grantee had to clear three acres of the land per year for every 100 acres received. In 1783, Godsend Ruff and his wife, Elizabeth, sold two of these tracts. Land records continue, and in 1794 and 1797, Godsend Ruff was a juror in Newberry County (created from Craven County). No further records exist in South Carolina for Godsend, and by 1820 he had moved to Giles County, Tennessee, where he was listed on that census.

John Ruff (c. 1790–1841), son of Godsend and Elizabeth Ruff, and next in this line, married Elizabeth Goodnight from Kentucky, and by 1820 were also in Giles County, Tennessee, where their eleven children were born. Continuing the quest to move west, John and Elizabeth moved their family to Searcy County, Arkansas. Next in this line, Jonathan Wesley Ruff (1823, Giles County, Tennessee – 1862, Searcy County, Arkansas), fourth son of John and Elizabeth (Goodnight) Ruff, was probably about 16 when his family moved to Searcy County. He married on 22 August 1845 to Cynthia Ann Robertson (1828–1880), daughter of Vincent and Charlotte (Reddell) Robertson. Their eldest child, William Riley Ruff (1846, Searcy County, Arkansas – 1920, Grady County, Oklahoma), married Paralee Robertson (1849, Searcy County, Arkansas – 1924, Grady County, Oklahoma) in Searcy County, daughter of John P. and Mary Ann (Young) Robertson, and thought by their descendants to be Cherokee Indian. William Riley Ruff was the father of Harvey Paxton Ruff and grandfather of Glen Paxton Ruff.

Glen Ruff married on 20 March 1931, in Medford, Oklahoma, Edith Wilma Johnson (1922, Woodward County, Oklahoma–1991, Longview), daughter of Clarence Arthur Johnson (1884-1954) and Laura Evelyn Gaines (1879-1954). Glen, Wilma and daughter, Sue Ann, moved to Longview in 1935 from Coffeyville, Kansas. Twins Jon and Jere were born in Longview in 1935, and another daughter, Mary, was born there in 1946. Glen established his first business, the Central Finance Company in 1935, and in 1959 he formed Ruff Real Estate.

Glen and Wilma enjoyed entertaining family and friends in their Lake Cherokee home. They were members of First Christian Church where Wilma served many years on the Minister's Aid Committee.

In 1937, Glen Ruff was elected president of the Longview Junior Chamber of Commerce. (Previous presidents were Oscar B. Jones, 1933; Davis Glover, John Moore, 1934; S.G. Khoury, M.D., Roy I. Tennant, Jr., 1935; Bish Mathis, R.B. Williams, 1936; and Leslie E. Sigmund, James R. Curtis, 1937.) In 1938, Glen Ruff received the Distinguished Service Award.

He was instrumental in forming, in 1938, the Tom Harris Hunting Club, whose hunters went to the Texas hill country near Mason, Texas. Through the years a group of about 20 or so men became close, life-long friends as they hunted together.

On 22 March 1981, on the occasion of their Fiftieth Wedding Anniversary, Wilma and Glen Ruff were honored at a party by their children

and spouses: Sue Ann and Tom Cocke, Martha and Jere Ruff, Nancy and Jon Ruff, and Mary Laura Ruff. Glen Paxton Ruff died 11 April 1984, in Longview and is buried in Memory Park Cemetery, Longview, with his wife Wilma, mother Mary Braswell Ruff and grandson David Ruff Harrison.

– Submitted by Jon Ruff

RUTHVEN-JARRETT

Douglas John Ruthven, Sr. was born in Donna, Texas, in the Rio Grand Valley on 20 October 1900. His father, Edwin Mortimer Ruthven, was born 26 April 1862, in McMinnville, Tennessee. His mother, Dora A. Smith, was born 13 February 1867, in Smith Springs, Lee County, Texas. They owned the first mercantile store in the area.

Edwin and Dora had thirteen children: Edwin, Ernest, Stella Norton, Vernon, Julius, Buel Charles, Rosa, Julia, Edward, Joseph Leland, Dora Myrtle, Elwyn V. and Douglas.

Early Ruthven ancestors include three brothers who came to America from Scotland. There was a Ruthven Castle in Perth, Scotland. It is now called Huntingtower.

Douglas received an appointment to West Point. While living there he met Florence Jarrett (born 11 May 1899, in Bordentown, New Jersey). Florence was the daughter of Israel Jarrett (born 26 April 1866) and Anna Emmons Burns (born 31 October 1867, Freehold, New Jersey). Douglas and Florence were married in Trenton, New Jersey, on 12 July 1922.

Doug and Florence settled in Longview in 1935. He was a barnstormer and had his own red Waco Place. He taught people to fly and took them up for hops. He flew drill bits to West Texas for Hughes Tool and knew Howard Hughes. He knew Charles Lindbergh and helped get the airplane on the field the day Lindbergh took off for Paris. The Ruthven family has movies of this event. Doug, Jr. was a babe in his mother's arms at the take off. Doug, Sr. was good friends with Gen. Claire Chenault of the Flying Tigers, Eric Schillings, Tom Potter of Kilgore, Dr. E.L. Jones, and Judge Merritt Gibson and Fred Erisman. He became the Sanitation Engineer for Gregg County with an office in the courthouse.

Doug, Sr. was teaching a friend to fly when a wind shear flipped the airplane upside down. He and Roy Baker were killed instantly at Elders Field, Kilgore on 11 February 1940. He was a member of Masonic Lodge #404. His relative, Archiebald St. Claire Ruthven, was Second Grand Master of Texas in the Ruthven Lodge in Houston (1847–1856).

Florence remained in Longview. She raised the children and saw them receive their college educations. She had graduated from Rider College in New Jersey. She was employed by Harmon General Hospital, East Texas Chamber of Commerce and retired from Le Tourneau College in 1966.

Red Waco Cabin airplane, Odessa, Texas, Oil Field, 1938. Doug Ruthven, Frank Davis (Alice, Texas) and mechanic.

Florence and Doug had three children. Daughter Elizabeth Goettle (born 5 June 1923) is a retired biology teacher from Longview High School. She has four children.

Daughter Elaine Margaret (born 13 May 1929) was an elementary school teacher in Longview. She died 11 November 1953, with a defective heart.

Son Douglas John, Jr. (22 September 1926) was in the United States Navy in the South Pacific during World War II. He married Dorothy Crowley 15 March 1952. Dorothy was born 17 April 1930, in Cleburne, Texas. Doug, Jr. retired from Lone Star Steel in 1993 after thirty years. Doug and Dorothy have two children, Brian Lynn and Debbie F. King of Kilgore; both are college graduates and teachers. There are three great grandchildren: Katie Claire (born 17 September 1985), Carried Jane (born 14 April 1987) and Clint Douglas (born 7 December 1990).

Florence, Doug, Sr. and Elaine Margaret are buried in Memory Park, Longview. They were members of Trinity Episcopal Church for many years.

The name Ruthven is almost extinct – there are few left in the world.

– Submitted by Dorothy Ruthven

ALEXANDER BOGGS & REVA HARRISON RYAN

Alexander (Alex) Boggs Ryan was born in Lawrence County, Illinois, on 27 May 1901. Mr. Ryan later moved with his family to Vincennes, Indiana, where he graduated from high school. He attended the University of Illinois. Reva Merle Harrison Ryan was born in Wynnewood, Indian Territory, Oklahoma, on 19 August 1904.

Mr. and Mrs. Ryan both moved to Forth Worth, Texas, with their families in 1920. Mr. Ryan was employed in the oil field machine business. They married on 12 February 1927, in Fort Worth, Texas, and moved to Longview, Texas, in 1931. While he was employed by the Hercules Supply Co, he furnished a string of oil well tubing for the completion of Dad Joiner's Daisy Mae Bradford No. 2, the discovery well of the East Texas Oil Field. Mr. Ryan was an independent oil operator and a partner in Federal Machine and Supply Co. in Kilgore, Texas, which supplied the casing for the Crim No. 1 discovery well.

Alexander Boggs and Reva Harrison Ryan

Mr. and Mrs. Ryan were active in church, civic and social activities. For many years they were members of the First Methodist Church (First United Methodist Church). In the 1970s, they became members of Trinity Episcopal Church, home of the Ryan Memorial Organ named in honor of Mrs. and Mrs. Ryan and their son, Alexander Boggs Ryan, Jr.

Mr. Ryan was a member of the Masonic Lodge, a Paul Harris Fellow of the Longview Rotary Club, which he joined in 1937 and remained a member until his death. He was elected to the Board of Trustees of the Longview Independent School District in 1947 and served as president of the board for three years. He served as board member and President of the Pinecrest Country Club, and the President of the Round-Up Club Youth Center. In addition, he served as a district committeeman of the Boys Scouts of America. He supported the Civic Music Association, Good Shepherd Hospital, Trinity Day School (Trinity School of Texas), Longview Symphony Orchestra, Kilgore College, the United Way and numerous other charitable organizations.

Mrs. Ryan's primary philanthropic endeavors and recipients included her church, education, genealogy and music. She was a past president and charter member of the Charity League (Junior League of Longview); a charter member and past president of the Garden Study Club; a member of the Aaron Burleson Chapter, Daughters of the American Revolution, a member of Colonial Dames of America, and a member of the Sabine River Chapter Daughters of the American Colonists. She supported, in addition to the above charities, the Gregg Historical Foundation and the Longview Independent School District Foundation.

Mr. and Mrs. Ryan had two children, Alexander Boggs, Ryan, Jr. DMA, born 3 June 1928, in Fort Worth, Texas, and Linda Jane Ryan Butter, born 6 May 1937, in Longview, Texas. Dr. Ryan graduated from Longview High School in 1945 and attended Southern Methodist University. He graduated from the University of North Texas with a Bachelor's and Master's of Music Degrees. He received his Doctor of Musical Arts from the University of Michigan at Ann Arbor, Michigan, and lived and taught at the University of Western Michigan in Kalamazoo, Michigan, until his death in 1979. He was the Cathedral Organist at Christ the King Cathedral and performed concerts all over the United States.

Linda Ryan Butter graduated from Longview High School in 1954, and returned to Longview after graduation from the University of Texas at Austin in 1958. She was married to Stephen Robert Butter of Longview whose family, Leo Edison and Billie Potts Butter, were owners of East Texas Plumbing Supply Co. (later to become International Supply Company). Four children were born to Linda and Stephen Butter: Leo Ryan Butter, born 15 June 1959; Zane Ryan Butter, born 29 December 1962; Alexis Ryan Butter Combest, born 12 September 1968; and Stephen Robert Butter, Jr., born 24 June 1970. There are eight great grandchildren. Linda Butter resides in Longview and continues the family tradition of community service. Mr. Ryan died on 20 April 1985, and Mrs. Ryan died on 3 October 1999.

– Submitted by Linda Ryan Butter

PATRICK WASHINGTON SANDEFUR

Patrick Washington (P.W.) Sandefur was born in Ashdown, Arkansas, on 18 January 1855. He was the son of Patrick Jackson Sandefur and Mary Jane Mallow. They lived on a farm about 20 miles outside of Texarkana, Arkansas. He was the next to the oldest of eight children.

Mr. Sandefur went into the cotton business in Jefferson, Texas. In 1881, he met Miss Lela Frances Pegues, born 2 March 1860, in Danville, Texas. She was the daughter of Mr. and Mrs. P.A. Pegues. They married 13 October 1881, in Danville. They made their home on a farm in Arkansas until 1893. Then moving back near the little community of Danville, the family farmed for eight years before they moved to a farm three miles out of Gladewater. Two years later they moved to a farm near Judson and remained there for a year before moving to Earpville, Texas, in 1902. This city later changed its name to Longview. As it grew, there was a need for more housing and part of his farm became Sandefur subdivision with a street named for Mr. Sandefur.

P.W. and Lela were the parents of eight children: LuRye (or Lula) born 1885, married first to James Oliver Campbell, Sr. and second to Edward Jasper Kennedy; Gussie Pegues, born 1890, married to Lawrence Chaney; Mollie born 1897, married to Arthur Brisbane Busby; Chaytor Orion; Mary Louise, born 1903, married to A.C. Numsen; Lela Belle, born 1895, married to Joel Dickson Mitchell; Emma, born 1882; and Patrick Jackson, born 1892.

Lela Frances, P.W.'s wife, died 20 October 1935, in Longview, Texas. P.W. died 28 October 1957, also in Longview, Texas. During an interview with a Longview *News-Journal* reporter, he remembered, at the age of 10, welcoming his grandfather home from the Civil War. Two of his uncles died in the Mansfield battle in Louisiana. He regretted being too old to join the fighting forces during World War II. At 101 years of age, he was described as a sprightly little man, with a slim figure and bright blue eyes that fairly sparkled as he talked. He was known for wearing his black bow tie every day. At 102 years, he said the he had always wanted to live to 100. "Now that I am 102, I hope to be here for many years to come." He had a wonderful memory and enjoyed spending time in the parlor playing Pitch. He was known to say that he drank his beer, not because he liked it, but because it was good for him. Many a time, he crossed the highway near his home to get his beer. He also said he voted for the man, and not the party! He was a strong Democrat. He enjoyed his friends and felt sorry that today's businessman does not have enough time to devote to developing good and lasting friendships.

P.W. was a life long member of the First Presbyterian Church in Longview.

– Submitted by Carol Dunn

SATTERWHITE

Lawrence Bud "Lonnie" Satterwhite (born 5 July 1903, died 20 March 1991) was born in Hope, Arkansas. His marriage to Rosa Maud Hinkson (born 13 December1905, died 13 April 1974), an Oklahoman of native American bloodlines, produced five offspring. In 1932, during the Great Depression, they migrated to Gregg County where Lonnie, a carpenter by trade, rebuilt a house on Melton Street in Longview that became their family home.

The Satterwhites and their five children were active members of the First Baptist Church. The three daughters and two sons each graduated from Longview high School. The eldest daughter, Charline "Buddy" (born 6 July 1925, died 8 April 1985), married a gentleman who also carried the surname Satterwhite. Buddy and her husband, Joe, settled in rural Anderson County outside of Palestine. Each Thanksgiving the clan would gather for a feast of fine home-cooked food, "touch" football, and fellowship at the country home they had made with their five children: Jerry Linda, Charline "Sandy," Joseph Edward, Jr. "Chip," Lawrence Edward "Lonnie" and Luke Wayne.

The second eldest daughter, Katherine (21 December1926), married Roy Charles Ingram. This union produced three children, Charles Lawrence "Larry," Martha Lynn and Mary Ann. This branch of the family settled in the Dallas/Fort Worth area where "Kat" retired after a successful career in the real estate business.

Patrick Washington (P.W.) Sandefur at 93 years of age.

The Satterwhites, 2003. (l.-r.) Standing: James "Lefty" Fuller, Beckie Fuller, Kirby Wilson, Tawny Wilson, Bob Satterwhite, Bene Satterwhite, Nancy Morris, Gene Morris, Joanie Thornton, Gerald Thornton and Dempsey Thornton. Middle: Daryl Jones, Mandie Jones, Bill Satterwhite, Susan Satterwhite, Sybil Satterwhite, Rosalynn Morris and Schuyler Thornton. Front: Mann Fuller, Jesse Fuller and Wil Morris.

Geraldine "Jerry" Satterwhite (born 27 October 1928) met and married Charlie Joe Propes while they were students at Kilgore Junior College where Jerry was a Rangerette and Charlie starred on the football team. They raised their family of four children in Nederland, Texas. Their three sons are Michael David, Joe Pat and Timothy Lynn and their daughter is Tere Lee. After retirement, Jerry and Charlie returned to Gregg County to reside in the area of Kilgore and actively serve in First Baptist Church, Longview.

William Lynn "Bill" Satterwhite (born18 January 1930) was the only one of the five offspring to settle in Gregg County. In 1949, he married Sybil Ann Shelton (born 2 February 1932), a native of Longview (see "Shelton" entry). Bill and Sybil have five children all born at Markham Hospital.

Rebecca Ann "Beckie," (born 23 July 1950) married James Manuel "Lefty" Fuller (born 30 September 1930). They have three children: William Mann (born 21 August 1975), Amanda Ann "Mandie" (born 18 October 1978), married to Daryl Russell Jones; and Jesse James (born 21 March 1981).

The only son, Robert William "Bob" (born 24 November 1951), now of Austin, married Benette Meadows (born 13 March 1956) and has one daughter, Tawney Susan Kneese (born 5-May 1978), who with her husband Kirby Wilson, is expecting their first child in April 2004.

Nancy Lynn (born 13 March 1953) married Ghenie "Gene" Wilburn Morris III (14 September 1949) and has two children, Ghenie Wilburn "Wil" IV (born 20 August 1981) and Rosalynn Olivia (born 26 June 1984).

Joan Elizabeth "Joanie" (born 30 December 1954), now of Corpus Christi, married Gerald Edward Thornton, Jr. (born 22 November 1952) and has two children, Schuyler Satterwhite (born 9 September 1989) and Dempsey Joan (born 5 February 1993).

The youngest Satterwhite, Susan Elaine (born 15 July 1958) resides in Corpus Christi

where she provides unconditional love to various homeless four-legged creatures. The two elder daughters, Beckie and Nancy, both returned after college to live and raise their families in Longview and teach in the Longview Independent School District.

The youngest of Lonnie and Rosa's children, Lawrence Edward "Sonny" Satterwhite (born 22 September 1931), wed Rose Marie Bounds of Panola County. Their daughter, Melodise, was the youngest of the eighteen grandchildren. Sonny and his family settled outside of Conroe near Houston.

Lonnie passed away at the age of 87 of prostate cancer after a long, full life. At the age of 69, Rosa died of ovarian cancer, which also claimed the life of her mother, her sister and her daughter Charline. Charline's oldest daughter, Jerry Linda, died of breast cancer. Lonnie and Rosa's remains are interred in the Memory Park Cemetery on Highway 80 east of Longview. Lonnie tried to teach his children and his grandchildren to "get shed of" the negative things in their lives and to always "take care of" the things that needed to be taken care of. Together he and Rosa left a legacy of heart-felt, hand-holding love and persevering faith.

– Submitted by Nancy S. Morris

DICK & OMALEE SCHERER

Dick and Omalee Scherer were married in June 1931, in Primera, Texas. In 1933, Dick hitch-hiked to Longview for a job in the oil field. Upon arrival, he stayed with a family on Silver Falls Road near Pine Tree School.

He had been born in Chicago, Illinois, immigrated to Texas in 1926, and then to Gregg County in 1933. His first job was in a filling station, and then he was hired by the old Simms Co. In 1935, Tidal Oil bought the old Simms Co., and it became Tidewater Oil Co.

The family was moved to the "Big Woods" in 1935, just north of the Judson Grove School. Dick was a switcher. This meant that he turned the wells off and on so that they could flow into the "tank batteries." Aside from the former, he kept the wells and tank battery free of brush in order to keep down the risk of fire.

In early 1942, Dick was transferred

Dick and Omalee Scherer, 1942

to Burras, Louisiana. He had to go to work by car, tugboat and putt-putt boat. They did not like the place where they were, so when the first Battalion of Seabees was formed in New Orleans, Dick enlisted. Not only did he join up to defend his country, but to get his family out of south Louisiana.

After three months of basic training, he was sent overseas to the South Pacific. At that time, the Seabees were attached to the Marines. In 1943, he was captured by the Japanese and put on a very small atoll with his men. They were not penned up as other captives were because the atoll was so small there was no place to go.

One day, he found a small piece of metal. This he shaped into the form of a fishhook. He then braided strands of palm fronds for fishing line. Always a fisherman in Gregg County, he helped to feed his men something besides rice. The commandant found out how good he was and agreed to let him fish all he wanted if he (the commandant) got his choice of fish; the Seabees could have the rest. Others started fishing, and thus these Seabees fared better than most.

Upon his return from the war, he went back to work for Tidewater in Kilgore, where he continued to work until his retirement at age 65.

As said before, Dick and Omalee were consummate fishermen. When they had the chance to have a lot on Lake Cherokee in 1948, they paid their $500 and drew lot number SR-50. It was a pretty big lot. They built their little house and a boathouse; Omalee planted her garden and orchard. There were plans to retire there, but someone offered them too much money and they sold. The same thing happened a year or so later in the NP section of the lake.

Finally, in 1955, Omalee found a small lot on Lee's Creek and bought it. She would not let Dick sell it. After Dick's death in 1973, Omalee lived and fished there until her death in 1976.

– Submitted by R.L. Scherer

DUSHEE SHAW

It has been said of Dushee Shaw that he wore out two court houses before he started on his third. He served as Gregg County Clerk for 24 terms, or 48 years, before his death on 26 November 1945. Shaw was a third generation Texan, having been born near Longview (then Rusk County), Texas, on 18 July 1871. He was the second child and first son of Dr. Daniel and Esther Louise Wadsworth Shaw (born 15 June 1845, Randolph County, Alabama, and died 8 February1891, in Longview, Texas). Dush had one sister, Effie, born 1868, died 31 October 1938, and one brother, Daniel, Jr., born 20 June 1874, died 24 June 1907. Neither sibling married, and both are buried in Longview at Greenwood Cemetery.

Dushee's father, Dr. Daniel (Dan) Shaw, served the Confederacy as Regimental Surgeon, Co. B, 3rd Cavalry, was wounded and taken prisoner. He died, when Dushee was just 4 years old, in April 1875, and is buried in Greenwood Cemetery in Longview, beside his wife Esther Louise and other family members. His widow remarried on 23 December 1880, to D.D. Durham. The Durhams had one child, Lewis.

Dushee went to live with his uncle, Dr. Angus Gilchrist Shaw, in Harmony Hill near Tatum soon after his father's death. He spent his summers there, returning in the fall to attend Longview Schools. "He attended College in Longview in an old frame school which for many years, was considered an outstanding educational institution in East Texas." (*Longview Daily News*, by Syril A. Parker).

On 16 January 1896, he married Miss Ida Sparke Rule of Shreveport, member of a prominent Louisiana family. Her mother, Julia Sparke Rule, was the first newspaper lady in Louisiana and was chosen to drive the golden spike when the first railroad came into Shreveport. Ida Rule and Dushee had five children, all born in Longview. They were Julia Rule, born 22 November 1896, married Dr. B.H. Acker on 21 March 1917; Effie Kate, born 13 February 1898, married C.F. Peyton, 20 March 1922; Louise Durham, born 14 February 1900, married Bill N. Taylor, 23 December 1924; Angus Gilchrist, born 20 April 1902, married Sally Haynes, 24 October 1923; and Alice Pauline, born 8 March 1904, married M.P. Blacknall, 16 April 1927.

Mr. Shaw's paternal grandfather was also named Dushee Shaw. He and his wife, Effie Gilchrist Shaw (daughter of Angus and Margaret McKay Gilchrist), were members of prominent Scots families from the Lumber River section of North Carolina. The families emigrated from Campbelltown, Cantyre/Kantyre, Scotland.

Dushee's sister, Apes Shaw, married her first cousin, Hector McKay, and along with Dushee's and Apes' mother, Rebecca Bowie/Buie Shaw, moved their families to Haywood County, Tennessee, for a few years, where Hector McKay died. They moved to Harrison County, Texas, in 1845. The families settled on land bought when they arrived in Texas. Their plantations were several miles northwest of Elysian Fields on the Marshal Road. In 1949, Mr. Shaw was made first Master of the Masonic Lodge No. 65 and in January 1851, became the first elder of the Golden Rule Presbyterian Church whose first building was built on the Shaw plantation. Dushee (born 19 July 1792, Cumberland County, North Carolina, died 22 May 1863, Harrison County) and Effie Gilchrist Shaw (born 20 November 1801, Richmond County, North Carolina, died 6 June 1883, Harrison County, Texas) are buried in the Shaw -Mackay Cemetery near Elysian Fields. Nine of the ten children were born in North Carolina; Archibald was born in Tennessee: 1. Rebecca Shaw, born 1821, married Thomas (Tom) Stewart, her cousin; 2. Margaret McKay Shaw, born 17 January 1823, died 4 September 1867, Texas, married Col. Sterling B. Hendricks; 3. Dr. Angus Gilchrist Shaw, born 23 April 1824, married Lola Caroline Tatum, widow of Pilsir Miller; 4. Dushee Shaw, born 1827, married Margaret A. Langhorne; 5. Dr. Daniel Shaw, born 1828, married Esther Louise Wadsworth; 6. Agnes Shaw, born 28 October 1831, married Col. Sterling B. Hendricks, 10 January 1868, after her sister Margaret's death; 7. Mary Catherine Shaw, born

1835, married Dushee McKay, her first cousin; 8. Sarah Elizabeth Shaw, born 27 January 1836, died 15 August 1855, Harrison County, Texas; 9. Belle Shaw, born 28 March 1838, married William Gladney of Rusk County, Texas; and 10. Archibald Shaw, born 1841, and was killed in the Civil War

– Submitted by Ann Price Mackenzie

DUSHEE & IDA RULE SHAW

Dushee Shaw was born 16 July 1869, in Rusk County, Texas, near Easton on the west bank of the Sabine River. At that time, the place was called Camden, a relay station on the stage line between Marshall and Henderson. His father, Dr. Daniel W. Shaw, who interned in Bellevue Hospital in New York City, had moved from North Carolina to Texas prior to the Civil War. In 1861, Dr. Daniel Shaw enlisted as a surgeon in the 3rd Texas Calvary and later died in Longview in 1875.

Dush Shaw

Elected in 1898 to the office of county clerk in Gregg County, Dush, as he was called, was commonly known as the man who wore out the court house. He served as county clerk for almost 50 years. An editorial in *The Shreveport Journal* in 1940 stated, "When the great East Texas oil field was discovered a few years ago, Gregg County found it necessary to erect a handsome new building, and it begins to appear that Clerk Shaw will stay on the job until that too is outmoded."

On 16 January 1896, Dush married Ida Rule, born 8 July 1873, in Shreveport, Louisiana. She was the society editor of *The Longview*

Ida Rule Shaw

News-Journal for many years, following the tradition of her mother, Julia Sparke Rule, who was the society editor of *The Times* in Shreveport. At a later date one of Ida's daughters, Julia Acker, also was the society editor of the Longview paper, continuing the tradition for a third generation.

Dush died 26 November 1945, and Ida on 9 November 1943. They are buried in Greenwood Cemetery.

Another of Dush and Ida's daughters, Louise Durham, was born 14 February 1900, and married Bill Northcutt Taylor in Longview on 23 December 1924. They had three children: Gloria Wismar of Baytown, Texas; Nancy Kennedy of San Mateo, California; and Charles Shaw Taylor of Longview.

Louise died on 15 December 1992, and is buried in Memory Park along side her husband.

– Submitted by Charles S. Shaw

SHELTON

Charles Reed "Charley" Shelton, Sr. (born 23 April 1891, died 11 February 1949) was born and grew up in Cass County. After serving his country during World War I in France, Charley returned home to teach, farm and work for the civil service as a railroad postal clerk on the Santa Fe Railroad. It was while traveling the Longview/Beaumont route that he met and fell in love with the beautiful Sybil Olivia McGown (born 22 September 1905, died 5 April 1985), born to Jefferson Henderson and Mary Ella McGown in Hemphill. At the age of 16, Sybil was a graduate of the University of Texas in Austin and teaching in Pineland. She also taught at Campus Ward Elementary in Longview. Charley and Sybil married on 2 July 1923, and settled in Gregg County where, in 1931, they built a home at 409 Shelton Street in Longview.

Their first born child was a curly-headed baby girl who was given the name Mary Ellen (born 2 October 1926, died 28 August 1929). Her brief life came to an abrupt end when she died of a ruptured appendix before her third birthday. She left behind her grieving parents and younger brother, Charles Reed, Jr. (born 1 October 1928) who missed her terribly. On 2 February 1932, another daughter was born and named Sybil Ann. Charles Reed and Sybil Ann both graduated from Longview High School and are members of First Baptist Church.

Charles Reed settled in Longview and worked as an engineer for the Union Pacific Railroad. He married Martha Jeanne Whitehead (born 28 May 1931), and they have four children. Charles Thomas (born 23 January 1952) married Deborah O'Neal Ellsworth (born 13 July 1953) and they have two sons, Brandon Lee Ellsworth (born 7 August 1975) and Christopher Reed (born 6 November 1983). Martha Alice (born 14 January 1955) married Don Laster (born 11 September 1951) and has two sons, Bradford Roscoe (born 15 April 1977) and Dustin Thomas (born 29 November 1980). Leesa Carol (born 6 November 1956) married Gary Lynn Broussard (born 19 June 1952) and had two daughters, Carol Lynn (born 1 January 1980, died 5 October 1993), who was killed in a car accident, and Sarah Beth (born 1 May 1982) who, with her husband James Smith (born 24 January 1981), has one daughter, Kristin Carol (born 14 August 2002). The youngest Shelton, William Reed (born 1 October 1967), along with his siblings, graduated from Longview High School and settled in the Gregg County area.

Sybil Ann married William Lynn "Bill" Satterwhite and has five children. (See "Satterwhite" entry.)

During the Great Depression, Charley managed to take care of not only his immediate family but his extended family as well, providing much needed dental and medical care for his many nieces and nephews. His generosity did not stop at bloodlines but reached past social and racial barriers to include the needs of a handicapped neighbor boy and the Negro couple that lived and worked on the Shelton farm. During the war when young women would draw imitation hosiery seam lines on their legs, Charley surprised his delighted nieces with genuine nylons for graduation. Never fully recovering from the loss of his first-born baby girl, Charley died with a broken heart on 11 February 1949. Sybil later married Frank Kunz and continued her career for many years as credit manager at Riff's, a distinctive women's apparel store in downtown Longview. Whether she was recruiting her eager grandchildren to sell "poppies," or snatching the annoyingly shrill whistle from the surprised traffic policeman in downtown Longview, handling the demanding business finances at Riff's, or sacrificing luxuries for herself in order to help those less fortunate, "Mama" was a woman ahead of her time. She did it all and left a legacy of overcoming adversity.

– Submitted by Sybil Satterwhite

SHEPPERD, MACKEY & PHILLIPS

John Ben Shepperd was born on 19 October 1915, in Gladewater, Texas, and died on 8 March 1990, in Gladewater. He married Mamie E. Strieber on 6 October 1938. She was born 30 December 1918, in Yorktown, Texas. They were parents of four children: Alfred Lewis, John Ben Jr., and twins Marianne Blanton Morse and Suzanne McCarver McIntosh. Alfred was born 19 March 1940, and practices law in San Antonio. John Ben Jr. was born 13 November 1942, died 18 June 1970. Marianne and Suzanne were born 2 September 1948. Marianne lives in Roanoke, Virginia, and Suzanne in Austin, Texas. John Ben and Mamie's descendants include nine grandchildren and nine great grandchildren.

John Ben graduated from The University of Texas with a B.A. in 1938, and an L.L.B. in 1941. Mamie received her B.J. in 1938 from The University of Texas. After college, they moved to Gladewater and he became a partner in the law firm of Kenley, Sharp and Shepperd of Longview. He served two years in the army during World War II, and upon returning to Gladewater served as a Gregg County Commissioner for the last ten months of 1946 to complete the unexpired term of his father, Doc Shepperd, who resigned. During the late 1940s, John Ben served briefly on the State Board of Education, organized the Texas

Economy Commission, and was chair of the election laws reform committee. He was state and national president of the Junior Chamber of Commerce (Jaycees), being named one of the Ten Outstanding Young Men of America in 1949. On 9 February 1950, John Ben was appointed Texas Secretary of State, at the age of thirty-four, by Governor Allan Shivers. He was elected Attorney General of Texas in 1952, and reelected in 1954. He was president of the National Association of Attorneys General and was Outstanding Citizen of Gladewater several times. John Ben moved to Odessa, Texas, in 1957 to become general counsel of Odessa Natural Gasoline Company, later a subsidiary of The El Paso Company. He led the campaign to establish the University of Texas of the Permian Basin in Odessa which opened in 1973. In 1984, he was named Texan of the Year by the Texas Chambers of Commerce. John Ben and Mamie began restoration of his parents' Gladewater properties in 1984 where they preserved several farm buildings at PineWay Farms and re-forested the land with pine trees. His death was noted by the *New York Times* and *U.S.A. Today*.

John Ben Shepperd was the son of Alfred Fulton "Doc" Shepperd who was born 9 November 1885, in Gladewater, Texas, and died 21 November 1957, in Gladewater. He married Berthal Frances Phillips on 30 December 1912, in Benjamin, Knox County, Texas. Berthal was born 9 December 1886, and died 14 April 1975. Berthal and Doc had two sons: John Ben and Alfred E. Shepperd, who was born 22 February 1921, and died 8 July 1994.

Alfred E. Shepperd graduated from Gladewater High School and received his degree from Texas Christian University. He worked and lived in Dallas until he retired to the hill country near Hunt, Texas. His place on FM 1340 is renowned as the site of Stonehenge II, a half-size, to-scale replica of England's famous monolith which Alfred and his neighbor constructed.

Doc Shepperd completed a business course at Tyler Commercial College. Berthal Shepperd attended Texas Christian University and worked as a bookkeeper, teacher and court reporter before marrying. Doc Shepperd was a mail carrier from 1904-1909, delivering mail south of the Sabine River on horseback and in a buggy. He was also a "free delivery boy" for medicine, groceries and messages from town. His first business venture was as owner of a livery stable from 1906-1912. He owned Shepperd's Hardware in Gladewater from 1912-1922, and sold all manner of goods including caskets. As the town's only funeral director, he provided a hearse which was pulled by a pair of matched blacks. He owned the first filling station in Gladewater, consisting of a single hand-operated gasoline pump. He opened A.F. "Doc" Shepperd General Merchandise in 1922. He and Berthal owned a large tract of farmland bordering the south bank of the Sabine River about two miles south of Gladewater. The Gladewater Municipal Airport, known as Doc Shepperd Field, is located on land once owned by them. He served in many

important positions including Gladewater precinct's Gregg County Commissioner for 23 years. He was known as "the father of good roads in Gregg County."

Berthal Phillips Shepperd was the daughter of Benjamin Franklin Phillips, who was born 22 April 1845, in Wilson County, Tennessee, and died 31 May 1927, at West Mountain in Upshur County, Texas. Her mother was Martha Jane "Mattie" Fambrough, who was born 21 April 1856, in Rusk County, Texas, and died 20 June 1937, in Upshur County. Ben and Mattie Phillips were married 25 June 1874, in Rusk County. Ben Phillips was the son of Alpha and Elizabeth "Betsy" Edwards Phillips, who settled in the West Mountain community, near Gladewater, Upshur County, Texas, in 1851. Mattie Fambrough was the daughter of John Edmund and Mary Jane Long Fambrough, who came to Texas from Georgia around 1851. John and Mary Jane farmed approximately ten miles north of Henderson in Cross Roads, a farming community near Pirtle in Rusk County which became part of Gregg County when it was created in 1874. Ben and Mattie Phillips had six children: David (by Ben's first wife, Mary E. Blakeley of Rusk County, who died on 5 April 1873, near Longview, Upshur County, Texas), Flora Almeda, Mary Pearl, Eula Jane, Lucy Bell, Mattye Lea, Sallie Viola, Berthal Frances, Jewel Mamie and Nina Kathleen.

Ben Phillips served as a private in the 34th Texas Brigade Cavalry Unit from 1863-65. He was an elder in the West Mountain Church of Christ and a founder of the First Christian Church in Longview in 1875. He was elected to two terms in the Texas House of Representatives, 1891-95, serving Upshur and Camp Counties.

Doc Shepperd was the son of John Henry Shepperd, who was born 5 May 1862, in Upshur County, Texas, and died on 21 September 1945, in Blum, Johnson County, Texas. John Henry married Ella Rebecca Mackey in Upshur County. She was born 21 September 1865, in Upshur County and died 11 January 1909, in Gladewater. Both are buried in the historic Rosedale Cemetery in Gladewater, Texas. Ella Mackey Shepperd was the daughter of Lewis Terrell Mackey, who was born 26 March 1828, in Maury County, Tennessee, and died 16 January 1868, in Upshur County. Lewis served as a soldier in the Confederate Army. He was the son of Joel Lewis and Mary Fonville Mackey, both buried in the Union Grove Cemetery in Upshur County north of Gladewater.

John Henry and Ella Mackey Shepperd were parents of 12 children: A.F. "Doc," Florence Bell, Alice Jane Dickson, Ivey, Daisy Dunaway, Jennifer Lynn Perdue, Vasta Elizabeth Hawkins, Mary Watkins, Terrell C., John Foy, Dora Ella Glenn Dake and Frank Lewis.

John Henry Shepperd was the son of Alfred Fulton Shepperd, who was born 13 November 1817, in Jefferson County, Georgia, and died 24 July 1876, in Upshur County, Texas. Alfred Fulton married Florence Elverse Hardin on 11 January 1843, in Montgomery County, Alabama. She was born 9 November 1825, in South

Carolina, and died on 8 September 1907, in Gladewater. Both are buried in Gay Cemetery within the Gladewater city limit in Upshur County. Alfred and Florence had five children: Gemmette F., Alfred Eleazor, Mary Lavinia Foshee, Rubannah Victory and John Henry.

Alfred Fulton Shepperd, father of John Henry, came to Upshur County, Texas, in 1845 during the time of the Republic of Texas. He and his eight grown siblings emigrated with their widowed mother, Elvey Anderson Shepperd. She was born in 1779 in Onslow County, North Carolina. Elvey married William Shepperd on 22 February 1802, after moving to Richmond County, Georgia, with her parents, Elijah and Lavinia Brack Anderson. William Shepperd was born in 1777 and died c.1828 in Montgomery County, Alabama. The Anderson and Shepperd families moved to Jefferson County, Georgia, where Elijah died before 1807. In the 1820s, the families and their ten children relocated to Tyson, Montgomery County, Alabama, where William Shepperd was killed, probably in 1828 because Elvey received title to land in her name in 1829. Later, she moved about ten miles south to Davenport, Alabama. In the fall of 1845, Elvey and eight of her grown children and grandchildren all came to East Texas and settled in what would become Upshur County. Elvey's boys and their slaves built one of the first log cabins in the area. She died of cancer in April 1860.

John Ben Shepperd, who was chairman of the Texas State Historical Survey Committee (now the Texas Historical Commission) was responsible for placing an official historical marker on her grave. Descendants have been able to join the Daughters of the Republic of Texas based on this documentation.

William and Elvey Anderson Shepperd were parents of ten children: Charity Bonham, Elizabeth Brady, William Jr., Lavinia Mildred Moseley, Mary "Polly" Phillips, Elijah Bird, Eleazor, Alfred Fulton, Robert A. and Allen Martin.

Charity Bonham and Elizabeth Brady remained in Alabama. William Jr. was the administrator of his father's estate in Alabama and came to Upshur County in late 1850; he later moved to Limestone County, Texas. Lavinia Mildred and her husband, Mason Moseley, are buried in the Moseley Cemetery near Warren City, Gregg County, Texas. Mary "Polly" and her husband, William Phillips, lived in the Union Grove vicinity and are buried in the Union Grove Cemetery; Jack Phillips and many others from Gladewater are their descendants. Elijah Bird went to Hunt County, Texas. Eleazor married Mary Ann Butler in Alabama and they settled in Upshur County. Alfred Fulton stayed in Upshur County, while Robert A. went to Falls County, Texas.

John Ben Shepperd had a keen interest in his family history. His enthusiasm, along with that of Virginia Coffey, a descendant of Mary "Polly" and William Phillips, encouraged distant cousin, Carl Venoy Wright, also a Shepperd descendant and native of Gladewater, to write a book on the family, *The Doty, Anderson, Shepperd and Allied Families*. It can be found in

the Lee Library in Gladewater; five other copies are located in genealogical libraries including the Latter Day Saints Library, Salt Lake City, Utah.

John Ben Shepperd was a member of The Pintlala Historical Association, which publishes a quarterly newsletter on the families and history of southern Montgomery County, Alabama. The Shepperd ancestors lived in that area before coming to The Republic of Texas in 1845.

John Ben Shepperd was also a member of The Edward Doty Society, where he served as councilor. He was a descendant of Edward Doty, Edward Fuller and Samuel Fuller, passengers on the *Mayflower* in 1620. Several relatives have joined the Mayflower Society on this well documented line.

(Sources: *The Doty, Anderson, Shepperd, and Allied Families*, by Carl V. Wright; *Ben Phillips of West Mountain: A Story of Faith and Integrity*, by John Ben Shepperd; and *The Handbook of Texas*, published by the Texas State Historical Association.)

– Submitted by Alfred L. Shepperd, San Antonio, Texas

KAREN SILKWOOD

Union activist Karen Gay Silkwood, the daughter of William and Merle Silkwood, was born on 19 February 1946, in Longview, Texas. She was raised at Nederland and studied medical technology at Lamar State College in Beaumont, Texas. In 1965, she married William Meadows and they had three children. After leaving Meadows in 1972, she went to Oklahoma City, where she worked for a short time before being hired as a metallography laboratory technician at the Cimarron River plutonium plant of Kerr-McGee Nuclear Corporation. Silkwood soon joined the Oil, Chemical and Atomic Workers Union and took part in the union's strike against the company. In 1974, she was the first female member of the union bargaining committee in Kerr-McGee history. On her first assignment to study health and safety issues at the plant, she discovered evidence of spills, leaks, and missing plutonium. In the 1970s, Kerr-McGee faced litigation involving worker safety and environmental contamination, and Silkwood testified before the Atomic Energy Commission that she had suffered radiation exposure in a series of unexplained incidents. On 13 November 1974, she was killed in an automobile accident on her way to meet with an Atomic Energy Commission official and a *New York Times* reporter. Her death led to speculations over foul play that were never substantiated. Her death caused investigations into plant security and safety, and a National Public Radio report about forty-four to sixty-six pounds of misplaced plutonium. An autopsy showed Silkwood's body had been contaminated by plutonium. Her case, which began in 1974, pointed to the hazards of nuclear energy and raised questions about corporate accountability and responsibility. According to the Oil, Chemical and Atomic Workers Union, the Kerr-McGee plant had manufactured faulty fuel rods, falsified

product inspection records and risked employee safety. Kerr-McGee closed the plant. Silkwood was the subject of a motion picture, *Silkwood*, released in 1984. Karen Silkwood was buried in Danville Cemetery, Kilgore, Texas.

SMITH: From Georgia to East Texas and Gregg County

JAMES MADISON SMITH, 1828, Franklin Co., Georgia, married Harriett C. Bryan, 24 July 1845. She was born 5 September 1830, Carnesville, Georgia, died 26 September 1874, Jordan Valley, Tennessee. He died 16 June 1866, Franklin Co., Texas. They had nine children who moved to Texas and other states. They were Royal David, John M., Sarah C., Robert Thomas, Mary Elizabeth, Benjamin Franklin and George Callaway Smith.

1. **ROYAL DAVID SMITH**, 28 June 1846, married Maria Emily Dean on 22 August 1869, died 23 November 1910, buried in Judson Cemetery, Gregg Co., Texas. They had Henry Stuart, Amanda Vannie, James Madison, Eliza Jane, Benjamin Franklin, Mary Elizabeth, John Robert, Effie A. and Riley Marshall Smith. (Note: This family came to Texas and Gregg Co., between 1870 and 1880.)

Henry Stuart Smith married Leila Frances Thomas and had Hughey C., Donnie Essie, Orvie O., Euel Jackson and Jessie Lee Smith.

Amanda Vannie Smith married William Lee Fuller and had Willie Lee "Leedie" Fuller and James Ollie Manuel "Mann" Fuller.

James Madison Smith II married Lela Ophelia Sparks and had Ollie, Mae Dee, Bertha Nellie, Irene and Mildred Smith.

Eliza Jane Smith married Jess M. Farmer.

Benjamin Franklin Smith married Emma Bell Morgan in Tennessee and went to Texas. They had Hoyt George, Mattie Sarah and Stanley Truant Smith.

Mary Elizabeth Smith married George Starling Mattox and had Blanche Iola (married Elmer Stone), Gladys DeLoise (married Howard Harris), Vera Essie Smith (married John Calloway), Georgia (married first Oliver Johnson, second Carl Barnett).

John Robert Smith married Mary Jane Stephens and had Ivol Alice (married Robert L. McLendon), who had Mary Alice (married first

Harriet C. (Bryan) and James Madison Smith

Four sons of James Madison Smith, b. 1828, Franklin Co., Georgia, d. June 14, 1856, Franklin Co. (l.-r.) Back: Royal "Riley" David Smith, b. June 28, 1846, d. October 21, 1924, and Robert "Bob" T. Smith, b. May 2, 1852, d. April 11, 1924. Front: Benjamin "Ben" Franklin Smith, b. May 17, 1856, d. unknown, and George "Doc" Calloway Smith, b. May 15, 1862, d. February 21, 1935.

Robert Lane, second Malcolm Hill, third Dean Steele); Sylvia (married Jack M. Thompson); and Robbie Lynn (married Ronnie Norvell).

Effie A. Smith (unknown).

Riley Marshall Smith married Maude Pressley.

2. **JOHN H. SMITH**, 1848, stayed in Georgia. He married Clarkie Carroll and Fannie Gillespie and fathered 16 children: James M., Henry Thomas, Richard B., Norman L., Martha Fay, Newton W., Walter Haden, Samuel Oscar Lee, Sarah Tulula and Minnie by first wife; John H. Jr., Johnny Justice, Ethel, Riley D., Robert T. and Dock Smith by second wife.

3. **SARAH C. SMITH** married first James M. Dean, second Thomas G. Pressley.

4. **ROBERT THOMAS SMITH** married Sarah Evelyn Brannon and had James Madison (married Lela Ophelia Sparks), William Henry, Susan Myrtle, Frances Cordelia, Ivy Magnolia, Lester Lewis, Beulah Catherine, Dora and Emma Smith.

5. **MARY ELIZABETH SMITH** married Harrison Cornelius Murray, settled in Memphis, Tennessee, had Mary Nola, Lena, George Ernest, Ollie Riley, Pearl Birdie, Jewell Cornelius, Arthur McKinley and Violet Katherine Murray.

6. **BENJAMIN FRANKLIN SMITH** married Emma Bell Morgan, settled in Dallas Co., Texas, had Hoyt George, Mattie Sarah and Stanley Truant Smith.

7. **GEORGE CALLOWAY SMITH** married Ida Leila Stephens (the grandparents of Bennie DonGene Smith). They had Richard Benjamin Turner Smith (married Flora Lillian Morton), Vera Lorene (married Johnnie Hamby), Irma Valeene (married Morris Ruggles) and Mamie Anderson (married Charlie T. Benson).

– Submitted by Bennie DonGene Smith

DON & MARY ANN SMITH

Donald Edward Smith is the son of Guy Edward Smith (7 June 1907, Ellis County, Texas-21 February 1991, Houston, Texas) and Juanita Alice Nolen (29 October 1911, Fort Worth, Texas-24 October 1980, Houston). Don, a fourth generation Texan, was born 4 August 1941, in Houston.

Mary Ann Puhl, born 5 October 1943, in Houston, is the daughter of Rudolph William "Rudy" Puhl (born 5 November 1911, Haugen, Wisconsin) and Carolina Ludmilla "Carrie" Chumchal (25 February 1917, Dillworth, Gonzales County, Texas-23 April 2004, Houston).

Don and Mary Ann were joined in Holy Matrimony on 8 June 1963, at St. Vincent de Paul Catholic Church in Houston. Three children were born in Houston to this marriage: Katherine Ann (born 19 December 1964), Douglas Edward (born 6 January 1968) and Suzanne Marie (born 24 June 1969).

In 1980, the Smiths moved to Longview, joined St. Mary's Catholic Church and became involved in many church and civic activities. Don was employed by Schlitz Container, a subsidiary of Joseph Schlitz Brewing Company. The three Smith children all graduated from Pine Tree High School.

Katherine, a graduate of Texas Christian University, was married on 23 May 1987, at St. Mary's to Wayde Charles Toups (born 12 May 1964, New Orleans, Louisiana). Their children are Madeleine Marie (born 4 July 1994, Fort Worth) and Benjamin Charles (born 15 September 2000, Houston). The Toups family lives in Spring, Texas.

Douglas, a Stephen F. Austin University graduate, married in Silsbee, Texas, on 8 June 1991, Kelley Jan Smith (born 20 December 1968, Hereford, Texas). They have three sons, all born in Houston: Matthew Edward (born 21 September 1994), Gregory Douglas (born 8 August 1997) and Nicholas Garry (born 8 April 1999). These Smiths reside in Katy, Texas.

Suzanne, a Texas A&M graduate, married Jeffry Scott Griffin (born 11 October 1967, Commerce, Texas) at St. Mary's on 5 January 1991. The four sons born to them are Patrick James (born 1 August 1995, Odessa, Texas), Zachary William (born 14 August 1996, Odessa), Anthony Scott (born 7 April 1998, Katy) and Michael Edward (born 1 December 1999, Aurora, Illinois). The Griffin family calls Charleston, West Virginia, home.

The Smith family

Don's heritage goes back to the American Revolutionary hero, John McKinney (2 September 1760, Camden District, South Carolina-1843, Macoupin County, Illinois). McKinney was Don's fourth great grandfather. At the age of sixteen, John McKinney served under General Francis Marion of the South Carolina Militia. At the time of his discharge, Marion presented him with two silver spurs for his patriotism and bravery.

John married Catherine Eaves (1776, Rutherford County, North Carolina–8 November 1846, Madison County, Illinois) in 1795 in Rutherford County. Seven children were born to this union: Hampton, Susan, Jefferson C., Mary, Diadema, Jubilee Lafayette and Nancy E. (20 May 1814, Madison County-22 November 1896, Ennis, Texas). The youngest, Nancy, married Fenwick Robbins Kendell (21 March 1808, Adams County, Ohio-5 June 1854, Navarro County, Texas) on 22 November 1831, in Madison County.

After John McKinney died in Macoupin County, Illinois, four of his children, with their families, traveled by wagon train to Texas in 1846. This was a remarkable and memorable journey made by Hampton, Jefferson, Jubilee and Nancy with their spouses and children. They settled in Corsicana where the family's Texas heritage began.

– Submitted by Don and Mary Ann Smith

GEORGE CALLOWAY SMITH: Descendants

GEORGE CALLOWAY SMITH, 15 May 1862, married **IDA LEILA STEPHENS** and settled in northern Gregg County after 1880. This is a brief report of their descendants.

Children:

RICHARD BENJAMIN TURNER SMITH (nickname "Bennie"), 1900, married Flora Lillian Morton, born 1905. He died 1977. She died 1998, buried in Judson Cemetery, Gregg Co., Texas. They had Bennie DonGene Smith and Betty Jane Smith.

VERA LORENE SMITH, 1902, married **JOHNNIE HAMBY**. They had no children.

IRMA VALEENE SMITH married Morris Ruggles. They had Morris Smith Ruggles (married Martha Laird) and Richard Donald Ruggles (married first Bonnie Lee Remmick, second Suellen Lynn Chapman).

MAMIE ANDERSON SMITH married Charles T. Benson. They had Tommy Gene Benson.

Grandchildren:

BENNIE DONGENE SMITH, 1926, Gregg Co., Texas; he married Ina Gayle Turman of Tyler, Texas, and have Donald Reagan Smith (married Sharon Hope Fabriz) and Nikki Gayle Smith.

BETTY JANE SMITH, 1928, Ft. Worth, Texas. She married Billy Joe Cabbiness of Longview, Texas, and had Billy Ray Cabbiness, 1926 (married Janet Carol James), Brenda Jane Cabbiness (married Ronald Lester McKinney), Bennie Ralph Cabbiness (married first Carla

Ida Leila (Stephen) Smith family. Photo taken c. 1944 in Leila's front yard in Omega, Gregg Co., Texas. (l.-r.) Flora Lillian (Morton) Smith, Joyce Kathryn Pyeatt, Richard Benjamin "Bennie" Turner Smith, Ida Leila Stephen Smith, Johnnie Hamby, Vera Lorene (Smith) Hamby, Morris Ruggles, Irma Valene (Smith) Ruggles, Joseph Ewing Pyeatt, Mamie Anderson (Smith) Benson, Bennie DonGene Smith, Willie Mae (McLendon) Pyeatt, Betty Jane Smith (Cabbiness), Joe Ewing Pyeatt, and children Morris Smith Ruggles and Richard Donald Ruggles.

Ann Lloyd, second Lynn Magee), Becky Jo Cabbiness (only lived 16 hours), and Bruce Wayne Cabbiness [married first Mary Ann Phillips Lawrence, second Robin Christina Laney (Seidel)].

MORRIS SMITH RUGGLES married Martha Laird. They had three children: Maury, Mark and Kim Ruggles.

RICHARD DONALD RUGGLES married first Bonnie Lee Remmick. They had two children: Trace and Mark Ruggles. He married second Suellen Chapman. They had two children: Melissa and Joshua.

Great grandchildren:

DONALD REAGAN SMITH and Sharon Hope Fabriz had Dylan and Hannah Smith.

NIKKI GAYLE SMITH.

BILLY RAY CABBINESS married Janet Carol James.

BRENDA JANE CABBINESS married Ronald Lester McKinney and have two children: Kathryn May "Kit" 'McKinney and Jeffery Kyle McKinney.

BENNIE RALPH CABBINESS married first Carla Case and had two children: Jason Lloyd Cabbiness and Amanda Dianne Cabbiness. He married second Lynn Sunski Magee, had three children: David, Catherine and Jennifer.

BECKY JO CABBINESS, born and died 29 October 1952.

BRUCE WAYNE CABBINESS married first Mary Phillips (Lawrence), second Robin Laney (Seidel). Bruce has one step child by his first marriage, Pamela Reneé Lawrence Green. He has two step children by his second wife: Robert Joe and Thomas Ray Seidel. He is the natural father of one daughter, Brianna Lynn Cabbiness.

KATHRYN MAY MCKINNEY married first Bill LaGrange, second Ruben Garza, and third Patrick McCarron.

JASON LLOYD CABBINESS married Kristen Kuehl.

JEFFERY KYLE MCKINNEY.

PAMELA RENEE´ LAWRENCE married Preston Green and has Natalie and Taylor Green.

AMANDA CABBINESS married Joseph Herndon and has Katie and Olivia Herndon.

ROBERT JOE SEIDEL has son, Jeffery Seidel.

Other great grandchildren are Maury, Mark, Kemmie, Tracy, Heath, Melissa and Joshua Ruggles, David, Cathy, Jennifer, Christopher and Caroline Magee, Ron, Hannah, Jacklynn and Katelyn Glunt, Mackenzie, Kylee Fleitman, Thomas Seidel, Briana Cabbiness, Natalie and Taylor Green, and Katie and Olivia Herndon.

(This is a continuation to the article "SMITH: From Georgia to East Texas and Gregg County.")

– Submitted by Kit McKinley

JOHN LONG & CLARA HARDIN SMITH

John Long Smith (31 July 1877) married Clara Hardin Smith (1 April 1874). They were both born in Crockett, Texas. After their marriage they moved to Palestine, Texas, and then to Longview in 1913. Their two-story family home was across the street from the Longview Museum of Arts (formerly the Holly Lawrence home) on the corner of Center and College Street. This house later burned down and was replaced by a yellow brick home owned by the George Kelly family.

John Long Smith

John Smith owned and operated a Grain and Elevator Company. Clara was active in civic affairs. They were members of the First Christian Church where John (Jack) taught the Loyal Men's Sunday School Class. John died on 30 May 1924, and Clara on 25 December 1919. Both are buried at Grace Hill Cemetery, Longview. Children of John and Grace Smith were Jack Ike Smith, Grace Smith and Luther Eastham Smith.

Jack Ike Smith (born 28 April 1902, died 9 October 1965) married Ozelle Haltom Smith (born 27 October 1906, died 21 May 1997). Jack and Ozelle Haltom Smith's daughter, Helen Grace Smith (5 December 1938), married first John Stafford and married second to Charles Cairns. Helen Grace's children are Rick Stafford

Clara Hardin Smith

(11 November 1959), Helene Stafford (11 October 1961) and Stewart Cairns (21 January 1969).

Grace Smith (born 19 August 1901, died 26 September 1969) married Julian Harrison Hurst (born 13 June 1901, died 26 September 1969). Grace and Julian met when her father, John Long (Jack) Smith, bought a car from J.G. Pegues Motor Company and Mr. Pegues sent Julian Hurst to teach Grace to drive. Julian began by bringing his then-girlfriend with him, but soon Grace stole Julian away. They eloped to Pittsburg, Texas, on 18 July 1923, and planned to keep the marriage a secret, but the County Clerk in Pittsburg told Dush Shaw, Longview's County Clerk, who then told Grace's father, Jack Smith. They were accompanied by Lou Sandifer and A.C. Numsen, who married also. A double wedding! Lou always said that if it had been the next night, she would have married a different boy. She always said that she kept the date the next night. The marriages were both very happy ones and both couples were married till their deaths.

The children of Grace Smith and Julian Harrison Hurst were Julian Garland Hurst and Clara Maude Hurst. Julian Garland Hurst (born 10 May 1925, died 7 May 1978) married on 5 December 1944, to Jane Jo Medley (born 5 December 1923, died 27 April 1969). Julian Harrison Hurst married second to Sue McDade on 10 September 1971.

Clara Maude Hurst (5 January 1932) married 2 February 1951, to William Burke Patterson (born 19 October 1931, died 10 December 1970). She married 2 December 1972, to William Brant Payne (3 December 1930. (See "John Henry Hurst," "Julian Harrison Hurst" and "William Brant Payne" family histories.)

Luther Eastham Smith, the third child of Grace Smith and Julian Harrison Hurst (14 October 1912, died 13 August 1973) married 25 December 1938, to Mary Louise Todd (25 December 1916). Their daughters were Grace Smith (26 January 1940) and Dorothy June Smith (24 March 1943).

– Submitted by Burke Patterson

JUDGE JOHN TYSON SMITH & NANCY MELVINA SKAGGS SMITH

Judge John Tyson Smith was born near Anniston, Alabama, 29 October 1846. His parents, both born in Alabama, were John A. Smith, in 1828, and Louisa Caroline Kennard, in 1823. Early ancestors came from the British Isles.

At age nine, John Tyson came with his parents to Upshur County, Texas, where they settled on a farm 15 miles east of Gilmer.

In 1864, at age 18, he entered the Confederate Army under General John Magruder's command in Texas. After the Confederate surrender in 1865, he returned home in 1865 and in 1869 he married Elladora Ann Kesseler. They came to Longview, Gregg County, about 1872 and lived on North Center Street. By 1876, his wife and both children, a boy, Volney, and a girl, Willie, had died.

On 19 December 1883, John Tyson Smith and Mrs. Robert M. Keasler (Nancy Melvina Skaggs Keasler) were married. They had been in-laws, having married brother and sister.

Nancy had been born in Lee County, Virginia, 12 December 1859. Her father, John Henry Skaggs, born in 1833, and mother, Martha Davis, born in 1840, both in Virginia, were married 30 December 1858, after John Henry Skaggs' graduation as a Baptist ministerial student from Mossy Creek College, Jefferson City, Tennessee. He died three months before Nancy's birth. Their early ancestors came to America from the British Isles.

Nancy's mother, Martha Davis Skaggs, widow, and Reverend William H. McCelland, widower, were married in 1864, in Lee County Virginia. In the summer of 1865, Reverend and Mrs. McClelland, five-year old Nancy Melvina Skaggs, and Reverend McClelland's three-year-old son rode horse back to Hannibal, Missouri, and picked up his other four children. They then took the Mississippi steamboat to Red River, then up to Shreveport, Louisiana. They went overland to Glenwood, Texas, in Upshur County. He established the Parson McClelland School for day and boarding pupils. Nancy attended the school and, it is thought, so did her future first husband, Robert Marion Keasler, before he went to Tahaucana Hills College at Waxahachie, Texas, to become a lawyer. Nancy and Robert were married 17 December 1876. The night they were married, her stepsister had a baby; Troy,

John Tyson Smith and
Nancy Melvina Skaggs

her stepbrother, died in the fire that destroyed the home and school; and the bride lost all her clothes. The couple went to Longview to live and had three daughters, Ethel May, Roxie Lee and Roberta Marian. All died young.

On 16 April 1882, Robert Marion Keasler died at their home at 435 North Fredonia Street.

After their marriage in 1883, Mr. and Mrs. John Tyson Smith lived in a house he had recently built at 410 North Center Street. They had six children: Ruby Ione Johnson, Lilla May Spinks, Virgie Belle Wood, Nancy Skaggs Hoenshell, John Tyson Jr. and Earl Davis. All lived to adulthood. There were five grandchildren: Edward Spinks Jr., Laura Virginia Wood Ellsworth, Charlotte Johnson Bowie, Jane Wood Lockett Witt and Ann Smith Lowman.

In 1880, John Tyson Smith served as City Tax Assessor of Longview. He was elected to two terms as Justice of the Peace. About 1890, He was admitted to the Texas Bar Association. He was elected to five terms as Gregg County Judge 1888-98. The former old red brick courthouse was built while he was judge. It was told in the family that Judge Smith said that it will never be paid for.

He built three two-story buildings, two on Methvin Street and one on Tyler St. The first floor of one housed the first picture show, "The Park Theater," in Longview. Governor Campbell built the building on the corner. The two buildings had a common stairwell, the second floors were used for doctors' and lawyers' offices. Then he built a one-story store building on Bank Street. Nancy owned a one-story store building which her first husband had built on Fredonia Street. Also, John Tyson built two adjoining two-story stores on Fredonia Street. The second floor of these was finished for a theater, "The Opera House," which he operated. It opened in 1902 with a week of grand operas by the San Carlos Opera Company. Minstrels and road show plays performed there on regular tours. It was also used for various local presentations.

On 15 May 1916, Judge John Tyson Smith died at his home and is buried on the Keasler-Smith joint lot in Greenwood Cemetery. There is a Texas Historical Marker on his grave.

After the North Center Street home was destroyed by fire in 1922, a house was built for the family at 419 North Fredonia Street. Only the three youngest children were unmarried and still at home. It was here that Nancy Melvina Skaggs Smith died 26 March 1934.

– Submitted by Ann Lowman

ROYCE & OTHODELL SMITH

Some of Othodell Smith's early Texas ancestors were Able Boles, Matthew Anderson, Felix Allen Eaton Anderson, William Goodwyn and Capt. James Chessher. Her father was Otho Jack Ellis, and her mother was Adell Tine Doggett. They were born in Shelby County, Texas. After Jack and Adell married in 1920, Jack went to barber school. He worked first in Center, and then heard of the oil boom and went to Kilgore in 1931. He worked there a while, but

Othodell and Royce Smith, 16 August 2003

there was no housing for Adell. He went to work in Longview and moved his wife from Shelby County. Jack Ellis and Forrest Hooper bought a shop on Highway 80 in the Greggton area called the Greggton Barber Shop. Jack and Adell lived close by in a tent with wooden sides and floor. Othodell was born in 1934, and was reared in Gregg County. About 1940, Jack moved his shop to the Greggton business buildings.

When World War II started, he worked in defense until 1945. He helped build the Atomic Energy Center at Oak Ridge, Tennessee. During the war the school children saved money to buy defense stamps to put into a book; when the book was filled the child was issued a War Bond to help with the war effort. After the war Jack came home; he worked on constructing the Knox Lee Power Plant. He went back to work in the barber shop and worked there until his death in 1955.

Othodell went to Pine Tree School until the eighth grade, when her parents moved to Longview. While attending Longview Junior High, she visited Nicholson Memorial Library (now Longview Public Library) where they had stereoscopic viewers with hundreds of pictures. After she graduated from Longview High, she went to work in the Southwestern Bell Telephone office on Methvin Street as secretary and teletype operator.

Royce Smith and Othodell Ellis married in 1953 in the Longview Missionary Baptist Church. They have three daughters: Lynda, Sharon and Betty. Lynda Harris has two daughters, Jennifer Tapia Lliebowitz and Lori Meagly. Lori has a daughter, Kirsten. Sharon Peters had two sons: Aaron and Lance Bailey (Lance died in 1997 at age nine), and one daughter, Hannah. All of these grandchildren attend Pine Tree School. Sharon and her husband, Kenney, adopted a newborn baby girl, Molly. Betty Lusby has one son, Jacob, and two daughters, Amanda and Sarah Burke. Betty and her family live in Nixa, Missouri.

Royce Smith family, 16 August 2003

Royce's father, Arthur W. Smith, and mother, Jewel Armstrong, were from Rusk County. Arthur was a carpenter and then became a Missionary Baptist preacher. Royce attended school in Longview. The family lived in the Pea Town Community near the Gregg County Airport. Royce has one brother, Alton and two sisters, Virginia Oldham and Helen Taylor. He graduated from Kilgore High School in 1953. He worked with Safeway Grocery Store. He went to work for Sears, Roebuck & Company in Longview in 1970, and retired in 1994 after 35 years.

Othodell and Lynda participated in the Centennial celebration in Longview in 1970. All the girls graduated from Pine Tree High School. Royce and Othodell are charter members of Parkway Baptist Church where he is a deacon. She is a member of the Daughters of the Republic of Texas, UDC and the Colonial Dames.

On 16 August 2003, Royce and Othodell celebrated their 50th wedding anniversary.

– Submitted by Othodell Smith

WAYNE MALCOLM SMITH & SHARON DERA WHADFORD

Wayne Malcolm Smith and Sharon Dera Whadford wed 6 April 1968, in Lubbock, Texas. They arrived in Gregg County, Texas, in November 1968, which marked the beginning of Wayne's long, interesting career as a law enforcement officer with the Texas Department of Public Safety, stationed in Kilgore as a state trooper. The couple worshiped with the Church of Christ. Both attended Kilgore College.

While residing in Kilgore, two sons were born to them, delivered by Dr. William Ott. Rex Vernon Smith arrived 1 January 1970, the First Baby of Kilgore for the New Year and decade. Snow blanketed the ground the day he was brought home. Over three years later, on 16 June 1973, the day before Father's Day, Troy Noble Smith was born.

At age 4, Rex enjoyed attending the Gingerbread House and Nelson's Playschool, both owned and directed by Bobbye Nelson, a talented artist. Later Rex attended Presbyterian Day School taught by Mrs. Weist. His 1975-1976 Kilgore Heights Elementary School kindergarten teacher was Lilla Peace, with Mr. Kennedy as principal. Classmates included Byron Lane Bosley, Chase Dorman, Ronald Brown, Kenneth Copeland and Kelly Custer.

Rex, Sharon, Wayne and Troy Smith, November 1978

A favorite childhood friend to Rex and Troy was Karen Anette Murphy, daughter of Kilgore neighbors Joe Don and Ertis (White) Murphy. Karen married Mark Berry, moved to Longview, and was employed with an insurance agency.

In summer 1976, the Smith family moved. Rex graduated from high school in Garland, Dallas County, Texas (1988), attended college and managed a computer store in Waco. He married Christine Wright in Waco (1994). Then he returned to Dallas County and began a custom screen printing business called "Tees and Things." They have three daughters: Kayla (1995), Amber (1998) and Robin (1999).

Troy enlisted in the United States Marine Corps. He married Kristi Hill (1990), and they have two daughters, Brittany (1991, in Dallas) and Ashlee (1992, in Cherry Point, North Carolina). Troy was stationed in Cherry Point with an aircraft fire and rescue unit. Troy later developed a moving company in Dallas County, Texas.

Grandparents to Rex and Troy Smith are Delvin Fred Smith and Arbrea Fae Jones and Chesley Orval Whadford and Francys Estelle Chance. Both grandmothers were born in Crosby County, Texas, to early west Texas pioneer families. Ancestral records exist in over thirty states and in the Texas counties of Upshur, Camp, Smith, Rains, Fannin, Red River, Smith, Lubbock, Floyd, Bailey, Lamb, Kaufman, Denton, Dallas, Dickens, Coleman, Erath, Falls, DeWitt, Hamilton, Cherokee, Rusk and Hams. Included are gospel ministers, missionaries, teachers, farmer, ranchers, soldiers, businessmen, school superintendents, law enforcement officials and dedicated homemakers. Additional family surnames include Jones, Gaddy, Morgan, Phillips, Hatchett, Savage, Garrison, Woolsey, Turner, Carpenter, Chance, Benton, Hardaway, Snow, Hinson, Matlock, Basham, Pearce, Collins, Carrico and Lewis.

By 1996, Wayne and Sharon resided in Upshur County, Texas; Rex, Troy and their families remained near Dallas. The eight years spent in lovely Gregg County remain cherished memories.

– Submitted by Sharon Smith

WILLIAM L SMITH & JEANETTE LOUISE ADAMS

William "Bill" Lawson Smith was born 6 August 1937, in Mountain Park, New Mexico, to William Renfro and Lela Walter Hedrick Smith. Carlsbad was home for the first ten years of life, and the family moved to the Dallas area in 1950 where they resided until Bill entered the Air Force in 1956.

In 1954, Bill met Jeanette Louise Adams and married her in 1956, and af-

ter serving in such places as Greenland; Roswell, New Mexico; Germany; Florida; Tripoli, Libya; Hawaii; and Tacoma, Washington, Bill was finally stationed in Altus, Oklahoma, in 1973. In 1976, Bill retired from the Air Force and moved to Gregg County to be nearer Jeanette's family who lived at Lake Callendar in Van Zandt County.

Bill went to work for Southwest Steel Casting until the business downsized, then went to work for Pine Tree Schools as part of the football maintenance crew until Southwest Casting started rebuilding in 1979. He stayed until 1985, when he went to work for Glo, Inc. selling fire extinguishers and maintenance equipment. In 1997, Bill went to work for a transport company pulling RVs; two years later he decided to subcontract out of Indiana so Jeanette could accompany him on trips. Jeanette began working for Pine Tree Schools driving a bus in 1977, but did not retire until 1998.

Now fully retired, Bill and Jeanette enjoy traveling, church work and camping. Jeanette has enjoyed genealogy research in such places as Greenville, Ohio, and Nebraska searching for her Simmons families.

– Submitted by William L. Smith

MELVIN DONALD "DONNIE" SNODDY, SR.

Melvin was born 22 October 1955, to parents M.T. Rhodes and Betty Joe Snoddy. He was born in Longview, Texas, in the County of Gregg. At the age of about 18 months, he was given to his father's sister to raise. She was Dillie Rhodes-Sanders. With her husband Bert Sanders, she raised him into adulthood. He would always refer to them as "momma and daddy." Siblings were Charlotte, Bert Wayne, Sharon, Michael, Cheryl Rhodes-Johnson and Fred Sanders.

Julia Mosely-Snoddy, wife of Thadeus P. Snoddy

The Snoddys have been in Longview, Texas, since 1866, moving from the T.B. Erwin and L.B. Snoddy Plantations around the Mt. Sylvan area of Smith County, near Tyler, Texas. L.B. Snoddy was the owner of about fourteen slaves. L.B. Snoddy (Lewis Bonaparte Snoddy) married T.B. Erwin's daughter Catherine around 1850. Their children were Thomas and Jane Snoddy. Both

*Thomas Snoddy, son of
Thad and Julia*

children were deceased by 1866. The slave schedule of 1860 Smith County, Texas, lists Thad as a 10-year-old black male. The inventory of the L.B. Snoddy estate in 1850 in Smith County, Texas, listed Mark, Rachel, Thad, Francis and Harrell — appraised at $3,000.00. Other slaves listed were Lucinda, Dan, Allen, Huston, Ace, Green and Martha — appraised at $2,700.00.

After slavery, Thad moved to Longview, living with his Aunt Mary Smith in 1870, in Upshur County later known as Gregg County. He married Julia Moseley on 2 May 1875.

(l.-r.) Front: Melvin D. Snoddy Jr. and Natassha R. Carrington. Middle: Melvin D. Snoddy Sr., Zanyah (being held), Gloria, Meisha D. Snoddy and Doneyll Y. Snoddy. Back: Delton Lamar Hollins.

(l.-r.) Front: Tommy, Jeanette, Rufus, Jr., Alice, Cecile Yvonne and Finis. Back: Betty Joe, Rufus, Sr., Catherine, Jason, Carl, Dorothy and Kay Francis.

They had 13 children: Annie, Laurecia, Francis, Amanda, Acy, Racheal, Minnie, Thadeus, Jr., Thomas, Emmett, Conway, Maidee Josie and Eddie.

Melvin descends from Thomas Snoddy. Thomas married Carrie Belle Davis, daughter of William "Bill" Davis and Sarah Andrews-Davis, on 19 December 1901, in Gregg County, Texas. Children were Wailie, Finis, Julious, Rufus, Lawrence, Gracie B., Annie May and Warness Lee.

Rufus was Melvin's grandfather. Rufus married Catherine Peterson. Their children were Finis, Tommy, Dorothy, Kaye Francis, Cecile Evon, Jannette Ann, Carl, Jason, Rufus, Jr., Betty Joe and Alice.

Melvin attended Ned E. Williams Elementary School, Foster Jr. High, Longview High and Kilgore College. Melvin married Tondalaya Sims in Dallas, Texas, in April 1973. They had one child, Donyell Y. Snoddy; Donyell has two children, Melvin Thomas and Serena DéAnn. He married Erica Brown from Marshall, Texas. Melvin later married Sheryl D. Jones; their child is Meisha Danielle Snoddy. Meisha attended Harvard, and Lesley. Melvin, Sr. later married Tonia Denise Harrison From Shreveport, Louisiana; they have Melvin D. Snoddy, Jr. Melvin, Sr. also has another daughter from Lufkin, Texas, Natassha René Carrington by Elaine Carrington. Natassha's daughter is named Zynyah Carrington. Melvin married Gloria Nell Hollins of Pittsburg on 4 May 2002. Gloria's son is Delton Lamar Hollins.

Employed with the Union Pacific Railroad for 28 years, Melvin is co-founder and Chairman of BEBO, Founder and Chairman of Greenville Project, and Deacon at Pleasant Green Baptist Church in Longview, Texas. He is also family historian. His library contains a plethora of information on family genealogy including original slave records, marriage licenses, etc.

– Submitted by Melvin Donald
"Donnie" Snoddy, Sr.

SPRINGSTEEN–WOOD–CARGILL: From Groeningen to Longview

Thomas D. and Dolly Ann (ROACH) HARRISS came in 1846 to what became Gregg County where they operated a stage stop near the intersection of present Rockwall Drive and U.S. Highway 80. Dolly Ann was the granddaughter of Samuel ROACH and Eleanor SPRINGS, a shortened version of the original family name, SPRINGSTEEN. The SPRINGS family founded the textile firm Springs Mills in Fort Mill, South Carolina. The widow Gertrude SPRINGSTEEN, her daughter and her three sons sailed from Groeningen, Holland, to New Amsterdam in 1652. This family had migrated south to the vicinity of Charlotte, North Carolina, by 1766. Samuel ROACH was a friend of the family of President James K. Polk, as is evidenced by his burial (1781) in the small Polk Family Cemetery in Pineville, North Carolina. Thomas ROACH, a son of Samuel and Eleanor, and a major in the War of 1812, married Ann Abigail GARRISON. Dolly Ann (See above.) was the first-born (1800) child of Thomas and Ann Abigail. After her marriage to Thomas HARRISS, the couple moved to Lawrence County, Alabama, where the first seven of eight children were born between 1831 and 1845. They were in East Texas in 1846. Pleasant S. HARRISS, first born of Thomas and Dolly (married Susan PEELER) was a constable when Gregg County was formed in 1873. T.B. (Buck) HARRIS (the final 's' was dropped around the turn of the century), second child of Pleasant and Susan, born in then Upshur County in 1858, acquired substantial land holdings in the White Oak area, and constructed Lake Harris. He also re-acquired a tract that his father had lost in bankruptcy, conveyed it to his son and son-in-law, who also went broke. Their brother-in-law, Martin HAYS, paid their debts in exchange for the land that eventually held 93 oil wells producing from the prolific East Texas Oil Field. Buck HARRIS married Willie LITTLE, the daughter of S. Miles and Mollie (BIGGERS) LITTLE. They had six children, four of whom survived to adulthood and married. Most of the Harris(s) family is buried in the White Oak Cemetery. The youngest of the survivors, Ida Dee, wed Bob WOOD in 1910. His family members were sharecroppers who immigrated to the Danville area from the vicinity of Iuka, Mississippi, around 1900. Bob and Dee had two children, Pauline and Thomas. Pauline lived with her aunt and uncle, Clara HARRIS and Gregg County Sheriff Martin HAYS, while she established a reputation as an excellent basketball player at Longview High School. She married Robert CARGILL, a salesman from Marshall. This couple became prosperous and contributed to the betterment of Longview and Gregg County. They had two children, Robert and Paula, both of whom live in Longview. Thomas WOOD married Fay MILLER of Mag-

Thomas Buckner Harriss

nolia, Arkansas. He was known as a calf-roper and as an oilfield worker. He served on the Pine Tree School Board. Thomas and Fay had two sons, Thomas and Steve, both of Longview.

– Submitted by Robert Cargill, Jr.
(August 25, 2003)

THOMAS, VANESSA & TAMSYN SPROTT

On 1 November 1980, Thomas Benjamin Sprott of Falls County, Texas, was transferred by Smith Industries Oil & Gas in Houston to Gregg County with his wife Vanessa Bennett Sprott, a native of Harris County, Texas. Thomas was born 23 September 1950, in Mountain Home, Arkansas. He was hired by Smith Industries following his graduation from San Houston State University with a BBA. Vanessa was born 11 October 1952, and graduated from M.D. Anderson Cancer & Tumor Institute in 1971, as a registered x-ray technician. They married 27 December 1975, at Heights Presbyterian Church in Houston. Their only child, a daughter they named Tamsyn Danielle Sprott, was born 10 November 1982, at Good Shepherd Hospital in Gregg County. All three are members of Alpine Presbyterian Church. Tamsyn, a graduate of Pine Tree High School, is attending Texas A&M University, majoring in Biomedical Science in pursuit of a career as a veterinarian.

– Submitted by Thomas Benjamin Sprott, III

Thomas, Tamsyn and Vanessa Sprott

STALL / STAHL

Henry Otis "Sonny" Stall was born 25 September 1907, in Red River Parish, Louisiana. He was the youngest son of Frederick August Stall, born 6 November 1864, in Webster Parish, Louisiana. On 1 March 1888, Frederick August married Anna Lee Newman in Webster Parish. Anna had been born 4 September 1870, in Heflin, Louisiana. August was the manager of a cotton plantation. He died 30 November 1907. Anna Lee died 31 March 1960, in Longview, Texas.

Frederick August Stall was the son of Frederick Augustus Stall born 28 October 1829, in Brochterbach, Prussia. He immigrated to America in 1852, settling in New Orleans, Louisiana. He enlisted in the Confederate Army in 1862. A shoemaker by trade, he detailed as shoemaker for Polignac's Brigade.

After the war he moved to Coushatta, Louisiana, and on 30 November 1890, he was sworn in as Mayor. Frederick was a 33rd degree Mason, Deputy Grand Master and was presented an ebony cane with a gold head as a fifty-year member. College educated, he read and spoke seven languages, including Greek and Hebrew. He wrote many articles for the Masonic magazine. He died 26 April 1904, and is buried in Wellington, Texas. Frederick was a Methodist for over fifty years. In Germany the family were members of the Protestant Evangelical Reform Church.

Frederick married Walburgis Caroline Kuhlman Beckler 6 April 1856, in New Orleans, Louisiana. She was born 6 August 1836, in Linden, Bavaria, and died 1 August 1866, in Sparta, Louisiana.

On the 29th of April 1929, in Shreveport, Louisiana, Sonny married Myrtle Elizabeth Detro, who was born 4 May 1910, in Red River Parish, Louisiana. Elizabeth was the only child of Louis Benjamin Detro and Lena Mae Norman Detro.

In 1941, the family moved to Gregg County where Sonny worked for Mabee Oil and Gas. They later, in 1945, moved to New London and then, in 1956, back to Longview where Sonny worked for the City of Longview Water Treatment Plant. Myrtle worked at Good Shepherd and did private duty nursing.

Active members of the Valley View Baptist Church, Sonny died 3 November 1978, in Longview, and Myrtle died 3 December 1988, also in Longview, Texas.

Descendants are (1) Frederick Henry Stahl (1933) who married Mary Dryden (1935). Their children are (i) Rebecca Lee Stahl (1959), married to Philip John Brunwald (1959), whose children are Taylor Hawkins Brunwald (1988) and Hunter Fergusson Brunwald (1992); (ii) Elizabeth Ann Stahl (1963), married to Michael Edwin Yeager with one child, William Michael Yeager (1998); and (iii) Frederick Henry Stahl, Jr. (1964). (2) Hertha Ann Stahl (1936) married

Mary and Frederick Stahl's 40th Wedding Anniversary, May 1997. (l.-r.) Elizabeth Ann, Frederick, Jr., Mary, Frederick and Rebecca Lee.

Ulysses Grant Whatley (1935). Their children are (i) Terry Grant Whatley (1959), married to Lisa Goar (1962), whose children are Christopher Grant Whatley (1983) and Matthew Joe Whatley (1986); and (ii) Shannon Kay Whatley (1968), married to Clifton Shelby Powers, whose children are Chelsea Ann Powers (1998) and Grant Michael Powers (1998). (3) Charles Hubert Stahl (1937) married Janice Louise Ramey (1940) and their children are (i) Shelly Suzanne Stahl (1964), married to John Guthrie Greene, whose child is William Charlton Greene (1997); and (ii) Stephen Lane Stahl (1968), married to Angela Leigh Edmonson, whose child is Tanner Jake Stahl (2001). (4) Mae Jeanette Stahl (1939) married Thomas James Kirkindoll (1938) and their children are (i) Gary Thomas Kirkindoll (1958), married first Kelly Denise Keys and second Lee Ann Myers Motley (1965), whose children are Lauren Ashley Kirkindoll (1988) and Brittany Dawn Kirkindoll (1992); (ii) Mark Charles Kirkindoll (1960); and (iii) Michael J. Kirkindoll (1965) married to Dawn Michelle McChristian (1965). (5) Patsy Carol Stahl (1946) married to Kenneth Wayne McGinnis (1943) whose children are (i) Traci Annette McGinnis (1966), married to Roger Neil Gillette, whose children are Sarah Elizabeth Gillette (1989) and Jacklyn Rose Gillette (1999); (ii) Karen Elizabeth McGinnis (1969), whose child is Ethan Kohl McGinnis-Land (1994); and (iii) Kenneth Wayne McGinnis, Jr. (1973).

Descendants raised in the Baptist faith.

– Submitted by Mary Stahl,
Henderson, Texas

STARR

Larry and Nancy Starr moved to Longview in 1966 with their two-year-old, Mike. Larry came to Longview to become a partner in the Kenley, Boyland, Hawthorn, Starr & Coghlan law firm. The family rounded out with the additions of Jeff and Jenny. Nancy then continued her teaching career as a sixth grade language arts teacher at Judson Middle School. Each family member joined the First Baptist Church of Longview.

After twenty years of trial law practice, Larry was appointed the first Judge of the Gregg County at Law in 1981. He was elected the second judge of the 188th District Court of Gregg County in 1986. In 1996, Governor George W. Bush appointed Larry to the Texas Court of Appeals. He was the first Republican to serve on the Texarkana Court of Appeals and the first Gregg County Resident to serve on any state appellate court for several decades.

The children brought honor to Larry and Nancy. Mike attended Baylor University on a National Merit Scholarship where he was Phi Beta Kappa and graduated Magna Cum Laude. Mike received a scholarship to Baylor Law School where he was on the Baylor Law Review. He attended the University of Nottingham Law School in England on a Rotary Scholarship where he received a master's degree in international law. He married Sarah Joyce Rutherford of Longview and they became the parents of Martha Elizabeth Starr, Emily Joyce Starr and Matthew Rutherford Starr. Sarah has both graduate and undergraduate degrees from Baylor. Mike now practices in Tyler.

Jeff attended Texas A&M University on a National Merit Scholarship, a Presidential Scholarship and the Crisman Endowed Scholarship. He graduated with honors. He was a member of the Fightin' Texas Aggie Band and Silver Taps, Ross Volunteers and a member of the student senate. He then attended Dartmouth College where he was a Tuck Scholar and received an MBA from the Tuck School of Business and a Master of Engineering from Thayer School of Engineering. He married Ellen Marie Bullock of Houston. They became the parent of Emma Marie Starr, Anna Mary Starr and Rebecca Ellen Starr. Ellen also graduated from Texas A&M and the University of Texas School of Pharmacy. Jeff has been vice-president of several companies and now lives with his family in Walnut Creek, California.

Jenny was a National Merit commended student and attended Baylor University on a Presidential Scholarship. Jenny then received her Juris Doctor degree from Baylor Law School, which she entered on a Hope Pierce Tartt Scholarship. She also was on the Baylor Law Review. Jenny married David Eric McCumber of Mexico, Missouri, a graduate in Jenny's law school class. They became the parents of William David McCumber, Michael Jeffrey McCumber and Andrew Edward McCumber. Before family duties required her full time attention, Jenny worked as Assistant General

Counsel for the New Mexico Energy, Minerals, and Natural Resources Department in Santa Fe, New Mexico, while David worked as General Counsel and Chief of Staff for the Governor of New Mexico, Gary Johnson. David and Jenny are now building their home in Los Alamos, where David works for the Los Alamos National Laboratory.

Nancy's parents were Edward Eugene Ogletree and Flora Terrell Ogletree of Griffin, Georgia. The Georgia Ogletrees present an interesting genealogical find. It is said that nearly all of the Ogletrees in the United States are descended from one of two brothers.

Nancy is descended from William Ogletree, father of John Ogletree, Sr. (1740-1822), the father of William Ogletree (recognized in Ptomy, at 311, as a Revolutionary War Veteran) (1765-1835), the father of Absolom Ogletree (1811-1861), the father of John Franklin Ogletree (1843-1930), the father of Edward Eugene Ogletree, Sr. (1870-1951), the father of Nancy's father, Ed (1908-2002).

Larry is descended from Casper Starr (as listed in the Rowan County, North Carolina, first federal census), the father of Jasper Starr, Jr. (1772-1850), the father of John Starr (1797-1872), Larry's great grandfather who settled near Elkhart in Anderson County, Texas. John Starr married Susannah Parker, the daughter of Elder John Parker, who among others, was maimed, scalped and killed by Comanche, Kiowa and Caddou Indians at the massacre at Fort Parker near the Navasota River on May 18, 1836. Elder Parker's granddaughter, Cynthia Ann, and others were kidnapped. (See Rachel Plummer, http://www.oldbooksonline.com/plummer1.html.) Elder Parker was also the father of Daniel Parker, who established the Pilgrim Primitive Baptist Church near Elkhart, the first such church in Texas, and said by many to be the first non-catholic church in Texas, Senator Isaac Parkers (for whom Parker County was named) and Silas Parker, one of the first Texas Rangers. (See Walter Prescott Webb, p.22.) John and Susannah Parker Starr, Larry's great grandparents, are also ancestors of Kenneth Starr, the Whitewater Special Prosecutor. John and Susannah were the parents of Thomas J. Starr, Larry's grandfather, who was the father of Alonzo R. Starr, Larry's father.

Larry is retired from the judiciary and Nancy is retired from teaching, but many former Longview students approach with a smile and good word for their former teacher.

– Submitted by Larry Starr

BRADLEY HOWARD STEGALL SR. (1941-1991)

Bradley Howard Stegall Sr. was born in Upshur County, Texas, in 1941 to Duard Hencle Stegall, born in 1920. Duard served in World War II. Bradley's mother, Modena Hilton, born in 1921, was the daughter of John Henry Hilton and Billie Carrl Bray.

Bradley married Betty Jean Thomas in 1963 and had two children, Bradley Howard Stegall Jr. and Bretta Katherine. When he died

Bradley Howard Stegall, Sr. and Betty Jean Thomas Stegall

in 1991, he was a well known and respected businessman in Gladewater. Bradley owned and operated Glade Appliance and Radio Repair Co. in Gladewater, where he had worked from the age of seventeen.

His ancestors have been traced back to 160 A.D. to Fornjotur, King Of Kvenland. His line includes William "The Conquer," Duke of Normandy, 1024-1087; Henry I "Beauclerc," King of England, 1068-1135; Henry II "Plantagenet," King of England, 1132-1189; John "Lackland," King of England, 1166-1216; Henry III, King of England, 1206-1272; Edward I "Longshanks," King of England, 1239-1307; Edward II, King of England, 1284-1327; and Edward III, King of England, 1312-1377.

Bradley's grandfather, Ples Stegall, born in 1889, married Emily Eugina Bumbgardener. His great grandfather, William Franklin Stegall, was born in 1852. He married Virginia Bell Patrick (1861-1941).

– Submitted by Bradley H. Stegall Jr.

ALEXANDER CALVITT STEVENS

Dr. Alexander Calvitt Stevens, physician in Longview from 1959 to 1989, was born 22 February 1928, in Mobile, Alabama. He was the only child of Alexander Campbell Luveta (Huxford) Stevens. His father, born in Burnet, Texas, in 1891, was the son of Mary Florence Crowder and James Alfred Stevens (1840-1922), newspaper editor and publisher, a native of Columbus, Mississippi, who moved to Burnet, Texas, about 1879. His mother was the daughter of Camilla Calvitt Huxford, a Mobile businessman, and his wife, Clara Hurley.

The Starr family: standing Jeff and Mike; seated, Larry, Nancy and Jenny.

Dr. Alexander C. Stevens

Dr. Stevens attended schools in Austin, Texas; he graduated from Gulf Coast Military Academy, Biloxi, Mississippi in 1944, Texas A&M University in 1948, and the University of Texas Medical Branch, Galveston, in 1952, where he was a member of Phi Beta Pi medical fraternity. He took a medical internship at University Hospital, Birmingham, Alabama, 1925-52, served in the U.S. Air Force from 1953 to 1955, attaining the rank of Captain and took a four-year surgical residency at University Hospital from 1955-1959, serving as Chief Resident in 1958-59.

Dr. Stevens and his partner, Dr. Harold A. Wood, moved to Longview in 1959 and opened their practice for general surgery with offices in the First National Bank building. He retired in 1989 after 30 years of practice. He is a Fellow of the American College of Surgeons, Diplomat of the American Board of Surgery, member of the American Medical Association, the Texas Medical Association (of which he is a member of the Fifty Year Club), the Gregg County Medical Society and the Texas Surgical Society. He served as Chief of Staff at Good Shepherd Medical Center in 1963. He is also a member of the First Christian Church and the Rocks Creek Hunting Club.

Dr. Stevens was married 6 August 1960, at the First Presbyterian Church, Longview, to Floreid Francis, daughter of Dr. Thomas Bramlette and Eugenia English (Tunstall) Francis of Longview. Born 3 February 1938, in Longview, she graduated from Longview High School, 1955, and received a B.A. degree from Southern Methodist University, 1959. She was a third grade teacher at Bramlette Elementary School from 1959-1962. She is a member of the First Christian Church, the Junior League of Longview, the Gregg County Medical Society Alliance, serving as president in 1982-83, and the Texas Medical Association Alliance. She was a charter member of Good Shepherd Medical Center Guild, 1984, and has served on the Longview Public Library Advisory Board and the Longview Public Library Foundation Board.

Dr. Stevens and his wife are the parents of three sons:

1) Alexander Calvitt Stevens, Jr., born 10 March 1963, Longview, lives in Milton, Massachusetts;

2) Thomas Huxford Stevens, born 26 September 1966, Longview, lives in Cumming, Georgia; and

3) Scott English Stevens, a Longview attorney, born 15 April 1969, Longview, married Emily Elaine "Lainey" Godsey of Longview, 15 November 1995. They are the parents of two children, Campbell Fox Stevens and Ella English Stevens.

– Submitted by Scott English Stevens

WILLIAM ARTHUR STEWART, JR. & GLADYS JEWELL HUNT STEWART

Bill was a U.S. Postal employee and rural route letter carrier in Gregg County. He also owned a café in Henderson, Texas, in the 1920s.

William Arthur "Bill" Stewart, Jr.

He served in the U.S. Navy from 1907 to 1909 aboard the U.S.S. *Virginia* as part of the "Great White Fleet" world cruise that was part of President Theodore Roosevelt's "Big Stick" policy. Honorably discharged from the Navy, he enlisted as a soldier during World War I from 1917 to 1919, attaining the rank of sergeant in Company M, 359th Infantry, U.S. Army. He saw action at St. Milheil and the Argonne Forest in France where he was exposed to and treated for gas attacks that affected his health later in life. He was part of the Army of Occupation of Germany in 1918 and 1919. He was a member of the Veterans of Foreign Wars Post 4002 and of the National Association of Letter Carriers Branch 1398.

Gladys Jewell Hunt Stewart

Gladys and Bill married in 17 November 1931, in Shreveport, Louisiana. She was a housewife and member of the First Baptist Church of Longview and the Colonial Dames.

Bill was born 2 October 1888, in Longview, the son of William Arthur Stewart, Sr. and Tommie Tankersley. Bill died 5 January 1969, in Longview. Gladys was born 19 October 1900, in Rusk County, Texas, the daughter of Joseph Lafayette Hunt and Anne Elizabeth Fears. Gladys died 11 June 1985, in Carthage, Texas. Bill and Gladys are buried in Grace Hill Cemetery in Longview.

– Submitted by Martha Hunt

CHARLES G. & LYDIA STOVALL

Charles Green Stovall was born in Panola County, Texas, on 4 March 1875, to Albert Green Stovall and Julia Adams Stovall. Albert, born in

Mississippi, came to Panola County. Charles settled in Gregg County.

While working at Kirby Lumber Mill in Kirbyville, Jasper County, Texas, he married Lydia Gibson Willett on 4 April 1921. One daughter, Callie Mae Stovall, was born there on 21 January 1922. Charlie, as he was called, moved his family, including his step-daughter Jewell Willett, to Gladewater the same year. Lydia was most insistent that her child should be able to attend school. Education was a very important thing to her. Being self-educated, she had no opportunity for formal schooling.

They worked very hard to provide for their children. Charlie worked at the old B.F. Phillips Sawmill in Gladewater for wages of one dollar per day. Not being landowners, the oil boom did little to improve their financial situation. He did what work he could, including some carpentry. Later, he was employed as a royalty gauger for a time by the Gladewater School District. Lydia contributed to the family income by doing sewing and alterations. During the boom years she also rented out some of the rooms in the house. From 1945 until her retirement, she was employed by Honey Togs, a manufacturer of children's clothing in Gladewater. Charlie died on 24 February 1936; Lydia died 30 October 1960. Both of them are buried at Rosedale Cemetery in Gladewater.

Charles was first married to Annie Jane Alexander, daughter of James Henry and Amanda McFarland Alexander on 1 March 1900, in Longview, Texas. She was born on 18 January 1881, and died on 18 June 1906. There were two children: Alice Lydia Stovall, born 27 November 1901, died 1 September 1980; and James Henry Stovall, born 19 January 1904, died 9 December 1912.

Charlie and Lydia are affectionately remembered by family members as honest, hard-working, fun-loving and always willing to help those less fortunate than themselves. Both were faithful members of Quitman & Center Church of Christ in Gladewater.

Charles Green Stovall is a direct descendant of Bartholomew Stovall, who was the first Stovall to emigrate from England, arriving in Virginia in 1684. On 7 July 1684, he signed, with his mark, an indenture to John Bright, a merchant, for a term of four years as payment for his passage.

Charles G. and Lydia Stovall

Regardless of the circumstances of the beginning of the Stovalls in America, they represent roots that succeeding generations may point to with pride. They were a brave, adventurous, patriotic and mobile group, moving on, always seeking a better life for themselves and their families. They moved south and westward with the frontier from Virginia to North Carolina, to Tennessee, to Georgia, to Mississippi, and finally to East Texas.

Callie Stovall Bloomberg, daughter of Charles and Lydia Stovall, now resides in Longview, Texas, and is very interested in preserving her family's history.

– Submitted by Callie Bloomberg

WINTON & VIRGINIA STUDT

Winton and Virginia Studt moved to Longview, Gregg County, in March 1951. They came from Kingsport, Tennessee, when Winton transferred from Tennessee Eastman Company to the Texas Eastman Company. The plant was being built at that time, and Winton continued to work there until he retired.

Winton received his degree from the University of Kansas as a Chemical Engineer. Virginia graduated from the same university majoring in Art Education.

All three of their children were born in Longview. They went to Longview Schools and graduated from Longview High.

Daughter Joyce, born in 1951, graduated from Stephen F. Austin University and majored in Home Economics. She now lives in Longview with her husband, Bob Moomau. They have two children, James Barnhill and Jenna Moomau. Both children graduated from Pine Tree High School. Jenna is now a senior at the University of Oklahoma, and James is in the Air Force. James attended Kilgore College before going into the service. Joyce teaches first grade in Pine Tree School District, and Bob works for Dillard's Department Store.

Son Brad Studt was born in 1952. He received his degree in Chemical Engineering at the University of Texas in Austin. He now lives in Houston and works as a Process Engineer.

Their youngest son, James Studt, was born in 1957. He also graduated from the University of Texas, Austin in Biochemistry. He went to Southwestern Medical School in Dallas and is an oncologist in San Angelo, Texas. He lives there with his wife, Mary Studt, and his children, Anna and twins Andrew and Camille.

Winton, Virginia and family have been active members in the First Presbyterian Church during the years of living in Longview. The children were involved in many activities while in school

Winton was a Marine dive-bomber pilot during World War II.

– Submitted by Virginia R. Studt

RICHARD KESTER & MILDRED CHRISTENE ROBERTSON SWIMM

Richard Kester Swimm was born in Jordan, New York, 13 December 1921. His parents were Kester John (29 May 1899 to 3 June 1975) and Ruth May Mahannah Swimm (18 October 1902 to June 1990). They were married 24 February 1920, in Memphis, New York. Kester and Ruth had five children: Richard Kester, Robert Earl, Stuart Jay, Donna and Shirley.

Richard and Mildred Swimm

Richard Kester was a master machinist. He went to work for Camillis Cutlery right out of high school and was working there when the United States joined World War II. In 1943, he decided he wanted to join the service and no longer take the deferments his employer was applying for. Camillis Cutlery had a contract with the government to make bayonets for the war effort. He joined the Army Air Corp in 1943.

While he was stationed in Pratt, Kansas, he met Mildred Christene Robertson. They married on 19 December 1944. Shortly thereafter he was shipped overseas, first to Tinian Saipan, and then to Okinawa, Japan. He was in Japan during the bombing of Japan and when peace was declared. From Okinawa, he flew supply missions until he was sent back to California to be discharged in 1946.

Richard was in the 20th Air Force, attached to the 8th Air Force, the 316 Wing, 346 Bomber Group, 463 Squadron.

He and Mildred have four daughters and one son. Charlotte Christene was born 13 October 1945, in Pratt, Kansas. She married Billy Wayne Spencer in Gregg County. They have three children, Tracye, Troy and Trampus. Ruth Ann was born 3 December, 1947, in Baldwinsville, New York. She married Gerald Wayne Cochran in Marshall, Texas. They have two children, Jerry and Rusty. Ruth Ann and Cochran divorced, and she is now married to Robert Still. Rickye Dossene was born 18 September 1951, in Longview. She married Joe Aldaco in Longview, Texas, and they have two children, Shelly and Jennifer. She and Aldaco are divorced. Richard Dec was born 14 January 1957, in Longview. He married Ruth Ann Gilbert in Longview, Texas, and they have three children, Sarah, Rachel and Catie.

Richard also raised Mildred's daughter and son from her first marriage, Lillian Edith Garrison (b. 13 September 1940) and Lou Clifton Garrison (3 May 1942 to 21 February 1977).

After being discharged from the service in 1946, Richard and Mildred moved to Memphis, New York. In 1950, they brought their family back to Texas. Richard went to work for R.G. LeTourneau Co. and worked there until he retired. During World War II, Mildred worked at the Air Base in Pratt in the office; she also worked at Camp Fannin helping with the soldiers who were being discharged and at Tinker Field in Oklahoma City. There she worked on the B-29 bombers doing the electrical wiring on the planes. In later years, Mildred was a waitress for several restaurants in Longview, El Chico's, Romeo's and the Petroleum Club. Mildred died 20 January 1972.

Richard married Inita Orr Cochran (born 3 September 1923 in Carter, Oklahoma) on 21 April 1972. At this writing they are living in Kilgore, Texas

– Submitted by Rickye Aldaco

TANKERSLEY/SPARKMAN

Absalom Booth Tankersley was descended from a Yorkshire family whose immigrants were Richard (1686, Yorkshire–1744 Caroline, Virginia) and his wife Margaret Rowland, and from the Huguenot Fountain (de la Fontaine) family by way of Ireland. Elizabeth Clark Sparkman was descended from John and Dorothy Sparkman, who immigrated to Virginia in 1635, and from Marcus Anthony, a Genoese reared in Holland, who, with his brother, was captured by pirates, escaped to be sold as bond servants in Virginia, and bought free to prosper and furnish descendants to fight in the American Revolution.

Absalom B. Tankersley and Elizabeth Clark Tankersley

Absalom was born 17 March 1833, in Jonesboro, Clayton County, Georgia. Elizabeth was born in the same community on June 14 of the same year. She came with her parents, William and Sarah Tate (Anthony) Sparkman, and her brother, Joseph Marc Sparkman, to this area before 1857. Absalom followed and the young couple married in Rusk County on 6 March 1859. Their first child, Sarah Ardecia (Deedie), was born 16 August 1860. Secession of the southern states found the family on the road back to Georgia, where they remained until about 1869, increasing the family by the births of Lavonia Francis (Voney), on 18 December 1861, and Mary Tommie on 30 March 1863.

A.B. Tankersley enlisted and served with Captain J.W. Mann's (F) Company, Neely's Battalion, 7th Regiment of the Georgia State Guards, at various times during 1863 and 1864. We have no documentation of his business or other activities during the war and reconstruction, only stories about service as a major on the staff during the battle of Atlanta and the family being in the path of Sherman's march.

The Tankersleys returned to Texas by mule-drawn wagon and settled on a farm near Pine Tree, having liquidated all that was left of their property in Georgia and hiding the specie in the wagon. A.B. and Elizabeth were charter members of First Baptist Church in Longview and active in civic affairs. In 1885, they moved into a home at 108 West Cotton. A.B. was a patternmaker in the forging and foundry trade and an astute businessman, associated with several early manufacturing businesses. He furnished farms or town houses to each of his daughters when they married.

A.B. Tankersley died on 8 June 1887, just past fifty-four years of age. Elizabeth lived until 8 March 1904. Sarah Ardecia Tankersley married Franklin Pierce Fisher, son of Silas McBee "Luke" Fisher and Martha Killingsworth, daughter of John Sweet Killingsworth and Emmaline Abney. Two children died as unnamed infants. Mattie, Rayburn and Tommy died in childhood. The children who survived to adulthood were –

Absalom McBee Fisher, who married Dovie Houston, and died young leaving three small sons: Joseph Weldon first married Thelma Oney, and his daughters by her are Dorothy Jean, who married Archie Granberry and had one daughter, Lee, who married Andrew Crews and has son Fisher Andrew Crews; and Maryann Fisher, who married Richard Dorsey, by whom she has three daughters; Dewana, who has adopted two sons, Jonathan and Jacob Rogers; Candance, who married Tommy Bagnoli; and Karina, who married Matthew Holmes.

Joseph Weldon Fisher then married Katherine Speights (who had one daughter, Darlynn Grounds, now Jones) and whose daughter by her was Vicki Jo, now deceased leaving no children.

Franklin Fisher married but had no children; and Abb Merle never married.

Lavonia Edna Fisher, who married Norman C. Ogilvie, and whose children were Norman ("Son"), who left no children; and Nina, who married Jimmy Oden and then Robert C. McDonald, and whose daughter, Jeannine Alexia, adopted by R.C. McDonald, married Arkie Monroe Knight and had no children; Clyde, a daughter who never married; Ernest, who married Sarah Wood, but had no children; Herbert, who married Maxine Carter, but had no children; May, who married William Frederick Farmer, and whose only child, Frankie Judith Farmer, married William Clifford Martin, Jr. and whose only child is Wm. C. Martin, III, who married Janet Marie Geist and has two children, Melissa Marie and Charles William, and three grandchildren, Alexander William through Melissa, Charles Garrett though Charles and Anna Jan Brannon, and Charla Richelle through Charles and Tuesday Hall; and Ralph, who married Rosa Bette Bumpus, and had two children, Kenneth, who married Thelma Churchill, and has three sons: Craig Kenneth, who married Sarah Webb, whose son, John David Webb has legally adopted the Fisher surname, and they have a son Zachary George; Paul Kevin, who married Pamela Early and has two sons, Clinton Paul and Chad William; and Derek, who married Kristi Duke, and they have a daughter and son, Elizabeth Christine and Luke Churchill; and Kirk, who married Marlene Goehring and has Laurie, who married first Matthew Bradford Perry, by whom she has a daughter, Sarah Elise, and then married Mark Lewis.

Lavonia Frances Tankersley married Luther Granville Calvin. This family and its accomplishments are so well chronicled in the article herein by B.F. Martin, Jr., that we defer to his account. (See "Luther Granville Calvin.") The recollections of childhood and migration differ with the telling by the two sisters, "Deedie" and "Voney."

Tommie Tankersley married William A. Stewart and had two sons, Bryant, who died as an infant, and William A. Stewart, Jr., who married twice, but had no children.

Malaria and the other fevers and jaundices and infections of the times in eastern Texas ravaged this family through all ages and generations as they did their neighbors. Lye Soap and water, coal oil and turpentine, muslin curtains and covers for wells and food storage and the best sanitation of the day were no match for them. The ones who died childless or way too young were often remembered and talked about and well loved.

– Submitted by William C. Martin, III

ANDREW SHAFTUCK & JOSEPHINE CHADICK TAYLOR

Andrew Shattuck Taylor was born in Mississippi on 12 December 1844. On 7 October 1868, in Pine Tree, he married Josephine Malinda (Chadick), born 13 September 1848, in Limestone County, Alabama.

Andrew Shattuck and Josephine Chadick Taylor

When Andrew was four years old, his father, Dr. Job Taylor, a practicing physician and Methodist preacher, moved the family to Texas and eventually settled in Earpville. About 1860, Dr. Job built a frame building for the First Methodist Church on the Marshall-Tyler stage road near Marshall Avenue and Eighth Street, when the original meeting house was abandoned. In 1873, the building was moved to Fredonia and Whaley and was replaced by a brick edifice because the rooting and grunting of hogs under the old frame building disturbed the services. Andrew, as the first county surveyor in Gregg County, staked out the ground for the new church. Andrew's wife, Josephine, was the first president of the church's women's society, organized in 1885.

In the 1870s, Andrew organized the field notes when Gregg County was formed and also laid out Greenwood Cemetery, Longview's oldest burial ground. He died 21 February 1890, in Longview, and Josephine on 28 February 1928. Both were interred in the cemetery beside his parents.

Andrew's son, Charles Lee Taylor, was born 29 November 1870, in Longview. His wife, Iba (Northcutt), was born 31 December 1871, in Harrison County. Iba was somewhat of a rebel. She decided as a young girl that she would go to dances, even though her father, W.G. Northcutt, was a trustee and deacon in the First Baptist Church. As a result, she was dismissed from the church. She was later reinstated and at her wedding in the church she was attired in purple and black and wore a large purple, black and white hat.

Charles was president of the Longview Chamber of Commerce, president of the Credit Bureau of Longview, and the first Longview mayor under the council-manager plan of government, which he helped to install in 1923. Charles died 16 January 1954, and Iba on 11 February 1958. They are buried in Memory Park.

Their son, Bill Northcutt Taylor, was born 10 September 1898. He graduated from Texas A&M in 1919, and worked in Venezuela for an oil company until his marriage on 23 December 1924, to Louise Durham (Shaw), who was born 14 February 1900, in Longview. They had three children: Gloria Wismar of Baytown, Texas; Nancy Kennedy of San Mateo, California; and Charles Shaw Taylor of Longview. Bill served as city manager of several towns over the years, including Longview, Tyler, McAllen, Port Arthur, Wichita Falls and Columbia, Missouri. He retired to Longview in 1955. In 1967, he compiled for each of his six grandchildren a comprehensive biographical and historical book of memories of the Taylor and allied families. He wrote, "There is no end to genealogical research, for a case is never closed." He died 14 May 1981, and Louise on 15 December 1992. They are buried at Memory Park.

– Submitted by Charles L. Taylor

TEMPLE

Edwin Fussell Temple, son of Thomas and Annie (West) Temple, was born in the Philadelphia, Pennsylvania, area in 1860. The Temples moved to Illinois in 1867. By 1888, E.F. was mar-

Temple family, c. 1917. Standing Edwin Vernon Temple; (l.-r.) seated: Thomas Temple, Edwin Fussell Temple and baby Louise Temple.

ried to Ida Ellen Looker and living in Chicago. They had four children. Edwin Vernon was born in Chicago in 1888. Elva was born in 1891. Twins Ida Floy and LaRoy were born in 1905. Between 1888 and 1905, the Temple family moved to Springfield, Illinois. E.F., a carpenter by trade, worked on the renovation of Abraham Lincoln's house and helped build the main staircase in the Illinois capitol building.

Vernon began working for the Illinois Central Railroad around 1902. During that time he took many trips to the 1904 St. Louis World Fair. He also saw President Theodore Roosevelt during the 1904 Presidential campaign. Vernon enjoyed telling stories of Pinkerton men, traveling musical shows and life on the Illinois Central.

Vernon moved with his family to Texas in 1905. His first meal in Texas was a bowl of chili at the Longview Junction. Not being familiar with chili, Vernon often told how unexpectedly hot it was! He and his father built their home in the Peatown Community. Edwin Fussel and Vernon farmed the land of their new home. Vernon was a self-taught photographer and calligrapher, or "fancy penwork," as he called it. Vernon put in the first telephone line and telephones in the Peatown area.

Vernon married Mary Ellen Graybill in Longview on 24 December 1915. Mary, the daughter of Michael and Dora (Rosson) Graybill, worked as a schoolteacher at the Tryon School at the time of her marriage. They built their home in Peatown and resided there the rest of their lives. Vernon owned the first Model T in Longview. He often bemoaned the fact that "small town Longview" only had five cars when he moved here in 1905. Vernon continued to farm, and during the Oil Boom he bought and sold oil leases for area companies. Mary died in 1983 at the age of 92. Vernon died in 1989 at the age of 101.

Vernon and Mary raised five children: Louise, Robert, Edward Rayburn, Lorraine and Vernon Maurice. All three sons served during World War II. Edward, a butcher for the A&P Grocery store at the outbreak of the war, re-

ceived a letter from the citizens of Longview that measured 1,942 feet long. It was the longest letter ever received by a United States Serviceman. Edward served as sergeant in the United States Medical Corps.

Louise, who married John B. Moore, continued to live in Longview. They had two children, Mary Elizabeth "Libby" (Novy) and John Temple Moore.

Edward married Thresa Arnold 1 March 1952. They resided in New Braunfels, Texas, for many years before returning to live in Longview. They had five children: Thresa Ann (Kuehler), Susan (Green), Edward Rayburn, Jr., Amy (Harriss) and David Alan.

Vernon and Mary have many other grandchildren and great grandchildren in Texas, Illinois, Missouri, California and Oregon.

– Submitted by Amy Harriss, Longview, Texas

WILLIAM L. TERRY & OLA LOGAN

William L. Terry was born July 1868, St. Michael's Township, Fredericktown, Madison County, Missouri, a mining community near the Illinois border, to Sarah Elizabeth Price and William T. Terry. His father, a miner, died before 1880. Sarah and children, John, Martha, William, Charles, Alice, Edward and Effie, moved to Camp County, Texas, where they lived with her widowed father, Richard C. Price.

William L. Terry married Ola Logan about 1894. Ola was born September 1879, Daingerfield, Morris County, Texas, to James "Robert" Logan and Martha Susan Weaver Graves. They married 22 November 1877, Upshur County; both were widowed with two children each: Sarah Magdalene, 11, and George Logan, 5; Mary, 7, and Joseph Graves, 5. Laura Logan, was born 1881.

James Robert Logan died 1885 of measles at age 40. Martha supported the family cooking for railroad crews. She remarried to W.H.

Left: William L. Terry

William L. Terry, Longview, Texas, 1901

William, Wanda and Ola Terry

Norwood, 4 May 1887, Upshur County. Norwood suffered from a head injury, went crazy, shot and killed Martha and some children; then killed himself.

James Robert Logan was born 1845, Lincoln County, Kentucky, to James Alexander Logan (1821-1880) and Sarah Combs Hickman (1819-1856), who had married in 1838. Their children were Susan, 1839; Sarah, 1841; Lidia, 1842; William, 1844; James Robert, 1845; and

Robert, Willie May and Richard Terry

Ira J., 1848. The Logan family removed to Titus County, Texas, about 1854. Logan was descended from Scotch-Irish who came to Pennsylvania, 1734; fought the Indians in Virginia; served in the Revolutionary War; and pioneered Kentucky, building Logan's Fort.

Martha Susan Weaver, born 1856, Randolph County, Alabama, was born to Nancy and John Thomas Weaver, (1832-1912). They removed to Upshur County about 1870. Their children were Anna, 1852; Martha Susan, 1856; Sarah, 1858; Seaborn, 1860; Adam, 1861; Joseph, 1866; and Mary, 1870.

John Thomas was born to Seaborn Jackson Weaver, Sr. (1811-1849) and Sarah Carroll (1812-1870) from Georgia. John Thomas Weaver removed to Little River County, Arkansas, where he died.

Mabel, William Terry, Don, Ola and Wanda, Ft. Worth, Texas, 1906

Ola and William Terry lived in Cass County, Texas, 1900, where he worked as a mill-laborer. Married for six years and had four children, three still living: Wanda, January 1896; Mabel, October 1897 (twin, Hazel died); and Marvin, April 1900. By 1901, Marvin had died. In 1910, William worked repairing railroad cars in Fort Worth. Children: Wanda; Mabel; Don, born 1903; and Willie May, 1907. Another child had died about 1905. Twins, Robert Joe and Richard Lee, were born 25 December 1910.

William Terry died in a smallpox epidemic about 1912, age 43. Ola supported the family working in the meat-packing plant in Fort Worth, where she caught the flu and died about 1916, age 36.

Robert and Richard lived with their grandmother, Sarah Elizabeth Terry, and Aunt Effie Wilson Grimes in Gum Springs. Willie May lived with Uncle Ed Terry and wife, Carrie, in Longview. Wanda married Raymond Cassidy in Fort Worth. Mabel married in Breckenridge; divorced, and moved to California. Willie May married Jimmie Ira Pray and moved to Oregon. Richard married Josephine Syfan, 1935, in Harris County, Texas. Children: Charles Richard Terry and Gene Melvin Terry.

Robert Joe Terry and Madeline Annie Nelms drove to Texarkana, Arkansas, 28 January 1931, and married. They had one night of honeymoon, then lived with her parents, William Mark and Annie Lou Nelms, in Longview. Later, they moved to Gum Springs, where their children, Bobby Joe, Carl Theron and Gloria Juanita, were born. Robert and Madeline lived in La Porte, Harris County, for 40 years; returned to Gum Springs and built a house in 1982. In January 2004, they were married for 73 years.

WILLIAM T. TERRY & SARAH ELIZABETH PRICE

Sarah Elizabeth Price was in born Cannon County, Tennessee, 1843, to Richard C. Price and Martha Jane Rains. Richard was born in Virginia, 1810, enlisted in Jackson County, Alabama, for the Second Seminole Campaign, 1836-1837, under Captain Meredith Price. Martha, called Polly, was born in Warren County, Tennessee, to Elizabeth Jackson (1780-1871) and James Jackson Rains, born 1775, North Carolina.

The Price family removed to Newton County, Missouri, bought property in 1854, and opened grocery stores in the great mining camp of Granby. By 1855, there were 8,000 people in the high-level lead-region township. Children born in Tennessee were James; Jasper; William; Parrelee; Martha; Sarah; America; and Mary; born Missouri: Richard; Pernicia; and Sterling. By 1870, Richard and Martha were in Elysian Fields, Harrison County, Texas.

Madeline and Robert Terry, 25th Wedding Anniversary

William T. Terry, born 1835, Valle Township, Jefferson County, Missouri, and brother, Thomas, left home, where they worked as miners, and joined the Granby stampede. William married Sarah Elizabeth Price in Granby, 1858. By 1860, William, 24, and Sarah, 16, were parents of John. At the breakout of the Civil War, Granby was classed as one of the greatest lead mines in the country. Early in 1862, the eyes of the furnaces were blown out. The Price and Terry families left Granby.

William's father, William M. Terry, Sr., born 1796, Virginia, lived in Kentucky before settling in Valle Township, where he had 3,000 acres of farmland. William, Sr.'s first wife died before 1833; they had one son, James (father of Francis). About 1837, William, Sr. married Sarah, born 1817. Children: William; Thomas; George; Mary; Synthia (Cintha); and Elizabeth. Sarah died before 1860. William, Sr. married young widow, Catherine Brown, 12 August 1860. He died in-

testate before 8 December 1864, and final settlement of probate was 21 September 1868. Heirs named: William; Thomas; George; Mary; Cintha; Elizabeth; and Francis Terry.

By 1870, William T. Terry was laboring in the lead mines at St. Michael's Township, Fredericktown, Madison County, Missouri. Sarah had five children: John, 11; Mary, 8; Martha, 6; William, 2; and Charles, 7 months. After 1870, Alice, Edwin, and Effie were born. William Terry and daughter, Mary, died before 1880; Sarah and children lived with her widower father, Richard C. Price, in Camp County, Texas.

John Franklin Terry (1858-1929) married R.A. before leaving Missouri, and already had two children, Rosa and George. John married second, 23 February 1890, Cora Cox, Morris County, Texas. Children: Swan; Willie; Percy; and Madeline. John married third to Adelle. He ran a boarding house and restaurant in Longview.

Carl, Bobby and Gloria Terry

Martha Jerusha Terry, "Mattie," (1864-1929) married Joseph Cope, 9 December 1880, Camp County. Children: Calvin; Ava-Pearl; Carrie; Knox; Onie-Belle; Hattie; Bryant; Otis; and Jodie. Mattie married Frank Pierce, 1909.

Charles Jefferson Terry (1869-1943) married Ada Lee Martin, 10 December 1891. Chil-

John Terry behind the bar in the restaurant in Longview, Texas, 1920

dren: Alvie; Samuel; EulaMae; Maxine; and Lola. He lived in Hughes Springs, Cass County.

Alice LunaMae Terry (1872-1938) married William Caver, 27 October 1891. Children: DunaMae and Mabel. She lived in Dallas and Longview.

Edward D. Terry (1874-1942) served in the Spanish-American War, 1893. His first wife was Lulu. He married second, Carrie. Children: Eddie and Maxine. Ed Terry ran a restaurant in Longview near the railroad station for many years.

Effie Terry (1878-1964) married Joseph Wilson about 1904. Children: Rosalie and Harold Wilson. She married second, William Grimes. Effie lived in Gum Springs.

William L. Terry (1867-1912) married Ola Logan (1879-1916) about 1894. Children: Wanda, 1896; Mabel (twin Hazel died), 1897; Marvin, 1900; Don, 1903; baby, d.y.1905; WillieMay, 1907; and Robert Joe and Richard Lee (twins), 1910.

– Submitted by Gloria Terry

CHARLES EDWARD THOMAS (1915-1994)

Charles Edward Thomas was born in Nacogdoches County, Texas, in 1915 to James Edward Thomas and Marqurite Katherine Belk. Charles married Dorothy Grace Drew in 1940 and had two children, Galen Edward and Betty Jean. Charles was a licensed electrician who worked and raised his family in Gladewater, Texas.

Charles Edward Thomas and
Dorothy Drew Thomas

Dorothy was born in Texas City, Texas, in 1925 to Willie Leon Drew and Frances Ellen Wood. Dorothy died in 1986. W.L. and Ellen had eight children. W.L. was born in 1899, and died in 1978. W.L.'s father was Albert T. Drew and his mother was Jodie Elsie Brown. Ellen was born in 1902, and died in 1989. Ellen's parents were Joseph Henry Wood and Della Lee Hudson. Ellen's grandparents were John Wood and Ellen Wilson Wood and Hal Hudson and Fannie Mosley Hudson.

Charles' grandfather was Charles Marion Thomas, 1851-1915. He was in the War Between the States, Regular Army. In 1876, he married Mary Emma Corley, 1856-1949. They had ten children. Three of their children became educators. Charles' father, James Edward, taught school in a one-room schoolhouse with all ages in attendance, including Charles.

Charles' mother died after childbirth when he was only ten years old. Marqurite Katherine

Belk was the daughter of Joseph F. Belk and Hattie Roquemore.

The Roquemore line has been traced back to 1280. The first Roquemores in Texas were French Hugenot refugees. On 29 January 1764, the Roquemore ancestors boarded Capt. Gregory Perkins' *Friendship*, which anchored in Charleston, South Carolina, 12 April 1764. Receiving land grants near Long Cane Creek, Hillsborough Township, New Bordeaux settlement, South Carolina, they hoped to establish a successful silk colony, but the climate was not suitable and it failed.

Sometime between 1776 and 1781, the Roquemores moved into Georgia. James Roquemore became a Revolutionary soldier. In 1783, he received a 287-1/2-acre land grant, survey #254, and an additional 250-acre grant, #558, in Washington County, Georgia, for faithful service in the war.

In the 1840s, the Roquemore family joined a wagon train from Georgia to Texas. Catherine Murphy Roquemore died on the journey and was buried in Russell County, Alabama, July 1847. The family continued their journey and settled in Panola County Texas.

– Submitted by Betty Jean Thomas Stegall

EZEKIEL THOMAS

Ezekiel Thomas and Vander Artimissie Clark were married in Franklin County, Georgia, on 11 August 1861. Ten years later, in December of 1871, they arrived in the Judson Community just north of Longview, Texas.

Soon after their marriage, the Civil War commenced and Ezekiel served in the Confederate Army as part of Co. G, 34th Georgia Regiment from May 1862 until his discharge in April 1865. It has been related that he was with Lee's army at the time of the surrender after having served through strenuous fighting in Tennessee and West Virginia.

Life was not easy in Franklin County, Georgia, after the war ended. Much of the countryside had been ravaged during the fighting and it was difficult for the farms and plantations to support multiple families. Thus, began the westward movement, including Ezekiel, his wife and four children.

Other relatives and friends who accompanied the Thomas family were Smiths, Randalls, Crawfords, Stones and Hambys. It isn't known what route and mode of transportation was taken from Georgia, but at least part of the journey was by covered wagon. Upon arriving in their new community, the remainder of the winter was spent living in the covered wagons while land was bought or homesteaded and houses were built. Two months after arriving, their fifth child was born and was followed by six more children. Only one, Ida Dorothy, died young; the other ten

Ezekiel and Vander Thomas

grew up, married and had families. Ezekiel and Van Thomas belonged to the Summerfield Methodist Church and are buried in the Summerfield Cemetery. Vander Artimissie Clark Thomas was born on 20 February 1844, and died on 21 November 1916. Ezekiel Thomas was born 2 July 1840, and died 30 October 1917.

Many of the descendants of this couple married and remained in Gregg County. The oldest daughter, Martha Ellen, married Russell Randall and moved to Dallas, Texas. The second daughter, Desta Monia Antlet, married William Butler Taylor. They operated a dry goods store plus the Judson Post Office. Later, they moved to Camp Switch near Gladewater where they continued to operate a store until her death. Their son, Arthur, continued with the store business for the rest of his life. Emily Angeline married Henry Taylor Hardy. They remained in the Judson community or in nearby Harrison County for most of their lives. John Elijah Thomas married Willie T. Whaley. When he was young, he taught school at Judson and had four of his younger sisters in his classroom. He later moved to Grand Saline, Texas, where he owned a grocery store for many years. William Joseph Thomas married Drucilla Younts. They remained in Gregg County, where they farmed for a while but then moved to Grand Saline, Texas. Mae Elizabeth married Edward Stone and they lived in the Judson area. After Mae's death in 1914, their children went to live with their Thomas grandparents and some of Mae's sisters. Jessie Arlee married Rev. William J. Fears. They first went to the Indian Territory (now Oklahoma), where he was a missionary. She returned to Judson for the birth of her first child and then they lived in Panola and Rusk counties

Ezekiel Thomas family

until his death in 1926. Jessie later returned to Longview and married William Jones. They lived on Tryon Road for the rest of their lives. (Subject of related article) Louella Rhoda married Thomas Edward Killingsworth and they stayed in Gregg County their entire lives. They farmed and operated a dairy for many years. Sarah Virginia married William Rankin Morris and, later, Joseph H. Bayless. They lived in Houston, Texas.

There are many descendants of this large Thomas family who still reside in Gregg County. They have and continue to contribute to the community as farmers, teachers, doctors, dentists and attorneys.

GEORGE & VICTORIA THOMAS

George Thomas (born 27 October 1886) came to the United States through Ellis Island from Beirut, Lebanon, in 1905, at the age of 19. He stayed in America for five years, working odd jobs in Altoona, Pennsylvania, and Gadsden, Alabama, and traveling throughout the states visiting friends. Upon his return to Beirut in 1910, he found his sweetheart, Victoria Curi, (born 15 November 1895). They were married in Beirut, but were experiencing difficulties at that time under the occupation by Turkey, much as the area today is suffering under the occupation by the Israelis. Having limited funds and all their earthly possessions in a footlocker and two suitcases, they booked passage on the cheapest level of a ship sailing to Ellis Island. This ship was rerouted, however, to Vera Cruz, Mexico, because of an epidemic closing Ellis Island to immigrants at that time.

George and Victoria took a train from Vera Cruz to the United States and got off the train in Shreveport, Louisiana. While living in Shreveport, their first child, Mary Thomas, was born on 31 August 1912, and their second child, Sam George Thomas, was born on 3 February 1916.

From Shreveport, the family moved to Cleveland, Ohio, in 1917, with George finding work in a foundry sweeping floors, working his way through the ranks to foreman of his division in the company. The third child, Selma Thomas, was born in Cleveland on 8 March 1918.

George did not like the harsh winters of Cleveland, and desired to return to the southern part of the United States, so the family moved to Henderson, Texas, in 1919. A fourth child was born in Henderson and died as an infant of pneumonia.

George worked as a peddler and was the only candy maker in the East Texas area.

From Henderson, the Thomas family moved to Longview in 1920, and has been here since that time. In 1921, George and Victoria bought the first piece of property they ever owned. This was the original home place of George and Victoria in Longview, and was located on the northeast corner of High Street and Marshall Avenue, where Eckerd Drug is currently located, which property is still owned by heirs of George and Victoria Thomas.

Three more children were born to George and Victoria in Longview: A.G. Thomas (born 29 April 1923); Tommy Thomas (born 31 August 1924); and Edd Thomas (born 16 April 1927). Mary died of typhoid fever on 7 November 1928.

George and Victoria sold the house that was located on their property at High and Marshall Avenue, and it was moved and still stands near the intersection of McCann Road and 1844. They built the fourth home in the Brookwood Subdivision in the 1940s. All of the children finished school, with A.G. and Tommy graduating from Baylor Dental School. Selma married Mose Andrew Naifeh in 1946, and they are the parents of two children. Mose was a World War II veteran, having served in the European and Pacific theaters of operation, and he is now deceased. The four Thomas sons enlisted and served in the military during World War II, and all were in uniform at the same time. After the war was over, the boys returned to Longview and made their homes. Sam and Edd returned to the grocery business with their father, George, on the original property at High and Marshall Avenue. A.G. and Tommy practiced dentistry together over forty years.

Sam married Marian Brown, whom he met while he was on active duty in England and she was serving with the military service of Great Britain, and they had two children.

Tommy married Ann Tuley from Dallas, Texas, and they had two children.

A.G. married Nadyne Bussey from Longview, and they had three children.

Edd still lives in the family home in the Brookwood division.

In the early 1970s, Ward Drug Stores of Dallas contacted George wanting to lease the property at high and Marshall Avenue for a new drug store in Longview. The family grocery business (Food City) closed in 1971, and Ward Drug Store leased the land and the building from the Thomas family. Ward Drug operated four years, selling the business to Eckerd Drug in 1975. A new building was built by the owners in 1997, to accommodate a larger Eckerd Drug, and the business is still in operation today.

George and Victoria were of the Eastern Orthodox religion and encouraged their children to attend church services. A.G. and Nadyne married at Trinity Episcopal Church in 1946, and began to worship there. All of the siblings are members of Trinity Episcopal Church.

George died on 24 December 1978, and Victoria died on 27 July 1985. Sam died on 15 August 2001. All are buried in the family plot at Grace Hill Cemetery in Longview.

– Submitted by A.G. Thomas

JOHN THOMAS

The story of the John Thomas family began in Lebanon, where John was born in 1882. Throughout his formative years, his parents schooled him in the values of hard work, honest living, and dedication to family and God. He was raised in the Christian Orthodox faith.

This John Thomas family photo was taken in 1929 by C.B. Culpepper. (l.-r.) Front: Alyce, Isaac, John and Naseep. Back: Philip, Maggie and Azizie.

As a young adult who had acquired just a fifth grade education, John sought a quality of life he could realize only in America. His yearning took him to Pennsylvania in 1901; there he found employment in the coal mines. After some time, he returned to Lebanon and married Maggie Mack, a woman his parents deemed "a very charming young lady." She was born in 1886.

Maggie gave birth to Isaac John in 1905, and to Naseep John in 1910. It was only a matter of time before John decided to revisit America. During World War I, Isaac was not permitted to accompany his family because children ages 3-14 were not allowed to leave the country at that time. He remained in the care of his grandparents. Lebanon was devastated by the war, and it took the intervention of the church and the Red Cross to reunite Isaac with his parents and brother.

After traveling through Mexico, the family boarded the train in Laredo, their destination being East Texas. They decided to disembark in Longview. The year was 1912, and although they knew not a soul, they perceived the tiny settlement as a place of promise. John rented a house on Cotton Street and, after purchasing furnishings and food, found himself with only $65.00 to his name.

John managed to eke out a living for his growing family by peddling much-needed household

Victoria Thomas   *George Thomas*

items by foot. Being a gregarious man by nature, people along his route grew to trust him as a man of integrity. His business thrived, and John graduated to a horse-drawn buggy. Eventually, he opened his own store at 131 Tyler Street.

The family increased by three more children with the births of Philip John (1914), Azizie (1917) and Alyce (1920). The years were good to John and Maggie, and with success they were able to complete a number of lucrative investments, which included real estate development and contributing to the bringing in of a discovery oil well. John was part of a group of citizens responsible for the creation of Cherokee Lake. In the early 1930s, he was one of the first to own a home in Nuggett Hill, an area which recently has been officially designated a National Register Historic Addition in Longview.

Slowly, John's health deteriorated and his life came to an end in 1959 at the age of 77. He had turned over many of his business affairs to Isaac and Naseep, who went on to forge careers in the fields of real estate development and investments.

Isaac (deceased) married Lucille Barro, and Naseep (deceased) wed Margaret Jabour. Philip (deceased) married Alice Barkett (deceased). Azizie married Michael Jabour (deceased) and lives in Vicksburg. Alyce married Fred Monsour and lives in Longview. Maggie passed away in 1979 at the age of 93. The children of Isaac and Lucille Thomas are Jeanette, Marlene and Dianne. The children of Naseep and Margaret Thomas are Barbara, John Nay (deceased) and George Preston. The children of Philip and Alice Thomas are Philip John, Jr. and Charles Bradford. The children of Michael and Azizie Jabour are John Wayne, Pamela and Michele. The children of Fred and Alyce Monsour are Gayle and Garland.

History has shown that John and Maggie made a wise decision that day back in 1912 when they departed the train in Longview. They saw in the town a place of promise and opportunity and committed themselves to building a bright, secure future for both them and their family. They were proud to have played a role in the development of Longview.

– Submitted by Alyce Monsour

DAN THOMPSON

King Daniel (Dan) Thompson Jr. was born in McKinney, Texas, 15 May 1907. He was the youngest child and only son of Dan Sr. and Frances Abernathy Thompson. Young Dan had red hair and two older sisters. He grew up somewhat used to having his own way about things. Due to some of his antics, he was expelled from high school and had to repeat that whole year, graduating a year late. He attended both Texas Tech and SMU, but did not graduate.

Dan first lived in Gregg County shortly after the discovery of oil. He worked as a lineman for Southwestern Gas and Electric Company. Dan met his future wife when Dan and her father were both working for that company. Dan and Lucile Irene Reaney were married on 20 June 1934. Lucile was born 16 February 1912, in Oklahoma City. She and Dan lived in Henderson near her parents for a while.

Dan briefly left the power company to work

for Westinghouse selling appliances, tough work in the depression years. Dan was able to get a job with Southwestern Gas and Electric Company doing vacation relief for local managers. There were moves every two weeks all over East Texas until Dan was made local manager of the Daingerfield office about 1939. By this time Dan and Lucile had two sons. Dan Charles resides in Gregg County with his wife of 44 years, Martha. Dan and Martha have two sons and five grandchildren. James William married Verdine Ford of Kilgore. Jim and Verdine now live in Athens, Tennessee.

In 1945, a daughter, Nancy, was born and Dan was given a transfer to the Grand Saline office. In 1948, Dan was able to become distribution engineer in the Engineering Division in Longview. The family moved to Longview and Dan continued to work for the company, which changed its name to Southwestern Electric Power Company (now AEP SWEPCO) until he retired in 1972. However, when the chief engineer died, Dan was told that to remain an engineer he would have to have an Electrical Engineering degree. Dan then embarked on an International Correspondence Schools course in Electrical Engineering. This was a major task to accomplish and took more than six years to complete. Dan was active in Longview noon Lions club and other community activities. Dan and Lucile and the whole family were active in Wesley Methodist Church (now Wesley McCabe United Methodist Church).

Dan and Lucile Thompson, seated; Jim, Nancy and Dan C., standing – 1984.

In 1972, when Dan retired from SWEPCO, he and Lucile moved into their new travel trailer for the winter months and lived in Weslaco part of each year. Eventually, they moved to Carrollton to be close to their daughter, Nancy Johnson. Nancy's husband, Art, is a graduate of LeTourneau University. Lucile died in April 1988, and Dan in October 1992. Both are buried in Memory Park, Longview.

– Submitted by Dan C. Thompson, Longview, Texas

GREENE SMITH THREADGILL

Greene Smith Threadgill was born to Allen and Anna Threadgill in Anson County, North Carolina, on 7 November, 1832. He married Martha Ann Taylor on 20 January 1853, in Lexington, Henderson County, Tennessee. Sometime

Green Smith Threadgill, 1832-1905, and Martha Ann (Taylor) Threadgill, 18??-1886

between 1885 and 1886, they moved to Upshur County, Texas, from Henderson County Tennessee. Martha died on 3 November 1886, and is buried in the Concord cemetery in Upshur County. After Martha's death, Greene married Octavia Alread. He preceded her in death on 10 November 1905, and was buried in the Concord cemetery. When Octavia died, she also was buried there.

All of the Threadgill children were from the first wife and were born in Henderson County Tennessee. Several of the children died in Tennessee. Three of whom researchers are sure came to Texas are Mary Amy (26 December 1861–15 November 1928), Mattie (26 December 1861–5 August 1930) and Zemariah Tig (12 November 1869–15 October 1939).

Mary was already married at the time of arrival in Texas. Her husband was Robert Washington Williams (10 March 1856–16 July 1933). They already had one child, William Ernest (5 November 1883–24 January 1934) born in Henderson County, Tennessee. Later they had two other children: Martha Ann Frances (26 July 1892–15 January 1964) and Green Smith, called "Pete," (1 November 1898–20 March 1964). Mattie, Mary's twin, married Timothy Powell. Zemeriah married Martha Ross on 13 December 1891, in Gilmer, Texas. After her death, he married Claudie Payne about 1927. There are still many descendants of these families living in the East Texas area, as well as other parts of Texas. Many of the ancestors are buried in the Concord cemetery and in the Willow Oak cemetery in Upshur County. A Threadgill reunion is held every year in July in Gilmer, Texas.

– Submitted by Lolita Marie (Williams) Lloyd

SOLON & AUGUSTA TODD

Solon D. Todd, born 9 January 1871, to Mary Pelina Phillips and John Morgan Todd, grew up in West Mountain in Upshur County. Pelina's and John's parents had traveled from Tennessee in the same wagon train. Pelina was descended from Alpha and William Phillips from North Carolina. Solon became a gifted carpenter and enjoyed playing the fiddle and calling square dances. He married Augusta Elizabeth Johnston, born 9 August 1883, to Sarah Della E. Armstrong and O.G. Johnston, on 14 October 1906. Three daughters were born to them: Adele on 11 October 1908; Estelle on 28 June 1911; and Mary Ella on 28 June 1915.

Solon D. Todd, 1952   *Augusta Johnston Todd, 1953*

Solon was Station Master for the T&P Railroad in Gladewater until his retirement in 1932. He was known by railroad men for his soft touch on the teletype. Solon was a school board member who diligently sought the installation of an electric kitchen in Gladewater's new high school, in the wake of the New London, Texas, school explosion. Construction was completed on the new Gladewater school on Melba Avenue in 1935.

As a young child, Augusta played games with her uncle Frank Armstrong. By age four, she was making biscuits for the family meals. She often recalled her father hitching the mules to the wagon and floating it across the Sabine River to attend church. Augusta graduated from Tyler (Texas) Business College in 1900. Being skilled in shorthand, she became the court reporter for her father, Justice of the Peace O.G. Johnston. Believing that a woman should take a leadership role in community affairs, Augusta was active in the Gladewater Fine Arts Club, Library Board, first Rodeo Association, Rosedale Cemetery Association, First Baptist Church, China Painting Guild, Daleth Study Club and Garden Club. She created many types of flower gardens to have blooms year round at their home on Mill Street in Gladewater.

Adele Todd married Ancil Mason. She gave birth to Cecil Ann, Paul Todd and James Allen. Adele died in Trenton, Texas, in 1999. Cecil Ann, who lived there with her husband Ray Pierce, preceded her in death.

Estelle Todd married attorney Harold Kermit Smith and had two sons: Dr. Kermit Smith Jr., residing in Houston with wife Susan; and James Robert Smith, who married Diane, producing two children. The elder Kermit's father, D.T. Smith, was superintendent of Gladewater schools. Estelle died in Fort Worth, Texas, 7 April 1969.

Mary Ella Todd married Floyd Raymond McDowell, 3 March 1935, and had daughter LaRue on 5 January 1936. Mary Ella divorced Floyd; she married Earl B. Hamner in 1952, and divorced in 1960. She lived in

Mary Ella Todd Hamner, 1984

Bossier City, Louisiana, until 1960, moving to Kansas City, Missouri, where she was a statistician for the L&A–KCS railroad. She retired in Longview to be near her family, especially her grandchildren. Mary Ella died there 26 July 1989.

LaRue McDowell attended Gladewater schools until January 1951, when she moved to Bossier City; she enrolled at Texas Christian University (Fort Worth) in 1954. The following year, she flew to Australia to join her father and stepmother. In 1956, she and her family departed from Melbourne, touring the East, Egypt and Europe. LaRue married Richard M. Bolin in 1957, and had two children, Karen Richea (born 20 February 1960) and Kyle Wayne (born 13 November 1962). She divorced Richard in 1969 and married Carroll V. Guice 28 September 1974. Carroll is a doctor of chiropractic and LaRue was his office manager and x-ray technician in their Longview clinic until their retirement in 2003. They live in Longview.

(l.-r.) Kyle Bolin, Michael Robertson, Carroll Guice, LaRue Guice and Karen Malkey.

Karen Bolin is a graduate of the University of Houston (Texas). Married to and divorced from David Robertson and also Steve Malkey, Karen is the mother of Michael David Robertson (born 25 February 1989), a student at Clear Lake (Texas) High School. Karen is a senior accountant with Center Point Energy in Houston.

Kyle Bolin graduated from Texas A&M (College Station) in 1985. He married Lori Boaz, 12 October 2002; their son is Collin Boaz. Kyle, Systems Administrator with Children's Hospital in Dallas, Texas, created the driving safety program for teens, Guardian Voice. Lori is the paralegal manager with Thompson and Knight Law Firm in Dallas. They reside in Lewisville, Texas.

Solon's grave is in Gladewater's Rosedale Cemetery. He died on 11 October 1953. Augusta

died on 15 July 1976, at age 93; burial was beside Solon. She lived in her beloved home surrounded by her flower gardens until 1975, when she went to a nursing home. Daughters Estelle and Mary Ella are also interred in Rosedale Cemetery.

– Submitted by LaRue Guice

JOE V. & BARBARA S. TOLLESON

Joe Vernon Tolleson was born 14 August 1944, in Atlanta, Texas. His parents were Hubert J. Tolleson, a World War II veteran, and LaVerne (Capps) Tolleson. Hubert was born 12 July 1917, in Lena, Louisiana, and died 18 July 2001, in Texarkana, Texas. LaVerne was born 16 July 1917, in Ashdown, Arkansas, and died 27 February 1998, in Texarkana, Texas. Joe has a sister, Judy Tolleson Stanley (born 5 August 1950). Joe graduated from Atlanta High School and married Jimmie Leigh Harden in June 1964. They had two sons, John Daren Tolleson (born 27 February 1965) and Joe Don Tolleson (born 9 October 1968), before they divorced in January 1974.

Joe V. Tolleson and Barbara S. Harris were married 30 June 1979, in Atlanta, Texas. Barbara was born 22 April 1938, in Panola County, Texas. Her father was Grady Harris, who was born 5 December 1913, in Shelby County, Texas, and died 19 July 2002, in Longview. Mr. Harris was retired from Foremost Dairies, and then was self-employed for almost twenty years refinishing and repairing antique furniture in Longview. Barbara's mother is Syble (Pitts) Harris, who was born 29 December 1918. Barbara and her parents moved from Tenaha, Shelby County, to Longview in April 1950.

Barbara graduated from Longview High School in 1955 and married Farol Taylor in June 1955. This marriage produced two children, Kenneth Lee Taylor (born 11 March 1956) and Kimberly Ann Taylor (born 19 May 1961), before they divorced in February 1976. Kenneth and Kimberly both graduated from Longview High School, in 1974 and 1979 respectively. Barbara graduated from BMI business school in Longview. She worked for Messner Electric Supply and J.C. Penney Co. at Longview Mall. She is an image consultant for BeautiControl Cosmetics. Joe and Barbara are long-time members of Mobberly Baptist Church.

Kenneth Taylor married Julie Ann Bechtold on 4 October 1974. They had two children, Karrie Lynn Taylor (born 19 January 1977) and Ryan Lee Taylor (born 15 July 1980). After a divorce in 1982, Kenneth married Mary Ann McCaskill, 13 January 1985, and daughter Nicole Taylor was born to them, 9 March 1995. They were divorced in July 2000. Ryan Taylor married Sarah George on 7 August 2002.

Kimberly Taylor married Steven E. Gray on 7 February 1981, and two children were born to them before their divorce in 1991, Taylor Andrew Gray (born 13 January 1984) and Allison Ann Gray (born 20 March 1986). Kimberly married Jamie Davies in May 1992.

Joe V. worked at Texas Eastman Company in Longview for 31 years before retiring in 1996. He graduated from Kilgore College with high honors in 2002, and is now a student at the University of Texas–Tyler and working at Hurwitz in Longview.

Kyle and Lori Bolin on their wedding day.

John D. and Joe D. Tolleson graduated from Longview High School in 1983 and 1988 respectively. John graduated from Texas A&M University in 1988. He married Ginette Struck, 19 September 1998. They have two children, Kate Lauren Tolleson (born 12 July 2000) and Jack Matthew Tolleson (born 3 October 2003).

Joe D. Tolleson graduated from LeTourneau University in May 2002. Joe married Susan Worley, 5 September 1992, and they also have two children, Trent Andrew Tolleson (born 17 January 1997) and Trey Hunter Tolleson (born 9 April 1998).

All children and grandchildren of Joe and Barbara Tolleson live in the Longview area.

– Submitted by Joe V. Tolleson

CHARLES TOMBERLAIN

Charles Waymon Tomberlain and wife, Barbara Ann Hubbard Tomberlain, moved to Longview, 1 June 1956. Charles opened Charles Tomberlain Insurance Agency at 1214 South Mobberly on 8 May 1958. In August of 1981, he moved the agency to its present location at 424 North High. Barbara worked from 1956-1961 for N.E. Loomis & W.B. Johnson Oil Company. They have owned and operated the T-3 Beefmaster Ranch on FM449 since 1966.

(l.-r.) Standing: Charles Tomberlain and wife Barbara, Chuck Tomberlain and wife Babette. Front: Charles William Coleman Tomberlain and Morgan Abbigail Tomberlain, December

Charles was born 22 December 1929, in Hughes Springs, Texas, to Broud Waymon and Lola Mae Morgan Tomberlain. His father was a farmer and service station owner. His siblings are Mary Virginia Quarles, James Marvin Tomberlain, Wanda Jean Riggins and Carrie June Walls. Charles attended school there, where he was an outstanding athlete. After his Navy duty in the Korean War, he returned to the States and played football for Paris Junior College, where he met and eventually married Barbara on 30 May 1954. They lived in Lubbock while he attended Texas Tech University. Their son, Charles "Chuck" Morgan Tomberlain, was born 3 May 1961.

They both were very involved in community activities over the years, giving of their time and financial support to the YMCA, Civic Music, United Fund and numerous organizations and charities. Charles served as a Deacon of First Baptist Church, President of the Junior Chamber of Commerce and

Daybreak Kiwanis Club. They were both listed in *Outstanding People in Our Community*. They held charter memberships in Longview Community Theatre, Longview Parent's League, East Texas Fine Arts Association and Longview Mental Health Association. They joined Pinecrest Country Club in 1965. Charles was appointed to the Draft Board by President Lyndon B. Johnson.

Barbara was born 25 October 1936, at Ben Franklin, Texas, to William Edgar Hubbard and Ruby Endsley Hubbard. Her father was an electrician and her mother a nurse. Barbara attended school at Paris. Her sister was Zelma Raye Hubbard Walker.

Barbara was listed in *Outstanding Young Women in America*. She served as President of Longview Museum of Fine Arts, Longview Symphony Prelude, Longview Federations of Women's Clubs, Ivy League Garden Club and Longview Jaycettes. She served as Chair of Good Shepherd Medical Center Gold Rush 2002, Chair of 2000 American Heart Ball and Chair of the first annual Spring Arts Festival. She was a member of the Junior League of Longview, serving as Ledger Editor, Cultural Arts Chair, Student Art Show Chair and she preformed in Children's Theatre and Charity Ball Cabaret. She was the founder and Coordinator of the Longview Cotillion. She was involved in Forever Friends and served as Sunday school teacher for youth, Girl's Auxiliary Leader and Intercessory Prayer Chair at First Baptist Church. Barbara enjoys bridge, tennis, golf and travel. They visited England, France, Germany, Italy, Ireland, The Netherlands, Belgium, Greece, Spain, Mexico, Belize, Alaska, Hawaii and much of the United States.

After the death of Barbara's sister in 1981, she and Charles reared two of their nieces, Angela Ann Anderson Hilz (14) and Shelly Rene Anderson Dean (12).

Their son, Chuck, and Babette, daughter of Clifford Ray Coleman and Marla Sue King Coleman, married 19 May 1984. A granddaughter, Morgan Abbigail Tomberlain, was born 15 March 1987, and a grandson, Charles William Coleman Tomberlain, was born 2 February 1989. Chuck joined his father in the insurance business and he also owns many rental properties. Babette owns the Mud Hut, the first pottery studio in Longview. Their family is also active at First Baptist Church.

– Submitted by Barbara Tomberlain

LEE TRAMEL

Lee Tramel came to Longview in 1930 and worked as a mechanic for Pegues-Hurst Ford through

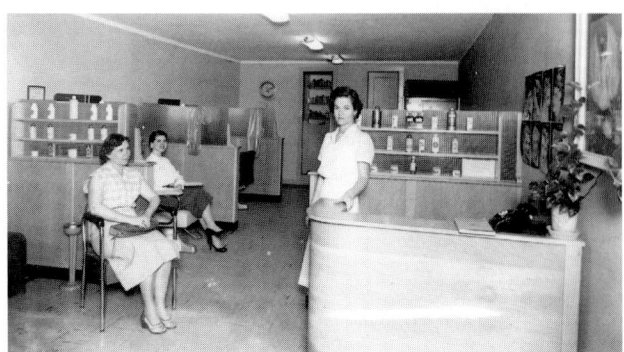

Margaret's Beauty Shop, 1954-55, South Mobberly at South Green. Margaret Tramel, standing.

1937. In 1947, Lee and his wife, Margaret, and children, Nancy and James, came back to Longview. Lee worked as an auto body repairman for Harris Olds-Cadillac until 1968. Margaret owned a beauty shop on South Mobberly for several years, then operated a shop at her home on Alpine Street in the late 1950s. Lee retired for good in 1977 after working for the Mercury and Ford dealerships. After several Cherokee Lake homes, the Tramels moved to White Oak where Lee died in 1986. Margaret lived in Longview until she died in 1998.

Nancy Tramel Culbertson graduated from Longview High School in 1960. She was in the band and was one of the first girls to earn a State Degree in High School homemaking. She and her husband, Lawrence, are now retired and live in Colorado.

James E. Tramel graduated from Pine Tree High School in 1962. He attended South Ward Elementary; then, Valley View, when in it opened in 1953. Junior high was at Foster and then the new Forest Park in 1957. After James' sophomore year at Longview, the Tramel family moved to a new house in the Everett subdivision in the Pine Tree area. It was in his senior year that James met his future wife, Christene Luman. James Tramel and Christene Luman married in 1966. He worked as a map draftsman for Gregg County when the tax rolls were put on computer and all property was given a lot and block number. Christene worked in the proof department at Longview National Bank.

After moving to Commerce, Texas, James earned a B.S. degree in 1970. He began teaching Industrial Arts at Spring Hill High School, and taught sixteen years. He then switched to the maintenance area and retired as Director of Main-

Pegues-Hurst Ford, 1930. Lee Tramel, fifth from right.

tenance in 1998 after a total of twenty-eight years. Christene also worked at Spring Hill School District for twenty-five years. She retired as the superintendent's secretary in 1998. The James Tramels have resided on George Richey Road in Spring Hill since 1974.

– Submitted by James Tramel

KIMBERLY BOLTON TSOUMBOS

Kimberly, daughter of John and Carroll Bolton, was born 19 August 1963, in Dallas, Texas. She attended Kilgore public schools until 1975, when she moved with her family to North Carolina. After graduating from Cary High School in 1981, she attended Louisburg Junior College in Louisburg, North Carolina, where she was on the Dean's List. Upon graduation, she attended North Carolina State University, and graduated from Wake Technical College. She was listed in *Who's Who Among Students in American Junior Colleges* in 1986.

Kim Bolton Tsoumbos and sons (l.-r.) Tyler, Sawyer and Spencer Tsoumbos.

While in Louisburg, Kim met Thanos Tsoumbos, son of Telly and Foto Tsoumbos. Thanos was born in Athens, Greece, on 17 June 1963. They were married, 5 September 1987, in Cary, North Carolina.

Kim worked for the North Carolina Parole Commission and North Carolina State University. In 1996, Kim and her family moved to Bryson City, North Carolina, in the Smoky Mountains. There they opened a very successful restaurant, The Mountain Steak House. Kim also worked in Swain County, North Carolina, schools with exceptional children. She was active in her church, Bryson City United Methodist, serving on several committees and teaching Sunday School.

In 2003, Kim, now a single mother, moved to Murfreesboro, Tennessee, with her children. She is manager of Applebee's Restaurant in Murfreesboro.

Kim is the mother of three sons: Tyler Aristotelis, born 20 July 1990, and Sawyer Lee and Spencer Lee, born 20 August 1994.

– Submitted by Kim Tsoumbos

BENNIE LEE TURNER

Bennie (Ben) Lee Turner is the twelfth child of James Jackson Turner and Permelia Tacora McFarland. They arrived in

Turner family, 1934. (l.-r.) Front: Ida holding Frances, Bennie Dee and Ben holding Clyde Albert. Back: General James Edgar and Glenna.

Emory, Texas, from Spartanburg, South Carolina, around 1900. Ben was the first child of James J. and Permelia Turner born in Texas. He was born 3 February 1901, at home in Point Texas.

Ben married Ida Frances Hunsinger, the daughter of Nathaniel Edgar and Lacy Lee (Echols) Hunsinger. Ida was born 20 December 1897, in McKinney, Texas. Ida's grandmother was Mary Jane (McFarland) Hunsinger. Mary Jane and Permelia were sisters. This makes Ben and Ida second cousins.

Ben and Ida moved with their five children from Chamberville, Texas, to Gladewater in August 1934. Their children are Glenna Winell, born 14 May 1919, in Commerce, Texas; General James Edgar, born 30 January 1921, in McKinney, Texas; Lemelia, born in 1922, died in 1932; Margie, born 1925, died in 1926, both buried in Dunbar Cemetery, Emory, Texas; Bennie Dee, born 19 January 1927, in Emory, Texas; Clyde Albert, born 24 January 1930, in Emory, Texas; and Willie Frances, born 15 June 1932, in Emory, Texas.

With the Oil Boom of the 1930s, many families moved to Gladewater. There were no houses to be found; like many others, they lived in tents at what was called the Old Soldiers Camp.

Ben and Ida had another son, Kenneth Harold, born 1 May 1935.

Ben worked with the well-known Dad Joyner during the 1930s Oil Boom in East Texas. In the middle 1940s, Ben purchased land on the corner of Pine Street and Highway 271 South.

Ben, son Edgar, and son-in-law Eartie Bee Weatherford built an auto garage and radiator shop. The auto shop was disbanded when the son and

Ben and Ida Turner children, 2000: (l.-r.) Glenna, General, Bonnie Dee, Frances, Kenneth, Gloria and Archie.

son-in-law moved on to other jobs. In the early 1950s, the state of Texas purchased part of Ben's garage property for the purpose of widening Highway 271 for the construction of Loop 485. Ben dismantled the garage and moved back further and built only the Radiator Shop in 1954. He moved the family into a house that was moved from another location, directly behind the shop. Ben and Ida had been living in the Shell Camp before moving to this location. They had two other children that were born in Longview Gregg Memorial Hospital. Gloria Mae was born 3 January 1939, their first child to be born in a hospital. Archie Troyce was born on 5 July 1940.

Ben and Ida had four of their children graduate from Gladewater High School. Bennie died 20 October 1972, and Ida died 8 July 1964. Both died in Gladewater and are buried in Dunbar Cemetery in Emory, Texas.

– Submitted by Gloria Mae Turner

GEORGE BENTON TURNER

George Benton Turner was born on 27 June 1899, at Longview, the son of Gaines and Emme (Riche) Turner. In 1918, Turner joined the military and served during World War I. About 1928, he moved to Los Angeles County, California, where he worked as a secretary in a law office and filled orders in a wholesale grocery chain store. In 1942, he joined the army. Private Turner was a member of Battery C, 499th Armored Field Artillery Battalion, Fourteenth Armored Division. On 3 January 1945, at Philippsbourg, France, he was cut off from his artillery unit by an enemy armored infantry attack. He joined up with a friendly infantry company, which was withdrawing. Seeing two German tanks and approximately seventy-five supporting foot soldiers, he seized a rocket launcher and, while under intense small arms fire, advanced to meet the tanks. Standing in the middle of the road he fired at them, destroying one and disabling the other. From a nearby half-track he then dismounted a light machine gun, placed it in the open street and opened fire on the advancing infantrymen, killing or wounding many and breaking up the attack. In the American counterattack that followed, two American tanks were disabled. Firing a light machine gun from the hip, Turner held off the enemy so that the crews of the disabled vehicles could extricate themselves. One of the tanks was on fire, and Turner ran through a hail of enemy fire to assist one of the crew. The tank exploded and wounded him. Refusing to be evacuated, he remained with the infantry until the following day, driving off an enemy patrol, assisting in capturing a hostile strong point and driving a truck through heavy enemy fire to deliver wounded men to a rear aid station. The courage and heroic initiative of Private Turner contributed to the defense of the French town. For his courageous actions, Turner was awarded the Medal of Honor. Turner died on 29 June 1963, in Encino, California, his ashes were buried in Arlington National Cemetery in Washington, D.C. He was survived by his wife, Lucille K. Turner.

TUTT-COOK

Millie Tutt, eldest child of Richard Hardy and Cordelia Warlick, was born in August 1869. Having decided to become a teacher, she graduated from what is now Sam Houston State University in the early 1890s. Shortly thereafter she married Samuel Francis Cook, a widower with four children, of Albany, Texas, and lived there until just after 1900. They had five children: Sam Tutt (born 1898), Hardy Rhodes (born 1900), Ida Ruth (born 1903), Sallie Mildred (born 1905) and Clara Francis Louise (born 1908). Sam Cook had founded the *Albany News* in the 1870s or 1880s, a newspaper which is still in existence, but they decided to return to Longview shortly after 1900 and open the *Gregg County News*. Millie taught both in the Longview public schools and her own private school. She was the sole support of her family after Sam died in October 1911. Her father, Richard, had died the previous February of pneumonia contracted when he went to a friend's house in the cold to pay a debt of no more than a few dollars.

In the summer of 1924, the Cooks moved to Houston so Mildred and Clara could attend Rice Institute while Millie and Ruth (who had graduated from Milford, now part of Austin College) began their long careers with the Houston Independent School District. Sam worked as the organist in the Majestic Theater in Houston when it opened that year. Rhodes worked as an independent musician. All of the children were gifted musicians. Clara, Sam and Rhodes worked professionally in that field for many years.

In the early 1930s, change came quickly to the family. Clara married Charles William Gribble, Jr. in 1931. Gribble operated Gribble Stamp and Stencil Company, bought by his father in 1910, and currently operated by his son, Bill. Clara had three children: Clara Cook (born 1936); Millie Ruth (born 1938); and Charles William, Jr. (born 1944). Ruth married Alva Eugene Jackson. Jackson was a teacher and coach in Pasadena Independent School District, but became a lawyer with Sam, who had given up professional music when vaudeville and silent movies disappeared. Ruth had one son, Alva Eugene, Jr. (born 1935). In 2003, Clara lived in Saratoga, New York; Millie, Boulder, Colorado; William, Houston; and Eugene in Portland, Oregon.

During World War I, Sam served in France. He was badly wounded on Armistice. He then served as a courier at the Versailles Peace Conference, making a long lasting friendship with Ignace Paderewski. He also served three years in the Pacific for the navy, first in combat then as a lawyer at Pearl Harbor.

Millie Tutt Cook retired in 1945 and died in December 1953. Her children raised their children, sent them all to college, and retired from their professions in the 1970s, except for Clara who worked for the stamp company until 1996.

Rhodes died in 1974, Sam in 1976, Ruth in 1992, Mildred in 1991, and Clara on 13 May 1999.
– Submitted by Bill Gribble,
Houston, Texas

CLEMENT & MILLIE TUTT

Clement Tutt was born in South Carolina, 10 March 1798, in the Edgefield District, South Carolina. His wife Millie (maiden name not known) was born 12 August 1799, either in Tennessee or South Carolina.

Millie Tutt

The arrival date in Texas for Clement is uncertain. Records have conflicting dates from 1820 until 1827. As early as 1820 appears to be correct if the birthplaces of his children on later census are correct. One list of early Texas settlers recorded that Clement came in 1824 and received one *sitio* of grazing land (4,428 acres) and one *labor* of farming land (177 acres) and declared themselves to be Catholic under the colonization law of Mexico. Another source stated he arrived with a family of nine in 1827 and that he was a native of South Carolina. On 24 September 1834, Clement bought land in the Free State of Coahuila and Texas, Municipality of San Augustine. He paid B.X. Mudd $1,990.00 for land.

In 1839, Clement was living in Shelbyville, Shelby County, Republic of Texas. In 1845, Clement's oldest son, James B. Tutt, was murdered by Joseph Simmons in Shelby County.

By 1847, Clement had purchased land in and moved his family to Rusk County, Texas, in the part that would become Gregg County in 1871.

Clement Tutt filed a claim in 1851 with the state of Texas. He stated that although he had not fought during the Texas War for Independence, that he had supported the cause. He had furnished a substitute, Arthur Tyne, outfitted him and provided him with a horse. Tyne served in Captain John A. Bradley's Company.

Clement had written his will on 4 January 1847. His estate papers state that he had died about the 5th or 6th day of December 1855. At the time of his death his assets included 84 acres of land in Rusk County and his total estate was valued at $7,183.50. The will named children at this time Elizabeth Rosaline, Jo Minor, Gabriel Jackson, Pierce Butler, Sydney O. Pennington, Mary Ann, Julia Ann, Richard Hardy and James Benjamin, "eldest daughter Lucy Ann who was the wife of John Vanripper having died and leaving children named William T., Jane, and James. My oldest son James B. being also dead without heirs..."

All of his sons, two sons-in-law, Thomas N. Tutt and John Wilson, along with grandson William T. Lane would serve in the Confederate Army. James Benjamin and John Wilson would both be killed during the war, and Pierce Butler would die later as a result of wounds sustained in the war.

Millie bought land in her own right that was to be part of Fredonia, a town that Hayden Edwards hoped to establish on the Sabine River (1839-1840) not far from where she lived. She also sold milk and butter to various neighbors. As evidenced by letters from her sons during the Civil War, she continued to run the farm.

Clement and Millie Tutt have hundreds of descendents in the East Texas area.
– Submitted by Sid Tutt

JAMES A. TUTT

James Alvin Tutt, son of Thomas Robert (Tom) and Amanda Pearl Davis, was born 16 April 1917, in Gregg County. He died 2 November 1994, in Gregg County and is buried in the Winterfield Cemetery, Gregg County, along with his parents and grandparents. James worked for Texas Eastman Company. He was a charter member and past president of the Gregg County Farm Bureau, a board member of the Agriculture Soil Conservation Service, served on the Gregg County Appraisal Board and was a member of the Longview Home Builders Association. He enjoyed fishing and hunting.

James and CarleneTutt

James married Carlene Mitchell, daughter of Benjamin E. Mitchell and Mary Caroline Bland. Carlene was born in Upshur County, Texas, 1920. She was an active three-year-old Sunday School teacher and Bible School worker for more than thirty years. Carlene was a member and officer of the Tuesday Bible Study Club.

Carlene and James were both active members of Macedonia Baptist Church. Both were involved in Dad's Clubs and P.T.A.s as well as being avid supporters for their three children and eleven grand-children's activities from sports to church.

Carlene and James' oldest son, James Sidney Tutt, Sr., was born in Gregg County, 9 September 1937. Sid served in the United States Marine Corps and is retired from Texas Eastman Company. He coached some level of boys' baseball for more than twenty-five years. Sid enjoys hunting and fishing. He married Marybelle Bolger in 1958. Marybelle has a Bachelor of Science and a Master of Arts from University of Texas at Tyler. They have four children and four grandchildren: Jim (married Margaret Ann VanBurkleo); Teri married Troy Cooper – they have daughter Teresa Sydney (Tera); Tim married Amy Prichard – they have Benjamin Pritchard and Mary-Austin; Tom married Karen Pierett and they have a son, Jonathan Thomas.

David Eiland Tutt was the second child of James and Carlene. He was born 28 November 1940, in Gregg County. He died in 1986 and is buried in Grace Hill Cemetery, Longview. David attended Southern Methodist University and East Texas State University (Texas A&M–Commerce) where he played football. He was a fireman for the city of Longview. He married Patricia Ann Stracner in 1962. They had five sons: David Benjamin, Matthew Kelly, Joel Hunter, Jason Eli and Daniel Ethan. Jason graduated from Baylor Law School. He died in 1997 and is buried next to his father. Daniel graduated from Stephen F. Austin University. Daniel married Sarah Ann Smyser in June 2004.

James and Carlene's daughter, Jamie Lynn, was born 2 November 1950, in Longview. She married Ray Wright. Ray graduated from Texas Tech University and Jamie from the University of Texas at Tyler. They both teach at Pine Tree Schools in Longview. They have two children, Jeffrey Ray and Jennifer Lynn. Jennifer graduated from Stephen F. Austin University and is a kindergarten teacher in Allen, Texas.

– Submitted by Tom Tutt

JIM, TERI, TIM & TOM TUTT

Jim, Teri, Tim and Tom Tutt attended Judson Middle School and Longview High School where they participated in many activities. They, their parents and grandparents were all members of First Baptist Church, Longview. Their parents are Sid and Marybelle Tutt. Their grandparents are James and Carlene Mitchell Tutt, Robert Cruess and Lillie Pearl Madden Bolger.

James (Jim) Sidney Tutt, Jr. married Margaret Ann VanBurkleo in December 2000. Jim graduated from the University of Texas–Austin with a B.S. in business management. He is a professional bass fisherman on the Kellogg's fishing team. He fishes the FLW and Everstart Fishing Circuits. Margaret, an R.N., has a Bachelor of Science in Nursing from Texas Women's University. She works as her mother's office nurse. Margaret is the daughter of Hoyle VanBurkleo and Dr. Julia Beville VanBurkleo.

Teresa (Teri) Elizabeth Tutt married Troy Ware Cooper, 30 May 1981. She has been a member of the Junior League of Garland, held many PTA offices, and a member of handbell choirs, a director for children's handbell choirs and a choir accompanist. Teri is a realtor in the Garland, Texas, area. Troy graduated from Baylor University where he played football. He is a computer/software consultant. Troy is the son of Troy Ware Cooper, Sr. and Virginia Ward Cooper. Teri and Troy have one daughter, Teresa Sydney (Tera), born 3 September 1983. Tera is a student at Belmont University and is majoring in music business. She is a member of Alpha Sigma Tau sorority and is a member of Gamma Beta Phi and Phi Eta Sigma honor societies. While attending Garland High School, Tera made Texas All-State Choir for three years, was class president two years, and an honor graduate.

Timothy Bolger Tutt married Amy Beth Prichard on 20 August 1994. Amy is the daughter of Dr. Charles H. Prichard and Doris Girty Prichard. Tim attended Aangenomen College in Sint-Truiden, Belguim as a Rotary International Exchange Student. He graduated from Baylor University and earned a Master's degree from the Baptist Theological Seminary, Richmond, Virginia. He worked in Washington, D.C., as a Legislative Assistant to Congressman Ralph

Back: Benjamin Tutt and Tera Cooper. Front: Jonathan Tutt and Mary-Austin Tutt.

Hall. Tim was the associate pastor of Briggs Memorial Baptist Church, Bethesda, Maryland, and is the pastor of the United Christian Church, Austin. He is president of the Austin Area Interreligious Ministries and the Northeast Austin Rotary Club, and a member of the Texas Conference of Churches' Commission on Christian Unity and Interfaith Relations. Amy graduated from Baylor where she was a member of Delta Delta Delta and earned a master's from Georgetown University, Washington, D.C. She worked on Capitol Hill and at Georgetown University. She is currently development director of Campaigns for People. She was a member of the Junior League of Washington, D.C., and Austin, Texas. She is a member of the Cherokee Nation of Oklahoma. Tim and Amy have two children Benjamin Prichard Tutt, born 29 February 2000, and Mary-Austin Tutt, born 9 October 2002.

Thomas Mitchell Tutt married Karen Denise Pieratt, daughter of Kelly and Doris Pieratt, 7 October 2000. They have one son, Jonathan Thomas, born 16 March 2003.

Tom graduated from the University of Texas Tyler and works with his dad in the Paint Contracting business. Tom's hobby is playing softball. Karen, an elementary school teacher, graduated from the University of Texas Tyler, and is pursuing a Master's in Early Childhood Development. Karen taught kindergarten until Jonathan was born. They are members of the Church of Christ, Ore City, Texas.

– Submitted by Tera Cooper

SIDNEY O. PENNINGTON TUTT & DESCENDANTS

Sidney was born about 1838, likely in Shelby County, Texas. He was the ninth child of Clement C. Tutt and wife, Millie, and was named after Sidney O. Pennington, a Shelby County resident and one of the signers of the Texas Declaration of Independence. He married his cousin, Harriett Catherine Tutt, in 1858. They had two sons, Sidney O.P. Tutt Junior, who died at about age 12, and Andrew Leon Tutt. Sidney was a Confederate veteran of the Civil War. He died young on 14 May 1868, in Rusk County, Texas, perhaps from injury or illness sustained in the war.

Tutt family. (l.-r.) Standing: Teri, Troy and Teri Cooper; Jonathan, Karen and Tom, and Margaret Ann and Jim Tutt. Kneeling: Tim and Sid. Seated: Marybelle holding Mary-Austin and Carlene. On ground: Amy and Benjamin.

Andrew Leon Tutt and Maggie Lollar about 1903. (l.-r.) Back: John Sidney, Eva Dove and Eunice Leon. Middle: Andrew and Maggie. Front: Ortie Bay, Bertha Ann and Millie Francis.

Andrew Leon Tutt was born 11 March 1866, in Rusk County, Texas. He and his mother were living with relatives in Red River County, Texas, in 1880, and not too far from his eventual wife, Maggie Lollar. The Lollars moved to Johnson County, Texas, around 1889. On 3 August 1892, Andrew sold 82 acres of Gregg County land from his grandfather's estate, and on 21 August 1892, he married Maggie Lollar in Johnson County. The couple lived in Red River County, Texas, for a short time before finally settling in Johnson County. They had seven children: John Sidney, Eva Dove, Eunice Leon, Bertha Catherine Ann, Ortie Mae, Millie Francis and Lona Ethel. All reached adulthood and had children. Maggie died in 1908, but Andrew never remarried. It is said that Andrew liked dipping snuff, whittling, and singing church songs while rocking in his favorite chair. He died in Alvarado, Johnson, County, Texas, 30 July 1940.

John Sidney Tutt was born 10 July 1893, near Clarksville, Red River County, Texas. He married Laura Gentry Orr in Alvarado, Johnson County, Texas, on 16 December 1916. John and Gentry had five children: Roxie Margaret Jane, Howard Louis, twins Hazel May and Mable Fay, and Helen Maime "Babe" Ruth, all born in Johnson County.

Mable Fay died at birth while the others reached adulthood. All but "Babe" Ruth had children. The family moved to Hidalgo County, Texas, before 1930. John was a self-educated man and a voracious reader. He died on 31 December 1967, in Corpus Christi, Nueces County, Texas.

Howard Louis Tutt was born 21 February 1920, near Lillian, Johnson County, Texas. He married Martha Etta Mullens in Mercedes, Hidalgo County, Texas, on 24 June 1940. Their children are Louis Garret "Gary," Barbara Jean, and Debra Sue. All reached adulthood and have children. Louis, as he is known, served in the U.S. Navy during World War II, and, afterwards, worked as a bookkeeper and accountant, mostly as a civilian employee of the U.S. Air Force. He is a Christian man, likes to read, and, in his younger years, was a talented artist. During the 1960s, he became expert in the artificial language, Esperanto, and, for several years, taught the language and corresponded with other Esperantists all over the world. Louis retired around 1975 and has seven grandchildren and eight great grandchildren.

– Submitted by Gary Tutt

THOMAS NEELEY TUTT & MARY ANN TUTT DESCENDANTS

Thomas Neeley Tutt and Mary Ann Tutt were cousins who married about 1859 in Arkansas. Their ancestry can be traced to Richard Tutt, who arrived in Virginia Colony about 1690, and William Underwood, whose family came to Virginia about 1630. William's daughter Mary married Richard Tutt.

Thomas Neeley Tutt, son of Richard Tutt and Mary Neeley, was born about 1832, Rankin County, Mississippi, and died in Gregg County about 1870. Thomas fought in the Civil War along side his brothers, Richard C. and Sidney, and Ross Webb, who married their sister Susan.

After the war Thomas joined Mary Ann in the Danville Community, Gregg County, where her parents, Clement and Millie Tutt, had settled about 1845. The couple farmed the land that had been left to Mary Ann by her father. Thomas died before 1870. He is believed to have been buried in the Danville Cemetery. His family placed a Civil War marker next to his wife and honored him with a Civil War reenactment.

Mary Ann was born in Shelby County, Republic of Texas, in 1839, and died in Danville at age 64. She is buried in the Danville Cemetery. Mary Ann and Thomas had seven children: John Z., died young; James Sidney; Gabriel Hansford; William Thomas; Julia Ann; Mary Evelyn; and Milly, died young.

James Sidney (1859, Arkansas–1900, Gregg County) married Hulda Elizabeth Mitchell, daughter of John Mitchell and Susan Jane Gee, in 1883, Gregg County. They had four children: Eunice Barnett, James Solon, Elizabeth Viola and Lucille Zelma.

Mary Ann Tutt

Gabriel Hansford (1861, Arkansas–1938, Gregg County) never married.

William Thomas (1863, Arkansas–1936, Gregg County) married Mary Cansadie Mitchell, (1865, Texas–1945, Gregg County), daughter of John Mitchell and Susan Jane Gee. In 1908, he and his family moved to Rowena, Texas, where they lived for two years before returning to Longview. They had fourteen children: Willie Mae, John Elbert, Thomas Robert, Henry Silvester, Ira Columbus, Emma Susan, Slade Barnett, James Solon, Mittie Erma, Odel, Charles Walter and Zellie Irene, and three children who died very young.

Julia Ann (1866, Rusk County– 1942) married Robert Barton, Sr. in Gregg County. They had eight children: Carra Bonnie, Eureka, Ethyl, Virgie Alice, Angus Bailey, Earle and Robert.

Mary Evelyn (1871, Rusk County–1952, Gregg County) married John W. Tutt, son of Pierce Butler Tutt and Martha E. Dungan. Mary and John had five children: Mattie, Julia Kate, Libby Inez, Thomas Pierce and John Howard.

– Submitted by Jamie Tutt Wright

THOMAS ROBERT TUTT & AMANDA PEARL DAVIS

Thomas Robert Tutt was the son of William Thomas Tutt and Mary Cansadie Mitchell Tutt. Tom was born 29 December 1886, in Danville, and died 4 August 1967, in Longview. He is buried along side his wife Pearl (died 2 May 1977) at Winterfield Cemetery. Tom was a life-long farmer.

Amanda Pearl Davis, was the daughter of William H. and Amanda Reese Davis. She was born 14 December 1888, in the Winterfield area of Gregg County. Pearl and Tom were married by Rev. J.W. Bergan at the Methodist parsonage, Gregg County, on 7 September 1909. Pearl sold butter, milk and eggs to supplement the family income. She was a wonderful cook.

Tom and Pearl Tutt had twelve children: Ruby Elizabeth (1910-1985) married Jewel Delbert Crawford in 1935 and had sons Marvin Douglas, Leonard Ellis and Delbert Troy, and daughter Reba Annette; Georgie Pearl (1911-1989) married Tom Clemens in 1930, and they had daughter Margie Frances, and sons Melvin Ray, Tomie Joe and C.C.; William Robert Tutt (1912-1996) married Doris McFarland in 1941, and they had one daughter, Cynthia Ann; Henry Otis (1914-1981) married Olga Pratt, and they had three sons Carlos Brian, William Thomas and George Everett; Lottie Bell (1916-2002) married Grady Gene Eugene Mobbs and had three children: Peggy Jean, Bernard Eugene and Larry Glenn; James A. Tutt (see "James A. Tutt" article); Tommie (1919-) married James Perkins and had two children, Patricia Rose and Ronald Tracy; Joseph Erskin (1921-) married Mary Maxine Patrick and they had five children: Jerrie Lane, Joe Michael, Thomas Patrick, Sharon Ann and Todd Gordon; Charles Edward (Pete) (1923-1966) married Lona Lorraine Thornton and had two children, Charlotte Ann and Robert Edward; Katie Lee (1925-1986) married James Durwood Bryant and had three chil-

Tom and Pearl Tutt family. (l.-r.) Men: Tom, Buck, Robert, Pete, Otis, James and Joe. Women: Pearl, Ruby, Betty Jean, Georgie, Katie Lee, Tommie and Lottie Bell.

dren: Glenda Gail, Kenneth Ray and Nelda Sue; Betty Jean (1927-1999) married first Howard Rodrique, and second Cliff Wyble; and J.W. (Buck) (1933-) married Rosie Lee Brown and had five children: Cathy Jeanne, Donald Mick, Ronald Wayne, Terry Allen and Chris Andrew.

In 1931, Thomas Robert Tutt and his family were living on a farm (located about the corner of Texas State Highway 300 and Blueridge Parkway, Longview, Texas). At that time the area was part of the Spring Hill community and that is where the children were going to school. It was a very rainy fall. The dirt road in front of the house was commonly called Spring Hill Road. The county road crews had worked on the road and when it rained the loose dirt quickly turned to mud in the low place in front of the house. Thomas Robert and the older boys made a "corduroy" road and charged a toll. A corduroy road is one made of logs placed crossways around the "low spot." They had a three- to four-acre pine thicket, where pine saplings grew up to 50 to 60 feet tall and were about three to six inches in diameter. Thomas Robert and Otis and Robert (the two oldest boys) cut about 300 fifteen-foot long pine poles. The younger boys laid the poles to make a road through the front yard from just past the bridge – it left the yard up by the garden. The toll was a quarter for cars and fifty cents for trucks. The bread man gave them two loaves of bread every morning to use the road. For a family with twelve children two loaves of bread did not go very far. This was during the oil boom in Gregg County. Oil field equipment was being hauled by twenty-mule teams. These were not allowed to use the road because they were so heavy they would have crushed the logs. Thomas Robert ran the road from October until April when it was time to make the spring crop. Amanda Pearl and the girls ran it from spring until July when it dried up. They made enough to buy new furniture plus had enough money to put in the crop. Several days they made fifty dollars. The most they made in one day was about seventy dollars. (This story was told by James A. Tutt, 1980.)

– Submitted by Jim Tutt

THOMAS ANDREW JACKSON TUTTLE

Thomas Andrew Jackson Tuttle was born in Talladega, Alabama, on 22 November 1853. His parents, with their children, came to Texas and settled near Hallsville. The parents died when the five children were fairly young. Thomas was 10 years old when he went to live with his Uncle Plez and Aunt Susan Harris in Gregg County. Their home was located where the White Oak Bank is now. He received the customary education of the times, attending school during the winter months, and helping on the farm through the spring, summer and fall, thus learning the virtues of industry and thrift and honesty as a lad. As a young man, he bought a tract of uncleared land in the Castleberry Survey, and himself cleared the place and put it in cultivation. This place, under his careful farming, became one of the fertile farm homes of the county, and he one of the substantial farmers of this section Then came the oil boom, and the property greatly increased in value, as developments came this way, and was the source of additional revenue, Mr. Tuttle witnessing the first oil activities on his place.

Mr. Tuttle was married in Gregg County on 7 November 1875, to Nancy Jane Bumpas, a native of Mississippi, in which state she was born on 14 October 1858, later coming to Gregg County with her parents and family. Thomas and Nancy eventually met because the Harris and

Bumpas families lived fairly close together. They raised a family of ten children, they being Julius Tuttle, Julia (Mrs. Charles Newton), Thomas Tuttle, Lee Tuttle, Jack Tuttle, Ruby (Mrs J.L. Spurrier), Fred Tuttle, Nobie Tuttle, Effie (Mrs. Floyd Jones) and Exa (Mrs. Joe Bander). There are numerous descendants in the East Texas area.

Mrs. Tuttle, who shared with her husband the pioneer spirit and stood his side during those early days when the county was a part of the frontier of the state, passed away on 11 March 1915. Her kindly nature and sympathetic spirit had endeared her to all who knew her, and although a home loving woman, she had that neighborly spirit that had made her many friends among the farm women of her community.

Mr. Tuttle died on 14 December 1933. He combined rare ability as an agriculturist, and real citizenship, he doing his full share toward community development, with a kindly and friendly nature, and his life was an inspiration to all who knew him, and he will be recalled as one of the influential men of his county, and one who did his part toward its development. He was a charter member of the White Oak Baptist Church.

– Submitted by Joyce B. Johnson

BLANCHE ANN MEAD ULLRICH

Blanche, a sweet bundle of happiness, was brought into the home of Harry Wilford and Carol Rude Mead in Patterson, New Jersey, 2 June 1940. Older sister, Shirley, was waiting to see her sister. They were joined years later by younger sister Roberta.

They grew up in Hawthorne, New Jersey, and attended Roosevelt, Washington, and Hawthorne High Schools. Summer times, Blanche stayed with her grandparents, cut their grass, trimmed hedge, helped with housework and was spoiled.

Blanche also spent time with her Aunt Bell and cousins Mark and Linda, helping them while her Uncle Everett served in the Seabee's of the United States Navy for our country. He served twice.

Blanche left high school her sophomore year and attended Sherwood Business School nights and worked days, so she could better myself. She also sang in the church choir of First Baptist Church and taught Sunday School.

When she was eighteen, she met the most handsome young man at church. They started dating and six months later married as he had really stolen her heart, and God had put them together. They married 30 May 1959. This was when Memorial Day was celebrated on its real day, when people did hang out the flag of our country to honor our servicemen who had given their lives for us to live.

In the spring of 1961, the couple loaded their Ford station wagon and, along with a wirehaired puppy, headed for Texas. Blanche's family tried to stop her from leaving New Jersey. She told them she truly loved her "honey" and that she would go to the ends of the world with him. Then they thought he was a millionaire because he came from Texas.

The Tuttle family

Oh, how they wished! Blanche and Bob have been together forty-four wonderful years and say God knew His plan when he put them together.

Their son was born 6-1/2 years later. He was one of the last babies born at Gladewater Municipal Hospital in 1965. If those walls could talk now, they could tell many stories. Blanche also worked within those walls. The family moved from Mary to Maple by the old Gladewater track in 1974. They sold out and bought the Marvin Pursell home at Union Grove.

Blanche moved from a big county in New Jersey to East Texas, where she will live until God has other plans for her. She was President of the Gladewater Jaycettes and, in 1976, Worthy Matron, Order of the Eastern Star.

She taught Sunday School and sang in the Choir at Gladewater First Baptist Church (Irby Bates, pastor; B.B. Fields, choir director). She was custodian at Union Grove schools for 13 years. She attended Kilgore College, earning her GED and later a nurse aide license.

Blanche worked for 17 great years for Good Shepherd Medical Center, Longview, Texas. She watched the hospital grow from small to big. She also received different awards and honors. A plaque in the hospital lobby as well as the Heart window in the Emergency Room will always display her name for contributions to this great place.She also worked on the oncology floor, which was very challenging.

Blanche is doing God's work more for the White Oak Community church. These are great people who love their Lord and she is glad to worship with them.

– Submitted by Blanche Ullrich

JENNIE LYNN BONHAM ULLRICH

A sweet bundle of joy was born at Good Shepherd Hospital on 7 April 1955, to Dorothy Smith. Jennie was adopted by Robert and Mandie Capps. She grew up in the Longview area and attended Longview schools through 1972.

She married 31 August 1972, to Michael Eugene Bonham, who had stolen her heart. Their first daughter, Patty Lynn Bonham, was born on 12 February 1974. Patty was a beautiful baby and brought much joy into their lives. Patty grew up and attended Longview schools through the fourth grade. She moved to the Pine Tree area and graduated in 1993. She now lives at Union Grove.

A second daughter, Eugenia Michelle Bonham, joined the household on 20 October 1982. She was also a beautiful baby and received much love. She attended Pine Tree schools and is being home schooled to graduate. Michelle married John Lee Woodcock on 16 August 2002. They now reside in Union Grove.

Jennie and Michael Bonham divorced in 1996. Jennie lived in the Pine Tree area for about nine years.

Jennie had not planned to remarry, but the love bug bit, and she met the cutie pie of her life: Robert Olin Ullrich. Robert and Jennie dated in 2002, and decided they wanted to spend the rest of their lives together. He was cute, religious and really made her heart skip beats. On 28 March 2003, they repeated their wedding vows. They are very much in love. They reside in Union Grove.

She married Robert Olin, and now she has the most wonderful, happy, religious helpful mother-in-law, Blanche, and father-in-law, Bob, that a girl could want.

Jennie and Robert have four great children: Austin Dakota and Sierra Cheyenne are Robert's children, and Patty Lynn and Eugenia Michelle are Jennie's children. The girls adore their stepfather Robert very much as Jennie adores his children.

Robert and Jennie remain friends.

– Submitted by Jennie Ullrich

ROBERT EDWARD ULLRICH

Robert Edward Ullrich was born in Patterson, New Jersey, at St. Joseph's Hospital 19 February 1938, to Clara Tuthill Coleman. Bob attended Public School #6, Devitts, Carson Long Institute. He came to East Texas in 1952, and graduated in 1956 from Union Grove High School. Bob served in the United States Army from 1956 to 1958, and received an Honorable Discharge. He worked in New Jersey for a time at the Manhattan Shirt Company.

Bob met his lifetime sweetheart in 1958 at church, dated six months, married in May 1959, and moved back to East Texas in 1961. Bob and Blanche Ann Mead have spent 44 years together and love each other more now than before.

Bob began his work career in East Texas working for R.G. LeTourneau as a machinist. He then became an Assistant Personnel Manager. Mr. R.G. was alive and going full steam ahead in 1964. (R.G. LeTourneau is known for building the largest earth moving machinery in the world.)

For 35 years, Bob has announced football games at Union Grove High School. For ten years, he wrote a column for the Gladewater Mirror. He wrote "The Lions Den" by the Old Lion (Bob). He coached little league baseball for ten years. Bob belonged to the Kiwanis and Lions for ten years. He held the second highest office in the Jaycees as Texas State Vice President National Director. He played Santa Claus for the Jaycee's Christmas visiting programs at Gladewater Municipal hospital and Union Grove and Gladewater Schools.

Bob coached young men's church softball.

Robert E. Ullrich family. (l.-r.) Standing: Jeannie Ullrich, Robert O. Ullrich and Austin Dakota Ullrich. Seated: Blanche Ann Ullrich, Sierra Cheyenne Ullrich and Bob Ullrich.

He was very instrumental in helping to set up the city of Union Grove. He was president of the Union Grove athletic boosters.

Bob Ullrich is a wonderful husband and father. He enjoys people, lives life to its fullest and loves helping people. He loves God and enjoys learning all he can about God.

Bob married Blanche Ann Mead at her parents' home (Harry Wilford Mead and Carol Rude Mead) in Hawthorne, New Jersey. They had a beautiful garden wedding. Blanche is the love of Bob's life. His favorite saying to her is, "I love you more than you love me." She answers, "No! You don't." They make this a game and truly love each other. After 6-1/2 years of marriage, she presented Bob with a son. He was, and is, their true bundle of joy and remains in their hearts.

Bob enjoys collecting. At home, he has school memorabilia that dates back to 1938. He has a two-story building and a double car garage that holds his collection. His biggest past time is genealogy. He was 61 when he decided to find out who his relatives were. In 2003, he organized the Gladewater Genealogy Club. It keeps his mind active and his hands busy.

Bob is now doing God's work at White Oak Community Church. These are great people who love their Lord, and he is glad to worship with them.

– Submitted by Robert E. Ullrich

ROBERT OLIN ULLRICH

Robert Olin Ullrich began life on 5 October 1965. He was welcomed into the home of Bob and Blanche Ullrich. Their wish had finally been answered from above. They now had their son they had waited for so long. God blessed them with a healthy, handsome young man. Robert was one of the last babies born at the Gladewater Municipal Hospital.

Robert grew up in a fine Christian home, attended Sunday school and church, and received many Sunday school and Bible school awards. He had a pony named Lady that he loved to ride. Only one hitch, Lady would not move unless someone led her by the rein. So guess who spent lots of time with Lady and Robert? You guessed right – dear mom.

When Robert was three he flew to New Jersey to meet his grandparents and other relatives. Although he does not remember the trip, it must have been exciting as they flew on a 757 jet. His Grandpa Harry W. Mead was very sick and dying with cancer. Robert also made his first bus trip from New Jersey to Texas – another trip he does not remember.

The family lived in Gladewater near the bus barn when he began school. Every morning Robert went early to help his favorite bus driver sweep the bus. When Robert was in the fourth grade, the family moved to Union Grove. In the summer, he played Little League Baseball. His father, Bob, was the umpire; sometimes he called Robert out when Robert did not think he should have been called out. But Robert loved him anyway, he was his Dad.

One hot summer Saturday afternoon he talked his Dad into taking him to the pool. Robert had a blast, jumping up and down on the 12-foot high diving board. That's right and guess what? He was getting his face wet and did not mind a bit.

Growing up Robert was very accident prone—an accident waiting to happen. He braved them all and is still here. He played football in school. His dad told Robert whatever he started he had to finish, whether he liked it or not.

Robert has completed a Basic plus-Be Tex Site Specific Training. He has a certificate for participating in the National Household Survey on Drug Abuse. He also took a certified Nurse's Aide course through Kilgore College and was a member of the Union Grove Fire Department. Robert has experienced many trades, but his favorites are the oil field and nurse's aid work.

Robert is the father of two beautiful children: Austin Dakota and Sierra Cheyenne. Both are enjoyable and fun to be around. They are the loves of his life.

Robert married Jennie Bonham in 2003. She has two daughters, Patty and Michelle. He is proud to be their stepfather. They are happy and plan to spend many good years together.

– Submitted by Robert O. Ullrich

SIERRA CHEYENNE ULLRICH & AUSTIN DAKOTA ULLRICH

Born 19 October 1993, at Good Shepherd Medical Center, Longview, Texas, Austin is the son of Robert Olin and Ragena Gay Boone. His parents are divorced but remain friends. He met his dad for the first time when four years old, and they get along well. Austin is a fine ten-year-old attending Hallsville public schools, placing above average in his grade level. He loves to read and has received awards for the number of books he has completed. Austin enjoys going and doing different things like watching movies, roller skating, bicycle riding, moving grass, watching TV and playing games. He likes using his mind. His grandmother was the late Patricia Jackson Boone. She was a good grandma but very sick, and God took her to be with Him on 14 July 2001.

His great-grandmother, Nellie Jackson, lives in Hallsville, and Austin has many aunts and uncles living there, too. His cousin Toni took Austin on small trips to see many things. He's been to the zoo, amusement parks, car races, Six Flags and lots more. Austin has been an honor student through his school years—he loves school.

This fine young man is the grandson of Robert E. (Bob) and Blanche A. Ullrich.

Born 7 July 2000, at Good Shepherd Medical Center, Longview Texas, Sierra Cheyenne is the daughter of Robert Olin Boone and Regena Boone Ullrich. She met Daddy when she was about eighteen months old. They like each other, and she follows him like a shadow. Sierra's a sweetheart, 3 years old, full of energy and beautiful naturally curly hair. She's just learning many new things and has lots more to learn.

Sierra loves her brother, Austin Dakota, or as she calls him, "Kota." She does not like him to be out of her sight for very long. Her maternal grandmother was Patricia Jackson Boone. When Sierra entered the world she was grandma's girl. At that time grandma was a very sick lady and wanted Sierra with her all the time. God took Grandma to be with Him and live in heaven on the fourteenth of July 2001.

Sierra's great grandma, Nellie Jackson, lives in Hallsville, Texas. She has many aunts and uncles living there too. She loves to go, go, go and get into mischief; that's her real name: Mischief Go-Go-Girl. Every other weekend is spent with her father and her paternal grandparents, Paw and Maw, otherwise known as Bob and Blanche Mead Ullrich. They love her so much. She enjoys getting into Paw's desk and stuff, the telephone, blood pressure cuff and whatever she can find.

She loves maw and is always telling her "eat," and then gives her cakes, cookies or fresh fruit. Sierra delights in tasting Maw's and Paw's drink. They both think she's "just the cat's pajamas" since she is so cute.

GEORGE V. UTZMAN, JR.

Johannes Utzman emigrated to this country from the Palatines in Germany in 1738, and settled in Pennsylvania where he lived the remainder of his life. Some of his descendants moved to Rowan County, North Carolina, and later to Tennessee and Texas. Among them was Jacob Utzman, grandson of Johannes.

Jacob Utzman married Mary Beard, daughter of John Lewis Beard. One of their sons, Lewis Utzman, was the first realtor in Salisbury, although he was a cabinet maker by trade.

Another son, John Utzman, was also prominent. He was elected to the Town Board in 1827 by his fellow townsman.

George Utzman, another son, served as Coroner of Rowan County and was a copper and tinsmith by trade.

Jacob Utzman, Jr. was left an orphan in 1807, and was apprenticed to Joseph Brown to learn the carpenter trade.

Mary Utzman, a daughter of Jacob and Mary, married George Vogler. George's uncle, Christopher Vogler, was the leading gunsmith in the Carolinas in the 18th century and his brother, John Vogler, was the leading silversmith.

Eight generations of Utzmans have lived in Gregg County since Jacob, Jr. migrated from Blount County, Tennessee, in the late 1840s with his family. He was born in 1802, and in 1820 was married to Nancy Gillespie. Children born to them were Thomas, George Vogler, John L., Mumford, William, Mary Jane, Martha, Jacob, James and Margaret. Jacob died 5 January 1852.

Jacob's second son was George Vogler Utzman who was a farmer and sawmill operator. He was born in Tennessee in 1823, and in 1846 was married to Emily Laird.

Emily was born 18 October 1825, and was the daughter of Andrew Jordan and Nancy Penn Laird. George and Emily's children were Francis Marion, George, Jr., James Monroe, Nancy and William D. "Dick" Utzman.

George V. Utzman, Jr. was born 6 February 1859, in the Danville Community, and in 1879 he married Mollie Tennessee Lee. She was the daughter of William and Sarah Adams Lee and was born 6 November 1859, in Maryville, Tennessee. Mollie came to the Danville Community when she was three months old. Her father had died before she was born and her 17-year old brother, Sam, brought the family to Texas in a covered wagon to be near her mother's parents, Lemuel and Elizabeth Brewer Adams.

Children born to George, Jr. and Mollie:

1. Eula Mae, born 7 November 1880, died 15 April 1975, married John Justice;

2. Ora Lee, born 26 September 1883, died 17 November 1978, married Lemuel Adams;

3. William Wayne, born 9 September 1885, died 25 September 1970, married Annie Lou Mitcham;

4. Cordie Alice, born 6 July 1887, died 26 September 1942, married Claude Bailey;

5. Georgia Flo, born 10 August 1889, died 28 October 1980, married Thomas Landers;

6. Henry Curtis, born 24 January 1891, died 22 September 1986;

7. Thomas Marvin, born 23 February 1894, died 17 December 1977, married Lois Dobbs;

8. Olive Emily Belle, born 13 September 1899, died 8 April 1985, married Rev. William C. Jones.

George Utzman, Jr. was a farmer, and the Utzman farm was located at Cotton Street and Spur 63, where there are presently three car dealerships. He owned a cotton gin in Danville and was also a sawmill operator. He was a fox hunter and for many years was the county champion fiddle player. He died in an automobile accident 1 May 1938, and Mollie died 31 May 1949.

George V. Utzman, Jr. Family, c. 1911. (l.-r.) Front: George Utzman, Jr., Olive Emily Belle and Mollie Tennessee. Back: Thomas Marvin, Georgia Flo, Henry Curtis, Cordie Alice, William Wayne, Ora Lee and Eula Mae.

Grandchildren of Mollie and George Utzman, Jr. now living in Gregg County are Tom Landers, Jr., William Utzman and Lou Gene Utzman Henderson.

– Submitted by Tom Landers, Jr.

WILLIAM E. & NORCIE MORGAN WADE

The Texas and Pacific Railroad transferred the Wade family with their eight children to Longview in 1923. William E. Wade was born in Clinton, Missouri, on 14 December 1879 (died 1972).

William's father, William Richard Wade (2 May 1852, place unknown–May 1938), made three trips as Wagon Master and blacksmith to Texas from Missouri. He had a federal land grant in Belle Plains, Texas. He was unable to make a living there and moved to Baird, Texas.

W.E. Wade worked as a water boy for the T&P, and later as a fireman throwing coal in the boiler of the locomotive. He worked for the T&P for fifty years.

W.E. married Norcie Morgan in Albany, Texas, on 26 February 1906. Norcie was born near the Llano River, Kerr County, Texas, on 2 May 1852 (there is no record of her birth), and died in 1978.

W.E. and Norcie had eight children. Arthur E. Wade was born 15 December 1906 (died 1991), in Big Springs, Texas, in a boxcar apartment! The second child, Irene Wade Henderson, was born 2 June 1908 in Baird, Texas. (The Henderson family were native Gregg Countians.) The third child, Vernon Richard Wade, was born in Baird on 24 August 1909. The fourth child, Rosa Mae Wade Wilson, was born 6 August 1911, and died 1994. The next four children were born in Cisco, Texas. Ica Belle Wade Byars was born 20 March 1914. (Her husband's family, the Byars, moved to Longview from Alma, Arkansas, in 1908.) Bernice Wade Evans (24 December 1916–June 1981) married into a family who were natives of the Hallsville, Texas, area. Wilma Wade Ottman (the Ottmans were a long-time Longview family) was born 9 November 1918. Buck J. Wade (29 June 1921–31 July 1987) was a member of the famous state champion Longview Football team.

Five members of the family, Irene, Ica Belle, Bernice, Wilma and Buck, graduated from Longview High School.

In 1923, the Junction was where the railroad families lived and this area was separate from Longview. There were train stations in both locations where the passenger trains stopped. A favorite past time for children was to watch the big locomotives come and go. All children walked a mile or more to attend school. The Pea Town children (a community south of Longview) attended Longview schools. The town band played on the courthouse lawn. Ica Belle and her friend Marie Boyd played hide'n'seek among the caskets at the Edward and Young Casket Company!

– Submitted by Ica Belle Byars

ALTON EDGAR "JACK" & MARY EULA (WATSON) WALKER

Alton Edgar "Jack" Walker, son of Montgomery Hamilton "Gum" and Annie America (Blythe) Walker, was born 3 October 1877, in Monroe Community, Rusk County, Texas. He married Mary Eula Watson, daughter of Henry Lark and Mary Jane (Robertson) Watson, 4 April 1900, in Monroe Community. Mary Eula was born 23 February 1885, in Monroe Community. Jack was a farmer.

Mary Eula (Watson) Walker, c. 1960

Jack and Mary Eula produced nine children, eight of which lived to adulthood. Lawrence Wesley (1902-1987) married Patricia Cleopatra "Cleo" Boswell (1908-1999), daughter of Royal Grant (1867-1949) and Lucy Ellen (Wisdom) (1872-1948) Boswell. Franky (1903-1903) died in her third day. Bonnie Cleo (1904-1922) married Julius Lackey Tillery (?-?). Annie Florence (1907-1992) married George Alton Ingram, Sr. (1908-1962), son of Frank Zollicoffer (1881-1933) and Katherine Elizabeth (Alexander) Ingram (1886-1908). Kenneth Haskell "Hack" (1910-1962) married Hallie Lee Wallace (1911-1992), daughter of Spurgeon Wilborn and Jennie (Davis) Wallace. Gracie Lorene (1911-1976) married Ira Leonard "Ike" Bowen (1908-1987), son of Marvin David and Alice Virginia (Brown) Bowen. Frankie Pearl (living, California) married William Troy Medlin (1912-1987), his parents are unknown. Merideth Edgar "Bill" (1916-1995) married Hazel Ila Wallace (living, New Mexico), daughter of Spurgeon Wilborn and Jennie (Davis) Wallace. William Robert Sid "John" (1918-1950) married Lucille Brooks (unknown), her parents are unknown.

Alton Edgar "Jack" Walker died 28 October 1939; Mary Eula (Watson) Walker died 7 May 1969. Both died in Longview, Gregg County, Texas, and are buried at Hickory Grove Cemetery, Cross Roads Community, Rusk County, Texas.

Lawrence Wesley and Cleo Walker made their home in Las Cruces, New Mexico. They produced three children, all residing in New Mexico. Wesley Lawrence "Wes," married 1) Sally Maxine Boyce, 2) Young Hui Chin. Betty Nell married Darrell Wall. Patricia Ann "Tita" married 1) Ralph Brown, 2) Robert E. "Bob" Crews.

Annie Florence married George Alton Ingram, Sr. (see separate article for descendants).

Kenneth Haskell "Hack" and Hallie Walker reared three children. Kenneth Bobby married Alice Ann Houghton (1941-2000). He resides in Las Cruces, New Mexico. Jackie Lee (1939-1981) married Sylvia Vescovi (living). Cheryl Lynn married 1) Frederick Andrew Gerber, 2) Mark Rabon West, 3) Henri Edward "Hank" Castela. Cheryl and Hank are enjoying retirement in Florida.

Gracie Lorene and Ike Bowen had one daughter, Peggy Jean (1931-1987), who married Cyril Reginald Johnson (1928-1975). Their daughter, Tresha Jan, and husband, Doug Carpenter, reside in The Woodlands, Texas. Their son, Lawrence Bruce, wife, Christy, and family reside in Wimberley, Texas.

Pearl and Troy Medlin produced two children. Joan "Patsy" married Ira Leslie Jones. Eugene Ross "Gene" married Anna Vanderwuall. Pearl and her descendants all reside in Stanislaus County, California.

Merideth Edgar "Bill" and Hazel Walker reared two children. Gale Davis married Judy Matkin. Nancy Ann married David Harley Finley. Hazel and her descendants all reside in Dona Ana County, New Mexico.

William Robert Sid "John" and Lucille Walker produced three children: Robert, Bill Thomas and Timothy Lawrence. Their whereabouts are unknown.

Although geographically scattered, these Walker/Watson descendants enjoy a richly significant heritage in Gregg County, Texas.

– Submitted by Lawrence Bruce Johnson, Wimberley, Texas (great grandson of Alton Edgar "Jack" and Mary Eula (Watson) Walker)

WILLIAM W. WALTERS

William W. Walters was born 1806 in Halifax County, Virginia, the son of Abraham Walters and Judith Thomas who had married in 1802. William's grandfather, Thomas Walters, Sr., born in Ireland, took Oath of Allegiance to the United States in 1777, and served as a Patriot in the War of the Revolution.

Abraham and Judith Walters moved to Henry County, Tennessee, in 1820. It was there that William married first Marietta Swift on 1 November 1830. They had six children born in Henry County.

William W. Walters moved his family to Texas in the 1840s, where they settled just east of the Sabine River. He had been in Texas as early as 1832, and many of his original papers are in possession of family members. Along with other great men of Tennessee, he helped free Texas from Mexico, establish the Republic of Texas, and played a major role as surveyor, postmaster, stagecoach/trading post owner and citizen. Here, he and Marietta had three more children. She died in early 1865, and is buried in Moseley Cemetery near their old homeplace.

In October 1865, William W. Walters married second Mary T. (Johnson) Stone, widow of Manoah F. Stone (CSA) of Rusk (now Gregg)

County, Texas. William and Mary had two children, Sarah Ann, born 2 January 1868, married E.W. Clements, formerly of Alabama, died 27 December 1915, and had a son, James Henry, born 1870.

William W. Walters died in 1885 in the home he had built in present day Gregg County, Texas, near Moody Creek, some two miles north of where it flows into the Sabine River. He is buried beside his first wife, Marietta, in Moseley Cemetery.

The widow, Mary Walters, and children, Sarah Ann and James Henry, continued to live on and work the farm. In time the son moved away, but when Mary died in 1906, Sarah and her husband, E.W. Clements, remained on the land. Their six children, Quincy Edward, Minnie Mae (who married William Riley Phillips who descended from an early Wilson County, Tennessee, family), Annice, Ida, Mamie and Jack K. grew up in the shadow of William W. Walters and all he had been. The tradition has been passed on through the generations.

In 1984, an official Texas Historical Marker was placed on old Highway 80 east of Gladewater, Gregg County, Texas, in honor of a community called Point Pleasant, Texas. This was done by Hershel Miles, William Marshall, Edward Wesley Phillips and Murle Phillips Rhodes, children of Minnie Mae Clements Phillips. The name and accomplishments of their great grandfather, William W. Walters, is inscribed thereon for future generations to see. On the back of the marker, in loving pride, is inscribed: "In memory of our mother, Minnie Mae Clements Phillips 1892-1973".
– Submitted by Edward Wesley "Eddy" Phillips

DANIEL RANDY & JOYCELYN (DAVIS) WARD

Daniel Randy Ward and Joycelyn (Davis) Ward moved into their home in the summer of 1978. The whole family belongs to the Church of Jesus Christ Of Latter-Day Saints. Randy was born 19 February 1951, in Gilmer, Upshur County, Texas. Randy was raised in the Kelsey community and graduated from Harmony High School in 1970. He has been a self-employed paint contractor for over thirty years. He was married in the LDS Provo, Utah, Temple, 1 June 1974, to Joycelyn Davis (born 20 January 1956, in Pittsburg, Camp County, Texas). Joycelyn moved to Longview in 1969 with her parents. She graduated from Pine Tree High School in 1974, and in 1975 she received her Cosmetology License. Joycelyn was a stay-at-home mom until her last child started first grade. She then went to work for the Pine Tree School food service, so she could be home when her children returned from school. They have four children, starting with the oldest, Daniel, Michael, Shawna and Landon; all were born in Longview, Gregg County.

Daniel Arleigh Ward was born 6 January 1976. He earned his Eagle Scout Rank in 1991. He graduated from Pine Tree high School in 1995, then served a two-year Spanish-speaking mission for the LDS church in rural San Jose, Costa Rica, from 1995 to 1997. Daniel graduated from BYU with a B.A. in American Studies and a minor in Business in 2002. He is the business manager at

The Wards. (l.-r.) First row: Lillian, Caden and Elizabeth. Second row: Landon, Joycelyn and Randy. Third row: Shawna, Priscilla and Suzanne. Fourth row: Michael and Daniel.

Sam's Club in Logan, Utah. He was married in the LDS Mount Timpanogos, Utah, Temple 13 March 1999, to Suzanne Marie Reis born 16 October 1979, St. Paul, Minnesota. Suzanne graduated from Centennial High School in 1998. She attended college for three years, studying Dental Assisting and General Studies, starting at Century College in St. Paul before transferring to Provo College in Utah for an additional two years. She is a stay-at-home mom. They have two children, Lillian Marie (born 3 September 2000) and Elizabeth Marie (born 1 April 2002). They are expecting their third child in 2004.

Michael Davis Ward was born 24 January 1977. He earned his Eagle Scout rank in 1991. He graduated from Pine Tree High School in 1996, served a two-year mission for the LDS church in Salt Lake City, Utah, from 1996 to 1998. Michael graduated from TSTC in 1999. He works for Wal-Mart. He was married in the LDS Houston, Texas, Temple, 12 January 2002, to Priscilla Marguierite White (born 25 October 1979). She graduated from Burnet High School in Burnet, Texas, in 1998. Priscilla is a senior at SFA University, currently seeking a teaching degree in Kinesiology. She works part time as a manager of Pizza Hut. They have a son, Caden Nicholas (born 13 March 2003, in Nacogdoches).

Shawna Lynn Ward (born 1 September 1979) earned her LDS Religious Young Women Recognition Award in 1997. Shawna graduated from Pine Tree High School in 1998. She is a senior at Lamar University in Beaumont, Texas. She is seeking her teaching degree in Kinesiology. She works part time at Tinsel Town Theaters.

Landon Keith Ward, born 17 December 1985, earned his Eagle Scout rank in 1999; he will graduate from Pine Tree High School in 2004. He works part time for Quest Pharmacy.
– Submitted by D.R. Ward

WARREN

James Thomas Warren, Sr. was born 27 May 1866, Forest, Mississippi, to William Samuel and Elmira Jane Rushing Warren. About 1884, William and Elmira came to Terrell, Texas, by train, bringing their son James and his eleven brothers and sisters. William Samuel died in 1892, and was buried in Lone Elm Cemetery, Kaufman County, Texas. Elmira moved to Winona with son Robert, where she died and was buried at Harris Creek Cemetery. On 13 June 1886, James married Nancy Harriet Knox, born 20 June 1871, Kentucky, daughter of James and Rhoda Smith Knox of Tennessee.

In 1901, James and Nancy moved from Kaufman County, Texas, to Smith County, Texas, where he farmed land in Winona and Starrville. They were the parents of ten children: Birdie Ophelia married Tom Bass; William Clayton married JeRusha Ann Terrell; James Thomas married first Verna Gilliam, second Sarah Jewel Hosch; Alice Gertrude married Corrie Pounders; Ida Lou married Luther Lambert; Myrtle Elmira married H.C. Gunter; Jessie Hamilton; Johnny Brown married Margaret Seay; Grady Lee; and Charles Alonzo.

Around 1920, James and Nancy moved to the Friendship Community. Within a few years they moved into Gregg County, just south of Gladewater. Nancy died 26 July 1939, and James died 1 July 1947. Both are buried in Harris Creek Cemetery, Winona, Texas.

James Thomas, Jr. (Jim) was born 17 December 1893, Lone Elm, Kaufman County, Texas. After moving to Smith County, he married Verna Gilliam the 16 December 1916. She was the daughter of James and Mary Gilliam. A son, Lexa Knox, was born 22 June 1918, to James and Verna. She never recovered from his birth and died very soon afterwards.

On the 13 February 1926, James (Jim) married Sarah Jewel Hosch, daughter of Lonnie Stenson and Frances Melinda Rutherford Hosch. James and Jewel lived in Forney, Texas, for the first few months. In the fall of 1926, they moved to the Starne's place just west of Winona in Smith County. About 1930, James moved his family to the Pounder's place in the Friendship Community. The summer of 1935 they moved

James T. Warren family, 1945. (l.-r.) Back: Nancy, Cullen and Jimmie. Middle: Joyce Velma. Front: Jewel, Clayton and James (Jim).

to Gladewater. James bought a small house from Mrs. Baker that was on the Everett land. In 1954, James and Jewel built a home on 105 East Gay in Gladewater, where they lived until they died. James worked as the Gladewater Street Superintendent from 1949 until 1968. He was also an ordained minister of the United Pentecostal Church International. He was pastor of the Gladewater United Pentecostal Church from 1951 through 1956. Jewel died 7 October 1982, and James died 12 February 1986. Both are buried in Gladewater Memorial Park Cemetery.

The children of James and Jewel are Jimmie Frances, married Joel McKinley; Nancy Verdell, married Walter Marrs; Cullen Bunyan, married Diane Elaine Gentry; Velma Jean, married William George; Mary Joyce, married Donald Gentry; and Clayton Roy, married Darlene Macon. All six of the Warren children graduated from Gladewater High School.

Cullen and Diane Warren, 2003

Cullen was born 3 August 1931. He never missed a day of school in twelve years. He graduated from Kilgore College and the Apostolic Bible Institute of St. Paul, Minnesota. The 15 October 1955, Cullen married Diane Elaine Gentry, born 24 February 1937. She is the daughter of Bernard and Margaret Wadlington Gentry of Hobbs, New Mexico. Between the years of 1956 and 1960, Cullen was pastor of the United Pentecostal Churches of Corsicana and DeLeon. On 12 April 1960, he became pastor of the Gladewater United Pentecostal Church, of which he continues to pastor now, forty-three years later. Cullen is an ordained minister of the United Pentecostal Church International.

The family of Cullen and Diane are Cynthia Diane, married Roy Price; Cullen Mark, married Vickie Richardson – their son is Marcus Landon; Sheila Elaine, married Kerry Lee – their children are Kerry Dwayne, Jr. who married Lara L. Barnoske, Sean Alan and Kara D'Nae; Sherry Beth, married Thomas Henry Ainsworth – their children are Elizabeth Diane and Bethany Anna. The four Warren children graduated from Gladewater High School.

– Submitted by Diane Warren

CRAIG ANTHONY WASHINGTON

Craig Anthony Washington was born in Longview on 12 October 1941. He earned a B.S. from Prairie View A&M University in 1966, and a J.D. from Texas Southern University Law School in 1969. He was elected a Texas state representative, 1973-1982, and Texas state senator, 1983-1989. Washington was elected as a Democrat to the One Hundred First Congress, by special election, 9 December 1989, to fill the vacancy caused by the death of George T. (Mickey) Leland, and reelected to the One Hundred Second and One Hundred Third Congresses, serving from 9 December 1989 to 3 January 1995. He was defeated in the election to the One Hundred Fourth Congress.

MARGARET WEBB-BARNES

Carey Edward Webb and wife, Elizabeth Blakely, married 22 May 1922, and lived in Dallas, Texas. Two children were born in Dallas: Eugene Edward (June 1921) and Mildred Eunice (July 1925). In 1930, the old Dallas National Bank folded and Carey took a train to Longview and got the job as a bookkeeper with the First National Bank. He retired as a Senior Vice-President in 1962, after 32 years in the same bank (unheard of in this day and time). After school was out in the spring, Elizabeth joined Carey in Longview and enrolled the children at First Ward Elementary School. Mildred died suddenly in 1932. A year later, 20 January 1933, Margaret Alice and Marian Louis were born. Eugene and the twins attended Longview schools. The family first lived in a small house 4-1/2 miles out in the country on the Winterfield Road, which is now Tryon Road and in the Longview city limits. In 1941, they moved to 718 East Melton Street in town.

Eugene graduated from Texas A&M in 1943, and immediately went into the Army. He was discharged in 1946, and returned to Longview and went to work as a design engineer for General Dynamics, Lone Star branch. He transferred to GD in Ft. Worth and remained there until he retired after 44 years.

Marian married Paul Boozman in 1954 after graduating from TSCW in Denton, now TWU. They have two daughters, Claudia, born March 1956, and Cynthia, born August 1957. Paul and Marian are now divorced after 22 years of marriage. Marian has three granddaughters and two grandsons.

Margaret graduated from the University of North Texas in Denton and married Bobby C. Barnes in October 1957. Bob and Margaret have lived in Longview all their married life. Bob, a Certified Professional Landman, formed BOMAR Enterprises, Inc., oil and gas exploration, and semi-retired in 2001. Margaret retired as education coordinator at the Gregg County Historical Museum after 13 years on staff and as a volunteer since the museum opened.

Bob and Margaret Barnes have three daughters: twins Rebecca Jane and Pamela Elaine, born 14 October 1958, and Kelly Louise, born 19 September 1964. They all went through the Longview Public schools. Rebecca married Steven Fahle in November 1982, and has two daughters: Stephanie, born September 1989, and Evelyn, born February 1991. The Fahle's live in Southlake, Texas, as of 2003. Pamela mar-

The Webb family, 1950. Sitting: Carey E. and Elizabeth B. Webb. Standing: Marian, Eugene and Margaret.

ried Bradley Hall in August 1980, and they live in Whitehouse, Texas. They have four daughters: Amber, born March 1984; Audrey, born September 1988; Adrienne, born September 1990; and Alexis, born November 1992. Kelly married Matthew Hand in August 1988, and has two daughters: Haley, born July 1990, and Madeline, born October 1992. They are currently living in Longview. All three daughters graduated from Longview High School.

Carey E. Webb died in September 1965, and Elizabeth B. Webb died in May 1986. Eugene E. Webb died February 1996, and all are buried in Memory Park, Longview, Texas.
– Submitted by Margaret Webb Barnes

WERTZ

Mr. and Mrs. Forest Wertz came to Gregg County in September 1931, and settled at White Oak. Mr. Wertz was born 16 March 1896, in Tionesta, Pennsylvania. He served in the Army and went to France during World War I and then attended college. After college he came west to Oklahoma to work in the oilfield. He worked in the Tulsa area, and then in Osage County where he met Evelyn J. Smith at Shidler, Oklahoma. Evelyn was born 10 April 1903, Tahlequah, Indian Territory. She was an original Dawes enrollee with the Cherokee Nation. After they married 18 June 1926, they moved to Borger, Texas. Dorothy Jane was born 29 May 1931.

Forest went to work for Shell Pipe Line in 1932, and he worked in White Oak, Kilgore, Huffman and Livingston. After retirement in 1961, they moved to Kilgore. Forest died 12 January 1977, and Evelyn died 14 December 1986.

Dorothy Jane started school at White Oak in 1937. She transferred to Gladewater her fresh-

Evelyn, Dorothy Jane and Forest Wertz

man year and then the family moved to Kilgore in 1947, where she finished school in 1948. She attended Kilgore College and then married Henry E. Mitchell, from Navarro County, 8 August 1949. At this time they moved to Cayuga, Texas, where he was employed by Tidewater Oil, which later became Getty Oil Company. They moved to Venice, Louisiana, 1955, and moved back to Kilgore in 1976. Dorothy worked for Acid Engineering, Inc. and they both retired in 1986 to fulfill their dream of traveling.

A daughter, Terry Jane, was born 29 December 1953, while they were living in Cayuga. Henry went to work in southern Louisiana in 1955, and Dorothy stayed with her parents in Livingston. During this time another daughter, Linda Kaye, was born, 13 November 1955. Both girls grew up in Louisiana, received their degrees from Southeastern University, married and continue to live there; both are teachers.

Terry married Darrell Guidroz, 22 November 1975, and they have two sons: Tanner, born 30 September 1983, and Tate, born 30 October 1986.

Linda married Darrell Rabalais, 3 June 1978, and they have a son, Grant, born 27 May 1982, and a daughter, Maggie Jane, born 30 October 1987.

Forest and Evelyn Wertz were members of the First Baptist Church in Kilgore at the time of their deaths. Mr. Wertz was a deacon and a 32nd Degree Mason. Evelyn was active in the church and had been a Sunday School teacher, President of the W.M.U. and Past Matron of Kilgore Chapter #630, Order of the Eastern Star.

Henry and Dorothy Mitchell are members of Forest Home Baptist Church and Henry is a 32nd Degree Mason and a Shriner. Dorothy and Henry are members of Longview Eastern Star Chapter #610 and Dorothy is Past Matron of Triumph Chapter #203, Order of the Eastern Star in Buras, Louisiana.

– Submitted by Dorothy Jane Wertz Mitchell

HIRAM & GEORGIANA "GEORGIA" WHATLEY

Hiram Whatley was born in 1841, and Georgiana Stone in 1844, in Henry County, Alabama. They married in 1862. He was a farmer, merchant and served in the 44th Alabama Infantry during the War Between the States. Harsh conditions during Reconstruction caused them to move to Texas in 1870. Hiram then purchased 1,000 acres of land bordering Highway 1844, Judson Road to Forest Lake and west to Judson Church.

On 14 September 1883, a Missionary Baptist Church was organized. Upon the recommendation of "Georgia" Whatley, the church was named "Judson" in honor of Adoniram Judson, America's first foreign missionary. The church met at Lawrenceville School until 1893. Hiram gave one acre of land on which the church was built. The present building is located on the same plot of land.

Since its humble beginning, this church has seen the community, six miles north of Longview, become known as Judson. Lawrenceville School changed its name to Judson before 1900. Later,

Hiram and Georgiana Whatley, c. 1906

Omega, Alpine, Tryon and Winterfield schools consolidated with Judson. The highway north of Longview, the Post Office and many businesses bear the name of Judson.

The Whatleys had nine children to grow to maturity. The six girls and their married names are Anna Attlesey, Ellen Whitehurst, "Nobie" Ponder, "Ala" Adrian, "Cordie" Maddox and Eula McQueen. The boys and their mates are William "Bud" and Mary Gibson, Hiram A. "Gus" and Ora Lea Dickinson, Edmund "Eddie" and Nannie Rector (Whatley Road in White Oak is named after Eddie). Hiram and Georgia were blessed with sixty grandchildren. There are hundreds of their descendents living in Gregg County. The following families are related to the descendents of Hiram and Georgia by marriage: Richardson, Killingsworth, Henderson, McKnight, Briley, Graves, Smith, Hunt, Honea, Visage, McAfee, Page, Baggett, Gibson, Stillman, Rhinehart, Caldwell and Winningham.

Hiram was a successful cotton farmer, mule trader and raised hogs. He received a teaching certificate from County Judge John Kilgore in 1884, and taught school at Lawrenceville (name later changed to Judson) for several years. In 1894, County Judge J.T. Smith appointed Hiram as presiding officer of precinct 2, Gregg County at the Judson Courthouse for primary and general elections. The polling place was located at the Judson Church and, years later, at the Judson schoolhouse.

Hiram's great great grandfather, Michael Whatley Jr., was a patriot from North Carolina who fought for American independence from Great Britain during the American Revolution. His great great great grandfather, Shirley Whatley Sr., was born circa 1685-1690, in Jamestown, Virginia.

Hiram died from cancer of the jaw on 13 September 1911, and is buried in the Judson Cemetery. "Georgia" lived 92 years, dying 9 January 1936, and is buried next to Hiram.

Hiram A. "Gus" Whatley gave one acre of land for the cemetery before 1900. The First Baptist Church of Judson MBA has a State Historical Marker.

– Submitted by Wesley Whatley, Longview, Texas

HIRAM J. WHATLEY & GEORGIA F. STONE

The ancestry of Hiram J. Whatley has revealed a long and distinguished heritage. Hiram J. Whatley was born in Henry County, Alabama 27 February 1841, and was the son of William B. Whatley, who was listed at 43 years of age in the 1850 Henry County, Alabama, census. Most researchers of this line believe that William B. Whatley was the son of John H. Whatley, aged 71 in the 1850 Henry County, Alabama, census, who was the son of Michael Whatley, Jr., who was the son of Michael Whatley Sr., who was the son of Shirley Whatley, Sr., who was born in Jamestown, Hanover County, Virginia, in 1692, and died in Warren County, North Carolina, 27 August 1779. The wills of Shirley Whatley, Sr., Michael Whatley, Sr. and Michael Whatley, Jr. tied these lines together. Documentation showed Michael Whatley, Jr. was a Revolutionary Soldier and his son, John H. Whatley, was the administrator of his father's estate.

By 1860, Hiram Whatley had moved out of his father's household and was a clerk. He served as a 2nd Corporal, in Guilford's Cavalry, Henry County, Alabama Reserves during the Civil War and never applied for a CSA pension. On 4 May 1862, Hiram J. Whatley married Georgia F. Stone in Henry County, Alabama. Their marriage certificate was found in the Henry County, Alabama, court records. Georgia F. Stone was born 10 January 1844, in Alabama, the daughter of Thomas Wesley Stone and his wife, and was listed on the 1850 and 1860 Henry County, Alabama, censuses. Wesley Stone served as a private from Henry County, Alabama, in the Civil War.

Hiram and Georgia Whatley moved from Lawrenceville, Henry County, Alabama, to Longview, Gregg County, Texas, before 1874 because the 1880 Gregg County, Texas, census revealed their last four children were born in Texas and the other children were born in Alabama. They were farmers and lived in the Judson area of Longview after their arrival in Texas.

Children of Hiram J. Whatley and Georgia F. Stone: Emma V. (3 October 1863, Alabama–14 June 1872); Lucy Lee (5 October 1864, Alabama–16 January 1865, Henry County, Alabama – infant death); Anna Fariette (1866, Alabama–1949, Reilly Springs, Texas) married Robert E. Attlesey; Mineva Ellen (12 April 1867, Alabama–30 March 1944, Texas) married Francis Marion Whitehurst and is buried Summerfield Cemetery, Longview, Texas; William Wesley (12 October 1868, Alabama–

Hiram J. Whatley and Georgia F. Stone

14 August 1961, Texas) married Mary; Hiram Augustus (1868, Alabama–1934, Texas) married Leora Dickerson and is buried Judson Cemetery, Longview, Texas; Thomas McAlister (18 May 1871, Alabama–26 June 1872, Alabama) – infant death; Georgia Zenobia (24 December 1874, Texas–1944, Texas) married Lias Eitt Page, then married Frank Ponder; Alabama (1875, Texas–1957, Texas) married Bob Adrian and is buried Summerfield Cemetery, Longview, Texas; Edmund "Eddie" M. (1877, Texas–1955, Texas) married Nannie Rester and is buried Judson Cemetery, Longview, Texas; Cordelia "Cordie" (1879, Texas–1965, Texas) married Ahas Mattox and is buried Judson Cemetery, Longview, Texas; and Eulah Florence (1 February 1881, Texas–24 July 1944, Texas) married Daniel W. McQueen and is buried Judson Cemetery, Longview, Texas.

In the 1870s, the people of the Judson community met in the Lawrenceville School for Christian worship services. In 1883, Georgia Whatley, wife of Hiram Whatley, suggested the name Judson Missionary Baptist Church for a church she had attended in Lawrenceville, Henry County, Alabama. Georgia and Hiram Whatley donated a plot of land for a church, and the structure was erected in 1894. Baptisms were held on a member's property, and then at nearby Whitehurst Lake. In the late 1890s, Hiram Augustus Whatley, a son of Hiram and Georgia Whatley, gave one acre for a cemetery. The cemetery is located next to the church.

In 1891, Hiram J. Whatley's father died in Henry County, Alabama, and his son Michael was administrator of his father's estate. As an heir, Hiram was given land that his father owned, and Hiram resold the land to his brother Michael, so the property remained in the family. The court document stated that Hiram J. Whatley lived in Longview, Gregg County, Texas.

The 1910 census revealed Hiram and Georgia had been married 47 years and had 12 children, nine of whom were living at the time. Hiram Whatley died 13 September 1911, and was buried at Judson Cemetery, Longview, Gregg County, Texas. The 1920 Gregg County, Texas, census listed Georgia Whatley living with her son-in-law Dan McQueen. Georgia Francis Stone died 9 January 1936, and was buried alongside her husband at Judson Cemetery.

Recently a Historical Marker was placed at the Judson Baptist Church and a dedication ceremony was held. The Whatley family was instrumental in the development of the Judson community and their descendants continue to live in the Gregg County area.

– Submitted by Wayne Whitehurst; prepared by Linda Whitehurst, Frisco, Texas

WESLEY LEWIS & SHARON CALDWELL WHATLEY

Wesley Lewis Whatley was born 29 January 1929, in Longview, Texas. Wesley was the only child of Wesley William "Pritt" Whatley and Bernice Rebecca Richardson. His wife Sharon Caldwell was born in San Antonio,

Wesley Whatley family

Texas, 12 September 1930. Sharon and her twin sister were daughters of Pat Caldwell and Carmen Jenkins. (See "Claude Patrick Caldwell" family biography.)

Wesley's paternal grandparents were Hiram Augustus "Gus" Whatley and Lea Ora Dickinson. Maternal grandparents were Lewis Hamilton Richardson (former County Clerk of Gregg County) and Rebecca Jane Killingsworth. His great grandparents, W. Hiram Whatley and Georgiana Stone (see "Hiram and Georgiana Whatley" family biography) and Goin Bell Richardson and Frances Virginia Tincher, were early settlers in Rusk and Upshur Counties before Gregg County was formed.

Wesley and Sharon married 24 November 1956, in Longview and have one son William Clayton "Clay" Whatley born 19 July 1961, in Longview. All three are graduates of Longview High School.

Wesley received a B.S. degree from East Texas Baptist in 1949, and a M.A. degree from Stephen F. Austin in 1950. He taught at White Oak High School several years, and was Junior High Principal at Judson Independent School District. After Judson and Longview consolidated school districts in June 1965, Wesley remained at Judson until 1977, when he became principal at Foster Middle School. In 1980, he became the Director of Professional Personnel for Longview ISD and retired in 1987. He was employed by the University of Texas at Tyler as Field Supervisor of Student Teachers from 1987-1994.

Sharon was graduated from Stephen F. Austin in 1951, worked at Pan American Petroleum and retired with 25 years of service in 1992 as Secretary to the Director of Public Relations at Texas Eastman. She was an avid tennis player, being nationally ranked in Junior Singles and Doubles (with her twin sister) in 1948. She is a Bronze Life Master in the American Contract Bridge League. She is a member of the Aaron Burleson Chapter of the Daughters of the American Revolution, Longview. She is also a member of the Thomas Noble Chapter, National So-

ciety Daughters of the American Colonists, New Orleans, the Robert Ruffin Chapter, National Society Colonial Dames XVII Century, New Orleans and the Chalmette Chapter, U.S. Daughters of 1812, New Orleans.

Clay received a B.S. degree in Chemical Engineering from the University of Texas in Austin in 1984, a degree in Computer Science from the University of Texas in Tyler in 1987, and a Master of Software Engineering from Seattle University in 1992. Clay lives in Seattle, Washington, and is a project manager for Boeing Aircraft.

Wesley was active in competitive pistol shooting, having won over 700 pistol matches including two National Pistol Championships, and several State and Regional Pistol Championships. He set three National .45 caliber records in 1960, 1962 and 1963. He was named to the All Army Pistol Team in 1961-1962, All National Guard Pistol Team in 1958, 1959 and 1960, all Army Reserve Pistol Team in 1963 and 1964. He is classified as a Lifetime Master and was stationed at Ft. Benning, Georgia, assigned to the U.S. Army Advanced Marksmanship Training Unit in 1961-62 as a shooter-coach. He is a member of the Elite National Rifle Association "2600" Club, and holds the prestigious Distinguished Pistol Shot Badge (awarded only 562 times since 1879) for Excellence in Competition.

He served in the U.S. Army, Army National Guard and Army Reserve, and was honorably discharged from the Army of the United States in 1968 with the rank of Captain.

Wesley is a member of the First Baptist Church in Longview, and is past President of the Business Men's Bible Class. Sharon is a member of Trinity Episcopal Church in Longview.

Wesley was past President of the Mordecai Baldwin Chapter, Sons of the American Revolution in Jefferson, and is a charter member and past president of the East Texas Chapter #57, Sons of the American Revolution in Longview. He was past president of the Gregg County Texas State Teachers Association and Charter Member of the General John Gregg Sons of Confederate Veterans. He also is a past president of the History Club of East Texas, and East Texas Rifle and Pistol Club.

The following great, great, great grandparents of Wesley fought for Independence during the American Revolution: Michael Whatley Jr., North Carolina; Samuel Abney Jr., South Carolina; and John Richardson, North Carolina.

The following great grandparents of Wesley fought for the South during the War Between The States: W. Hiram Whatley, 44th Alabama Infantry; Goin B. Richardson, 12th Texas Cavalry Regiment; and William Dickinson, 19th Tennessee Cavalry Regiment, serving as part of Lt. General Nathan Bedford Forrest's Cavalry Command.

– Submitted by Sharon Whatley

I.S. WHITE: Life and Times, 1886-1960

Israel Scott White came up at a time when blacks had few opportunities beyond farming. That didn't stop White, the youngest of Noah and Susie White's four sons, from envisioning

Israel Scott White

something quite different for his life. A native of Camp Switch in Pleasant Hill, Gregg County, "I.S.," as he was called, was a man of purpose. He educated himself and pursued his passions in the business world with zeal. Equally as important, if not more, was his devotion to his community and the public good.

A graduate of Bishop College in Marshall, White earned his law degree from Howard University in 1926. He passed the bar in Oklahoma but found the practice of law unfulfilling. After teaching in Oklahoma, practicing journalism in Louisiana, and speculating in oil in East Texas, White built and operated Peoples Funeral Home on Roosevelt Street in the 1930s. He organized one of the town's first funeral insurance plans, Longview Burial Association, in the 1940s.

As an independent businessman, White took responsibility and great pride in working for the betterment of Longview's African-American citizens. He helped establish the first black medical facility, Camp Normal Hospital, on Methvin Street. He was an organizer of the Price Hall Masonic Lodge, the American Woodmen, and served in the state and national funeral directors' associations. He also gave time to the Longview Safety Council, the Boy Scouts, the Negro Chamber of Commerce and the Longview Voters' League. (At his office, White displayed a miniature voting booth that residents used to practice pulling the lever.) Throughout his life he served tirelessly on his church trustee board and helped the community secure a modern library and community center on Harrison and Luckett streets. In the early 1940s, he organized the first black high school Parent Teacher Association, and he is still remembered for trying to enroll his daughter, in 1957, in the all-white junior high school. Seven years later, a junior high school was built for African American students, Maggie B. Hudson Junior High, on Lilly Street.

What came to define the man, though, was his dedication to civil rights. Affectionately called "Judge," he understood the urgency of equal rights and Longview's unique history within that context. Texas' early laws prohibited NAACP chapters, but White served as president of the local branch and maintained confidential membership lists. He worked with national strategists, including Thurgood Marshall, to help overturn the Texas prohibition. The chapter subsequently supported

lawsuits to integrate the University of Texas and Kilgore College, and repeal the Texas poll tax voting restriction, among other struggles. During the 1959 sit-in at the Longview Walgreen's soda counter, White and his brother were the first called to negotiate bail to release the students.

Not only a dedicated community activist, White was also a strong family man. He married Velma Isam, an accomplished musician and Harrison County schoolteacher, in 1937. The couple had a daughter, Agnes Sue, and lived on High Street. For years, their home served as a meeting place for cultural and social gatherings in the community.

Among his varied interests, White was a natural foods enthusiast. He favored brown (whole wheat) bread and used a clunky industrial model juicer to make fresh carrot juice. In his backyard, he raised chickens, fruit trees and honeybees. His exercise equipment and therapeutic gizmos garnered light-hearted teasing, but he was not deterred.

Although not terribly successful in convincing others to follow his health habits, the "Judge" never stopped cajoling and prodding citizens to stand up and fight for what was right.

His life was a testament to his determination that the world could, and should, be a better place for all people.

– Submitted by Sue White Lione

DEACON R.B. (ROBERT BOB) WHITE: Beloved Servant of God, Family Man and Businessman

Deacon R.B. White, a well respected and loved gentleman of Gregg County, the state and the nation. Everyone was welcomed into his home. He followed and lived each day by the following lines from his favorite poem:

Let me live in my house by the side of road – It's here the race of men go by.
They are good, they are bad, they are weak, they are strong, wise wise, foolish – so am I,
Then why should I sit in the scorner's seat, Or hurl the cynic's ban?
Let me live in my house by the side of the road And be a friend to man.
– Sam Walter Foss

Deacon White was born 13 June 1881, in Upshur County to Noah and Susan White. He graduated from Pleasant Hill County Schools and furthered his studies at Bishop College. He was the third son of Mr. and Mrs. Noah White. His brothers were Sam White, Ben White and I.S. White. They were also established businessmen in Longview and Palestine, Texas.

He was a Christian man who gave generously of his time, influence and means to the support of Center Baptist Church, Sabine Valley Baptist Church and Bethel Baptist Church. He served in the capacity of deacon and treasurer in all three churches. He was deacon and treasurer for Bethel Baptist Church until his death 4 July 1975.

Deacon R.B. White, Longview businessman and farmer.

He was a life-long member of St. Luke Masonic Lodge 173, served as Worshipful Master and was the recipient of a fifty-year service award.

He was a member of the Board of Directors of Camp Normal Industrial Hospital, which was built on the property he donated for the building of the hospital on Methvin Street. He was a member of the Trustee Board of Butler College in Tyler, Texas; a life-long member of the Boy Scouts of America; and served as the treasurer for the State Convention for many years and was a well established businessman of Longview, Texas, and Gregg County.

He married Julia Williams in January 1907, and was married to her for fifty years until her death. To this union three daughters and one son were born: Perilla Horton, Izora Scott, Alta Charles and Roscoe White. He had five grandchildren: Joyce Williams, Peggy Scott, Patsy Franklin, Dwayne Bullock and Robert Charles; three great grandchildren: Dionne Johnson, Stephanie DeLoach and Kim Franklin; and two great great grandchildren: Krystal Johnson and Audriana Johnson.

Later, he married Mrs. Alma McCullough and they remained united until his death.

His Christianity extended into his life in many ways – through his love and affection for God, his family, church, community and to the many friends who frequented his home with a feeling of welcome and love at all times.

– Submitted by Joyce Williams

FRANCIS MARION WHITEHURST & MINERVA ELLEN WHATLEY

Francis Marion Whitehurst (3 March 1845–26 August 1916) was born in Henry County, Alabama, the son of Seaborn S. Whitehurst (1820-1877) and his wife Martha (maiden name unknown). The 1850 Henry County, Alabama, census lists F. M. as a child of 5 years of age born in Alabama. Seaborn S. Whitehurst was the son of John W. Whitehurst (10 March 1793–25 September 1875). John W. Whitehurst went from North Carolina to Alabama in 1819, when the land was very unsettled. He became a wealthy landowner in Henry County, Alabama, and was a member of the Methodist Episcopal Church for 53 years in Lawrenceville, Henry County, Ala-

Minerva Ellen Whatley and sons. Back: Emmitt, Theo, Travis, Elbert and Roy. Front: Hiram F. Minerva Ellen and Morgan.

bama. He was buried in the Lawrenceville Cemetery next to the church. The will of John W. Whitehurst was quite lengthy and named his son, Seaborn S., and numerous other heirs. Francis Marion Whitehurst was not mentioned as a grandchild, although most of the grandchildren seemed to be mentioned. No one knows why this occurred, but speculation is that either the family thought he was deceased because of his capture by the Union Army during the Civil War, or they had no idea where he was at the time of John W. Whitehurst's death.

Francis Marion Whitehurst enlisted in the Confederate Army at about the age of 16 on 1 August 1861. He was a private in Company E, 19th Battalion Georgia Cavalry, formerly known as 2nd Battalion Georgia Partisan Rangers. As a sergeant in Company K, 10th Confederate Cavalry, CSA, he was captured 28 December 1863, at Charleston, Tennessee. He was sent to Louisville, Kentucky, then Rock Island, Illinois. He was released 13 March 1865, at Boulwares & Cox's Wharf, James River, Virginia. What an irony that the first Whitehurst in the colonies was William Richard Whitehurst, who arrived in 1636 to help settle the Virginia Plantation. William Richard Whitehurst and his wife, Ellen, made their home at a place called "Three Runs" in the 1640s on the south shore of the eastern branch of the Elizabeth River, a tributary of the James River in Lower Norfolk County, Virginia. There was a place called "Whitehurst Landing" which still exists today. F.M. Whitehurst was back in the home of his colonial ancestors! No one knows where F.M. Whitehurst went when he left Virginia. He ultimately made his way to Bell County, Texas.

Francis Marion Whitehurst married Emily "Emma" Dickson 10 September 1871, in Bell County, Texas. She had a daughter from her first marriage, and she and F.M. Whitehurst had four children together. They were Effie Allene (22 June 1872–15 June 1886), who drowned in the Salado River, was buried at Hillcrest Cemetery in Temple, Texas; Ollie Monroe (21 March 1874–13 July, 1954) was buried at DeLeon Cemetery, DeLeon, Texas; Margie (17 January 1879–17 April 1880) and Ella Amanda (27 May 1881–14 August 1881) were both buried at Eulogy Cemetery in Bell County.

Emily (22 February, 1852–6 November 1881), F.M.'s wife, died about three months after she gave birth to their last child. She was

also buried at Eulogy Cemetery in Bell County. At one time there was a large Whitehurst standard in the cemetery, but it no longer exists. After the death of his wife, F.M. Whitehurst had two remaining natural children, Ollie Monroe and Effie Allene, and they moved to Longview, Gregg County, Texas.

Francis Marion Whitehurst married Minerva Ellen Whatley (12 April 1867–30 March 1944) in Longview, Gregg County, Texas, 16 January 1883. This was recorded in the Gregg County Court House. They lived north of Longview in the area known as Judson. Minerva Ellen Whatley, daughter of Hiram J. Whatley and Georgia Stone was also born in Alabama. The censuses for Henry County, Alabama, indicated that both the Whitehurst and Whatley families were in Henry County at the same time and probably knew each other. Francis Marion Whitehurst was only about four years younger than Minerva's father. Fifteen children were born to this union.

They were Alvin Morgan (30 June 1888– 30 September 1941); Georgia Ethel (24 November 1889–3 February 1955) married Lee Reinhart; Jewel (18 April 1891–22 September 1895) was buried at Summerfield Cemetery, Longview, Texas; Lola Myrtle (15 November 1892–17 September 1951) married William Knox Smith, buried Summerfield Cemetery, Longview, Texas; Howard Gould (24 December 1893– 7 September 1894), buried at Summerfield Cemetery, Longview, Texas; Hiram Francis (30 March 1895–3 June 1964) married Ruby Ozzelle Reynolds, buried at Summerfield Cemetery, Longview, Texas; Roy Turner (8 June 1896–10 February 1964) married Ernestine McAfee, buried at Summerfield Cemetery, Longview, Texas; Theo (12 February 1898–3 March 1971), never married, buried at Summerfield Cemetery, Longview, Texas; Gilbert (8 September 1899–21 June 1901) was buried at Summerfield Cemetery, Longview,

Daughters of Francis Marion Whitehurst and Minerva Ellen Whatley. Back: Lola, Georgia Ethel and Willie. Front: Girlie and Hazel.

Texas; Elbert (8 September 1899–14 April 1936) married Mamie McLendon, buried at Summerfield Cemetery, Longview, Texas; Emmett (20 October 1901–10 September 1975) married Beatrice McLendon, buried at Judson Cemetery, Longview, Texas; Travis F. (15 April 1902–12 April 1958) married Odie Oline Johnson, buried at Summerfield Cemetery, Longview, Texas; Martha Delila "Girlie" (15 July 1906–) married William Houston "Bill" Quinn, and then Angus Gibson; Willie Mamie (29 May 1908–3 July 1982) married Eugene Carlton McAfee, buried at Summer-field Cemetery, Longview, Texas; and Hazel Lorene (11 April 1910–19 October 1989) married Clyde Austin Briley, buried at Judson Cemetery, Longview, Texas.

Francis Marion Whitehurst began serving as Postmaster at the Judson Post Office on 4 March 1890. The Post Office was discontinued for a time, and then re-established 26 April 1893, and he continued as Postmaster until 13 December 1894.

Francis Marion Whitehurst died at the age of 71; however, there is no death certificate for him as none was required at the time. Minerva Ellen (Whatley) Whitehurst died in a horrible stove fire in her home. She suffered first, second and third degree burns and had an agonizing death at age 77. The Longview newspaper covered her death with a front-page story. Both F.M. and Minerva Ellen were buried at Summerfield Cemetery on the property she sold to the Summerfield Methodist Church for $1.00. She left behind a large and loving family. Most of F.M. and Minerva's children called Longview home, and today many of their descendants are still found in Longview.

– Submitted by Linda Whitehurst, Frisco, Texas

HIRAM FRANCIS WHITEHURST & RUBY OZZELLE REYNOLDS

Hiram Francis Whitehurst was the sixth child of Francis Marion Whitehurst and Minerva Ellen Whatley Whitehurst. He was born in Longview, Gregg County, Texas, 30 March 1895. He lived with his parents north of Longview in the area known as Judson and eventually bought property there himself. Hiram Francis Whitehurst was named for his grandfather, Hiram J. Whatley, and his father, Francis Marion Whitehurst.

Hiram Whitehurst married Ruby Ozzelle Reynolds 27 August 1921, in Longview, and the marriage certificate was recorded in the Gregg County Courthouse. Ruby Ozzelle Reynolds was the daughter of Henry S. Reynolds and Dora "Missie" Brown, who came by covered wagon from Randolph, Bibb County, Alabama. Hiram and Ozzelle struggled, like others of their day, with farming and rearing a growing family. Eventually, Hiram left farming and took positions in Longview to better support his family during the Depression. Hiram worked for the County Commissioner, and then he served as cook for the prisoners at the county courthouse. For a time he was a jailer. He also worked at Boedeker Ice Cream Company, and later started

*Hiram Francis Whitehurst and
Ruby Ozzelle Reynolds*

a career in demolition of old homes. He sold the architectural antiques from these homes to others in town who were building newer homes or refurbishing existing homes. Hiram and Ozzelle had eight children, and most of them have lived, worked and been involved in Longview activities the majority of their lives.

Their children include: Hiram Falvey Whitehurst (29 July 1922—22 June 1987) married Mollie Wayne Schaffer, buried Summerfield Cemetery, Longview, Texas; Ruby Nelwyn Whitehurst (1 November 1924—25 August 1991) married Edward Fuller, buried Memory Park, Longview, Texas; Franklin Henry Whitehurst (10 December 1926—13 August 1953), never married, died in oil field accident, buried Summerfield Cemetery, Longview, Texas; Doyle Mack Whitehurst (26 December 1928–) married Evelyn Hendry; Milam Carroll Whitehurst (9 November 1930–) married Ann Pollard; Derrell Beatty Whitehurst (29 July 1932–) married Ann Sherman; Bonnie Gail Whitehurst (6 October 1934–) married Stan Glenn; and Gladys Murlean Whitehurst (21 May 1939–) married Michael Post.

Serving in the military was not unfamiliar to the Whitehurst family. Hiram F. Whitehurst's father, Francis Marion Whitehurst, was a soldier in the Civil War. Hiram served his country during World War I, and even sent his military money home to his widowed mother, Minerva Ellen Whatley Whitehurst. Love of country and patriotism was of great importance to Hiram Whitehurst, and he passed that dedication down to his sons: Hiram Falvey, who served in World War II, and Franklin, Milam and Derrell, who served during the Korean War.

Hiram and Ozzelle's home on Main Street was the one most remembered by his grandchildren because that was where his whole family gathered. He often handed one of his grandchildren a dime and told him/her to walk to the store to buy a "soda pop" or a popsicle. Sometimes on a hot summer day he would put one or more of his grandchildren in his pickup truck and off they would go to "Whitehurst Lake" to "cool off."

Hiram and Ozzelle doted on their grandchildren. Memories may fade with time, but the laughter and joy still lingers with thoughts of those wonderful times.

Hiram F. Whitehurst died 3 June 1964, in Longview, Gregg County, Texas, and was buried in Summerfield Cemetery where his father, mother and son Franklin were buried. On 8 July 1977, Ruby Ozzelle died in Longview and was buried alongside her husband of forty-three years at Summerfield Cemetery. Both left a large family legacy. Every Thanksgiving the children, grandchildren and, now, great grandchildren of Hiram Francis Whitehurst and Ruby Ozzelle Reynolds Whitehurst gather to count their blessings and remember their wonderful heritage. The treasured stories, the family recipes, the laughter—all are a part of what is still remembered about these dear, dear people who worked hard all their lives to make a better life for their children and grandchildren. They succeed beyond their wildest dream, for all of his children and grandchildren are successful and happy. What a testament to family love and devotion!

– Submitted by Bonnie Glenn;
prepared by Linda Whitehurst,
Frisco, Texas

TOM WILKERSON

Tom Wilkerson was born around 1866, in Gilmer, Upshur County, Texas, and died around 1911. He had one brother whose name was John. He met and married Elveney Stinson of Gregg County, Texas. To this union, eleven children were born: three boys, James F., Elbert, and Collie, and eight girls: Texana, Julie, Mary, Carrie, Frances, Minnie, Jeanie and Arie. Tom was a very industrious man. He bought about 250 acres of land in rural Gregg County and about 50 acres of land in the city of Longview, Gregg County, Texas. He was part of the establishment of the Willow Springs Baptist Church and Bethel Baptist Church in the city of Longview, Gregg County, Texas.

– Submitted by Mrs. Artelia Perry

**JOHN HAROLD "BILL" WILLIAMS &
ADDIJO WHITAKER WILLIAMS**

J. Harold "Bill" Williams, only son of John Tom and Bernice Cook Williams, was born 13 February 1921, in Bernice, Union Parish, Louisiana.

His family moved to Gregg County, Texas, in 1938. During the early summers, he worked in the oilfield as a roustabout. He graduated Gladewater High School, 1940, and in 1941, he graduated Curtis Wright Technical Institute, Glendale, California. He was employed by Consolidated Aircraft, San Diego, California, for the years 1941-1943. He served as an aircraft mechanic in the Army Air Corps from 1943-1946. While on leave in 1945, he met Addijo Whitaker, a teacher in Longview High School.

After World War II, he was employed in Longview for Olsco Mfg. Co. as a construction supervisor, King Tool Company in sales and service, Garrett Oil Tools with the relief valve, U.S. Industries as supervisor in the warehouse and Stemco Mfg. Co. as production engineer in the leather department. He retired in May 1982.

He was instinctively curious about mechanical devices. He had patience required to complete tedious work and an innate ability to explain intricate procedures involved in construction, operation and maintenance of anything mechanical.

Addijo Whitaker Williams was the youngest in a family of nine. She was born 3 September 1919, to Charles Richard "Dick" Whitaker and Addie Hogan Whitaker in the Central Heights Community, Nacogdoches County, Texas. There were six girls: Ethel, Kittie, Goldine, Ruth, Irwyn and Addijo. The three boys were Paul, John C. and Eugene Hogan.

Education was held as a high priority in the Whitaker family, and all of the children attended college. Of the nine children, eight became teachers.

Addijo attended Stephen F. Austin where she received a Bachelor's Degree in 1939, and a Master's Degree in 1960.

*J. Harold Williams and
Addijo Whitaker Williams*

Her teaching career began in Long Branch I.S.D. in 1939, and in 1940, she was employed by Longview Schools where she worked until her retirement in 1980, after 41 years in public school education. Various assignments in Longview I.S.D. included teaching 6th grade at First Ward Elementary, teaching government, biology, and Senior English in Longview High School, and sponsoring the "Lobo" Longview High School Yearbook. She completed her career by serving as Secondary Consultant for Longview Schools, a liaison between teachers and administrators.

On Sunday, 29 December 1946, she married J. Harold "Bill" Williams, a service man she had met in September 1945, while he was home on leave. Their marriage spanned more than 43 years. Though they had no children, there were many they claimed and enjoyed as their own.

There were eight beautiful years of retirement together to enjoy personal hobbies and shared hobbies of gardening, cooking, reading and traveling before Bill's death 18 December 1990.

The retirement years alone for Addijo have focused on community affairs, volunteer work, club work in Zonta and Retired Teachers, and continued gardening, cooking, reading, and more extended traveling and lots of bridge playing.

Addijo has been recipient of many significant honors, among which is the scholarship fund created by students in the Longview High School graduating classes 1947 through 1950, and named in her honor at Stephen F. Austin University. So many additional contributions by family and friends have made the fund grow rapidly. Indeed, a gift to the fund is a gift that keeps giving.

Another honor for Addijo was in 1999 when the Zonta Club of Longview presented the "Woman of Achievement" award to her.

– Submitted by Addijo Williams

ROBERT WASHINGTON WILLIAMS

Robert Washington (Wash) Williams (born 20 March 1856, died 16 July 1933) and his wife, Mary Amy (Threadgill) Williams (born 26 December 1861, died 15 November 1928) were both born in Tennessee, and were married in Henderson County, Tennessee. They moved to East Texas before 1885 with her parents, Greene Smith Threadgill and Martha Threadgill, and settled in the Ewell community in Upshur County. Wash's father-in-law had a store in that area, but Wash was a farmer. Most people who remembered Wash said that he did not talk much about his family left behind in Tennessee, but his father was probably Hampton W. Williams, who lived in the Lexington, Tennessee, area for many years.

Mary (Threadgill) Williams and her twin sister, Mattie (Threadgill) Powell

Wash and Mary had one child at the time of the move to Texas. He was William Ernest. At one time, he ran for the office of representative of the fourth district, Upshur and Camp counties; but, he was also a school teacher. Two more children were born to Wash and Mary in Texas. They were Martha Ann Frances (Fanny) and Green Smith (Pete). Pete was always in some business of his own. Like his grandfather Threadgill, he had a country store for a time. He would travel to a different part of the state and trade produce grown in East Texas for produce grown other places. He also had a sawmill, and during World War II he sold lumber to the government. It is said that during the Great Depression he gave work to as many people as he could. Although they did not get much pay, they could at least not be idle.

W.E. Williams (born 5 November 1883, died 24 January 1934) married Emma B. Maloney (born 12 June 1889, died 2 December 1950) on 5 August 1905. They continued to live in the Ewell area. Both are buried in the Willow Oak cemetery in Upshur County. They had three children: Jewel Irene (born 3 January 1907, died January 1979); Hubert Leroy (born 4 July 1915, died 1999); Olan Troy (born 25 August 1918, died 13 June 1960).

Fanny (born 26 July 1892, died 15 January 1964) married William Isaac Fink. They had no children. Isaac worked for many years as custodian at the Union Ridge School and was loved by all the children there. They were both loved by nieces and nephews.

Pete (born 1 November 1898, died 20 March 1964) married Jesse Verda Alexander (born 4 June 1903, died 28 December 1977) on 31 December 1919, in Gilmer, Texas. Pete and Verda had six children. They were Carleton Omar (born 28 June 1921, died 15 December 1968); Edwin Glen (born 27 October 1922); Billy Don (born 28 October 1923); Frances Louise (born 1 April 1929); Lolita Marie (born 25 February 1936); and James Ernest Earl (born 27 July 1938).

Pete and Verda were separated in 1939. He lived in Gladewater, Texas, until his death and is buried in the Willow Oak cemetery in Upshur County. Verda lived for a while in Dallas, Texas, but moved back to Gilmer for several years. She moved again to Dallas for a time, but lived last in Eustace, Texas. She died in Athens, Texas, on 28 December 1977, with pneumonia and is buried in the Moorehead cemetery in Henderson County.

– Submitted by Tammie Lynn (Lloyd) Olson

TAYLOR GEORGE WILLIAMS – CLARA D. KILLINGSWORTH

Taylor George (Tad) Williams (8 November 1879–5 August 1964) proved that good things do come in small packages. His life began in the Tryon area of Gregg County, 8 November 1879, on land he would call home for almost 85 years. Taylor's small stature from childhood was said to be the source of his nickname "Tad." He was "only a tad" growing up, according to his mother, Rebecca Jane Williams. And grow he did. He courted and married Clara D. Killingsworth (11 April 1878–21 December 1961) on 19 December 1901, daughter of James W. Killingsworth (26 December 1849) and Eliza Smitherman (11 August 1849) who, like Rebecca Williams, were early settlers in the Tryon community.

The T.G. Williams family: Gene, Mary Alice Whittington, T.G., Clara, J.T., Annie D. Pliler and Lewis, 1951.

Lewis and Edith Williams

Tad and Clara's home and family grew to include seven children: James Willie (20 September 1902); Emmett Eugene (19 February 1904); Hugh G. (10 September 1905); Annie D. Rebecca (17 May 1907); Mary Alive (24 July 1909); John Taylor (J.T.) (23 March 1914); and Lewis Edward (8 August 1918). Hugh G. died before his first birthday; and when Willie was 18, he was struck and killed by lightening. Of the siblings, all except Annie D. established their homes near the Williams homestead on Tryon Road. Annie D. married Fred Marshall Pliler in April 1932, and they established their home on Judson Road near the Pliler Cotton Gin, lumber mill and the Russ Pliler homestead.

Tad was a grocery man, cotton grower, dairyman and farmer who supplied vegetables for local grocers. Clara was a homemaker; both were tireless workers in the Alpine Presbyterian Church where he served as an elder for many years. Clara taught Sunday School classes and was the first President of the Ladies Aid Society, a forerunner of today's Presbyterian Women.

The Williams home was filled with the newest inventions of the day, one of which was a player piano, and occasionally the family "boarded" local teachers or preachers. The parlor rooms were often filled with ladies who quilted and visited. Grandchildren fondly remember Grandpa Williams' great skill as a farmer — he could grow anything! Clara amazed her grandchildren with stories of seeing the Dalton Gang, who staged their daring bank robbery in Longview when she was in her early teens. Clara was a sweet, gentle woman who could work wonders with little babies, always had something special in her purse for little ones, and kept goodies on the stove for any errant grandchild who could not wait until dinner. Their home was a gathering place for children and grandchildren.

The Williams Lake on T.G. Williams' farm was a popular community gathering place for church outings, fishing, picnicking and swimming. Today the lake is still a popular fishing spot and is owned and operated by Tad's youngest son, Lewis (born 8 August 1918), a retired dairyman, and his wife, Edith (born 25 March 1918). Lewis married Edith Carroll Walker (30 October 1937), and they have made the "Williams Place" their home for the last 66 years.

Tad and Clara are buried in Alpine Presbyterian Cemetery.

– Submitted by Lewis Williams

WILLOUGHBY

The Willoughby family originated in England and migrated from Maryland to Alabama. The son of James Madison Willoughby, Michael Andrew Willoughby was born in 1844, in Opelika, Alabama. He married Mary Elizabeth Louise Sommerkamp, who was born in Glennville, Alabama, in 1851. Michael Andrew served in the Civil War, enlisting in Montgomery Alabama, in 1861. At the time, he was 17 years old and single. After several battles, he was captured during the Wilderness Campaign in Virginia, and was held for the duration of the war, most likely at a federal prison camp in Elmira, New York. He was called Captain Willoughby by his fellow soldiers, although he probably only attained the rank of Sergeant Major. After the war he and Mary Elizabeth married in Dadeville, Alabama, in 1872, and came to Rusk County, Texas, circa 1876.

Mary Elizabeth Louise Sommerkamp Willoughby came to Gregg County about 1897, after the death of her husband in 1893. Earlier she came to Smith County to live near a brother, Charlie Sommerkamp, who operated a saloon in Tyler. According to her obituary in 1939, she had lived in Gregg County for 42 years. She sewed for Mrs. Lou Della Crim for 50 cents a day to make ends meet as she had eight children. She lost her husband just two weeks before her last child was born.

The children of Michael Andrew and "Lizzie" (a name she hated) were Mary Hope, 1873-1968; Francis A., 1875-1950, married Cordelia Tutt and later lived in Walters, Oklahoma; Edgar Wyche, 1877-1967, married Franklyn Lenora Reynolds and lived in Shreveport, Louisiana; Charles M., 1879-1956, married

Willouhby brothers and sisters about 1941 (l.-r.): Minnie Willoughby Elder, Charlie Willoughby, Hope Willoughby Lackey and Wyche Willoughby.

Ebon Strickland and lived in Liberty City, Texas; Minnie Mae, 1882-1970, married Frank Elder, Sr. and lived in Kilgore, Texas; Kenner Sommerkamp, 1888-1967; Jessie Love Wills, 1889-1923, who lived in Dallas, Texas; and Michael Andrew, Jr., 1893-1974, married Minnie Woods. Hope Willoughby Lackey lived in both San Angelo, Texas, and Kilgore, Texas. Minnie Willoughby Elder became a telephone operator in Kilgore and met her future husband, Frank Elder, Sr. there. She married Frank Elder, Sr. on 25 November 1906. As adults, the children who lived at least a few years in Kilgore were Frank Al, Wyche, Hope, and of course, Minnie who married Frank Elder, Sr. and lived in Kilgore until her death in 1970. (See "Elder" history.)

One interesting facet of the history of the Mary Elizabeth Louise Sommerkamp Willoughby family is she is a descendent of John Frederick Amelung who was a glassmaker in the mid 1700s in New Bremen, Maryland. The chemistry and technical methods employed in the factory, as well as the patterns and decorations have been studied by glassmakers for many years. There are pieces of his glass in the Smithsonian Institute in Washington, D.C., and the Corning Museum of Glass in Corning, New York.

Wyche Willoughby's granddaughter, Francye Willoughby Phillips, lives in Kilgore with her husband Dan. Her daughter, Shannon Maledon, who married Robert Guttry, lives in Longview with her husband and their children, Robert King and Mary Shannon. Stayce Lee Maledon McCollum lives in Lewisville with her husband and two sons, the oldest being Wesley Willoughby McCollum and the youngest, Aaron Edwards McCollum.

Other descendants of the Willoughby's are also the descendants of Frank Elder, Sr. and Minnie W. Elder. (See "Elder" history.)

– Submitted by Frank Elder, III

WOMACK

Jacob Pryor Womack and his wife, Nancy Ann Faddis, came to Texas in 1840, primarily buy land in East Texas. Many surveys in Panola County, Texas, today carry his name. The couple settled at Potter's Point.

Jacob's son, Major John F. Womack, came to Texas in 1842, and also settled at Potter's Point near Port Caddo in Harrison County. Port Caddo was a thriving commercial center with barges, paddle wheel steamers and even Indians in canoes plying along the string of lakes from New Orleans to Jefferson and Nacogdoches. There was heavy cotton trading there for him as a cotton factor.

John F. Womack was on the staff of Confederate President Jefferson Davis. He served as quartermaster for all army supplies from the Mississippi River to Texas. He was under the command of a unit under General Grier

John F. Womack's son, A.A. Womack, was sixteen years old when he climbed out of his bedroom window and ran away to join the Confederate forces. A.A. was taken prisoner at the Battle of Spring Hill, and re-

Womack-Lacy House built at a cost of $1,561.00.

mained a prisoner of war in the New Orleans prison camp until the war ended.

After the war, and learning the business from his father, A.A. Womack came to Longview after a stay in Galveston. A family picture shows him at the Port of Galveston in 1868. A letter to Kathryn Lacy Keene's mother indicates A.A. came to Longview in 1872. He, his brother Julian and sister Mary Josephine Womack Luckett opened a family business. Julian and Mary Josephine Luckett left the firm in 1880.

In 1890, Womack and Perry incorporated as Green Perry joined the firm. He had no management duties in the business but represented his wife, Medora Womack Perry, sister of A.A. Womack.

In 1874, A.A. Womack married Eliza Harris Thweatt Flewellen of Longview. In 1876, the couple built the first "Gingerbread" trimmed house in East Texas. The material was brought from St. Louis. Every Christmas a barrel of oysters was shipped from New Orleans for family entertaining.

A.A. Womack died in 1910, and the business was terminated at his death.

In 1916, the only surviving child of A.A. and Eliza Womack, Kate Perry Womack, married Judge Edwin Lacy. Their house was known as the Womack-Lacy House. Their family and descendants occupied the house for three generations until it was torn down. Permission was given to demolish house by the Texas State Historical Society. The descendents of Kate and Edwin Lacy are John Edwin Lacy (deceased), Elizabeth Lacy Bond and Kathryn Lacy Keane.

Albert Alonzo Womack (called Lonzo by family and friends) was remembered by his friends for his character that endeared him to all and served as an example of excellent judgment, ability, honor and experience. He left behind a wonderful company that traded from St. Louis to Galveston to New Orleans and as a cotton factor.

– Submitted by Kathryn Lacy Keane

WOMACK – REMBERT

John Faddis Womack was born in Hillsboro, North Carolina, 22 April 1819. He married Lockey Ann Wagnon (from Gallatin, Tennessee) in Memphis, Tennessee, 8 March 1843. They lived in Mississippi for two or three years, then moved to the Caddo Lake area north of Marshall, Texas, in 1846.

John Womack was sheriff of Harrison County in 1854. He was a quartermaster with the rank of major in the Confederate army.

John and Lockey had nine children: 1) Albert Alonzo Womack, who married second Eliza Flewellen and their children were Kate, John, Elizabeth and Katherine; 2) Mary Josephine Womack married Major C.J. Luckett–the Luckett's daughter, Jewel M., married Dr. Cochran; 3) Julian O. Womack; 4) Medora A. Womack married Dr. W.S. Mayfield; 5) Susan A. Womack married Dr. W.S. Mayfield–their daughter, Erma Mayfield, married Dell Everett and the Everett's daughter had a daughter, Dorothy; 6) Walter Orville Womack; 7) Kate Womack married Frank T. Rembert; 8) John Faddis Womack, Jr.; and 9) Chase Lane Womack married Yancy D. Harrison and had three sons–Yancy had moved to Marshall from Anniston, Alabama, to "cast his lot with Texas."

Mrs. Frank Taylor Rembert (Kate Womack)

Frank Taylor Rembert

Several Womack brothers and sisters moved to Longview and had their own businesses. The Womack-Perry Mercantile Co. was located in the brick building in downtown, where the Bistro and Travel Station are located.

Daughter Kate Womack and Frank Taylor Rembert had married in 1878 in Marshall. Kate and Frank moved to Longview in 1879, and bought a house at 316 South Fredonia, which was a magnificent gingerbread gem.

Mr. Rembert became active in the cotton business. (Cotton Street was named for the bales of cotton lining the street.) He had a mercantile business and owned an entire block on South Fredonia Street known as the Rembert Block. He built the Palace Hotel and the Rembert Theatre.

Mr. and Mrs. Rembert traveled to Europe, where he became enchanted with Loch Lomond

Rembert-Harrison House, 316 South Fredonia, Longview.

in Scotland. On their return he built his own Loch Lomond a mile or so out of town. It was a popular swimming and boating area.

The Remberts built and operated Rembert Park and Race Track that was popular in East Texas and became the site for the annual East Texas Derby. The Fourth of July Races drew crowds each year. Mr. Rembert bought the first car, a 1910 Buick, in Longview. In 1918, he bought the old Guaranty State Bank, that became the Rembert National Bank. He served as mayor from 1896-1898. Frank Rembert was Longview's first millionaire and a real wheeler-dealer.

Kate Rembert was a gracious first lady of Longview. She entertained lavishly in their beautiful home. On one occasion, she wore a purple velvet gown made exclusively for her. She served the first molded ice cream flowers. These were brought from Dallas.

The Rembert's had two little girls, both of whom died as infants. They are all buried in the Rembert Mausoleum in Greenwood Cemetery.

Frank Rembert died in the summer of 1926.

– Submitted by Marjorie Bivins

MR. & MRS. A.L. WOOD

Both Amos Wood (born 15 December 1891) and his wife, Ollie (born 25 October 1896), were born in the area of Tioga, Texas. They had one daughter, Reta Mae, born 30 April 1914, in Pike, Texas. Later, they moved to Electra, Texas. Mr. Wood worked for the Cities Service Oil Co. and was transferred to East Texas in 1931. First they lived in a one-room house in Willow Springs, which later became Greggton. Many not as fortunate as the Wood family were

R.O. and Reta Mae Shaw and Ollie and Amos Wood

living in tents. After Reta Mae finished high school in Electra in 1932, she joined her parents in Greggton. Later, Amos found another house on Highway 80 and lived there until 1936.

Reta Mae worked at the 5 & 10 cent store in Gladewater until she married R.O. Shaw on 14 June 1936. They moved to Longview. R.O. worked for the Marcus Wood Gulf Product Distributors. At that time there was a park on the corner of Fredonia and Tyler Streets where they could enjoy relaxing. Later the Glover Crim Building was built there. Across from there was Perry's Variety Store on the corner. A carnival wagon served hamburgers. Boedecker Ice Cream Parlor was behind the Masonic home on Methvin Street. On Center Street was the Dolson (Dalston) Hotel, where later the first city hall and fire station were built. The Arlyne Theatre was on Methvin Street.

When World War II began, the Shaws moved to Sausalito, California, where R.O. worked in the shipyard for three years. After the war, they returned to Gladewater, and R.O. built his shop, S&W Repair Shop, in Clarksville City. Reta Mae worked for Brookshire's for 33 years until January, 1985, when she retired to care for R.O., who was ill.

Mr. Shaw died on 13 March 1985. Amos L. Wood died on 28 April 1977, and Ollie Wood died on 22 September 1988. They are all buried in the Lakeview Cemetery, Longview.

– Submitted by Reta Mae Shaw

WRIGHT, YOUNG & BOWLES

James Samuel "Sam" Wright, born 8 June 1891, near Gladewater, Gregg County, died 31 August 1974, Gladewater, Texas, married on 18 September 1912, Gladewater, to Lillie Maude Young, born 9 January 1896, Harrison County, Texas, died 27 June 1977, Farmers Branch, a part of the multiplex of Dallas, Texas. Both are buried in the Gladewater Memorial Park Cemetery.

Maude came to Gladewater in the summer of 1911, with her widowed mother, Missie E. (Bowles) Young (daughter of William Henry Bowles and Miss Elvey Shepperd). Maude's father (Charles L. Young) died of tuberculosis in 1911, Steep Creek, San Augustine County, Texas. Missie was advised to move back to Gladewater to be near her family. Missie's brothers, Jimmette and John F. Bowles, sent wagons to move Missie and her seven orphaned children back to Gladewater, where Missie purchased 54-plus acres of land near Moody Creek, just east of Gladewater, Texas, on 11 November 1911.

Missie's farm, situated on the Old Longview Highway, was out of the H.R. Edwards survey and the J.R. Crosby survey and 2-1/2 acres out of the Cartwright head right. An old log barn, built in 1857, a long time landmark that was on the original farm that Missie purchased in 1911, survived until the late 1980s. Some of Maude's grandchildren, and one of her sons, Howard Wright, and a daughter, Ruby Stewart Torres, still own part of the original property.

Sam Wright, the grandson of Anderson T. and Sarah Ann (Barnes) Wright Anderson, was born in Georgia in 1811; his wife, Sara, was born

1812, Edgefield District, South Carolina. She was the daughter of Henry Barnes, born 1762, Maryland, died 1818, Edgefield District, South Carolina. Henry was a soldier of the American Revolution; he married after the war to Ann Roby Lanham and later moved his family to Edgefield District, South Carolina, where he died in 1818. His family then moved to Montgomery County, Alabama, in 1819.

The earliest Wright ancestor was Richard, born about 1699, Virginia; his grandson, John, was a veteran of the American Revolution. The Wrights moved to Montgomery County, Alabama, in the 1820s, where William B. Wright purchased land in 1823. William B. Wright returned to Georgia, and died there in 1856. His son, Anderson, and his wife and six children moved to East Texas in 1845, during the time of the Republic. Anderson Wright purchased 382 acres of land situated one half mile west of the Wm. Castelberry line, running west to the H.H. Edwards line, on 6 February 1849.

This land was in Upshur County at that time and later was included in Gregg County when it was formed in April of 1873, and is located in what is now Warren City, a few miles northeast of Gladewater.

Both Maude and Sam Wright are descendants of early settlers of East Texas, arriving before Texas was admitted into the union. Maude, a descendant of the Shepperds who came to what was later, Upshur County in 1845, was a descendant of Edward Doty and Edward Fuller, and his son, Samuel, passengers on the *Mayflower*. Elvey (Anderson) Shepperd, born 1779, North Carolina, who was widowed in about 1828, Alabama, accompanied her grown children and grandchildren, with the exception of two of her older daughters, Charity Bonham and Elizabeth Brady, to Upshur County in 1845. Her children, William, Shepperd, Jr.; Lavinia Moseley; Mary (Polly) Phillips, Elijah Bird; Eleazor; Alfred F.; Robert Alexander; and Allen Martin Shepperd, all are listed on the 1850 census of Upshur County, Texas, Eleazor Shepperd, born 15 March 1815, Georgia, was the son of William and Elvey (Anderson) Shepperd. Eleazor and his wife, Mary Ann Butler, born 20 March 1817, South Carolina, were married 5 September 1832, Alabama, came to Texas with his widowed mother. Elvey and her family built one of the first log cabins in Upshur County.

Elvey died of cancer in April of 1860, and is buried in the Gay Cemetery, Upshur County, Texas. An historical marker was placed on her grave by the Texas Historical Commission chaired by one of her descendants, John Ben Shepperd.

Elvey Shepperd, daughter of Eleazor and Mary (Butler) Shepperd, was born in Alabama on 5 June 1841, came to Texas in 1845, with her parents and the large Shepperd clan. She married 10 July 1857, Harrison County, Texas, to William Henry Bowles, born 1836, Mississippi. Their children were Pearlie Rogers; John F. Bowles; Jimmette; and Patsy Ruth Todd and Missie E. Young.

Missie E. Bowles, born 15 August 1874, Upshur County, Texas, died 27 May —, married Charles Leonard Young, born 27 June 1866, Alabama, died 28 June 1911, San Augustine County, Texas. They were parents of Harvey

Alvin; Preston Arthur; Lillie Maude Wright; Clifford Carl; Claude Lee; Hazel Bernice Goolsby; and Addie Belle Marsh Heimann.

Sam Wright was the son of James Franklin Wright, 1840-1910, a veteran of the Confederate Army, who came to Texas with his parents in 1845. Sam's mother, Mariah Dean, 1855-1942, was the daughter of another early settler of Gladewater, Jarrett Dean, 1813-1883. The Deans came to Texas with the Wrights. Also traveling with them was Hezekiah Barnes and his family. One of his daughters married Martin Armstrong, son of John K. Armstrong, who was a neighbor to the Wrights, Deans and Shepperds back in Davenport, Montgomery, Alabama. John Armstrong came to Upshur County in 1843/44.

On 30 December 1872, Jarrett Dean conveyed to the Texas and Pacific Railroad Company certain parcels of land to encourage the placement of the railroad through his property. Dean Street in Gladewater was named for Jarrett Dean. Jarrett's wife, Mary Jane Phillips, was a half sister to William Phillips (children of George Phillips). Jarrett Dean and Mary Jane lived in Gladewater the remainder of their lives. Citizens of an obscure community, which was later named Gladewater, met under a large oak tree at the home of William H. and Bellona (Dean) Victory (Bellona was a daughter of Jarrett Dean), once the home of Jarrett Dean, to select the name of this community. The new county of Gregg was named for a slain Confederate General, John Gregg. These three events became official on 13 April 1873, the naming of Gladewater, the forming of Gregg County, and the day the first train came through Longview to Gladewater.

The eight children of James Samuel "Sam" and Lillie Maude (Young) Wright are Helen Brown, 1915-1996; May Dean Hunt, 1918-1940; James Leonard Wright, 1919-2001; Nelwyn Louise Sims, 1921-1986; Franklin Leon, 1922-1953; Ruby Olean Stewart Torres, born 1930; Howard G., born 1933; and Carl Venoy Wright, born 1935.

(Note: Information taken from census records; probate records; *Mayflower Families Through Five Generations*, Vol. II, Part II, by the General Mayflower Society, 1996, pp. 45, & 127 (Carl is a member of the Society of Mayflower Descendants.); birth and death certificates; and mortality records, cemetery records and other records.) – Submitted by Carl V. Wright, Ganado, Texas (son of Maude and Sam Wright)

BERNICE BRADLE & EUGENE S. ZINSER

Bernice Meyer Bradle graduated from high school in 1926, and Eugene S. Zinser in 1927, both in Washington, Illinois. Bernice's mother was widowed as her husband, Bernice's father, had died in the influenza epidemic of 1917. Eugene's father, Dr. Harley Zinser, was a prosperous physician. Eugene's only sister, Caroline, married August Martini, and they had two daughters, Marilyn and Roslyn.

When Bernice and Eugene graduated from high school, this country was in a terrible depression and economic downfall. There were no jobs; people in every walk of life were desper-

Bernice and Eugene S. Zinser, daughter Patricia, and sons, Steele and Jon Edward.

ate. Both students were very bright and had aspired to college. Nevertheless, in spite of no formal education, both found employment: she was employed as a cosmetologist and he worked in a service station. They married in 1930.

In 1935, hearing there were jobs in the East Texas oil boom, Bernice and Eugene traveled from Illinois to Gladewater, Gregg County, Texas, with their first child, daughter Patricia.

Eugene went to work for General American Oil Company, owned by Algar Meadows from Vidalia, Georgia. Meadows started his business in Shreveport, Louisiana, and subsequently moved it to Gladewater, and finally to Dallas, Texas, on Mockingbird Lane, where it presently exists today. The General American Oil Company interests were in drilling, purchasing land, and producing and properties.

Eugene S. Zinser was a gauger. His job was to monitor the wells, tanks and leases throughout the oil fields. Daughter Patricia recalls how she often traveled with him to these fields and leases, of which, she says there were many. Camp Switch and Sun Camp are two that still exist today. She also remembers many of the workers, no matter what job they held in the oil business. D.V. "Red" Loflin, Rae Hollis, Tom Terrell, Doyle Gregory, Mr. Presly (Dana Jo), Bill Peed, Miss Kitty, Charlie Adams and Shane O'Neil.

With the coming of black gold, Gregg County in the 1940s was a booming and bustling place. The oilfield crews and workers enjoyed good commingle and camaraderie spirit. They had their hangouts where they drank "mulebach" beer in green bottles. The Green Hut, Minute Café and Hatley's were some of the many. There was the Carter newsstand in Greggton where they went for the newspaper and ice cream. The "Big Grocery" was next door. (The Carter family all drowned in a boating accident on Lake Harris.) The many faceted activities building was built in Greggton with Texas rock and still exists today.

Eugene and Bernice had two more children, sons, Steele and Jon. Their only daughter, Patricia, graduated from White Oak High School in 1953, and then nursing school. She married Travis Lloyd Nevels of Gregg County in June 1956. Patricia and Travis have two children, Travis III and Angela (Nicholas), and three grandchildren. They presently reside in Johnson City, Tennessee.

– Submitted by Travis L. Nevels, Johnson City, Tennessee

Index

A

Aaron, Fran 109, Janean 86, 109, Kristen 109, Shirah 109

Abbot, Ann Dunbar 241, Bertha 40

Abernathy, Clay Madison 234, Curtis Mark 234, Curtis Quentin 234, Jaclyn Gail Pickens Martin 234, Leslie Anne 234, Luella 187, Marvin D. 30, Nancy Claire 234, Nancy Elmine Cheek 187, Nancy Jane Phillips 234, Peggy 234, Vicki 120, William Henry 187

Abernethy, Eleanor Horsman 98, F.E. 196, Isabella 98, William David 98, William H. 98

Abney, Alexander Hamilton 194, Blanche Killingsworth 195, Emmaline 193, 198, 236, Samuel Jr. 280, Thomas Hamilton 194, Zach, Jr. 171

Abnott, Louise Graybill 157

Acker, B.H. 249, Julia Rule 249

Acorn, Lucinda 179

Adam, Edna Eleanor Stricker 122, Eleanor 122, John Frederick 122

Adams, C.W. 23, Charlie 287, Darlina Calvin 112, Donna Whitaker 113, Elizabeth 101, 275, Gladys 100, 101, J.N. III 113, Jack 17, James Nathaniel 112, James Nathaniel, Jr. 112, James Quincy 101, Judith Amanda Mercer 101, Julia 259, Lavonia Lorraine 112, Lemuel 101, 275, Madge 230, Margaret DeLoach 64, Natilla McNairy 101, Ora Lee 275, Sarah 275, William Russell 101, Zack 113

Adamson 109

Adcock, Marilyn 242

Addison, Irvin K. 40

Adkins, Allyne 110

Adrian, Alabama Frances "Ala" Whatley 78, 79, 89, 279, 280, Amy Estelle 80, Benjamin J. 78, 89, Bob 280, Charles 78, 80, Chellie Parrish 79, Cora Matilda Brooks 80, David 79, David, Sr. 78, E.V.A. Williams 78, 79, Eliza 78, Elizabeth M. 78, Ella McCreary 78, Eugene 78, 79, 89, Fleming Fowler 78, Frederick L. 78, Gladys Lattimore 79, 89, Hannah 79, Harold 78, 79, 89, Henry D. 78, "J.C." Justin 78, James 79, James Beauregard 80, James Costin 78, James Fowler 78, 80, Jeremy 79, Jerilyn 78, John David 78, 80, John German 78, Joseph

David 78, Leila 78, Luther P. 80, Mamie 89, Marilyn 79, Mark 79, Martha Mackey 78, Marvin E. 78, Mary A. 80, Mary A. Elizabeth "Lizzie" Chastain 78, Mary E. 78, Mary Louise 78, Mattie 78, Michael 79, Nan 78, Nancy Jane 78, Nannie B. 80, Nina Bassett 78, Olivia 78, Rachel 78, 80, Ralph Dewey 78, Robbie 78, 79, 89, 90, 150, 161, Robert David 78, 79, 89, Robert DeKalb 78, Ruby Mildred 80, Russell DeKalb 78, Sallie B. 78, Sallie F. 80, Sally 214, Samantha 78, Sarah Elizabeth Pearson 78, 80, Sarah Vinson 89, Van(n) Pomeroy "Brick" 80, Vester 78, William Harvey 78, William Robert "Bob" 80

Agee, Anna 80, 165, 189, Arphie 80, Beatrice 80, Flossie 80, 165, Frank 80, Lois Beatrice 189, Mathieu 80, 99, 165, 166, 189, Nancy Eller Christian 80, William Nathan 80, William Wisemon 80, 165, 189, Zella 80

Aikman, Dora Ann 121, John David 121, Mary Elizabeth 121, Mary McLaughlin 121

Ainslie, Philip 241

Ainsworth, Bethany Anna 278, Elizabeth Diane 278, Sherry Beth 278, Thomas Henry 278

Akard, Christian 139, Rebecca Sue Shipman 139, Rick 139, Sean 139

Akers, Dane Webster 81, LaLita Yvonne 81, Myrtle Isabel Bilyeu 80, Patsy Ruth 81, Shirley Lea 81, William Webster 80

Akin, J.O. 50, Paul 93, Ruth 93

Akins, Eva Mae 105

Alba, Javier 41

Aldaco, Jennifer 260, Joe 260, Rickye Dossene 260, Shelly 260

Alden, John 83, Priscilla Mullins 83

Alexander 106, Amanda Tinsley, McFarland 81, 82, 183, 259, Annie Jane 82, 259, Ashley Erwin 81, Barbara Gail Tekell 81, 187, Brenda Park 230, Caitlyn 94, Catherine Ferguson 82, 182, Catherine Duke 94, Charles C. 147, Clinton Douglas 81, 187, Cynthia Kay 81, 187, David 81, 82, 94, David Gregory 82, Elias 147, Elizabeth Caroline Tamson "Carrie"

182, Eula Mae 82, Gregory 94, Henry 82, 182, Hester Rush 82, Isaac 81, 92, 237, Isabella Jane 182, James Clyde 81, 83, James David 81, James Henry 81, 82, 182, 183, 259, Jesse Verda 284, Katherine Elizabeth 82, 183, 276, Laura Fay Potts 81, Lillie Dell 82, Lizzy 82, Malcolm Erwin 82, 83, Margaret Gilmore 81, Margaret Lockens 81, Martha Blanton 147, Martha Sydney Ingram 182, Mary 82, Mattie Elizabeth 81, Megan 94, Michael Erwin 81, 187, Millicent 82, 94, Nancy Agnes McCall 147, Oscar Benjamin 82, 83, Rosie Mae Magrill 82, 83, Sandy Bingham 81, 94, Stella Mae Thomas 82, 83, Victoria Wachtel 81, Virginia 82, 147, William M. 82, 182, Willie Dee "Shug" 82, 83, Zelda 40

Alfred, Polly Elizabeth 182

Allen, Ala Jane 83, Araminta Pink 127, Betty 167, Bob 167, Charity 83, Cody 83, Dorothy Jean 83, Dura Smith 83, Elizabeth Nell 83, Florene Hale 83, Florine Cody 83, Horace Vaughn 83, Jane 97, 100, Jasper James 84, Jerry Ann 83, Jesse Killingsworth 5, Jimmie 83, Joanna Maxine 84, John William 83, Johnny James 83, Letitia Davis 130, Lil 83, Lucy 83, Margaret Kathryn 83, Mary Alice 84, Mary Frances 84, Mary Killingsworth 5, Mary Margaret "Mollie" Ellis 83, Morris Everett 83, Nellie Surat (Rolf) 83, Ray 83, Rebecca 202, Ricky 83, Rosemary 84, Royal Polk "Roy" 83, Rufus 5, Russell Fleming 83, Sarah Ann Tedder 84, Savannah Taylor 84, Thomas Andrew 84, Vaudis 83, Vernette 83, Virginia Lee Hardy 167, W.M. 44, Will 130, William 5, William Andrew 84, William David 84, William Edwin 84, William W. 97, Winfred Vernet 83, Woodrow Wilson 83, Zella Agee 80, Zoie Mae Bradley 83

Allison, Ada Dell 84, Angeline 84, Berry 84, Ela Lee 84, Elizabeth Brown Smitherman 84, Ena Naoma 84, Eula Lee 84, Frank 84, Ida Dorinder 84, Ima Mae 84, J.N. 25, Joan R. Fisher 84, 147, John N. 8, 84, 147, Martha Price 84, Mary Ann Morgan 84, Minnie Elizabeth 84, Oma Marshall 84,

Pugh 84, Sophronia 84, Thomas Jefferson, Jr. 16, 84, 133, Thomas Jefferson, Sr. 11, 84, Virgil Clyde 84, William 84

Allred, James V. 217

Alread, Octavia 266

Alsup, Molly 126

Alurins, Sussanah 94

Alverson, Mary Louella 84

Alvice, W.C. 169

Amelung, John Frederick 285

Amos, Sallie Elizabeth 240

Anderson 143, 244, 251, A.M. 198, Abraham 108, Ada Louise 187, Bailey 223, Bessie Mae 188, Bob 164, C.M. 207, Cora Blanche 207, Dora Georgia Pond 85, Doris 7, Dorothy Letterman 85, Elijah 98, 235, 251, Elisha 235, Elizabeth Brack 235, Elmore 235, Elvey 97, 98, 235, 251, 287, Eveylyn 134, Fannie 130, Felix Allen Eaton 254, Glendon 85, Glendon Sylvester 84, 234, Jane 97, Jannie Marie Herndon 173, Jerry Meitzen 153, Josephine Griffin 159, Judy Lynn Hale 164, Julie Hale 164, Lavinia Brack 98, 235, 251, Lola Irene Elizabeth Faulk 146, Lyndy Karen 153, Matthew 254, Mattie Ellen 245, Patricia Duke 153, Ronald 164, W.D. 159, Wanda Jean Phillips 85, 234, William 85, 245

Andrews, Annie Myrtle 137, Benneta Ann 137, Sam 137

Andrews-Davis, Sarah 256

Angel, Amy Burt 106, 108, Ben 108, Fernando 108, Nando 108, Sam 108

Angell, Mary Helen 109

Ansley, Wesley Sole 8

Anthony, Sarah Tate 260

Apple, Caitlin Cheyane 137, Colton Tyrel 137, Daphyna Dawn Dryden 137, Nolan Stafford 137, Wilburn 137

Armour 179

Armstrong, Dellah 85, 133, 188, 226, Elizabeth Barnes 188, 226, Emma Stovall 98, Frank 267, Gertie 98, Jewel 255, John K. 49, 85, 133, 188, 226, 287, Joni Lee 224, Louis 230, Martin 85, 188, 226, 287, Mary Elizabeth Barnes 85, Sarah Della E. 266, Sarah Poland 85, 188, 226

Arnold, Bessie Lea 212, 213, Edward 38, Fannie Wyatt 96, Harrell 97, Jordan 97, Joseph Council 212, Katie Herndon 173, Mamie E. Rees 212, Robert, Jr. 173, Robert, Sr. 173, Roger 127, Sarah Caroline Culpepper 97, Sarah Mims 97, Thresa 262

Arradaza, Arthur Dioso 232, Jane Devereux Boone 232, Michaela Boone 232

Asaff, Matilda 223

Asberry 206

Asbury 206

Ash, Maurice 103

Ashby, Lucy Vdell Wright 133, Wanda Lee Doss 135, William 133

Ashcraft, Brenda 221, Frances 172

Ashton, Ruth 231

Ashurst, Sarah Clay 176

Askins, Cooper 170, Mary Jane 136, Mason 170, Susan Elizabeth 170

Astaire, Fred 191

Aston, Brenda 97

Astorudd, Valerie Ann 121

Ater, Jennifer Alisse 85, 87, Jesse Jewel 86, Jonas Sanford 87, Kimberly Ann 85, 86, 87, 109, Marita Ann Chanler 85, 86, 87, 109, Nora Belle Johnson 86, Stanley 85, 86, 87, 109, Stephanie Kelly 85, 86, 87

Athon, Mary Wilmoth 237

Atkins, Nancy Ann 180

Atkinson, Elizabeth 158, Fred 30, Hattie 30, Helen 30, James Henry 30, Jewel 30, Mary 30

Attlesey, Anna 279, Robert E. 279

Audibert 75

Aultman, Donna 49, Jessica 49, Joel 49, Larry 49

Austin, Alvin "Bud" 35, Stephen F. 189, 271, 280, 283, Teddy R. 41

Auten, Nellie 187

Autry, Gene 38

Avant, Ava 60

Avery, Anne 88, Danny 88, David 88, Dottie Mae Fowler 87, 88, Jessie Taylor 88, John 88, Karen 88, Kathryn 88, Kendall 96, 110, Lennie 88, Maggie 88, Mamie 88, Margaret Alyce 88, Mark 88, Mary Vanita Harlow 88, 178, Mohan 88, Patsy Homeyer 88, Paul 88, Stephen 88, Susan 88, Tim 88, Tommy 88, Tressie 88, Virginia Thorn 88, W.S. 88, William Oliver 88, William Oliver III 88, William Oliver, Jr. 88

Awalt, Ann E. 51, 244, Fanny 147, Solomon 11, 18, 25, 51, 54, 141, 244

B

Bachtell, David 154, Dorothy Garrett 154, Michael 154

Bacon 225, Dorothy 241

Baggett 279, Ader Bell 89, Ann 78, Beulah 89, David

Jesey 212, David Jesey, Jr. 89, David Jesey, Sr. 89, David Lenard 89, Fannie 89, 212, Gennifer Patricia 90, Jesey E. 89, Jess 89, Joa Byron "Joe" 79, 89, 90, Joe 78, 150, 161, Joe Adrian 89, 90, Joy 78, 79, 89, 161, 162, Lettie Udora Mathews 89, Lewis 89, Margaret Vinson 89, Mary Ann 89, 212, Minnie Bell Osburn 89, Myrtle 89, Ophealia Fay 89, Robbie Adrian 78, 79, 89, 90, 150, 161, Robbie Ann 89, 150, Sarah 90, Tricia 90

Bagnoli, Candance 261

Bagwell, Charleen Elder 64, 90, 142, Deanne 90, 143, J. 143, J.J., Jr. 143, Jane 143, John 90, John Judson, Jr. 90, John Judson "Jud" III 90, John Judson, Sr. 90, Jonathon Judson 90, Jud 143, Judson 90, 142, 143, Mary Deanne 90, Peter 90, Rosemary 90, 143, Tootsie 90,143, Tracy Gowan 90

Bahadory, Carol Holloway 218, Jerry 218

Bailey, Claude 275, Cordie Alice 275, Joe 87

Baird, Barbara Ann 91, 135, Benjamin W. 91, Billy Joe 91, 135, Billy Joe, Jr. 91, Dorothy Claire Drew 91, Drew William 91, Elizabeth Claire 91, 135, Helen Mathis 91, Jack Forest 91, John Thomas 91, John Thomas III 91, John Thomas, Jr. 91, Johnnie Lois 91, Kathleen Ann Christensen 91, Lorena Runette 91, Lula Mae Satterwhite 91, Mary Bays 135, Mary Cox 91, Mary Lee Epperson 91, Mary Virginia Bays 91, Nancy J. Hoover 91, William Jefferson 91, William P. 91

Baker, Arthur Lee 130r, Jessie Estelle 182, Nathaniel Beauregard 182, Polly Elizabeth Alfred 182, Roy 24, William O. 25

Baldwin, Renvie 216

Bales, Bill 238, Dorothy Reeh 238, Gary 238, Richard 238, Tom 238

Ball, Esther 147

Ballow, Andrew Wilburn 91, Artie Elizabeth 91, Audrey Faye 91, Edna Mae 91, Ernest Love 91, Eunice Marie 91, Ira Willard 91, Mattie Lou Vail 91, Sidney Love 91, Steward 91, William Wyatt 91

Bander, Exa 273, Joe 273

Banks, Winona 66

Baptist, John 27

Barbee, Geraldine Van Allen 64

Barber, P.B. 8, Sallie P. 180

Barclay, Connie 161

Baremore, Garland 237, Gaynell Ratliff 237

Barge, Caitlin Rebecca 163, Melinda Guttry 163, Patrick 163, Shaughn Patrick 163, Stephen Alexander 163

Barker, Kaye 159, Mildred 233, Minnie Florence Foshee 149

Barkett, Alice 266, Betty 71

Barksdale, Arley 41

Barnes, Ada 92, Aletha 235, Amanda Caroline 209, Anderson 201, Ann Roby 287, Arthur D. 92, Bob 92, Bobby C. 92, 278, C.A. 92, Elizabeth 133, 226, 235, Henry 287, Hezekiah 133, 235, 287, J.W. 51, Kelly Louise 92, 278, Mabel 92, 214, Margaret 92, 278, Mary 85, 97, 235, Nancy Lockett 201, Pamela Elaine 92, 278, Rebecca Jane 92, 278, Sarah Ann 133, 286

Barnett 24, Frances 193, Georgia Smith 251, Mary E. Kilgore 92, Pamela 96, 110, S. Slade 18, 92, Talitha Cumi Woods 92

Barnette 84

Barnoske, Lara L. 278

Barrett, John 66, Nicholas 99, 189

Barro, Lucille 266

Barron, Julie 61

Barrow, Charles Austin 97, Elizabeth Ashley 97, Elizabeth Ruth Boles 97, Kenneth Wayne 97, Margie Marie Upchurch 97, Martha Kansas 135, Mollie Brock 97, Wayne Austin 97

Barry, Andrew 214, Elizabeth Watson 213, 214, John 213, Margaret Catherine Moore 214, Mary 171, 213, 216

Bartlett, Jim 67

Barton, Andrew 93, Angus Bailey 272, Augustin 93, Bryan Marsh Erwin 92, 93, Carra Bonnie 178, 272, Carrie Bell Meadows 217, Earle 272, Emily Belle 93, Emily Miller Erwin 92, Ethyl 272, Eureka 272, Hugh 93, Jack C. 93, James Madison 92, John Andrew Virgil 92, 93, Josie B. 93, Julia Ann 178, 272, Julian W. 93, Mabel 90, Pheriba 93, Philip E. 93, Robert 178, 217, 272, Robert Sr. 272, V. Henry 93, Virgie Alice 272, William Robert 217

Basham 255

Basie, Count 230

Baskin, Renee Carroll 115

Bass, Birdie Ophelia 277, Dana 102, John E. 8, Marina Howard 102, Tom 277, Wyatt Roland 102

Bassett, Agatha B. 206, Nina 78, Rebecca 175, 176

Bateman, Ed 29, Treacy 222

Bates, Ann 49, Clara Blair 95, Irby 49, 274, John 49, Luara

Deck 197, Nina 147, Tammy 95, Terry 95, Tully Democrat 197, Virginia 49

Baucum, Andrew Thomas 93, Barbara 93, 155, Davis Joesph 93, Helen Hines 93, Henry 93, Joseph Bevill, Jr. 93, Joseph Bevill, Sr. 93, Molly Ann Davis 93, Robert Jayson 93, Stacy Elizabeth 93

Baudain, Marie Louise 135

Baum, Kenneth 66

Bauman, Percy Charles "Joe" 233, Sybil Edna Phillips 233

Baxter, Henry 180, Nancy Ligon Hughey 180

Bayless, Joseph H. 265, Sarah Virginia 265

Bays, Joel Hugh 91, Mary 91, 135, Verna Beatrice Buckner 91

Beach 122

Beard, Ida Ophella 229, John Lewis 275, Lula Essie 167, Mable D. 146, Mary 275

Bebee, Thomas J. 45

Bechtold, Julie Ann 267, Lurlie Dee 190

Beckham, Elizabeth 118, William 118

Beckler, Walburgis Caroline Kuhlman 257

Beckman, Brenda 191

Beckwith, Mary 160

Beckworth, Lindley Garrison, Sr. 93

Becton, Eleanor Sharp 93, Fannie 93, Frederick Edwin 93, John May 93

Bedford, Nathan 280

Beebe, Edwin 242, Jane 242, Margaret 243, Mary 242, Samuel 242, Waldo 242, 243

Beiler, Katie 147

Bekal, Jewel Yoder 97

Belcher, Abner 96, Mary Jane 96, Nancy Emiline Grubbs 96, Obadiah 97

Belding, Amelia Castleberry 64, Paul B. 227

Belew, Itura 210

Belflower, Bertha 94, Carolyn Sue Milford 94, Edmund Wayne 94, Irmon 94, Kenneth 94, Milton 94 Belflower, Milton Luther 218, Pamela Marie Hare 94, Patsy 93, 94, 218, Spencer Lee 94, Stephen Douglas 94, Susan Eileen Stone 94, Tina Ruth 94

Belisle, J. Milton 40

Belk, Hattie Roquemore 264, Joseph F. 264, Marqurite Katherine 264

Bell, Corrinna Maud 132, Kenneth 41, Mary Alice McWhorter 214, Thomas Shook 214

Belvin, Ann 198

Bennet, Mary Elizabeth 124

Bennett, Alice 118, Alice Ethel 75, 174, Anne 118, Benjamin Harrison 118, Elizabeth Beckham 118, James 118,

Jim 29, 178, Lavensor Saperonia Sims 118, Mary Rogers 118, Reubin 118, Reubin Sr. 118, Richard 118, Richard Jr. 118, Rubye Evelyn Phillips 233, Sara Jane 118, Simon 118, Thomas 118, Vanessa 257, Walter H., Sr. 233

Benson, Charlie T. 252, Mamie Anderson Smith 252, 253, Tommy Gene 252

Benton 255

Bentson, Marty 63

Berg, Chuck 89, Josie Lee Harris 89, Norman 89, Robert 89

Bergan, J.W. 272

Bergen, Edgar 69

Berger, Catherine Patience 229

Berry, Don 50, Doyle 224, Karen Anette Murphy 255, Mark 255, Thelma 224, William David 66

Berwick, Lee 170

Bevill, Arthur 93

Beville, Julia 271

Bibb, Robin 85

Bickley, Ken 126

Biedenharn, Joseph 68

Biggers, Mollie 256

Billingsley, Mitch 63

Bilyeu, Lon A. 80, Myrtle Isabel 80

Bingham, Aline 81, 94, Bill 94, C.W. 94, H.E. 81, 94, Janice 81, Janis 94, Laura Shrum 94, Lola 94, Sandra 94, Sandy 81

Binnion, Naomi 126

Binotti 204

Bird, Jay 106, Mahala Williamson 136

Birdsong, Amelia Emma 95, Daniel Jefferson 95, Elvy Ann Skipper 95, Eunice Ann 95, Ex 154, Exie Augustus 95, Ferdinand Lafayette 95, 216, Fredrick Morris 95, George Washington 95, Georgia Ann 95, Homer F. 95, James H. 94, 95, James Monroe 95, Joseph B. 94, Maggie Morris 95, Mary Elizabeth "Dolly" Meadows 216, Mary Goins 95, Mary M. 95, Nancy Eunice P. Law 95, Oscar Prentice 95, Robert Milton 95, Samuel Johnson 95, Sarah Frances 95, Sarah S. 95, Sussanah Alurins 94, Thomas Franklin 95, Thomas J. 95, William Hopson 95, William Monroe 95, Willie L. Fuller 154

Birdwell, Frances Jo 101, Jane 89

Bivins, Craig Harrison 167, Effie Rule Durham 64, Jim 167, Louise Durham 167, Marjorie 167, 286, Viola 65

Black, Amanda 175, Elizabeth Shipley 175, Fannie 150, Florence 150, Jack 179, John

175, Nathaniel 175, Sarah 95, T.P. 150

Blackard, Mary Bell 229

Blackburn, George 203, James A. 108

Blacknall, M.P. 249

Blair, Clara 95, Gertrude 170, Jessie Mae Stouard 95, John Houston 95, Robert L. 95, Robert W. 95, Samuel 95, Samuel, Jr. 95, Texanna Walker 95

Blakeley, Mary E. 250

Blakely, Elizabeth 92, 278, Kelly Elder 143

Blalack, Alta Lera Willard 129, Nathan Armstrong 129, Patsy Louise Jean 129

Blalock, Anne 95, Anne Christian Scott 95, Charles 95, Charles Dickens 96, Charles Elijah 96, Charles Richard 95, Charles Thomas 96, Daniel 97, David 95, Elijah Brazier 96, Elizabeth 95, Fannie 96, Floy 96, Frances 95, George Dewey 96, Hannah 96, Ida Mae 96, 110, Ida Ruth 96, James Dewey 96, James Stuart 96, James William 96, John 95, John Wesley 96, John William, Jr. 95, John William, Sr. 95, Josephine 96, 110, Kate 96, Lela Pearl McCook 96, Lucy 96, Lucy Ann Womack 96, Lucy Margaret 96, Marshall Howard 96, Marshall Manuel 96, Martha Ellen 96, Mary Ann 96, Mary Terrell 95, Melissa Janelle Boles 97, Melvina 96, Nancy Alice 96, Rachel 95, Rebecca 96, Richard 95, Richard Brazier 96, Richard Womack 96, Russell H. 96, Sarah 96, Sarah Ann Brazier 96, Sarah Black 95, Sarah Francis 96, Sarah Jane 96, Susan Elizabeth 96, Thomas Henry 96, Thomas III 95, Thomas, Jr. 95, Thomas, Sr. 95, Vashti Russell 96, William 95, 96, William, Jr. 96, William Millington 95, William, Sr. 95, Zachary Todd 97

Bland, Abner 96, Alva Hamilton 96, Chloe Mizell 96, David 96, Elizabeth Wood 96, Elton Ray 96, Exchier 96, Fannie 96, Harper Lee 96, Harrison Jones 96, Hazel Camp 96, Hazel Watson 96, Howard Lee 96, James Presley 96, Lila Mae 96, Mary Caroline 96, 220, 270, Mary Jane Belcher 96, Maye Hendrix 96, Nellie May Jones 96, Robert Lee 96, Roxie Pauline 96, Samantha Thompson 96, William 96

Blann, William 166

Blanton, A.L. 66

Blcknall, Alice Pauline 249

Blocker, Samuel J. 16

Blodgett, Ruth 126

Bloomberg, Callie Stovall 260

Blount, Eva Jean 204, Helen 180, Peppy 204, Sarah 169, Verna Louise 139

Bluhm, Paul Larue 182, Paula 182, Wanda Joyce Husband 182

Blythe, Annie America 276

Boatner, Fred 61

Boaz, Lori 267

Bodenheim, Gabriel Augustus 20, 24, 29

Bodine 95

Boles, Able 254, Annie Lee King 97, Brenda Aston 97, Ciji 97, Elizabeth Ruth 97, Elsie Fern Skelton 97, Geneva Nell 97, James E. 97, 98, James Henry 97, James Henry II 97, Jewel Yoder Bekal 97, John Phelps 97, Johnette Nathan 97, Melissa Janelle 97, Mollie Stovall 97, 98, Mollie Tubbs 97, Odel 97, Preston Courtney 97, Rebecca Jane Howard 97, Selmer Jimett 97, Selmer John 97, Sherry Lynn Dobbins 97, Thelma Lee 97

Bolger, Bob 98, Carlisle Rose 98, Crosdella Elizabeth Cruess 98, Daniel James 98, Daniel Patrick 98, David Edward 98, Elizabeth Shay 98, George Albert 98, Isabella Cruess 98, James Michael 98, James Peter 98, Joseph William 98, Katherine Erin McKenna 98, 205, Lillie Pearl Madden 98, 205, Marybelle 3, 7, 98, 205, 206, 270, Robert Cruess 98, 205, Ruben Francis 98, Rufus Hunt 98, Samuel Robert 98, Samuel Robert, Jr. 98, Timothy Robert 98, William Robert 98, 205

Bolin, Karen Richea 267, Kyle 267, LaRue McDowell 267, Lori 267, Richard M. 267

Bolls, Marguerite 61

Bolton, Adam Christian 99, Bonnie Norwood 99, Bryson Alan 99, Carroll 98, 99, 269, Courtney Michelle 99, Etta 25, 54, Evan Blake 99, Feenie 25, 54, Ida 25, 54, J. 80, J.J. 99, James 99, James Seguine 98, Jeannie Jones 99, John 99, 269, John Seguine 98, 99, Joshua Seguine 99, Kerry 99, Kim 99, Kimberly 269, May 25, 54, Pat 99, Patricia Earp 98, Sonja Carroll Jones 99

Bommarito, S. 60

Bond, Betty Jean 134, Billy 100, Elizabeth 285, James B. 99, James Benjamin 100, James Bradford 100, Jane Allen 100, Katherine Beatrix Thurmon 99, Mark Deakins 100, Theodocia Gallatt 99,

William Frederick II 99, William James 99, 100, Yyvonne Lodell Deakins 100

Bonds, April Cecelia Johnston 189, Britt Gregory 189, Lucas Avery 189, Reece Cameron 189

Bonham, Charity 251, 235, 287, Eugenia Michelle 274, Jennie 274, 275, Michael Eugene 274, Michelle 275, Patty 274, 275

Bonner, Janet Louise King 152, Lydia Velma Ingram 183, Thomas Earl 183

Bonser, Rebecca Patton 243, Abigail Burt 243, Ellen 243, Hannah 243, Isaac 243, Jane 243, Jasper 243, Joseph 243, Rhoda 243, Samuel 243

Boom, Garrett E. 180, Mary Virginia 180, Nancy Fletcher 180

Boone, Benjamin Hayden 232, Daniel 160, Daphnie Leander 232, Elizabeth Lee Martin 165, 207, Jane Devereux 232, Julia Elizabeth 232, Martin Hayden, Jr. 232, Mary 160, Michael Brett 165, Michaela 232, Patricia 275, Regena 275, Robert Olin 275, Rose Ann 232, Rosemarie Pelphrey 232, Theodore 165, Theodore, Jr. 165, Tyler Hayden 232, William Allman 232

Booth, Aldo 100, Anna Elizabeth Cain 100, Beverly 100, Claudie 100, Edwin Russell 100, Frances Jo Birdwell 101, Frances Monigold Liston 101, Gladys Laressa Adams 100, 101, Henry T. 245, Horace Kenneth 100, J. Willis 100, James Willis 100, 101, James Willis, Jr. 100, Leanne Elizabeth 101, Leila Nancy 245, Mary Elizabeth 100, Robert 100, 101, Stuart Lee 101, Talmadge 66, 100, 101, Varina 100, Victoria Lynn 101, Willis Early 100, Woodie C. Woods 100

Boothe, Armenda Jane Henderson 172, Barry 172, Billy 172, William Henry 172

Boozman, Claudia 278, Cynthia 278, Marian 278, Paul 278

Borders, Augusta 155, William R. 8

Boren, Alonzo Baber 156, Carrie Christine 242, Daisie Lee 156, Dan Little 242, David 242, Janna Little 242, Sally Elizabeth Johnson 156

Boring, E.R. 67, Emma 67, 102, 104, Emory 104, Helen 61, 104, J.R. 192, J.W. 8, Jessie Olivia 102, 104, Joseph 102, 104

Bosley, Byron Lane 255

Bosner, Detner 243, Joseph 243

Boswell, Audie Imogene Null 101, 102, Christi Lynn 102, Christopher 102, Clara Nabors 101, Clay Scott 102, Debra 231, Elton Clay 101, Gary Clay 101, John Thomas 101, John W. Riley 101, Justin 102, Larry 102, Larry Joe 101, Lucy Ellen 276, Patricia Cleopatra 276, Rachel 102, Royal Grant 276, Shelli 102, Virginia 101, 102, 236

Bottolfson, Linda Ann 147

Bounds, Rose Marie 248

Bourchier 241

Boussard, Sarah Beth 250

Boutell, Jamee 171

Bowden, Rebecca 200, 225

Bowen, Alice Virginia 276, Gracie Lorene 276, Ira Leonard "Ike" 276, Marvin David 276, Peggy Jean 276, Rosetta 147

Bowers, R.S. 40

Bowie, Charlotte Johnson 254, Rebecca 249

Bowl 116

Bowles, Elvey 97, 286, James Henry 97, Jimmette 286, 287, John F. 286, 287, Margaret 234, Missie 97, 98, 133, 286, 287, Patsy Ruth 287, Pearlie Rogers 287, William Henry 97, 286, 287

Bowlin, Lydia 157, Norma Jean 240

Bowring, Benjamin Leon 40

Boyce, Sally Maxine 276

Boyd, Iris 104, Marie 276, Tennessee Virginia 103, 150

Bozman, Benjamin M. 49, 235, James Denzil 97, John Henry 97, Margaret Bumpus 97, Mariah Phillips 235

Brack, Eleazor 235, Elizabeth 235, Lavinia 98, 235

Bradle, Bernice Meyer 287

Bradley, Carl 50, John A. 270, Johnnie Virginia Foshee 149, Zoie Mae 83

Brady, Elizabeth 251, 235, 287

Brame, Fabia 230

Bramlette, Ada Chaney 102, Annie Eliza Miller 102, 150, 151, Annie France 103, Annie Hibernia 103, Claribel McCord 103, Clementine Miller 102, Dana Bass 102, Erskine Miller 28, 114, 102, 104, 217, Esther Wellborn 102, Floreid 103, 150, 151, Frederick E. 103, Frederick Leavenworth 103, Gloria 103, Grace A. Jones 103, Hazel Branthoffer 102, Ione Perry Pegues 103, Jack Howard 102, Jesse Hughes 102, Jesse Morgan 102, Jessie 67, 102, 104, Joan Docherty 102, John Edwin 102, John Edwin, Jr. 102, John Woodson 102, Josephine Helen "Dot" Keener 102, Josephine M. 102, Kathryne Clementine 102, Lawrence

Miller 102, Lida Lee Denney 103, Mary Ann 103, Nancy Taylor 102, Nannie Mae 103, Paul Miller 103, Paula 103, Pauline 102, 103, Thomas Anderson 102, 150, Thomas Leander 102, William Howard 103, William Howard, Jr. 103

Brandon 90

Brannon, Anna Jan 261, Clift 123, Madlyn 123, Sarah Eveline 152, Sarah Evelyn 252

Branthoffer, Hazel 102

Brashear, Aubrey 66

Brasher 26

Brasier, Cindy 124

Brasswell 90

Braswell, Mary Laura 245, Randolph 245

Braudaway, Audra Gladys 83, Dorothy Alice 83, Flora Dee "Fordie" 83, James William "Bill" 83, Jesse Albert 82, 83, Malcolm Travis 83, Willie Dee "Shug" Alexander 82, 83

Brawner 90

Bray, Billie Carrl 258

Brazier, Sarah Ann 96

Breaux, Alexis 161, Eula 161

Brennan, John 55, 103

Brent, Jim 136

Brewer, Celita 136, Doris Irlene Dozier 136, Doyle 26, Elizabeth 101, 275, Garl 136, Jon Garl 136, Kelton 17, Mable 26, Sadie Jane 167, Wallace 136

Brewton, Ada Louise Anderson 187

Brian, Eva Lorene Rathburn 103, Judith Pauline 104, Karen 103, Leo 103, Leon, Sr. 103, Mark Wendell 103, Mary Elizabeth Keese 104, Matthew Elijah 104, Sarah Catherine 104, Susan Cigainero 103

Brick, Blanche Henderson 171, Hannah Grace 171, Jamee Boutell 171, John 171, Kathleen 171, Robert 171

Bridges, Ann 231

Brigance, Clinton 187, Elvia Arrena 187, Henry C. 187

Briggs, E.J. 48

Bright, Joel S. 28, John 259

Briley 279, Clyde Austin 282, Hazel Lorene 282, Tracy 63

Brinkley, Kathleen 126

Brittain, Bonnie 96, 110

Broadwell, Kate 99

Brogdon, Frances 126

Brooks, Bazzie Wilbur 193, Cora Matilda 80, Emily Hoskins 177, Frances Asbury 177, Lucille 276, Lula Marie 177, Ophelia Key 192, Stephen 177

Brookshire, Blake 161, Britt 161, Caroline 161, Chad 161, Ross 161, Sunni Feather 161

Brothers, W.C. 37

Broussard, Carol Lynn 249, Gary Lynn 249, Leesa Carol 249

Brown 22, Acme Elberta 105, Alan Ridley 228, Alice Virginia 276, Anderson 202, Anna 104, 173, Annie Lee Taylor 64, Annie Lou 45, 105, 223, 224, Arthur Northcutt 228, B.W. 11, 27, Barbara 228, Bernice Hemperly 105, Betty 228, Bev E. 105, Bluford W. 8, 100, 104, Bruce E. 228, Catherine 263, Chester Adams 105, Danny 182, David 133, 228, Docia Jane Hill 106, Donnie Leon 105, Dora "Missie" 282, Edward A. 228, Eely 173, Elizabeth 84, Ellen Marie 106, Elmo 104, Elsie Hendricks 105, Emily 228, Emma Reancy 102, 104, Erica 256, Ethel 104, Eva Mae Akins 105, Fannie Isabell Cock 105, Francine 105, Frank 105, Fred 104, George Melvin 228, Grace 139, Heather Lauren 223, Helen 98, 133, 287, Henry Lewis 105, Hilton 193, 194, Hitson 84, 104, I.L. 8, Ida Cora 104, Iris Boyd 104, Isaac 104, Isaiah 104, 105, 106, James Isaac 106, Janet Tienry 228, Jessie Mae Prothro 64, Jessie Northcutt 228, Joanna R. Clark 104, Jodie Elsie 264, John Garland 105, 119, John William 8, 105, Johnny Mack 38, Joseph 275, Josie Rawls 104, Lavonn 50, Lena Kennedy 105, Lewis Edwin 45, 104, 105, 106, Lewis Edwin, Jr. 105, 223, Lewis Edwin, Sr. 223, Lula Frances 104, M. Methvin 104, 105, Mabel 64, Margaret 45, 105, Marian 265, Martha 104, Mary A. 104, 105, Mary Louise Delmas 106, 108, Matilda Omega Husband 182, Minnie Morris 104, 105, 223, Mittie Florence 104, Nancy Caroline Cox 104, Oscar F. 104, P.M. 49, Pam Posey 228, Patricia Ann "Tita" 276, Paul 45, 105, Peaches 105, Pearl Lee 105, Perry 98, R.G. 48, Ralph 276, Robert E. Lee 104, Romaine 104, Ronald 255, Rosie Lee 273, Rowena 52, Russell E. 174, Sallie Turner 105, Sally Irene Hewell 173, Sue 241, Suzanne 228, Suzy 106, 108, Taylor 105, Tressie May 105, Walter Ney 104, William I. 45, 105, Willie Ray 84, Wilton Elmo 106, 108, Windford Ray 104, Zellie Ineza 105

Browning, Alexander Mead 195, Lula Viola 195, Sarah 195, Tom 195

Broyles, Mary Penelope 103

Bruce, Carrie 64, 104, 148, Eloyse 49, Gretchen Giels 195, Ingram 104, Jake 195,

Laurie 195, May Dee 104, Mittie Brown 104, Robert 195, Robert H. 104, Shannon 195

Brumble, Mabel 202

Brumfield, Emily Anne Lancaster 197, John Olen 197, Michael Olen 197, Nettie Louise Newman 197

Brumit, Kim 139

Bruner, Bennie 117, Fannie Irene 113, Tempa 145, William Isaac 8

Brunwald, Hunter Fergusson 137, 257, Philip John 137, 257, Rebecca Lee Stahl 137, 257, Taylor Hawkins 137, 257

Bryan, Frances Killingsworth 167, Hanna 160, Harriet C. 251, Lily 143, Louis 167, Mary Boone 160, Sarah Wolf 228, William 160

Bryant, Barbara 107, Betty Jean 273, Beverly 107, Billy Oneal 184, Carl 107, Genevieve Green 107, Glenda Gail 273, James Durwood 272, Julia 107, Julie 107, Katie Lee 272, Kenneth Ray 273, Kimberly 107, Lawrence Derrill, Sr. 107, Lawrence, Jr. 107, Louises 245, Mary Nell Ingram 183, 184, Nelda Sue 273, Nina 163, Reba 197, Wanda 126

Bryson, Martha Fisher 147, William 147

Buchanan, Jack T. 60

Buck, Jana 170

Buckner 88, Murrell L. 37, Verna Beatrice 91

Buie, Laura 177, 178

Bukingham, George 29

Buley, Vicki 223

Bullock, Dwayne 281, Ellen Marie 258

Bumbgardener, Emily Eugina 258

Bumpas 115, Juan Minerva 227, Nancy Jane 273

Bumpus 148, Alice Ray Coleman 122, Caleb 28, Ethel May 122, James 122, Jane Allen 97, John 28, 97, Margaret 97, Martha Ann 97, Nettie 122, Rosa Bette 261, William E. 97

Bundren, George 210, Novie Ree Mauldin 210

Bunt, Birda Inez 171

Burk 95

Burke, Archibald T. 8, LoIda 107, Minnie Elaine 154, Sarah 254, Wendy J. 107, William 107

Burkett, Ila 179

Burleson, Aaron 223, Aaron II 58

Burlew, Fannie Mae 64

Burnett, Dale Jeter 107, P.C. 158, Richard Wesley 107, Susan Alvina Hill 158, William Preston 158, Worthy Pauline 158

Burney, Clare Denman 151, Floreid Francis 103, 151, Henry P., Sr. 151, Henry Prather III 151, Henry Prather, Jr. 103, 151

Burns, Anna Emmons 246

Burr, Lillie Zelika 242

Burrell, Mary Ann Saphonie Storey 84

Burrous, Deborah Kay Hollers 175

Burt, Abigail 243, Alan 107, 108, Amy 108, Carl 108, Helen 108, Joseph 108, Sam 108, Suzy B. 4, 108, Tammy 5, 108

Busby, Arthur Brisbane 247, Mollie 247

Bush, A.D. 208, George W. 258, Marion 29, Patricia Arlee 240

Bussell, Eva Lillian 213

Bussey, Bill 30, Lillian Belle 116, Nadyne 265

Butler, Aletha Barnes 235, James Anthony 97, Mary 97, 235, 251, 287, Thomas 235, Ulletta Ann 131, 132

Butrill, Virginia Beall 118

Butter, Alexis Ryan 247, Bettye Frances Fears 146, Billie Potts 247, Dallas F. 146, Leo Edison 247, Leo Ryan 247, Linda Jane Ryan 247, Stephen Robert 247, Stephen Robert Jr. 247, Virginia 146, Zane Ryan 247

Buttrill, Britton 11, 229, Ruth Emmaline McCord 229, Virginia Beall 229

Butts, Annie 109, 203, Carrie M. 109, Charles M. 8, Ethel Fambrough 109, Harvey J. 109, 203, Jesse J. 109, Jesse Lafayette 109, Judith 156, Mary 203, Mary Angell 109, Mary Catherine Price 109, Mary Ethel 109, Nellie Milam 109, Sallie M. 109, Sarah Hunt 156, Thomas Clements 156, Washington L. 109

Byars, Ica Belle 276

Byers, Homer 86, 109, Lillie Beatrice 86, 109, Margaret Alice Dunn 109, Sarah "Sallie" Priscilla 238

C

Cabaniss, Carol 198, Charles Davis 198, Kathryn Landers 198, Kristin 198, Mary Kathryn 198

Cabbiness, Janet Carol James 110, Kristen Kuehl 110, Mary Phillips Lawrence 110, Robin Laney Seidel 1 1 0 , Allyne Adkins 110, Amanda 96, 110, 253, Becky Jo 96, 110, 253, Bennie Ralph 96, 110, 252, Bessie Sanford 110, Bettie L. Witcher 110, Betty 96, 110, 222, 223, 238, 253, Billy 63, Billy Joe 96, 110, 223, 252, Billy Ray 96,

110, 252, Bonnie Brittain 96, 110, Brenda Jane 96, 110, 252, Briana 96, 110, 253, Bruce Wayne 96, 110, 253, Carla Ann Lloyd 96, 110, 252, Carla Case 253, Carol Cearley 96, 110, Catherine 253, David 253, Dianne 253, Elbert Monroe 110, Ella D. Dunbar 110, Gaynelle 96, 110, Hayden 110, Henry Daniel 110, Hershell 110, Ida Mae Blalock 110, James R. 110, Janet Carol James 96, 252, Jason Lloyd 96, 110, 253, Jennifer 253, Johnnie Mae 96, 110, Josephine Melvina Blalock 96, 110, Joshua 109, 110, Kristen Kuehl 96, 253, Leoni F. 110, Lula W. Marshall 110, Lynn Magee 96, 253, Margie Ann 96, 110, Marla Gayle 96, 110, Mary Ann Phillips Lawrence 253, Mary J. 110, Mary Phillips 96, 110, 253, Mattie Dee 110, Maud 110, 126, Milton III 96, 110, Milton, Jr. 96, 110, Milton, Sr. 96, 110, Orline Sayer 110, Patsy Sue 96, 110, Ralph Herman 110, Ralph Herman, Jr. 96, 110, Robin Laney 96, 253, Sarah A.E. Mings 110, Sarah Caroline 110, Staci Nicole 96, 110, Sterling Price 96, 110, Walter Laurence 110, William Bryan 110

Cabines, Kevin 198

Cabiness, Kathryn Landers 198

Caddell, Lily June 179, Mary 147

Cadell, Lena 176

Caffey, Dorothy Stephens Nunnally 228

Cahill, Alice 110, Charles 110, Bob 110, 111, 157, Georgina 110, 157, Jack 110, Jana 110, 111, 157, Jessica 110, 111, 157, John 110, 157, Joyce 110, 157, Rose 110

Cain, Anna Elizabeth 100, Donnie 170

Cairns, Charles 253, Helen Grace Smith 253, Stewart 253

Caldwell 279, Robert John 112, Carmen 111, 112, 280, Catherine Mary 111, Claude Patrick 111, 280, Jennie 112, Katherine Mary 112, Margaret 112, Mary Anne Pinkerton 111, Pat 280, Sharon 111, 280, Shirley 111, 112, Simon Claudius 111, Susan Frances 111, 112, William 111, 112

Calhoun 214, Rebecca 167

Callaway, Alvin J. 233, Betty Virginia 121, Carrie Fisher 112, Charles Ashley 112, Dora 121, Elizabeth Ann 112, George Newton 112, George William 121, John A. 112, John Roy 121, Marga-

ret Ann 112, Mary Jane 112, Mattie Lavinia 130, Mattie Person 233, Ollie 112, Robert E. 112, Robert Merrell 112, Sallie Eliza 112, Sanders Eugene 112, Sarah Ann Elizabeth Walker 112, Sarah Wicker 112, Vera 112

Callihan, Mary M. 238

Calloway, Dick 25, 54, Grace Jane 154, Jane 25, 54, John 251, Pearl 25, 54, Raz 25, 54, Ruth 25, 54, Vera Essie Smith 251

Calvin, Absalom 112, Bettie 64, Charlotte Elizabeth 112, Charlotte Jane Pollock 112, Granville Perry 112, Lavonia Frances 112, 261, Lorraine 64, 113, 208, Luther Granville 112, 113, 261, Stephen Parker 112, Vere Lorraine 112

Cameron, Rod 38

Cammack, James 63, James Milton, Jr. 118, Sara Finch 118

Camp, Cecil 225, Daniel 186, E.A. 45, Gloria Marceal Nevels 225, Hazel 96, Jessica 186, Joy Denise 225, Julia B. 147, Steve Alan 225, Vicki Susan 225

Campbell 254, Ann 167, Annie Mae DeLoach 64, Brice 167, Charles 167, Elizabeth 206, Fannie Irene Bruner 113, James Oliver, Sr. 247, Jessie 199, Katherine Harrison 167, L.T. 6, LuRye 247, Margaret 167, Rachel Moore 113, Thomas Duncan 8, 113, Thomas Mitchell 113

Candler, Asa G. 68

Canion, Donnie 94, Janice Bingham 81, Janis Bingham 94, Laci Laird 94, Roger Bingham 94

Cannon, Amanda Elmina Haley Hinkle 114, Burrell 114, Gilbert 202, Ginger Elder 143, Goalman 119, Jakie 119, Lawrence, Jr. 114, Margaret 114, 201, Ora 202, Rebecca 202, Ron 143, Ruff 201, William 114

Cantrell, John 108, Shirley 7

Cantwell, Conan Westmoreland 102, Pauline Feagle Bramlette 102

Capps, Jennie Lynn 274, LaVerne 267, Mandie 274, Robert 274

Caradoc 125

Caraway, Abney Edwin 194, Agnes 194, 195, Archie Edwin 194, Ed 194, Eliza Jane 116, Emma Agnes 194, 195, Laura Ann 194, Laura Kate 194

Cardenas, Abigail 192

Cargile, Jonathan Wayne 175, Paula Hubbard 175

Cargill, Paula 256, Pauline 169, 256, Robert 169, 170, 256, 257

Carlisle 90

Carlson, Hollis Xan Pugsley 105

Carlton, Asa 115, Bill 115, Dolores Jean 115, Durold Dean 115, Mary Lucille 115, Mike 115

Carpenter 255, Christy 276, Claude W. 218, Claudette Alyce 218, Doug 276, Kenneth 150, Lawrence Bruce 276, Ollie Beatrice 134, Tresha Jan 276, Victoria Bernice Miller 218

Carr, Jenny 110, Quenton 110

Carrico 255

Carrington, Elaine 256, Natassha 256, René 256, Zynyah 256

Carrol, Frank 65

Carroll, Daniel 115, Gwendolyn Blodwyn Ellis 115, Isabelle Dunseath McKeag 115, Jack A. III 115, Charles 115, Charlotte 115, Clarkie 252, Donald Thomas 115, Emma Ora 101, Harvey Floyd 115, Jack A. 115, Jean Frances MacTavish 1 1 5 , Jennifer 115, Lara 115, Margaret Charlotte Peterson 115, Martha Brown 104, Patricia 115, Salathiel J. 115, Sarah 115, 262, Thomas Floyd 115, W.G. 104, Walter Lowrey 115

Carson, Sarah 161

Carter 287, Anna Marie 168, Carol Jane 116, Eliza Jane 116, Ewing Clayton 116, Gladys Marie Carter 168, Hiram H. 110, Howard Glenn 168, John H. 176, Margaret 116, Mary Claire 116, Mary Louisa 116, Mary Nell 116, 125, 176, Maxine 261, Paula Elaine Harroff 168, Raenell 116, 125, Randy Eugene 168, Ray H. 116, 125, 176, Robert Daniel 116, Sarah 147, Sarah Battle 123, Sarah Hoskins 176, Walter 176

Cartmell, Catherine Compton 152, Eugenia Francis 151, 152, Philip Martin, Jr. 152, Thomas Philip 152

Cartwright, Alma 172, 184, William Davis 172

Case, Carla 253

Caskey, Eleanor Jane 118

Casselberg, Hendrick 244

Cassidy, Raymond 263, Wanda 263

Casteberry, Mattie 70

Casteel, Hallie 218

Castela, Cheryl Lynn 276, Henri Edward 276

Castleberry, William 287

Castleberry, Aaron 116, 199, 244, Ada 116, Agnes Lodeema 199, Amelia 64, 243, Ann 64, 244, Asa 25, Cora 116, Cynthia Lawrence 199, Elmira 44, 51, 116, 244, Elmyra 116, 206, George

Aaron 116, J.R. 56, J.T. 51, James Herman 199, James Rodden 44, 199, Joseph 25, 54, 199, Lillian Belle Bussey 116, Mae Dee 199, Maggie 116, 206, Mary Frances 116, Maud 199, Richard 44, 116, 244, Sarah Craven 244, William 233

Castles, Minnie 186

Cathey, H. Mark 222, Mary Ellen 222

Catterton, Benjamin N. 8

Causey, Andrew J. 121, Georgia Coleman Graves 121, Jessie Zebelon 153, Sarah Dixie Morse 153

Cauthen, Mary 118

Cave, Don 38

Caver, Alice LunaMae Terry 264, DunaMae 264, Mabel 264, William 264

Cearley, Carol 96, 110

Chadick, Josephine Malinda 261, Martha Margaret Fisher 147, Stokley Rowan 147

Chance, Anne 206, Francys Estelle 255

Chandler, Emma Caroline 109

Chaney, Ada 102, France Ellen Johnson 103, Gussie Pegues 247, Lawrence 247, Nancy Lucinda 209, 218, R.R. 103

Chanler, Arthur Leroy, Jr. 86, 109, Arthur Leroy, Sr. 86, 109, Candace Brooke 109, Christopher Bryce 109, Dennis 109, Henry David 86, 109, Janean 86, Leroy, Sr. 86, Lillie Beatrice Byers 86, 109, Marcia Janean 109, Marita Ann 85, 86, 87, 109, Myrtis 109

Chapman 153, 154, 191, B.F. 24, Derek Luell 130, Francis Ellen Huston 130, Laura A. 121, Nevonda Jean, Davidson 130, Robert Obie 130, Suellen 252, 253, Vernon Luell 130

Charles, Alta 281, Robert 281

Chastain, Mary A. Elizabeth 78

Cheek, Mary Catherine Masters 187, Nancy Elmine 187, Solomon 187

Chenault, Claire 246

Chessher, James 254

Chevalier, E.L. 128

Childers, Amanda Caroline Barnes 209, Ethel 209, John Ellison, Jr. 209

Childress, Ethel 209, Jackson Scott 216, Jessie Ellen Lynn 216, Laura Wellington 216, Mary 61

Chisum, Charlotte 26, William P. 24

Choice 109, Andrew Earl 116, 117, Ann Nancy 156, Carrie Jane Clinkscales 116, Earline 117, Frank C. 116, Harry Tully 116, Horace 116,

Jane Eleanor 116, John 116, 117, Karry Augusta 117, Lorine 117, Marybelle Crews 116, Mavis Pauline 117, Olly Darby 116, Orion 142, Ruth 117, Tully 8

Christensen, Brian 41, Clay Charles 91, Kathleen Ann 91

Christian, Alec 118, Ann 117, Annie B. Jones 118, Albert W. 117, Alec 117, Amanda Susan Lester 152, Ann 118, Burger 118, Butcher 117, 118, Carrie 117, Channey 118, Channie 118, Chester 117, Christina 118, Dianne 85, 188, Early Sessum 117, Edgar 152, Edward Lewis 117, Ella Rhee 117, Ethel 152, Georgia 152, Gertrude Howell 117, Gideon 27, 117, Hulda 118, Ida 152, Ila Mae 117, Isa Dora 152, 245, J.R. 49, Janet Rhea Shepard 85, Jim 56, 152, Linnie 85, Mariah McCollum 117, Muriel 117, 118, Nan Roberts 117, Nancy Eller 80, Ollive Wilhite 118, Rachael Snoddy 118, Rachel 85, Randle 117, Rebecca Jones 118, Steve 85, Susan 152, Thomas 117, 152, Tommie Thadeus 117, 118, William 80, 99, 165, 166, 189

Chumchal, Carolina Ludmilla 252

Churchill, Thelma 261

Cigainero, Albert 103, Florine Whalen 103, Susan 103

Clafferty, Bill 70

Clairmont, Madeline 147

Clanton, B. Reid 37, Benjamin Reid 118, Elaine Markham 118, Emily Jane Hilton 118, Princess Louise Markham 121, R. 60, 118, 121, Sara Jane Bennett 118, Sarah Finch 118, 121, Virginia Elaine 118, 121, 206, William Marr 118

Clapp, A.E. 178, Charlotte 178, Natalie 178

Clark, Billie Francis 17, Bobby 90, Darlina Calvin Adams 112, David 90, Emma 118, 127, George W. 20, Gloria Marceal Nevels Camp 225, Guy P. 235, Ivey Jewel 225, Joanna R. 104, Joe 90, Keith W. 225, Kriss 113, Kyle 113, Lillie Gertrude Phillips 235, Mabel Barton 90, Mike 112, R.S. 118, Reecc Buttrill 229, Rosemary 90, S.B. 118, Stella Maud Wood 127, 229, T.J. 118, 229, Thomas Britton 127, 229, Vander Artimissie 146, 264, Virginia Beall Butrill 118, 229

Clarke, Elijah 156

Clay, André 119, Arula 118, 202, Candice 119, Claudette 119, Denise 119, DeQuence 119, 202, JaHarial 119, Jer-

emy 119, Leon 119, Leon 119, Marvin Henry 118, Noah 119, Rachard 119, Royce 119, Sudie 119, Valencetta 119, Bennie 119

Cleland, Carol Sue 138, Nellie Angie Moss 138, Pelham Jackson 138

Clem, Amecia Gaile Dryden 137, Cyndell Grace 137, Samuel Travis 137, Timothy Lee 137

Clemens, Claude Caesar 116, 272, Margie Frances 272, Melvin Ray 272, Tomie Joe 272

Clements, Annice 277, E.W. 277, Ida 277, Jack K. 277, Mamie 277, Martha Ann Bumpus 97, Miner 97, Minnie Mae 277, Quincy Edward 277, Sarah Ann 277

Clemmons, Andrew E. 42, 43

Clemons, Joseph 29

Clendenen, Wade 163

Cleveland, Benjamin 180, Grover 193

Cliburn, Harvey Lavan Jr. 118, Rilda Bee 118, Van 118

Clifton, I.O. 27

Clinkscales, Carrie Jane 116, Emma Stillwell 116, Frank B. 116

Clinton, John 241

Clymore, Carol 230

Coan, Mary 206

Coats, Henry R. 237, Malinda Elizabeth 237, Malinda Evelyn Reed 237, Morris 91, Sudie 119

Cobb, David 182, Lillie Mae 61, Maude 60, 61, 63, 119, Paula Bluhm 182, Robert Edward 197, Roy C. 197, Ruby Lanagan 197

Coby, Clemmie 202, John L. 202

Cochran, Gerald Wayne 260, Inita Orr 260, Jerry 260, Jewel M. 286, Rusty 260, Ruth Ann 260

Cock, Edward William 119, Fannie Isabella 105, 119, George Washington 119, Joseph 105, 119, Kate 119, Mary Ella 119, Pleas 119, Ria 119, Sally 119, Turner 119

Cocke, Sue Ann 246, Tom 246

Cockerall, Sara H. 207

Cockerell, Azure 120, Ben 120, Brian 120, Cameron 120, Candice 120, Casey 120, Cinnamon 120, Clint 120, Elizabeth 119, Garth 119, 120, Gayleen White 120, Gloria 120, Janis Ford 120, L.L. 119, Leslie 120, Phillip 120, Sylvia 120, Tina 119, 120, Vicki Abernathy 120

Cocteau, Jean 188

Cody, Florine 83

Coe, Benjamin F. 120, M.L. McLendon 120, Mary Lou

Melton McLendon 120, 212, 213

Cofer, Margaret 141

Coffman, Jacob 147, Susannah Fisher 147

Coggins, Gary Neal 213, Julius 213, Mamie Eloise McLendon 212

Coghlan, Emma Inez Watts 64

Coke, Nancy Kay 214

Colburn, Archie 148

Cole 70, 179, 229, Edna 40, Gay Keener 64, Martha Ann Elizabeth 206

Coleman, Elizabeth Ann Roper 121, Louisa Alabama 120, Louisa Elizabeth Ledford 121, Martin 120, Alice Lenora E. Johnson 121, Alice Ray 120, 121, 122, Ann Roper 206, Annie 121, Babette 268, Beatrice Southern Parker 121, Bobb 121, Charles S. 121, Clara 274, Clifford Ray 268, Cornelia S. 121, Eddie J. 121, Ethel 122, Evonne 121, Frank 121, Georgia Ann Harrison 121, Horatio Jefferson 120, 121, Coleman, Isham 121, 122, 206, James S. 121, Jeff 120, 121, John Washington 121, Lavinia Wilkins 121, Lillie 121, Louisa Alabama 122, Louisa Elizabeth Ledford 120, 121, Louisa Marie 121, Louisiana 122, Lu 122, Marilah Francis 121, Marla Sue King 268, Martha Ann Elizabeth 121, Martin Turner 121, 122, Mary Elizabeth Ray 121, 206, Mary Ethel Schofield 183, Mary Ray 120, 121, Mary Winifred 121, Mena Ethel Estella 120, 121, Mollie 121, Nora 121, Otis Edgar 183, Sarah Adaline 121, T.K. 11, Thames 121, Thomas 120, Thomas Alton 121, Thomas Marion 121, William 120, William Edgar 121, William Goodwin 121, 122

Collier, Aaron Bruce 131, Bruce 131, Clayton Barclay 131, Courtney Blaine 131, Lanna Rosalin Davis 131, Stacy Lynn Klunkert 131

Collins 255, Arnold Dale 243, Jackie Ray 243, Lillian Jarrelline 243, Otis Lee 243, Robert Lee 243, Tommy Joe 243

Colquitt, Carol 122, Eleanor Adam 122, Landon A. 60, 122

Combs, Greg 209, Linda 209, 218, Melina 209, T.M. 173, Vera 173

Compton, Danette 170

Conaway, Charity Allen 83, John 83

Conerly, Wilmuth Octavia 242

Conley, Danielle Moore 221, Michael 221, Murray 41

Conlin, Max J. 41

Conner, Elizabeth Caroline 177

Conway, Jill Townes 97, Shelley Ann 164, Traye Bradley 164

Cook 206, Allyene Elizabeth Fears 146, Bernice 283, Clara Francis Louise 270, Doris Alma 103, Fred W. 146, Hardy Rhodes 270, Huldah 220, Ida Ruth 270, Jane Elizabeth 178, Judy 146, Millie Tutt 270, R.B. 71, Sallie Mildred 270, Sam Tutt 270, Samuel Francis 270, Stephen Lucas 46, Terri 219, Tiana M. 173, W.H. 146

Cooke, Elias Green 220, Josh 29, Martha B. Prater 220

Cookman, Gwendolyn Wood 112

Coolidge, Carol 87

Coones, Dorothy 122, 123

Cooper, Amy Beth 271, Glynda Gilley 175, Keith 175, Nicholas Allen 175, Phebe 222, Phillip Ryan 175, Tera 271, Teresa Elizabeth Tutt 98, Teresa Sydney 98, 271, Teri 220, 270, Troy 98, 270, 271, Virginia 271

Cope, Ava-Pearl 263, Bryant 263, Calvin 263, Carrie 263, Hattie 263, Jodie 263, Joseph 263, Knox 263, Martha Jerusha Terry 263, Onie-Belle 263, Otis 263

Copeland, Kenneth 255

Copes, John 117, Kaaran 117

Corbin, Carlton 202

Cordell, David 83, Floyd 83, Lucy Pearl Allen 83, Mary Ann 83, Nancy 83, Sid 83

Corley, Charles Jesse 132, Katie Lee Davis 132, Mary Emma 264

Cornelius, Betty Louise Hardy 166, Gina 167, William Calvin 166

Costlow, Kathryn Malise Hafner 163, Madison 163, Morgan 163

Couch, Jake 199, Mary Beth 199

Coupland, Martha White Sloan 124, Andrew Adams 123, Andrew Jackson 123, Gladys 123, 124, Harold 124, Laura 123, 124, Margaret 124, Martha White Sloan 123, Philip 124, Sarah Battle Carter 123, Thomas Dodson 114, 123, 124

Cousins, Dora M. Kelly 124, Isaac William 124, Lucinda 216, Mary Elizabeth 124, Robert Bartow 124

Covin, David Reid 118, Jack Michael 118, Jonathan Scott 118, Virginia Elaine 118

Cowan, Syntha Evalene 180, Virginia Jane 103

Cowart, Ola Mae 196

Cowles, Louretta 80

Cox 90, Adam Michael 195, Casey Leanne 195, Cora 263, Delores Ann 201, Margaret 91, Mary 91, Mary Estella 173, Mary Joe 97, Nancy Caroline 104, Tom 67, William 91

Coxe, Richard 90

Crabtree, Clara Elizabeth 181, 182, Evelyn Anne 181, 182, John William 181, 182, Julianne Patterson 181, 182, Pat 181, 182

Craddock, Bettye 124, 125, Catherine Anne 125, Dorothy 124, Van 47, 124, 125

Craft, A.J. 125, Carol Claire 125, Kimberly Nell 125, Leighann Elizabeth 125, 176, Mary Elizabeth 125, Raenell 116, 125, 176, Russell 116, 125, 176

Craig, Eddy 17, William D. 41

Crain, B.W. 104, 140, Ed 104, Hattie May Griffin 159, Joel 159, John Richard 104, 159, Lillo 104, Lula Brown 104, Mattie Patience Rogers 159

Crane, Austen Barrow 125, Corbin Hodges 125, Curtis Wayne 125, Ernest James 125, Glyn 125, Jackson Kelly 125, Janice Ellen 125, June 125, Kathleen June 125, Kelly 125, Leona Beatrice Goad 125, Lucretia Lynn Langston 125, Nannie 56, Nettie 56

Crank, Grace Anne Hurst 181, 182, John Clyde 181, 182, Medley Jane 181, 182

Craven, Sarah 244

Crawford, 264, Allie 183, Delbert Troy 272, Ellis 132, James 183, Jewel Delbert 272, Leonard Ellis 272, Lorena Tincher 183, Marvin Douglas 272, Reba Annette 272, Ruby Elizabeth 272

Crawley, Ethel DeLoach 64, Henry K. 140

Crews, Andrew 261, C.C. 27, Cordie Lee 216, Doris Jean 186, Ernestine Ham 186, Fisher Andrew 261, George Henry 216, Jenea Augusta "Anna" Meadows 216, Jesse Calvin 186, Lee 261, Marybelle 116, Patricia Ann "Tita" 276, Robert E. "Bob" 276

Crim, Elizabeth 61, Liggett 35, Lou Della 159, 285

Crocker, Byron A. 214, Mary Alice McWhorter 214

Crosby, J.R. 286

Cross, Leon 45, Martha Elizabeth 131

Crossland, Mike 56

Crouch, Anna Frances 218

Crow, Bobby Joe 126, Ivy Myrtle Moore 126, Joe David 126, Marilyn Kilgore 126, Martha Elizabeth White 126, Naomi Binnion 126,

Raymond, Jr. 126, Raymond Marshall 126, Raymond Robert 126, Sarah Annie Miller 126, Wroland Green 126

Crowder, Mary Florence 258

Crowley, Ardie 126, Carl 126, Cordelia Belle Watkins 126, Dorothy 126, 246, E. Rufford 126, Elizabeth 126, Evelyn 126, Frances 126, Jack 126, James Joseph 126, Jennie 126, Joseph 126, Kathleen 126, Molly 126, Robert Lee 126, Ruth 126, Teen 126, Tom 126, Wanda 126, William 126

Cruess, Crosdella Elizabeth 98, Florence L'Estrange 98, Isabella 98, M. Thomas 98, M. William 98, Mary Ann Hunt 98, Robert 271, Samuel Robert 98, William Vere, Sr. 98

Cruice 98

Cruise 98

Cuberley, Martha 64

Culberson, Theresa 227

Culbertson, Lawrence 268, Nancy Tramel 268

Culpepper 96, 143, C.B. 265, Charles Thomas 171, Cody 110, 126, 127, David Bartow 127, Elbert 118, 126, 127, Emma Katherine 127, Gladys 171, 172, Inez 127, Joseph 97, 128, Katherine Inez 128, Letta Belle 127, Luisa Elizabeth Ferguson 171, Martha Blanche 118, 127, 128, Martha Etta 127, Maud 110, 126, Sarah 97, Teruko I. 128, Thomas Elbert 127, 128, Thomas Jefferson 127, Willa Koehler 128

Cunningham, Martha Virginia 206

Cunyus, Jesse Julia Graybill 156, Lou 160

Curi, Victoria 265

Curry, Ann 230

Curtis, Colista Ann Hughey 180, James R. 246, Mary S. 206, Robert A. 180, Ruth 241

Custer, Cora Vemelle Martin 207, Kelly 255, T. Ray 207

Cyrena, Martha 244

D

Dabney, Gladys Marie 168

Daccache, Anna Marie 93, Jean Pierre 93, Lauren Elizabeth 93, Stacy Baucum 93

Daiches, Max 189

Dailey, J.C. 228, Nannie Odom 228

Dalston, J.W. 36, R.T. 36, Sharlie Peck 36, Turley 70

Dalton, Bill 13, 29, 177, 178

Daniel, Beatrice 229, Beecher 151, Daphne Rushing 145, Deborah 128, Edith Darlene Watson 128, Elizabeth M. 129, Hester Elizabeth 164, James Rushing 145, Josiah

Goodson 128, Oliver 151, Robert 60, Robert Hiram 128, Robert S. 128, 145, Sondra 128, Theophilus Smith 128, Theresa 128

Daniels 49, 97, Aaron 129, Algie 129, Algie Perry 230, Brenda 230, Carol 239, Cattrell 129, Cullen David 129, Dancy 129, Dearcie 129, Dorothy Patillo 230, Eddie Lee 129, Emma Ida 129, Eva Jane Hamilton 129, Fred 129, Glover 129, Gracie 129, Inez 129, J.C. 129, James 129, Janie Holt 129, Jesse 129, Lenora 129, Lola Bell 129, Loueaser Young 229, Mable 129, Mamie 129, Margaret 129, Margery 129, Mary Ellen Lewis 129, Myrtle 129, Noble 129, Norman 129, Ona 129, Ormond 129, Oscar 129, Roscoe 129, Sadie 129, Virginia 129, Walter Charlsey 129, Wendell David 129, William 129, Willie 129

Danvers, Reba Onean Doss 135

Darby, John 185, Olly 116

Darnell, Daisy 238, James M. 179, Mary Jane 179

Darst, Almeda 132

Daubler, Dianne Elizabeth Dobbs 143

Davenport, Douglas 238, Frances Reeh 238, June 238, Karl Douglas 238

Davidson, Allyene Elizabeth Fears 146, Atchley "Pete" 146, Bruce Cates 129, Edward Nevon 129, Edwinna Lynn 130, John 78, Martha Magrill 206, Nevonda Jean 130, Patsy Louise Jean 129, Rachel Adrian 78, T.J. 129, Veda 146, Wade Hampton 206

Davies, Jamie 267

Davis 6, 241, Alice 130, 139, Allie 138, Almeda 132, Amanda 132, 270, 272, Beatrice Daniel 229, Bennie Wayne 210, Betty Joyce 241, Calvin P. 28, Cameron Blake 132, Carrie Belle 256, Charles 63, 241, 242, Corrinna Maud 132, Dale 173, Delton Wade 131, Doy Herbert 131, 132, Edmund J. 148, Efella 202, Eliza Belle "Mam" 183, Elizabeth Joyce 241, Emma Elizabeth Hall 209, Ethel Jenkins 132, Etta Griffin 132, Frank 246, Gussie Nell 35, 130, Hilton Joycel 131, Horace Gray 210, Ida Cora Brown 104, Jack S., Sr. 139, James B. 104, James D. 139, James R. 132, Janice 179, Jannie 130, Jeannie 210, Jefferson 285, Jennie 276, Jerry Ann 224, Jewel 132, Jimmie Virginia 132, Jo Ann Harris 132, 167, John 130, 132, 137, Joseph Moore 132, Joycelyn 131, 277, Judy

190, Karen Elaine 132, Katie Lee 132, Kimberly Taylor 267, Lanna Rosalin 131, Lanny 131, Lauri Alicia 131, 132, Lear 130, Letitia 130, Lillie Zelmodene 131, Louis W. 104, Margaret 132, Martha 131, 254, Mary Brook 242, Mary Ella 139, Mary Jeanette 139, Matthew Cameron 131, Mattie Lavinia 130, Molly Ann 93, Narciss 130, 218, 219, Novie Ree 210, Pamela 242, Patsy Sue 210, Robert Augustus 130, Robert Dee 132, Roberta 130, Rosa D. 130, Roy 241, Ruby Elvira 130, Ruth 241, Sarah Jane 132, Shawna Dene 131, Susan Caledonia 208, 209, Susanna 130, Tamara Denise 131, Thomas 167, Thomas Jefferson 132, Thomas Sidney 209, Ulletta Ann Butler 131, 132, Victoria Kemp 130, Walter Henry 132, Watson 119, Wesley Christine 242, William 132, 256, 272

Dawson, Carol Lynn 121, Donna 121, John Matthew 121, Louis Markham 121, Princess Louise 121, Ralph Matthew 121, Rebecca Alice 121, Robert 40

Day, David A. 50

de Warren, William 156

Deakins, Homer Lodell 100

Deakins, Kathryn Beatrice 100, Yvvonne Lodell 100

Dean 179, Ann Jeter Hatley 132, Bellona 133, 287, Daniel 132, Emily Emma 154, Emma Eliza 180, James M. 132, 252, Jarrett 16, 49, 132, 133, 287, Jarrette 235, John F. 133, John M. 132, Malinda 132, Maria Emily 251, Mariah 133, 287, Mary Jane 132, 235, 287, May 287, Nancy Mathis 132, Sarah C. Smith 252, Shelly Rene Anderson 268, Thomas Jefferson 132, Vandorah 152

Dearion, Eliza 202, Willie 202

Dearker, Anna 220

Dearmore, N.B. 127

Deason, Tressie Avery 88

DeBerry, A.W. 177

Deen, Duane 164, Jared 164, Jesse 164, Justin 164, Martha 164

Dees, Marie 235

DeFrance, Laura Kay 194, Lauren Ruth 194, Roland 194

DeGraffenreid, Reese Calhoun 133

Delaney, Claudine 109

Deleon, Charlie Ray "B.J." 184, Karen Lynn 184

Delmas, Adela J.E. 106, Amanda Luisa 106, Catarina Amanda Luisa 106, Charles Francis 108, Emilio Charles 106, Mary Louise 106

DeLoach, Annie Mae 64, Ethel 64, Margaret 64, Mary 64, Stephanie 281

DeLoy, Anna Brown 104, Frank 104

Democoeur, Joellyn 98

Denison, Gene 155, Kelsey 155, Lindsey 155, Regan 155, Taylor 155, Tina 155, 245

Denman, Clare 151, Ethel "Jeanne" 164, Lola Elma 197

Denney, Lida Lee 103

Denson, Cora 116, W.I. 116

Denton, Blanche 40, David Lee 134, James David 133, James Keys 134, Margaret Elizabeth 134, Margaret Katherine 134, Rosannah Keys 133, Thomas Warren 134

Deteau, Bradley Alan 134, Clarence Harold 134, Denise Marie 134, Diana Kay 134, Donna Gail 134, John Mark 134, Ollie Beatrice 134, Paul, Jr. 134, Richard Roland 134, Rita Pat 134, Shirley Hall 134, Stephanie Kay 134

Detro, Lena Mae 257, Louis Benjamin 257, Myrtle Elizabeth 257

Detweiter, Barbara Fisher 147, Christian 147

DeuPree, Grace Fisher 147

Devereux, Sallie Griffin Mills 159

Dewberry, Martha 26

Dexter, Mary 222

Dickard, Adella 170, 171, Bonnie Rachel 183, Maudie 27, Robert Pierce 183, Ruth 171

Dickerson, Leora 280

Dickinson, Ora Lea 279, 280, William 280

Dickson, Elbert 21, Emily "Emma" 282, Lucy 156, Mary Frances 156, Star 119, Stella 128, William 156, Wilson 119, Winter 142, 143

Dildy, Agnes Kay Caraway 194, Walter 194

Dillard, E.D. 64, Vivian 64

Dilley, Judith 193, Ophelia Key 192, Orville 193

Dinkins, Samuel Paul 66

Dixon, Chessa 131, Harold 131, James 50

Doane, Patricia Eugenia 163

Dobbins, Sherry Lynn 97

Dobbs, David Ellis 143, Dianne Elizabeth 143, James Robert, Jr. 143, Lois 275, Sally Ellis 143

Docherty, Joan 102

Dodson, Ann 218, Beth 175, Beth Holloway 76, 218, Bill W. 218, Gary 218 Lauren 76, 218, Shannon 76, 218, William Harrington 43

Doggett, Adell Tine 254, Jerry 83

Doherty, Genevieve Wood 112

Dolive, Agnes Laurindine 135, Billie Jean 134, 135, Brian Bruce 134, 135, Caitlin Christine 134, Daniel Bruce 134, David Wayne 134, 135, Dominique 135, Don Edward 135, Edward Daniel 135, Emily Jean 134, Evan Mathew 134, Haley Katherine 134, Jean 135, Jim Morgan 135, Louis 135, Louisa Le Fleau 135, Marie Louise Baudain 135, Marie Savabos 135, Martha Jane 135, Mary Baird 91, 135, Mary Lois 135, Mary Lucretia May 135, Mattie Lee Kane 135, Maurice 135, Melanie Jeanne Perkins 134, Morgan Joseph 135, Naneline 135, Peggy Elaine Payne 134, Reuben H. 135, Silas Sedoin 135, Wayne Bruce 91, 134, 135

Dollahite, Sam 49

Dollison, Jill 224

Donaghey, Emmie McDaniel Hendricks 241, John 241, Mary Lee 241

Donaho, Anne Chance 206, Augustine 207, Blackston 207, Charles H. 207, Daniel 206, 207, David T. 207, Dora Martin 207, Henry 207, Jarvis 207, Louis 207, Lula 207, Mollie 207, Moses 206, Ollie 207, Sallie Bell 207, Sara H. 207, Travis Fanning 207, William 206, 207

Donald, Scott Harroff 168

Dorflinger, Jean 157

Dorman, Chase 255

Dorsey, Candance 261, Dewana 261, Karina 261, Maryann 261, Richard 261

Doss, Burl 135, Carolyn Lajuan 135, Dorothy Marie 135, Earl 135, Hershel Lane 135, Janice 7, 136, Larry Noble 135, Leonard Uland 135, Leonard Young 135, Ludie Blanche 135, Martha Kansas Barrow 135, Norma Jean 135, Reba Onean 135, Wanda Lee 135, William 135

Dossman, Michelle C. 199

Dotson, Josiah 143, Margaret Ann 143, Paul 63

Doty 251, Edward 98, 235, 251, 287

Douthitt, Julian Patrick 107

Douwes, Styntje 196

Dowell, C.C. 56, Julie Holloway 176, Meghan 176

Downman, Million 147

Dozier, Doris Irline 136, Elinor Jane 136, Elsie Huffman 136, Florence Addie Wallace 136, James Thomas Fletcher 136, John Fletcher 136, John Raymond 136, Laura Monique 136, Laurance "Adrian" 136, Laurance Arvell 136, Lee O'Neal 136, Linda Lee 136,

Margaret Robinson 136, Mary Zelda Knowles 136, Mattie Lucielle 136, Wallace Duane 136

Drake, Bill 136, 230, Bobby Wayne 136, Charles 136, 230, Frances M. 148, Jewell Kathryn 136, Jim 136, 230, Mary Eleanor 136, 230, Sidney J. 136, Virginia 136

Draper, Annie Edmondson 179, Callie Spence 179, Doris Janel 179, Goldie 179, Jack 179, M.L. "Billy," 179, Mamie Ruth 179, Marion LeRoy 179, Olive 179, Timothy A. 180

Drew, Adele Fieve 91, Albert T. 264, Carl William 91, Dorothy Claire 91, Dorothy Grace 264, Frances Ellen Wood 264, Jodie Elsie Brown 264, Willie Leon 264

Drewry 49

Dryden, Alice Grace McWhorter 137, Amecia Gaile 137, Charles 136, 137, Daphyna Dawn 137, Hannah Mae 137, Lillie Mae 136, Lisa Kaye 137, Marvin Henry 136, Mary 136, 257, Myrtie Neal 136, Robert Marvin 136, Sophie Linn 137

Dudley 138, Benetta Inez 216, Benneta Ann 137, Houston Russell 137, Issac Alexander 137, John 137, John Carroll 137, 138, John Leon 137, Kate 137, 138, Mary Catherine Russell 137, Wayman Carroll 137, William Carroll 137, William Gardiner 137

Duff, Barry Napoleon 138, Delila Thompson 138, Edward 138, Elizabeth Strother 138, Ida Bell Mobberly 138, James 138, John 138, Mildred Tutt 138, Roseanna Paillett 138, Sarah Nash 138, William Hiram 138

Duff-Neal, Bonnie 138

Dugan, Ida Annelle 190

Duggan, Dan 66

Duke, Catherine 94, 175, David 175, Ellen Yarbrough 175, John P. 175, John William 175, Kristi 261, Patricia 153, Robert Edward 175, Stella Lassophene 175

Dulaney, Arthur A., Sr. 43

Dunaway, Carol Anne 165, Elizabeth Lee Martin 165, James Monroe 216, James Roland 165, John Malcolm 165, John Ronell 165, Lucinda Cousins 216, Robert Lee 165

Dunbar, Ella D. 110

Duncan, Allie Davis 138, Asa A. 43, Caroline 138, Franklin 138, John Martin 138, Ray 109, Reba Nell 223

Dungan, Martha E. 272

Dunn, A.E. 86, Carol 138, 247, James 115, Jimmy Lee 138, Lee Roy 138, Margaret Alice 109, Ola Mae Smith 138

Dunnavant, Ada Louise 240, Mattie Gertrude 143

Dunnaway, Eliza Ann 216, Elizabeth Ann 216

Dupree, Mary Jane 192

Durham 138, Alexander Paxton 139, D.D. 8, 248, David Lawton 139, Effie Rule 64, Eloise Hutchison 139, Emma 139, Esther Louise 248, Grace 139, Hannah 139, 140, Jeff 139, Joel 139, John P. 139, Julie Jaffee 139, Justin 139, Ken 29, 34, 35, Kenneth R. 139, Kim Brumit 139, Lewis 248, Mark Hutchison 139, Mary Jeanette 139, Minnie Estes 139, Rebekah Holmes 139, Reuben 139, Tess 139

Durr, Louisa Christina 239

Duwali 116

Dworin 230

Dyal, Verna 163

Dyche, Christine 154

Dyches, Lucinda 95

Dyer, Bob 74

E

Eakin, Gretta 143, Joseph 143, Meriam 143

Early, Pamela 261

Earnest, Elizabeth 119

Earp, James 21, 155, John 98, Louisa 155, Patricia 98, Suveter 98, Wyatt 21

Eason 148

Eastep, Dewey Jackson 139, Edythe Eleanor 139, Lillie Mae 139, Wesley Thomas 139

Easter, Kris Pitts 162

Eastland, Alice Lydia 82, Charles Sidney 82, Lewis William 82, Robert Lewis 82

Eaves, Burrel 95, Catherine 252

Echols 69, Alabama Zeigler 141, 142, Amelia Alabama 141, 142, Amelia Ann 140, 142, 244, Ann 199, Beverly Anne 140, Billie Anne Reynolds 141, Bob 141, 244, Bradley R. 140, Bruce Alan 140, Fannie 141, 142, Fay 141, George C. 140, George W. 140, Hannah 140, Harry 140, Hugh 141, 215, J.T. 51, James 140, 141, 215, 244, John 140, John Herbert 141, John Wicker 141, Josh 140, Lacy Lee 269, Margaret 141, Martha 51, 140, 141, 244, Millie 141, Nancy Winbush 140, Nicholas 140, Ola 141, Patricia Southerland 140, Paul 141, Pearl Smith 5, 141, Robert B. 140, Robert Finis 8, 140, 141, 142, 215, 243, Robert Templeton 141, Ross 140, 141, Temp 244, Thomas Jefferson 140, Vera

Ellis 140, Vesta 67, 141, 214, 215, William Homer 141

Ecker, Wolfert 241

Eckford, Elizabeth Fisher 147, John F. 147

Eddins, Elizabeth Flewellen Miller 148, Lacy 148

Edelman, Audrey Mae Ingram 183, Marvin Ray 183

Edington, Doris Viola 224

Edmonds, Mollie Maxine McCoy 142

Edmondson, Annie 179

Edmonson, Angela Leigh 257

Edney, Edna 182

Edwards 22, Dick 17, Elizabeth 250, H. 21, 40, 270, 287, H.R. 286, James A. 104, John Tilley 223, Karen Brian 103, Maxie 133, Ruth 222

Eisenhower, Dwight D. 69

Elder 49, Camie Wilkins 142, Carey 143, Charleen 64, 90, 142, D.H. 142, Elizabeth 84, Frank III 142, 143, 285, Ginger 143, Gretta 142, 143, Henry T. 22, 142, Jack 142, 143, James Z. 142, Jan 143, John Samuel 142, Joseph 142, Kelly 143, Kristin 143, Lee 143, Leon "Bo" 143, Matilda Eudora 142, Meriam 143, Minnette 143, Minnie 142, 143, 285, Nancy Elizabeth 142, Orion Choice 142, Sallie 142, Sarah 142, 175, 176, 211, Susie 143, Tara 143, Tiffany 143, Tootsie 143, Victoria 142, William Wesley 142, Winter Dickson 142, 143, Zipporah Harris 142

Elkins, O.W. 38

Ellender, Charity 104, Frederick 104, Julia Ann 104

Elliott, Emily Kay Hunt 139, Kaylee Danielle 139, Nancy 117

Ellis, Adell Tine Doggett 254, Barney Hobson 143, Carlton 49, David P. 115, Eldene 49, G.E. 49, Gwendolyn Blodwyn 115, John Garrison 143, John Wesley, Jr. 143, Joy 65, 143, Linda 143, Margaret Ann 143, Mary Margaret "Mollie" 83, Mattie Gertrude 143, Maude 49, Michaela Grace 193, Otho Jack 254, Othodell 254, Ruth May 115, Sally 143, Vera 140

Ellsworth, Brandon Lee 249, Charles 173, Deborah O'Neal 249, Laura Virginia 173, 254, Robert 41

Elmore, Lucy 67

Emberlin, Billy Carol 143, Darlene 143, Dorothy 143, Frances Woods 143, Fred 143, Lily Bryan 143, Mabel 143, Minnie 143, Patsy Ruth 143, Richard Lee 143, Roy 143, W.E. "Bill" 143, Zora 143

Emerson, Gouverneur V. 31

Emmons, Jamie Karol 193, Judith 193, Kristi Diane 193, Mark Timothy 193

Endsley, Ruby 268

England, Fannie Mae 217

Engleman, Bruce 66

English, E.H. 147, Emma Virginia 151, John 198, 223, Julia Agnes 147

Enox, Araminta Pink 127, Martha Etta 127, Squire J. 127

Epperson, Mary Lee 91

Erisman, Fred 246, Fred R. 194

Erwin, Bryan Marsh 92, Catherine 255, Emily Miller 92, Glenn 41, T.B. 255

Estes, Carl 16, 31, 35, 144, Della Marshall 144, Joseph Guinn 144, Margaret 35, 144, Minnie 139

Evans, Alyson 155, Bernice 276, Danesa Gayle 200, 225, Danyta Kay 200, 225, John 155, Kiel 155, Kristen 155, Lanyta Dianne 225, Lanyta Kayann 200, 225, Linda Faye 200, 225, Mary Oates 200, 225, Milton Todd 200, 225, Milton William 200, 225, Susan 152, 155, 245

Everett, Annie Mae 25, 54, Carl Bussey, Jr. 146, Carl Bussey, Sr. 145, Clarence 25, 54, Dell 144, 145, 286, Dorothy 145, 146, 286, Elizabeth 146, Erma 286, Howard 25, 54, Irma Sue 144, 146, J.B. 25, 54, Jane 146, Josiah 145, Katie Lea 145, L.J. 16, 49, 97, 144, 145, Martha Ann 144, 145, Tempa Bruner 145, Tommy 25, 54, William C. 43

Evers, Anne 116

F

Fabriz, Sharon Hope 252, 253

Facer, Norman 41

Faddis, Nancy Ann 285

Fahle, Evelyn 92, 278, Rebecca 92, 278, Stephanie 92, 278, Steven 92, 278

Faircloth, Irene Jones 216

Fall, Ethel Mae 219, Mary 219, W.S. 219

Fambrough 7, Ethel 109, John Edmund 250, Martha Jane 250, Mary Jane 250, S.B. 67

Fanelli, Anne Stuart 215

Farmer, Eliza Jane 251, Frankie Judith 261, Gwen 61, Jess M. 251, May 261, Shirley 154, William Frederick 261

Farrell, J.E. 29

Fason, Ceedie Elizabeth 209, Georgia Martin 209, Marie Delphine 210, William 209

Faulk, Fannie Clara 146, Jessie Elree 146, Lola Irene Elizabeth 146, Mable Dee Nellie Dee 146, Manilla Mae 146, Mary Dell Sena Head 146, 240, Mary Jane 146, Phillip Marion 146, Robert

Charles 146, Robert Edward 146, 240, Robert Grady 146, Ruby Lena 146, Thomas Leslie 146, Winnie Toy 146, 240

Faulkner 104

Feagle, Alice 103, Balfour 103, Pauline Bramlette 103, W.M. 103

Fears, Allyene Elizabeth 146, Anne Elizabeth 259, Barbara Harroff 168, Bettye Frances 146, Bonnie 146, Gracie Loucille 146, James 168, Jessie 146, 264, Joe Wallace 146, Oren W. 146, Veda Davidson 146, William J. 264, Winston J. 146

Feather, Betty Carolyn Grigsby 160, Lisa Sawyer 161, Robert 161, Sunni 161, Susanna 161, Victoria 161

Featherstone 214, L.P. 37, Lewis L. 37

Feemster, Johnnie Lee 25, 54

Felps, Sarah 132

Fendley, Milley Phillips 235

Fenley, Charles 147, Elizabeth Ann 147

Fennell, Doris Darline 130, Edwinna Lynn 130, Gary Randall 130, Horace Randall 130, Starlia D'Lynn 130

Fenton, Mary Lynn 152, Milton Ray 152, Patricia Ann 152, Rayford 152, Thelma Helen 152

Ferguson, Catherine 82, 182, Luisa Elizabeth 171

Ferkovich, Inez Culpepper 127

Ferrell, Oscar 49

Fielding, Bertha Stone 201, Jerry 201, Leslie 201, Mike 201, Naomi 201, Patsy 201, Peggy 201

Fields, B.B. 274, Virginia Butter 146

Fieve, Adele 91

Finch 204, Eugenia Althea 206, John 8, 190, 206, John Smith 206, Mary Coan 206, Princess Emma 121, 206

Findley, Minnie 230

Fink, Laura 162, Martha Ann Frances 284, William Isaac 284

Finley, Ann Norris 147, Carol Faith 147, Clyde 147, David Harley 276, David Taylor 147, Eleven Norman 147, John 147, Linda Ann 147, Lizzie Estelle 171, Mary 147, 240, Maryann "Addie" 147, Myrtle O. 147, Nancy Ann 276, Norman Estis 147, Rachel 147, Rosetta Bowen 147, Sarah Carter 147, Willis 147

Fischer, Christian 147, Magdelena Yoder 147

Fish, Stanley 188

Fisher, Clinton Paul 261, Thelma Churchill 261, Abb Merle 261, Absalom McBee

261, Alice 233, Ann Elizabeth 147, Anna 147, Barbara 147, Bertha 227, Caroline Hawkins 147, Carrie 112, Chad William 261, Christian 147, Clyde 261, Cora Belle 166, Craig Kenneth 261, David K. 147, Derek 261, Dorothy Jean 261, Dovie Houston 261, Elizabeth 147, Elizabeth Christine 261, Ernest 261, Fanny Awalt 147, Franklin 261, George Alexander 147, George W. 147, Gladys 25, 54, Grace 147, Hattie 30, Henry Peter 147, Herbert 25, 54, 176, 261, Jacob 112, 147, Joan 84, 147, John 113, 147, John David Webb 261, Joseph Weldon 261, Josephine Howell 147, Juan Minerva 227, Julia Agnes 147, Julia B. Camp 147, Kenneth 261, Kirk 261, Kristi Duke 261, Laurie 261, Lavonia Edna 261, Loraine 25, 54, Luke Churchill 261, Madeline Clairmont 147, Mae 25, 54, Magdelena 147, Malinda Jane 147, Margaret T. Garrison 147, Marlene Goehring 261, Martha Blanton 147, Martha 147, 233, 261, Marvel 25, 54, Mary Blanton 147, Maryann 261, Mattie 25, 54, 261, Maxine Carter 261, May 261, Minnie Burr 217, Oliver Hazard Perry 147, Pamela Early 261, Pat 25, 54, Paul Kevin 261, Perry 25, 54, Peter 147, Ralph 261, Rayburn 261, Robert Donnell 147, Rosa Bette 261, Roy L. 184, Sarah Ardecia 261, Sarah Webb 261, Sarah Wood 261, Shirley Lea Akers 81, Silas McBee 147, 227, 233, 261, Susan Spratt 147, Susannah 147, Thelma Oney 261, Tommy 261, Veronica 147, Vicki Jo 261, William Decatur 147, Willie 25, 54, Zachary George 261

Fitzgerald 69, Ella 232, Fred 96, 110, Freddie Ray 96, 110, Freddie Wayne 110, Gaynelle 96, 110, Pamela 96, 110

Flanagan, Charles 147, Elizabeth 147, 148, James W. 147, Joyce 63, M. Tracy 38, Polly Miller 147, Webster 148

Flannery, O'Connor 188

Fleetwood, Jane 103

Fleitman, Anne 110, Jennifer 96, 110, Kenneth 96, 110, Kylee 253, McKenzie 110

Fleming, Pheroba 78, Rachel 78, 80, Robert 78

Flemister, Octavia 178

Fletcher, Ed 150, Essie 150, Gary 66, Hanna 239, Nancy 180

Flewelen, Iris 143, Junius 143

Flewellen, Ada Johnson 148, Antoinette 64, Carrie Bruce 64, 148, Eliza 148, 285, 286, Elizabeth 148, Eugene 148, Frances M. Drake 148, Hettie Marshall 148, Junius 148, Margaret Showalter 148, Maria Antoinette 148, Nettie 148, T.A. 11, Theo 148, Thomas 8, 148, Victoria Monroe 148, Wilbur 148

Flinnoy, Minerva A. 186

Florence, Carroll 217, Leslie 217, Sim J. 8

Florey 7

Flournoy, Carroll 63

Floyd, Dolphin Ward 160, John Manuel Sr. 202, John W. 160, Mary 160, Temperance 160, Thomas Penuel 160, Y.D. 230

Flynt, Jason 161, Lindsay Harrell 161, Macy 161

Fogartie, Arthur Finley 46

Foggleson, Buddy 212

Foirriestier, Adaline 148, Alice Perkins 148, Aline 150, Alvin Fonnie 148, Benjamin 148, Beval 150, Billie Nell 150, Essie 150, Ethel 148, George 148, Iva Mae 148, James Lonnie 148, John 148, Josephine 148, Lonnie Bryant 150, Martha 148, Mary 148, Minnie 148, Molly 150, Newton J. 148, Norma Jean 148, Oma Elizabeth 148, Owen 150, Rita Kelley 150, Ruby 150, 229, William 148

Foistier, Alvin Fonnie 148, Ethel 148, Minnie 148, Oma 148

Fontana, Amelia 162, Evelyn Joy 162, Francis 162, Michael 162, Peter 162, Sara Ruth 162

Fopay, Rickey 176

Ford, Janis 120, John F. 110, Morris 203, Sarah Caroline 110, Tara Elder 143, Verdine 266, W. Morris 42, 43, 209

Forman, Dolly 206, 228, S.C. 228, Steve 206

Formby, Lena 230

Forrester 150

Fort, Mary Janet 197

Foshee, Albert Martin 149

Foshee, Alfred Franklin 149, Azar Beryl 149, Edgar Leon 149, James M. 149, John 149, Johnnie Virginia 149, Mary Elizabeth Claudia 149, Mary R. 149, Minnie Florence 149, Nathaniel 149, Noah 149, William 133, 149

Foster, Della Gomer 150, Dora Warren 150, Faye 234, Florence Black 150, Florine 150, Henry L. 53, 150, Owen 150, R.D. 150

Fournet, Ann Baggett 78, Bill 150, Carmen 150, Daniel 89, 150, Jacque 150, Jason 150,

John 150, Jonelle 150, Linda 150, Robbie Adrian 150, Robbie Ann 89, 150, Terri 150, Trevor 150, William Daniel 150

Fournett, Ann 150

Fowler, Albertine 41, Angeline 200, Bud 123, Dorothy 88, Dottie Mae 87, 88, Joshua 108, Juliette 158, Littleton 8, 177, M.E. 87, Mary Belle 177, 178, Ola Lindsay 87

Fox, Lela 171, Tom 56

Frances, Abernathy 266, Lavonia 261, Martha Ann 266

Francis, Edith 103, 151, Eugenia 103, 151, 259, Floreid 103, 150, 151, 259, James Carlton, Jr. 103, 150, 151, John Woodson 103, 150, Tennessee Virginia 103, 150, Thomas A. 151, Thomas B. 103, 151, 259, Traci 63

Franklin, Benjamin 207, James Emmons 193, Kim 281, Patsy 281

Franks, Elizabeth 206, Jonita 237

Frantz, Marlene 239

Franz, Elizabeth Joyce Davis 241, Jimmy 242

Frazier, Claudine Delaney 109, Milton 109

Fredrick, Beulah Irene 224, Jefferson Davis 224, Mandy Lea 224

Freeman, Belton Ward 152, Carl 152, Carrie Lee 152, Edgar Preston 152, Frances Cordelia 152, Isa Dora Christian 152, 245, Jewell Violet 152, Jodie Lavinna 152, Joe 152, Lila Vermelle 152, Maggie 183, Mary Susan 152, 155, 245, Myrtle Smith 152, Rachael 152, Raleigh 152, Rasial Mattison 152, Robert H. 245, Robert Hamil-ton 152, Robert Homer 152, Samuel 152, Thelma Helen 152, Tom Gerome 152, Van-dorah Dean 152, Von W. 41, William G. 152, Willie Irene 152

Freeze, Jessie 51, Margaret 51

Friddell, Bunnie 180

Fritts, William Jack 50

Frost, Anderson 153, Caroline 153, David Anderson Winslow 153, David Wayne, Jr. 152, 153, 191, David Wayne, Sr. 152, 153, 191, Freida 152, 153, 191, Henry Franklin 152, Lena Mae Pierce 152, Lyndy Karen Anderson 153, Mary Elizabeth Morse 153, Robin 85, Sharla Elizabeth 152, 153, 191, Shelly Lorene 152, 153, 190, 191, Victoria 153, Wayne 152

Fry, Cora 110, Nancy Addie 179, Philip 108

Fulgham, Nancy Ellen 233

Fulgium, Donald 45

Fuller, Amanda Ann 248, 251, Autrie McLendon 120, Beckie 248, Benjamin 51, Charles 163, Edward 98, 235, 251, 283, 287, Elizabeth Gilmer 154, Gabriella 103, Grace Jane Calloway 154, James 248, James Manuel 154, 248, 251, Jesse James 248, John Judson 154, Mann 248, Mary 51, Mary F. 154, Rebecca Ann 248, Rhoda Antenette 154, Ruby Nelwyn 283, Samuel 98, 154, 235, 251, 287, Vannie Smith 154, William L. 154, 251, William M. 154, William Mann 248, Willie L. 154

Funderburk, Marsha 165

Furrh, Alice 170

G

Gaddy 255, Nancy 180

Gaines 214, Laura Evelyn 246, Richard 84, Victoria 84

Gains, Mary 95

Gallatt, Theodocia 99

Galloway, Joe 226

Galyon, Maureen 61

Ganshaw, Richard D. 41

Garcia, Adela J.E. 106

Gardner, Alice Elisabeth 206, Ila Burkett 179, Lester Lee 143, Minnie Emberlin 143, Roberta 143, Whitey 143, Zelta 143

Garner, Jill Elizabeth 189, Kristopher Wayne 189, Martha Howard 28, Mary Rebecca 194, 198, Nancy Latham 194, William 194

Garrett, Belle Wyatt 154, Betty 154, Christine Dyche 154, Dorothy 154, Eddie 154, Evelyn 52, Henry Udell 154, John 154

Garrison 255, Ann Abigail 256, Carol Gregg 243, James Oscar 243, James Ray 243, Lillian Edith 182, 243, 260, Lou Clifton 243, 260, Margaret T. 147, Mildred Christene 243, Susan Spratt 147

Garson, Greer 212

Garst, Kathryn Ann 184

Garvey, A.B. 245, Adam Burney 152, 154, Billie Sue Rothwell 152, 154, Diane 155, Minnie Elaine Burke 154, Osborn Conrad 154, Susan 155, Tina 155

Garza, Brian 139, Briana 139, Kathryn May 253, Ruben 110, 253

Gee, Ann E. 220, George William 220, Hershal 220, Huldah Cook 220, James 220, John L. 220, Lemuel Merrill 220, Martha B. 220, Phillip 220, Robert M. 220, Susan Jane 219, 272

Geers, Patti 199

Gehlen, Sandra 201

Geist, Janet Marie 261

Gentry 84, Bernard 278,

Diane Elaine 278, Donald 278, Margaret 278, Mary Joyce 278, Octavia Jones 66
George, Arthur 112, Sarah 267, Velma Jean 278, William 278
Gerber, Cheryl Lynn 276, Frederick Andrew 276
Gerera, David 85, Lynn 85, So Yong 85
Geter, E.E. 45
Gibson 279, Angus 282, Martha Delila "Girlie" 282, Mary 279, Mel 214, Merritt 246, Shirley Odom 229
Giels, Gretchen 195
Giese, Cindy Lou 155, Jenny Frances 155, Lara Lee 155, Wayne 155
Gilbert, Barbara 65, Ruth Ann 260
Gilchrist, Angus 249, Effie 249, Margaret 249
Giles, Darrell Henry 187, Martha Diane 187, Robert Shawn 187, Shannon Leigh 187
Gillespie, Fannie 252, Julia Cordelia 199, Nancy 140, 275, William 140
Gillette, Jacklyn Rose 257, Roger Neil 257, Sarah Elizabeth 257, Traci Annette 257
Gilley, Glynda 175
Gilliam 49, James 277, Mary 277, Verna 277
Gillock, R.F. 45
Gilmer, Elizabeth 154, Elsie 235
Gilmore, Elizabeth 154, Margaret 81
Gipson, Mary Lou 199
Girty, Doris 271
Giuce, LaRue McDowell 267
Gladney, Belle Shaw 249, William 21, 249
Glardon 90
Glasco, Jesse Martin 155, Louisa 155
Glasscock, Ann Nichols 147, Benjamin 147, Dewey Gadston 147, 197, Esther Ball 147, George 147, Gladys Nina 197, Jane Juett 147, John Milton 147, Margaret 147, Martha 147, Mary 147, Million 147, Nancy Sarah Elizabeth 147, Nina Bates 147, 197, Rachel Faith 147, Thomas 147, William 147
Glenn, Bonnie 283, Stan 283
Glover 150, Augusta Borders 155, Barbara Ann 93, 155, Davis 246, Hattie Thomas 93, 155, Jackson Franklin 155, Lina 93, 155, Millard Franklin 93, 155, Susan 148
Glunt, Magee 110, Catherine Anne Magee 96, Hannah 110, 253, Jacklynn 110, 253, Jeffery 96, 110, Katelyn 110, 253, Ron 110, 253
Goad, Leona Beatrice 125
Goar, Lisa 257

Gober, Jefferson Davis 205, Sarah Roxanne Patterson 205, Sarah. E. 180
Godsey, Emily Elaine 259
Goehring, Marlene 261
Goetfle, Elizabeth 246
Goforth, Rueben 8
Goins, Mary 95
Gomer, Della 150
Gonzaullas, Manuel T. 30
Goode 49
Goodnight, Elizabeth 246
Goodrich, Benjamin Franklin 243, Ida Mae 243, Jane 243, Lucinda Johnson 243, Richard 243
Goodson, Courtney Anne 156, 232, Durwood 83, Henry Louis 155, 156, 232, James Henry 155, 156, 232, James Rush 156, 232, Lasca Minnette 156, 232, M. Hampton 156, Vera Elizabeth 155, 156, 232, Wanda Minnette 155, 156, 232
Goodwyn, William 254
Goolsby, Hazel Bernice 287
Gordon, Anna 114, Glenn 114, Julius 38, Sol 38
Gore, David 215
Gorman, T.K. 55
Gossett, Mary Lucille 190
Gosson, Martha Lillian Wright 133
Gowan, Tracy 90
Gowder, Frederick M. 78, Olivia Adrian 78
Grace, Sidney 176, Sophie 176
Graham 31, Alice Pearl Hays 169, Joseph M. 169
Granberry, Archie 261, Dorothy Jean 261, Lee 261
Granger, Aline Foirriestier 150, Odell Warren 150
Grant, Ulysses S. 174
Granville, Bonita 38
Graves 122, 279, Doris 236, Georgia Ann 121, John 121, Joseph 262, Lela 121, Lillian 121, Maggie V. 121, Martha Susan 262, Mary 262, Mattie 121, Natalie 178, Noel F. 236, Sidney Eugene 121
Gravey, Billie Sue Rothwell 245
Gray 24, Allison Ann 267, Kimberly Taylor 267, Steven E. 267, Taylor Andrew 267
Graybill, Ann Nancy 156, Annie 157, 245, Caroline Emily 156, Dora 156, 157, 245, 262, Elizabeth 156, Frances 156, George 156, Henry 156, Jesse Goodwin Butts 156, Jesse Julia 156, John Frank 157, 245, John W. 156, Judith Butts 156, Leonidas Josephus 156, Louise 157, 245, Lucy Virginia Juanita 157, 245, Martha 156, Mary 156, Mary Ellen 157, 245, 262, Mary Frances Dickson 156, Mary

Gregory 156, Mary Jopetra 156, Michael 156, 262, Michael "Don" Adoniram 156, Michael Hal 157, 245, Michael Hamilton 156, 245, Phillip 156, Sarah Tyler 156, Silas M. 156, Thomas 156, William 156
Grayson, C.C. 45
Grebe, Robert 41
Green 49, Barbara Jean 157, Bo 157, Brandon 111, 157, Charlotte 157, Dixie Odom 228, Genevieve 107, H.G. 228, J.M. 12, Jack Michael 157, Jennie 157, Jerry 157, Jessica 111, 157, John Perry 157, Juanita Rhodes 157, Kevin 157, Mable Dee Nellie Dee 146, Manvel 157, Marshall 96, Mike 157, Nancy 96, 110, Natalie 96, 110, 253, Nubern 157, Pamela 96, 110, 253, Pearl Weir 157, Preston 96, 110, 253, Roxie Pauline 96, Ruth 157, Scott 157, Susan 245, 262, Taylor 96, 110, 111, 157, 253, Tempie 157
Greene, John Guthrie 257, Shelly Suzanne 257, William Charlton 257
Greer, Annie 230
Gregg, Anna 192, Carol 243, Emma Belle 200, Hubert 158, John 11, 66, 158, 159, 280, 287, William 245
Gregory, Aline 94, Barbara 158, Beth Suzan 159, "Buddy" 94, Claudia 94, Cody 159, Collin 159, Doyle 287, Evelyn 94, Gerald 158, Gertrude Rogers 94, Heywood 158, Irene Hitt 158, Isaac 159, Jack 158, Jacob 158, Janet 158, Jennie Miller 158, John 94, Kaye 159, Ky 159, Marion Williamson 158, Mary 156, Miller 158, Rebecca Jane 158, Rita 94, Robert Jackson, Jr. 159, Robert Jackson, Sr. 158, Ronald H. 158, Rubye Cute Miller 159, Samuel Benjamin 158, Sybol Elizabeth 158, Thalia Rebecca 158, Thomas 94, "Tincy" 94, Worth 158, Worthy Pauline 158
Gresley 241
Gribble, Bill 270, Charles William, Jr. 270, Clara 270, Millie Ruth 270
Grier 285
Griffin, Anthony Scott 252, Charles T. 160, Clyde 159, Daniel Boone 159, 160, Ella A. 160, Emily Belle Barton 93, Fannie L. 160, George Washington 43, Goldie Gray 159, 160, Hattie May 159, 160, Helen 93, 159, 211, 237, Henry Clay 159, 160, J.D. 160, Jacob 160, James 93, 159, Janie B. 160, Jeffry

Scott 252, John Early 160, John Ross 159, Josephine 159, Larkin Porter, Jr. 93, 159, Larkin Porter, Sr. 159, Leon 159, Lorenzo W. 160, Lou Cunyus 160, Mary 159, 160, Mary G. Martinez 159, Mary Susan 159, Mays 159, Michael Edward 252, Minnie 160, Orra A. 160, Patrick James 252, Pheriba Barton 93, Radonia Alabama Lee 160, Roy 159, Sallie 159, Sarah 159, 160, Sudie R. 160, Susan Ann Stoker 160, Susan Rilda 159, 160, Suzanne Smith 252, Temperance Floyd 160, Tony 160, William Elisha 160, William F. 160, Wyman 159, 160, Zachary William 252
Griffith, Bettie Calvin 64, Charlotte Elizabeth 112, Earl Calvin 112, Hallie 218, John S. 174, Lavonia Lorraine 112
Grigsby, Amanda 161, Annie Lou Ray 161, Betty Carolyn 160, Blanche Alice 160, Brent 161, Frances Ellan 160, Jacklyn 161, James Louis 160, Kaitlyn 161, Louis 161, Matthew 161, Nelda Faye 160, Robyn 161, Staci 161, Teri 161, Trey 161, Wilena Vick 161
Grimes, Alice Elizabeth 172, Billy Eugene 224, Bryan 172, Charity 104, Effie 263, 264, Henry Herman 224, Margaret Jane 224, Marguerite Ellen 45, 224, Teresa Mitchell 115, William 264
Grisham, Ashley Kayann 200, 225, Trinity Wade 200, 225
Grounds, Darlynn 261
Grubbs 97, April 161, Debby Jane 161, Deidra 161, Emily 161, Hannah 161, Helen 161, Jeffrey 161, Jennifer 161, Jerry Mack 161, Joy 161, Julie 161, Kaye 161, Kimberly 161, Leslie 161, Nancy Emiline 96, Ryan 161, Sarah 161, Shane 161, Shawn 161, Stephanie 161, Tammy Kay 161, Todd 161, Tommy Ray 161, Trevor 161, William E. 41, 161
Grund, Barbara 228
Guerniere 161
Guerro, Clara 139
Guice, Carroll 267, LaRue 267
Guidroz, Abraham 161, Brenda 161, 162, Charles 161, Darrell 279, Earl 161, Ethan Patrick 162, Eula Breaux 161, Gwendolynn Denise 162, Holly Hill 162, John William 162, Joy 78, 79, 89, 161, 162, Kris Pitts Easter 162, Laura 161, 162, Mallory 162, Paul 89, 162, Ralph 78, 89, 161, 162, Sara 161, 162, Sydney 162, Tan-

ner 279, Tate 279, Terry 279, Theresa 161
Guild, Vanita Howard 177
Gunter, H.C. 277, Myrtle Elmira 277
Guttry, Carlos Byron 162, John Dabney 163, John Sutherlin 163, 201, John Wilson 162, Lala Sutherlin 162, Lottie 163, 196, 200, Mary Shannon 163, 285, Melinda 163, Murtilda Jane Sanders 162, Nancy McNeil 162, Rachel Lyn 163, Rebecca Elizabeth 163, Robert 285, Robert Byron 163, Robert King 163, Shannon Maledon 163, 285, Sherie Rivenbark 163
Guy, Bonnie Mae 233, Warren Keith 233
Guzak, Frank 226

H
Hackney, Howard 74
Haden, Lucy 242
Hafner, Brenda 163, Brittany 163, Clynton Leroy 163, Cortney 163, Donna 163, Kathryn Malise 163, Michael 163, Neva Inez Todd 163, Patricia Eugenia 163, William Kirk 163
Hagler, David G. 122, Elizabeth Ann 164, Francis Marion 122, Glenda Gaye 164, James Walter 163, Louisiana 122, Lucille Elizabeth 163, Mary J. 122, Nellie Mae 163, Newton 122, R.A. 52, Robert 122, Robert Velver 163, Rosalee 122
Hagood, Anniebell Hays, 169, Asberry Talmage 169
Halbert, Charlotte Clapp 178
Hale, Amy 164, Anne 164, Eddie 164, Ellen 157, 245, Ethel "Jeanne" 164, Florene 83, Howell Holt 164, Howell Pope 164, Howell Pope II 164, Howell Pope III 164, Joel 164, Judy Lynn 164, Julie 164, Larry 164, Louis F., Jr. 164, Louis France 164, Louis III 164, Martha 164, Mary Emma Holt 164, Max Edwin 164, Mollie McHaney 164, Nancy 164, Ruth 164, Sarah 164, William Denman 164
Hall 81, Adrienne 92, 278, Alexis 92, 278, Alice 164, Amber 92, 278, Audrey 92, 278, Ben 176, Bessie 164, Bradley 92, 278, Dorothy 17, Eleanor 123, Emma Elizabeth 209, Ermine 92, Hester Elizabeth 164, James 40, Joseph 40, Kenneth Lane 43, Kristi 176, Lizzie Kay 176, Nellie 164, Pamela 92, 278, R.L. 22, Ralph 271, Robert McAlpine 46, 164, Ruth 164, 207, Sam 6, Sarah 164, 238, Shirley 134, Tuesday 261, William 164

Halliday, Camilla Charlotte 64, Tricia 179
Haltom, Ozelle 253
Ham, Ernestine 186
Hamberlin, Joy 161
Hamby, 264, Johnnie 252, 253, Mary Jane "Molly" 148, Rhoda Antenette 154, Vera Lorene 252, 253
Hamilton 51, Alva 96, Anna Marie 96, Christopher 170, Darlene 210, Eva Jane 129, Ida Mae 210, John 100, Linda Jean 210, Marion Mosley 152, Steven 170, Terry 63, William Scott 210, Winnie D. 167
Hamman, Annie Clementine 102, Clementine 102, James Newton 102
Hammett, Billy Wayne 224, Brandon Lee 224, Joni Lee Armstrong 224, Levi Joel 224, Michael Wayne 224, Ronald Dow 224, Sandra Lea Nelms 224, Shawn Hood 224, Stormy 224
Hamner, Earl B. 267, Mary Ella Todd 267
Hampton, Benjamin N. 133, Mary Beaulah 201
Hamvasy, Emer 148, Nettie Flewellen 148
Hand, Haley 92, 278, Kelly 92, 278, Madeline 92, 278, Matthew 92, 278
Handy, Elva 143, John, Jr. 143, John, Sr. 143, Mabel Emberlin 143
Hane, Paul 161, Tammy Kay 161, Tiffany 161
Hanes, Abraham Empson Smith 237, Margaret Catherine 237
Hanivasy, Antoinette 64
Hankins 109, Bobby Dale 165, 166, Flossie 80, 165, Heather 165, 166, Jack Merrill 165, James Alexander 165, Joanne Rambo 166, Johnny 166, Marsha 165, Robert Wesley 165, Ryan 165, 166, Shirley 166, Starley 166, Weltha Jane 165, Wesley 166
Hanna, Jean Marie 80
Hansen, Branden Ray 225, Danesa Gayle 225, Gayle 240, Ray C. 225
Hanson, Alex 202, Branden Ray 200, Clinton 186, Danesa Gayle 200, Ethel, 235, Eula 186, Lum Turner 235, Martha J. 235, Minnie McDaniel 186, Ray C. 200
Harachuck, Doris Janel Draper 179
Hardaway 255
Harden, Jimmie Leigh 267, Rachel 95
Hardin 90, Clara 253, Florence Elverse 250, John 66
Harding, Kay 144, Warren G. 234
Hardwick, Harry T. 35

Hardy, Barbara Ann 224, Benjamin Kyle 224, Betty Louise 166, Bobby Lee 224, Bradlee Kent 224, Brian Keith 224, Emily Angeline 264, Emma Evadna 166, Henry Leroy 166, Henry Taylor 264, Michelle 224, Richard 270, Virginia Lee 166
Hare, Pamela Marie 94
Harlow, Gladys Howard 177, Mary Vanita 88, 178
Harmon, Daniel Warrick 31
Harpe, Corene 202
Harper, Wendal 155
Harrell, Bill 161, Billy Bob 161, Connie Barclay 161, Denise 161, Frances Ellan 160, Lindsay 161, Michael Wayne 161, Rebecca 161, Sam 161, Troy 161
Harris 97, 102, Alto 25, 54, Barbara S. 267, Charles 167, 190, 236, Clara 25, 54, 169, 256, Elizabeth Ann 147, Emma Virginia 167, 236, Essie Francis 167, Fannie "Faye" 89, Frank 25, 54, Gladys DeLoise 251, Grady 267, Houston Exl 242, Howard 251, Ida Dee 25, 54, Ila Mae Christian 117, J.K. Polk 113, James Leslie 167, Jerry Strickland 242, Jo Ann 132, 167, John 167, Josie Lee 89, Kathryn 117, 167, Lillie 158, Lula Essie Beard 167, Martha 167, 236, Mary 167, 171, Mary Pickens 167, Melissa 242, Miriam 242, Missouri 226, Novie Belle 167, Paul 89, Perry Lee 117, Pleas 28, Plez 273, Polk 113, Sabrina Morgan 167, Sadie Jane 167, Sarah Catherine 167, 171, Spencer 187, Stella 167, Susan 273, Syble 267, T.A. 11, T.B. 256, Tom 25, 54, 208, 246, Vannie 54, Vonnie 25, Willie Little 256, Wilma 121, Zipporah 142
Harrison, Ann Louise 167, Carol 167, Chase Lane 286, Chase Love 167, David 167, 246, F.J. 177, Jean Ramey 167, John W. Jr. 167, John Womack 167, Katherine 167, Kelly 167, M.A. 8, Marjorie 167, Martha 167, Reva Merle 246, Tonia Denise 256, Winnie D. Hamilton 167, Yancy D. 167, 286
Harriss, Amy 262, Dolly Ann 256, Pleasant S. 256, Susan Peeler 256, Thomas Buckner 257, Thomas D. 256, Tommy 157
Harroff, Barbara 168, Caroline Sue 168, George Henry 167, George Pierce 167, Iva Jean 168, Kristen Michelle 168, Lory Christopher 167, 168, Lynette Faye 168, Mary Ada

167, Meayrene 168, Paula Elaine 168, Pauline 167, 168, Samantha Kay 168, Samuel Kevin 168, Scott Donald 168, William Christopher 168
Hart, Gary L. 41, Nancy 5
Hartwell, John 245
Harvey, Gayle Johnston 182, Laura Gayle 181, 182
Harville, Emily Ann 231, John 231, Katherine Ann 231, Molly Frances 231, Sarah Ellen 231
Haskine, Joe M. 10
Hastie, Daniel 172, David 171, 172, George 172, Marilyn 172, Mary Ruth 171, 172
Hasty, Benjamin 206, James 206, Mary Fernetta 206, Polly Roden 206
Hatcher, Anne Burton 225, Benjamin 225, Edward 225, Henry 225, MaryBeth 225, Nancy 225, Sarah E. 225, William 225
Hatchett 255
Hatley, Ann Jeter 132
Hauk, Ben 50
Hauskins, Jesse, Sr. 176
Havard, Jessie 48
Hawkins, Caroline 147, E.C. 52, Lillie Mae 136, Mary Jane 136, Minnie 148, Oma Elizabeth 148, William John 136
Hawley, Della 202, Florence 202, Robert 202, Sandy 202
Hawthorne, Neal 60
Hayden, Brigette 49, Ellis 49, Jackie 49, Jamie 49, Lance 49
Hayes 49, Margie Mittie 236
Haynes, Florette 136, Helen 169, James Martin 169, Marcus P. 169, Mary Ellen 169, Mary Lester 169, Sally 249
Hays, Alice B 169, Alice Pearl 169, Anniebell 169, Bonnie Fears 146, Clara 169, 256, Daniel Francis 217, Douglas 169, Emma 169, 217, Feriby Isabella 169, Hollis Beryl 169, Jesse 169, John 169, Martin 169, 256, Nancy C. 169, Sarah Blount 169, William W. 169
Head, Mable D. 146, Mary Dell Sena 146, 240, T.R. 146
Heaney, Seamus 188
Hearne, Jim 142, Sallie Elder 142, W.A. 56
Hedges, Harold 70, Michael 70
Hedrick, Anna Bess 170, Anna Marie 170, Bill 170, Bobby Dale 170, Bret Daniel 170, Brittany Katherine 170, Bruce Don 170, Byron David 170, Danette Compton 170, Gertrude Blair 170, Jana Buck 170, Jena Leigh 170, Laura Anne 170, Leanne Joy 170, Lela Walter 255, Lem

170, Lisa Michelle 170, William Karl 170
Heffner, Fred 244, Nancy Ella 244
Heidler, Alice Ethel Bennett 75, 174, Mary Ellen 75, 174, Maximillion George 75, 174
Heidtman, Frank Henry 240, Nellie 240, Ralph Malcom 240
Heimann, Addie Belle 287
Heitt, Ogie 125, Talitha Cumi 170
Heller, Nancy Howard 228, Robert 228
Helm, Mary Louisa 116
Hemperly, Bernice 105
Henderson 27, 279, Ada Adelia 171, Adella Dickard 170, 171, Alice Elizabeth 172, Alice Elvira 213, 214, 215, 216, Alice Ida 171, 172, Alice Keeton 170, Armenda Jane 172, Arminda Smith 171, Arthur Albert 171, Augusta Eugenia 171, Barry 63, Betty Jean 172, Birda Inez 171, Blanche 170, 171, 184, 195, Charles N. 167, 171, Elizabeth Ann McHaney 170, Elma Jean 170, George Taylor 172, Gladys Mae 171, 172, Gladys Rebecca 170, Grace 171, 172, Hattie Belle 172, Irene 276, James Lawson 170, 171, Jasper Lewis 170, 184, John 213, John B. 171, John Dewitt 171, 172, Joseph Scippio 171, Laura Alice 172, Lawson Pursley 170, 171, 213, Lela 171, Lizzie Estelle Finley 171, Lonnie 183, Lou Gene 276, Lucy 244, Marion 172, Mary Barry 171, 213, 216, Mary Elizabeth 171, Mary Ethel 183, Mary Lou 171, Mary McWhorter 213, Mary Morrison 171, Mary Ruth 171, 172, Morgan Barry, Jr. 172, Morgan Barry, Sr. 171, Nancy Luella 171, Nanny Alice 172, Pete 170, R.T. 172, Rebecca Jane 171, 204, 205, 214, Richard Eanes 170, Richard Lewis 170, Robert Taylor 171, 172, Ruth 171, Sarah Catherine Harris 167, 171, Shirley Potz Neilson 172, Sidney Franklin 171, 172, Susan Elizabeth 170, Sylvester Fair 171, Talitha Cumi 170, 171, Thomas Newton 171, Tijuana Jordan 172, W.K. 152, William Barry 171, 213, 216, William Harris 171, 172, William Reed "Pete" 170, Willie Cumi 172, Charles Newton 171
Hendricks, Agnes Shaw 249, Elsie 105, Emmie McDaniel 241, Margaret McKay Shaw 249, Sterling B. 249
Hendrix, Maye 96

Hendry, Evelyn 283
Henry, Susan 195
Hensley, R.G. 56
Henson, Ann Holder 180, William H. 180
Herbold, Sue Ellen Hughes 83
Herndon, Albert 173, Alma 172, 184, Amanda 96, 110, 253, Anna Brown 173, Darba Gay 172, 184, 185, Forrest Albert 172, 184, George 173, James William 173, 218, Jannie Marie 173, 218, Jimmie 173, 218, Jimmy Gerald 173, 218, Joseph 96, 253, Katie 96, 110, 173, 253, Mary Estella 173, Olivia 96, 110, 253, Samuel Forrest 172, Samuel Rodney 172, Scottie Malott 172, Willie May 173, 218
Herrera, Norberto 41
Herrin, Hoy 63
Herrington, Bettye 124
Hester, Georgia Ruth 183
Hewell, Bill 174, Dale 173, 174, Sally Irene 173, Walter Robert 173, William Albert 173, William Marvin 173
Hickey, Hazel 74
Hickman, Sarah Combs 262
Hicks, Salina 222
Hidte, Peter 158
Hiett, Margaret Ann 194, Mary Elizabeth 125, Talitha Cumi 171
Hilbern, John 23
Hilburn, Barney 66, 158, Hunter Hines 66
Hill, Alice Estell 190, Atha Allen 224, Carolyn Kay 224, Docia Jane 106, Fannie 233, Holly 162, James Alexander 108, Joseph A. 124, Kristi 255, Malcolm 252, Margaret 61, Martha Anne 224, Mary Alice 251, Michael B. 41, Naomi Ruth Nelms 224, Richard Cabell "Dick" 8, Sue Jackson 185, 186, Susan Alvina 158, Verna Sue 224
Hillis, Adeline Rhodes 174, Charles Lee 75, 174, Charles Max 75, 174, Dixon Naylor 174, Flora Johnson 174, Jana Alice 75, 174, John Leeton 75, 174, Leeton 174, Leigh Ellen 75, 174, Lydia Logue 174, Mary Ellen 75, 174, Murphy 174, Nancy Johnson 174, Robert 174, Sally Poston 174, Sampson 174, Samuel 174, Stephen Henry 174, Vickie Anne 75, 174
Hilton, Billie Carrl Bray 258, Emily Jane 118, John Henry 258, Modena 258
Hilz, Angela Ann Anderson 268
Hines, Helen 93, Kathryn Harris 117, 167, RoxiAnna 222
Hinkle, Amanda Elmina Haley 114, Anna 114
Hinkson, Rosa Maud 247
Hinson 255

Hise, Conrad 99, 189, Thomas J. 99

Hitt, Alfred 158, Alice Jarman 158, Evie Leona 220, Fred 158, Irene 158, Jasper Price 220, Lillie Harris 158, Nancy Land 158, Zellar Khun 221

Hobby, William 13, 28

Hodge, Eely Brown 173, Jessie 173

Hoenshell, Nancy Skaggs 254

Hogan, Addie 283

Hogg 179, James S. 12, 113, 138, 174, Joseph Lewis 174, Lucanda 174, Sallie 174

Hoke, Billie Jean 134, 135, Edna 135

Hoke, Weyman Jefferson 135

Holbert, Bob 125, Carrol D. 234, Clairborn 16, 234, Mary Elizabeth 234, Matilda Talley 234, Mike 125

Holder, Ann 180, Barbara Ann 85, 187, Eldice Head 187, Gaylard Wesley 187

Holht, Annie Virginia 245, J.F. 245

Holland, Charles L., Jr. 43, Ernest 82, Eula Mae 82, Eva Mae 82, John 82

Hollandsworth, Earl 231

Hollaway, Rebecca 175

Hollers, Albert 175, Albertson 175, Amanda Black 175, Billie Joyce 175, Bobbie Jo 175, Deborah Kay 175, James Lemuel 175, Mattie Elizabeth 175, Richard William 175, Stella Lassophene 175, William Arthur 175

Holley, B.D. 226, Janice 226, Tobie 226

Holliday, Virginia 176

Hollins, Delton Lamar 256, Gloria Nell 256

Hollis, Rae 287

Holloman, Ashley Kayann 200, Dustin Dallas 200, Lanyta Kayann 200, Ronald Dale 200

Hollomon, Ashley Kayann 225, Dustin Dallas 225, Lanyta Kayann 225, Ronald Dale 225

Holloway, Allyson Kimberly 176, Ann 218, Beth 76, 218, C.C. 60, Carol 211, 218, Crawford Omer 176, D. Paul 125, 175, David 175, 176, Delbert Thomas 175, Delores 176, Erna 176, Ethan Thomas 176, Geraldine 175, Heather 176, James A. 31, 175, 176, 218, James Lowell 176, James P. 175, 176, 210, 211, Julia 176, 210, 211, Kenneth Hugh 175, Kristi 176, Laura 176, Lauren Elizabeth 176, Leighann 125, 176, Leonard Russell 175, Lizzie Harrison 175, 176, 218, Logan Paul 176, Lowell Jr. 176, MaeBeth 175, 218, Marci 176, Mary Polly 175, 176, Rachel Leah 176, Rebecca 175, 176, Robert 176, Roy Coleman 176, Sarah 175, 176, 211, Shirley 176, Sidney Omer 176, Thomas 175, William Alton 175, 176, William Carroll 175, 176, William Carroll 8

Holly, David Randall 228, Joe Franklin, Jr. 228, Johnnie Bell 40, Johnnie Mae 228, Larry Stephens 228, Nancy Teresa 228

Holman, John 114, 115

Holmes, Cornie Louana 125, Karina 261, Matthew 261, Rebekah 139

Holt, Carrie 117, Dorothy R. 244, Greg 117, Heath 117, Janie 129, Kaaran 117, Karry Augusta 117, Laura 117, Marcene Nathan 117, Mary Emma 164, Nancy Elliott 117, Nathan M Jr. 117, Romaldus Edwin 164

Homeyer, Patsy 88

Honea 279

Hood, Shawn 224, Stormy 224

Hooks, Dorothy Ruth 97

Hooper, Forrest 254

Hoover, Nancy Ann 91, Nancy J. 91, William 91

Hope, Bob 38, 69

Hopkins, J.N. 45, Margaret 116

Hopper, Gustavis C. 182, Matilda Josephine "Mattie" 182, 183, Minnie Mae 183, Rachel 182

Horaney, Albert 71, Betty 71, Harry S. 71, Lorene 71, Ron 71

Horgan, Alice Bell Martin 207

Horn, Alice 121, Deidra 161, E.R. 121, Emma E. 121, Joseph A. 121, Lola Irene Elizabeth 146, Lucy A. 121, Mattie J. 121, Mittie A. 121, Robert T. Sanford 121, Samuel 121, Sarah Adaline 121, William W. 121

Hornbuckle 179

Horner, Margaret Jonelle 217, Nathan 108

Horridge, Alison Leon 110, Brooks 96, 110, Debbie 96, 110, Haley 96, 110, Mary Leon 96, Ralph 96, 110

Horsman, Eleanor 98

Horton, Perilla 281

Hosch, Fannie 48, Frances Melinda 277, L.J. 48, Lonnie 48, 277, Sarah Jewel 277

Hoskins, Arra Lee 176, Bethena Johnson 176, Burke J. 177, Ella 176, Emily 177, Jack 177, Jesse F., Jr. 176, Jesse, Sr. 176, Joseph Martin 176, Joy 177, Julia 177, Malissa 177, Margaret Ann Euphemia Reasonova 176, Mary Pearl 176, Milton Tate 177, Oran West 177, Penelope 176, Pleasant Hill 177, Sarah 176, Selina 177,

Virginia Holliday 176, West 176

Houghton, Alice Ann 276

Houston, Dovie 261, John 177, Letitia Talbot 140, Luther 140, 244, Maria 177, Martha Cyrena 140, 141, Martha Jackson 140, Mary Jane 244, Mary Rodden 140, Matthew 140, Nancy Gillespie 140, Robert 140, Sam 20, 100, 106, 116, 140, 148, 211, 270

Hovatter, Jerry 45

Howard, Abner Perry 177, 178, Belle 177, Dorothy Ruth 97, Elizabeth Caroline 177, Gay Cole 228, Gladys 177, J.C. 67, Jackson Conner 8, 177, 178, July G. 28, L.L. "Luke" 10, Laura Buie 177, 178, Marina 102, Martha 28, 147, Mary Belle Fowler 177, 178, Rebecca Jane 97, Vanita 177

Howell 90, Gertrude 117, Josephine 147

Hoy, Theresa Holton 241

Hoyler, J.D. 100

Hubbard, Barbara Ann 268, Paula 175, Ruby Endsley 268, William Edgar 268, Zelma Raye 268

Hudgins, Ada Elizabeth 178, Albert 122, Archie Lee 178, Carra Bonnie 178, Dorothy 122, Geraldine Geneva 178, Jane Elizabeth Cook 178, John Wilson, Jr. 178, John Wilson, Sr. 178, Judy Nan 178, Julia Ann 178, Leonidas Green 178, Lillian Lucretia 178, Lottie Baker 122, Lucretia 178, Maggie Bertice 178, Octavia LeNeille 178, Rachel Elise 178, Rebecca Elizabeth 178, Richard Earl 178, Richard Elice 178, Richard Elton 178

Hudson, Anna 61, Della Lee 264, Ellen 214, Fannie 119, 264, Hal 264, J.J. 114, Maggie B. 281

Hudspeth, Abigail Kay 92, Brian Ray 92, Elizabeth Jean 92, Ermine Hall 92, Joshua Brian 92, Kimberly Jo 91, 92, Morgan Kimberly 92, Ray 92

Huffman, Elsie 136, Willie Opal 183

Hug, Roland 70

Huger 104

Hughes, Bettye Jo 82, 183, 184, Charles Herbert 184, Dietra Ann 184, Dona Elyse 184, George Washington 242, Howard 246, James Eaton 43, Jay Weldon 184, John William 184, Karen Lynn 184, Keli Rianna 184, Kevin Scott 184, Mary Ella 242, Melanie Marie 184, Missouri 175, Sue Ellen 83, 184, W.B. 242, Wanda Jean 183, 184, Wilmuth Octavia 242

Hughey, A.A. 179, Achsah 180, Anna 180, Annie Belle 180, Aurbon Acey 178, 179, Blanche 180, Bunnie 180, Callie Draper 179, Carla 179, Charles W. 180, Charlotte 179, Colista Ann 180, Curtis 180, Dena 179, Earl 179, Edna Ann 180, Effa 180, Ella Christine 179, Floria Estelle 178, 179, Haywood 180, Herschel 179, Horace 180, Ila Burkett 179, James C. 180, Janice Davis 179, Jesse 179, Jimmie 180, John F. 180, John Stacey 179, John W. 180, Joseph P. 180, Josephine 180, Josephus Brock 180, Kelly 179, Lawrence 180, Lily June 179, Linda 3, 7, 179, Loretta 179, Mary B. 61, 180, Mary Jane 179, 180, Meshac 180, Nancy Addie 179, Nancy Ann 180, Phillip Jerome 179, Roy 179, 180, Sallie P. 180, Sarah. E. 180, Scott 179, Selena 180, Selina 179, Sherry 179, Stacy 179, Steven 179, Thomas 180, Thomas Ace 179, Thomas Madison 179, Tricia 179, Wanda 179, William H. 180, William R. 180, William W. 180, Willis Hinton 180

Hull, Betty 242

Humphrey, Barbara 142, Bobby 142, Judy 142, Melinda 142, Mollie Maxine 142, U.D., Jr. 142, U.D., Sr. 142

Humphreys, Robert 221, Will 221, William 221

Humphries, Edith Joyce 187, Elinor Jane 136, Jeffrey Lynn 187, Katie Brooke 187, Lee Ann 187, Luke Van 187, Ronnie Van 187, Samuel Curtis 187, Sarah Jane 187, Thomas Calhoun 187, Thomas Chad 187, William Pelham 224

Hunsinger, Ida Frances 269, Lacy Lee 269, Mary Jane 269, Nathaniel Edgar 269

Hunt 279, Albert L. 180, Anne Elizabeth 259, Burr H. 180, Charles Logan 180, Clifford T. 180, Cynthia 180, Deason L., Jr. 139, Emily Kay 139, George P. 180, Gerald G. 180, Gladys Jewell 259, Gordon N. 180, Harriet Moss 180, Henry Maxwell 223, Hugh J. 180, Ida B. 180, James 180, John A. 180, Joseph Lafayette 259, Judkins 223, Kindal Shores 139, Larry Wayne 180, Lydia M. 180, Mabel A. 180, Martha 139, 259, Mary A. 98, 180, Mary L. 180, Mary "Polly" 180, May 287,

Maydean Wright 133, Michael Allen 139, Monroe 180, Mordilla 180, Nancy 180, Noah J. 180, Peggy 223, Reba Nell Duncan 223, Sarah 156, Sedley M. 180, Susan F. 180, Susan J. 180, Syntha Evalene 180, Thomas 180, Warren 66, Wilkins Wallace 223, William 98, 180

Hurley, Clara 258

Hurst, Clara 181, 182, 231, 253, Edith Isabella 181, Grace Anne 181, 182, 253, Henry Eugene 181, J.H. 181, James Garland 181, 182, James H. 72, 180, 181, Jane Jo 180, 181, 253, Jay Harrison 181, 182, John Henry 181, John Russell 181, 182, Julia 72, 180, 181, 253, Julian H. 72, 180, 181, 231, 253, Lena Walker 181, Lewis Charles 181, Linda Sue Ray 180, 181, 182, Sara Alice 223, Sue McDade 253, Vesse Reeves 116

Husband, Connie 243, David 182, 243, Earnest 182, Eligah Franklin 182, Ida Louise 182, James Obed 182, Jessie 182, Lillian 182, 243, Matilda Omega 182, Mavilene Redding 182, Polly Anne 182, Suzanne Rigby 182, Wanda Joyce 182

Huston, Francis Ellen 130

Hutchings, Frankie Lyno Miller 219, James 219, Judge 219

Hutchins 90

Hutchison, Eloise 139, James S. 139

Huxford, Camilla Calvitt 258, Clara Hurley 258

Hynson, S.J. 24

I

Ingram, Abner Clark 182, 183, Allie Crawford 183, Annie Dee 183, Annie Florence 82, 183, 184, 276, Aubrey Davis "Dat" 183, Audrey Mae 183, Bettye Jo 82, 183, 184, Billie Frank 183, Bonnie Rachel 183, Caryl Susan 184, Charles Lawrence 247, Clark Terrell 182, Dana Lea 184, Edna Edney 182, Eliza Belle "Mam" 183, Elizabeth Caroline 182, Eva Mae 183, 187, Frank Zollicoffer 82, 183, 276, Garland Gustavos 183, George Alton, Jr. 82, 183, 184, George Alton Sr. 82, 183, 184, 276, Herman Roy 183, Isabella Jane 182, John Wright 182, Katherine Elizabeth 82, 183, 247, Kathryn Ann 184, L.C. Ransome 183, Lula Tanner

183, Lydia Elizabeth "'Liddy" 183, Lydia Velma 82, 183, Maggie Freeman 183, Margie M. Tucker 183, Martha Caroline 182, 183, Martha Lynn 247, Martha Sydney 182, Mary Ann 247, Mary Josephine "Jocie" 183, Mary Katherine 183, Mary Nell 82, 183, 184, Matilda Josephine "Mattie" 182, 183, Mattie Lee 183, Minnie Mae 183, Roy 82, 183, 247, Samuel Davis 182, Sean Charles 183, 184, Stonewall Jackson 182, Susan Jane 182, Susan Jean 184, Sylvia 183, Velma 82, Wanda Jean 82, 183, 184, William Garrett 182, 183, Willie Opal Huffman 183

Inman, Myrtle O. 147
Inzer, Judy 242
Irons, Vesta Evelyn 231
Irvine 213
Irving, Washington 241
Isam, Velma 281
Isbell, Nancy Jane 126
Isham, Christian Anthony 193, Emily Katherine 193, James Anthony 193, Lee Allen 193, Lisa Deanna 193, Shirley 193
Ivie, Geneva Jasmine 213

J

Jabour, Azizie 266, John Wayne 266, Margaret 266, Michele 266, Pamela 266
Jacks, David 94, Laura 94, Millicent Alexander 82, 94
Jackson, Alva Eugene Jr. 270, Andrew 20, Andrew Columbus 184, Andrew Craig 184, C.B. 227, Darba Gay 184, 185, Darren 186, Elizabeth 263, Eric 186, F.R. 91, 171, Forrest Leath 185, Forrest Milan 185, Frank Richie 184, 185, Frank Worth 185, Jennie Caldwell 112, Jere Langdon 184, Jessie Evelyn 227, Laura Ann 184, Laura Blanche 185, Lauralee Elizabeth 185, Lora Ethel 111, Margaret Frances 185, Margaret Lois 184, 195, Mary Augusta 185, Monroe Franklin 186, Monroe Homer 185, Nellie 275, Patricia 275, Ruth 270, Samuel H. 185, 195, Sue 185, 186, Tom 185, William 112
Jaffee, Julie 139
James, Elizabeth 121, Isabella 98, Janet Carol 96, 110, 253, Margaret 98
Jameson, James B. 84, Lulah Fields 84, Victoria Gaines 84
Jamison, M.F. 52, Minerva A. Flinnoy 186, Robert 186
Jarman, Alice 158, Berry 158, Mary Wrenn 158
Jarrell, Laura 243, Lillian

Edith 243, Simeon Barton 243
Jarrett, Anna Emmons Burns 246, Elma Jean 170, Ethel Cliff 226, Florence 246, Israel 246
Jeffries, Anne 38
Jehorek, Jonathan Edward 46
Jenkins, Carmen 111, 280, Carmen Lorene 111, Charlie 186, Dan Moody 186, Doris Jean 186, Eldoras B. 186, Elva Laura 112, Ethel 112, 132, Eula Hanson 186, J.J. 109, Jeanna 186, Lora Ethel 111, Minnie Castles 186, Oran Thomas 111, Rebecca 186, Thomas 186
Jennings, Andrew Burton 179, Annie Edmondson Draper 179
Jenson, Hilma Margaret 91
Jeter, A.E. 49, Ann Elizabeth 145, Anna 132, Dale 107, Edmond 145, Eleazor 132, George Washington 132, J.T. 145, John 133, Malinda Dean 132, Martha Ann 144, 145
Jhass, Jeremiah 88, Mary Grace 88, Mohan 88
Johns, Alice 139, Charles 139, Grace Brown 139
Johnsey, John 182, Martha Caroline 182, 183, Nancy Pardue 182
Johnson, A. Odell 45, Ada 148, Alice Lenora E. 121, Art 266, Atha Odell 186, Audriana 281, Barbara 186, Ben 106, Bethena 176, Burke Randall 234, Charlotte 254, Clarence Arthur 246, Collier F. 169, "Cyclone" 25, Cyril Reginald 276, Dionne 281, Douglas 186, Edith Joyce 187, Edith Wilma 246, Eli 187, Elvia Arrena 187, Flavius Josephus 86, Flora 174, France Ellen 103, Frank 169, Gary 258, Georgia Smith 251, Gilford 187, Gwendolynn Denise 162, Helen 234, Idabell 148, Ira 26, Jack 176, Janie B. 160, Janis 186, Jess Franklin 110, Jessie Lillian 186, Joyce B. 273, Julia 186, Krystal 281, Lawrence Bruce 276, Leslie Anne 234, Lillian 186, Lucinda 243, Luella Abernathy 187, Lyndon B. 268, Marion 52, Martha Winn 237, Mary T. 276, Mattie Arlene 81, 187, Mattie Myrtle 81, 187, Nancy 174, 266, Nancy C. 169, Nettie Belle 160, Nora Belle 86, Odell 186, Odie Oline 282, Peggy Jean 276, Penelope 176, Randolph Keets 81, 187, Ruby Ione 254, Sally Elizabeth 156, Sherwood 187, Stephen M. 187, Tresha Jan 276, Willie 176

Johnston, April Nanette 189, Dellah 188, Mary Shirey 187, April Cecelia 189, Augusta Elizabeth 266, Barbara 187, 188, Billy Ray 85, 187, 188, 235, Bryan 143, Camryn 85, 188, Carol Ann 85, 188, 189, Charles 85, 187, Charles Bert 188, 226, Charles Michael 189, Christian Andrew 189, Della Armstrong 133, Dellah Armstrong 85, 188, 226,, Dianne Christian 85, 188, Donna Lynn 85, 189, 226, E.C. 182, 230, Gayle 182, Georgia Ruth 49, 64, 85, 188, 189, 226, Helen 182, Jill Elizabeth 189, Juliana Michelle 189, Marion Cecelia 189, Mary Pearle Shirey 85, 188, 226, Mozelle 63, 185, O.G. 85, 188, 189, 226, 235, 266, 267, Ogie 133, Richard 41, Robbie Nell 85, 235, Robert 41, Robert Marshall 189, Robert Marshall II 189, Robert Marshall III 189, Rosa Elvira Solari 189, Sarah Della E. 266, Taylor 85, Taylor Marie 188, Tiffany Elder 143, Victoria Nanette 189, Wendy 85, 188, Wesley Ray 85, 188
Joiner, C.M. "Dad" 29
Jones 90, Arthur 189, Adrew Leroy 229, Alice Estell Hill 190, Amanda Ann 248, Annie 118, 229, Arbrea Fae 255, Beatrice 80, 99, 189, 190, Billie Joyce Hollers 175, Bruce 99, Channey Christian 118, Daisy Mildred 221, Daniel 190, Darlynn Grounds 261, Daryl Russell 248, Dewey 182, E.L. 246, Ed 190, Effie 273, Florence 189, Floyd 273, Frances 99, Frank 174, Grace A. 103, Grady 5, Harris 242, Huldy 118, Ida Louise 182, Ira Leslie 276, Irene 216, J.H. 22, Jack 99, 189, 190, James Edward 190, James Eugene 190, Jeannie 99, Jerry M. 60, Jessie Arlee 146, 264, Joan "Patsy" 276, Josephine Tate 190, Josie 25, Judy 190, Kathleen 64, Lois Beatrice 189, Louisa L. 243, Mandie 248, Marion Cecelia 189, Mary 190, Mary Lee 121, Melvin 164, Mike 164, Miriam Harris 242, Muriel Glenn 118, Nancy 199, Nell 190, Nellie May 96, Octavia 66, Olive Emily Belle 275, Oscar B. 246, Rebecca 118, 160, Roland 99, 189, Ronnie 190, Samuel L. 28, Sheryl D. 256, Simon 118, Sonja Carroll 99, 190, Thomas 190, William 265, William C. 275, William Robert 146

Jordan, George R. 136, Tijuana 172
Jorgenson, Christine 190, Geneva Jean 190, Jacob Syverine 190, Jorgen Gustav 190, Lou 63, Lurlie Dee 190, Raymond Earl 190
Joseph, Amelia 191, Eric 191, Aaron 191, Adal 190, Ed 190, Eric 153, 191, George Aaron 153, 190, 191, George Eric 190, 191, Helen 190, Joe 190, John 190, Martha 190, 191, Rose Samuel 229, Sadie Lee 153, 191, Shelly 152, 153, 190, 191, Sydney 153, 191
Josephson, Kent 40, 41
Joslin, Helen 104
Joyce, Emily Starr 258
Joyner, Dad 269, William Hutcheson 43
Judkins, Brenda Beckman 191, Mark 191
Judson, Adoniram 279, Adonirum 23
Juett, Jane 147
June, Mary Miller 203
Justice, Eula Mae 275, John 275

K

Kalam, Tonu 65
Kane, Jennie 121, Mattie Lee 135
Kaplan, Paula 170
Kauffman, Anna Fisher 147, Christian 147
Keadle, George 148
Keane, Kathryn 285
Keasler, Ethel May 254, Nancy Melvina Skaggs 254, Robert Marion 254, Roxie Lee 254
Keegan, G. Kearnie 43
Keenan, Eric 85, 234
Keener, Gay 64, George 102, Josephine Helen "Dot" 102, Lawson Jefferson 8, Lucretia 102
Keese, Mary Elizabeth 104
Keeton, Alice 170
Keller, Helen 232, P.B. 232
Kelley, Beval Foirriestier 150, John 150, Rita 150, T.A. 10
Kelly, Anna 192, Arra Lee Hoskins 176, Buford Troy 125, Carey Elder 143, Cornie Louana 125, Dora M. 124, Euphemia 176, G.A. 47, 238, George 176, 192, 253, George Addison 34, Jacob 192, June Nelwyn 125, LeGrand D. 34, Lucy Anne 192, R.M. 176, Robert Marvin 34, T.A. 10, Virginia 64, 67, W.L. 134
Kemp, Edward 130, Jane 130, Victoria 130
Kendell, Fenwick Robbins 252, Nancy E. 252
Kennard, Homer 192, Ann Sandefur 192, Charles Henry 192, Charles R. 41, D.C. 192, Don 192, Elizabeth 192, H.

German 192, James Jones 192, Leo 192, Louisa Caroline 253, Love 192, Mary Jane 192, Nathaniel 192, Nona Pauline 192, 211, Sara Elizabeth 192, Taylor 192, Thomas E. 10, Zoe 192
Kennedy 255, Carson 84, Derek Robbins 242, Dorothy 241, 242, Edward Jasper 247, George 241, George Ernest III 242, George Ernest IV 242, George Ernest Jr. 242, George Ernest Sr. 241, 242, Lena 105, Lucy 242, LuRye 247, Marilyn Adcock 242, Nancy 249, 261, Neina Mead 242, Stacia Michelle 242
Keppler, Barbara Letitia 219, Harry 219, Jacques 219
Kerns, Carolyn Lajuan Doss 135
Kerr, Ada 176, Catherine Compton 152, Gladys Bertha 176, Will 176
Kesselberg, Heinrich 116
Kesseler, Elladora Ann 254
Key, Abigail Cardenas 192, Charlie 203, Francis Scott 192, Frank Murray 192, George Edward 192, Judith 192, Mamie 60, 61, Ophelia 192, Patrick Henry 192, Shirley 192, William H. 8
Keys, Cecil 134, John Henry 133, Kelly Denise 257, Maxie Edwards 133, Rosannah 133, Warren F., Sr. 133
Keyton, Cecil 143, Mattie Gertrude 143
Khoury, S.G. 246
Khun, Zellar 221
Kilgore, C.B. "Buck" 24, Constantine Buckley 18, 92, 137, 193, Frances Barnett 193, John 10, 279, Marilyn 126, Mary E. 92, Willis 193
Killett 180
Killingsworth 84, 102, 279, Amanda 194, 198, Anderson 5, 193, 194, Blanche 170, 184, 195, Charles Lee 195, Clara D. 284, Donnie Cain 170, Eliza 284, Emma Agnes 195, Emmaline Abney 193, 194, 198, 236, 261, Eudera Minnie 194, Florence Ann Leath 170, 184, 194, Frances 167, Gladys Rebecca 170, Henry Newt 194, Ida R. 194, Isaac Gordon 194, James 167, James A. 194, James W. 194, 284, John 24, 193, John Albert 194, 198, John L. 194, John Sweet 193, 194, 198, 236, 261, Leroy Lee 194, Louella Rhoda 265, Margaret 184, 194, 195, Martha 147, 167, 233, 236, 261, Mary 5, 194, 198, Mary Sweet 5, 193, 194, Molly Antoinette 194, Nancy 5, 194, Rebecca 194, 280,

Samuel Abney 170, 184, 194, Samuel Hardy 195, Sarah Jane 194, Stephen 5, Thomas Edward 265, Willey T. 194

Killingsworths, Alice 193, Bennie 193, Clara 193, Eddie 193, Eliza 193, James W. 193, Lucy 193, Rebecca 193, Robert 193, Tera 193

Killingsworth, Amanda 198, Emma Agnes 194

Kilpatrick 78, Alta Beatrice 183, Martha Jane 196, Windell Clarence 183

Kimball, Spencer W. 40

Kimberling, Benjamin Franklin 206, Emily Knight 206, Nancy Jane 206

Kimble 204, Aaron 204, Cornelia 204, Easter Lundy 204, George 204, Hampton 204, Henderson 204, Lewis 204, Minnie Lee 204, Sam 204

Kimbrough, Linnie Moore 195, Gindy Propes 195, Ginny Rae 195, Julie Marjorie 195, Kenneth 195, Kevin 195, Kristy Kay 195, Lanny 195, Laurel 195, Marjorie 195, O.L. 66, 195, Orman 195, Susan Henry 195

Kimmel, Diane 201

Kincheloe, Ann 204

King, Asbury Alexander 196, A.A. 196, Alice 103, Annie 97, 230, Asbury 195, 196, 200, Debbie F. 246, Dura 196, Edward Berry 196, Esther 196, Jacob Solon 195, 196, 200, Janet Louise 152, Jewell Violet 152, Joanna Maxine 84, John 195, 196, 200, Juliana Ray 195, Lecta 196, Lottie 196, 200, Lula Viola 195, Mamie 196, Marla Sue 268, Mossie 196, Myrtle 196, Nancy 195, Paulina 195, Reba 230, Sam 230, Solon 196, Viola 196, 200, William Carleton 152, Willie May 196

Kinsey, Hollis 200, Viola 200, 201

Kipp, Shara Park 230

Kirk, Margaret 132

Kirkindoll, Brittany Dawn 257, Dawn Michelle 257, Gary Thomas 257, Kelly Denise 257, Lauren Ashley 257, Lee Ann 257, Mae Jeanette 257, Mark Charles 257, Michael J. 257

Kirkpatrick, Mary "Polly" 234

Kiser, Ollie Donaho 207

Kittle, John 188

Kittner, Courtney Blaine 131, Michael Myles 131

Klunkert, Stacy Lynn 131

Knackstedt, Gerald 40, 41

Knight, Arkie Monroe 261, Emily 206, Jeannine Alexia 261

Knighton, Caroline Sue 168, Lillie Mae 139, Stephen 168

Knowles, J.A. 136, Mary Zelda 136

Knox, Alvah 196, Annie 196, Claudia 196, Debbie 196, Dee 196, Esther Mack 196, 204, Galen 196, J. Roy 16, J.M. 60, J.W. 196, James 277, James D. 196, Jennie 196, Joe 196, John W. 196, Judy 196, Kenneth 196, Kirk 196, Linda Sue 204, Lula 196, Martha Jane 196, Mattie Lee 196, Murray 196, Nancy Harriet 277, Rhoda 277, Robert Lane 196, Robert Rhodes 196, Sam 196, Sidney Earl 196, 204, Walter 196

Koehler, Willa 128

Koonce, James Phillip 242, Lillie Zelika 242, Mary Ella 242

Kouba, Karen Elaine 132

Krutza, Cheryl 196

Kuehl, Kristen 96, 110, 253

Kuehler, Thresa Ann 262

Kunkell, Kate 224, Mellisa 224, Tommy 224

Kunz, Frank 250, Sybil Olivia 249

Kutzer, Mary Ethel 219, Ralph 219

Kuykendaal, Carroll 196, Cheryl Krutza 196, David 196, Dee 196, Don 196, Emily Sarah 196, Julie 196, Linda 196, Lori 196, Mark 196, Monica 196, Ola Mae 196, Rachel Alyse 196, Tessie Reese 196

Kuykendall, Joe G. 196, Joe Henry 196, John William 196, Joseph A. 196, Ola Mae 196

Kyle 229

L

Labatt, Blair Plowman 103, Gloria 103

Lackey, Hope 285

Lacy, Edwin 285, Elizabeth 285, John Edwin 285, Kate Perry 285, Kate Womack 64, 148, Kathryn 285, R. 213, Rogers 227, T.E. 31, Thomas Edwin 148

LaGrange, Bill 110, 253, Kathryn May 253

Laine, J. Gary 80

Laird, Andrew Jordan 275, Dickson Henderson 10, Emily 275, Laci 94, Libby Terrell 103, Martha 252, 253, Maude 86, Nancy 275, Roy H. 109

Lama, Tony 204

LaMaster, Dennis 181, 182, Grace Elisabeth 181, 182, Jane Anne 181, 182, John Clark 181, 182, Julie Katherine 181, 182, Laura Grace 181, 182, Leslie Claire 181, 182, Scott William 181, 182

Lamb, Judy Nan 178, Margaret 114, Rosa 240

Lambert, Clarissa Anne 140, Ida Lou 277, Luther 277

Laminack, Jerry 179, Linda 3, 7, Linda Janelle 179, Stacy 179

Lamour, Dorothy 38, 159

Lanagan, Bill 197, David Mayo 197, Eddie Irene 197, Elizabeth Sean 197, Jane Carol 197, Jena Renee 197, John Antonio 197, John Matthew 197, John Mayo 197, John Mercer 197, John William 197, Judith Lynn 197, Mary Etta 197, Mary Janet 197, Mayo 38, Mike 197, Reba Bryant 197, Ruby 197, Tony 197, Tracy Willam 197, W.A. 38, 197

Lancaster, Emily Anne 197, Ernest A. 197, Gladys 197, Jan Alberta 197, John Albert 197, Lola Elma Denman 197

Land, Nancy 158

Landers, Amanda 198, Christopher Columbus 198, Effie 197, 198, Georgia Flo 275, James Clarience 198, James Rayburn 198, Jim 197, 198, Jo Ann 197, 198, Kathryn 197, Mary Kathryn 198, Paulina 195, Ray 197, Thomas 275, Tom Jr. 276

Landis, Julia Ann Hudgins 178

Landreth, Andrew 229, Annie 229, Ida Ophella 229, Sammy 229

Landtroop, Jennie 126

Lane, Betsy 237, Charles 157, Charlotte 157, Elizabeth 148, Isaac 186, J.A. 10, Jean 157, Mary Alice 251, Robert 252, William T. 10, 270

Laney, Nancy Sarah Elizabeth 147, Robin Christina 253

Langford, Phoebe 222

Langham, Earl 45

Langhorne, Margaret A. 249

Langston, Lucretia Lynn 125

Lanham, Ann Roby 287

Lanier, Asa 180, Margaret 61, Norma 180

LaPrade, Allen 83, Bobby 83, Janis 83, Margaret Kathryn 83

Larkin, Kimberly Shipman 139

Larkins, Doris Darline 130

Lasseter, Mary Ann 103, William Lee 103

Laster, Bradford Roscoe 249, Don 249, Dustin Thomas 249, Martha Alice 249

Latch, Lola Bingham 94, Sarah 186

Latimer, Dorothy Jane 124

Lattimore, Gladys 79

Laurindine, Agnes 135

Law, John 95, Nancy Eunice P. 95, Sarah Maxey 95

Lawndes 68

Lawrence, Agnes Lodeema 199, Ann Belvin 198, Betsy Kim 199, Bobbie Jo 175, C.W. 114, Callye Renee 199, Christopher Michael 199, Clay Edward 199, Cynthia Jane 198, Edward Joseph 199, Elizabeth Belvin 198, Enoch 198, Fred Parker 199, Garland Belvin 199, Henry Winfred 199, Hollie Middleton 199, Hollis Dee 199, Hollis Lloyd 199, Holly 253, Holly M. Jr. 199, Jeremy Dee 199, Jessie Campbell 199, Joey Kemp 199, John Wesley 198, Jonathan Chance 199, Julia Cordelia Gillespie 199, Kathryn 60, Kemp G. 199, Lillie 64, 199, Margaret Clementine 102, Mary Ann Phillips 253, Mary Lou Gipson 199, Mary Phillips 96, 110, Michael Lloyd 199, Michelle C. 199, Nancy Elizabeth 199, Pamela Renee 96, 110, 253, Patti Geers 199, Ruth 199, Suzanne Taylor 199, Tommy 173, William Warren 199, Willie May Miller 173

Lawson, Anna 80, 165, David 50, Louretta Cowles 80, Thomas 80

Le Fleau, Louisa 135

Le Tourneau, Mary Evelyn Peterson 200

League, Angeline Fowler 200, Bessie 200, Ciccero C. 200, Earl 200, Harriett Williams 199, James 199, Joab 199, Joe Luther Perry 200, Joel 199, Joel Perry 199, John 200, Lela Lois 200, 225, Lois 200, Luther 200, Mary Ann 199, Minnie 200, Morgan 200, Nancy Jones 199, Patience 199

Leahy, Bill 162, Erin Nicole 162, Jessica Joy 162, Laura Ann 162, Sean Patrick 162, Thomas Daniel 162, William Joseph 162

Leak 12

Learned, Charles 29

Leath, Florence Ann 170, 184, 194, Josiah S. 194, Margaret Ann 194

Leatherman, Sallie 100

LeBlanc 161

Ledbetter, Elestial 17

Ledford, Alfred 122, Louisa Elizabeth 120, 121, Lu 122, Nancy 165, Samuel Jackson 165, Weltha Jane 165

Lee, Annie 64, Clarence 137, Dona Small 222, E.L. 60, 61, George Thomas 222, Harold B. 40, Jerry 25, 54, Julia Ann Gertrude 222, Kara D'Nae 278, Kerry 278, Lara L. 278, Mattie Gertrude 137, Mollie Tennessee 275, Nathan 160, Pearl 105, Radonia Alabama 160, Robert E. 20, 95, 158, Sam 275, Sarah 160, 275, Sean Alan 278, Sheila Elaine 278, William 275

Leford, Franklin 122, Fuller 122, William J. 121

Leland, George T. "Mickey" 278

Lemmon, Mark 200

Leon, Alison 110, Mary 96

Leslie, Arenva 228

Lester, Amanda Susan 152, Mary 169

L'Estrange, Florence 98

Letcher, Lafayette 10

LeTourneau, Robert Gilmour 35

LeTourneau, Caleb T. 200, Elizabeth 200, Evelyn 35, Mary 30, R.G. 16, 34, 200, 201, 216, 274, Richard 35

Letterman, Dorothy 85

Lettice, Amy Hale 164, Jeff 164

Levy, Mary DeLoach 64, R.B. 65, 101, 223, 227, Richard B. 10

Lewis 255, Benjamin Franklin 10, Bennett 10, Carroll Denman 197, Eldridge 48, Ella Rhee 117, Helen Jean 197, Jan Alberta 197, Jerald Wayne 197, Laurie 261, Mark 261, Marla Gayle 96, 110, Mary Ellen 129, Michael 96, 110, Willard 117

Light, Jimmie Oree Odom 229, Robert 229

Ligon, Nancy Gaddy 180, Willis 180

Lile, Karen 213, Kaye Barker 159, Margie Nell 213

Lincoln, Abraham 262

Lindbergh, Charles 246

Linder, Blane 169, Brittany 169, Carolyn 169, Jennifer 169, John G. 169, Paige 169

Lindley, Dick B. 66, Robert 66

Lindsey, Carolyn C. 46, Charlotte Jane 187, Joseph 40, Mattie Myrtle 187

Lindwall, David 47

Lione, Sue 281

Lipcomb, Viola King 200

Lippeatt, Floyd 170, Linda 170

Lipscomb, Cuvier 200, Diane King 200, Emma Belle 200, Lottie 163, 196, 200, Mary A. 200, Robert Dabney 196, 200, Sandra 201, Viola King 196, 201

Liston, Frances Monigold 101, Thomas Walter "Pat" 101

Little, Allen 83, Annie Mae 25, 54, Dorothy Jean 83, Gayle 83, Harvey 201, Helen 234, Ida Dee 256, Irene Pickett 201, Jack 83, Janice Ellen 125, Jennie K. 196, Mike 83, Mollie 256, S. Miles 8, 256, Willie 256, Zack 196

Lliebowitz, Jennifer Tapia 254

Lloyd, Betty 241, 242, Bob Motley 242, Carla 96, 252, 110, Donald Parker 242,

Kelley Sidney 242, Lolita 7, 266, Tammie Lynn 284
Lockens, Margaret 81
Lockett, Arula 118, 202, Asbury 202, Bevin 202, Clemmie 202, Connie Mae 202, Dell 202, Della 202, Efella 202, Eliza 201, Ellison Smart 202, Essek 201, 202, Exora 202, Florence 202, Ira 118, 202, Jane Wood 254, Lenora 201, Mattie 202, Nancy 201, Oliver 202, Ora 118, 202, Roscoe C. 202, Ruby Lee 202, Thelma 202, William 201, Zachariah 34
Loden, Suzanna P. 209
Loflin, D.V. "Red" 287
Loftis-Heleum, Connie Mae 202
Logan, George 262, Ira J. 262, James Alexander 262, James Robert 262, John 128, Laura 262, Lidia 262, Martha Susan 262, Ola 262, 264, Sarah Magdalene 262, Susan 262, William 262
Logue, Lydia 174
Lollar, Maggie 272
Lon, Alice 202
Long, Alice 203, Daniel 203, David 202, 203, 218, Eliza 203, Emmitt 203, Ernest 202, Essie 203, Gary Martin 203, James David 203, Jimmie Lee 203, JoAnn 202, John Alan 203, Karen Anne 203, Mabel 202, Mary Ella 139, Mary Jane 250, Mary June 203, 218, Sandra 202, Susan Kay 203, Thomas Edward 203, Viola 203, Walter 221
Longacre, Aubrey Sienna 232, James Evan 232, James Kinney 232, Lasca Minnette 156, 232
Looker, Ida Ellen 262
Looney, Martha DeLeice 223
Lorimer, Elizabeth 200
Loudon, Arthur 41
Louise, Jeanette Adams 255
Lovell, Mary 137
Lowe, Elizabeth 161, Laura 161, Lindsey 161, Mark 161, Robyn Grigsby 161
Lowke, Adrienne 79, Brock 79, Kelsey 79, Kyle 79, Marilyn Adrian 79, Richard 79
Lowman, Ann 254
Loy, Della Marshall 144
Lucas, Judson M. 219, Roberta Letitia 219
Lucenay, Harry 43
Luckel, L.C. 37
Luckett, C. J. 10, 286, Mary Josephine 285, 286
Luckey, Robert 174
Lucy, Ann 109, 204, Annie Helen Butts 109, 204, Betty Nalley 204, Dan 203, 204, Ethel 109, Frank 203, Jerry 205, Jerry Joseph 109, 203, Jerry Lester 203, Julia Ann 203, Mary Beth 203, Rebecca

Ann 203, Stephen Harvey 204, Woodie Mackey 203, 205
Luman, Christene 268
Lummus, Francis 220, Robert 220
Lundy, Easter 204, Henry 204, Lewis 204
Lupton, John Thomas 68, 69, Ruby 69
Lusby, Amanda 254, Betty 254, Jacob 254
Luursen, Jacob 196, Styntje 196
Lynn, Jessie Ellen 216

M

MacCurdy, Alexander Bowles 42, 43
Mack, Bena Thomas 204, George 204, Maggie 265, Peter Butrous McChoil 204, Sam 204, Saydie 204
Mackenzie, Ann Price 249
Mackey, Anna Cora 205, Audrey Faye 91, Caleb Reece 92, Cora 30, 204, Curtis 171, 186, 204, 205, Ella Rebecca 250, Faye 91, Jessie 204, 205, Joel Lewis 250, Kerry Reece 91, 92, Kimberly Jo 91, 92, L.L. 186, 204, Lester Losson 205, Lewis Terrell 250, Lou Ann 186, 204, 205, Lula 204, 205, Lynelle 204, Martha "Mattie" 78, Mary Fonville 250, Nancy 205, Nona Lynelle 205, Norbert Reece 91, Rebecca Jane 171, 204, 205, Robert Kent 91, 92, Stephanie 92, William Claude 205, William Lester 204, 205, Winnie 204, Woodie 203, 204, 205
Macon, Darlene 278
MacTavish, Jean Frances 115
Madden, Amanda Ozella 205, Charles 205, Lillie Pearl 98, 205, Mary Sylvester 205, Sarah Roxanne 205, Susannah 205, William Harvey 205, William Henry 205
Maddox, "Cordie" 279
Magee, Caroline 110, 253, Catherine 96, 110, Cathy 253, Christopher 110, 253, David 96, 110, 253, Jennifer 96, 110, 253, Kendall Avery 96, 110, Lynn 96, 110, 253, Sarah 228, William 228
Magill, James Rankin 43
Magrill 220, Agatha B. Bassett 206, Alex Young 160, Alexander R. 160, 206, Amanda C. 206, Benjamin 206, C.D. 206, Dennis Lawrence 116, 206, Dora 206, Elizabeth A. 206, Elmyra 116, 206, George F. 206, J.T. 20, James Monroe 206, Jim 116, John 36, 52, John B. 206, John R. 10, 206, Laura J. 206, Maggie 116,

206, Malcolm Erwin Alexander 82, Margaret 160, 206, Martha 206, Mary E. Orr 206, Mary S. Curtis 206, Nettie Belle Johnson 160, Richard 206, 116, Rosie Mae 82, 83, S. Elizabeth 206, Samuel D. 36, Samuel Dee 206, Samuel Devall 206, Temperance Annie 206, William B. 206, William E. 206
Magruder, John 254
Mahan 95
Mahannah, Ruth May 260
Mahler, Dietra Ann 184
Mahlman, Adrianne 150, Robbie Adrian Fournet 150, Robert 150, Thomas 150
Makham, Elaine 155
Malcolm, J. 18
Maledon, Shannon 163
Malkey, Karen 267, Steve 267
Mallory, Annie D. Rebecca 236, Haskell Lee 236
Mallow, Mary Jane 247
Malone, A.A. 128, Elizabeth 128, Francis David 128, Jessie Robertson 128, Mariah 128, Viola 128
Maloney, Emma B. 284
Malott, Scottie 172
Maness, Evelyn 61
Maney, Nancy Tioletto 165
Mangrum, Joel A. 104, Jolie Ashling 104, Judith Pauline Brian 104
Manhollan, Charles 110, Cora 110, Georgina 110, 157
Mann, J.W. 261, Mary Beth 205
Marchbanks, George 199, Ann Echols 199, George 199, John 199, Joseph 199, Lucy 199, Mary Ann 199, Patience 199, Sarah 199, Ursula 199, William 199
Marion, Francis 99, 252
Marjoribanks, George 199
Markham 120, E.C. 121, Elaine 118, 206, Elizabeth Campbell 206, Essie L. 121, L.N. 228, Laura A. Chapman 121, Lewis S. 206, Louis Napoleon 121, 206, Louis Northcutt 37, 121, 206, Louis S. 121, Martha Ann Elizabeth 121, 206, Mary Elizabeth 121, Princess Emma 121, 206, Sarah Mayo 121, 206, Sarah Northcutt 228, Thomas L. 206, Tommy S. 121, Virginia Elaine 121, 206
Marrs, Nancy 278, Walter 278
Marsh, Addie Belle 287
Marshal, Frank Hart 91
Marshal, Johnnie Lois 91
Marshall, Erminie 64, Hettie 148, Lula W. 110, Thurgood 281, W.K. 46, William 277
Martin, Ada Lee 263, Alexander William 261, Alice Bell 207, Anna Jan 261, Arthur 207, B.F. Jr. 261, Bazely 206, Bell 206, Ben-

jamin Franklin 60, 69, 70, 113, 165, 207, 208, Caroline 206, Charla Richelle 261, Charles Garrett 261, Charles William 261, Charlotte Elizabeth 113, 208, Chester 207, Cora Blanche 207, Cora Vemelle 207, Dock J. 206, Dora 206, Elizabeth Lee 165, 207, Emily 237, Emma Lee 207, 237, Emmit 198, Essie 207, Florence 219, Frankie Judith 261, Franklin 80, 110, 113, George Wesley 206, Georgia 209, Grace 60, 208, 219, Harriet 206, Henry Clay 222, Herbert Esten 207, Jaclyn Gail 234, Janet Marie 261, Jennie 222, Jessie Lee 207, Jim 196, Joe 206, John Robert 206, Johnnie Mae 110, Joseph Elijah 206, L.M. 49, Lorraine 64, 70, 208, Lynn 73, Malcolm M. 70, 165, 207, 219, Margaret 64, 116, Marshall Allan 207, Martha Virginia 206, Mary Elizabeth 206, Mary Evelyn 165, 207, 219, Mary Frances 116, Max H. 41, Melissa Marie 261, Minnie 222, Mollie Morris 207, Morris Billing 207, Newt 206, Nora 206, Ora Beatrice 236, Patricia Anne 165, 207, Robert Newton 207, Roy E. 206, Ruth 165, 207, 219, Sallie Bell Donaho 207, Sandra 196, Thomas G. 207, Thomas S. 207, 208, Thompson J. 116, Travis Wesley 207, Tuesday Hall 261, Una Mae 198, Walter Coleman 207, William 206, 219, William Clifford 261, William Jessie 206, Williams 23
Martinez, Alfugia Cucca Refugio 159, John Lasco 159, Mary G. 159
Martini, August 287, Caroline 287, Marilyn 287, Roslyn 287
Mason, Adele Todd 267, Ancil 267, Cecil Ann 267, James Allen 267, Paul Todd 267
Massengill, Mary Etta 197
Massey, Carrie M. 109, Lena Formby 230, U.A. 48, William Thomas 229, Wilna 229
Masters, B.E. 35, Mary Catherine 187
Mathews, Lettie Udora 89
Mathis, Ada 176, Alison Woodville 208, 209, Bish 246, Dessie Lee Williams 208, 209, Dewey O. 208, 209, Edmond 209, Elizabeth Ann 209, Helen 91, James 208, James Allison 209, James Otto 209, 218, Linda Sue 209, Nancy 132, 209, Peggy Sue 209, 218, Rebecca 208, Susan 208, 209, Sybil 208
Matkin, Judy 276

Matlock 255, Stevanna 244
Matthews, Nancy C. 169, Richard H. 169, Sarah 169
Mattox, Ahas 280, Cordelia "Cordie" 280, Effie 198, George Starling 198, 251, Mary Elizabeth 198, 251
Mauldin, Ceedie Elizabeth 209, Clarence Whitfield 210, Eleanor Jean 210, Elizabeth 210, Ethel 209, Ida Mae 210, J.W. 210, James Cole 210, James Ellison 210, James Loden 209, Janice 210, Jimmie Eleson 209, Margaret Woods 210, Marie Delphine Fason 210, Medaline Easter 209, Melvin 210, Mollie Whitley 210, Nathaniel Whitfield 209, Novie Ree 210, Obie Hendrick 209, Preston Leon 210, Rocky 210, Ronald 210, Shirley Ree 210, Suzanna P. 209
Mauthe, Barbara Grund 228, Eda 227, 228, Jacob 228
Maxey, Sarah 95
May, Fannie 93, Mary Lucretia 135
Mayer, Beth McCrea 143, Gordon J. 232, 233, Nauty Byrd Pelphrey 232, 233, Patricia 233
Mayes, James Harvey 175, Mattie Elizabeth 175, Missouri 175
Mayfield, Erma 286, Irma Sue 144, 146, Medora A. 286, Susan 144, W.S. 10, 286, William Sidney 144
Mayo 40, Eddie Irene 197
McAfee 279, Ernestine 282, Eugene Carlton 282, Willie Mamie 282
McAlister, Ed 210, Itura Belew 210, Joseph E.J. 210, Dorothy Pearl 121
McAlpine, Sarah 164
McAnnelly, Caroline 138
McArthur, Ann Byrd 217
McBride, Derek 195, Gail 107, Johnnie 61, Kristy Kay 195
McBroom, C.J. Jr. 112, Elizabeth Ann 112
McCaleb, Lois 194
McCall, Callie 12, Nancy Agnes 147
McCann, Jimmie Virginia 132
McCarley, R.S. 69
McCarron, Kathryn May McKinney 253, Patrick 110, 253
McCary, Thelma Lee Boles 97
McCaskill, Mary Ann 267
McCay, Bill 66
McCelland, William H. 254
McChristian, Dawn Michelle 257
McClellan, L.L. 45
McClelland 49, Ann 103, Annie Hibernia 103, Chalmer Kirk 103, Clement Bramlette 103, Doris Alma 103, Grace 103, James Ed-

ward 103, Martha Davis 254, Mary Josephine 103, Maurice Ash 103, Nancy 244, Robert Clement 103, Thomas Bramlette 103, Virginia Jane 103

McClendon, Augusta Eugenia 171, Mary Lou 171

McCleskey, Doris McClung 214

McClung, Doris 214

McClure 102, Allison 129, Jodie 186, Robert F. 129, Scott 129, Theresa Daniel 129

McCollum, Aaron Edwards 285, Mariah 117, Stayce Lee Maledon 285, Wesley Willoughby 285

McConkie, Bruce R. 40

McConnell, Franz Marshall 43

McCook, Elizabeth Brown 84, Joe 84, Lela Pearl 96

McCord, Claribel 103, Felix J. 103, Gabriella 103, Ruth Emmaline 229

McCoy, Charles Worth 142, James Lawrence 142, Janie 142, Mollie Maxine 142, Rhodes 142, Roxie Ray Rhodes 142

McCracken, John Brownlow 99

McCranie, Mable Dee Nellie Dee 146

McCrea, Beth 143, Jane 90, 143, Winn 143

McCreary, Ella 78

McCullough, Alma 281, Mary Ethel 221

McCumber, Andrew Edward 258, David Eric 258, Jenny Starr 258, Michael Jeffrey 258, William David 258

McCurry, Corey Wayne 222, Jeffery Martin 222, Terry Paul 222

McCutcheon, Ronald 66

McDade, Sue 253

McDaniel, Mavis Pauline 117, Minnie 186, Theodore 117

McDaniels, Richard 123

McDill, R.H. 29

McDonald, Alexis 242, Darlene 83, Elizabeth M. Adrian 78, Jeannine Alexia 261, Julia 242, Laura Agnes 162, Margaret 117, Melissa 242, Nina 261, Patsy Ruth 81, Robert C. 261, William 78

McDowell 213, Billie Nell 150, Floyd Raymond 267, LaRue 267, Lenn 150, Mary Ella 267

McDuffie, Moses David 8

McElroy, Alice B. 169, Mary Louella 84, Venia 84, Walter 84

McEntire, Octavia 230

McFadin, H.A. 137, 138, Kate 137, 138

McFarland, Amanda 81, 82, 183, 259, Angela Gaye 164, Barbara 158, Diane Garvey 155, 272, Elizabeth Atkinson 158, Elizabeth "Betty" 82, J. Daniel 82, James 158, John Wesley 158, Malcom 155, Mary 183, Mary Jane 180, 269, Paul Noel 164, Permelia Tacora 269

McFarlin, Mariah Amanda Dean 133, William Edward 133

McGaugh, Clementine 210, Robert W. 210

McGaughey, Anthony Dale 132, Emily Anne 132, Lauri Alicia Davis 132, Madison Davis 132, Mason Davis 132, Lois Leland 217

McGaw, Clarence Emory 210, Clarence, Jr. 210, Cornelia Tomlinson 210, Dorothy Bearce Richards 210, Grace 210, Robert James 210, Robert William 210, Rose Marie 210

McGee, David 49, Donna 49, Faye 49, John 49, Prentis 49, Susan 49

McGinnis, Karen Elizabeth 257, Kenneth Wayne 257, Patsy Carol Stahl 257, Traci Annette 257

McGinnis-Land, Ethan Kohl 257

McGowen, Wanda 60

McGown, Jefferson Henderson 249, Mary Ella 249, Sybil Olivia 249

McGrede, Edith Eloise 82, 183, Eva Mae 183, 187, George Ernest 82, 183, Georgia Ruth 82, 183, Henry 91, 167, John Robert 183, Lydia Velma 82, 183, Novie Belle 167

McHanery, Nona Pauline 192

McHaney, Annie Belle 211, Dee 211, Elizabeth Ann 170, James Cornelius 210, 211, Judson Holloway 192, 211, Julia Barclay 210, 211, Katie May 211, MaeBeth 175, 218, Mary Ann 210, 211, Mollie 164, Nona Pauline 211, Vallie 211, Will Eanes 211, William Edwin 210, 211

McIntyre, Aris Deney 236, Duncan 237, Lorissa 237, Martha Ann 237

McKaig, H.L. 64, Lillie Mae 64

McKain, Harry 17

McKay, Apes Shaw 249, Dushee 249, Hector 249, Margaret 249, Mary Catherine 249

McKeag, Isabelle Dunseath 115

McKee, Temperance Annie 206, Thomas Alonzo 206

McKelvey, Lula Cumi 205, Sam 205

McKenna, Katherine Erin 98, 205

McKenzie, Jerry 63

McKinley, "Butch" 155, Jenny Frances 155, Joel 278, Kit 253, Margurite Eloise 211, Mary E. 206, Sexton Lando 211

McKinney, Brenda Jane 96, 253, Catherine Eaves 252, Diadema 252, Hampton 252, Jefferson C. 252, Jeffery Kyle 96, 110, Jeffery Kyle 253, John 252, Jubilee Lafayette 252, Kathryn May 96, 110, 253, Martha Jane 126, Mary 252, Nancy E. 252, Ronald Lester 96, 110, 252, 253, Ronnie 63, Susan 252

McKinney, Brenda Jane 110

McKinnon 143

McKittrick, Julius Michael 89, 212, Mary Ann Jane "Mollie" 89, 212, Mary Louise 212, Peter Michael 212

McKnight 279

McLaren, Etta Francis 95

McLaughlin, Willy Coleman 121, Bailey Jean 121, 122, Boone James 121, 122, Charles Fredrick 121, Charles Ronan 121, David 121, Dora 121, Dorothy Pearl 121, Elizabeth 121, George 121, Gwenda Darlene 121, James, 121, James Patrick 121, Jennie Kane 121, Kelly Jean Wyatt 121, Mark Coleman 121, Mary 121, Mary Elizabeth 121, Mary Lee 121, Melissa Michell 121, Mena Ethel Estella 121, Milton Cannon 121, P.J. 121, Sallie Edmiston Williamson 121, Scott 121, Timothy David 121, Valerie Ann Astorudd 121, Willy Coleman, Jr. 121, Wilma Harris 121

McLemore, Benjamin Reagan 143, Beverly Ann 242, Katheryn Keyton 143, Stephen Insley 143

McLendon, Alice Cormie 120, Augusta Eugenia 120, Autrie 120, Beatrice 282, Bessie Allene 212, 213, Bessie Lea 212, 213, Carl Lea 212, Carol 213, Charles Daniel 213, Charles David 212, Donna Jean 213, Eliza Louvenia 120, Eva Lillian 213, Frances Jane 213, Geneva Jasmine Ivie 213, Gladys Opal Moody 213, Harriet Mary Lou 120, Idus Simpson 120, Ivol Alice Smith 251, James Allan 213, James Alpheus 120, 212, 213, James Isum 120, 212, James Louis 213, James Melton 212, 213, Jo Carol 213, John L. 213, Johnnie Louis 212, Johnnie Randall 213, Joseph Franklin 212, Juddie Annelle Reel 213, Judith Ann 213, Larry William 213, Mamie 212, 282, Margie Nell 213,

Mary Alice 213, 251, Mary Anne 213, Mary Florence Terry 213, Mary Lou Melton 120, 212, 213, Michael Bryan 213, Nancy Carolyn 213, Patsy Elizabeth 213, Peggy Elaine 213, Robert L. 251, Roger Glenn 213, Roger Neil 212, Roger Terry 213, William Bryan 212, Willie Mae 253

McLeod, Margaret Virginia 144

McManus, Rebecca Jane 158

McMath, Lucanda 174

McMeans, Rita Pat 134

McMichael, Dorothy Ruth 97, Francis 17, James Calvin 97

McMillan, Nancy E. 84

McMurry, Amy Estelle 80, Jill 80, John 80

McNairy, Francis 100, 101, John Hamilton 100, 101, Natilla 101, Sallie 100, Susan (Susannah) 100, 101

McNeil, Nancy 162

McNew, Sophia Ellen 237

McNutt, Hamilton 25

McQueen, Beverly Ann 152, Daniel Cole 152, Daniel L. 152, Daniel W. 280, Doris 63, Eula 279, Eulah 280, Jodie Lavinna 152, Norma Jo 152

McWhorter, Alice Elvira 213, 214, 215, 216, Alice Grace 137, Andrew G. 140, Anne Stuart 215, Charlotte Vesta 216, Claude Fleming 213, 214, David 216, 244, Doris McClung McCleskey 214, E.W. 140, 142, Elizabeth 214, Ellen Hudson 214, Eugene Osborne 140, 141, 213, 214, 215, 216, 243, Eugene Rodden 140, 141, 213, 214, 215, 216, 243, Eugene Warren 215, 216, Frank Ripy 214, Helen Ripy 214, James Barry 215, Jennie V. 215, John Barry 213, 214, John Charles Thompson 215, Laurence Stansel 214, Lottie 142, 215, 216, Louise 214, Mabel Barnes 214, Marian Helen 214, Mary 213, 214, 216, Mary Alice 214, Mary Frances 215, Maxine Mohon 216, Nancy 214, 216, Robert Frank 214, Robert Warren 213, 215, Ruth 214, Sallie 78, 214, Thomas Afton 213, 214, 215, Thomas Duvall 215, Thomas Osborne 214, Vesta 67, 141, 214, 215, Warren Echols 215, Warren Osburn 213, 214, William A. 78, 213, 214, William P. 215, 216

McWilliam 99

McWilliams, Eva Elizabeth 209, 218, Gerald Reginald 218, Irby I. 218, John Howell 218, Lela 218, Loyce Elora 218, Maggie Oline 218, Marion Kellis 218, Marion Lafayette 209, 218, Mary Ann Sousin 218, Maude Katherine 218, Nettie Bernice 218, Perry Joseph Linston 218, Ruby Opal 209, 218, Virgil Andrew 218, William Warren 218

Meacham, Andrea 96, 110, Bob 110, Jenny 96, 110, Pamela 96, 110, Pamela Sue 96, Robert 96

Mead, Blanche 274, 275, Carol 273, 274, Edward 241, Harry Wilford 273, 274, Neina 64, 241, Roberta 273, Shirley 273, Theresa Holton 241, William Ecker 241

Meadows, Alene Watkins 217, Algar 287, Alice Corene 216, Benetta Inez 137, Benetta Inez 216, 248, Calvin Mays "Dick" 216, 217, Carrie Bell 216, 217, Charles Andrew Jackson 216, Chesley Hobson 216, 217, Cordie Lee Crews 216, Curtis W. 58, Darry 137, Delores 216, Eliza Ann 216, Elizabeth 216, 217, Emma 216, 217, Fannie Mae 217, George Franklin 216, Glenn Curtis 216, Irene Jones 216, James Kinchion 216, 217, Janie Lubreta 216, Jenea Augusta "Anna" 216, Jesse Green 216, John Dudley 216, John Henry 216, 217, Julia Elizabeth 216, Julie Elizabeth 217, Karen Gay 251, Katie Belle 216, 217, Lottie Mae 217, Lucretia 216, Mary Elizabeth 216, 217, Mary Virginia 216, Nancy 217, Naoma Mae Belle 217, Naoma Utzman 216, Nathaniel Christopher Green 216, Paulina Lee 216, Renvie Baldwin 216, Sam Edwin 216, 217, Shirley Jean 216, Stella Mae 216, 217, Tenza Minta 217, Van Oliver "Bill" 216, 217, Virginia Dare 216, Wayne Nathaniel 216, William 251, Willie Mae Standard 217

Meagly, Kirsten 254, Lori 254

Mears, Kathy 63

Mecey, David 221, Jimmy 221, Opal Moore 221

Mediate, Frank 110, Mary 110, 157, Teresa 111

Medley, Harold David 222, Jane Jo 180, 181, 253, Rosemary Morris 222

Medlin, Anna 276, Eugene Ross "Gene" 276, Frankie Pearl 276, Joan "Patsy" 276, Pearl 276, Troy 276, William Troy 276

Meeks, Elizabeth 84

Mefford, Lila Mae Bland 96, Robert Lee 96

Megaughey 99

Melton, Ann Crews 186, Elizabeth Michael 186,

Emily Mackey 186, Grady 186, 205, John Ernest 128, Letta Belle 128, Lou Ann 186, 205, Mary Lou 120, 212, 213, Michael Mackey 186, Mickey 171, Rebecca Jenkins 186

Melville, Jennie V. 215

Mercer, Joanna Whittington 101, Judith Amanda 101, Marion 101, Paulina Lee 216, Sam 66

Merchant, Elvey Shepperd, Jr. 235, Mathis B. 235

Meredith, Ann Byrd 217, Corinne Leland 217, D.S. 28, David Sutton 217, Henry McGaughy 217, John McGaughy 217, Leigh Ellen 217, Lois Leland 217, Margaret Jonelle 217, Minnie Burr 217, Monroe Mays 217, Olivia Gee 217, Perry Reynolds 217, Sara Ann 217, Steven Parker 217, Thomas Stuart 217, Van Patterson 217, Will Gordon 217, William Quinn 217, Wilmer Thomas 217

Merlos, Julio 41

Merrill 40, Helen Muston 223, Robert T. Winnifred 43

Merritt, A.P., Jr. 143, Susie Elder 143

Methvin, Anna Frances 218, Lizzie 175, 176, 218, M. 104, 105, Margaret 217, Nathan 217, O.H. 46, 76, 176, Ossamus Hitch 12, 217, 218, Richard R. 217, William Alton 218

Meyer, Daniel 129, Deborah Daniel 129, Kelly 129, Kenneth B. 129, Mary Kathryn 205, Nona Lynelle 205, Wilbur 205

Meyers, L.E. 179

Middlebrooks, Jimmy 66

Mifflin, Bertha 187

Mikeska, Josephine 60, Marvin, Sr. 60

Miles, Hershel 277

Milford, Carolyn Sue 94

Miller, Andrew 199, Angus 148, Ann 64, Annie E. 102, 150, 151, Barbara Letitia 130, 219, Brandon 198, Celia Neal 199, Clarence William 130, 219, Dan L. 47, Ebenezer Erskine 102, Elizabeth Flew-ellen 148, Fay 256, Francis 224, Frankie Lyno 130, 219, Franklin R. 158, Fred Eugene 218, Hallie 218, Hattie Irene "Patsy" 218, Helen Evelyn 218, Henry 22, Jack Martin 203, 218, Janet 143, Jay 114, Jennie 158, Jerry 198, Jo Ann 198, Katherine Mary 218, Lola Caroline Tatum 249, Margaret Clementine 102, Margery 102, Martin 93, 203, 209, 218, Martin Marion 209, 218, Mary June

218, Mason 198, Nancy Elizabeth 203, 218, Nancy Lucinda 209, 218, Narciss Davis 130, 218, 219, Ollie Margaret 218, Opal 93, 203, 209, Patsy Ruth 93, 203, 218, Peggy Sue 203, 209, 218, Pilsir 249, Preston Jesse 218, Roberta Letitia 130, 219, Ruby Opal 209, 218, Rubye Cute 159, Sadie Agness 218, Sarah Annie 126, Steve 257, Thomas 257, Victoria Bernice 130, 218, Viola 130, 218, William 130, 209, 218, 219, Willie May 130, 173, 218

Milligan, Mindy 233, Mitzi 233, Patricia Mayer 233

Millington, Elizabeth 95

Mills, Debra JoRene 240, Sallie Griffin 159

Mims, Sarah 97

Mings, Jesse Daniel 109, John Wesley 98, Sarah 98, 109, 110

Mirach, John 132

Mistrot, Kate 119, Mabry 119

Mitcham, Annie Lou 275, Nell 219

Mitchell, A.S. 10, Almedea 219, Benjamin 96, 220, 270, Blanche Alice 160, Carlene 220, 270, 271, Carrie 219, Charlotte Carroll 115, David Gardiner 165, Dorothy Jane 278, 279, Eiland Callen 220, Elizabeth 219, Ethel Mae 219, Frances 219, Gardiner 203, Grace Lee Martin 219, Henry E. 279, Hulda Elizabeth 219, 272, Jack P. 115, James 219, Jeremy 159, Jesse 219, Joel Dickson 247, John 219, 272, Joy Ellis 65, 143, Laura 201, Lela Belle 247, Linda Kaye 279, Martha A. 219, Mary 219, 272, Mary Anna 219, Mary Caroline 96, 220, 270, Mary Ella 119, Mary Ethel 219, Mary Evelyn Martin 165, 207, 219, Mary Hollan 239, Nancy Karen 219, Nat 159, Nell Mitcham 219, O. Clayton 143, Pleas J. 219, Raven 159, Reagan 159, Rebecca 219, Ronald Hall 165, 219, Sarah 219, Sarah Jane 233, Susan Ellen 219, Susan Jane 219, 272, Teresa 115, Terry Jane 279, Thomas W. 152, Vandorah Dean 152, Walter 219, William Augustus 239, William Gardiner, Willis Wilson 219, Zack Fall 165, 219

Mix, Tom 38

Mizell, Chloe 96

Mizer, Ashley Gail 234, Barbara Gail 234, Stephen Charles 234, Stephen Jack 234, Whitney Phillips 234

Mobberly, Ida Bell 138, Mary Noel 104, Sam 10, 23, 37

Mobbs, Bernard Eugene 272, Grady Gene Eugene 272,

Larry Glenn 272, Lottie Bell 272, Peggy Jean 272

Mobley, Geraldine Geneva 178, Lucy C. 20, Melanie Marie 184

Moeschle, Cecile 119

Moffett, Beckey 205

Mohon, Maxine 216

Moland, Henry 202

Moncrief, W.A. 29

Mondrik, Dana Bass 102, Frank V. 102

Monigold, Frances 101

Monroe, Elliott 110, Thomas J. 50

Monsour, Alyce 266, Fred 266, Garland 266, Gayle 266

Montgomery, Andrew 147, Malinda Jane Fisher 147, Mark 167, Matthew 167

Moody, Andrew Alan 184, Dana Lea Ingram 184, Gladys Opal 213

Moomau, James Barnhill 260, Jenna 260, Joyce Studt 260

Moore, Ann Holloway 218, Bennie 119, Bonnie 202, Brad 218, Brenda 221, Bridget 119, Calvin 220, Carol 213, Charles 220, 221, Danielle 221, David 221, Dixie 220, 221, Dorothy Fae 221, Doug 218, Elizabeth 218, Emmit 220, Ethel 220, Evie Leona 220, Fern Paul 221, Frances 220, Francis Lummus 220, G.W. 8, George Emmit 220, George Washington 220, Gilbert J. 218, Hal 226, Ivy Myrtle 126, James 163, 220, 221, James Kenneth 221, James Melton 221, James Patrick 220, James Warren 221, James Washington 221, James Winford 221, Jeremiah 206, 228, Jerrilyn 221, Jerry 221, Joe 221, John 246, 262, John Temple 262, Johnny 220, Josphine 220, Joyce 221, Julia 206, 220, 228, Kathleen Jones 64, Landon 218, Linnie 195, Louise 262, Lucille Elizabeth 163, Margaret 214, 220, Mary 220, Mary Elizabeth 262, Mary Ethel 221, Mary Frances 221, Nettie 220, Nina Bryant 163, Obra Jesuit 31, Opal 221, Pat 221, Pearl Florence 64, Portia 119, Rachel 113, Ray 221, Robert 220, 221, Sam Houston 220, Sarah 220, Susannah 206, 228, Thomas 220, 221, Thomson 220, Timothy 221, Vannie 221, Vickie 221, William 220, 221

Moorman, Lottie Mae 217, Polly Miller 147

Morgan 90, 133, 255, Adiline 234, Albert 187, Carrie Ellen 234, Daniel McCowan 234, Eleanor 187, Elizabeth 84, Emma Bell 251, 252, Fannie Mae 64, Florrie 234,

George 187, Gertie 25, 54, Isaac 187, Jessie Lillian 186, John 234, John Monroe 171, Knox 234, Lawrence 25, 54, Lola Mae 268, Loufreshie 234, Louis 125, Margaret 234, Mary Ann 84, Mary J. 234, Mary Maude 64, Nancy Luella 171, Nellie Auten 187, Norcie 276, Richard 84, Sabrina 167, Wendel 234

Morley, Essie Foirriestier 150, Hugh 150

Morning, Jasper 25, 54

Morris, Alice 136, Anna 221, Daisy Mildred 221, Daniel Boone 104, 105, Gene 248, Ghenie Wilburn 248, Judy 55, 146, Margaret 105, Mary Emily 104, 105, Minnie 104, 105, 223, Mollie 207, Molly 150, Nancy Lynn 248, Nancy S. 248, Ralph Curtis 221, Ralph Curtis, Jr. 221, Rosalynn 248, Rosemary 221, Sarah Virginia 265, Wade 221, Wil 248, William Rankin 265

Morrison 190, J.J. 45, Lewis 48, Mary 171

Morrow, Ada 222, Arch 222, Cecil 222, Elizabeth 214, Faye 222, Florence 222, George 222, Gertrude 222, Gladys 222, Harold Edward 193, Henry 222, Inez 222, Irene 222, James 222, Johnnie 222, Julia Ann Gertrude Lee 222, Lee 222, Louise 222, Mary Lou 222, Mattie Goldie 222, Minnie 222, Robbie 222, Robert 222, Ronnie 222, Shirley 193, Steven Edward 193, Vonda Lee 193, William 222, Willie 222, Zelpher 222

Morse 154, 191, Jane Rogers 153, Kendall Q. 153, Mary Elizabeth 153, Sarah Dixie 153

Morton, Abraham 222, Annie Lou Lorena 222, Annie May 222, Azuba 222, Benjamin 222, Bonnie Bernice 222, Clark 222, Delilah 222, Dimple Marjorie 223, Dorothy Marie 223, Ebenezer 222, Elizabeth 222, Ennis Melton 223, Eunice 222, Evelyn 126, Flora Lillian 222, 223, 252, 253, Frank P. 222, George 222, Gracie Beatrice 222, Hannah 222, James 222, John 222, John Luke 222, John William 222, Jonathan 222, Joseph 222, Josephine Evelyn 223, Laura E. 222, Leila 222, Lenora Bell 222, Lou Kinney 222, Lou Treacy 222, Louisa 222, Maggy 222, Mary 222, Metta 222, Nolly 222, Phoebe 222, Phoebe Lang-ford 222, Richard 222, Robert Solomon 222, Roy William 222, Ruth Edwards

222, Salina Hicks 222, Sally 222, Sammy 222, Sarah 222, Thomas 222, Virginia Adele 222, William 222, William Arthur 222, 238, Woodrow Wilson 223

Moseley, Amos 206, Anna 132, Arcenith Rodgers 206, Jesse 206, Julia 256, Laurina Phillips 235, Lavinia 235, 251, 287, Mary 205, 206, Mason 235, 251, H.G. 142

Mosely-Snoddy, Julia 255

Moses, M.E. 146, 221

Mosley, Fannie 264, Harold 150, Mase 49

Moss, Harriet 180, Ira E. 40, Nellie Angie 138

Motley 180, Lee Ann Myers 257

Mott, Abby 176, Monica 176, Olivia 176

Mottley, Ruth McWhorter 214

Mount, Helen Jean 197

Mouser, Easther Arlene 201

Muckleroy 29, Louis K. 41

Mueller 218

Mullens, Martha Etta 272

Mullins, Priscilla 83, W.H. 141

Munden, Georgia Person 233, Gertrude Person 233, Harry 233, Jose 233

Munford, Barbara Brown 228, Robert 228

Muray, George Ernest 252

Murchison, Anna Elizabeth 100

Murdoch, Mary 60

Murdock, Mary 176

Murphy, Ann Louise 167, David 167, Ertis 255, Joe Don 255, Karen Anette 255, Katherine 167, M.A. 121, Marilah Francis 121, Mary Francis 121, Warren 167, William 121

Murray, Arthur McKinley 252, Harrison Cornelius 252, Jewell Cornelius 252, Lena 252, Mary Nola 252, Ollie Riley 252, Pearl Birdie 252, Violet Katherine 252

Murrell, Agnes Kay Caraway 194, George W. 10, Grant 194, Laura Kay 194

Murry, Samatha Jane Odom 229, Thaxton 229

Muse, Eleanor 66

Muston, Helen 223, Robert Nelson 223, Sara 223

Myers, Annie 40, Beatrice 40, Lee Ann 257, Mary Augusta 185, W.D. 37

N

Nabors, Clara 101, Emogene 61

Nader, Martha DeLeice 223, Matilda Asaff 223, Peggy Hunt 223, Ron 223, Tom 223

Naifeh, Mose Andrew 265, Selma 265

Nalley, Betty 204, Jonathan 204, Kevin 204, Leisa 204

Narramore, Ludie Blanche 135

Nash, Sarah 138

Navy, Mary Elizabeth 262

Neal, Daniel 134, Garrett 134, Kelsea 134, Lauren 134, Myrtie 136

Nealy, Kathryn 88

Neeley, Mary Ada 167

Nefus, Glenn 49

Neighbors, Margaret Renfro 105, Mary Emily 104, 105, Thomas 105

Neilson, Shirley Potz 172

Nelms, Abner Carroll 223, Annie Lou 105, 263, Annie Lou Brown 45, 223, 224, Armintia Minervia Rhodes 223, Barbara Ann 224, Billie Faye Ridings 224, Bobby Joe 263, Calvin J. 223, 224, Carl Theron 263, Carmen Estella Shott 224, Dewey Mark 224, Francis Miller 224, Gloria Juanita 263, Jerry Ann Davis 224, Jill Dollison 224, Joyce Ann 224, Leon Dow 224, Lovisie 224, Madeline Annie 45, 223, 224, 263, Mandy Lea Fredrick 224, Marcus 45, 223, 224, Marguerite Ellen 45, 223, 224, Naomi Ruth 223, 224, Pamela 224, Randall Lee 224, Richard Wayne 224, Ronald Calvin 224, Sandra Lea 224, Tom 224, Walter Leon 224, Walter Orvil 224, William Arthur 223, 224, William Carroll 223, William Mark 45, 105, 223, 224, 263, William Randolph 223

Nelson, Bobbye 255, Christine 190, Daisy Dean Smith 235, Joseph Franklin 235, Marie Dees 235, Orlando Burl 235, Tom 61

Nemec, Cezanne 120, Chad 120, Chili 120, Cinnamon 120, Colista 120

Neu, Brian Andrew 232, Christopher Thomas 232, Leo Thomas III 232, Michelle Ann 232, Rose Ann Boone 232

Neundorfer, O.J. 199, Ruth 199

Nevels, Angela 225, 287, Doris Viola Edington 224, Gloria Marceal 225, Martin Simeon 224, Patricia 225, 287, Travis 224, 225, 287 Travis III 225, 287

Nevill, Edith Robinson 103, 151, Les 151

Neville, Ruthene Samuel 229

Newman, Angela 120, Anna Lee 257, Katie 120, Mike 120, Nettie Louise 197, Sylvia 120

Newsom, J.W. 24, 26, Olive 24, 26

Newton, Charles 180, 273, Emma Eliza Dean 180, John Bishop 180, Julia 273, Mary Virginia Boom 180

Nicholas, Angela 225, 287

Nichols, Ann 147, Christopher Jared 200, 225, Debbie Sullivan 200, 225, Flayle 225,

Ivey Jewel Clark 225, James Garland 200, 225, James Garland, Jr. 200, 225, James Michael 200, 225, Jon Mark 200, 225, Kevin Scot 200, 225, Lanyta Dianne 200, 225, Lela Lois League 225, Linda F. Evans 200, 225, Nancy Hatcher 225, Rebecca Bowden 200, 225, Richard F. 45, Robert Benjamin Hamilton 225, Samuel John Wesley McCook 225, Sarah E. Hatcher 225, Thomas Cecil 200, 225

Nicholson, Daisy Bell 180, Dana Clare 226, Dora 226, Edna Ann Hughey 180, Edward 226, Ethel Cliff Jarrett 226, Ethel Frances 226, James Brack 180, John Walter 226, John Wesley 226, Margaret A. 226, Mary Virginia 226, Missouri Harris 226, Norma 180, Ruth L. 226, Walter Reuben 226, 231, Walter Ronald 226

Niehus, Donna 85, 189, 226, Joe Lawrence 189, 226, Judy 226, Karlie 85, 189, 226, Katie 85, 189, 226, Larry 226

Nimtz, Harry 41

Nite, Bill 29, 178, Jim 29, 177, 178

Nixon, Richard M. 69

Noble, Elma Jean 170, Michael Scott 97, Paxton 97

Noland 179

Nolen, Juanita Alice 252

Noon, Alice 226, Elmer 226, Janice Holley Stone 226, Joel Wayne 227, Patrick Paul 226, Rylee Mackenzie 227, Susan Renee Wallace 227

Norman, E.D. 45, Jessie 50, 227, Lena Mae 257, McKinley 227, Melanie Ruth 227, Paul Jackson 227, Wayman 50, 88, 227

Norris, Ann 147, Charlotte 179

Northcutt 69, Bernice 64, Bertha Fisher 227, Dolly 64, 227, 228, Eda Mauthe 227, 228, Emma 64, 228, Erminie 64, Flossie 228, Gordon 227, Iba 228, 261, Ida 64, Jere E. 228, Jessie Vada 228, John Thomas 228, Josephine 64, 116, Julia Ann Moore 206, 228, LeGrand 228, Leon 227, 228, Sarah 121, 206, 228, W.D. 113, W.D., Jr. 60, 116, W.D., III 163, W.G. 261, William Davis 227, 228, William Davis, Jr. 228, William Fisher 227, William George 10, 206, 228

Northen, Mary Alice 213

Norton, H.W. 31, Lucille 91, Lynne Smith 64

Norvell, Robbie Lynn Smith 252

Norwood, Bonnie 99, John 99, Martha 262, W.H. 262

Null, Audie Imogene 101, 102, Emma Ora Carroll 101, G. Cleveland 101

Numsen, A.C. 247, 253, Mary Louise 247, Lou Sandifer 253

Nunn, Richard 224, Sandra Lea Nelms 224

Nunnally, Dorothy Stephens 228, John Henry 228, Nancy Teresa 228, Randall Jay 228

Nusbaum, Mildred 195

O

Oanschow 40

Oates, Mary 200, 225

Oberg, Susan 85

Obermeyer, Alex 139, Austin 139, Stacia 139

Obethier, F.D. 93, Josie B. Barton 93

O'Brian, Sarah Roxanne Patterson 205

O'Bryan, Andrew Franklin 10

Oden, Caroline Elizabeth 208, Jimmy 261, Madison Lee 113, 208, Martha 167, Martin Blair 113, 208, Nina 261

Odom, Ada Williams 228, Arenva Leslie 228, Arron 228, 229, Audry Arenva 229, Beatrice 229, Charlie 228, 229, Dixie 228, Edgar 228, Frank 229, Henry 228, Jimmie Oree 229, John 228, Johnny Edward 229, Kyle Bryan 228, Marie 229, Martha Waldrop 228, Marylyn 229, Maxine 229, Moses 228, Nannie 228, Nash 150, 229, Richard Cole 229, Ruby Foirriestier 150, 229, Samatha Jane 229, Sarah Wolf Bryan 228, Shirley 229, Terrell Jack 229, Thomas G. 228, Thomas Henry 229, William 228, Willie 229

Ogilvie, Lavonia Edna Fisher 261, N.C. 13, Nina 261, Norman 261

Ogletree, Absolom 258, Edward Eugene 258, Edward Eugene Sr. 258, Flora Terrell 258, John Franklin 258, John Sr. 258, William 258

Ogungbade, Annie Landreth Jones 229, Ladipo A. 229

Oldham, Virginia 255

Olejnik, Daniel 150, Jacob 150, Linda Fournet 150, Mark 150

Oliver, Ruth Edward 199

Olivier 161

Olson, Kenneth 195, Marjorie 195, Mildred Nusbaum 195, Tammie Lynn 284

O'Neal, William Daniel 46

O'Neil, Sally 84, Shane 287

Oney, Thelma 261

Orendorff, Charles William 176, Donald Ray 176, Eloise 176, Geraldine 175, Gladys Bertha (Kerr) 176, James Weldon 176, Larry Gene 176, Lena 176, Lillian 176, Ray Cooper 176, Waynell 176

Orgeron, Don 63

Ormuz, Brandon 108, Bronco 108, Tammy Burt 108

Orr, Laura Gentry 272, Mary E. 206, O.W. 214

Osburn, Minnie Bell 89

Osteen, Elizabeth 233

O'Toole, Anna Dearker 220, Margaret 220, Patrick 220

Ott, William 255

Ottman, Wilma 276

Ouzts, Samuel 82, Virginia 82

Overton, Emma 103

Owens, Debra 41, J.P. 172, Lennie Avery 88, Wanda 179, Willie Cumi Henderson 172

P

Pace, Henry 25, 54

Pace, Marshall 25, 54

Packer, Catherine Elizabeth 175

Paderewski, Ignace 270

Paganini 113

Page 279, Georgia Zenobia 280, John 11, Lias Eitt 280

Paillett, Roseanna 138

Palmer, Luther C. 229, Stella Maud Wood Clark 229

Pardue, Nancy 182

Park, Ann Curry 230, Brenda 230, Carol Clymore 230, David 230, F.D.G. 229, Fabia Brame 230, Jerald Gomer 230, Kristi 230, Mary Bell Blackard 229, Mary Eleanor 136, 230, Samuel Jackson 230, Samuel S. 229, Shara 230, Tom 230, Tracey 230, William Thomas 230, Wilna Massey 229

Parker, Beatrice Southern 121, Cynthia Ann 258, Daniel 258, Elder John 258, Florence 202, Karen Lile 213, Mary Maude Morgan 64, Sara Ann 217, Silas 258, Susannah 258, Syril A. 249

Parkers, Isaac 258

Parmer 97

Parpal, Della 245

Parr, Erastus 195, Sarah Browning 195

Parrish, Chellie 79, Sylvia 183, Virginia 136

Parrott, Eliza F. 245, William 245

Parsons, Eva Elizabeth 209, 218

Pate, Aubrey 49, Norma 49, Pauline 123

Paterson, Mary Wood 112

Patillo, Almarine 230, Ardelia Sowells 230, Brenda Daniels 230, Daneshia 230, Danielle 230, Dorothy 230, Ed 230, Erica 230, Joe Anderson 230, Joe Davis 230, John 230, Johnnie Lawrence 230, Johnny Lawrence 230, Joseph 230, Margaret 230, Octavia McEntire 230, Reba King 230

Patrick, Elbert Vinson 230, Linda Rae 231, Mary Maxine 272, Minnie Findley 230, Virginia Bell 258

Patten, Helen 161

Patterson, Burke 253, Clara Hurst 181, 182, 231, 253, Eliza Jane 237, Grace Hurst 181, 182, Julianne 181, 182, Laura Gayle Harvey 181,

182, Letitia 205, Mary-Margaret 181, 182, Russell D. 230, Sarah Jane 237, Sarah Roxanne 205, William 205, 231, William Burke 181, 182, 253, William Burke, Jr. 181, 182, William Payne 181, 182

Patton, David V. 52, Mary 244, Rebecca 243

Paul, Aaron 222, Anna Maria Snyder 222, Fern 221, 222, Gertrude Morrow 222, John 222, Terry 222, William 222

Paxton, Eloise 139, Rebecca 138, William Edwards 138

Payne 90, Ann Bridges 231, Austin Mitchell 231, Betty Jean Bond Womack 134, Charlotte Elizabeth 113, 208, Clara 182, 231, 253, Claudie 266, Debra Boswell 231, Donna 231, James Alan 231, Katherine Ann 231, Lee Bridges 231, Lee Francis 231, Michael Alan 231, Pam Terry 231, Peggy Elaine 134, Robert Daniel 134, Timothy Andrew 231, Vesta Evelyn Irons 231, Walton H., Sr. 180, William B. 8, 181, 182, 231, 253, William Brant III 231, William Brant, Jr. 231, William Collin 231, William Crogan 231

Peace, Alice Corene Meadows 216, John Wesley 216, Lilla 255

Peals, Lenora 129

Pearce 255, Bill 191, David Fritz 190, Florence Elizabeth Truelove 190, Jim 191, Martha 190, 191, Pat 191

Pearl, Minnie 123

Pearson, Sarah Elizabeth 78, 80

Peck, Elizabeth Dodson 36, Franklin 36, Sharlie 36

Peebles, David 199

Peed, Bill 287

Peeler, Susan 256

Pegues, Dock 177, Emma Overton 103, Ione Perry 103, J. Garland 72, 253, Lela Frances 247, O.H. 12, Oliver 177, 211, Oliver Hazard, Jr. 103, P.A. 247

Pelphrey, Lasco Wheeler 20, 231, 232, 233, Mary Alice Wheeler 233, Nauty Byrd 231, 232, 233, Nauty Byrd Wornel 231, 232, 233, Rosemarie 231, 232, Samuel 233, Wanda Minnette 155, 156, 231, 232, William 232

Pemberton 158, John Smith 68

Pender, H.B. 49

Pendleton 214

Penn, Nancy 275, William 199

Pennick, Annie 157, 245, Thomas H. 157, 245

Pennington, Rhoda 235

Penny, Morris M. 80

Percy, Thomas 245

Perdue, Connie Wallace 160

Perkins 150, Alice 148, Eveylyn Anderson 134, Gregory 264, James 272, John 148, John Cameron 134, Melanie Jeanne 134, Patricia Rose 272, Ronald Tracy 272, Susan Glover 148, Tillman 159, Winona Banks 66

Perreau, Margaret 217

Perry, Artelia 283, Betty 52, Chris 167, Gina Cornelius 167, Green 144, 285, Green P. 10, Laurie 261, Matthew Bradford 261, Medora 285, Medora Womack 144, Richard 52, Sarah Elise 261

Person, Alice Fisher 233, Cassie 233, Emma 233, Fannie Hill 233, Frank Clark 233, Georgia 233, Gertrude 233, James Sydney 233, John J. 233, Joseph Crow 233, Louis 233, Mattie 233, Nancy Ellen Fulgham 233

Peters, Aaron 254, Hannah 254, Kenney 254, Lance Bailey 254, Molly 254, Sharon 254

Peterson, Betty 51, Catherine 256, Gabriel 115, Harvey Heth 115, Margaret Charlotte 115, Mary Evelyn 200

Petro, Brenda 78, 162, Jason Michael Charles 162, Kealie Amera 162, Kenneth 162, Laura Fink 162, Robbie Adrian 162

Petty, Charles 51, Elisha 89, Evelyn 186, Fannie Lucindy 89, 212, Gene 50, Jane Birdwell 89

Peurifoy 45

Peyton, C.F. 249, Effie Kate 249

Pharris, Charlotte Jane Lindsey 187, Nancy Ann 187, Sydney 187

Phelps, Gennifer Patricia Baggett 90, John 90, Josiah Barron Glardon Nelson 90, Lynette Faye 168, Sarah 132, Tricia Baggett 90

Philips, Lavon Inez Phillips 234, Susan Scarle 234, Verne Douglas 234, Vincent Darby 234

Phillips 255, Aldon 45, Alfred Mason 49, 234, Alpha 250, 266, Augusta Stevenson 85, 233, 235, Azor Holbert 234, B.F. 10, B.F., Sr. 128, Barbara Gail 234, Barbara Gene Wampler 234, Ben 251, Benjamin Franklin 250, Berthal Frances 250, Bobby Joe 234, Bonnie Mae 233, Carrie Ellen Morgan 234, Daisy Dean Smith 233, 235, Dan 285, David 250, Dillard J. 233, Edward Wesley 277, Eliza Jane Simms 235, Elizabeth 132, 133, 234, 235, 250, Ellen 234, Elsie Gilmer 235, Ethel Eliza 235, Eula Jane 250, Ezra 234, 235, Faye Foster 234, Flora Almeda 250, Floyd 85, 233, 235, Floye Anne 234, Francye 285, George 132, 234, 287, Glenn 125, Helen Johnson 234, Helen Little 234, Inez Elizabeth Scarborough 234, Jack 251, Jack Loyce 234, 235, James A. 235, Jewel 49, 250, Joseph Marion 233, 235, Laurina 235, Lavon Inez 234, Lillie Gertrude 235, Loyce 234, Lucy Bell 250, Mariah 235, Martha Jane 250, Mary 96, 251, 253, Mary E. Blakeley 250, Mary Elizabeth Holbert 234, Mary Jane 132, 235, 287, Mary Palistine 110, Mary Pearl 250, Mary Pelina 266, Mary 132, 234, 235, 287, Mason 133, Mattye Lea 250, Medea Ann 235, Milley 235, Minnie Mae 277, Nancy Jane 234, Nina Kathleen 250, Oma Lee 235, Rubye Evelyn 233, 235, Sallie Viola 250, Shannon Maledon 285, Sybil Edna 233, Wanda Jean 85, 234, William 132, 234, 251, 266, 287, William Riley 277

Pickens, Andrew 167, Jaclyn Gail 234, Mary 167, Rebecca Calhoun 167

Pickett, Betty 201, Brenda Fulton 201, Easther Arlene Mouser 201, Eugene 201, Irene 201, James 201, Jo Ann 201, Joseph Preston 201, Mamie Stone 201, Mary Beaulah Hampton 201, Mearl A. 201, Robert 201, Ronnie 201, Ross 201, Syble 201, Winford 201

Pieratt, Doris 271, Jonathan Thomas 271, Karen Denise 98, 271, Kelly 271

Pierce 153, 191, Carolyn 169, Cecil Ann 267, Don 169, Elizabeth 154, Elmira 44, 116, Frank 263, George 154, Helen Haynes 169, Hugh 154, John 106, Lena Mae 152, Martha Jerusha Terry 263, Ray 267, Roy L. 169, Sophia 154

Pike, Tempie Green 157

Pillsbury, Timothy 193

Pilsbury 137

Pinkerton, Ali 161, Aliceson Wallace 161, Jeffrey 161, John 161, Mary Anne 111, Reed 161

Pirkey, Russell Johnson 43

Pirtle, Calab III 177

Pitcock, Eleanor Hall 123, Gladys Edith Coupland 123, James Douglas 123, James Douglas, Jr. 123, Martha 12, Patricia 123

Pitts, Kris 162, Syble 267

Plaster, Angela 161, Brandon 161, Camron 161, Debby Jane Grubbs 161, James 161, Lindsey 161, Tyler 161

Pliler, Annie D. 284, 236, 101, Charlie 236, Conrad Russell 236, Conrad, Sr. 236, Doris

Henri 236, Emanuel 236, Emma Virginia Harris 167, 236, Fred M. 101, 236, 284, George Merriweather 236, Margie Mittie Hayes 236, Marion Emanuel 236, Mary Allen Williams 236, Robert Russell 236, Russ 167, 284, Virginia Ann 101, 236, Wiley 236

Plummer, C.E. 25, Linda Rae Patrick 231, Patricia Rae 231, Rachel 258, Sherry Kay 231

Plyler, Dee 133

Poe, John T. 10, Minnie 32

Poesy, Charles 40, William B. 40

Poland, Sarah 85, 226

Polk, James K. 256, Mamie Frances 238

Pollard, Ann 283

Pollock, Charlotte Jane 112

Polser, Francis W. 128, Mariah Malone 128

Pond, Dora Georgia 85

Ponder, Emma Person 233, Frank 280, Georgia Zenobia 280, Henry 233, "Nobie" 279

Poole, Brenda 201, Eliza Tines 206, Eugenia Althea 206, Mamie Avery 88, Merry Sedley 206, Nancy Jane Kimberling 206, Robert 206

Pope, Gene Paul, Jr. 97, Henry 223, Jane E. 91, Melissa Janelle Boles 97, Rogers 74, Rogers, Jr. 74

Porter 213, Elmer 170, Jonnie 83, Martha Ann 237, Rebecca 97

Posey, Pam 228, William 41

Post, Gladys Murlean 283, Michael 283

Posten 214

Poston 214, Mary 216, Sally 174

Potter, John 113, Tom 246

Potts, Billie 247, Laura Fay 81

Potz, Shirley 172

Pouncy, Lenora Lockett 201, Medea Ann Phillips 235, Peter 235

Pounders, Alice Gertrude 277, C.W. 48, Corrie 277

Powdrill, Brent 96, 110, Hillary 96, 110, Jeff 110, Jeffery 96, Robert 96, 110, Terri Lynn Snider 96, 110

Powell, Ben 202l, Earl 50, Emma 202, Mattie 266, Ruth 157, Timothy 266

Powers, Bertha Mifflin 187, Chelsea Ann 257, Clifton Shelby 257, Freida 187, George Washington 187, Grant Michael 257, Luther Jesse 187, Nancy Ann Pharris 187, Shannon Kay Whatley 257

Prall, Clyde 69

Prater, Martha B. 220

Pratt, Olga 272

Pray, Jimmie Ira 263, Willie May 263

Prescott, F.W. 68

Presly, Dana Jo 287

Pressley, Maude 252, Sarah C. Smith 252, Thomas G. 252

Price, William 263, America 263, Cynthia Diane 278, Denise 119, James 263, Jasper 263, Martha 84, 263, Mary 263, Mary Catherine 109, Meredith 263, Parrelee 263, Pernicia 263, Richard 262, 263, Roy 278, Sarah Elizabeth 262, 263, Sterling 263

Prichard, Amy 271, Charles H. 271, Doris 271

Prickett, Nellie Mae 163

Prince, Kevin 45, Wayne 63

Prior, Janie Ethel 213

Pritchard, Amy Beth 98

Proctor, Ethel Moore 48, Preston 186

Propes, Charlie Joe 248, Geraldine 248, Gindy 195, Michael David 248, Tere Lee 248, Joe Pat 248, Timothy Lynn 248

Protho, E.B. 228, Jessie Northcutt 228

Prothro, George E. 129, Jessie Mae 64

Pruett, Aaron Clinton 131, James Clinton 131, Lanna Rosalin Davis 131

Puhl, Carolina Ludmilla 252, Mary Ann 252, Rudolph William 252

Pumphrey, Mavis Lucille 239

Pursell, Marvin 274

Puthuff, A.E. 43

Pyburn, Delilah 84

Pyeatt, Joseph Ewing 253, Joyce Kathryn 253, Willie Mae McLendon 253

Q

Quarles, Mary Virginia 268

Quinn, Arthur 217, Bobby Joe 217, Grace Lynn 217, Marion 217, Martha Delila 282, Pauline 217, Stella Mae Meadows 217, William Houston 282

R

Rabalais, Darrell 279, Grant 279, Linda 279, Maggie Jane 279

Raby, Louise 138

Rachael Garner 7

Rader, Betty 73, Charles 73, LeRoy 73, Lynn 73

Raines, C.W. 174

Rains, Elizabeth Jackson 26, James Jackson 263, Martha Jane 263

Ralston, Arphie Agee 80

Rambo, Billierae 166, Joanne 155, 166

Ramey, Janice Louise 257, Jean 167

Randall, Martha Ellen 264, Russell 264

Rathburn, Eva Lorene 103

Rathert, Mel 70

Ratliff, Aris Deney McIntyre 236, Benjamin Alan 237,

Bessie 237, Dewey 236, Elnora 237, Emily Martin 237, Emma Lee Martin 207, 237, Gary Wayne 207, 237, Gaynell 237, Ima Lee 237, Jacob Anderson 237, Jonita Franks 237, Jordan Michael 237, Lorenza 236, Lorissa McIntyre 237, Mary Schwalbe 237, Ora Beatrice Martin 236, Oscar 236, Shirley Maudine 237, Vernon Alan 207, 237, Vernon L. 207, 237

Rawls, Josie 104

Ray 49, 122, Alice 242, Andrew Cannon 237, Annie Lou 161, Anthony Tucker 190, Earline 117, Elizabeth 206, Elizabeth Ann Roper 121, Frank 242, Gabriel 222, Gerald 117, Grace 237, H. Grady 237, Helen 180, 237, James 237, 242, Juliana 195, L.C. 180, Leonard Phouts 237, Linda Sue 180, 181, 182, Lou Treacy 222, Mary Elizabeth 121, 206, Mary Frances Strong 237, Mary 237, Mary Wilmoth Athon 237, Michael Crow 126, Myra Lynn 242, Treacy Bateman 222, William 121, 206, 237, Willie 84, Windford 104

Ream, Christi Boswell 102, Emma 102, Grayson 102, Michael 102

Reaney, Lucile Irene 266

Reasonova, Benson 176, Margaret Ann Euphemia 176

Rebouche, Laura Monique Dozier 136, Tim 136

Rector, Mable 92, Nannie 279

Reddick, William 8

Redding, Mavilene 182

Redford 109

Reed, Alcey Elizabeth 237, Alfred 237, Alice 170, Amanda 237, Andrew 237, Andrew Jackson 237, Andrew Jackson, Jr. 237, Bell 237, Betsy Lane 237, Clayborn 237, Claybourne 237, Clayton Clayborne 237, Cynthia 237, Daniel David 237, Eliza Jane Patterson 237, Elizabeth 237, Ellen 237, Emily 237, General Gano 237, Isaac Kansas 237, James Madison 237, John A. 237, John N. 237, Josephine 237, Joshua 237, Judith Silver 237, Laura 85, Malinda Elizabeth Coats 237, Malinda Evelyn 237, Malinda Lucinda 237, Manuel Thomas 237, Margaret Catherine 237, Mary Ann 237, Mary M. Callihan 238, Nancy Walker 222, 238, Patsy 237, Pauline Mae 167, 168, Robert 237, Samuel Dill 237, Sarah Jane Patterson 237, Sarah Priscilla 238, Solomon 222, 237, 238, Sophia Ellen McNew 237, Virginia Adele 222, 237, 238,

William 237, William III 237, William, Jr. 237, William Martin 237, William, Sr. 237, Wilson Carol 237

Reeh, Daryl 238, Dorothy 238, Douglas 238, Florence 238, Frances 238, Galen 238, Karl August 238, Karl Joseph 238, Kathlyn 238, Kathy 238, Mamie Frances Polk 238, Rebecca 238, Thomas 238

Reel, Janie Ethel Prior 213, Juddie Annelle 213, William Henry 213

Rees, Mamie E. 212

Reese, Amanda 132, 272, Franklin McClure 109, John 132, Nellie Milam Butts 109, Sarah Phelps 132, Tessie 196, Thelma 202

Reetz, Rudolph 120

Refugio, Alfugia Cucca 159

Reid, Margery 102

Reinhart, Georgia Ethel 282, Lee 282

Reis, Suzanne Marie 277

Rell, Henry 132

Rembert, F.T. 144, 215, 217, Frank 142, 167, 286, Kate 144, 167, 286

Remmick, Bonnie Lee 252, 253

Renfro, James, Jr. 45, Margaret 105

Rester, Nannie 280

Retort, Joyce 110, 111, 157, Louie 110, 157, Mary 110, 157, Mary Lou 111, Roxanne 111

Reyburn, Mary Blanton Fisher 147, W.W. 147

Reynolds, Allie Blake 231, Anna Golightly 140, Bill 238, Billie Anne 140, Clarissa Anne Lambert 140, Daisy Darnell 238, Dennis Wells 140, Dennis Wells II 140, Dock 238, Don 209, Elizabeth 140, 238, Emily Ann Harville 231, Forrest 238, Frankie Lee Richardson 209, Franklyn Lenora 285, Gary 231, Harmon 238, Henry Clay 209, Henry S. 282, Hez Bussie 238, Hughleen 238, Irene 238, James Madison 140, John Franklin 10, Lenord 238, Marlene 239, Mary Elizabeth 171, Ruby Ozzelle 282, 283, Samuel Ervin 140, Sybil Mathis 209

Rhinehart 279

Rhodes, Adeline 174, Armintia Minervia 223, Jennie Green 157, Juanita 157, Lydia Bowlin 157, Mary Jane 229, Mattie Lee 196, Murle Phillips 277, Roxie Ray 142, William Thomas 157

Rhodes-Johnson, Cheryl 255

Rhodes-Sanders, Dillie 255

Rice, Bill 161, Joe A. 41, Tammy Kay Grubbs 161

Richard 40

Richards, Carol Daniels 239, David 239, David Eugene 239, David Marr 239, Dor-

othy Bearce 210, Golda 239, Hanna Fletcher 239, Holland 239, Jacob 239, John 239, Laura 240, Louisa Christina 239, Mary 239, Mary Hollan Mitchell Stephens 239, Mavis Lucille Pumphrey 239, Noah 239, Otho Elba 239, Patricia Arlee Bush 240, Rachel 239, Ralph Wayne 239, Randy 240, Sam 239, Ulan G. 239, William 239, Zula Marie 239

Richardson 279, Ada Louise Dunnavant 240, Bernice Rebecca 280, Bobby Gene 240, Carol Diane 240, Clarence 61, Debra JoRene 240, Douglas Lafayette 240, Douglas Laverne, Jr. 240, Fannie L. Griffin 160, Frances Virginia 280, Frankie Lee 209, George Washington 132, Goin B. 280, Goin C. 21, Jefferson Davis 240, Jessie Elree Faulk 146, John 280, John L. 160, Lewis Hamilton 280, Louis 194, Margaret Ada Davis 132, Norma Jean Bowlin 240, Rebecca Jane 280, Sallie Elizabeth Amos 240, Sunni Michelle 240, Sybil Loraine 240, Vickie 278, Winnie Toy Faulk 146, 240

Richburg, Laura Ann 184

Riche, Emme 269

Richkie, Louis 240, Mary 240, Nellie Heidtman 240, Rosa 240, Sara 240

Riddell 97

Riddle 97, Jack 70

Ridings, Billie Faye 224

Ridley, Amelia 228

Riehl, Louis 147, Veronica Fisher 147

Rigby, Suzanne 182

Riggins, Frankie Parson 30, Wanda Jean 268

Rilda, Susan 160

Riles, Sarah Ann Elizer 109

Riley, Amelia Young 118, Hattie Belle 172, William 118

Ripy, Helen 214

Risinger, Andrew 49, B.F. 49, Jan 49, Mark 49

Ritter, Jane Allen 100, Melvin 100

Rivenbark, Sherie 163

Roach, Ann Abigail Garrison 256, Anna Bess 170, Belinda Arleen 213, Bessie Allene McLendon 213, Bessie Staggs 170, David Edwin 213, Debra 224, Dolly Ann 256, Eleanor Springs 256, Gregory Mark 213, James Victor, Sr. 170, Linda Elaine 213, Lisa Gayle 213, Lloyd Edwin 213, Samuel 256, Thomas 256

Roard, Reggie 63

Roark, Edith Eloise McGrede 183

Robbins, Ann Dunbar Abbot 241, Betty Joyce 241, Bever-

ly Ann McLemore 242, Dorothy Bacon 241, Dorothy Mae 242, Dorothy Mary 241, Georgia 241, Henry 241, Janna Little Boren 242, John 184, John C. 241, John C. Jr. 241, John Clinton 242, John Cyril 241, John George Clinton Sr. 241, Lila Gail 242, Mary 64, 241, Mary Lee 7, Mary Lee Donaghey 241, Mary Susan 242, Neina Mead 241, Neina Mead 64, Rebecca Lynn 242, Thomas 241

Roberson, Carol Diane Richardson 240, Thomas Rae 50

Roberts 106, Betty Hull 242, Cameron 242, Caroline 24, Claire 242, David 242, Earl Jr. 242, Earl Sr. 242, Ellen 242, George Stanton 242, 243, James 242, Jane Beebe 242, Jason 242, Joan Marbeth 243, Jonas 242, Judy Inzer 242, Marbeth 242, Margaret McDonald 117, Mary Ellen 243, Mary Margaret 242, Meredith Earl 242, Murray 242, Myra Lynn Ray 242, Nan 117, Stan 242, 243, William Perry 117, Williams 26, Wythe 242

Robertson, Louisa L. Jones 243, Cynthia Ann 246, David 267, Doss 243, Ethel Pauline 243, J.M. 44, James Clifton 243, Jessie 128, John P. 246, Julie Elizabeth Meadows 217, Karen Bolin 267, Lillian Edith Jarrell 243, Lillian Jarrelline 243, Mary Jane 276, Michael David 267, Mildred Christene 243, 260, Paralee 246, Robbie 63, Theda Lestine 243, Waddie Dolphus 217

Robins, John 241, Thomas 241, William 241

Robinson, Edith 151, Frank Mason 68, Margaret 136, Mary Mitchell 190

Robyns, Thomas 241

Rodden, Aaron Jasper 244, Nancy Ella 244, Aaron Castleberry 140, 243, 244, Aaron Jasper 141, Amelia 51, 140, 142, 243, 244, Anna Eliza 244, Bun 6, Caddie 198, Cynthia Jane Lawrence 198, Dorothy R. Holt 244, I.P. William 19, James Howard 244, John 51, 140, 141, 215, 243, 244, John David 244, John Howard 244, Joseph 244, Lawrence 198, Leona Walker 244, Lucy Henderson 244, Mary 140, 244, Nancy, Newton Wood 244, Stevanna Matlock 244, William James 198, William Jasper 244, William M. 244

Roden, Goldie Marie 234, Polly 206

Rodgers, Arcenith 206

Rodrique, Betty Jean 273, Howard 273

Roe, John G. 11

Rogers, Dewana 261, Gertrude 94, Ginger 191, Ina Killgore 214, Jacob 261, Jane 153, Jonathan 261, Mary 118, Mattie Patience 159

Rolf, Katy 83, Nellie Surat 83, Walter 83

Roosevelt, Franklin D. 37, Theodore 210, 259, 262

Roper, Ann 206, Charles, Sr. 206, Elizabeth Ann 121

Roquemore, Catherine Murphy 264, Hattie 264, James 264

Rose, Deanne Bagwell 143, Mary Deanne Bagwell 90, Peter 90

Rosemond 84

Roshto, Martha 123, Virgil 123

Ross, Eliza 201, John 201, 202, Martha 266

Rosser, John 201

Rosson, Annie Virginia 245, Della Parpal 245, Della Tigner 245, Dora 157, 245, 262, Ellen Hale 157, 245, Henry H. 245, James Madison 244, Joseph Barkley 245, Leila Nancy 245, Louises Bryant 245, Mary Elizabeth 244, 245, Mattie Ellen 245, Rebecca Jane 245, Thomas Jefferson 157, 245, Vick Wilson 245, William Henry Harrison 244

Roth, Martha Blanche Culpepper 118, 127

Rothwell, Alma 245, Billie Sue 152, 154, 245, John P. 245, John R. 245, John Samuel 245, John W. 152, 155, 245, Lillie K. Smith 245, Lucy Mae 245, Mary Susan 152, 155, 245, Randolph 245, Ruby 245, Sonora Anne White 245

Rotundo 161

Rouche, Peter 41

Rountree, Nancy 205

Rouse 49

Rowden, Mary Jane 146

Rowland, Brenda 201, Dianne 201, Gail 201, Helen Stone 201, Kenneth B. 201, Margaret 260

Rucker, Eliza 233, J.K. 233, James Howard 10, Margaret C. 160, 206

Rude, Carol 273, 274

Ruff, Martha 246, Cynthia Ann Robertson 246, Edith Wilma Johnson 246, Elizabeth 246, Glen Paxton 245, 246, Godsend 245, Harvey Paxton 245, 246, Hudson 245, Jere 246, Jon 246, Jonathan Wesley 246, Laura Evelyn Gaines 246, Mary Laura 245, 246, Nancy 5, 127, 246, Paralee Robert-son 245, 246, Sue Ann 246, William Riley 245, 246

Ruggles, Bonnie Lee Remmick 252, 253, Heath 253, Irma Valene Smith 252, 253, Joshua 253, Kemmie 253, Kim 253, Mark 253, Martha Laird 252, 253, Maury 253, Melissa 253, Morris 252, 253, Richard Donald 252, 253, Suellen Chapman 252, 253, Trace 253, Tracy 253

Rule, Effie 64, Ida 64, 249, Julia Sparke 249

Rundell, Charlotte Vesta McWhorter 216, Thomas Gardner 216

Runnels, Henry 100, Margaret Smith 100, Susan (Susannah) 100, 101

Rush, Hester 82

Rushing, Daphne 145, Diana 145, 146, Dorothy Everett 145, Elmira Jane 277, Garland S. 145

Russell, Anna 64, Annie 137, Burr Davis 137, Charles M. 241, Henry Crew 137, Mary Catherine 137, Mary Elizabeth 125, Minnie 137, Rachel 182, Vashti 96

Rutherford, Frances Melinda 277, Sarah Joyce 258

Ruthven, Dora A. Smith 246, Brian Lynn 246, Buel Charles 246, Debbie F. 246, Dora Myrtle 246, Dorothy 246, Dorothy Crowley 126, Doug, Jr. 246, Douglas John Sr. 246, Edward 246, Elaine Margaret 246, Elizabeth 246, Elwyn V. 246, Ernest 246, Florence Jarrett 246, Joseph Leland 246, Julia 246, Julius 246, Rosa 246, Stella Norton 246, Vernon 246

Ryan, Alexander Boggs 246, 247, Alexander Boggs Jr. 247, Linda Jane 247, Reva Harrison 246, 247

S

Sabin, Dona Elyse Hughes 184, Gary George 184

Sadler, Debbie 63

Sample 84

Sample(s), Martha A. 141

Samuel, Billy Ray 229, Earnest 229, Oscar, Sr. 229, Rose 229, Rozzell 229, Ruthene 229

Sanby, Ann 241

Sandau, Marcy John 91

Sandberg, Mary 63

Sandberg, Sandy 63

Sandby, William 241

Sandefur, Ann 192, Chaytor Orion 247, Emma 247, Gussie Pegues 247, Lela Belle 247, Lela Frances Pegues 247, LuRye 247, Mary Jane Mallow 247, Mary Louise 247, Mollie 247, Patrick Jackson 247, Patrick Washington 247

Sanders, Bert 255, Bert Wayne 255, Charlotte 255, Fred 255, Michael 255, Murtilda Jane 162, Sharon 255, Teen 126

Sandifer, Lou 253
Sanford, Bessie 110
Sang, James 70
Sanger, James 70, 208, Joe 69, Mamie 69, Minerva 69
Sanov, Loraine 17
Sassar, Mary Frances 221
Satterwhite, Ada L. 119, Bene 248, Benette Meadows 248, Bill 248, Bob 248, Charline 247, Geraldine 248, Isaac W. 91, Jerry Linda 247, Joan Elizabeth 248, Joe 247, Joseph A. 91, Joseph Edward, Jr. 247, Katherine 247, Lawrence Bud 247, Lawrence Edward 247, 248, Luke Wayne 247, Lula Mae 91, M.C. 119, Martha Ann Stringer 91, Mary Elizabeth Snow 91, Mary Katherine 183, Melodise 248, Michael 91, Nancy Lynn 248, Rebecca Ann 248, Robert William 248, Rosa Maud Hinkson 247, Rose Marie Bounds 248, Susan 248, Sybil 248, 250, Tawney Susan Kneese 248, Tina Colista 119, William Lynn 248, 250
Saunders, Elizabeth 147
Savabos, Marie 135
Savage 255
Sawyer, Lisa 161
Saylor, Bryan 162, Erin Nicole Leahy 162
Scarborough, Inez Elizabeth 234
Schaffer, Mollie Wayne 283, Red 229
Schardt, A.E. 190
Scherer, Dick 248, Jenny 155, 166, Omalee 248, R.L. 248
Schillings, Eric 246
Schleicher, Karl 91
Schlitz, Joseph 161
Schloer, Ruby Lena Faulk 146
Schofield, Alta Beatrice 183, Mary Ethel 183, Mary Josephine Ingram 183, William Daniel 183
Schoonover-Mizer, Thomas Sutton 234
Schrader, R.J. 198
Schroeder, Carolyn 41, Charles W. 41
Schuler, Carol Faith Finley 147, Jetre Alan 147
Schultz, Andrea 110, Marcus 110
Schwalbe, Mary 237
Scott, Anne Christian 95, Eugene 109, 152, Geneva Nell Boles 97, Izora 281, James B. 244, Jodie Lavinna Freeman 152, Mary 244, Peggy 281, Portia 119, Sallie M. Butts 109
Scurry, Susannah 206, 228
Seay, Margaret 277
Seidel, Jeffery 110, 253, Robert Joe 110, 253, Robert Joseph 96l, Robin Laney 96, 110, Thomas 253, Thomas Joe 110, Thomas Ray 96
Sellers, Cora Belle Fisher 166, Elbert 146, Emma Evadna

166, Fannie Clara Faulk 146, Isaac 166, John 146, Martha Porter 188, Marvin Bell 166
Sessums, Tommie M. Coleman 121, William Dancy 121
Setzer, Frank 181, 182, Julianne Patterson 181, 182
Sewell, Henry Levi 160, Orra A. Griffin 160
Shaddock, Elizabeth 82
Shanholtz, Caryl Susan 184
Shappell, Michael 195, Shannon 195
Sharp, Eleanor 93, Gretta Eakin 143, Scott 48
Shattuck, Andrew 261
Shaw, Alice Pauline 249, Daniel Jr. 248, Angus Gilchrist 249, Apes 249, Archibald 249, Belle 249, Buie 249, Charles S. 249, Daniel 248, 249, Dush 249, 253, Dushee 248, 249, Effie 248, 249, Effie Kate 249, Esther Louise Wadsworth 248, 249, Ida Sparks Rule 64, 249, J.R. 50, Joe 45, Julia Rule 249, Lola Caroline Tatum 249, Louise 64, Louise Durham 249, 261, Margaret A. Langhorne 249, Margaret McKay 249, Mary Catherine 249, R.O. 286, Rebecca 249, Reta Mae 286, Sally Haynes 249, Sarah Elizabeth 249
Shawn, Eddie P. 136, Linda Lee Dozier 136, Phillip Michael 136, Will Alex 136
Sheegog, Mary Carlisle 90
Shelby, Isaac 244, Lillie Iona 199
Shelton 97, Brandon Lee Ellsworth 249, Charles Reed, Jr. 249, Charles Reed Sr. 249, Charles Thomas 249, Christopher Reed 249, Deborah O'Neal Ellsworth 249, J.E. 28, Leesa Carol 249, Martha Alice 249, Martha Jeanne Whitehead 249, Mary Ellen 249, Sybil Ann 248, 249, Sybil Olivia McGown 249, William Reed 250
Shepard 97, Janet Rhea 85, Robbie Nell Johnston 85, 235, Robert R. 85, Robert Ray 85, Susan Oberg 85
Shepperd 287, Alfred E. 250, 251, Alfred Fulton 235, 250, 251, 287, Alfred L. 250, 251, Allen Martin 235, 287, Alice Jane Dickson 250, Allen Martin 251, Ben Cranfield 97, Berthal Frances Phillips 250, Charity 235, 251, 287, Daisy Dunaway 250, Dora Ella Glenn Dak 250, Eleazor 97, 251, 287, Elijah Bird 251, 287, Elijah Byrd 235, Elisha Eleazor 235, Elizabeth 97, 235, 251, 287, Ella Rebecca Mackey 250, Elvey 97, 286, 287, Elvey Anderson 97, 98, 235, 251, Elvey, Jr. 235, Florence Bell 250, Florence Elverse Hardin 250, Frank

Lewis 250, Gemmette F. 251, Ivey 250, James Norton 97, Jennifer Lynn Perdue 250, John Ben 98, 235, 250, 251, 287, John Ben, Jr. 250, John Foy 250, John Henry 250, 251, Lavinia 235, 251, 287, Mamie E. Strieber 250, Marianne Blanton Morse 250, Mary 132, Mary Ann 97, 235, 251, Mary Barnes 97, Mary Joe Cox 97, Mary Lavinia Foshee 251, Mary "Polly" 234, 235, 287, Mary R. 149, Mary Watkins 250, Rebecca Porter 97, Robert A. 235, 251, 287, Rubannah Victory 251, Suzanne McCarver McIntosh 250, Terrell C. 250, Vasta Elizabeth Hawkins 250, William 98, 235, 251, 287, William, Jr. 97, 235, 287, William, Sr. 97
Sheridan, Phil 160
Sherman 261, Ann 283
Sherrill, David W. 20
Sherwood, Sallie Griffin Mills Devereux 159
Shettlesworth 84
Shipley, Elizabeth 175
Shipman, John Robert 139, Kimberly 139, Martha Ann 139, Rebecca Sue 139, Sara Jane 139
Shipp 60, Grady 38, Ola Nancy Echols 141, Sam C. 141
Shirey, Elizabeth 210, Mary Pearle 226, Mary Pearle 85, 188
Shivers, Allan 250, Melvin 159
Shobert, Brian 50
Shook 179
Shopka, Edward 55
Shores, Kindal 139
Shott, Carmen Estella 224
Showalter, Margaret 148
Shows, Feriby Isabella 169
Shrum, Laura 94
Sigler, John P. 141, Martha A. Sample(s) 141
Sigmund, Leslie E. 246
Silkwood, Karen Gay 251, Merle 251, William 251
Silver, Judith 237
Simmons 255, Joseph 270
Simms, Eliza Jane 235
Simpson 17, H.G. 31, Terri Lynn Snider 96, 110, William 96, 110
Sims, Lavensor Saperonia 118, Nelwyn Louise 287, Nelwyn Louise Wright 133, Tondalaya 256
Sistrunk, Elizabeth Ann Hagler 164
Sjoerdsma, Courtney Anne Goodson 232, Dustin James 232, Paige Allison 232
Skaggs, John Henry 254, Martha Davis 254, Nancy Melvina 254
Skelton, Elsie Fern 97, Melissa 167
Skipper, B.A. 82, E.D. 142, Elvy Ann 95, Matilda Eudora Elder 142, Sion 95
Sloan, Martha White 123, 124, Trula 204

Small, Dona 222, James P. 222, RoxiAnna Hines 222
Smallwood, W.G. 26
Smith 219, 279, 264, Adam 95, Albert 235, Alton 255, Amanda Vannie 251, Amber 255, Ann 254, Ann Castleberry Miller 64, Annie Dee 183, April Nanette 189, Arabella 26, Arminda 171, Arthur W. 255, Ashlee 255, Benjamin 110, Benjamin Franklin 251, 252, Bennie Dongene 223, 252, 253, Bertha Nellie 251, Betty 254, Betty Jane 96, 110, 222, 223, 252, 253, Beulah Catherine 152, 252, Blanche Iola 251, Bob 152, 154, Bonnie Duff-Neal 138, Brittany 255, Byron 83, Charles D. 148, Charlotte Chisum 26, Christine Wright 255, Clara Hardin 253, Clarkie Carroll 252, Crawford 224, D.T. 267, Daisy Dean 233, 235, Delvin Fred 255, Diane 267, Dock 252, Don 252, Donald Edward 252, Donald Reagan 252, Donnie Essie 251, Dora 246, 252, Dorothy 253, 274, Douglas Edward 252, Dura 83, Dylan 253, Earl Davis 254, Effie A. 251, 252, Eleanor Jean 210, Eliska 5, Eliza F. 245, Eliza Jane 251, Elizabeth Ann 170, Elizabeth Blalock 95, Elladora Ann Kesseler 254, Emily Emma Dean 154, Emma Bell Morgan 251, 25, Estelle Todd 267, Ethel 252, Euel Jackson 251, Evelyn J. 278, Fannie Gillespie 252, Flora Lillian 252, 253, Frances Cordelia 152, 252, Gayle Turman 223, 252, George Calloway 223, 251, 252, Georgia 251, Gladys DeLoise 251, Glen 17, Glenn Grosbeak 40, Grace 181, 253, Gregory Douglas 252, Guy Edward 252, Hannah 253, Harold Kermit 267, Harriet C. 251, Helen Grace 253, Henry Stuart 251, Henry Thomas 252, Hoyt George 251, 252, Hughey C. 251, Hughie L. 78, Ida Leila Stephens 223, 252, 253, Irene 251, Irma Valene 252, 253, Ivol Alice 251, Ivy Magnolia 152, 252, J.T. 279, Jack 253, James 250, James M. 251, 252, James Madison C. 152, James Madison II 251, James Robert 267, Jana 174, Jeanette Louise Adams 255, Jessie Lee 251, Jewel Armstrong 255, Joel 26, John 26, 207, John A. 253, John Burns 218, John H. 252, John H. Jr. 252, John Long 180, 181, 253, John M. 251, John Robert 251, John Tyson 10, 253, John Tyson Jr. 254, John

W. 26, Johnny Justice 252, Juanita Alice Nolen 252, Juddie Annelle Reel McLendon 213, Katherine Ann 252, Kayla 255, Kelley Jan 252, Kendall 170, Kermit Jr. 267, Kristi Hill 255, Kristin Carol 250, Leila Adrian 78, Leila Frances Thomas 251, Lela Ophelia Sparks 251, 252, Lela Walter Hedrick 255, Lester Lewis 252, Lester Louis 152, Lilla May 254, Lillie K. 245, Lola Myrtle 282, Louisa Caroline Kennard 253, Luther Eastham 253, Lynda 254, Lynn 25, 54, Lynne 64, Mae Dee 251, Mamie Anderson 252, 253, Mandy Lea Fredrick 224, Margaret 100, Maria Emily Dean 251, Martha Dewberry 26, Martha Fay 252, Marvin 83, Mary 256, Mary Ann 7, 252, Mary Elizabeth 198, 251, Mary F. Fuller 154, Mary Jane Stephens 251, Mary Louise Todd 253, Matthew 26, 252, Mattie Dee 110, Mattie Sarah 251, 252, Maude Pressley 252, Melton 26, Mildred 251, Minnie 252, Myrtle 152, Nancy Elizabeth Miller 218, Nancy Melvina Skaggs Keasler 254, Newton W. 252, Nicholas Garry 252, Nikki Gayle 252, Norman L. 252, Ola Mae 138, Ollie 251, Orvie O. 251, Oscar Lee 43, Othodell 254, 255, Ozelle Haltom 253, Pamela 242, Pearl 5, 141, R.H. 60, Rex 255, Rhoda 235, 277, Richard Benjamin Turner 223, 252, 253, Riley D. 154, 252, Riley Marshall 251, 252, Robbie Lynn 252, Robert R. 245, Robert T. 152, 251, 252, Robin 255, Ron 63, Royal David 251, 252, Royce 254, Ruby Ione 254, Russell 170, Samuel 26, 252, Sarah Beth 250, Sarah C. 251, 252, Sarah Evelyn Brannon 152, 252, Sarah Tulula 252, Sharon Dera Whadford 255, Sharon Hope Fabriz 253, Stanley Truant 252, Steve 63, Susan 252, 267, Suzanne Marie 252, Sylvia 252, Theo Flewellen 148, Thomas P. 78, Troy 255, Vannie 154, Vera Essie 251, Vera Lorene 252, 253, Virgie Belle 254, Volney 254, Wade Hampton 213, Walter Haden 252, Wayne 255, William Henry 152, 252, William Knox 282, William L. 255, William Renfro 255, Willie 254
Smitherman, Eliza 284, Elizabeth Brown 84, Mary 84, Newton 84, Robert 84, Wiley 84
Smyser, Sarah Ann 271
Sneed, Nora 97, W.R. 97

Snider, Debbie 96, 110, Gaylon 96, 110, Gaylynne 96, 110, Jason 96, 110, Kelly 96, 110, Margie Ann 96, 110, Pamela 96, 110, Terri 96, 110

Snoddy, Dorothy 256, Ace 256, Acy 256, Alice 256, Allen 256, Amanda 256, Annie 256, Betty Joe 255, 256, Carl 256, Carrie Belle Davis 256, Catherine 255, Cecile Evon 256, Conway 256, Dan 256, Donyell Y. 256, Eddie 256, Emmett 256, Erica Brown 256, Finis 256, Francis 256, Gloria 256, Green 256, Harrell 256, Huston 256, Jane 255, Jannette Ann 256, Jason 256, Julia 256, Julious 256, Kaye Francis 256, L.B. 255, Laurecia 256, Lawrence 256, Lewis Bonaparte 255, Lucinda 256, M.T. Rhodes 255, Maidee Josie 256, Mark 256, Martha 256, Meisha D. 256, Melvin D. Jr. 256, Melvin D. Sr. 255, 256, Melvin Thomas 256, Minnie 256, Rachael 118, Rachel 256, Rufus 256, Rufus Jr. 256, Serena DéAnn 256, Sheryl D. Jones 256, Thad 256, Thadeus 118, 255, Thadeus, Jr. 256, Thomas 256, Tommie 118, Tommy 256, Tonia Denise Harrison 256, Wailie 256, Warness Lee 256, Zanyah 256

Snodgrass, David 42, 43

Snow 255, Elizabeth 91, James 91, Karl Anthony 40, Mary Elizabeth 91

Snowden, James 59, 60, 65, 186, Shirley 60

Snyder, Anna Maria 222

Solari, Rosa Elvira 189

Sommerkamp, Charlie 285, Mary Elizabeth Louise 285

Souder, Barbara 147, Henry 147, Susannah 147

Southerland, Patricia 140

Southern, E.H. 177

Sowells, Ardelia 230

Sparkman, Sarah Tate 260, Dorothy 260, Edythe Eleanor 139, Elizabeth 112, 260, Homer Ansel, Sr. 139, John 260, Joseph M. 25, 141, 260, Ruth 64, Verna Louise Blount 139, William 260

Sparks, Charles E. 45, D.G. 23, Daril 41, Ida 64, J.W. 177, Julia Hoskins 177, Lela Ophelia 251, 252

Speed, Jennifer Adaine 97, Jeromey Dwight 97, Larry 97, Mollie Boles 97

Speights, Katherine 261

Spence, Callie 179, Emily Ann Harville 231, Frank 180, George C. 180, John Henry 180, Micah 231

Spencer, Billy Wayne 260, Charlotte Christene 260, Tracye 260, Trampus 260, Troy 260, Vonseal 17

Spinks, Edward Jr. 254, James Monroe 8, Lilla May 254, Victoria 142

Spottswood 158

Sprayberry, Mary Ann Harris 167, Mary Harris 171, W.L. 167

Springer 90

Springs, Eleanor 256

Springsteen 256, Gertrude 256

Sprott, Tamsyn 257, Thomas 257, Vanessa 257

Spruell, Robert 17

Spunner, Margaret 98, William 98

Spurrier, J.L. 273, Ruby 273

St. Denis 223

Stacha, Joe, Jr. 240, Sybil Loraine Richardson 240, Waynette Elain 240

Stack, Bill 63, Keith 107

Stafford, Helen Grace Smith 253, Helene 253, John 253, Rick 253

Staggs, Bessie 170

Stahl, Angela Leigh Edmonson 257, Charles Hubert 257, Elizabeth Ann 137, 257, Frederick Henry 136, 257, Frederick Henry Jr. 137, 257, Hertha Ann 257, Janice Louise Ramey 257, Mae Jeanette 257, Mary Yvonne Dryden 136, 257, Patsy Carol 257, Rebecca Lee 137, 257, Shelly Suzanne 257, Stephen Lane 257, Tanner Jake 257

Stall, Anna Lee Newman 257, Frederick August 257, Henry Otis 257, Myrtle Elizabeth Detro 257, Walburgis Caroline Kuhlman Beckler 257

Stallcup, John C. 138

Stanbridge, Venia Blane McElroy 84

Standard, Willie Mae 217

Standish, Miles 83

Standridge, Ersle Wroten 84, Mary Alice 84

Standsbury, L.D. 10, M.D. 10

Stanley, Artie 217, John 85, 188, 217, Judy Tolleson 267, Julie Kay 217, Larry Gene 217, Lloyd 7, Lola Irene Elizabeth Faulk Anderson 146, Minnie Heavel 233, Naoma Mae Belle Meadows 217, Wendy Gail 85, 188

Stansbury, Leander Dexter 206, S. Elizabeth Magrill 206

Stark, Robert E. 45

Starks, June 41

Starnes, Ann 51, Milton 51

Starr, Alonzo R. 258, Anna Mary 258, Casper 258, Elizabeth Martha 258, Ellen Marie Bullock 258, Emma Marie 258, Jasper Jr. 258, Jeff 258, Jenny 258, John 258, Kenneth 258, Larry 257, 258, Matthew Rutherford 258, Medaline Easter 209, Mike 257, 258, Nancy 257, 258, Rebecca Ellen 258, Sarah Joyce Rutherford 258, Susannah Parker 258, Thomas J. 258

Steele, Dean 252, Mary Alice McLendon 251

Stegall, Betty Jean Thomas 258, 264, Bradley Howard Sr. 258, Bretta Katherine 258, Duard Hencle 258, Emily Eugina Bumbgardener 258, Modena Hilton 258, Ples 258, Virginia Bell Patrick 258, William Franklin 258

Steinmetz, Callie Ann 179, Linda Janelle Hughey 179, Ron 179, Ronald, Jr. 179

Stephens 90, Dorothy 228, Ida Leila 223, 252, 253, Jane Carol 197, Mary Hollan Mitchell 239, Mary Jane 251, Minnie Teressa 200, Neylon 239

Stephenson, Charles A. 70, Charles V. 70, Frank 70

Sterling, Ross 29, 169, Ruth Sparkman 64

Stetson, John B. Hat 122

Stevens, Alexander Calvitt, Jr. 151, 259, Alexander Calvitt 151, 258, Campbell Fox 259, Ella English 259, Flo 118, Floreid Francis 103, 151, 259, James Alfred 258, John Edward 192, L.L. 48, Mary Florence Crowder 258, Nina 25, 54, Ophelia Key 192, Rembert 25, 54, Sam 25, 54, Scott English 151, 259, Shirley Carole 192, 193, Thomas Huxford 151, 259

Stevenson, Andrew Paul 233, Augusta 85, 233, 235, James 209, Jane Everett 146, Lucille 51, Rebecca Mathis 209, Sarah Jane Mitchell 233, Ward 146

Stewart, Bryant 261, Cynthia Reed 237, Gladys Jewell Hunt 259, James M. 237, John A. 34, 192, Lucy Anne 192, Rebecca Shaw 249, Ruby 133, 286, 287, Thomas 249, Tommie Tankersley 259, 261, William A. 261, William A., Jr. 259, 261, William A., Sr. 259

Still, Josephine 64, Robert 260, Ruth Ann 260

Stillman 279

Stinchcomb 230, Mary A. Brown 104, Mary Noel Mobberly 104, T.B. 37, Tad 104, Thomas B. 104

Stine, Nancy Jane 160

Stinson, Elveney 283, Sallie 174

Stoinoff, Huntington 79

Stoker, Arnold 160, Rebecca Leander Jones 160, Susan Ann 160

Stokes, Robert 128

Stone, 264, Ann M. 137, Bertha 201, Blanche Iola Smith 251, Connor Harrison 227, Debra 201, Delores Ann Cox 201, Dylan Cody 227, Edward 264, Elmer 251, Georgia 78, 279, 280, 282, Georgiana 279, 280, Harold 201,

Helen 201, Janice Holley 226, Jeffery 201, Joe Neal 226, Mae Elizabeth 264, Mamie 201, Manoah F. 276, Mary Beth 201, Mary T. 276, R.W. 137, Roger Allen 226, Susan Eileen 94, Theresa Culberson 227, Thomas Wesley 279

Storey, Loretta 7, Mary Ann Saphonie 84

Storm, Gail 38

Stouard, Etta Francis McLaren 95, Jesse Lee 95, Jessie Mae 95, John William 95, W.D. "Tom" 95

Stoudt, Bill 30, 70

Stoval, Charles G. 82

Stovall, Albert 98, 259, Alice Lydia 82, 259, Annie Jane Alexander 82, 259, Bartholomew 259, Beverly Anne Echols 140, Brittany Anne 140, Callie 259, 260, Charles 82, 98, 259, Emma 98, Eva 98, James Henry 82, 259, Jewel 132, John 98, Julia Adams 259, Julian 98, Julie 98, Lydia Gibson Willett 259, Mollie 97, 98, Perry Daniel 140, Ruth 98, Samuel 98, William 98

Stracner, Patricia Ann 271

Strait, Christopher 108

Strauss, Freida Hamilton 152, 153, 191, Marion Mosley Hamilton 152, William Isadore 152

Stricker, Edna Eleanor 122

Strickland, Ebon 285

Strieber, Mamie E. 250

Stringer, Jane E. Pope 91, Jefferson 91, Martha Ann 91, William 91

Stripling, Ben R. 49, Carolyn 49, Lorene 49, Paul 49

Strong, Jack B. 161, Martha Winn 237, Mary Frances 237, Nelda Faye Grigsby 160, William Benjamin 237

Strother, Elizabeth 138

Stroud, Tenza Minta 217

Struck, Ginette 268

Struffolino, Charles Michael 154, Elizabeth 153, 154, Lauren Hamilton 153, 154, Marion Rose 154, Michael Anthony 153, Michael Pierce 153, 154, Sharla Elizabeth Frost 152, 153, Shirley Farmer 154

Stuaffer, Barbara 147

Studt, Andrew 260, Anna 260, Brad 260, Camille 260, James 260, Joyce 260, Mary 260, Virginia 260, Winton 260

Sullivan, Debbie 200, 225, Lula Marie Brooks 177

Summers, Jennie 222

Sundby, Brian 96, Bryan 110, John 96, John Jr. 110, John William Sr. 110, Johnnie Mae 96, 110, Steve 96, 110

Sunski, Lynn 96

Sustaita, Mark James Emmons 193, Sarah 193, Tiffany Nicole 193

Sutherland, Ala Jane Allen 83, Nevil 83, Pam 83, Pat 83, Toy 83, Toy, Jr. 83

Sutherlin, E.W. 163, John Arthur 162, Lala 162, Laura Agnes McDonald 162, W.K. 163

Swafford, Johnnie Mae Williams Holly 228

Sweeney, Eva 69, 208, Payton 69, 208, Thomas H. 69, 70, 207, 208, Thomas H., Jr. 69, 208

Sweet, John 5, Mary 5, 194

Swift, Marietta 276

Swimm, Catie 260, Charlotte Christene 243, 260, Donna 260, Inita Orr Cochran 260, Kester John 260, Mildred Christene 243, 260, Rachel 260, Richard 243, 260, Rickye Dossene 243, 260, Robert Earl 260, Ruth Ann 243, 260, Ruth May Mahannah 260, Sarah 260, Shirley 260, Stuart Jay 260, Josephine 263

T

Tabler, G.M. 36

Tadlock, Edna 135

Taft, William Howard 106

Talbot, J.O. 176, Letitia 140, Thomas Hardy 46

Talley, Elizabeth 132, 234, James Obie 234, Mary Kirkpatrick 234, Matilda 234, O.B. 49

Tanguma, John Noe 94, Tina Ruth Belflower 94

Tankersley, Absalom B. 10, 112, 260, Elizabeth Clark 260, Elizabeth Sparkman 112, Lavonia Frances 112, 261, Margaret Rowland 260, Mary Tommie 261, Richard 260, Sarah Ardecia 260, 261, Tommie 259, 261

Tanner, Lula 183

Tardy, William Thomas 43

Tarpley, John H. 235

Tate, Joseph Newell 190, Josephine 190, Mary Lucille Gossett 190, Thomas Marvin 10

Tatum, Alto 188, 232, Lola Caroline 249, Sara Elizabeth 192

Taylor, Andrew 10, 11, 261, Annie Lee 64, Arthur 264, Barbara S. Harris 267, Bill M. 147, Bill Northcutt 249, 261, C.L. 228, Casper J. 160, Charles Lee 261, Charles Shaw 249, 261, Desta Monia Antlet 264, Dora 49, Elbert C. 121, Farol 267, Gloria 249, 261, Helen 255, Hugh Donald 165, Iba 261, Iba Northcutt 228, Ida Luticia 182, Ida Northcutt 64, James W. 160, Jessie 88, Job 20, 21, 261, John 167, Josephine Chadick 261, Josephine Malinda 261, Julie Ann Bechtold 267, Karrie Lynn 267, Kenneth Lee 267, Kim-

308 *Index*

berly 267, LaLita Yvonne Akers 81, Louise Durham 249, 261, Louise Shaw 64, Martha Ann 266, Martin Duke 165, Mary 147, Mary Ann McCaskill 267, Mary Lee 165, Maye Bell 49, Melissa 49, Michael 49, Nancy 84, 102, 249, 261, Nancy Jane Stine 160, Nicole 267, Nora C. Coleman 121, Norman 74, Patricia Anne Martin 165, 207, Roy 49, Ryan 267, Samuel Alan 165, Sarah George 267, Savannah 84, Stella Harris 167, Susan Rilda 159, 160, Suzanne 199, William Butler 264, William W. 84, Zachary 20, 96

Taylor-Sparks, Ira Mae 202

Teague, Bernadine 113, George 219, Latimus 21, 113, Mary 21, Mary Mitchell 219, Molly 12, Patsy Elizabeth McLendon 213, Sally 245, Sarah 12, Shannon 123

Tedder, Delilah Pyburn 84, Elizabeth Meeks 84, Farrington 84, James A. 84, Mary Ann Saphonie Storey Burrell 84, Sarah Ann 84

Teel, Peter 128

Tekell, Barbara Gail 81, 187, Katie Bell 81, Martha Diane 187, Mattie Arlene Johnson 187, R.Q. 81, Robert Douglas 81, 187

Temple, Amy 262, Annie 261, David Alan 262, Edward Rayburn 262, Edward Rayburn, Jr. 262, Edwin Fussell 261, 262, Edwin Vernon 157, 245, 262, Elva 262, Ida Ellen Looker 262, Ida Floy 262, LaRoy 262, Lorraine 262, Louise 262, Mary Ellen 157, 245, 262, Robert 262, Susan 262, Thomas 261, 262, Thresa 262, Vernon 262

Tenery, G.B. 27

Tennant, Roy I. Jr. 246

Tenner, Catherine Anne 125, Matthew Richard 125

Tenney, Mary Frances McWhorter 215, Robert Paul Warfield 215, Samuel McWhorter 215, Samuel Mills 215, Warren William 215

Terrell, Bill 103, Billy Bob 163, James Robert 103, Jane Fleetwood 103, Jean 103, JeRusha Ann 277, Libby 103, Mary 95, 103, Nannie Mae Bramlette 103, Tom 287, William Hughes 103, William Robert 103

Terry, Ada Lee Martin 263, Adelle 263, Alice 262, 263, 264, Alvie 264, Bobby 263, Bobby Joe 224, Carl 224, 263, Carrie 264, Catherine Brown 263, Charles 262, Charles Jefferson 263, Charles Richard 263, Cintha 263,

Cora Cox 263, Don 263, 264, Ed 263, Eddie 264, Edward 262, 264, Edwin 263, Effie 262, 263, 264, Elizabeth 263, EulaMae 264, Francis 263, Gene Melvin 263, George 263, Gloria 263, 264 Gloria Juanita 224, Hazel 263, 264, J.L. 12, James 263, James H. 10, John 262, 263, Josephine Syfan 263, Lola 264, Lulu 264, Mabel 263, 264, Madeline 45, 224, 263, Martha 262, 263, Marvin 263, 264, Mary 263, Mary Florence 213, Maxine 264, Ola 262, 264, Pam 231, Percy 263, R.A. 263, Richard Lee 263, 264, Robert Joe 224, 263, 264, Rosa 263, Samuel 264, Sarah 262, 263, Swan 263, Synthia 263, Tamara 104, Thomas 263, Wanda 262, 263, 264, William L. 262, 264, William M., Sr. 263, William T. 262, 263, Willie 263, 264

Teruko, I. 128

Theis, Lee Ann 187

Thomas, A.G. 204, 265, Alice Barkett 266, Alyce 265, 266, Ann Tuley 265, Azizie 265, 266, Barbara 266, Bena 204, Benjamin Franklin 68, Betty Jean 258, 264, Beulah Irene 224, Charles Bradford 266, Charles Edward 264, Charles Marion 264, Desta Monia Antlet 264, Dianne 266, Dorothy Drew 264, Dorothy Grace Drew 264, Drucilla Younts 264, Edd 265, Elizabeth A. 206, Emily Angeline 264, Ezekiel 146, 264, Galen 84, 264, Garry 96, 110, Gaylynne Snider 96, 110, George 265, 266, Harriet Tweedle 155, Hattie 93, 155, Ida Dorothy 264, Isaac 265, James Edward 155, 264, Jeanette 266, Jennifer Blane 169, Jesse Earl 84, Jessica 96, 110, Jessie Arlee 146, 264, John 264, 265, 266, Judith 276, Leila Frances 251, Louella Rhoda 265, Lucille Barro 266, Mae Elizabeth 264, Maggie 265, Margaret Jabour 266, Marian Brown 265, Marlene 266, Marqurite Katherine Belk 264, Martha Ellen 264, Mary 264, 265, Mary Alice 84, Nadyne Bussey 265, Naseep 265, Philip 265, 266, Philip John, Jr. 266, Rosemary Allen 84, Ruth May 115, Sam George 265, Sarah Virginia 265, Selma 265, Stella Mae 82, 83, Tommy 265, Vander Artimissie Clark 146, 264, Victoria 265, William Joseph 264, Willie T. Whaley 264

Thompkins, Samuel 202

Thompson, Dan, Sr. 266, James William 266, Dan 266, Delila 138, Frances Abernathy 266, J.B. 70, J.M. 159, James Henry 84, Jim 266, Joe 63, King Daniel, Jr. 266, Lou Della 159, Louise Day 214, Lucile 266, Lulah Fields Jameson 84, Martha 266, Nancy 266, Nikki 115, Patricia Carroll 115, Permelia F. 84, Rosie 25, 54, Sally O'Neil 84, Samantha 96, Steven Arthur 84, Sylvia Smith 252, Verdine Ford 266

Thorn, Mary J. 234, Virginia 88

Thornton, Dempsey 248, Gerald 248, Gerald Edward Jr. 248, J.A. 13, Joan Elizabeth 248, Joanie 248, Lona Lorraine 272, Schuyler 248

Threadgill, Allen 266, Anna 266, Claudie Payne 266, Greene Smith 266, 284, Martha 266, 284, Mary Amy 266, 284, Mattie 266, Octavia Alread 266, Zemariah Tig 266

Thurmon, Kate Broadwell 99, Katherine Beatrix 99, Robert A. 100, William Mitchell 99

Thweatt, Eliza Harris 285, Victoria Monroe 148

Tienry, Janet 228

Tillery, Bonnie Cleo 276, Julius Lackey 276

Timmons, Coma 26

Tincher, Frances Virginia 280, Lorena 183

Tines, Eliza 206

Tipton, James 63

Titus, Amos Jackson Jr. 243, Amos Jackson 243, Theda Lestine 243

Todd, Adele 266, 267, Augusta Johnston 266, 267, Estelle 266, 267, John Morgan 266, Katie Dee 61, Mary Ella 266, 267, Mary Louise 253, Mary Pelina Phillips 266, Neva Inez 163, Patsy Ruth 287, Solon D. 266, 267

Tolbert, Amy Ruth 80, Jean Marie 80, Joyce Omega 80, Ruby Mildred Adrian 80

Toler, Mabel 51, Shirley Hall 134

Tolleson, Barbara S. Harris 267, Ginette Struck 268, Hubert J. 267, Jack Matthew 268, Jimmie Leigh Harden 267, Joe D. 267, 268, Joe V. 267, 268, Judy 267, Kate Lauren 268, LaVerne 267, Susan Worley 268, Trent Andrew 268, Trey Hunter 268

Tomberlain, Babette 268, Barbara 60, 268, Broud Waymon 268, Carrie June 268, Charles Morgan 268, Charles Waymon 268, Charles William Coleman 268, Chuck 268, James Marvin 268, Lola Mae Morgan 268, Mary Virginia 268, Morgan Abbigail 268, Wanda Jean 268, Barbara 268

Tomlinson, Cornelia 210, J. Clyde, Sr. 74, 116, Mitt 116

Toothaker, Tom 83

Torres, Ruby 286, 287, Ruby Olean Wright Stewart 133

Torrez, Joy Denise Camp 225

Toups, Benjamin Charles 252, Madeleine Marie 252, Suzanne Marie Smith 252, Wayde Charles 252

Townes, Jill 97, Terri 97

Townsend, Michelle 224

Traherne, Thomas 188

Tramel, Christene Luman 268, James 268, 269, Lee 268, Margaret 268, Nancy 268

Traughber, J.J. 64, Lavon Wood 64

Travis, Roy 135, William Barrett 91

Treadwell, Gretta 142, 143

Trice, Ann 244

Truelove, Florence Elizabeth 190

Truett, George W. 167

Tsoumbos, Foto 269, Kim 99, 269, Sawyer 99, 269, Spencer 99, 269, Telly 269, Thanos 269, Tyler 99, 269

Tubbs, A.H. 97, Albert Glenn 83, Albert Henry 82, Atha Grace 83, J.S. 97, James Archie 82, Joseph Malcolm 83, Lillie Dell Alexander 82, Mollie 97, Otis Dement 8, P.J. 97

Tucker, Geneva Jean 190, Jackie Lee 143, John 183, Linda Ellis 143, Margaret 147, Margie M. 183, Mary McFarland 183, Ray 190, Samuel Scott 143

Tucker-Click, Renea 190

Tuel, Mary Frances Allen 84

Tugwell, Billy 17

Tuley, Ann 265

Tunstall, Beecher 151, Emma Virginia English 151, Eugenia 103, 151, 259, Vicory Barker 151

Turman, Gayle 223, 252

Turner 255, Ann Elizabeth 145, Archie 269, Ben 269, Benjamine 145, Bennie Dee 269, Bennie Lee 269, Billie Sue 64, Bonnie Dee 269, Clyde Albert 269, Edgar 269, Elizabeth 145, Emme 269, Frances 269, Gaines 269, General 269, George Benton 269, Glenna Winell 269, Gloria Mae 269, Harold 61, Ida 269, James Edgar 269, James Jackson 269, Jerry 47, Katheryn Keyton McLemore 143, Kenneth Harold 269, Lemelia 269, Lucille K. 269, Margie 269, Mary Louise 78, Permelia Tacora McFarland 269, Sallie 105, Tyriska 119, Willie Frances 269

Tuthill, Clara 274

Tutt 92, Amanda Pearl 132, 270, 272, Amy 98, 271, Andrew Leon 271, Barbara Jean 272, Benjamin Prichard 98, Benjamin Pritchard 271,

Bertha Catherine Ann 272, Carlene 270, 271, Carlene Mitchell 220, Carlos Brian 272, Cathy Jeanne 273, Charles Edward "Pete" 272, Charles Walter 272, Charlotte Ann 272, Chris Andrew 273, Clement 270, 271, 272, Cordelia 285, Cynthia Ann 272, Daniel Ethan 271, David Benjamin 271, David Eiland 271, Debra Sue 272, Donald Mick 273, Elizabeth Rosaline 270, Elizabeth Viola 272, Emma Susan 272, Eunice Barnett 272, Eunice Leon 272, Eva Dove 272, Gabriel Hans 11, Gabriel Hansford 272, Gabriel Jackson 270, Gary 272, George Everett 272, Georgie Pearl 272, Harriett Catherine 271, Hazel May 272, Helen Maime "Babe" Ruth 272, Henry Otis 272, Henry Silvester 272, Howard Louis 272, Hulda Elizabeth 219, 272, Ira Columbus 272, J.W. "Buck" 273, James 220, 271, James Alvin 270, 272, 273, James B. 270, James Sidney 205, 219, 272, James Sidney, Jr. 98, 271, James Sidney, Sr. 98, 270, James Solon 272, Jamie Lynn 271, 272, Jason Eli 271, Jerrie Lane 272, Jo Minor 270, Joe Michael 272, Joel Hunter 271, John Elbert 272, John Howard 272, John Sidney 272, John W. 272, John Z. 272, Jonathan Thomas 98, 271, Joseph Erskin 272, Julia Ann 178, 270, 272, Julia Kate 272, Karen 98, 271, Katie Lee 272, Laura Gentry 272, Libby Inez 272, Lona Ethel 272, Lona Lorraine 272, Lottie Bell 272, Louis Garret "Gary" 272, Lucille Zelma 272, Lucy Ann 270, Mable Fay 272, Maggie 272, Margaret Ann 98, 270, Martha E. 272, Mary Ann 270, 272, Mary Cansadie 219, 272, Mary Evelyn 272, Mary Maxine 272, Mary-Austin 98, 271, , Marybelle Bolger 3, 7, 98, 205, 206, 270, 271, Matthew Kelly 271, Mattie 272, Mildred 138, Millie 270, 271, 272, Milly 272, Mittie Erma 272, Odel 272, Olga 272, Ortie Mae 272, Patricia Ann 271, Pierce B. 11, Pierce Butler 270, 272, Richard 272, Richard H. 8, Richard Hardy 270, Robert Edward 272, Ronald Wayne 273, Rosie Lee 273, Roxie Margaret Jane 272, Ruby Elizabeth 272, Sarah Ann 271, Sharon Ann 272, Sid 270, 271, Sidney 272, Sidney O. Pennington 270, 271, Sidney O.P., Jr. 271, Slade Barnett

272, Susan 272, Teresa Elizabeth 98, 220, 270, 271, Terry Allen 273, Thomas Mitchell 98, 271, Thomas N. 11, 270, 272, Thomas Patrick 272, Thomas Pierce 272, Thomas Robert 132, 270, 272, 273, Tim 271, Timothy Bolger 98, 271, Todd Gordon 272, Tom 271, Tommie 272, William Robert 272, William Thomas 219, 272, Willie Mae 272, Zellie Irene 272

Tuttle, Andrew Jackson 172, Dan 172, Dimple 172, Effie 273, Exa 273, Fred 273, George 172, Jack 273, Jenelle 80, Julia 273, Julius 273, Lee 273, Nancy 172, 273, Nobie 273, Polly 172, Robert 172, Roy 172, Ruby 273, Shirley Cantrell 7, T.J. 28, Thomas 273, Thomas Andrew Jackson 273

Tweedle, Harriet 155

Tyl, Sissy 150

Tyndell, Terri Townes 97

Tyne, Arthur 270

Tyre, J.W. 230

U

Ullrich, Austin Dakota 274, 275, Austin Dakota 275, Blanche 274, 275, Bob 274, 275, Jennie 275, Lynn Bonham 274, Ragena Gay 275, Regena 275, Robert E. 274, 275, Robert O. 274, 275, Sierra Cheyenne 274, 275

Underwood, Mary 272, William 272

Upchurch, Margie Marie 97

Utzman, Annie Lou 275, Bernice 86, Cordie Alice 275, Emily 275, Eula Mae 275, Francis Marion 275, George 275, Georgia Flo 275, Henry Curtis 275, Jacob 8, 275, Jacob Jr. 275, James 275, Janet 86, Jennifer 85, 86, 87, 109, Jessica-Alisse Ater 86, 87, 109, Johannes 275, John 275, Lewis 275, Lois 275, Lou Gene 276, Margaret 275, Martha 275, Mary 275, Mollie Tennessee 275, Mumford 275, Nancy 275, Naoma 216, Olive Emily Belle 275, Ora Lee 275, Richard 87, Richard, Jr. 86, Richard, Sr. 86, Thomas 275, Tommy 86, William 275, 276, William Wayne 275

V

Vail, Martin Luther 91, Mattie Lou 91, Melinda 91

Van Allen, Geraldine 64

Van Burkleo, Hoyle 271, Julia 271, Margaret Ann 98, 270, 271

Van Kuykendaal, Luur Jacobsen 196

Van Landingham, Georgia 64

Van Sickle, Lina Glover 93, Lina Hardin Glover 155, R.J. 93, 155

Van Zandt, Khleber Miller 200

Vance, Arthur H. 8

Vanderwuall, Anna 276

Vanoy, Isaac 16

Vanripper, James 270, Jane 270, John 270, Lucy Ann 270, William T. 270

Vaughn, Albert Bell 43

Vaverek, Gavin 55

Veale, Martha Cuberley 64

Vela, Eileen 118, 127, 128, 229

Veneable 68

Vernon, James Crawford 48, Sam L. 26

Vescovi, Sylvia 276

Vick, Wilena 161

Vickers, Darrell C. 40, 41

Victory, Bellona 133, 287, J.T. 11, Warren P. 20, William H. 133, 287

Vinson, Genevieve 90, James Glardon "Don" 90, John 90, Mary Carlisle Sheegog 90, Patricia 90, Richard 90, Sarah 89, 90

Visage 279

Vogler, Christopher 275, George 275, John 275, Mary 275

Vulgamore, Margurite Eloise 211

W

Wachtel, Victoria 81

Wade, Arthur E. 276, Bernice 276, Buck J. 276, Floria Estelle 179, Ica Belle 276, Irene 276, Lillie Zelmodene 131, Norcie 276, Rosa Mae 276, Vernon Richard 276, William E. 276, William Richard 276, Wilma 276

Wadlington, Margaret 278

Wadsworth, Esther Louise 248, 249

Waggoner 190

Wagley, Charles A. 41

Wagner, Jenny Frances 155, Shelley Ann Conway 164

Wagnon, Lockey Ann 285

Waid, J.P. 105

Waide 22

Waite, Mary 222

Wakely, Jimmy 38

Walden, Betty Garrett 154, Douglas 154, Garrett, 154, Mary A. 200

Waldrop, Martha 228

Walgren, Carolyn Ann Wallace 161, Ellen 161, Laura 161, Mark 161

Walker, Kenneth Bobby 276, Alice Ann 276, Alton Edgar "Jack" 183, 184, 276, Annie America 276, Annie Florence 82, 183, 184, 276, B.F. 6, B.P. 26, Betty Nell 276, Bill Thomas 276, Bonnie Cleo 276, Cheryl Lynn 276, Edith Carroll 285, Frankie Pearl 276, Franky 276, Gale Davis 276, Garrett 195, Ginny Rae 195, Gracie Lorene 276, Hallie Lee 276, Hayden 195, Hazel 276, J.B. 142, Jackie Lee 276, Judy 276, Kenneth Haskell

"Hack" 276, Lawrence Wesley 276, Lena 181, Leona 244, Lillie Lawrence 64, Lloyd H. 33, Lucille 276, Mabel Brown 64, Mary Eula 183, 184, 276, Maryann "Addie" 147, Merideth Edgar "Bill" 276, Montgomery Hamilton 276, Nancy 222, 238, Nancy Ann 276, Nancy Elizabeth Elder 142, Patricia Ann "Tita" 276, Patricia Cleopatra "Cleo" 276, Robert 276, Sally Maxine 276, Samuel 95, Sarah Ann Elizabeth 112, Steven 195, Sylvanious 199, Sylvia 276, Texanna 95, Timothy Lawrence 276, Wesley Lawrence 276, William Robert Sid "John" 276, Young Hui Chin 276, Zelma Raye Hubbard 268

Wall, Betty Nell 276, Darrell 276

Wallace, Alice Morris 136, Aliceson 161, Bob 227, Carolyn Ann 161, Connie 160, Florence Addie 136, Hallie Lee 276, Hazel Ila 276, James D. 66, Jennie 276, Jim 161, Joseph Reid 136, Nelda Faye Grigsby 161, Paul 139, Sara Jane Shipman 139, Shirley 227, Spurgeon Wilborn 276, Susan Renee 227

Walling, John 20

Walls, Carrie June 268

Walquist, Kaye 161

Walters, Abraham 276, James Henry 277, Judith 276, Lemuel 28, Marietta 276, Mary T. 276, Sarah Ann 277, Thomas, Sr. 276, William W. 20, 26, 276, 277

Walton, Sam 134

Wampler, Barbara Gene 234, Floyd 234, Goldie Marie Roden 234

Ward, Caden Nicholas 277, Daisy Bell Nicholson 180, Daniel 131, 277, Daniel Randy 131, 277, Dorothy Ruth 172, Elizabeth Marie 277, Essie Francis Harris 167, Floria Estelle 178, George 167, J.W. 17, James S. 180, Joycelyn 131, 277, Landon 131, 277, Lillian Marie 277, Margaret Alice 172, Michael 131, 277, Oscar Watson 172, Priscilla Marguierite 277, Sarah 97, Shawna 131, 277, Suzanne Marie 277, Virginia 271, Willie Cumi Henderson 172

Wardlaw, Annie France Bramlette 103, Lerone Edgar 103

Ware, Cecil 50, Elizabeth 148

Warlick, Cordelia 270

Warren 206, Alice Gertrude 277, Birdie Ophelia 277, C.B. 48, Charles Alonzo 277, Clayton Roy 278, Cullen 17, Cullen Bunyan 278, Cullen Mark 278, Cynthia Diane 278, Daisie Lee Boren 156,

Darlene 278, Diane 17, 278, Dora 150, Elmira Jane 277, Grady Lee 277, Gustavus Earickson 156, Humphrey, Sr. 156, Ida Lou 277, J.T. 4, James 48, James Rush 156, James Thomas 277, JeRusha Ann 277, Jessie Hamilton 277, Jimmie Frances 278, Johnny Brown 277, Lexa Knox 277, Marcus Landon 278, Margaret 277, Mary Joyce 278, Myrtle Elmira 277, Nancy 48, 277, Nancy Verdell 278, Robert 156, 277, Sarah Jewel 277, Sheila Elaine 278, Sherry Beth 278, Velma Jean 278, Vera Elizabeth 155, 156, 232, Verna 277, Vickie 278, William Clayton 277, William Samuel 277

Warrick, Gwenda Darlene 121

Washburn, Matilda Omega Husband 182, Robert 182

Washington 115, Craig Anthony 278, George 207

Wathen, Ben 203, Dan 203, John 203, Julia Ann 203, Thurman 203

Watkins, Nancy Jane Vaught Isbell 126, Alene 217, Barbara 17, Cordelia Belle 126, E.O. 6, Glass 204, Melinda 204, Minnie Lee 204, Monroe 126

Watson 213, Edith Darlene 128, Elizabeth 213, 214, Hazel 96, Henry Lark 276, John 21, Mary Eula 183, 184, 276, Mary Jane 276, Samuel 214, Sarah 160, Timothy E. 43

Watts, Emma Inez 64

Weatherford, Eartie Bee 269

Weaver, Adam 262, Anna 262, John Thomas 262, Joseph 262, Martha Susan 262, Mary 262, Nancy 262, Sarah 262, Seaborn 262

Webb, Carey E. 92, 278, Chick 232, Elizabeth 92, 278, Eugene E. 278, Eugene Edward 278, Jessie L. 28, John David 261, Margaret 278, Margaret Alice 92, 278, Marian Louise 92, 278, Mildred Eunice 278, Ross 272, Sarah 261, Susan 272, Walter Prescott 258

Webster, J.J. 234

Wedemeyer, Henry 74

Weil, Simone 188

Weir, Pearl 157, Richard N. 10, Richard W. 10

Weist 255

Welborn, John 29

Welborne, William 11

Welbourne, William 25

Welch, Alta Rita 61, Florette Haynes 136, Jewell Kathryn 136, John W. 136, O. Thomas, Sr. 61, Thomas 73, Thomas, Jr. 50, Vicki Susan Camp 225

Welge, Ava Avant 60

Welk, Lawrence 202

Wellborn, Esther 102

Wells, Henry 137

Welty, Eudora 188

Wensley, John 201

Wertz, Dorothy Jane 278, 279, Evelyn J. 278, Forest 278

Wesley, Anna 104

West, Annie 261, Cheryl Lynn 276, Freda 61, Laura 243, Mark Rabon 276, Mary Josephine 103

Westley, Anna 104

Westmoreland, Sarah Elizabeth 159

Westrope, Hanna Bryan 160, John 160, Mary 160, William 160

Weyel, Elmo 123, Patricia 123

Whadford, Chesley Orval 255, Sharon Dera 255

Whalen, Florine 103

Whaley, Willie T. 264

Wharton 88, Adoniram Judson 43

Whatley, Alabama Frances 78, 79, 89, 279, 280, Anna 279, Bernice Rebecca 280, Christopher Grant 257, Cordelia 279, 280, Edmund 279, 280, Ellen 279, Emma V. 279, Eula 279, Eulah Florence 280, Georgia 23, 280, 282, Georgia F. 78, 279, Georgia Zenobia 280, Georgiana 279, 280, Grace Henderson 172, Hertha Ann Stahl 257, Hiram 23, 78, 279, 280, Hiram J. 279, 282, John H. 279, Lea Ora 280, Leora 172, 280, Lisa Goar 257, Lucy Lee 279, Mary 279, 280, Mary Alice 172, Matthew Joe 257, Michael, Jr. 279, 280, Michael, Sr. 279, Minerva Ellen 279, 282, 283, Nannie 279, 280, "Nobie" 279, Ora Lea 279, Rowan A. 172, Rowan A., Jr. 172, Shannon Kay 257, Sharon 111, 112, 280, Shirley, Sr. 279, Terry Grant 257, Thomas McAlister 280, Ulysses Grant 257, W. Hiram 280, Wesley 66, 279, Wesley Lewis 111, 112, 280, Wesley William "Pritt" 280, William B. 279, William Clayton 111, 112, William Clayton "Clay" 280, William Wesley 279

Wheat, Amy Ruth Tolbert 80, Bruce Edwin 80

Wheatley, Alma 173, Anna Brown Herndon 173, Anna May 173

Wheeler, Amelia Ridley 228, Barbara Frances 228, Flossie Northcutt 228, Franklin Clay 228, Gay Cole Howard 228, Joseph 91, 171, Lorena Runette Baird 91, Mary Alice 233, Nancy Howard 228, Ridley Northcutt 228, Sarah Northcutt 228, William Ridley 228

Wheeley, Bob 226

Wherry, Laura Wellington Childress 216, Lottie Maicel 215, 216, Samuel 108, Walter Thomas 216

Whiddon, Eva Elizabeth 218, Lela Ann 218, William Ernest 218

Whitaker, Addie 283, Addijo 283, Charles Richard "Dick" 283, Donna 113, Ethel 283, Eugene Hogan 283, Goldine 283, Irwyn 283, John C. 283, Kittie 283, Paul 283, Ruth 283

Whitakers, Mary Polly Hardigree 175

White, Agnes Sue 281, Alma 281, Alta 281, Anderson 16, Ben 281, Bessie Mae Anderson 188, Ertis 255, Gayleen 120, George Cleveland 188, Georgia Ruth 85, 188, Israel Scott 31, 280, 281, James R. 51, Julia 281, Lee "Lasses" 38, Martha Elizabeth 126, Noah 280, 281, Perilla 281, Priscilla Marguierite 277, R.B. 281, Roscoe 281, Sam 281, Sonora Anne 245, Sue 281, Susan 281, Susie 280, Velma 281

Whitehead, James M. 10, Joseph Brown 68, Martha Jeanne 249

Whitehorn, Alina 143, Ashley 144, Darlene Emberlin 143, Deanna 143, Garrett 143, Gary 143, Hunter 144, Janet Miller 143, Kay Harding 144, Norman 143, Stan 143, Zach 144

Whitehurst, Alvin Morgan 282, Ann 283, Beatrice 282, Bonnie Gail 283, Derrell 283, Doyle Mack 283, Effie Allene 282, Elbert 213, 282, Ella Amanda 282, Ellen 279, 282, Emmett 282, Ernestine 282, Evelyn 283, Francis 23, 279, 281, 282, 283, Franklin 283, Gayle 240, Geneva Inez 213, Georgia Ethel 282, Gilbert 282, Gladys Murlean 283, Hazel Lorene 282, Hiram F. 283, Hiram Falvey 283, Hiram Francis 282, Howard Gould 282, Jewel 282, John W. 281, Linda 280, 282, 283, Lola Myrtle 282, Mamie 282, Mamie Eloise McLendon 212, Mamie Ethlyn 213, Margie 282, Martha 281, 282, Milam 283, Minerva Ellen 279, 282, 283, Mollie Wayne 283, Odie Oline 282, Ollie Monroe 282, Ouida Florine 213, Roy Turner 282, Ruby Nelwyn 283, Ruby Ozzelle 282, 283, Sara Richkie 240, Seaborn S. 281, Theo 282, Travis F. 282, Wayne 280, William Richard 282, Willie Mamie 282

Whitelock, Amanda C. Magrill 206, William T. 206

Whitenack, Becky 63, Brian 63

Whitfield, Kelly 96, Lucretia 178

Whitley, Mollie 210

Whitlock, Kelly 110

Whitten, Dean 94

Whittington, Joanna 101, Lottie 196

Whorter, Ina Killgore Rogers 214

Whorton, John L. 198, John Lacy 42, 43

Wickman, Loretta 179

Wicoff, Mary 160

Wieber, Susan Jean 184

Wiggins, J.W. 46

Wilburn, Perry 202

Wilcox, Darlene McDonald 83, Julia Ann Ellender 104, Mary Ann 104, 105, Peter 104

Wilder 114, E.M. 96, George Lawrence 122, Lu 122

Wilhite, Hardy 118

Wilkerson, Arie 283, Carrie 283, Collie 283, Elbert 283, Elveney 283, Frances 283, James F. 283, Jeanie 283, John 283, Julie 283, Mary 283, Minnie 283, Texana 283, Tom 283

Wilkes, A.B. 27, Ada Adelia Henderson 171, Josiah 171, Nancy Jane 27, 78

Wilkins, Camie 142, Lavinia 121, Mortimer 8

Wilkinson, Nancy 209, Norma Jean Doss 135

Willard, Alta Lera 129, Joyce Omega Tolbert 80

Willett, Jewell 259, Lydia Gibson 259

William, Annie D. 101, Robert 80

Williams 49, Ada 228

Williams, Addijo 87, 283, 284, Alice Perkins Foirriestier 148, Annie D. Rebecca 236, 284, Bernice 283, Billy Don 284, Carleton Omar 284, Charles T. 148, Clara 208, 284, Dessie Lee 208, 209, E.V.A. 78, 79, Edith Carroll 285, Edwin Glen 284, Eleanor Jane Caskey 118, Eli J. 118, Emma B. 284, Emmett Eugene 284, Evelyn Garrett 52, Exora 202, Frances Louise 284, Green Smith 266, 284, H.G. 11, Hampton W. 284, Harriett 199, Hubert Leroy 284, Hugh G. 284, J. Harold "Bill" 283, J.O. 85, J.S. 148, James Ernest Earl 284, James Willie 284, Jerry 85, Jesse Verda 284, Jewel Irene 284, John Taylor 284, John Tom 283, John W. 229, Johnnie Mae 228, Joyce 281, Julia 281, Kenneth Wayne 85, Laura Reed 85, Lewis 284, 285, Linda 154, Lolita Marie 266, 284, M.G. 228, Martha Ann 266, 284, Martha Jane 135, Mary 214, Mary Alive 284, Mary Allen 236, Mary Amy 266, 284, Mary Jane 148, Mary Jane Rhodes 229, Ned E. 129, Ned E. 22, Nicolas Tyler 85, Olan Troy 284, Oma Elizabeth 148, Otis 114, R.B. 246, Rebecca Jane 214, 284, Riley 148, Robert

Washington 266, 284, Robin Frost 85, Sarah Lenorah 118, So Yong Gerera 85, Taylor George 84, Timothy Matthew 85, Trula Sloan 204, Wanda Jean Phillips 85, 234, William Ernest 266, 284, Willie A. 204, Willis Edmond III 85, Willis Edmond, Jr. 85, 234

Williamson, Ann 107, John 50, Louie L. 56, Mahala 136, Mary 107, Nan 107, Salliem Edmiston 121

Willingham, L.A. 49

Willoughby, Charles M. 285, Cordelia 285, Ebon 285, Edgar Wyche 285, Eleanor 187, Francis A. 285, Francye 285, Franklin Lenora 285, James Madison 285, Jessie Love 285, Kenner Sommerkamp 285, Mary Elizabeth Louise 285, Mary Hope 285, Michael Andrew 285, Michael Andrew, Jr. 285, Minnie 142, 285, Wyche 285

Wills, Chill 38, Jessie Love 285

Willson, Elizabeth 214, James 214

Wilson 22, 171, Doby 224, Effie Terry 264, Elizabeth 219, Ellen 264, Eugene A. 37, Harold 264, John 270, Joseph 264, Julia Elizabeth Boone 232, Kirby 248, Laura Anne 170, Mamie Ruth Draper 179, Maria Willis 219, Mary Anna 219, Mattie 202, Meghan Rose 232, Mitchell Reagan 232, Rosa Mae 276, Rosalie 264, Tawney Susan Kneese 248, Vick 245, William 219, 232, Willis 219

Winbush, Nancy 140

Wingfield, W.W. 10

Winn, Edward F. 160, Nettie Belle Johnson Magrill 160

Winnie, Fox 37

Winningham 279

Winsley 213

Winslow 213

Wisdom, Lucy Ellen 276

Wismar, Gloria 249, 261

Witcher, Bettie L. 110

Withers, Elmer J. 53

Witherspoon, John F. 11

Witt, Jane Wood 254

Wolens, Kalman 128

Womac, Albert Alonzo 285

Womack, Albert Alonzo 10, 285, 286, Alonzo 144, 148, Betty Jean Bond 134, Chase Lane 286, Chase Love 167, Eliza 148, 285, 286, Elizabeth 286, Jacob Pryor 285, Jewel M. 286, John 286, John Faddis 285, John Faddis Jr. 286, Julian 285, 286, Kate 64, 144, 148, 167, 285, 286, Katherine 286, Lockey Ann 285, Lucy Ann 96, Mary Josephine 285, 286, Medora 144, 285, 286, Nancy Ann 285, O.T. 52,

Susan 144, 286, Walter Orville 286

Womble, Harold 17

Wood, Ellen Wilson 264, Alvie Tuney 183, Amos 286, Angela Gaye 164, Bob 256, Catherine Patience Berger 229, Charles Clinton 243, Della Lee Hudson 264, Elizabeth 96, Fay Miller 256, Frances Ellen 264, Glenda Gaye Hagler 164, Harold A. 259, Ida Dee 256, Ida Mae 243, Ina 25, 54, James Edwin 229, Jane 254, John 210, 211, 264, Joseph Henry 264, Josie 54, Kid 25, 54, Laura Virginia 173, 254, Lavon 64, Leck 5, 25, 54, Leila 61, Margaret 243, Mary Ann 210, 211, Mary Claire 116, Mattie Lee Ingram 183, Mima Jean 17, Ollie 286, Pauline 169, 256, Pigeon 5, R.M. 128, Reta Mae 286, Sarah 261, Stella Maud 127, 229, Susan Francis Caldwell 112, Thomas 256, Virgie Belle 254

Woodall, Irena Hope 204, William Troy 204, Winnie 204, 205

Woodbury, Vernon 41

Woodcock, Eugenia Michelle 274, John Lee 274

Woodman, John F. 41

Woodruff, Bob 69, Earnest 69

Woods, Anna Elizabeth Murchison 100, Caleb Nelson 100, Donald 182, Frances 143, Jeanette 210, Margaret 210, Minnie 285, Polly Anne Husband 182, Talitha Cumi 92, Woodie C. 100

Woodson, Sam 69

Wooldridge, Sybil Edna Phillips 233, Woodrow 233

Woolley, Mary Louise McKittrick 212

Woolsey 255

Wooten, Lester 125

Worley, Susan 268

Wornel, Elisha William 233, Minnie Heavel Stanley 233, Nauty Byrd 231, 232, 233, Richard 232, William Richard 232

Worsham, Amanda 176, Emily 176, John 225, Marci Holloway 176

Wortham, John 199, Katrina 179, Robert 179, Sherry Hughey 179, Stephanie 179

Wren, Denny 6

Wrenn, Mary 158

Wright, Allison McClure 129, Anderson 133, 286, 287, Carl V. 98, 133, 235, Carl V. 251, 287, Christine 255, Curtis 283, Franklin Leon 133, 287, Harvey 233, Helen 98, 133, 287, Howard 133, 286, 287, James Franklin 133, 287, James Leonard 133, 287, James R. 158, James Samuel 133, 286, 287, Jamie 271,

272, Jeffrey Ray 271, Jennifer Lynn 97, John 287, Lillie Maude 133, 286, 287, Lucy Vdell 133, Mariah 133, 287, Martha Lillian 133, Maude 98, 287, May 287, Maydean 133, Nelwyn Louise 133, 287, Ray 271, Richard 287, Ruby Olean 133, 287, Rubye Evelyn Phillips 233, 235, Sam 98, 286, 287, Sara 133, 286, Will C. 129, William B. 133, 287

Wyatt, Belle 154, Floye Anne Phillips 234, James Robert 234, Kelly Jean 121, Susan Jane 182

Wyble, Betty Jean 273

Wyche, Lois 202, Robert D. 20

Wylie, Caroline Elizabeth 113, 208

Wynn, Beulah Baggett 89

Y

Yarbrough, A.C. 175, Ellen 175

Yeager, Elizabeth Ann Stahl 137, 257, Erna 176, Michael 137, 257, William Michael 137, 257

Yielding, Elizabeth 209, Paul 209

Yockey, Lisa Kaye 137

Yoder, Jewel 97, Magdelena 147

Young, Addie Belle 287, Amelia 118, Barbara 158, Charles L. 98, 286, 287, Claude Lee 287, Clifford Carl 287, Earlene 115, Grace 103, Harvey Alvin 287, Hazel Bernice 287, James H., Sr. 229, Lillie Maude 133, 287, Lillie Maude 286, Loueaser 229, Martha D. 147, Mary Ann 246, Mary Elizabeth 206, Mary Nell 116, 125, Missie E. 97, 98, 133, 286, 287, Preston Arthur 287, W. Francis "Frank" 10, William 64, 216, 227, 228, 231

Younts, Drucilla 264

Youse, Bob 201, Syble 201

Z

Zeigler, Alabama 141, 142, John Philip 141

Zimmerman, Aaron 131, Cassidie 131, Dee 86, 87, Ethel Pauline 243, Jacob 131, Kelly 86, 87, Leland 86, Makinzie 131, Marguerite 86, Michael John 131, Percy 70, Robert 243, Robert Dee 86, Stephanie Kelly 86, 109, Tamara Denise Davis 131, Tamira 131, Zachary 131, Zachry Ater Albertson 86, 87, 109, Zane Austin Ater 86, 87, 109

Zinser, Bernice Meyer 287, Caroline 287, Eugene S. 287, Harley 287, Jon 287, Patricia 225, 287, Steele 287

Zollicoffer, Felix Kirk 183

Zook, John 147, Magdelena Fisher 147

Family Tree

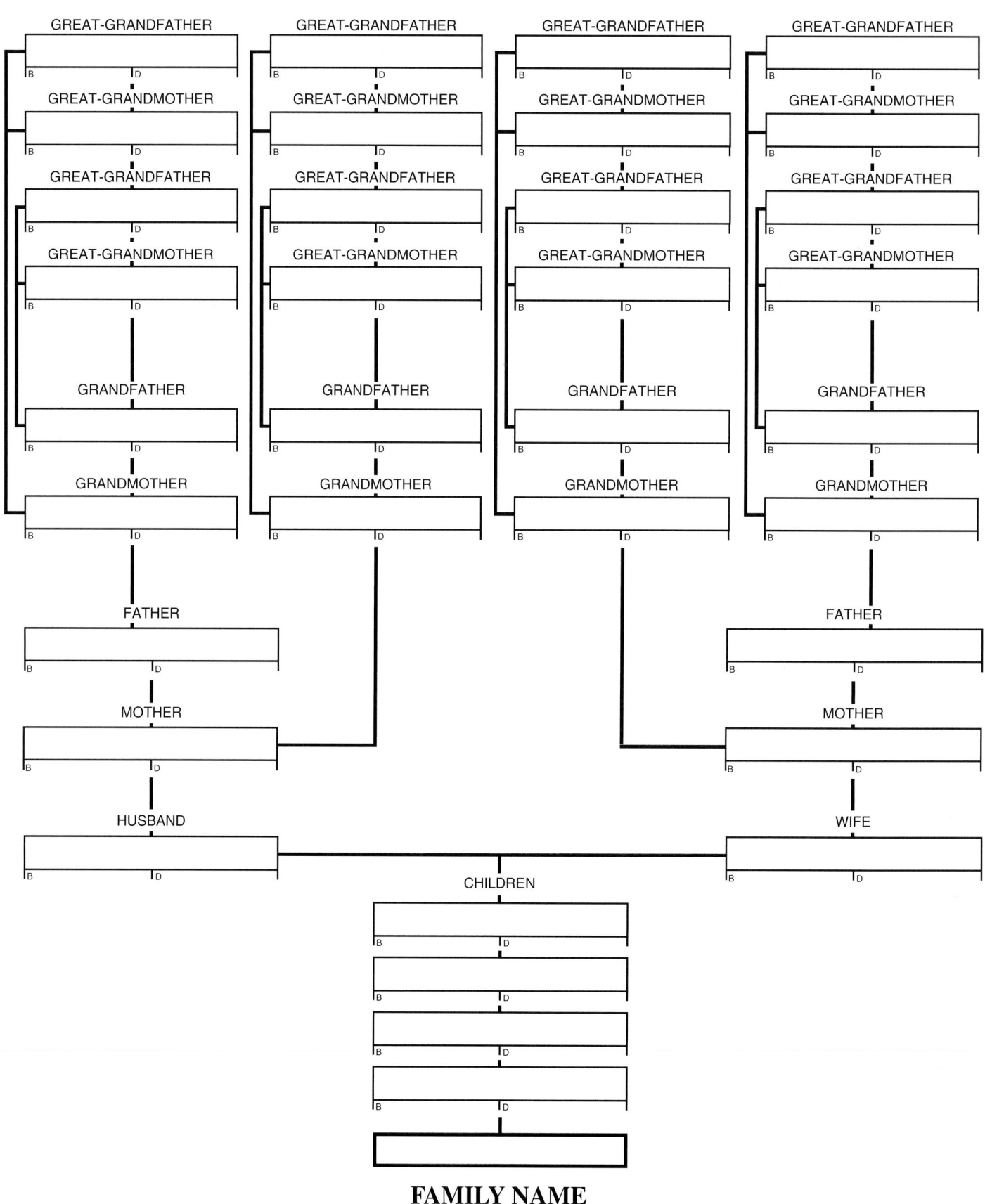

GREAT-GRANDFATHER

B   D

GREAT-GRANDMOTHER

B   D

GREAT-GRANDFATHER

B   D

GREAT-GRANDMOTHER

B   D

GREAT-GRANDFATHER

B   D

GREAT-GRANDMOTHER

B   D

GREAT-GRANDFATHER

B   D

GREAT-GRANDMOTHER

B   D

GREAT-GRANDFATHER

B   D

GREAT-GRANDMOTHER

B   D

GREAT-GRANDFATHER

B   D

GREAT-GRANDMOTHER

B   D

GREAT-GRANDFATHER

B   D

GREAT-GRANDMOTHER

B   D

GREAT-GRANDFATHER

B   D

GREAT-GRANDMOTHER

B   D

GRANDFATHER

B   D

GRANDMOTHER

B   D

GRANDFATHER

B   D

GRANDMOTHER

B   D

GRANDFATHER

B   D

GRANDMOTHER

B   D

GRANDFATHER

B   D

GRANDMOTHER

B   D

FATHER

B   D

MOTHER

B   D

HUSBAND

B   D

FATHER

B   D

MOTHER

B   D

WIFE

B   D

CHILDREN

B   D

B   D

B   D

B   D

FAMILY NAME

Gladewater Depot, 1903

Kilgore Depot